BLACK BELT
B·O·O·K·S®

THE ULTIMATE GUIDE TO
MARTIAL ARTS
MOVIES OF THE 1970s

500+ FILMS LOADED WITH ACTION, WEAPONS AND WARRIORS

BY DR. CRAIG D. REID

Edited by Sarah Dzida, Oliver Gettell, Raymond Horwitz,
Jeannine Santiago and Jon Sattler

Graphic design by John Bodine

Pictures by Celestial

Library of Congress Control Number: 2010909855
ISBN-10: 0-89750-192-6
ISBN-13: 978-0-89750-192-7

First Printing 2010

BLACK BELT BOOKS
A Division of **OHARA ⏻ PUBLICATIONS, INC.**
World Leader in Martial Arts Publications

DEDICATION

This book is dedicated to my wife of more than 29 years, Dr. Silvia Nien Mei Reid (aka Sil), the greatest wife in the universe, before and after infinity. Thank you for supporting all my writing endeavors throughout the years, especially during the writing of this book. She was unfairly made an early victim of the 2008 financial crisis, and our finances dwindled away faster than ice on a sunny day. Even though we did not know how long this depression was going to last, having me finish my first book was still a priority to her. Marriage is truly a partnership, through good times and bad and through sickness and health. I had less than a year to live when I proposed to Silvia in 1979, and when I told her that I might soon be dead, she said, "Moment with you, better than no time with you."

Love is not just about looking at each other but looking in the same direction. Communicate and always remember why you love someone in the first place.

I also dedicate this book to my mum and dad, Kathleen E.M. Reid and James W. Reid. They refused to let me waste away and die from cystic fibrosis when doctors in the 1950s advised them to make me as comfortable as possible for the "last" few years I had remaining. It is good they did not live to see me die. To my two older brothers, Graeme and Blair, who did not treat me with kid gloves or act like I was ever on my last leg. Instead, they gave me more legs to stand on.

Photo courtesy of Craig D. Reid

ACKNOWLEDGMENTS

Thank you to the good folks at Black Belt Communications who made this book possible—Robert W. Young, Cheryl Angelheart, Raymond Horwitz, Rachelle Lagnado, Ed Pollard, art man John Bodine—and to the book editors for their much-appreciated efforts: Jon Sattler, Oliver Gettell and Jeannine Santiago. Many thanks also go to the proofreaders Rebecca Dzida, Sara Hudson, Amanda Zeitler and Kristin Barrett. Special thanks to senior book editor Sarah Dzida who worked around many Craigisms, British sensibilities and my pun-and-verse narratives with a positive eye. A big *xie xie nimen* (thank you) goes to Celestial Pictures for its support, with special nods to Vicky Chung, Debi Yang and former CEO William Pfeiffer. Long live Shaw Brothers films!

This book would have fallen short cinematically without the unselfish love of martial arts films from the following people: George Yuan and Jeff Stockton at hkflix.com, who have the best DVD mix of martial arts films for purchase anywhere; my pal John Kreng, who is the awesome owner of new martial arts DVDs and old VHS tapes; Wiwat K. at ethaicd.com, who has an amazing old Thai martial films for purchase; the magic of Merlin David, who is the director of subtitling services and a distributor of Japanese samurai films at samuraidvd.com, which sells the most dynamic choice of classic Japanese martial arts films available; and Larry Edelstein at medimark.com, who was more than happy to blow the dust off of his ancient videotape collection for the benefit of martial arts movie fans everywhere—VHS tapes that have never been viewed in more than 25 years. I also want to acknowledge Celestial Pictures, which truly treats the Shaw Brothers films with the respect they deserve, and my ancient Betamax VCR and tapes for holding up— man I've got a few films most people don't have … yet.

Many deep, heartfelt thanks and respect go to Bruce Lee, *sensei* Nantambu Bomani, my great friend Lee Li-chwuin and my *sifu* Zhao Bao-fu. They shaped me as a martial artist and pointed the way to the mountain, which ultimately saved my life.

I would like to thank the following people for giving me the time of day. They shared their wisdom and experience of 1970s Chinese film with me over the years: Jimmy Wong Yu, Cheng Pei-pei, Gordon Liu Chia-hui, Yuen De (Yuen Tak), Chen Kuan-tai, Jackie Chan, Robert Lee, Phoebe Lee, Chia Lin, Yuen Bing, Sammo Hung, Danny Lee and Kuo Chue, as well as the late Ding Shan-xi, Evelyne Kraft and Ho Meng-hua. Thank you also to Shin Koyamada for coining the term "martialogy" and for translating many Japanese film titles into English, to Roberta Chow for her words of encouragement and to Curtis Wong for his words of wisdom … *Arigato, m'goi, do jie*. Many awesome thanks to my soul mate and wife Silvia for listening and laughing at many of my freaky jokes, wordplay and Craigisms. English is her second language, so if she got them, most English speakers should, too. I also thank her for translating the Chinese film titles into English … *duo xie*.

Gracious thanks to my writing brother and editor at kungfumagazine.com, Gene Ching, for giving me the freedom to express my views on martial arts and martial arts cinema. Thanks also go to editor Steve Biodrowski for giving me my writing breaks with the magazine *Imagi-Movies* and letting me go Fant-Asia-film nuts with enthusiasm on the now-defunct fandom.com and the still-roaring cinefantastiqueonline.com.

Lastly, to John Fusco, my spirit brother in life and martial arts. Thank you laddie for your martial arts and martial arts film passions, and for writing the foreword.

TABLE OF CONTENTS

PREFACE

I am a man that believes in fate, and fate takes us on predestined journeys in life as we eventually learn that coincidence is not a coincidence. The first "martial arts" film per se that I ever saw was in 1961. I was 5 years old. It was a Japanese movie adapted from a Chinese kung fu novel, and it was in a theater in the middle of nowhere in England (Tadley), a country still living in the past distrust of the Japanese via World War II. But there in the middle of anti-Japanese England it was—an *anime* film called *Alakazam the Great* (1960), based on a Chinese kung fu novel about the legend of the Monkey King. Of further coincidence, I was born in the Year of the Monkey. (Or were these coincidences?)

Adding to the numerological curiosity of life is when I was 16; my doctor said I would be dead in five years because of the deadly effects of cystic fibrosis. At the time, I was taking 30 pills a day, undergoing up to two hours of therapy a day and going to the hospital every three months. It was a major time of depression, and so rather than deal with the angst of waiting for death, I had decided to quit my medications and simply die. Then about 15 days later, an event happened that changed my life forever: I saw my first official kung fu film at the V Drive-In in Vestal, New York, Bruce Lee's *Fists of Fury* (aka *The Big Boss*; 1971). In an instant, I wanted to live to learn kung fu and watch every kung fu film ever made.

At the time, I thought kung fu movies were a brand-new genre of film. Of course, I did not realize that martial arts films had been around since 1905—so much for that dream! But then again, dreaming is free and I have since watched close to 5,000 martial arts films. My quest to watch every martial arts films ever made took on a new direction in 1975. It was the year I decided to start a martial arts movie collection, and once again, Lee was the casual factor.

The first film I ever collected was Lee's *Return of the Dragon* (aka *Way of the Dragon*; 1972). I was a freshman at SUNY Cobleskill in upstate New York, which is an agricultural and technical school about an hour's drive east of Cooperstown—home of the Baseball Hall of Fame. I had learned that the movie was going to be on that new funky, commercial-less channel HBO. The only place I knew that had the channel was my home in Endicott, New York (the city where IBM was born), which was a three-hour drive away. The previous summer, I had learned that by jamming a thick piece of paper behind the channel switch on my parent's TV switch between the 3 and 4 on the dial, HBO would phase onto the screen. Armed with such knowledge and my training pal telling me that Lee's film was going to be on that channel, an elaborate plan was hatched.

I became friends with a lady at the college's audio-visual department so that I could easily check out one of five humongous 60-pound Sony reel-to-reel videotape machines and one of two 30-pound black-and-white cameras. Every weekend, I would carry the equipment about a mile back to my dorm (no campus buses back then) to film how my friend and I would train and spar with each other. (Ouch, man.) But now, it would be a lugging of about 150 miles.

Weeks in advance of the big HBO show, I reserved the equipment and talked my roommate Terry into making a three-hour drive to Endicott with his pickup truck. At home, I jammed in that thick piece of paper into the TV channel changer, set up the black-and-white camera in front of the screen, and bingo, my kung fu film collection had begun. (I later purchased the reel-to-reel tapes; I still have them today.) Keep in mind that back in the 1970s, for a simple poor person like myself—my father gave me $16 per college semester for spending money—the thought of owning any copy of a movie, never mind having a collection of martial arts films, was as outlandish as trying to watch every kung fu film ever made. But then again, dreaming is for free and the pursuit is more important than just talking about it.

Because every kung fu film in American theaters (including the one on HBO) in the '70s was dubbed into English, it was fascinating and shocking to find and watch one of these kung fu films in its original language, most of which were in Mandarin. So when I became an undergraduate at Cornell University, I was in heaven because Cornell's Chinese Student Association (1,200-plus members) occasionally had a kung fu movie night. The events featured the now-classic Shaw Brothers kung fu films in Chinese from the 1960s and 1970s, which had never been shown in mainstream American theaters. Seeing them in Chinese made the films more exciting to watch and increased my interest in learning more about these great movies. The way I found out more about these films was as crazy as it was bizarre.

In 1978, I was elected president of the Chinese Student Association and immediately changed Kung Fu Film Night to every two to three weeks. The original black-and-white,16 mm Shaw Productions catalog given to me by Mrs. Wong from the Music Palace in New York City's Chinatown was filled with a wealth of great information about kung fu films. With my knowledge about these films growing, a year later, several things happened that made me appreciate kung fu movies even more, and it also put me into a better position to slowly increase my personal collection.

In 1979, while I was a graduate student at National Taiwan University in Taiwan (known then as the Republic of China), I became an actor/stuntman/fight choreographer in Chinese kung fu films and Chinese TV kung fu soap operas. Over the next few years, I would also watch up to three kung fu films a week (mostly with my stunning wife-to-be Silvia) in theaters. In fact, working in the industry and watching movies is mostly how I learned to speak Chinese. In learning Chinese, I was able to watch the films without subtitles and understand linguistic and cultural nuances. It opened up a whole new level of understanding to the genre.

In early 1981 (I'm still in Taiwan), some of the kung fu film stars who I had become close friends with began flashing around Betamax videotapes of Jackie Chan and other kung fu films. Borrowing my sister-in-law's Betamax machine, I spent hours at these friends' houses making my own Betamax copies of just the films' fight scenes. I figured it would be a great learning tool for the shows I worked on. When I returned home to the States in late 1981, I had accrued the fight scenes of about 20 kung fu movies on two Betamax tapes. It may not seem like much by today's standards, but back then, there were no video stores and 20 were a lot of films. Unfortunately, I had nothing to play them on, and VCRs in the 1980s were considered a luxury item, therefore, very expensive.

By 1982, my wife Silvia and I had become Ph.D. graduate students at the University of Illinois. We both agreed that to be able to watch those 20 collected films, it was important enough to fork out a combined one-month's salary to buy our first Betamax VCR—it was the low-end model, by the way. This is how strong the passion for watching kung fu films was, even though I was just watching the same 20 films over and over.

Then one Saturday afternoon in 1982 … WOW!!! The Shaw Brothers' kung fu film *The Kid With the Golden Arm* (1979) was on USA Network. Fortunately, married student housing at the University of Illinois had free cable television. I could not get my Beta machine on quick enough. Then lo and behold, every weekend a new kung fu film was on television. The thought of now making my miniscule martial arts film collection larger was exhilarating.

The following year, my wife discovered Chang's Oriental Mart in Champaign, Illinois, where they rented out original language, third-generation (copy of a copy of a copy) VHS videotapes copies of Chinese kung fu films. A what? VHS? Are you kidding me? Each tape rental cost $1. The only problem was that Silvia and I did not have a VHS machine. However, at least that format's machine only cost us about half our month's salaries combined. As you can see, being a research or teaching assistant as a graduate student didn't earn much money. The cool thing about Chang's, however, was that the employees had never met anyone like me who knew so much about kung fu films. So when they asked me for film recommendations that they could get in Chicago, I always gave them a toilet-roll list of great films I had always wanted to collect and watch.

Over the next six years, I found several video-rental stores, one of which had more than 300 kung fu films (the badly dubbed, pan-and-scan ones). I was also meeting tons of other kung fu film fans who had also started that long path of collecting kung fu movies. Rentals were an expensive $3 a shot, so I'm deeply indebted to my wife for being cool with my film-collecting hobby. With rentals being so expensive, it always bugged me when three different films I rented would actually turn out to be the same one. The film's titles were different, yet they were the same film. Today, this still happens. I actually have 10 copies of many of the same films because of these title changes, as well as having them on Betamax, VHS, CVD and DVD. Who knows what format is next? We've got Blu-ray, so maybe the future holds red ray or death ray.

Even the synopses of these varying titles for the same film were different. Of course, it is about sucking you in to watch or buy the tape. Yet what's also misleading is that video distributors would hire a film critic to churn out clichéd one-liners like "Wall to Wall Action," "More Fights Than You Have Ever Seen Before," "Action Packed" or other tag lines on the video covers, making you think that the film is just one, continuous great fight scene. Furthermore, synopses were often historically incorrect and were written by someone who had no clue about which martial art is real or cinematically created. The writers also used the same tired adjectives to describe similar plotlines and action. The stars and directors had tons of different spellings on each film, leaving me wondering who is who when in fact it was the same person.

Back in the day when I was collecting and watching martial arts films, I had always thought how cool it would be if there was an all-inclusive book that did the following: list every kung fu film title, list every alternative title to these films, list what the Chinese titles mean and how they relate to the English titles, and list how much action is really in these films; in other words, how much fight am I getting for my buck. I also hoped for a book that would give me a correct film synopsis, tell me about the cinematic histories of a film, explain why actors had so many different names, and analyze the fight choreography because, after all, this is the main reason we watch these movies in the first place.

Therefore, after a 38-year dedication to martial arts training, martial arts film watching and martial arts film collecting, as well as 31 years of working in the martial arts film industry, 30 years of practicing *chi gong (qigong)*, 22 years of *chi* (qi) healing and 18 years of writing, and using the 1970s as my initial focal point, I thought now is that time.

So within an intense eight-month period, I collected more than 900 films, watched more than 600 of them but only had space to write about 500 of them. More than 40 of the films I watched did not feature enough martial arts to be included in this book as a "martialogy." (See Introduction for explanation of this term.) With a book of this magnitude covering so many different aspects of martial arts, marital arts history and martial arts cinema history, I relied on my personal extensive library of martial arts books (in English and Chinese) and more than 1,000 published magazine articles for references and thus the reason for opting not to include a bibliography at the end of the book. It not only would be more than 60 pages of references, but also many references would be from my own work. This would come across as too self-aggrandizing. Plus, after all, this is not a book about my literary collection but a collection of literary verse … Craig vs. martial arts cinema.

It is also important to point out that this is not a book of recommendations but a book of knowledge. However, after watching and writing about so many films, I was compelled to create the section "The Best 20 Martial Arts Films of the 1970s Before and After the Book." In that section, I share my top 20 choices of films before and after I wrote this book, which at the end of the day illustrates that you can't really make a final list of the "Best of Anything" until you have literally seen everything.

As is becoming quite evident, one of my original goals in life after seeing Lee's *Fists of Fury* in watching every martial arts film ever made is obviously never going to happen. But maybe if the chi (qi) is with me, I'll be able to watch every martial arts film made in the 1970s from every country. Or at the very least, I'll be able to write about each one that I find. So what about the 1980s, 1990s and 2000s? I am in the hands of fate and destiny.

Lastly, if it were not for Chinese kung fu films that inspired me to learn martial arts and to journey to Taiwan in search of a mystical cure for my terminal illness, I would have died during the 1970s. Therefore, with this book, I would like to think that I am giving a little bit back to the martial arts film genre. For those who take the time to read and use this book and to find out or learn more about these great movies, it is you who are the heroes.

Cheers, Craig

FOREWORD

The Western world has always been fascinated by the mystique of Asian fighting styles. Of all my dad's war stories, his tales about a little Korean mechanic named Papa-*San* and his "secret killing karate" held me the most spellbound, likely triggering my boyish thirst for all things martial arts. This was the early 1970s. I was barely a teen, and a Chinese film called *Fists of Fury* (aka *The Big Boss*; 1971) would soon roll into the local drive-in at Watertown, Connecticut.

I would never be the same.

In the way that Western movie heroes fired the imagination of my grandfather and war movies captivated my dad, I was enamored with Chinese guys who didn't need guns to fight for justice and who inhabited an exotic, mystical landscape far more wondrous than Oz and far more deadly than Tombstone. I had never seen anything like it: wandering monks, secret societies, arcane fighting systems named after animals, legends like White Eye Brow, or mysterious internal forces called *chi* (*qi*). The strokes of peculiar humor—so different from our own—constantly caught me off-guard and added to the magic.

My Saturday mornings became dedicated to training at a local *dojang* (Korean training hall), a practice that made me feel connected to the furtive mysteries of the kung fu movie universe. Barefoot, I'd make my way home to watch *Black Belt Theater* with my friends. Nights were spent trying to beg my way to another trip to the drive-in to see a Shaw Brothers triple feature. One might say that that first, long-ago viewing of *Fists of Fury* changed my direction and lit the fuse for a discipline and career in movies. For another young man, it would literally save his life.

British-born Craig Reid was 16 when doctors told him he'd be dead in five years because of the debilitating effects of cystic fibrosis. A few weeks later, his brothers took him to the V Drive-In upstate New York to see *Fists of Fury* (originally called *The Big Boss*, but I'll let this book tell the fascinating story of that title caper). The Bruce Lee film inspired young Craig, incurable disease or not, to pursue the path of martial arts—a path that would restore his health and prove the Western doctors wrong.

Craig Reid's unlikely journey to Asia to investigate the healing powers of chi—a central spiritual force in the kung fu movies he so much loved—could be an epic movie in itself. In the Taiwan of the early 1970s, Reid built on his martial arts foundation and studied what the masters call "deep *gong fu*." Through the rigorous, traditional practice of *qigong*, Reid not only overcame his illness but also overcame the prejudice of the time to become the first Caucasian stuntman in the kung fu movie industry in Taiwan. He would return to the United States to earn college degrees from Cornell and the University of Illinois. While his doctorate is in entomology (the study of insects), it is fitting that an early thesis of his was on the fighting techniques of the praying mantis; he essentially replicated the findings of Ming patriot Wong Long, the legendary Shaolin father of the praying mantis fighting system. His knowledge of such systems and their applications—both practical and cinematic—would lead to his becoming a Hollywood fight choreographer and fight director from 1996 to 2007. Highly regarded as a reviewer and curator of kung fu cinema history, he would also write the box covers for 160 DVDs from the Shaw Brothers martial arts collection.

Like most of us Western kids raised on the Hong Kong movies of the 1970s, Reid never lost his passion for the genre. Unlike most of us, however, he's been able to combine that passion with incisive scholarship, a fluency in Chinese language (his qigong master had actually encouraged him to watch early kung fu movies to learn the old style of Chinese), a deep understanding of martial arts on myriad levels, and a working knowledge of combat choreography. I got my first true glimpse of this a few years back when Harvey Weinstein, producer and studio head, asked me to consider writing a remake of *The Avenging Eagle*, the 1978 gem by Chung Sun. I wrote to Reid and asked for his take on the film. His reply came back quickly in an e-mail:

Actors Ti Lung and Alexander Fu Sheng do not play your typical "wuxia" heroes like in Chang Cheh's films and many of the other wandering swordsman, knight-errant movies. In this film, to be a loner is not a goal and to find love and female companionship is also worth dying for. Fu Sheng is also getting to know his opponent (Ti Lung), which is the whole tenet of Swuin Zi's (or as most folks write Sun Tzu) *The Art of War* wherein by ultimately knowing yourself and your enemy, there is no fear in battle. Adding in a touch of revenge for the loss of a wife makes for some interesting pious pay back. In fact, Ti Lung dies for this at the end of the film (maybe not in the way one would think), but again, this is something Chang Cheh would never do.

I really like how director Chung Sun weaves in the whole philosophy of yin yang into the movie, such as when Ti Lung is running away from his enemy while Fu Sheng is running toward them. It creates a balance, and as it turns out, they have the same enemy.

Although as is typical of Chinese scripts, wherein the rules of inciting incidences occur at the midpoint and end of Act 1 and Act 2 are not set in stone, this is one of those few times where the plot points kind of fall into place at the right moments. The screenplay also has some good plot twists that keep the interest moving forward where we want to see how the things are going to work out. And as is true of many "wuxia" stories (and this film is based on a kung fu novel), major plot points occur right down to the last minutes of the film.

The fights are actually pretty good in this film. What I really like is the use of many different kinds of martial arts weapons for all the main fighting characters, and this brings out interesting information about who these characters are. Certain weapons have a history as to who would use them in real life, a reflection of one's personality. The audience may not know these things, but they subliminally work their way into their psyche based on what they see over many years of watching kung fu films.

Reid would go on to identify these weapons and their unique histories and how they reflected character and theme. After reading his e-mail, watching the film again was like listening to Italian composer Giuseppe Domenico Scarlatti after a day at the piano with an admirer of his talents Frédéric Chopin. Not only did elements such as structure and character emerge with deeper layers, but also the entire movie was a richer experience to see as a martial artist, and far more enjoyable as a fan. That, I think, is what makes Reid's approach to martial arts cinema so remarkable and long overdue. Unlike all the kung fu movie reviews out there, Reid's "martialogies" cover aspects of the films commonly not seen. He doesn't just understand this sub-genre as a scholar but shares our passion and affection for it as a fan. Many of the martialogies include obscure trivia and lost kung fu lore that will delight lovers of the genre. If you're one of those fans, this first volume will get your old-school memories reeling and introduce you to hidden 1970s gems missing from your DVD library. If you're new to kung fu cinema, Reid is the perfect guide to lead you through the Jiang Hu world of monks, thieves, one-armed swordsmen and drunken masters; I envy you the experience. Calling this comprehensive encyclopedia *The Ultimate Guide to Martial Arts Movies of the 1970s* is an apt description. Like the treasure trove of the 500-plus titles it celebrates, the book is a feast.

Read and savor, and, if I can borrow Reid's own valediction from his *Avenging Eagle* e-mail … may the chi be with you.

—John Fusco
Mud City, Vermont
2010

Screenwriter John Fusco has written 10 major movies and a miniseries. Among his credits are *Young Guns* (1988), *Thunderheart* (1992), *Hidalgo* (2004), and *The Forbidden Kingdom* (2008)—the first motion picture to team Jackie Chan and Jet Li, as choreographed by Yuen Woo-ping. He is a longtime student of northern Shaolin praying mantis kung fu and, more recently, *jeet kune do*.

ABOUT THE AUTHOR

Photo by Monique Ozimkowski

Born in Reading, England, Dr. Craig D. Reid began practicing martial arts in 1972. He is one of America's most respected martial arts film historians and critics. His extensive knowledge of martial arts history, martial arts cinema history and experience as a fight choreographer in Asia and Hollywood lend unique insights into his film articles and reviews. Reid has also appeared as an interviewee on many international TV shows dealing with martial arts, such as on a Japanese TV special about Bruce Lee and The History Channel of Asia's special 2008 Olympic show *Ancient Chinese Sports*. Reid was also the curator of the Shaolin Kung Fu Film Festival held by the National Geographic Society in 2008 at its national headquarters in Washington, D.C. At the festival, Reid spoke to a cumulative audience of more than 1,000 about the history of the Shaolin Temple, how that intertwined with the history of martial arts cinema, and discussed the evolution of fight choreography in the Chinese film industry. In 2010, Reid not only was the *chi gong* (qigong) and animal kung fu styles expert for two episodes of National Geographic's *Fight Science* TV show but he was also the curator for a second film festival for National Geographic based on its Terra Cotta Warriors exhibit.

In 1979, he became the first regular Caucasian and American stuntman in Chinese kung fu movies and kung fu TV soap operas in Taiwan. Besides being a guest lecturer on combat choreography at Yale School of Drama, Reid did fight choreography on Sam Raimi's ABC TV show *Spy Game* and was a fight-directing apprentice with the Hong Kong action crew on CBS's *Martial Law* for two years. He also wrote the screenplay for the award-winning docudrama *Red Trousers: Life of the Hong Kong Stuntman*, which was directed by Robin Shou.

With 18 years of freelance writing experience, Reid has accrued more than 1,000 published articles. More than half are related to film and martial arts and have appeared in magazines such as *Black Belt*, *Karate Illustrated*, *The Hollywood Reporter*, *Emmy*, *Boxoffice*, *Fangoria*, *Femme Fatales*, *Masters of Kung Fu*, *Inside Kung-Fu*, *Location Update*, *Wu Shu Kung Fu*, *Asian Trash Cinema*, *In Camera*, *Kung Fu Qigong*, *Bright Lights Film Journal*, *Imagi-Movies*, *Cinefantastique*, *Sci-Fi Universe*, *Impact* and *Kung Fu Tai Chi*. Reid's 1993 article "Fighting Without Fighting: Film Action Fight Choreography" published in *Film Quarterly* was the first scholarly approach to analyzing Hong Kong action fight choreography that was published in any academic film journal. Besides covering action and martial arts movies for old cinema-film sites like fandom.com and cinescape.com, Reid still writes for solid, surviving sites such as kungfumagazine.com, fangoria.com, cinefantastiqueonline.com and his own established *the-filmfiles.com*. He was the Los Angeles film correspondent for Reuters of Asia. Although that branch phased out a year later, Reid continued to write on Asian film for Reuters through the Los Angeles bureau. With this, Reid's articles were not only read worldwide by more than 55 million readers but the articles also appeared in prestigious newspapers such as *The Wall Street Journal*, *The New York Times*, *Los Angeles Times* and *Chicago Tribune*.

When Celestial Pictures bought the rights to the entire Shaw Brothers library, Celestial hired Reid as one of its Shaw Brothers film experts. He wrote the film synopses for more than 160 films, as well as many of the actor and director bios that appear within the DVD's "Special Features" section. Since 2007, Reid has become the official blogger for the San Diego Asian Film Festival, one of the largest and important Asian film festivals in North America. For what it is worth, at last count, Reid's martial arts film collection now exceeds 4,300, the only problem is that more than 1,200 of them are on Betamax.

Reid and his wife Silvia have been doing chi healing for more than 22 years. They founded Vivalachi Health and Wellness Services and vivalachi.com, in which their goal is to bring health, happiness and harmony through chi gong and chi healing to the world.

Photos courtesy of Craig D. Reid

INTRODUCTION

The two most important things about martial arts are that a person should practice martial arts not to fight and that a person should learn to use martial arts to heal rather than hurt. Over the decades, both these virtues in martial arts films and martial arts schools are slowly disappearing. But one of the beauties of the films of the 1970s is that these martial arts ideals come through loud and clear. I have written this book as a martial artist, a historian, a fight choreographer and as a major fan of these films. This is not a book of reviews or recommendations but a collection of 500-plus film *martialogies*. A martialogy is basically a biological review of a film, if you will, a living entity wherein we dissect a movie down to its anatomical components: plot, actors, fight choreography secrets, tidbits of "I didn't know that" cool information, and discussions on comparing the reel and real histories of the story, characters and various martial arts styles. (I guess that would make a martialogy about cartoons a study of "cel" biology.) That's why there is an advantage to being the sole author and film watcher of this book; I'm able to refer back and forth to the various films as references to each other, which gives the book a sense of unity, the kind of thing I hope can happen over time to the international martial arts community.

1970s—Best Decade for Martial Arts Films?

Yes. Bruce Lee, Jackie Chan, Sonny Chiba, the Liu family (Liu Chia-liang, Gordon Liu Chia-hui, Liu Chia-rong), Jimmy Wong Yu, the Five Venoms plus one, Ti Lung, David Chiang, Chen Kuan-tai, Chang Cheh, Chu Yuan, Amitabh Bachchan, Angela Mao Ying, Wen Chiang-lung, Sammo Hung, the Yuen family (Yuen Xiao-tian, Yuen Woo-ping, Yuen Cheung-yan, Yuen Shen-yi), Alexander Fu Sheng and a cast of thousands. What more really needs to be said?

Without being too biased, Bruce Lee really says it all. No other single martial artist and martial arts star in any other decade has come close to accomplishing what Lee has done. As a martial artist, he has done more than any one person in the history of martial arts to spread the word of kung fu, and as a martial arts film star, he legitimized kung fu films worldwide. But when it comes to making martial arts films during the 1970s, how worldwide is worldwide?

What if I told you that Wales and Scotland made martial arts films in the 1970s? Excuse me, are you kidding? Well … yes and no. Officially, Wales and Scotland didn't make any martial arts films in the 1970s. However, the United Kingdom, which encompasses the two, did co-produce 10 martial arts films during the decade.

Number of Martial Arts Films Made in the 1970s	
Hong Kong/Taiwan (Chinese martial arts films):	1,245 (1,366)
Japan:	288 (315)
South Korea:	244 (87)
India:	122
Philippines:	112
United States of America:	69
Turkey:	43
Thailand:	18
Indonesia:	15
Italy:	12
United Kingdom:	10
Spain:	5
Australia:	3
West Germany:	3
France:	2
Mexico:	2
Communist China:	1
Sweden:	1
Pakistan:	1
Total:	2,196

The list shows countries that made martial arts movies in the 1970s and the number of films they made that featured martial arts. Because films made in Taiwan and Hong Kong are considered Chinese kung fu films, I've lumped their film totals as one. (Plus, many are co-productions between Hong Kong and Taiwan anyway.) For example, if a film is a co-production of four countries (*The Stranger and the Gunfighter*—Hong Kong, USA, Spain, Italy), I've counted it as a production of each country, but for the final tally of all films made in the 1970s, it will only be counted once. Oh yes, I've also noted the total number of alternative titles for films made in Hong Kong/Taiwan, Japan and South Korea.

As is quite evident, Hong Kong and Taiwan made the most martial arts movies during the 1970s. Actually, every decade since the 1900s and up until the 1990s, Chinese-made kung fu films reigned supreme. This is why you'll notice that most of the information in this book discusses Chinese films. In fact, the first martial-arts-influenced movie made was the 1905 Chinese film production of *Ding Jun Shan* (Ding Jun Mountain), which starred Beijing opera great Tan Xin-pei. From this movie, Chinese kung fu films blossomed into five different genres that have influenced the various styles of martial arts films made throughout the world, which came to its first major proliferation head in the 1970s. During this decade, 20 countries got involved in making martial arts films as compared to four countries before the 1970s (Hong Kong, Taiwan, Japan, and a handful of films made in South Korea during the late 1960s).

The first genre is known as the *wuxia pian* and originated in Shanghai back in the 1920s when the city was known as the Chinese Hollywood. Loosely translated as "martial chivalrous-hero film," wuxia movies are so named because of the Chinese literary genre *Wu Xia Xiao Shuo* (wuxia novels). These literary masterpieces written during the Tang Dynasty (A.D. 618-907, when the Vikings were coming of age) were saturated in classical tales, heroic stories and legends of superhuman swordsmen and magical feats. Several important wuxia films from that silent era include *The Lady Killer* (1921), *The Boxer From Shandong* (1927), *Burning of the Red Lotus Monastery* (1928) and *Red Heroine* (1929). What's interesting about these silent films is that they essentially look like American silent films but with Chinese actors in which the actors' well-conceived and somewhat over-the-top facial expressions tell the whole story.

Hong Kong's Cantonese cinema arose when the Nationalist government laid down the law that all films made in Shanghai had to be shot in Mandarin. This spurred a mass exodus of Cantonese-speaking talent to Hong Kong. The martial arts genre was heavily censored in the 1930s by the Nationalist government because they believed the films would cause political upheaval. When the Communist People's Republic of China was established in 1949, leader Mao Ze-dong had these wuxia films destroyed, saying that they could incite the masses to rebel. There are only 20 pre-1949 films known to have survived the destructive cleansing of the Chinese Proletarian Cultural Revolution. Wuxia novels were also banned in China and Taiwan.

As Hong Kong's Cantonese cinema (no martial arts films then) was waning, in 1949, filmmaker Wu Peng sought to revive the dying industry by making a film about legendary folk hero Huang Fei-hung. The first film about Huang starred Cantonese opera star Kwan Tak-hing in *Story of Huang Feihong Part 1* (1949). Kwan went on to star as Huang in about 100 films. The film series ushered in the next genre of martial arts film known as the *gong fu pian* (kung fu films).

The term "kung fu" is derived from the Cantonese dialect (mandarin *gong fu*), which literally means "working man"; its meaning implies "hard work." For example, a painter, writer or singer can put a lot of "kung fu" into what they are doing. The genre therefore had more of a metaphorical association with the common folk, wherein anyone could understand the notion of hard work but not everyone could associate with the superhero characters of the wuxia films. Thus, the kung fu films presented characters and fight choreography of a more supposedly realistic nature. In other words, it was less fantastical.

As Mandarin filmmakers began arriving in Hong Kong in the early 1950s, they abhorred wuxia and kung fu films and considered them crass. However, the notion of making martial arts films about a country's martial arts and historical heroes did not go unnoticed. In the 1950s, Japanese director Akira Kurosawa created *chambara* (sword fighting) films, many of which starred his prime discovery Toshiro Mifune in movies such as *Rashomon* (1950) and *Seven Samurai* (1954).

Over the next decade, the influence of chambara movies began to filter into Hong Kong-made wuxia films with their simple fight choreography and somewhat slow cinematic pacing. By the mid-1960s, Mandarin filmmakers working for Shaw Brothers Studio like King Hu (Hu Jing-chuen) directing Cheng Pei-pei in *Come Drink With Me* (1966) and Chang Cheh directing Jimmy Wong Yu in *One-Armed Swordsman* (1967) made their marks making martial arts films. Their works not only led to the reversal of Mandarin filmmakers' prejudice against the wuxia genre but also broke away from the chambara film mode by having more and longer fight scenes. In the late 1960s, Korea also began making wuxia-style marital arts films, in which the fights, costumes and story lines mirrored Chinese wuxia movies—*A Fierce Animal* (1969) being one of the better-known films in the West.

While Sir Run Run Shaw, head of the legendary movie studio Shaw Brothers, stuck to the popularity of wuxia films, a Shaw Brothers film executive named Raymond Chow broke away from the studio and created Golden Harvest in 1970. Chow's first major signing was Bruce Lee. (Although kung fu films had been around since 1949, they were brought to international prominence by Lee in 1971 with his first film *The Big Boss*, aka *Fists of Fury*.)

With the growth and worldwide spread of kung fu films in the 1970s, other countries began to feature martial-arts-stylized fights in their movies. These films would usually star an actor who practiced an Asian martial art—Chuck Norris in America,

Cüneyt Arkin in Turkey—or feature a country's specific style of martial arts with an actor versed in the art—Sonny Chiba in Japan with karate, Bobby Kim in South Korea with *taekwondo*, Roland Dantes in Philippines with *escrima*, Amitabh Bachchan in India with *kalaripayit*, etc.

Because of the overpowering success of Jackie Chan's kung fu films made at Golden Harvest studios in the late 1970s, specifically *Snake in the Eagle's Shadow* (1978) and *Drunken Master* (1978), rival studio Shaw Brothers financed the creation of a new third genre of martial art film called *guo shu pian* to counter Golden Harvest's popularity. Although literally translated as "national art film," thus implying the national art as being marital arts, guo shu films were designated as neo-hero movies (new style of hero). Director Chang Cheh and Hong Kong's most prolific fight choreographer at the time Liu Chia-liang are credited with developing this new genre, which eloquently mixes the fight choreography of the kung fu films with the mythos of wuxia films. Early examples include *The 36th Chamber of Shaolin* (1978) and *The Five Venoms* (1978), in which realistic fights blend with fantastical sets and period-piece sensibilities.

As the kung fu and guo shu films started to lose their luster, partly because of Hong Kong's industry-destroying copycat mentality in which the martial arts fight action became repetitive, the 1980s saw the birth of the final two martial arts film genres. At the turn of the decade, Jackie Chan's film characters began to move away from being a practitioner of traditional kung fu and became more of an extreme athlete like in *Dragon Lord* (1982). With his next film *Project A* (1983) and more officially with *Police Story* (1985), he created the *wu da pian* (fight films using martial arts). This genre combined athleticism, martial-arts-influenced fights and dangerously outrageous stunts wrapped in more contemporary themes and settings. Instead of using traditional kung fu movements, the fights also incorporated more Western-style boxing punches with karatelike kicks.

Finally, in 1983, Western-trained, new-wave filmmaker Tsui Hark with his movie *Zu: Warriors From Magic Mountain* ushered in a fifth martial arts film genre that ironically was not officially named until the genre had ran its course. In 1995, in several major magazine articles, I coined the term Fant-Asia film to describe the genre of Hong Kong martial arts movies made during the early 1980s up to the mid-1990s. The genre uniquely combined elements of sex, fantasy, sci-fi and horror with high-flying wire work and over-the-top martial arts choreography. A year later, my term inspired Pierre Corbeil, Martin Sauvageau and André Dubois to create the magnificently successful Fantasia Film Festival, which is now one of North America's premier and largest film festivals. Fant-Asia films are basically revamped and highly stylized wuxia movies injected with what most people associate as Hong Kong cinema: frenetic-paced over-the-top action mixed in with far-out sight gags and gravity-defying wire fu. So films like *Crouching Tiger, Hidden Dragon* and Jet Li's *Hero* are Fant-Asia films. In fact, since the late 1990s, the term has grown to include just about any Asian genre film that has one or more of the aforementioned elements. Furthermore, even if the film does not have any martial-arts-stylized action in it, it still generally receives the Fant-Asia label, like the popular Hong Kong/Singapore horror film *The Eye* (2002).

Although there are five main genres of Chinese martial arts films, the three genres most prominent in the 1970s (*wuxia,* kung fu and *guo shu*) are ultimately responsible for influencing just about every single martial arts film made from that decade on. For example, the groundbreaking Japanese samurai movie *Azumi* (2003) is basically a wuxia pian with samurai swords. And the pioneering Thai production of *Ong Bak* (2003)? That's really a gong fu pian movie, Thailand style.

However, the 1970s also gave rise to some sub-genres, if you will, which essentially came and went within the decade. There was Bruceploitation, which describes Bruce Lee rip-off films that used a variety of actors that looked like Lee and tried to act and fight like him. There was America's blaxploitation films, movies that featured black actors as cinematic heroes, wherein cool male characters often ended up sticking it to the man (white authority figures) or foxy females would outdo and outwit bumbling idiotic white characters. There was the pinky-violence sub-genre of Japanese sexploitation thriller pictures so named because of the color of certain naughty body parts that were heavily censored by the government but were smartly hidden during the framing of nude shots. There was Suexploitation, films that copied the Beggar Su character made famous by Yuen Xiao-tian in Jackie Chan's *Drunken Master* (1978) and the similar character in *Snake in the Eagle's Shadow* (1978).

Yet the unifying factor of all martial arts films made during the 1970s, regardless of genre, country, year of production, bad dubbing, story confusions or misleading Western-marketing ploys (changing the titles, gross misinformation) is of course the martial arts action.

Themes, Schemes and Scenes

Most Asian countries have a tendency to feature their native martial arts and common thematic devices to reflect their culture, and non-Asian countries have characters who know an Asian martial art, which makes that character a force to be reckoned with. What can be useful before watching these films that can help a person to understand where these movies are coming from is to become familiar with the common themes, schemes and scenes that flourished during the 1970s. Apart from the details shared within each of the 500-plus martialogies written in this book, here are some of the more common elements that are most frequently seen in the top four countries who made the greatest number of martial arts films during the 1970s: Hong Kong/Taiwan, Japan, South Korea and India.

In Chinese martial arts movies, many films were set during the Ching Dynasty (1644-1911) or in the early days of the Republic of China (post-1911). Plotlines usually focus on good vs. evil; revenge as a powerful motivational factor; or nationalist struggles against foreign invaders, such as the Shaolin heroes fighting against the Chings (aka Manchus) or martial artists of the early Republic fighting Japanese invaders. Other common story devices evolve around the world of Jiang Hu and its for-martial-artists-only microcosm world of Wu Lin; the fall of the Song Dynasty via the Jins; and revenge for the death of a family member or *sifu* (kung fu teacher), in which the hero needs to learn martial arts in preparation for the ultimate showdown.

Common sequences in these films include scenes in an inn, restaurant, brothel, gambling house and/or teahouse in the middle of nowhere. The movies also often feature a white-haired villain—the notion of this originates from Shaolin Temple lore

in which former Shaolin monk Bai Mei (see *Executioners From Shaolin*) traitorously became a Wu Dung monk and helped the Chings destroy Jiu Lian Shan Shaolin Temple during the Ching Dynasty. The Wu Dung was a rival school of martial arts created by former Shaolin monk Zhan San-fung in 1365 after he left Shaolin and set up shop on Wu Dung Mountain.

Jiang Hu and Wu Lin stories often feature opposing clans trying to be the head of these worlds, which sometimes boil down to one of the clans finding a special weapon or kung fu manual before the other. Translated as "river and lakes," the world of Jiang Hu was an alternative society made up of beggars, martial heroes, martial arts villains and outcasts who coexisted with normal society but lived by their own laws, systems of brotherhood and morality code of ethics. Within the Jiang Hu world is a sub-community known as Wu Lin, where martial inhabitants often vie to be the head fighter, swordsman or clan leader and attain that position by adhering to the unwritten but respected ethical codes of righteousness, loyalty, chivalry and gallantry.

In films in which the hero ends up training with some old kung fu teacher, you know the hero is ready when, during a training sequence, the camera zooms in on the kung fu teacher's muted grunt or slight nod. This subtle acknowledgment is the greatest affirmation from a teacher that a student is excelling. Traditional kung fu training is not about tons of positive reinforcement, pats on the back or showering a student with compliments of improvement. Instead, it is about a student training his guts into the ground during which a simple visual cue from the teacher is enough to sustain one's positive attitude. Ultimately, if a student wants to quit because the training is too hard or the teacher is not supportive enough, then he/she should leave.

During the 1970s, most Japanese martial arts productions were *jidaigeki* (period piece) films, its sub-genre chambara (sword fighting) movies, karate flicks, pinky-violent soirées, or movies about the Yakuza (mobsters). Jidaigeki and chambara films were usually set during the Tokugawa period, aka Edo period (1600-1868), which involved ninja, corrupt officials, warring clans, heroic samurai swordsmen battling their personal obligations and honoring the code of *bushido* (warrior code of the samurai), and the lives of *ronins* (masterless samurai). These films also featured varying stories about the Japanese shoguns (head of the Japanese military) and emperors (leader of Japan). There were also several chambara films set during the Meiji period (1868-1912). What made samurai films so popular with American audiences were the obvious parallels between the samurai warriors and the Wild West gunfighter heroes seen in American Westerns. In Britain, the samurai characters were akin to the English knights and various other sword-wielding heroes who fought for the good of the king (or queen) and the country. The decade saw the arrival of karate films, which were set post-World War II up to contemporary times, many dealing with karate heroes battling Yakuza gangs.

Many South Korean films of the decade focused on the struggles and battles between downtrodden Korean freedom fighters and martial arts heroes who battle Japanese forces and karate villains during the Japanese occupation of Korea (1910-1945). One of the more famous freedom fighters during this time was the real-life hero Kim Du-han, of which four films in the 1970s focused on his exploits against the Japanese. Other films focused on heroes learning taekwondo as a means to overcome great odds, defeat killers and beat criminals (many of which were in cahoots with the Japanese Yakuza).

From the few films made in India that I watched, apart from the extravagant musical and dance numbers, it seemed love, family values and a strong sense of morality were common themes in which heroes would always end up trying to do the right moral thing. It was not always about killing the villains so much as trying to make them see the error of their ways.

Ha-Ha-Ha-Ha. But Still … I Have This Movie.

Peculiarly, an effective measure of the popularity of these old martial arts films, especially the ones made in Hong Kong and Taiwan, is that many of them have several alternative titles. Regardless of this fact, fans (especially me in the distant past) would buy the same film over and over, not realizing it was the same one. Fortunately, many of the Shaw Brothers' kung fu films were put in storage vaults after their original runs and were not sold as legal English dubs or distributed under more than one name. Thus, many of the Shaw's films have not been tainted by tons of different titles for the same film.

It is amazing how these Chinese distribution companies came up with English titles and really did not give a crap about how or what they looked like. For example: Here is a great film, *Dynamite Shaolin Heroes*. To most folks, it is confusing to think that a single batch of these films were shipped to the West, slipped through somebody's fingers, and were released with the blatantly misspelled and totally grammatically wrong title *Dynamit Shaolin Heroer*. Now, add to that the outrageously funny and weird English dubbing, and it has just become part of the whole grand scheme of kung fu film pop culture and film lore. It is just so charmingly wrong that you can't help but to love it.

So how come the English dubbings sound the way that they do and how did alternative titles come about? Well, as it turns out, a few months after arriving in Taiwan in 1979, one of my first jobs was dubbing kung fu films into English. I would work with the same three or four voice-over artists and dub 60 films per month, two per day, for $30 per film. Most of the times, there was not a complete script, thus creating the opening for implanting weeds of extemporaneous chatter. The producers did not speak English. They just cared about that when the actor's mouth on-screen moved, there was a voice, and when the mouth stopped, the voice stopped. We dubbers were not professional actors or translators, and because we each had three to five different voices to forge per film, we quickly ran out of voices to parrot after the second film. So we would develop a good-guy voice, a villain voice, an innkeeper voice, etc, and that is why the films all sound alike. There were also no rehearsals. We would watch the scene in Chinese with sound, then once without sound, then dub the scene. Speed was of the essence.

Furthermore, in Chinese period-piece films, Mandarin was spoken in an old-fashioned way, comparable to modern English vs. Shakespearean English. The language has its own cinematic rhythm, and certain words were dubbed in a fashion to fill in the gaps of the dialogue. For example, the word *ke shi*, which literally translated means "but," we dubbers would have to make up a two-syllable word to match the mouth movements of the Chinese actor. Thus, the birth of the ubiquitous *but still* in all those dubbed films.

But still … the dubbed films and alternative titles have led to mass headaches and confusion. Sadly, they also may have cheapened the legitimacy of the kung fu film genre. Adding to the malicious misfit of title-monkeying around is when distributors often do not check to see what titles have already been used, or they make subtle adjustments to a previously used title that sold well at some point. Classic example: *Big Boss 2* and *Big Boss II*. One is ultimately the *Lone Shaolin Avenger* with Casanova Wong. The other stars Dragon Lee, Bolo Yeung and Gao Fei. The titles imply that they're sequels to Bruce Lee's *The Big Boss*, but they're not. At the end of the day, for old kung fu films, it was the title that sells. This is why so many films in the 1970s used words like "Shaolin" and "Kung Fu" in their English titles, even though the film has nothing to do with either subject. In the 1980s, "Ninja" was the new mantra in film titles.

So how did words like "Shaolin" and "Kung Fu" become so popular? When I was dubbing these films, the producer in charge of dubbing would ask me whether I had any neat English film-title ideas he could use for film sales overseas. Back then, I had no idea about what was going on and how it would eventually be a confusing mess, but I rattled off a bunch of key words that might be eye-catching to fans in the United States. Yes, as you might have guessed, I did indeed suggest the use of the words "Shaolin," "Kung Fu" and "Dragon" (knowing that many would think of China and Bruce Lee by using the word) and a whole bunch of other words that I thought would make a film stick out. I am not saying that I am responsible for all those film titles, but I think it shows that if Chinese distributors, whether in Hong Kong or Taiwan, asked their other dubbers for suggestions, we as kung fu film fans were all on the same page.

As an aside, when I worked on Chinese film and TV shows and met an actor whose voice I had dubbed into English, it was a great way to break the ice to share with them how I was a dubber. Back then, the actors had no clue that this was going on. Anyhow, the actors would ask me what kind of voice I used for them. Of course, I always demonstrated it to them in my deepest, manly hero voice.

Did We Just Watch the Same Movie?

Speaking of having the same film, there is another interesting phenomenon that mystifies the innocent onlooker and puzzles the experienced. It actually struck me when I was trying to hunt down South-Korean-made kung fu films. Here are two synopses as taken from the Internet:

Synopsis 1: "The cruel Tien Hu, with his many powerful alliances, oppresses an entire Chinese province, killing many of the hard-working citizens. A wise Shaolin monk trains the brave Kang and Kao Yin to become kung fu masters and free their town and seek revenge. The time has finally come for the deadly mission to begin!"

Synopsis 2: "In order to earn the title as the greatest warrior, Sa-haeng Chu-myung of the country Yuan opens a fighting contest. At this contest, the Koryo man, Go-chul, beats everyone with his taekwondo martial arts and receives the 'sword of the greatest warrior.' Having lost the sword, Sa-haeng Chu-myung attacks Go-chul's home. Only Go-chul's daughter, Eun-pyo, escapes with her life with the help of a Koryo Buddhist monk who had been passing by. Twenty so years pass by and Sa-haeng

Chu-myung has committed many atrocious acts during that time. Having grown up into a warrior, Eun-pyo reappears before Sa-haeng Chu-myung. With the help of a warrior named Sim Seung-ui, Eun-pyo succeeds in having her revenge."

Can you believe this is the same film? So which is the right synopsis? When I found the Korean Movie Database, I was shocked to discover that during the 1970s, South Korea made almost 300 martial arts films. What was even more amazing is that, according to the site, actors like Jackie Chan, Lo Lieh (under a different name) and Jimmy Wong Yu starred in several South-Korean-made kung fu films. As Curly would sometimes say in the Three Stooges movies, "Nyeeeh, fooled ya." I was sucked into the pseudo-hype. On further scrutiny, it became evident that when a Hong Kong or Taiwanese kung fu film was directed by or starred a South Korean national, those films were often listed as being South-Korean-made kung fu films. Also, when a Chinese film was dubbed into Korean, the Chinese names were dubbed into Korean names and the story was changed to fit the personality of the country. You can certainly surmise which of the above synopses is the South Korean version of the film *4 Clans of Death*.

To some extent, this also happens in the English-dubbed version of the film. In March 2008, I presented a kung fu film festival at the Otis College of Art and Design in Los Angeles. One of the films was *The Eight Diagram Pole Fighter* (1983). The film was not in Chinese but had English dubbing and English subtitles, of which also appeared on the screen. So the audience and I had a great laugh because the English subtitles rarely matched the dubbed English; each seemed to be telling different stories.

Which reminds me of a nonrelated but relevant story. When I was living in Taiwan during the late 1970s, I took my fiancee Silvia to the movies to watch the hit science-fiction film *Laserblast* (1978). At the time, she spoke very little English and my Chinese was worse. The film was in English and had Chinese subtitles. For those of you not in the know, *Laserblast* is about alien creatures accidentally leaving behind a deadly weapon on Earth. Halfway through the film, while speeding home on their flying saucer, the aliens suddenly realize they left the weapon on Earth. For about two minutes, the aliens argue in their native tongue with garbled sounds that of course made no sense … but the film had Chinese subtitles that were not jibberish. Silvia was shocked when I asked her for a translation of what the aliens were talking about. We just laughed our heads off.

And here's one final example: An Internet site that sells the South Korean movie *Thirteen Year Old Boy* as a kung fu film is listed on the Korean Movie Database as the drama *A Boy at His Age of 13* (1974) with the following synopsis:

Synopsis: "Second lieutenant Kang, who led a mobile unit in battlefields during Korean War, attacks a village to stir up the rear of the enemy. A 13-year-old boy Kim Hong-kil persistently resists at first but returns as a naive little boy thanks to Kang's devotion. As Kang's unit is totally under siege due to the enemy's attack one day, Hong-kil runs into the enemy and falls down with a shooting sound. Kang sets his steps with the boy in his arms screaming."

Does this read like a kung fu film? Not to me, but that does not mean that it could not be a kung fu film because the reverse is also true; insipid titles sometimes turn out to be great martial arts films. The bottom line is that to know what something is, you have got to ultimately watch it. Incidentally, this was not a martial arts film.

Final Notes

The one thing I have discovered over time is that every film has its moments. Even though a film may truly suck the royal bird or be at the low end of the spectrum, if there is one moment of martial glory, a great kick, a series of punches or a fighter against a group of baddies that for some reason just clicks, then that film is always worthy to be watched, even just for that moment. It is like watching a cool film or TV show (the reruns of the original *Star Trek* series come to mind) in which you end up waiting for that one line, facial expression, body posture, a musical bite or a totally awesome sound effect or visual image. Often times, it is one or two of those small things that make you remember that TV episode or cinema moment forever. To me, kung fu films hold this same kind of fascination. Sadly, however, there will be some movies that will be so bad that there is truly nothing positive to say about them, and for that I apologize.

Also, please keep in mind that a single martialogy is not enough to discuss at great length all the exacting details of an event in history or all the varying versions that surround the creation of each particular martial art. In regard to the history of a martial art, it is rare to have everyone agree on everything about the style, whether it is the founder(s), the date, the lineage or even how the style was named. In many instances, one martialogy will discuss one version of a style's history and a second martialogy will discuss another version of the history, each proposed not as "the one" but as "a version." In-depth analyses of these histories is a book in itself of which I leave to those who wish to challenge these dynamic subjects.

KEY TO THE MARTIALOGIES

Martialogy Breakdown: This section explains the anatomy of each martialogy—what each part tells you and, where applicable, how the information was derived. The martialogy breakdown is rather detailed, but as a scientist, I have learned to be as meticulous as possible. I don't want to leave any questions on the table about what is being said. Furthermore, in order for a film to appear as a martialogy in the book, the movie needed to have at least **1m 55s** worth of martial arts action. (See the martialogy for *Good Guys Wear Black* for details.)

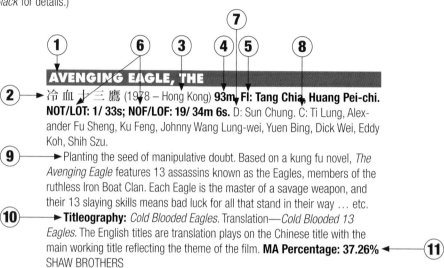

AVENGING EAGLE, THE

冷血十三鷹 (1978 – Hong Kong) **93m. FI: Tang Chia, Huang Pei-chi. NOT/LOT: 1/ 33s; NOF/LOF: 19/ 34m 6s.** D: Sun Chung. C: Ti Lung, Alexander Fu Sheng, Ku Feng, Johnny Wang Lung-wei, Yuen Bing, Dick Wei, Eddy Koh, Shih Szu.

Planting the seed of manipulative doubt. Based on a kung fu novel, *The Avenging Eagle* features 13 assassins known as the Eagles, members of the ruthless Iron Boat Clan. Each Eagle is the master of a savage weapon, and their 13 slaying skills means bad luck for all that stand in their way … etc.

Titleography: *Cold Blooded Eagles*. Translation—*Cold Blooded 13 Eagles*. The English titles are translation plays on the Chinese title with the main working title reflecting the theme of the film. **MA Percentage: 37.26%**
SHAW BROTHERS

1) Avenging Eagle, The: English titles of Chinese films will be chosen and listed by three criteria of descending importance:

- For a Shaw Brothers film, the English title used by the Celestial Pictures release
- Based on the English title of the film version I watched
- Based on the English title as presented by the HKMDB (Hong Kong Movie Database)

All titles are listed alphabetically. Articles of speech—a, an, the—are placed after the main title. So the film *The Avenging Eagle* will be listed under *Avenging Eagle, The.*

If titles begin with the same word, all the titles that begin with that common word will be listed first, then followed by apostrophe versions of that word, then followed by derivations of the word. For example, titles starting with "Hero" will be listed in alphabetical order, followed by titles with "Hero's" followed alphabetically by derivations of "Hero" (Heroes, Heroic, Heroine). Titles with the word "of" will come before titles with the words "of the." (*Hero From Shanghai*; *Hero of Kwantung*; *Hero of the Wild*; *Hero's Tear*; *Heroes Behind Enemy Lines*; etc.)

Titles beginning with *Mister* shall appear before titles with Mr., and films with numbers at the beginning of their titles like *18 Disciples of Buddha* will be listed as if the number was spelled *Eighteen*.

Romanized titles of Korean and Japanese films that do not have English titles will be listed using the Romanized letter-by-letter format.

2) 冷血十三鷹: Because most films made in the 1970s are Chinese, I decided to provide the titles in Chinese characters when possible. Also, because many Chinese films have similar English alternative titles, knowing the Chinese title is always the ultimate way to tell which film is which. Other Asian language films will just include their language titles using Romanization. Although there are several different ways that the Japanese and Korean language can be Romanized into English, this book will only use one version per title.

3) (1978 – Hong Kong): The information in the parentheses refers to the year of theatrical release in the country the film is listed under.

I have often been asked why there are so many different years that a film is listed under. It is often quite tricky to decipher through this because some books and/or Web sites use different years based on different criteria: year of the theatrical release in the movie's country of origin; year the film was made in the movie's country of origin; year the video of the film was released in the United States (and the same for other countries that released their home-language dubbed version of the film); and the release date of the newest distributor's version of the same film that has already been distributed many other times under different release dates.

In this book, for the Shaw Brothers kung fu films, I have tried to list the year based on the information distributed by Celestial Pictures in Hong Kong or its information in regard to the first theatrical run of the film in Hong Kong. For other films, I used the same date that can be corroborated by at least two other sources that list the same year based on each film's first theatrical run in the movie's country of origin. Yet admittedly so, there are so many films made in the late 1960s and early 1980s that have been listed as the 1970s, I can only hope that the *chi* (not the force) is with me on my final decision on the year a film is listed. For this, I beg your indulgence.

It is way freaky to think that you could own 40 or so versions of the same film even though it is listed under six totally nonrelated titles. It would be great if a distributor or even the various Internet rental companies (Netflix and Blockbuster that rent quite a number of these same films under several different titles) could include on their box covers all the other known titles and have the right synopsis for the right title. Thus, there is a present and probably future need to use this book to double-check everything.

4) 93m: Running time of the movie in minutes.

5) FI: This part of the martialogy describes the credit followed by the person(s) who are credited in the film for doing the fight choreography. In the early days of kung fu cinema, the English credit for fight choreographers was listed as "Martial Arts Instructor" or "Kung Fu Instructor." During the 1970s, as fight choreography evolved, the English credit got chopped and changed depending on the production company, the year, the country and the skill level of the choreographer. For Chinese films, production companies would credit the martial arts choreographer using four Chinese characters, which in Romanization can be written as *wu shu zhi dao*. In the 1970s Shaw Brothers films, the wu shu zhi dao was always listed in English as the "Fight Instructor," thus the sample *Avenging Eagle* martialogy uses the acronym "FI." (Note: the acronym "FI" does not appear in the film's opening credits).

List of Acronyms

AC:	Action Coordinator
AD:	Action Director
AS:	Action Scene Arranged (staged) By
ASAB:	Action Scenes Arranged By
F:	Fight Instructor
FC:	Fight Choreographer
FCO-CO:	Fight Co-Coordinator
FCom:	Fight Composer
FD:	Fight Director
FSC:	Fight Scene Coordinator
FS:	Fight Staged By
FSS:	Fight Sequences Staged By
KA:	Karate Adviser
KFCO:	Kung Fu Counselor
KF-Cou:	Kung Fu Counselor
KFD:	Kung Fu Director
KFI:	Kung Fu Instructor
MAA:	Martial Arts Advisor
MAC:	Martial Arts Consultant
MAD:	Martial Arts Director
MAI:	Martial Arts Instructor
MAS:	Martial Arts Sequences Designed By
MAT:	Martial Arts Trainer
SAD:	Stunt Action Director
SC:	Stunt Coordinator
SS:	Stunt Supervisor
SWC:	Sword Choreographer
TA:	Technical Advisor
TD:	Thrill Director
Uncredited:	No English Credit Available

That is the list of all acronyms that I used in the martialogies as well as what they stand for. They reflect the various English credits used for a film's fight choreographer based on how the role was presented.

6) NOT/LOT: 1/ 33s; NOF/LOF: 19/ 34m 6s: These are the film's fight statistics.

- **NOT/LOT** - **N**umber **o**f **T**raining sequences/cumulative **L**ength **o**f **T**raining sequences.
- **NOF/LOF** - **N**umber **o**f **F**ight sequences/cumulative **L**ength **o**f **F**ight sequences.

So out of **93 minutes**, *The Avenging Eagle* has **1** training sequence that lasted **33 seconds**. It had **19** fight scenes that lasted **34 minutes** and **6 seconds**. This means that the film has a combined fight total of **34 minutes** and **39 seconds**. That means 37.263% of this film is purely kung fu action.

Rules of the Training Sequences (NOT/LOT): Training sequences times were calculated based on whether the scenes include the following: when a character is learning martial arts; when a character is practicing martial arts, like doing a few seconds to several minutes worth of weapon or empty-hand routines; when a character is undergoing spiritual or philosophical training, like when San Te's head is between two piece of burning incense in *The 36th Chamber of Shaolin*; when a character is performing any kind of physical exercise in preparation for learning martial arts such as doing upside-down sit-ups, running with weights, stretching, etc.; any sequence that shows any kind of Beijing-opera stage-combat performance that is not part of a real fight in the film; when two or more characters are fighting for training purposes in which the intention is not to hurt each other but improve their martial arts; and when two or more characters who are part of the same martial arts school are asked to spar with each other.

When Kuo Chue's character in *Shaolin Temple* (1976) tries to jump out of a pit wearing leg weights, all the separate shots showing him trying to jump out of the pit until he successfully leaps out of the pit are classified as one training sequence. In a film like *10 Brothers of Shaolin* (1979) in which each of the 10 brothers does a five- to 10-second kung fu training routine during the opening credits, that is classified as 10 training sequences. Then, if another sequence shows the same brothers doing additional movements of the same form, that is still considered part of the original 10 training sequences. If a character does three different kinds of training sequences within the same shot (like training with three different kinds of weapons), as a fight choreographer, I would view this as three separate training sequences that an actor had to learn. Thus in this book, I would quantify this as three training sequences. Although maybe confusing, suffice it to say that the total **LOT** would always work out to be the same.

Rules of the Fight Sequences (NOF/LOF): If one main hero fights 30 baddies in one scene, that is one fight. If two main heroes fight the same 30 people in one scene, there are two fights (one fight for each hero). Three heroes against the same 30 means three fights and so on.

If six main heroes fight six main villains in one scene, then that would be six fights. It would be easy to imagine that the number of fights could escalate exponentially if each hero or villain were to constantly split into differing numbers of groups to fight each other, but amazingly this doesn't happen. Choreographers know that if there is too much splitting up and coming back together of the characters during a fight sequence, it becomes a nightmare for the choreographers to keep up with the various fight pairings. Plus, with too many different fights and changes of who is fighting whom, it makes editing a nightmare. Let me illustrate a 15-minute fight-scene example between three heroes. (Tom, Dick, Harry) and two villains (Joe, Ed) and break it down into their respective number of fights.

If hero Tom does hand-to-hand combat with villain Joe for 15 minutes, no matter how many times during the fight they change scenery (i.e., start in an inn, run outside and fight in a courtyard, jump onto a mountain and continue to fight, etc.), this is Fight 1. If Tom picks up a sword and fights Joe, who is still weaponless, that would be Fight 2 because the dynamics of the choreography changes. Joe picks up a weapon; that's Fight 3. Dick helps Tom fight Joe; there's Fight 4. Harry joins Tom and Dick to fight Joe; here comes Fight 5. Tom is injured and leaves the fight, so now Harry and Dick fight Joe; hello, Fight 6. Tom recovers and joins the fight, but because this is the same dynamic as Fight 4, it is not considered a different fight. Ed arrives to help Joe fight Tom, Dick and Harry, starting Fight 7. Ed and Tom fight on their own and enter Fight 8. If at the end of the fight, Tom is back to fighting Joe, which is the same dynamic as Fight 1, then there are no further combat sequences. To fight choreographers, this scene has eight fights.

You can see how that with all the possible combinations of who is fighting whom how the number of fights per scene can grow. Although it may seem a bit difficult to follow the above scenario and the fight number derived from the fight sequence, at the end of the day, regardless of how many combinations of individuals are fighting in a fight scene, the **LOF** of the above sequence is always going to be 15 minutes.

Except for Japanese samurai films, all fights from all other countries officially begin with whichever of the following happens first: initial scream and/or run at each other, or after the first kick or punch. A fight finishes at the end of the death scene or a surrendering opponent scene. Japanese sword fights typically comprise of one to three sword strokes, so a fight scene is technically over in a second or two. With this scenario, a film could have 10 fights and only 10 seconds of fight scenes. Because the buildup toward those few strokes is an essential part of the samurai fight scene, the fight officially begins when the two warriors face-off and have their classic stare down.

The NOT/LOT and NOF/LOF for documentaries are both listed as "None."

7) D: Indicates the film's director(s); see "Rules of the Name" below.

8) C: Indicates the film's major cast members; see "Rules of the Name" below.

9) Main Body of the Martialogy: Plot, history, neat tidbits

about the film, the humor of yours truly, etc. Also, not every character is identified by their actor.

10) Titleography: All known English alternative titles will be listed. Whenever possible for foreign films, a translation of the title will be provided. A few words will describe the potential reasoning behind the English titles. A special acknowledgment for Shaw Brothers productions is noted for each of its films.

Rules of the Titleography: As most of you know, many Hong Kong, Taiwan and Korean kung fu films have more than one title. For example, the 1977 *The Last of Jung-mu Martial Arts Hall* has 13 other known release titles: *Dragon Lee Does Dallas*; *Real Bruce Lee*; *Ultimate Lee*; *Bruce Lei - König der Todeskralle*; *Bruce Lee - O Dragão*; *Choihui Jeongmumun*; *The Last Martial Artist*; *The Last Fist of Fury*; *The Last of the Ching Wu School: Righteous Martial Party*; *Dragon Bruce Lee*; *Choehu-ui Jeongmumun*; and *Bruce Lee El Dragon Indestructible*.

Each year, Chinese kung fu films are being released in more foreign countries outside of Hong Kong/Taiwan and renamed using that foreign country's native language. For example, *Eroberer, Die* is the German DVD title for *All Men Are Brothers* (1973). Listing each foreign-dub title of every kung fu film and including that language's film title is impossible, to say the least. The same holds true for all the various Romanization systems for Chinese (which can be more difficult because there are also differing systems for the various dialects), Japanese and Korean films. Therefore, the titleographies will only include all known alternative English titles that I was able to track down. Therefore, the titleography for *The Last of Jung-mu Martial Arts Hall* will only include the following alternative titles: *Dragon Lee Does Dallas*; *Real Bruce Lee*; *Ultimate Lee*; *The Last Martial Artist*; *The Last of the Ching Wu School: Righteous Martial Party*; *The Last Fist of Fury*; and *Dragon Bruce Lee*.

A final note: The reason that one film has so many different titles is when a new company buys the distribution rights, it will rename the film to separate itself from the same film's other titles.

11) MA Percentage: 37.26%: This is the percentage of the film that is dedicated to martial arts training and fights put together—i.e., the amount of kung fu for your buck.

12) Rules of the Name: Unless a Chinese, Japanese and Korean actor, director or fight choreographer is more well-known by his or her English name (Jackie Chan, Sonny Chiba, Bobby Kim), I will use the Romanized names from his or her respective languages. Chinese and Korean names will be listed surname first and given name last. Japanese cast and crew will be presented like English names—first name first and surname last—. while Japanese characters will be listed as how they are referred to in the movie. For most Chinese names, I will use the talent's Romanized Mandarin name. All other talent listed from the other countries will be listed with their surnames last. In regard to the use of aliases in the *Index of Talent and Aliases* section, please see "Rules of the Name 2" below.

Rules of the Name 2: Chinese and Korean names are generally Romanized into three names, starting with surname last and given name second. (Chinese actress Cheng Pei-pei and Korean actress Lee Tso-nam.) To eliminate redundancy, alias combinations with the surname last or first, differing ways of uppercase and lowercase letters, and with or without hyphens, if the Romanized lettering are all similar, then only one alias name will be listed in standardized format. So Cheng Pei-Pei, Cheng Pei-pei, Pei Pei Cheng, Pei-Pei Cheng; and Pei-pei Cheng will be listed as Cheng Pei-pei.

For Chinese actors, directors and fight choreographers, alias names will also include known credits in a film of the Romanized names of the varying dialects. Therefore:

Lee, Danny: Li Hsiu-hsien / Li Hsiu-Hsien / Li Hsiu Hsien / Li Hsiu-Shien / Li Hsui-Hsien / Lee Sau Yin / Danny Li Hsiu-Hsien / Danny Li Sau-Yin / Li Xiu Xian / Li Xiu-xian / Xiuxian Li / Li Sau Yin / Li Sau-yin / Danny Lee Sau-Yin / Lee Sau-yin / Lee Sau-Yin / Lee Shou-Hsien / Lee Shou-hsien / Lee Hsiu-Hsien / Lee Hsiu-hsien / Lee Hsiu Hsien / Lee Siu-Yin / Danny S. Y. Lee.

. . . becomes . . .

Lee Danny: Li Hsiu-hsien / Li Hsiu-shien / Li Hsui-hsien / Danny Li Hsiu-hsien / Danny Li Sau-yin / Li Xiu-xian / Li Sau-yin / Danny Lee Sau-Yin / Lee Sau-yin / Lee Shou-hsien / Lee Hsiu-hsien / Lee Siu-yin / Danny S. Y. Lee.

13) Kung Fu, Shaolin, Translation Travesties and Martialogy Fun Stats: This is a "fun fact" section. Below is a "laundry" list of cool statistics that ultimately speak for themselves. This list, in many cases, also reflects how Chinese kung fu films (Hong Kong/Taiwan) have run amuck because distributors and title makers have gone barmy and bonkers, as we would say in England.

Of the 354 Chinese kung fu films that appear as martialogies in this book:

- 45 of the films have two Chinese titles.
- 3 of the films have three Chinese titles.
- 112 main English titles match the translated Chinese titles.
- 243 main English titles do not match the translated Chinese titles.
- 14 main English titles have "Shaolin" in them, but "Shaolin" (少林) is not in the Chinese titles.
- 4 main English titles don't have the word "Shaolin" in them, but the Chinese titles do.
- 11 main English and Chinese titles have the word "Shaolin" in it.
- 17 main English titles have "Kung Fu" in them, but "Kung Fu" (功夫) is not in the Chinese titles.
- 2 main English titles don't have the word "Kung Fu" in them, but the Chinese titles do.
- 6 main English and Chinese titles have the word "Kung Fu" in both titles.
- 45 alternative English titles have "Shaolin" in them, but "Shaolin" is not in the Chinese titles.
- 43 alternative English titles have "Kung Fu" in them, but "Kung Fu" is not in the Chinese titles.

Of the 1,245 Chinese kung fu films made during the 1970s, here is a list and number of times certain common words have been used in the original English titles and in the alternative titles:

Word	Original	Alternative
Kung Fu	82	131
Shaolin	60	108
Dragon	66	119
Tiger	58	52
Monkey	11	21
Mantis	7	11
Crane	4	10
Snake	21	24
Eagle	12	25
Big	17	9
Black	17	24
Boxer	34	44
Blood	16	32
Bruce	26	54
Chinese	23	18
Crazy	11	2
Deadly	14	33
Fist	48	113
Hero	48	39
Invincible	21	15
Iron	27	36
Magnificent	11	12
Master	26	54
Ninja	4	20
Revenge	17	23
Return	9	13
Sword	65	39
Young	11	10
One	20	18
Two	11	11
Three	6	10
Four	5	1
Five	9	10
Six	3	2
Seven	5	12
Eight	8	7
Nine	2	4
Ten	4	1
Eighteen	8	24
Thirty Six	6	3

The most popular English word found in the original English and alternative titles are "Kung Fu" followed by "Dragon" (also the most popular animal word). In terms of the next 18 subsequent most popular words found in the original English titles in descending order, they are the following: Sword; Shaolin; Tiger; Fist; Hero; Boxer; Iron; Master; Bruce; Chinese; Snake; Invincible; One, the most often used number; Big; Black, the most often used color; Blood; Deadly; and Two. In terms of the next 18 subsequent most popular words found in the alternative English titles in descending order, they are the following: Fist; Shaolin; Master; Bruce; Tiger; Boxer; Hero; Sword; Iron; Deadly; Blood; Eagle; Snake; Eighteen, the most often used number; Revenge; Black, the most often used color; Monkey; and Ninja.

For the six Japanese *Lone Wolf and Cub* films, there are **41** alternative titles. *Good Guys Wear Black* has the minimum fight time allowed for this book: **1m 55s**. *Beach of the War Gods* has the longest single fight scene: **25m 43s**. *The Cavalier* and *Shaolin Rescuers* had the most number of fights: **45**.

Trivia: Which of the following eight films had the greatest amount of screen time devoted to martial arts, in other words the most martial arts for the buck? *Secret Rivals*; *Master of the Flying Guillotine*; *The Magnificent*; *Kung Fu vs. Yoga*; *Goose Boxer*; *Fearless Hyena*; *Dance of Death* and *Enter the Game of Death*. Hint: They all have more than 50 percent of the film devoted to kung fu.

Trivia: Which of the following six films had the greatest amount of screen time devoted to kung fu training sequences? *Snake in the Eagle's Shadow*; *Shaolin Temple*; *Invincible Shaolin*; *The 36th Chamber of Shaolin*; *Executioners From Shaolin* or *Mad Monkey Kung Fu*.

14) Spellings: Spellings of many martial arts' names and other English romanized spellings of foreign terms are in line with Black Belt's format of spelling. For example BB's format for the spelling of the Indian martial art is *kilaripayit*, where other existing spellings of the art are *kalaripayat*, *kalari payatta* and *kalari payatt*.

Some Chinese words are written in old romanization with today's standard romanization in parentheses afterwords. For example, chi (qi) and chi gong (qigong).

Also, the Chinese people are made up of five distinct races—the Han, or the "real" Chinese; the Man or the Manchus; the Mong, or the Mongolians; the Hui, or the Muslims; and the Tsang, or the Tibetans. Many martialogies delineate which Chinese race a character belongs to as part of the story setup. Knowing the ethnicity of the characters tells the audiences why certain characters are good, bad, friends or enemies. Today, the contemporary Chinese government recognizes an additional 55 ethnic groups in China.

15) Leaps of Faith: Two major questions that may come to mind: Besides based on availability, how did I decide which films to write a martialogy on? Plus, if I haven't seen a film, how do I know that it has martial arts in it and thus included the film in the *Complete Martial Arts Film Reference List by Country* section? For the first question, please see the martialogy for *Good Guys Wear Black*. The second question's answer is, for the most part, a leap of faith.

When it came to Hong Kong/Taiwan, South Korean and Japanese films, if I found a listing that included a fight choreographer—or anything related such as fight instructor, stunt coordinator, fight instructor, etc.—I would include that in the reference list, regardless of whether the genres were horror, science fiction, drama, erotic, *huang mei* opera, pinky violence, Yakuza, gambling, period piece, war or comedy. Most Yakuza films I watched (including contemporary ones) had some martial arts action in it, where the fights often times used *tanto* (knife or dagger), knives or *shoto* (short swords; *wakizashi* or *kodachi*). Therefore, all Yakuza genre film listings that I could find are on the list, except for four of the five *Battles Without Honor and Humanity* series. Although Amitabh Bachchan was the golden-boy action star in Indian action films of the 1970s, films listed for India were based on the pedigree of India's more well-known thrill directors (or anything related) such as A. Mansoor, S. Azim, Mohan, Mohammed Ali, Nishan Singh, Veeru Devgun, M.S. Dass or Ravi Khanna. Their action sequences were always dwarfed by the song and dance choreography of these films, but not in this book. One of Turkey's all-time greatest cinematic martial arts action heroes was Cuneyt Arkin, so any film he starred in during the 1970s was included in the list. Philippine action films that starred Roberto Gonzales, Eddie Garcia, Vic Vargas and Roland Dantes, or were directed by Armando A. Herrara, Eddie Romero, Jose Pepe Wenceslao or Jun Gallardo, were also included on the list.

If I ever get to do *The Ultimate Guide to the Martial Arts Movie of the 1980s*, *1990s* and/or *2000s*, I will be able to use my name as one of those leaps of faith, which to me would be jumping to the right conclusion.

Just like writing, watching films must be seeped in passion. As previously mentioned, I have seen about 5,000 martial arts films, with representative movies from about 50 countries and films dating back to the 1920s when the genre began. So when you watch martial arts films and look at the actors' faces, reflect on the fact that more than 105 years of martial arts cinema history is staring back at you. Like writing this book, watching martial arts movies is an intensely spiritual and awe-inducing experience for me. Thanks for reading and may the chi (qi) be with you.

ADVENTURE, THE

狂風沙 (1972—Taiwan) **87m. KFI: Shan Mao. NOT/LOT: None; NOF/LOF: 7/ 17m 3s.** D: Li Su. C: Jimmy Wong Yu, Tian Ye, Paul Chang Chung, Li Xiang, Lei Jun, Xie Han, Shan Mao.

The heroically exaggerated punishment dished out on actor Jimmy Wong Yu at the end of *Golden Swallow* (1968) is peanuts compared to the well-orchestrated, emotional and bloody finale of *The Adventure* with its spurts of arterial magma more riveting than the number of rivets on a Manhattan skyscraper.

From the gritty and highly ambient opening of a lone knight-errant coursing over a desolate sand-stormed panorama, we bear witness to the tight-lipped Ti Si-guan (Jimmy Wong Yu) mourning the decade-old massacre at Seven Willows in which his good friend Two Gun Lo and the Brothers of the Six Union were gunned down, sliced up and killed by the ruthless vagabond Xiao Chu (Tian Ye) and his band of mercenaries. Rumors abound that Xiao Chu and some unknown traitor are planning to wipe out the families of the current Six Union leaders and take over Man Ke mansion. Ti vows to unearth the traitor and bury Xiao.

The showdown between Ti and Xiao is a marvelous *mano a mano* rendition that combines the intensity of a samurai classic, the rustic cool of a *High Noon* gunfight, and the hot flair of a Chinese martial arts duel. And like in *High Noon*, the showdown is soaked with enduring long shots similar to the classic gunfighter walk wherein the adversaries slowly move toward each other. Then BAM! The fight starts with guns blasting, knives gouging and climaxes with fists and feet tearing.

But it is the movie's big finale that will bludgeon your brain into submissive awe. Even after Ti gets both his eyes gouged out by a blade when he's accused of being a traitor, he still takes on the real one. The blind Ti faces the true traitor who is armed with a razor-sharp knife that slices deeply into Ti's flesh an unrelenting 23 times … before the final deathblow for one of them is dealt.

The carefully picked soundtrack truly adds to the film's overall mood. It also adds to Jimmy Wong Yu's staccato fight rhythm in which he looks like he's slightly jumping up and down between high-and-low strike attacks even though he's still rooted to the ground.

Titleography: *Iron Fist Adventure*; *Iron Fist Adventures*; *Adventure Sandstorm*. Translation—*The Incredible Sandstorm*. *The Adventure* is a somewhat generic word in several of the English titles, but ultimately it fits the film's mood. Like the sandstorm at the beginning of the picture, the film has a gritty feel about it. **MA Percentage: 19.6%**

ADVENTURES OF EMPEROR CHIEN LUNG, THE

乾隆下江南 (1977—Hong Kong) **100m. FI: Tang Chia, Huang Pei-ji. NOT/LOT: 1/ 2m 16s; NOF/LOF: 2/ 3m 43s.** D: Li Han-hsiang. C: Liu Yong, Wang Yu, Ching Miao, Li Kun.

One of the famous legends told about the kung fu emperor Chien Lung was that he secretly visited the area of Chiang Nan in southern China six times dressed as a commoner because he wanted to blend in and learn what his subjects thought about him. In this way, Chien Lung was similar to King Richard I (1157-1199), better known as Richard the Lionheart. Although he only spent six months of his reign on British soil—otherwise, he was off fighting in the Christian Crusades—Richard did don peasant clothes six times to walk among his subjects. Six months in England and six secret visits by Chien Lung—that's something for those who like numerology to think about.

The Adventures of Emperor Chien Lung is the second of four Shaw Brothers films that star Liu Yong, who also played the character Tony in Bruce Lee's *Way of the Dragon* (1972). In this movie, Yong plays Emperor Chien Lung who, on another one of his excursions, wants to understand the subculture, if you will, of tea.

The film starts with an in-depth discussion of Chien Lung's life as a child, his love for literature and his fascination with collecting things like snuff bottles. It is shot like one of those historical re-enactment stories one can see on The History Channel. Although it is not mentioned in the film that Chien Lung was known as the kung fu emperor, the movie shows how he learned to defend himself while growing up in the cold Mulan lands of Heilongjiang province in the most northeastern part of China. As a young teen, he won the favor of his grandfather, Emperor Kang Xi (1654-1722), the third emperor of the Ching Dynasty (and second Ching emperor to rule all of China) when Chien Lung saved him from a ferocious black bear during a hunting trip. Of course in this film, the attacker is a dude dressed in a bear suit who looks a lot like the bear on *The Andy Williams Show* (1969). The film then flows into a scene that shows Chien

Lung enjoying a battle of wits between his two top advisers.

But the crux of the film is Chien Lung's extreme interest in understanding the social importance and daily routines that revolve around the various kinds and noted teas of Chiang Nan. The disguised emperor hooks up with a waiter who is extremely patient with Chien Lung's tea ignorance. He also runs into Zhou Ri-ching (Wang Yu), who loves to read literature and practice martial arts, which makes him someone Chien Lung can connect with. Then Chien Lung learns that local Ching officials are raising exorbitant taxes against the people while claiming to do so in the name of the emperor. This leads to a fun "oh shit!" moment in the film when Chien Lung reveals himself as the emperor and the corrupt officials have to eat humble pie. In good-guy land, the waiter and Zhou are rewarded and become part of Chien Lung's procession because Chien Lung values the waiter's honesty and respects Zhou's love for martial arts and literature.

During the only fight in the film, Chien Lung cheers for Zhou when the young lit-lover fights the bumbling Manchu soldiers. When things get unfair, Chien Lung is captured by the emotion of the moment and gleefully joins in the fray. Compared to the first Shaw Brothers Chien Lung film, *Emperor Chien Lung*, the fights are much better staged because they flow more smoothly and the moves are less hesitant looking. But this martial artist's eye notices that Liu Yong still looks uncomfortable when fighting because he leans forward at the waist. If he kept his back straight, the scene would look classier— like he really was the kung fu emperor and not an actor trying to look like one.

Titleography: As of this writing, no alternative titles could be found. Translation—*Chien Lung's Visit Down to Southern China*. The titles pretty much tell it all. **MA Percentage: 5.98%** SHAW BROTHERS

ALL MEN ARE BROTHERS

蕩寇誌 (1975—Hong Kong) **101m. FI: Liu Chia-liang, Liu Chia-rong, Chan Chuen, Tang Chia. NOT/LOT: None; NOF/LOF: 38/ 34m 40s.** D: Chang Cheh, Wu Ma. C: David Chiang, Fan Mei-sheng, Chen Kuan-tai, Wong Ching, Danny Lee, Wang Guang-yu, Yu Fung, Ti Lung, Bolo Yeung, Ku Feng, Tong Lin, Zhu Mu, Chin Feng, Michael Chan, Tetsuro Tanba.

Three years after the sparkling success of *The Water Margin*, director Chang Cheh and many of the film's original stars reprised their roles and revisited this classic tale to complete the story in a sequel that was more bloody, sad and violent than the first.

All Men Are Brothers is the title given by American author Pearl S. Buck to her English translation of one of China's most enduring *wuxia* novels *Shui Hu Zhuan*.

(See *The Water Margin*.) The historically based Chinese novel focused on a group of 108 Heroes who called themselves a "gallant fraternity" and lived in the Liang Shan (Mountain) Marshes. Founded by Chao Gai, they defiantly opposed corrupt officials during the final years of the North Song Dynasty (A.D. 907-960).

The novel is a yarn that truly embraces and romanticizes the spirit of the world of Jiang Hu. (Translated, Jiang Hu means "rivers and lakes.") This alternative society is made up of beggars, martial heroes, martial arts villains and outcasts who coexisted with normal society but lived by their own laws, systems of brotherhood and morality code of ethics. The 108 Heroes (105 men and three women) were known as the Stars of Destiny, and in the book, they are broken down into the 36 Heavenly Spirits and the 72 Earthly Friends, reflecting the *yin-yang* philosophical view that there must be balance between heaven and earth. While many of these heroes play a minor role in *The Water Margin* and this film, they are critical in other parts of the original story.

The movie begins with the emperor of China when he hears a beautiful *pipa* (a Chinese instrument that's similar to a lute) from behind a curtain. He emotionally cries out that such a player must be a righteous and upright person. When he finds out the player is one of the outlawed 108 Heroes, Yen Ching (David Chiang), he is moved to give the Heroes a pardon, but only if they can help him eliminate the armies of Fang La (Zhu Mu), who is trying to usurp the emperor while taking control of many southern territories. Yen Ching agrees that he and the other 107 Heroes will do it.

With the mission accepted, the leaders of the 108 Heroes hatch a plan to attack Fang La's stronghold at Hang Chow. Because the city has 10 gates, four of which are blocked by sea and coastline, the 108 Heroes plan to open the two least-guarded water gates. Because doing this is all about timing, seven heroes—Yen Ching, Li Kuei (Fan Mei-sheng), Shih Hsiu (Wong Ching), Shi Jin (Chen Kuan-tai), Chang Sun (Danny Lee), Zhang Qing (Wang Guang-yu) and his wife Sun (Yu Fung)—are chosen to infiltrate the city and figure out a strategy to attack from the inside. While the other six heroes die heroic and bloody deaths, Yen Ching (he's the seventh hero) runs into the famous Chinese wrestler General Si Xing-fang (Bolo Yeung) and his men. Si Xing-fang cannot pass up the opportunity to challenge Yen Ching to a wrestling match. He declares that if Yen Ching wins, he can go free. But if he loses, then death.

After winning, Yen Ching speeds back to Liang Shan to be greeted by his bosom buddy Wu Song (Ti Lung) with the villain Fang La and his men in pursuit. In a final blaze of 108-Hero glory, Yen Ching and the Liang Shan Bandits truly become heroes because they get their pardons from the emperor. But it comes at a great expense because the heroes no longer number 108.

Chang Cheh elicits varying emotions of heroic loss as revealed by either the 108 Heroes' overt defiance or memorable deaths. Big-mouth Li Kuei is the most amusing of the 108 Heroes, especially while he tornadoes his axes through fields of enemies constantly screaming, "Li Kuei is here!" Actor Chen Kuan-tai as Shi Jin has the most heroic postures and facial expressions—his taut, sullen

face is accentuated even more by the dragon tattoos on his torso. With his body soaked death red from wounds gouged by Fang La's lackeys that continue to attack, Shi Jin wipes the blood away from his chest to expose his dragon tattoo, then dies. It is a grand gesture of defiance. Chang Cheh also creates a great moment for the sole female who infiltrates the city. With her back against a wall, Sun uses it for protection as she slides along it toward the camera, slashing and hacking without oodles of gushing blood. Her dramatic face glares powerfully, showing the strength of a female heroine who is worthy to be one of the 108 Heroes. And of course, Chang Cheh includes that touching brotherhood between actors Ti Lung and David Chiang—two of his all-time favorite lads—as the final twinkle for Yen Ching is the signatory sound bite of "chica-chica-chaaa."

Titleography: *Seven Soldiers of Kung Fu*; *7 Soldiers of Kung Fu*; *Seven Blows of the Dragon II*; *7 Blows of the Dragon II*; *Seven Kung Fu Assassins*; *The Story of Punishment*; *Water Margin 2*; *108 Heroes*. Translation—*The Record of Eliminating the Bandits*. See above martialogy and *Water Margin's* martialogy. The *Seven* in the titles refer to the seven heroes who infiltrate Hang Chow: Li, Shih, Shi, Chang, Zhang, Sun and Yen Ching. The Chinese title refers to the record or story of the death of the 108 Heroes. **MA Percentage: 34.32%** SHAW BROTHERS

AMBITIOUS, THE

Bakumatsu (1970—Japan) **120m. FI: Uncredited. NOT/LOT: 1/ 33s; NOF/ LOF: 4/ 7m 4s.** D: Daisuke Ito. C: Kinnosuke Nakamura, Toshiro Mifune, Keiju Kobayashi, Tatsuya Nakadai, Shintaro Nakaoka, Sayuri Yoshinaga, Katsuo Nakamura, Noboru Nakaya, Eitaro Matsuyama, Shigeru Koyama, Shinsuke Mikimoto.

The Japanese title of this film refers to the Bakumatsu, the final years of the Tokugawa or Edo era (1853-1867). During this time, the Tokugawa shogunate and the age of the samurai came to a screeching halt, and Japan ended its isolationist policy. The shogunate forces, headed by the Shinsengumi, a group of *ronin* created to protect the shogun (see *Shinsengumi* for details), vied with the imperial forces for supreme power. Ultimately, Tokugawa shogun Yoshinobu relinquished power to Emperor Komei. After Komei's sudden death, Emperor Mejii ascended to the throne, thus beginning the Meiji Restoration. The English title of this film refers to the ambitions of certain individuals during the Bakumatsu, particularly those of the historically based character of Ryoma Sakamoto.

The Ambitious stars Kinnosuke Nakamura, Shigeru Koyama, Toshiro Mifune and Tatsuya Nakadai as Shinsengumi members Ryoma Sakamoto, Kaishu Katsu, Shojiro Goto and Shintaro Nakaoka. The main story is about Ryoma's rise, accomplishments and fall during the Bakumatsu. As with most Japanese samurai films, the fights are few and far between. This film features only seven minutes of swordplay. The final skirmish offers plenty of blood and gore, like when Ryoma, as the master of *hokushin itto-ryu*, wields his sword with his left hand after his right arm is injured. Overall, the action in the film has lots of scuffling, or "sword wrestling." The actors lock blades and grimace, grunt and push at each other. To make the clashes more dynamic, the director uses eye-catching visual elements. For example, a ceiling light sways back and forth on an electric wire, adding motion to the final fight that would otherwise look static.

Otherwise, the movie follows the exploits of the father of the Imperial Japanese Navy: Ryoma Sakamoto. As happened in real life, after the arrival of Commodore Matthew Perry's "Black Ships" in Japan, Ryoma is ordered by his feudal lord, Takechi Hanpieta, to assassinate Kaishu Katsu, an officer in the shogun's navy, but Katsu dissuades him. Katsu explains to Ryoma that it is futile for Japan to resist and isolate itself from Western incursion. He also tells Ryoma that Japan needs to learn from the West in order to deal with it, and Ryoma agrees and decides to become Katsu's assistant. Ryoma goes on to successfully negotiate an alliance between the rival Choshu and Satsuma clans—these two clans were and will be instrumental in toppling the Tokugawa shogunate. The Satsuma clan then helps Ryoma create a private navy and trading company, which later becomes known as Kaientai, Japan's first modern corporation and the precursor to Mitsubishi. But after the Choshu clan defeats the Tokugawa army, Ryoma and his friend Shojiro Goto persuade shogun Yoshinobu to peacefully resign and hand over political power to Emperor Komei. The

film ends when Ryoma and his good friend Shintaro Nakaoka are assassinated by the Shinsengumi on Ryoma's birthday, November 15, 1867.

Titleography: As of this writing, no alternative titles could be found. **MA Percentage: 6.35%**

AMBUSH

埋伏 (1972—Hong Kong) 94m. FI: Xu Er-niu. NOT/LOT: None; NOF/LOF: 18/ 24m 59s. D: Ho Meng-hua. C: Li Ching, Zhao Xiong, Yang Chi-ching, Wang Xia, Dean Shek.

It is *Monty Python and the Holy Grail* meets Miguel de Cervantes' *Don Quixote* without the humor and ass (donkey). This film is about a run-of-the-windmill man accused of robbery and then accused of being the master behind a murder plot. Our protagonist, constable Wang Chao-fan (Zhao Xiong), must find the culprits before the law finds him. A better title for this film would actually have been *Framed*.

One thing that you may not know about martial arts films is that oftentimes the stories and the fights are shot in sequential order of the scripts. This is why the fights in kung fu films progressively get better as the plots move along. This is especially advantageous when the actors do not know martial arts, but they get used to each other and the fighting instructors and are able to get into some sort of choreographic rhythm. *Ambush* is a prime example of a film in which the fights not only get better as the film moves along but also the level of bizarreness sweeps you off your feet like a broom pushing tons of dust on a windy day.

Still from *Ambush* © Celestial Pictures Ltd. All rights reserved.

Because of the impressive novelty of the teahouse/inn fight scene in *Come Drink With Me* (1966), it quickly became a standard in Chinese kung fu films, and noted directors scrambled to add their own visual and emotional take to it. Usually, the obvious differences would be the speed of the fight as well as the number of attackers.

Ambush's fight instructor Xu Er-niu—who worked with and was heavily influenced by Han Ying-chieh, the fight instructor from *Come Drink With Me*—pays homage to his teacher with a rousing one-against-50 teahouse super fracas. Later on, he ups the ante—and keeps the odds the same—with a barmy two against 100. What sells these fights is a lot of motion on the set: Stuntmen run here and there while lead actor Zhao Xiong, who knows no martial arts, windmills his swords with brazen and reckless abandonment. He mows down the enemy who listens to his commands to die, but they can't hear him anymore because they are all not alive. As the others scream and the blood squirts, it is over for those wretched warriors who have fallen to the dirt.

The little-used windmill set on the Shaw Brothers lot was prominently featured in this film to create a weird combination of Cervantes' classic windmill fight from *Don Quixote* with the infamous Black Knight vs. King Arthur in *Monty Python and the Holy Grail*. The difference here is that the fight is not for laughs.

The villain (played by Yang Chi-ching) and the hero battle each other on the wings of the windmill as it spins around, creating a gruesome bloodletting of disarmament. Wow, man.

Titleography: As of this writing, no alternative titles could be found. Translation—*Ambush*. It is indeed an *Ambush* for the hero. **MA Percentage: 26.58%** SHAW BROTHERS

AMSTERDAM CONNECTION

荷蘭賭人頭 (1978—Hong Kong) 90m. FI: Bai Biao, Bolo Yeung, Huang Ha. NOT/LOT: None; NOF/LOF: 10/ 12m 18s. D: Fan Mei-sheng, Lo Ke. C: Chen Hsing, Bai Biao, Mi Lan, Bolo Yeung, Fan Mei-sheng, Huang Yuan-shen.

Based on a true story in Amsterdam's Chinatown, *Amsterdam Connection* goes to show that no matter how good a gambler you are, one day your luck will run out.

Gambling Triad bosses Big Louie (Bolo Yeung) and Chui Tung (Fan Mei-sheng) vie for the "goods" from Mr. Hong (Chen Hsing). Each tries to play the other and come across as innocent in the eyes of the Dutch police. At the same time, Louie's right-hand man Ah Bun (Bai Biao) and Chui's right-hand man Wing (Huang Yuan-shen), who used to be buddies, get torn apart when each one tries to woo the same woman. (She eventually chooses Wing.)

One of the many problems with this film is that there are no good guys, so you have no idea who to cheer for. It is not until the last 20 minutes that some of the characters decide to turn good and take down their Triad bosses.

The opening fight takes place in a *wing chun* kung fu school in Hong Kong, but it just does not look right having big, tense, biceps-bulging Bolo be the *sifu* of an art partially based on relaxation. His sticking-hand sensitivity drills, which should be relaxed and fluid, look more like tense bear-wrestling fists. The fights are somewhat funny because all the characters wear too-small, three-piece, John Travolta-like disco clothes while flailing their arms like windmills and kicking like a bunch of Kick'Em Stick'Em Robots, my mental martial arts version of the 1970s popular Rock'Em Sock'Em Robots.

There is one intriguing aspect about the film. When bosses Big Louie and Chui Tung call for peace talks, we are introduced to the Chinese Triad world of hand signs and handshakes, wherein the signs you flash show who you know and where you are in the hierarchy. And in real life, flashing a certain hand sign at the right time can save your life or get you killed.

Titleography: As of this writing, no alternative titles could be found. Translation—*Holland Gambling the Human Head*. This film was shot in Amsterdam, France and Hong Kong, and because the titles of *The Chinese Connection* and *The French Connection* were already used, that left the makers with Amsterdam. The film is also about opposing gambling dens with one delving into prostitutes trafficking, in which each prostitute is considered a head, as in head count. **MA Percentage: 13.67%**

ANGRY GUEST, THE

惡客 (1972—Hong Kong) 89m. FI: Liu Chia-liang, Tang Chia. NOT/LOT: 6/ 3m 4s; NOF/LOF: 24/ 12m 3s. D: Chang Cheh. C: David Chiang, Ti Lung, Ching Li, Yasuaki Kurata, Fong Yan-ji, Chen Hsing, Bolo Yeung, Jie Yuen, Chang Cheh.

The Angry Guest, a direct sequel to *Duel of Fist* (see martialogy), revisits the lives of our heroes Wen Lieh (Ti Lung) and Fan Ke (David Chiang), two brothers who once were lost but now are found. (See *Duel of Fist*.) They were also blind, but eventually they do see. In fact, it is from the amazing grace of their brotherhood that they recover from losing sight of their future and those that defy or cheat them.

Chiang Ren (Chen Hsing), the Thai kickboxing fight fixer and big gang boss of Bangkok, whose leg was mangled by Wen and Fan in *Duel of Fist*, escapes from Thai prison only to be demoted by his superior, Boss Yamaguchi (Chang Cheh). With a limp in his leg and a pain with a cane, Chiang heads to Hong Kong to dish out his own version of amazing un-grace: to send the brothers all the way to Dante's Inferno, but in the end, it is he who becomes hell bound. Meanwhile, Boss Yamaguchi also fumes over Wen and Fan's antics in Thailand

and sends his luscious lad and lass hit dyad, the karate kicking Katsu (Yasuaki Kurata) and judo-flipping Akiko (Fong Yan-ji), to Thailand. He gives them orders to kill Wen's mother and kidnap his girlfriend, Yu Lan (Ching Li), bring Yu Lan to Japan, then blackmail Fan and Wen into working for him. Yet back in Japan, the plan backfires because Akiko has a yen for Fan and does what she can to help them flee from Japan, and Katsu is told to pursue them but doesn't realize he will end up like fodder at the zoo.

There are two bizarre shots in this film, which both occur in the final fight at Fan's construction site. One reeks of the 1985 MTV video hit *Tough Enough* by the Fabulous Thunderbirds. If you have seen the video and this film, to use Master Kan's catchphrase to Kwai Chang Caine in *Kung Fu* the TV series, "Then you will know." During the first unedited shot, director Chang Cheh pans the camera to the left to show 19 men, one by one, violently strip off their jackets and toss them to the ground with angry machismo. In the second sequence, when Katsu fights Fan's construction employees, the karate hit man wears a headband and the bottom of his unbuttoned shirt tied in a knot just above his bellybutton. It's like *I Dream of Jeannie* meets Olivia Newton-John in her music video *Physical*.

Of nostalgic value, this film features a rare cameo from director Chang Cheh as Boss Yamaguchi. His only other on-screen time can be found in *The Call Girls* (1977), which is not a martial arts film.

Many Western film reviewers often lament that someone as scrawny as David Chiang became popular because he looks so weak compared to other martial arts stars. Furthermore, his early kung fu fight postures appear diluted and insipid. But before becoming one of Shaw Brothers' leading men, he was a highly sought-after stuntman that would do anything to be on camera. Well-known for doing awkward falls and landings, Chiang earned the nickname "Elastic Double." Also, when he was ultra-popular, Chiang's physical stature was similar to the average Chinese male of the time, which must have been uplifting to the average "Zhou" or "Joe" to see someone so lithe and thin exuding pure fighting physicality.

Titleography: *The Annoyed Guest*. Translation—*Vicious Guest*. The *Guest* and his emotional content is Ti Lung's character of Wen Lieh. Each title fits his persona and his driving force.
MA Percentage: 16.99% SHAW BROTHERS

ANONYMOUS HEROES, THE

無名英雄 (1971—Hong Kong) 100m. FI: Liu Chia-liang, Tang Chia, Yuen Cheung-yan. NOT/LOT: None; NOF/LOF: 13/ 10m 31s. D: Chang Cheh. C: David Chiang, Ti Lung, Ching Li, Ku Feng, Ching Miao, Wang Chung, Chen Hsing, Zheng Lei.

In 1916, after the death of Yuan Shi-kai, the man who tried to become the last emperor of China and who strong-armed Sun Yat-sen out of being the president of the Republic of China (see *Five Tough Guys*), China plummeted into an era of war-

lordism. That ended in 1928 after Chiang Kai-shek's successful military campaign known as the Northern Expedition. The goals of Chiang's Kuomintang Party were to rid the country of three powerful warlords—Zhang Zuo-lin in Manchuria, Wu Pei-fu in the central plains and Sun Chuan-fang on the eastern seaboard—and unify China.

During this period, many of those who tried to quell the power of these warlords were anonymous heroes. Their names have been forgotten, but their successes are remembered. In this film set in this period of anarchy, Kuomintang loyalist Wan Tai (Ku Feng) recruits three rambunctious youths: thief Meng Kang (David Chiang), who beats up and steals from warlord soldiers to fund his brothel habit; fight-happy gambler Tieh (Ti Lung); and their friend Hung Yin-fung, also known as Pepper (Ching Li), the daughter of a ranking officer in warlord Marshall Chin's army. The plan is to steal 3,000 long-range rifles and 280,000 rounds from Chin and deliver them to troops loyal to unifying China. Because they are young and restless, they agree to take on Wan Tai's mission.

Acting lighthearted like they're in a Bob Hope-Bing Crosby road movie, the three friends weasel, fib and fast-talk their way through the warlord's upper-echelon commanding ranks. The jolly-wolly tone of the movie shifts to a rambling, Sam Peckinpah-esque shootout sort of flick when the three heroes bamboozle the warlord Chin, get the rifles, steal a train, become targets for every soldier loyal to Chin and have a major run-in with a violent crime boss (Chen Hsing). Of course, it's best to ignore the 1940s and '50s cars in this 1910s-era film.

When Bruce Lee wanted to pursue a film career in Hong Kong, he was first approached by Sir Run Run Shaw in 1971 and invited to visit the set of a non-*wuxia* film being shot at the Shaw Brothers studios by director Chang Cheh. The only non-wuxia film Chang made in Hong Kong that year was *The Anonymous Heroes*. Lee reportedly said to Shaw, "Is that all you have got?" That must have been quite a blow. Apparently, Lee considered Shaw Brothers' Iron Triangle—the nickname for actors Ti Lung and David Chiang and director Chang Cheh—to be a case of "three strikes, you're out." Lee was not impressed and ended up at Golden Harvest working for former Shaw executive Raymond Chow.

What Lee saw was not necessarily kung fu fighting so much as smash-'em, crash-'em choreography. The main in-studio fight in the film between David Chiang and Ti Lung involves their two characters destroying every piece of furniture in a small, ruined house. One strikes the other, who then flies back and crashes on or through something, or he picks up an object and whacks the other into next week with it. It is actually rather entertaining to see them body-roll and collide all over the place, and it might have been Chang Cheh's way of letting the audience see that his two new young stars loved romping around with stuntman craziness. Most of the other fights involve shootouts and bloody bayonet impalings. The film is also a rarity in that Chang's leading lady, Ching Li, who plays Pepper, has a relatively strong and almost equal role to the lead men. The soundtrack is also peppered with the overly pervasive refrain from the Marlon Brando film *The Chase* (1966), which also has a train scene like *Anonymous Heroes*.

Titleography: As of this writing, no alternative titles could be found. Translation—*Anonymous Heroes*. **MA Percentage: 10.52%** SHAW BROTHERS

APE GIRL

醉 猴 女 (1979—Taiwan) **81m. MAD: Wang Tai-lung. NOT/LOT: 3/ 5m 28s; NOF/LOF: 14/ 19m 57s. D:** Chen Zhi-hua. **C:** Chen Hsing, Lo Lieh, Miao Tian, Jin Feng-ling, Li Wen-tai.

You have got to love a film as barmy as this that does not even try to justify its storyline by explaining how a girl looks and acts like a chimpanzee in the forests of China. The bottom line is that she just exists, learns monkey-style kung fu from the elderly couple that found her as a chimp girl, and grows up to be a fighting ape woman bent on foiling emperor (Chen Hsing) in the name of saving the Ming Dynasty. It really is an astonishing "tail."

Ape-teen Ming Li-shi (Jin Feng-ling) asks her "mom" to turn her into a beautiful young lady so she can win the heart of the emperor. Although his name is not specifically mentioned, it's implied that it's Yong Zheng, as he becomes a Ching emperor by changing the official will of the recently deceased emperor. (See *Return of the 18 Bronzemen*.) The problem is that as the ape lass sits in a large vat of boiling magical herbs, her beauty blossoms more than any botanical wonder of the world. And as her hair sheds, she grows a long tail. Her father laments that his little Li-shi will suffer because now she will learn about human love, which may cause her heartbreak because it is often shallow.

Although actress Jin Feng-ling only did two films in her career—the other being *Iron Bridge Kung Fu* (1979)—her monkey kung fu performance and simian antics are not too bad. She rolls and flips around with ease among the nasty human kung fu generals and soldiers who are trying to kill her, all the while avoiding vicious attacks while grinning and snickering as if it were a game. It can be difficult to memorize fight sequences when the technique count goes beyond 10 moves per shot. This is why most American martial arts stars keep the fights simple and shoot only a few techniques per shot. They rely on the editing to make them look good. Imagine how hard it must have been to perform the fights with a certain lightheartedness when the temperature is above 100 degrees and your body is covered in fake fur. My hat goes off to the young lass jumping around in the monkey suit.

And speaking of women doing monkey martial arts, there is an Indonesian legend about a woman who created a form of monkey fighting. As the story goes, a young woman was doing her laundry down by the river and became so enamored by how a monkey evaded a snake attack that she returned home late. When her husband tried to beat her, she defended herself by using what she saw the monkey do against the snake, successfully thwarting his attacks. This is the foundation for the development of Indonesia's national martial art of *pentjak silat*.

Titleography: *Fighting Justice*; *Lady Iron Monkey*. Translations—*Drunken Monkey Woman* or *Girl*. Monkey girl is fighting for justice for the Mings against the Chings, and there is also a sequence in which she gets drunk to impress the emperor, but her fights do not revolve around drunken monkey kung fu. The film was shot when drunken boxing was popular because of Jackie Chan's *Drunken Master* (1978). Thus, *Drunken Monkey* is in the Chinese title. **MA Percentage: 31.38%**

ASSASSIN, THE

Yakuza Deka: Marifana Mitsubai Soshiki (1970—Japan) **86m. FI: Uncredited. NOT/LOT: None; NOF/LOF: 9/ 4m 43s. D:** Yukio Noda. **C:** Sonny Chiba, Fumio Watanabe, Jiro Chiba, Toshiaki Minami, Ryohei Uchida, Osman Yusuf, Koji Hio, King Stone.

How do you beat a drug rap in Japan? Beats me. Oh, right! Hide the dope in a drum. That's how Yakuza gangster Sudo (Koji Hio) of the Saiwa Organization brings drugs into Japan from his Hong Kong distributors. But the snare of undercover narcotics officer Hayata (Sonny Chiba) posing as Sudo's getaway driver and drumming up some trouble for the Yakuza gangs makes the Yakuza go bongos. Hayata's orders are to crash down on Sudo and a rival gang led by Boss Natsui, who is backed by the Chicago Mafia, like high hat cymbals by using his karate kicking feet to control the pedal's rhythm and beat. Yet before the music starts, Hayata becomes the bodyguard of Sudo's boss, Maruda. However, just as Sudo is warming up to his new pal Hayata, he learns that Hayata is an undercover cop, and things start to cool down between them. Hayata gets

captured and tortured by Natsui's gang but gets out because of a surprise save by one of Hayata's enemies. Bound by honor to destroy the Yakuza but bound by friendship to let one live, Hayata faces some heavy dilemmas. Yet the crescendo arrives only after the skinny karate man sings … kicks.

The fights in *The Assassin* are very simple, but they were meant to bring out Chiba's karate and gymnastic skills. (At one time, Chiba missed out on being a Japanese Olympic gymnast because of an injury.) The action scenes consist of simple karate-like sparring drills against stuntmen not trained enough to sell everything effectively. But then again, this was the first karate-stylized movie in Japan and something new for everyone, including Chiba.

Later in 1970, Chiba established his own training school for martial arts film actors, known as the Japan Action Club. Actors Sue Shihomi, Yasuaki Kurata, Hiroyuki Sanada and Chiba's brother Jiro became some of his prize pupils. Interesting as well, none of the characteristics that define Chiba as a martial arts actor appear in this film. There are no demonstrative faces, *sanchin*-style breathing sounds or contorted *shorinji kenpo* hand postures—his signature moves in his signature movie, *Street Fighter* (1974).

Titleography: *Yakuza Deka II*. Translation—*Yakuza Detective: Marijuana Black Market Group*. **MA Percentage: 5.48%**

ASSAULT OF FINAL RIVAL

奔 出 江湖路 (1978—Hong Kong) **87m. AD: Ken Yuen. NOT/LOT: 1/ 15s; NOF/LOF: 13/ 14m 52s. D:** Li Su. **C:** Wong Dao, Lin Yi-wa, Lung Fei, Li Long-yin, Susan Tsang Siu-san, Hui Man-yu.

With a Chinese twist on the Samson and Delilah parable, "Samson" learns, as all martial artists should but many do not, that you should not egotistically flaunt your kung fu skills for fame and fortune. Instead, the real power of kung fu comes from a clear mind and spiritual purity.

When the longhaired Chen Wai (Wong Dao) outshines everyone in the kung fu world, he becomes a threat to Ma Tien-po (Lung Fei, who also played Betty in the 2002 film *Kung Pow: Enter the Fist*) because as head of the Dragon Clan, Ma must also become the supreme leader of the kung fu world. Realizing that Chen's hurricane hair is the harbinger of his handiness and hardiness, Ma forces Chen's fiancee, Ah Ming (enter the Delilah; Lin Yi-wa), into cutting Chen's hair. If she doesn't, Ma will kill her mother. So to borrow the tune that's sung when the Cowardly Lion gets his haircut in *The Wizard of Oz*: Snip, snip here. Snip, snip there. In the merry old land of Jiang Hu. Chen's marriage goes down the drain and so does his kung fu.

And this is as funny as it gets. It seems that each actor throughout their kung fu film careers make a handful of films that you can just feel their hearts are not in it. Because of that, the fights come across as uninspiring and hackneyed. Elements are tossed together like a rotten salad with a dressing that tastes like dirty socks.

The dead giveaway for this sensibility is the final fight scene and how it compares to the rest of the film's fights. As I have seen on many a set when wrapping up a movie, actors get fed up, the production has run out of money, and it becomes more about finishing it up and covering one's losses than quality. The final sequence, which is a group of five fights, lasts a tad more than five minutes, and most of it is in slow motion. If it were shot at normal speed, this 87-minute film would barely have had 10 minutes of fights. On the positive front, it is interesting that before protagonist Chen's hair being cut, actor Wong Dao does a lot of kicking combinations during his battles. Yet after the hair is cut, there is barely a kick for the rest of the film. Also, two main fighting characters who appear at the film's end merely watch Chen fight, then walk away without lifting a foot.

Titleography: As of this writing, no alternative titles could be found. Translation—*Sprinting Out of the Jiang Hu Road*. Chen is the final rival in the way of Ma's plans to become the head of Jiang Hu, so he sends five fighters to assault him. The Chinese title refers to the fact that Chen is aware that he has become a target and leaves the world or road of Jiang Hu to hide in a Buddhist temple. **MA Percentage: 17.38%**

AVENGER, THE

仇 (1972—Hong Kong) **74m. KFI: Wen Min-xiong. NOT/LOT: 2/ 1m 12s; NOF/LOF: 9/ 22m 20s. D:** Florence Yu Fung-chi. **C:** Chia Ling, Peter Yang Kwan, Lee Ying, Ma Chang, Cai Hong, Xue Han, Lan Yun.

With the success of *The Boxer From Shantung* earlier in 1972 (eee martialogy), the Taiwanese kung fu film industry's response to the Shaw Brothers' true story of Ma Yong-zhen was *Brave Girl Boxer in Shanghai*. (See martialogy.) Doris Long Chun-er starred as Ma Yong-zhen's sister Ma Su-zhen in *Brave Girl Boxer*, who comes from Shantung to Shanghai to find her brother's killer. In *The Avenger*, which opens with the theme music from *Shaft*, the exquisite Chia Ling makes her film debut in a remake of *Brave Girl Boxer* playing Ma Su-zhen looking for the gangsters that killed her brother. Chia enters the kung fu genre like a bat out of hell on a freakazoid chopper while high on Meat Loaf. She also throws down a groovy gauntlet in front of female kung fu stars Angela Mao Ying and Doris Long Chun-er's challenge to become the next kung fu screen queen after Cheng Pei-pei. In what has to be the most men killed by any kung fu female star in any film in the history of martial arts cinema, maybe even in film history, the final fight is as mesmerizing as it is relentless. For nine-and-a-half minutes straight, Chia Ling is surrounded by knife-wielding warriors and hatchet men trying to feed-frenzy her into oblivion. Ultimately, it is the lady who axes the questions, and when they try to lie and cheat her, she becomes the cheetah and makes them lie on the ground.

In one of his best and final efforts as a fight choreographer in film, Wen Min-xiong uses 1960s, old-school fight choreography in this movie. Yet he shoots the fights with tight camera angles to create a strained sense of pugilistic claustrophobia that gives the feeling that Ma Su-zhen and Chia Ling are literally fighting for their lives. In the Chinese opera style of stage combat choreography and this being Chia's first kung fu film, it was fitting to not disrupt Chia's expectations of what the fight might look and feel like. Thus the use of 1960s choreography in which baddies would form tight circles around the hero and the nonattackers would excessively move to add motion and commotion to the fight. Chia was then instructed to throw nonstop kicks and punches in all directions while spinning around like a female Olympic skater—except doing it with knives and hatchets in hand.

One of my greatest regrets in working on Chinese kung fu films and TV shows back in the late 1970s is that at the time, I knew very little about the rich history of these filmmakers and stars and the stuff they had done. In my first kung fu film, Chia Ling was the lead actress, spoke great English, and although we spoke about kung fu films, martial arts and opera training, if I had known what I knew now, I would have asked much, much more. Of even greater note, the director of this film is a woman, a rarity during any era of kung fu cinema time … fight on sister.

Titleography: *Queen Boxer*; *Kung Fu Queen*. Translation—*Feud*. Each title fits the noir of the movie. **MA Percentage: 31.8%**

AVENGING EAGLE, THE

冷血十三鷹 (1978—Hong Kong) **93m. FI: Tang Chia, Huang Pei-chi. NOT/LOT: 1/ 33s; NOF/LOF: 19/ 34m 6s. D:** Sun Chung. **C:** Ti Lung, Alexander Fu Sheng, Ku Feng, Johnny Wang Lung-wei, Yuen Bing, Dick Wei, Eddy Koh, Shih Szu.

Based on a kung fu novel, *The Avenging Eagle* features 13 assassins known as the Eagles who are members of the ruthless Iron Boat Clan. Each Eagle is the master of a savage weapon, and their 13 slaying skills means bad luck for all who stand in their way. But for one of the 13, Chi Ming-sing (Ti Lung), who is master of the three-sectional staff, his luck has run out. Chi's gusto for causing death waivers when his 12 Eagle brothers kill the woman he loves and forces him to execute a pregnant woman. Now on the lam, Chi flees from the pursuing talons of his former fellows, who are led by Yu Xi-hong (Ku Feng). Dehydrated and almost dead, Chi is befriended by a lone warrior, Chao Yi-fan (Alexander Fu Sheng). But by sharing each other's troubled dark pasts, they see the line between friend and foe blur, especially as their intertwined destinies come to a head because eventually only one can become the Avenging Eagle.

Inevitably, when a great Shaw Brothers kung fu masterpiece blankets the silver screen with pure gold, one would expect to see Chang Cheh's name attached as the director. But *The Avenging Eagle* is directed by Sun Chung, the first Hong Kong director to use the steadicam during a fight scene, and this film is nothing like a Chang product. Sun's views on love and the hero are different from Chang's, and this film brings that out. Chi is a badass killer but becomes a man with feeling, and that comes from the kindness of a woman who tells him that she is willing to ignore his past (as should he). She tells him that it is the action of his present and future that will essentially be the judge of who he is.

Chi and Chao are also not your typical *wuxia* heroes like in Chang Cheh's wandering knight-errant films. In this movie, to be a loner is not a goal, and finding love and female companionship is worth dying for. Chi also gets to know his opponent Chao, which embodies the central tenet of *The Art of War* by Sun Tzu's (pronounced "Soo-in Zi"): By knowing yourself and your enemy, there is no fear in battle. Adding in a touch of revenge for the loss of a wife makes for some pious payback. Also, Sun Chung intelligently weaves in a *yin-yang* philosophy by having Chi run away from his enemy while Chao runs toward his, thus achieving a balance because, as it turns out, they have the same enemy.

Sun uses elaborate slow-motion effects and freeze-frame furor to accentuate martial technique and emotional weapon moments. His unique approach to extreme close-ups, wherein the zoom-ins mimic the shifting objective lenses of a microscope that click onto a specimen, are great. However, the fantastical kung fu weapon roll call is a real joy to watch. Southern and standard broadswords, scimitar-bladed and standard spears, short-staff tridents, butterfly knives, chain hammers, iron shields, three-sectional staffs, knife whip chains, double axes, brass and fire-bladed rings, iron-clawed gloves, a gashing queue (a queue is the hair style of the Ching Dynasty), and a club with a giant gold candle snuffer at the end of it make for some very exciting and freaky fight choreography. Fight instructors Tang Chia (who cameos as the spear-wielding head of the gold consignment) and Huang Pei-chi eloquently show off their many years of opera training on the Shaw Brothers lot.

Titleography: *Cold Blooded Eagles*. Translation—*Cold Blooded 13 Eagles*. The English titles are translation plays on the Chinese title with the main working title reflecting the theme of the film. **MA Percentage: 37.26%** SHAW BROTHERS

AWAKEN PUNCH, THE

石破天驚 (1973—Hong Kong) **96m. AD: Yuen Woo-ping, Yuen Cheung-yan. NOT/LOT: 1/ 16s; NOF/LOF: 11/ 15m 10s. D:** Fang Long-xiang. **C:** Henry Yu Yung, Ou-Yang Pei-Shan, Tien Feng, Kenneth Tsang Kong, Fang Ye, Sun Lan, Fung Ke-an, Li Chao, Shan Guai.

If your reason for learning martial arts is purely about fighting, then you will be labeled as such (a fighter rather than a martial artist) once that goal is attained. The only way to break the vicious cycle of violence is to look under the rock of righteousness in search of freedom as happens in *The Awaken Punch*.

Lei tai (fighting duels on a raised stage originating during the Song Dynasty circa A.D. 960) champion Chen Da-gang (Henry Yu Yung) is summoned home to hear his father's dying words: "Settle down, become a farmer and give up fighting." He painstakingly follows this advice. Local ruthless land-grabber and expert knife thrower Mr. Wong (Tien Feng) wants to buy Chen's property because, unbeknownst to Chen, a new north-south railway line is going to be built through their property, making the land a gold mine. Chen's promise to not fight is put to task after Wong sends two hit men (Li Chao and Fung Ke-an) and several fan-fighters, meaning fighters who use fans, to kill him. But the straw that breaks Chen's back is when his sister, mother and future brother-in-law are brutally murdered and his home is burned to the ground. Against the climactic theme from *Once Upon a Time in the West* with sounds of loud thunder and streaks of lightning, Chen vows revenge as he destroys a series of trees with his fists … his punch is now awakened.

The soundtrack features music from all of Bruce Lee's Chinese-made films, a bursting-at-the-seams rendition of Van Morrison's *Wild Night* and a peculiar use of *The Godfather* (1972) theme. But using a go-go version of the theme song from the critically acclaimed film about Jesus, *King of Kings* (1961), is more far-out than the star formerly known as the planet Pluto.

What sets this film apart from other films made at this time is the fight choreography created by the duo of Yuen Woo-ping (made world famous by the *Matrix* trilogy) and younger brother Yuen Cheung-yan (the *Charlie's Angels* movies of the 2000s). They pay meticulous attention to camera angle (mostly tight angles) and position to make sure that all kicks, punches and blocks look like they make contact, even if the fights at times look sloppy. To add intensity to the fights, the brothers make liberal use of Dutch angles (tilted image), have the actors run across and through the frame of the camera, and track the attacker on close-ups when they move across the set during a fight. This was all pretty experimental stuff for the early 1970s.

Most of the final fights are unwatchable (at least on the DVD I saw) because the film is so dark that you can't see a thing. I initially thought that it might have been the film transfer until clues like night lanterns and then a specific shot of a sunrise that switches to bright sunlight confirmed that the fights were shot at early dawn. Back then, when shooting outside at the beginning or at the end of the day through a viewfinder under ambient light, the image is fine, but it comes out dark after the film has been developed. Keep in mind that when shooting outside, most Chinese productions do not have lighting equipment, and so at dusk, it becomes a race against time. A final thing that you may also not know is that all these fights are shot using just one camera, which was common for exterior shooting late into the 1970s.

Titleography: *The Awaken Fist; Village on Fire; Buddhist Shaolin Avengers.* Translation—*The Rock Broke and Shattered the Sky.* The Chinese title is a Chinese idiom that means, "the story is a shocker." The *Awaken* aspects of the English titles refer to when the house burns down (thus *Village on Fire*) and the hero essentially wakes up and decides to fight. No Shaolin monks in the film, just a ruse to sell the video. **MA Percentage: 16.08%**

BAMBOO HOUSE OF DOLLS, THE

女集中營 (1973—Hong Kong) **110. FI: Yasuyoshi Shikamura. NOT/LOT: None; NOF/LOF: 9/ 6m 41s.** D: Kuei Chi-hung. C: Lo Lieh, Birte Tove, Wang Xia, Li Hai-shu, Liu Hui-ru, Chen Feng-chen, Chan Shen, Dana.

This is one of the odder films made by Shaw Brothers. It's not because of some fantastical approach to action or a weird kung fu monster, and it's not because it contains some bizarre erotic situations. It is unusual in that it is about Chinese women and a few foreign women being tortured and sexually abused by Japanese soldiers at a POW camp during World War II. When you consider the historical angst about the atrocities committed by the Japanese against the Chinese during the war—for instance, the Rape of Nanking or the horrific experimentation of Japanese scientists and doctors on Chinese prisoners at Camp 731, as depicted in the film *Men Behind the Sun* (1988)—it seems very daring or blatantly wrong to make this 1973 film because it exploits the abuse on such a gut-wrenching level. To say this is a women-in-prison film also seems a bit off-kilter, but based on what those films present, it is understandable why it is labeled as such.

In the film, Japanese soldiers break into a Chinese hospital and shoot all the helpless sick and injured men and children. The women are sent to the 13th Women Concentration Camp; among them is a foreign concession of nurses led by Jennifer (Danish actress Birte Tove). The camp is run by the Japanese commander (Wang Xia); his alluring but dangerous lesbian sergeant, Mako (Liu Hui-ru); and the commander's traitorous Chinese assistant, Kuo Tung (Lo Lieh). The women are immediately instructed what will happen to them if they should try to escape: torture, defamation and death. A group of Japanese troops arrives, and sexual abuse becomes a daily nightmare that the prisoners must endure. There is one special prisoner, Hung Yu-lan (Li Hai-shu), who must somehow escape before the Japanese find out who she is and what she knows.

Before Hung's husband died, he told her where a major consignment of

gold was hidden. The gold was stolen from Chinese cities occupied by the Japanese but retrieved by Chinese soldiers as a means to fund their war efforts. The problem is that Hung has lost her memory, but if she can escape, something might jog it.

Six prisoners, led by Jennifer and helped by a Chinese patriot close to the commander (any guesses who that might be?), make a daring and explosive escape, and the film switches from the claustrophobic confines of the camp to the wide landscapes of China, rife with open fields, storming rivers and jagged cliffs. However, among the six is a traitor working for the Japanese who is trying to find out Hung's secret. One by one, the escaped women mysteriously die, and the traitor leaves a trail of clues for the commander to follow. Everything comes to a head at the White Cloud Peak. Chinese rebels and Japanese samurai meet, the female traitor is exposed, Jennifer and Mako get it on combat-style, and the evil commander faces and fights … guess who?

The film does not include many fights to speak of, but Lo Lieh does have a few decent moments of glory, and the uncanny demise of Mako is priceless.

Titleography: *Bamboo Women's Prison.* Translation—*Female Concentration Camp.* **MA Percentage: 6.08%** SHAW BROTHERS

BANDIT VS. SAMURAI SQUAD

Kumokiri Nizaemon (1978—Japan) **162m. FI: Uncredited. NOT/LOT: None; NOF/LOF: 12/ 17m 20s.** D: Hideo Gosha. C: Tatsuya Nakadai, Shima Iwashita, Shogoro Ichikawa, Takashi Yamaguchi, Koshiro Matsumoto, Tetsuro Tanba, Keiko Matsuzaka, Teruhiko Aoi, Mitsuko Baisho, Shôji Ishibashi, Takuzo Kawatani, Junko Miyashita, Hiroyuki Nagato, Isao Natsuyagi, Jo Shishido, Shingo Yamashiro.

Every country has "glue" techniques or plot devices to propel the story in a new direction. In Hong Kong and Taiwanese films, there are lots of main characters who simply pop out of nowhere when the story needs a jolt or a fight scene. In Japan, films are stuffed with twists so unpredictable that they're sometimes impossible to follow, but they hold the audience's attention like glue on paper. (It's no wonder so many characters find themselves in a sticky wicket.)

Bandit vs. Samurai Squad opens when Shikubu Abe (Shogoro Ichikawa) arrives in town. He's the head of a special police force known as the Arson and Theft Investigation Arm, and his goal is to bring down the Kumokiri gang. Meanwhile, Kumokiri Nizaemon (Tatsuya Nakadai), a former samurai warrior who now leads a gang of thieves, has told his men that he will retire from crime after their next job—robbing the castle of the Owari clan, to which he once belonged. But Shikubu catches wind of this scheme from a masseur who used to be a samurai with the Owari clan and overheard the plot. The masseur was part of an eight-samurai assassin group hired to find the Tsuji brothers, who were ordered by the head of Owari to commit seppuku but didn't. The brothers were never found, but word has it they are coming together to attack Lord Owari. But as it turns out, only one brother is willing to die in the attack, while the other is not. Regardless, something is going to happen at Owari castle, and Kumokiri and one or both of the Tsuji brothers are involved. Shikubu has also been informed that whatever is going to happen will start at a secret tunnel entrance to the castle. It shows you that just because your masseuse may not be good, don't rub him the wrong way, because if he's bad, he is the one that can create a lot of friction for you.

Long, grandiose movies that are set during Japan's Edo period are known as *jidaigeki.* They are filled with contrived capers, enigmatic escapes and great performances. Western critics have plenty to sink their teeth into with these period dramas. That's all fine and dandy for Japanophile film critics, but as a fight choreographer, I can tell you that substantive action scenes, actors' fight skills and creative choreography are equally important. So if you hoped that *Bandit vs. Samurai Squad* would be loaded with breathtaking sword fights, I'm sorry to burst your bubble, because this film has bad and little action. In all fairness, Nakadai is his usual dour and dastardly self. He brings a sense of cool to the movie.

Most of the fights in *Bandits vs. Samurai Squad* are basically brawls in the dark. People run chaotically in and out of frame, and it's very difficult to tell who is who and who is doing what other than dying and screaming.

There is one bizarre fight sequence that just about says it all for this film. In the dark secret passageway of Owari castle, actors Nakadai and Ishikawa are locked in battle. One charges, the other moves back. It is a collection of over-the-shoulder and reverse-angle shots. Then, with one last magnificent effort, Ishikawa clashes swords with Nakadai, but in the next shot, Nakadai is facing the masseur. Ishikawa is gone. Where did he go? I don't know. Maybe it's just an editing error. In any case, the next shot is of Nakadai wading through water outside the castle. It's no wonder the title of this film sounds like a World War II movie—Ishikawa pulled one great escape!

Titleography: *Bandits vs. Samurai Squadron.* **MA Percentage: 10.7%**

BARE KNUCKLES

(1977—USA) **90m. SC: Jim Winburn. NOT/LOT: None; NOF/LOF: 6/ 8m 41s.** D: Don Edmonds. C: Robert Viharo, Sherry Jackson, Michael Heit, Gloria Hendry, John Daniels, Karen Kondazian, Essex Smith, Richard Kennedy, Patrick M. Wright, Jace Khan.

Kane (Robert Viharo) is a bounty hunter who plays the flute to stay calm, but when the music stops, it usually means the fat lady is about to sing for the criminal he's after. It's interesting that Caine from the American TV series *Kung Fu* is another character who plays the flute to free his mind of distraction. But whereas peace and harmony reign with Caine, violence and brutality rule the life of Kane. He is on the trail of Richard Devlin (Michael Heit), an insane masked serial killer trained in kung fu who murders innocent women and learns killer martial arts from his deranged *sifu*, Kido (Jace Khan from *Black Samurai*). Kane gets help from his friend Black (John Daniels), and his only clue lies in locating a beautiful nightclub singer before the police do. If they do, they will prevent him from collecting the $15,000 bounty.

Most of the fights are shot using point-of-view and over-the-shoulder angles, which guarantees that each front shot of someone getting punched, kicked and kneed away or toward camera is a perfect sell. It is lazy choreography and such shots are painfully simple to set up, but they serve Kane's violent fisticuff skills well. I found myself grimacing at some of Kido's neck craning, hunched postures and weird hand positions because I used to do the same thing back in 1973 (and I have the rotten photos to prove it). However, the stunt coordinator and the director's cluelessness when it comes to featuring the martial arts aspects of the action make those sequences goofily audacious, such as when Devlin screams like a banshee, does freaky heavy breathing and then begins to hiss like a snake with a sore throat. But the moment that really takes the cake has to be when the Asian girl in the apartment complex is about to get "hissed" on by Devlin. Then from nowhere, her Chinese boyfriend shows up and chases Devlin onto the roof. The boyfriend then uses chopsticks like *escrima* sticks against the knife-wielding Devlin, who goes praying mantis with more guttural hisses. The final fight goes on far too long and is undoubtedly there to dramatize the rivalry between Kane and Devlin. Ultimately, it's kind of a drag.

Titleography: As of this writing, no alternative titles could be found. **MA Percentage: 3.65%**

BASTARD, THE

小雜種 (1973—Hong Kong) **102m. FI: Yuen Woo-ping, Yuen Cheung-yan. NOT/LOT: 2/ 1m 5s; NOF/LOF: 26/ 14m 26.** D: Chu Yuan. C: Tsung Hua, Lily Li, Liu Dan, Ching Miao, Jiang Ling, Lu Di, Chan Shen, Zheng Lei, Wu Chi-chin.

Still from *The Bastard* © Celestial Pictures Ltd. All rights reserved.

After watching 17 of director Chu Yuan's extravagant, colorful, often mind-boggling *wuxia* films about the worlds of Jiang Hu and Wu Lin, this film is a real change of pace. Following the success of Bruce Lee, films with naïve country-bumpkin characters became popular. These characters would have good kung fu and good hearts, and they represented an offshoot of the typical stories featuring downtrodden Chinese peasants being oppressed by an evil government or foreign power while still being able to rise up, be victorious and remain righteous.

The hero of this film was left at the foot of a temple as a nameless baby. Eighteen years later, the name (or lack thereof) has stuck, and Nameless (Tsung Hua) heads out into the cruel world with a lot of kung fu under his belt and angst in his head. He is on a mission to find his parents and learn why he was an abandoned. Along the way, he befriends the street-smart Hsiao Yi (Lily Li). She's nicknamed Little Beggar, and she gives him the nickname Little Bastard.

Together they learn the truth about Little Bastard's background. They locate his real father, Gu Chang-bo (Ching Miao), and find out why he left his son at the temple. Yet it turns out that Gu is shadier than the forest floor in the Amazon, and he and his goons are trying to get Little Bastard thrown in jail for a higher purpose. Little Bastard tries to remain upright, but when Little Beggar is killed, he unleashes 18 years of pent-up anger at Gu and all his new so-called friends.

The point of the film is obvious, but the message is well worth revisiting as the on-screen narrative tells, "Some people trade life for money, not all educated people are virtuous, a father may renounce his son, and a beauty can sometimes be deceiving." We have all run into such people, but as Little Bastard—whose real name is Xia Za-zhong—learns, if you know yourself, then there is nothing to fear from them.

Actor Tsung Hua is the perfect example in this film of how to recognize whether an actor knows martial arts. Techniques such as undercranking the camera can help disguise poor form, but only to a point. Observe when Tsung kicks. Notice how he sometimes pushes with his feet rather than snapping them, or how he takes little skips (aka skip kicks) to give a dimension of power. These are things fight instructors would usually tell actors to do. What an actor would not be instructed to do is kick with both arms above his head or look away from his opponent when kicking, both of which Tsung does in this film. These tendencies reveal his lack of expertise. But what does help sell Tsung in this movie is the skillful team of stuntmen. They fly or dive into various objects upon being struck, like true professionals. The gag Tsung performs with a thin bamboo stick twice in the film is also novel without being overused.

Titleography: *Little Hero.* Translations—*Bastard* or *Little Bastard.* **MA Percentage: 15.21%** SHAW BROTHERS

BATTLE WIZARD

天龍八部 (1977—Hong Kong) **72m. FI: Huang Pei-ji, Tang Chia. NOT/LOT: 2/ 8s; NOF/LOF: 14/ 9m 35s.** D: Pao Hsueh-li. C: Danny Lee, Lin Chen-chi, Tanny Tien-ni, Frankie Wei Hong, Jiang Dao, Shi Zhong-tian, Si Wei, Jiang Han, Jin Lou, Hung Ling-ling.

For a film with less than 10 minutes of martial arts, there's is a lot going on, including a fight with a giant snake, freaky monsters doing freaky things, and kung fu wizards shooting a variety of laser beams at each other, which are not included in the martial arts fight statistics. And when these fighters have run out of everything, even the kitchen sink … it is time … to bring in a kung fu fighting gorilla … again. (If you have gone through a good many of these martialogies, you probably know exactly what I mean about the gorilla statement. And if you haven't, I encourage you to keep reading.)

Battle Wizard begins when Yellow Robe Man (Shi Zhong-tian) catches his adulterous wife Shu Bai-feng (Hung Ling-ling) with her illicit lover Tuan Zheng-chu (Si Wei), who is betrothed to Chin Hong-mian (Jin Lou). Illicit lover Tuan uses his Yi Yang Finger skills to shoot laser beams out of his hands and sever off Yellow Robe Man's legs. The crippled man crawls off into the moonset vowing revenge against his ex and the phalange-fighting Tuan, who dumps Hong-mian and marries Bai-feng. Twenty years later, the stars have aligned and the pieces of freaky come together.

Scholar Tuan Yu (Danny Lee), son of Tuan and Bai-feng, goes out into the world trying to discover the value of martial arts and whether it's necessary to study them to get anywhere in life. Meanwhile,

Yellow Robe Man has sunk into the most sunken sinkhole of metaphorical pits, but he's learned powerful magic and has prosthetic telescoping legs that look as if they belong to *Sesame Street*'s Big Bird. Yellow Robe Man has also picked up an assistant, Tsang Long (Jiang Dao), who is a green-faced monster with fangs, mad-scientist white hair and hands that have been replaced with a round-tipped smashing device and a vicious steel hook that resembles a 1970s can opener; he is quite the Chinese Frankenstein. Elsewhere, the jilted fiancee Hong-mian had a daughter out of wedlock who is known as Mu Wang-qing (Tanny Tien-ni), the master of the Bone Cutting Sword. She's become so feared in the Jiang Hu world that if someone should call her by her real name, Xiang Yao-cha, death would be easier to deal with than her.

On his journey, Tuan Yu meets Snake Lady Zhong Ling-er (Lin Chen-chi), who uses snakes as weapons that can enter into a man's body to wriggle and wriggle and wriggle inside him. And perhaps, like the old lady that swallowed the proverbial spider to catch the fly, he'll die. But she takes a liking to Tuan Yu and talks him into finding the humongous Red Python—who is red because it has been feeding on ginseng and deer antlers for thousands of years. By sucking out its blood, Tuan Yu then can attain Red Dragon Soul kung fu, thereby making him invincible. After Ling-er hooks up Tuan Yu with her godsister Mu Wang-qing, Yu and Mu fall in love and not a moment too soon. Tuan Yu's Red Dragon Soul kung fu and Mu's Bone Cutting Sword must unite to rescue Ling-er from the Poisonous Moth Clan, fight the bloodsucking Tsang Long, duel a vicious kung fu gorilla and finally come to the bitter realization that their histories are intertwined as everyone's parents meets everyone's parents, and more than all hell lets loose.

It becomes an intense battle between wizards. And sometimes it seems like the only way to get out of the mess is to call out, "Help me, Mr. Wizarrrrd," like Tooter Turtle in the 1960s cartoon. So when you hear the German-English accented Dragon Wizard cast his "home-drome" spell, "Drizzle, drazzle, druzzle, drome," then you'll know it's safe for you to come home.

Titleography: *The Battle Wizard*. Translation—*Heavenly Dragon Eight Volumes*. The English title should have been *Battle Wizards* because there is more than one magical wizard and witch doing battle in this film. The Chinese title is merely the name of the kung fu novel that started out in a newspaper, penned by Jin Yong, of which this film is based on. **MA Percentage: 13.5%** SHAW BROTHERS

BATTLES WITHOUT HONOR AND HUMANITY: DEADLY FIGHT IN HIROSHIMA

Jingi Naki Tatakai: Hiroshima Shito Hen (1973—Japan) **99m. FI: Uncredited. NOT/LOT: None; NOF/LOF: 1/ 3m 3s.** D: Kinji Fukasaku. C: Sonny Chiba, Bunta Sugawara, Seizo Fukumoto, Meiko Kaji, Toshie Kimura, Kunya Kitaoji, Asao Koike, Nobu Yana.

The origin of the Yakuza (Japanese gangsters) is seeped in a Robin Hood-like folklore, at least according to many Yakuza themselves. But in real life, the Yakuza evolved into robbing hoods, which decomposed into their negative Yakuza caricature that became the impetus behind a series of five films based on newspaper articles written by former Yakuza Koichi Iboshi. The dark and brutally violent *Battles Without Honor and Humanity* series follows the life of a post-World War II soldier Hirono Shozo (Bunta Sugawara), who returns to his destroyed home city of Hiroshima, Japan. He moves up the Yakuza ranks from a fed-up street punk dealing with arrogant low-level Yakuza and evading American MPs to one of the most influential Yakuza bosses in Hiroshima.

Most Yakuza films shot before the 1970s hailed the pre-World War II Yakuza underworld as an organization consisting of upright heroes, like the chivalrous knight-errants of the Chinese Jiang Hu world so vividly portrayed in *wuxia* novels and films. However, this movie series, grittily directed by Kinji Fukasaku, erased that myth. Even Fukasaku's titles reflect the "without" honor and humanity view that public cynicism viewed the neo-Yakuza with—a view the Yakuza disagreed with.

For the most part, the "mob" hits, assassinations and gang confrontations are a collection of messy, chaotic fights heavily dispersed with excessive handgun fire, blood and squawking men who die in painful, gut-wrenching agony. Rattling and shaking camera movements add to the lack of intricate fight choreography. It seems that mass mayhem and movement makes the action look more complex than what it actually is: men kinetically rolling around and popping or squeezing blood pouches. However, in this film, *Deadly Fight in Hiroshima*, up-and-coming karate film star Sonny Chiba adds a different dimension to the squabbles with an almost choreographed brutality with a samurai sword in one hand and a gun in the other—instead of the usual second sword or short *tanto* knife. So it was slice, shoot, slice, kick, shoot, shoot, slice—a hidden rhythmic choreography style I call hack'n'whack'n'bang.

The success of the film series led to a three-part sequel, *New Battles Without Honor and Humanity*, and a subsequent final installment, *Aftermath of Battles Without Honor and Humanity*. But perhaps the most memorable part of the original series is that daunting and haunting guitar shtick. Throughout the five films, it repeats itself almost every five minutes whenever somebody is about to suffer an agonizing and violent death.

Titleography: *Battles Without Honor and Humanity: Deathmatch in Hiroshima*; *Deadly Fight in Hiroshima*; *The Yakuza Papers, Vol. 2: Deadly Fight in Hiroshima*; *Yakuza Papers 2*; *Battles Without Honor and Humanity 2: Deadly Fight in Hiroshima*. Translation—*Battles Without Honor and Humanity: Deadly Fight in Hiroshima*. *The Yakuza Papers* title comes from the notion that the stories were derived from the previously mentioned newspaper articles that appeared in the Japanese newspaper *Yomiuri Shinbun*. **MA Percentage: 3.08%**

BEACH OF THE WAR GODS

戰神灘 (1973—Hong Kong) **96m. FI: Guan Hong, Siu Bo. NOT/LOT:1/ 38s; NOF/LOF: 23/ 36m 10s.** D: Jimmy Wong Yu. C: Jimmy Wong Yu, Lung Fei, Shan Mao, Tian Ye, Xue Han, Cai Hong, Guan Hong, Zhang Yi-gui, Su Zhen-ping, Hsieh Hsing, Wang Yong-sheng, Shi Ting-General

This film features the longest martial arts fight and probably the longest fight of any kind in cinema history. It begins an hour into the movie and clocks in at a whopping 25 minutes and 43 seconds. Jimmy Wong Yu must have been sipping 30 cups of espresso a day just to keep going. Imagine shooting a long, hectic sword-fight scene for two weeks, from dawn to dusk, and in 100-degree heat and high humidity. There were probably no water breaks—unless the tea lady came around—and the cast and crew probably only got a half an hour for a meal break on a slow day. There were likely no toilets, no trailers and no changing out of sweaty clothes. To top it off, the actors probably got paid diddly-squat. Welcome to the real *Beach of the War Gods*.

The film is set in 1556 during the late Ming Dynasty. *Wokou* (Japanese pirates) have been attacking Chinese shores for 250 years, and the Ming emperor's continued refusal to allow civil trade with Japan as a means to curb pirate activity has only exacerbated the situation. Over the years pirate bands have grown larger, more bloodthirsty and more intrepid by invading villages from Korea to the South China Sea.

Jimmy Wong Yu plays the noble Hsiao Feng. Like in Akira Kurosawa's *Seven Samurai*, he recruits men to defend and train the villagers for an upcoming invasion by the most fearsome Wokou pirate ever: Shinobu Hashimoto (Lung Fe); Betty in 2002's *Kung Pow: Enter the Fist*). The grand garrison of guards includes Iron Man Chow (Xue Han), Dagger Vest Leng Ping (Tian Ye), Giant Shield Lightning Fist Hung (Zhang Yi-gui) and Spear Man Li (Guan Hong).

This movie is mythical in its dimensions. The manpower and organization required for the 25-minute fight scene alone must have been daunting. There is a cast of hundreds fighting in the background while lead heroes and villains scrap away in the foreground, and the cast and crew manage to do it all in a way that does not look like a free-for-all. And throughout all the action sequences and scenarios, the camera is almost invisible in that it weaves among the various combatants without getting in the way. There are three especially memorable visuals in the epic fight. The first is a great piece of physics: A Japanese fighter whips a chain around that lodges around a tree and holds taut. Jimmy Wong Yu then kicks another attacker into the chain, causing the chain holder to catapult toward Wong Yu and be dispatched by him. The second and third are two great tracking shots. The first is of Wong Yu moving right to left while killing 17 attackers. The second is when actor Lung Fei moves from left to right while killing 13 attackers.

A fun history note: The film was inspired by the true story of Chinese hero Yu Da-you, an exceptional martial artist and expert of the Chinese sword. In 1556, the historical Yu killed 2,000 pirates while defending Jiaxing in Zhejiang province. It was considered the greatest victory of the Wokou wars.

Titleography: As of this writing, no alternative titles could be found. Translation—*Beach of the War Gods*. On the night before the final epic battle, Japanese *taiko* drummers wearing scary Bishamon masks (representing the Japanese god of war) are on the beach pounding their drums, thus *Beach of the War Gods*. **MA Percentage: 38.33%**

BEST OF SHAOLIN KUNG FU, THE

萬法歸宗一少林 (1976—Hong Kong) 78m. **AD: Chen Shao-peng. NOT/LOT: 13/ 1m 43s; NOF/LOF: 17/ 34m 3s. D:** Chen Shao-peng, Zhang Ren-dao. **C:** Cliff Lok, Carter Wong, Bai Ying, Doris Lung Chun-er, Jin Gang, Gao Fei, Qin Zhi-min, Chen Shao-peng, David Tong Wai.

The Chinese people are made up of five races: Han (the Chinese), Man (Manchus), Mong (Mongolians), Hui (Muslims) and Tsang (Tibetans). When the Manchus took over China and established the Ching Dynasty, that made the Han and Manchus bitter enemies.

In this film, mouse-faced actor Cliff Lok plays a righteous martial artist who is determined to prove that an heir to the Ching throne, Chien Lung (Bai Ying), is his blood brother, which would mean Chien is Chinese (a Han) and not a Manchu (a Man). Chien refuses to believe he's not of the imperial line unless he's shown written proof, which exists in the Shaolin Temple.

Lok's character must traverse to the Shaolin Temple and face several adversaries on his path. Arriving at Shaolin, he then proves his worth to the abbot of Shaolin and gains access to the document by defeating the abbot-assigned guardians of the documents, the fabled Bronzemen of Shaolin who attack him in varying groups of weapon-wielding fury and weaponless pugilistic pandemonium. The final test of the 12 Styles of Kung Fu against the abbot is an epic battle, which cinematicwise led to the truth about Chien Lung. However, on a historic note, Chien Lung (1735-1796) did become the emperor of China, and that led to the zenith of the Ching Dynasty and the subsequent spiraling of the empire.

In this film, Cliff Lok is a contradiction in martial arts. On the one hand, during most of his fights, he has weak stances and is constantly off-balance. Rather than using proper posture, he hunches his back and fights like a hero from early kung fu films. Yet the scope of the choreography is very broad, and he tackles some difficult fight sequences—such as sword fighting on swinging vines, fighting four monks armed with three-sectional staffs, and being involved in an interesting meditative battle in which the monks use poles and Lok uses a giant *mu yu*. Here's

a cultural note for you: The mu yu, which is translated as "wooden fish," is the drum you usually see Buddhist monks rhythmically beating during meditation. Its significance in Buddhism is that it represents living without the fear of drowning in the ocean of suffering.

Carter Wong's character (the nameless bodyguard of Chien Lung) was not as convincing with his fights compared to his other *Bronzemen* films. (See *The Blazing Temple*.) Wong also did a lot of off-kilter eye glares, a sign that it was probably unclear as to what his character was supposed to be glaring about, or close-ups of his face were shot in one go and the various faces were edited into the final cut to keep him "in the film" so to speak. The slow-motion, wide-angle single unedited shot of Lok rolling down a long hill and splashing into the water was eerily marvelous. But as a former choreographer in Chinese kung fu films and Hollywood, I was most impressed that in several instances, Lok and his foes filmed more than 50 techniques in one unedited shot. My limit was about 15 techniques in one shot before making an error or forgetting the correct fight sequence.

Titleography: As of this writing, no alternative titles could be found. Translation—*Of a Million Kung Fu Styles, Shaolin Is the Best*. The English title is the Chinese title paraphrased, but it probably reflects the opinion of the filmmakers because the film's story does not indicate that Shaolin is the best. **MA Percentage: 45.85%**

BIG BAD SIS

沙胆英 (1976—Hong Kong) 93m. **FI: Tang Chia, Huang Pei-ji. NOT/LOT: 1/ 11s; NOF/LOF: 12/ 12m 6s. D:** Sun Chung. **C:** Chen Ping, Wong Chung, Shaw Yin-yin, Wang Xia, Chen Kuan-tai, Chong Li, Yang Chi-ching.

Pinky violence meets contemporary kung fu as one of Hong Kong's 1970s female exploitation starlets Chen Ping rivets the screen with sex, violence and a Helen Reddy "I am woman, hear me roar" attitude. Chen also growls and bares her body wares, scars and flair on the screen with energetic panache and flappable feet and hands. With a title undoubtedly influenced by female-starring American blaxploitation films, *Big Bad Sis* is about Chinese female empowerment in a male-dominated society. Although the femmes must give into the lewd whims of men at certain points in their lives, they turn the tables and become the fatales. Of course, it never hurts when a strong, understanding male character who is comfortable with his masculinity supports these fem-macho mavens of autonomy.

In the opening scene, a feared lesbian factory worker tries to seduce unwilling garment workers in the bathroom between stitches and britches. The film's heroine, Ah Ying (Chen Ping), saves Ah Fong (Chong Li) and Sai Chu (Shaw

Still from *Big Bad Sis* © Celestial Pictures Ltd. All rights reserved.

Yin-yin) by shoving her moxie into the lesbian's face and giving her a toilet-bowl cleansing. Ah Ying is able to do this because she possesses a luminous and looming presence that does not come from making clothes in a factory; it is a gift that evolved from her past life.

Years ago, Ah Ying was a card dealer at a Triad casino and knew how to cheat customers, but one night, she had a change of heart and helped an in-debt old man win some money. When big boss Dai Gi-luk (Wang Xia) and his right-hand man Ah Wei (Wong Chung), who loves Ah Ying, try to get the money back from the old man, she exchanges slashes and gashes with the gang. Her own wounds awash with gobs of blood, she finds sanctuary in a restaurant owned by the highly respected, Triad-neutral Brother Cheng (Chen Kuan-tai), who plays the same character originally in *The Tea House* (1974) and *Big Brother Cheng* (1975). Cheng convinces Triad casino boss Dai to let Ah Ying leave Dai's gang.

In her current incarnation as a factory girl, Ah Ying teaches Ah Fong and Sai how to defend and assert themselves into not taking crap from men. But it is Ah Ying who gets crapped on when she tries to save factory owner Boss Wong (Yang Chi-ching) from Dai Gi-luk's desire to buy the building by cheating Wong at the casino and driving him into debt. After Ah Ying threatens Dai with gasoline-filled balloons, which forces Dai to return Wong's IOU to Ah Ying, Dai kidnaps Ah Ying and drags her to an isolated quarry where he plans to burn her.

Although not trained in martial arts, actress Chen Ping sells her intensity with facial expressions that make you feel like her life is truly in danger, especially during the machete fights.

The final fight at the rock quarry makes superb use of the whole environment. It starts off in a large, open space followed by motorcycle and car stunts that whittle the environment down into tight hand-to-hand confrontations filled with stunts and dramatic tension. The choreography uses overemphasized wide-swinging punches with big overdone reactions that cause the stuntmen to leap into the air, jump backward, or frantically spin around onto the ground or land on an object with a crash, clang and clatter. It is, as you can imagine, pretty cool looking.

Sun Chung was the first director in Hong Kong to use the steadicam, and he blatantly makes sure that the audience can see his expertise with the equipment. He is quickly able to smoothly shift the camera during the fights from high to low to high again so the audience can see each technique of the fight. Chen Ping's "shovel *fu*" is equally engaging and enhanced by Sun's framing of each shot, which removes any sloppiness and adds more motion and emotion to the fight sequences.

Titleography: As of this writing, no alternative titles could be found. Translation—*Xia Dan Hero. Xia Dan* is a place, and Ying is the hero of that place. *Big Bad Sis* is an inspired blaxploitation title nod. **MA Percentage: 13.21%** SHAW BROTHERS

BIG BOSS, THE

唐山大兄 (1971—Hong Kong) **99m. FI: Han Ying-chieh. NOT/LOT: 3/ 50s; NOF/LOF: 8/ 20m 45s.** D: Lo Wei. C: Bruce Lee, James Tien, Han Ying-chieh, Maria Yi Yi, Lam Ching-ying, Tony Liu Yung, Nora Miao.

The film that literally saved my life. In the early 1970s, several weeks after my doctor said I would be dead in five years, my brothers took me to the Vestal Drive-In to see *The Big Boss*. I had already resigned myself to death and was just sulking in the inevitable, until Bruce Lee did those two, amazing, fast-as-greased-lightning kicks after the jade got ripped away from his neck, which stimulated him to fight. I literally screamed out. In a split second, I went from waiting to die to going to live because it led me up the path of martial arts and *chi gong* (*qigong*). Lee saved my life that day. Thanks, man.

The Big Boss is not the best martial arts film ever made—not even in my top 20—but it is without a doubt the most important martial arts film in the world for one reason: It introduced the cinema universe to Bruce Lee, which launches a martial arts craze in the West and revitalizes a waning kung fu film industry in the East.

It also features a straightforward plot and pioneers a novel style of street-fighting heroism in Hong Kong cinema. Lee plays a lad named Cheng, a bumpkin Chinese worker at a Thai ice factory who is perplexed by the disappearance of his co-workers until he discovers that Boss Mi (Han Ying-chieh) is using the factory as a front to smuggle heroin. Around Cheng's neck is a jade amulet, which he wears as a reminder to keep his solemn vow to refrain from fighting.

The "emotional content" of the film builds while Cheng helplessly stands by and watches his friends getting more beaten into pulverized pulp than apples at a cider mill. Suddenly, Cheng gets whacked across his face. Rage boiling through his veins, the jade reminds him not to fight. Although we've never seen Bruce Lee before and don't understand the nature of the action, we know that we are in for something special when Cheng realizes the jade has been broken and he cradles the broken pieces like a newborn baby. What follows is more explosive than opening a can of beer after it has been cooked up in the back of a speeding truck at the Baja 500. Lee's patented snarling face is pure elation as he deals out what everyone gets what's coming to them.

Although Han Ying-chieh was the fight instructor, Lee formed a close bond with Han's assistant, Lam Ching-ying, who understood the boxing/kung fu combos that Lee insisted on spattering on-screen—a way of movement that Han was averse to incorporating into "his" film. Han was old school, Lee was new school, and we know which school had the superior graduation rate.

Titleography: *King of the Boxers*; *Fists of Glory*; *Fists of Fury*. Translation—*The Big Brother from Tang Mountain*. Originally *King of the Boxers*, then changed to *Fists of Fury* for the American market and *Fists of Glory* in other parts of the world, was Golden Harvest's fifth released film. All titles are appropriate for the film, the above three alternative titles referring to Cheng; *The Big Boss* and the Chinese title referring to the villain Boss Mi, the Chinese title telling where he is from. **MA Percentage: 21.8%**

BIG BROTHER CHENG

大哥成 (1975—Hong Kong) **107m. FI: Tang Chia. NOT/LOT: None; NOF/ LOF: 8/ 4m 11s.** D: Kuei Chih-hung. C: Chen Kuan-tai, Karen Yeh Ling-zhu, Wang Yu, Karen Yip Leng-chi, Tong Lin, Frankie Wei Hong, Tsung Chang-chih, Feng Jing-wen, Liu Liu-hua, Lin Wei-tu.

This film reminds me of a teahouse I once visited in Taipei in 1979. A bunch of foreigners and I were sipping tea when we spotted a film star drinking coffee in a corner. Three guys walked in with broadswords, told everyone not to move and said no one would get hurt. Then they slashed several parts of the actor's body and left. The actor calmly finished his coffee, slowly got up and also left. Weird.

Chen Kuan-tai reprises his roll as boss Wang Cheng from *The Tea House* (1974), a film about a transplanted Chinese mainlander who opens a successful teahouse in Hong Kong and hires immigrants like himself. In *Tea House*, Wang converts juvenile delinquent Darkie Wen (Wang Yu) into a hard worker, but Darkie has a run-in with Prince Ji (Tsung Chang-chih), an important member of the 18K Triads. Prince Ji is sent to prison, and Darkie is now his enemy for life. The film shows the ludicrous nature of Hong Kong's court system at the time— teen felons get probation, adults who spit on the ground get a month in jail— and the daily struggles of real people. Although Ching Siu-tung was the fight instructor in *Tea House*, there was no kung fu per se in the film, just a fleeting

Triad skirmish. The film does, however, detail some Triad rituals, but since Hong Kong was handed back to Communist China in 1997, the Chinese government has usually censored these images.

In *Big Brother Cheng*, Cheng seeks peace in the new territories, but as criminal activity increases around the area of the teahouse, he returns to protect his employees from the new racketeers and various neighborhood riffraff. Despite Cheng's Charles Bronson-ish *Death Wish* (1974) vigilante tendencies, the cops secretly support his efforts after he saves the life of the head local police inspector (Tong Lin). After Prince Ji is released from prison and comes looking to avenge his incarceration at the hands of Darkie, the stakes get higher because the violence and brutality escalate. It all comes to a head when Cheng is injured and recuperating in a large apartment complex. Prince Ji finds out where he is and storms the complex with his Triad gang. Cheng is trapped. Only one will survive, and the other will meet an oily end.

There are a couple of brawls in the film, but they are not much to speak of beyond the usual flails, wails, knives and steel-bar whacking associated with contemporary Hong Kong street fights. However, the mop, broom and kitchen utensil attack at the film's end is rather funny (although not intended to be) when a group of old fogies decide to rise up and go after Prince Ji. It looks like a scene from a film in which a village mob chases Frankenstein, who frantically limps to escape.

Chen would reprise his the role of Cheng a year later in *Big Bad Sis* (1976). (See martialogy.)

Titleography: As of this writing, no alternative titles could be found. Translation—*Big Brother Cheng*. **MA Percentage: 3.91%** SHAW BROTHERS

BIG LAND FLYING EAGLES

大 地 飛 鷹 (1978—Taiwan) **84m. FI: Chan Chuen. NOT/LOT: None; NOF/LOF: 17/ 13m 45s.** D: Ulysses Au-Yeung Jun. C: Wang Guan-xiong, Lin Yun, Paul Chang Chung, Shi Feng, Liu Ping, Zhang Xiang, Lan Yu-li, O Yau-man.

I first saw this film back in 1979, and to this day, it has one of the best fight scenes of all from the more than 5,000 martial arts films I have watched throughout my life. Yet it is not because of the great choreography, camerawork or sword skills from the actors who did the scene, but the deep-seated philosophical significance of the fight itself, something I have not seen in any other film.

Big Land Flying Eagles is an ambitious attempt to adapt another one of Gu Long's famous novels, *Soaring Eagle of the Land* (aka *Land of the Condors*), a typical *wuxia* work loaded with characters, double- and triple-crosses, love duets and triangles, mixed loyalties, clan rivalries, avenging villains, and a lot of poisonings. On the whole, the complexity can make this film a tough watch, and if you end up being interrupted for just a minute or so, you might get lost.

In a nutshell, Fang Wei (Wang Guan-xiong) is the best swordsman in the world of Wu Lin. He kills Lu Tian-bao, the lewd and lustful son of Lu San, the most vicious man known to mankind. Lu San (Paul Chang Chung), who was banished from the Hani Clan, has vowed to kill Fang and wipe out the whole Hani Clan. Fang is in a sticky situation because he is running out of shoulders to look over. Why? Lu wants to assassinate him; that's one shoulder. Famous swordsman Du Bu-chi (Lin Yun) keeps repeatedly challenging Fang to a duel, but the sick part is that Du anonymously pays Fang 3,000 taels of gold to assassinate Du. Yes, Du pays his rival to assassinate himself, that's shoulder two. Then Ban Cha Ba Na (Shi Feng) is hot on Fang's trail for something Fang does not know about yet, and that's shoulder three. Talk about trying to shoulder responsibility.

One of Du's behavioral quirks is that he likes to get into duels. One night he ends up fighting a Buddhist monk (O Yau-man) who holds the high-ranking position of Luin Si Ma, which means he has been a monk for 20 years or more. When their swords collide, sparks literally fly, and we hear a loud, echoing ringing sound. Suddenly, a glorious chorus of voices wells up with ceremonious music. The monk lowers his sword, and his face becomes incredibly calm. Du attacks for all he is worth, but the monk, as if in a trance, effortlessly blocks each attack with his sword. With their final sword clash, the force of the impact knocks Du to the ground. As Du looks up at the monk, he sees the monk's head silhouetted against a bright light as dramatic smoke passes over his body. Chinese characters appear on screen that read, "While hearing the sound of the swords clashing, the Luin Si Ma monk understands Ch'an [the way of Buddhism], and has received the way." In total reverence, Du gets on one knee and recites in Chinese, "*Gong xi Fa Shi, ni cong jian zhong wu dao*" ("From the sword, you have realized the way.") The scene comes right out of left field, and

there is no warning that this could even remotely happen. In reality, that is just the way this would happen, because "the way" finds you, not the other way around. Because the way is something that finds you, it is thought that those who constantly talk about being or finding spiritualism are really the ones still looking. For those whom the way has found, the individual does not need to boast or speak of it because it is not about the words, but the deeds.

Titleography: As of this writing, no alternative titles could be found. Translation—*Big Land Flying Eagle*, an alternative English translation for the novel. **MA Percentage: 16.37%**

BIG RASCAL, THE

大 惡 客 (1979—Taiwan) **89m. FD: Ah Choi, Lai Kan, Fook Chow. NOT/LOT: 6/ 4m 3s; NOF/LOF: 17/ 35m 28s.** D: Chi Kuan-chun. C: Chi Kuan-chun, Zhang Tai-lun, Wang Chen, Jin Gang, Lu Di, Ma Jin-gu.

This movie is like Jackie Chan's *Drunken Master* without the alcohol. Chi Kuan-chun—the legendary Shaw Brothers' star borne out of the popularity of the groundbreaking Chang Cheh *Shaolin Temple* films—breaks away from Shaw Brothers to direct his first and only film, *The Big Rascal*. The main character, Shanghai coolie (a term originally used to describe a dockworker who unloaded goods from Dutch ships at Nagasaki) Ho (Chi Kuan-chun), rises to the heights of gang boss while still keeping a righteous heart. When three thugs threateningly scream his name, "Ho, Ho, Ho," it is our hero that gets the last laugh. He figures out that the man who arranges for him to be the bouncer at a respectable brothel-gambling den (if there is really such a thing in any kung fu film) is the evil force who killed Ho's brother and tried to place the blame on a competing brothel owner.

After *Drunken Master* hit box-office heights with Chan's novel fight choreography formula of precise martial techniques delivered with body-bouncing rhythm, Hong Kong had a new action-fight blueprint to copy. Actor Chi Kuan-chun's solid foundation in *hong jia* (*hung gar*) kung fu and postage-stamp delivery of action rescues the ludicrous nature of this film. The film's solid fight sequences include a bar brawl using benches, a terrific tussle between protagonist Ho and his opponent on galloping horses, and a finale fight against evil Boss Wen's brother (Ma Jin-gu) that looks like the end sequence between Jackie Chan and Hwang Jang-lee in *Drunken Master*. Not only were most of the techniques similar but also the trees, dirt, grass, bushes and costumes were the same, except that from Chi Kuan-chun's roots, there exudes solid heroic amber rather than soft comedic sap.

Titleography: *Dragon Warrior*; *Macho Man*; *Mackoman*; *Dragon Force*; *Death for Death*; *Shanghai Beach*. Translation—*Big Bad Guy*. Titles with *Dragon* in them imbue an image of windlike ferocity, and at the end of the day, Chi Kuan-chun's character is indeed a macho man. *Mackoman* is probably a misspelling of a box cover that escaped the notice of an Asian executive who was too embarrassed to admit that he couldn't read the title. This happens a lot in Asia. Certainly the distributors chose *The Big Rascal* as a play on Bruce Lee's *The Big Boss*. **MA Percentage: 44.4%**

BIG RISK, THE

虎 鬥 虎 (1974—Hong Kong) **89m. FI: Lee Chiu. NOT/LOT: 1/ 53s; NOF/LOF: 16/ 29m 35s.** D: Joseph Kong Hung. C: Cheung Lik, Lee Chiu, Queenie Kong Hoh-Yan, Dean Shek, Tong Tin-hei, Eddy Koh.

Set in Japanese-occupied Macao and Hong Kong during World War II, *The Big Risk* stumbles and trips along. Cheung Lik plays a heroic Chinese patriot who takes on Japanese collaborators while trying to find a secret list of Chinese patriots and deliver it to China before the local Japanese officials can find it and execute the rebels. Although the film is an obvious consequence of the anti-Japanese theme borne from Bruce Lee's *Fist of Fury* (aka *The Chinese Connection*), Lik and his *Risk* do not have the same energy and ferocity as Lee and his *Fury*.

Lik tries too hard to match the power and intensity of Lee's blocks and punches. As a result, he sacrifices solid stances by trying to be quick and light on his feet, which actually makes him come across weaker than he probably is. However, Lik does get good licks in that he is able to effortlessly put together consistent combinations of successive spinning kicks either against one or several opponents at a time. Although everyone else in the film fights worse than your average grandmother, you have to take your hat off to these stars because they're doing 10-minute fight scenes in hot and humid weather and really giving it a go. Their energy and commitment is far superior to more than 90 percent of the American martial arts stars who grace the made-for-video productions collecting dust at the local video stores.

Titleography: *Kung Fu Conspiracy*; *When Tough Guys Meet*. Translation—*Tiger Butts Head With Tiger*. They got me, I have two copies of this film. The *Kung Fu Conspiracy* title sounds attractive and reflects part of the plot. A new distributor must have dreamed up *When Tough Guys Meet* when he was eating an overcooked steak. **MA Percentage: 34.23%**

BIG SHOWDOWN, THE

猛虎鬥狂龍 and 跆拳龍虎鬥 (1974—Hong Kong) **85m. KFI: Yuen Woo-ping. NOT/LOT: 5/ 1m 30s; NOF/LOF: 16/ 21m.** D: Wang Tian-lin. C: Xiang Hua-jiang, Tina Chin Fei, Lily Chen Ching, Liang Shao-hua, Chin Chun, Gam Fook-man.

It is an old plot device in which a man finds a dead body and picks up the knife lying next to the body. Someone arrives in the nick of time to see it, and immediately, everyone and their pet parrot believe the man holding the knife is guilty until proven innocent. We always wonder when this happens: Does the idiot who finds the body have any sense? Of course not, and it is these sorts of cinematic plot points that make a film like *The Big Showdown* frustrating to watch. However, just when you think this movie is doldrums city, something magical happens that puts wind into the film's sails.

When young, naïve Tang King-ku (Liang Shao-hua) returns home from overseas, he learns that his house no longer exists, his sister who he has not seen for many years is missing, and he finds his uncle's dead body with a knife in it. As he picks up the knife, passers-by appear from nowhere and label him a murderer. On the lam, Tang ends up working for local casino boss Mr. Tuan (Xiang Hua-jiang), who takes Tang under his wing but plans to make Tang a dupe for a future purpose.

It is about one-third of the way into this film, during a typical gambling scene, when a seemingly incongruous and wimpy character shows up at Tuan's casino and loses his money. Instead of this downtrodden man becoming the usual faltering-under-pressure loser who bends under the threats from the casino heavies, he rises to the challenge and confronts the cheating dealer. He then lets loose a stunning and unexpected array of sharp *taekwondo* kicks. It turns out he's Pao Pu-ping (Gam Fook-man), a man framed for "murdering" his wife and stealing her money, a plot that Mr. Tuan and Pao's wife devised so they could be together while Pao serves a long prison sentence. When Pao and Tang share their stories, they realize they have a common enemy in Tuan, whose deadly Steel Fingers of Death skill (basically a pair of concealed *nunchaku*) is tough to beat. Pao teaches Tang how to kick, and the two put the boot on Tuan and his immoral miscreants.

The fight scenes come across like constructively choreographed street fights with actor Gam Fook-man's kicks being the center of attraction. Kung fu fight instructor Yuen Woo-ping liberally adds quick zoom-ins and zoom-outs to medium shots during the fights. On many occasions, the main fight characters are not always center framed, which adds an interesting touch to the action. The fights are slightly undercranked or filmed at a slower frame speed to remove the pauses created by the actors when they wind up too much before delivering their techniques. Add in quick edits and the action looks pretty good. As it turns out, Gam Fook-man only made two films in his short career, both in 1974: this one and *Challenge of the Dragon* (1974).

Titleography: *Kung Fu Massacre*. Translations—*Vicious Tiger Fights With Crazy Dragon* and *Tai Chuan (Tae Kwon Do) Dragon Fights With the Tai Chuan Tiger*. The *Tiger* and the *Dragon* refer to Pao and Tang, respectively. Pao teaches Tang how to kick. Although the kicks are obviously from taekwondo, the film does not mention that Pao's martial art is taekwondo, but the Chinese title does. *Kung Fu Massacre* and *The Big Showdown* are generic titles that seem to fit the billing, especially because all kung fu films usually have, at some point, a massacre of innocents that leads to the big showdown between the antagonist and the protagonist. **MA Percentage: 26.47%**

BILLY JACK

(1971—USA) **114m. FC: Bong Soo-han. NOT/LOT: None; NOF/LOF: 2/ 1m 24s.** D: Tom Laughlin. C: Tom Laughlin, Delores Taylor, Clark Howat, Victor Izay, Julie Webb, Debbie Schock, Teresa Kelly, Lynn Baker, Stan Rice, David Roya, John McClure, Susan Foster, Susan Sosa.

Before the first Hong Kong kung fu film landed in America in 1972 (*King Boxer*; aka *Five Fingers of Death*), before Bruce Lee changed the face of martial arts on- and off-screen, and before Kwai Chang Caine introduced the true martial artist's way of peace and non-violence, there was Billy Jack. The brainchild of Tom Laughlin, the character Billy Jack first appeared in the movie *Born Losers* (1967) as a half-white, half-Native American loner trained in judo; he walked a path of pacifism but wandered off the road to defeat a biker gang terrorizing a California town. Billy Jack's path changed again on July 4, 1969, the day Laughlin met Bong Soo-han during a *hapkido* demonstration at a park in Pacific Palisades, California. Laughlin was so moved by Han's skills that he asked Han to work with him on his next film, *Billy Jack*, which also introduced America to the Korean martial art of hapkido. Although Choi Yong-sul (1899-1986) is credited with founding hapkido, which was largely influenced by his background in *daito-ryu aikijujutsu*, the art arose more out of a collaborative effort between a small group of Korean nationals—including Ji Han-jae, Kim Moo-hong, Suh Bok-sub and Myung Jae-nam—following the period of Japanese colonialism in Korea.

Although the cutoff point for this book is 115 seconds of martial arts (see *Good Guys Wear Black*), *Billy Jack* had such an impact on both the social awareness issues of the time and the fundamental techniques necessary for creating an engaging fight scene that it deserves to be a sort of special guest star.

In a nutshell, the film is about Billy Jack (Tom Laughlin), a half-Cherokee ex-Green Beret who helps prevent the slaughter of wild horses from becoming canned dog food and fights to save a peace-loving art school in Arizona run by Jean Roberts (Delores Taylor; Laughlin's wife). The racist, close-minded members of a nearby town who have a problem with youth counterculture and Native Americans are antagonizing the school.

When I was learning fight choreography on the set of *Once Upon a Time in China V* (1994), Tsui Hark had me watch a video of a lion stalking a gazelle. He commented on the nature of the emotions—the stalking; the buildup of tension; then at the height of the hunt, the final death moment. To him, this was the essence of setting up fights. Both of Billy Jack's fights are derived from a scene that reflected America's discrimination against Native Americans at the time.

In the first fight, dialogue perfectly builds the tension. When some Native American children try to buy ice cream and are refused and abused, Billy Jack enters. And so it goes that Billy Jack says to the son of an influential man about town: "Bernard, I want you to know that I try. When Jean and the kids at the school tell me that I'm supposed to control my violent temper and be passive and nonviolent like they are, I try. I really try. Though when I see this girl of such a beautiful spirit so degraded, and this boy that I love sprawled out by this big ape here, and this little girl who is so special to us we call her 'God's little gift of sunshine,' and I think of the number of years that she's going to have to carry in her memory the savagery of this idiotic moment of yours, I just go berserk!"

Then a classic shot happens. In preparation for a fight with Bernard's father, Mr. Posner, and his goons in the park, Billy Jack slowly and methodically removes his shoes and socks, which would become part of Billy Jack's signature pre-fight routine in his sequels, *The Trial of Billy Jack* (1974) and *Billy Jack Goes to Washington* (1977). Posner and his thugs quickly surround Billy Jack when he enters the park. Billy Jack says to Posner: "You wanna know what I think I'm gonna do then, just for the hell of it? I'm gonna take this right foot, and I'm gonna whop you on that side of your face. And you wanna know something? There's not a damn thing you're gonna be able to do about it." Posner blurts, "Really?" and Billy Jack replies matter-of-factly, "Really." Then he throws a well-executed inside crescent kick (shot from two angles), and Posner crumbles to the ground in slow motion. Bong Soo-han then steps in for Laughlin to perform some of the trickier kick combos, but it doesn't and didn't matter, because in the 1970s, anyone watching this film was taken aback by the simplicity and effectiveness of the fight.

Titleography: As of this writing, no alternative titles could be found. **MA Percentage: 1.23%**

BLACK BELT JONES

(1974—USA) **87m. FC: Robert Wall. NOT/LOT: 2/ 47s; NOF/LOF: 16/ 15m 35s.** D: Robert Clouse. C: Jim Kelly, Gloria Hendry, Scatman Crothers, Eric Laneuville, Alan Weeks, Andre Philippe, Vincent Barbi, Mel Novak, Malik Carter.

This movie is more like *Bruce Lee Jones*, but that's OK. Riding the crest of Bruce Lee's successful *Enter the Dragon* wave, Warner Bros. had the same production team come up with a film that could not only tap into the current lucrative blaxploitation genre but would also create a part for Jim Kelly that closely resembled his popular Williams character from *Enter the Dragon*. The result was a sort of Lee-like *Fist of Fury* (1972) in the ghetto that centered around Kelly playing a cool karate cat named Black Belt Jones who saves a martial arts school from the clutches of the Mafia because they have more than land grabbing on their minds.

The mob hires Pinky (Malik Carter) to coerce Papa Byrd (Scatman Crothers) into selling his karate school, which happens to be on a piece of land the mob wants, but Papa refuses. Pinky accidentally kills him, but that incurs the wrath of Byrd's daughter Sydney (Gloria Hendry) and Jones. Worried sick that Jones and Sydney are in the mix, the mob leans on Pinky, who calmly and coolly states that everything will be fine. "I have a couple of Bogarts coming in from Frisco." After the Don asks what they are, Pinky grins and stalwartly says, "Treacherous n****rs." I saw this film in college back in 1974 or 1975 in a mixed crowd, and everyone laughed. At the time, such a line was just not shocking, but today it would have a deeper impact.

The fights in this film are rehashed tidbits of the action between Lee and Kelly from *Enter the Dragon*, probably because that was the only kind of action that director Robert Clouse was familiar with. Fight choreographer Robert Wall was similarly limited by what he saw Lee choreograph during the two films he worked on with Lee (*Enter the Dragon* and *Way of the Dragon*). But at the end of the day, the approach still works. It is like seeing the rebirth of the Williams character on a larger scale because Kelly gives more nods to Lee than a bobbing-head doll. Although he delivers his dialogue like Williams, Kelly fights, walks, creeps and wields *escrima* sticks like Lee. He also uses a rubber hose as if it were a *nunchaku*.

Two main things to point out: Throughout his fights, Kelly developed the bad habit of not fully extending his legs when he kicked—something that he would do throughout the rest of his martial arts films. It makes his fights feel cramped and hurried. Kelly also created the obscure power strike, wherein he tries to sell the illusion of a powerful punch by striking his opponent while tensing every muscle in his upper torso. Jean Claude Van Damme took this bad idea to a worse level in his early films. I don't mean to disparage Kelly, it's just that he's a legitimate martial artist and had the good fortune to work with Lee, and I believe he could have done better.

Titleography: As of this writing, no alternative titles could be found. **MA Percentage: 18.81%**

BLACK BELT KARATE

黑帶空手道 / *Karate Sabuk Hitam* (1979—Hong Kong/Indonesia) **91m. MAI: Larry Lee, Bruce Leung. NOT/LOT: 11/ 8m 48s; NOF/LOF: 27/ 29m 21s. D: Wisjnu Mouradhy. C: Larry Lee, Bruce Leung, Lo Lieh, Billy Chong, Jiang Dao, Peter Chan Lung, Tony Leung, R.D. Mochtar, David Sembel, Kies Slamet, Toto Soegianto, Deasy Surachman.**

Karate teaches that ego must be checked in at the door, and those who forget this virtue of humility will be humbled into deadly submission.

Wide-eyed and bushy-tailed country-bumpkin Tommy (Larry Lee) travels to Indonesia in search of a karate teacher only to find a great *sensei* at the Golden Eagle *dojo*. Unfortunately, a senior student in Tommy's school switches to the dark side, in this case the Dragon dojo, and plots with the egotistical loser who Tommy beats in a tournament earlier in the film. They plan to destroy the Golden Eagle dojo while Tommy is in Hong Kong training for his fifth-degree black-belt test. Based on one of the *kata*, it looks to me like Tommy is learning Okinawan *goju-ryu* karate.

Black Belt Karate is one of those films that opens with the often-used star performing the martial art of the day against a solid-red background during the opening credits. In this case, it's karate man Larry Lee wielding a bevy of Okinawan weapons like the *sai* and *nunchaku*. Although neat-looking, these opening credit sequences ruin the plot as we now know the downtrodden dude is going to become a great fighter.

The fights occur in two locations in this film: Hong Kong and Indonesia. You know that Larry Lee is choreographing the Indonesia fights because those fights look like karateka are going at each other. You know Bruce Leung is choreographing the fights in Hong Kong because they have a more Chinese kung fu flavor. Along with helping Lee do the fight choreography, Leung also cameos with some interesting combinations of karate and northern Shaolin kung fu with just a few hints of his Bruce Lee alter ego. The karate fights at times border on dummied-down kung fu techniques, but the swift, solid kicks add a certain level of authenticity to main actor Larry Lee's karate background. For the martial arts

film debut of Indonesian-born actor Billy Chong, he shows sturdy stances and focused kicks while playing his part as Tommy's karate *sempai* (senior student). Actor Lo Lieh plays the visiting Japanese fighting representative, but the lessons he learned from doing kung fu films in Hong Kong seems to overshadow Lo's karate foundation, and he only shines through with his physical demeanor rather than skill.

Titleography: *Bad Guys Wear Black.* Translation—*Black Belt Karate.* This film was released in America after Chuck Norris' *Good Guys Wear Black,* which the distributor thought was a recognizable enough film to warrant the paraphrased title. **MA Percentage: 41.92%**

BLACK SAMURAI

(1977—USA) **88m. FSS: Jim Kelly, Jace Khan. NOT/LOT: 3/56s; NOF/LOF: 10/ 11m 12s. D: Al Adamson. C: Jim Kelly, Bill Roy, Roberto Contreras, Marilyn Joi, Essie Lin Chia, Biff Yeager, Charles Grant, Jace Khan, Erwin Fuller.**

Four years after teaming up with Bruce Lee, Jim Kelly was still unable to let go of his *Enter the Dragon* alter ego. In this film, he borrows from Lee, his own character from *Enter the Dragon* named Williams, and even Chuck Norris. Watching the fight scenes, I couldn't help feeling bad for Kelly, wondering how he was able to stomach what the choreographers wanted him to do; Kelly is a legitimate martial artist, after all.

Kelly plays Robert Sand, an agent of DRAGON (which might as well stand for Down-Right Awful Gung fu and Outlandishly Nasty). His former lover Toki (Shaw Brothers actress Essie Lin Chia) is kidnapped by a voodoo villain, Janicot, who holds the girl for ransom so her ambassador father will fund his "freeze bomb" weapon. Sand cuts his vacation short and uncovers drug dealing, prostitution and a California condor in the process of trying to rescue Toki. Of the ambassador father, Sand says, "He is the minister of samurai code—he won't give in that easy." I never knew there was such a government position in Japan that has representation in America; sign me up.

After the film, my heart lowered further when the credits revealed Kelly specifically staged and choreographed his own fight sequences. For a man with his caliber of martial arts skills and experience in film, it is disappointing to see him do the Ali shuffle and Bruce Lee fidgety fists and footwork in just about every fight scene. He even does his footwork in the payload of a pickup truck in preparation for a fight with a guy standing six inches away from him.

His flash training sequences, which are little snippets of martial arts movements to show off Kelly's skills, look like they were done off the cuff. In Chinese films, a director would commonly ask an actor to fire off a few movements for the camera. Unfortunately, in cases when there was no fighting instructor present to ensure quality, the actor would sometimes end up waving his arms haphazardly. When Sand picks up a samurai sword like a tennis racket—you will note that in most of his contemporary films, Kelly has a scene playing tennis or holding a racket—he begins to shadowbox with the sword. It could have been a cool scene, but it falls as flat as U.S. President Gerald Ford did when he fell down the steps of Air Force One on national TV in the mid-70s. You have got to love when Kelly does a *nunchaku* sequence because the weapon's sound effects are lifted directly from Lee's performance in *Way of the Dragon* (1973). As if that were not crazy enough, another fight cribs the sound effects from the Lee-Norris Colosseum battle from the same film.

The group fights also leave something to be desired because each fight is really just a series of one-on-one confrontations in which each adversary goes down after one technique. There are a lot of stunts involving jumping down from balconies, and Kelly swaggers around the set while preening for camera. Ultimately, like Norris, Kelly's best cinematic fight for his entire career would be in a Lee film.

Titleography: *Black Terminator; The Freeze Bomb.* Not to be confused with Kelly's *Death Dimension,* which also had the alternative title *Freeze Bomb.* **MA Percentage: 13.79%**

BLACK TAVERN, THE

黑店 (1972—Hong Kong) **81m. FI: Xu Er-niu, Xu Song-hao. NOT/LOT: None; NOF/LOF: 40/ 30m 36s. D: Yeh Yung-tsu. C: Shih Szu, Ku feng, Tung Li, Dean Shek, Wang Xia, Yu Feng, Jiang Ling. Guo Chu-qing, Barry Chan, Lio Hao, Wu Ma, Yang Chi-ching, Yang Zi-lin, Jiang Nan, Lu Wei.**

They do not make films like this anymore. *The Black Tavern* is simply the best whip movie in the history of whip-moviedom. My mouth was so agape watching this film that I swallowed a few thousand flies. Whip master Zhang Shou-shan (Ku Feng) is like a flamethrower full of rocket fuel, and this movie is on my list of must-see films of the 1970s. It is on the list not for the story, which isn't very far from the typical revenge method of action, but the fight scenes are cooler than liquid nitrogen freezing the T-1000 in *Terminator 2* (1991). One such fight scene features a minor character named Hu (Lu Wei) wearing a Viking helmet and terrorizing the Gao Family Inn. He's like an enraged bull in a ring filled with blind matadors who forgot their capes and swords.

The story begins after a drunken monk (Dean Shek) performs a *shu xiao ban* (a sort of Chinese rap music dating back to the 11th century) in a restaurant full of vagabonds, thieves and a mysterious swordswoman named Zhang Cui-ping (Shih Szu). (Does her name ring a bell? Hint: She's a character Shih Szu played in an earlier film in which Cheng Pei-pei was her teacher.) The monk raps that there is a chest full of treasure heading to the Black Tavern. The loot belongs to Hai Gong-fong, a corrupt official who amassed a fortune by accepting bribes and now wants to retire. The patrons all leave the restaurant with gleams in their eyes, greed on their brains and leers on their faces. They head to the mysterious inn to grab the spoils for themselves.

Any film that has great snow shots always grabs my attention, and this is one example. It then moves to an inn, following the footsteps of *Come Drink With Me* (1966), and eventually erupts with a bunch of baddies trying to get their hands on a secret consignment of jewels. Things get increasingly lethal, resulting in some inventive death scenes. It is a menagerie of Chekhovian pseudo-heroes and back-stabbing villains, plus zombie men, ghosts, leopard-skin lackeys, switched women and, of course, actor Lu Wei in the Viking helmet.

The whip choreography for actor Ku Feng goes far beyond similar films in which characters twirl the whip in circles above their heads or in figure eights, occasionally injecting a whip crack or two. Ku is sharp, crisp and quick, and he continually performs different moves and gags. In one scene, he uniquely beheads a woman with his whip. Then there is Lu Wei's whacked-out piece: He carries a pole for one kooky fight sequence featuring a wicked reverse-angle point-of-view shot of him holding onto his weapon for dear life while being flipped around. He is lifted up, travels in a semicircle and then lands on his back; his face grimaces into camera the whole time. Lu is then whipped into a coffin and dragged across the ground toward several swords waiting to put a stop to his antics. The final fight between heroine Cui-ping and villain Zhang Shao-shan is a combo whip-in-a-whip-in-a-whip crescendo with a headless horse and carriage. The two jockey for life against a crushing, rolling wheel, and the visuals of two warriors at night facing each other while surrounded by falling snow is just glorious.

Titleography: As of this writing, no alternative titles could be found. Translation—*Black Tavern*. **MA Percentage: 37.78%** SHAW BROTHERS

BLAZING TEMPLE, THE

火燒少林寺 (1976—Hong Kong) 87m. MAI: Chen Shao-peng. NOT/LOT: 17/ 3m 27s; NOF/LOF: 15/ 15m 17s. D: Chen Shiao-peng. C: Carter Wong, Chia Ling, Zhang Yi, Barry Chan, Yi Yuan, Huang Fei-long, Jin Gang, Liu Ping, Jia Kai, David Tong Wai, Zhang Zhong-gui, O Yau-man.

The conflagration of hatred can be distinguished by the waters of time, which begins when the flames of the torch are understood. The fire of hatred that Ching Emperor Yong Zhen held toward the Shaolin Temple led him to burning down the temple. As time flowed by like water, the monks learned why the emperor did it, and by knowing this, they could extinguish the torch that started the blazing temple.

The Blazing Temple was made and released after *Return of the 18 Bronzemen*, which was a film that accentuated the failed attempt of a young swordswoman (Polly Kuan) to assassinate Ching Emperor Yong Zheng (Carter Wong), who is saved by his secret sword-resisting vest. *Blazing Temple* begins with the same failed attempt of a female warrior (played by Chia Ling in this film) trying to assassinate Yong Zheng (played by actor Yi Yuan) who retaliates by wholeheartedly attacking and destroying Song Shan Shaolin Temple. Although the film does not explicitly state which temple is destroyed, historically, Yong Zheng razed Song Shan to the ground in 1735 during the 13th and last year of his reign.

Blazing Temple is basically a sequel to *Return of the 18 Bronzemen*. It follows the story of how the Shaolin monks, who escaped the burning temple via their Yuen Kung garden's secret tunnel, hid in the mountains and vengefully plotted to assassinate the emperor. Unlike in *ROT-18*, Carter Wong stars in this film as a Shaolin monk that is given the secret Ta Mo's 18 Principles kung fu manual. After learning the technique, he is accompanied by a handful of monks to storm Yong Zheng's palace. Of note, this is the same kung fu style that Wong's Yong Zheng character wanted so desperately to learn in *ROT-18*. I guess one could say *ROT-18* was the "Wong" film for Carter to do Ta Mo's kung fu.

This film also solidified actor O Yau Man's place in martial arts cinema history as the heroic and highly principled abbot of Song Shan Shaolin, where he, like Gordon Liu, would typically become typecast as a Shaolin monk. In O's case, he was often the ancient sage monk who would transcend the martial aspects of training, so fantastically shown in *Big Land, Flying Eagles* (1978).

The coveted techniques from Ta Mo's 18 Principles featured in this film stem from historical reality. After arriving at Song Shan Shaolin Temple in A.D. 520, real-life Indian Buddhist monk Ta Mo meditated while facing a wall for nine years. During that time, he wrote the 18 Buddhist Fists (one of the written treasures of Shaolin), which outlined a series of exercises that improved the health of the monks and provided a means of self-defense against bandits during long pilgrimages or while foraging for food. These movements are considered the beginning of Shaolin martial arts. Over time, the techniques were constantly revised or improved on, one of the most famous delineations being the mid-17th century creation of the Five Animal Styles of Shaolin by Shaolin monk Zhue Yang and fellow martial artists Li Sou and Bai Yu-feng.

Although official records claim that Emperor Yong Zheng died peacefully, it is strongly believed that the daughter of a family that Yong Zheng had executed assassinated him. Whether she was helped by a handful of Shaolin priests bent on revenge (like this film alludes to) is like many things in Chinese martial arts history: It's as bright as the moon from the earth and the luminescence differs pending on time, place and the weather.

During the scene with the invading Ching army and the temple burning, the background music from composer Gustav Holst's *The Planets,* specifically the first movement, *Mars, the Bringer of War,* captures the resonance of the mood perfectly.

Titleography: As of this writing, no alternative titles could be found. Translation—*Burning Shaolin Temple*. **MA Percentage: 21.53%**

BLIND WOMAN'S CURSE, THE

Kaidan Nobori Ryu (1970—Japan) **85m. MAT: Nakase Masatoshi. NOT/ LOT: None; NOF/LOF: 11/ 10m 9s.** D: Teruo Ishii. C: Meiko Kaji, Hoki Tokuda, Makoto Sato, Yoshi Kato, Yuzo Harumi, Toru Abe, Shiro Otsuji, Hideo Sunazuka, Yoko Takagi, Ryohei Uchida.

Imagine Zatoichi the blind swordsman meets Yojimbo (Toshiro Mifune's famous *ronin* role) in drag, certainly a samurai swords slice-of-life film to be gored at.

When the dragon-tattooed, female Yakuza boss Akemi (Meiko Kaji) kills the rival Yakuza clan's leader, she inadvertently swipes her razor-sharp sword across the eyes of the leader's sister, Aiko (Hoki Tokuda), thus blinding her in an ocular slice of rod-and-cone frenzy. The camera then focuses on a black cat licking the profusely bleeding eyes of Aiko, which sets off a series of superstitious and gruesome events that leads Akemi to believe she has been cursed. Everything boils down to a showdown between Akemi's gang and a second rival gang trying to usurp her reputation and territory, and the personal vendetta that has driven blind woman Aiko to use the next five years to learn the art of guillotine swordplay in order to give Akemi the Marie Antoinette treatment.

This movie is a rarity in *ninkyo* (chivalrous Yakuza) films because of the addition of the macabre and surreal Grand Guignol (a Parisian theater that specialized in graphic amoral horror) sensibilities and imagery, which categorized *The Blind Woman's Curse* as a horror film.

The movie ends with Yakuza crusading unto war. They prepare for glorified gore in a final venge-filled massacre that all parties believe is for a righteous purpose. "Pop!" goes the Yakuza world.

The ending duel between Akemi and Aiko is purposely shot in low light with a snow-covered ground. The combatants are placed in specific areas on the set where the artificial light source reflects off the shiny silver samurai sword blades and tracks along with the fighters as they move within the set. Furthermore, whenever they move or strike a snow-covered object, swirling flakes of snow float into the air. These things subliminally force the audience to focus on the sword flashes, which creates a sense of speed in the choreography and makes the fight appear dramatic and kinetic. In reality, the actors mostly pose and use little footwork.

Titleography: *Black Cat's Revenge*; *Strange Tales of Dragon Tattoo*; *The Haunted Life of a Dragon-Tattooed Lass*; *The Tattooed Swordswoman*. Translation—*Story of Strange Things (Ghost Story) Rising Dragon*. All the titles are inferred from the film. **MA Percentage: 11.34%**

BLOOD BROTHERS

刺 馬 (1973—Hong Kong) **118m. FI: Liu Chia-liang, Tang Chia. NOT/LOT: 4/ 2m 22s; NOF/LOF: 24/ 22m 13s.** D: Chang Cheh. C: Ti Lung, David Chiang, Chen Kuan-tai, Ching Li, Ching Miao, Tian Ching, Yang Zi-lin, Wang Kuan-yu, Fan Mie-sheng, Tong Yen-san, Jiang Dao, Danny Lee.

"Blood brothers" can refer to two or more males related by birth, or it can refer to males not related by birth who swear a lifetime oath of loyalty to each other, otherwise known as a blood oath. In such a ceremony, each man cuts himself and then exchanges blood with the other. This can involve dripping blood into a bowl of water and drinking it or shaking cut hands, thereby mixing the blood. Blood oaths were a common practice among Norsemen, Mongols, Native Americans and Chinese warriors such as those portrayed in this film, specifically the historically true-life characters of Chang Wen-hsiang (David Chiang), Ma Hsin-I (Ti Lung) and Huang Chung (Chen Kuan-tai).

When Chang is accused of treason and appears before a Ching tribunal, the judge asks him to detail all the events that conspired over a nine-year period. Chained in iron and with a death penalty looming above his head as big as the sharp ax his executioner holds, Chang tells his story to the tribunal in a series of flashbacks.

Chang explains how, many moons earlier, he and his fellow robber Huang waited for their next victim, who turns out to be Ma, a righteous and well-honed martial artist. As the three fight, each comes to respect the other's abilities, and Ma hands over his money without a fight. Ma then decides to follow Huang and Chang back to their hideout to convince the robbers to change their criminal ways and become good men. The three quickly

become friends. Because Ma aspires to pass the royal exam and realizes he will need a good martial arts army to support his future goals, Ma begins to train an army of loyal fighters. The problem is that Huang's wife, Mi Lan (Ching Li), really respects Ma's ambitions for future wealth and power and thus develops a yen for him. After passing the exam, Ma joins the Xiang army. Alongside Zeng Guo-fang, the Ching general, he fights long and hard to destroy the rebel "Long Hairs." Ma moves up the ranks and recruits his blood brothers, Chang and Huang, and together they bring the Taiping Rebellion to a violent end.

However, drunk with power and position, Ma has an affair with Mi Lan and then conspires to get rid of Huang, which he does. Chang learns that Ma's hands are dirty with the blood of Huang and confronts him. He ends up having to clean his own hands of Ma's blood, which brings the story back to the Ching court, where Chang is sentenced to death. It is a tragic love-triangle story about honor, brotherhood and, ultimately, dishonor.

Co-directed by John Woo, the fights start out oversimplified, reflecting the initial simplicity of the relationship between the three brothers. The fights use one-step choreography, in which the movements are overly rhythmic and delivered one at a time, making the fight sequences a lesson in memory rather than continuity. Even the group fights are a series of single movements against each opponent. Each member of the triumvirate takes out one rebellious Long Hair at a time with one technique, using a metronomic rhythm. As the film moves toward the end, similar to the plot and the growing complex relationships between the three blood brothers, the fight scenes also become more complex. It's as if director Chang was using increasingly elaborate fight scenes to reflect Ma, Chang and Huang's entangled friendship. An odd eccentricity about the fights is that there are a lot of bodies rolling down hills—as many as 15—putting European soccer players to shame. (Many of these athletes are famous for rolling all over the field after being fouled.) Ti Lung won a Golden Horse award (the Hong Kong version of an Academy Award) for his outstanding performance in this film.

A note on the Taiping Rebellion: It was led by Christian convert Hong Xiu-chuen, who believed he was the younger brother of Jesus. The rebellion occurred between 1850 and 1864. Rebels fought the Ching government in an effort to abolish foot binding, introduce land socialization, and replace Chinese folk religion and philosophies like Buddhism and Confucianism with Christianity. The rebels were called Long Hairs because they wore their queues differently than what the law demanded. Of note, American sailor Frederick Townsend Ward was a successful military leader for the Ching army.

Titleography: *Dynasty of Blood*; *Chinese Vengeance*. Translation—*Kill Ma*. *Dynasty of Blood* refers to the blood spilled as a result of the Ching Dynasty killing Han Chinese. *Chinese Vengeance* refers to hero Chang, a Han Chinese, who kills Ma, a Manchu by heritage, in revenge for murdering their blood brother, Huang. The Chings were Manchus and not Han Chinese; the distinction between these various races of Chinese peoples is important in Chinese history. **MA Percentage: 20.83%** SHAW BROTHERS

Still from *Blood Brothers* © Celestial Pictures Ltd. All rights reserved.

BLOODED TREASURY FIGHT

血 肉 磨 坊 (1979—Hong Kong) **90m. FD:** Yuen Cheung-yan. **NOT/ LOT:** 1/ 9s; **NOF/LOF:** 23/ 21m 19s. **D:** Pao Hsueh-li. **C:** David Chiang, Tan Dao-liang, Michael Chan, Wang Chung, Cai Hong, Chen Bi-feng, Zhang Yi-dao (Bruce Lai).

Knit one, "pearl" two—the making of *Blooded Treasury Fight* is partially woven in a run-of-the-mill maelstrom of lost pearls and the fights that ensue to get to them. If someone ever knitted you a sweater, the audio cadence for knitting is, "Knit one, purl two," where purl is simply a reverse stitch skill. Yet the screaming screech and stitch you hear at the end of the film is not the destruction of the mill's grindstone going in reverse but the fights fading from gritty sand to liquid white-out.

As the theme from the TV series *Battlestar Galactica* (1978) blares in the background, and in the vein of *The Dirty Dozen* (1967), perennial Shaw Brothers' hero David Chiang plays Ying Kan-tao who is recruited out of prison by Marshall Chao Kwan-han (Tan Dao-liang) to assist him on a dangerous mission to find the lost treasure of the Bai Ling Sect. Problem: The treasure was hidden in the sect's secret lair after the leader committed suicide. Bigger problem: If Ying refuses Chao's offer, he dies; if he accepts, he will probably die during the mission. But if he does survive, he will win his dream of freedom. But like any dream, the dream can fade.

With such a high degree of pedigree martial artists—like David Chiang, Michael Chan, Tan Dao-liang, Wang Chung, Bruce Lai and Shaw Brothers' regular villain Cai Hong—in this finicky flick, it is a blush of misplaced rouge for a kung film to begin with fights as colorfully plush as a $2,000 cashmere sweater only to unravel into a pile of white used wool. Because fights in kung fu films are mostly shot in order of their appearance, early fights usually are the worst, and as the actors become attuned with each other and the fight choreographers, the fights typically elevate to new levels by the end of the film, but not in this movie.

And it is interesting that even though some of David Chiang's best fights occur in his earlier films, he is arguably doing some of his best pure kung fu performances to date during the first half of this movie. His stances are solid, he uses correct kung fu posture (meaning his back is straight) and his hand positions during the choreography are well-placed and not dropping away from his body (like in most of his films). Actor Tan Dao-liang's kicks also appear more powerful looking than usual. But at the final fight, when all the main martial arts stars are vying to grab the treasure chest amid a finale of twists, turns and trying anything they can do to pull a red herring over their plot, the action is so disjointed and poorly choreographed that the showdown at Blood Mill is more of a bloody mess.

Titleography: *Dragon Devils Die.* Translation—*Blood Meat Mill.* Assuming that because everyone in the film is practically a villain (the *Devils* in the title) and most of them die, *Dragon* was probably tagged on to complete the alliteration. *Blood Meat Mill* is the Chinese name of the mill where the final fight occurs. At the end of the day, as the blood flows, they are all fighting for the treasure, which is why the original English title makes sense. **MA Percentage: 23.85%**

BLOODY ESCAPE, THE

逃 亡 (1974—Hong Kong) **84m. FI:** Liu Chia-rong, Huang Pei-ji. **NOT/LOT: None; NOF/LOF:** 13/ 12m 15s. **D:** Sun Chung, Chang Cheh. **C:** Chen Kuan-tai, Shih Szu, Wu Chi-chin, Frankie Wei Hong, Jiang Dao, Chan Shen, Li Min-lang.

Peer pressure is one of the many evils we all have to deal with. It can cause us to make stupid and unhealthy decisions such as smoking cigarettes, drinking alcohol and taking drugs. At its extreme, peer pressure can force one to commit treachery and murder. It takes a strong-willed person to be his own man, and in both life and this film, the way of martial arts can provide the key to unlock the door to one's freedom of individuality and decision.

While director Chang Cheh was busy trying to establish his own production company in Taiwan and still fulfill his directorial duties for Shaw Brothers,

sometimes a project had to be sacrificed. Although Chang started *The Bloody Escape* in early 1975, other commitments took precedence (possibly his next Shaolin epic *Disciples of Shaolin*). Therefore, all shot footage was handed to co-director Sun Chung, who shot the rest of the film, edited it and got it into the can in eight weeks.

Chief Du (Wu Chi-chin), the head of the Wolf Head Gang, took a liking to the naive Gu Hui (Chen Kuan-tai) and taught him all the kung fu he knows. But Du, who learned kung fu to be a better ruthless bandit and wanted Gu to follow in his footsteps, never dreamt that Gu would truly understand the righteousness and fair play that martial artists should follow. One day when Du tries to cheat in a fight, much to Du's anger, Gu points out the incorrectness of doing that and so Du begins fighting Gu for real. Yet Gu refuses to hit back because Du is his mentor. Du recently became chief after the old leader mysteriously died, and Du started to make changes that Gu disagreed with.

Still from *The Bloody Escape* © Celestial Pictures Ltd. All rights reserved.

Economic times are tough for the common people, so when the Wolf Head Gang raids a village, their original rules were to only take half the money and to never kill or rape. However, things change under the new leadership of Du. So when Gu is assigned to head a raiding party and sees his gang members begin to rape and kill, then kidnap the beautiful Tang Li (Shih Szu), who is police Commissioner Zhang's (Frankie Wei Hong) fiancee, Gu defiantly disobeys Du's new unjust rules. Gu rescues Tang, gets several of the gang members caught by the police (who get executed by the commissioner's firing squad), and now Gu goes into hiding from Du and also the police. In order to clear his name, Gu must weed out Du, and so begins his journey of retribution, redemption and revenge. In other words, he does not want to Du bad, only Gu-d.

Sun Chung directs an effective story about a rising hero who refuses to bend under peer pressure and, in fact, uses that negativity to make a positive impact on his own life. The fights are below Chen's usual solid legitimate martial arts sharpness and appeal when comparing it to some of his previous powerful works. Each technique is overemphasized, which indicates that the fighters are trying to create the illusion of power and emotion rather than being powerful and emotional during a struggle. Although the fighters try to make the windups look logical, they come across as sloppy. But in their defense, it can be difficult to get one's blood up when a new director takes over. Most of the fights become second hat (not as important), whereas Chang Cheh would have scrounged for every bit of blood and guts in this kind of revenge-laden film. The change of director may also explain why a film that has *The Boxer From Shantung* written all over it only has a meager 12 minutes of fights.

Titleography: As of this writing, no alternative titles could be found. Translation—*Escape.* Both titles reflect Gu's plight away from Du. **MA Percentage: 14.58%** SHAW BROTHERS

BLOODY FISTS, THE

蕩 寇 灘 (1972—Hong Kong) **86m. FD: Yuen Woo-ping, Yuen Cheung-yan. NOT/LOT: 1/ 19s; NOF/LOF: 23/ 32m 10s.** D: Ng See-yuen. C: Chen Kuan-tai, Chen Hsing, Henry Yu Yung, Fang Ye, San Kuai, Liu Ta-chuan, Hon Gwok-choi.

During the 1920s, many regions in China were not only hit with cholera, a plague caused by a gastrointestinal bacterial infection that caused death by dehydration, but also had to contend with the growing presence of Japan militarism.

When fugitive Chang Wu-ge (Chen Hsing) passes through a seaside community, he finds himself forced to take sides between a local Chinese martial arts school and the masked, cruel killer Takeo Okagawa (Chen Kuan-tai). The school is trying to prevent Okagawa from opening a Japanese gym and finding the village's secret warehouse that holds the special herbs needed to cure the plague hurting the Japanese troops. Two brothers, Yu Yang (Henry Yu Yung) and Yu Chang (Liu Ta-chuan), successfully stand up to the Japanese fighters until Okagawa threatens to behead all the Chinese men on the beach unless he is given the herbs. Fortunately, Chang has a change of patriotic heart when he comes down with the plague and when the bumbling local mute (Hon Gwok-choi), who selflessly saved Chang's life from the plague, is sliced down by Okagawa's Japanese swordsmen. Our protagonist runs to the beach to take on Okagawa and his Nippon nasties. The showdown will decide the fate of the village and undoubtedly southern China.

I occasionally slight Chen Hsing's kung fu ability for his poor posture, yet I finally realized why I still like the guy (apart from meeting him in Taipei, China, where he actually lived in the apartment complex across the street from my dormitory). He has got the best gritting-teeth face in the industry, which is comparable to anything Jack Elam (popular villain in Westerns, his psychotic screen presence accentuated by an off-centered, lazy left eye) can throw at you. Plus in this film, Chen has a nice touch with a comb, which adds new life to the phrase "combing the beach."

Overall, there is a certain powerful sloppiness to the fights that makes them seem real to the average movie viewer rather than phony. Furthermore, the choices of camera angle and camera movement by Yuen Woo-ping gives added motion to create the illusion that more is going on than really is. Woo-ping also limits the number of martial techniques to less than 10 per shot. He must have finally realized that having actors perform too many techniques in a row when shot in wide angle slows down the fight and increases the risk of revealing "misses."

Titleography: *Death Beach.* Translation—*Wiping Out Bandits Beach. The Bloody Fists* shares the notion of bloody fists, which was often the case in all those anti-Japanese films of that era, so it is a generic title. The Chinese title is the name of the beach, whereas the English title *Death Beach* is closer to the literal meaning to the Chinese title. However, I can't tell whether the distributor called it *Death Beach* because people are dying on the beach or whether they knew that *Wiping Out Bandits Beach* was the actual name of the beach. **MA Percentage: 37.77%**

BOHACHI, CLAN OF THE FORGOTTEN EIGHT

Bohachi Bushido (1973—Japan) **80m. FI: Uncredited. NOT/LOT: None; NOF/LOF: 12/ 6m 20s.** D: Teruo Ishii. C: Tetsuro Tanba, Goro Ibuki, Tatsuo Endo, Ryohei Uchida, Yuriko Hishimi, Keiko Aikawa, Rena Ichinose, Emi Katsura, Ruriko Ikejima, Shiro Kuno, Koichi Sato.

"If dying is hell, then how is that any different from the hell that is life?" So grunts the assassin Shiro (Tetsuro Tanba) while he fights government samurai on a quaint footbridge against the setting sun. Being a *ronin* on the run for so long has drained him of his spirit and his will to live, so during the fight Shiro hurls himself into the waters below in a suicide attempt. But a samurai from the Bohachi Clan named Kesazo Shirakuba saves him and throws Shiro into an even more hellish struggle than he ever could have imagined.

Kesazo wants Shiro to join the Bohachi Clan as a fellow sword-wielding enforcer, and in return, the clan will protect him from the police. Despite the fact that the Tokugawa shogunate is taking over lands and businesses to maintain power, the shogun is powerless against the Yakuza-based flesh peddlers known as the Bohachi Mono. It's important to know that the Bohachi Clan doesn't just sell women as sex slaves. They also coerce them to do the clan's bidding, even if it means sacrificing their lives.

Shiro reluctantly agrees. To become one of the clan members, he must live outside the law and forget eight virtues: godliness, obedience and fidelity to elders, loyalty to friends, giving trust to allies, modesty, justice, conscience and shame. But Shiro fails his test, which is to force an innocent woman who owes the Bohachi money to pay the clan back with sexual servitude. Before the Bohachi have the chance to hand him over to the police, an elderly Bohachi boss arrives. He saves Shiro and gives him the job of killing feudal lords, samurai and any official who intervenes in Bohachi business. The audience also learns that the old man possesses a special bell, which was given to him by Ieyasu, the former Tokugawa shogun. The bell gives the old man the power to run his nefarious business without any interference from the shogunate powers that be—representative and actual.

Shiro once again agrees. He is given eight beautiful and deadly fighting women to do with as he pleases. They also serve as his protection. But the Bohachi code has taught Shiro that he can trust no one. So like the water under the bridge at the beginning of the film, he simply goes with the flow and sees where fate takes him.

The film's opening fight on the bridge with the setting red sun is beautifully accented, while severed limbs fly about and melt into the blood-soaked opening credits. The simple and steady long shots and wide angles contrast with the sheer brutality of the bloodletting and stylistic romanticism of slow-motion samurai slices. Then a later fight in which Shiro's nude Bohachi babes manhandle—in slow motion—an opposing ninja foolish enough to try to kill Shiro is as mesmerizing as it is disturbing. The fights are glorified gore and gory with glory. They are filled with a cool combination of steely determination and praiseworthy fight altercations that culminate in the film's final showdown between Shiro and the policemen.

The final fight is series of steps and chops, where Shiro simply steps toward an opponent with his sword and does one of three strikes: chop down, slice up or slice horizontally. It is up to the stuntmen to sell the reactions of each of the three strikes. They are aided by blood hoses, blood pouches and even a little wire work, but the wires are not on the actors. On several occasions wires are attached to various severed limbs that mystically float and fly away. The effect is superb and gives the action a surreal, dreamlike quality. Another cool visual is using multicolored spotlights that beam on Shiro as he moves methodically around the courtyard. It's also interesting because although it is a group fight, for Shiro it personalizes each individual battle—not only with his opponent, but also with himself.

A Shiro-influenced character returned the following year in the similarly themed film *Saburai: The Way of the Bohachi* (1974).

Titleography: *Code of the Forgotten Eight.* Translation—*Way of the Bohachi Samurai.* **MA Percentage: 7.92%**

BORN INVINCIBLE

太 極 氣 功 (1978—Hong Kong) **83m. SC: Yuen Woo-ping. NOT/LOT: 9/ 10m 51s; NOF/LOF: 18/ 29m 51s.** D: Joseph Kuo. C: Carter Wong, Lo Lieh, Yan Nan-xi, Long Guan-wu, Jack Long, Yuen Kwei, Lung Fei, Yuen Shen-yi, Alan Hsu, Su Chen-ping, Yuan Sen.

The film's Chinese title, *Tai Chi Chi Gong* (*Taiji Chi Gong*), is the exact name of the style of *chi gong* (*qigong*) that a *tai chi* (*taiji*) practitioner must do in order to reap the benefits of the style. Notice that the "chi" (極) in tai chi and the "chi" (氣) in chi gong are different characters and are not related. This is why "tai chi" should be pronounced "taiji" (which by the way is the correct pronunciation). If one does not practice taiji chi gong, then taiji is but a series of exercises that will not strengthen the chi, and it becomes more of a dance or simple calisthenics. Chi (*qi* or *ki*) means "life force," "spiritual energy" or "air." This energy is not fully understood by the West and is therefore not always accepted as real, yet chi is the fount of Eastern medicine and has been used as a healing tool for more than 2000 years. The first physical evidence of chi's existence in Asian healing was found on a Chinese Neolithic pot dating back to 3000 or 5000 B.C. It depicts a person practicing the "post" or "hugging the tree stance," which is one of the foundations for practicing taiji. With good chi flow comes good health; with bad chi flow comes bad health. Chi gong means "the working of air" and is a series of breathing techniques that can be done standing or lying down.

Depending on whom you ask, taiji chi gong is a series of exercises that consist of 13 or 18 movements. These movements are done clockwise and counterclockwise in all four directions. Although there are many different kinds of chi gong, two of the many unifying factors for all real chi gong is that during practice, the eyes are open and the mouth is shut. Some chi gong practitioners can master *jing zhong zhao* (golden bell), in which their chi is used to protect themselves against strikes and weapon blows. However, due to the focusing of chi all over the body, there is usually at least one weak point on the body that is vulnerable at a specific time of day. (Chi is affected by diurnal rhythms. Like the immune system, chi is weaker at certain times of the day.)

Now on to the movie! When the Bei Pai killers (Yuen Kwei and Yuen Shen-yi) try to kill Lu Ching (Yuan Sen), Lu is saved by Yu Ming-tu (Jack Long) and then finds sanction at Yu's kung fu school, which is headed by Lei Ping (Lung Fei), master of the nine-ringed broadsword. Yet the Bei Pai killers are only assassin pawns of the real baddies, the caustic Chin Ying chiefs, jing zhong zhao expert Tian Wu-sing (Carter Wong) and master of the *tonfa* saw blade Chi Chin-fa (Lo Lieh). When the Chin Ying chiefs show up at the kung fu school and kill the teacher, Yu is bitten by the vengeance bug and goes into training seclusion to later emerge and defend his teacher and school's honor. Unable to defeat Wu-sing, he leaves a dying message in blood that reveals Wu-sing's weak spot: "Strike when he is not himself." Only one student is capable of defeating Wu-sing, and his name is Tien (Long Guan-wu).

The problem with the English dub is that it omits the notion that the fatal strike on Wu-sing must be done at a specific time (thus the stick in the ground and the ensuing shorter shadow indicating the time to strike. The dub also keeps calling Wu-sing's ability tai chi gong fu. Although he does practice tai chi, it is the chi gong that is the key to the film. Furthermore, each dubber has a different way of saying the character names, which at times can be confusing. I like that Wu-sing's vulnerable point is related to when he does something chi gong practitioners are not supposed to do, so it is his overconfidence in ignoring that simple rule that leads to his demise. The penny whistle sound effect also represents Wu-sing sinking his chi down to the *dan tian* (chi center), but it comes off more humorous than the scary impending doom it is supposed to show.

Titleography: *Shaolin's Born Invincible.* Translations—*Tai Chi Chi Gong* or *Taiji Chi Gong*, depending on which romanization one uses. As a note, Cantonese romanization for the film would be *Taai Gik Hei Gung. Born Invincible* refers to Wu-sing's kung fu skill that makes his body invincible against attacks. The use of *Shaolin* is only to attract buyers; the film has nothing to do with Shaolin martial arts. Wu Dung monk Zhang San-fung created tai chi. (See *The Shadow Boxer.*) **MA Percentage: 49.04%**

BOXER FROM SHANTUNG, THE

馬 永 貞 (1972—Hong Kong) **123m. Fl: Liu Chia-liang, Liu Chia-rong, Chan Chuen, Tang Chia. NOT/LOT: None; NOF/LOF: 20/ 22m 40s.** D: Chang Cheh, Pao Hsueh-li. C: Chen Kuan-tai, Ching Li, David Chiang, Cheng Kang-yeh, Jiang Nan, Chia, Feng Yi, Ku Feng, Wong Ching, Mario Milano.

After the burning of the Song Shan Shaolin Temple, the five monks who survived became known as the Five Ancestors of Shaolin and pledged their brotherhood at the Red Flower Pavilion. (See *Five Shaolin Masters.*) The monks organized what is known as the Hong League or Hong Men ("Hong" is a family and does not mean "red," and "Men" means "door" or "entrance") and vowed vengeance against the Ching Dynasty. This was the birth of the Chinese Triads, whose initial purpose was to fight for the good of the Chinese people. Either as offshoots of Hong Men or arising independently, Triad gangs evolved and branched into devious organized criminal activity. Before World War II, Shanghai became a major hub for their negative and rampant activities. But not every Triad boss was evil; many were, in fact, righteous men who upheld a strict martial code of honor and morality in which they used their influence to the betterment of China and its people.

The Boxer From Shantung was co-directed by newcomer John Woo (he is unlisted in the credits above) and is a highly explosive film based on the real-life rise and violent fall of one such good Triad leader, Ma Yong-zhen (Chen Kuan-tai). The movie begins when Ma and his loyal friend Xiao Jiang-bei (Cheng Kang-yeh) arrive in Shanghai from Shantung and inadvertently cross fists with the feared and loathed Boss Yang (Jiang Nan). Afterward, Ma finds an ally with the respected crime boss Tan Si (David Chiang). Ma aspires to be like Tan and uses him as a role model to become a rich but fair protector of the locals, who not only gladly pay for his protection against Boss Yang but also become the foundation for Ma's own syndicate. Determined to put a stop to Yang's killing ambi-

tions and become the head boss in Shanghai, Ma has the ultimate showdown with Boss Yang and his hatchet men at the Green Lotus Pavilion Tea House.

This film was Chen's first major lead, and he earned it because of his martial arts tournament victories. Initially scheduled to be a 60-day shoot, Shaw Brothers wanted the film done before the Chinese New Year, thus the 60 days was squeezed into 30 all-day shoots. Because of his tournament background, Chen once told me that his biggest challenge was to not use too much power in his techniques during the fight scenes. During rehearsals, he even split fellow actor Ku Feng's lip. When you watch Chen fight in this film, notice that his back is very straight and that he uses his waist and hips during each technique. He also extends his punches straight out, which is a signatory strike in many kung fu styles. Chen even has a major fight scene, albeit a wee bit hokey, with a Russian wrestling champion who was played by the Italian-born and 1967 IWA world heavyweight wrestling champion Mario Bulfone, notably known by his ring name Mario Milano. Milano started as a wrestler in Venezuela who wore a mask and was called "Black Diablo." His signature move, the atomic drop—which he performed by lifting an opponent above his head, then dropping him tailbone first over his bent knee—was prominently featured in the film.

What is most interesting and perhaps little known is that Bruce Lee's Tang Lung character in *Way of the Dragon* is heavily influenced by the real-life Ma Yong-zhen. The country-bumpkin Tang Lung comes to Italy, inadvertently crosses the local crime boss, becomes the protector to the Chinese restaurant and takes on a large foreign fighter.

The Boxer From Shantung not only spawned the pseudo-sequel *Man of Iron* and other films about Ma and his sister (see *Ma Su Chen*), but also Yuen Kwei shot a remake titled *Hero* (1997) with Jet Li.

Titleography: *Killer From Shantung.* Translation—*Ma Yong-zhen. Boxer* and *Killer From Shantung* are appropriate in that Ma Yong-zhen is from Shantung province and the Chinese title is the main character. **MA Percentage: 18.43%** SHAW BROTHERS

BOXER REBELLION

八 國 聯 軍 and 神 拳 三 壯 士 (1975—Hong Kong) **90m. Fl: Liu Chia-liang. NOT/LOT: 4/ 9m 25s; NOF/LOF: 10/ 19m 20s.** D: Chang Cheh. C: Alexander Fu Sheng, Chi Kuan-chun, Jenny Tseng, Wang Lung-wei, Richard Harrison, Liang Chia-ren, Li Li-hua, Tang Yen-tsan.

The true-life event known as the Boxer Rebellion is actually a sad footnote in martial arts history because it was the first time in Chinese history that supposedly honorable kung fu men banded together to indiscriminately kill innocent women, defenseless pacifist clergymen and children. The film *Boxer Rebellion* follows the stories of three patriotic heroes played by actors Chi Kuan-chun, Alexander Fu Sheng and Liang Chia-ren who rally martial artists to fight nearby

German, American and Japanese forces.

When Chi's character fights Alfred Graf von Waldersee (Richard Harrison), a real-life German general field marshal, it's a proud moment of the Chinese determination to free their country. It also shows that they are not weak people. In reality, the Boxer Rebellion or Boxer Movement (1899-1901) was an uprising of martial artists loyal to the Society of Right and Harmonious Fists (a Chinese Triad sect), and their initial purpose was to overthrow the Chings and kill all foreign devils. However, that soon changed, and their slogan then became "Support the Ching; destroy the foreigner!" Despite this, both the film and today's Chinese communist government portray the Boxers as patriotic heroes. Furthermore, the Boxers were led to believe that through martial arts and spiritual training they could withstand the foreign bullets.

Like most early martial arts films, this one was not intended for non-Chinese audiences. One problem with old Chinese films was the lack of historical correctness, especially when it came to foreign characters, especially their costumes. The same is true for Hollywood films that feature Asian characters because the costumes are often based on what an American thinks an Asian should look like rather than how they actually do look. However, Chinese studios did not have the budget to make unique costumes for foreign soldiers from different periods. In this film, American, Japanese and German soldiers have the same uniforms for any period. But there is no excuse for blatant Chinese historical inaccuracy.

Still from *Boxer Rebellion* © Celestial Pictures Ltd. All rights reserved.

For example, the film justifies the Boxers' killings in the name of Sun Yat-sen and in support of his new Chinese Republic (1912-1916), which again, in reality, the Boxers were in support of the Ching government, the same government that Sun wanted to defeat. It is unclear why director Chang Cheh, who was such a proponent of Chinese history, chose to inject such glaring mistakes. As a footnote, General von Waldersee arrived after the Boxer Rebellion.

Fortunately, Liu Chia-liang's *Legendary Weapons of China* (1982) and Tsui Hark's *Once Upon a Time in China* films series (1991-1997) tried to point out the true problems of the Boxers and how their actions were not in the name of true martial artists.

Titleography: *Bloody Avengers*; *Spiritual Fists*. Translations—*Eight Nation Alliance* and *Incredible Boxer Three Heroes*. The English title is logical because the film is about the Boxer Rebellion. Part of the film deals with the Boxer spiritualism and subsequent immunity to strikes and bullets, thus *Spiritual Fists* is a plausible alternative title. They are also fighting to avenge their kung fu brothers, so *Bloody Avengers* also works. The literal title derives from what the U.S., French, Russian, Japanese, U.K., German, Austrian-Hungarian and Italian alliance was actually called. The alternative Chinese title reflects the three main characters in their efforts to fight for China. **MA Percentage: 31.94%** SHAW BROTHERS

BOXER'S ADVENTURE

旅 and 神拳霸腿追魂手 (1979—Taiwan) 95m. AD: Blacky Ko. NOT/LOT: 2/ 1m 48s; NOF/LOF: 28/ 30m 43s. D: Tyrone Hsu. C: Tan Dao-liang, Meng Fei, Jack Long, Blacky Ko, Lung Tien-hsiang, Zhang Ji-ping, Wang Hsieh, Long Xuan.

The Battle Hymn of the Republic … of China. After Sun Yat-sen was elected as the first provisional president of the Republic of China in 1912, he relinquished the presidency to ruthless warlord Yuan Shi-kai in lieu of Yuan using his military might to arrange for the abdication of the last emperor of China, Pu Yi. However, four years later and under the auspices of a fair democratic vote, Yuan proclaimed himself the emperor of China. With Yuan's powerful authoritarian rule backed by his military dictatorship, the exiled Sun was seeing his dream for the republic dying. Yet Tsai Ao, the military governor of Yunnan, rose up against Yuan in an effort to usurp Yuan and bring back the republic.

The film *Boxer's Adventure* opens with the news that Yuan Shi-kai has taken over the country, and Yuan wants Minister Tai (Long Xuan) assassinated before he can get to Yunnan, where it is believed that Tai will use his righteous influence to raise an army to fight Yuan. Tai's bodyguard, Li Tao-wei (Tan Dao-liang), handpicks three men—the cheeky Chang Lu (Meng Fei), nancy-boy Li Ching-gong (Jack Long) and the dorky Chao San (Blacky Ko)—to help him protect the minister from assassins loyal to Yuan. On paper, this has the makings of a great film. Ideally, it would introduce a romanticized view of an important time in Chinese history and show how maybe Minister Tai weathered countless assassination attempts under the umbrella of four brave heroes. Instead, the film quickly breaks down into a story about the three handpicked protectors and how the three friends constantly bicker among each other about who is the most efficient womanizer inside and outside the local brothels and who is the best gambler.

There is an interesting sequence that features actor Meng Fei, who plays the cheeky Chang, training while rolling around on marbles on a slippery sheet of steel; it ties into a fight later on in the film. But the movie's fights by Jack Long, who is a real smooth technician of the arts in this film, really stole the show. The bloody groin-grip scene is scary as sin, and it also occurs during one of the film's mistakes. A large table covered with a bright pink tablecloth stands in a secluded pool of shallow water. It is there in one shot, then disappears and reappears throughout the fight.

As Meng Fei gets a bit older and loses his cute appearance and gains weight, his fight scenes improve. Although he started out with no martial arts experience in film, he quickly improved over the years by working with many of the top fight choreographers. The English credit for fight choreographers chopped and changed depending on the production company. See "Martialogy Breakdown" under "Key to the Martialogy" after this book's Introduction. Shaw Brothers stuck mostly to FI (fight instructor) throughout most of the 1970s. Yet for the most part, the Chinese credit of *wu shu zhi dao* was fairly constant for most films.

Titleography: As of this writing, no alternative titles could be found. Translations—*Adventure* and *Mighty Fist, Powerful Leg, Soul Chasing Hand*. The film is an adventure, and because the four heroes are boxers, the English title bodes well with the movie's spirit. The second Chinese title refers to the martial arts technique specialties of the three bodyguards who Tan Dao-liang's character chooses to help him. **MA Percentage: 34.23%**

BRAVE ARCHER, THE

射鵰英雄傳 (1977—Hong Kong) 117m. FI: Robert Tai Chi-hsien, Li Gu-ding. NOT/LOT: 7/ 2m 18s; NOF/LOF: 24/ 13m 45s. D: Chang Cheh. C: Alexander Fu Sheng, Tien Niu, Ku Feng, Kuo Chue, Wang Lung-wei, Danny Lee, Gu Guan-zhong, Lee Yi-min, Yu Rong, Dik Wei, Fan Mei-sheng, Chan Shen, Hui Ying-hung, Cai Hong, Helen Yu, Yang Xiong, Tong Yen-san, Ti Lung.

The Legend of the Condor Heroes (1957) is the first part of famous *wuxia* novelist Jing Yong's (aka Louis Cha) *Condor Trilogy*, the second part being *The Return of the Condor Heroes* (1959), and the third part being *The Heavenly Sword and the Dragon Sabre* (1961; see *Heaven Sword and Dragon Sabre*). The characters of each novel play important roles in the rise and fall of several

Chinese dynasties. The movies *The Brave Archer, The Brave Archer 2* (1978) and *The Brave Archer 3* (1981) cover the first part. *The Brave Archer and His Mate* (1982) covers the second.

For bird buffs: Although the novel's title *Condor Heroes* refers to legendary condors twice as big as humans, the literal translation "The Legend of the Bird of Prey Shooting Heroes" implies that the bird is actually an eagle. Condors are New World vultures only found in parts of North America (California, Arizona) and South America (the Andes Mountains). Old World vultures are the vultures we are familiar with, whereas the cinereous and redheaded vultures—the two main species in China—are not condors.

Set during the waning years of the Song Dynasty, in a country beset by Jin invaders, *The Brave Archer* begins with one of the Seven Disciples of Quan Zhen, You Chu-ji (Yang Xiong), naming two children. One is named Yang Gang. He is the son of Yang Tie-xin who is a Yang descendant. (See *14 Amazons* to learn about the Yangs.) The other child is named Guo Jing. He is the son of Guo Xia-tian and a descendant of Guo Sheng who is one of the 108 Heroes in *The Water Margin*. (See martialogy.) Jin soldiers suddenly appear, kill Yang Tie-xin and kidnap his wife and son Yang Gang. As Guo Xia-tian is mortally wounded and barely escapes, his wife and son Guo Sheng are saved by the Seven Freaks of Jiangnan, headed by Flying Bat (Cai Hong). When opposition to the Seven Freaks Taoist You returns to where the Jin soldiers killed Yang Tie-xin and the Seven Freaks saved Guo Sheng, Flying Bat and Taoist You agree that instead of fighting each other, You will find Yang Gang and teach him kung fu, and the Seven Freaks will teach Guo Jing. If things go according to plan, the two sons will meet and fight at the Drunken Fairy Restaurant in 18 years, where the winner will reflect who is the best kung fu teacher.

Also important to the film (and the novel) are The 5 Greats: Eastern Evil Hung Yao-shi (Gu Guan-zhong), who lives alone on Peach Blossom Island; villainous Western Poison Ouyang Feng (Wang Lung-wei), a master of venoms and poisons; Southern King Duan Zhi-xing (Ti Lung), who leaves the world of Jiang Hu and becomes a monk; Northern Beggar Hong Chi-gong (Ku Feng), who is the king of the beggars and lover of good food; and the Pope, the teacher of the Seven Disciples of Quan Zhen. Before dying, the Pope passed on his kung fu to the most powerful martial artist alive, the immature Zhou Bai-tong (Kuo Chue), who is trapped in the Peach Blossom Maze of Peach Blossom Island. He's caught because Eastern Evil wants to know the contents of two secret kung fu manuals Zhou memorized then destroyed, and Zhou refuses to give him the knowledge.

Part of the film's story also centers on the famous lost books of war that

Yue Fei wrote before he died. (See *Heaven Sword and Dragon Sabre* as to where the manuals turn up.) According to the Jins, the book must never get into the hands of the Songs.

Guo Jing learns various martial arts from the Seven Freaks and grows up to be a dimwitted, righteous young man, who is played by actor Alexander Fu Sheng. Yang Gang, on the other hand, is raised by the Jin's sixth prince Wanyan Honglie (Yu Rong) and a disciple of You Chu-ji, who originally named him. Yang Gang grows up to be a treacherous, conniving and immoral young man (played by Lee Yi-min) and learns evil kung fu on the side from Mei Chao-fung (Helen Yu), a former student of Eastern Evil.

Guo Jing's adventure takes off after he treats a street beggar with kindness and respect. The beggar turns out to be the beautiful Huang Ying (Tien Niu), daughter of Eastern Evil. As Guo Jing and Huang Ying break into the palace where Yang Gang lives, Guo Jing gets attacked by a giant snake and drinks its blood, which gives him more powerful kung fu. Hand in hand, Huang and Guo cook chicken and win over the heart of Northern Beggar, who then teaches Guo the coveted Dragon 18 Palms. In hopes of convincing her father to allow them to marry, Guo and Huang go to Peach Blossom Island to confront Eastern Evil, who has already betrothed Huang to Western Poison's student Ouyang Ke (Danny Lee). While walking around the island, Guo gets lost and runs into Zhou Bai-tong, who takes a liking to Guo and gleefully teaches him the kung fu that Eastern Evil wants to learn.

Eastern Evil wants his daughter to be happy, so he sets up a contest between Guo and Ouyang Ke to determine who will marry Huang. In the end, it comes down to Guo putting his life's kung fu lessons into action if he is to win the hand of Huang.

Titleography: *Kung Fu Warlords.* Translation—*Legend of the Bird of Prey (Eagle) Shooting Hero.* See above martiology and *The Brave Archer 2.* **MA Percentage: 13.72%** SHAW BROTHERS

BRAVE ARCHER 2, THE

射鵰英雄傳續集 (1978—Hong Kong) 110m. Fl: Robert Tai Chi-hsien, Liang Ting, Lu Feng. NOT/LOT: 1/ 52s; NOF/LOF: 17/ 10m 43s. D: Chang Cheh. C: Alexander Fu Sheng, Niu Niu, Ku Feng, Kuo Chue, Wang Lung-wei, Danny Lee, Gu Guan-zhong, Lee Yi-min, Hui Ying-hung, Yu Rong, Shirley Yu, Cai Hong, Helen Yu, Lo Meng, Sun Chien, Lin Zhen-ji, Wang Ching-ho.

The Brave Archer 2 is more of a filler film in readiness for the big finale, *The Brave Archer 3* (1981), which came out almost three-and-a-half years later and featured less characters and more fights than the previous two installments.

Part 2 begins where Part 1 ends, with the marriage of Guo Jing (Alexander Fu Sheng) and Huang Ying (Niu Niu; different actress). However, something is amiss. Eastern Evil believes that Guo cheated (although he did not) by memorizing pages from his wife's book; she died writing it. All marriage bets are off as everyone leaves the island on different boats: Guo, Northern Beggar (Ku Feng) and Zhou Bai-tong (Kuo Chue) in one boat; Ouyang Ke (Danny Lee) and Western Poison (Wang Lung-wei) in another; and Huang on another. During a severe storm, Guo's boat sinks, but everyone lives. Huang's boat sinks and Western Poison picks her up. When they all meet on shore, Western Poison will only hand over Huang Ying if Guo writes him a copy of the Nine Yin manual. After writing a fake manual, Western Poison injures Northern Beggar, Guo injures Ouyang Ke, and Guo, Huang and Northern Beggar must get a jump on Western Poison and flee.

Mortally wounded, Northern Beggar makes Huang the leader of the Beggar Clan, gives her the mark of the clan leader (a thin, long green bamboo rod), and tells her she must attend their next gathering and tell them what is going on. Being hungry, the trio go to Lin An Palace, not knowing that Wanyan Honglie (Yu Rong)—the sixth prince of Jin—and Yang Gang (Lee Yi-min) are there with Western Poison to steal the war strategy/kung fu manual that Yue Fei (real-life founder of Eagle Claw kung fu) wrote before the Jin killed him. After a fight with Western Poison, Yang Gang stabs Guo, who is left to die. The only way he can live is if Huang and Guo connect hands for seven days and not speak to any third party during the connection. So they sneak off to a secret room in an abandoned restaurant that they found earlier on and begin.

While hidden, many events occur in front of their eyes. Yang Gang kills Ouyang Ke and takes the Beggar Clan rod (Ouyang ripped it away from Huang when he tried to expose them) while the Seven Disciples of Quan Zhen and Eastern Evil fight. The Six (originally Seven) Freaks show up and begin fighting Eastern Evil. Although Guo's healing is not complete, he cannot watch his teachers get killed, so Guo and Huang reveal themselves. But Eastern Evil is so happy that Huang is alive that he agrees to heal Guo, recognize their marriage and treat the Six Freaks like brothers.

At the meeting, Yang Gang pretends to be the beggars' leader and orders them to kill Guo and Huang. As Guo looks at the stars in the sky, Chief of the Iron Palm, Chio Chian-ren (Lo Meng), appears and demands that the beggars help the Jins, and Yang agrees. The beggars are upset, and just when all seems lost, Guo has an epiphany about the Nine Yin kung fu manual and steps in to save the day. Huang takes her rightful place as head of the beggars, and Yang skulks off with Chio.

Still from *The Brave Archer 2* © Celestial Pictures Ltd. All rights reserved.

Here's the real timeline of the film. The Jin invaded Northern Song and established the Jin Dynasty in 1125 (the year Montezuma Castle was built near Sedona, Arizona). By 1141, the Northern Song Dynasty disappeared and Song General Yue Fei was executed. In 1161 (four years after the birth of England's King Richard the Lionheart), Prince Wanyan Honglie wanted to be the emperor of China and invaded the Southern Song (as in the film). He failed and was assassinated by his own generals later that year.

There's not much action in either of the *Brave Archer* films, which is odd considering that they were both directed by Chang Cheh and had large casts of legitimate fighting talent. A lot of the action, per se, revolves around the various characters using super *chi*-powered kung fu techniques that display firm stances and solid hand postures amid sizzling palms, voracious sound effects and skill-initiated puffs of wind.

Titleography: *The Brave Archer Part II*; *Kung Fu Warlords 2*. Translation—*Continuation of the Legend of the Bird of Prey (Eagle) Shooting Hero*. *Kung Fu Warlords* is a generic title for any *wuxia* film in which multiple sects vie for position. There are two glaring omissions from the book not in the films: Guo Jing was raised in Mongolia by Genghis Khan, and Guo Jing was an expert archer known for killing two eagles with one arrow, thus the *Brave Archer* titles and the condor connotation being an eagle, a bird of prey. **MA Percentage: 10.53%** SHAW BROTHERS

上 海 灘 and 十 面 威 風 (1972—Taiwan) **80m. KFI: Yen Yu-lung, Wu Dong-qiao. NOT/LOT: None; NOF/LOF: 22/ 31m 50s.** D: Yu Han-hsiang, Fu Ching-wa. C: Doris Lung Chun-er, Wen Jiang-long, Yang Yang, Chen Hung-lie, Yee Yuen.

With the glorious success of the Shaw Brothers film *The Boxer From Shantung* earlier in 1972, the Taiwanese kung fu film industry's almost immediate answer to the true story of Ma Yong-zhen was *Brave Girl Boxer in Shanghai*, which starred the rising queen of the Taiwanese kung fu film Doris Lung Chun-er as Ma's sister, Ma Su-zhen, who traveled from Shantung to Shanghai to find out who killed her brother and why. Accompanied by Ma Yong-zhen's disciple Hsiao Pu (Wen Jiang-long; in his first lead role) and befriended by Pai La-li (Yang Yang), Su-zhen strives to take down the wicked Boss Liu because of his criminal extortion rackets in Shanghai and because he is the prime suspect in her brother's murder.

Of the short-lived career of Taiwanese fight choreographer Yen Yu-lung, *Brave Girl Boxer in Shanghai* was his best work because his camerawork makes the fights in this film perhaps better than they were. When new kung fu action star Wen Jiang-long fought, Yan mostly used tight medium shots to ensure that each strike and block looked like it connected. Within the same shot, he added a quick Dutch tilt for a higher degree of motion and depth to the fight, making the area within the shot look bigger. During her fight scenes, Doris Lung Chun-er's straight-backed posture was very good for someone who does not practice martial arts. Also, the choreography enhanced her cinematic kung fu expertise on camera so that most kicks, punches and blocks landed between her bellybutton and head. Doing so made it easier for the actress to memorize the movements because she didn't have to perform spins or move in and out of varying stance heights. There were also some neat over-the-shoulder shots that showed Wen and Doris rapidly retreating while attacking and defending at the same time.

Finally, in what is a true level of commitment to do good fights, Wen's character would throw 20 to 30 different techniques per shot in many of his sequences. Keep in mind that these fights were created on the set with just a few rehearsals before shooting. Furthermore, these sequences could be shot over and over until the fight director was happy. Plus, back then, there were no monitors for immediate playback and all the fights were shot with just one camera. This is why in Chinese-choreographed kung fu films each shot of a fight scene is considered to be a master shot.

Titleography: *Boxer in Shanghai*; *Shanghai Boxer*; *Brave Girl Boxer From Shanghai*. Translations—*Shanghai Beach* and *All Powerful in Ten Directions* (meaning *All Directions*). With the Chinese titles both referring to Shanghai and a female main character, the English titles all make sense, except the *Brave Girl Boxer From Shanghai* title, which reveals that whoever created that title probably did not watch the film because it explicitly states she is from Shantung, not Shanghai. **MA Percentage: 39.79%**

(1977—USA) **86m. FC: Chuck Norris. NOT/LOT: None; NOF/LOF: 6/ 4m 21s.** D: Don Hulette. C: Chuck Norris, George Murdock, Terry O'Connor, Don Gentry, John Di Fusco, Ron Cedillos, Michael Augenstein.

Convoy Chuck cruises with CB commotion. At a time when America was losing sight of 8-track tapes, Chuck Norris made his American debut in a film that tapped into the road culture of CB (citizens band radio) truckers, who would ease on down the arterial roads of America back when semis and 18-wheelers were the lifeblood of American manufacturing.

Citizens from Texas Town, Califor-nai-ay, claim independence from California state laws and create their own justice system to rationalize the legality of illegal moonshine. But when J.D. Dawes (Norris) John Waynes his way into town looking for his lost and maybe dead hijacked brother, the proverbial feces hits the spurs. J.D. dishes out Korean martial art spinning kicks with clean-cut, all-American, explosive canonized justice.

"Breaker, breaker" is a CB slang term that tells a specific user (as called by his or her "handle" or CB nickname) on a specific radio channel that one would like to speak with him or her. With this film, Norris was able to speak to enough of an audience to officially launch a successful 30-year film career in Hollywood. The final fight scene is shot entirely in slow motion, which is why it feels like a long fight. Like most of Norris' fight scenes in all his movies and TV appearances, this film is no different and features the usual spinning heel kicks, jumping side kicks (with no height on his leaps), spinning backfists and overall lack of emotional intensity. Yet the metaphor of the horse after the final deathblow is potent and similar to Bruce Lee setting free two birds at the end of *The Big Boss* (1971). "10-100 good buddy … over and out."

Titleography: *Cindy Jo & the Texas Turnaround*. It is beyond me why this film is also called *Cindy Jo & the Texas Turnaround*. Although the film takes place in California, some of the "back hill" characters seem to have Texas accents, so maybe the distributor keyed in on Texas. The *Cindy Jo* has that Texas feel to it, or the title may be a CB name for someone at the distributor company. **MA Percentage: 5.06%**

BRIGHT RED FLOWER OF COURAGE

Nihon Jokyou-den, Makkana Dokyoban (1970—Japan) **96m. FI: Uncredited. NOT/LOT: None; NOF/LOF: 11/ 2m 55s.** D: Yasuo Furuhata. C: Junko Fuji, Ken Takakura, Shingo Yamashiro, Bin Amatsu, Rinichi Yamamoto, Eitarô Ozawa, Kôtarô Ôkôchi.

No horsing around here, not one bit. It's the early 1900s, and the resettlement program of the cold northern island of Hokkaido is in full swing. When the elderly horse union leader Matsuo catches some Yakuza illegally gambling away horses, the film goes the route of the horse-head-in-bed-scene from *The Godfather* (1972), and Matsuo ends up dead. But killing Matsuo is just the beginning. The Yakuza want to take over the union and make tons of money by controlling the yearly horse auction. The only problem is that Matsuo's daughter Yuki (Junko Fuji) arrives on the island to take his place. Though she appears to be demure and mannerly, Yuki is in fact a martial arts practitioner who won't take nonsense from anyone. The Yakuza want to insert their puppet as the head of the union, but the senior island official says the verdict depends on the uncounted vote of Mr. Kazami, who incidentally blames Matsuo and the horse association for the death of his own father.

The Yakuza are aware of this but decide not to kill Yuki. Instead they go after the other horse association members, burn their houses and destroy their properties. Meanwhile, Yuki rides around on the desolate plains of Hokkaido looking for horses that are lost because of the Yakuza burning their homes. One night, Yuki gets lost, but is eventually confronted by a handsome outdoorsman named Moro the Wind (Ken Takakura). Like in any good Japanese soap opera, they pitch a tent and stay close to keep warm and survive the night. Moro turns out to be Mr. Kazami. He speaks of his hatred for Yuki's father, and Yuki apologizes for her father. He speaks of his hatred for Yuki's father, and Yuki apologizes for her father. She explains that her father left her and her mother alone when she was a child because he believed that helping the emperor's resettlement of Hokkaido was important. As the Yakuza step up their efforts to scare the horse union reps and coerce Moro's vote in their favor, Moro and Yuki put aside their differences and team up to kick the Yakuza out of Hokkaido.

This film is low on action, and although actress Junko Fuji's karate-ish fights are simple, she does the movements with proper posture and confidence. The shocker scene is when a female lead gets shot in the neck, resulting in an incredible over-the-top blood gush that truly impresses. The film is also shot like a Western, and the soundtrack is inundated with jew's-harp "boings." Although not a noodle Western per se, did you also know that the jew's-harp is not Jewish but was created by the Chinese in 300 B.C.?

Titleography: *Brave Red Flower of the North*. Translation—*Tale of the Japanese Swordswoman*. **MA Percentage: 3.04%**

BRONSON LEE, CHAMPION

Za Karate 3: Denkô Sekka (1975—Japan) **81m. FI: Uncredited. NOT/LOT: 9/ 5m 59s; NOF/LOF: 24/ 17m 24s.** D: Yukio Noda. C: Tadashi Yamashita, Chong Men-jo, Dale Ferguson, Steve Fisher, Horikoshi, Gorian Huddert, Suzuki Masafumi, Albert Taso, Jimmy Yamashiro, Shingo Yamashiro.

The unlikely hero of this film is a Japanese-American in Ohio who wears pure-white cowboy duds (including a white cowboy hat) and has the taut, rugged face of Charles Bronson. He also has a grandmother who looks like she just got off the boat from Eastern Europe, and he fights like a clumsy Bruce Lee with good balance. His name is Bronson Lee (Tadashi Yamashita).

After discovering that his grandmother might lose her farm, Bronson decides to fight foreclosure by zipping over to Japan, zeroing in on master Suzuki's international karate tournament and winning the $50,000 prize. What he doesn't count on is getting mixed up with a seedy tournament organizer, a Mexican hatchet man, a blowpipe-wielding Hong Kong kung fu practitioner, a sadistic Japanese *sai* user and a Singaporean sword swinger. Contrary to what a few Internet sites contend, Yamashita doesn't run into Bolo Yeung, who is not in this film.

The action is more about brutality than beauty because Yamashita goes way overboard in trying to show his power, focus and chutzpah in *shorin-ryu* karate. He does one of his popular real-life weapon routines—swinging a *kama* attached to a string and chopping a watermelon in half as it rests on a person's stomach, all while blindfolded, which was a popular demonstration gag many a karate *sensei* did in America during the 1970s. But the rest of his fights make him look more like a person with facial tics than the smooth, flowing *karateka* he is, and his squawks and screeches are more distracting than engaging. On the positive front, Yamashita sticks to his Okinawan karate. His shorin-ryu movements and *nunchaku* techniques look nothing like Bruce Lee's fluid way of moving, which is good because they show off the rough and rugged ferocity of the Okinawan art. But you have to wonder the meaning of when Yamashita throws a chopstick at a bad guy in a Japanese tempura bar but misses him, and the chopstick sticks into a Bruce Lee poster hanging on the wall, right in the solar plexus. No message there, right?

Titleography: *The Karate*. **MA Percentage: 28.87%**

BROTHERHOOD

江湖子弟 (1976—Hong Kong) **94m. FI: Yuen Woo-ping, Yuen Cheung-yan. NOT/LOT: None; NOF/LOF: 10/ 8m 26s.** D: Hua Shan. C: Liu Yong, Hu Jin, Lily Li, Ching Miao, Wang Xia, Shi Zhong-tian, Jiang Dao, Chan Shen.

The Chinese title, which translates to *Next Generation of Jiang Hu*, indicates that this is a contemporary tale using the milieu or subworld of Jiang Hu in a nontraditional *wuxia* setting. As a result, the story is geared more toward the

criminal element of Hong Kong's triads. On a very surface level, there are two kinds of triads: the bad triads, which is the one most people are familiar with and that deal with the kind of criminal activities we associate with the Italian Mafia; and the "good" triads, the kung fu triads if you will, that operate within the realms and moralities of martial arts. The good triads include organizations such as Hong Men, Hong Bang and the Ching Bang. Wuxia films that talk about Jiang Hu and Wu Lin all refer to the martial underworlds. But *Brotherhood* infers that the new generation of Jiang Hu is about the bad triads that do not have ties with the martial underworld, thereby trying to create a new dimension of Jiang Hu, which is traditionally incorrect.

When four brothers (by relationship, not family) pull off a major jewel heist, greed gets the best of them; they dwindle down to a sole survivor, Liao Da-jiang (Liu Yong). After he melts the stolen jewels into gold bars, he is robbed by Guo Ming-tuo (Shi Zhong-tian), who plans to take over Boss Zhang Lao-hai's (Ching Miao) syndicate. Liao is more pissed off than someone who just drank a gallon of cola at a movie screening and needs to go to the bathroom. He gets protection from rival Triad Boss Ou Yang-hsiung (Wang Xia), then he marches up to Zhang screaming. Liao's guts and savvy impress Zhang. At the fray, Zhang's daughter Rose (Hu Jin) gets the hots for Liao. After Guo secretly kills Zhang, thinking he will get to run the family, Rose becomes the new head. She then goes on a rampage of revenge, lusts for Liao and double-crosses Ou, which culminates with some serious Jiang Hu heavies harassing and haranguing each other's various houses of corruption.

Oftentimes actors or fight directors get to do a "day off" martial arts film, which is not so much about doing martial arts as it is about throwing a few punches and kicks around and tossing in remote movements of kung fu to appease audience expectations. For the Yuen brother fight choreographers, this film was one of those "day off" movies, which is revealed by only having about eight minutes of fights. The fights they did are sloppier than a sloppy Joe with extra tomato sauce. Although the fights do not even look like a bad street fight, there are a couple of scary, hanging-high-off-the-ground stunts. In the finale fight, Liu uses a weapon like a meteor ball, and the scene's shot really, really, really tight so we cannot see errors. Many of the shots are just people falling away from a hand-held camera, which is a lazy way to shoot a fight scene, but it is quick, efficient and let's-go-home-early shooting.

Titleography: As of this writing, no alternative titles could be found. Translation—*Next Generation of Jiang Hu*. See above martialogy. **MA Percentage: 8.97%** SHAW BROTHERS

BROTHERS, THE

差人大佬搏命仔 and 龍兄虎弟 (1979—Hong Kong) **89m. FI: Yuen Cheung-yan, Yuen Shen-yi. NOT/LOT: 1/ 43s; NOF/LOF: 13/ 10m 32s.** D: Hua Shan. C: Liu Yong, Danny Lee, Zhou Li-juen, Ku Feng, Nan Gong, Jiang Dao, Harada Riki, Chan Shen.

A 1979 film can offer great comparative analysis of an actor or filmmaker's range of work throughout the decade. It can also give a glimpse of the future for these respective talents. This film is one example.

When German land grabber William wants to buy a pier on the seafront of a Chinese village, owner Zhang (Harada Riki) refuses to sell. William hires some local thugs to do his dirty work and beat up Zhang and his workers. Almost dead from the beating and under threat of William killing his wife and two children, Zhang loses his will to fight. He hands over the lease but is branded a traitor by the unhelpful villagers. When his wife and kids face public humiliation and shame, the family moves away and Zhang dies. With no money and a grim future ahead of him, the eldest son, Zhi-gang, is now the man of the family. He quits school, finds work and insists that younger brother Zhi-chiang stay in school. This goes on for 15 years, during which Zhi-gang (Liu Yong) continues to find work and pays for Zhi-chiang (Danny Lee) to enter a prestigious military academy.

When a fight over wages at the docks escalates into a violent fracas, Zhi-gang steps in and effortlessly handles gang boss Qian Lao-san's (Ku Feng) men. Impressed with his skills, Qian hires Zhi-gang to be the new dock foreman. Zhi-gang is a fair man, and he instills a more efficient work ethic in his workers. He eventually becomes Qian's right-hand man and a threat to rival gang boss Huang (Chan Shen), who puts a hit on Zhi-gang. After that fails and Zhi-gang saves Qian's life, Qian retires and makes Zhi-gang head of the gang.

Meanwhile, Zhi-chiang has graduated with honors and been assigned to clean up organized crime in the city where his brother just became a major

player in the underworld. What started as a typical gangland rivalry becomes a family affair, and the two brothers are forced to clash, breaking their mother's heart because in this world of guns and knives, only one can survive.

Although the fights in this film are short and infrequent, they make use of some interesting camerawork, such as slow in-and-out zooms, which draw viewers into the fight, give them a moment's respite, and then put them back into it. They are also used to emphasize or focus on particular emotional and physical moments of the fights. The choreography has a street-fight aesthetic without being too sloppy, which many earlier films done by the Yuen brothers failed to achieve. When I first watched this film, I didn't recognize actor Liu Yong—partly because of his groovy long hair, mustache and denim, but also because his fights are so good. Liu's usual hunched posture, wobbly neck and bad stances are kept to a minimum, and he delivers great extension of his kicks, making them look fast and powerful.

For actor Danny Lee, *The Brothers* was a hint of what was to come. He would soon start his own production company and move away from martial arts films to do police-genre roles, which the judo black belt and former bouncer found more comfortable.

Titleography: As of this writing, no alternative titles could be found. Translation—*Big Hillbilly Official and the Life Fighting Lad* and *Elder Brother Dragon, Younger Brother Tiger*. The Chinese titles refer to boss Qian and Zhi-gang, and to brothers Zhi-gang and Zhi-chiang. **MA Percentage: 12.64%** SHAW BROTHERS

BROTHERS FIVE

五虎屠龍 (1970—Hong Kong) **101m. FI: Sammo Hung, Xu Er-niu. NOT/LOT: 2/ 2m 42s; NOF/LOF: 26/ 34m.** D: Lo Wei. C: Cheng Pei-pei, Chin Han, Zhang Yi, Yueh Hua, Lo Lieh, Gao Yuan, Tien Feng, Ku Feng.

In Chinese numerology, the No. 5 is associated with the five elements (earth, fire, metal, water and wood), and each element is associated with a specific virtue. In order for you to achieve harmony in life, you need an equal distribution of these elements. However, when five brothers who have been separated since childhood unite as one, that spells an element of disaster and danger for the cause behind the separation. This leads to harmony for the five brothers who must become one in order to defeat the enemy.

When the head of Flying Dragon Villa, Long Zheng-feng (Tien Feng), wants to find and kill the five children of Gao Shi-tu, Long can't find them because a swordsman saves them and sends them to different places to be raised. Twenty-some years later, the Flying Dragon Villa has become an even more feared lair. Meanwhile, swordsman Yen's daughter, Miss Yen (Cheng Pei-pei), takes it upon herself to find the five brothers to end Long's reign and make Flying Dragon Villa an honorable and upright place once again. When she finally unites Gao Wei, Gao Hao, Gao Zhi, Gao Yong and Gao Xia (Yueh Hua, Chin Han, Zhang Yi, Gao Yuan and Lo Lieh, respectively), Miss Yen teaches them the Five Tigers with One Heart kung fu skill to give them a fighting chance against Long. Seeing this technique will help you understand why the Chinese are known for those amazing balancing acts and people-pyramid shows.

This movie offers yet another reason why Cheng Pei-pei is considered the first queen of kung fu films, a title she earned during the 1960s and held onto until her retirement in the mid-1970s. It has been discussed in several martialogies that many of these early kung fu films put out by Shaw Brothers often do not have many fights, partially because the actors do not know anything about martial arts, do not have the endurance to withstand the punishment of doing many fights (especially the actresses), and/or do not wish to get hurt. In *Brothers Five*, there are a lot of fights for a film made in 1970. If you observe Pei-pei's stances and movements closely, you will realize that she does all her own fights and sequences. Plus, I have known Pei-pei for many years and have had long conversations with her about most of her films. She has joyfully shared with me that she did all her own fights, which if you develop an eye for fights, obviously differentiates the way an actor moves compared to a stunt double. The only time she used a double was when the director would not allow her to perform dangerous stunts because she had once insisted on performing a particular stunt during the filming of *Golden Swallow* (1968) and got injured.

When Pei-pei fights Tien Feng's stunt double, her with a sword and him with a large *guan dao*, they rock the screen with lengthy weapon exchanges captured in the same shot. In my opinion, this is Pei-pei's best fight scene. She is relentless, smooth and graceful, which is a difficult thing to do when fighting

someone with a guan dao, a large blade on top of a long pole—even the fake versions for movies are pretty heavy. (The weapon is named in honor of General Guan, a hero during the Three Kingdoms period from 265-220 B.C.)

Titleography: As of this writing, no alternative titles could be found. Translation—*Five Tigers Slay the Dragon*. The *Five Tigers* are metaphors for the five brothers and the secret kung fu technique they learn that is used to *Slay the Dragon*, the dragon being Long Zheng-feng. **MA Percentage: 36.34%** SHAW BROTHERS

BRUCE AND SHAOLIN KUNG FU

達魔鐵指功 (1978—Hong Kong) **90m. KF-Cou: Deng De-xiang. NOT/LOT: 10/ 7m 35s; NOF/LOF: 11/ 32m 38s.** D: James Nam Gung-fan. C: Bruce Le, Chen Hsing, James Nam Gung-fan, Kim Jeong-ran, Bae Su-cheon, Bolo Yeung, Jiang Dao.

Bruce Le vs. the Hunchback of Bolo Dame à la Chen Kuan-tai. Many fans were disappointed that John Saxon and not Bruce Lee fought Bolo in *Enter the Dragon* (1973). Because of this martial letdown, Bolo became a popular villain (nabbing 16 roles in the 1970s) who would end up fighting the various Bruce Lee copycats, like in this film.

This film keys in on the two elements that made Lee's *Fist of Fury* an important statement in Hong Kong kung fu cinema: the anti-Japanese sentiment and the heroic feats of a Huo Yuen-jia disciple. During the Japanese occupation of China and Korea, Lee Ching-lung (Bruce Le) travels from Shanghai to Korea to learn *taekwondo* to supplement his Shaolin kung fu skills, protect the honor of Huo's Ching Wu Athletic Association and to wreak revenge on the Japanese brass who killed his brother and the assassins who killed his Shaolin monk mentor (Chen Hsing).

It is through training sequences that Le gets to reveal for the first time his true kung fu background in the tiger-crane form, which was created by the fabled Chinese hero and one of the Ten Tigers of Shaolin, Hong Xi-guan. Coincidently (but probably not), the year before *Bruce and Shaolin Kung Fu* was made and released, Chen Kuan-tai starred in the Shaw Brothers mischievous chronicle of Hong Xi-guan in *Executioners From Shaolin*. (See martialogy.) The film intriguingly revealed two of the secrets of Hong's art: using a bronze dummy and specialized training techniques that focused on striking the various acupuncture points of the body. Le uses a similar approach to training by hanging stuffed dummies. Although not as effective as his fellow actor Chen's film, Le makes his point to bring out the spirit of Hong Xi-guan.

Director and co-star James Nam Gung-fan has a background in taekwondo, and it's highlighted when his Master Po character explains to Le's character that the spirit of the important Korean art is secretly hidden in the written calligraphy of the words. According to Nam, the words of the art create the motion of the strikes and blocks based on the strokes' order and the way the word is written from left to right and up and down. It is actually a rather creative way to explain the art and is the only time I have seen it featured in a film in this manner.

The fight scenes run the usual gamut of Bruce Lee look-a-like films, editing in sound bites from *Enter the Dragon,* with copycat Le brushing his thumb against his nose while screeching like a Bruce Lee banshee and flexing his striated muscles. Like many low-pecuniary and peculiar-made Hong Kong films that were shot in South Korea with most extras being Korean and having a South Korean production value, part of its charm is the various outlandish villains and the equally freaky way they bite the dust. The filmmakers even had the gall to create an ultra-cheap poor rendition of Sonny Chiba's *Street Fighter* (1974) X-ray striking method. Seeing Bolo romp, roll and hunchback himself around like Quasimodo doing monkey kung fu (thus the German title *Der Gelbe Gorilla*) as he fights Le, well, that just takes the banana … cake.

Titleography: *Bruce and Shao-lin Kung Fu*; *Bruce vs. Black Dragon*; *Shadow of the Snake Wizard*; *Ching Wu & Shaolin Kung Fu*. Translation—*Achieving Evil Iron Finger Kung Fu*. Based on the film's various plot points, it is obvious how *Bruce*, *Shaolin* (*Shao-lin*), *Ching Wu* and *Kung Fu* found their way into the various titles, but everything else is up in the air. Although, I must admit that *Shadow of the Snake Wizard* sounds like it should be a far-out film. There's no shadow or shadowy figure, no snakes or someone doing snake kung fu, and no magic or characters with magical skills. There are also no black characters or dragon kung fu. **MA Percentage: 44.69%**

BRUCE AND SHAOLIN KUNG FU 2

火燒少林門 (1978—Hong Kong) **75m. MAI: Tang Jin-tang. NOT/LOT: 2/ 1m 05s; NOF/LOF: 13/ 16m 38s.** D: James Nam Gung-fan. C: Bruce Le, Bae Su-cheon, Jiang Dao, Lee Hang.

Whatever Lee Ching-lung practices, I want to learn. At the end of *Bruce and Shaolin Kung Fu*, Lee Ching-lung (Bruce Le) is shot to pieces by a brigade of Japanese soldiers led by General Kawasaki, who wanted Lee dead for killing Kawasaki's son. Bruce Le reprises his Lee character in *Bruce and Shaolin Kung Fu* in this sequel. (See martialogy.) The film opens with Kawasaki (Bae Su-cheon) pining the death of his son and blaming himself for the loss of his family honor at the hands of Lee Ching-lung. When Kawasaki hears that Lee somehow survives the 100 bullet wounds, we cut to the sound track of *The Young and the Restless* and watch Lee being nursed back to health by a Chinese man and his daughter somewhere in Korea.

Meanwhile, the Japanese government assigns Xi Sha (Jiang Dao) as the official samurai instructor to the Japanese forces in Korea. Xi Sha is also searching for Korean freedom fighter Po Su-pai, who Sha lost to in an earlier fight; now Sha wants a rematch. After Mao Yi (Lee Hang), captain of the Japanese secret agents in Korea, kills the Chinese family taking care of Lee Ching-lung, he vows to avenge the family by learning the secret kung fu art of *taekwondo* from Po. Lee learns taekwondo and wreaks karmic revenge on all those who have offended his makeshift family and the Shaolin Temple, where we saw his Shaolin monk teacher slain by the Japanese in the first movie.

The film contains strong moral messages about taekwondo. It is not about killing or revenge and should be used to help the sick and poor. Once Lee Ching-lung realizes this, Po teaches him. However, what he learns and uses against the Japanese is far from real taekwondo. Also, of course, taekwondo is not a style of kung fu.

This is one of Le's less-inspired films, and it was shot right after the first movie as an afterthought. Most of its fights were shot at 18 frames per second to make it look like everyone is moving faster than the declining stocks during the 2008 financial crisis. Too much shaky camerawork, lower camera speeds and offbeat editing further reflect that this film never had a sense of belief. In fact, the final two fights, which take up about seven minutes, are only that long because six minutes of it is shot in sloooooow motion. Yet the movie had a few funny-cool moments, such as when Lee Ching-lung takes to the air, flaps his hands like a giant white crane, and flies across the screen to wing his opponents.

In case you are wondering, at the end of the day in many low-budget films, the various actors stand in close-up before the camera and flash various emotional faces. These faces are then intermittently edited in throughout the fight scenes, and that is why facial expressions often do not match the action circumstance, like with Kawasaki's reactions to Lee's white crane kung fu. (Maybe Kawasaki was thinking that taekwondo looks nothing like this.)

The finale death scene is peculiar because the two "deathees" end up hugging each other and because the music sounds more like they are two young teens finally discovering love. Bolo is not in this film, and you have got to love the screenwriter's name ... Zacky Chan.

Titleography: *Bruce and Shaolin Kung Fu*; *Bruce and the Shaolin Fist*; *Ching Wu & Shaolin Kung Fu Part 2 (II)*. Translation—*Fire Burns Down the Shaolin Temple*. It's pretty obvious about the English titles when you look at the alternative titles for *Bruce and Shaolin Kung Fu*. The Chinese titles of these two *Bruce and Shaolin Kung Fu* films are different. Because this is an inferior film, the fact that to the Chinese audience it is not titled as a sequel, it removes the comparative expectation that comes with a sequel. **MA Percentage: 23.62%**

BRUCE LEE: A DRAGON STORY

一代猛龍 (1974—Taiwan) **90m. FI: Uncredited. NOT/LOT: None; NOF/ LOF: 10/ 8m 53s.** D: Shi Di. C: Bruce Li, Na Yan-sau, Tang Pei, Zheng Fu-xiong.

This is the film that started the Bruceploitation era—an era full of half-truths, half-lies, and one of the things that has cheapened and oftentimes threatened the legitimacy of the martial arts genre: the ubiquitous copycat mentality of the Hong Kong film industry.

Bruce Li's first of many incarnations of Bruce Lee begins with the anti-legend of Lee delivering newspapers for the *Washington Post* (assume a paper in the state of Washington). He then rapidly proceeds to kick the tar out of two black guys, fall in love and marry Linda Emery, and win a martial arts tournament, which inspires him to open a kung fu school. He next gets challenged by evil Japanese samurai swordsmen in a local San Francisco park (like that would happen), receives a contract from BBC to star in the TV show *The Green Hornet* (ABC in real life), moves to Hong Kong, snubs Run Run Shaw, gets headaches, cheats on his wife with Betty the prostitute, protects Betty from bad guys, then dies in her bed.

This film is a bit similar to Chuck Norris' CBS TV show. Like *Walker, Texas Ranger,* it is beyond reason how more films about Bruce Lee were made based on this first "episode" if you will. There are barely nine minutes of fights. If Li was trying to emulate Lee with looks and action, he fails miserably, and the fight choreography was sub-par even for a low-budget, poorly shot film. Li exhibits weak technique, his kicks are off-balance, and there is too much windup for his punches.

In the introduction, I shared that usually every film has its moments, something memorable in the movie that strikes you, even if a film sucks the royal bird. This is one of those rare instances that really has zero moments. However, after this movie, every Li, Le, Leung and Lai jumped on the Lee bandwagon, and a few made some decent music. But speaking of music, this film featured the soundtrack from Cantonese Opera's greatest opera, *Tai Noi Fa,* so in retrospect, it did indeed have its moment.

Titleography: *Bruce Lee, Superdragon*; *Bruce Lee, We Miss You*; *Bruce Li, Super Dragon*; *The Bruce Lee Story*; *Superdragon: The Bruce Lee Story*; *The Dragon Dies Hard*; *Bruce Lee: A Dragon's Story*. Translation—*This Generation's Powerful Dragon*. Just creating any title using the words *Bruce, Lee* or the fake Bruce star's last name with varying combinations of *Dragon* is a popular mode of action for many Bruceploitation films. **MA Percentage: 9.87%**

BRUCE LEE & I

李小龍與我 (1976—Hong Kong) **84m. FI: Yuen Woo-ping, Tang Chia. NOT/LOT: 1/ 33s; NOF/LOF: 9/ 12m 3s.** D: Luo Ma. C: Danny Lee, Betty Ting Pei, Huang Shin, Yuen Cheung-yan, Jin Di, Si Ma Hua Long.

Do you promise to tell the truth, the whole truth and nothing but the truth, so help you Buddha? If you do, then you may remove your hand from the Bible. But what is the truth? We may never know, yet maybe in the words of Jack Nicholson's Col. Nathan R. Jessup from *A Few Good Men* (1992), "You can't handle the truth." So with this film, we are faced with the possibility of handling the truth as told by the last person who saw Bruce Lee alive, Betty Ting Pei. Because if for some reason she was telling truth, it might just pop a lot of Bruce Lee bubbles.

In the world of Bruceploitation, this is perhaps one of the most disturbing films because Betty Ting Pei was the last person to see Bruce Lee alive. She tells her side of the story to a bartender who is protecting her from what appears to be a group of thugs bent on avenging their hero's death and blaming her for it. Ting Pei paints a picture of Lee that makes him up to be a hero, a woman beater, an unfaithful husband, a great philosopher, an extreme martial artist, a caring man, a bad father, and a man who inspires loyalty. She creates a list of *yin-yang* virtues, the good and the bad, which creates an awkward balance that the viewer can choose to accept or decline.

This movie's leading man Danny Lee once told me that the film embarrassed him, but his contract dictated that he had to act in whatever film he was told to do. Ironically, although he was trying to do a Bruce Lee impersonation, he comes across more like a young Robin Shou. It is unclear just who the thugs are in the bar trying to beat up Betty Ting Pei. If you watch carefully, the thugs are the stuntmen who Danny Lee (as Bruce Lee) battles during this film's re-enactments of fights from Bruce Lee's *Fist of Fury*. That would make the thugs in the bar Bruce Lee's stunt people, which could symbolize an attempt by Golden Harvest, the studio that made the Bruce Lee films, to pressure Ting Pei not to make this film, especially because it was also shot at their enemy studio, Shaw Brothers.

As was common for the times when a contemporary film used fight instructors experienced with period-piece films, even with the pedigree of Yuen Woo-ping and Tang Chia, the fights are relegated to a mixture of Bruce Lee style kicks, punches and poses as well as those old traditional straight-arm and helicopter-fist-and-arm maneuvers from *hong jia* kung fu and Beijing opera school. The old-school techniques are as obvious and out of place in the fight as a tall pine tree in the middle of a desert. This creates the image that the fighters seem to be flailing their arms. When they begin to hunch their backs to give the impression of power and intensity, it merely adds to the fight's sloppiness.

Titleography: *Bruce Lee: His Last Days, His Last Nights*; *I Love You, Bruce Lee*; *The Superstar*; *Bruce Lee His Last Days*; *Sex Life of Bruce Lee*; *Bruce Lee—His Last Days*. Translation—*Bruce Lee and I*. Based on the film, one can easily grasp how these alternative English titles were created to be either more exploitive than normal (*Sex Life of Bruce Lee*) or overly generic (*The Superstar*). That's why it would be easy to purchase this movie at least four or five times without realizing you already have it. **MA Percentage: 15%** SHAW BROTHERS

BRUCE LEE'S DEADLY KUNG FU

詠春截拳 (1976—Hong Kong) **93m. KFI: Huang Fei-long. NOT/LOT: 7/ 2m 11s; NOF/LOF: 16/ 32m 33s.** D: Chan Wa, Zhang Qi. C: Bruce Li, Carter Wong, Hwang Jang-lee, Robert Kerver, Roy Horan, Chin Chi-min.

Jeet kune do (in Mandarin, *jei chuin dao*), the way of the intercepting fist, now becomes the way of the intercepting slap. The Bruces keep marching on as this slice of Bruce Lee's life deals with Lee's job as a busboy/waiter in Ruby Dee's (a close family friend of the Lee family) restaurant in San Francisco. It also deals with how he began teaching foreigners *wing chun* (*yong chuin*), the time he beat up a local kung fu master who disapproved of Lee teaching foreigners, and that epiphanous moment when Lee created his art of fighting without fighting.

When I used to dub Chinese kung fu films into English in Taiwan in 1979, I discovered that dubbers spoke varying levels of Chinese, which led to translation problems. Oftentimes, each dubber would pronounce the romanized names of the characters, kung fu styles and places of interest differently, which can make watching these films unbearable because the main character seemingly has four or five different names. In this film, when Bob Li (Bruce Li) is explaining to his foreign kung fu pupils the name of his kung fu style, he calls it, "*Yi Chuan sum chun sung de yong chuin.*" Although the confusion is mild (and I have no idea what style this is by the way; although I know it is supposed to be wing chun), the dubber used romanized Cantonese and Mandarin in the same sentence, which in the unwritten rules of dubbing is freaky.

As with any film that is about Lee or copies him, you must never expect it to even remotely look or feel like a Lee film, especially the fights. With that in mind, this film does not fail. The fights are pretty bad and use a style of choreography called slapping choreography, in which lead fighters and inexperienced stuntmen use open hands to literally strike their opponents with a gentle slap; they let the sound effect create the illusion of power. The technique is excellent for giving the appearance of making contact and rarely hurts the individual being struck. Someone as powerful as Carter Wong often uses this method against fighters who he is afraid of hurting or who are afraid of being hurt. Yet in a movies-mirror-real-life moment, we see Bob sitting on the edge of a creek poking a stick into the water after he is beaten by Chin Yung-chi (Hwang Jang-lee). He suddenly has an epiphany about his training, and the next thing you know, Bob is fighting just like Lee does in his films, and with all those famous Lee mannerisms.

In real life, one day Bruce Lee was drifting around in a small rowboat in the middle of a pond, his hand feeling the cool water speeding between his fingers. It then hit him. Inspired by this aqueous moment, Bruce sped back to shore and told his brother Robert how one needs to be like water in martial arts.

Titleography: *Story of the Dragon*; *Bruce Lee's Secret*; *Bruce Li's Jeet Kune Do*; *A Dragon Story*; *Bruce Lee: A Dragon Story*; *He's a Legend, He's a Hero*; *Master of Jeet Kun Do*; *Wing Chun Big Brother*. Translation—*Wing Chun Jeet Kune*. Basically, any title that can tap into the name of Bruce Lee or his martial arts suffices, even if the titles have already been used (as you can read in the indexes in the back of this book). *Wing Chung Jeet Kune*, of course, refers to wing chun, the style Lee first practiced (actually *hung gar* kung fu was the first, but that was more of playing around), which led to the style he created, jeet kune do. Warning: There's a film with the title *He's a Hero, He's a Legend* listed on some Internet sites that has all the same alternative titles as *Bruce Lee's Deadly Kung Fu* but claims to be a different film. However, the Chinese titles are the same, and they are the same film. Yet there is another film called *He's a Hero, He's a Legend* (1977), and it is different from *Bruce Lee's Deadly Kung Fu*. **MA Percentage: 37.35%**

BRUCE LI IN NEW GUINEA

蛇女慾潮 (1978—Hong Kong) **80m. MAI: Huang Mei. NOT/LOT: 3/ 2m 3s; NOF/LOF: 23/ 23m 19s.** D: Yang Yi-jiao. C: Bruce Li, Dana, Chen Hsing, Shan Guai, Larry Lee, Lee Hoi-san, Bolo Yeung, Cheung Lik.

What happened to Keela the gorilla? By this time, Bruceploitation was beginning to lose its luster, and perhaps the stars of these films believed they could get away with minimal impersonations but still cash in on the Bruce Lee phenomenon. In this totally uninspiring Bruce Li vehicle, he plays archaeologist Wan Li. Wan travels to New Guinea in search of the magical Snake Pearl only to fall in love with the beautiful Snake Sect Princess Ankawa, who is about to be sacrificed by the Great Wizard (Chen Hsing) and leader of the Devil Sect because she won't marry his son. Cheung Lik co-stars more as a fight-filler character than anything else. Of course, there is the princess's bodyguard protector Keela, an Abbott-and-Costello-like man in a monkey suit.

After Wan loses a fight to the Great Wizard, he disappears only to suddenly show up in Hong Kong and have visions of Ankawa. At this point, the film begins to play a lot like an episode from the 1965 to 1969 show *The Wild Wild West* "The Night of Montezuma's Revenge," in which secret agent Jim West falls in love with the Aztec Sun Goddess when he starts having visions of her showing up on inanimate objects.

Chen Hsing is relegated to doing his usual flexing armed lower tiger claw kung fu while striking snakelike poses. There are pits of creepy snakes to fall into and actor Bolo Yeung looks as out of place as in any film with muscles bulging out everywhere. There is also a bit of racism in the film. The black American traveling with the white American evildoers is referred to as "the Negro" and is dubbed by a Chinese actor trying to talk like a soul brother. It is also curious that some of the Grand Wizard's henchmen fought with a *Fo Shou* (Buddha hand), (a peculiar weapon originating in the Buddhist monasteries, where it is simply a hand on a pole).

Titleography: *Bruce Li (Lee) in Snake Island*; *Bruce in New Guinea*; *Last Fist of Fury*. Translation—*The Tidal Wave of Sexual Desires From the Snake Lady*. Most of the English titles are obviously tapping into the Bruce Lee name, and the English-dubbed constant referrals to *Snakes* and *New Guinea*. The Chinese title reflects Li's dreams of being with Ankawa the *Snake Lady*, which of course has nothing to do with Bruce Lee. *Last Fist of Fury* is a redundancy of Lee's *Fist of Fury*. **MA Percentage: 31.71%**

BUDO: THE ART OF KILLING

(1977—Japan) **101m. FI: Uncredited. NOT/LOT: None; NOF/LOF: None.** D: Masayoshi Nemoto. C: Because this is a documentary, there is no main cast.

In a nutshell, this is a Japanese documentary with a dubbed English narra-tive that discusses *budo*, what it is and how it applies to all the major Japanese martial arts. The documentary features karate, judo, *naginata*, *aikido*, sumo, *iaido* and *kendo* practitioners demonstrating their skills for the camera.

As a general rule of thumb, movies are about feelings and emotion, while documentaries are about knowledge and learning. With that in mind, there are several glaring mistakes and omissions that *Budo: The Art of Killing* makes. First is the film's title. Budo refers to the art of being a martial artist rather than the art of killing. Also, the point of many Japanese martial arts is to not inflict harm on another person unless necessary. Even karate is presented as being a deadly art and able to kill a man with a single blow. Second, the film doesn't distinguish between budo and *bushido*; it confuses them as the same concept. This makes me think that the original Japanese must be different from the English dub, because equating bushido and budo is like saying Ghandi and U.S. General George Patton are alike. And third, several times in the film, a *karateka* demonstrates *sanchin* (tension) *kata*, but nothing is said as to what it is called or what its purpose is. It is such an integral part of karate training that it deserves explanation now. Sanchin is a form created by Okinawan karate stylists as a way of strengthening *ki* (in Chinese, *chi* or *qi*). Compared to Chinese martial arts that stress relaxation to build up chi, karate principles state that ki is built up and strengthened with tension.

It is great, however, to see traditional karate training methods in the documentary, such as training in bare feet on the beach and in snow, which is all part of the art's mental discipline. The section on iaido (sword drawing) was probably the first time Westerners had seen real samurai sword demonstrations, in which the practitioners sliced matted straw wrapped around bamboo using correct angular cuts (as compared to baseball-swing slices seen in American films, even today). During this section, we see an elderly man making a samurai sword from start to finish. Although not mentioned in the film, Masamune (1264-1343) was Japan's greatest swordsmith of all time. It is said that in the hands of the right samurai, his swords were durable enough to kill 10,000 Mongols. Of important historical note: The one-sided *jian* (Chinese straight sword) created during the Tang Dynasty was the blueprint for the samurai sword, something Masamune may have learned from his father, Muramasa Sengo.

The notion of bushido explains why thousands of British, American and other POWs were killed or treated badly by the Japanese during World War II—because surrender to the samurai was shameful and looked down upon. It would seem that after Japan surrendered the war, the code of bushido would plainly dictate that everyone should commit suicide. Of course, that was a ridiculous notion. Thus the way of peace and non-violence that comes with the notion of budo is certainly a better and more humane philosophical martial way of life.

Titleography: As of this writing, no alternative titles could be found.

BUTTERFLY MURDERS, THE

蝶變 (1979—Hong Kong) **86m. AD: Huang Shu-tang. NOT/LOT: None; NOF/LOF: 7/ 8m 36s.** D: Tsui Hark. C: Liu Zhao-ming, Mi Xue, Chen Qi-qi, Zhang Guo-zhu, Huang Shu-ying, Eddy Ko, Tino Wong-cheung, Liu Zhen-hui. Danny Chow.

Growing up in Vietnam, future Hong Kong film director Tsui Hark wrote and drew *wuxia* cartoons for the local newspaper, romanticizing the world of Jiang Hu. (See *The Water Margin*.) He later studied film at and graduated from the University of Texas in Austin. It's no surprise then that in his directorial debut, *The Butterfly Murders*, he combines Western elements with wuxia and Jiang Hu sensibilities. His new approach to wuxia films spawned the birth of a new genre of movies in Hong Kong known as Fant-Asia films.

Butterfly Murders kicks off with—you guessed it—a murder. A copier is found dead after a man visits and shares with him chilling stories as witnessed and documented by a scholar named Fung. The stories discuss the bloodthirsty butterfly swarms that attack the tenants of Shum Castle. While the police determine that the scholar's documents are fake, the truth is that the butterflies and the castle are real. Information comes to light that the leader of Shum Castle is alive. This causes several famous fighters to investigate the dark happenings and solve the butterfly mystery. The fighters are lead by Tien Lung (Huang Shu-ying) of the Tien Clan and the Green Shadow (Mi Xue). They arrive at and enter Shum Castle, where they find Fung, his wife and a mute servant hiding in the dungeon-like labyrinth. Hiding from what? The mystery deepens.

Later, butterfly swarms kill some fighters, much like when Tippi Hedren is attacked in Alfred Hitchcock's thriller *The Birds* (1963). The intensity increases when an assassin in black armor suddenly appears. He is a member of a gang of three killers known as the Thunders—the other two being 1,000 Hands and Magic Fire—who terrorize those entering the castle. Once the Thunders smell blood, it's up to the remaining heroes to survive the bad weather and put an end to the entomological nightmares that have been bugging the castle.

As would become Tsui's signature and the blueprint for many Fant-Asia filmmakers, the action is a conglomeration of flashing images and quick edits, which at first added a new dimension to the fights due to their frenetic pace, wondrous wire work and fast cuts. This style of fight choreography also made it easier to hide an actor's lack of martial arts abilities. Thus when fights with nonmartial artists and martial artists were shot in a similar fashion, it put each character on the same level. Tsui's camerawork is very much involved in the fights, with smooth moving camera angles. We also see a shift in wire work from just showing a character's leaping and fighting abilities to adding a romantic-looking dimension to various images. The best example is a shot in which an actor in the foreground holds a butterfly in his hand and Green Shadow speedily flies by in the background. This captivating, high-flying wire work was a taste of things to come in the 1980s. Tsui went on to become one of the most important Hong Kong directors in the 1980s and '90s.

Titleography: As of this writing, no alternative titles could be found. Translation—*Butterfly Metamorphosis*. **MA Percentage: 10%**

CALL HIM MR. SHATTER

奪命刺客 (1974—UK/Hong Kong) **90m. FI: Uncredited. NOT/LOT: 1/ 2m 6s; NOF/LOF: 7/ 8m.** D: Michael Carreras, Monte Hellman. C: Stuart Whitman, Ti Lung, Lily Li, Peter Cushing, Anton Diffring, Gao Xiong, James Ma Chim-si, Jiang Han.

This is another Shaw Brothers/Hammer Films co-production starring Peter Cushing in which he got to star with Shaw's biggest box office draw at the time. The other film was *Dracula and the 7 Golden Vampires*. In *Golden Vampires*, the star was David Chiang; in this film, it's Ti Lung. It is too coincidental that around the time of making these international productions, which were shot one after the other, Chiang and Ti Lung were also both given the chance to direct each other in the beginning stages of their respective directing careers. Furthermore, *Golden Vampires* and *Mr. Shatter* were the only two films Shaw Brothers and Hammer did together.

This film stars former Army lightweight boxing champ Stuart Whitman as a sorehead assassin named Shatter. He is duped out of his payment for assassinating President M'Goya, the corrupt puppet leader of the East African nation of Badawi, because he wrongly killed someone who got in his way during the assassination.

Shatter sets out to find out who really hired him to kill the president and to collect his money. However, he becomes a target for assassination by an international drug cartel. When he returns to Hong Kong, matters get worse because the local Hong Kong authorities, headed by Paul Rattwood (Cushing), want Shatter out by the next morning or they will kill him on sight. After Chinese hit men beat Shatter to a pulp, he hobbles down an alley to find sanctuary with massage parlor and bar owner Tai Bao (Ti Lung) and his companion and head masseuse who goes the extra mile when needed (if you know what I mean), Mei Li (Lily Li).

After going that extra mile with Mei Li, Shatter goes underground, only to surface at a fighting tournament where Tai is the man to beat for three champion martial artists, one from Japan, one from Korea and the other from Thailand. After the tournament, Mei Li and Tai agree to help Shatter extort $1 million from the syndicate by threatening to hand over a list of names and addresses of all the syndicate bosses in the world and expose how the nation of Badawi is involved with the syndicate to Rattwood. As the screws tighten from all directions (Rattwood, the syndicate, the disastrous assassination in Badawi), Shatter and Tai must fight to avoid getting squeezed.

The fights were not directed or edited by a Hong Kong fight instructor, and actor Ti Lung's honed fighting talent was put to the test. Each fight is shot in a really tight and Euro-

pean style with a ton of coverage. This at times makes the fights seem disjointed because there is no way an English editor would know how to piece together a good kung fu fight. Thus the fights use simple camera angles and are usually static; there is no hand-held camerawork or fancy choreography. However, in editor Eric Boyd-Perkins' defense, he used sound effects differently than Hong Kong films, which gives the fights a different sense of life and power.

Fortunately, the film did not shatter Ti Lung's kung fu stardom or bankable reputation, and he was able to sell his emotional anger and kung fu viciousness without doing any Bruce Lee faces.

Titleography: *Shatter*. Translation—*Life Taken Assassin*. *Shatter* is the title character. *Life Taken* refers to Shatter, the assassin whose life could be taken. **MA Percentage: 11.22%** SHAW BROTHERS

CALL TO ARMS

盜兵符 (1972—Hong Kong) **79m. FI: Yuen Woo-ping, Yuen Cheung-yan. NOT/LOT: None; NOF/LOF: 20/ 10m 25s.** D: Shen Chiang. C: Tsung Hua, Hsia Fan, Chang Pin, Chan Shen, Wang Xia, Yang Chi-ching.

It is sad in history and life when a person believes that sacrificing his love for honor will help the country or the person he loves. Although having 20/20 vision is easy in hindsight, the obscurity of foresight is usually compounded by blind loyalty.

This film takes place during the Warring States period (476-221 B.C.) when seven states arose from the Zhou Dynasty: Chu, Han, Qi (Chi), Qin (Chin), Wei, Yan and Zhao (Chao). The Zhao state succumbs to the tyrannical invasion of the Qin. However, because the Wei emperor desires anonymity and seclusion from the conflict (think ostrich-head-in-the-sand mentality), he does not believe there is any threat from the Qin to his kingdom. But Prince Shun Ling (Tsung Hua) of the Wei is determined to gain control of the Wei troops and save the Zhou, believing an allegiance with the Zhou could ultimately defeat the powerful and cruel Qin.

Worried about Shun's plans to align the Wei with the Zhou, the Qin emperor sends spy Zhu Hai (Chang Pin) to assassinate Shun's most trusted adviser Su Song (Yang Chi-ching) and infiltrate Shun Ling's ranks. Shun's plan is to gain control of the Wei troops, and to do so, he sends the love of his life, Su Yu (Hsia Fan), to marry the Wei emperor in order for her to win his confidence and steal the Military Tally from his secret vault. The Military Tally is the official insignia of the emperor. Whoever carries it automatically controls the Wei military because every soldier is duty bound to follow the Tally regardless of who carries it. In the West, it may be a strange thing to blindly do something like this, but it was just the way it was back then in China. After the Tally is stolen, Su Yu is found out and put to death, and Shun's eventual plan to control the military is stopped.

Call to Arms is partially inspired by the life of Wang Zhao-zhuen, who lived during the Western Han Dynasty (206 B.C. to A.D. 220). Known as one of China's legendary ancient beauties, she put her country before the expense

Still from *Call to Arms* © Celestial Pictures Ltd. All rights reserved.

of her interests, much like Su Yu. In Wang Zhao-zhuen's life, the Han Emperor Xuan's (91-49 B.C.) biggest fear was an invasion from China's vicious northern neighbors, the Huns. (In Chinese, the Huns are known as the Xiong Nu.) Eventually, Xuan and the leader of one of the five Hun kingdoms, Shan Yu Khukenye, decided to put aside their differences and become allies. After Xuan died, his son Yuan took over as emperor. To maintain peace and solidify the relationship between China and Khukenye, Wang Zhao-zhuen gave up her much-desired palace existence and volunteered to spend the rest of her life in a barbaric land for the sake of China by marrying Khukenye. This is the way of Confucius, put your country before family and yourself, thus she lived a lonely life of sadness never to return to China for the sake of peace.

History reveals that the Qin eventually won. Their leader, Qin Shi Huang Di—later shortened to the typical three-character name of Qin Shi Huang—established China's first imperial dynasty, making him the first official emperor of an entire China (221-210 B.C.).

Titleography: As of this writing, no alternative titles could be found. Translation—*Steal the Military Tally*. The *Call to Arms* is Shun Ling's beckoning that never happened and the Chinese translation is obvious. **MA Percentage: 13.19%** SHAW BROTHERS

CANNONBALL

(1976—USA) 93m. FC: David Carradine. NOT/LOT: None; NOF/LOF: 3/ 2m 41s. D: Paul Bartel. C: David Carradine, Bill McKinney, Veronica Hamel, Gerrit Graham, Robert Carradine.

One year after David Carradine left his passive and peaceful Kwai Chang Caine role from the *Kung Fu* TV series, he played a deranged race-car driver in *Death Race 2000* (1975), in which the winner was decided by points collected from running over people during a cross-country car race. Carradine once told me he purposely chose a violent film to distance himself away from Caine. But he eventually returned to that path because, just like Leonard Nimoy is Spock, Carradine was Caine. But with *Cannonball,* Carradine continued his jumping front kick habit in which he not only accepted his first foray into choreographing a martial arts fight scene but also was able to unite his fascination with autos and martial arts into a demolition-derby-style, cars-across-America race.

The film features more fight time than in Chuck Norris' *Good Guys Wear Black* (1978; see martialogy), which is the gauge film that determines whether a movie is written about in this book. According to *Cannonball's* DVD, Carradine reveals that his favorite scene from *Cannonball* was the one he choreographed a fight in. During that particular fight, he uses the same parry, roll to one side and then elbow strike five times throughout the fight, with each sequence shot from a different angle. This is considered dull fight choreography, but at least he tried something new. The only problem is that he did it five times. Carradine has his character perform kung fu kicks like he is kicking a soccer ball. He also delivers two jumping front kicks while resting his hand on a tall set of shelves in order to maintain balance. Of note, the fight scene that features Veronica Hamel protecting Carradine's real half brother Robert is surprisingly effective, and she, too, throws that ubiquitous jumping front kick, but it works for her, probably because we've never seen her do it before.

Titleography: *Carquake.* A climactic scene on a bridge that looks like it has been damaged by an earthquake may have been the reason British distributors decided to rename the film *Carquake.* Back in the U.K. while I was growing up, Los Angeles was dubbed "Quake Town." **MA Percentage: 2.89%**

CASINO, THE

吉祥賭坊 (1972—Hong Kong) **77m. FI: Liang Shao-song. NOT/LOT: None; NOF/LOF: 12/ 8m 15s.** D: Chang Tseng-chai. C: Lily Ho, Yueh Hua, Chin Feng, Fan Mei-sheng, Shiek Khan, Wu Ma, Jiang Nan.

It is great to have good friends in high places because, when you deal with corruption in the government and police force, only a name can literally save face. However, when it gets to the point that you do not mind literally losing your face, then it is about putting your life into your enemy's hands because you have nothing to lose and the enemy has everything to lose. Yes, life is a gamble. Welcome to *The Casino*.

When Xiao Wang (Wu Ma) needs money to continue gambling, he bets his hand, unaware that the gambling is fixed. Losing the gamble, he cuts off his fingers and runs out of the casino screaming. The sly and sneaky Zhao Fu (Jiang Nan) revels in his wicked victory, while the real casino boss, Ms. Cui (Lily Ho)—a

master of the 1,000 Hand Buddha skill (meaning she can accurately throw many knives at the same time)—is not aware of his simmering subterfuge and that the gambling is fixed. Still fuming over the "finger" incident, in walks the gentleman gambler Luo Tian-guang (Yueh Hua), which adds pressure to her day. Insulted by Luo's presence, she attacks him, but Cui meets her kung fu match, and he calms her down. Then surprise! Although Cui and Luo were betrothed as children, Luo does the decent thing and proposes to her instead, proving he is an uncommon Chinese man who does not stick to an assumption based on tradition. After they marry, they agree to work hard to make the gambling hall an upright establishment.

Luo's best friend, Master Lun Liu (Chin Feng), invites Luo over to his place for a gambling match in the hope that Luo's good ears and eyes will catch the shifty, never-seems-to-lose gambler Hao Li-shan (Shiek Khan). When Hao loses, which causes him to lose face with his peers, he conspires with the local superintendent to arrest Luo during a scam gambling competition. After Luo's way with words and logic makes the superintendent feel like he's the criminal, the two-faced Zhao has Hao and his hit men kill Ms. Cui and frame Luo for it. Luo subsequently gets tossed into prison and beaten to within an inch of his life. At the eleventh hour, Master Lun uses his influence to free Luo, who then goes on a sadistic rampage of revenge, causing each man who was part of the conspiracy to kill his wife to splinter like soft wood whittled away by a Ginsu knife.

In case it's not familiar, the Ginsu knife was made famous by a series of 1970s TV ads that coined catchphrases like "But wait, there's more" and "how much would you pay—don't answer." These commercials paved the way for the infomercials of the today.

This film is low on fights, and that is a pity because the action is sharp, enjoyable and brought to life with keen tracking camerawork and reverse-angle shots. Fight instructor Liang Shao-song further perfected his look of obliteration and camera choreography, which later rocketed Taiwan's Wen Jiang-long into kung fu film stardom.

Titleography: As of this writing, no alternative titles could be found. Translation—*Good Fortune Casino*. The Chinese title is the name of the casino in the film run by Ms. Cui and Luo. **MA Percentage: 10.71%** SHAW BROTHERS

CAVALIER, THE

鬼馬大俠；鬼馬雙俠闖江潮 and 大俠客 (1978—Hong Kong) **91m. MAA: Huang Fei-lung. NOT/LOT: None; NOF/LOF: 45/ 29m 23s.** D: Joseph Kuo. C: Si Ma-long, Doris Lung Chun-er, Yan Nan-xi, Lo Lieh, Tang Wei, Lung Fei, Yee Yuen, Tsang Chiu.

What do you get when you cross the classic 1946 Droopy the cartoon dog's *Northwest Hounded Police* with its Monty Python-esque humor and the bludgeoning viciousness of a kung fu film about the Mings fighting the Chings? I don't know, but *The Cavalier* is crawling up your leg.

The film begins when Wu Lung-san (Yee Yuen) announces that any man who can defeat his granddaughter, the street-performer Ping Er (Doris Lung Chun-er), in a fight will marry her. In answer to his challenge, every Tang, Ding and Ha Rei comes out of the woodwork to do battle against her and lose.

An elderly suitor next tries his hand at the maybe marriage. As Ping beats the old man into fresh pulp, anti-Ching rebel Kang Fang-si (Si Ma-long) steps in to save the old man not realizing that the old man is a suitor. After Kang easily fends off Ping, she instantly falls in love with Kang, and the grandfather summarily announces that he has finally found a new son-in-law. Throughout the rest of the film, Kang and his partner (Tang Wei) run, boat and leap through forests to get away from Wu and Ping, who comically pop up in the middle of nowhere to claim that Kang must marry Ping.

While still on the run from Ping and her grandfather, Kang meets up with fellow pro-Ming loyalists who have three missions to accomplish: 1) Kill Ching Emperor Yong Zhen, 2) kill the evil Minister Kung Tai-pu (Lo Lieh), and 3) hide the list of anti-Ching rebels in a secret Taoist temple before Minister Kung or his cohorts get their grubby Manchu mitts on it.

With a whopping 45 fights, it just seems that actor Si Ma-long's fight scenes get better with each successive movie. Si only made 11 movies, and his career was peculiarly intertwined with Hong Kong's martial arts superstar Alexander Fu Sheng's. Si's excellent kung fu stances, postures and technique delivery mirror Fu Sheng's movements and on-screen fighting persona very closely. This was done on purpose because Si was once touted as the Taiwanese Fu Sheng. Ironically, when Fu Sheng passed away, Si also disappeared from film.

Some of this film's fights are just wild and wacky. One running gag is that whenever Kang is in the middle of trouble with Ching soldiers, Wu and Ping pop up to bother Kang, which changes the complexion of the fights from violent to Monty Pythonesque stupidity. And the even sillier thing is that it works for the movie.

In one scene, old man Wu bonks 20 lined-up soldiers with his clublike walking stick while running in a straight line. During another grand moment, a rebel screams and runs toward the sitting Minister Kung. The rebel thrusts his forefinger into Kung's mouth, who catches it in his teeth, bites off the finger and spits it out at the rebel who now dies as the finger pierces his throat. Ack—bloody marvelous if you ask me.

Titleography: *Dancing Kung Fu*; *The Smart Cavalier*; *The Hero Kang Feng Chih*; *Smart Kung Fu*. Translations—*Ghost Horse Heroes*; *Ghost Horse Two Heroes Adventure in Jiang Hu*; *Great Heroes*. As with many *wuxia*-inspired films, the titles are somewhat romanticized to create a feeling of the mysterious Jiang Hu world. The Chinese titles are metaphors for Kang and his partner who travel through the world of Jiang Hu in search of ways to fight the Chings. A cavalier is a chivalrous hero who usually serves as an escort for a woman, thus *Cavalier* does technically fit into one of the movie's subplots. However, *Dancing Kung Fu* is a stretch and perhaps stems from the street-performing Ping Er. Or it comes from Si's fighting rhythm, which uses spins and moves from high-to-low stances, so he comes across more like a dancer than a fighter. **MA Percentage: 32.29%**

CHALLENGE OF THE MASTERS

陸阿采與黃飛鴻 (1976—Hong Kong) **92m. FI: Liu Chia-liang. NOT/LOT: 1/ 14m 55s; NOF/LOF: 17/ 16m 11s.** D: Liu Chia-liang. C: Gordon Liu Chia-hui, Chen Kuan-tai, Liu Chia-liang, Liu Chia-rong, Jiang Yang, Lily Li, Ricky Hui, Jiang Dao, Wong Yu, Wilson Tong, John Cheung, Peter Chan Lung, Fung Ke-an, Eric Tsang, Chien Yueh-sheng, Shi Zhong-tian.

It's Bao Festival time, when all the local martial arts schools come together and scramble to get the *bao*—translated as "envelope" or "package"—which are believed to bring fame and fortune to the holder over the coming year. After the competition, the gods are honored with a feast. In this film, the bao are short red stick-shaped packages that are thrown into the air, and the schools try to make sure they have as many sticks as possible when the contest is over. If one school gets a stick, the other school uses martial arts techniques to wrestle it away. These tussles often lead to fights.

Although the brattish Huang Fei-hung (Gordon Liu Chia-hui) has the heart to enter the bao contest, he does not know martial arts. His father, Huang Chi-ying, was afraid that kung fu in the hands of someone with his son's bad temper would be too dangerous. Regardless, Fei-hung secretly dresses up and enters the contest with his father's other kung fu students. Because of his lack of skill, he not only gets beaten up but also causes the school to lose the only bao it got. Great shame befalls the family and school. However, realizing Fei-hung's potential to be a great martial artist, his uncle Officer Yuan Ching (Liu Chia-rong) introduces Fei-hung to his good friend Lu A-tsai (Chen Kuan-tai). Lu takes on Fei-hung as his student and teaches him *hong jia* kung fu and the Eight Diagram Pole Technique. Lu instructs Fei-hung that it is important to always try to win over the heart of one's enemies rather than just kill them, believing that everyone has the potential to be a good person.

Meanwhile, Yuan is looking for escaped criminal Ho Fu (Liu Chia-liang), a murderer who uses the *mei hua* spear and the Deadly Sharp Kick skill, which uses iron claws attached to the tips of his shoes. Ho Fu kills Yuan, which makes Fei-hung thirst for revenge and leads us to one of the film's fantastic final fights (there are actually two). This was the first time fight instructor and actor Liu Chia-liang would fight his younger kung fu and adopted brother Gordon. During this fight, as well as the last bao competition sequence following it, Fei-hung emerges as a true hero. The confrontations are not about revenge, hurting or killing, but trying to make friends of his enemies. He follows the words of Lu: "Forgiveness and less aggression."

In real life, Lu A-tsai was a Manchu who was orphaned at an early age and raised by an abusive uncle. His fortunes changed when he met Shaolin monk Li Bai-fu at a Cantonese opera performance; Li taught him flower fist and introduced Lu to monk Zhi Shan at Jiu Lian Shan Shaolin. After perfecting the little-known Eight Diagram Pole Technique (created by Yang Wu-lung during the Song Dynasty; it could also be used with a spear), Zhi sent Lu to Fa Cheng to study with Hong Xi-guan and help him set up a new martial arts school. As it turns out, contrary to the film, Lu's first, last and only student was Fei-hung's father, Huang

Chi-ying, who then passed on his knowledge to Fei-hung. One story says Lu, while propped up by pillows on his deathbed and using a pair of chopsticks to represent poles, taught Chi-ying his final secret, Eight Diagram Pole Technique, so he could fight Big Kam, an expert left-handed fishing pole fighter. If Chi-ying lost, he would have to end his medical practice and close down his martial arts school. Lu died at age 68 at his home, Lei Shan lodge, never knowing that Chi-ying was successful. Lu and Chi-ying were both members of the fabled 10 Tigers of Canton heroes.

When the Liu brothers do fight scenes, precise kung fu is important, especially stances and postures. Tracking shots were particularly difficult because the whole body would be under the scrutiny and watchful eye of Chia-liang, which sometimes proved to be unnerving to Gordon. He once told me that Chia-liang's perfectionist attitude back then was very intimidating, especially during their first cinematic fight. Shot after shot was rejected, and sweat seemed to be draining his very soul dry. But obviously he survived and the fight was excellent—film and family-wise. Note that there are no fancy flips or splits, just pure solid contact with wrists and weapons, where one mistake could mean injury. Chia-liang was also the first fight director to specifically have close shots on the legs and feet to show the importance and intricacy of footwork and proper stance foundation.

Titleography: As of this writing, no alternative titles could be found. Translation—*Lu A-tsai and Huang Fei-hung*. **MA Percentage: 33.8%** SHAW BROTHERS

CHAMPION OF DEATH

Kenka Karate Kyokushinken (1975—Japan) **88m. FI: Uncredited. NOT/LOT: 6/ 5m 29s; NOF/LOF: 18/ 18m 579s.** D: Kazuhiko Yamaguchi. C: Sonny Chiba, Jiro Chiba, Kenji Imai, Masashi Ishibashi, Mikio Narita, Yumi Takigawa.

Champion of Death is the first of three Sonny Chiba films that are an ode to real-life martial arts hero Masutatsu Oyama (1923-1994). Better known as Mas Oyama, the founder of *kyokushinkai* karate was also Chiba's most influential teacher.

The film begins in post-World War II Japan, when U.S. military forces are still present. A young and long-haired Oyama (Sonny Chiba) arrives in tattered clothes to Japan's first national martial arts championship. But the national tournament is actually a secret because the U.S. occupiers have forbidden the practice of karate.

Chiba's Oyama makes mincemeat out of the competition before facing tournament favorite Nanba (Masashi Ishibashi) and event organizer Nakasone (Mikio Narita) on the mat. Both Nanba and Nakasone don't see Oyama as a threat because they don't believe he is a true practitioner of karate. Also, he looks weird. So Oyama whomps them. He doesn't accept his trophy, says karate isn't just a dance and then leaves. From here on out, the movie follows Oyama through a few adventures—he saves a village from a crazy bull running rampant on the streets; begins teaching his first student, Shogo Ariake (Jiro Chiba); goes on a drinking binge when that student fails him; and crosses some local Yakuza bosses. All this and more trouble culminates in a violent rematch against Nanba and Nakasone.

Although the fights are shot with shaky camera choreography, the karate techniques are refreshingly clear. Chiba successfully portrays Oyama's sense of power and efficiency of movement. Chiba is obviously enthusiastic to play his karate teacher. As is normal for biopics, some of the film is fictional, but for the most part, it really captures the spirit of Oyama's background and training mentality.

In real life, Mas Oyama was born Choi Yeong-eui in Korea, but he went under the name Choi Bae-dal. He began studying kung fu at 9 years old. By 12, he was practicing Korean *kenpo*. During World War II, he became a fighter pilot in Japan and was labeled a *zainichi* (Korean resident in Japan). After the war, Oyama practiced *shotokan*, then *goju-ryu* karate under Korean martial artist So Nei-chu. Nei-chu convinced the 20-something Oyama to study karate alone in the mountains for three years. One story goes that after 18 months of training on Mount Kiyozumi, Oyama came down from the mountain and hit and killed a charging bull with one blow. Was it a bunch of bull? Some say yes. Yet over time it was recorded that Oyama fought 52 other bulls—three died, 49 had their horns removed by a knife-hand strike. Why did Oyama fight bulls? His goal was to become the epitome of the samurai warrior who lived by the words, "*ichi geki hissatsu*" or "one strike, certain death." His fame as a bullfighter spread, earning him the nickname "The Godhand." The non-smoking Oyama died in 1994 from lung cancer at age 70.

A cultural note: It's interesting that the Japanese tournament organizers are upset that the American occupation forces have banned karate, especially if you consider that Japan forbade the practice of martial arts when occupying Okinawa and China.

Titleography: *Karate Bullfighter*; *Karate Bull Fighter*; *Kyokushin Karate Fist*. Translation—*Fight Karate Kyokashinken*. See above martialogy. **MA Percentage: 27.77%**

CHINATOWN KID

唐人街小子；唐人街功夫小子 and 以毒攻毒 (1977—Hong Kong) 86m. FI: Li Gu-ding, Robert Tai Chi-hsien. NOT/LOT: 2/ 1m 29s; NOF/LOF: 14/ 10m 47s. D: Chang Cheh. C: Alexander Fu Sheng, Kuo Chue, Shaw Yin-yin, Sun Chien, Wang Lung-wei, Jenny Tseng, Lo Meng, Chiang Sheng, Lu Feng.

Similar to how Jackie Chan's *Rumble in the Bronx* (1994) was shot in Vancouver, Canada, and not in the Bronx, *Chinatown Kid* "takes place" in San Francisco's Chinatown, but barring a few stock shots of familiar landmarks, it actually was all shot in the Shaw Brothers studio back lot. I will undoubtedly repeat this elsewhere in the book, but this film does not feature or even star the Five Venoms (see *The Five Venoms*); only four appear in this film. Without sounding like an exam, which one is missing?

Apart from being a rumble in San Francisco, this movie is also about the unity and inherent brotherhood of Chinese youth from Hong Kong and Taiwan (referred to as the Republic of China in the movie), especially between martial artists. When poor, down-on-his-luck, street-vendor Tan Dung (Alexander Fu Sheng) impresses local Hong Kong crime boss Shu Hao (Wang Lung-wei) with his ability to squeeze the juice out of oranges, Shu lures Tan into a friendly fight by promising Tan his watch if he can defeat him. Bim-bam-boom later, Tan has Shu's watch, and Shu loses face. To avenge his loss, Shu plants cocaine on Tan. The police arrest Tan, but he escapes and finds himself on a one-way boat trip to San Fran.

Meanwhile, fresh from serving the required three years in the Republic of China's army where he was a *taekwondo* champion, Jian Wen (Sun Chien) opts to pursue an education in America. To raise money to stay in school abroad, he ends up in San Francisco working in a Chinese restaurant. When the on-the-run Tan and the walk-about Jian meet in San Francisco, they form a brotherhood through their martial arts abilities. Although starting up on opposite sides of the

track, Tan and Jian eventually jump on the same train to derail the local San Fran Triad protection rackets and drug-running schemes.

Like several early Shaw Brothers films that featured the stars from *The Five Venoms*, *Chinatown Kid* also became a cult classic of sorts in America. However, compared to the choreography and fight performances of these established kung fu superstars in their other films, this movie actually ranks pretty low in the action department because the style of fights look awkward and out of place in this contemporary setting. I once asked actor Kuo Chue about this, and he agreed. He relayed to me that everyone in the production was so attuned to the *wuxia*-style fights that contemporary fights felt foreign and that it was tough to find the right balance between the two conflicting methods of kung fu timelines.

Some fun facts: Although today's Chinese military now teaches soldiers unique combinations of Chinese kung fu styles for hand-to-hand combat, taekwondo was indeed the preferred style of the armed forces back when I was in Taiwan in the 1970s and 1980s. Also, Americans will notice that the San Francisco cars have the steering column on the right side rather than the left. And also similar to Great Britain, Japan and Australia, the characters drive on the left side of the road. From this, there can be no doubt as to why San Francisco has the highest rate of car accidents in the country!

Titleography: As of this writing, no alternative titles could be found. Translations—*Chinatown Lad*; *Chinatown Kung Fu Lad* and *Use Poison to Fight Poison*. The word *Lad* implies someone older than a *Kid*. Of course, director Chang Cheh was a student of the American Old West, so perhaps it's some kind of Billy the Kid reference. Chang's 1969 film title *Have Sword Will Travel* was adapted from the Richard Boone's 1957 TV Western *Have Gun Will Travel*, where incidentally Boone's Palladin character's assistant was a Chinese coolie named Hey Boy played by Kam Tong. **MA Percentage: 14.26%** SHAW BROTHERS

CHINESE CONNECTION 2

唐山大兄 2 and 精武門續集 (1977—Hong Kong) 95m. MAD: Tommy Lee. NOT/LOT: 1/ 21s; NOF/LOF: 19/ 25m 1s. D: Jimmy Shaw Feng, Lee Tso-nam. C: Bruce Li, Lo Lieh, Chen Hui-lou, Tien Fung, Nan Gong-xun, Xue Han, Jimmy Lung Fong, Gao Fei, Yasuaki Kurata.

Before World War II, the Japanese sphere of influence was strong in China because the Japanese had strong authoritarian control over several provinces and cities. Shanghai was one such area, where outside the various foreign concessions in the city, Japan had relatively free reign. Bruce Lee's *The Chinese Connection* (aka *Fist of Fury*) took place in Shanghai during this time of Japanese occupation. *Chinese Connection 2* begins where *Chinese Connection* ends.

The film opens with a funeral procession for Chen Chen (played by Bruce Lee in the prequel) that features a real framed picture of Bruce Lee. The Japanese authorities brutally destroy all Chinese kung fu schools in Shanghai, but they will spare the schools that agree to recognize the new Japanese martial arts leader (Lo Lieh) as the head of their schools. With Japanese disrespect toward the Chinese taking on an even greater "kicking a dead horse when its down" mentality, it is prime time for Chen Shen (Bruce Li) to avenge his brother Chen Chen and destroy the Japanese karate school. When one character tells Chen Shen, "You even look like Chen Chen," it is beautifully blatant, clearly telling the audience that Bruce Li is the spitting image of Bruce Lee, thus all is logical in the film and in the world of Bruceploitation. The film repeats the *Chinese Connection* plot, in which the Japanese this time want to find Chen Shen, who goes on a killing spree in the name of the Chinese people and their martial arts.

Although the Bruce-*Enter-the-Dragon*-Lee body and facial cuts are prominent, the director resisted having Li act and fight much like the legendary man. And it was good that Li did not use the *nunchaku* or touch his bleeding wounds, then lick the blood, like Lee did in *Enter the Dragon*. Although lacking Lee's intensity, the fights in *Chinese Connection 2* appear to be similar in style to *Chinese Connection* in the way they were shot, thus making the time to look and feel the same from one Bruce to the other.

This film even had the audacity to have Lo Lieh's character's hand turn red when he claws the Japanese up, right out of *King Boxer* (aka *Five Fingers of Death*, which made Lo an international star). I can only imagine Shaw Brothers wishing that there were copyright laws on things like this, especially when you had one of its franchise actors doing what made him famous in the West (like Alpha Motion Pictures did not know this).

With all the Bruce Lee fakery going on, there is an interesting fight aberration in this film: an old man who plays a small fighting role. I have never seen this actor before, but his snake fist kung fu really sticks out, and choreographer Tommy Lee made sure he was prominently featured in a major fight scene. Nice touch Tommy.

Titleography: *Fist of Fury 2*; *Fist of Fury Part Two*. Translations—*The Big Brother From Tang Mountain 2* and *Entry Into the Ching Wu Martial Arts School, the Continuation*. The faux pas English release titles of Lee's first two films haunt us again. The *Big Brother From Tang Mountain 2* Chinese title uses the same characters (except for the *2*) as Lee's first film, *The Big Boss*, insinuating in Chinese that this film is a sequel to *The Big Boss*, which was released in America as *Fists of Fury*. So based on the Chinese character title and the English release title *Fists of Fury*, the alternative title of this film is *Fist of Fury 2*. The *Entry Into the Ching Wu Martial Arts School, the Continuation* Chinese title uses the same characters (except for *the Continuation*) as Lee's second film *Fist of Fury*, implying in Chinese that this film is a sequel to Lee's *Fist of Fury*, which was released in America as *The Chinese Connection*. So based on the Chinese character title and the English release title *Chinese Connection*, this film was released as *Chinese Connection 2*. However, based on the original Hong Kong English title of Lee's second film, *Fist of Fury*, it makes sense that this film is *Fists of Fury 2*. There are also other films that were released under the English titles *Big Boss 2*, *Fist of Fury 3* and *The Big Boss Part 2*. As the Chinese would say, AYAH! **MA Percentage: 26.7%**

CHINESE BOXER, THE

龍虎鬥 (1970—Hong Kong) 75m. FI: Tang Chia. NOT/LOT: 6/ 4m 45s; NOF/LOF: 23/ 21m 3s. D: Jimmy Wong Yu. C: Jimmy Wong Yu, Lo Lieh, Wang Ping, Chao Xiong, Fang Mian, Chen Hsing, Cheng Lei, Wang Chung.

For his last Shaw Brothers production, *Chinese Boxer* was the first film Jimmy Wong Yu wrote and directed, in which he started a new trend of Mandarin unarmed-combat films. The movie is a revenge tale filled with morbid acts of senseless violence against Chinese hero Lei Ming (Jimmy Wong Yu). His martial arts school is wiped out, and his friend's wife is raped by Japanese villains who run a crooked casino, swindle men out of their money, and force those men's wives to beg for mercy and submit to sexual abuse. The film is a cross between common *wuxia* motifs and storylines, including the rival school, the crippled hero, the threatened martial arts school, the master's words of wisdom, the rebellious hero and the secret technique. However, Wong Yu's approach as to how the audience sees Lei Ming prepare for his revenge against the Japanese was new for 1970.

Wong Yu once shared with me that at the time he made the film, Japanese movies began to feature judo stylists battling karate practitioners—it wasn't all samurai sword fighting. Wong Yu thought it would be interesting to do a Chinese film that featured kung fu fighters against karate fighters. He drew on his past films and created the story, taking 10 days to complete the plot. This film also marks the first time audiences got a glimpse of how to practice *ching gong* (the technique that gives one the ability to leap high), although Wong shows the real way to practice ching gong in *Master of the Flying Guillotine* (1976). It also marks the first time audiences saw iron palm, which was made famous in the West two years later by actor Lo Lieh in *King Boxer*, aka *Five Fingers of Death*. In this film, Lo stars as the Japanese killer samurai master Kita, whom Lei Ming faces in a beautiful snowy landscape. Although Lei Ming is the hero, Wong Yu chose to make himself a seemingly unimportant character in the first third of the film. This was an effective choice because it reflects how you can become a hero from humble origins if you practice kung fu with all your heart.

Wong Yu also explained to me that as the director, it was initially difficult to decide where to place the camera during a shot, but after one scene he was confident enough to actually take control of shooting the action (most directors leave that to the fight instructors). He intelligently used different camera choreography for different fights, something again that was novel in earlier films. In the big casino fight, he used a lot of hand-held camerawork, almost to the point of looking clumsy, but keeping the angles tight and maneuvering the camera quickly. The camera choreography really sold Lei Ming's cool demeanor and the claustrophobic feel of the scene. The shrinking room sense manifests itself onto a personal level as Lei's hands are tightly wrapped in cotton and he wears a surgeon's mask due to him recovering from his iron palm training.

This was also the first film to actually deal with the torturous physical hardship the hero endures during his training for ultimate revenge.

The final fight, shot in a wide, open, snow-laden landscape, is slowed down and uses open-hand techniques. It's also worth noting that in earlier fights, the sound was ramped up in editing, but during the final fight, the sound was toned down, revealing the virtue of stealth, something that is inherent in iron palm and kung fu training, where silence of what you know is a weapon in itself. (Stealth is an important aspect of martial arts rarely expressed as a virtue.)

As a director, Jimmy Wong Yu has always been a solid proponent of martial arts. In many of his films, including this one, he tries to bring out the spirit of martial arts history. In one scene, a kung fu teacher is instructing his students while protagonist Lei Ming listens intently. The *sifu* says that karate came from China via the Tang Dynasty, but in the past, it was called *tang shou dao* (the Tang hand). No other film prior to this that I have seen discusses this. It is partially true too.

In actuality, Shaolin martial artists arrived in Okinawa in 1372 to teach martial arts, which led to the development of the Okinawan arts of *naha te*, *shuri te* and *tomari te*. These martial arts were combined and introduced into Japan as karate in 1922 by Gosei Yamaguchi. The term "karate" was first used in 1722 by Okinawan martial artist Sakugawa. "Kara" referred to China, while "te" refers to a person's hand. So "karate" means "Chinese hand" or "Tang hand." When karate was introduced into Japan, the meaning of "kara" was changed to "empty." The Tangs introduced martial arts into Korea around A.D. 663, after the Tangs helped the Silla Kingdom defeat the Japanese-backed Paetcha Kingdom. In honor of the Tang emperor, the Silla called the martial art *tang su*, and the art evolved into *tang soo do*.

Titleography: *Hammer of God*. Translation—*Dragon Tiger Fight*. The title *Dragon Tiger Fight* refers to the Chinese, represented by the dragon, fighting the Japanese, represented by the tiger. *Hammer of God* refers to Lei Ming's training; he makes his fists hard like a hammer and strikes with the wrath of God. **MA Percentage: 34.4%** SHAW BROTHERS

CHINESE IRON MAN

中國鈇人 and 中國鐵人 (1973—Taiwan) **87m. FI: Lin You-chuan. NOT/LOT: None; NOF/LOF: 19/ 26m 52s.** D: Joseph Kuo. C: Wen Jiang-long, Yan Nan-xi, Liu Ping, Yee Yuen, Liu Li-zu, Bruce Li, Shi Zhong-tian, Chen Sen-lin, Wu Dong-qiao.

The plot occurs before the Rape of Nanking in World War II, so the evil Japanese are still hell bent on destroying all martial arts schools in Shanghai. The hell bending continues with *Chinese Iron Man*, Taiwan's answer to Bruce Lee's *The Chinese Connection* (aka *Fist of Fury*).

When Chinese chef Little Tiger Liang Xiao-hu (Wen Jiang-long in a large French chef hat) sees the Japanese karate students from the Musashi Martial Club enter his restaurant, bully the Chinese patrons and call them dogs, he breaks out his rolling pin and clubs every one of them, forcing the head *karateka* to admit that it is the Japanese who are dogs. The stage is set. The Japanese force the Shanghai police chief to find Liang and shut down the Zhong Hua Martial Arts school. (The Republic of China, which is now known as Taiwan, in Chinese romanization is Zhong Hua Ming Guo. Therefore, calling the kung fu school Zhong Hua infers that it is China's martial arts school).

The Japanese martial artists challenge the Chinese martial artists to an open-air tournament. Of course, the Japanese believe that they will make mincemeat of the Chinese kung fu students and force Chinese patriot Liang to come out of hiding to defend the honor of the Chinese. Their plan works because Liang does come to fight, but they pay a dear price for their misplaced loss of face.

Fight instructor Lin You-chuan is one of those hidden gems in kung fu cinema. He is known for creating relentless, fast-paced fights that don't dwell on perfect technique, posture or real kung fu fighting.

My hat also goes off to actor Wen Jiang-long. In his earlier films, he put his body on maniacal overdrive and just kicked and scrapped his way all over the screen; he didn't care a crap about what the kung fu folks thought of him. When Wen takes on multiple attackers in this film, so much goes on in every single shot. He is as intense as he is fun to watch, regardless of the haphazard nature of the choreography and the somewhat sloppy kung fu. The key to Lin's choreography is that he had Wen throw his leg in the direction of his attackers, and they would just react to the leg placement. As a result, Wen was not actually kicking. Instead, he just rapidly lifted his leg in several directions. Wen never actually extends his kicks because he is not kicking per se.

The "Bruce Lee *nunchaku* fight in the Japanese school" rip-off scene that features Wen using a piece of rope is so blatant that you have got to admire the audacity of the filmmakers. They use the same sound effects for Wen's rope that were used for Lee's nunchaku. They choreograph the fight so Wen strikes the heads of the Japanese and rolls on the ground while hitting their feet with his rope. It looks like the way Lee did it with his nunchaku. And they even use the same camera angles.

With all the exhausting, high-energy fights this film had, the final fights lacked the same juice; they just seem to run out of steam. This was probably because of the fights being one-on-one confrontations in which the flail-on-flail choreography lacks the animalistic luster of the previous group fights. Plus, one-on-one fights are more difficult to hide a star's lack of skills because the audience focuses on just two fighters rather than stuntmen running all over the place when the star really only has to keep moving around to sell the fight. But the film's climax is poignant. Echoing how Lee broke the Shanghai Park sign in *Chinese Connection*, Wen grabs the Japanese martial club's sign, tosses it skyward, leaps up and splinters the board with a kick. The last Bruce-Lee borrow of

the film I want to bring up is a young Bruce Li playing an insignificant Japanese thug. Who could have predicted what was around the corner for Li. He became a major player in the Bruceploitation industry.

Titleography: *Iron Man*; *Young Hero of the Shaolin II*. Translation—Both Chinese titles translate into *Chinese Iron Man*. There are two films with the title *Young Hero of Shaolin* (1975 and 1984) and another film with the title of *Young Hero of Shaolin II* (1986). All three are about the legendary folk-hero Fang Shi-yu. However, there is no *Young Hero of the Shaolin* film out there. Also, because *Chinese Iron Man* is about a character named Liang Xiao-hu who does not train at Shaolin, *Young Hero of the Shaolin II* is one of those pull-a-rabbit-out-of-the-hat titles that have no rhyme or reason. **MA Percentage: 30.88%**

CHINESE KUNG FU

唐山功夫 (1974—Taiwan) **84m. FI: Uncredited. NOT/LOT: None; NOF/LOF: 14/ 25m 8s.** D: Artis Chow A-chi. C: Shi Feng, Joan Lin Feng-chiao, Li Zhen-hua, Li Xin-hua, Xue Han, Li Jiang, Cho Kin.

Do "ore" die. When Lo Wu-wen's (Shi Feng) mother died, he was taken at age 5 to the Shaolin Temple where he was raised and taught kung fu. Twenty years later, he is on a mission to find his long-lost aunt. Before leaving the temple, the abbot of Shaolin tells Lo that he can only use his kung fu to defend his home or country, which sets up the obvious plot. On his arrival home, he discovers that noxious Nippon nasties are trying to strong-arm a local shipping company in Fujian province to ship iron ore to Japanese steamships waiting off the coast. (Fujian is a Chinese province near Taiwan, which was under Japanese rule between 1895 to 1945.)

The owners of the Fujian Union of Boats, Mr. Chu (Cho Kin) and Mr. Yeh (Li Xin-hua) refuse to help because they know the Japanese will use the ore to make weapons with which to attack China. When the chief of the Eagle School, Ho Lao-chu (Xue Han), and his local Chinese traitors force Mr. Chu to obey the Japanese will, Lo arrives on the scene. Although he badly wants to fight the traitors and help his Chinese brethren, he is torn by his kung fu philosophy never to fight. Fortunately, Lo is saved when Mr. Chu's American-educated son who is also a kung fu expert, Chu Shao-hua (Li Zhen-hua), arrives to thump the thugs into submission.

Foaming at the mouth, the head Japanese brewer of trouble, Mr. Taro, sends his head hit man Mr. Sukata (Li Jiang) to weed out the son and plant extra fear into Chinese hearts by breaking Chu Shao-hua's legs. Fifty-six minutes into the film, Lo finally sees that enough is enough. With the help of the lovingly upright Miss Lao Si (Joan Lin Feng-chiao), Lo—and behold!—gets all Bruce Lee's *Big Boss* on them.

Lao Si is the first major role for Jackie Chan's wife of many years, Joan Lin Feng-chiao. (Lin is also the mother of Chan's son Jaycee Chan. Chan never publicly revealed he had a son until the 1990s.) Some of the film's many memorable visuals occur when several fights end up by the sea. The soothing shots of the ocean beautifully juxtaposed with the violent fights are all very *yin-yang*. Late in the final fight, there is a truly freakazoid upside-down camera shot that stays with you in a good way once you've seen it. Yet most fighters would wind up for a strike too much; these windups made the fights look even more awkward when they would raise their foot off the ground before punching. The choreographers also use many low-angle heroic-looking shots that make it look like someone is trying to find his car in a giant parking lot. There is also the old hero-drowning-in-the-water shot, in which the villain stupidly guffaws at the hero's final sinking air bubbles only to be caught off-guard when the hero amazingly leaps 10 feet out of the water and birds down on the flabbergasted flunky who was fooled by the fearless and now flying victor.

Titleography: *Super Dynamo*; *Duel of the Masters*; *Shaolin Long Arm*. Translation—*Tang Shan Kung Fu*. Tang Shan is a mountain in China and is also found in the Chinese title of Bruce Lee's first film, *The Big Boss*, which translates to the *Big Brother From Tang Mountain*. *Duel of the Masters* and *Super Dynamo* are rather generic titles. Because Lo practices Shaolin long fist kung fu, the title *Shaolin Long Arm* makes sense, although I would guess the distributors might not have known it. **MA Percentage: 29.92%**

CIRCLE OF IRON

(1978—USA) **102m. MAC: Kam Yuen, Joe Lewis. NOT/LOT: None; NOF/LOF: 7/ 10m 4s.** D: Richard Moore. C: David Carradine, Jeff Cooper, Christopher Lee, Roddy McDowall, Eli Wallach, Anthony De Longis, Earl Maynard, Erica Creer.

This film was made in the wrong decade. Today's audiences would be more receptive to the premise and philosophical messages that it evoked. The disadvantage of watching any martial arts film back in the 1970s with Bruce Lee's name attached to it (see next paragraph) was the expectation of seeing good martial arts in the movie. This film does not deliver on the martial arts fight scenes on any level. If Bruce Lee had lived to star in this film, the fights would have been better choreographed and shot with a martial arts eye for good skill. Yet, as it was, this movie was not ultimately about the fights but the philosophy.

Based on an idea that Lee shared with actor James Coburn in 1969, the final shooting script of Lee's wise tale was edited by Academy-Award-winning screenwriter Stirling Silliphant. The film spins a yarn about a fighter named Cord (Jeff Cooper) on a quest to find a mysterious fighter named Zetan (Christopher Lee) who is the keeper of the *Book of Enlightenment*, which holds the key to understanding one's self. Shot in Israel under the original title *The Silent Flute*, the film initially comes across as a sword-and-sandal film. (This is the genre of films that refer to Italian mythology movies like *Hercules* (1958) and *Jason and the Argonauts* (1963). They have a specific feel to them with costumes, togas, etc.) It then quickly melts into something more along the lines of the classic Chinese kung fu novel *Journey to the West*, which is about a monk who searches for ancient Buddhist scriptures with the help of the Monkey King. Lee's childhood fascination with Chinese kung fu and *wuxia* novels—which his sister Phoebe Lee told me he read by the droves during his upbringing in Hong Kong—may have helped shape *The Silent Flute,* which is an amalgamation of Lee's martial arts philosophy translated for Westerners through the cultural influence of Chinese literature. For example, one of the main characters in the film is a monkey that fights using praying mantis kung fu, an art known for incorporating monkey-style footwork.

In his first fight as the character of the Blind Man, David Carradine gently defeats a gaggle of ne'er-do-wells in a cave with his pole-length flute that whistles as he wields it. Mainstream audiences in the late '70s were not attuned into the film's themes unless they were heavily into martial arts philosophy and/or Buddhism, which ultimately was a very narrow audience. Perhaps the filmmakers were merely trying to cash in on Lee's name, but I would like to believe that the movie tried to make audiences understand how Lee viewed the tight marriage of martial arts and life. To watch this film is to understand a bit more about Bruce Lee, and how to him, martial arts was a path to knowledge and understanding of one's self.

With today's broad and heavy acceptance of Eastern thought pervading Western society, *Circle of Iron* would have been a more accepted, meaningful and less airy-fairy story to contemporary audiences. Carradine's performance as the Blind Man, Monkeyman, Death (a black panther) and Changsha all came across like Kwai Chang Caine in four different costumes. Caine was Carradine's character in the *Kung Fu* TV series. However, if Lee was alive to play the same roles, as was the intention, perhaps his portrayal would have been compared to Tony Randall's role in the Oscar-winning film *The Seven Faces of Dr. Lao* (1964), and it would have been the first time an Asian actor played (at least in the original inception) four distinct separate roles. As Lee would probably have said, "Cool man."

Titleography: *Silent Flute.* The original title of *The Silent Flute* was a reflection of Bruce Lee's philosophical conundrum of having no limit as limit. In the movie, Lee equates music to one's philosophical understanding of the self, as prescribed through hearing without listening and speaking without talking—both of which are a tangential verse of Lee's classic martial arts tenet that he practices the art of fighting without fighting. *Circle of Iron* could reflect the nature of the book that Cord seeks as the ultimate knowledge, which is framed within a circle of iron on each page of the book. **MA Percentage: 9.87%**

CLAN OF AMAZONS

秀花大盜 and 陸小鳳傳奇之一繡花大盜 (1978—Hong Kong) 85m. FI: Huang Pei-ji, Tang Chia. NOF/LOF: 31/ 15m 25s. D: Chu Yuan. C: Liu Yong, Ling Yun, Yueh Hua, Ching Li, Shih Szu, Zhang Ying, Ai Fei, Xu Hsao-chiang, Chan Man-na, Zhuang Li, Di Bo-la, Gu Guan-zhong.

As the Chinese title indicates, this film is not about a clan of Amazons but about the legend of Lu Xiao-feng and the Embroidery Thief. In a way, it is also a sort of backward twist on *Snow White and the Seven Dwarfs*, a story about Lu Xiao-feng and the Seven Beauties. In place of the wicked queen with her deadly apple and misleading mirror is an evil drag queen with deadly embroidery needles and misleading red shoes.

The film begins with a string of bizarre events involving a veiled highwayperson who wears red shoes and sits in the middle of a road waiting to rob someone blind. The robber always finishes a piece of embroidery just before preying on his victim and says, "I don't embroider flowers, but I embroider blind." At that moment, the killer pierces the victim's eyes with the embroidery needles, grabs the loot and disappears. Thus the world of Jiang Hu has a new tenant, and the red-shoe killer is someone that the old tenants need to keep their eyes open for because if they don't, the killer may shut their eyes for good.

Still from *Clan of Amazons* © Celestial Pictures Ltd. All rights reserved.

Charming and arrogant detective Lu Xiao-feng (Liu Yong) is asked by the dour Jin Jiu-ling (Ling Yun), head of the murder and theft investigation, to help with the case. After Lu finishes a Chinese chess match with his blind swordsman pal, Hua Man-lou (Yueh Hua)—whose chess strategy is a gamble (a gambit of things to come) and who uses his *chi* to move the pieces without touching them—Lu goes off to investigate. His only lead is a red silk scarf with an embroidered flower on it. Lu and his lover, Xue Bing (Ching Li), go in search of the Red Shoe Society, a secret sect of swordswomen who are believed to be at the bottom of the needle and thread murder caper.

Though Lu and Xue's initial efforts are thwarted, they manage to slither some information about the society from for the mysterious "king of the street," Mr. Serpent (Zhang Ying). But after Xue goes missing, Lu is left alone to match wits and swords with the Red Shoe members and their fearless leader, Gong Sun-lan (Chan Man-na). She challenges him to three competitions that will determine his success or doom: poetry, swordplay and *ching gong* (the ability to leap high and run on treetops).

Two plot conventions used in many *wuxia* films appear in this film, and they are having someone deliver a letter that provides important information for the characters and audience, and having a character whisper something in someone's ear, which keeps the audience's curiosity and can be used to explain plot inconsistencies later in the film. They are simple story devices that can be filled in later for some desired effect.

As all these letters are being delivered and people are whispering in the ears of others, it is only a matter of time before Hua, Lu's blind swordsman friend, shows up. He does so when the heroes are trapped in a dark room being sliced and diced by the baddies. Then, in what seems like a snap of the fingers, the underlying ruse of the film is re-vealed. Before you know it, all the main villains and heroes end up fighting on a large burning boat before the fight moves to dry land, where the film literally and suddenly comes to an abrupt halt. Case closed.

Since this film is about a villain who uses embroidery as a weapon of sorts, here's a final "Did you know?" tidbit of history: The earliest records about the art of embroidery have been traced back to China's Shang Dynasty (1766 B.C.). Just thought I'd point it out.

Titleography: As of this writing, no alternative titles could be found. Translations—*Embroidery Thief*; *The Legend of Lu Xiao-feng and the Embroidery Thief*. *Clan of Amazons* implicitly compares the Red Shoe Society to the Amazons, a female warrior tribe originating in Greek my-thology. But it is a stretch since Amazons originated from Greek mythology, the warriors of Scythia, who burned off their right breasts to become better archers. None of that in this film. **MA Percentage: 18.84%** SHAW BROTHERS

Still from *Clan of the White Lotus* © Celestial Pictures Ltd. All rights reserved.

CLAN OF THE WHITE LOTUS

洪文定三破白蓮教 (1979—Hong Kong) **90m. FI: Liu Chia-liang. NOT/LOT: 9/ 13m 11s; NOF/LOF: 24/ 31m 36s. D:** Lo Lieh. **C:** Gordon Liu Chia-hui, Hui Ying-hong, Lo Lieh, Wang Lung-wei, Lin Hui-huang, Li Qing-xhu, Yang Jing-jing, Hsiao Ho, Ching Miao, Shen Xian, Wilson Tong.

According to history, two of Shaolin's Five Ancestors named Hu Dei-di and Tsai De-zhong, as well as two of Tsai De zhong's students, established Jiu Lian Shan Shaolin Temple in Fujian province after the burning of Song Shan Shaolin Temple. Five important figures arrived at Jiu Lian and became the Five Elders of Shaolin: Zhi Shan, Wu Mei, Miao Xian, Feng Dao-de and Bai Mei. Feng and Bai left that Shaolin temple to join the Wu Dung Taoist school of martial arts, the Wu Dung being an enemy of the Shaolin. They were then recruited by the Chings to plan the burning of Jiu Lian. In the film *Executioners From Shaolin* (1977), the character Bai Mei kills Shaolin hero Hong Xi-guan only to be defeated by Hong's son Wen-ding, who combined his father's tiger kung fu with his mother's white crane kung fu. Although *Clan of the White Lotus* is an unofficial sequel to *Executioners From Shaolin,* the reel and real histories of each film are inconsistent with history and even with each other, which off the bat is apparent in the opening scene.

This film opens with Hong Wen-ding (Gordon Liu Chia-hui) and Ah Biao (Lin Hui-huang) defeating the white-haired priest Bai Mei. It was only Wen-ding in *Executioners.* When Bai's brother, chief of the White Lotus Sect (Lo Lieh) and who is also the spitting image of Bai Mei, is asked by Gov. Kao Ting-chun (Wang Lung-wei) to avenge Bai's death and destroy the rest of Shaolin, he agrees. Bai's brother and his Ching cohorts attack Wen-ding's house, but Wen-ding manages to barely escape with Ah Biao's pregnant wife Mei Ha (Hui Ying-hong). Strike one.

Although Wen-ding combines white crane and tiger kung fu in the *Execu-tioners,* this film depicts Wen-ding as not having learned the techniques yet. So after Wen-ding combines his father's tiger kung fu with Mei's white crane, he loses to Bai's brother because the brother uses the air created by the force of Wen-ding's attacks to avoid the strikes. It is like when you grab for a mosquito in flight, you create an air puff that the mosquito uses to escape. Wen-ding barely escapes. Strike two.

After Mei teaches Wen-ding how to strike paper dummies without pushing them back, Wen-ding returns to the White Lotus Sect. Although he is able to successfully hit the white-haired priest, Wen-ding is still ineffective and almost dies. Strike three but not yet out.

Hobbling home, Mei next teaches Wen-ding embroidery kung fu, and Wen-ding learns to act like a lady and use needles to strike acupuncture points. Wen-ding is ready for a fourth and final strike with the White Lotus chief, whereby

constantly needling him, Wen-ding might be able to find the home-run bloody weakness. If not, he's out for good.

Executioners and *Clan* tell a different story about how Bai Mei died, which brings to mind, How did Bai Mei really die? One theory explains that after Jiu Lian Temple burned, the Five Elders (four because Bai Mei left Shaolin; three if you consider that Feng Dao-de left Shaolin, but because this theory considers Feng nontraitorous, let's call it four) were aware of Bai Mei's traitorous acts and made their way to Er Mei Mountain in Sichuan province where they plotted their revenge against Bai. In order to avoid the Chings, they became Taoists in appearance and adopted many Taoist philosophies. During the process of the Four Elders seeking revenge, Bai Mei killed Miao Xian and Zhi Shan but was killed by Feng Dao-de. After Bai's death Feng Dao-de and Wu Mei went their separate ways. This story seems to indicate that although Feng Dao-de defected to Wu Dung, it was maybe a rouse to win Bai Mei's confidence, wait for the right moment, then bam—Shaolin revenge.

Three memorable scenes: 1) Actor Lo Lieh smoothly walks and defends himself against many attackers and strikes without breaking stride in one uned-ited shot; 2) while leaving his bath nude, Lo's White Lotus chief fights off Wen-ding while smoothly getting dressed—it's not so much a funny scene as it is creative; and 3) when the White Lotus chief's body is covered in acupuncture needles, he uses his *chi* to explode the needles away from his body. Gordon Liu told me that the needles were individually glued onto Lo Lieh's body and were constantly being retouched or reattached.

Titleography: *Fist of the White Lotus.* Translation—*Hong Wen-ding Defeated Three Times by the White Lotus Sect.* See above martialogy. **MA Percentage: 49.76%** SHAW BROTHERS

CLANS OF INTRIGUE

楚留香 (1977—Hong Kong) **98m. FI: Huang Pei-ji, Tang Chia. NOT/LOT: None; NOF/LOF: 24/ 14m 5s. D:** Chu Yuen. **C:** Ti Lung, Yueh Hua, Nora Miao, Ling Yun, Li Ching, Pei Ti.

Lesbians, hermaphrodites and sword fights—what a mixed-up kung fu world we live in. Because of actress Pei Ti's mesmerizing role in director Chu Yuen's dazzling *Intimate Confessions of a Chinese Courtesan* (1972), many legitimate actresses found mainstream box-office success doing kung fu erotica during the 1970s. For actress Nora Miao, the year was 1977 when she decided to leave her good-girl image behind. It was also the year she left the clutches of Golden Harvest and producer Raymond Chow for Shaw Brothers. In Jim Mor-rison and The Doors' psychedelic words, Miao decided to "break on through to the other side."

Clans of Intrigue is an adaptation of a kung fu novel that features an expert swordsman named Chu Liu-hsiang (Ti Lung), an upright detective who prestigiously treads the line between the normal and *wuxia* worlds. He is trying to solve the mystery of why three major clan leaders have been brutally murdered. Peppered with sexual ambiguity (erotica Miao for one) and more back-stabbing intensity than what occurs in politics and academia, Chu's use of the fabled Triple-Sword Technique, Soul-Returning Strike and Pole Trellis Maneuver beautifully bonds with some curious-looking scenery. For example, one set is filled with flower-covered swings and a large wicker chair hanging over water that is used to drown people. It looks like something out of *The Wild Wild West* color episode that featured Victor Bueno as the villain Count Carlos Mario Vincenzo Robespierre Manzeppi.

According to the film, the Yi Her people from Fujian were the progenitors of the ninja. Historically, people with the surname Her immigrated into Fujian during the Western Jin and Southern Dynasty periods (A.D. 420 to A.D. 589). However, because of the rugged terrain and its subsequence isolation, Fujian became a penal province for exiled prisoners and dissidents. While other powerful families (Chen, Huang, Lin and Zheng) replaced the Her family, the Hers became targets for the aforementioned exiles. They fled into the uninhabitable Wuyi Mountain for protection. Meanwhile, Shaolin martial arts was being introduced throughout China, and as legend implies, several of the Her mountain people learned these arts and formed secret fighting groups to defend themselves. Eventually, no one would dare enter Wuyi Mountain. Whether their little-known stealth-fighting abilities are associated with the ninja (who appeared in Japan in the 1400s), the history of one art, whether for assassination or defense, ultimately influences another.

You could easily think that this is indeed a film laced with wall-to-wall action because director Chu opted to feature 24 short fights evenly distributed throughout the film rather than the usual strategy of placing most of the action in the third part of it. In actuality, 14 minutes worth of kung fu in a Shaw Brothers production is considered very small, but the story is as engaging as the shocking lesbian love scene between Miao and Pei.

Titleography: As of this writing, no alternative titles could be found. Translation—*Chu Liu-hsiang*, the lead character's name. The only known English title to date aptly reflects the story. **MA Percentage: 14.37%** SHAW BROTHERS

Still from *Clans of Intrigue* © Celestial Pictures Ltd. All rights reserved.

CLEOPATRA JONES

(1973—USA) 88m. SC: Paul Nuckles, Ernest Robinson. NOT/LOT: 1/ 3s; NOF/LOF: 9/ 2m 27s. D: Jack Starret. C: Tamara Dobson, Bernie Casey, Brenda Sykes, Antonio Fargas, Shelley Winters, Dan Frazer, Bill McKinney, Stafford Morgan, Michael Warren, Albert Popwell, Caro Kenyatta.

Once regarded as the tallest leading lady ever in film, the 6-foot-2-inch Tamara Dobson flails and wails into martial arts blaxploitation as U.S. Special Agent Cleopatra Jones. Soul sister Jones takes on the jive turkey Mother (Shelley Winters), who is out to get Jones because Jones destroyed $30 million worth of opium she was getting from Turkey. Surrounded by corrupt cops and assorted mudslide brothers such as Doodlebug Simkins (Antonio Fargas), Jones finds allies in the karate Johnson brothers. She also has special guns hidden in a secret compartment in her car (inspired by the secret stash of guns in *The Wild Wild West* TV show, thus the inclusion of similar music from the show) and, of course, her long, lanky karate-kicking legs and fastidious fists. And even though they usually miss their targets, the villains still bite the dust.

I loved the final fight on the rock escalator at the quarry, which is right out of what was considered one of the most violent detective series in TV history, *Mannix* (1967). The fights truly are pathetic, but what can you expect from a film that has no trained martial artists and instead has stunt coordinators raised on bar brawls and fisticuff fights? It's clear neither group knew the difference between kung fu and karate because, back then, the terms were synonymous. At least they tried … right on!

Titleography: As of this writing, no alternative titles could be found. **MA Percentage: 2.84%**

CLEOPATRA JONES AND THE CASINO OF GOLD

女金剛鬥狂龍女 (1975—Hong Kong) 97m. FI: Tang Chia, Yuen Cheung-yan. NOT/LOT: None; NOF/LOF: 10/ 8m 11s. D: Chuck Bail. C: Tamara Dobson, Tanny Tien Ni, Stella Stevens, Chan Shen, John Cheung, Lin Zhen-ji, Liu Liu-hua, Norman Fell, Albert Popwell, Caro Kenyatta, Christopher Hunt, Eddy Donno, Bobby Canavarro.

It is one martialogy down but two years later in this *Cleopatra Jones* sequel, and the seemingly taller and skinnier Cleopatra Jones (Tamara Dobson) is back with six more minutes of kung fu fighting to take down another honky female drug lord, Dragon Lady (Stella Stevens). Higher on fashion and makeup, faster with innuendo and humor, sleeker than a speeding cheetah, able to take down any cheater, Cleopatra is the woman with the plan. In this film, she flashes more glitz, glamour, bling and clamor while enlisting the help of Hong Kong hottie Mi Ling (Tanny Tien Ni) and motorcycle daredevil David Chang (John Cheung) to infiltrate the Casino of Gold. It's a shoot-'em-up, flip-'em-over and knock-'em-down extravaganza as they try to send Dragon Lady to the big reptile farm in the sky.

It is amazing how in so many movies dealing with drugs, including this one, every time the buy is going down or the drug stash is found, either the hero or villain takes a finger full of the drug and jams it into his mouth. If one really did that, he would probably end up dead or incredibly intoxicated. During the final attack on the casino, it suddenly hit me that this is the female version of *Rush Hour*. Sure, there's the obvious partnership between black cop Cleo and Chinese cop Mi Ling, but especially during one shot when Cleo is speeding around in a motorcycle sidecar and shooting up the whole place, her grimacing face and bug-eyed stare are the spitting image of Chris Tucker. Actress Stella Stevens does a reasonable job in her sword fight against actor Chan Shen in the pit of swords as well as in her final clash with Tamara Dobson, during which the two ladies destroy a fanciful boudoir by crashing through curtains, screens, dividers and doors and smashing every piece of furniture in sight. It is all shot in close-up with a lot of low angles, which accentuates their larger-than-life personas.

Titleography: *Cleopatra Jones Meets the Dragon Lady.* Translation—*Iron Woman Fights Crazy Dragon Woman.* That would be Tamara Dobson versus Stella Stevens. **MA Percentage: 8.44%**

CONDEMNED, THE

死囚 (1976—Hong Kong) 103m. FI: Tang Chia, Huang Pei-ji. NOT/LOT: 3/ 34s; NOF/LOF: 17/ 21m 19s. D: David Chiang. C: David Chiang, Lily Li, Cai Hong, Chan Shen, Bai Ying, Lee Hoi-san, Ku Feng, Hu Jin, Jiang Nan.

When a vicious gang of bandits headed by the mellow Lung Wen-xian (Bai Ying) pillages villages and molests the women, Boss Shi hires kung fu fighter Feng Da-gang (Cai Hong) for protection. When wolf-in-sheep's-clothing Mr. Sheng (Ku Feng) visits his friend Shi to "pay his respects" and discuss the current state of evil, he's really paving the way for the mellow Lung and his low-down marauders to loot Shi's land and estate. Naturally, with a wicked weasel like the shifty Sheng lurking in the shadows, kung fu fighter Feng is framed for all the pilfering and murders. He's summarily shackled and stuck in the darkest, dankest prison cell where he is chained to a moldy wall. But even the darkest place can shed light.

Cheeky street thief Yang Lin (David Chiang) picks the wrong pocket one day. He steals Mr. Liang's (Chan Shen) wallet, but Mr. Liang is the sandy-as-soot Sheng's associate. Sheng arranges for Yang to be Feng's cellmate. Feng is incensed that he has to share his cell. As if things couldn't get worse, Feng strains at his chains and tries to wring Yang's neck while Yang cowers in the corner and makes wisecracks about Feng's temper. After the two eventually become friends, Sheng approaches Yang and tells him that if he kills Feng in prison, he can arrange for Yang's release and will leave his girlfriend Bao Ying (Lily Li) alone.

Yang tells Feng about the arrangement and admits that Bao Ying is in danger, but he values their friendship too much to do Sheng's dirty work. Hearing that, Feng musters up all his kung fu powers, rips away the chains and helps Yang break out of prison. Once free, Feng goes after all those who have done him wrong, and Yang goes to save Bao Ying. But sadly, Yang's raw emotion and guts are not enough to defeat Bao's kidnappers as they pummel him into the ground like a tent stake in granite. All seems lost for Yang, but everything is found when Feng comes back to help his little buddy rescue Bao. But the happy reunion is short-lived as the livid Lung appears and seeks to take away their last breaths.

Watching this film is a little bit like watching Sylvester Stallone in *Cop Land* (1997). Stallone's acting is rather good, but you can't help but wait for Stallone to lash out as his usual action-hero persona. When he needs to step up and fight back, the physically brutal Rocky or Rambo spirit never comes to light. Similarly, as the story builds in *The Condemned* and the chips are down, you end up waiting for Yang, played by kung fu superstar David Chiang, to ante up and wow the table with a hidden full house—but it does not happen. On the other hand, Cai's brooding wrong-place, wrong-time man-on-death-row portrayal of Feng is his best acting performance. It's a step away from his usual kung fu assassin, hit man or villain roles.

During a powerful moment in the film when Yang delivers his first kill, blood slowly oozes down over the camera lens, creating an effective visual that reveals the shock Yang feels. The choreography also mostly uses open-hand fighting, meaning the actors use their palms to block arm attacks, which causes less pain on an actor's arms compared to wrist-on-wrist blocks. It is also easier to strike an opponent with a slap compared to a fist in terms of hand-and-power control. Keep in mind that when many actors do several films simultaneously, or one right after the other, there usually is not enough recovery time to heal, so open-hand choreography is a good way to work around injuries.

Titleography: As of this writing, no alternative titles could be found. Translation—*Death Row Prisoner*. All titles are referring to Cai Hong's character Feng. **MA Percentage: 21.25%** SHAW BROTHERS

CRAZY GUY WITH SUPER KUNG FU

頭呆佬笨徒弟 (1978—Taiwan) 82m. FI: Huang Long. KFI: Huang Long. NOT/LOT: 2/ 1m 32s; NOF/LOF: 17/ 26m 48s. D: Huang Long. C: Lee Yi-min, Peng Gang, Dean Shek, Zheng Fu-xiong, Wong Chi-sang, Li Wen-tai, Tsang Chiu, Wei Ping-ao, Sun Rong-ge.

It is my belief that if everyone in this world could find someone they really love (not infatuation) and find true happiness, there would be no evil in their hearts, thus perhaps no killing. Such is the story of this film's villain as he tries to find love. But because that does not happen, his evil grows deeper and there is only one thing that can stop him, and it is not fighting.

A gang of four vile villains headed by Dead Eye (Peng Gang; his debut)

inflict fear on a trembling town. In response, a down-on-their-luck trio of tofu traffickers led by Ah Ching (Lee Yi-min) become barmy bounty hunters. With hopes of collecting a large reward, the trio plans to bag the four philanderers. As you might expect from a Lee Yi-min movie with *Crazy* in its title, the thickheaded threesome stand no chance until they get the typical daily dose of Suexploitation. (See *Dance of the Drunk Mantis*.)

We next learn that because of facial disfigurement and the inner turmoil that arises from that, Dead Eye believes that the only way he can find true love and attention is through violence. So he kidnaps a beautiful lady and threatens to kill her unless she falls in love with him, but she refuses. As Dead Eye laments about his ugliness and we feel bad for him, our intrepid trio arrives to rescue her. Yet in a neat twist (I applaud the filmmakers for this), Dead Eye realizes that violence is not the way to find love, and in a sense, he finds true love at the very end.

The film is actually a peculiar yo-yo of film genres: comedy one moment, tragic love story the next, followed by martial arts, drama and tragedy. It was the first, last and only film that Huang Long got to direct and choreograph. The fights were actually pretty well-choreographed. Peng Gang's movements and postures reflect the soul of a well-trained martial artist. Unfortunately, each technique is delivered too slowly, and the result comes across like an Alvin and the Chipmunks record that had not been sped up.

Here's what I mean by this: When the voice actors for the Chipmunks delivered their lines to be recorded at a normal speed, they spoke very slowly. So when the recording speed was sped up, their voices were not insanely fast but came across as normal sounding for a high-pitched chipmunk. Many kung fu film directors wanted the audience to see perfect kung fu techniques. To achieve this, each technique would be performed slowly and precisely, and shot at a lower speed like 20 frames per second. So when the film was played back at the normal film projector speed of 24 fps, the fighters look crisp and believably fast. In this film, it looks like the cameraman either forgot to undercrank the camera or the director refused to undercrank it (which is always a director's choice). But if the fights were performed slow, at the normal 24 fps, then they would look slow and boring on-screen. As a fight choreographer, I thought the fights were pretty good, but the slowness distracts from the energy of the action.

In Huang Long's defense, he had actor Peng Gang wear a bright-red flowing tunic while the three heroes wore drab white-with-black kung fu pants during the final fight. As a result, you can't help but focus on Peng Gang because he sticks out like a bright flame dancing with three translucent ice cubes. Plus, actor Dean Shek's Five-Fighting Female kung fu, where he impersonates five different women doing different kinds of kung fu, is simply ingenious.

Bit of trivia: Hong Kong film projectors operate at 25 fps, so when Hong Kong films were shown in America where the projector run at 24 fps, the fights automatically look faster. But even that couldn't help this film.

Titleography: *Crazy Guy With the Super Kung Fu*; *Three Donkeys*. Translation—*Stupid Man and Stupid Disciples*. The Chinese title refers to the idiot who teaches the film's three goofy heroes. The *Three Donkeys* is probably meant to be *Three Asses*, but many years ago, that title would be offensive to put on a tape box. Yet the *Crazy Guy With Super Kung Fu* title seems to be about Dead Eye because he is the one who goes nuts as he falls in love. **MA Percentage: 34.55%**

CRAZY INSTRUCTOR, THE

烏龍教一 (1974—Hong Kong) 84m. MAD: Chan Chuen. NOT/LOT: 3/ 3m 31s; NOF/LOF: 13/ 15m 17s. D: Luo Qi. C: James Yi Lui, Liang Lan-si, Li Xiao-tian, Li Gu-ding, Chien Yueh-sheng.

Kung "zoo" man? Children's kung fu teacher Ho Tung (James Yi Lui), who pretends to be a master martial artist, accidentally wins a fight, and the loser's kung fu elders want revenge. To escape, Ho lies to the children, telling them that it is time for him to move on and spread his art. Along his journey, he stumbles on a sachet of hidden gold, so all the local scum want to win him over so he will lead them to the gold. One righteous fighter/policeman in disguise (Li Gu-ding, who starred in Jean-Claude Van Damme's 1989 *Kickboxer*) sees through Ho's nonsense kung fu. However, because Ho is a good-hearted slacker, the policeman always covers Ho's back and jails the thugs who try to kill Ho.

While Yi Lui looks a bit like Vin Diesel, action is definitely not the actor's forte. However, Yi Lui once worked at the Hong Kong Zoological and Botanical Gardens, so there's a peculiar short segment early in the film in which he tries to pick a fight with a real giant white crane, a boa constrictor, two cobras and a bunch of other snakes; they just try to peck, bite and strangle him, instead. Although he looks like Diesel, he has the gumption of the Crocodile Hunter Steve Irwin. However, what's gross is that after rolling around on top of about 20 snakes, a lizard clings to his jacket. He grabs the lizard (which is a living lizard, folks, and not a special effect), puts it in his mouth and bites it in half. Ooooooh. Other than those freaky highlights, this film offers less than run-of-the-mill bad fights.

Titleography: *Iron Head*; *Snake Fist Dynamo*; *The Dragon's Snake Fist*. Translation—*Black Dragon Number on Teacher*. Although the first two Chinese characters in the title translate as "black dragon," they mean "not good" as in "idiot." On several occasions, the "hero" plays with snakes and wears an iron wok on his head like the lone swordsmen wear bamboo hats in the *wuxia* films, thus the use of S*nake, Iron Head* and *Dragon* in the English titles. **MA Percentage: 22.38%**

CRIMINALS, THE

香港奇案 (1976—Hong Kong) **92m. MAI: Yuen Cheung-yan. NOT/LOT: 1/ 5s; NOF/LOF: 5/ 2m 43s.** D: Ho Meng-hua. C: Lo Lieh, Yueh Hua, Tanny Tien Ni, Wang Yu, Ku Feng, Chan Shen.

Years before the Italian Mafia infiltrated Hollywood during the 1940s, sex, organized crime and violence were the norm on and off the set at Hong Kong's film studios. So on the set of a Chinese kung fu film, you never know who is who or who knows whom. Therefore, it is important to always be respectful to everyone because your on-set tantrum could also be your last.

The Criminals is a trilogy of short films that were melded into one, and the stories are based on real crimes that occurred in Hong Kong during the early part of the 1970s. The short films include *Hidden Torsos*, *Valley of the Hanged*, and the one relevant to this book, *The Stuntmen* (aka *The Stuntmen*). Although various movie Web sites advertise that the original crime in *Criminals* took place inside a Shaw Brothers' martial arts film unit, in actuality, the murders took place outside the studio. But the bad blood between the respective perpetrators did begin during a choreographed kung fu sequence on a Shaw Brothers film. Which film you ask? It is not mentioned, but actors Yueh Hua and Tanny Tien Ni play themselves in the film inside this film, so you can extrapolate from that.

Chen Zhong (Lo Lieh) is a down-on-his-luck lad looking for a job, so a good friend introduces him to a film stunt coordinator (Chan Shen) who offers him a job on a Shaw Brothers kung film that stars Yueh Hua and Tanny Tien Ni. He secretly falls in love with Tanny, but she is out of his league. Instead, he ends up in bed with a prostitute who looks like Tanny. Chen decides to pimp off the imposter to rich men to make them believe they are having sex with a film-star goddess. He inadvertently pimps on a street run by a local crime boss (Ku Feng). As it turns out, some of his "boys" work on the same film as Chen, and the three genuinely beat Chen to a pulp during what is supposed to be a staged fight scene. Via the stunt coordinator, Chen is introduced to a rival boss who gives Chen protection and hires him to take over the other bosses' street-protection racket. As knives slash, fists fly and Chen proves his street worth, he runs into an adversary out of left field who comes into his inner circle to end his whole ball game for life.

The fights in the film are nothing to speak of. However, it is quite cool going behind the scenes, so to speak, of a Shaw Brothers kung fu film production and seeing a young Yuen Cheung-yan (Yuen Woo-ping's brother) choreograph a fight.

Titleography: As of this writing, no alternative titles could be found. Translation—*Hong Kong Odd Cases*. And indeed the crimes are odd. **MA Percentage: 3.04%** SHAW BROTHERS

CRIMSON CHARM, THE

血符門 (1970—Hong Kong) **95m. FI: Han Kuo. NOT/LOT: None; NOF/LOF: 25/ 20m 13s.** D: Huang Feng. C: Ivy Ling Po, Zhang Yi, Shih Szu, Ku Feng, Wang Chin-ho, James Nam Gung-fan, James Tien, Wang Xia, Fang Mian, Li Gu-ding, Hong Liu.

It's a well-known fact that the third time's a charm—but not if it is the Crimson Charm Gang. When you're trying to protect a loved one, it is not uncommon to act mean and nasty in order to drive that person away from danger.

Such is the travesty and heartbreak of swordsman Chiang Zi-chao (Fang Mian), head of the Chung Chow Sword School. He must feign disappointment and anger toward his top, favorite student, Han Yu (Zhang Yi), in order to expel him from school. But why?

After Chiang kills the despicably evil son of the gang's Yellow-Gown Chief Tsao Kong (Wang Xia), Tsao sends White-Faced King of Hades Guo Xiao-wei (Hong Liu) and his two ungodly assassin colleagues to kill Chiang and his daughter, Shang-ching (Shih Szu). By the way, the ungodly assassins are green guys who jump out of coffins. One is a ruffian whose weapon is a large skull attached to a vertebral column, and the other is a mad man who wields a cudgel with a hand holding a large pen attached on top of the pole. At the midnight hour, Blood Master Ling Hu-lei (James Nam Gung-fan) saves Chiang and his daughter Shang-ching, who promptly falls in love with Blood Master Ling. Further losing face, the Crimson Charm Gang plots to kill everyone associated with the Chung Chow Sword School, Han Yu being a major target.

Chiang knows that the gang killed Han Yu's parents, and in order to seek revenge against the gang, he needs to improve his sword skills, and the only one to teach him is the sword master Ungodly Sword (Wang Chin-ho). As the Crimson Charm Gang closes in, under fabricated pretenses and for Han's own safety, Chiang banishes Han from the school just in the nick of time. As the school is getting wiped out, Chiang dies, Blood Master Ling saves Shang-ching again, and Han's secret admirer, Yu Fang-fang (Ivy Ling Po), gets her arm cut off. At the last moment, the long-lost Taoist nun grand teacher of the sword school suddenly appears, rescues Yu, and arms her with a powerful one-armed style of kung fu.

Still from *The Crimson Charm* © Celestial Pictures Ltd. All rights reserved.

Once Han learns the Ching Gong Light Jumping skill (which is a real technique, see *Master of the Flying Guillotine* for details), the Bird Pouncing on a Shadow technique and the Three-Dragon style of swordplay, he unites with the one-armed boxerette. They take on the head cheese Li Han-su (Ku Feng), "e-dam" good fighter, and his two secret weapons known as the Crimson Charm: a sword that looks like an aboriginal gut-stripping pike and a shield that spits out lung-deforming red smoke amid a flurry of poisoned darts.

The fights are kept interesting by the wild menagerie of peculiar adversaries, far-out weapons and the foreboding or romantic environments. Han practices his secret ways of kung fu in a bamboo forest during a snowstorm—very memorable indeed. Plus, for a 1970s film, it is refreshing to see that everyone does not die at the end of the movie.

Interesting fact: Whenever a great kung fu fighter is introduced in the film, the camera is undercranked so the fighter can appear faster and more deadly than the regular hero he is about to teach, whose fights up to that point are shot at a normal frame speed.

Titleography: As of this writing, no alternative titles could be found. Translation—*Bloody Talisman Gate*. Both titles basically refer to the same thing. Instead of magic, the charm represents a gang, in this case the Crimson Charm Gang. **MA Percentage: 21.28%** SHAW BROTHERS

CRIPPLED AVENGERS

殘缺 (1978—Hong Kong) **106m. FI: Chiang Sheng, Lu Feng, Robert Tai Chi-hsien. NOT/LOT: 8/ 9m 41s; NOF/LOF: 32/ 28m 11s. D:** Chang Cheh. **C:** Chen Kuan-tai, Chiang Sheng, Kuo Chue, Lo Meng, Lu Feng, Sun Chien, Dik Wei, Liu Jian-ming, Ching Miao.

Chang Cheh and screenwriter Ni Kuang, who also wrote this film, got a taste for disabled heroes when they made the Jimmy Wong Yu film *One Armed Swordsman*, featuring a character patterned after Yang Guo, the protagonist of Jin Yong's 1957 serialized novel *Legend of the Condor Heroes* (aka *Legend of the Brave Archer*). The presence of disabled heroes in *wuxia* novels and Chinese martial arts cinema speaks to the notion that regardless of your physical abilities, you can overcome any problem if your dedicate yourself to practicing kung fu. I am a firm believer in this philosophy. Because of martial arts, I was able to overcome cystic fibrosis, a deadly genetic lung disease with an average life expectancy of 21 years. In 1986, with 30 percent of both of my lungs deteriorated, I walked 3,000 miles across America to show the power of a positive mental attitude and the strength of kung fu and *chi gong* (*qigong*).

This film is like a Chinese version of the story of Ivan IV, who in the 16th century was one of Russia's most beloved czars—until his wife died. He then became one of Russia's most feared czars, known as Ivan the Terrible, for without his wife, there was no good left in him. In this film, the righteous Dao Tian-du (Chen Kuan-tai) returns home one day to find that his wife has been senselessly murdered and his son, Du Chang, has had his arms cut off. Dao finds the culprits and brutally kills them, but he is not satisfied. Rather than trying to find balance, he dedicates his life to being a menace to all mankind; if someone so much as looks at him the wrong way, Tian-du will maim or kill him. He arranges for a special pair of metal hands to be made for Du Chang (Lu Feng), who also grows up with a twisted mind and is hell-bent on using his kung fu skills to hurt others. His two arms of death can rip a man to shreds and shoot deadly darts from his fingertips.

Three innocent street lads annoy the Daos. As a result, Chen Shuen (Kuo Chue) is blinded, Wei Jia-jie (Lo Meng) is rendered deaf and mute, and Hu Ah-kuei (Sun Chien) gets his feet chopped off. When the well-off Wang Yi (Chiang Sheng) tries to avenge them, he is beaten and suffers brain damage. Wang's famous kung fu teacher, master Li (Ching Miao), adopts the three wayward wanderers and takes it upon himself to teach them special kung fu skills. He says, "Cripples can be remedied and can adapt." Three years later, the four avengers combine their abilities to take down Tian-du and Du Chang.

Although this film had a release under the English title *Return of the Five Deadly Venoms* in an attempt to cash in on the financial success of *The Five Venoms* (1978), it actually only stars four of the original venoms and Chiang Sheng (who played a sixth venom). There's no way this could be a true *Return of the Five Deadly Venoms* because there is no Wei Bai. Wei suffered from Tourette's syndrome, a genetic disorder that causes sudden uncontrollable motor and vocal tics. It was becoming increasingly difficult for Wei to control the tics and outbursts on camera, so he slowly faded from cinema. His four *Five Venoms* co-stars—Kuo Chue, Lo Meng, Lu Fung and Sun Chien—and Chiang Sheng continued making films together, and in Taiwan, they became known as the Five Weapon Guys because their films featured extended weapon fights.

Chiang Sheng became known as a double-weapon guy for often using paired weapons, but he was also an excellent tumbler. Lu Fung's specialty was the *guan dao* (a long pole weapon with a giant blade on one end and a spear point at the other), which he does not use in this film. Lo Meng was known for his strength and brute physical force from traditional hard kung fu training, Sun Chien was known for his kicking, and Kuo Chue was known for doing everything the others could do. Because the fights with the Five Weapon Guys were inspired mostly by opera training, weapons and kung fu skills, *taekwondo* specialist Sun quickly became the odd man out and kept getting less and less fight time. Due to his limited skills, Sun did not always blend well into the flowing operatic choreography, which often featured a lot of spins and fancy acrobatics. Even in this film, he was already being relegated to waiting for a kick with short bursts of techniques, as the camera would quickly pan or cut to the one of the other Five Weapon Guys.

Titleography: *Mortal Combat*; *Return of the Five Deadly Venoms*; *Avengers Handicapped*. Translation—*Handicapped*. A distributor released this film as *Mortal Combat* after the success of *Mortal Kombat* in America. **MA Percentage: 35.72%** SHAW BROTHERS

CUB TIGER FROM KWANGTUNG, THE

廣東小老虎 and 刁手怪招 (1973/1979—Hong Kong) **78m. FI: Jackie Chan, Yuen Kwei, Li Chao-jun, Jiang Jin, Zhu Gang. NOT/LOT: 14/ 11m 13s; NOF/LOF: 16/ 22m 21s. D:** Wei Hai-fung, Tommy Lee. **C:** 1973—Jackie Chan, Chen Hong-lieh, Shu Pei-pei, Tien Fung, Hong Kwok-choi, Guan Cong. 1979—The 1973 cast, plus Yuen Xiao-tien, Dean Shek, Jiang Jin, Kwan Yung-moon.

To avoid confusion right off the bat, I'm just going share with you right now that there are three versions of this film—a 1973 version, a 1979 re-edit and a 1979 re-re-edit. It's like Rick James used to sing: It's a super freak, super freak. It's super-freaky. (Well, James uses the word "she" instead.)

When *The Cub Tiger From Kwangtung* was originally made in 1973, producer Lo Wei was determined to make Jackie Chan the next Bruce Lee, as is evident from all the kicking and non-kung fu choreography Chan had to do in the fights.

Ever since making this film, Chan has rarely been able to do *taekwondo*-style side kicks and roundhouse kicks well, as is evident based on his body position, posture and ending foot position while performing them. While filming this movie, he was probably taught how to do these kicks on the fly but never made them part of his training or kicking arsenal. The film was rapidly shelved because Lo was trying to determine what to do with the film; he needed to decide if or when he should release it. What fell in his lap was Chan becoming famous after Lo lent him out to Ng See-yuen to make *Snake in the Eagle's Shadow* and *Drunken Master*. After the success of those 1978 films, Lo hired Yuen Xiao-tien to play a similar beggar character he portrayed in the aforementioned films, found a body double for Chan, took the 1973 footage and created a whole new film. When shot in wide angle, the double wore a blindfold during fight and training sequences, and when he was not wearing a blindfold, all the shots were over-the-shoulder shots as to hide his face. Lo filmed additional training and fighting footage, did a re-re-edit and re-released the film with a different ending in 1979 and released it as *Master With Cracked Fingers*.

1973 version: Ah Lung's (Jackie Chan) father and kung

fu teacher (Tien Fung) forbids him from fighting, so every time he comes home from working in the restaurant, regardless if a fight is warranted—like protecting his sister (Shu Pei-pei) or his good friend Little Frog from a band of thugs who work for dock owner Chow Bin (Chen Hong-lieh)—he has to endure corporal punishment. When Chow loses face because his thugs can't defeat Ah Lung, he burns down Ah Lung's home with his sick father still inside and ties Little Frog to a ship's mast, then defies Ah Lung to fight for Little Frog, his sister and his own life.

1979 re-edit: Big boss Master, who fights his duels blindfolded to prove how good he is, decides to kill two traitorous hooded assassins in his employ. One dies and begs the other assassin to escape and look after his little son, Ah Lung. The assassin who gets away becomes a righteous man (Yuen Xiao-tien; I will refer to the character as Yuen) and teaches Ah Lung praying mantis kung fu. When Ah Lung is older, he becomes the adopted son (he's the biological son in the 1973 version) of a kung fu teacher who forbids him from fighting. Ah Lung fights to protect the daughter of his adopted father (his real sister in the 1973 version) and his good friend Little Frog from a band of thugs led by Chow Bin (the big boss in the 1973 version). Chow, who in this version works for the Master (Kwan Yung-moon), burns down the house with the sick adopted father inside and ties Little Frog to a ship's mast, then defies Ah Lung to fight for Little Frog, his adopted father's daughter and his own life.

This version of the film edits narrative (under different character relationships as indicated above) and fight footage from *Cub Tiger* with new footage featuring shots of Yuen teaching a little boy kung fu, then mixes in 1973 shots of Ah Lung training with shots of Yuen "teaching" him. (Note: The 1979 version was called *Master With Cracked Fingers,* which uses the original footage called *Cub Tiger from Canton.*) Ah Lung is not allowed to fight, and when he does—as when saving his adopted father's daughter and Little Frog from thugs who work for the Master—Ah Lung is subjected to corporal punishment. After Ah Lung kills all the thugs at the docks, the Master challenges Ah Lung to a death match during the day that includes weapons and must be done blindfolded. Yuen teaches Ah Lung the trident and uses a giant blue flag to increase his awareness while learning to fight with a blindfold, and there is a clip of Chan from *Drunken Master* doing the eight immortal forms. Prior to defeating the Master with praying mantis strikes to his neck, Ah Lung fights the Master's assistant, Fats.

1979 re-re-edit: After Ah Lung kills all the thugs at the dock, the Master challenges him to a death match at night, outside near a cliff. Prior to fighting the Master, whose hair is now puffier looking from the re-edit, Ah Lung fights two assassins at the same time, one assassin using a broadsword and the other using a spear. Ah Lung defeats the Master by a final deathblow that sends the Master over the cliff's edge.

Titleography: 1973—*Little Tiger from Kwantung; Little Tiger of Canton.* Translation—*Little Tiger from Canton.* 1979 re-edit—*Master With Cracked Fingers; Snake Fist Fighter; Ten Fingers of Death; Stranger in Hong Kong; Shaolin Death Kicks; Marvelous Fists.* Translation—*Hook Hand Odd Style.* Producer Lo Wei made like Ah Lung was a hero in the vein of the 10 Tigers of Canton, but since he was still a young lad, a little tiger if you will, then he is a *Little Tiger of Canton. Master With Cracked Fingers* is a reference to the 1973 footage, which features Ah Lung dipping his hands in buckets of broken glass. *Snake Fighter* and the Chinese title imply a pseudo-sequel to *Snake in the Eagle's Shadow* (1978). *10 Fingers of Death* is undoubtedly a play on Lo Lieh's *Five Fingers of Death* (1971). *Stranger in Hong Kong* is a generic title but it probably refers to Canton-native Little Tiger, who is a stranger in Hong Kong. *Shaolin Death Kicks* is a stretch—the film has nothing to do with Shaolin—although Chan does throw more kicks than usual. **MA Percentage: 43.03%**

CUTE FOSTER SISTER

女少林寺 and 俏師妹 (1979—Hong Kong) **92m. MAI: Chin Lung. NOT/LOT: 10/ 16m 9s; NOF/LOF: 18/ 22m 21s.** D: Huang Chong-kuang. C: Liu Hao-yi, Wang Tai-lung, Wang Guan-xiong, Lung Fei, Ma Jing-gu, Su Yuan-feng, Yuen Xiao-tian.

In the 16th century, Francois Rabelais gave birth to the idiom "don't judge a book by its cover," but the second part, "yet after you look you can judge the book," seems to have faded into the annals of history.

Such is the life of Su Mei (Liu Hao-yi), a cute and lovable kung fu princess who learns swallow boxing from her doting, scraggly-looking grandfather (Wang Tai-lung). On her 18th birthday, Su Mei is told that she must now obey

her family honor and marry Chao Yun-hai's son Chen Kang (Wang Guan-xiong) in an arranged agreement between her grandfather and Chao. Following the news, she has visions that Chen is a fat, crazy and freaky-looking guy, so she cuts her long pretty hair and runs away. Meanwhile, ultra-handsome Chen is having trouble holding down a job because he wants to be a righteous kung fu hero who always protects people in trouble, but his kung fu is at the low end of the spectrum. He is befriended by a street beggar (Yuen Xiao-tian in yet another Suexploitation film) and is subsequently taught the Eight Immortal Style. Unfortunately, he still does not gain enough skill to become a great fighter. He then meets Su Mei, who takes a liking to him and shows him swallow boxing. After the two learn that the banefully beastly Bai Ying (Lung Fei) has killed Su's grandfather, they unite for the biggest battle that will eclipse any future spousal problems the two will ever face.

This is a surprising film on many fronts. It is Liu Hao-yi's film debut, and she really rocks the kung fu cinema boat with good form, posture and power. She's also one of the only female stars of that era who was able to successfully sell *fa jing*—that moment when it looks like the strike could kill. It is also the first film that veteran stuntman Chin Lung oversees the martial arts choreography, which begins with a fantastic routine by Liu, who flashes her flexibility and strength by doing her swallow boxing form on top of 6-foot-tall wooden posts. (Also, as seen in *Secret of the Shaolin Poles.*) Following that, she leaps off and runs through a gauntlet of wooden dummies with sliding dowel "hands," then climaxes her training session with a stick fight with the rarely seen 10-foot-long pole. The film also features some of the best fights I have seen done by actor Lung Fei (Betty in the 2002 *Kung Pow: Enter the Fist*). Most of that can be attributed to how Lung maintains good hand and body posture while smoothly transitioning from lower-than-usual stances up to delivering solid blocks and strikes.

It is a pity that Liu went on to star in only six more kung fu films, based on *Cute Foster Sister.* She had the pizzazz and kung fu skills to be one of the top kung fu actresses in the 1980s. Even though it was Chin Lung's debut as a fight choreographer, it just goes to show that you don't have to be a veteran fight choreographer to do amazing martial arts fights. You just need to think with the brain and not with the actors' skill levels, which is the problem with Hollywood fight choreographers who usually limit their imagination based on what the actor can and cannot do … major error.

Titleography: *Kung Fu Terminator; Horse Boxing Killer.* Translations—*Female Shaolin Temple* and *Cute Kung Fu Sister. Female Shaolin Temple* probably derives from Su training on the Shaolin posts at the film's beginning, and she is a cute kung fu sister. She is not adopted, so *Foster* is inappropriate. The *Horse Boxing* may be derived from Wang Tai-lung playing a similar character in *Dance of Death,* in which he teaches Angela Mao Ying how to kill a master of horse boxing. **MA Percentage: 41.85%**

DAMNED, THE

博命; 三千大洋; and 強盜,妓女,錢 (1977—Hong Kong) **82m. FI: Yasuyoshi Shikamura, Blacky Ko. NOT/LOT: 3/ 1m 37s NOF/LOF: 15/ 21m 38s.** D: Gao Bao-shu. C: Wong Dao, Angela Mao Ying, Lo Lieh, Xue Fang, Gao Fei, Wang Xia, Wen Jiang-long, Xue Han, Lin Hsiao-hu.

To quote the orders of American Civil War admiral David Glasgow Farragut during the Battle of Mobile Bay: "Damn the torpedoes, full speed ahead!" This line sort of reflects this film because the words, like the characters in this film, are not always what they appear to be.

When horse carriage driver and whip expert Shang Li (Wong Dao) falls in love with a prostitute at the local brothel, he vows to buy out her contract. Unfortunately, the cruel brothel madam threatens to sell her to Wu (Wang Xia), who is the rich head of a security transportation company and has it out for Shang. Shang's only recourse is to join up with the seemingly righteous kung fu fighter and thief Sparrow (Wen Jiang-long) to steal a shipment of silver being escorted by Wu's company. The sticky wicket arises when we find out Wu is in cahoots with Pao Cheng-feng (Lo Lieh), the ultimate ringmaster behind a robbery scam. Pao plans to steal the silver that Wu is transporting so Wu can report it robbed. Wu then will gives half the haul to Pao for arranging the robbery in the first place. But not everyone is playing bad cricket because a band of upright outlaws led by Mao (Angela Mao Ying) and Three-Scars (Gao Fei) also vie for the silver shipment, and they may throw a wicked googly at Wu and Pao to bowl them out. (In cricket, a wicked googly occurs when the bowler knocks off the bails that rest on top of the three wooden stumps with the first pitch.)

Gao Bao-shu is one of only a few female directors who was able to make a small mark in the predominantly male-controlled kung fu film industry of the 1970s. Like her name implies (Gao in English means "big"), it was a huge challenge for any woman to break out of the actress ranks and become the director. We would certainly never see director Chang Cheh care about a kung fu hero falling in love with a prostitute and risk all to rescue her.

The fights are a great mix of *hapkido* and *taekwondo* kicks with kung fu that's like flummery with flavor, something sure to please the average flan … I mean fan. It is always refreshing when the action is shot slightly off to one side in the frame because it forces the eye to move with the action rather than remain static when the actors are centered. When I saw that Mao Ying's silk shoes had three, razor-sharp circular saw blades sticking out of the toes, I kept thinking of Don Adams in the TV show *Get Smart* (1965-1970) because each time the saws spun, it sounded like her shoe phone was ringing.

Although this is one of actor Wong Dao's top five best fighting performances and Lo Lieh uses a rip-off flying guillotinelike weapon to great brutal effectiveness, the film's ending is like Farragut's order. When you think of torpedoes, you think that Farragut's ship the USS Hartford was under attack by submarines or ships firing an underwater ship-to-ship bomb. Back during the Civil War, though, torpedoes were tethered naval mines. So things are not what they seem until you see below the surface, and Wong and Lo are heading for something you are not expecting. The film is essentially Gao's nod to *Romeo and Juliet,* with a kung fu twist, spin and beheading.

Titleography: *Battle of Shaolin*; *Snake in Eagle's Shadow 2*; *Bandits, Prostitutes and (&) Silver*; *Robber, Pros & Money*; *Wu Tang Ho's, Thugs & Scrillah*. Translations—*Fight for Life*; *Three Thousand Big Dollars*; *A Robber, Prostitute and Money*. There is nothing in the film about Shaolin, thus *Battle of Shaolin* is just selling words. *Damned* reflects the characters' situation in the film. Wong's *Snaky Knight Fight Against Mantis* (1978) was released in the States as *Snake in Eagle's Shadow 2*, and the same distributor, therefore, released *Damned* as *Snake in Eagle's Shadow 3* (although it is not a sequel). For the Chinese titles, Wong's character Shang Li is in a *Fight for Life*; it will cost $3,000 dollars to buy the prostitute's freedom (English dub says $125); and it is a story about a *Robber, Prostitute and Money*, which reflects the other English titles—the *Wu Tang* title uses the street vernacular. **MA Percentage: 28.35%**

DANCE OF DEATH

舞拳 (1976—Hong Kong) **86m. KFD: Jackie Chan. NOT/LOT: 14/ 9m 30s; NOF/LOF: 22/ 36m 18s.** D: Chen Zhi-hua. C: Angela Mao Ying, Qin Pei, Wang Tai-lung, Dean Shek, Shiao Bou-lo, Hui Bat-liu, Jia Kai, Sun Rong-zhi.

Spunky, charming, flippant, silly-willy, quirky and flirty describe this film, and you might be tempted to do a few name switcheroos to finally determine who is the subliminal or obvious star of this film: kung fu director Jackie Chan or lead actress Angela Mao Ying?

Female country-bumpkin Fei Fei (Angela Mao Ying) stumbles on two old kung fu masters, Ku (Qin Pei) and Hu (Wang Tai-lung), arguing over whose kung fu is better. To settle the argument, she tricks them into thinking she is a he and tells them that if they teach her kung fu, they can see who is better based on whose techniques she uses when she fights. Meanwhile, Ma Fu-shan (Jia Kai), the leader of the 100 Bird Clan and a master of the Upside Down Horse style, wants to eliminate every member of the Five Forms School. When righteous Fei Fei stumbles on a handful of Ma's Birds trying to kill one of the Five Forms leaders, she rescues him by making the Bird fighters look like a gang of flighty chickens and clay pigeons. In response, Ma sets out to personally ruffle and tar Fei Fei's feathers and kill her newfound teachers.

With its incessant silly overacting, camera mugging and Walt Disney film antics, this movie would probably be funny and a wee bit more digestible if it were made for children. Yet when Fei Fei (which incidentally means "Fly Fly") continues picking comedic fights, it becomes more like a female version of a Jackie Chan comedy while trying to smudge in feminine cuteness and boy-girl charm. Although Mao Ying appears comfortable in the roll, it seems more out of place than in sync.

But like a piece of bread, Mao Ying does get on a roll as the fights begin to lean more toward femininity than "Chan-inity." As Fei Fei continues to struggle against more powerful opponents, the masters realize that he is a she and begin teaching Fei Fei forms of kung fu that conform to her femaleness such as the Six Dancing Phoenix Fist. It is the payoff for the opening credit music of female

sounding bells, which sets a marvelously beautiful tone for the film.

What might go over some heads is that the masters are teaching Fei Fei martial movements extrapolated from the dancing movements associated with six legendary women in Chinese history. Hua Mu-lan, known for her bow-and-arrow abilities, disguised herself as a man to take her elderly father's place in the Northern Wei army (A.D. 386 to A.D. 534). Pan Jin-lian, a character from the books *The Water Margin* and *The Plum in the Golden Vase*, is famous for her dance on Golden Lotuses for Emperor Xiao Bao-zhuan of the Southern Qi Dynasty (A.D. 479 to A.D. 502). The other movements are based on the Four Beauties of China: Xi Shi, from the Spring and Autumn period (seventh century to sixth century B.C.), who was so beautiful that fish would forget to swim when she walked by; Wang Zhao-zhuen, from Western Han Dynasty (206 B.C. to A.D. 220), known for playing the pipa and for being so beautiful that birds in flight would fall to the ground; Diao Chan from the Three Kingdoms period (A.D. 220 to A.D. 280), whose face was so luminous that the moon would hide to save its face from embarrassment; and Yang Gui-fei, from the Tang Dynasty (A.D. 719 to A.D. 756), who had a face that would shame any flower on the face of the earth.

During Fei Fei's finale fight with the bucking bronco Ma ("horse" in Chinese) and his high-kicking Upside Down Horse kung fu, the masters tell the audience which beauty actress Mao Ying is doing as a reminder of whose kung fu Fei Fei is using.

Titleography: *Eternal Conflict*. Translation—*Dancing Fist*. The *Eternal Conflict* could be one of several meanings: the conflict between the two masters to decide who is better or the conflict between the 100 Bird Clan and the Five Forms School. The *Dancing Fist* inference is discussed in the martialogy. **MA Percentage: 53.26%**

DANCE OF THE DRUNK MANTIS

南北醉拳 (1979—Hong Kong) **94m. MAC: Yuen Shen-yi, Chien Yueh-sheng, Brandy Yuen, Yuen Kwei. NOT/LOT: 13/ 12m 38s; NOF/LOF: 16/ 33m 19s.** D: Yuen Woo-ping. C: Yuen Xiao-tian, Hwang Jang-lee, Yuen Shen-yi, Yuen Kwei, Linda Lin Ying, Yen Shi-kwan, Chien Yueh-sheng, Brandy Yuen.

Most readers are probably familiar with blaxploitation, Bruceploitation and sexploitation, now let me introduce you to Suexploitation—that's right, Suexploitation. Ever since the introduction of Yuen Xiao-tian's Beggar Bai character in *Snake in the Eagle's Shadow* (1978), a character based on the legend of Beggar Su (see *Drunken Master* (1978) for history of this real-life hero), Yuen has reprised his manifestation of the old, gray-haired sot, dressed in a floppy hat, holey kung fu shoes and raggedy-Andy clothing in several other films as have other actors in similar kung fu teacher-student relationship movies. Thus, Suexploitation.

Unfortunately, English dubbing of these films has now insultingly renamed the famous Beggar Su character to Sam Seed. Before you get on my case, that it is just a movie, reverse the role. Imagine if the Chinese dubbed a film like John Wayne's *The Alamo* (1960) into Chinese with the American iconic heroes of Davy Crockett and Jim Bowie renamed to Dorky Dave and Babbling Bowie. Do you think the average American would be happy with that? I didn't think so.

Similar to *Drunken Master*, *Dance of the Drunk Mantis* is a story about a well-to-do evil northern drunk mantis kung fu master Rubber Legs (Hwang Jang-lee) who wants to defeat the aging, minding-his-own-business, good-hearted southern drunk boxer master Sam Seed (Yuen Xiao-tian). The good master ends up teaching a being-taken-advantage-of bumpkin Froggy (Yuen Shen-yi). And although the Biffo-like buffoon Froggy knows no kung fu, he leaps in to save Sam from Rubber Legs. Rubber Legs now wants his student (Yuen Kwei) to metaphorically make Froggy part of a French restaurant's menu that accepts pickup … like frog legs to go. What Rubber Legs does not know is that Froggy has a second kung fu teacher, Sam's friend, a man who lives in a coffin (Yen Shi-kwan), who teaches Froggy sick kung fu.

To quote the famous American funk-band Sly & the Family Stone, "It's a family affair." Yuen family patriarch Xiao-tian stars, oldest son Woo-ping directs, younger son Shen-yi co-stars and does choreography, and youngest son Brandy does choreography and doubles for dad in the fight scenes. Shen-yi has good stances and overall good drunken form. Compared to the fights with Jackie Chan's Huang Fei-hung drunken character, Shen-yi's early fights in *Dance of the Drunk Mantis* begin like Jackie's fight in *Drunken Master,* but then Shen-yi's action dynamic changes to a faster pace as more environmental creativity takes over. The major difference in choreography is that Jackie Chan creates a bouncing rhythmic cadence as he bobs up and down. Shen-yi's fights are faster because the bobbing is eliminated so the movements are more rapid. However, Jackie Chan's stances, overall postures and presentation of the drunken fist is much more palatable and cooler looking.

Hwang's drunken mantis is contrived because he's only doing a mantis stance and mantis hand postures, and the rest is made up of shaking his body like he is drunk. However, his kicks are well-balanced and powerful looking. Hwang has been referred to as Rubber Legs in this film. (It's distracting when dubbed English films create stupid names for these characters, just like Sam Seed for Yuen Xiao-tian). But it seems to me that well-known *taekwondo*-trained actor John Liu (see *Secret Rivals*) should be called Rubber Legs because Hwang's kicks are firm whereas Liu's twang here and there like a rubber band.

Although praying mantis and drunken boxing styles of kung fu exist, traditional styles specifically called northern drunken mantis or southern drunken boxing do not exist. Instead, they arose because of kung fu films' popularity of the drunken style. The filmmakers made the distinction between northern and southern kung fu to make this film's styles feel more authentic. But martial artists are flexible, so I'm sure someone can stretch things and say something like: Because parts of drunken boxing originated in the south, that means it is southern drunken boxing. Perhaps western drunken boxing is just a Chuck Norris film away.

Titleography: *Drunken Master Part 2*; *Drunken Master Part 2: Dance of the Drunken Mantis*. Translation—*South North Drunken Fist*. The titleography is pretty obvious considering the actors and what the film looks like. **MA Percentage: 48.88%**

Still from *The Daredevils* © Celestial Pictures Ltd. All rights reserved.

DAREDEVILS, THE

雜技亡命隊 (1979—Hong Kong) **99m. FI: Lu Feng, Robert Tai Chi-hsien, Chiang Sheng, Kuo Chue. NOT/LOT: 21/ 15m 44s; NOF/LOF: 38/ 19m 9s.** D: Chang Cheh. C: Lo Meng, Chiang Sheng, Kuo Chue, Sun Chien, Lu Feng, Wang Li, Chan Shen, Tan Zhen-dong, Tu Tai-ping, Yang Xiong, Wu Hung-sheng, Xiao Yu.

Although Sun Yat-sen was the face of the Republic of China after the fall of the Ching Dynasty, it seemed that powerful military man Yuan Shi-kai held the true power. In fact, he forced Sun Yat-san out of the presidency. But when Yuan died in 1916, China fell into an era of warlordism. The country split into regions controlled by various power-hungry militias. One of the major forces to be reckoned with throughout the era was the Beiyang Army, a formidable Western-style army conscripted during the Ching Dynasty that was involved in a Chinese political tug-of-war until 1949.

In this film, powerful bandit Han Pei-chang (Wang Li) instigates a military coup and kills Yang Da-ying's (Lo Meng) father and family. He then becomes an evil warlord. Distraught, angry and bubbling with vengeful angst, Yang tries to talk four friends—Liang Guo-ren (Kuo Chue), Fu Guan-yi (Lu Feng), Chen Feng (Chiang Sheng) and Xin Zheng (Sun Chien)—into helping him take revenge against Han. When they all try to talk him out of this suicide mission, Yang's thirst for vengeance seems to be subdued, only for him to realize that he was asking too much of his friends. One night, Yang goes to Han's house and tries to take care of things on his own, but he fails and is killed.

Awed by their friend's spirit, the four friends devise a plan to go after Han. Liang and Chen act like street performers looking for work. They get invited to give a performance for Han at his home. Fu masquerades as the son of a field marshal of the Combined Army (the Beiyang Army) with Xin as his second in command. Xin tells Han that Fu is planning an uprising, and the hook goes deeper when Fu says he will gladly give Han machine guns if he can rely on Han's allegiance to help his father, the field marshal, take over the region. Han happily agrees, and they plan to meet at a large warehouse to finalize the deal. As is typical of a Chang Cheh movie that features his latest young batch of martial arts actors, all four of our heroes eventually show up at the warehouse for the final 15 minutes of straight action.

After *The Five Venoms* (1978) became a cult classic in the West, the five actors Wei Bai, Kuo Chue, Lo Meng, Lu Fung and Sun Chiang became known as the Five Venoms. However, because actor Chiang Sheng was, for all intents and purposes, a sixth venom in that film, he was still labeled as one of the Five Venoms. So for films that starred combinations of these actors, Western distributors often advertised them as a Five Venoms film. This Five Venom mentality also caught on in Hong Kong, and even today, Chinese distributors will call films with these actors Five Venom films. The irony is that one of the "real" Five Venoms, Wei Bai, rarely appeared with the other Five Venom actors, and instead Chiang made up the quintet. When Chiang was in those films, in Taiwan, their movies were called Five Weapon Guy films and not Five Venom movies. (See *Crippled Avengers* and *Shaolin Rescuers*.) Anyway, their films always ended with long, intricately choreographed fights that featured heavy helpings of acrobatics and weaponry.

In Chang's eyes, the film was a vehicle for the opera-trained members of what I like to call the Chang Gang (Hong Kong's Brat Pack). Actors Kuo Chue, Chiang Sheng and Lu Feng had free reign to feature their acrobatic opera routines combined with flipping, flopping and spinning stunt gags. They show off some of their movements while playing street performers, and then during the final fight, all these street skills and demonstration sets are all nimbly and neatly applied to combat scenarios, making the plausible conclusion that if you practiced Chinese opera combat, you could apply it to a street fight. Lo Meng's only fight, against Han and his three bodyguards, is straight kung fu and simple weaponry without the fanciful nature of opera. As was becoming the trend, Sun Chien's contributions were minimal because his kicking skills did not blend in with the type of fights featured in the film. The action sequences are mostly filmed from the side using wide-angle or medium shots to clearly show all the actors' skills. You feel as if you are an audience member watching a live opera performance.

Titleography: *Magnificent Acrobats*; *Daredevils of Kung Fu*; *Shaolin Daredevils*; *The Kings of Kung Fu*; *Venom Warriors*. Translation—*Street Performers Suicide Team*. *Acrobats*, *Daredevils* and *Suicide* fit the bill because they aptly describe the nature and abilities of the main heroes. The movie has nothing to do with Shaolin, however, which is another example of a generic marketing buzzword. *Venom Warriors* is a reference to the cast because it features most of the main actors from *The Five Venoms*. **MA Percentage: 35.24% SHAW BROTHERS**

DEADLY ANGELS

俏探女嬌娃 and 女神探 (1977—Hong Kong/ S. Korea) **85m. FI: Yuen Chiang-yan, Tang Chia. NOT/LOT: None; NOF/LOF: 30/ 14m 24s.** D: Pao Hsueh-li. C: Liu Yong, Yan Nan-xi, Shao Yin-yin, Evelyne Kraft, Dana, Yuko Mizuno, James Nan Gung-fan, Kim Jeong-ran, Shi Zhong-tian, Si Wei, Ching Miao, Lee Hoi-san.

Whereas the 1976 opening episode of the American TV show *Charlie's Angels* could be accused of being a watered-down blaxploitation production starring three white chicks from Suffragette City, *Deadly Angels* would've gotten a "yea" vote for political correctness even in a time when nobody new what that meant.

A team of three female detectives, the Chinese Yang Chi-shin (Yan Nan-xi), the Korean Kao Chen-chen (Kim Jeong-ran) and the Japanese Lu Ping (Yuko Mizu-no), take on a diamond smuggling ring headed by Hong Kong crime boss Xia Hu-tian (Shi Zhong-tian) who uses showgirls as diamond mules. The girls hide diamonds in their bras, but after making their delivery, they become fodder for Xia Hu-tian's assistant Fan Feng and his knife habit. So who is the Charlie of these deadly angels? The hot-pants-wearing female British chief of detectives in Hong Kong played by the late Swiss actress Evelyne Kraft. (Also note that having a Chinese, Japanese and Korean working together as friends in a 1977 film in Asia is as a powerful statement as if a 1960s American film had black-and-white heroes working together to overcome racism in the deep South.)

Kraft (later Evelyne Matthys) once told me that do-ing *Deadly Angels* and *Mighty Peking Man* (1977) was a lifesaver for her. She was a classically trained stage actress, and it pained her to be in "stupid movies" like *Lady Dracula* (1975). When studio head Run Run Shaw called her to come to Hong Kong and do two films, she was ecstatic. She shared that she still had negative emotional childhood issues on both sets, and you can see this angst served her characters on camera. With great glee, she also loved the fact that she did all her own fights and stunts in the films.

And speaking of the fights in *Angels,* there are two things that stick out visually about all four of the battling babes. First, there are several high kicks that purposefully show the ladies' underwear. (Hong Kong films were praised for this in the late 1980s.) Second, and although the fights were shot tight, the cameras beautifully use floating angles that move high-to-low and around with many swish pans and rapid tilts. This adds depth to the simplicity of the choreography and more speed to the actors' movements without using too much undercranking of the camera speed. In Evelyne's case, it adds a touch of "witch-Kraft" to her fights.

In 1999, *Fangoria* magazine asked me to interview Kraft. She agreed under the condition that the whole interview be published. She spoke in-depth about her sad childhood and how she was treated after her rich parents died when she was 9. It was a heartfelt story, and for some reason, she wanted to share it with the world. What was supposed to be a 20-minute phone call to Switzerland was a two-hour epic. However, when *Fangoria* only published an 800-word sidebar, I still needed to honor my word to Kraft, so I wrote a 4,000-word article for *Femme Fatales* magazine, which got me into some trouble with *Fangoria*. After Kraft read the *Femme Fatales* piece, she called me from Switzerland to thank me for keeping my word, wondering how come the article was not in *Fangoria.* When I told her that I had gotten in trouble, she sadly shared that this was why she didn't trust the media and only trusted animals. A pause later, she added that she trusted me. I thanked her. This martiaology is for her.

Titleography: *Bod Squad*; *Women Detective.* Translation —*Cute Detective Babes*; *Extraordinary Female Detectives.* All English and Chinese title transla-tions fit the notion of the film, *Bod Squad* being a rather nifty rhyming title. *Deadly Angels* is a play on the 1976 to 1981 American TV show *Charlie's Angels.* **MA Percentage: 16.9%** SHAW BROTHERS

DEADLY BREAKING SWORD, THE

風流斷劍小小刀 (1979—Hong Kong) **101m. FI: Tang Chia, Huang Pei-ji. NOT/LOT: 2/ 1m 35s; NOF/LOF: 23/ 25m. D:** Sun Chung. **C:** Ti Lung, Alexander Fu Sheng, Shih Szu, Ku Feng, Michael Chan, Lily Li.

The "pin" is mightier than the sword—almost. Tuan Chang-ching (Ti Lung) is the kind of swordsman you would not want to be a waiter for at a restaurant because, when it comes time to leave a tip, the point will not be well-taken. The world of Jiang Hu rolls along, and as the decade passes, the number of major characters in these films got fewer. This is a good thing because it not only made following the stories easier (for the Chinese audience too by the way) but

also gave directors more time to flesh out the characters and the actors more opportunities to create new caricatures based on old thematic devices. With the popularity of Jackie Chan's forced floppy and cute physical comedy, Shaw Brothers injected cheeky, wisenheimer drollery a la actor Alexander Fu Sheng in an effort to be unique and keep up with the current entertainment landscape.

Duels in the world of Jiang Hu are just a way of life, and Tuan, who is confident of his abilities to win, brings a coffin along to put his opponents in. When two evenly matched martial folks cross paths and have at it, it opens the doors for a new adventure. Lian San's (Michael Chan) Throat-Piercing Halberd clangs and bangs against Tuan's Deadly Breaking Sword, but Lian loses. Using his signature death strike, Tuan lodges his sword point into his opponent's bone. Then, with a snap of his wrist, Tuan breaks the point of his sword, leaving the tip in Lian's body, which usually causes a slow, agonizing death. Before Tuan can put his port-a-coffin to use, Lian staggers away. As Lian's blood gushes away, he finds the Killer Dr. Guo Tian-sheng (Ku Feng), who then cures him. The doctor uses voodoo acupuncture to zombify Lian into a white-haired wayfaring warrior who we just know Tuan will meet again.

Meanwhile, bungling, knife-juggling and IOU-gambling Xiao Dao (Alexan-der Fu Sheng; Xiao Dao means "Tiny Sword" in Mandarin) pays back casino owner Luo Jin-hua (Lily Li) by becoming Luo's bouncer. Xiao Dao doesn't real-ize that Luo loves him and made him lose in dominoes in order to keep him around. Instead, Xiao Dao has his beady eyes on the new brothel babe Liu Yin-xiu (Shih Szu). With a little ba da bing ba da boom, Liu seduces Xiao Dao into getting Tuan to visit her so she can hire Tuan to kill Dr. Guo, who she believes betrayed her brother and got him locked up in jail. As the tiles fall into place and the domino effect takes over, Xiao Dao and Tuan team up against zombie Lian and the evil doc as Lian becomes a puppet on a needle for the doc. Xiao Dao bamboozles Lian by attacking him with a bamboo tree, and Tuan's deadly breaking sword must successfully smoke the pipe of halberd hell on this film's Doctor Doom.

During the fights, the director uses bird's-eye shots and then slams into medium-tight shots. What makes the fights more engaging is that actors Ti and Chan, who play enemies Tuan and Lian, exchange techniques exceedingly close to each other during their actual fights. This adds a truer sense of danger with-out the rhythmic "barely missed me" fights Golden Harvest usually did. There's also a cool little shot in which actor Fu Sheng leaps through a window. It's these tongue-in-cheek, physical moments that add a touch of magic to the film.

Actor Ti Lung also "takes the mickey" out of himself (pokes fun at himself) in this film by combining his oft chest-swelling hero stance with what became known as the "Ti Lung Skip." In this and later Shaw Brothers films, Ti would slightly jump up or skip when running into a room or something. By acting like there was an invisible barrier to hurdle, the effect was hilariously abstract. It looks like the footwork you might see when someone is trying to avoid stepping on a pavement crack. It is subtle but becomes more prevalent in the 1980s.

Dr. Craig D. Reid

Titleography: As of this writing, no alternative titles could be found. Translation—*Elegant Style Broken Sword Little Tiny Sword*. The English title is based on Tuan's sword skill, and the Chinese title refers to Liu (*Elegant Style*), Tuan (*Broken Sword*) and Tiny Sword (*Xiao Dao*). **MA Percentage: 26.32%** SHAW BROTHERS

DEADLY DUO

雙俠 (1971—Hong Kong) **77m. FI: Liu Chia-liang, Tang Chia. NOT/LOT: 1/ 3s; NOF/LOF: 28/ 24m 26s.** D: Chang Cheh. C: David Chiang, Ti Lung, Ku Feng, Wang Chung, Chen Hsing, Wang Kuang-yu, Tong Yen-san, Stan Fung Sui-fan, Yang Zi-lin, You Lung, Liu Chia-rong, Bolo Yeung.

Toward the end of the Song Dynasty (1126), the Jin army invaded China, captured Prince Kang and established the Jin Dynasty. A group of loyal martial fighters rescued Kang and helped him escape to the south, where he founded the Southern Song Dynasty and under the Jing Kang era became known as Emperor Qin Zong. *Deadly Duo* is the story of the brave warriors who risked their live to save the prince.

After Prince Kang was captured, the Jins announced that anyone connected with the Song or who tried to help Song loyalists would be tortured to death. In this film, the opening scene depicts nine prisoners being gruesomely put to death. With the last prisoner/hero, Gao Shun (Wang Chung), clinging to life, the cavalry arrives to save him. Bao Ting-Tien (Ti Lung) charges over the hill with a score of kung fu fighters to rescue Gao and kill several famous fighters under the command of the traitorous Wan Tien-kuei (Ku Feng), such as the Five Element Great Fighters. However, the Fire Demon Lui (Yang Zi-lin) escapes, and he's a fighter who may burn the heroes later.

Once Gao is saved, the Song loyalists hatch a plan to rescue Prince Kang. Their mission is to scale a steep cliff, then cross the long, rickety bridge across a dangerous gorge that leads to the back entrance of Wan's lair. To do that, they need someone with great *ching gong* skills, which give the user the ability to leap high and run on top of reeds. The only man they know who can accomplish this is Yuan Lu-yan (Stan Fung Sui-fan). Meanwhile, 30 minutes into the film, we meet Little Bat (David Chiang), Yuan's younger kung fu brother, a Song loyalist through and through who is suspicious of Bao's insistance that Yuan join his group of heroes. But when Yuan pledges his allegiance to Fire Demon Lui and the Jin empire, Little Bat and Bao join forces to kill Yuan and eventually Lui. With Yuan dead, their plan seems doomed until Little Bat smugly shares that there is one person in the Jiang Hu world with better ching gong than Yuan—him.

The day of reckoning arrives. Time is running out for Kang, and Wan has posted savage fighting sentries all around Kang's prison. Wan also booby-traps the bridge, and many Song heroes plummet to their death. Only Bao and Bat remain. The two bow to each other and step up to bat for the Song Dynasty, but with their backs to the wall, odds are that they will probably strike out. However, Little Bat has a secret weapon that on the outside looks like a short hooked spear. They also have the mark (an identification plaque of sorts) of the Jin, which they took off Fire Demon Lui's body after they killed him. So the game is still not over.

The phenomenal bridge set cost $400,000 and first appeared in the exciting finale of *The New One Armed Swordsman*. It went on to become an iconic structure on the studio lot area known as Tiger Hill and appeared in almost every Shaw film for the next two years.

In the forest fight with actor Wang Chung, there is an awesome shot of Wang in which the camera first tracks him in close-up, and then while still fighting, Wang moves away from the camera into a wide angle shot. It's very nifty piece of camera choreography. The opening rescue fight also has great camerawork that is apparent when the actors overreach their fighting marks; when the camera pans around to different groups of fighting heroes, it adds motion the fight. These kinds of pans to groups of fighters create the feeling that there is more than just the two main stars fighting on-screen. It also adds to the epic nature of the scenes. If you watch carefully, even on wide-angle or bird's-eye-view shots, everyone is fighting well, which is a sign of a fight instructor's important eye for detail. The only setback of this film is that the fights get a bit sloppy toward the end of the movie rather than the norm of improving over the course of the film.

Titleography: *The Deadly Duo.* Translation—*The Two Swordsmen.* The titles refer to Little Bat and Bao. **MA Percentage: 31.80%** SHAW BROTHERS.

Still from *Deadly Duo* © Celestial Pictures Ltd. All rights reserved.

DEADLY KNIVES, THE

落葉飛刀 (1972—Hong Kong) **82m. FI: Yuen Woo-ping, Yuen Cheung-yan. NOT/LOT: 2/ 1m 12s; NOF/LOF: 22/ 15m 4s.** D: Chang Yi-hu. C: Ling Yun, Ching Li, Lily Li, Ching Miao, Chen Yan-yan, Chan Shen, Dean Shek, Liu Gang, Gu Wen-zhong, Chen Feng-chen.

Although this is an anti-Japanese film, parts of this film are clearly Japanese-influenced. And what that shows is that people involved in the film industry often find common ground and have the gumption to move forward. When I lived in Taiwan back in 1979, for example, the United States had just broken relations with Taiwan and recognized Communist China. While a good many people treated me like a pariah, the folks I worked with in the film industry had no qualms with me—with the exception of the hundreds of extras on my first film. They were all soldiers from the Chinese army who were ordered to be on set.

This film is set in China during the years of Japanese occupation before World War II. Yen Zi-fei (Ling Yun) is heading home from college on a train when a group of Japanese martial arts drunks attack a Chinese woman and behave lewdly toward her. As the other Chinese cower in fear, Yen steps in. As I have mentioned in other martialogies, in most Chinese kung fu films, the fights improve as the movie goes along because actors and stuntmen get attuned with each other. Because the opening fight in this film is shot beautifully and the fight looks good too, this is a good omen.

When Japanese land grabber Omura (Ching Miao) decides he wants the Chinese trees on Yen Zi-fei's valued forest property for the Japanese empire, Yen refuses to sell. The implied meaning, of course, is that he will not sell China out to Japan. Omura brings in three Edo executioners from the old country. However, Omura's groveling Chinese assistant—there always has to be a traitorous Chinese guy working for the Japanese—suggests they buy out the mayor and get Xu Qian (Yen's accountant, who tries to rape Yen's good friend Jiao Jiao but is stopped by Yen) to steal the deed and family seal. Then the mayor can legally register the land to the Japanese. The plan almost works, until Yen hides the seal. But his girlfriend, Guan Yue-hua (Ching Li), is about to be forcibly married off to Japanese hit man Ishigawa (Chan Shen). Just as Ishigawa is about to rape Guan, Yen enters and rescues her. But it is short-lived, as the Japanese capture Yen, coerce him into giving up the seal and then leave him to die on the drowning water torture wheel. Luckily, Guan's father saves Yen, after which Yen and Guan hide in the mountains. Yen learns and hones his Deadly Knives skills and finally crashes the official opening party of the Ogawa Forest Company.

The fights are exciting and energetic, with plenty of smashing and crashing and slicing and springing. Samurai swords are swung like baseball bats, and stuntmen fly about and wreck every object on set. It's all glued together with hand-held camera shots from just about every angle imaginable. Although

65

actor Ling Yun does not practice martial arts, fight instructors create a great attack rhythm for him (block, counter, block, counter, block, etc.). It is a pleasing cadence to watch and hear. During the final fight, a lot goes on in each shot, with people running in and out of frame while fighting as the camera tracks and pans in close-ups. The final confrontation is a knife-versus-gun duel shot and played out like an American Western. It's effective, intense and a bit corny, but it works well.

The Chinese title of this film translates to *Fallen Leaves, Flying Knives* because the hero of the film, who has been severely injured, must train himself to be able to throw knives well enough that he can impale a moving leaf on the floor. So what Japanese film is that from? Hint: It's a 1961 Toshiro Mifune movie. But not all the borrowed elements in the film make sense. Unless I'm mistaken, during the opening credits and the hero's training scenes of throwing knives into the leaves, the soundtrack is taken from the '70s television show *Charlie's Angels*. On a final production note, for some insane reason it is also enjoyable to watch the view of the scenery painted on a large piece of paper scrolling by the train's window, giving the illusion of movement.

Still from *The Deadly Knives* © Celestial Pictures Ltd. All rights reserved.

Titleography: *Fists of Vengeance*. Translation—*Fallen Leaves, Flying Knives*. *Fists of Vengeance* is a typical generic title for a revenge film; a better choice might have been *Knives of Vengeance*. **MA Percentage: 19.84%** SHAW BROTHERS

DEADLY ROULETTE

國際警察 / *Gugje Gyeonchal* (1976—S. Korea) **73m. FC:** Suk Joo-lee. **NOT/LOT: None; NOF/LOF: 5/ 7m 8s.** D: Lo Lieh. C: Bobby Kim, Lo Lieh, Chang Il-sik, Chen Feng-zhen, Park Dong-ryong, Kim Kee-joo, Chiu Chun.

There's a kill, an overkill and then way too much kill as the final kill blow in this film consists of 10 side kicks to the neck of the villain as he sits there and takes them one at a time. That has to be a record. Talk about sticking your neck out for someone.

Actor Bobby Kim (who looks like a Korean Charles Bronson) plays Interpol Agent Bobby, who is sent to Hong Kong to foil the plans of the Syndicate, which is headed by a Chinese arms dealer who gets weapons shipped from the Philippines to Japan and then into Communist China. Along the way, Bobby enlists the help of his good friend Darion (Lo Lieh), and together they hunt down the Syndicate's elusive prize assassin, a master of the deadly Finger-Bullets technique: a finger thrust that leaves a bullet-size cavity in the victim's head.

This is a surprisingly well-shot film—very dark, very noir—and Kim's performance as the stoic Korean Interpol agent blends well with actor Lo Lieh's rustic, pseudo-sleazy persona. There is also an interesting *yin-yang* combative balance in the film with Kim mostly kicking and Lo mostly punching. Further-

more, although used to death in this movie, the Dutch camera angles enhance the mood of the fights and the film in general.

Titleography: *Interpol*; *International Police*; (*The*) *Deadly Kick*. Translation—*Interpol*. Because the unknown assassin's deadly Finger-Bullets strike leaves a bullet-size wound in the temple of his victims—not unlike a game of Russian roulette in which you point a gun at your own temple—*Deadly Roulette* could be some sort of extrapolation of this notion. Furthermore, gambling words like roulette or casino seem to wreak with international intrigue, like the 1967 film *Casino Royale*. Look no further for those 10 damaging side kicks to the assassin's neck to justify the title *Deadly Kick*. **MA Percentage: 9.77%**

DEADLY SNAIL VS. KUNG FU KILLERS

天螺大破五行陣 (1977—Hong Kong) **88m. FI:** Little Unicorn. **NOT/LOT: None; NOF/LOF: 11/ 11m 6s.** D: Xiang Ling. C: Huang Yuan-shen, Yu An-an, Yuen Xiao-tian, Little Unicorn, Tian Qing, Wu Jia-xiang.

When Cheung Fu (Huang Yuan-shen) inadvertently saves a large snail shell from a blue-and-yellow snake, he does not understand that within the snail shell lives a 1,000-year-old beautiful fairy (Yu An-an). She now takes it upon herself to return to the mortal world to fall in love and protect Cheung from the ridicule and anger of rich patriarch Chow (Wu Jia-xiang) and his cronies who hate Cheung for being poor and wanting to marry the woman that Chow's son wants. Unfortunately, the venomous blue-and-yellow snake is the spirit incarnation of a snake demon (Little Unicorn) who loves the snail fairy. He gets permission from Head Snake Demon (Yuen Xiao-tian) to ascend to the world of mortals disguised as a Taoist priest to wreak treacherous spiritual revenge against Cheung. Yellow Snake is then assisted by five creatures: Wood Block, Acorn Head Spirit, Red Fire Demon, Green Demon (who looks like a small version of the Jolly Green Giant) and Water Spirit, as well as the evil trickery of Cheung's former fiancee. Only Snail Fairy's kung fu stands between eternal damnation or a mortal's lifetime of love and happiness.

In the animal kingdom, especially among insects and snakes, bright obvious colors are a survival strategy known as warning coloration, which signals other creatures to stay away because they are either poisonous or very bad tasting. Such is the case for Yellow Snake, who first appears as a blue-and-yellow snake. In the realms of the Chinese spirit world, some spirits desire to become mortal and live with mankind. However, according to the tenets of Taoism, spirits are not allowed to walk around or fall in love with man. So when a spirit tries to do this, a Taoist priest is usually called on to exorcise a person who is haunted, pursued or possessed by the spirit or ghost. Thus, Yellow Snake is posing as a Taoist priest under the guise of killing Snail Fairy who wants to be with Cheung. Starting with Tsui Hark's *Zu: Warrior From the Magic Mountain* (1983), films about Chinese fox spirits, fairies and vampires became popular in the 1980s and eventually evolved into a new genre of martial arts movies called Fant-Asia film. A few movies touched on the subject in the 1970s, and *Deadly Snail* is one of them.

Titleography: As of this writing, no alternative titles could be found. Translation—*Heavenly Snail Defeats the Five Shapes Tactics*. The *Five Shapes* are the five creatures the Snake Demon brought from hell to Earth. **MA Percentage: 12.61%**

DEATH DIMENSION

(1978—USA) **84m. FI:** Uncredited. **NOT/LOT: 1/ 22s; NOF/LOF: 9/ 10m 20s.** D: Al Adamson. C: Jim Kelly, Harold "Odd Job" Sakata, George Lazenby, Bob Minor, Myron Bruce Lee.

Blaxploitation meets Bruceploitation vs. James Bond. Bond's most famous hit man opponent (Harold "Odd Job" Sakata as The Pig) teams up with Sean Connery's James Bond replacement (George Lazenby as Captain Gallagher) to take on Jim Kelly and Myron Bruce Lee in an effort to freeze the sale of a snow-inducing bomb.

Actor Jim Kelly tries to broaden his martial arts ability and cinematic horizons by jockeying between a Bruce Lee impersonation and his Williams character from *Enter the Dragon* (1973). He also tosses in a few junior-level approaches to staff fighting and whippy *nunchaku* swings. Like many American-made martial arts films from the 1970s (and as painstakingly still continues today), there's the almost required training sequence in the *dojo* that gives the actors a chance to brandish their views on martial combat, self-defense or martial arts philosophy and to teach the American audience about martial arts. It can sometimes come across as preachy, but it does reflect an intention to spread the positive virtues of the martial arts. There was also a novel introduction of *escrima* in one fight scene. It's a pity that the filmmakers did not establish what escrima was all about because if the audience understands what they are seeing, it adds a new dimension to the feeling. Back then, audiences probably thought it was someone trying to look impressive by twiddling a simple stick in the air.

The fights were probably choreographed by Jim Kelly because of his martial arts film experience and Bob Minor who was one of the first black stunt coordinators in the industry. Minor worked on two important Pam Grier flicks: *Coffy* (1973) and *Foxy Brown* (1974). *Coffy* has no martial arts action. *Foxy Brown* has a few seconds of martial arts poses snuck in as psychedelic shadows during the film's opening credits, which is why it is included in the index of martial arts films at the back of this book but not written as a martialogy.

The film was more than a cheap shot at Bruceploitation. Myron Lee, who was blatantly credited as Myron "Bruce" Lee, looked so lost in the fights that it seemed like he was told to just stand there and wait for an opening to throw a punch or kick. I can feel for the guy because in my first kung fu film shot in Taiwan in 1979, there were giant 20-foot billboards all over Taipei calling me the American Bruce Lee: *ayah*! Or for you English speakers: OMG!

On a neat note: There was a fight scene done in a particular wooded area outside Los Angeles that looks exactly like the place where we shot the two-part episode of the TV show *Martial Law* (2000) where Arsenio Hall gets trapped in the trunk of a car. In England, you could say that Hall got the boot.

Titleography: *Black Eliminator*; *Dead Dimension*; *Death Dimensions*; *Freeze Bomb*; *Icy Death*; *The Kill Factor*. The fact that this movie has so many alternative titles—with most of them reflecting one of the film's plot devices—shows its distribution popularity. **MA Percentage: 12.74%**

DEATH DUEL

三少爺的劍 (1977—Hong Kong) **91m. FI: Huang Pei-ji, Tang Chia. NOT/LOT: None; NOF/LOF: 16/ 9m 42s. D:** Chu Yuan. **C:** Derek Yee, Ling Yun, David Chiang, Ti Lung, Lo Lieh, Chen Si-jia, Liu Liu-hua, Yan Nan-xi, Yueh Hua, Ku Feng, Yu An-an, Fan Mie-sheng, Chen Ping, Yang Chi-ching.

When Yen Shi-san (Ling Yun) kills the Jiang Hu world's six best swordsmen in 13 strokes with his Divine Sword, it is a lucky number for Yen but not for the six bodies. However, Yen's luck runs out after Lady Mu-Yung Chiu-Ti (Chen Ping) approaches him. She tells him that he can only be the No. 1 sword fighter if he can defeat the Third Young Master or Prince, who is not only nicknamed the Divine Sword but also is Lady Mu's family's mortal enemy. Determined to be the best, Yen sets out to find Third Young Master but learns that he died several weeks before his arrival. Distraught and running out of luck, Yen becomes a hermit and shuts himself out from Jiang Hu.

Elsewhere, street rambling-man Ah Chi (Derek Yee; David Chiang's real brother), who is just a "u" away from a sneeze, runs into a different ill, meaning the Tiger Society who oversees a prostitution ring and protection racket. It all comes about when Ah Chi rescues night-walking woman Hsiao Li (Yu An-an) from a belligerent john. He ends up living with street-peddler Miao Zi (Ku Feng) and his mother, who also happen to look after Hsiao Li. The four quickly become a happy surrogate family until the Tiger Society comes a knocking on their door. After the Tiger Society kills the mother, beats up Miao Zi and grabs Hsiao Li, Ah Chi goes Billy Jack on them, meaning he gooooooeees ber-SERK. Punching, crunching and pummeling, Ah Chi causes each Tiger to lose his stripes as they crash and bash through walls, doors and windows.

As word gets out about Ah Chi, Lady Mu puts the "muves" on him. She tells him that if they get married, Ah Chi would rule alongside her as head of Wu Lin (that part of Jiang Hu that is for martial artists only). But Ah Chi declares that he must now become a wanderer, so Lady Mu tries to kill him for the 47th time by putting a hit out on him and letting the cat out of the bag that whoever can kill

the Third Prince Ah Chi can be famous. So yes, Third Master is alive, and once Yen Shi-san—the guy who wants to be the best swordsman from the film's beginning—finds out, the hunt is on.

Although during a battle between Ah Chi and Eight Spirit Catcher (Yueh Hua), Ah Chi wins by using the same silver-attached halberd weapon featured in *Killer Clans* (see martialogy), Eight Spirit Catcher seriously poisons Ah Chi. However, instead of wishing to die for real, he wants to live and marry Hsiao Li, so he tells her that he knows a descendant of the famous physician Hua Tuo and that the descendant might be able to help cure him from the poison. Then we are privy to a unique scene in which the famous swordsmen Han Tang (Lo Lieh) and Fu Hong-xue (Ti Lung) tell Ah Chi he cannot escape the past by avoiding the responsibility for his actions. Fu, being an expert herbalist, saves Ah Chi. The stage is set for the final fight between Third Young Master Ah Chi and Yen Shi-san of which Ah Chi calls the confrontation the final death duel but with an added surprise: Lady Mu roles out a cage with her crazy swordsman brother Mu-Yung Chien-Lung (David Chiang) stuffed into it. It is the last film that Ti Lung and David Chiang both appear in.

On a real historic note, the aforementioned physician Hua Tuo was a Shaolin monk in A.D. 220 (before the arrival of Ta Mo who introduced martial arts into Shaolin) who created the Five Animal Frolic, a set of exercises for strengthening *chi* and increasing your health.

Compared to other Chu Yuan films, this one has among the least amount of screen time dedicated to fights. Although this is Derek Yee's debut film, his fighting ability looks sharp. He has good on-balance spins that are accentuated by some tricky camera choreography in which the camera pans and tracks his movements at the same time, which is not easy to do smoothly. As Yee did more action in other films, his lack of martial skills becomes more apparent.

Trivia: Characters Han Tang and Fu Hong-xue have appeared together in another film by director Chu Yuan. But which one? Hint: The clue is within the martialogy.

Titleography: *The Peerless Swordsman*. Translation—*Sword of the Third Young Master*. See above martialogy. *Peerless Swordsman* is a good generic title that reflects Ah Chi's abilities and the fact that his peers wish to dethrone him as the No. 1 swordsman. **MA Percentage: 10.66%** SHAW BROTHERS

DEATH DUEL, THE

惡報 and 單刀赴會 (1972—Taiwan) **92m. FI: Huang Pei-ji, Tang Chia. NOT/LOT: None; NOF/LOF: 16/ 9m 42s. D:** Joseph Kuo. **C:** Jiang Nan, Yee Yuen, Wen Jiang-long, Lu Ping, Su Zhen-ping, Shi Zhong-tian, O Yau-man, Bruce Li.

The Death Duel is the first Bruceploitation film ever made (before Bruce Lee died) and arguably the quickest. The strange thing is that it is also the first film that Bruce Li appeared in—albeit an extra, but talk about a portent of things to come.

On the surface, the story plays a little bit like Bruce Lee's *Fist of Fury* (aka *The Chinese Connection*) in which a Chinese kung fu man takes on some local traitorous Chinese and Japanese martial artists who are trying to shut down the Chinese school and capture the Chinese hero fighter. Then further solidifying that it is like Lee's movie is that according to some English synopses, it is written that this film is about the Ching Wu School and takes place in Shanghai … not exactly.

In *The Death Duel*, the film's hero, Lao Tao-san (Jiang Nan), is blinded in one eye by the eye-gouging technique of the heartless Wu Xu-tian (Yee Yuen), who was similarly blinded by Lao's teacher Tang Hou-yin (Lu Ping) many moons ago. It is Wu's mission in life to shut down the Tang Family Kung Fu School that is headed by Tang Hou-yin. Wu recruits three Japanese samurai to help kill several of Tang's top students.

Meanwhile, the blinded Lao is off in the mountains recovering from his injury and training to compensate for vision loss. One day, he sees his midget helper kicking a wee cuddly kitten and observes how the cat always lands on its feet. Lao proceeds to fling the kitten repeatedly into the sky and watches it safely land on all fours. From this, Lao creates a new leaping kicking technique, a superlative skill that prepares him for the final battle against the hired samurai assassins and the wicked Wu.

The American Humane Association has ensured the proper safety and care of animal actors and stunt animals in Hollywood film and TV productions since 1940. However, no such association existed in Hong Kong or Taiwan back in the 1970s, so sometimes these films can have some unsettling animal images.

The film does not imply that the events take place in Shanghai. It is mentioned that one of the fighters is from Shantung, so perhaps there was a leap of faith that the story took place in Shanghai because other films have indicated that fighters from Shantung go to Shanghai. (See *Boxer From Shantung*.) Furthermore, the Chinese characters above the kung fu school that is the target for Wu and his samurai killers is "Tang Jia Guan" (Tang Family Kung Fu School) and not "Ching Wu."

The fighting is very lazy looking. Except for Bruce Li and future Shaw Brothers star Lung Tian-hsiang—they worked as stuntmen extras in the film—most of the performers had never practiced martial arts. This was the norm for most film actors during the 1960s and early '70s until directors like Chang Cheh and Liu Chia-liang demanded that practitioners be in shape and be prepared to fight 15 to 18 hours a day, which was normal for film productions in Hong Kong and Taiwan.

Titleography: *Revenge of Fist of Fury*; *Revenge of Kung Fu*; *Revenge of Fury*. Translations—*Vicious Revenge* and *Went Into Battle Alone*. Using one of the two literal translations and adding in the words *Fist* and *Fury*, the film is aligning itself with Bruce Lee's *Fist of Fury*. *Death Duel* is also just a generic-sounding title that could be used by other films. In fact, several other films have been released under the same title, including another in the 1970s. **MA Percentage: 28.68%**

DEATH'S JOURNEY

(1976—USA) 90m. FI: Uncredited. NOT/LOT: 1/ 3m 4s; NOF/LOF: 5/ 1m 57s. D: Fred Williamson. C: Fred Williamson, Bernard Kirby, Art Maier, Lou Bedford, Heidi Dobbs, Stephanie Faulkner, Emil Farkas.

With Chinese kung fu films from the 1970s, it was very common for viewers to press the fast-forward button on their Betamax VCRs until the next fight. For this film, hold the FF button down for the whole movie.

This is the second film in the Jesse Crowder trilogy, after *No Way Back* in 1976 and before *Blind Rage* in 1978. If it is anything like the other two, in which Crowder (Fred Williamson) is touted as "one bad cat"… perhaps "one ill cat" would have been more appropriate.

Two New York attorneys hire protector Crowder to escort their star witness from Los Angeles to New York. With clinched fists and a stogie clenched in his mouth, Crowder lives up to the film poster's promise of "sudden death in each fist" when he knocks out a Bobby-Knight-looking hit man with a punch that can only be compared to the famous May 1965 Muhammad Ali invisible punch that knocked out Sonny Liston 104 seconds into the first round.

However, in keeping with his promotion of the martial arts, Williamson featured European black-belt karate champion Emil Farkas in the film as Crowder's karate teacher. Most of the martial arts time is taken up during a three-minute slow-motion charge toward a punching bag and the subsequent kick by Crowder at Farkas' *dojo*.

Williamson also featured *goju-ryu* stylist Aaron Banks—known for getting his martial arts promotional show *Oriental World of Self Defense* on ABC's *Wide World of Sports* five times in 1974—in a 30-second fight scene against

Williamson in *Mean Johnny Barrows* (1976). However, because the movie did not have the prerequisite one minute and 55 second total amount of martial arts action as dictated by Chuck Norris' cutoff point film *Good Guys Wear Black*, it is not written as a martialogy in this book.

Titleography: As of this writing, no alternative titles could be found. **MA Percentage: 5.57%**

DEATH MACHINES

(1976—USA) 92m. FI: Uncredited. NOT/LOT: 1/ 1m 26s; NOF/LOF: 8/ 4m 40s. D: Paul Kynazi. C: Ronald L. Marchini, Michael Chong, Joshua Johnson, Mari Honjo, Ron Ackerman, Eric Lee.

After the death of Bruce Lee, the notoriety that American martial artists Chuck Norris, Bob Wall and Jim Kelly received from starring alongside Lee increased their status in the martial arts world, and this prompted other martial artists to dip their feet in the film world. It did not matter if their films weren't very good because back then it was about a different outlet for martial artists to get publicity for their egos and a way to get more students into the schools. Martial arts magazines sucked this stuff up back then too, but because they could only do so many stories on Bruce Lee per month, all these other films became fillers. No matter if the films were good or bad—and most people never got to see them anyway—being a so-called martial arts star didn't hurt anyone's resume or ego. After all, you never knew just whose eye in Hollywood you might catch.

Here is another résumé film for three legitimate martial artists: Ron Marchini, Michael Chong and Joshua Johnson, who play the white, Asian and black Death Machines. The fake-bad-English-accented dragon lady Madame Lee (Mari Honjo) injects the three with a serum to make them superhuman. (No Asian stereotyping here folks … not.) They are part of a plan for the unseen, cat-stroking villain (obviously influenced by James Bond villain Ernst Stavro Blofeld), who wants to corner the assassination market by killing off all other competition. To prove their abilities, the Death Machines are ordered to kill three marks before another assassination organization in town can do it. But Madame Lee loses control of her assassins, and the three begin doing their own thing. One of the targets avoids being killed and helps the police find Lee and close down the operation. But what happens to the three assassins? To borrow from singer-songwriter John Denver, they're leaving on a jet plane.

The opening fights see a three-sectional staff versus two broadswords, a Chinese *jian* versus a spear, and a karate fighter versus a kung fu fighter. For anyone who saw this film back then, it was probably the first time you had ever seen this sort of sideshow—a three-ring circus of martial artists who were not clowning around but sure looked that way. Even the noted kung fu stylist Eric Lee stepped into the ring for a brief moment: All his karate students get sliced into oblivion while his character helplessly stands and watches. The only decent fight, if you want to call it that, is when Marchini's character brutally fights his way out of a police station. This film demonstrates one of the challenges encountered by many American martial arts films: Black belts and tournament champions are rarely good on film. Better to get a good choreographer and a couple of decent martial arts students with no ego. I would recommend Dr. Craig Reid, who I hear was a stuntman in Chinese kung fu films in the 1970s and '80s, and also worked in Hollywood and is familiar with fight choreography on both sides of the Pacific Ocean. Hey, wait a minute—that's me.

Titleography: As of this writing, no alternative titles could be found. **MA Percentage: 6.63%**

DEATH PROMISE

(1977—USA) 89m. AD: Thompson Kao Kang, Charles Bonet, Bill Louie. NOT/LOT: 9/ 3m 28s; NOF/LOF: 18/ 11m 24s. D: Robert Warmflash. C: Charles Bonet, Speedy Leacock, Bill Louie, Gao Gang, Abe Hendy, Vincent Van Lynn, Thom Kendell, Tony Liu, Bob O'Connell, Bob Long, Jason Lau. Jerry Ng.

When a group of corrupt community leaders and officials who are basically slumlords try to oust their tenants to build a huge complex, the tenants refuse to leave, causing the officials to resort to extortion and murder. Their problem is that they murder the father of Charlie (Charles Bonet), and Charlie is a black belt in karate. On the advice of his *sensei*, Shibata (Gao Gang), who was also a good friend of his father's, Charlie heads to upstate New York to receive special martial arts training from the venerable master Ying (Tony Liu; a young man made to look older). Along with his new skills, his pal Speedy (Speedy Leacock) and the friendship of Ying's top student, Sup Kim (Bill Louie), Charlie ends up taking on the slumlords and the villains ultimately at the core of the scheme: the Japanese mob, or Yakuza.

What is refreshing about this American-made martial arts film is that it does not follow the usual Hollywood conventions. In many 1970s Hollywood martial arts films, you get the sense that the martial arts actors are merely trying to pad their résumés. They wear tons of makeup, have fluffy hairdos, try to look good for the camera, and do very little fighting because they are somehow convinced they are actors rather than martial artists. Charles Bonet and the other martial arts talents in this film know they are not actors—and probably have no inclination to be—but have all gotten together to make a martial arts film mostly for posterity. There are no fancy hairdos or costumes, just an honestly made film and an attempt to take a *dojo kumite* mentality and apply it to cinematic fighting scenarios. Although the choreography is somewhat mechanical and there is a bit too much blood-curdling screaming before an attack, most of the techniques are delivered from good karate stances, and Bonet has a couple of effective kicks and punch combinations. Bill Louie backs himself into a Bruce Lee-like corner with his prancing and footwork, but he still has a repertoire of original movements that belong to him. Overall, the fighters all have pretty good stances and solid karate kicks. So even when a fight scene essentially comprises a series of well-rehearsed one-two-step sparring drills strung together and delivered with intensity, the results don't look half bad on camera.

Titleography: *Enter the White Dragon*; *Pay-Off Time*; *Slumfighter*. Four different titles show that this film has gotten several distribution deals. *Enter the White Dragon* is obviously a play on Bruce Lee's *Enter the Dragon* and refers to Charlie. **MA Percentage: 16.7%**

DEFENSIVE POWER OF AIKIDO, THE

Gekitosu! Aikido (1975—Japan) **81m. FI: Uncredited. NOT/LOT: 11/ 10m 22s; NOF/LOF: 14/ 14m 22s. D:** Shigehiro Ozawa. **C:** Jiro Chiba, Sonny Chiba, Yoko Koizumi, Ryunosuke Kaneda, Tsunehiko Watase, Etsuko Shihomi.

Inspired by Hong Kong cinema's martial arts biopics, Sonny Chiba set out to bring Japanese martial arts heroes to the big screen. *The Defensive Power of Aikido* is Chiba's first venture into that genre. It's about the founder of *aikido*, Morihei Uyeshiba (1883-1969). It's also one of my must-see picks for martial artists!

The film opens with Uyeshiba (Jiro Chiba) relocating to Hokkaido and losing a fight to karate expert Natori Shinbei (Sonny Chiba). After being defeated by the *bokken*-wielding (wooden sword) sword master Okita, Uyeshiba puts great faith in learning karate from Soubei Honda. When he receives his license to teach from Honda, Uyeshiba heads to Tokyo to re-challenge Natori Shinbei and Okita. He inadvertently ends up fighting Shinbei's brother and easily defeats him. Suffering a loss of face, the brother commits suicide, causing his school to lose face too. The brother's students hire Okita to help avenge the brother's death. During Uyeshiba's bout with Okita and the students, the priest Onisaburo Deguchi is so impressed by Uyeshiba's calm demeanor that he stops the fight and takes Uyeshiba on to be his religious disciple. Word gets back to Shinbei that Uyeshiba caused his brother's death, and although they have great respect for each other, Uyehsiba understands that Shinbei must fight for the honor of his fallen brother. They agree to meet as martial artists, and what happens next is a beautifully orchestrated fight scene between two real martial artists, Chiba versus Chiba, as well as hard-style karate versus soft-style aikido.

The reason this film is one of my favorite 1970s discoveries is not so much for the action but for the martial arts principles it displays. For example, when Honda presents Uyeshiba with a teacher's certificate, Uyeshiba must decline it because he can't afford it. But Honda (who represents Uyeshiba's real-life teacher, Takeda Sokaku) says: "I don't take money when I give lessons to a man I trust. Though I can sell my skills, I cannot sell my martial heart. The money you paid for all lessons was for training to test the heart." On saying that, Honda returns all the money Uyeshiba had paid him for lessons over the years. As a martial artist, I really appreciate seeing the true spirit of a style communicated to an audience.

Actor Jiro Chiba also does a great job portraying Uyeshiba, especially when he adjusts his martial arts movements from one teacher and fight scene to the next. His techniques subtly change and improve over the film's duration, and this shows how Uyeshiba gradually evolves *jujutsu* to aikido's basic hand-guard fight-ready position that is modeled

after the way a samurai holds his samurai sword.

In real life, Uyeshiba started practicing *tenjin shinyo-ryu jujutsu* with Tozawa Tokusaburo in 1901. Yet his true martial calling began in 1911 when he learned the code of *budo* (the martial way) and *daito-ryu aikijujutsu* under Takeda Sokaku in Hokkaido. As Uyeshiba replaced linear approaches to techniques and striking vital points with softer, more circular movements, he developed a more spiritual outlook on life under Onisaburo Deguchi. Three spiritual events lead to Uyeshiba's new philosophy of aikido: In 1925, a fight with a navy officer who attacked him with a bokken; in 1940, while practicing the Shinto practice of *misogi* (purification rituals, such as standing under waterfalls), his martial knowledge became vehicles of life, knowledge and virtue; and in 1942 during World War II, he had a vision of the "Great Spirit of Peace" and prophesized that the warrior's way should not be about killing but about peace, love and preserving life, which are the spiritual foundations and philosophical tenets of today's aikido.

Titleography: *The Power of Aikido.* **MA Percentage: 30.53%**

DELIGHTFUL FOREST, THE

快活林 (1972—Hong Kong) **91m. MAI: Tang Chia, Liu Chia-liang, Liu Chia-rong, Chan Chuen. NOT/LOT: 2/17s; NOF/LOF: 17/ 17m 35s. D:** Chang Cheh, Pao Hsueh-li. **C:** Ti Lung, Tien Ching, Yu Feng, Zhu Mu, Jiang Nan.

This is the third of five Shaw Brothers films that feature the heroic figure Wu Song; the other four are *The Amorous Lotus Pan* (1963), *The Water Margin* (1972), *All Men Are Brothers* (1975) and *Tiger Killer* (1982).

Wu Song is one of the legendary 108 Heroes of the Liang Shan marshes. (See *The Water Margin*.) He is known for killing a man-eating tiger on Jing Yang Ridge with his bare hands and avenging his brother's death by murdering his adulterous sister-in-law, then hunting down her illicit lover and killing him at Lion's Pavilion. *The Delightful Forest* begins as Wu Song mercilessly eradicates those cheating hearts.

Wearing a cangue (a kind of pillory) around his neck that looks like a bad turtleneck sweater, Wu Song (Ti Lung) is walked off to An Ping Fortress Prison by two security guards. When they stop at a restaurant along the way, two would-be killers befriend Wu Song, telling him that he should kill the guards and flee into the marshes. Wu Song righteously states that he only fights tough guys and that the guards have been good to him. He does not want them to lose their jobs or get in trouble or, you know, die.

When he arrives at prison, the warden's son, Shih En (Tien Ching), arranges for Wu Song to forgo the usual 100 lashes entry "fee." He also gets Wu a single cell with a view and plenty of food. In return, Shih En asks Wu Song to fight God of the Door Jiang Zhong (Zhu Mu), who beat him up and took over Delightful Forest, his gambling den. Wu Song agrees but only if he can have three drinks of wine at each wine shop along the way to Delightful Forest. Wu explains that the drunker he gets, the stronger he becomes.

When he arrives at Delightful Forest drunk as a skunk, Wu Song beats the

Still from *The Delightful Forest* © Celestial Pictures Ltd. All rights reserved.

living crap out of Jiang Zhong, who is merely a stinking token protector of the gambling den. The casino is really run by the local magistrate (Jiang Nan) who frames Wu Song for a robbery in order to get him tortured, dishonorably dragged back to prison and treated like the lowest of lows prisoner ... no more respect or special treatment for Wu Song. Wu Song is tied up, covered in a heavy rope net and gang-beaten into a pulp. But on his way back to prison, he rises up from the "pulp-it," slaps his enemies with a sermon and smites those who have sinned against him. His next chapter in life, as well as in the book *The Water Margin*, sees him hooking up with the 108 Heroes of the Liang Shan marshes.

Actor Ti Lung's action sequences in which he fends off several attackers while being confined in the large wooded cangue around his neck are exquisite. Next, he fights a maniacal witch who is armed with a pole and her husband who is armed with a broadsword. Ti effortlessly moves around the weapons, countering with his feet and cangue. If he tripped or fell to the ground with his hands and head locked in place, the cangue would hit the ground first and seriously damage his neck, even if it was not made of heavy wood. His finale sword fight reveals his martial arts expertise by the way he shifts his body in and out of low front stances. There is also a great emotional builder when the swords slice thick bamboo in half, leaving a proverbial giant punji stick ominously waiting for someone to get impaled.

Note: A pillory is a set of stocks that forces the wearer to stand, and in the case of a cangue, the wearer can walk around with it on. A stock is a wooden board with one or more semicircles cut along the edges, so when two stocks connect, the semicircles form holes around the neck and hands.

Titleography: *Happy Forest*; *Outlaw of the Forest*. Translation—*The Delightful Forest*. *Outlaw of the Forest* indicates that the distributor did not watch the film and realize that the film's title refers to a gambling den and not someone in or from a forest. **MA Percentage: 19.63%** SHAW BROTHERS

DELINQUENT, THE

憤怒青年 (1973—Hong Kong) 100m. FI: Liu Chia-liang, Tang Chia. NOT/LOT: 3/ 2m 35s; NOF/LOF: 10/ 16m 24s. D: Chang Cheh, Kuei Chih-hung. C: Wang Chung, Lily Li, Bei Di, Tung Lin, Fan Mei-sheng, Dean Shek, Lu Di.

Everybody Wang Chung tonight! Director Chang Cheh went through a period when he was interested in Hong Kong's teens and the influence of Western youth subcultures, specifically British youth movements like the Teddy Boys (see *Singing Killer*) and the Mods and Rockers (see *Generation Gap*). In *The Delinquent*, Chang focuses on the day-to-day life of troubled street fighter and noodle delivery boy John Sum (Wang Chung), who tries to gain acceptance among his shady peers while trying to accept the boring life and Chinese traditional values taught to him by his single dad (Lu Di). The movie also is about the identity crisis Hong Kong youth faced while trying to balance the influence of Chinese and British cultures in their lives. The fact that our protagonist's name is John already establishes that he's leaning toward one over the other. John's father is in charge of the Wing Kee Warehouse, and the loathsome Boss Lam wants to rob the place. In the wink of an eye, John is suddenly the center of attention of Boss Lam because he wants John to steal the warehouse's key from his father. He lures John into his world with wine, women and fast cars.

After giving in to the dark side, John is ashamed of what he did and can only imagine what is happening to his dad on the night of the robbery. Although his father practices kung fu, he is old and there are too many thugs to fight. Even a strong old lion like Mr. Sum cannot fight 50 conniving and bloodthirsty hyenas. After a sudden epiphany of wrong vs. right, John speeds to the warehouse to help his father, but he is too late. Revenge in his heart, John stalks Boss Lam's lame-excuse-for-allies like a young lion, getting the last laugh on the hyenas. He then prepares to make mutton out of Boss Lam, who is ready to tame the beast with four fly-kicking lion tamers who are armed with more than just whips and chairs.

One particular fight is more dangerous than meets the eye. Back in the 1970s, there were still remnants of the old open sewer system in Hong Kong

Still from *The Delinquent* © Celestial Pictures Ltd. All rights reserved.

that look like drainage ditches. Actor Wang Chung fights a band of ruffians in a ditch that still has large puddles of standing water, and you can bet that it's not clean. Rolling around and being splashed with this water is really dangerous. The risk of infection could be fatal, especially if there were any injuries or scrapes from rolling around on the concrete surfaces.

There was also an interesting setup at the Wing Kee Warehouse in which John's hands are trapped under large steel staples and his body is draped over the cut end of a large log. As the log speeds along on a conveyer belt toward the foreboding giant buzz saw and is only inches away— a scene right out of a 1960s *Batman* TV episode—the scene cuts to daytime, and John is walking around. How did he escape?

Although the fights are sloppy in the beginning, the later fights are better. It is the old problem of the choreographers not finding that right mix of old-style kung fu choreography in a contemporary setting. No one really did it right until Jackie Chan created his *wu da pian* style of films like *Project A* (1983) in the 1980s and that he further refined with *Police Story* (1985). The four kick fighters mentioned earlier come across a lot like the four battling amazons Jackie Chan fights in *Armour of God* (1987).

Titleography: *Street Gangs of Hong Kong*. Translation—*Angry Young Man*. Each title fits the character studies brought out in the film. **MA Percentage: 18.98%** SHAW BROTHERS

DELINQUENT GIRL BOSS: BLOSSOMING NIGHT DREAMS

Zubko Bancho: Yume Wa Yoru Hiraku (1970—Japan) 87m. FC: Hio Koj. NOT/LOT: None; NOF/LOF: 5/ 4m 55s. D: Kazuhiko Yamaguchi. C: Reiko Oshida, Junko Miyazano.

If blood is thicker than water, what happens when the Yakuza code is thicker than the family? Happy-go-lucky juvenile delinquent Rika (Reiko Oshida) is released from reform school and ends up working at a lounge bar owned by her eventual protector Shinjiro (Junko Miyazano, who played the insanely sane female samurai in the *Yoen Dokufuden Okatsu* series of the 1960s). Shinjiro loved Rika's father but had to kill him because of Yakuza law. When local gang boss Ohya wants Shinjiro's bar and Rika finds out Shinjiro killed her father, Rika's nice nature slides into vengeful remorse that will destroy either Shinjiro or Boss Ohya, depending on who gets in her blood-lusting way first.

Although the fights lack the bloody, lewd intensity associated with pinky violent films, the final fight in Ohya's headquarters creates a good sense of doubt and claustrophobia as Shinjiro chases down Ohya through the narrow spaces between Japanese-style slot machines. Pinky violence movies are Japanese action, sexploitation thriller pics made during the late '60 and early '70s. Compared to later pinky violent films, *Delinquent Girl Boss: Blossoming Night Dreams* is rather mellow because it has less bloodletting and arterial squirts and is lighter on the nudity.

Samurai short sword and knife fights in narrow spaces are simpler for actors and filmmakers to work with because they are usually shot with medium or close shots that require fewer attacks and counterattacks for the actors to remember. Furthermore, using a short sword compared to a long sword in tight spaces is also easier for the actors because wielding a long sword would require more skill and precision in avoiding hitting pieces of the environment and makes spinning more difficult. From a lighting perspective, fights in narrow spaces are easier to deal with because less light is needed, which means less time is spent setting up the shots.

Titleography: As of this writing, no alternative titles could be found. Translation—*Delinquent Girl Boss: Blossoming Night Dreams.* **MA Percentage: 5.65%**

DELINQUENT GIRL BOSS: WORTHLESS TO CONFESS

Zubeko Bancho: Zange No Neuchi Mo (1971—Japan) **86m. FI: Uncredited. NOT/LOT: 1/ 10s; NOF/LOF: 2/ 4m 26s.** D: Kazuhiko Yamaguchi. C: Reiko Oshida, Junzaburo Ban, Nobuo Kaneko, Yumiko Katayama, Yukie Kagawa, Tsunehiko Watase, Ichiro Nakatani, Tonpei Hidari, Yôko Ichiji, Shizuko Kasagi, Masumi Tachibana, Mieko Tsudoi.

The late 1960s arrive in Japan a few years late in this psychedelic bubblegum romp, which is full of miniskirts, colorful wigs and pinky violence. As the second film in the *Delinquent Girl Boss* series, *Worthless to Confess* tells the story of how five teenage and 20-something girls in prison become friends. Once out of the slammer, they form a gang of femme fatales. Of course, they cross paths with the Yakuza and eventually reach that "enough is enough" moment.

After baby-faced Rika (Reiko Oshida) is released from prison, she walks the streets of her home city with glee. After a run-in with some Yakuza who own a penny arcade, during which Rika openly chastises them for cheating, she finds work at a garage owned by Muraki (Junzaburo Ban). He's the estranged father of Midori (Yumiko Katayama), one of her former prison mates whose lame boyfriend owes money to the local scar-faced Yakuza boss, Ohya. We quickly realize it was Ohya's men whom Rika had the earlier troubles with, and now that trouble is about to grow exponentially.

Muraki gives Midori money to help bail out her boyfriend, but Ohya wants the garage, which is not for sale. Rika helps out with the situation, and because Ohya has the hots for her, she offers to strip for Ohya if he agrees to leave Muraki's garage alone. However, Ohya wants the garage and Rika. When Midori steps in to help she is captured by Ohya. Suddenly the doors burst open, and in flies Muraki, who was once a powerful Yakuza known as Tetsu the Razor; he frees the girls. Midori and Muraki patch up their past differences and become a family again. Yet Ohya remembers that the scar on his face was given to him by Muraki years ago, and so he gives the order to have Muraki killed. Ohya enlists a down-and-out Yakuza dying from tuberculosis to do the dirty work. Muraki's killer does it for the money so his wife, Mari, can stop working at Ohya's sleazy nightclub. However, Mari is one of the aforementioned five friends from prison.

When word gets out that Muraki is dead, the five girls retrieve his body. Dressed in long red leather overcoats and respectively flashing Yakuza-style stances in front of his body, the girls make a solemn vow to avenge Muraki's death. After the obligatory shots of long hair wafting in the wind and heroic side-by-side strutting through the streets, the five arrive at Ohya's place, cast off their coats and brandish their samurai swords.

Heroine Rika is a delinquent version of the character April Dancer (played by Stefanie Powers) from the TV show *The Girl From U.N.C.L.E.* (1966-1967). This makes sense considering the movie's melancholy soap-operatic rhythm and a Yakuza-like beat. The movie ends with a four-minute fight scene that comes across like a go-go dancer party that rollicks and frolics on a floor of bloody revenge. The five heroines kick butt with simple sword techniques delivered in short bursts and shot in tight places. The treatment is similar to the typical way *chambara* films (sword movies) were shot, but there is a unique sensibility to the fights because moving colored lights direct the audience's attention to who is doing the killing. Positioning the camera under a glass floor also adds to the novel flavor of the fights, with swords slashing and blood oozing across the floor like Jell-O. Yum.

Titleography: *Delinquent Girl Boss: Unworthy of Penance.* Translation— *Delinquent Girl Boss: Worthless to Confess.* **MA Percentage: 5.35%**

DEMON STRIKE

茅山道人 and 茅山道士 (1979—Hong Kong) **89m. MAI: Alan Hsu, Wong Chi-sang. NOT/LOT: 1/ 54s; NOF/LOF: 23/ 28m 21s.** D: Mun Yiu-wa. C: Hwang Jang-lee, Liang Chia-ren, Bai Biao, Xue Han, Zhu Ke, Alan Hsu, Zhou Shao-dong, Zhang Fu-jian, Wong Chi-sang, Lin Yi-wa.

To roughly paraphrase Harry Belafonte's 1957 Jamaican folk song, "Come Mister Talisman, talis me my Mao-ntain. Daylight come an me don't wan' t'do magic."

Demon Strike is an early film that deals with Taoist sorcery and the magic of the Mao Shan Mountain, which was the center of many 1980s Fant-Asia films like Sammo Hung's *Encounters of the Spooky Kind* and parts of the *Mr. Vampire* series. Fant-Asia is the term used to describe the genre of martial arts films made during the 1980s up to the mid-1990s that uniquely combined elements of sex, fantasy, sci-fi and horror with high-flying wire work and over-the-top martial arts choreography.

Mao Shan, a famous school of Taoist magic, is split into three levels: high, for positive and good; middle, for magic that can be used to make someone fall in love with you; and low, which is evil and negative magic. In order to either invoke a magic spell or protect yourself from an evil spell, you need to use a talisman, which can be some kind of an amulet, piece of jewelry or handwritten mantra written on yellow paper.

When valuable gold is stolen from the emperor's palace, the emperor gives the distorted and contorted white-haired official Shui Chao-tian (Hwang Jang-lee) three months to get it back and wipe out the gang responsible for the robbery. Shui then orders the trusted Lord Pao Chang-yi (Bai Biao) to complete the mission and find the missing collection of Mao Shan spells that the gang also stole. However, when the leader of the Beggar Gang, Master Chiao (Liang Chia-ren), is warned by Lama Priests that something evil is in the air and that Shui wants the Mao Shan spells for his own devious purposes, Chiao sets off after Lord Pao in hopes of beating him to the punch.

When the magic spells are unwittingly returned to Shui, all hell breaks loose. Chiao and Pao unite with the wife (Lin Yi-wa) of one of the slain gold robbers to prevent Shui from drinking virgin menstrual blood, which would allow him to shoot blue laser beams and explosive lights out of his hands.

When it comes to demonstrating precise kung fu technique on camera, Liang Chia-ren is one of the best. He specializes in perfect posture and stances, even at the risk of fighting and moving slower than his contemporaries. Of course, this is covered up when the camera is slightly undercranked, which fortunately takes nothing away from his cinematic look. The fights in this film are well-choreographed and use very little undercranking, so Liang moves a wee bit quicker than in his previous famous "posture" looking film *Warriors Two* (1978). The choreographers toss in a short, extremely nifty cameo fight for actor Alan Hsu. He takes on Shui's men and ends up in a confined Chinese-style gazebo wherein Hsu nimbly jumps and flips around the gazebo's supporting structures.

Hwang Jang-lee's skills are somewhat overshadowed by his newfound powers (hand-shooting blue beams and explosions), but at the end of the day, everyone still looks like they are having a blast on the film.

Titleography: *Death Duel of Silver Fox.* Translations— *Mao Shan Taoist Monk* and *Mao Shan Taoist Monk.* (The second translated title uses a different Chinese character for monk). *Mao Shan* is the name of a mountain. The film is about an evil "monk" who wants to do things using Mao Shan magic. *Demon Strike* is appropriate because the "monk" develops evil and inhuman striking power. Hwang Jang-lee, who is well-known for his Silver Fox character in *Secret Rivals* (1976), plays the monk, so the distributor is advertising that Silver Fox— or at least the actor who plays him and who also happens to have white hair like in *Secret Rivals*—is in the film. **MA Percentage: 32.87%**

DEVIL'S EXPRESS

(1976—USA) **00m. FI: Uncredited. NOT/LOT: None; NOT/LOF: None.** D: None. C: None.

The DVD *Tales of Voodoo: The Rapist / Devil's Express* advertises that *Devil's Express* is a 1976 American-made martial arts film starring black martial artist Warhawk Tanzania, who fights a beastly force that has surfaced in the East and is now wreaking havoc in the New York City subway system. In actuality, the movie on this DVD is the Hong Kong horror movie *The Devil* (1981), which actually stars a good pal of mine, Taiwanese actor Liu De-kai. Because *The Devil* is a 1981 film, it is not in this book. And now you know not to rent this DVD with the hopes of watching *Devil's Express* like me!

Titleography: As of this writing, no alternative titles could be found.

DEVIL'S MIRROR, THE

風雷魔鏡 (1972—Hong Kong) **86m. FI: Xu-Er-niu, Xu Song-hao. NOT/ LOT: None; NOF/LOF: 31/ 25m 42s.** D: Sun Chung. C: Shu Pei-pei, Liu Tan, Li Chia-hsien, Ching Miao, Wang Xia, Tong Lin.

Sun Chung was the first Chinese director in Hong Kong to use a steadicam, and four years after his directorial debut with *Wild Girl* (1968), he finally got the chance to tackle the hush world of Jiang Hu. *The Devil's Mirror* is his first *wuxia* film, which delves into the secretive Jiang Hu sub-society of beggars, transients, martial heroes and anti-government insurgents who lived nowhere but everywhere.

When Witch Jiu Xuen (Li Chia-hsien) and her Bloody Ghost Gang come and go like ghosts, no one can do anything about it because they fear her magic. The heads of the Tai Shen Clans—Chief Wen (Ching Miao) and his good peg-legged friend Chief Bai Tian-xiong (Wang Xia)—recognize that the evil Witch must be stopped. Each chief possesses a magic mirror: Chief Wen has the Wind Magic Mirror and Chief Bai Tian-xiong has the Thunder Magic Mirror. However, they agree not use the mirrors against the Witch because the mirrors could hurt the environment when used together. The Witch builds an army of obedient kung fu men by feeding them poisonous Corpse Worm Pills and then threatening to withhold the antidote if they disobey her. This manic measure for magically marauding the Jiang Hu world is put together at her giant, green skull-shaped, etched-into-a-mountain lair. With the help of Chief Bai's traitorous assistant Leng Yun (Tong Lin), she plans to steal the magic mirrors to open the gates to Emperor Wu's tomb and obtain the Fish Intestine Sword to become invincible and the thousand-year-old Ganoderma to attain longevity. Note: Ganoderma is a genus of fungi that grows on wood and has been used in traditional Chinese medicine for thousands of years.

But standing in the Witch's way is Chief Wen's son Wen Jian-feng (Liu Tan) and Chief Bai's daughter (Shu Pei-pei). Both are outstanding in their fields but not like the Scarecrow in Oz who was out standing in his cornfield. Instead, the children of the chiefs are amazing sword fighters who will follow the green-rock road to Emperor Wu's magical tomb wherein they will not ignore that traitorous man behind the curtain.

The film's opening fight is very good and gets you on board the magical mystery tour that the filmmakers are dying to take you away on. The sequences comprise fast sword cuts, stab blocks, and spinning rhythms intermingled with tight camera shots to increase the excitement. Actor Wang Xia often uses a weapon attached to a long chain, and there is a unique twist to this film: When he is crawling on the ground, he begins to use his peg leg like a sword. Any guesses as to the climactic weapon that Wang Xia whips out to save his life?

Yep, the old chain gag with something attached at the end. And what is attached at the end of the chain? Hint: In this paragraph.

A note on wire work in these early films: It was all done by hand with extremely thin wires. It was also shot using lighting and camera angles to hide the wire. The wires were attached to a piece of cloth, or rope and people off-camera jumped off ladders to make the actors fly up. When you watch these old movies, try not to compare the wire work with the stuff that evolved in the 1980s. It is like trying to compare a high-school football team with a professional football team. Each understands the foundations and principles of the game, but they're on totally different levels when it comes to age, experience, physical ability and talent.

Titleography: As of this writing, no alternative titles could be found. Translation—*Wind Thunder Magic Mirrors*. See above martialogy. **MA Percentage: 29.88%** SHAW BROTHERS

DIRTY HO

爛頭何 (1979—Hong Kong) **97m. FI: Liu Chia-liang. NOT/LOT: 4/ 5m 21s; NOF/LOF: 26/ 5m 21s.** D: Liu Chia-liang. C: Wang Yu, Gordon Liu Chia-hui, Lo Lieh, Wang Lung-wei, Hui Ying-hong, Hsiao Ho, Wilson Tong, Lin Ke-min.

After watching this film three times, several things hit me. The first was the 1970s jingle "From the valley of the (ho, ho, ho) Green Giant" because this was a jolly big film. The second was the Santa Claus catchphrase "Ho, ho, ho. Merry Christmas" because the movie is a gift to fight choreography. The third was with the title *Dirty Ho* because I'm sure no malicious flip-flop political correctness was intended. But these allusions and delusions were nothing compared to the three amazing fights discussed further below.

When it comes to fight choreography and creativity, this film is a prime example of simplicity meeting complexity. Some of the sequences are like nothing seen before or since; they look effortlessly performed, but the complexity of proper timing and avoiding errors during filming cannot be ignored. Because they're so simple, it is perhaps difficult to realize how much effort was put into making them look so awesome. Like a beaver building its home, the choreographers were "dam" busy. The scenes are also shot in a way to bring out the authenticity of the actors' movements and reveal to the audience that the stars are actually pulling these things off. What is even more impressive is that the intricacies and subtle nuances are distinctly translated from kung fu skills, hidden by the nonchalant attitudes of the fighters involved. It is, as Bruce Lee would say, fighting without fighting.

The film is partially inspired by the life of Emperor Chien Lung, who made six secret visits to Chiang Nan dressed as a commoner in order to blend in and learn how his subjects felt about him. (See *Adventures of Emperor Chien Lung*.) Gordon Liu plays the son of the Ching emperor known as 11th Prince, who enjoys gallivanting around the country in disguise as Wang Chin-chen, a wine connoisseur, art collector, jeweler and visitor of brothels. After a few run-ins with the overgrown rug rat and jewel thief Dirty Ho Ching (Wang Yu), Wang admires his chutzpah and takes a liking to him. He even saves Ho on a few occasions by flashing the imperial seal to make the Ching police rapidly disappear. Wang also plans to make Ho his student and bodyguard because Wang's life is in danger.

Elsewhere, the emperor is about to announce his heir. The Fourth Prince is concerned about Wang's popularity with the emperor, so he hires General Liang Jing-cheng (Lo Lieh) to do whatever it takes to prevent Wang from arriving on time at the palace for the announcement. Liang's plan? Assassinate Wang. During one such attempt, Wang's leg is severely injured, making him a cripple. Wang then decides to teach Ho kung fu and make Ho his bodyguard. Although Wang is crippled, during their elaborate training sequences, the two cook up a way to get Wang safely back to the palace on time. While en route to the palace with Wang in a wheelchair, they run into hapless hit men hired by Liang, like the transvestite-ninja-looking Seven Tigresses and their merry archer men. At the palace, Liang and his dastardly kung fu assassins prepare to drive our two heroes batty with a large *guan dao* (a

Still from *The Devil's Mirror* © Celestial Pictures Ltd. All rights reserved.

long-poled weapon with a huge blade at one end and a spear point at the other). Wang and Ho must drive home a "crutch" single to save the game.

There are three amazing fight sequences to watch out for in this film: the wicked wine-tasting scene, the art-inspecting sight gag and the courtesan-manipulating set piece. Throughout each of these three skirmishes, Ho is clueless about Wang's superb kung fu skills because the prince cleverly disguises them. Take a look at the first fight against Liang's wine-loving assassins—Mr. Fan (Wang Lung-wei) and his assistant (Hsiao Ho). As the assistant pours the wine, it looks like Fan and Wang are just enjoying themselves while drinking it. However, between the pouring and sipping, the imbibing is interspersed with deadly kung fu attacks. In the second fight, Wang is having a friendly discussion with fellow art lover Mr. Chu (Wilson Tong) who is also one of Liang's assassins. While admiring a painting of ancient Chinese strokes, they begin to exchange deadlier strokes with a sword hidden inside one of the paintings. While they fight, Ho has no idea that Wang is beating up one of Liang's assassins because Wang disguises the violence with a calm and cool demeanor. In the third fight, Ho and Wang are at a brothel with the courtesan Tsui Hung (Hui Ying-hong). Wang warns Ho that Tsui is also his bodyguard. When Ho sneers at this statement and attacks him, Wang pretends to cower behind Tsui but really controls her arms, feet and weapon work by pushing and pulling on her limbs at the right moment. Tsui is also confused as to what is going on, but she easily beats up Ho at the same time. It is simply marvelous.

Still from *Dirty Ho* © Celestial Pictures Ltd. All rights reserved.

On a curious note, I surmised that Wang may have been the son of Emperor Kang Xi. Historically, the 14th Prince was supposedly the heir to the throne, but because Fourth Prince Yong Zheng got his hands on Kang Xi's secret will and changed a few characters to make the will read that Fourth Prince was the heir, Yong Zheng became emperor. Of course after Kang Xi died, no one was around to contest the will since only Kang Xi knew of its original contents. Also, Kang Xi's 11th son died early in life, and fatefully, so did Yong Zheng's 11th son.

Notice during the last fight that actor Lo Lieh's posture is slightly hunch-backed with his neck forward, similar to actor Chen Hsing's bad habit of always hunching his back during fights, as mentioned in several martialogies; for an example, see *Iron Fisted Monk* (1977). You can tell when Lo's double is in a shot because his posture is straight.

Titleography: As of this writing, no alternative titles could be found. Translation—*Rotten Head Ho*. In parts of the film, Ho has a patch on his head with a black circle in the center, which is often seen in Chinese films and represents a sick character, usually with scabies. That patch is called a *lan tou*. The first two

Chinese characters in the Chinese title are *lan tou*, and they translate as "rotten head." **MA Percentage: 32.56%** SHAW BROTHERS

DIRTY KUNG FU

鬼馬功夫 and 奇招怪腿 (1978—Hong Kong) **85m. FD: Liu Chia-liang, Liu Chia-rong. NOT/LOT: 4/ 2m 2s; NOF/LOF: 11/ 23m. D: Liu Chia-rong. C: Wang Yu, Liu Chia-rong, Wilson Tong, Xu Hsao-chiang, Dean Shek.**

After being involved in Chinese martial art films for years, I've learned lots of things. I know which actors are real martial artists and whether their technique looks good or bad on-screen. I know which actors picked up martial arts skills because they were in so many films and, in doing so, can manage to look like martial artists on camera. I know which actors are opera-trained and how many of them are not martial artists per se. And I can recognize the actors who know no martial arts and look like they don't know it on-screen. This last category is the trickiest because there are many traditionally trained martial artists that, for some reason, look like beginners when they fight in a film. Throughout the book, I have tried to politely point out the various kinds of actors and their skill levels. In this film, when you watch the fight between Wilson Tong and Xu Hsao-chiang, take a moment to use your newfound knowledge from this book to answer: Who do you think really knows how to use the sword?

In *Dirty Kung Fu*, Li Dao-tai or Gao Jai (Wang Yu) fancies himself a bounty hunter, and one of his get-rich-quick schemes is to hunt down criminals and collect the reward. However, he wisely knows his kung fu shortcomings, so when the criminal who he's hunting turns out to be a dangerous kung fu man, Li elicits the help of various experienced fighters such as Lu Pao (Liu Chia-rong) or swordsman Flashing Blade Yip (Xu). The three of them agree to split the reward money. However, when the far-out and freaky voodoo kung fu felon Hu Lan (Wilson Tong) proves too dangerous for Lu Pao and too good for blade master Yip, Li must figure out a way to learn new martial tricks and create a new style of martial arts called eel kung fu. Li hopes the style's slip-sliding and slithering will keep him from withering under Hu Lan's blade.

This film features some very good straight-sword fights. In Chinese, the double-bladed Chinese sword is called the *jian*, but many know it simply as the *taiji* (*tai chi*) sword. This term actually hides the history of the weapon, considering that the art of taiji has only been around since 1365, and bronze versions of the jian are proven to have existed before the iron taiji jian as far back as the Zhao Dynasty (B.C. 1122 to B.C. 256).

Many taiji jians have tassels attached to the base of the handle. In combat, the tassels' bright colors can distract the opponent. In training, the tassels help students learn proper twirling and sword strikes because the goal is to never have the tassel wrap around the sword's hilt or user's hand during use of the weapon. Swords are usually custom-made for their users, and the blade's balance is more important than its weight. The correct balance point is found by measuring the width of the user's three fingers (forefinger, middle finger and ring finger), and it is that width from the sword hilt up the blade that the blade should balance like an "evenly weighted on both sides" seesaw on a fulcrum.

The film's title song is the *Tea (Chinese Dance)* from Pyotr Ilyich Tchaikovsky's ballet *The Nutcracker*. This is a curious choice considering that this piece is also in the Walt Disney film *Fantasia* (1940) and features dancing Chinese mushrooms.

Titleography: *Kung Fu Expert*. Translations—*Ghost Horse Kung Fu; Odd Strike, Strange Leg Technique. Ghost Horse Kung Fu* and the *Strange Leg Technique* refer to Hu Lan's voodoo kung fu. In order to conjure a fighting spirit up from the ground and into his body, Hu Lan must stomp his foot on the ground like a horse. Thus, we get the scene in which our hero Li tries to prevent Hu's foot from connecting with the ground. The *Odd Strike* title part also refers to the kung fu that Hu uses—the odd strike being from whatever spirit Hu invokes into his own body. *Kung Fu Expert* is just a generic title referring to the main character's eventual mastering of eel kung fu. **MA Percentage: 29.45%**

DIRTY TIGER CRAZY FROG

老虎田雞 and 大鱷鬥蝦蟆 (1978—Hong Kong) 97m. **MAD:** Liu Chia-rong, Sammo Hung. **NOT/LOT:** None; **NOF/LOF:** 19/ 29m 14s. **D:** Karl Maka. **C:** Sammo Hung, Liu Chia-rong, Meg Lam Kin-ming, Karl Maka, Dean Shek, Bai Biao, Lee Hoi-san, Du Xiao-ming.

Many famous comedians in history played funny characters on-screen, but in real life, the humor is just a persona. When you watch the over-the-top visual gags in Sammo Hung's films, they are presented with a grain of salt, peppered with camera muggings filled with "Hehe, haha, hoho." (Think of the song, *They're Coming to Take Me Away, Ha-Haaa!* by Napoleon XIV.) The comedy bits attached to the fights are as painful to watch as they were to shoot. Sammo Hung and his opera brothers used fight scenes as a way to share their experiences in growing up in opera school. This is why many of Hung's 1970s films had little character development beyond going from point A to point B, where by the end of the film, it was always about how good the character's fighting abilities got, i.e., a reflection of their opera-based martial arts training. Hung once told me that from his perspective, if the fights were great, regardless of whether the the movie was not that good, the film would still be successful.

As a dowry for marrying into a prestigious family, Crazy Frog (Sammo Hung) gets a most coveted prize: the Invincible Armor, which is a white, sleeveless chain mail shirt that renders the wearer immune to strikes and weapon blows—provided that the strikes hit the armor. The catch is that his new wife is 65 years old—gaaaaak! Crazy Frog runs away with the armor, and the geriatric granny hires the shady-as-an-elm-tree Tiger (Liu Chia-rong) to track Frog down and bring him home. However, everyone and their pet chicken are after the armor, including the double-crossing female pickpocket Multi-Hand Chick (Meg Lam Kin-ming). But because Frog is like the toad-in-the-hole (courtesy of the British dish), she needs to stir the sausage out of the pastry by luring him into the bedroom to steal the Invincible Armor. The film becomes a mishmash of cons vs. cons, double-dealings and some farcical (albeit not too creative) fights like with villain White Brow Monk (Lee Hoi-san), a master of crab kung fu (no such kung fu style in real life) who dwindles into a heap of crustacean crackers under the crushing kung fu of our two crackpot heroes, the amphibious Frog and the mammalian Tiger. This is certainly a film rendering itself well for the animal kingdom. Where are Marlin Perkins and his gutsy assistant Jim from the popular TV show *Animal Kingdom* when you need them?

The best fight in the film is the three-sectional staff battle between Liu and Sammo. If you have a good eye, you can distinguish between Liu's classic weapons training and Hung's flamboyant opera rendition. Historically, the three-sectional staff was invented in A.D. 360 by Chao Hong-yin when he was a bodyguard for the royal family and before he became first emperor of the Song Dynasty. After his wooden staff broke during a fight, he had a blacksmith link the broken ends with two iron rings. During another fight, the pole broke again, and two more iron rings were added. He now had a three-sectional staff, which could break a horse's legs to bring down the rider.

Titleography: *Dirty Tiger and Crazy Frog.* Translations—*Old Tiger and Frog* and *Big Crocodile Fights Toad. Tiger* and *Frog* refer to the characters played by Liu Chia-rong and Sammo Hung, respectively. *Crocodile Fights Toad* infers that two water creatures fight each other. The creatures are metaphors for White Brow Monk and Frog. Although White Brow Monk practices crab style, both crabs and crocodiles have thick skin. **MA Percentage: 30.14%**

DISCIPLES OF SHAOLIN

洪拳小子 (1975—Hong Kong) 101m. **FI:** Liu Chia-liang. **NOT/LOT:** 6/ 7m 18s; **NOF/LOF:** 15/ 21m 26s. **D:** Chang Cheh. **C:** Alexander Fu Sheng, Chi Kuan-chun, Jiang Dao, Chiang Tao, Feng Ke-an, Wang Jing-ping, Cheng Ming-li, Lu Di.

As the Chinese title indicates, this film is about a young man, Guan Feng-yi

(Alexander Fu Sheng), who learns *hong jia* kung fu, the martial arts of the Hong family. He teaches his kung fu to embittered workers at the Fa Long factory who are being forced to work for a rival factory run by underhanded Chings. Although his older kung fu brother and best friend, Wang Hong (Chi Kuan-chun), initially refuses to get involved in the battle, he eventually joins the cause.

On the surface, the film has nothing to do with being a disciple of Shaolin or with Shaolin martial arts in general because Alexander Fu Sheng and Chi Kuan-chun are not playing any of the famed martial arts heroes of old. Yet the martial arts action is classic Fu Sheng at his best; he is a good martial arts technician with a cheeky personality, and he manages not to overdo it or distract from the seriousness of the intention behind the fights. Like many martial arts movies of the 1970s, this film's opening credits feature its star performing the title martial art, which sets the tone of the story and introduces the character before the film begins. With his wrists and forearms weighed down by heavy silver rings, Fu Sheng performs the famed hong jia form of iron wire fist.

Still from *Disciples of Shaolin* © Celestial Pictures Ltd. All rights reserved.

One of the key emotional threads in this film is protagonist Guan's desire for a watch, which he eventually earns and carries around like a badge of honor. Director Chang Cheh revisited this theme with Fu Sheng's character in *Chinatown Kid* (1977). Chang is also known for being a bit off-kilter with his visual devises and demises, such as the scene in which a hero flip-flops on-screen in slow motion while his life and blood slowly drain from his body. In another scene, it takes one of Chang's impaled heroes five pity-inducing minutes to meet his bloody end. It's like a scene in *The Duel* (1971), but shot in black and white with orchestral music that sounds like it was borrowed from a 1960s European film. It's bizarre, to say the least.

The beauty of this film is that choreographer Liu Chia-liang often has Fu Sheng, a trained martial artist, doing more than 30 techniques per shot so the camera can follow him all over the room with tracking and hand-held camera choreography. There are also point-of-view shots of both fighters in one unedited take. The camera moves around behind each fighter, which makes the fight feel more engaging, as if you were in the fight.

Now for some history: Although Hong Xi-guan is usually credited as the founder of hong jia, a lot of credit goes to his teacher, Monk Zhi Shan, one of the Five Elders of Shaolin. Zhi Shan's lineage as a student traces back to Tsai De-zhong, one of the Five Ancestors of Shaolin. Zhi Shan taught many famous students, eight of them belonging to the legendary 10 Tigers of Shaolin. Hong, alongside Fan Shi-yu, was one of Zhi Shan's top disciples.

The iron wire fist (aka iron thread set) is one of the most advanced hong jia forms. It was created by Tie Qiao-san (whose name literally means "iron bridge three" or "Sam the Iron Bridge") while he was at the Hai Chuang Monastery.

Dedicated to the Shaolin way, Tie taught martial arts at the Guang Zhi Dye Works at Rainbow Bridge in Guangdong. A longtime opium smoker, Tie died at age 70 in 1888 because of overexertion while practicing what is known as the 36 Point Copper Ring Pole technique, which he hoped would help him break his opium addiction. Tie was known to be able to lift up to six men with one hand and carry them more than 100 steps without changing pace.

When fight instructor Liu Chia-liang cast his adopted family member and young kung fu brother Gordon Liu Chia-hui in *The 36th Chamber of Shaolin* (1977), that film also began with opening credits featuring the iron wire fist (as performed by Chia-hui). The form is about creating a balance of technique in which the hard "iron" movements represent power and the soft "thread" skills represent calm.

Titleography: *Invincible One*; *The Hung Boxing Kid*; *Disciples of Shao-Lin*. Translation—*Hong Fist Kid*. The main English titles refer to Fu Sheng and Chi Kuan-chun's characters being practitioners of martial arts that originated from Shaolin. Both actors have also played Shaolin heroes in past films, so the titles could also have a marketing component. The Chinese and alternate English titles refer to Fu Sheng's character practicing hong jia. **MA Percentage: 28.45%** SHAW BROTHERS

DISCO GODFATHER

(1979—USA) 96m. **FSC: Howard Jackson, Cliff Stewart. NOT/LOT: None; NOF/LOF: 8/ 3m 7s.** D: J. Robert Wagoner. C: Rudy Ray Moore, Carol Speed, Jimmy Lynch, Jerry Jones, Lady Reed, Frank Finn, Julius Carry.

Saturday Night Fever meets *Soul Train*, but there is more hustle than tussle, more disco than dialogue and more boogieing than brawling. Ex-cop Disco Godfather (Rudy Ray Moore) leads a crusade against the drug angel dust, which is killing the black brothers in the projects. Besides a trippy exorcism sequence, it is also the last on-screen appearance of *Black Belt* Hall of Fame member Howard Jackson in the '70s. Although Moore does less fighting and more preaching in this movie, he still firmly establishes his signature kung fu move when he crosses his arms in front of his face, shakes his head and flaps his lips like a grumbling bear.

Titleography: *Avenging Disco Godfather*; *Avenging Godfather*. **MA Percentage: 3.25%**

DOC SAVAGE: THE MAN OF BRONZE

(1975—USA) 101m. **SC: Toni Eppers. NOT/LOT: None; NOF/LOF: 8/ 4m 27s.** D: Michael Anderson. C: Ron Ely, Paul Gleason, William Lucking, Michael Miller, Eldon Quick, Darrell Zwerling, Paul Wexler, Janice Heiden.

Created by Henry Ralston and John Nanovic, Doc Savage was an American pulp comic book hero that appeared in *Doc Savage Magazine*, printed by Street and Smith Publications from 1933 to 1949. Savage become more well known when Bantam Books reprinted the magazine stories as novels with shiny book covers that featured Savage sporting blond hair styled into a widow's peak, which was accented by his golden tanned skin and a torn khaki shirt exposing his muscular body.

This film based on that character stars Ron Ely of NBC's *Tarzan* (1966-1968) as Doc Savage. Along with his brain trust, the Fabulous Five, Doc takes on the demented Captain Seas (Paul Wexler) and the ghostly, snakelike Green Death while trying to find out the cause of his father's death in the jungles of Hidalgo.

I remember seeing Ron Ely on the cover of some martial arts magazine a long time ago in which he spoke about *Doc Savage* and how they did all kinds of martial arts in the film. He was not lying. The final fight between the Doc and Captain Seas features a number of different martial arts. As is common in Chinese kung fu films, each time a different fighting style is used, the name of the respective style flashes on screen. Within a two-minute time period, the following arts are demonstrated: sumo; kung fu, which is shot with extreme close-ups and features a few chops and one takedown; *tai chi chuan*, featuring Doc using a crane beak hand strike (half-right, when you consider that tai chi was first inspired by Zhang San-feng observing a snake and crane fighting); karate, which has Savage doing a front kick-spinning kick combination; *bo jijsu* (I've never heard of bo jijsu, but perhaps it is a misspelling of *bo jujutsu*); and fisticuffs. Despite the variety, the film failed miserably, as does the look of each fight. The fights were shot too tight, and whenever Ely throws a fist, he uses an overextended neck-jerk to sell speed and power. Ultimately, nothing was sold—except producer's George Pal's house when he tried to get enough funds

together to finish the film.

In 2000, Arnold Schwarzenegger told me on the set of *The 6th Day* that he would be starring in a new Doc Savage film, then in the early stages of development. Of course, that project fell through after he became the governor of California.

Titleography: As of this writing, no alternative titles could be found. **MA Percentage: 4.41%**.

DOLEMITE

(1975—USA) 90m. **FS: Gene Davis. NOT/LOT: 19s; NOF/LOF: 7/ 4m 14s.** D: D'Urville Martin. C: Rudy Ray Moore, D'Urville Martin. Jerry Jones, Lady Reed, Brenda DeLong, Terri Mosley, Marilyn Shaw, Lynell Smith, Dolemite Girl, Vera Howard, Joy Martin, Jana Bisbing, Brenda Banks, Pat Haywood, René Van Clief, Pat Jones.

Great martial arts action—say what!? The beauty of early martial arts films made in America, especially blaxploitation films, is that the Western audience truly had no clue what a good fight scene looked like. Back then, no one cared as long as someone's butt got kicked and the hero looked cool doing it. What was truly far-out about watching blaxploitation movies in the inner-city theaters in the 1970s was that audiences actually talked to the screen and shouted warnings to the hero. I guess we are too sophisticated nowadays to openly enjoy ourselves because we're afraid of being labeled uncool. It's such a drag, man. (It's also interesting to note that while many people seem unoffended by the genre name, today's politically correct culture dictates that you call blaxploitation films an "urban movie.")

Pimp hero Dolemite (Rudy Ray Moore) goes to the local karate studio and hand-picks a harem of "fiiiine women" to help him karate-kick the racist cops who framed him for drug dealing and stealing furs. He also wants revenge against opponent pimp Willie Greene (D'Urville Martin), who mowed his little nephew down in cold blood on the streets. Mostly, the "suck the royal bird" fight scenes seem too bad to be true, but we still like them—back then.

But you have got to admire Moore's "pimp and circumstance" because he truly embraces the spirit of the kung fu and blaxploitation genres. It is no easy task to put yourself out there and go for it. I tip my ultra-furry hat to him.

Titleography: As of this writing, no alternative titles could be found. **MA Percentage: 5.06%**

DON

(1978—India) 166m. **TD: A. Mansoor. NOT/LOT: 1/ 55s; NOF/LOF: 8/ 10m 57s.** D: Chandra Barot. C: Amitabh Bachchan, Zeenat Aman, Pran, Iftekhar, Om Shivpuri, Satyendra Kapoor, P. Jairaj.

Jackie Chan in India. Oops, I mean Bachchan in India. Embittered sister Roma (Zeenat Aman) learns judo and karate, then joins the police force so she can go undercover to avenge the death of her brother and his fiancee, who were executed gangland style by a ruthless don named Don (Amitabh Bachchan). During a bizarre car chase, Don dies, but the Chief of the Police is the only person who witnesses it. Following that, the Chief stumbles on a street bum named Vijay (Bachchan), a Don look-alike. In exchange for helping his two adopted orphan children get an education, Vijay reluctantly infiltrates the Mafia as their leader and becomes Roma's target; she's positioned herself as Don's girl and is now waiting for the right moment to kill him. It's like a battle between a black widow spider (Roma) that kills its mate (Vijay who is now Don) and a ghost mantis (Vijay), which looks like a vicious army ant (Don) and can walk freely among the deadly ants (Don's gang).

Although not trained in martial arts, Zeenat (a former Miss Asia Pacific) was praised for taking on "less than pure" roles, which revolutionized the portrayal of women in Indian films; her fighting role in *Don* added to her legendary status. Thrill director Mansoor—a veteran fight instructor and choreographer who has often worked with star Bachchan—smartly Xeroxed Jackie Chan's *Drunken Master* success in a very Indian way. Mansoor is also a *kalaripayit* practitioner, which is evident in a few well-executed pole fights that you won't see in Chinese or Japanese martial arts films.

An interesting cultural point: Vijay hails from the northern city of Benaras, which is one of India's oldest and holiest cities because it is near the place that the Buddha gave his first sermon. It's also a place where simple folks like Vijay chew betel leaves. These leaves contain betel oil, a mild stimulant. The film makes use of this plant. After Vijay chews a ton of the leaves, his martial arts prowess goes through the roof, especially his kalaripayit pole skills. It is quite similar to what happens when Jackie Chan's Huang Fei-hong character drinks too much wine and his kung fu improves.

Furthermore, the final fight at the cemetery is filled with some unique and exciting choreography. Our heroes and the Mafia hit men vie for a red book of Mafia secrets, which is kicked, flipped, spun, Frisbeed and helicoptered in a novel "catch it if you can" sequence. With some fights in this film, it also sounds like they took the sound effects from a Hong Kong kung fu film and then looped them into their own fight scenes.

One last comment about contemporary Indian films: It is rather kooky that in the middle of Hindi dialogue, English catchphrases like "what are you doing here" are intermittently dispersed throughout the films. But English catchphrases mixed in with dance-and-song routines add to the novelty of India's gifted production packages.

Titleography: As of this writing, no alternative titles could be found. **MA Percentage: 7.15%**

DRACULA AND THE 7 GOLDEN VAMPIRES

七金屍 (1974—Hong Kong/U.K.) **98m. MAS: Liu Chia-liang, Tang Jia. NOT/LOT: None; NOF/LOF: 22/ 16m 42s. D:** Roy Ward Baker. **C:** Peter Cushing, David Chiang, Robin Stewart, Julie Ege, Shih Szu, Chan Shen, John Forbes-Robertson, Liu Chia-rong, Tino Wong.

What a wacky idea: Vampires of the East and West unite to take over the world! The place: Transylvania. The time: 1804. Count Dracula (John Forbes-Robertson) kills the mortal Chinese High Priest Kah (Chan Shen; *Five Fingers of Death*) and then secretly takes his place. Kah wanted Dracula to help him resurrect the legend of the Golden Vampires, but now Dracula as Kah has designs to take over China as part of a more sinister plan.

Fast-forward 100 years to 1904 in the city of Chun King. The stalwart vampire-hunter Van Helsing (Peter Cushing) and the fighting Hsi family led by Hsi Ching (David Chiang) embark on a dangerous journey to the remote village of Ping Kwei, middle of nowhere, Sichuan province, for humanity's last stand against the Golden Vampires. Along the way, they face macabre mishaps, biting bats and undead kung fu fighters—things that dampen their spirits and physically weaken them for the final battle of mankind vs. Dracula unkind.

After the original director Gordon Hessler quit at the eleventh hour, Hammer veteran director Roy Ward Baker (who directed Christopher Lee in the 1970 Hammer film *Scars of Dracula*) and the legendary Chang Cheh (uncredited) stepped in to save the day. Chang convinced the impressive martial arts instructor duo of Liu Chia-liang and Tang Jia to put together some face-saving action that blends relatively well with the Hammer horror mien.

There are two interesting and glaring problems with this film that no one has ever pointed out. None of the Chinese characters have queues, which was the standard, required-by-law hairstyle for all Chinese men during this era. Also, when Van Helsing is lecturing at Chun King University, he indicates that the Chinese believe that vampires and ghosts are nonsense. In reality, Chinese culture is heavily steeped in ghosts and spiritualism. This is basically the Western screenwriter expounding on what he thinks Chinese characters should be rather than who they really are.

It is interesting that the title is *7 Golden Vampires* because the number is considered unlucky in Chinese numerology because of its association with ghosts and spirits. In addition, Ghost Month—when the gates of hell are opened and the ghosts walk the mortal world—is the seventh month of the Chinese calendar. So at least that's spot on with the plotline.

Titleography: *The Legend of the Seven (7) Golden Vampires*; *Seven Brothers Meet Dracula*; *The 7 Brothers & Their One Sister Meet Dracula*. Translation—*Seven Golden Corpses*. Only the sister meets Dracula; none of the seven fighting Hsi brothers do. **MA Percentage: 17.04%** SHAW BROTHERS

DRAGON FIST

龍拳 (1978—Hong Kong) **93m. FC: Jackie Chan. NOT/LOT: None; NOF/LOF: 26/ 23m 3s. D:** Lo Wei. **C:** Jackie Chan, Nora Miao, Yen Shi-kwan, Pearl Lin Yin-zhu, Hsu Hsia, Ou-Yang Sha-Fei, James Tien, Han Ying, Gao Chiang.

Similar to *Spiritual Kung Fu* (1978), *Dragon Fist* was shot in 1978 after Jackie Chan had recovered from his eyelid surgery in Japan. However, because Lo Wei's production company ran out of money, *Dragon Fist* was released in April 1979, after receiving money for loaning Chan out to Ng See-yuen at Seasonal Films for a two-picture deal. Ironically, it turned out to be a smart move

for Lo because Chan's pedigree as an actor and choreographer skyrocketed after those films (*Snake in the Eagle Shadow* and *Drunken Master*). Lo made a financial killing, and he had in his hands unreleased films and other footage of Chan, which he released after Chan became famous, such as *Dragon Fist*.

After the righteous dragon fist kung fu teacher Wang San-tai (Hsu Hsia) wins a prestigious kung fu tournament that brings honor to his martial arts and his school, he is challenged and slain by the uninvited bad-seed kung fu killer Chung Chien-guan (Yen Shi-kwan). Wang's top student, Tang Hao-yuen (Jackie Chan), is angered beyond belief and jumps into the fray, but it proves to be a frail attempt. Chung quickly dispatches him. With flippant laughter and disrespect, Chung leaves Wang's crumpled body on the ground and exits the school unscathed.

Tang, Wang's wife and his daughter (Nora Miao and Pearl Lin Yin-zhu) plan their revenge and go after Chung, only to find that he has seen the error of his ways. In honor of Wang, Chung has chopped off one of his legs as a form of penitence, thereby preventing him from ever fighting and killing anyone of good moral character again. However, the seed of the deception goes deeper than Chung; it is revealed that a traitorous student of Wang's is responsible for poisoning Wang's wife and is set on taking down dragon fist as a whole. Once the truth is out, Tang goes ballistic, especially in a *tonfa*-versus-crutch duel, and his final death march is loaded with the same over-the-top emotional angst revealed after Chan's character gets drunk at the end of *Drunken Master II*, though this film lacks the humorous overtones.

Two major differences in this film for Chan are that the movie has a more serious tone and that Chan has none of his patented kung fu training sequences. Audiences had become enthralled with watching Chan perform these grueling tasks. In terms of choreography, Chan uses fewer side angles in this film but uses strikes toward and away from camera to sell the hits. He also begins one of his signature kung fu moves (it is subtle) in which he would begin to strike, stop, then continue the strike on the same path. It is not supposed to be a fake or a feint, just a momentary respite to build the emotion of the technique. Furthermore, his back posture is straighter than usual compared to his previous films, something that looked better when he started doing more fancy fist maneuvers and gave the movements a better rhythmic cadence. He almost got to the point of appearing mechanical, which Yuen Woo-ping would smooth out in Chan's next two films.

The origins of dragon fist kung fu are not well known, but the movements derive from Shaolin martial arts as one of the animal styles of kung fu that originated from Ta Mo's 18 Luo Han fists. Sometime during the Ming Dynasty in the mid-1600s (although some historians believe the 13th century is more correct), Shaolin monk Zhue Yang wandered around China and met fellow martial artists Li Sou and Bai Yu-feng. Together, they improved Ta Mo's 18 movements to 173 and created the five animal styles of Shaolin, which combined their observations and theories of the animal fighting strategies of the tiger, leopard, snake, white crane and dragon. The dragon style has roots in *hakka cheun*, a style of kung fu from the Hakka people who live in the inland eastern area of Guangdong (Canton). Their movements were combined with the kung fu taught to them by Zhi Shan, one of the Five Elders of Shaolin. Similar to tiger claw kung fu, the dragon style uses clawed hands as part of its repertoire of movements. The dragon claw can be distinguished from the tiger claw in that the dragon-claw hand has the fingers arched back at the knuckles.

Titleography: *In Eagle Dragon Fist*. Translation—*Dragon Fist*. After *Snake in the Eagle's Shadow* came out, other English titles for kung fu films began using the word "in" with combinations of animal styles of kung fu. In many cases, like for this film, the use of "in" makes little grammatical sense, but admittedly, it does make the title sound kind of cool. **MA Percentage: 24.78%**

DRAGON FORCE OPERATION

狂龍雪恥 (1976—Taiwan) **84m. KFI: Chen Shen-yi. NOT/LOT: 1/ 37s; NOF/LOF: 23/ 37m 52s. D:** Tyrone Hsu. **C:** Yan Nan-xi, Lung Tien-hsiang, Shi Ting-gen, Li Jiang, Zhang Peng, Chen Shen-yi, Zhang Peng, Wang Re-ping.

When man's best friend is more valuable than any individual, then a dog-eat-dog world becomes a "dog ruthlessly maims, eats, defecates, then lights it on fire" world. When it is a Japanese dog in occupied China, mercy does not exist—ever. This is why the opening instrumental version of Bob Dylan's 1963 hit *Blowin' in the Wind*, a song that poses philosophical questions about war, peace and freedom, is appropriate for the film's mood and subsequent hate-induced bloodletting between the Chinese and Japanese.

After a Japanese big boss (Shi Ting-gen) takes over a local Chinese delivery company, his right-hand man (Li Jiang) sets his vicious dog on Wang Lung (Chen Shen-yi), one of the three Lung brothers who used to do security work for the company. Wang kills the dog in self-defense. The slaying becomes the firecracker that sets off a fireworks display of devious back-stabbing and death. When the dust settles, youngest brother Pai Lung (Lung Tien-hsiang) and his newfound anti-philandering, fighting-female friend Nan Ying (Yan Nan-xi) make sure that the message is loud and clear: Chinese are not dogs, and one day the Japanese will suffer for their cruelty.

The film is a worn-out statement about Chinese feelings toward the Japanese a la Bruce Lee's *Fist of Fury* (1971), and when the fight scenes lack any kind of punch, so does the statement. While watching the film, I waited for any good fight. Because the agonizing visuals of the two older brothers' cruel, dehumanizing and tortuous deaths are so disturbing, you want the younger brother and girlfriend to deliver the appropriate pugilistic and emotional payoff—but it never happens.

However, actor Lung Tien-hsiang deserves recognition for fighting shirtless on a craggy mountain. Even the simplest fall, flip or landing on the sharp rocks must be painful but to do it bareback is lacerating beyond belief. I have done similar things fully dressed and still bled. Rolling around on such rocky and backbreaking terrain probably felt worse than being in a real fight. Even without facing the music, rolling on rocks can be painful indeed … rock on dudes … I mean, on rock. Ouch.

Titleography: *The Revenge Dragon*; *The God Father of Hong Kong*. Translation—*Wild Dragon Snow Little*. The three brothers all have Lung (Dragon) in their names, thus the use of *Dragon* in the titles. Besides the *God Father* title making no sense, the story does not take place in Hong Kong. Furthermore, the *God Father of Hong Kong* is an alternative title for *The Mandarin* (1973), but there is no relation between the films and no similar cast members. The Chinese title's use of *Snow Little* is also a non sequitur because there is neither snow nor a character named Snow or any metaphorical connection about snow that I could deduce, unless it is an inference to the cold hearts of the Japanese characters. **MA Percentage: 45.81%**

DRAGON FURY

火拱楓林渡 (1974—Taiwan) **75m. AD: Wang Yong-sheng. NOT/LOT: None; NOF/LOF: 18/ 28m 35s.** D: Zhong Guo-heng. C: Wen Jiang-long, Hsu Feng, Chen Sha-li, Yang Lun, Zhang Ji-ping, Robameice Deimikor, Lee Jiang, Robert Tai Chi-hsien.

In most Chinese films, foreigners usually play the bad guys and are therefore ripe for the pickings. We got our asses whooped tomato red, and that red was oftentimes blood because no one wore pads or had any protection in the 1970s. Getting injured on camera was normal and became a badge of honor for we white stuntmen who were trying to earn respect from our Chinese counterparts. In *Dragon Fury*, I was impressed by how much damage Robameice Deimikor had to endure during his final six-minute fight against the former king of taking-a-licking-and-keep-on-ticking: Wen Jiang-long. When you fight an actor who gets hurt and hit as much as Wen does, you don't mind getting hit by him, because similar to Jackie Chan, he can dish it out as well as he can take it.

After serving a prison sentence for accidentally killing his foreman during a lumberyard mishap, Pai Lung (Wen Jiang-long) returns home to find that his fiancee, Snow, has pity-married the foreman's lackadaisical son, Shu Hu (Zhang Ji-ping). Shu Hu's sister Miss Chu (Hsu Feng) is out for revenge against Pai, and the lumberyard has fallen under the greedy control of an evil white ghost (which is what Caucasians are called in China) who cheatingly bought the property because he discovered gold "in them thar hills." Because of the underhanded way he got the deed and subsequent way he beat Shu Hu to death, the foreigner frames Pai for the murder. Pai becomes a fugitive and must expose the white mangler to prove his innocence before the local Inspector or Miss Chu catches up and remangles Pai back to prison.

After word spread that Bruce Lee's fights were shot at normal speed, other successful fighting actors like Wen Jiang-long decided to follow suit. The problem with this is that it exposes sloppy kung fu, and that's what happens with this film. Perhaps because he accepts that the experiment failed, Wen reverts back to undercranking the camera toward the film's end. This change is apparent during his fight with Deimikor, but that's fine because the fight looks exhausting.

In kung fu films, it's a popular gag to have the hero get lassoed by several ropes and have to come up with a great and smooth way to escape the bondage while being treated like a hogtied cow. Rope-fighting choreography reveals the creativity of the kung fu instructor and his understanding of rope trapping, which can look spectacular on-screen.

When Wen reverse neck-flips a thug up and over his shoulder, it caught my eye. The stuntman's neck and head are facing skyward when Wen grabs his neck and forces the stuntman's body to roll up and over Wen's back. The stuntman's gasping face says it all—a simple yet dangerous move. Hong Kong's stuntmen back then didn't always get the recognition they deserved: ultra-low wages, terrible working conditions, wearing the same costumes weeks on end without the clothes being washed, and taking a lot of physical punishment from actors who didn't know how to fight or control their power. It's never too late to show appreciation to anyone for anything. Way to go, men! You guys are the backbone of the kung fu industry, and that is one reason kung fu films have so many spine-tingling moments.

Because Bruce Lee was the ultimate heroic star when he died at an early age, we never, ever saw him take a licking on camera as bad as Jackie Chan and Wen Jiang-long. To me, Wen is one of the little-known action-star heroes who never got the praise he deserves for his efforts and physical sacrifices in his early films.

Titleography: *Duel in Forest*; *Duel at Forest*; *Forest Duel*. Translation—*Fire Encircles the Maple Forest River Crossing*. Based on the Chinese translation, the use of *Forest* in the English titles makes sense (although it is really a lumberyard). There is a major duel at the end of the film that is partially shot in a forest, but the trees are not maple. *River Crossing* refers to the foreigner crossing into China. **MA Percentage: 38.11%**

DRAGON LEE VS. THE 5 BROTHERS

五大弟子 (1978—S. Korea) **89m. FI: Cui Min-kui. NOT/LOT: None; NOF/LOF: 13/ 21m 39s.** D: Kim Si-hyeon. C: Dragon Lee, Yuen Qiu, Lee Ye-min, Cui Min-kui, Kim Kee-joo, Kwon Il-su, Han Myeong-hwan, Hong Xing-zhong.

Bruce Lee in a Korean period-piece film … I don't think so.

In the late 1880s in China, an anti-Ching rebel who is dying gives Mr. Han (Dragon Lee) a secret bracelet with the hope that it will eventually lead Han to Mr. Chong, who is protecting a special list of anti-Ching rebels from Ching military official Yuan Shi-kai. Standing in Han's path is the ruthless Lee Xiao-shang (Lee Ye-min) and the master-of-disguise and killing-machine Silver Hand (Cui Min-kui), who leads his three harbinger-of-death henchmen. Silver Hand and his henchmen are apparently four of five former kung fu brothers from the Shaolin Temple. Just when Han is harrowed by hoards of hit men, the odds even out when in comes the fifth "good" brother, a swordswoman (Yuen Qiu; the cigarette landlady in *Kung Fu Hustle*) who is part Angela Mao Ying and part Cheng Pei-pei.

Although not a Korean-themed film per se, the Korean connection to Yuan Shi-kai is valid. In 1885, Yuan was appointed by the Chinese as the Imperial Resident of Seoul with orders to basically protect Korea and Chinese interests from the Japanese. Japan eventually became dissatisfied with their holdings in Korea, and that led Yuan to essentially skulk back to China. Because of Yuan's lack of spine in Korea, it opened the doors for the First Sino-Japanese War and left Korea at the merciless mercy of the Japanese.

One thing that is barmy with South Korean and Taiwanese kung fu films is their horrendous hokeyness, which bends your mind and makes your eyes laugh. In this film, there are several flying steel-fan gags and flying hat tricks. They occur three times each—it's almost as if they did it three times to make it a hat trick!

Seeing Dragon Lee in a Chinese period-piece costume, sporting a queue and doing a Bruce Lee impersonation is just as out of place as a skunk in a perfume factory. Of all the Bruceploitation actors in the Lee-ward winds of copycat-dom, Dragon Lee's facial features resemble Bruce Lee's the most, but Dragon overdoes the patented Bruce neck-craning movements.

As the film's saving grace, actress Yuen Qiu's swordswoman uses twin swords like Pei-pei's Golden Swallow character in *Come Drink With Me* (1966) and kicks with Mao Ying's signature wide-eyed gaze in *Enter the Dragon*. When Han and the good Shaolin 'brother" unite to fight the senior local Manchu official Xiao-shang, with wire-enhanced head stomping, Xiao-shang is suddenly faced with 10 opponents—five Hans and five female swordswomen. It is simple, effective and as funny as a nickel-and-dime store selling you X-ray specs. You swear you can see your bones by wearing them but you're actually just seeing double like Xiao-shang is seeing quintuple. How many of you out there bought X-ray specs just to look at your hands?

Titleography: *The Angry Dragon*; *The Five Brothers*. Translation—*The Five Principle Disciples*. *The 5 Brothers* is in reference to five kung fu brothers and not blood relations. Because it is a Dragon Lee film, he fights with excessive Bruce Lee-like scowls and definitely looks like an angry dragon. **MA Percentage: 24.33%**

DRAGON LIVES AGAIN, THE

李三腳威震地獄門 (1977—Hong Kong) **87m. MAI: Bruce Leung, Liang Shao-song. NOT/LOT: 2/ 1m 48s; NOF/LOF: 28/ 30m 43s.** D: Luo Qi. C: Bruce Leung, Shen Yi-long, Tang Ching, Alexander, Cheung Lik, Hon Gwok-choi, Yuen Xiao-tian, Fang Ye, Gera.

If there were ever a Bruceploitation film that would make Bruce Lee roll over in his grave, this is the one. As it turns out, the opening credit sequences of this kung fu fantasy/comedy film parodies several genres of martial arts films (as well as a few in Hollywood) and inspired the opening credit sequence for Jackie Chan's *Half a Loaf of Kung Fu* (1978).

The film opens with Bruce Lee's (Bruce Leung) sheet-covered corpse lying at the Chinese Gates of Hell as various concubines of emperors past admire the large bulge protruding at groin level from Lee's sheet. The Hong Kong industry insiders were well aware of Lee's "affairs," so the bulge and the Chinese title are analogies to express Lee's alleged indiscretions. The English translation of the Chinese title is *Lee's Famous Third Leg Shakes the Gates of Hell*. This notion is further exasperated when Lee realizes his weakness and apologizes to his wife Linda. The "third leg" joke appears in a different incarnation later in the movie.

When the bad spirits of the underworld are unhappy with the way things are being run, the Exorcist plans to usurp the God of the Underworld. To stop the Exorcist, he enlists the help of James Bond, Zatoichi, Emmanuelle (title character from many European soft-porn films), The Godfather, Clint Eastwood's spaghetti Western alter ego and Dracula. With the promise of being able to return to Earth, Lee agrees to help the God of the Underworld and begins to teach *wing chun* kung fu to his helpers, such as the One-Armed Swordsman, Popeye and Kwai Chang Caine.

Compared to many other Leung films, the choreography in this movie is not up to par, especially compared to the *Incredible Master Beggars* (1979), which contains some of his best stuff from the 1970s. Leung experimented too much with the hand-held camera, and there are a lot of shifty camera movements. The sea-sickness-inducing motions are further compounded by Leung's shifty body motions, which are similar to the Tourette's syndrome character in the Thai action film *Chocolate* (2008). The choreography also featured too many sequences that use a tight angle to capture Leung running and rapidly punching his opponents at the same time. It is supposed to give the illusion of speed, power and intensity, but over-use of the technique makes the fights look ragged and piecemeal. Wackiness reaches unprecedented lunacy when Lee must fight a hoard of murderous mummies. Unfortunately, this spoof poofs.

Titleography: *Deadly Hands of Kung Fu*. Translation—see above martial-ogy. The English titles are pretty generic, but the *Deadly Hands of Kung Fu* title is similar to the Bruceploitation film *Bruce Lee's Deadly Kung Fu* (1976). **MA Percentage: 37.38%**

DRAGON MISSILE, THE

飛龍斬 (1976—Hong Kong) **82m. FI: Tang Chia, Yuen Cheung-yan. NOT/LOT: None; NOF/LOF: 15/ 10m 6s.** D: Ho Meng-hua. C: Liu Yung, Lo Lieh, Yan Nan-xi, Ku Feng, Jiang Yang, Liu Hui-ru, Yang Chi-ching, Xu Hsao-chiang, Fan Mei-sheng, Hao Lu-ren, Ou-Yang Sha-Fei.

The road sign "Landscaping Ahead" usually means someone is cutting down trees, shrubbery and/or grass, but it could also mean someone is cutting a person's hair. In *Dragon Missile*, "Landscaping a Head" takes on a new meaning.

Si Ma-zhuen (Lo Lieh) is a personal bodyguard and killing machine for a heartless Lord (Ku Feng), who has seven days left to live unless he can procure the Longevity Rattan of a Thousand Years herb to cure the Two Birds Worship-

ping the Phoenix boil on his back. It certainly sounds like a super-serious health problem requiring a bizarre cure to boot, and the venerable Dr. Fu (Hao Lu-ren) tells the Lord that his good friend Hermit Tan (Yang Chi-ching) is the only man he knows who possesses the herb. Si is sent to find the honorable hermit, but before he leaves, he is told to kill Dr. Fu.

Si wears two long-bladed weapons like an "X" on his back called Flying Beheaders. When he throws them, the blades helicopter around and boomerang back into his hands. While in flight, the razor-sharp blades sound like Kilaak spacecraft from the Japanese *kaiju* monster film *Destroy All Monsters* (1968), ending with an eerie Moog synthesizer riff as they nestle back into Si's hands.

The ruthless Lord trusts no one and sends six assassins to accompany Si, telling them to do whatever it takes to get the herb, even if it means killing Si. The seven killers find the Hermit, kill him and steal the herb. Moments later, the herb is nabbed from Si by a masked man with powerful Iron Fingers kung fu, who turns out to be Hermit Tan's kung fu student and longtime student in herbology Er Long (Liu Yung). Er Long and Si are former kung fu brothers, and Si recognizes his signature moves. When Si visits Er Long and his blind mother (Ou-Yang Sha-Fei), Si retrieves the herb and beheads the mother.

Meanwhile, the six assassins sent to monitor Si have all greedily outwitted themselves. However, the female killer Miss Sha (Liu Hui-ru), who can summon three knife blades from her hands like X-Men's Wolverine, decides to team up with Er Long and Hermit Tan's daughter Tan Xiao-li to figure out a way to defeat Si's spinning swords of silent termination. The answer lies with the village fisherman.

Still from *The Dragon Missile* © Celestial Pictures Ltd. All rights reserved.

Director Ho Meng-hua told me that *The Flying Guillotine* was one of his favorite films to make, partially because he dug Chinese history and the tumultuous times of Ching Emperor Yong Zhen. Yong Zhen burned down the Shaolin Temples and commissioned secret weapons to use against his opponents. Nobody really knows what the weapons looked like because those who saw them never lived to talk about it. Ho's fascination for this kind of secret weaponry once again comes to a head as he creates another new-fangled beheading weapon in this film.

A final note: When Ming loyalists were fleeing the Chings, many of them hid with fishermen. Based on how the fishermen interacted with the fish, the Ming loyalists developed the Fish Gate style of kung fu (*yue men chuen*) by mimicking how the fishermen cast their nets on the water. One wonders whether director Ho had this in mind at the film's end.

Titleography: *The Guillotine*; *Flying Dragon Cat*; *Flying Dragon Sword*. Translation— *Flying Dragon Beheader*. The Chinese title is the title weapon Si uses. *The Guillotine* taps into Ho's cult classic *The Flying Guillotine* (1975). Titles with *Flying Dragon* in them and the Chinese title infer the film is about some kind of weapon. **MA Percentage: 12.32%** SHAW BROTHERS

DRAGON PRINCESS

Hissatsu Onna Kenshi (1976—Japan) **79m. FI: Uncredited. NOT/LOT: 6/ 6m 49s; NOF/LOF: 17/ 16m 39s.** D: Yutaka Kohira. C: Etsuko Shihomi, Sonny Chiba, Yasuaki Kurata, Jiro Chiba, Bin Amatsu, Masashi Ishibashi, Tatsuya Kameyama, Shunsuke Kariya, Yoshi Kato.

When I first saw this title, I assumed the film might be one of those Japanese fantasy samurai movies in the vein of *Legend of the Eight Samurai* (1983), but it is essentially a story about the spirit of karate and just how far a father will go to make sure his daughter studies as hard as possible. It is similar to a famous Chinese legend about a father who tied his son to a tree and would beat him with a cane every day. Over time, the son became immune to the beatings, and eventually he was able to take the stick away and defend himself.

In this film, Nikaido (Bin Amatsu) wants to be the top karate instructor, and he corners karate expert Higaki (Sonny Chiba) and his daughter, Yumi, in a grain house to find out who's best. Higaki is clearly the superior fighter, but Nikaido then summons a group of eccentrically evil weapon-wielding hit men to his side, putting Yumi in harm's way. With a dart in his eye, a *sai* stuck through his hand and a samurai sword piercing his shoulder, Higaki is put in a pretty bleak place. But just when Nikaido is about to administer the killing blow, he looks into the innocent eyes of Yumi, has a change of heart and warns Higaki to get out of town. Nikaido leaves. Yumi must pull the dart out of her father's eye, and it becomes the eye-opening moment in Yumi's life that leads her down a path of revenge. But who is the revenge for, her father or herself?

Years pass filled with intense karate training and her father's constant challenges to have Yumi (Etsuko Shihomi) beat him up. Yumi doesn't quite understand the purpose of all the training and writes in her diary that she hates karate. One night, Higaki reads the diary and is deeply hurt because he loves Yumi. But regardless of her heart and crippled karate spirit, he must continue to push her to become better in karate than himself and Nikaido. One day during training, Yumi cracks and lets loose at her father in a blind rage, defeating him. It is a moment of great pride for Higaki, whose weary body can now die in peace, knowing that he has taught her the skills necessary to avenge him. While snowflakes fall outside, Higaki lies on his deathbed inside with Yumi by his side. His dying words help her understand why he worked her so hard. Yumi accepts that her path is the path of revenge.

Yumi's chance for vengeance comes when Nikaido holds a karate tournament. When Nikaido learns Yumi is back in town, he worries that if he or any of his men lose to Yumi in the tournament, it would be a great loss of face. To be safe, Nikaido plans to kill her before the tournament. But Yumi finds an ally in *karateka* Masahiko Okizaki (Yasuaki Kurata). They unite like Godzilla and Rodan did to defeat the dreaded three-headed creature Ghidoral, but this time the monsters are the deadly triad of Nikaido bodyguards, tournament competitors and Nikaido himself. It's a fight of monstrous proportions.

Unfortunately, the choreography is monstrously bad. The fights are shot in close-up with the oft-used shaky hand-held camera, which after a while can give you a headache. It is made more painful when the filmmakers zoom in and out during the same shot and incorporate Dutch angles to emphasize heroic moments. But like any film that features talent like Sonny Chiba, Etsuko Shihomi and Yasuaki Kurata, there are many wonderful karate moments, even if they often get lost in the camerawork.

Titleography: *Sonny Chiba's Dragon Princess*; *Which Is Stronger, Karate or the Tiger?* When stars are especially famous, distributors will sometimes stick their names in the title to attract audiences, thus the title *Sonny Chiba's Dragon Princess*. Yumi is the eponymous *Dragon Princess*. *Karate* probably refers to Chiba and Yumi, while the *Tiger* is Nikaido. **MA Percentage: 29.70%**

DRAGON, THE HERO

雜家高手 (1979—Taiwan) **80m. MAI: Deng De-xiang. NOT/LOT: 16/ 4m 35s; NOF/LOF: 22/ 32m 33s.** D: Godfrey Ho. C: John Liu, Tino Wong Cheung, Gao Fei, Dragon Lee, Bolo Yeung, Chen Lou.

Hate and bickering can lead to the death of people, countries and kung fu, which consequently can often shape the children of these conflicts. Although the children may grow up in the presence of ignorance, they can move down the path of forgiveness.

About 1200 years ago, there existed a little-known technique called Shaolin rock fist. Whether this film is about that is unclear, but it does reveal one of the many ways that kung fu styles have disappeared over the centuries. *Dragon, the*

Hero opens by explaining the friendship between Shaolin-trained martial artists Du Gang (John Liu) and Tang Xiong (Tino Wong Cheung). The pair learn the Shaolin Rock Hitting Fist from Monk Shan Ling, who lives on Kuei Mountain. Shan Ling may be based on Kuei Shang Ling Lu (A.D. 771 to A.D. 853), who was a master of Ch'an (Zen), a major movement in Chinese Buddhism. The two friends become martial arts champions by combining their knowledge to create the Double Rock Hitting Fist skill. Later in life, they become bitter enemies. During a fight, Du kills Tang, and the art supposedly dies with him. Yet each man has a son, Du Wu-shen (Liu again) and Tang Jia-lu (Wong again). Twenty years after the death of Tang, the sons reunite to keep the style alive for one more generation.

Du is in town to investigate a man named Tien, not knowing that Tang has been tracking him and plans to kill him to avenge his father's death. However, Du has elevated his kung fu by combining what his father taught him with cobra leg kicks and *mi zhong chuen*. However, something big is going down in town, and it is the kind of thing that would make a clown frown. Enter the vermin villains. Mad Dog Tien Hou (Chen Lou) is a pale, Dracula-looking scallywag who is wheelchair-ridden because a dog bit off his private parts after Tien raped the daughter of the dog's master. Tien partners with Ma Ti (Gao Fei)—a borderline psychotic who uses an egg timer and black magic to improve his kung fu—to form a Chinese antique smuggling ring with a bunch of sleazy foreigners. So when the sons reunite against Mad Dog and Ma's black-magic-induced Intermingle kung fu, barmy outrageousness steals the film.

Actor Bolo Yeung revisits his gorilla ways from *Bruce and Shaolin Kung Fu* with a small role as King Kong. With fake hair stuck on his chest, Bolo frets and struts his five minutes on the screen and is heard from no more. This is one of John Liu's better martial arts performances; he does so much more than just his patented *taekwondo* techniques or usual kicking maneuvers. (See *Mar's Villa.*) What also really enhances the action is the almost subtle use of hand-held camerawork and creative track shots in several of the fight scenes. But there is one major point of "what were they thinking" contention. Dragon Lee's character in this movie goes beyond the definition of non sequitur. While doing a poor Bruce Lee impersonation, he fights using two *nuns*—he uses two pairs of *nunchaku*, but each has only one stick (half a nunchaku, hence nun) connected to a piece of chain. Time to use that fast-forward button on your DVD.

Titleography: *Dragon on Fire*; *Dragon the Great*; *Muscle of the Dragon*; *The Dragon, the Hero*. Translation—*Not a Specialist But Big in Martial Arts* (i.e., meaning like a jack-of-all-trades and a master of none). I can only assume that because Dragon Lee is in this film, all the English titles use *Dragon,* which is ironic considering Lee is as important to this film as watering your lawn is during a hurricane. The Chinese title refers to Gao Fei's character wanting to understand as many kung fu styles as possible to create his own Intermingle Fist skill. **MA Percentage: 46.42%**

DREAMING FISTS WITH SLENDER HANDS

夢拳蘭花手 and 師娘怪拳 (1979—Taiwan) **90m. KFD: Sun Xin-xiang, Sun Shu-pei. NOT/LOT: 13/ 10m 48s; NOF/LOF: 10/ 18m 37s.** D: Liao Chiang-lin. C: Lung Fei, Hu Jin, Sun Xin-xiang, Liu Li-zu, Dai Liang, Wu Chia-xiang, Liu De-kai, Jing Guo-zhong, Hou Ba-wei.

It is the Taiwanese version of *Clan of the White Lotus* (1979) meets *Drunken Master* (1979) a la *Buddhist Fist* (1979). In the film, everyone's kung fu is a notch below the Hong Kong heroes but a notch above the ridiculous and the sublime, including an overweight bungler learning an art that's a cross between embroidery kung fu (white lotus kung fu) and the kung fu of He Xiang-gu, the female drunken god who Jackie Chan's character in *Drunken Master* does not take seriously. It's yet another film joining the ranks of Suexploitation. (See *Dance of the Drunk Mantis.*)

When the inscrutable Shen Piao (Lung Fei; Betty in the 2002 film *Kung Pow: Enter the Fist*) wants to be the supreme master of Chao Village and sends out his hooligans to soccer-kick everybody into the net, two street-bum brothers—the scruffy Ho Hu (Sun Xin-xiang) and portly Sun Lung (Jing Guo-zhong)—pathetically try to fight back. Ho gets arrested and sent to prison, but he is befriended by a Beggar Su-like cellmate (Hou Ba-wei) who teaches him sleeping fist kung fu. Sun is on the run and ends up under the gun, learning fun fu from the local brothel owner and queen prostitute Miss Ho (Hu Jin), which is not intended to be a slangy 2008 pun.

The action is the often-seen Taiwanese tracing fight affairs using chintzy-looking slip slaps that vaguely look like the zippity-whippety worn sequences from countless Hong Kong films. The training sequences drag on a bit too long, especially when the dumpy disciple Sun has to have his feet bound, wear traditional female shoes in which the sole of the shoe is a round piece of raised rubber in the middle of the shoe, dress up in drag and act effeminate.

When the two brothers unite for the final battle against Shen Piao, they combine their sleeping and effeminate kung fu to defeat Shen. The creativity of the choreographers made this film enjoyable to watch. They use the exact same bouncing fight rhythm that Jackie Chan uses in his later 1970s kung fu films. A major difference between this film and the many others before it is that the male student learns kung fu from a female teacher.

An interesting historical note: Chinese foot binding originated in the Tang Dynasty (A.D. 618 to A.D. 907) and was inspired by a Tang emperor who fell in love with a concubine who wrapped her wee feet in silk and then cutely danced around the court. Foot size then became a measure of a woman's beauty, so the four small toes were wrapped under the boot and tightly bound by material. Over time, the bones would break and eventually the woman would have a pointy foot with a protruding big toe that looked like a knife point.

Titleography: *Kung Fu Kids.* Translations—*Dreaming Fist and Orchid Hands; The Kung Fu Teacher's Wife's Strange Fist Technique.* There are actually several films made in the 1980s that are titled *Kung Fu Kids* because they are about children doing martial arts, so this film really does not fit the bill. However, the two heroes act like immature kids by pouting, getting in trouble and whining. The Chinese titles reflect the notion of sleep and something female (*Orchid* and *Slender Hands* or *Wife's Strange Fist*). **MA Percentage: 32.69%**

DRUG ADDICTS, THE

吸毒者 (1973—Hong Kong) **95m. FI: Liu Chia-rong, Chan Chuen, Huang Pei-ji. NOT/LOT: 4/ 1m 58s; NOF/LOF: 10/ 10m 38s.** D: David Chiang. C: Ti Lung, Wang Chung, Li Si-chi, Qin Pei, Lu Di, Jiang Dao, Lee Hoi-san, Feng Yi, Deng Di-xiang.

Around the time of this film, actors Ti Lung and David Chiang, who were once Shaw Brothers' most successful cinematic duo, were starting to exchange words. In a few years, these once-close friends would split up. Before that happened, in an effort to mend the rift, Shaw Brothers had the two actors begin directing careers. However, two things pretty much ended their excursion into film directing: For some reason, Ti and Chiang would cast the other as the lead in their respective films (director Chiang cast Ti as his lead, and vice-versa). Ti and Chiang's early efforts, such as this film, veered away from what they were good at and known for—martial arts. These early works were hard-pressed for fights and action, which also undoubtedly helped bring their careers as directors to a halt. Although over the next 35 years Chiang did direct 12 more films (two in the 1970s), his eye for directing martial arts did not evolve, and he turned to comedy and drama.

In this film, opium addict Kuan Cheng-chun (Ti Lung) has a Bruce Lee haircut and also teaches kung fu at a police station, which is certainly a peculiar set of circumstances. In addition, Tseng Chien (Wang Chung), his drug dealer friend, is a man with a conscience and is devastated by what the drugs are doing to Kuan's mind and body. I can't resist pointing out the gaps in logic: Don't Kuan's police friends notice something is wrong him? And what's with his best friend being a drug dealer who is upset that he's taking drugs? Something is wrong with this picture.

In any case, Tseng locks Kuan in a room, where he flips out for about 10 minutes. The next morning, he is off drugs and vows to work with the police inspector (Feng Yi, who plays the judo teacher with Coke-bottle glasses in the 1972 film *Fist of Fury*) to take down the head of the drug ring, who happens to be Tseng's boss (Lu Di). Meanwhile, realizing that Kuan is going to be a problem, the boss makes all his associates and Tseng take a blood oath of brotherhood. He then orders Tseng to kill Kuan, or else the drug addict girl that everyone in the film seems concerned about, Yuan Li (Li Si-chi), will be killed. The heroes hatch a plan to fake Kuan's death so Tseng can look good in the boss's eyes, which would allow Kuan and Tseng to find Yuan and eventually expose the boss. But it is their plan that gets exposed first, leading to a race against the clock for

Yuan, Kuan and Tseng to save each other.

After avidly studying kickboxing for the film *Duel of Fists* (1971), Ti got to use his newly acquired skills in this film. On some occasions, his new techniques do add a certain animalistic intensity to his fights, especially when Yuan's life is a stake. But to me, his best action moment is a stunt in which he rolls down a long cement staircase; each stair drop-off is rather high, and to do this without wearing any protective padding and with very little training or prep time is very impressive. In Hong Kong film, when it is time for a stunt, it is discussed, practiced (if you are lucky and there is time), and then you just do it. That's fine for a stuntman, but tough for a leading man.

Titleography: *Drug Addict.* Translation—*Drug Addict.* **MA Percentage: 13.26%** SHAW BROTHERS

DRUNKEN MASTER

醉拳 (1979—Hong Kong) **111m. MAI: Hsu Hsia, Yuen Woo-ping. NOT/LOT: 14/ 15m; NOF/LOF: 13/ 35m 47s.** D: Yuen Woo-ping. C: Jackie Chan, Yuen Xiao-tian, Hwang Jang-lee, Yuen Shen-yi, Dean Shek, Hsu Hsia, Brandy Yuen, Linda Lin Ying, Tino Wong, Shan Guai, Huang Ha, Lee Chun-wa, Lin Jiao.

Drunken Master is a landmark movie in the kung fu film genre and arguably one of Jackie Chan's best films. Chan plays Chinese folk hero Huang Fei-hung who is not a heroic defender of the downtrodden, a healer of the poor or a king of the lion dance. These hero stereotypes come from portrayals by actors like Kwan Tak-hing's Cantonese Huang Fei-hung movies (99 of them between 1949 and 1970), Ku Feng (see *Master of Kung Fu*) and Shi Zhong-tian (see *Rivals of Kung Fu*). Chan's version is a cheeky, fun-loving upstart teen whose kung fu skills often inadvertently land him in trouble. The serious overtones are further distanced when the film's characters lack the traditional queue hairstyle required by law during the Ching Dynasty. It is comparable to a Wild West American hero driving a car instead of riding a horse—it gives a comedic feel. Yuen Xiao-tian portrays the legendary Su Qi-er, aka Beggar Su (one of the 10 Tigers of Canton), who teaches Huang drunken fist kung fu as a means of learning to control his aberrant behavior. Of course, Huang resists with all the teenage angst he can muster. However, after he has a humiliating kung fu run-in with a strange kick fighter, Huang takes his drunken kung fu more seriously than an English fan cheering for his country in the 1966 World Cup final against Germany. Huang gets to use his newfound drunken fist skills to fight for his father's life because the mysterious kicker turns out to be the abominable iceman assassin. Undoubtedly hired by a Ching official, Yan is hired to kill Huang's father, Huang Chi-ying (Lin Jiao), who is also one of the 10 Tigers of Canton. The hand-flapping that Yan does is an advanced white crane skill, which Jackie uses in *Snake and Crane Arts of Shaolin* (1978).

The key scene in the film is when Jackie Chan performs the respective movements that are associated with the Eight Immortals. These Chinese mythological gods or fairies are able to transfer their power into a tool that can give life or destroy evil. The allegorical immortal leader of drunken kung fu is Lu Don-bin, who bears a sword behind his back, which he uses to ward off evil. He is also known for having a famous dream that has become known as his Yellow Millet Dream. The other seven immortals are Chuan Zhong-li, who carries a fan; Cao Guo-ji, the newest of the immortals, known for his jade tablet; Iron-Crutch Li, who after being reincarnated into a crippled beggar became known for fighting with a limp; Lan Cai-he, maybe a boy or a girl who is always depicted as wearing one shoe; Han Xiang-zi, known for holding a flute; Elder Zhang Guo, the only immortal considered to be a *chi gong* (*qigong*) master; and He Xiang-gu, the only true female immortal, who carries a lotus flower and practices the one style our protagonist Huang has difficulty with. As a side note, Chan's character in *The Forbidden Kingdom* (2008) is Lu Dong Bin.

Yuen's Beggar Su is an old, gray-haired sot dressed in a floppy hat, holey kung fu shoes and ragged clothing. He fights best when he's drunk as a skunk. In real life he was born Su Tsao in Hunan and made a living by performing martial arts in the street with his sister. When they eventually arrived in Canton, he opened a martial arts school. An expert of Shaolin pole techniques, he preferred the life of a wanderer. Historically, Su never taught Huang kung fu. That fell on the shoulder of Huang Chi-ying.

Titleography: *Drunk Monkey in the Tiger's Eye*; *Drunken Monkey in the Tiger's Eyes*; *Eagle Claw, Snake Fist, Cat's Paw, Part 2*; *Drunk Monkey*; *Challenge*. Translation—*Drunken Fist*. When Huang Fei-hung confronts Beggar Su, he flashes some monkey kung fu. Also, assassin Yan appears to the untrained eye to be doing tiger kung fu. *Drunk Monkey in the Tiger's Eyes* is also an attempt to mimic the rhythm of *Snake in the Eagle's Shadow*. The *Eagle Claw* title is a further embellishment positioning the film as a sequel to *Snake in the Eagle's Shadow*. The Chinese translation refers to the titular kung fu style. Unfortunately, this film's clout is diluted by the English dub version renaming Huang Fei-hung as Freddy, Yan as Thunderfoot and Beggar Su as Sam Seed. We should "Su" them. **MA Percentage: 45.75%**

DUEL, THE

大決鬥 (1971—Hong Kong) 105m. Fl: Yuen Cheung-yan, Tang Chia. **NOT/ LOT: None; NOF/LOF: 26/ 25m 42s.** D: Chang Cheh. C: Ti Lung, David Chiang, Yang Chi-ching, Ku Feng, Cheng Kang-yeh, Chuan Yuan, Hong Liu, Wang Ping, Yu Hui, Li Yun-zhong.

Back in 1978, when I was president of the Chinese Student Association at Cornell University, one of the first things I initiated was Kung Fu Film Night. My roommates and I would get 16 mm Shaw Brothers films from New York City's Chinatown, and one of the first films we rented was *The Duel*. Back then I did not know how famous Ti Lung, David Chiang and director Chang Cheh were, or that they were known as the Iron Triangle. The most memorable parts of the film were Chiang's character coughing and covering his mouth with a white handkerchief while the haunting music of the *gu zhen* twanged in the background, Ti Lung slashing and knifing his way out of a building while protecting his prostitute girlfriend, and the final bloodbath in the rain. Watching the film 30 years later, those same images still stick out, but I have a different appreciation for the fights and how they tell an emotional story.

The film is set in the Roaring '20s during the era of warlordism in China (see *The Anonymous Heroes*), when the country was split into military cliques. Two rival groups are at odds: the good guys, led by Shen Tian-hung (Yang Chi-ching), and the bad guys, who until recently were led by Liu Hsing-bang. He was assassinated by Liao Xiao-yi, his nephew. At Liu's funeral, there are scores to settle. Shen goes to the funeral and is joined by his trusted right-hand man, Gan Wen-bin (Chuan Yuan); his loyal adopted son, Tang Ren-jie (Ti Lung); and hired assassin Jian Nan the Rambler (David Chiang). Toting funeral wreaths with hidden knives, they march over to the funeral, which becomes an even bigger celebration of death when Shen's men win the day and become the No. 1 clan around. During the melee, Rambler and Ren-jie find mutual respect for each other's *dao fa* (knife skills), and Ren-jie saves Rambler's life.

However, Shen and his men don't have much time to enjoy their victory because during a celebratory feast, Liao and his lackeys crash the meal. The lights go out, and by the time they're back on, Shen has been assassinated. But by whom? If word gets out that the opposing warlord succeeded, it would make Shen's clan appear weak. After much convincing, Ren-jie agrees to take

the blame (as though he had committed a traitorous act), and Gan takes over the operation. Gan tells Ren-jie with great reverence that he should head down south and stay there for a few years until things have cleared.

But as money from the family dries up and attempts are made on Ren-jie's life, he senses something is awry. He heads home to find that Gan has united with the enemy and become a ruthless warlord. Gan has turned the love of Ren-jie's life, Hu Dieh (Wang Ping), into a prostitute and set his sights on killing Ren-jie and his latest ally, the Rambler, who in fact killed Ren-jie's stepfather. It's an unlikely pairing, but Ren-jie respects the Rambler and will do anything to save Hu Dieh. Ren-jie and the Rambler therefore try to take out Gan and an even bigger enemy, and we learn that Rambler is a nationalist who just wants to save and unite China.

A film character's introduction can add a chord of electricity to a movie. Although Ti is the main actor, Chiang's on-screen arrival is the most memorable. The audience first sees a hand catch an airborne knife, and then Chiang's character steps out from behind an object into frame. Glorious. Also note the metaphorical crushed-tomato scene when Shen's gang all march to attend Liu's funeral. The gang destroys a vegetable vendor's baskets of tomatoes, and the blood-red mess spews on the ground like the blood these men will soon spill at the funeral. The knife fights that feature David Chiang and Ti Lung hacking and whacking their way through legions of enemies are stimulating for the audience. The choreography is smooth as glass because Ti and Chiang seem to flow around their enemies like water running. Blood squirts, jugulars burst, and Chang Cheh's hand-held camera amplifies the energy of the visuals. There is also good use of tracking shots, in which the camera often moves from one fight to another within the same shot. Some of the characters fight with their jackets open, and the loose material flaps around, providing more motion to the action. And of course the severed arteries, impalings, and blood and guts resulting from giant bamboo spear wounds—culminating in a two-and-a-half-minute slow-motion death crawl of Ti and Chiang fighting for their lives—are to die for.

Titleography: *Duel of the Iron Fists*; *Iron Fist Pillage*; *Duel of the Shaolin Fist*. Translation—*The Big Duel*. *The Duel* is the most appropriate title; it refers to the eventual big duel between the Rambler and Tang Ren-jie. Using *Shaolin* and *Iron Fist* in the titles is a weak attempt at using generic keywords to lure viewers. **MA Percentage: 24.48%** SHAW BROTHERS

Still from *The Duel* © Celestial Pictures Ltd. All rights reserved.

DUEL FOR GOLD

火併 (1971—Hong Kong) **93m. FI: Xu Er-niu, Xu Song-hao. NOT/LOT: 1/ 1m 39s; NOF/LOF: 33/ 29m 40s.** D: Chu Yuan. C: Ivy Ling Po, Wang Ping, Chin Han, Lo Lieh, Tsung Hua, Fan Mei-sheng, Richard Chan Chun.

In real life and in this film, it does not matter how good you are with the sword when dealing with back-stabbers. Things go beyond being a pain in the neck if you can not block what you can not see.

Duel for Gold is one of a handful of early Shaw Brothers *wuxia* films that boldly feature the prominent seven-story pagoda on the Shaw Brothers' back lot; its use began to slowly disappear from the film limelight because it became too recognized as a landmark. Then perhaps, in a small way, this is a landmark film.

Two street-performing acrobatic sisters, Yu Ying (Wang Ping) and Yu Yin (Ivy Ling Po), weasel their way into the local Fu Lai Money Bureau (an old Chinese-style bank) headed by the ethical Wen Li-hsien (Richard Chan Chun). They are soon discovered to be dirty rats who try to gnaw their way out of trouble like beavers in a collapsing dam. Once they break through and escape, trouble flows like water from a dike that has lost the little Dutch boy's finger. The leader of the acrobatic sisters, Hua Dieh-er (Tsung Hua), and the Invisible Loner Teng Chi-ying (Lo Lieh), join the flood of betrayals, two-faced facades and misleading trails. The river of greed ends with blood-squirting intrigue that spills over silver and gold.

The film begins with bodies strewn on the ground and a voice-over describing what had happened and that the film is about the events leading up to the bodies on the ground. It is almost like watching *Titanic* (1997). You already know the ending, but the journey is still interesting as long as there are still things to discover. Such is the case for screenwriter Ni Kuang's wuxia works, which weave in more red herrings than a packet of kippers eaten during an English breakfast.

Still from *Duel for Gold* © Celestial Pictures Ltd. All rights reserved

This film beautifully features a form of fight choreography known as the swish-crash-fly method, which became popular as movie budgets increased and the stuntmen got better. In many of the fights, there are fewer actual sword techniques per shot because the action would get broken down into shorter sequences. The lead actor who was also the lead fighter would simply swish his or her sword through the air, which was then usually followed by a stuntman flying back and subsequently crashing onto a table, through various kinds of wooden windows and folding screens, or any other object on set that a stuntman could crash through or over. There are also a lot of "cute" gags like using chopsticks as darts at the restaurant or tossing cups of hot tea into the air and catching them still full on the end of a sword. These little vaudevillian bits are always fun to watch.

On a final note, several times throughout the movie, you will hear guitar and-drum riffs that sound like they are from Bob Kane Batman-and-Robin influenced, 1960 cartoon *Courageous Cat and Minute Mouse*. Is there no limit to the wildness of the soundtracks? Talk about stretching the copycat mentality.

Titleography: As of this writing, no alternative titles could be found. Translation—*Fiery Feud. Fiery* in respect to fierce. **MA Percentage: 33.67%** SHAW BROTHERS

DUEL OF FIST

拳擊 (1971—Hong Kong) **104m. FI: Liu Chia-liang, Tang Chia. NOT/LOT: 2/ 1m 51s; NOF/LOF: 27/ 19m 1s.** D: Chang Cheh. C: Ti Lung, David Chiang, Li Ching, Chen Hsing, Wang Chung, Liu Lan-ying, Ku Feng.

This is Hong Kong's first film that delves into the world of Thai kickboxing. It's a movie that actor Ti Lung practiced kickboxing for several months before shooting, and when the fights were being shot, much of the choreography ended up using heavy contact for authenticity. It is also one of the few kung fu films that Ti Lung has done in which he openly admits that he was proud of his fighting work.

Dressed in loud, clear and somewhat queer clothes (see *Singing Killer* and the discussion on Teddy Boys), Fan Ke (David Chiang) travelogues to Thailand in search of his long-lost brother Wen Lieh (Ti Lung) who he has never met. Fan carries Wen's childhood picture around with him and is told that the grown-up Wen has an anchor tattoo on his left arm. Fan Ke eventually ends up at a kickboxing match and spots an anchor tattoo on the arm of a fighter. The unknown man, who of course turns out to be Wen, refuses to take a dive against an opponent aptly named Killer (Ku Feng)—the main moneymaking face masher for the local fight fixer and "your dead if you disobey me" gang boss Chiang Ren (Chen Hsing). After Killer bites the dust, Fan and Wen go after the sleazy Chiang before he can hang his dirty laundry out to dry.

Muay Thai is considered a sport and not a martial art and has only been around since 1930. It is actually a watered-down version of a more vigorous and lethal form of the ancient martial art called *muay boran*, which comes from an even older version of *pahuyuth* (systems of Thai martial arts) called *ling lom,* which means "air monkey" and has its foundations in *krabi krabong.* Although the ancient forms of Thai's pahuyuth are seeped in Buddhist notions, the ling lom aspect of muay boran has its foundation in the Hindu monkey god Hanuman. Traditional muay boran fights were actually dances to honor the story *The Legend of Ramayana.* These dances portrayed fights between the various deities involved, which of course include the hero Hanuman.

Although many parts of the boxing matches in the movie have an authentic ring to them, there's a peculiar image that resonates with contradiction: Moments before a bout, Wen is seen smoking a cigarette. It is similar to how Jackie Chan acts on set, choreographing and demonstrating a fight scene with a cigarette hanging out of his mouth.

The nonboxing ring fights use a lot of wide-angle shots, and the group fights use many hand-slapping and hand-placement moves. Rather than block the attack, the lead actor places his open hand on the leg or arm he has to block, then uses a slapping hand to "punch" the attacker out of the way. To sell this kind of choreography requires great timing by the stuntmen, and they do it in this film. Watch as David Chiang quickly and effortlessly flows from one opponent to the next, which can cloak the sloppiness of the fights because there is no sense of windups or delays. The success of this film spawned a true sequel, *The Angry Guest.*

Titleography: *Striking Fist; Duel of Fists.* Translation—*Boxing.* Although *Duel of Death* and *Striking Fist* are generic, they fit the premise of the film. The Chinese title is indeed about boxing, just not the kind of boxing a Westerner would envision back in 1971. **MA Percentage: 20.06%** SHAW BROTHERS

DUEL OF THE BRAVE ONES

踢寶 (1978—Hong Kong) **89m. FI: Wilson Tong. NOT/LOT: None; NOF/ LOF: 12/ 21m 46s.** D: Wai Man. C: Wilson Tong, John Cheung, Liu Chia-yung, Lin Wen-wei, Feng Jing-wen, Yu Tou-yun, King Lee.

As Chinese cinema started to move from old-style *wuxia* films to contemporary movies, the classic clan-vs.-clan motif gave way to the gang-vs.-gang theme. To the outside eye, the gang-vs.-gang brawl has never been as artistically pleasing or engaging as the clan-vs.-clan kung fu showdowns. This is mostly because in period pieces the costumes and weapons flow like a dance,

the fights have more spins, and the loose clothing can hide the imperfection of poor stances and awkward body and hand postures.

Thus, the English title of this film, *Duel of the Brave Ones*, has an old-style sensibility about it, but the movie does not rock and roll. Instead, it pebbles and flops.

Wilson Tong plays former gang-member Ah Sing, who turns "Queen's evidence" on his boss, Fa Kai-lung (John Cheung), for double-crossing his father. In response, Fa kidnaps Ah Sing's girlfriend, which forces Ah Sing to join a rival gang for protection, giving him the oomph to approach Fa and say, "This time, you have gone too Fa." It comes down to Ah vs. Fa, a battle of the bench warmer vs. the leave-it-to-meat cleaver.

Like many gang-vs.-gang films, they are not so much kung fu films as they are street slugfests that lose the kung fu film translation because the fighters are decked out in blue jeans and Hawaiian shirts. Furthermore, the fights often look like the bad boxing matches from the China-vs.-Japan-themed films created during the early '70s. In those, nobody looks like they know what they are doing and just flip and flop around like dying fishes stranded on the beach.

The film also reveals the importance of having an experienced fight choreographer that can make the necessary adjustments between the differing films' sets and styles of fights used in wuxia and contemporary films. In this film, the transitions of the various fighting actors experienced in period-piece films and that style of action seemed to be in limbo because Tong had not found the correct balance between his period-piece expertise and contemporary fiddle-faddle. Yet the final showdown between actors Tong and Cheung has its moments, albeit out of context with the film's overall feel—but who cares about that as long as the fight is decent.

Titleography: *Revenge of the Dragon*; *Shadow Killers*; *Struggle*; *Hong Kong Karate Hatchet Men*. Translation—*Kicking a Hole in the Ground*. The English titles are simply generic titles that make the film sound like the kind of movie you want to buy, but there are no characters named *Dragon*, or ninja-like *Shadow Killers* or even secret assassins. Sure, it is a *Struggle* (as the distributor had none when dreaming up these titles), and *Karate Hatchet Men* could not be further from the truth. The Chinese title refers to how getting out of deep trouble can be as futile as kicking a hole in the ground. **MA Percentage: 24.46%**

DYNAMITE BROTHERS

(1974—USA) **90m. KFD: Lin Zheng-yin. NOT/LOT: 1/ 49s; NOF/LOF: 6/ 8m 35s.** D: Al Adamson. C: Alan Tang, Timothy Brown, Aldo Ray, James Hong, Don Oliver, Al Richardson, Lam Ching-ying, Billy Chen Hui-yi.

Dynamite Brothers is a blast from the past, but for kung fu director Lam Ching-ying, the explosion into Hollywood would not last. With a title like this from the 1970s, it is a pity they did not call it *Dyn-o-mite*, but then again, this movie did not have many *Good Times* (1970s TV show).

Chinese illegal alien Larry Chin (Alan Tang) gets arrested and handcuffed to a recent racist cop's bust named Stud Brown (Timothy Brown). Thus begins what the filmmakers would like to think was the first *Rush Hour* motif in Hollywood. Larry must find his brother in Los Angeles, and Stud wants to help his mudslide brother Smiling Man prevent the deviously depraved Wei Chin (James Hong) from hassling him.

After working as a fight choreographer on all four of Bruce Lee's films, Lee

promised Lam that he would take him to Hollywood. Unfortunately, Lee passed away, which destroyed Lam's dreams. Because Lam was working with such a low budget, had no time to plan the fights, and the performers weren't skilled enough to fulfill his vision, Lam decided to toss in the towel and do mediocre work rather than use the film to showcase his abilities. The film was never noticed in the United States, nor was Lam. At least he had a successful career in Hong Kong, but when you get that break, regardless of the circumstances, you've got to do your best.

The opening fight on the docks when Larry sneaks into America is actually pretty smooth and flows well between the several attackers, but the fights got worse from there. Usually in Hong Kong films, the fights get better as the film proceeds because they are usually filmed in the order of the script. By the end of the movie, everyone is clicking. But in this film, the clicking was more like clucking. In the final fight, people jump off a tall castle turret one at a time but try to make the stunts look like part of the fight. During the same fight, there are several camera angles that were right out of the final *Enter the Dragon* fight. Also, similar to the final crowd melee in *Enter the Dragon*, this film takes shot sequences from earlier on in the fight and loops them several times into the final edited sequence of the same fight. So we see the same camera shot several times during the same fight.

Titleography: *Dynamite Brown*; *Killing of a Chinese Bookie*; *Stud Brown*. *Stud Brown* was the original title with the notion it would be a blaxploitation film, and in that genre the lead black hero's name was the film's title (*Dolemite, Cleopatra Jones, Foxy Brown*). But the Chinese fighter was featured more prominently so the idea was scrapped. It is possible the studios inserted *Dynamite* into the title as a means to beat *T.N.T. Jackson* to the punch because female blaxploitation hero films were popular. It is also common for studios to release films with similar titles before their competitors to steal the limelight. *Killing of a Chinese Bookie* was the Australian release title. Because back then immigration and visa policies for minorities were very strict and racist, an indication of "blackness" in the title would mean instant doom and added censorship. **MA Percentage: 10.44%**

DYNAMO

不擇手段 (1978—Hong Kong) **87m. MAI: Yuen Cheung-yan. NOT/LOT: 7/ 3m 42s; NOF/LOF: 21/ 27m 47s.** D: Wa Yat-wang. C: Bruce Li, Ku Feng, James Griffith, Jiang Dao, Peter Chan Lung, Mary Hon Ma-lee.

Please, not another film with a story about a Bruce Lee look-alike! In this case, Lee Ting-yee (Bruce Li) is discovered for some reason or another and is then primed to do Bruce Lee-ish films under a new moniker. Are we supposed to believe that he is Bruce Lee because he wears the old yellow one-piece tracksuit with black stripes? To bolster the legitimacy of the next Bruce Lee's martial arts skills, the head of the Pacific Agency, Mary, hires a kung fu teacher (Ku Feng) to train Ting-yee to win the ultimate martial arts fighting competition in the United States. To do that, he has to defeat the American champion (James Griffith), who fights for the opposing Cosmo Agency, which is owned by a two-faced white American. However, Ting-yee must throw the fight in order to save his kidnapped girlfriend. Mary is just as devious as the two-faced white American, but she claims that the ends justify the means. A man of morals, Ting-yee quits the industry—it is a pity that his morals did not lead him to quit the industry for real or at least quit doing Bruce Lee rip-offs.

Although the fights slightly improve as the film progresses, the filmmakers decide to create the illusion of more fights by editing two major fight scenes from Danny Lee's Shaw Brothers film *Bruce Lee and I* (1976). Is there no limit to the shame? The final ring fight between Lee and his American nemesis is choreographed like a wrestling match with kicks. It's shot close-up and uses dark background lighting to hide the fact that there is no crowd, although the match is supposedly taking place at a sold-out fighting venue. This technique was used in many low-budget American martial arts movies from the 1980s, many of which were made by Ng See-yuan's Seasonal Films productions.

Titleography: As of this writing, no alternative titles could be found. Translation—*Winning at All Costs*. The Chinese title reflects the attitudes of both agency heads, so it is befitting for the film. Although dynamo can refer to an extremely energetic person, there really was no real *Dynamo* in the film, but I am sure the distributors saw otherwise, thus the English title. **MA Percentage: 36.19%**

EAGLE'S CLAW

鷹爪螳螂 (1977—Hong Kong) **86m. FI: Tommy Lee. NOT/LOT: 6/ 1m 11s; NOF/LOF: 28/ 24m 7s.** D: Lee Tso-nam. C: Chi Kuan-chun, Wong Dao, Zhang Yi, Goa Fei, Liang Chia-ren, Ma Chang, Jimmy Lung Fong, Hua Lin.

In most film industries in any country, certain actors are always good guys or villains, while other actors tread the line between the opposing worlds. But when an actor like Chi Kuan-chun, who consistently plays an upright and righteous fighter, is the villain, it can be a hard sell to the audience. Despite all the red herrings in a movie in which he is the evil double-crossing kung fu bad guy, you know it is going to be too fishy. And when the fish is found, it's Chi's former roles that make the ending too predictable, as the audience is not taken in hook, line and sinker—instead the film loses a bit of its "sole."

When senior student Chen Tien-chun (Chi Kuan-chun) of China's northern eagle claw kung fu school is not chosen by his teacher to be the next master of the style, which includes marriage to his dueling daughter (Hua Lin), Chen goes beserk. He kills his teacher; beats up the new master, Li Chi (Wong Dao); and subsequently is cast out of the school as a scandalous traitor. Meanwhile, Chao Ma-wu's (Zhang Yi) mission is to kill the head of the Chinese eagle claw school and take over the school. By doing so, he will dampen the spirits of the Chinese people and use that weakness as an inroad to invade China.

Because Chen killed his own teacher, Chao persuades him to set his sights on ousting Li and taking over the school. In order to do that, Chao agrees to teach Chen his combination of eagle claw and praying mantis fist kung fu.

Despite the film's martial arts star power, the actors lack the intensity and martial skills they've brought to previous works. Actor Liang Chia-ren, for example, winds up too much before delivering his strikes. It also looks like some of the stars may have been nursing injuries because Chi, Wong Dao and Zhang Yi were unable to hold their stances and deliver full motion strikes. This is common in films when actors get charley horses or pull muscles early in filming. Often when this happens, filmmakers resort to over-the-top deaths, extreme close-up death strikes and more blood to take the focus away from the injuries.

However, this movie does try to engage the Chinese audience on a higher emotional level via the student-teacher relationship between Chen and his two kung fu teachers, where due to the circumstances, each teacher is his friend and foe. Regardless of whether or not someone practices kung fu, viewers will understand the true dynamics of the student-teacher relationship and the consequences of a student becoming a traitor to the school as well as the ultra-blasphemous nature of a student killing his fatherly *sifu*.

If you are wondering why the cruel villain Chao looks a bit like Merlin the Magician—with long white hair draping down his back, white facial hair, a tall pointed hat and boots that curl like arthritic fingers—then wonder no more. Actor Zhang Yi's Merlin-like appearance is actually an acknowledgement of Yue Fei, a Song Dynasty general. In A.D. 1250, Yue Fei used his observations of eagles fighting and capturing prey to teach his soldiers a new way to fight against the invading northern Jin armies. Chao's attire looks marginally like something a northern Jin official would wear, and Chao is defeated by the eagle claw (as the Jin were). The film's opening credits explain that there are seven specific skills involved in practicing eagle claw kung fu and vividly describe how to apply each of the skills.

On a historic note, there are actually 10 skills used by eagle claw stylists. Perhaps the three missing in the film are a reminder to the audience that when a master dies, so does a bit of the style, especially if the master does not find a fitting replacement to be the head of the school. A master would rather die than teach everything to the wrong person.

Titleography: *Eagle Fist*; *Eagle's Claws*. Translation—*Eagle Claw Praying Mantis*. The English titles refer to eagle claw stylists Chen and Li. The Chinese title refers to the combination of the two animal fighting styles that Chao uses. **MA Percentage: 29.42%**

EAGLE'S CLAW AND BUTTERFLY PALM

神鷹飛燕蝴蝶掌 (1978—Hong Kong) **89m. MAI: Yu Tien-lung, Ma Jin-gu. NOT/LOT: None; NOF/LOF: 24/ 21m 47s.** D: Yu Tien-lung. C: Lo Lieh, Yueh Hua, Chi Kuan-chun, Sun Jia-lin, Tsung Hua, Yu Tien-lung, Jin Gang, Tsang

Chiu, Jiang Bin, Liang Jia-ren, Li Jiang, Liu Chun-hua.

If there is a clan of martial artists who can defeat the Shaolin and Wu Dung schools of kung fu, what evil conquering power would not want to have them in their court?

In this film, China has defeated the Mongols, thus ending the Yuan Dynasty. A nameless Chinese patriot (Chi Kuan-chun in a cameo) mortally wounds the final khan, but before he dies, the khan makes his final commands. He orders his personal bodyguard (Yueh Hua), who is also head of the Butterfly Clan, to take back China and establish his daughter (Sun Jia-lin) as the empress. The film references that the Butterfly Clan has already destroyed the Shaolin Temple, the Wu Dung Clan and the Yang Family. (See *The 14 Amazons*.)

Three Chinese heroes—Eagle, Flying Swallow (Flying Legs in the English dub), and Swallow's daughter—aim to destroy the Butterfly Clan and stop the would-be empress from using black magic to transform Chinese soldiers into deadly Mongolian zombie warriors.

On paper this sounds like an ambitious film, but it quickly devolves into one of those films that benefit from the fast-forward button on your remote. There are a lot of good fights featuring crisp choreography, but there's nothing visually spectacular. The only exceptions are the Butterfly Clan's spiked shields and the opening fight, in which actor Chi Kuan-chun uses the nine-ring broadsword—a large broadsword with nine rings along the dull side of the blade. The rings are used to temporarily trap the points of spears or similar weapons. They then break the opponent's weapon tip or create an opening for the heavy blade to slice into the opponent's flesh. If the wound is deep enough, the rings can make the gash even nastier. Furthermore, nine in Chinese numerology can represent a long period of life and also denotes the element of fire, which is the element of energy and inspiration.

The final moments of the story whittle down to a conclusion that features a bunch of out-of-left-field quirks that peel off like a *Mission: Impossible* face mask. But on a higher level, it's really a battle between the birds and the bees in the sycamore trees, so to speak. We have three characters named after birds taking on a clan named after an insect that does not sting like a bee, but floats like a butterfly, and what is at stake is the freedom of a coun-tree … I mean, country.

Titleography: *Eagle Claw vs. Butterfly Palm*. Translation—*Incredible Eagle Flying Swallow Butterfly Palm*. *Eagle* and *Flying Swallow* are the names of the heroes fighting against the Butterfly Clan; the clan uses the Butterfly Palm Killing technique, the reason behind the animal-insect English title. *Flying Swallow* may have been dropped because it does not sound as deadly as *Eagle* and makes the English title too long. The Butterfly Clan run around dressed in black with black hoods, so it is surprising that there is no English title with the word "ninja" in it. **MA Percentage: 24.48%**

EBONY, IVORY AND JADE

(1976—USA/Philippines) **80m. FI: Uncredited. NOT/LOT: None; NOF/LOF: 14/ 4m 34s.** D: Cirio H. Santiago. C: Rosanne Katon, Colleen Camp, Sylvia Anderson, Ken Washington, Jun Aristorenas.

What a politically correct film made at a politically incorrect time—because of one race, three races of women unite to battle sex-slave traders to prove that the most superior race in the world is the 100-meter dash.

Compared to *The Muthers* (1976), which included many members from the same production crew, this has much more action, but in a very surprising way. The fights come across like many found in the early Hong Kong *wu da pian* films, which are a genre of martial arts movies created by Jackie Chan in the 1980s that replaced traditional kung fu movements with dangerous and acrobatic stunts and stylized street-fighting kicks and punches. There are more excessive wide-swinging punches in this film than traditional kung fu strikes. There are also more overhead shots to emphasize the deeper, wider stances of the actors and to make the punches look more dangerous. Add in flips, spins, wider angles and Filipino stuntmen doubling for the multi-race battling babes, the result is fights with a dab of soul sistahood and foxy mamas who are as sly as the family stone and can put any beagle boy to doggone shame. What distracts from the fights, though, is that most of the fights were shot at dusk without additional lighting, probably because artificial lighting was too expensive and it was too hot to shoot outdoors during the day. Still, it gives an almost provocative bite to the film.

In case something did not sound right a few sentences earlier, I did indeed write that Filipino men doubled for the rather buxom American actresses. Even

I, a 6-foot white dude, doubled for Chinese women in kung fu TV soap operas when I was in Taiwan (1979-1981).

Titleography: *American Beauty Hostages*; *Foxfire*; *Foxforce*. The titles are all logical based on the film because the sex slaves are indeed foxy, beautiful American hostages, and three of the four main female characters are named Ebony, Ivory and Jade. **MA Percentage: 5.71%**

EDGE OF FURY

撈家撈女撈上; 大亨 and 黑色家變 (1978—Hong Kong) **85m. FC:** Tommy Lee. **NOT/LOT:** 1/ 25s; **NOF/LOF:** 11/ 17m 52s. D: Lee Tso-nam. C: Bruce Li, Yasuaki Kurata, Tommy Lee, Michelle Yim, Dana.

At this point in Hong Kong cinema, the Bruceploitation genre was in high gear, and Lee impersonators were making the grade (albeit a low grade) doing the same thing over and over and over. Though many of these films were low-budget, hackneyed, and as in the case of this film, full of tired fight choreography, the popularity of the genre reflected that Bruce Lee fans were still enamored and content to see even a pseudo-version of their hero on screen.

In this film set in contemporary Hong Kong, Ah Lung (Bruce Li) is a chauffeur to rich man Mr. Chan, who is going on a trip to Thailand, where he will be executed on charges of drug smuggling. Before Mr. Chan leaves, he hands Ah Lung a letter revealing that Chan's cheating wife is determined to get revenge, even at the cost of her stepson's welfare, a young lad who really likes Ah Lung. Meanwhile, King Fei-fei (Yasuaki Kurata) is twisting the arms and tightening the screws on Ah Lung's finances, family and romances because he's certain that Ah Lung must know where Chan hid the drugs, although the film refers to the stash simply as "the goods."

Because Chinese audiences would not accept that street-fighting thugs would use traditional stylized kung fu movements—the fights and the actors would be too out of place from the usual *wuxia* and period films—the choreography in modern-day films lacked creativity. It quickly became mundane because actors simply brawled while throwing kicks and flashing simplified stances and postures. Choreographing these fights was easy and required minimal skill or effort from actors and fight instructors, which eventually gave rise to complacency in certain circles of the industry, like Bruceploitation films. But this is what makes the real Bruce Lee's films even more amazing: He essentially fought in contemporary settings and pulled it off with grandeur.

Titleography: *Blood on His Hands*. Translation—*Rescue the Family, The Women and Salvage the Rescue* and *The Big Rich Guy* and *Black Tragedy in the Family*. All the Chinese titles reflect certain plot points of the film, but it is the English titles that are as generic as they come. The *Edge of Fury* title is Bruce Lee's *Fist of Fury* title in disguise. **MA Percentage: 21.51%**

EIGHT HUNDRED HEROES

八百壯士 (1975—Taiwan) **101m. FI:** Uncredited. **NOT/LOT:** None; **NOF/LOF:** 6/ 2m 5s. D: Ding Shan-xi. C: Ke Jun-xiong, Hsu Feng, Brigitte Lin Ching-hsia, Chen Jin-han, Cho Kin, Carter Wong, Zhang yi, Wong Dao.

Eight Hundred Heroes is more of a war movie than a martial arts film, although it still falls within that gauge of having more martial arts fighting than Chuck Norris' *Good Guys Wear Black*. This Taiwanese war movie brandishes its hero with a gun in one hand and a Chinese broadsword in the other. The hero simultaneously shoots, slashes and kicks through masses of Japanese soldiers. Director Ding Shan-xi was arguably the best Chinese director during the 1970s known for his wild and woolly World War II war epics, in which Chinese heroes were as real as they were fantastical.

This film is based on a true story. History says that prior to the start of World War II, the Chinese 524th Regiment, 88th Division, under the leadership of Lt. Col. Xie Jin-yuen (Ke Jun-xiong), set up a final defensive line at the Si Hang Warehouse from Oct. 25 to Nov. 1, 1937. From that position, they held out against a vicious onslaught of Japanese troops. This stand not only marked the beginning of the end of the three-month Battle of Shanghai but also protected Chinese forces as they retreated across Suzhou Creek to the safety of the foreign concessions in Shanghai.

The film pretty much runs the gamut of what happened during the Warehouse War. Because the defenses are running out of supplies and morale, Girl Scout-like Yang Hui-min (Brigette Lin Ching-hsia) arranges for the delivery of supplies to the surrounded Chinese forces. Later, in a selfless act of courage, the teenager swims across Suzhou Creek from the foreign concessions

into Japanese-occupied Shanghai at the height of the onslaught and delivers a Chinese flag to the defenders of the warehouse. She inspires the Chinese defenders to raise the flag Iwo Jima-style, which makes the Japanese lose face and lifts Chinese morale. At the end of the day, the events blare out a warning to the foreign powers in Shanghai of the impending cruelty and aggression that Japan was going to unleash upon the world.

Although in real life the 88th Division initially had 800 men at the beginning of the Battle of Shanghai, there were actually only 423 soldiers left alive before the warehouse battle. Final death count? More than 200 Japanese, 10 Chinese.

My first film in Taiwan was a World War II movie directed by Ding Dao Yen. Watching this movie by Ding Shan-xi brought back memories of that experience and the vivid way that Ding Dao Yen directed the action. Because Ding Dao Yen was highly respected by the Republic of China military at the time, he had an inexhaustible supply of extras. Each day, real soldiers were ordered to work on the film. In fact, on my film, the producer was a four-star general in the Chinese Army. Stay tuned for 1980.

Titleography: *800 Heroes*. Translation—800 Heroes. **MA Percentage: 2.08%**

EIGHTEEN JADE ARHATS

十八玉羅漢 (1978—Hong Kong) **85m. KFD:** Lee Chiu, Zhou Ran-jian. **NOT/LOT:** 3/ 4m 43s; **NOF/LOF:** 20/ 22m 58s. D: Zhang Jie. C: Polly Kuan, Li Zhen-hua, Lo Lieh, Lung Fei, Zhang Yi, Gao Fei, Chuan Yuan, Fang Fang, Jiang Qing-xia, Li Jiang.

This film has more jabs than a boxing match—jabs with punji sticks (sharpened bamboo stakes), that is. While Chinese *wuxia* novels can be simple stories about revenge, patriotism, and martial or familial honor on the surface, their story structures and plot designs can be quite intricate. They have a vast supply of rich characters, red herrings and sometimes too many twists, which come so far out of left field that not even Willie Mays could see them coming. *Eighteen Jade Arhats* is as highfalutin as these stories get, with characters dying who are not dead, back stories popping up to stump the hero (and the audience), and names tossed around like baseballs at a baseball camp, further exasperated when each dubber in the English version seems to say the same Chinese name differently.

Kung Xi-yao (played by short-lived kung fu star Li Zhen-hua) is a wandering and wondering swordsman roaming the world of Jiang Hu who doesn't understand why so many fighters are trying to kill him. He befriends the seemingly innocent warrior woman Xi Pei-pei (Polly Kuan), who is searching for her father's killer and the thief who stole nine of the 18 jade *arhats* from their family's collection. Literally meaning "worthy one," an arhat is a Buddhist who has attained enlightenment, so these jade arhats are small green jade statuettes of Buddhist monks in various meditative and kung fu poses. Along their jaded path, truths and untruths are revealed as Kung and Xi confront a menagerie of skilled swordsmen and kung fu fighters, such as the undaunted Ku Ying-pung (Lo Lieh), the head of the Assassins from North Temple (Gao Fei), and the doesn't-telegraph-his-punches-or-kicks stalwart Wang Chung-wei (Zhang Yi).

In a lot of kung fu films, stars perform cameos for terrific kung fu set pieces that make the film more marketable or memorable. This movie is chock-full of good fights that are made even more exciting because of the camera choreography. During the fights, the camera uses many close shots that zoom in for tighter angles while the camera tilts up and down, all within the same shot. The emotion is further heightened when the choreographers use explosive martial techniques in conjunction with good body reactions. Although good body reactions may be a no-brainer for a good fight, they are not always an easy thing to pull of.

When you watch a lot of kung fu films, sometimes a technique misses by a mile and you wonder how it sneaked past the editors or choreographers. The answer is that back then, these fights where shot with one camera, without video feed or playback capabilities, so the choreographers could often only go by what the cameramen told them about how the fights looked on camera.

Titleography: *Eighteen Jade Pearls*; *The 18 Jade Arhats*; *18 Jade Pearls*; *Jade Killer*; *The Eighteen (18) Claws of Shaolin*. Translation—*18 Jade Buddhas*. The words *Jade* and *18* in the titles are based on the Chinese title and what is seen in the film, but there are no pearls—perhaps pearls are a metaphor for something special like arhats? The only indication of claws in the film would be the bronze-fighting statue at the film's beginning that our heroes practice against, which has 14 clawed hands and not 18. **MA Percentage: 32.57%**

EIGHTEEN SWIRLING RIDERS

旋風十八騎 (1977—Taiwan) **85m. MAI: He Ming-xiao. NOT/LOT: None; NOF/LOF: 18/ 19m 39s.** D: Lin Fu-di. C: Wong Dao, Chia Ling, Chen Hsing, Lo Lieh, Wen Chiang-long, Chen Hui-lou, O Yao-man, Yi Yuan, Fun Dan-fung.

In Chinese folklore, because carp are known to leap over the rapids of the Yellow River, the fish have become a symbol of perseverance and endurance. From Chinese society's perspective, the carp is also a representation of how businessmen and scholars outdo their competition. In Chinese numerology, the number eight is associated with fortune, so possessing an artistic masterpiece portraying eight carp in a pond remains a powerful symbol of success.

In this film, a group known as the 18 Whirlwind Riders, led by the veil-hat-wearing Hu Yu-han (Wong Dao), gallops about like Robin Hood and his Merry Men. Like those famous outlaws, they steal from the corrupt government and give to the poor and downtrodden. As a signature, Hu leaves behind a small dart shaped like a *dao* (a Chinese broadsword). However, these small darts begin appearing in the dead bodies of righteous men who attended a special auction for a coveted antique called the Eight Carp. Determined to get to the bottom of this murder mystery, Hu and his fellow Riders devise a plan to trap the imposter; they eventually find out he is the vengeful Dr. Chao (Chen Hsing). Chao's mission in life is to discredit the Whirlwind Riders and kill them off one by one because they stole an evil sword from a nefarious killer: Chao's father.

Of interest, one of the heroes uses an ancient healing art known as pulse reading, which is a medical diagnostic tool used by traditional Chinese doctors, Tibetan lamas and Ayurveda specialists from India. By lightly placing your left fore-, middle and ring fingers on a patient's right wrist and then pressing them in deeper, a pulse reader can "listen" to the state of the health of a patient's organs.

This movie is loaded with freaky sound effects, wicked weapons, far-out flying darts, and off-kilter flips and rolls. The snappy fight choreography contains no extended exchange of techniques in a single take and uses mostly close shots strung together by quick edits, which makes the fights rather enjoyable to watch. The final bamboo forest showdown—perhaps a final nod to the fight between Robin Hood and the Sheriff of Nottingham in Sherwood Forest—is as confusing to watch as it is bloody fun.

Titleography: *18 Swirling Riders*; *18 Riders for Justice*; *Eighteen Riders to Justice*; *18 Shaolin Riders*; *Eighteen Shaolin Riders*; *Eighteen Shaolin Brave Men*; *18 Shaolin Brave Men*. Translation—*18 Whirlwind (Cyclone) Riders*. The Chinese title is simply the name of the gang, and the English title with *Swirling* is basically the same as *Whirlwind*. The *Riders for Justice* title aptly describes what these heroes do, but the *Shaolin* implication is definitely pure distributor sales pitching because there is nothing about Shaolin in the film—although the film does star O Yao-man, who became Taiwan's go-to Shaolin priest character in the '70s. **MA Percentage: 23.12%**

EMPEROR CHIEN LUNG

乾隆皇奇遇記 (1976—Hong Kong) **98m. FI: Uncredited. NOT/LOT: None; NOF/LOF: 8/ 4m 28s.** D: Wang Feng. C: Liu Yong, Wang Yu, Chiang Yang, Lin Feng, Tien Ching, Shi Zhong-tain, Xia Ping, Chan Shen, Jiang Nan.

Historically, after the brutal 13-year reign of Emperor Yong Zheng (see *Flying Guillotine*, *Blazing Temple* and *Return of the 18 Bronzemen*), his fourth son, Hong Li, ascended to the throne and became Emperor Chien Lung, the fifth emperor of the Ching Dynasty (but the fourth to rule over China). He officially ruled China for 60 years (1736-1796), making him the longest-serving emperor in China's history. Because of his expertise in martial arts, Chien Lung was known as the kung fu emperor. During his fabled six visits to the region of Chiang Nan in southern China, he disguised himself as a commoner to learn how his subjects felt about him and how he could improve the country.

Emperor Chien Lung is the first of four Shaw Brothers films starring Liu Yong (son of the big boss in Bruce Lee's *The Big Boss*) as the kung fu emperor. Chien Lung is so bored with his mundane life—eating the same fancy food and sleeping with concubines—that he decides to leave the Forbidden City. He trades places with his tailor and sneaks past the palace guards. On the outside, he disguises himself as a silk trader named Gao and walks among his subjects. He is befriended by Chau Yi-ching (Wang Yu), and he learns some harsh lessons about how people view him and how his local officials take advantage of the populace under the guise of carrying out his orders. This is the kind of film you can enjoy because you know that at some point, the corrupt characters who abuse the poor, simple folks—the same folks who help Chien Lung survive—

will get what's coming to them. That moment occurs when Chien Lung finally reveals who he is and the bad guys melt like the Wicked Witch of the East. At that moment, one of Chien Lung's favorite advisors, Lord Jiang (Jiang Nan), appears to announce the edicts of change. Everyone who matters gets to be happy: The masses have food in their bellies, and the dynasty is in good hands.

Unfortunately, the fights are not much to speak of. Liu is awkward and unsure, and he lacks any kind of proper martial arts stance, so the minutes all fall on actor Wang Yu's shoulders to give the film at least a moment of pizzazz, but that fizzles and frazzles without any razzle or dazzle. But one shouldn't expect good fights in this film. There is no choreographer, and the fights were probably haphazardly put together at the last minute by the film's stuntmen, who included Yuen Kwei, Hsu Xia and Yuen Hua.

Although the film depicts Chien Lung as a righteous, fair man with an open mind, the real Chien Lung became overly conservative and extremely Sinocentric (viewing China as the center of the universe) as he aged. He thought Western culture and its inventions were all—for lack of a better word—lame. It was this sort of attitude that eventually led to the decline of the Ching Dynasty.

Titleography: As of this writing, no alternative titles could be found. Translation—*The Story of Emperor Chien Long's Adventures*. The titles both pretty much tell it all. **MA Percentage: 4.56%** SHAW BROTHERS

EMPEROR CHIEN LUNG AND THE BEAUTY

乾隆皇與三姑娘 (1979—Hong Kong) **100m. FI: Tang Chia, Huang Pei-ji. NOT/LOT: None; NOF/LOF: 2/ 4m 39s.** D: Li Han-hsiang. C: Liu Yong, Pan Ping-chang, Hui Ying-hong, Lun Gu-jun, Lee Kwan, Jiang Nan, Chan Shun.

Emperor Chien Lung and the Beauty is the last of four Shaw Brothers films starring Liu Yong as Emperor Chien Lung. (Liu Yong is the fighter in yellow whom John Saxon defeats in his opening-round bout in Bruce Lee's *Enter the Dragon*.) The series is based on Chien Lung's six famous visits to Chiang Nan; he would secretly dress up as a commoner, mingle with his subjects, learn about their lives and ultimately expose the rampant corruption caused by having power without responsibility. However, Shaw Brothers did make a final fifth film about Chien Lung, *The Emperor and His Brother*, in 1981, starring Bai Biao as a more serious emperor. *Dirty Ho* (1979) was also inspired by Chien Lung's life.

This film opens during the aftermath of the terrible Chiang Nan earthquake, when the visiting Emperor Chien Lung arrives in the area to help the quake's victims. With the recovery going well and things settling down, Chien Lung dons his secret simpleton disguise and discovers an exciting new world outside the castle. His first experience is the phenomenon of gambling, which he begins to understand the evils of. The owner of a gambling den, Miss San (Pan Ping-chang), tries to force Li Pao-er (Hui Ying-hong) to return her sizable winnings by hiring a large man to pretend to be Li's husband and demand the money. After arguing that the man is not her husband, Li reveals her martial arts expertise and claims that only her real husband could defeat her in a fight. As Li makes mincemeat of the imposter, Miss San orders her other cronies to beat Li up and get the money back. Chien Lung sticks his nose into their business, joins in the fracas and has the utmost respect for Li's fighting ability. After the enjoyable moment in the film when Chien Lung reveals who he is, he brings down Miss San and proposes the edict "Betting less is enjoyable."

The fights feature actress Hui's smooth transitions between kung fu master and demure lady. She fights with the power of a man hidden behind the grace of a lady, and that feminine grace is befitting to who her character is. The fight choreographers accentuate this sensibility using familiar low-angle and medium shots of people running in and out of frame as the heroine effortlessly (using good postures, mind you) takes care of herself. Again, though, like all the Chien Lung films, the fights are minimal.

Titleography: As of this writing, no alternative titles could be found. Translation—*Chien Lung and the Third Daughter*. The English title refers to Hui Ying-hong's character, and the Chinese title refers to Miss San, the owner of the casino. **MA Percentage: 4.65%** SHAW BROTHERS

END OF THE WICKED TIGERS

老虎燕星 and 猛虎鬥肥龍 (1976—Hong Kong) **85m. MAD: Han Ying-chieh, Sammo Hung, Chan Cheun. NOT/LOT: None; NOF/LOF: 19/ 28m 48s.** D: Luo Qi. C: Charles Heung Wah-keung, Sammo Hung, Han Ying-chieh, Li Gu-ding, Eric Tsang, Wilson Tong, Hsu Hsia, Eddy Ko.

It is hard to teach an old dog new tricks, and in the martial arts choreography world, that can lead to fights that look terrible. Five years after choreographing Bruce Lee in *The Big Boss* (aka *Fists of Fury*), Han Ying-chieh—an early innovator in kung fu fight choreography—was still churning out the same kind of fights in *End of the Wicked Tigers*. The film also plays like Lee's masterpiece because Han portrays a similar big-boss character, Boss Chang, who runs a protection racket and oversees a bunch of hooligans that pick on locals. After one of Hang's sons commits murder and the other son, Chang Xiao-fu (Wilson Tong), murders and rapes a local woman, hero Ma Sung (Charles Heung) and visiting police official Captain Ling (Li Gu-ding) team up to shrink the big boss down to size and lay the boss's right-hand man, Lau (Sammo Hung), low.

For cinematic fighters like Wilson Tong and Sammo Hung, this film is one giant leap backward for kung-fu-kind. When you get right down to it, these are not kung fu fights at all. Rather, they're brawls filled with slaps, whiffle and windmill punches, karate reverse punches and chops, boxing-style right hooks, and off-balance kicks. Lead actor Heung wears the same clothing (black pants, white T-shirt open at the neck, sash hanging around his hip) as Bruce Lee from *Big Boss*. In fact, the final fight between Heung and Han is shot in the same way as the final fight between Bruce Lee and Han from that same movie. Although Heung fights like Lee (or tries to), at least he does not act like Lee or try to do any of Lee's typical faces and screams.

Titleography: *End of Wicked Tiger*. Translations—*Tiger Swallow Star* and *Vicious Tiger Fights Fat Dragon*. In reality, Han Ying-chieh is known for his tiger claw kung fu, and often it appears as if he uses that background when he choreographs himself. In essence, he is the *Wicked Tiger* who comes to an *End*. The Chinese titles do not make sense. However, using animal characters in Chinese titles always gives the film a Jiang Hu and kung-fu-like feel to a film that appeals to Chinese audiences. Although Sammo Hung was in the film *Enter the Fat Dragon* (1978), the second title could be a later re-titling of the film in which the *Tiger* (Han) fights the *Fat Dragon* (Hung). But that is a stretch, considering that Sammo Hung's character works for Han's character in *End of the Wicked Tiger*. **MA Percentage: 33.88%**

ENTER THE DRAGON

龍爭虎鬥 (1973—Hong Kong/USA) **102m. MAI: Bruce Lee. NOT/LOT: 4/ 3m 44s; NOF/LOF: 15/ 30m 46s.** D: Robert Clouse. C: Bruce Lee, John Saxon, Jim Kelly, Shiek Khan, Bolo Yeung, Peter Archer, Sammo Hung, Tony Liu Yung, Ahna Capri, Angela Mao Ying.

Bruce Lee officially unites Hong Kong and Hollywood under the parasol of kung fu. In this $500,000-budgeted gasp of fresh air in Tinseltown, Lee plays secret agent Lee. He's sent by the British to break up a suspected drug ring organized by the inscrutable Han (Shiek Khan), who uses martial arts tournaments to recruit bodyguards and lackeys. The idea of the tournament is actually based on the ancient Chinese sport *lei tai*, which first appeared during the Song Dynasty (A.D. 960 to A.D. 1279). The tournament winner would either become the emperor's bodyguard or a martial arts instructor for the imperial army.

You could make an argument that the film was politically correct 20 years before it was politically correct to do so. However, having a black, a white and an Oriental (or by today's PC terms, an African-American, a Caucasian and an Asian) hero working together was a way for Warner Bros. to appease the demographics and a tacit admission that an Asian lead still wasn't plausible.

When the film came out, Westerners had no idea about the pedigree of the Hong Kong cast. Shiek Khan had done more than 400 films, and most of them were martial arts movies that featured him as the villain. And with 18 films under her *hapkido* black belt, Angela Mao Ying was attaining cult status as a kung fu heroine, so the fights she did in *Enter the Dragon* were a walk in the park for her and her Vietnamese karate champion co-star. Bolo Yeung, a veteran of 28 kung fu films. By 1973, Sammo Hung had fought in 42 kung fu films and had been the head martial arts instructor for 17 of them.

It's impossible to deny that *Enter the Dragon* is a great film but the fights are very Hollywood. Although I respect John Saxon, he did not possess the martial savvy to fight convincingly against Bolo Yeung. There are also problems with the choreography, such as the dungeon scene when Bruce Lee is flexing his back while trying to open the elevator doors. He suddenly steps, turns around and is accosted by a handful of attackers. Talk about close-up—you can't see what anyone is doing, and a bad guy falls in the opposite direction after Lee throws his last sweeping backfist. Also, Lee's handspring and flip after the film's beginning fight scene with Sammo Hung were not performed by Lee but by Lam

Ching-ying, who found fame with his one-eyebrowed priest character in the *Mr. Vampire* films.

Then there's the final Hollywood glitter mirror room fight between Han and Lee. It has always been funny to me that director Robert Clouse never re-shot the scene when Lee throws the coat stand into the mirrors and no mirror breaks. A person could argue it shows how tough the mirrors are, so when Lee breaks them with his hands and "feet" (a hand in the shoe on close-up), we can feel his power. However, it's an awkward-feeling moment, though it is quickly replaced when Lee does his patented hunchbacked creeping walk around the mirror set. Lee's daughter, Shannon, once told me that she remembers often looking at the spear from that final Shiek-a-bob shot resting in the corner of her home as a child.

The irony about Lee's career and stardom in the West is that they came together at the wrong place at the wrong time. In 1972, the United States was in the midst of the Vietnam War, and anti-Asian sentiment had not been so high since World War II. Each week, racial tension was finding a new way to twist the psyche of a country floundering in gas lines and cold war. Traditionally, whenever the United States was at war, Hollywood would create characters and storylines based on the heroic efforts of the American soldier, trying to use films as a way to boost the country's morale and confidence that the troops were righteously defending the realm against the evils of the world. But during the Vietnam War, America was in no mood for war heroes. Furthermore, when you look at the five top-grossing films in descending order from 1972— *The Godfather*; *The Poseidon Adventure*; *What's Up, Doc?*; *Deliverance* and *Deep Throat*, with the brunt of the Academy Awards going to *The Godfather* and *Cabaret*—it was evident that the definition of the American cinematic champion of justice was undergoing a huge transition away from the glory of riding off into the sunset. Additionally, keep in mind that back in those days, to most Americans, someone who used their feet during a fight was considered a sissy. So for all intents and purposes, it was not only the wrong time for any Asian actor to make a mark in Hollywood, but it was also the wrong time for the hero to win a fight by kicking. Yet Bruce Lee came along, and with his dynamic facial contortions, rapid-fire punches, greased-lightning kicks and high-pitched phoenix screeches, he single-handedly gave Chinese martial arts cinema legitimacy and the Chinese people an identity. Lee has done more for spreading the word of martial arts throughout the world than anyone else in history. He was also the first martial artist to make mainstream the concept of cross training and combining the best attributes of many martial arts into one.

One neat thing about watching *Enter the Dragon* (and in fact, all of Lee's films) is being able to recognize many of the Chinese faces in the background—faces that are famous and recognizable to Chinese martial arts cinema fans. (Yep, Jackie Chan dies twice in the film.) I still don't know who the laughing guy was in the background after Lee kicks the same guy four times (similar to Lee kicking Chuck Norris in *Way of the Dragon*) in the final disorganized courtyard brawl. How did that sneak by Robert Clouse, the director of photography and the editor?

Titleography: *Iron Hand*; *Operation Dragon*; *Deadly Three*; *Blood and Steel*; *Han's Island*. Translation—*Dragons and Tigers Fight*. *Dragons* refers to Lee and his men, and *Tigers* refers to Han and his men. *Iron Hand* refers to Han's iron hand and other attachments. *Operation Dragon*, *Deadly Three* (Lee, Saxon, Kelly), *Blood and Steel*, and *Han's Island* were all at one point considered as alternative titles, and it is easy to see how they were created. What's the point of even trying to rename this film? **MA Percentage: 33.82%**

ENTER THE GAME OF DEATH

死亡魔塔 (1978—Hong Kong/S. Korea) **85m. FI: Uncredited. NOT/ LOT: 3/ 2m 48s; NOF/LOF: 28/ 43m 20s.** D: Lin Guo-xiang. C: Bruce Le, Park Dong-ryoon, Lee Hoi-san, Cheung Lik, Bolo Yeung, James Nan Gung-fan, Chu Chi-ling.

If you are going to do a Bruce Lee rip-off, you might as well do it all the way, show no shame and be as blatant as possible because the sheer audacity of it makes it work. Of all the Lee copycat actors, I bet Bruce Le took his personal homage to Lee most seriously, which is obvious through the evolution of his Bruceploitation films. He does the best overall impersonation of Lee, his muscle tone and build are the closest to Lee's (at least Lee's final years), he does a good job mirroring Lee's acting nuances, and he successfully copies Lee's idiosyncrasies when he fights.

Enter the Game of Death, obviously inspired by Lee's *Game of Death* and complete with a yellow tracksuit, is actually one of the better Lee borrowers. If you watch it without thinking about how these films cheapened and eroded Bruce Lee's legend, you'll discover that it has a lot of cool action sequences and old-style kung fu charm. It is always important to remind ourselves that character development is not important in kung fu films like this because they're all about imitation rather than plot, dialogue or acting. In fact, I did a film in 1980 in Taiwan for which we shot about two weeks of fighting before a script was written around the fights.

Mr. Ahn's (Bruce Le) only goal in life is to find the evil Japanese man who raped and murdered his cousin. When a female Chinese agent asks him to help the Chinese recover a secret stolen Chinese document that could mean doom for the country, he initially refuses. But when she appeals to his sense of loyalty to his country, Le agrees to enter the five-story pagoda where the document is reportedly hidden. At each level of the pagoda is a deadly martial artist, and out of all the evildoers who want the document, only Ahn is brave enough to climb this stairway to hell.

Still from *The Eunuch* © Celestial Pictures Ltd. All rights reserved.

Bolo Yeung appears as often in Bruceploitation films as hunters on the opening day of duck season. Many fans like me were disappointed that Bruce Lee did not fight Bolo in *Enter the Dragon*, so this is about as close to that pipe dream as we will ever get. And, in keeping with the cinematic reality of it all, each time Bolo appears in a film like this, the appropriate Lee impersonator easily wins because everyone knows that Bruce would have always beat him.

Although Le does too many of the patented Lee-finger-brushing-his-nose gestures, his fight performance and martial arts schooling are far superior to his Lee-act-alike counterpart Kim Tai-chung, who played Lee's character in the 1978 *Game of Death* debacle. The five floors of the pagoda are truly laced with some wild opponents from bottom to top: Lee Hoi-san with double butterfly knives, bordering on the Lee-versus-Dan Inosanto match; Snake Man, who bites off the head of a snake and squirts the leaking blood at Ahn (what is it with Chinese films and biting off snake heads?); Zhang Li with his double *nunchaku* attack; attack-of-the-equal-opportunity duo Black Tiger and White Tiger; and the last (sadly, the worst fight in the pagoda), the red-haired rival.

But just when you think the film might be over, Le tackles a large group of black and white guys protecting a German spy who is keen on using the secret document to destroy China. I have to applaud Steve James, who had a tough four-minute fight against Le. During several slow-motion shots, it's easy for the audience to plainly see Le whack the living daylights out of James. I salute the late Mr. James for his guts and martial arts prowess.

Titleography: *The King of Kung Fu*. Translation—*The Evil Death Pagoda*. Although generic, Bruce Lee could indeed be called the king of kung fu, but it is a statement about Lee rather than a translation of the title. Also, on another Bruceploitation film, the opening soundtrack was an original song created for the film *The King of Kung Fu*. Anyway, the distributors probably figured that the title was still available. Furthermore, the main padding of the story, like Lee's original story for *Game of Death*, is the five-story *Evil Death Pagoda* that Le has to climb. **MA Percentage: 54.27%**

EUNUCH, THE

鬼太監 (1970—Hong Kong) **90m. FI:** Xu Er-niu. **NOT/LOT:** 2/ 2m 16s; **NOF/LOF:** 15/ 14m 52s. **D:** Yeh Yung-tsu. **C:** Chiao Chiao, Tsung Hua, Bai Yin, Wang Hsia, Yang Chi-ching, Meng Jia, Yung Yuk-yi.

As discussed in *Eunuch of the Western Palace*, toward the end of the Ming Dynasty, the emperor employed about 70,000 eunuchs. After gaining the emperor's trust, many eunuchs would devise plans to overthrow the emperor. Dealing with them was difficult because they had no family to use as blackmail, and kicking one in the groin was a waste of time. This was part of the reason so many eunuchs were good martial artists.

But the penile codes at the palace don't stop eunuch Guei De-hai from trying to overthrow the regime. So when the emperor uncovers Guei's plot, the emperor plots to assassinate him. Unfortunately, when the plan backfires, Guei orders the royal family massacred. There is only one survivor, Prince Chu Jin (Tsung Hua), who manages to escape because of a good deed. Just before the eunuch's ball-busted baddies find him, he ends up chasing an old man who has just kidnapped a woman's baby. After following the old man into the woods, the prince discovers that his target is the legendary fighter Gong Shen, the Leisurely Old Man in the Bamboo Forest (Yang Chi-ching). Gong arranged the fake nabbing with his daughter as a means of getting Chu away from the palace in time.

What the world doesn't know is that during his final days as a farmer and before becoming a eunuch, Guei sowed his wild oats, and he now has a 20-year-old daughter. If word got out, it would be the end of his eunuch era. To avoid being caught by the government, Guei sends out his top assassins to track down and silence the three people who could jeopardize his position: His daughter, Yan Yan (Chiao Chiao); Yan Yan's mother; and Prince Jin, because as long as Jin is alive, the line of the emperor still exists.

As Guei's assassin is about to kill Yan Yan, a wandering old lady (Yung Yuk-yi) saves her. The wandering old lady turns out to be Gong's wife. In preparation for the inevitable, Gong teaches Jin the secret Wandering Soul Sword style and Yan Yan learns fencing from Gong's wife.

The two fights featuring Gong protecting Jin and Gong's wife defending Yan Yan are the best sequences in the film. These fights feature simple pole fights. As a choreographer, I can say that it is the simplicity and directness of the pole that can make any fight visually effective without having to be fancy. On a fight choreography side note, when sword fights look too simple, they can easily end up looking more like the kind of backyard fencing you see kids do when they're pretending to be Robin Hood.

This early film doesn't have many fights, mostly because most actors knew no martial arts, thus the fights are kept simple and quick. When a character learns a special technique like Jin's Wandering Soul Sword skill, the ultimate skill that can't be beat, then it makes his future fights pointless because all he has to do is use the ability right off the bat. I mean, what's the reason to have a long fight when all the hero has to do is use the skill? It's like in *The Matrix Reloaded* (2003)—what's the point of Neo fighting 100 Agents Smiths if he's just going to fly away anyway? Jin's sword skill only becomes necessary if the villain has a comparable skill or if after Jin uses this great skill, but only as a last resort, he endangers himself and the world of Jiang Hu. But neither of these things are set up in the film. The irony is that Hollywood films now use the old secret-technique trope, leaving you to wonder why the hero doesn't just use his fight-ending technique in the first place. *Hellboy II: The Golden Army* (2008) is another prime example of this.

Titleography: As of this writing, no alternative titles could be found. Translation—*The Conniving Eunuch*. Although the Chinese characters literally mean "ghostly eunuch," the meaning implies plotting or scheming. **MA Percentage: 19.04%** SHAW BROTHERS

EUNUCH OF THE WESTERN PALACE

白馬素車勾魂幡 (1979—Taiwan) **90m. MAD:** Zhan Long, Huang Fei-long, Xiao Huang-long. **NOT/LOT:** 3/ 2m 14s; **NOF/LOF:** 29/ 19m 31s. **D:** Wu Ma. **C:** Meng Fei, Wong Dao, Doris Lung Chun-er, Lo Lieh, Lung Fei, Tsung Hua.

It takes a lot of guts to go up against the emperor, but it doesn't take a lot of balls to go up against a eunuch—unless he is planning to secretly usurp the emperor and take over the Ming Dynasty. Although castration was a traditional form of punishment in ancient China (ending during the Sui Dynasty, A.D. 581 to

A.D. 618), planned eunuch-hood was also a way to gain entry into the imperial court. In these instances, castration was performed at an early age to produce the desired physiological effect of a seemingly demure, culled and passive man who would not be a threat to the emperor's concubines. Toward the end of the Ming Dynasty, there were an estimated 70,000 eunuchs employed by the emperor because he could trust these men to leave his concubines alone and rely on them to reflect his personal will. Because eunuchs could get so close to an emperor that they knew his every weakness, plots to overthrow emperors became as rampant as the number of kung fu movies made during the 1970s. This film explains how boys are picked to become eunuchs and then—squish!—cut to a bunch of high-pitched screaming kids getting the old castration scythe right between the legs. Ouch, man…or in this case ouch boy.

When eunuch Wang Zu secretly plots to overthrow the Ming emperor and hurt the Chinese people, Lai Chien-tin (Wong Dao) unwittingly takes up the mantle to deliver evidence of Wang's wily ways before the penile codes of the country change. To ensure the evidence is delivered, Lai enlists the help of Ke Xing-shu (Meng Fei) and two female warriors: Bai Yu-shang (Doris Lung Chun-er), master of the telescoping Killing Flag Spear, and Xiao Ling-ling, expert of the telescoping Invincible Sword. However, a Wang loyalist and supreme fighter of the court, master Hung (Tsung Hua)—who also calls in a favor from the legendary but righteous swordsman Hao Wu-bing (Lo Lieh)—stands in the way of Lai's mission, which snowballs into a white storm of crystalline killing at the end of the film.

Featuring some of actor Wong Dao's best fights and certainly reflecting his great aptitude with the sword, this film contains a brief musical interlude when Lai tackles a renegade Shaolin monk who fights with cymbals (ba). Often used by lion dancers and street performers, cymbals could double as throwing discs or be used like steel rings when passersby would challenge the martial arts demonstrators to fights. As previously mentioned in earlier martialogies, I love snow, and when the final fight occurs during a light snowstorm, it adds a unique blend of calm violence and virgin ferocity to what is already a good film.

Titleography: *Soldiers of Darkness*; *Royal Family*. Translation—*White Horse Funeral Wagon (Funeral Procession) Soul Hooking Flag*. Although the villain is a eunuch, he only briefly appears in the film during the opening credits. The main fighting villain is the white-haired Hung, who has fighters that jump out of coffins, thus the *White Horse* and *Funeral* references from the Chinese title. The *Soldiers of Darkness* may refer to the coffin soldiers, and the distributor might have been influenced by Sam Raimi's *Army of Darkness* title. **MA Percentage: 24.17%**

EXECUTIONER

Chokugeki! Jigo-ken (1974—Japan) **87m. FI: Uncredited. NOT/LOT: 8/ 6m 12s; NOF/LOF: 25/ 20m 36s.** D: Teruo Ishii. C: Sonny Chiba, Eiji Go, Makoto Sato, Yutaka Nakajima, Hiroyuki Sanada, Yasuaki Kurata, Ryo Ikebe, Masahiko Tsugawa, Michitaro Mizushima, Rikiya Yasuoka, Hideo Murota.

In *Executioner*, Koga, Sakura and Hayato (Sonny Chiba, Eiji Go and Makoto Sato) are a triumvirate of karate secret agents recruited by an ex-police captain bent on stopping drugs from being smuggled into Japan. One of their chief drug smuggling suspects is the daughter of a Latin American foreign diplomat. The trio gets sucked into a cloak-and-dagger martial arts mystery in which their mission is to mop up the Yakuza and Chicago Mafia gangsters led by Mario Mizuhara and send them to the cleaners.

Chiba's fights are filled with the brutal kicks that would become his signature later in his career. His kicks are exemplified in one fight in this film wherein he steps in paint and proceeds to leave his footprint on a variety of faces and bodies, making it quite clear that Chiba was making contact with his targets. Back in the 1970s, Chiba was similar to Bruce Lee in that making contact with the stuntman was simply par for the course. Lee would often strike the participants during an action scene, whether accidentally or on purpose, depending on the person and the intent of the scene. After Lee passed away, the Chinese stuntmen Lee fought in films would display their missing teeth and other injuries as badges of honor. Chiba's karate mentality was similar in that he would also make or take the contact during an action sequence, and no one would complain about being hit. It was part of the honor code of the *karateka* stuntmen.

Fights in films need to have a blend of hard and soft techniques like martial arts in real life. Sonny Chiba's personal style of cinematic violence is hard and intense, but he would temper that with the softer style of his fellow actors. In earlier Chiba films, the softer-looking violence fell to actress Etsuko Shihomi; her

karate technique had more fluidity. In *Executioner*, actor Yasuaki Kurata is the softer fighter. The difference in his technique and Chiba's is most likely due to Kurata's fight experience in 24 Hong Kong movies.

To further enhance this soft-and-hard feel, the filmmakers shot Chiba's fights with tighter angles. His choreography also had more straight-line attacks. In contrast, Kurata's fights were shot in wide angle in order to showcase the neatness of his skills and make the techniques seem less direct. Not only did this balance out the fight scenes, but it made both actor's action bits look different. Kurata also struck a good balance by using close arm and fist techniques to show power and extended kicks to show speed and skill momentum.

Of note, this was actor Hiroyuki Sanada's film debut. Sanada portrays a young Koga learning martial arts. Sanada's father was a Yakuza and died when Sanada was a child. Chiba was his surrogate father. Sanada also played the villain in Jackie Chan's *Rush Hour 3* (2007).

Titleography: *The Executioner*. Translation—*Direct Hit! Hell Fist*. The English titles probably specifically refer to Chiba's Koga character, and the translation relates to Koga's deadly fist strike, which always hits its target. **MA Percentage: 30.8%**

EXECUTIONER II

Chokugeki Jigoku-ken: Dai-gyakuten (1974—Japan) **86m. FI: Uncredited. NOT/LOT: None; NOF/LOF: 7/ 4m 31s.** D: Teruo Ishii. C: Sonny Chiba, Eiji Go, Makoto Sato, Etsuko Shihomi, Kanjuro Arashi, Ryo Ikebe, Tanba, Yasuko Matsui, Hideo Murota, Rikiya Yasuoka.

Action stars like Sonny Chiba often put their bodies on the line for projects worthy of their martial arts skills. So to recover from injuries and prep for the next hard-knock film, Chiba would occasionally star in a "relaxing" film. That's exactly what *Executioner II* was for him. Clocking in with four minutes of karate action—compared to the 27 minutes in *Executioner*—Chiba takes a fight break in this film. But he also used it as an opportunity to further distance himself from his popular but psychotic anti-hero character in the *Street Fighter* films; that way the audience could begin to associate him with a more likeable cinematic caricature.

Executioner II opens with foreigner Sabine Kaufman visiting her young daughter in Japan. Kaufman is a paraplegic and the honorary chairman of the International Philanthropic Organization. While in Japan, she plans to raise money for disabled Japanese people by exhibiting her family's priceless Star of Pharaoh diamond necklace and donating the proceeds. When the necklace is stolen and Kaufman's daughter is kidnapped, the heroic trio of Koga, Sakura and Hayato (Sonny Chiba, Eiji Go and Makoto Sato) get roped into recovering the diamond and the child to save the Japanese government's face. During the ransom exchange, the child is recovered but the jewelry is lost in a double-cross and re-stolen via a stunt with an advertising balloon. Our heroes must then re-recover the jewel or the insurance company will have to pay $1 billion to Kaufman.

At this point, the audience's collective eyebrows might rise because of the film's lowbrow humor when our heroes hatch a crazy, almost Disney-like comedic scheme to re-steal the diamond. Eventually they find out that the Chicago Mafia is involved—a common plot element in 1970s Japanese crime films. And although his action sets are played more for laughs than kicks, Chiba has a few violent moments in this comedic caper. For example, he pops out someone's eyeballs and then rips out a man's guts with one strike.

For me, this film raises two questions. First, is it possible to hit someone's head so hard that his eyes pop out? Second, why is it that so many of these films specifically state that the Chicago Mafia is involved in backing Yakuza activity in Japan?

In terms of the Chicago Mafia reference, all I can surmise is that the most notorious 1970s Chicago Mafia gangster was a Japanese American known as Tokyo Joe. He was so feared throughout the United States that mob bosses put a hit out on him. Tokyo Joe was shot three times in the skull, survived and went into witness protection. By the early 1980s, his testimonies single-handedly bought the Chicago Mafia to its knees.

In terms of my first question, under certain circumstances, if you hit the right place, you could pop someone's eyes out. But here's a fun and freaky fact: You can still see things even if your eyeball is out of your socket as long the optic nerve is still intact. So if you want to look around the corner without anyone seeing you, you could theoretically pop your eyeball out, stretch the nerve a few inches and take a peek. It'd probably really hurt, though.

Titleography: *Executioner 2*; *Executioner II: Karate Inferno*. **MA Percentage: 5.25%**

EXECUTIONERS FROM SHAOLIN

洪熙官 (1976—Hong Kong) 98m. FI: Liu Chia-liang. NOT/LOT: 11/ 12m 31s; NOF/LOF: 17/ 30m 48s. D: Liu Chia-liang. C: Chen Kuan-tai, Lo Lieh, Lily Li, Wang Yu, Hsiao Hou, Wilson Tong, Fung Ke-an, Lee Hoi-san, Dong Wei, Lam Ching-ying, Jiang Dao, Gordon Liu Chia-hui, John Cheung.

Still from *Executioners From Shaolin* © Celestial Pictures Ltd. All rights reserved.

After the burning of Song Shan Shaolin Temple (see *Shaolin Temple* and *Five Shaolin Masters*), two of the Five Ancestors of Shaolin, Tsai De-zhong and Hu De-di, and two of Hu's students, Yung Zong and Zhi Kong, established the Jiu Lian Shan Shaolin Temple in Fujian province, which became the base for the Five Elders of Shaolin (Wu Mei, Bai Mei, Feng Dao-de, Miao Xian and Zhi Shan). Zhi Shan had nine very important students, eight of whom were members of the fabled 10 Tigers of Shaolin, and the ninth would later become one of the 10 Tigers of Canton.

The Manchus eventually found Jiu Lian Shan Shaolin Temple. They attacked it with thousands of soldiers and razed it. However, during the great second conflagration, the Five Elders and 10 Tigers of Shaolin escaped the clutches of the enemy. Thus the manhunt began. One of the most famous 10 Tigers of Shaolin to escape was Hong Xi-guan, who ended up hiding out with an opera troupe. Cantonese opera troupes would typically travel to villages in Canton province on vessels known as red junks and phoenix junks. Shaolin refugees often sought shelter with these actors and also taught them martial arts. As it turns out, Shaolin elder Bai Mei conspired with the Manchus to burn down the temple, and he also switched his allegiance from the Shaolin way to the Wu Dung philosophical way and tradition of martial arts.

Chang Cheh's *Men From the Monastery* (1974) featured Chen Kuan-tai as Hong Xi-guan, who escaped the burning temple and vowed undying revenge. Several years later, director Liu Chia-liang intelligently cast Chen as Hong in *Executioners From Shaolin,* giving the audience a face they could associate with the hero.

Executioners begins where *Monastery* ends, with the Shaolin Temple burning and Hong escaping. Hong hides on a red junk, where he meets and marries street entertainer Ying Chun (Lily Li), who bears him a son named Wen Ting (Wang Yu). Director Liu really outdid himself with the fight between Hong and Ying, a bedroom brawl on their honeymoon night that leads to them consummating their marriage. Ultra-precious.

Hong diligently practices his tiger kung fu to prepare for his fight against Bai Mei (Lo Lieh) and repeatedly ignores Ying's pleas to combine her crane martial arts with his tiger. Instead he focuses on striking certain acupuncture points at a specific time of day on a bronze statue in hopes that he can break Bai Mei's *chi* control and expose Bai's weaknesses. Hong fails, and it is up to Wen Ting to accept his mother's idea of combining her crane with Hong's tiger techniques, thus giving birth to one of kung fu's important styles, *hong jia chuen* (hung gar

kung fu), one of its premier skills being the tiger crane form.

Of martial arts interest, Bai Mei practices a real kung fu technique that allows him to use his chi to withstand strikes and blows to vital points of his body. However, this technique's weakness is that there is at least one point on the body that is vulnerable at a particular time of day (thus the stick in the ground and the shortening shadow indicating the time to strike in the film). If timed properly, the attack can kill Bai. Hong trains for the fight by hitting a bronze statue covered with little holes, and each time he hits a particular hole, it releases a steel marble. Hong then performs a series of other strikes to make certain he understands Bai's chi flow, and he figures out where and when to strike that vulnerable point. When he strikes the vulnerable point, a particular steel ball drops out of the statue's groin. The only problem is that Bai Mei can move this vulnerable point around at will.

Mainstream American audiences were introduced to Bai Mei via Quentin Tarantino's *Kill Bill: Vol. 2* (2004). Because Lo Lieh had passed away, Tarantino asked Gordon Liu Chia-hui to play a descendant of Bai Mei: the white-haired and bearded kung fu teacher of the Bride (Uma Thurman) and Bill (David Carradine).

In reality, Hong welcomed his wife's white crane martial arts. In 1821, Hong died at the ripe old age of 93, and Wen Ting never killed Bai Mei. Recent evidence purports that fellow and former Five Elder of Shaolin brother Feng Dao-de feigned becoming a Wu Dung monk and waited for the right time to assassinate Bai.

Lo Lieh returns as Bai in *Clan of the White Lotus* (1979) and *Shaolin Abbot* (1979), and Bai appears in *The Shaolin Avengers* (1976) and *Ninja Hunter* (1984).

Titleography: *Executioners of Death*; *Shaolin Executioners*. Translation—*Hong Xi-guan. Executioner of Death* could mean that those who cause death are executed or that one is dealing in death as in the execution of a will. *Shaolin Executioners* is logical (and generic) because Bai Mei and the Chings are trying to execute all those associated with Shaolin. **MA Percentage: 44.20%** SHAW BROTHERS

EXIT THE DRAGON, ENTER THE TIGER

天皇巨星 (1976—Hong Kong) 86m. KFI: Lung Fei, Shan Mao. NOT/LOT: 1/ 1m 29s; NOF/LOF: 17/ 25m 47s. D: Lee Tso-nam. C: Bruce Li, Zhang Yi, Lung Fei, Shan Mao, Jin Gang, Zheng Fu-xiong.

Elvis has been spotted in Florida, while Bruce Lee has been spotted in Taiwan. Bruce Li's fifth consecutive Bruceploitation film during the 1970s tries to imply that the root of Lee's death is somehow related to someone or something that happened in Taiwan. Partially influenced by Max Caulfield's book *Bruce Lee Lives* (1976), which exploitatively tries to make the case that Bruce Lee's death was a ruse (in a similar vein to the notion of Elvis still being in the building), stories were twisted to insinuate that Lee was possibly still alive.

In *Exit the Dragon*, Bruce Lee's kung fu brother is Tang Lung (in the dubs he was called David and Tiger), which is also Lee's character name in *Way of the Dragon*. Tang is so distraught over Lee's death that he travels to Taiwan to find out how Lee really died. Because Tang looks like Lee and the local media reports that Lee's death is a publicity stunt for his next film, Tang convinces the policeman guarding the entrance to the apartment of Betty Chan (Lee's secret girlfriend) that he is indeed Lee and needs to get into the apartment, where Tang believes there are missing clues that could solve Lee's death. As it turns out, the Taiwanese Triads are after a secret cassette recording Betty made that would implicate the Triads' involvement in Lee's death as well as other criminal activities. It is a race against time to locate the tape before the elusive Triad gang leader tortures it out of Betty. After that, it's time to find the big Baron and take him out.

Li's fighting prowess is not bad in this film because the choreographers put together some creative fights, especially the ones against the film's fight instructors, perennial Taiwanese bad guys Lung Fei (most recognized by Western audiences as Betty in Steve Oedekerk's 2002 parody *Kung Pow: Enter the Fist*) and Shan Mao. There are two fights of particular note. During one, Li takes on a gaggle of nasty geezers in front of a wall of stacked oil drums; the other is the final confrontation between Li and Baron (Zhang Yi).

During the oil-drum fight, baddies fling drums down at Li like giant raindrops, and dodging them required incredible awareness for both Li and his adversaries. The final fight takes place on Taiwan's vicious South China Sea coastline, which is littered with rough terrain. Based on my experiences working there, and knowing how Taiwanese film crews work, I'm guessing that the fight was shot in one day, from the break of dawn to the final minute of sunlight. With only ambient light to work with and high winds, you can see that the crashing waves from the sea are literally upon Li and Zhang toward the end of the fight, and director Lee uses the setup to its best advantage.

Pink Floyd's songs are often used in these lower-budgeted kung fu films, but as far as I have seen, this is the only film that has used Floyd's *Shine on You Crazy Diamond* from their *Wish You Were Here* album.

Titleography: *Bruce Lee, Star of Stars; Bruce Lee, the Star of All Stars.* Translation—*Supreme Superstar.* One of the nicknames of Li's character in the film is Tiger, thus *Exit the Dragon* refers to Bruce Lee's death and *Enter the Tiger* refers to Tiger. *Star of Stars*, like any martial arts film about Lee, would be a logical title. **MA Percentage: 31.71%**

FALL OF AKO CASTLE, THE

Ako-Jo Danzetsu (1978—Japan) **159m. FI: Uncredited. NOT/LOT: 1/ 48s; NOF/LOF: 10/ 16m 44s.** D: Kinji Fukasaku. C: Sonny Chiba, Kinnosuke Nakamura, Tsunehiko Watase, Masaomi Kondo, Toshirô Mifune, Kyôko Enami, Kasho Nakamura, Shinsuke Mikimoto.

The truth shall lead to death and misery for you and everyone around you—this is the price of *bushido.*

Once director Kinji Fukasaku's Yakuza films had ran the gamut, he began to make films that featured heroes and heroic deeds or period-piece samurai movies (*jidai geki*). These movies told traditional tales of honor and virtue, stories that could re-instill a sense of national pride in postwar Japanese audiences. Fukasaku's *Fall of Ako Castle* was planned to be a neo-Confucian chronicle of the age-old tale of the 47 Ronin who filtered out Lord Asano. The film was intended to focus on Sonny Chiba's Fuwa Kazuemone character, with the idea of featuring more fights. However, the other lead, Nakamura Kinnosuke, was able to use his influence with the studio to keep the story on traditional par, which similar to past 47 Ronin films, would expectedly have minimal sword fights. Regardless of the film's direction change, the final 11-minute fight is infused with creative sword choreography and gags via Chiba and the Japan Action Club, a stunt club created by Chiba to train stuntmen for martial arts films, making this version of the 47 Ronin most memorable.

Based on the true story of when Lord Asano Naganori was forced to commit *seppuku* (ritual suicide) for trying to kill Kira Yoshinaka in the emperor's palace over disrespectful insults, Asano's 47 loyal samurai warriors became the 47 Ronin (masterless samurai). Because Kira was exempt from punishment, this was considered an insulting blow to Asano and his samurai. Instead of disbanding, the 47 Ronin, under the leadership of Oishi Kuranosuke, sought to avenge Asano. The dilemma for the ronin was that if they were to kill Kira, the code of bushido would force them to commit seppuku, and all their families would be put to death. They waited patiently for their moment, and two years after Asano took his own life, on Dec. 14, 1702 (the film says 1703), the ronin attacked Kira's palace, beheaded him and ceremoniously committed *seppuku.*

After Hong Kong sword-fighting films were influenced by Japanese samurai movies (circa 1954-1966), in regard to fight simplicity and slow buildup, Shaw Brothers elevated the simple one-on-one-duel format into high-flying mass-mania tornadoes of sword-and-knife bloodbaths. Japanese choreographers had to change their fighting ways in order to keep up with Chinese choreographers, while still maintaining the traditional simplicity of samurai sword fights. Although Japanese cinema maintained the slow buildup toward the climactic fights, the choreography began infusing more spins and better camerawork later in the '70s.

In this film, for example, fights occur inside narrow corridors leading to many rooms that were built with breakaway wood-framed paper screens and thin tatami walls—which were summarily tossed, ripped, torn and crashed through by the various fighters. This demolition-derby approach to the fights added layers of excitement to the action's pandemonium. Additionally, dozens of opponents constantly move in and out of frame to add motion to the shots. Also, attacks and strikes were still distilled into simple blocks, counters and an occasional spin, and the final deathblows used samurai sword cuts

from high to low or side to side.

Inasmuch as it was difficult for actors to come across as not looking like the same kind of samurai warrior of film, new dimensions cropped up over the years when actors would create novel ways to hold, draw and re-sheath their swords like Chiba does. In this film, Chiba uses an open-handed grip, which was a unique approach at the time.

Titleography: *Last of the Ako Clan; Swords of Vengeance.* Translation—*The Castle of Ako is Destroyed. Swords of Vengeance* seems to be a crossover title keying into one of the alternative titles of the *Lone Wolf and Cub* series, *Sword of Vengeance.* Back then, most people would not bother to check or would not know the difference and end up getting either title. **MA Percentage: 11.03%**

FANGS OF THE COBRA

人蛇鼠 (1977—Hong Kong) **95m. FI: Yuen Cheung-yan. NOT/LOT: None; NOF/LOF: 3/ 7m 15s.** D: Sun Chung. C: Tsung Hua, Hsia Yao, Frankie Wei Hong, Dana, Ching Miao, Yang Chi-ching, Fan Mei-sheng.

This film just ain't right. It's herpetology versus rodentology in this martial-ogy. Critics enjoyed actor Don Johnson in his 1975 film *A Boy and His Dog,* a kooky tale about a boy named Vic who uses ESP to talk to his dog, Blood, while they try to survive a cruel world. Two years later, Hong Kong brings the world a movie about a girl and her snake that is an even more disturbing and slithery love saga between a reptile and a human.

Ah Fan (Hsia Yao) is in love with her snake, Xi Xi (a real cobra), and it turns out that Xi Xi is in love with Ah Fan. We see them laughing and frolicking in the woods hand in "hand." Dare I say they listen to music and even have a picnic together? They are literally a happy couple. But this is no ordinary snake because Xi Xi also knows how to fight, and she is quick to protect Ah Fan when she is in trouble. Then one day Ah Fan falls in love with a landowner's son, Tang Shi-de (Tsung Hua). He's just returned home from school, and his father hopes he will take over the family business. Although the flirtatious Man-ling had her designs on Shi-de while he was away at school, she's secretly carried on an affair with Shi-de's black-sheep stepbrother, Hu Lin (Frankie Wei Hong), and is "hissed off" that Shi-de has a new girlfriend. Hu and Man hatch a plan to discredit Shi-de and make the father give the business to Hu. It does not work because the snake steps in to rescue Shi-de and Ah Fan from a gang of rascals. Later, the snake saves Ah Fan, who almost dies on her way to the wedding. Regardless, Shi-de still cannot accept Xi Xi as a friendly snake. What more proof does he need?

After Shi-de and Ah Fan marry, Xi Xi runs away, but Ah San chases after her and tells her everything will be OK. They also share tears when Ah Fan tells

Still from *Fangs of the Cobra* © Celestial Pictures Ltd. All rights reserved.

Xi Xi that she is going to have a baby and asks the snake to keep her distance. After the baby is born, Hu and Man feel they can disrupt their rivals' marriage by putting an enormous rat in the baby's room, hoping that the rat will kill and eat the child. As the gray beastie stalks the child in the crib and is about to have supper, Xi Xi comes out of nowhere and fights the rat, which incidentally is a large mongoose painted to look like a rat.

While not part of the movie's fight statistics, the film's best fight is the classic image of what a snake-versus-mongoose kind of confrontation looks like. You may have seen those animal kingdom battles between a snake and a mongoose in books and on film. Except in this movie, it is a personal battle for the snake against a huge gray rat. After the movie's biggest rat dies, Shi-de finally acknowledges Xi Xi's good character, and Xi Xi sets her sights on Hu and Man. The ending is as peculiar as it is unsettling. It is impressive, if not freaky, how each scene with Xi Xi involves a real snake and how the whole snake-human story kind of works.

Although the kung fu fights are at the low end of the spectrum, the real snake kung fu is crazy, and the cobra-and-mongoose—I mean, rat—confrontation in the baby's bedroom must have taken forever to shoot and been a nightmare to keep everybody safe, including the child in the crib. For details on snake kung fu, see *Snake in the Eagle's Shadow* (1978). However, this film does contain a lot of great shots that reveal how part of the style was created by studying the attacking and defensive behavior of the cobra.

Titleography: *Cobra Girl.* Translation—*Man, Snake, Mouse.* See above martialogy. **MA Percentage: 7.63%** SHAW BROTHERS

FANTASTIC MAGIC BABY, THE

紅孩兒 (1975—Hong Kong) **62m. FI: Li Tong-chun, Liu Chia-liang. NOT/LOT: 4/ 1m 24s; NOF/LOF: 29/ 27m 35s. D:** Chang Cheh. **C:** Ding Hua-chong, Liu Chong-chen, Shen Yi-he, Chang Chuan-li, Yang Kui-yu, Jiang Dao, Hu Jin, Cai Hong, Deng Jue-ren, Fung Ke-an, Chao Li-chuan.

You have read in this book about *wuxia* novels—stories soaked in traditional tales and legends of superhuman swordsmen and magical feats. But there is another genre of martial arts prose called *gung-fu xiao shuo* (kung fu novels)—books in which the characters use martial arts even though the heroes are not necessarily from the wuxia setting. One of the most famous kung fu novels was completed during the Ming Dynasty. Written by Wu Cheng-an, *Journey to the West* is the translated title of *The Monkey King*, aka *Xi You Ji.* The titular Monkey King, Swuin Wu-kung, is famous for riding around on a golden cloud and fighting with a pole magically made from a strand of his hair. He is also arguably the most important character in Beijing opera. Accompanied by his kung fu brothers Zhu Ba-jie (a rake-wielding pig) and Xia Wu-jing (a creature with a monk's spade), the Monkey King sets out to protect Tang San-tsang, a Buddhist monk, while he travels to India to get sacred scriptures.

Chang Cheh made this film with Beijing opera popularity in mind, and it is presented not so much as a movie as it is a stage production shot with cameras. The sets, costumes, choreography and fight scenes all emulate a rich stage-play

version of what you might have seen at the local Chinese opera theater during its heyday. I was fortunate enough to watch live Beijing opera performances in one of those musty, smoke-filled opera theaters in 1970s Taipei. Back then, I knew little about Beijing opera, and although I loved the essence of the martial arts, I did not fully understand the opera's meanings, metaphors and analogies. Still, it was glorious. What is also unique about this film is that Chang did not just rehash a Beijing opera performance; he also weaved in the stage production sensibility of the pantomime of musical-comedy theatrical productions traditionally found in Great Britain and usually performed during the Christmas holidays. They would feature extravagant costumes and were most often geared toward younger audiences. As you might guess, I watched pantomimes growing up as a kid in England.

In *Fantastic Magic Baby*, Princess Iron Fan (Hu Jin) and Ox Demon King (Jiang Dao) want to eat Monk Tang (Deng Jue-ren) so they can live for 1,000 years, but Tang is protected by Swuin Wu-kung (Liu Chong-chen), Zhu Ba-jie (Shen Yi-he) and Xia Wu-jing (Yang Kui-yu). However, because Iron Fan and Ox Demon King's son Red Boy (Ding Hua-chong) has mastered the Three Types of True Fire in Flaming Mountain, they order him to kill Swuin. But with the help of god Yang Jian Er-lang (Fung Ke-an) and Swuin's simian stick skills and sneakiness, Tang and his crew prove too much for Red Boy. The flaming mad and red-in-the-face Red Boy reciprocates his loss by capturing Zhu Ba-jie and threatening to eat him. Just when all the frantic frays and frenetic fights seem to be failing, Goddess of Mercy Guan Ying (Chao Li-chuan) and her helper Dragon Girl (Chang Chuan-li) descend from heaven to make peace on Earth.

The fights are relatively slow all around. Their timing is off, and some fighters hesitate with their techniques. However, most of the extra fighters are well-known Shaw Brothers choreographers. As a note, the film runs for 62 minutes but is immediately followed by a real opera version of the story, thus the DVD's reported 92-minute running time.

Titleography: *Red Boy.* Translation—*Hong Hai-er. Red Boy* is a loose literal English translation of *Hong Hai-er*, although "baby" is better. In essence, Hong Hai-er, who is the title character and son of Ox Demon King and Princess Iron Fan, is a *Fantastic Magic Baby.* **MA Percentage: 46.75%** SHAW BROTHERS

FAREWELL TO A WARRIOR

辭郎洲 (1976—Hong Kong) **87m. FI: Uncredited. NOT/LOT: 3/ 2m 38s; NOF/LOF: 4/ 3m 31s. D:** Chu Yuan. **C:** Hsiao Nan-ying, Ting Min, Yeh Feng, Lo Kwai-feng, Huang Su-yu, Chan Chun-tung.

What makes *Farewell to a Warrior* such an important film for the studio is that it is the only Shaw Brothers film that uses Chaozhou opera. It's based on the famous opera story about how Lady Chen Bi-niang says goodbye to the love of her life, General Zhang Da, as he heads off to war.

Chaozhou opera is a style with a 500-year history beginning in the city of Chaozhou in Canton, which faces the South China Sea. Its major influence comes from Nanxi opera, which originated during the Song Dynasty (A.D. 960 to A.D.1279).

The film is set in Chaozhou during the waning years of the Song Dynasty. News spreads that the Mongols (or Yuans) are winning the war, and the call goes out to find any hero willing to defend China. When the emperor's Minister Wen asks General Zhang Da (actress Ting Min) to fight for the emperor, he refuses and cites how the emperor has on several occasions been disloyal to him. Lady Chen Bi-niang (Hsiao Nan-ying) understands his refusal and insists that he is not fighting for the emperor, but for the people. She also brings up the Yang family, which for 20 years was at odds with the emperor, but Old Lady Yang set aside her differences to defend the country from danger. (See *The 14 Amazons.*) Zhang Da agrees to fight and gathers an army of volunteers. Heading off to war, Zhang and Chen say goodbye, and she takes a moment to remind him of historical heroes Lady Hua Mu-lan and General Yue Fei.

When Mongolian General Zhang Hong-fan captures Zhang Da, Chen leads an army against the Mongols to rescue him. But then Minister Wen, who is the Mongolian liaison, tells Chen that her husband will be set free if she gives up. Blurting that she will be righteous until she dies and will never give up, Chen kills Wen and defeats the Mongols. Following that, Hong-fan arrives

to fight Chen. Unable to beat her, he orders all his archers to fire. Prickled like a porcupine, she refuses to go down and ends up dying on her feet with her eyes wide open.

Similar to Chang Cheh's *Fantastic Magic Baby*, the fights are performed using opera-style choreography, but director Chu Yuan shot them like movie fights rather than stage combat. The action looks more intense because Chu incorporates several camera angles and camera movements during each major fray. Of note, star Hsiao Nan-ying became famous for her Chaozhou opera portrayal of Chen. In the hopes of preserving the art and recording her performance for posterity, Chu insisted the film could only be shot using Hsiao as Chen.

Of historical note: During the Wei Dynasty (A.D. 386 to A.D. 534), Hua Mu-lan was a seamstress, martial artist and archer. When her father was too sick to fight the Tu Jue (an ethnic group from the Mongol empire), she put on men's clothing, joined the army, became a general and saved China. Mu-lan has been played by Nancy Chan in *Maiden in Armor* (1939), Yam Kim-fair in *The Story of Hua Mulan* (1951), Ivy Ling-po in the Shaw Brothers film *Lady General Hua Mulan* (1964) and Deng Bi-yun in *Hua Mulan, The Girl That Went to War* (1957). In 1250, during the Song Dynasty General Yue Fei used his observations of eagles fighting to teach his soldiers a new way to fight against the invading northern Jin armies. And in reality, while cinematic Zhang Hong-fan is a Mongol, the historical general was really a Chinese Han who served the Yuan Dynasty. He crushed the last Song resistance at the Battle of Yamen in 1279.

Titleography: As of this writing, no alternative titles could be found. Translation—*Saying Goodbye to Your Man on an Island Near a River*. The final character of the Chinese title represents a location somewhere on an island near a body of water, and Chaozhou is by the South China Sea. **MA Percentage: 7.07%** SHAW BROTHERS

FAST FISTS

大盜 (1972—Taiwan) **78m. MAI: Shan Mao. NOT/LOT: 2/ 1m 42s; NOF/LOF: 15/ 15m 44s.** D: Ding Shan-xi. C: Jimmy Wong Yu, Guo Xiao-zhuang, Paul Chang Chung, Tian Ye, Yee Yuen, Cui Fu-sheng, Lung Fei, Shan Mao, Zhang Fu-xiong.

During China's warlord period (1916-1927), the dream of a Chinese republic vanished. Every province seceded from the country, which fragmented China into independent states that were under the control of military leaders who called themselves warlords and attacked neighboring provinces over trivial excuses and stupid logic. However, bands of righteous "villains" arose out of this dark period of chaos to shine light onto Sun Yat-sen's (founder of the modern Chinese government) vision for the Republic of China. One such slice of brightness was the Red Lantern Gang, headed by the righteous vagabond Hong Ching-pao (Jimmy Wong Yu).

Set during this tumultuous time in Chinese history, the film opens in northern China. When local chiefs Chang and Ho battle to convince the famous and eloquently beautiful Madam Yu Pei-chu (Guo Xiao-zhuang) to perform her

Chinese opera at their respective headquarters, she opts to spend her time with Hong because the local militia maintains some semblance of police authority in the area. The upright Captain Fang (Paul Chang Chung) and the brutal Captain Chang (Yee Yuen) plan to use the opera performance to capture Hong and his Red Lantern Gang. Fang and Hong are on opposite sides of the law, Hong considered a feared outlaw by the chieftains and Fang a puppet policeman, but they both fall for Madam Yu. Hong proves his love by getting kicked out of the Red Lantern Gang and leaving that life behind. Hong and Fang learn that they share common goals: to form the Republic of China and oust the devious Commander Lu from office.

As the righteous Hong, Wong Yu dons the same recognizable hat he wore in *Ma Su Chen* and *Furious Fists*. It's similar to Indiana Jones' hat, but 10 years earlier. Curious wide-angle shots are used in the fights, and one cool fight uses a tracking shot on Wong Yu, who fights from one side of the room to the other in one take. Director Ding filmed some of the fights from obscure angles—usually through a piece of furniture or a slat of space between gratings or railings. Ding's signature action shot makes you feel like you are secretly watching the fight from the safety of a hidden position, and then the violence and emotion suddenly ends up in your face, where there is no hiding from it.

Two cool things happen in this film that still stick out in my mind. First is the enigmatic fight with Madame Yu. While dressed in full opera regalia, she beguilingly spins, ducks and strikes out with her opera prop weapons against the various corrupt policemen and bad guys who are trying to disrupt her performance because of her close ties to Hong. It is very romantic in a violent sort of way. Second, within that fight on the stage, Madame Yu's fatherly assistant gets caught up in the brawl. While he tries to protect Yu, he does a neat little opera-arm stance that shines with Chinese pride and opera glory. It is a simple movement and shot, but it is this kind of subtlety that director Ding handles with grace.

Titleography: *The Fastest Fists*; *The Fast Fists*. Translations—*The Big Criminal* and *Jimmy Wong Yu's the Big Criminal*. With undercranking, many of the fist maneuvers look fast, but there really is no rhyme or reason as to why this film is titled *Fast Fists* or something similar. Because Hong is the head of a gang, regardless of how righteous he is, he is a *Big Criminal* in the eyes of the warlords. **MA Percentage: 22.35%**

FATAL FLYING GUILLOTINES, THE

陰陽血滴子 (1977—Hong Kong) **78m. AD: Chen Shao-peng. NOT/LOT: 1/ 15s; NOF/LOF: 17/ 29m 29s.** D: Lei Cheng-gong. C: Chen Hsing, Carter Wong, Mang Hoi, Ou-Yang Sha-Fei, Chen Shao-peng, Cheung Lik, Gao Chiang, Guan Cong, Hua Shan, Dong Wei.

What's the difference between "Look on the road ahead" and "Look on the road—a head"? One means you need to keep your eyes on the road, the other means you may have just seen the effects of the dreaded decapitating flying guillotine. The beauty of the real weapon known as the blood-dripping object (aka the flying guillotine, blood whirlwind or lightning strike) is that no one ever survived its attack or got to write about it, so filmmakers got to create its look. Director Ho Meng-hua in *The Flying Guillotines* first created the weapon design based on what he thought it might look like and then convinced the audience that this could have been the design that was commissioned by Emperor Yong Zheng as a way to behead honest politicians who stood in his way.

This film's version contends that Shen Mo-chao (Chen Hsing) designed the weapon while living in seclusion in No Return Valley because the vapors from the valley helped the insane man survive the injuries he suffered when he failed to get the Da Mo Holy Book of medicine from Shaolin 20 years earlier. Prince Yong Zheng sends emissaries to Shen Mo to convince him to join his side and help him become emperor. Aware of Yong Zheng's plans, Shaolin fighters are sent to warn Shen Mo that the Shaolin will be forced to kill him if he defects and helps Yong Zheng. But anyone who tries to bully the schizophrenic Shen Mo becomes the butt of a cruel joke in that his head will be able to see his backside as it rolls away. As you can see, it's "ass"-inine to bother Shen Mo.

While the emissaries get killed by Shen Mo, good-hearted warrior Shen Ping (Carter Wong) arrives at Shaolin and passes the three combative tests to attain the Da Mo Holy Book so he can save his dying mother. But then Yong Zheng steals the book from Shen Ping and uses it as a bargaining chip to bring the psychotic Shen Mo over to his dark side. Fearing the worst, the Shaolin abbot believes Shen Ping has the guts, courage and skills to convince Shen Mo not to reveal his secrets to Yong Zheng. On her deathbed, Shen Ping's mother tells him about his long lost father, who disappeared 20 years ago. Can you guess who the father is? The final fight becomes a family affair, but without classic characters Mr. French, Buffy, Jody, Cissy, Uncle Bill and of course Mrs. Beasley. But then, someone may end up being a puppet for Yong Zheng.

For such a serious film, there is one bit of perhaps inadvertent humor. When Shen Ping shares his sad childhood story with an accompanying monk, melancholy Chinese flute music plays in the background, which sets the tone for Shen Ping's grief. However, at the end of the story, Shen Ping and the monk look off to one side and see a fellow traveler sitting on a rock playing the flute music. I'm not sure if this was actually planned to be funny or not, but it came across as rather humorous.

Because Chen Hsing's character is a wild man, his usual hunchbacked and scrappy-looking posture fits his character and therefore the film. The fights use a lot of hand-held camerawork, and there are also a lot of quick pans and tracking shots, which add a new look and dimension to Chen Shao-peng's choreography. It is a good story with some predictable twists, but the overall look and feel of the film blends nicely with a somewhat different-looking weapon from Ho Meng-hua's cinematic version.

The flying guillotine first appeared in Ho's *The Flying Guillotine* (1975), then resurfaced in Jimmy Wong Yu's *Master of the Flying Guillotine* (1976), Ho's *Flying Guillotine Part II* (1978) and *Vengeful Beauty* (1978), and lastly (for now) in Ching Siu-tung's futuristic thriller *Heroic Trio* (1993).

Titleography: As of this writing, no alternative titles could be found. Translation—*The Yin-Yang Blood Dripping Object*. Once you are beheaded, your blood makes the weapon a blood-dripping object, thus part of the Chinese title is merely the Chinese name of the weapon. The *Yin-Yang* part of the title suggests that either Taoists are somehow involved or that because Shen Mo-chao was injured at Shaolin Temple (the inhabitants of which are mostly Buddhist), an iconic Taoist philosophical image was a way of being anti-Buddhist as far as Shen Mo-chao was concerned. **MA Percentage: 38.12%**

FAST SWORD, THE

奪命金劍 (1971—Hong Kong) **79m. KFI: Han Ying-chieh, Sammo Hung, Pan Yue-kun. NOT/LOT: None; NOF/LOF: 19/ 26m 24s.** D: Huang Feng. C: Zhang Yi, Han Hsiang-chin, Shih Jun, Miao Tian, Wang Lai, Gao Ming.

When you take the law into your own hands and your fingers do not grasp what the law is, you will end up on the wrong arm of the law in hand, and it will disarm you.

When Nan Kung-zhen (Shih Jun) avenges his father's death by killing Chief Tu Tien-bao in front of Tu's piers, Tu's brother (Miao Tian) vows bloody vengeance. However, Nan escapes their headquarters, makes his way back home and meets up with his whip-expert sister (Han Hsiang-chin) and blind mother (Wang Lai), who are concerned for Nan's life. Amid lots of horse riding, the audience once again hears spaghetti Western twangs and moaning chorus voices.

The righteous Master Yen (Zhang Yi) from the acclaimed Six Fan School is assigned to track Nan down and bring him in alive for trial. The whole Nan family bows to Yen's upright reputation, and Kung-zhen agrees to go quietly. But in a blind vengeful rage, Tu's brother sends a barrage of assassins to kill Yen and Nan as a means to hide the Tu family's true guilt over wrongly killing Nan's father 12 years earlier.

When you watch early Chinese kung fu films, it is always a great idea to watch with the gaze of wide-eyed wonder, ignore logic and wait for things you could never have predicted to happen. In the folklore of *wuxia* novels, everyone knew kung fu, but not everyone knew who knew kung fu, and understanding this makes it easier to suspend disbelief.

The Fast Sword is one of the last early-'70s films in which I recall seeing actors using sword strikes and blocks that look like regular punches and blocks; they are easier for actors to remember. The point was to teach the actors the fights as if it was their arms doing the fighting, then simply give them a sword and tell them to do the exact same movement as if they weren't holding a sword. This made the sword choreography more manageable, and actors did not have to bother having good sword technique. In a sense, it uses the idea that a weapon is really an extension of the arm. The only problem with this technique is that if you are holding a sword and can only do moves based on punches and blocks, the sword length quickly limits the nature of the choreography. Imagine having to throw an uppercut with a 36-inch sword attached to your hand. But the first fight between Nan and Yen exemplifies that it can work and look good.

There are a few well-orchestrated triple-trampoline stunts, in which an

actor jumps onto three different trampolines in one unedited shot, which by the way is very difficult to do in a controlled manner. Also, when the blind mother is threatened with disembowelment, her long walking stick springs into a nasty wooden pole and actress Wang Lai deftly transitions from decrepit blind mom to warrior woman who coldly disperses the enemy to the north and south poles. And look out for the Porcupine Arrow technique.

There are two creative set pieces that I just cannot get out of my mind. The first is when Yen proves his kung fu mettle at a teahouse by crushing a cup in his hand and throwing the broken pieces against the door. The shards stick into the door and form the Chinese character *fa*, which means "law." In the second, actor Miao Tian uses a giant pair of scissors as his weapon in the final fight.

An interesting side note: During most of his early film years, Zhang Yi was slated as the Chinese Toshiro Mifune because both actors have a similar jowly, dead-serious look. The comparisons faded, however, when Zhang became more popular as a bad guy. *Fast Sword* is one of his earlier films that beam with the legendary Mifune's facial seriousness.

Titleography: As of this writing, no alternative titles could be found. Translation—*Life Taking Gold Sword*. The title is the name of the sword Yen uses. Although generic, Yan is fast with his sword, so *Fast Sword* fits. **MA Percentage: 33.42%**

FEARLESS FIGHTERS

頭條好漢 (1971—Taiwan) **83m. MAI: Uncredited. NOT/LOT: 1/ 30s; NOF/LOF: 11/ 15m 34s.** D: Wu Min-xiong. C: Chen Lieh, Yee Yuen, Cheung Ching-ching, Chiang Ming, Huang Jin.

Hokey fights can be horrendous fun. Virtuous swordsman in this film, Lei Peng (Yee Yuen) refuses to follow in the wily ways of the Eagle Claw Clan. Under the leadership of Lei's former friend You Pa (Huang Jin), the Eagle Claw Clan wipes out Lei's family and takes back their gold—gold that was previously stolen by the clan and that Lei is determined to return to the government. Along his righteous path, Lei teams up with three people: a mysterious swordswoman (Cheung Ching-ching) and a brother-sister duo bent on killing Lei because they believe he killed their father while stealing the gold, though You Pa is the real culprit.

With villain names like Soul Pickers, Dragon Razor Brothers, White Claw Man and the ultimate one-man army, the Loner, the film is a stone's throw from crazy. But when things get rolling and the villains start using weapons such as flying sparrows (the Klingon bat'leth in *Star Trek* is based on this weapon), solar rays, devil rippers and angel swords, then the proverbial rock is really gathering moss. Yet when the heroes start to counter with high-jumping vaults across lakes and weapons with freaky detachable legs and arms that shoot out on chains, well, it's as wacky as trying to kill two birds with 10 stones. In the end, the film is not short on head-scratching fun.

Because the main cast members are mostly seasoned old-school opera stage performers and not the stereotypical martial arts relief players like Jackie Chan and his opera brothers, their fights tend to be more about spins, poses and excessive movements of grandeur. Although each of the fights' rhythm and pace is similar to the Chinese black-and-white kung fu films of yesteryear, the freaky sounds and cheap visual effects add a certain *je ne sais quoi* to all the haphazard symmetry of the sequences.

Titleography: *Ninja Killers*; *A Real Man*. Translation—*Bravest of the Brave*. There are no ninjas in this film. Released during the American ninja craze of the 1980s, *Ninja Killers* is really stretching the title and must be based on the 10-second scene in which hooded men enter Lei's house, only to remove their hoods immediately. It is like saying bank robbers with kerchiefs over their mouths in a Western are really *Ninja Cowboys*. Now that's a film title dying to be made—10 percent for the idea, please. **MA Percentage: 19.36%**

FEARLESS HYENA

笑拳怪招 (1979—Hong Kong) **97m. FD: Jackie Chan. NOT/LOT: 8/ 16m 25s; NOF/LOF: 16/ 36m 46s.** D: Jackie Chan. C: Jackie Chan, James Tien, Yen Shi-kwan, Li Kun, Chen Hui-lou, Zheng Fu-xiong, Ma Chang, Wang Chi-sheng, Ricky Cheng Tien-chi, Dean Shek, Han Ying.

Why mess with perfection? It makes perfect sense that for Jackie Chan's first script and directorial debut he would use the formulaic plot and story from *Snake in the Eagle's Shadow* and *Drunken Master,* the two films that essentially made him lovably famous and comically popular. It is a familiar premise: When bumpkin student Shing Lung's (Jackie Chan) teacher and grandfather (James

Tien) is killed by kung fu villain Yen Chuen-wong (Yen Shi-kwan) because Yen wants to wipe out the Hsing I Clan, Shing has no alternative but to get revenge. He learns kung fu from Unicorn (Chen Hui-lou), a surrogate *sifu*, fellow Hsing I Clan member and friend to his grandfather, so he can avenge his teacher's death. Everything boils down to Chan the man doing what he can to create great fights and set pieces. But the danger of formulas, like in this and many Chan films, is that the stories get tiresome quickly.

As the film begins, Shing enjoys fighting but is forbidden to do so by his grandfather. So he finds a job fighting for a kung fu school where he dresses up in various costumes and beats those who come to challenge the school's legitimacy. He starts off as a cross-eyed village idiot and uses avoidance-behavior techniques similar to those often seen in early Charlie Chaplin films. Next he's a pirate with a weird mustache who does some interesting catch-and-release weapon work that further develops in Chan's next directed film, *Young Master* (1980). His final alter ego sees Chan in drag, using his fake breasts (likely large oranges or small grapefruits) to pummel a guy into pulp. However, Shing's clowning around leads to his grandfather's death when someone recognizes the fighting style and the villain uses the information to locate and kill his grandfather and destroy his home. Shing is taught emotional kung fu and learns to use his emotions to call upon different fighting skills, which in turn gives him the ability to play with his opponents' emotions.

Chan devises several brutal training segments for his character—a nod to his grueling days at the opera school—such as the hanging upside-down sit-up that makes him forcibly smash his whole back against a wooden plank. But then that visceral sequence is balanced by an enjoyable chopstick food fight. There are several things that stick out in this film. One of the training sequences marks the first time we really get to see Chan flex his muscles for camera, but he does so in a way that does not come across as forced. His emotional kung fu forms are shot similarly to the Eight Drunken Immortal forms in *Drunken Master*. The fight he does with the three fighters using long-handled swords is influenced by the spear fight in *Snake and Crane Arts of Shaolin*, but Chan takes things to a higher level as you sit in awe waiting for a major injury to occur. Incidentally, it did, though back then, Chan didn't show his outtakes. There is also a very interesting split-second shot of his gut in which it is painfully distended to create the impression that his *chi* (*qi*) is strong. Jackie forcibly filled his stomach with air to get that look. As an aside, back then, Chan did not buy into things like chi.

During the shooting of the sequel *Fearless Hyena II* (1983), Chan walked off the set, and Lo Wei completed the film by mixing new stuff with old footage from this film.

Titleography: As of this writing, no alternative titles could be found. Translation—*Laughing Fist Odd Style*. Chan's character learns the odd emotional kung fu style, which also sometimes makes him laugh like a wild hyena, thus the English title. The style is fictional and was created for the film. **MA Percentage: 54.83%**

FEMALE YAKUZA TALE: INQUISITION AND TORTURE

Yasagure Anego Den Sokatsu Rinchi (1973—Japan) **84m. MAI: Uncredited. NOT/LOT: None; NOF/LOF: 5/ 6m 16s.** D: Teruo Ishii. C: Reiko Ike, Makoto Ashikawa, Arumi Kuri, Meika Seri, Jun Midorikawa, Emi Jo, Toru Abe, Tarô Bonten, Tatsuo Endo, Ryohei Uchida.

When filming on a threadbare budget, there's no better way to spice up a film than with bare swordswomen bouncing around the screen. It probably made a lot of gawking adolescents rave, "Who cares about the fight scenes with all the nude women running around!"

As American women were burning their bras in the 1970s (they didn't really, but the legend drew attention to a woman's right to reject male beauty standards in that they didn't want to wear it just to make men happy), on the other side of the Pacific, the rising popularity of Japanese pinky-violence films helped Japanese women explode out of their traditional restrictive societal notions of sex and nudity. Wielding samurai swords, young Japanese women played Yakuza members who made mincemeat out of men and used their sexual wiles to make men look like idiots—things that, strangely enough, should not have gone over well in a male-dominated society.

In this film set in 1904 Tokyo, Reiko Ike reprises the role of Ocho from *Sex and Fury*. The film is a sequel, in which Ocho seeks revenge against a Yakuza gang that framed her for being the Crotch-Gouge murderer because they

discovered that she did not fit their drug-mule requirements during a vile and degrading inspection of her female anatomy. Teaming up with lone-wolf Yakuza Jyoji (Ryohei Uchida), who owes loyalty to Ocho's old-school Yakuza boss, Ocho exposes the Yakuza's sordid drug-trafficking method of using prostitutes under the local Boss Lady's protection.

Ocho, Jyoji and Boss Lady unite under their code of nudity. It sounds bizarre, but it is the system under which the Yakuza used and abused these prostitutes. In a freakish and disjointed three-and-a-half minute final fight scene, dozens of fully nude women use samurai swords, *manrikigusari* (a chain with weighted ends) and steel-clawed gloves to take down these god-awful Yakuza.

It is as plain as blood on snow that little care was put into this sequel's fights. In the opening fight, Ike spins a bright red bamboo umbrella like a hypnowheel and draws a sword from the parasol's handle. While the pouring rain falls in slow motion, she cuts her opponents down. With each successive sequence, she loses clothing until she is completely naked. In one shot, Ike blocks and actually grabs the sword blade of her attacker—an indication that the director was not planning more than one take for the sequence. Although slow motion lends a mythic quality to a fight scene, in low-budget films or when time is limited, it is sometimes used to make the fights feel longer.

The final fight is, for the most part, a collection of single shots randomly edited together. They are filled with blood squirting, bodies being cut, and actors swinging a sword or some other weapon directly into or in front of the camera. But perhaps, as the opening line of this martiality states, the majority of viewers won't care how wrong the fights look when there are nude women on camera. However, there is one unique fight in this film: A women parades around like Meiko Kaji's character in *Female Prison Scorpion*—replete with the low, sultry voice and wide-brimmed black hat—and uses a hairpiece that telescopes out into a long sword. Sadly, the weapon does not reappear later in the film.

On several occasions, Ocho uses karate kicks, something that did not exist in 1904 Tokyo, unless she learned kicking in either northern Japan from Shaolin kung fu practitioners or in Okinawa after Chinese traders introduced *ba qua*, *tai chi* and Shaolin martial arts into the region.

Titleography: *Female Yakuza Tale*. Translation—*Story of a Wild Elder Sister: Widespread Lynch Law*. The titles pretty much reflect the film's plot and angst. **MA Percentage: 7.46%**

FIGHTING ACE

好小子的下一招 (1979—Hong Kong) **85m. FD: Ricky Cheng Tien-chi, Wong Chi-sang. NOT/LOT: 15/ 13m 32s; NOF/LOF: 20/ 22m 56s.** D: Zhang Zhi-chao. C: John Liu, Doris Lung Chun-er, Cliff Ching Ching, Kwan Yung-moon, Han Su, Wang Tai-lang, Li Min-lang, Wu Ma.

In the realm of real martial arts, not all films touch upon the tradition of a student only having one kung fu teacher. If they do, they do not always show the ceremony that symbolizes the birth (initiation) into a family. The *sifu* is the father, and the students are the brothers and sisters. Seniority is determined by how long someone has trained at the school rather than by age, so a 15-year-old student could be the older kung fu brother of a 20-year-old student. Traditionally, a student's acceptance into the school begins with the student kneeling before the teacher, who is sitting on a chair. The student offers a cup of tea, the teacher takes a sip, and then the teacher gives the student a *hong bao* (red envelope) with a small amount of money in it. Once the student takes the envelope, he or she is now a part of the family, an official student. I went through this ceremony in Taiwan. It was a big deal, and I was happy, humbled and fortunate to be a part of it. Nowadays it is often about signing contracts, down payments, and paying through the nose for uniforms and tests to move up in rank. This film brings out the old teacher-student spirit in that it relies on true heart but begins with the broken heart of a child.

Protagonist Chi Kao's mother is raped and killed by a corrupt bum-legged killer because she refused to hand over the family's secret kung fu books to him. Chi escapes with his uncle and resurfaces 20 years later, eager to find a kung fu teacher who will take him under his wing in his quest for revenge. Chi's uncle takes demeaning jobs to find kung fu teachers and becomes a petty laborer at a house where the famous Master Yen (Kwan Yung-moon) teaches kung fu to the rich owner's son, who is lazy and has no interest in the art. Chi (John Liu) convinces Master Yen to teach him and goes through the initiation ceremony. When the house owner finds out that Yen is teaching Chi, the uncle and Chi are kicked out of the house. Back on the streets and still yearning to learn, Chi finds two teachers but refuses to call them sifu because of his commitment to Yen. Chi ends up learning kung fu from a third great master, who instills such a strong sense of loyalty and uprightness in him that Chi goes out and beats up other kung fu people who are perceived as threats to the man. The only problem is that the third master is the one who killed and raped his mother. When the truth is out of the closet, Chi enters a room that he can never leave until death does him part.

Due to Liu's *taekwondo* background, the characters he plays are always kickers, so it's refreshing that Chi is taught by kicking teacher Master Yen. Thus, when Chi can suddenly do fancy kicks, it makes sense. The sad thing about this film is that Liu is right-footed and Kwan is left-footed, so their training fights look awkward, not unlike a southpaw fighting an orthodox boxer. Yen is the best thing about this film, but because it can be tough to do smooth choreography under these circumstances, Yen's character disappears from the film completely. This movie was Kwan's first, last and only film with Liu.

Titleography: *Kung Fu Ace*; *Master of Death*; *Kid's Ace in the Hole*. Translation—*Next Kung Fu Move of the Little Good Lad*. The Chinese title refers to the fact that although Chi learns kung fu from different teachers, he is still loyal to his first teacher. The English titles are generic: Chi is a *Kung Fu Ace*, the rapist/killer is the *Master of Death*, and *Kid's Ace in the Hole* captures the Chinese title's sense that Chi is a young lad. Maybe Chi's various kung fu abilities are the *Ace in the Hole* for his avenging heart. **MA Percentage: 42.90%**

FIGHTING BLACK KINGS

(1976—USA) 90m. TA: Mas Oyama. NOT/LOT: None; NOF/LOF: None. D: Goto Shuji. C: Because this is a documentary, there is no main cast.

This is an interesting documentary about the First World Open Karate Tournament held in Japan, and although the brunt of the information and tournament action is strongly biased toward the Japanese contestants, the filmmakers recognized the importance of the American market. From the U.S. perspective, the film follows four American *karateka*—William Oliver, Willie Williams, Frank Clark (the only white man on the American team) and Charles Martin—as they prepare for the *kumite* tournament in Japan, which also features 128 karate contestants from 35 countries.

Fighting Black Kings is an important documentary because it reflects an influential martial arts growth period in America and gave a 1970s American audience a peek into the intensity and straightforward beauty of karate. Along with some rather rousing kumite competitions based on *kyokushinkai* karate rules, there is the usual collage of heads, elbows, heels and kicks breaking boards, ice, concrete, roof tiles, cinder blocks, hand-size pebbles, watermelons and the top of a bottle. The film is all about promoting what the documentary calls the sport of karate, which has been around for about 1,000 years, and explains that the three major elements of karate are the thrust, catch and kick. To this, even I say, "What?"

Like anything that has to be a show-and-sell, there is also trickery. As we know now, breaking objects is not just about focus or karate but also techniques rooted in physics. One of the demonstrations shown several times involve a guy running full speed toward a speeding car. Just as he is about to be run over, he does a flying sidekick over the car. Of course, it is a camera perspective trick. While in the air, the guy's trailing leg disappears from view as the car drives by, so he was not exactly going over the car so much as jumping over to one side of the car. However, what I enjoyed most was the straightforward side, roundhouse and front kicks demonstrated by William Oliver. There's nothing gymnastic about it. Instead, it's just some old-school kicks—traditional, fast and powerfully simple.

On a sentimental note, I felt a tear welling up in my eye when they were showing footage of the Twin Towers in New York City. How could we ever guess back in 1976 that they would disappear from the Manhattan skyline?

Titleography: *The Strongest Karate*. During the 1970s, black America embraced the whole kung fu film pop-culture movement with greater passion than white America. Thus, *Fighting Black Kings* is an effort to focus on the black demographics.

FIGHTING MAD

(1978—USA) 90m. FI: Uncredited. NOT/LOT: 8/ 2m 44s; NOF/LOF: 10/ 4m 33s. D: Cirio Santiago. C: Leon Isaac Kennedy, Carmen Argenziano, Allen Arkus, Joe Mari Avellana, Tony Carreon, Ernie Carvajal, Vic Diaz, Ramon D'Salva, Elena Fortman-Waters, Jayne Kennedy.

This film is partially inspired by the true story of Japanese World War II

soldier Lt. Hiroo Onoda. It's a good concept for a film and also a surprise. Sure, it is another low-budget film featuring a protagonist who learns martial arts and then seeks revenge, but it offers a unique approach to the genre.

Three Vietnam War veterans steal a shipment of gold in the Philippines and are escaping via the many intertwining straits in the South China Sea, but Doug Russell (Leon Isaac Kennedy) is the odd man out. He is betrayed, brutally stabbed in the neck and flung overboard by his two false friends, Marelli and Maghee. The two revel in their riches, return to Los Angeles and become powerful, shady, feared businessmen. Marelli also sets his lascivious eyes on Russell's voluptuous wife and threatens to hurt her son if she doesn't reciprocate his lewd advances.

Meanwhile, the nearly dead Russell washes up on an uncharted island being defended by two holdout Japanese soldiers who believe that World War II is still going on. After they nurse Russell back to health, the commanding officer refuses to believe that the war is over. However, after repeated pleas from Russell, the officer agrees to teach him the way of the samurai so he can exact revenge against Marelli and Maghee. When American Marines stage a landing on the island, they find Russell and the commander, much to their surprise. After a few Marines get hacked by the commander, he disappears into the jungle. Russell is left with sword in hand and thumbs a ride back to the states, where he must now track his enemies, find his family and live up to the code of *bushido*.

In terms of the action, this film is a surprise—not only because the actors hold their samurai swords correctly but also because the fights are filled with motion and spinning. The actors also move in circles around each other during the fights, which is refreshing compared to most American films that use straight-line attacks and retreats. Furthermore, there are no static poses in which an actor is trying to look cool or ominous with the sword; they just jump right in and hack away. The actors are really trying to do some decent fights, and the use of wide and tight angles within the same sequences, plus undercranking the camera, adds a frenetic pace to the fights that separates them from the usual low-budget affairs seen in the 1970s. There are also many solid and memorable beheadings toward the film's end, and the barbershop duel is filled with wide, large motions and tight spins, which make for a closer shave than the villain bargained for.

The real-life Hiroo Onoda was a lieutenant in the Japanese army during World War II. In 1944 he was assigned to conduct guerrilla warfare in Lubang, a remote Philippine island. It was not until March 19, 1972, that he emerged from the dark jungles of the past to learn the war had ended in 1945.

Titleography: *Death Force*. Not to be confused with Peter Fonda's revenge-angst film *Fighting Mad*. **MA Percentage: 8.09%**

FINGER OF DOOM

太陰指 (1971—Hong Kong) 91m. FI: Xu Er-niu, Xu Song-hao. NOT/LOT: None; NOF/LOF: 22/ 15m 17s. D: Pao Hsueh-li. C: Chen Feng-chen, Chin Han, Ivy Ling Po, Chin-hsien, Tung Li, Yang Chi-ching, Hong Xing-zhong, Little Unicorn, Po Chi-yin.

For this film, understanding the Chinese title adds a new dimension to the viewing pleasure of *Finger of Doom*. The literal word-for-word translation of *Tai Ying Zher* is *Extreme Shadow Finger*, but when the characters *tai ying* are together, they describe an acupuncture term that refers to positions of certain *chi* meridians. These meridians run along the inside portions of the limbs and the sides of the abdomen. When you understand how all these chi meridians and acupuncture points work, then you can control a person's health or death. But the Finger of Doom skill is a bit more special in that it goes beyond life and death and into the dimension of zombies.

Finger of Doom is a supernatural thrill, spill and chill in which that coughing you hear in the background is a coffin filled with a ghostly looking but living maiden draped in a flowing white gown (reminiscent of Joey Wang in *A Chinese Ghost Story* (1987)). These maidens are part of a spectral clan of Jiang Hu women; some are good and some are bad. At night, when the maidens arise from their coffins and put on their steel-tipped fingers and poke someone in the nape of the neck (the secret Finger of Doom kung fu technique), that man turns into one of their sword-zapping zombies. (The maidens are poking points along the tai ying meridians.) The first duty of these undead men is to transport their ladies around in a coffin because the beauties inside prefer to do their deeds at night. However, depending on which woman in white emerges, the undead man can either be fodder for evil or a fighter for good, something the Four Hill Heroes will witness firsthand—or finger.

several unique technique pieces: the "tippy toes" fight, in which actor Li Jian-xiong is on his toes like the Greek god Pan and silently fights with Gordon over a stolen box belonging to the General (a character inspired by the hit Shaw Brothers' 1972 non-kung fu film *The Warlord*); the training sequences and subsequent use of the training to get through a corridor of bone-crushing, multi-positioned wooden posts; the sickening fight against the Leper King and his horde of sloughing slouches; and the final Lo vs. Liu/lama vs. Shaolin showdown, in which Lo looks a little disjointed but seems to suck it up as the fight moves along, ultimately rivaling some of the best stuff he's done.

The film also gives Gordon Liu another opportunity to demonstrate his butterfly knife skills. (See *Heroes of the East.*) The butterfly knife is a forearm-length, 3-inch-wide, single-edged broadsword with a knuckle guard that can be used as knuckle dusters and a parrying hook that can be used for either trapping weapons or as a second handle to hold the blade along the forearm.

Correctly called butterfly swords and usually used in pairs, the weapon first originated in southern China with the Shaolin Temple version, in which a 3-inch section from the tip of the blade down the curved surface was sharpened. After the burning of Song Shan Shaolin in 1735, the Secret Triad Society formed as a result of the conflagration and added a stabbing tip to the sword. During the 19th century, the entire blade was sharpened, and the subsequent introduction of a fourth version called the tiger's blade featured a curved distal part of the blade.

Titleography: *Fists and Guts.* Translations—*One is Guts, Second is Strength and Third is Kung Fu* and *Real Kung Fu.* One, two and three refer to the virtues of Ah Yung, Pin Peng and Ah San, respectively. A logical title for this film could have been *Shaolin vs. Lama* (although this title was used in a 1983 film starring Alexander Lo Rei). **MA Percentage: 31.96%**

FIST OF FURY

精武門 (1972—Hong Kong) **107m. FI: Han Ying-chieh. NOT/LOT: 2/ 3m 26s; NOF/LOF: 10/ 22m 15s.** D: Lo Wei. C: Bruce Lee, James Tien, Han Ying-chieh, Nora Miao, Maria Yi Yi, Lam Ching-ying, Tony Liu Yung, Robert Baker, Tien Feng, Wei Ping-ao, Hashimoto Riki, Lo Wei, Feng Yi.

Over the years, I have had the pleasure to interview a regular who's who of Chinese martial arts film directors, actors and fight choreographers. To every one of these cream-of-the-crop filmmakers, I always ask the same question: "What are your feelings toward Bruce Lee?" More than 95 percent have answered pretty much the same thing and made reference to this film, saying, "It gave our country an identity." I have also asked the same question to many of the top Asian-American martial arts and nonmartial arts actors, and they have also said, "He made me proud to be Asian." Those are pretty powerful words, and it says a lot about the influence of Bruce Lee on Chinese society, if not at least on the Chinese and Asian-American film communities.

It took the clout of Bruce Lee to overcome Hong Kong's fear of producing anti-Japanese films with *Fist of Fury.* The Mandarin title, *Ching Wu Men*, reflects the film's significance. "*Men*" means "gate" or "door," and in martial arts circles, it represents a gate to knowledge. So *Ching Wu Men* means entry into the Ching Wu martial arts school, which was created by Shanghai martial arts legend Huo Yuan-jia. Although three films have spotlighted Huo's life—*Legend of a Fighter* (1982), *Fist of Legend* (1994) and *Fearless* (2006)—*Fist of Fury* focuses on the events after his death.

Set during the Japanese occupation of Shanghai in 1909, the story revolves around Huo's student Chen Chen (Bruce Lee), who arrives late for the funeral and seeks to avenge his master's death. After Chen Chen endures ridicule from the visiting Japanese entourage, headed by the weak and effeminate Japanese interpreter, we are only minutes away from one of Hong Kong cinema's most important fight scenes. Of note, Wu Ping-ao, who played the wimpy interpreter, was imprisoned in real life for brutally stabbing his wife 10 times.

Although kung fu film fans now know that it was Jackie Chan who flew backward across the yard during the final stunt when he was doubling for Hashimoto Riki's villainous character Susuki, Lee's earlier fight in the Japanese school had

When a renegade member of the female Tai Ying cult, maiden Kung Suen Mao Neong (Po Chi-yin, who only made three films), uses her Finger of Doom skills to make many zombie men and use them as part of her plan to take over the cult, the high priestess orders her right-hand maiden (Ivy Ling Po) to create her own group of coffin-carrying cronies to stop Kung before she becomes drunk with power and her army of zombies flows like beer during a fraternity party. But it seems that the powder keg is about to explode, and so the "good" Finger of Doom damsel elicits the help from the leader of the Four Hill Heroes, Lu Tien-bao (Chin Han), who must first battle the Quasimodo-like Kung (Tung Li) and turn him into scoliosis sap before his fellow Hill Heroes literally become bubbling pools of blood.

Initially, flash pans of the camera are used to create the supernatural feel of the film. But as the creepiness subsides into more swordplay than finger poking, the static camera angles become more dynamic as unsung fight instructor Xu Er-niu incorporates more hand-held camera and tracking shots, culminating with quick zooms and pull-back camera choreography to add to the increasing intensity of the later fight sequences.

Titleography: As of this writing, no alternative titles could be found. Translation—*Extreme Shadow Finger Technique.* See above martialogy. **MA Percentage: 16.79%** SHAW BROTHERS

FIST AND GUTS

一膽二力三功夫 and 真功 (1979—Hong Kong) **92m. MAD: Liu Chia-liang, Liu Chia-rong. NOT/LOT: 2/ 3m 51s; NOF/LOF: 10/ 25m 33s.** D: Liu Chia-rong. C: Gordon Liu Chia-hui, Lo Lieh, Liu Chia-rong, Lee Hoi-san, Li Jian-xiong, Mars, Chen Ling-wei.

When jerks-of-all-trades and a master of disguise match up in *Fist and Guts*, everyone begins to look like an ash because we all get burned at least once in the urn of life and death. When Ah San (Gordon Liu Chia-hui) chases his former thieving housekeeper (Lo Lieh), a master of disguise, to a coastal town for stealing his family's legacy, he hooks up with two jerks-of-all-trades, Ah Yung (Liu Chia-rong) and his partner in cheesy crime, Pin Peng (Lee Hoi-san), under the guise of sharing his family's recovered treasure with them as payment. While Ah San starts the film with hair, he ends up with a shaved head, which makes him look like San De, Gordon Liu's Shaolin monk character in *The 36th Chamber of Shaolin.* Ah San tries to rescue the ashes of Ta Mo (the Buddhist monk responsible for establishing Shaolin kung fu in A.D. 520) from a lama high priest who hides the treasure within a menagerie of secret rooms and corridors rife with traps and gadgets. The setting makes for a great final fight between Gordon Liu and Lo Lieh.

Veteran martial arts directors Liu Chia-liang and his real younger brother Liu Chia-rong combine their kung fu talents with kung fu brother Gordon (who adopted the Liu name after becoming a kung fu disciple of Liu Zhan) to produce several impacts on Hong Kong cinema. First, after Lee is surrounded by the karate fighters, he kicks eight people with eight different kicks in one unedited wide-angle shot, so the audience can tell that Lee pulled off the stunts. It worked, and he used the same idea in the final mass-mayhem fight scene in *Enter the Dragon* (1973). Second, Lee introduced the world to the *nunchaku*, a weapon that swept through the imaginations of film fans and budding martial artists at that time. I saw this film as a college freshman at SUNY Cobleskill, and the crowd cheered when Lee whipped out the nunchaku during the final fight scene. Two weeks later, I hit my eye with a pair made from a lacrosse stick. Strangely, I did not get a black eye. Instead the skin turned green—a sign of bad *chi*.

After the first Sino-Japanese War (1894-1895), China was a fractured country that was sliced up, divided and handed out to Japan and European powers. The Japanese would play a large villainous role in Chinese history from this point on, so much so that a rift of hatred formed and grew out of the treatment Japanese forces inflicted on the occupied Chinese. One of the most notorious incidences from this period of history is the Rape of Nanking, in which Japanese troops killed 300,000 Chinese men, women and children and raped 20,000 Chinese women and girls. (See *Seven Man Army*). With the defeat of the Japanese in World War II, Hong Kong and the Republic of China (now Taiwan) kept silent on these sensitive matters. Because Japan's post-World War II economy was U.S.-supported, they feared a backlash if they spoke up. Bruce Lee's *Fist of Fury* changed all that because his character defiantly defeated the Japanese martial artists in the film's setting of 1909 Shanghai, when the city was under the strict rule of Japan. Lee single-handedly crashed through that barrier of silence, making sure no one forgot what it meant to be Chinese and to be a Chinese martial artist. He also gave his fellow Chinese a renewed sense of dignity and pride in the heritage of their martial arts, something that had been hurt during the Boxer Rebellion and missing since World War II.

It is no wonder that Chinese crowds reportedly cried and gave standing ovations at every showing. I saw this film in Taiwan in 1979, and even seven years after its initial release, the normally quiet Taiwanese moviegoers were still cheering during the moments when Bruce Lee was beating the crap out of the Japanese. There are also several subtle insults that reflected Lee's disdain toward the way foreign powers treated the Chinese people, specifically the Japanese. Some Japanese attackers wear their *hakama* backwards, which shows that the Japanese martial artists were not heeding the honor of their art. There is also a defining shot of a smug Lee proudly and defiantly posing in front of a portrait of Gichin Funakoshi, the father of Japanese karate.

There are a few major historical things to point out. Huo Yuan-jia died in 1910, and karate was introduced into Japan in 1921 by Gichin Funakoshi, so there is no way that a Japanese karate school could have existed in the early 1900s in Shanghai, certainly no martial arts school of any kind that would have a picture of Funakoshi. Furthermore, Huo's kung fu was mostly a melding of two martial arts styles: *mi zong chuen* and *luo han chuen,* which are cumulatively known as *mi zong yi* kung fu. However, after Huo died, other martial arts teachers introduced eagle claw, *hsing-i, wu jian chuen* and seven star praying mantis into Ching Wu's training regimen.

But the ultimate power of film and Lee's persuasive message that the Chinese are not sick people is brilliantly depicted when Lee takes out several Japanese fighters in front of Shanghai Park. Lee performs a flying kick that destroys a wooden sign that reads, "No Dogs or Chinese Allowed." To this day, based on this movie, millions believe that the sign really existed, while in reality it was merely a creation of the film.

Titleography: *The Chinese Connection; School of Chivalry.* Translation—*Ching Woo School of Kung Fu.* Although initially called *The School of Chivalry*, the film was released in Asia as *Fist of Fury*. However, due to a labeling mistake, when the prints were shipped overseas, the film was released as *The Chinese Connection* outside of Hong Kong, undoubtedly keying in on William Friedkin's 1971 crime thriller *The French Connection*. **MA Percentage: 24.00%**

FIST OF SHAOLIN

少林高徒 (1973—Taiwan) **85m. FI: Du Wei-he. NOT/LOT: 1/ 19s; NOF/ LOF: 9/ 19m 43s.** D: Lee Shun. C: Bai Ying, Han Ying-chieh, Pearl Zhang Ling, Lung Fei, Wan Chong-shan, Mario Milano.

Enter the revenge factor. Tiny tot Chin Wang-lee sees his family massacred by a silent shadow of a man, who then absconds on horseback with Chin's mother and disappears into the misty morn. Chin's only mementos are his fa-

ther's pocket watch, the attached chain and three thin, ax-blade-shaped knives that the killer left in his father's flesh. After 12 years of kung fu training in the Shaolin Temple, Chin (Bai Ying) leaves Shaolin on a mission of death, seeking revenge against the man who massacred his family. His path intertwines with a government investigator (Pearl Zhang Ling) who is investigating Chairman Lee (Han Ying-chieh), a shady businessman that cheats flood victims out of government rice. (Lee purportedly volunteered to distribute to the starving hoards.) Armed with secret board-breaking skills, kung fu kicks, blocks and punches, Chin must overcome black-market greed, rice robbers and gambling-hall hit men to track down his family's killer and find peace at the end of the rainbow.

Actor Han Ying-chieh is the villain and fight choreographer in Bruce Lee's *The Big Boss*, and in this film, he portrays a similar character in terms of fighting style and garb—he even carries around a bird cage. Actress Pearl Zhang Ling's straight-backed posture and *taekwondo* kicks (she trained in Taiwan) add a decent element to her fights, while Bai Ying's straight-armed flailing slaps and hunched posture detract from his expertise in martial arts. However, the manly-man artistry and sheer rat-tat-tat of his techniques saves the fight face of the film. The rhythm of the fights, which are mostly repetitive series of blocks and counterpunches or blocks and counter-kicks, make the sequences look relatively smooth. Watch for a thug appearance from Lung Fei, who plays Betty in *Kung Pow: Enter the Fist* (2002).

Although Du Wei-he is the kung fu instructor on the film, it is obvious that the final fight between Han and Bai was choreographed by Han and his assistant at the time, Lin Zhen-ying (whose face pops up as a lackey flattened by Pearl during the film's first fight). Han and Lin also choreographed the final fight scene between Han and Bruce Lee in *Big Boss,* which is why the fight looks almost the same, technique- and pace-wise, right down to the final deathblow.

Titleography: *Fist of Shao-Lin; Fists of Shaolin; Fists from Shaolin.* Translation—*Top of the Shaolin Class.* Only the film's English title taps into Han's appearance in *The Big Boss*, which was released stateside as *Fist of Fury*. In 1973 and probably today, Han's association with Bruce Lee would make him the most recognizable face in *Fist of Shaolin*, so the distributors created a marketable title that reminds us of Han's cinematic relationship with Lee. **MA Percentage: 23.57%**

FIST TO FIST

(1973—Hong Kong) **43m. FI: Uncredited. NOT/LOT: None; NOF/LOF: None.** D: John Woo. C: Because this is a documentary, there is no main cast.

The marketing information for this 1973 film boasts that through technological advances, this directorial debut from John Woo has created a "realistic confrontation in a bout coined 'The Match of the Millennium,' which compares the unique styles of both masters." The masters mentioned are Bruce Lee and Jackie Chan. Really? Wow, I must have this film—not.

Released by Westlake Video in 1999, the film is really just a collection of fight scenes from Lee's *Fist of Fury* (1972) and Chan's *The Cub Tiger From Kwangtung* (1973), *Drunken Master* (1978) and *The Twin Dragons* (1992). Obviously, with highlight clips from these films, this movie could not possibly be a John Woo directorial debut, let alone a 1973 film. Whether or not Woo directed this movie will remain a mystery until I speak to him next. The only redeeming factor is that it has several clips from Bruce Lee's lost 1971 interview with Pierre Berton from *The Pierre Berton Show*, which turned out to be Lee's only television interview.

Titleography: As of this writing, no alternative titles could be found.

FISTFUL OF YEN

from **Kentucky Fried Movie** (1977—USA) **31m. FC: Bong Soo Han. NOT/ LOT: 4/ 2m 32s; NOF/LOF: 8/ 6m 1s.** D: John Landis. C: Evan C. Kim, Eric Micklewood, Derek Murcott, Agneta Eckemyr, Bong Soo Han, Ingrid Wang, Nathan Jung, Dovie Boehms.

Sometimes the first is the best. American filmmakers have been parodying Chinese kung fu films since *Fistful of Yen* from *Kentucky Fried Movie*'s spoof of Bruce Lee's *Enter the Dragon*, but none seem to have done it as perfectly as the original, which was part of John Landis' poignant comedic take on the social issues of the late 1970s. The short film nails Asian and Asian-American stereotypes. The jokes, one-liners and sitcom humor come fast and hard, but also highlight and satirize the political incorrectness of the time. I remember seeing this film at Cornell University with my Chinese roommate, and he laughed harder than me. What more can I say?

Not only is Dr. Klahn (Bong Soo Han) recruiting an army on his private island, but he also has an opium and heroin racket going, along with schemes for biological and atomic weapons. Enter Loo (Evan C. Kim)—an appropriate name, given the bits of bathroom humor in the film—whose mission is to infiltrate Klahn's clan and put a stop to his evil ways. All the great memorable scenes from *Enter the Dragon* are present: the opening fight at the temple, the cobra and the dog, the training in Loo's room and holding the side kick, the *escrima* and *nunchaku* dungeon fight, the slow-motion stomp on "Ohara's" head, the climactic courtyard fight in which Klahn calls out the names of his fighters (all named after Korean dishes), and of course the clawed hand of death.

It does not matter if the fights are good, bad or mad. This film is a humorous homage from a time when political correctness did not exist. It is odd, though, that the ideology of political correctness was the foundation for Lenin's Communist philosophy; does that mean the United States, which is into the whole PC thing big time, is becoming Communist? Sen. Joseph McCarthy must be rolling in his grave.

A historical note: In 1950, McCarthy convinced Americans that their friends, neighbors or politicians could be Soviet agents. People turned in their friends, accusing them of being spies. This is how many filmmakers in Hollywood were blacklisted, because other filmmakers made false accusations against them. To paraphrase Loo, "This is not a chawade—we need to go back to the 1970s, open our minds and do things with more feewing!"

Titleography: As of this writing, no alternative titles could be found. **MA Percentage: 27.58%**

FISTS OF VENGEANCE, THE

狂龍出海 (1973—Taiwan) 86m. **MAI: Zhang Yi-gui. NOT/LOT: None; NOF/LOF: 23/ 40m 1s.** D: Chen Hong-min. C: Jiang Bin, Yasuaki Kurata, Barry Chan, Liu Ping, Cao Jian, Tu Song-zhao.

If there was ever a film that simply rocked 'n' rolled, this is it. It is also one of my surprise films of the book—something that on the surface looked like it was going to be run-of-the-mill but bowled me over with how good it really was. Similar to another one of my big surprise films of the book, *The Tongfather*, *The Fists of Vengeance* begins like a low-budget film with that typical early-'70s Taiwanese grittiness. Think Led Zeppelin's *Whole Lotta Love*, Def Leppard's *Let's Get Rocked* and Deep Purple's *Smoke on the Water* wrapped up into one group and one song, and you've got one hell of a group doing one hell of a song that if used as the soundtrack to the final fight of this film … Well, rock 'n' roll, baby.

Hero Zhen Zheng (Jiang Bin) returns home only to find out that he has been labeled a traitor and ostracized by his home village. Furthermore, his girlfriend has forsaken him for his brother, a traitor who mines red sand from the river for the Japanese, which the Japanese would use to forge high-grade steel to make guns so they can kill the Chinese.

Although the early fights look like they are performed by out-of-control windmills, they are in essence extremely raw. What really makes you watch them to the point of being out of breath are the actors' faces. They are filled with unabashed desperation, like those fantastic facial expressions associated with old silent-film stars. Like female fans of Rod Stewart who say he is so ugly that he's cute, Jiang's fights are so sloppy that they're great. Just when you think Jiang can't get any worse, the attack ante rises because actor Yasuaki Kurata skulks onto the screen as the nefarious nemesis from Nippon. Yasuaki brings the same kind of animalistic intensity Sonny Chiba exhibited in the first *Street Fighter* film (1974), but his *hapkido* kicks are tempered by his years of training with Chiba's Japanese Action Club, which elevates the film's fights and makes Jiang look like he was 20th degree black belt in everything. Midway through the final fray, for the first and only time in the film, Jiang's character performs the Buddha Prayer Fist. It is a bit cheesy, but an effective turning point that sends the battle onto a fast-moving freight train. The fight then takes on an *Emperor of the North Pole* (1973) appeal, similar to when Lee Marvin and Ernest Borgnine brutally battle on a moving train. In both of these battles, you really feel like they're fighting as though their lives depended on it, and the intensity makes it hard to breathe. To me, this is a rare accomplishment in Chinese martial arts cinema, and if I had never tackled this book,

I probably would never have found this film. Another unique touch is that the movie's soundtrack includes *Black Magic Woman* by Santana.

Titleography: As of this writing, no alternative titles could be found. Translation—*Mad Dragon From the Sea*. The main character is indeed a mad dragon from the sea. *Fists of Vengeance* is a reference to how the hero wants to kill the Japanese who killed his brother and many of his friends. **MA Percentage: 46.53%**

FIVE SHAOLIN MASTERS

少林五祖 (1974—Hong Kong) 105m. **FI: Liu Chia-liang, Kiu Chia-rong. NOT/LOT: 7/ 7m 32s; NOF/LOF: 36/ 32m 58s.** D: Chang Cheh. C: David Chiang, Chi Kuan-chun, Alexander Fu Sheng, Meng Fei, Ti Lung, Liang Chia-ren, Cai Hong, Wang Lung-wei, Jiang Dao, Tang Keung-mei, Tang Keung-ying, Fung Ke-an.

This is the third of Chang Cheh's five big films made in honor of the Shaolin Temple—the others are *Heroes Two* (1973), *Men From the Monastery* (1974), *Shaolin Martial Arts* (1974) and *Shaolin Temple* (1976).

Understanding the history of Shaolin in regard to the Ching and Ming Dynasties pretty much summarizes this film's plot. On April 25, 1644, Ming Emperor Chong Zhen hung himself as Beijing fell to Ming rebels led by Li Zu-cheng. Months later, Ching troops overtook China, Li was assassinated, and the Ching Dynasty began. However, anti-Ching sentiments pervaded the country, and in 1662, Taiwan-based Ming loyalist Zheng Chen-gong sent some troops to China to stir up an anti-Ching revolution and to seek refuge at Song Shan Temple, under Abbot Zhi Tong. Among Zheng's men were five young fighters: Tsai De-Zhong, Hu De-di, Li Shi-kai, Fang Da-Hong and Ma Chao-xing.

In 1685, during the reign of Ching Emperor Kang Xi, the Xilu people invaded China and overran the border patrols. When the call went out for help to save China, 128 Shaolin monks from Song Shan Shaolin answered the call and defeated the Xilu, despite being armed only with poles. Politely refusing offers of money and power, the monks accepted the emperor's imperial seal and returned to Song Shan. Word of their heroism spread, and though they were men of peace, they would use their martial skills to protect their country.

However, the Chings' gratitude eventually turned sour. Because many Han Chinese considered the Chings to be foreign invaders, there was a large movement to bring back the Ming Dynasty. So when the Shaolin monks began accepting students with fewer restrictions, the Ching court interpreted this as the Shaolin putting together a fighting force, and a fuse was lit.

In 1736, during the reign of Emperor Yong Zheng, as one story goes (see *Shaolin Temple* for another), Ching officials bribed a top Shaolin monk, Ma Lin-ge, to help plot the destruction of the temple at Song Shan. Of the 128

Still from *Five Shaolin Masters* © Celestial Pictures Ltd. All rights reserved.

monks who lived in Song Shan, Ma was ranked seventh, which is why the number seven now represents bad luck in some circles. Ma was being punished for breaking a valuable lamp, and perhaps he saw helping the Chings as a way to punish those who had punished him. Ma showed the commanding Ching generals the locations of all the temple's hidden passageways and traps, thereby paving the way for the destruction of the temple and the killing of the monks. Five monks survived, which brings us to the film.

Five Shaolin Masters is the story of those five young fighters from Taiwan who became monks and survived the destruction of Song Shan. After the temple is razed to the ground, monks Tsai De-Zhong, Hu De-di, Li Shi-kai, Fang Da-Hong and Ma Chao-xing (played by Ti Lung, David Chiang, Chi Kuan-chun, Meng Fei and Alexander Fu Sheng) pledge their brotherhood at the Red Flower Pavilion by organizing what is known as the Hong League (a precursor to the Chinese Triads) and vow to fight the Chings to the very end. Meanwhile, each of the five kung fu brothers is being chased by one of seven Ching assassins (played by Liang Chia-ren, Cai Hong, Wang Lung-wei, Jiang Dao, Tang Keung-mei, Tang Keung-ying and Fung Ke-an). The assassins have orders to kill the monks and anyone associated with them. In preparation for their assassins, each of the five Shaolin fighters practices a secret form of kung fu in hopes that his Ching opponent won't be expecting it. These five monks would go on to become the Five Ancestors of Shaolin.

In terms of the actors and their martial arts in this film, Chi and Liang are almost too tense, flexing every muscle in their bodies, but it works for their respective styles of fighting. Ti's pole work is relatively solid, and by the end of the decade in *Kung Fu Instructor* (1979), you can see how much he evolved as a pole fighter. Actor Meng Fei's kung fu is very weak because his fights having too many slaps as blocks, for example. He would continue fighting like this until later in the decade, when he finally put on some pounds and began practicing kung fu for real. Fu Sheng's patented snappy movements add speed to his fights and make him stand out most. In contrast, Chiang's movements are rather insipid; perhaps his costume and use of a small steel whip add to that appearance, which makes him look thinner than usual as the whip twirls around his body in short, tight circles. (A longer steel whip generally looks more flowing and circular, which can fill up a screen on medium and wide-angle shots.) Finally, actor Cai Hong's ax on a rope is a danger to behold, and his face and body really show the angry intent behind his vicious attacks.

Of note, the secret hand code used in the film is the reverse hand posture seen in *hong jia* kung fu, the martial art created by Shaolin Monk Zhi Shan but often credited to Hong Xi-guan, the art's namesake. Also, actor Wang Lung-wei's character, Ma Fu-yi, is representative of Ma Ling-ger (remember the seventh-ranked monk who is the Shaolin traitor). Wang also played Ma Fu-yi in *Shaolin Temple* (1976) and in Yuen Kwei's *The New Legend of Shaolin* (1994). A few years later, when Chang Cheh directed *Shaolin Temple*, only Ti Lung and David Chiang reprised their Five Ancestor roles. Chi Kuan-chun and Alexander Fu Sheng portrayed the Shaolin student friends Hu Hui-qian and Fang Shi-yu.

Between this film and *Shaolin Temple*, you pretty much get a good double dollop of Shaolin lore and the legendary Five Ancestors of Shaolin.

Titleography: *Five Masters of Death*; *5 Shaolin Masters*. Translation—*Five Ancestors of Shaolin*. **MA Percentage: 38.57%** SHAW BROTHERS

FIVE SUPERFIGHTERS

唐山五虎 (1979—Hong Kong) **94m. FI:** Hsu Hsia. **NOT/LOT:** 11/ 10m 15s; **NOF/LOF:** 30/ 23m 38s. **D:** John Lo Mar. **C:** Wu Yuan-chin, Hui Tien-si, Hou Chao-sheng, Guan Feng, Lin Hui-huang, Liu Jian-ming, Yin Fa, Jiang Han, Huang Wei-wei, Wu Yuan-jun, Tony Leung, Liu Hao-nian.

For those of you who like to advertise how good your kung fu is, there will always be someone around to challenge you. I saw this happen when I was a senior at Cornell University. A young man or was screaming and yelling while he performed kung fu outside in an open grass field. He was certainly attracting attention to himself. A few minutes later, a rather mean-spirited student walked past me, shook his head, went over to the other guy and showed him just how good he was not. I agree that kung fu is not for show, but I thought it was rather petty of the guy (who I later learned was a Hong Kong Triad member) to do that. Although you cannot put your own thoughts or philosophies into the hearts and minds of others, I partially understand why that guy called the young man out

after watching this film. It was to point out that showing off in public was, in a way, disrespectful to the art. Like I said, only to a point. But certainly the villain of this film would wholeheartedly support the Chinese guy's actions.

After the black-caped villain (Guan Feng) arrives in town and identifies himself with a cloth of writing that states "Specialist in Correcting Bad Kung Fu," he quickly beats the living tar out of anyone he sees doing bad-looking kung fu. His point is that if your kung fu is bad, you should not insult the art by practicing it in the open. When this caped un-crusader stumbles upon kung fu teacher Wan Tian-hang (Hou Chao-sheng) and his three street-performing students—Ah Fu, Ah Tian and Ah Chi (Hui Tien-si, Tony Leung and Wu Yuan-jun)—he summarily drops them all like a bag of wet cement. With their master's birthday quickly approaching, the three students decide to go off on their own to find a kung fu master to teach them more kung fu so they can defeat the villain as a gift to their teacher. Of course, they forgot to tell the teacher that they are leaving, so now the teacher feels that he has let his students down and that they have deserted him.

Ah Fu learns the Deadly Kick of the Yang Family from Madame Fung (Huang Wei-wei), Ah Tian studies crane kung fu from beggar Han He (Lin Hui-huang), and Ah Chi practices Fisherman's Stick with the Fisherman (Liu Jian-ming). Meanwhile, saddened by the loss of his students, Wan begins focusing on broadsword work.

After watching 50 or so older films with fights that look similar on the surface, this movie was a breath of fresh air because none of the fighting actors needed a double, and each fighter is technically different from the other. Furthermore, the kung fu in this film is exact; the actors deliver each technique clearly and show if the skill is offensive or defensive. The choreography demonstrates the meaning or intention behind each movement rather than worrying to create a fight that flows. But hey! The choreography succeeds in that too.

Also, each star uses good straight-backed postures and hand positions for each strike, and the camera follows each important skill and kung fu movement, revealing correct whole-body stances. The camera then goes into close-up to reveal the intricacy of correct finger positions for the various strikes, one of the many strong points and effective means of fight choreography that was heavily influenced by Liu Chia-liang. As you may well imagine, the story is pretty superficial and is of least importance to the film, but the final 12 minutes of the movie rocks better than the 1970s British rock group Humble Pie—well, almost.

Titleography: *The Super Fighters*. Translation—*Five Tigers of Tang Shan*. The *Five Superfighters*, who are all from Tang Shan, refers to the three students, their *sifu* and the fighter beating them all up. Tang Shan is the place mentioned in Bruce Lee's *The Big Boss*, the area where the main villain (Big Boss) is from. **MA Percentage: 36.05%** SHAW BROTHERS

FIVE TOUGH GUYS

五大漢 (1974—Hong Kong) **80m. FI:** Liu Chia-rong, Huang Pei-ji. **NOT/LOT:** 2/ 43s; **NOF/LOF:** 22/ 24m 55s. **D:** Pao Hsueh-li. **C:** Chen Kuan-tai, Ling Yun, Lily Ho, Frankie Wei Hong, Shi Zhong-tian, Ku Feng, Fan Mei-sheng, Wang Chung, Omae Hitoshi.

In May 1915, Japan sent Yuan Shi-kai a secret ultimatum known as the

21 Demands. (Yuan Shi-kai was the guileful Chinese general who got himself elected as the second president of the Republic of China and booted China's father of democracy, Sun Yat-sen, out of office in 1912.) On top of banning China from giving coastal or island concessions to any foreign power except Japan, the demands included the following: Japan would get free range of movement and expansion in China, control of China's police force and permission to spread Japanese Buddhism in China. When Yuan accepted a shorter version, the 13 Demands, it set off a series of events that led Yuan to declare himself as the new emperor of China on December 12, 1915. After Yuan announces the start of his reign, the titular five tough guys enter.

Yuan Shi-kai assigns Chief Hung (Ku Feng) to find and kill the resistance leader, General Tsai Song-po (Ling Yun), before Tsai can escape to the municipality of Tian Jin. Because Tsai can get protection at the British Concession there, it will be easier for Tsai to join his troops in Yunnan province in southwest China. But when Tsai goes missing in Beijing, his aide Shen Shi-xian (Frankie Wei Hong) hires martial arts master Wu Wen-yuan (Chen Kuan-tai)—who used to support Yuan but is now a fugitive on the lam—to find Tsai and help escort Tsai to Tian Jin. Wu recruits his old friend Da Chiang (Shi Zhong-tian), a former security guard trainer, and Wei Jin-bao (Fan Mei-sheng), who accepts the job to relive his old security-escort glory days when he was proudly known as a Li Fa spear expert and the son of 8-Arm Na Zha. Finding Tsai and traveling on the back roads, Chief Hung's hacking heavies try to cut them down. When all is lost, they run into Beijing college student Feng Hsieng (Wang Chung), who is eager to use his kung fu for the cause. With their number now at five—Shen, Wu, Da, Wei and Feng—the adventure can begin.

As Chief Hung's hordes of hapless fighters prove ineffective in fighting the five bodyguards, he seeks help from the Japanese. They send out the gigantic judo champion of Japan, Miyazaki (Omae Hitoshi), and he methodically whittles down the fighting five as each bodyguard tries his hand at defeating him. Wu is the most powerful and gets his licks on the judo champ, proving his Chinese kung fu mettle over the Japanese by showing that you don't have to be big to beat the enemy. The heroes stay united and eventually bring about the death of Chief Hung's heavies. Then, as they hang Hung out to dry, Tsui finds safety and security in the British Concession. (I guess England cannot be all that bad).

Actor Chen Kuan-tai is the tallest of all the stars in this film, not including the Japanese wrestler Omae, and he adjusts his height to accommodate the short fighters who oppose him, which is a difficult thing to do without looking off-balance. During Chen's real tournament fighting days, he had to adjust himself to his various-sized opponents, so it's a good reflection of his martial arts training. (See *Iron Monkey*.) It's also worth applauding the fact that most of the shots during his fights contain more than 10 separate fighting techniques, which is something choreographers of the day assumed trained kung fu stars should be able to do.

On a final historical note: Tsai got to Yunnan and defeated Yuan's army, which ended Yuan's dream of becoming the emperor and led to his eventual death a year later.

Titleography: *Kung Fu Hellcats*. Translation—*Five Tough Guys*. Although *Kung Fu Hellcats* sounds like a neat title, probably borrowing some inspiration from the American film *The Hellcats* (1968), it is a poor choice. A hellcat is a bad-tempered woman who is considered to be, or in reality is, a witch, and all the heroes in this film are men. **MA Percentage: 32.04%** SHAW BROTHERS

FIVE VENOMS, THE

五毒 (1978—Hong Kong) **97m. FI: Lu Feng, Liang Ting, Robert Tai Chi-hsien Ting. NOT/LOT: 6/ 3m 48s; NOF/LOF: 14/ 15m 13s.** D: Chang Cheh. C: Sun Chien, Kuo Chue, Wang Lung-wei, Lo Meng, Lu Feng, Chiang Sheng, Kuo Chue, Wei Bai, Dik Wei, Ku Feng, Sun Shu-pei, Liu Huang-shi.

Even in Chinese, this film is basically called *The Five Venoms*, which is strange because there are six venoms in the movie. And even though that's the truth, people still insist that there can be only five venoms because the title says there are only *Five Venoms*. But that's why it is sometimes important to watch *wuxia* and Jiang Hu films with a wary eye—they don't always align with Western logic and tastes in regards to plot. As this Eastern plot goes on, the audience will learn there is a seventh venom. What's going on? Here's what's up.

The sixth venom, Yang De (Chiang Sheng), is sent out into the world by his dying master (Dik Wei), the head of the Five Venoms House, who by the way is also a venom (that's seven now), to complete three missions. Yang De's first task is to find a bookkeeper and former house member (Ku Feng)—whoops, there's an eighth venom—who guards some ill-gotten treasure. Yang must convince the former venom to donate the treasure to charity before the master's former disciples, the titular Five Venoms, get their hands on it. The second mission is to determine which of the Five Venoms are good, and the third mission is to kill the bad ones. So if there are really eight venoms, then how are there only Five Venoms? It is a paradigm of conundrums that is counterintuitive.

Before I let the cat—I mean, poison—out of the bag, let's investigate an important question: How did this kung fu flick become an instant cult classic? Sure, it was shot by one of kung fu film's greatest directors. And yes, it did star five of the most prolific and athletic martial arts actors of the late 1970s. But here's the weird part: The film became popular without being shown in any American theaters. And it only has a measly 15 minutes of subpar fights. In turn, those five prolific and athletic martial arts actors have done much better stuff in their other films.

I suppose that like any cult classic, it's about timing, and there is no way to know when that will work out. In the early 1980s, the 1970s fervor for Hong Kong kung fu, Bruce Lee films and drive-in movies was wearing off in the United States. Lee had been dead for seven years, there were no viable replacement kung fu stars, and theatrical distribution of these films was also dying. Yet out of nowhere came cable TV. It was rapidly growing in America, as was the market for English-dubbed kung fu films on video. That's why in 1979 when I worked as a dubber, I would dub 60 kung fu films into English per month.

As a result, cable companies needed programs to attract audiences that network TV would never dream of acquiring. Independent networks gambled that the kung fu craze was not really dead, but on hold. They went back to the film that started it all in 1972, Shaw Brothers' *Five Fingers of Death* (aka *King Boxer*; see martiology). But it wasn't the film that distributors went back to, but the film company: Shaw Brothers. Because *guo shu pian* films—a new genre of martial arts films created at Shaw Brothers by fight director Liu Chia-liang and director Chang Cheh—were popular in Hong Kong in 1980, Shaw Brothers started distributing English-dubbed films such as *Five Venoms*, *The Kid With the Golden Arm* and *Chinatown Kid* outside of Hong Kong. These videos got lots of air time, filling weekend afternoon and late-night time slots on American cable TV.

Five Venoms, which was released on cable TV as *Five Deadly Venoms*, found a whole new fan base and immedi-

Still from *The Five Venoms* © Celestial Pictures Ltd. All rights reserved.

ately attained cult status. Again, it is curious because the film had few fights compared to other kung fu films, and the actors were performing well below their skill levels. However, it had a simple story, and the costumes and wire work were completely different from anything American audiences had seen up until that point. But the coolest parts of the film are the Five Venoms and their whole poisonous shtick.

First, there's Scorpion Gai Ji (Sun Chien). Even though he doesn't directly deal out poison, his kick is as potent as the venomous sting of a scorpion. In the animal kingdom, there are 25 species of scorpions with a sting that can kill humans, and all 1,500 species tend to crush their prey within their pinchers.

Second is Toad Liang Shen (Lo Meng). Although some real toads have poisonous skin glands in their backs that can release hallucinogens and neurotoxins that can be fatal to humans, Liang is a bit more direct. His skin is so tough that it absorbs body blows and powerful punches.

Next comes Centipede Zhang Yiao-tian (Lu Feng). He kicks and punches like he has 100 legs, much like a centipede. And although he can't inject poison through a pair of legs modified into fangs like his namesake creepy-crawly, Zhang does have a poisonous mind that can decide to kill a person just as quickly.

The fourth Venom is Snake Qi Dong (Wei Bai). He fights like a cross between a cobra and a viper. Like a cobra that bites with a paralyzing neurotoxin, Qi paralyzes opponents by hitting certain acupuncture points. And like the viper, whose bite releases a hemotoxin and causes internal bleeding, Qi's strikes draw blood.

Finally, there's Gecko Meng Tian-xia (Kuo Chue). Technically, the gecko is not poisonous, but it doesn't really matter. Like the little lizard, Meng tends to uncannily run up and down walls so he can launch surprise attacks from above and below.

While writing this martialogy, I wondered why none of the Five Venoms is a spider. Maybe within their secret society, there are more venoms. (Remember the sixth, seventh and eighth?) I bet they have nicknames like Jelly Fish, Spider or even Stingray. But only Five Venoms can exist in the Five Venoms House at the same time. The venoms all train while wearing masks to hide their identities, even from each other. But ultimately, a venom is just a kung fu fighter who has been taught a style of animal kung fu that uses aspects of behavior from a signature poisonous animal.

Yang De, the sixth venom, knows the techniques of all the other venoms and is on his own in a world full of poison—literally and figuratively. But Yang De

really has his work cut out for him because the Five Venoms are camouflaged, like any venomous creature, and the only time you know you have met one of these fighters is when you are about to die from the effects of his venomous kung fu skills.

On a final note, I have often wondered if the Five Venoms might be a metaphor for the Five Afflictions: ignorance, ego, attachment, aversion and fear. According to legend, Chinese esoteric hero Zhuang Yu destroyed the Five Afflic-tions to help the Chinese Buddhists attain peace and wisdom within themselves. Incidentally, this was not the first film in which the actors who play the Five Venoms appeared together—that honor goes to *The Brave Archer II* (1978). Of course, in that film they were not known as the Five Venoms. Instead, they were simply five actors in a large cast.

Titleography: *The Five (5) Deadly Venoms*. Translation—*The Five Poisons*. **MA Percentage: 19.6%** SHAW BROTHERS

FLIGHT MAN

馬蘭飛人 (1973—Taiwan) **90m. FI: Guan Hong. NOT/LOT: 1/ 33s; NOF/LOF: 12/ 12m 44s.** D: Ding Shan-xi. C: Ivy Ling Po, Wang Jung, Ling Yun, Shan Mao, Yee Yuan, Yuan Sen, Tian Ye.

Director Ding Shan-xi is highly regarded as a filmmaker who recounts lost stories of Chinese heroism that are often entangled with the ubiquitous Japanese Imperial Army. (As in real life, prior to and during World War II, the Japanese army had little regard for the Chinese.) Yet his films were not an at-tempt to breed hate for the Japanese. Instead, they were a reminder to Chinese audiences that no matter how insignificant someone might be or feel, everyone in China has the power within him or herself to rise up under the banner of Chinese nationalism and pride and ultimately make a difference.

Based on true events, *Flight Man* takes place in 1933 in Kaohsiung, Taiwan. The film is set during the Japanese occupation of Taiwan, which was ceded to Japan from China in 1895 when the Chinese lost the first Sino-Jap-anese war (1894-1895). After local martial artist Yang Ah-bao (Wang Jung) kills a Japanese commanding officer named Pan, Yang and his elderly kung fu teacher, Old Ghourd (Yuan Sen), go on the lam. Ghourd heads north to find recruits to fight the Japanese, and Yang finds refuge with the Ami people in the Malan Mountains. He eventually falls in love with the beautiful and brave native Taiwanese mountain girl San Mei (Ivy Ling Po). With the help of a snivel-ing Ami native (Shan Mao), the Japanese authorities and Chinese policemen finally find Yang and San, which sets up the typical climactic and tear-jerking melodramatic finale Ding is known for.

The story was inspired by the Tapani Incident, which was one of the largest uprisings against Japanese rule in the Chinese province of Taiwan. ("Tapani" is the local mountain dialect romanization of where the revolt took place.) It is also known as the Silai Temple Incident, after the place the revolt started, and the Yu Ching-fang Incident, which is based on the leader's name. In 1915, former police officer and rice merchant Yu partnered with Chiang Ting (who was wanted for murdering a Japanese official) to organize an army of Taiwanese aborigines and Han Chinese, which eventually overran many Japanese police stations in the mountains around Kaohsiung. The revolt was eventually quelled by the Japanese military.

The film is full of song-and-dance routines by actress Ivy Ling Po, who dressed in aboriginal garb for the part. At first, the film appears to be an old travelogue, but it is Ding's homage to the Ami people of the Malan Mountains, where singing is a part of everyday life. Ami songs do not express any outward meaning through lyrics. Instead, the songs are about the spirit within, and the sounds the songs intone represent different meanings. Ding also rightly knocks the *bushido* code when Yang confronts the Japanese military higher-ups and condemns them for lying and using women to trap him. Bushido is of course the same code that caused the Japanese to kill thousands of POWs during World War II, believing that it was a dishonor for a soldier to surrender.

Director Ding has an interesting eye for using obtuse and oblique camera angles, which are rarely found in other kung fu fight scenes. The camera is seemingly nowhere, somewhere and then everywhere. Ding gives a mythical dimension to Yang's fighting ability when he uses a special *da dao* (long-handled sword) with a telescoping shaft. Instead of undercranking the camera, Ding removes frames from the shots during the editing process, which creates a flickering image similar to that of a light trying to remain lit as the power fades in and out. It's a way to "undercrank" the speed of the final picture without

lowering the camera speed.

Titleography: *Flying Man of Ma Lan*; *The Daredevil*. Translation—*Flying Man of Malan*. The Chinese title implies that Yang is hard to catch, and the English title that uses *Flight* is from the Chinese translation. *Daredevil* describes the attitude of Yang. **MA Percentage: 14.76%** SHAW BROTHERS

FLYING GUILLOTINE II

清宮大刺殺 and 殘酷大刺殺 (1977—Hong Kong) **88m. FI: Tang Chia. NOT/LOT: 4/ 1m 49s; NOF/LOF: 22/ 15m 15s. D:** Cheng Kang, Hua Shan. **C:** Ti Lung, Shih Szu, Lo Lieh, Ku Feng, Frankie Wei Hong, Wang Chung, Yan Nan-xi, Fan Mei-sheng, Gu Guan-zhong, Ching Miao, Yang Chi-ching.

Besides the many films about the Shaolin Temple that mention Ching Emperor Yong Zheng's treachery in razing the temple and murdering all the martial monks, some films deal with his cruel nature, distrust of his officials and paranoia that everyone wanted him dead (he actually got that one right). This film's prequel, *The Flying Guillotine* (1976), is an example of the latter. After the movie's success, several films popped up with stories about why Yong Zheng hated Shaolin, such as *Return of the 18 Bronzemen* (1976), and about how he was assassinated, such as *The Blazing Temple* (1976). Shaw Brothers had trusted Chinese history buff and respected screenwriter Ni Kuang to come up with a sequel that further showed the development of Yong Zheng's brutal commissioned flying guillotine weapon and how he really died, thus the birth of *Flying Guillotine II*. However, Chen Kuan-tai, star of the first *Flying Guillotine*, and Shaw had venomous contract disputes—Chen refused to do what Lo Lieh did, which was agree to take half his salary when Shaw threatened to let him go—so Ti Lung was cast to play protagonist Ma Tang instead.

The sequel begins where *Flying Guillotine* ends. Ma Tang and his family are on the run as Emperor Yong Zheng (Ku Feng) orders lords Bao Ying (Lo Lieh) and Gang Jing-feng (Frankie Wei Hong) to find Ma and bring him in. Elsewhere, a group of four assassins—Li Sing-nan (Fan Mei-sheng); Tien Sin Dragon Sword Heroine (Yan Nan-xi); Brother Jin (Gu Guan-zhong); and swordswoman Na Lan (Shih Szu), whose father had to divorce her mother to prove loyalty to Yong Zheng, which lead her mother to commit suicide—ask Ma to join them. He refuses until Yong Zheng's assassins brutally murder his wife and child, after which he has nothing left to lose.

Because of Ma's iron umbrella and his voracious appetite for avenging his family, Yong's Zheng's beheading assassins are rapidly dwindling. Yong Zheng asks Tibetan lama Koupin (Ching Miao) to create two kinds of flying guillotine weapons to counter Ma's iron umbrella and then orders Bao Ying to recruit good kung fu men to learn how to use the new weapon. In order to figure out what Yong Zheng is up to, Ma's fellow assassin Na Lan gathers a group of women warriors with plans to become one of Yong Zheng's trusted flying guillotine assassins. By proving her great martial arts prowess, she is allowed to organize a group of female guillotine flickers. Yet to prove her loyalty to Yong Zheng, she

must kill her father. Biting her lip and fighting back her tears, Na does Yong Zheng's bidding, but her father volunteers to die in order to hide her cover. But all is not in vain, and the assassination plan comes together at the right time as the last three assassins Ma, Na and a man named Bai (Wang Chung), corner Yong Zheng in his palace. Many have been massacred in the palace before, but this time the victim might be Yong Zheng himself.

As one story goes, historically speaking, during the 13th year of his reign over the Ching Dynasty, Yong Zheng was killed by a female assassin named Lu Si-niang. She was the daughter of educator Lu Liu-liang, a mild-mannered man executed for literary crimes against the Chings. Other stories report that Yong Zheng poisoned himself while looking for the elixir of immortality.

In terms of action and choreography, the fights in this film are nothing special, though there is some interesting use of tracking shots, which were becoming standard for camera choreography.

Titleography: *Flying Guillotine Part II*. Translation—*Massive Massacre in the Ching Palace* and *Cruel Massive Massacre*. The massacres could refer to the people who have been killed in Yong Zheng's palace, because our heroes must kill many guards to make their way though the palace for the final fight with Yong Zheng. **MA Percentage: 19.39%** SHAW BROTHERS

FLYING GUILLOTINE, THE

血滴子 (1975—Hong Kong) **102m. MAI: Simon Chui. NOT/LOT: 7/ 4m 24s; NOF/LOF: 12/ 18m 18s. D:** Ho Meng-hua. **C:** Chen Kuan-tai, Ku Feng, Frankie Wei, Wang Yu, Liu Wu-chi.

Men with a conscience shall rise to victory, fueled by love and not money. But the realization of love can be soaked in enigmatic vagueness, like a love based on pure infatuation. This was the mind-set of director Ho Meng-hua when he recreated the nebulous development of how Ching Emperor Yong Zheng commissioned the ungodly weapon known as the flying guillotine in order to "decommission" honest politicians who were soft-hearted toward the Chinese people. It was Yong Zheng's way of getting ahead in life, literally. (See *The Fatal Flying Guillotines*.)

When the emperor's favorite assassin, Ma Tang (Chen Kuan-tai), realizes that the deadly beheading cage is spilling innocent blood, he goes on the lam only to become the prime target of the flying-guillotine assassination squad. One by one, Ma is forced to face his brothers in arms in deadly duels of survival, culminating in his creation of a malicious counter-weapon forged from the metal skeleton of an everyday object, which makes for some fascinating weapon fights.

Ho distinguishes his action filmmaking savvy from his fellow Shaw Brothers directors with a unique emotional approach to his fight sequences. He softens protagonist Ma's bludgeoning and blood-gushing blows of destruction with sounds of life and hope. For example, Ma chokes and gashes two of his former compatriots

during one fight scene, and the sounds of their death are masked by the melodious whining voice of Yu Ping (Liu Wu-chi), a beautiful street-performing wench who is purposely singing loudly so the other assassins cannot hear the back-alley slaughter. Later on, as Ma is defacing three other assailants, their cries of distorted pain are drowned out by the screams and moans of Ma's wife, Yu Ping, giving birth to his son. The climactic deathblows arrive as the baby begins to cry.

Although an anti-Ching film at heart, the anti-Communism theme is pervasive throughout *The Flying Guillotine*. Ma boldly disagrees with blind loyalty to the emperor and argues that love for your family is as important as love for your country. Ho was also an avid patron of Chinese history, so it is curious to note that in the film, 13 recruits are taught how to use the flying guillotine, but emperor Yong Zheng only ruled for 13 years before his untimely death. That's 13 years and 13 people he had his flying guillotine users kill. In an exclusive interview with Ho many years ago, he told me that anyone who saw or heard the flying guillotine always died; therefore there are no eyewitnesses or drawings of what the weapon really looked like. Filmmaking is about imagination.

The flying guillotine has resurfaced in other films such as *Master of the Flying Guillotine* (1976), *The Fatal Flying Guillotine* (1977), *Flying Guillotine Part II* (1978), *The Vengeful Beauty* (1978) and lastly (for now) in the far-out thriller *Heroic Trio* (1993).

Titleography: As of this writing, no alternative titles could be found. Translation—*The Blood Dripping Object*. Certainly once you are beheaded, your blood drips off this weapon, but ultimately, the Chinese title is just the Chinese name of the weapon. **MA Percentage: 22.25%** SHAW BROTHERS

FOR Y'UR HEIGHT ONLY

(1979—Philippines) 86m. SC: Eddie Nicart. NOT/LOT: None; NOF/LOF: 10/ 5m 22s. D: Eddie Nicart. C: Weng Weng, Yehlen Catral, Beth Sandoval, Mike Cohen, Tony Ferrer.

When wacky meets crazy, you may be tempted to say, "Oh, oh, this is some freaky film." But just "Weng" you thought a film could not get any nuttier, you realize that "kooky" is spelled with a "00"—double zero, that is.

Perhaps one of the most famous Filipino movie stars of the decade was the 2-foot-9-inch Weng Weng, a primordial dwarf who began practicing martial arts at an early age. In this bizarre James Bond spoof, Agent 00 (Weng Weng) must rescue Dr. Von Koler from the film's villain, Mr. Giant. While under duress, Von Koler hands over the secret N-bomb formula to Giant, who wants to conquer the world with the weapon. The film opens with the usual Bond musical shtick: Weng Weng shoots a gun and blood oozes over the gun barrel, and from there, the film becomes a bizarre journey of spy gadgets (e.g., a radio-controlled steel hat that kills like Oddjob's baneful bowler), beautiful women swooning over 00, lots and lots of gunfire (appear, stand, crouch, shoot), and a goofy smattering of rather interestingly choreographed martial

arts fights using samurai swords and karate.

Each fight, and for that matter each of the action gags, is put together in a way that makes perfect use of Weng Weng's height without looking contrived. Sure, there are lots of groin punches and kicks, but those are in fact the most logical targets and strikes available to Agent 00. Additionally, Weng Weng does all his own stunts. He climbs over tall gates, jumps from high places (up to a good 10 feet) and lands solidly on his feet. He even flies through the air using a mini jet pack.

This film ranks up there with *Kung Fu vs. Yoga* (1979) on the "you have got to watch this to believe it" scale.

Titleography: *For Your Height Only*. Obviously a play on the Bond film *For Your Eyes Only* (1981), so you have to wonder what the original title of *For Y'ur Height Only* was when it was released in 1979. Unless of course, the filmmakers caught wind that *For Your Eyes Only* was being filmed and pinched the title. Maybe the title was simply ripped from Ian Fleming's 1960 collection of short stories, *For Your Eyes Only*. **MA Percentage: 6.24%**

FORCE OF ONE, A

(1979—USA) 90m. FC: Chuck Norris, Aaron Norris. NOT/LOT: 2/ 2m 16s; NOF/LOF: 7/ 9m 16s. D: Paul Aaron. C: Chuck Norris, Jennifer O'Neill, Clu Gulager, Ron O'Neal, Bill Wallace, Eric Laneuville, James Whitmore Jr.

Six-time world karate champion Chuck Norris goes for seven, and this time Bill Wallace stands in the way in this *Rocky* (1976)-goes-karate film. For better or for worse, the movie introduces the tournament karate fighting hero Wallace into American cinema, paving the way for the likes of Jean Claude Van Damme and Don "The Dragon" Wilson to make their mark in the 1980s as heroes fighting for justice inside and outside the ring.

A karate killer sporting stealthy ninja attire is disrupting a Los Angles team of undercover narcotics officers who are investigating a drug distribution ring. The police turn to Vietnam veteran and kickboxer Matt Logan (Chuck Norris), who is preparing for an important fight against Sparks (Bill Wallace). Weeks before the bout, sparks fly when Logan's adopted son, Charlie (Eric Laneuville), is targeted for assassination and he's not there to protect him.

Perhaps finally realizing that the few minutes of fights scenes in his previous films were not really worthy of the label "martial arts movie," Norris intelligently returned to what made him a recognized name. In this film, he used karate tournament bouts to lengthen the duration of fight scenes. The choreography is simple: Two opponents bob and weave around a ring for three minutes or so, while intermittently throwing flashy high kicks, jabs and spinning backfists to the backdrop of a cheering crowd. To the karate tournament enthusiasts of the time, the fact that Norris' main pugilistic villain was the real-life undefeated world middleweight champion Bill "Superfoot" Wallace made the film's final showdown a nostalgic centerpiece—not unlike Jackie Chan and Jet Li getting it on in the 2008 hit film *The Forbidden Kingdom*. However, similar to *Breaker! Breaker!*, the final fight in this film is shot completely in slow motion, which instead of accentuating any particular piece of amazing skill or emotional beat, makes the final fight with Wallace more of a downer than an upper.

Titleography: The film was released as *Der Bulldozer* in West Germany, an appropriate characterization for a country known for its machine-like efficiency. The title indicates that Norris would methodically bulldoze over the bad guys. **MA Percentage: 12.82%**

FOUR CLANS OF DEATH

Sa Dae Tong Iue Moon (1978—S. Korea) 80m. FI: Uncredited. NOT/LOT: None; NOF/LOF: 16/ 25m 47s. D: Kim Jung-yong. C: Gang Yong, Seo Yeong-ran, Jang Mang, Nam Chung-il.

When the sword of gain causes the loss of innocent life, only a female Robin Hood has something up her sleeve to bring down the oppressive Sheriff of Notting-Korea.

Because he killed her father for attaining the Sword of the Greatest Warrior, the leader of the Tong Chan Clan is killed by the beautiful Mistress of Verity Lodge, Ka Gi-mien (Seo Yeong-ran). His orphaned son, Devil Killer Xi Hao (Jang Mang), is then raised by a Shaolin priest. Xia Hao counterplots to assassinate Ka and get the sword back. When things start to look really bad for Ka, the Wanderer (Gang Yong) appears from nowhere to save her from Xi Hao, but the two barely escape. Then the same Buddhist monk who raised Ka teaches her and the Wanderer a secret technique to defeat the Devil Killer.

Apart from the same short, shrill violin and trumpet musical shtick that is used at least 50 times throughout the film (mostly during the action scenes; I hummed it all night after watching it), other things abound that will also make you hum. For example, when Ka shoots out a long sleeve from her arms a la Joey Wang in *A Chinese Ghost Story* (1987) and the Wanderer fights the buzz-saw flying shields that hover around him like a mad swarm of killer bees, it is the audience who gets stung with barbed hilarity. Then there is the old *Mission: Impossible* masked switcheroo gag that seems to be popular in a lot of kung fu films: Someone is wearing a totally lifelike mask of another character and then—*schwipp!*—the mask is ripped off to reveal something you never saw coming. Further coming out of nowhere are the flying fans on chains that shoot poisonous darts and the far-out treetop pursuits. In the finale, Devil Killer's clawed metal gloves can only be rivaled by the mother of kicking techniques available at our heroes' toetips.

Of particular note, lead male actor Gang's fight scenes are shot at 18 frames per second, while the lead female actress Jang's fights are shot at 21 to 22 frames per second. This is to make him look like a better fighter than her.

Titleography: *Dragon From Shaolin*; *Death Fists of Shaolin*; *4 Clans of Death*. Translation—*The Four Big Political Doors*. The film has no dragons and only one clan, but words like *Death*, *Of*, *From* and *Fist* are as common in kung fu film titles as wordplay and puns are in this book. **MA Percentage: 32.23%**

FOUR RIDERS

四騎士 (1972—Hong Kong) 103m. FI: Liu Chia-liang, Tang Chia. NOT/LOT: None; NOF/LOF: 18/ 15m 14s. D: Chang Cheh. C: David Chiang, Ti Lung, Chen Kuan-tai, Wang Chung, Yasuaki Kurata, Ching Li, Lily Li, Tina Chin Fei, Andre Marquis.

Similar to the movie *Boxer Rebellion* (1975), *Four Riders* shows director Chang Cheh's sometimes skewered view of Chinese nationalism. Four nationalist Chinese soldiers serving in Korea during the Korean War (1950-1953)—Feng Xia, Guo Yih-han, Jin Yi and Li Wei-shi (Ti Lung, Wang Chung, David Chiang and Chen Kuan-tai)—who fought alongside South Koreans against the Communist North Koreans, get mixed up in cookie batter going bad. When the heat is turned up, the head chef is Lei Tai (Yasuaki Kurata), the malignant Japanese muscle behind the American drug smuggler Mr. Hawkes (Andre Marquis), who uses American soldiers returning home to transport drugs into the States.

When Feng Xia stumbles upon Lei Tai killing an American soldier who refuses to smuggle drugs, Feng is framed and arrested by Korean military police for the murder of the soldier and sent to the hospital (because he was injured while trying to save the American) under heavy guard. However, Feng is broken out of the hospital by Guo and Li and is later joined on the outside by Jin. The four riders ride again and are speedily galloping toward a confrontation with drug smugglers and the military. But in the steeplechase of life, only one horse can finish first, and the race is on.

The Chinese title of the movie and the four friends is Chang's metaphor for the Four Horsemen of the Apocalypse, who appear in Chapter 6 of the Book of

Revelation in the Christian Bible. In that book, the horsemen represent Conquest, Death, Famine and War. At one point in the film, the four heroes dress in period costumes and slay the invaders of China while riding on horses. It is all part of Chang's constant quest to aggrandize his male actors by shaping them into heroes, not only in mythical proportions but in biblical proportions.

Furthermore, the Republic of China, now known as Taiwan, was not allowed to participate in the Korean War because at the time the United States feared that it would encourage the People's Republic of China to get involved in the war. The People's Republic eventually got involved in the war to help out the North Koreans anyway. Chang Cheh must have missed this piece of history, as this film indicates in his vision that the Republic of China was indeed fighting in Korea.

On a historical side note, when 14,000 People's Republic prisoners of war declared hostility against Communism, the day of January 23, 1954, was declared World Freedom Day in the Republic of China in honor of the prisoners defecting to Taiwan.

It is original for a Chinese kung fu film to have one of the main characters be into Western classical music and then play those songs on a record player during the film. As a screenwriter, I am always curious about the choices a director makes, and the reasons for Chang's choices are often unclear. But because of my 1974 high school music appreciation class, I quickly recognized the following two pieces that Li plays on his record player while he recovers in the hospital. When Li has a mellow moment with his girlfriend (Ching Li), he listens to Beethoven's *Fifth Symphony*—not the opening stanza that most people know, but the second movement; later, Li listens to the "William Tell Overture" (which the *Lone Ranger* TV show used during the opening credits) while Feng breaks out of the hospital.

The final fight in the gymnasium—which is rife with trampolines, climbing ropes, rope ladders and weights—is shot mostly with close and medium shots to increase the dynamic emotion and motion of the action and to hide the fight's sloppiness. At that point, choreographers Liu and Tang had yet to find the right kung fu look for a contemporary setting. It is interesting that the exact same gymnasium scenario was used to better effect by Liu when he directed *The Lady is the Boss* some 10 years later.

Titleography: *Strike 4 Revenge*. Translation—*Four Riders*. *Strike 4 Revenge* is an intelligent play on words that acknowledges there are four heroes out for revenge. **MA Percentage: 14.79%** SHAW BROTHERS

14 AMAZONS, THE

十四女英豪 (1972—Hong Kong) 117m. FI: Ching Siu-tung, Charles Tung Shao-yung, Bolo Yeung. NOT/LOT: 1/ 2m 23s; NOF/LOF: 30/ 16m 26s. D: Cheng Kang, Tung Shu-yung. C: Ivy Ling Po, Lisa Lu, Lily Ho, Yueh Hua, Li Ching, Shu Pei-pei, Tina Chin Fei, Wang Ping, Betty Ting Pei, Tien Feng, Fan Mei-sheng, Lo Lieh, Bolo Yeung.

In A.D. 986, the second emperor of the Song Dynasty, Emperor Taizong, ordered Song General Pan Mei, Vice Commander Yang Ye (aka Yang Tsung-pao) and their armies to head to the northern territories of China and fight the invading Khitan Tartars. Their campaign was successful until Song General Cai Bin got beat and tossed into the garbage bin by the Tartars, which forced Yang and company to retreat south. En route, Yang Ye and his army were ambushed by Khitans, who completely wiped out Yang and many of his sons and sons-in-law.

The story then goes that the 14 Yang woman warriors—lead by matriarch Commander in Chief Shi Sai-hui, who was seconded by her daughter-in-law and Yang Ye's wife, Mu Gui-yang—became the default defenders of the realm because they took over the task of defending China in the name of their male family members. *The 14 Amazons* is based on how they patriotically and altruistically (in true Confucius fashion) put aside their squabbles with the emperor to fight and sacrifice themselves for the country.

In the film, Fifth Prince (Lo Lieh) of the Western Xia armies brutally kills Yang Ye with 19 arrows. (The Western Xia states were comprised of the Tanguts, tribes of people who lived in the northwestern part of China.) This sets the stage for Shi (Lisa Lu), Mu (Ivy Ling Po), the other 12 woman warriors and Yang Ye's youngest daughter, Yang Wen-guan, (Lily Ho) to march north. They don't know, however, that a major ambush awaits them at Twin Dragon Mountain.

Meanwhile, Lei Chao (Yueh Hua), a Han Chinese prisoner of the

Still from *The 14 Amazons* © Celestial Pictures Ltd. All rights reserved.

In the early 1970s, director Chang Cheh made a string of films about young people. In a sense, the "Chang Gang," as I like to call them, was a Hong Kong version of the Brat Pack. Twelve years before the teen-angst coming-of-age film *The Breakfast Club* (1985) was made, director Chang Cheh shot *Friends* with not only the same kind of melodrama, but also a smidgeon of martial arts gaiety and a palpable portion of pole-fighting pleasure with pigeons that really add some fight flight to the film. However, Chang's ultimate Chang Gang came together with *The Five Venoms*.

Friends opens with nine friends at a dinner party. They reminisce about their respective pasts and relationships and how it all started with a kidnapping, so to speak. Because spoiled teenage kung fu fanatic Du Jia-ji (Alexander Fu Sheng) is unhappy and bored with life, he tells his rich father that he is going out for a walk. He bumps into art student Hua Heng (David Chiang), who is in a street fight with a bunch of thugs. After beating the thugs with precise kung fu furor, Jia-ji is impressed and immediately forms a bond with Hua. He then accidentally ruins one of Hua's freshly finished artworks and purposely fails to mention that he has a very rich father. Hua takes Jia-ji back to his hangout, where he introduces him to all his close friends. Everyone chats, practices martial arts and jumps on a trampoline. In fact, there is one scene in which all the merry teens simultaneously jump on the trampoline. It is very reminiscent of Frodo and his fellow hobbits gleefully jumping up and down on a large bed together in *The Lord of the Rings: Return of the King* (2003). Yikes, man.

Xia, hears about the plan to wipe out Shi's advancing army and requests his freedom under the Rite of Combat, through which any slave can win freedom by fighting empty-handed and defeating a heavily armed warrior of the leader's choice. Lei must fight the vicious Xia champion wrestler (Bolo Yeung; a typical role for him in old Shaw films). Upon his victory, Lei rides like the wind to warn the women warriors. But Twin Dragon Mountain is the only way to the Xia base, and so a suicide plan is devised. A handful of women warriors climb up the mountain behind enemy lines to take on a few hundred Tanguts to give their sisters a chance to get through the mountain pass. The rest of the film is one battle scene after another. Shi's army overcomes incredible odds to end up face-to-face with the Xia leaders, and Mu must ignore her bleeding body to exact revenge against the Fifth Prince, who proudly boasts how he shot Mu's husband and watched the life drain out of him.

The fight in the woods is eye-catching, especially when Mu swings down from a tree in an effort to save Shi. At one point, she digs her spear into the ground while still hanging by the rope as 30 Xia men attack. This causes her to spin like a black widow spider dangling on silk, turning her prey into steak Tartar—oops, wrong northern tribe—I mean Tangut mincemeat. The human bridge scene over a deep gorge is incredibly wrong, looking sort of like red army ants connecting their bodies to traverse a creek, but it's utterly creative, and I have never seen a bloodier death than Lo Lieh's final gasp into camera. Of note, by 1972, actress Lisa Lu was an established Hollywood actress who made her mark as the dowager empress in the Shaw Brothers film *Empress Dowager* (1975; there are no martial arts in it) and reprised the role in Bernardo Bertolucci's *The Last Emperor* (1987). It is also amusing that the Queen and Fiona scene in *Shrek 3*, in which they take back the castle from Prince Charming, was inspired by the Yang women—the Queen being Shi and Fiona being Mu. Xmas comes early for xenophobes as the Xias look like Xerox copies of fighting Santa Clauses. It's wild to witness.

Of martial arts history relevance, Emperor Taizong was the brother of the first emperor of the Song Dynasty, Emperor Taizu. Taizu was an expert martial artist who created *tao zu chang chuan*, a Shaolin-based martial art that was the precursor for today's Shaolin long fist kung fu.

Titleography: *The Fourteen Amazons*. Translation—*Fourteen Female Heroines*. See martialogy. *14 Amazons* refers to the heroes being fighting female warriors. **MA Percentage: 16.08%** SHAW BROTHERS

FRIENDS

朋友 (1973—Hong Kong) **103m. FI:** Liu Chia-liang, Tang Chia. **NOT/ LOT: 1/ 53s; NOF/LOF: 17/ 13m 41s.** D: Chang Cheh. C: Alexander Fu Sheng, David Chiang, Lily Li, Lu Di, Frankie Wei Hong, Minoru Matsuoka, Li Rong-jie, Ko Ti-hua.

Still from *Friends* © Celestial Pictures Ltd. All rights reserved.

The film focuses mostly on the friendship between Jia-ji and Hua. Jia-ji tries to help Hua's art career by buying all of his paintings. To pay for the paintings, Jia-ji sends a ransom note to his father via Lin Si-bao (Li Rong-jie) and pretends to be kidnapped. When this proverbial cat gets out of the bag, things go from a purr to a roar because sleazy night club/brothel owner Ma Wei-hong (Minoru Matsuoka) really kidnaps Jia-ji. Ma Wei-hong plans to extort money from Jia-ji's father, kill Jia-ji and place the blame on the unknowing Hua and his friends. You have got to love the mass pole-vaulting scene during the last fight. If this was a horror film, it would be called *Pole-tergeist*.

What made Bruce Lee popular in the West, apart from his looks and obvious martial arts skills, was his build. A guy with muscles like that could be accepted as a hero in the West, but anyone as skinny as the friends in this film would be a hard sell. This is why David Chiang looks weak and wimpy rather than intimidating when he fights. However, Chiang's heroic attitudes and screen presence worked when he donned the sword and period costumes as seen in *wuxia* films. When all was said and done, and based on researched box office receipts, it was Chiang's wuxia films that earned most of the money for Shaw Brothers studios.

Interesting note: Although *Friends* was Alexander Fu Sheng's sixth film, his role won him the Best New Actor Award at the 20th Asian Film Festival.

Titleography: As of this writing, no alternative titles could be found. Translation—*Friend.* The English title encompasses all the friends, whereas the Chinese title refers to Jia-ji and his newfound friend Hua. **MA Percentage: 14.14%** SHAW BROTHERS

FUGITIVE, THE

亡命徒 (1972—Hong Kong) **76m. FI: Liang Shao-song. NOT/LOT: None; NOF/LOF: 10/ 6m 49s.** D: Chang Tseng-chai. C: Ku Feng, Li Ching, Lo Lieh, Li Chia-qian, Tang Di, Dean Shek, Ting Chien.

There is no Dr. Richard Kimble pursuing a one-armed killer like in the ultra-popular TV series *The Fugitive* (1963-67), but Xiao Liao (Lo Lieh) does go around disarming plenty of folks who try to stop him from getting revenge on his former best friend and partner, Ma Tien-piao (Ku Feng). Ma gladly let Xiao take the rap, prison time and torture for the shoot-'em-up bank robbery they committed to-gether. Xiao breaks out of jail, becomes a fugitive from the law and tracks down Ma. The final showdown will be determined by the luck of the draw, as each man unloads his six-shooter at each other in earnest (at times, they seem more like 600-shooters). Bullets fly with reckless abandon, and other spaghetti-Western elements are also present: stubbly beards, a gritty landscape, gritted teeth. Even the shrill harmonica from the film *Once Upon a Time in the West* (1968) is used to perfection when Xiao and Ma face off in Death Valley and the sands of time tick away. One thing is clear: The town ain't big enough for the two of them.

The film is filled with some very well-orchestrated tracking shots and makes use of snap zooms, a technique favored by Chang Cheh and Italian director Sergio Leone. It is also refreshing to watch a film that is a brisk 76 minutes. It moves along at a good pace and is not padded out to over 100 minutes with filler, unlike many other Shaw films.

Titleography: As of this writing, no alternative titles could be found. Translation—*Ending Life Person.* **MA Percentage: 8.97%** SHAW BROTHERS

FULL MOON SCIMITAR

圓月彎刀 (1979—Hong Kong) **93m. FI: Tang Chia, Huang Pei-ji. NOT/LOT: 1/ 1m 10s; NOF/LOF: 28/ 18m 36s.** D: Chu Yuan. C: Derek Yee, Lisa Wang, Wang Jung, Meg Lam, Pan Bing-chang, Yueh Hua, Gu Guan-zhong, Xu Hsao-chiang, Ching Miao, Xia Ping, Wang Lung-wei, Xu Hsao-chiang.

When there is a half moon, man is safe from the beasties within and without, but when there is a full moon, man can be affected by it without even knowing. Ow-ooo!

In the world of Wu Lin (the martial artist subdivision of Jiang Hu), the only way swordsman Ding Peng (Derek Yee) can become its head is to defeat Wu Dung's leader, Liu Ruo-song (Wang Jung). By mastering his father's Shooting Star Sword skill, Ding can defeat anyone, but Liu's wife tricks Ding into handing over the secret manual while on his way to the showdown with Liu. This has two major consequences for Ding. Because Liu has the manual and has learned the skill, he defeats Ding. Also, Liu can claim that because he has the manual, the skill has always belonged to his family. Therefore, since Ding knew the technique, that would indicate that Ding's family at some point stole the skill from the Liu family. So when Liu sneakily accuses Ding of stealing the Shooting Star skill, he shames Ding into considering suicide. Just prior to suicide, Ding is suddenly Wizard of Oz'd away to a magical, colorful underworld inhabited by fox spirits. While there, he falls in love with Ching Ching (Lisa Wang).

Ching teaches Ding how to wield the Full Moon Scimitar, which she carries around in what looks like an Easter basket. The weapon belonged to her aunt, who died after mourning her human lover, Xie Xiao-feng (Yueh Hua); he was a master swordsman who used his *nei gong* (an outward manifestation of inner *chi* strengthened by *chi gong*) to emblazon characters on the sword. Ding is told that the scimitar has a spirit. He is also told that if the bearer practices

without sincerity, he will never perfect it, but whoever masters the scimitar will be invincible in the human world. Bent on revenge against Liu and wanting to be head of Wu Lin, Ding returns to the human world with Ching Ching; his established Full Moon Villa could be the bastion of his dreams or the end of his marriage and reality.

A scimitar is a curved-blade sword and is possibly a descendant of the Persian *shamshir*, which means "lion's claw." Some experts argue that the scimitar came from the Egyptian *khopesh* sword, which was created in 1600 B.C. by using borrowed technology from the Asiatic Hyksos people. The origin of the curved-blade Chinese broadsword traces back to the Shang Dynasty (1600-1046 B.C.), when it was a straight sword with a blade on one side. The blade showed curvature in the Han Dynasty (202 B.C.-A.D. 220) and was perhaps influenced by the Chinese dignitaries who visited Persia in 115 B.C. Curiously, 17 years after the Chinese visited Persia, the Persians created *varzesh-e pahlavani*, an art using low stances and kicks. I wonder what kind of martial arts cultural exchanges might have occurred back then.

This film clearly shows why actor Xu Hsao-chiang is a favorite of fight choreographers, especially when he does sword fights. (This became even more evident in the 1980s.) Even if an actor does not practice martial arts, when they do tons of kung fu films, they either depend on stuntmen and become complacent, or they work hard to understand the martial arts and choreography. Cheng Pei-pei is a prime actress example, and Xu is the male version. When he fights with his sword, he leans toward his opponent, which not only shows no fear but also adds a special angst of danger to the fight. This kind of awareness and on-screen fighting skill, which creates a feeling of tension and danger during his fights, comes from training and understanding fight distance between one's opponent, something actors who rely on stuntmen usually don't bother to pick up.

Many of the film's fights rely on static camera positions that capture the choreography from multiple angles. The shots are often purposely obscured by sheer curtains, which add a somewhat romanticized element to the action. This is further compounded by the actors' flowing costumes. Adding in spins and flips accentuates the wow factor even more. This is the sort of action shooting style that gives *wuxia* films a certain savoir-faire.

Titleography: As of this writing, no alternative titles could be found. Translation—*Full Moon Curved Sword.* Although a scimitar is a half-moon shape, it becomes a full moon scimitar because of the title weapon's secret. Or as the film describes, it becomes a Rainbow Scimitar. **MA Percentage: 21.25%** SHAW BROTHERS

FURY IN STORM

大地龍種 (1974/1987—Taiwan) **78m. FC: Rick Pang; FI: Wang Yong (1987). NOT/LOT: None; NOF/LOF: 13/ 10m 37s.** D: 1974—Hsu Chin-liang. 1987—Godfrey Ho. C: 1974—Zhang Yi, Lung Fei, Wei Su, Jin Lou, Shan Mao, Zheng Fu-xiong. 1987—Richard Harrison, Stuart Smith, Kenneth Lundh.

Here is a movie in which there is a lot to say and not much to say. This is one of those freaky films packaged and re-released in the 1980s under a completely different title by the king of cut-and-paste kung fu filmmaking, Godfrey Ho. Ho shot many films using Caucasian actors with 1980s poofy hairstyles. He had them run around in brightly colored ninja costumes, edited in footage from old kung fu films that he either shot years ago or bought the rights to with producer Joseph Lai, dubbed in English dialogue completely different from the original film, and then usually put the word "ninja" in the title.

The original story mirrors the film *Red Sun* (1971), but it doesn't exactly mirror the premise of a Japanese samurai and a Western gunslinger pursuing a Western outlaw who stole a Japanese sword intended to be a gift to the U.S. president. Instead, *Fury in Storm* is about a Chinese kung fu fighter named Dragon or Lung (Zhang Yi) and an Italian Catholic monk named Antonio (who carries around a man-sized cross on his back like Jesus Christ). They pursue a Japanese samurai outlaw (Lung Fei) who stole a Chinese chop seal belonging to the royal court. To get the chop back, Lung and Antonio use the samurai's girlfriend as a means to find him and as a bargaining chip.

The revamped Godfrey Ho-directed version, which has all the added footage of an American running around in ninja costumes and was renamed *Ninja Avengers*, is about a man named Ringo who gets out of prison and vows revenge against the Catholic priest who put him there. A white ninja (Richard Harrison) stops him.

The choreography of the fights is fairly simple and is mostly a collection of individual shots of techniques delivered one at a time with overemphasized wind-ups of each movement. But in my opinion, the finale may have inspired Robert Rodriguez's gun-hidden-in-a-guitar trick, which the character El Mariachi uses in the films *El Mariachi* (1992), *Desperado* (1995) and in *Once Upon a Time in Mexico* (2003). If you have seen *Fury in Storm*, you will know exactly what I mean, and it is certainly nothing for Rodriguez to get "cross" about to admit the possibility that he got the idea from *Fury in Storm*. It would not be the first time a Western filmmaker has done it, and it will not be the last.

Titleography: *Shaolin Quick Draw*; *Champion on Fire*; *Ninja Avengers*. Translation—*The Big Earth Dragon Sort*. *Sort* here refers to ilk or type. The *Champion* and *Ninja* refer to the Godfrey Ho version of the film. Although there are no Shaolin monks or Shaolin Temple references in the film, the *Quick Draw* aspect stems from the bizarre gun footage at the end of the movie. The Chinese title draws from the man named Dragon and what he does for the *Big Earth*, i.e., China. *Fury in Storm* is a nice generic title that sounds like a great kung fu film and is perhaps a metaphor for the *Fury* of China within the *Storm* of Japanese invaders. **MA Percentage: 13.61%**

GALLANT, THE

一身是膽 (1972—Taiwan) **106m. FI: Zhang Yi-gui. NOT/LOT: None; NOF/LOF: 17/ 17m 55s.** D: Yang Su. C: Jimmy Wong Yu, Li Xiang, Yee Yuen, Sally Chen, Paul Chang Chung, Ling Yin, Chen Hung-lie.

In this ode to the age-old virtue of gallantry, Sir Jimmy Wong Yu stars in a trilogy of short films under the main film title *The Gallant*. In each story, he must rise to the challenge of the unjust behavior of various black knights and slay them to save three fair maidens.

In the first tale *The Stranger*, a woman (Li Xiang) runs away from crooked police and into a man's (Jimmy Wong Yu) apartment. Her nameless savior is part James Bond and part knight in shining armor. But rather than brandishing a pistol or a sword and shield, he uses flaming fists and combustible kicks to take down a nightclub full of Triads led by a kingpin (Yee Yuen) who has used and abused the woman. The final bar fight rocks like an avalanche, and Wong Yu's sweating, gritty demeanor and snarling face have the intensity of 10 tigers. With up to 25 techniques per shot, Wong Yu moves like a snapping dragonfly and displays a controlled mayhem that rivals any of his previous fights.

The second short, *The Stranger Attending the Tomb*, is a bit more somber. A heavy-hearted prodigal son (Jimmy Wong Yu) returns to his hamlet home to bury his rich father. While watching over the grave, he laments on his past as being a

bad son. His heart is now heavy from all the sins that pervade his conscience. To make matters worse, his younger sister (Sally Chen), who her brother considers as his last bastion of all that is good in his world, is threatened by a rebel (Paul Chang Chung) and his grave-robbing gang, who also want to loot the father's grave. The son goes berserk, which leads to a final confrontation reminiscent of the OK Corral; each gang member meets his demise by pitchfork, shovel or fists. Although not as fast-paced as in the first story, the fights are more brutal and delivered in a more methodical way. They are also laced with weapons, revenge and disdain.

In the final tale called *The Avenger*, a man (Jimmy Wong Yu) returns home from prison after taking the rap for a three-man heist of a treasure map in order to protect his accomplice and father-in-law. Their third partner in crime is the double-crossing Li San (Chen Hung-lie). The map was split in three, with each member getting a piece. While the man was away, Li killed the father-in-law, took his piece of the map, and then set his sights on our hero's wife, Hsiao Hung (Ling Yin). Li threatens to kill Hsiao Hung unless he gets the third piece of the map. Wong Yu breaks out his sword and does his one-man sword-slashing routine to save the woman he loves, avenge his father-in-law's death and recover the map.

Overall, the fights in *The Gallant* are intense and well-choreographed, and Wong Yu portrays each character and his fighting skills uniquely and with prowess.

Titleography: *The Gallant Boxer*. Translation—*One Body Is Courage*. The titles serve the film well because it is about gallantry, and each one of Jimmy's characters is a manifestation of courage wrapped into one body. **MA Percentage: 16.90%**

GAME OF DEATH, THE

死亡遊戲 (1973/1978—Hong Kong/USA) **100m. MAD: Bruce Lee, Sammo Hung. NOT/LOT: None; NOF/LOF: 13/ 26m 46s.** D: Bruce Lee, Robert Clouse. C: Bruce Lee, Kim Tai-chung, Danny Inosanto, Kareem Abdul-Jabbar, Chi Hon-joi, Bob Wall, Dean Jagger, Coleen Camp, Gig Young, Mel Novak, Cassanova Wong, Roy Chiao, Sammo Hung.

In 1972 and 1973, Bruce Lee wrote and shot 40 minutes (some say 90 minutes) of an idea originally titled *Song of the Knife*, which addressed his philosophy about the existence of martial arts. Lee was interested in separating the useful and nonessential elements of various martial arts, and in this film, that process is revealed via a hero's journey while he ascends a five-story pagoda to reveal each floor's treasure. In the story, each floor represents a step toward truth and is guarded by a certain type of martial artist: karate warriors, a *wing chun*/praying mantis artist, a Filipino fighter (Danny Inosanto), a *hapkido* stylist (Chi Hon-joi) and "the Unknown" (NBA star Kareem Abdul-Jabbar). What was the treasure? Perhaps knowledge, understanding, or the realization that the journey is never-ending, and that it is the pursuit of the journey that is important.

Five years after his death, Lee's final treasure, now called *The Game of Death*, manifested as something far less than he had envisioned. This version combines 11 minutes of Lee's directed footage and fight scenes with a highly convoluted story about a famous movie star, Billy Lo (Kim Tai-chung/Lee), who feigns his own death in order to exact revenge on those who were trying to destroy him.

Snippets of Lee from his other Golden Harvest films and a double (Kim) were used. Also, compared to legitimate kung fu films and in order to mask Kim's lack of Lee's finesse, speed and fluidity, the martial arts were kept to a minimum, and fight director Sammo Hung purposely made his fight with Bob Wall poor so Kim's fights would look better by comparison. Ultimately, anyone aware of Lee's legacy watched the film just to see those precious 11 minutes and 32 seconds because at that time, who knew if there would ever be another opportunity to see them? Just for posterity, stuntmen who wore Lee's famous yellow jumpsuit in the film were Yuen Biao, Feng Ke-on and Lam Ching-ying.

It's possible that Lee never intended for the footage to be part of a final cut, that it was shot and edited as a tool to convey his vision to get financing. Perhaps if the film were ever to be made, parts of the fights would have been re-shot to match his high expectations of quality and perfection. In the *nunchaku* sequence, for example, Lee's two mistakes are as obvious as an elephant running in a herd of buffalos, and you'll be in no doubt as to what they are when you watch the film. Next in line for what could have benefited from some re-shooting was Lee's bout with the 7-foot-plus, former NBA star Kareem Abdul-Jabbar. Although the contrast of height between the two combatants is a grand visual, Abdul-Jabbar was often off-balance; it seems as if he had not yet found his cinema legs. Also, what is with Lee and Chi's supposed kicking fight looking more like a judo bout? I have seen the behind-the-scenes footage shot by Lee, and it reveals that each time Chi blew a shot, Lee's frustration grew to the point at which the kicks became a no-go. The lesson learned is that good martial arts technicians are not always good movie fighters.

Lee accomplished a great deal in film and martial arts because he gave the Chinese people a sense of pride and national identity. He also essentially made the martial arts film genre a worldwide phenomenon. Unfortunately, at the end of the day, his name, films and images have largely been relegated to the dungeons of money and business for those who can tap into his success. *Game of Death* was merely a financial pawn in the Bruce Lee game of entertainment.

Titleography: As of this writing, no alternative titles could be found. Translation—*Game of Death.* **MA Percentage: 26.77%**

GANGA KI SAUGAND

(1978—India) **145m. TD: S. Azim. NOT/LOT: None; NOF/LOF: 5/ 3m 20s.**
D: Sultan Ahmed. C: Amitabh Bachchan, Rekha, Amjad Khan, Bindu, Inder Sen Johar, Anwar Hussain, Jagdeep, Iftekhar.

The Ten Commandments (1956) meets the Chinese kung fu god Guang Gong … sort of. Although it does not have many fights, *Ganga Ki Saugand* still has more than *Good Guys Wear Black* (see martialogy), and it has all the physical and spiritual elements often seen in Asian-made martial arts films.

Cult Indian action-star Amitabh Bachchan takes on a more downtrodden hero role as Jeeva, a man who crosses the corrupt regional ruler Jashwant Singh (perennial villain actor Amjad Khan). Jeeva's elderly mother Ramvati is Jashwant's maid. One day, after Jashwant slips on the wet floor Ramvati cleaned, he proceeds to beat her up. Jeeva arrives in the nick of time to rescue her, but for doing so, he is badly beaten and exiled from the region.

Although Bachchan's *kilaripayit* (an Indian martial art) cudgel play is weaker than in *Don* (1978), it is rare to see kilaripayit in film (famously exhibited in Jackie Chan's *The Myth* (2005)), but it is still exciting to watch despite its off-balance and awkward pole-fighting flaws. The most engaging moment occurs after Jeeva is almost cudgeled to death wherein the respected pole-fighting village guru, who is a Moses-like figure who leads the villagers away from Jashwant's lands, saves him. Jeeva's mother then drags her dying son away into the hinterlands.

Night falls, and it appears as if mother and son are in the middle of nowhere. Jeeva is seconds away from dying. Suddenly, a flash of lightning breaks the darkness to reveal a foreboding statue of Kali, the Hindu goddess of war and redeemer of the universe. (Some readers may recall Kali from the 1974 fantasy film *The Golden Voyage of Sinbad*). Ramvati pleads with Kali to take her life and spare Jeeva's. In the morning, Jeeva awakens to find his mother dead at the foot of Kali. While burning her body on a funeral pyre in the holy Ganges River, Jeeva vows vengeance for his mother's death. He finds the strength to rise up and stop Jashwant's unjust behavior and treatment of the people, regardless of the corrupt police and submissive villagers who blindly protect Jashwant.

The whole religious spiel is a classic moment right out of many Chinese kung fu films. When the odds are stacked against the hero, he will drop to his knees before an imposing statue of Guang Gong, the Chinese kung fu god; Guan Ying, the goddess of mercy; or Buddha to seek the strength to fight the villain and make a solemn vow of revenge. So in this film, it's the Hindu goddess Kali to which Jeeva prays.

On a silly note, the local tax collector from the village in the film is the spitting image of Ray Davies, the lead singer of the famous 1970s British rock group The Kinks.

Titleography: As of this writing, no alternative titles could be found. **MA Percentage: 2.30%**

GENERATION GAP, THE

叛逆 (1973—Hong Kong) **113m. FI: Liu Chia-liang, Tang Chia. NOT/LOT: 1/ 11s; NOF/LOF: 9/ 10m 41s.** D: Chang Cheh. C: David Chiang, Ti Lung, Agnes Chen Mei-ling, Chiang Ling, Lu Di, Yang Chi-ching, Jiang Dao.

In this film, director Chang Cheh investigates the problems of Chinese youth in the early 1970s—though they still feel relevant today. He explores the lack of communication between parents who grew up with traditional values, the memory of World War II and the arrival of Mao, and Chang investigates their children who were raised during the heavy influence of British pop culture and rock 'n' roll—a generation that wanted to pursue dreams. Instead of taking a stance one way or the other, Chang treads on neutral ground so that he can

speak to both sides of the generation about the issue.

The Generation Gap tells the story of high-school student Cindy (Agnes Chen Mei-ling), 15, who dreams of becoming a singer, and her 21-year-old boyfriend, Ling Xi (David Chiang). Ling Xi opts not to attend a university in England because he wants to become an auto mechanic and hang out with Cindy. When the two decide to live in the same pad together, their square parents become tighter than a pair of fluorescent-striped bell-bottoms on a sumo wrestler. Cindy is forced to return home, and the rifts between her and Ling Xi and their respective parents worsen. Even Ling Xi's older brother, Ling Zhao (Ti Lung), gets involved. The siblings have a bitter physical confrontation that makes any argument I had with my brothers look like a battle between Smurfs. During a moment of weakness and stupidity, Ling Xi hooks up with a roster of ruffians headed by the ultra-cocky Xiao Zhoa (Jiang Dao), which leads to fights, jail time, gun waving and death. Ling Xi goes down the tubes screaming, "I didn't do anything!"

But like Janis Joplin tells us, freedom is just another word for nothing else to lose, and in the case of Lin, he has everything to lose—everything being love. His life is lost unless he remembers that love is not always about looking directly at the one you love. Lovers also need to look toward the future in the same direction.

Chang's study of youth was influenced by the British youth cultures of the mods (those clean-cut motor-scooter riders) and the rockers (the macho bikers in leather jackets). The film's opening music mixes a Steppenwolf-like song with a Marianne Faithfull lament. The fight scenes are certainly below par for all actors and choreographers involved in the film, but to be fair, the movie is not focused on action (nor should it be). However, if my older brothers could fight like Ling Xi and Ling Zhao, I would have had the best seats in the house and would have charged my friends to watch.

The most memorable scene takes place in a singing club. During Cindy's rendition of Delaney and Bonnie Bramlett's 1971 hit *Never Ending Song of Love*, the camera follows a flamboyant Teddy boy dancing in the club, and it is scary to think that any of us ever danced like that during our high-school days in the early 1970s. But the best song they should have used in this film is *Don't Let Me Be Misunderstood* by the Animals.

Titleography: As of this writing, no alternative titles could be found. Translation—*Rebellion.* **MA Percentage: 9.62%** SHAW BROTHERS

G.I. SAMURAI

Sengoku Jieta (1979—Japan) **140m. FI: Uncredited. NOT/LOT: None; NOF/LOF: 5/ 4m 8s.** D: Mitsumasa Saito. C: Sonny Chiba, Ryo Hayami, Masashi Ishibashi, Haruki Kadokawa, Asao Koike, Kentaro Kudo, Isao Kuraishi, Isao Natsuyagi, Akira Nishikino, Mizuho Suzuki, Ken Takahashi, Hiroshi Tanaka, Hiroyuki Sanada.

This is another samurai sci-fi romp for Sonny Chiba. But unlike *Message From Space* (1978), *G.I. Samurai* is about going to the past rather than being in the future.

Chiba plays Lt. Yoshiaki Iba from the Ground Self-Defense Force. While leading soldiers on military drills, Iba and troop get sent back in time to the Warring States period of Japan, also known as the Sengoku period (circa 1467-1603). They arrive in the middle of a skirmish between opposing samurai warriors Nagao Kagetora (Isao Natsuyagi) and Takeda Shingen (Hiroshi Tanaka). Nagao sees the power of Iba's tanks, helicopters and machine guns and persuades Iba to join him on his quest to rule Japan.

The two new friends have a moment reminiscent of Chang Cheh (the Hong Kong director known for his martial brotherhood films) when they ride horses together on the beach and when Nagao teaches Iba how to shoot a bow and arrow. But from the bow and arrow to the straight and narrow, Iba's first mission is to destroy Takeda with his 20th century weapons and men. Several of Iba's Ground Self-Defense Force men oppose the decision, stage a mutiny and then are killed during a vicious gun battle. Other soldiers go AWOL, only to be hacked apart by Takeda's samurai. Iba convinces his remaining men that changing history by fighting might create a time paradox that would enable them to go home. After a long, bloody battle, Iba beheads Takeda and then is forced to kill Takeda's son Katsuyorie (Hiroyuki Sanada). Only a handful of Iba's men survive, and all their advanced machines of war are destroyed. Instead of creating a time paradox, they run out of time; Iba's friend Nagao is ordered by the shogun to kill Iba and his men. It is time to see if Nagao and Iba's time together can stand the test of time when they meet for one final time.

Historically, two of the most famous rivals during the Warring States period were Nagao Kagetora and Takeda Shin General Nagao was nicknamed "The Dragon of Echigo" because of his fearless martial arts abilities. Takeda was nicknamed "The Tiger of Kai" because of his ferocious fighting skills. It's also important to know that Nagao's historic name was actually Uesugi Kenshin, and most historical texts refer to these warriors as Uesugi and Takeda Shin General Takeda is believed to have died from an old sniper-induced war wound or pneumonia. His son Katsuyorie committed suicide three years later after losing the Battle of Temmokuzan. Akira Kurosawa's film *Kagemusha* (1980) relates the sniper version of Takeda's death.

One neat thing about watching a decade's worth of films is that you can see how certain stars grow. It is interesting how Sonny Chiba's first and last martial arts films of the 1970s—The Assassin and G.I. Samurai—each feature about four minutes of fight scenes. You might think that this would symbolize a lack of growth or even a step back, but in fact Chiba ages like a fine wine, and some of his best film are still to come in the 1990s and 2000s. After Chiba's last film about Mas Oyama (see *Karate for Life*), Chiba left the karate genre and shifted toward the sword, which would hold true in most of his later martial arts films and TV shows. Also of note, a year after *G.I. Samurai* was made, the USS Nimitz went back in time to World War II-era Japan in the American film *The Final Countdown* (1980).

Titleography: *Time Slip*; *Time Slip of an Okinawan Village*; *Time Slip of the Battleground*; *Day of the Apocalypse*. Translation—*The Warring States (Sengoku) Period Self-Defense Force*. **MA Percentage: 2.95%**

GOLDEN LION, THE

金毛獅王 (1973—Hong Kong) 84m. FI: Xu Er-niu. NOT/LOT: 1/ 3s; NOF/LOF: 27/ 20m 2s. D: Ho Meng-hua. C: Li Ching, Zhao Xiong, Wang Xia, James Nam Gung-fan, Fang Mien, Chan Shen.

When Golden Lion Dai Xiao-yao (Zhao Xiong) desperately needed money to help his sick mother, he admittedly took the wrong step in life and became a robber, regretting his decision each day. He now does the old Robin Hood routine, stealing from the rich and giving to the poor, until a rich official decides this lion must be killed.

The official hires Wang Jian-chao (Wang Xia) and his batch of big-game hunters, who first kill Golden Lion's parents as a way to lure him out of his den. When Wang finally corners Golden Lion in the forest, he breaks out his deadly Poison Claw and rips into Golden Lion's flesh, forcing him to search for the famous Dr. Lu Guo-jing (Fang Mien), who lives in seclusion with his daughter Wen Fang (Li Ching) and his wannabe kung fu hero son Wen Yeh (James Nam Gung-fan).

Regardless of Golden Lion's reputation as a ruthless bandit, the moral-minded doctor treats him and learns more about his truth and the poisonous words of the world. Risking his life and reputation to heal and protect Golden Lion, Dr. Lu ignores threats from Golden Lion's detractors to turn in Golden Lion to the authorities. However, Dr. Lu's nephew, who works for Wang, lures pseudo-

son Wen Yeh to the dark side. He promises Wen Yeh the world if he can tell his new friends how to defeat Dr. Lu's secret Dragon Sword skills and help them find Golden Lion. Wen Yeh unwittingly betrays his father but stays alive long enough to make amends. Meanwhile, Golden Lion intercepts a snake bite meant for Lu's daughter Wen Fang, which makes his health worse. But when Dr. Lu, Wen Feng and Golden Lion team up, the hunted now become the hunters.

There are several interesting talking points in this film. During actor Zhao Xiong's sword fights, he used a reverse grip on his weapon, similar to the character of blind Japanese swordsman Zatoichi. (See any Zatoichi martialogy like *Zatoichi Meets Yojimbo* (1971).) This grip was rarely used in earlier films, possibly because blatantly copying the fight choreography poses of a Japanese cinema icon would not go over well with Chinese audiences. What was even more rare at the time was that Zhao also used *taekwondo* hand and arm defensive postures during his nonweapon fights, which may have been influenced by the presence of Korean taekwondo practitioner James Nam Gung-fan as one of the film's fighting characters.

Choreographer Xu Er-niu cleverly accentuates the notion of great strength, which is a trait associated with lions, by having Zhao pick up and throw his attackers all over the place. Note that because the stuntmen do not jump at the right time, Zhao is still able to heave a guy out of frame with Herculean strength. Imagine that—a Chinese hero fighting like a Greek hero and a Chinese doctor upholding the oath of an ancient Greek physician (Hippocrates). The Greek and Chinese gods would be proud.

So even though the Chinese title of this film might evoke a popular Disney animated film, this movie does not feature a trio of friends like Simba, Timon and Pumbaa but a trio of warriors who uphold the conscience of a country and the Hippocratic oath. Although considered a rite of passage for doctors sincerely dedicated to moral treatment and healing the sick rather than financial gain, all physicians no longer take the oath—thus one of the reasons for the fight against instituting nationalized health care in America. 'Tis a sad state of affairs.

Titleography: As of this writing, no alternative titles could be found. Translation—*Golden Fur Lion King*. The title refers to the nickname of the main character. **MA Percentage: 23.91%** SHAW BROTHERS

GOLDEN SEAL, THE

金印仇 (1971—Hong Kong) 84m. FI: Liang Shao-song. NOT/LOT: None; NOF/LOF: 27/ 14m 24s. D: Tien Feng. C: Wang Ping, Tsung Hua, Ku Feng, Tien Feng, Yu Feng, Chan Shen, Bai Lu, Cliff Lok.

When a villain gets the *Good Housekeeping* "Seal of Disapproval" in a Shaw Brothers film, then it is a good thing. Take for example the libertine lowlife Lei Zhen-tian (Ku Feng), who wants to be the head of Jiang Hu. (See *The Water Margin*.) The only way he can do that is if he can get his grubby little saw-tooth-wheel-wielding paws on the fabled Golden Seal, the ultimate power of authority that is passed down from leader to leader of the righteous Green Dragon Clan, who are the current heads of Jiang Hu. When Lei stages a coup against the Green Dragons, the sole child survivor Dai Tian-chou escapes with his uncle and disappears. Lei creates the Sun Moon Sect and sets his sights on searching for the seal that has been carefully hidden before the Green Dragon Clan was destroyed.

Twenty years later, Lei has gone too far; his sect and he have burned a path of foreboding and fear. However, Dai (Tsung Hua) is now grown up and master of the Villain Avoid Sword technique. It's up to him to defeat Lei before Lei finds the seal and cements his authority as head of the Jiang Hu.

After an altercation wherein one of Lei's poisonous darts injures our hero, Dai ends up under the care of three women: a semi-nude jungle woman (Bai Lu) who swings around on vines; female assassin Wu Xiao-yan (Wang Ping) who was the intended target of the poisonous dart; and swordswoman Feng Jing-yi (Yu Feng) who is the daughter of a high-ranking Sun Moon swordsman. Once fully recovered and dealing with a pseudo-love-quadrangle, Dai hooks up with the three female fighters to eclipse Lei's Sun Moon Sect and restore order to the world of Jiang Hu.

The sword fights in this film are a throwback from the 1950s and early '60s style of choreography, a technique known as "giving a target to strike." For this technique, the lead fighter aims for a specific target, as set by the opponent, when swinging his swords. In other words, the opponent puts his sword in a place that directs the actor where to strike. It is an effective reminder for inexperienced actors, and the hesitation between strikes and cues can be partially covered by undercranking the camera (lowering the frames-per-second speed).

Still from The *Golden Lion* © Celestial Pictures Ltd. All rights reserved.

Still from *The Golden Seal* © Celestial Pictures Ltd. All rights reserved.

The main weakness is that such fights do little to create a sense of danger because you can tell that even if the strike were not blocked, the sword would simply swish through the air harmlessly.

As explained in other martialogies, many early Shaw Brothers films with inexperienced fighters (such as this movie) do not have a long length of fight time. However, because Ku Feng was working on many films, he became amazingly adept to adjusting to other actors' fight rhythms. This is probably why newly recruited Shaw Brothers actors were assigned to learn the ins and outs of doing fights on film from Ku. It's a testament to Ku's on- and off-camera dedication to his work.

On an interesting side note, the jungle-woman character would reappear later in director Ho Meng-hua's *Mighty Peking Man* (1977; not a *wuxia* film) in the form of actress Evelyne Kraft.

Titleography: As of this writing, no alternative titles could be found. Translation—*Golden Seal Feud*. Both English and Chinese titles are pretty much spot on in regard to the story line. **MA Percentage: 17.14%** SHAW BROTHERS

GOLGO 13: KOWLOON ASSIGNMENT

Golgo 13: Kuron no Kubi (1977—Japan) **92m. FI: Uncredited. NOT/LOT: 2/ 18s; NOF/LOF: 6/ 2m 39s.** D: Jia Lun, Yukio Noda. C: Sonny Chiba, Chia Lun, Etsuko Shihomi, Emi Shindo, Elaine Sung, Dana, Nick Lam Wai-kei, Jerry Ito, Lee Chi-chung, Chen Yao-lin, Bill Lake.

Golgo 13, aka Duke Togo, is a comic-book hero created by Takao Saito in 1969 for publisher Shogakukan's *Big Comic* magazine. Golgo is derived from Golgotha, the place where Jesus was crucified, and 13 is the number of people present at the Last Supper. Golgo's logo is a skeleton wearing a crown of thorns, similar to what Jesus wore during the Crucifixion. It also represents his bearing of all man's sins. But as we will see in this movie, Sonny Chiba's character Golgo 13 is the sin you are forced to bear, the thorn in the side you cannot reach. No wonder he is the man that makes men cross.

Golgo 13 (Sonny Chiba) is a hit man for hire. His next job, as instructed by a powerful drug syndicate, is to whack Chow Lui-fung (Nick Lam Wai-kei) before Chow rats out the syndicate to the Hong Kong police. Detective Smith (Chia Lun) is aware of Golgo 13's reputation and is determined to protect Chow so Smith can take down the syndicate. From there, Golgo 13 saves a woman from her abusive boyfriend and gets a hit put out on him by said boyfriend, who actually works for Chow. But there's someone even bigger in the background, and

that someone forces Golgo 13 to head to Tokyo, then Macao. He must kill that mysterious person before the person kills Golgo 13. Meanwhile, Detective Smith needs to protect a man from the Poranian Republic who is seeking asylum in the United States. This devious and heartless man Polansky's ticket is his list of syndicate connections, which he plans to expose for the right price. It is a list Smith must get before Golgo 13 kills Polansky.

Despite all the assassinations, this movie was another relaxation piece for Sonny Chiba, but it is imperative to note that this doesn't mean the film is bad. Instead, it only means that Chiba's martial arts efforts are minimal, for reasons described in *Karate Kiba* and *Executioner II*. It is something that Chinese and Japanese martial arts stars usually do, usually as a means to recover from fight-film related injuries while still fulfilling their movie contracts.

On an end note, Ken Takakura played a nonmartial arts version of good guy Golgo 13 in the failed 1973 film *Golgo 13*, directed by Junya Sato.

Titleography: *Golgo 13, International*; *Sniper 13*; *The Kowloon Assignment*; *Golgo 13: The Neck of Kowloon*. **MA Percentage: 3.21%**

GOOD GUYS WEAR BLACK

(1978—USA) **96m. FC: Chuck Norris, Aaron Norris. NOT/LOT: None; NOF/ LOF: 4/ 1m 55s.** D: Ted Post. C: Chuck Norris, Anne Archer, Lloyd Haynes, Dana Andrews, Jim Backus, James Franciscus, Oh Soon-Tek, Aaron Norris.

Chuck Norris versus the CIA, but in this case, CIA stands for "Chuck Ignores Action." Touted by several Web sites and a few books as a classic American-made martial arts film, *Good Guys Wear Black* became the gauge for what could be construed as a martial arts movie by me for this book. In 96 minutes, the film boasts a whopping four fight scenes that cumulatively last 115 seconds, which include 19 kicks, eight punches and two knee strikes. So to be presented as a martialogy in this film, I decided that any film I watched had to have at least the same length-of-time fight statistics and similarly simple martial arts choreography as this film. Of note, I watched more than 50 films that had martial arts in them but failed to meet this minimum standard. However, the films are mentioned in the Complete Martial Arts Film Reference List By Country at the end of the book.

After the Vietnam War, former Black Tigers commando members begin to lose their stripes in that they are being mysteriously killed. Former Tiger Commando John T. Booker (Chuck Norris) is sent to investigate why the State Department is killing them off.

This is Norris' second American-made martial arts film (see *Breaker! Breaker!*; that being his first one) that features a couple of decent *tang soo do* kicks. Formally called *soo bahk ki*, tang soo do is believed to have originated sometime around A.D. 663 during the Three Kingdoms of Korea (Koguryo, Paekche and Silla). After the Chinese-backed Silla defeated the Japanese-backed Paechta, the martial art of *tangsu*, which is a forerunner of tang soo do, was created in honor of China's Tang Dynasty emperor. Whether people realize it or not, Norris was the first to introduce tang soo do techniques into American martial arts cinema with *Breaker! Breaker!*. (Or did he? Check out Howard Jackson films to see if it's true!)

However, for a legitimate martial artist like Norris, the man who had an awesome fight scene against Bruce Lee in *Way of the Dragon*, you expect that his films would have superior martial arts and better fight choreography than in the films of his other American martial arts star counterparts. Yet it wasn't until 1980 when Norris starred in *The Octagon* that he finally did a martial arts film with any good martial arts worthy of his abilities. Probably the most engaging action moment in *Good Guys Wear Black* is when Booker plays chicken with a car trying to run him over; he does a flying side kick through the front windshield. Of course, it's generally well-known now that his stunt-double brother, Aaron Norris, delivered the kick.

Titleography: As of this writing, no alternative titles could be found. **MA Percentage: 2.00%**

GOODBYE BRUCE LEE: HIS LAST GAME OF DEATH

新死亡遊戲 (1975—Taiwan) **87m. SC: Chen Kee. NOT/LOT: 1/ 30s; NOF/LOF: 13/ 27m 30s.** D: Harold B. Swartz, Lin Bing. C: Bruce Li, Lung Fei, Shan Mao, Cai Hong, Li Jiang, Ma Chang, Zhang Yi-gui, Robert Kerver, Ronald Brown, Johnny Floyd, Zhang Yi-gui, Hou Ba-wei.

This film should have been named *Goodbye Bruce Li: His Last Film About Bruce Lee's Death ... Please*, but the Bruceploitation mentality trudged on like disco. (Also like disco, Bruce Lee spinoffs faded in the 1980s.)

After doing a pathetic-looking karate-like form, Bruce Lee look-alike Lee (Bruce Li) is hired to complete Bruce Lee's unfinished movie *The Game of Death*. Yet on his way home from signing the contract, Lee is duped into delivering a mysterious package. Once he realizes some seedy people are after it, he refuses to deliver the package and gets caught up in fighting a bunch of gangsters. When word gets out that Lee can really fight, he becomes a threat to rival studios. So before Lee can reap the benefits of his film career, he must kill Manager K (Lung Fei), who has captured his girlfriend.

In yet another angle on Bruce Lee's *Game of Death*, this film has Li donning the famed yellow tracksuit again, but instead of climbing a five-story tower and defeating a different fighter on each floor to reach martial virtue, Lee must climb a seven-story tower in order to save his girlfriend from certain death. The floors are guarded by the following fighters: two guys who look like Bruce Lee, a disappearing-and-reappearing samurai warrior, a karate black belt with a *bo*, a thin white wrestler who grunts like a dying dog, a *nunchaku* master from India, a black boxer and the whip-wielding Manager K.

What is most irritating about this film is the opening and closing credits song *The King of Kung Fu*. Hearing it is as disconcerting as hearing the song *Kung Fu Fighting* by Carl Douglas. Even a few days after viewing the film, I found myself constantly humming, "He's the king of kung fu."

Not unlike the film's beginning karate *kata*, Li's martial arts continue to struggle throughout the film's fights in a clumsy, awkward and technically unsound fashion. Besides lacking creativity, the martial arts sequences look like something a bunch of Cornell college students put together one weekend in the dormitory while preparing for a live kung fu fight performance for the Korean Student Association's year-end party. (Oops, gave the lads and me away on that one.) However, as is typical with many kung fu films, the fights do get a bit better toward the end, and you have got to whack yourself on the side of the head in disbelief when you see veteran Shaw Brothers star Cai Hong with a turban and dark skin imitating a fighting guru from India.

Titleography: *The New Game of Death*. Translation—*New Game of Death*. The Chinese and alternative English title make sense because the film is a rework of Bruce Lee's *Game of Death*, and *Goodbye Bruce Lee* is probably a farewell salute by Li to Lee. However, this film was not the last time that Li would don and prance around in the famous yellow tracksuit that Bruce Lee wore in *Game of Death*. **MA Percentage: 32.18%** SHAW BROTHERS

GOOSE BOXER

梁山怪招 and 野鵝烏龍招 (1978—Hong Kong) **79m. MAD: Jin Ming. NOT/LOT: 14/ 14m 5s; NOF/LOF: 14/ 27m 23s.** D: Tai Si-fu. C: Xiang Hua-jiang, Lee Hoi-sang, Gao Fei, Tian Qing, Da Xi-yan, Lee Chun-wa.

Who is the teacher? Who is the student? And who are they trying to kill and on whose behalf? Are you confused yet? But don't fret about it because even in Chinese, this goofy film is a challenge to follow.

A goose-rearing hero (Xiang Hua-jiang) is forced to learn white crane kung fu from one villain (Lee Hoi-sang) and some other unknown style from a second villain (Gao Fei). The hero also practices a third form of kung fu from a village idiot and the idiot's attacking dwarf who runs around biting groins and crying like a baby.

As it turns out, all the villains are teaching the hero so he will unconsciously use what he has learned from one villain during the training session of another and vice versa. That way, each villain will learn the kung fu techniques of the other. The film comes down to the hero teaching the villains a few lessons of his own, but of course, one villain reigns supreme, and it is up to the goose boxer to clip his wings. What results is an unsettling but dynamic fight between a metaphorical white crane and a goose, and at the end of the day, someone's goose will be cooked. For me, this kung fu comedy hits an all-time low because the comedy is so nonsensical and forced. It's like watching Jackie Chan mug to the camera just for the sake of mugging, in which you feel like someone should just come up and mug him. In case you were wondering, there is no such style as goose kung fu.

Dwarfs were treated very poorly in Chinese films, and it was not until the appearance of Teddy Luo Bin (aka Robin Luo) in the early 1980s that height-challenged actors gained respect in Chinese movies. Before his appearance, most roles were completely offensive and insulting. Even today, if the nonprofit organization Little People of America ever saw this film, it would probably be burned. (Note: Please observe "probably.")

Titleography: *Shaolin's Tough Kid*. Translation—*Strange Techniques From Liang Mountain*; *Wild Goose Black Dragon Technique*. *Goose Boxer* is the most

logical English title because there is no association with Shaolin in the film. *Liang Mountain* is from the famed *wuxia* novel *All Men Are Brothers* (see *All Men Are Brothers* martialogy), and apparently the area in Shandong province is known for its goose dishes. Perhaps whoever created the Chinese title was a Shandong person and knew the goose tie-in. **MA Percentage: 52.49%**

GREEN DRAGON INN

青龍客棧 (1977—Taiwan) **93m. FI: Wu Ming-xiong. NOT/LOT: None; NOF/LOF: 21/ 19m 17s.** D: Wu Ming-xiong. C: Lo Lieh, Yueh Hua, Polly Kuan, Si Ma-long, Cliff Ching Ching, Tien Ming, Jiang Qing-xia, O Yau-man, Huang Jun, Su Guo-liang.

No one should be above the law, but in the world of politics and money, some wealthy and powerful families literally get away with murder—unless a man of the law is righteous enough to discard the broom used to sweep things under the rug and bring these families back under the law's jurisdiction. In Chinese families, the oldest son is the most important and therefore has free rein to do what he likes, and if the father of this child is influential or important, the kid is above the law and holds the key to controlling that metaphorical broom.

Son of the feared local warlord or spoiled brat Hong Bing-chun (Huang Jun) runs amok and flippantly murders the Chu family, including all the children. Bold Dragon Marshall Luo (Yueh Hua) is ordered by the emperor to arrest Bing-chun and bring him to justice within seven days. Meanwhile, mysterious swordsman Silent Tracker Kung Fung-mien (Lo Lieh) has his own designs on Bing-chun, as does a masked, ninja-like assassin (Polly Kuan). When Luo makes the arrest, Bing-chun's father, Hong Di-er (Su Guo-liang), hires assassins and uses all means necessary to kill Luo and free his son. As Marshall Luo instigates his martial law and escorts Bing-chun back to the emperor's court, they have to stop for the night at the Green Dragon Inn. And this is where father Di-er makes his final move to free his son.

Luo makes his last stand inside the Green Dragon Inn. He hunkers down for a full-frontal assault by Hong Di-er and his vagabonds, while Silent Tracker and the masked assassin await their own opening to get at Bing-chun.

Influenced by *Dragon Gate Inn* (1967) and featuring fights more along the lines of *Come Drink With Me* (1966) in that it also has an "inn scene," this movie ups the "inn" ante with strange rope machinations and creative sword-laden booby traps. They spring up in Grand Guignol grandeur in an effort by Luo to even the odds, protect his prisoner from within and without the inn and complete his martial mission.

As with many of these types of swordplay films in which the villain's relentless ultra-martial arts reeks with the dastardliness of a Charles Manson crime, the final skirmish spirals out of control into a helter-skelter spectacular. Interestingly, the fight rhythm, cadence and posture of the warlord assassin played by Si Ma-long is reminiscent of the then-current Shaw sensation Alexander Fu Sheng. In fact, in most of Si's films, his choreographed fights mimic Fu Sheng. Furthermore, Si's career started a few months after Fu Sheng's and ended after Fu Sheng died—this is no accident. During the '60s and '70s, whenever a new Hong Kong film star was born, the Taiwanese created their own version; Si was Taiwan's answer to Fu Sheng. After Fu Sheng died, Si's career rapidly declined because it depended on the success of the Chinese star.

Titleography: *Bruce Is Loose*. Translation—*Inn of the Green Dragon*. How did this film get renamed *Bruce Is Loose*? It is one of the many mysteries of dubbed kung fu films. The poster of *Bruce Is Loose* boldly states that Bruce Lee stars in the film and that the movie is an "Official Chinese Black Belt Society film." Wow. **MA Percentage: 20.73%**

GREEN JADE STATUETTE

神刀流星拳 (1978—Hong Kong) **91m. FD: Tommy Lee. NOT/LOT: 1/ 30s; NOF/LOF: 21/ 24m 5s.** D: Lee Tso-nam. C: Chi Kuan-chun, Meng Fei, Hu Jin, Wang Guan-xiong, Tommy Lee, Lung Fei, Kitty Meng Chui, Shan Mao, Jimmy Lung Fong, Goa Fei, Liang Chia-ren.

As stated in this film, in the world of kung fu and Jiang Hu, a man's reputation is worth more than his life. That also means that the people who do not care about their reputations have a better chance to survive. With statements like these, you have to wonder about the reputations of some American presidents and how they would fare in this martial arts underworld. They would undoubtedly live a long time. Like singer Billy Joel sings, "Honesty is such a lonely word. Everyone is so untrue."

After three hooded robbers kill the family who they stole a green jade statuette from, they agree to meet one year later in Stone Village to divide the spoils. A year later, the dynamics of Stone Village erupt with intrigue because the local Wyatt Earp-like protector, Wu Kang (Chi Kuan-chun), won't allow anyone to interfere with the running of Madam Pearl's (Hu Jin) brothel.

The suave, James Bond-ish assassin Chen Chang (Meng Fei) arrives in town with the assignment to find the statue and kill anyone in his way. His prime suspect is Madam Pearl. When the three robbers return to the village, no one knows who's who, who is hired by whom to find out what, who has what and who did what. It sounds complicated, nay confusing, but for insane reasons that boggle the mind, somehow the ending makes sense and all the right martial arts stars fight against each other for maximum kung fu fighting glory.

In some martialogies, I have described the ultimate secret of how these Chinese fight choreographers put their fights together—the page flipping is now on for those wishing to know that ultimate secret—and as it turns out, one of the best "cadence callers" in the kung fu film industry is actor Meng Fei. I have been on set to witness his timing technique, and many stuntmen who I spoke with back then agreed he was easy to fight with because of his timing of technique delivery in response to his rhythmic screaming.

Fight director Tommy Lee makes good use of Meng Fei's cadence calling abilities and uses a lot of hand-held camerawork for the fights in this movie. Although the camera operator shakes a bit too much, the shots used during the fights follow the fighters' technique exchanges relatively well. Some fight directors would operate the camera during the fights back in the 1970s, but I am unable to tell in which films they did this. What is also enjoyable is that most of the fights are relatively short and evenly spaced out, giving the feeling that there is a lot of kung fu action. The short fights also prove the effectiveness of always leaving the audience wanting because when they are good, you want to see more. It is in line with one of the unwritten mantras of Hollywood: "Always leave the audience wanting more."

Of the several times I have seen Meng Fei on film sets, he often uses a fan as part of his character's habit as well as during his fights. During the 1970s, the fan became Meng's signature weapon; he always enjoyed spinning the closed fan in his hand during fights and slapping the fan in his other hand when he had dialogue. Although he does not use a fan in this film, you will note that his sticklike knife weapon is about the same size as a fan, and he also does all his usual closed-fan strikes and twirls with it.

Titleography: *Killer's Game*; *The Green Jade Statuette*. Translation—*Mystical* (i.e. *Immortal* or *God*) *Sword and Shooting Star Fist*. The Chinese title refers to how the the names of the signature kung fu skills of Cheng Chang and Wu Kang. *Mystical* in this case also implies immortal and godlike. There are several hired killers in the film, and being that the movie is a mystery and a veritable cat-and-mouse game, *Killer's Game* is an appropriate title. **MA Percentage: 27.01%**

HALF A LOAF OF KUNG FU

點止功夫咁簡單 and 一招半式闖江湖 (1978—Hong Kong) **93m. AD:** Jackie Chan. **NOT/LOT:** 2/ 1m 11s; **NOF/LOF:** 30/ 29m 59s. **D:** Chen Zhi-hua. **C:** Jackie Chan, James Tien, Dean Shek, Doris Lung Chun-er, Jin Zheng-lan, Jin Gang, Miao Tian, Li Zhi-lin, Li Wen-tai.

After director Liu Chia-liang's *Spiritual Boxer* (1975) was a hit (first official kung fu comedy) and director Chang Cheh successfully turned martial artist Alexander Fu Sheng into a lovable and heroic moppet, self-anointed prolific director Lo Wei was resolute in keeping up with the Changs, i.e., the Joneses. Lo's answer to these Shaw Brothers creations (kung fu comedy and the heroic moppet in Fu Sheng) was Jackie Chan. After Chan grew his hair longer, had his eye operation (made his face softer and not as "Oriental"), and hit kung fu comedy success in Ng See-yuen's *Snake in the Eagle's Shadow* (1978), Lo took full advantage of Chan's remaining multi-picture deal with Lo.

In this Lo-produced film, Lo let Chan develop his chicanery. Chan let the star apply approaches to fight choreography that Chan picked up from director Yuen Woo-ping from *Snake in the Eagle's Shadow* and *Drunken Master*.

Inspired by director Bruce Leung's *The Dragon Lives Again* (1977), Jackie Chan was also interested in parodying established kung fu genre films. Similar to that movie, the opening credits of *Half a Loaf of Kung Fu* begins with Chan making fun of how formulaic and far-fetched kung fu films had become.

In the film, a security company openly flaunts that it is transporting the

secretive cargo of the Evergreen Jade Piece and the Soul Pill. This starts a race between rival evil factions who want to steal the precious payload. Posing as a fake kung fu hero, the loveably gullible and determined Master Chang (Jackie Chan) finds himself sucked into this rivalry while winning the hearts of several kung fu masters. The martial arts men take it upon themselves to teach Chang some half real, half fake kung fu, which Chang eventually masters to save the day and the cargo. In the old days in Western society, up to about the end of the 1970s, the term "master" was a salutation to boys and young men before they became a "mister." Therefore, it can be misleading in kung fu films when a character is called master; he could be a kung fu expert or simply a young man. In this film, it is tricky to decipher what kind of master Chang is, kung fu or a young man who is still not a man. Either way, it is fodder for discussion that does eventually get resolved in the end.

This is the first film in which Chan constantly mugs for the camera. Disney family comedy films from the '50s, '60s and '70s were always known for the stars constantly having to do big double takes, wide-eyed glares of surprise and fear and over-the-top mugging for the camera. Chan would have fit perfectly into the Disney comedy style of filmmaking and acting. If Disney could have discovered Chan in the 1970s, who knows how far Chan could have gone?

Flashes of Chan's fighting prowess appear during the everyone-on-everyone final barrage. But it is curious that Chan pokes fun at director Liu Chia-liang's *hong jia chuan* kung fu, in which the signature hand posture is to have one arm outstretched, palm facing the opponent (like a traffic cop signaling you to stop) and fingers bent, except the forefinger is pointing to the sky. Dean Shek's kung fu master character teaches Chang the same hand posture, except that it is the middle finger that points to the sky.

Chan of course is as good at fight choreography as he is in using kung fu comedy to make a statement. In 1966, John Lennon stated that The Beatles were more popular than Jesus now. This caused uproar with leading religious zealots and Bible pushers in America who called for the mass burnings of The Beatles' records. Of course, Chan's shot at Lennon's comment did not go unnoticed when Chan had the artistic nerve or comedic gall to compare himself to Jesus without having to say it. This is the beauty of comedy, as concepts and contexts are like polluted water: In the beginning, only the chemical companies know exactly what is being dumped into the water, but those companies can always plead denial later.

Titleography: *Karate Bomber*. Translation—*Dim Mak Kung Fu Made Simple*; *With One Technique and Half a Form, One Can Travel in the Jiang Hu World*. If you went to China and knew two words in Chinese, you would get a sense of how successful you would be in China with such a limited vocabulary. It would be half-baked, or a half loaf of kung fu. The analogy also refers to learning one or two kung fu skills. The *Dim Mak* title refers to Chan's one-finger posture, and the *With One Technique,* refers to how it is easy to fake how good your kung fu is if you do one technique well. **MA Percentage: 33.51%**

HAND OF DEATH

少林門 (1976—Hong Kong) **91m. KFI:** Sammo Hung. **NOT/LOT:** 11/ 7m 26s; **NOF/LOF:** 21/ 29m 40s. **D:** John Woo. **C:** Tan Dao-liang, James Tien, Sammo Hung, Jackie Chan, Zhu Qing, Yang Wei.

Usually, if you are not in a queue, then you are not in a line, but during the Ching Dynasty, if you were not sporting a queue, then you were out of line—and that was punishable by death. The first emperor of the Ching Dynasty, Nu Er Ah Che (sometimes Nurhaci; ruled from 1616 to 1626), created the recognizable hairstyle in which the hair was shaved on the front of the head above the temple and the remaining hair was braided into a long ponytail. Back then, the law explicitly stated, "No queue, no head." That is why in *Hand of Death*, it is a strong message of freedom when actor Tan Dao-liang's character cuts his hair. He is being his own man and removing the shackles of oppression. (It was not until 1911 that the queue was abolished.)

When Shaolin Monk Xi Xiang-feng (James Tien) sells out the Shaolin Temple to the Chings, only one man has the skills to exact revenge against him: Yuin Fei (Tan Dao-liang), master of southern boxing, northern kicks, tiger dragon kung fu and the Shaolin pole. He also must protect Ming loyalist Mr. Shan who needs to get across the river because he is carrying a secret document that he must deliver to the right people, a document that the Chings so desperately want to intercept. Along the path of his important mission, two sword-and-spear heroes, the Wanderer (Yang Wei) and Little Tan (Jackie Chan), join Yuin, and all three protectors ponder their lives and loyalties.

Because it is not his martial arts foundation, actor Tan's weapon work is weak, but it's clear he is truly trying to nail the proper stances and postures. In complete contrast, Jackie Chan's spear technique is extremely smooth and full of rapid flashes of windmill wields and body spins. He fights for less than four minutes, but his performance outshines everyone else's. Ultimately, this is Chan's first movie in which he gets a real opportunity to demonstrate his martial skills, whereas before he only showed short snippets of off-balance awkwardness. Director John Woo was smart in making sure, however, that the final fight reveals Tan's strongest skills: a series of beautifully executed jumping spin kicks that, to the casual viewer, will leave positive last impressions.

Titleography: *Countdown in Kung Fu; Dragon Forever; Strike of Death; The Hand of Death.* Translation—*The Shaolin Door.* Most of the English titles make use of rather generic words that would attract Western fans. The Chinese title is more specific and fits because the film is about Shaolin and the doors to revenge. In kung fu terminology, when you enter a martial arts school of training, it is called entering the school's *men*, which means "door" in English. **MA Percentage: 40.77%**

HANZO THE RAZOR: SWORD OF JUSTICE

Goyokiba (1972—Japan) 89m. FC: Jun Katsumura. NOT/LOT: None; NOF/LOF: 4/ 3m 1s. D: Kenji Misumi. C: Shintaro Katsu, Yukiji Asaoka, Mari Atsumi, Ko Nishimura, Kamatari Fujiwara, Akira Yamauchi, Koji Kobayashi.

In this film, Shintaro Katsu leaves behind his role as the decent, righteous and often-passive criminal Zatoichi (see *Zatoichi and Yojimbo*) for the overactive, down-and-dirty lawman named Hanzo the Razor, who really should be called Hanzo the Rapist.

Along with the sword violence, there are several times per *Hanzo* picture in which he violently rapes women as an acceptable torture device to get the information he needs to catch the villains. The disturbing dystopia in the Stanley Kubrick film *A Clockwork Orange* (1971) is nothing compared to this film. If you imagine how a *karateka* toughens his wrists by pounding them with a solid object or how a kung fu man practices the beginning stages of iron palm buy thrusting his hands into a cauldron full of heated dried beans, you might be able to guess how Hanzo trains his phallus. Keep the fast-forward button handy on your remote control. Or I guess you could watch the film the way many men claim to read *Playboy*—I know, just for the articles, right?

The film is set during the Tokugawa period, and Hanzo "The Razor" Itami (Shintaro Katsu) is a no-nonsense samurai policeman for the Kitamachi Constabulary. He is not afraid to step on the toes of Tokugawa officials and stand against traditional samurai codes if they affect his duties to protect farmers and townsfolk. In this sense, he has some very heroic attributes that endear him to the good and strike fear into the corrupt. He works for the wimpy head of the constabulary, Magobei "Snake" Onishi (Ko Nishimura), who bows to bribes and false accolades faster than a boat going over Niagara Falls. But Onishi is sunk when Hanzo investigates his mistress. Hanzo believes the mistress has ties to a reputed criminal who was supposed to be on Hachijo Island, a penal prison that is supposedly impossible to escape from.

Although Katsu left the mild-mannered Zatoichi behind for the mantle of the ill-mannered Hanzo, he did not leave the lack of fights behind. Each Hanzo film has between three and seven minutes of fighting, which isn't a lot. The fights are performed slowly and make use of quick edits that make them appear dynamic. An interesting bit of trivia is that fight choreographer Jun Katsumura was in Bruce Lee's *Fist of Fury* (aka *The Chinese Connection*) as the bodyguard of lead villain Suzuki.

Titleography: *Sword of Justice; The Razor: Sword of Justice.* Translation— *Arresting Fang.* **MA Percentage: 3.39%**

HANZO THE RAZOR: THE SNARE

Goyokiba Kamisori Hanzo Jigoku Zeme (1973—Japan) 79m. FI: Uncredited. NOT/LOT: 1/ 30s; NOF/LOF: 9/ 6m 39s. D: Kenji Misumi. C: Shintaro Katsu, Keiko Aikawa, Kazuko Ineno. Keizô Kani'e, Shin Kishida, Hosei Komatsu, Toshio Kurosawa, Daigo Kusano, Ko Nishimura, Kei Sato.

Based on a *manga* character created by Kazuo Koike, Hanzo "The Razor" Itami is a rough-and-tumble Edo (or Tokugawa) period police officer who has no time for lordly lords, pompous chamberlains or stuffy magistrates with time-wasting protocols. Instead, he gets results by using his oversize member to tor-

ture women; the ladies can't help but cave in to his interrogations when under duress from his sexual advances. It is actually a rather disturbing premise when you consider the implications: It's like a police officer having lawful permission to rape any female suspect or witness into telling the truth.

After Hanzo (Shintaro Katsu) fails to bow down to Lord Okuba, a treasurer for the government, Okuba orders his head bodyguard, Junai (Toshio Kurosawa), to fight Hanzo. They fight to a standstill. Okuba is impressed, but Hanzo continues his defiance, blurting out that he has no time for officials and cheap ornaments because he is hot on the trail of a devious crime. His path leads him to a dead girl's body in a desolate water mill; she has died from a messy abortion. Hanzo learns that the abortion was performed by head priestess Nyokai at Kiazan Temple Convent. He learns that young virgin girls are lured there under the guise of learning the tea ceremony and flower arranging, only to have their virginity auctioned to rich merchants. When Nyokai refuses to tell Hanzo who is behind the scheme, he drags her back to his fortress and rapes her into submission.

Hanzo is caught with his kimono down when ninjas invade his home and interrupt his interrogation. The next thing you know, Hanzo wraps on his *obi* faster than Obi-Wan Kenobi's swings his light saber. He pushes buttons, pulls levers and punches the walls of his abode so it becomes something out of the TV show *The Wild Wild West* (1965–1969). Booby traps snap to life, sharp spikes protrude from the walls, spears drop from the ceiling, and secret weapon racks appear on the walls. The racks include swords, spiked knuckle-dusters and Hanzo's weapon of choice: the *jutte*. It must be breakfast time at Hanzo's house because those ninjas are toast.

Later on, just as Hanzo seems to be piecing the murder puzzle together, he is abruptly assigned to arrest the wicked thief Shobei Hamajima by his sleazy boss, Magobei "Snake" Onishi (Ko Nishimura). This is part of an effort by Onishi to quell Hanzo's rudeness toward Lord Okuba as well as Hanzo's illegal entry in Kiazan Shrine by posing as a dead body. The word on the street is that Shobei is planning to rob the National Treasury. However, Hanzo still finds out who the main villain is, and that the villain has a yen for money laundering. Having it up to here with all the bureaucracy, Hanzo harries the thief, hooks the villain and hacks the bodyguard Junai into hunks.

Hanzo's weapon of choice is derived from the Okinawan *sai*, a dagger-like baton with two side tines. The jutte only has one tine instead of two. Originally invented by legendary Japanese swordmaker Masamune, the jutte was also used to strike pressure points, and the prong was also handy in joint manipulation. Hanzo's jutte is also unique in that it has a weighted chain hidden inside the handle that he can use to block and ensnare sword attacks and to lasso fleeing criminals.

This second installment of the *Hanzo* trilogy has the most samurai fights. The first features a beautiful low-angle tracking shot from behind Hanzo as he mows down a bunch of government samurai, with the camera then zooming in on the character of Junai. Overall, the fights are better than the first installment, mainly due to less editing.

Titleography: *Razor 2: The Snare; Sword of Justice 2.* Translation—*Arresting Fang Razor Hanzo's Torture From Hell.* **MA Percentage: 9.05%**

HANZO THE RAZOR: WHO'S GOT THE GOLD?

Goyokiba Oni No Hanzo Yawahada Koban (1974—Japan) 83m. FI: Uncredited. NOT/LOT: 1/ 30s; NOF/LOF: 4/ 4m 49s. D: Yoshio Inoue. C: Shintaro Katsu, Ko Nishimura, Mako Midori, Mikio Narita, Asao Koike, Etsushi Takahashi, Daigo Kusano, Keizo Kanie, Hiroshi Nawa.

Although Shintaro Katsu played the character of Zatoichi in 26 movies, Katsu as Hanzo "The Razor" Itami sped to the finish line in three movies. A positive thing about the *Hanzo* films is that they show Katsu wasn't a one-note actor. Heck, if Hanzo's rape interrogation scenes, *jutte*, spiked knuckle dusters and true-bladed samurai sword fights aren't miles away from his Zatoichi character, then I don't know what is. (See some *Zatoichi* films!) This is the final installment in the *Hanzo* trilogy, and it contains the standard themes of money, corruption and rape.

While drinking and fishing down at the local lake, Hanzo's two loyal aides, Onibi (Daigo Kusano) and Mamushi (Keizo Kanie), see a female ghost that scares them sober. They whine to Hanzo, and his reaction sets up the requisite rape scene wherein he nonchalantly grunts that he's always wanted to interrogate a ghost. Anyway, Hanzo makes use of his spinning-net torture device to rape the "ghost" (really a lady posing as a ghost to scare people away from the lake).

Hanzo eventually discovers some bamboo poles filled with gold and learns that the lady's husband, a treasury guard, stole the money to pay poorly compensated samurai warriors. Hanzo believes a true samurai needs to be frugal, and he is contemptuous of the couple's plight. But after he hears that his close friend Takei Heisuke is being coerced into giving up his family's ancient spear to the blind high priest Ishiyama (Asao Koike) in order to pay his debts, Hanzo has a change of heart. When Takei is found dead and the spear goes missing, Hanzo knows something is awry and begins to investigate Ishiyama. But Ishiyama has some serious backup in the form of swaggering bodyguard Bansaku Tomami (Mikio Narita), who has a taut face and has been taught to kill without remorse.

Elsewhere, the patriotic but tuberculosis-stricken Dr. Sugino (Etsushi Takahashi) is trying to convince the shogunate that Japan needs to accept Western ways or it will be doomed. One of the shogun's corrupt advisers sees the good doctor as a dangerous man. Because supporting the acceptance of Western ways is punishable by death, he orders Hanzo to arrest and behead the doctor. Yet Hanzo is a patriot and wants to know more about Sugino's beliefs. Sugino has 30 days to live and plans to build a Western-style cannon to demonstrate its power, thus showing that Japan must not resist but accept the West. Hanzo hides the doctor and tells him to build his cannon. Hanzo tells his superiors that if he can't find Sugino in 30 days, he will forfeit his head. Thirty days later, with cannon in hand and proof of corruption stemming from Ishiyama and the shogun's adviser, it is time to break out the *jutte* and sword as Hanzo prepares for the last battles of his cinematic life.

As with all the Hanzo movies, there are not many fights, but *Who's Got the Gold?* does contain more self-defense gadgets hidden in Hanzo's home. Although all the Hanzo fights are shot with tight camera angles, which can sometimes hide an actor's movements or make them seem choppy, Katsu's moves are smoother in this movie. The reason for this is probably because unlike the first two *Hanzo* flicks, which use the typical shaky camera choreography (making the images hard to follow), this production keeps the camera steady, thereby making his movements less jumpy and the choreography clearer. The final fight shows more spinning by Hanzo and a few good long shots, which nicely break up the fight's rhythm and prevent the fights from becoming a collection of quick takes.

Titleography: *Haunted Gold*; *Razor 3: Who's Got the Gold?*; *Sword of Justice 3*. Translation—*Arresting Fang Evil of Hanzo Gold Coin*. **MA Percentage: 6.41%**

HEADS FOR SALE

女俠賣人頭 (1970—Hong Kong) 86m. FI; Yasuyoshi Shikamura. NOT/LOT: 1/ 28s; NOF/LOF: 31/ 19m. D: Cheng Chang-ho. C: Chiao Chiao, Chen Liang, Wang Xia, Ma Hai-lun, Ching Miao, Chen Yan-yan, Fan Mei-sheng, Gao Ming, Chen Hsing, Tung Li.

The moral of this film could be summed up as this: Don't renege on an agreement to marry a swordswoman unless you have a death wish. It is a lesson well learned by Luo Hong-xun (Chen Liang), who calls off his wedding with Hua Bi-lian (Chiao Chiao) because he feels he's not good enough for her family. Hua is outraged and throws a deadly temper tantrum, swinging her sword at any male who dares come near her. Fortunately for her, she runs into a bunch of thugs led by Wan San-ju (Fan Mei-sheng) and takes out some of her aggression on them. Wan complains about Hua to his boss, Huang Lun (Gao Ming). Huang is particularly upset because of Hua's association with Luo—Luo once scarred Huang's face after Luo caught him bullying a woman, killing her father and kidnapping her daughter.

Huang bribes a magistrate to charge Luo with any unsolved robbery and has him thrown in prison. Things get worse for Luo when he comes down with typhoid fever. Hua tries to talk a doctor into visiting the prison to see how Luo is doing, but the doctor refuses. Luckily, Hua has an ingenious plan to change the doctor's mind. I won't give it away, but I will say that part of the plan is the impetus behind the film's title. At one point, Hua goes to Huang's hangout and freaks everyone out when she decapitates two iron shirt bodyguards who were thought to be pretty tough. Hua's plan succeeds, and she and the doctor find themselves in prison. The only problem is that they can't get out.

With a bit of arm-twisting and some righteous logic, Bao Zian (Wang Xia), a friend of Hua's father, convinces the magistrate to transport Luo, the doctor and Hua outside his jurisdiction. Then Bao can rescue everyone. However, while they are en route, Huang sneakily intercepts the prisoners and takes them back to his lair. Fingering the scar on his face, Huang prepares a feast of dungeon

agony and stockade torture for his newly arrived guests. But amid the whipping, Hua's traitorous kung fu brother, Hao Tian-ping, comes back to the light side and rips away Luo's shackles. Luo frees Hua, who gives Huang another face wound, resulting in an X-shaped facial scar, thus completing what Luo started.

This is another example of a film in which none of the actors knew martial arts, which is amazing considering that it has 19 minutes of fight scenes. The coolest fight has to be the one on a mountain bridge; although it is not well executed by the actors, the environment really saves the day. The fight is short enough that you end up looking at the scenery more than the swordsmanship.

By the end of the decade, as the quality of fight scenes in these types of films tended to improve (thanks to better-trained martial arts stars and to non-martial arts stars improving with experience), the film sets generally became simpler and less pronounced, except in far-out *wuxia* films. The idea was for the audience to focus on the fighters and not the environment, unless the environment was an integral part of the film.

Titleography: As of this writing, no alternative titles could be found. Translation—*Swordswoman Selling Human Heads*. **MA Percentage: 22.64%** SHAW BROTHERS

HEAVEN AND HELL

第三類打鬥 and 殺出地獄門 (1978—Hong Kong) 88m. FI: Lu Feng, Robert Tai Chi-Hsien, Leung Ting. NOT/LOT: 1/ 14s; NOF/LOF: 34/ 26m 38s. D: Chang Cheh. C: Lee Yi-min, David Chiang, Kuo Chue, Lo Meng, Tong Yen-san, Alexander Fu Sheng, Jenny Tseng, Chiang Sheng, Lu Feng, Sun Chien, Jiang Dao, Wang Lung-wei.

When American film critics first saw Hong Kong's Fant-Asia genre films of the 1980s, one of the popular cinematic mantras written by these critics was, "Anything goes." It was immediately recognized that in Fant-Asia film, nothing was too offbeat as long as it added fun and entertainment. However, if these same critics had taken the time to go back a decade further and discover the *wuxia* films of the 1970s that dealt with the world of Jiang Hu, Wu Lin or even earlier wuxia movies, they would have had a similar reaction, especially with a film such as *Heaven and Hell*.

Similar to many elements of Fant-Asia, Chang Cheh's *Heaven and Hell* combines fantasy, kung fu, wuxia, musical theater, gangster noir, sci-fi, love story and pantomime. It is a film that teeters on the psychedelic and totters on the psychotic cycle of reincarnated restarts. Chang also blends religion, philosophy, and the cynicism of truth, deception and perception to create a world of film that became standard in many 1980s productions. Although film director Tsui Hark (see *The Butterfly Murders*) is considered the father of Fant-Asia, Chang most certainly was one of the grandfathers.

The film comprises three shorts melded into one; they are consecutively titled *Heaven*, *Earth* and *Hell*. The first, *Heaven*, initially looks like a karmic journey for two celestial lovers named Zhou Bao (David Chiang) and maiden Zi Xiao. They want to elope to the human world, so they go to the southern gate of heaven where they are met by Zhou's good friend Xin Ling (Lee Yi-min). Xin lets them past and is punished for that by the deities Na Zha (see *Na Cha the Great*) and his two godly brothers, Jin Zha and Mu Zha. In *Earth*, Xin is banished to the mortal world to be a taxi driver and saves two singing lovers—Chen Ding (Alexander Fu Sheng) and Shi Qi (Fu Sheng's wife Jenny Tseng)—who were on the run from dancing kung fu gangsters. Xin is then transported to hell. In *Hell*, Xin is given permission by the Divine Buddha to recruit four fighters. If they can fight their way out of hell, they shall all be reincarnated back to where they should be in the Buddhist cycle of life.

At the beginning of *Earth*, singing lovers Chen Ding and Shi Qi pine for each other on a typical British pantomime stage while four kung fu fighters attack Fu. They use contemporary and balletic dance movements, and no sound effects are heard during the fight. Although the fights look snappy, they are not crisp because the lack of sound removes the sense of power. An overly shaky hand-held camera feels like an attempt to add in that missing strength sensation. Another of this part's oddball oddities is the highly recognizable bass-guitar riff from Isaac Hayes' theme song from *Shaft* (1971) that breaks into a melodramatic Chinese song.

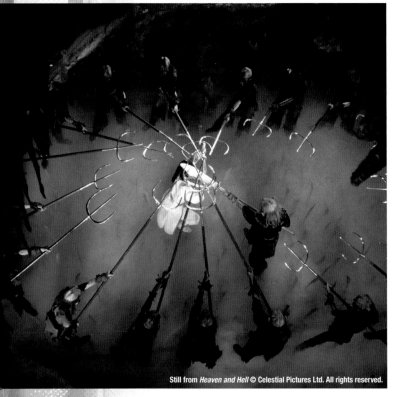

Still from *Heaven and Hell* © Celestial Pictures Ltd. All rights reserved.

Hell takes Dante's *Inferno* to the max; sinners are subjected to daily tortures resulting from their earthly weaknesses and nastiness. After each of the four freedom fighters (played by actors Sun Chien, Tong Yen-san, Lo Meng and Kuo Chue) share their story as to how he ended up in the place of lost souls, all hell breaks loose because they literally confront their demons (the ones responsible for killing them when their true karmic times were up). In the typical Five Venom (or Five Weapon Guys) fashion, each of the freedom fighters are spotlighted with a unique mixture of old-style kung fu and weapon choreography with contemporary fighting slugfests. This film could get away with this because Xin and the four heroes lived in different times in Chinese history during their previous lives. So the martial arts matched up with the fighting styles of their respective periods. Director Chang Cheh gave a special nod to his new golden boy, Alexander Fu Sheng, because Sun Chiang's character (one of the four freedom fighters recruited by Xin) died under the same circumstances as Fu Sheng's character in *Police Force* (1973). As it turns out, this was also the last film that director Chang Cheh did with one of his greatest protégés, David Chiang.

Titleography: *Shaolin Hell Gate*; *Heaven and Hell*; *Heaven and Hell Gate*. Translation—*Battle of the Third Kind*; *Killing Their Way Out of Hell Gate*. Each title fits the thematic devices of the film. However, as is common, *Shaolin* is

tagged on for marketing appeal. Although one of the four fighters is anti-Ching, it is not mentioned whether he is a Shaolin fighter. **MA Percentage: 30.53%** SHAW BROTHERS

HEAVEN SWORD AND DRAGON SABRE

倚天屠龍記 (1978—Hong Kong) **100m. FI: Tang Chia. NOT/LOT: None; NOF/LOF: 32/ 17m 22s** D: Chu Yuan. C: Ching Li, Derek Yee, Lo Lieh, Wang Jung, Wang Lai, Yu An-an, Tian Ching, Zhang Ying, Xu Hsao-chiang, Gu Guan-zhong, Pan Bing-chang, Zheng Li-fang, Candy Wen Xue-er, Chen Jia-yi, Ai Fei, Liu Hui-ling.

Written in 1961, *The Heavenly Sword and the Dragon Sabre* is the third entry in famous *wuxia* novelist Jing Yong's "Condor Trilogy." (Jing Yong also goes by the pen name Louis Cha.) The story centers on the fall of the Mongolian Yuan Dynasty and the rise of the Ming Dynasty. The first two parts of the trilogy, *Legend of the Condor Heroes* (1957) and *The Return of the Condor Heroes* (1959; see *The Brave Archer*), deal with the fall of the Jin and Song Dynasties and the rise of the Yuan Dynasty. Now let's get ready for a mouthful.

The Heaven Sword and Dragon Sabre are two legendary weapons in the world of Jiang Hu. (See *The Water Margin*.) They were created by amalgamating hero Guo Jing's (again, see *Brave Archer*) heavy sabre with the hardest quartz known to mankind. Although Guo Jing hid the Heaven Sword with the Er Mei Taoist nuns, the Dragon Sabre has been drifting from place to place for hundreds of years. A book of military strategies written by the famous Song Dynasty General Yue Fei is hidden in the hilt of one sword, and two scrolls describing powerful kung fu techniques are concealed in the other. It is said that whoever can possess the two swords and learn their secrets can rule the world of Wu Lin, which is the martial arts microcosm of Jiang Hu.

This film follows the path and story of the Dragon Sabre. Golden Hair Lion Xie Xun (Lo Lieh) is one of the four chiefs of the Ming Cult. (The cult originated in Persia, came to China and gained prominence toward the end of the Song Dynasty.) After his daughter and wife were raped and murdered by his kung fu teacher, Cheng Kun (Tian Ching), Xie went on an uncontrollable killing rampage and then disappeared with the Dragon Sabre. The only person who knows where Xie is hiding is his teen godson Zhang Wu-ji. However, besides being chased by Mongolian soldiers, Wu-ji has been hit by the Ice Palm skill and is slowly dying, which kills by interrupting *chi* (*qi*), and as the chi gets blocked, one's life fades away until death. (We see something like this in the 1970 film *The Jade Faced Assassin*.) At least for now, Wu-ji is under the protection of the famous Wu Dung monk Zhang San-feng (Zhang Ying). Anyone wanting to be head of Wu Lin knows that they must first get the Dragon Sabre, and the only way to do that is to find Xie, so Wu-ji becomes the center of attention. Yet because Wu-ji is dying from the Ice Palm strike, he is left in the care of Dr. Wu. Monk San-feng continues on by escorting Wu-ji's young girl traveling partner, Zhou Zhi-ruo, to Er Mei Mountain, where she will become a Taoist nun under the mentorship of Abbess Mie Jue (Wang Lai).

Ten years later, Wu-ji (Derek Yee) is not cured and has only two years left to live, so he sets out to find and say goodbye to his teacher San-feng. Along the way, he runs into the now-grown Zhou (Yu An-an; Chow Yun Fat's first wife) who is traveling with Abbess Mie Jue. They are out to kill a former Taoist nun, Ji Xiao-fu, because she ran out on her betrothed—a Wu Dung Sect member—because she was raped by Ming Cult chieftain Yang Siu (Wang Jung) and had a daughter, Bu Hui. After a long fight, Mie Jue kills Ji, and just as she is about to kill Ji's daughter Bu Hui, Wu-ji steps in and convinces Mie Jue to spare her life. Now on the road in search of his teacher, Wu-ji first helps Bu Hui find her father Yang Siu.

His health dwindling, Wu-ji stumbles on a passage via a house that is balanced on the edge of a cliff. While there, a gibbon (a kind of monkey) he helps heal gives him three stolen secret kung fu manuals from the Shaolin Temple that two thieves once tied to his back; the monkey subsequently hid them in this nowhere place. After learning the Nine Yang skills, Wu-ji is cured and full of power. He ends up going to Summit Bright Peak in an attempt to stop the Six Mighty Clans (Er Mei, Wu Dung and Shaolin being the most powerful ones) from wiping out the Ming Cult.

On his way to Bright Peak, Wu-ji skirmishes with Shaolin Monk Yuen Zhen. The monk is revealed to be Cheng Kun, who was Golden Lion Hair Xie Xun's kung fu teacher and who also killed Xie's wife. (Remember Xie? Wu-ji's godfather and the one who turned crazy and ran off with the Dragon Sabre?) Yuen was so upset that the love of his life was married off to the head of the Ming

Cult for money that he vowed to destroy the Ming Cult. In the middle of the fight between Yuen and Wu-ji, Yuen escapes, and as Wu-ji follows, he finds himself in an eerie crypt and discovers a piece of rag that explains how to master the secret Shifting Technique, which makes Wu-ji an even more formidable fighter.

Making it to Bright Peak, Wu-ji defeats five clan heads and exposes Yuen's plot to take out the Ming Cult by stirring up conflict between the six clans and the Mings. Wu-ji battles his childhood sweetheart, Zhou Zhi-ruo, who is not as righteous as he has been led to believe, a portent of things to come. (See *Heaven Sword and Dragon Sabre 2*.) But for now, Wu-ji still saves the day and becomes the head of the Ming Cult. Although he does not want to become the head, the other leaders of the Ming Cult insist that he remain the leader at least until the Holy Flame Medal can be found. Therefore, Wu-ji's first orders are that the Mings must bury the grudge against the other clans, find Golden Lion and locate the Holy Flame Medal so he can resign as the head. But a new problem arises in the shape of Mongolian Princess Zhao Min (Ching Li), who wants to acquire the Dragon Sabre, take out the Ming Cult and discredit Wu Dung by claiming that Zhang San-feng (the teacher that Wu-ji wanted to see before Wu-ji died from the Ice Palm technique; although he's cured now) is a fake martial artist. When her kung fu fails, she resorts to poison. With San-feng and the members of the six clans now dying agonizing deaths and Wu-ji at Zhao Min's lair begging for the antidote, the film ends on a cliffhanger.

So you might be thinking, "Was this the simplified rundown of the story?" Yup! Like a villain in any English-dubbed kung fu film, I tilt my head back at you and laugh: "Ha ha ha ha ha … I see. You're kung fu is no good, but still … you must read the second part of this martialogy if you wish to defeat my … (fight sound effects) … Plum Blossom Fist."

Because Parts 1 and 2 of *Heaven Sword and Dragon Sabre* were shot at the same time (similar to Tarantino's *Kill Bill* films), I will discuss the action for this martialogy during the sequel's martialogy.

Titleography: *Chivalrous Killer*. Translation—*The Tale of Heaven-Reliant and Dragon-Slayer*. See martialogy. *Chivalrous Killer* is a rather generic title but undoubtedly refers to Wu-ji. Other films adaptations of the novel *The Heavenly Sword and the Dragon Sabre* include the Cantonese four-part film series *Story of the Sword and Sabre* (1965), the Shaw Brothers film *Thundering Sword* (1967) and Jet Li's *Kung Fu Cult Master* (1993). **MA Percentage: 17.37%** SHAW BROTHERS

HEAVEN SWORD AND DRAGON SABRE 2

倚天屠龍記大結局 (1978—Hong Kong) **95m. FI: Tang Chia. NOT/ LOT: None; NOF/LOF: 38/ 23m.** D: Chu Yuan. C: Ching Li, Derek Yee, Lo Lieh, Wang Jung, Wang Lai, Yu An-an, Tian Ching, Zhang Yin, Xu Hsao-chiang, Gu Guan-zhong, Pan Bing-chang, Zheng Li-fang, Candy Wen Xue-er, Chen Jia-yi, Ai Fei, Liu Hui-ling, Yu Rong, Hu Hong-da, Yang Chi-ching, Teresa Ha Ping, Yueh Hua.

This film begins where *Heaven Sword and Dragon Sabre* ends: Wu-ji (Derek Yee) is at Zhao Min's (Ching Li) lair and gets the antidote for Zhang San-feng (Zhang Yin) and the six clan heads and their men, who have all been trapped by Zhao and her marauding Mongolians. After Wu-ji saves them, Zhao agrees not to kill Wu-ji's childhood sweetheart, Zhou Zhi-ruo (Yu An-an), who is also the new head of the Er Mei Sect (the Taoist nuns clan). In return, Wu-ji agrees to

fulfill three requests. As you can well imagine, these requests put Wu-ji under considerable stress and strain.

New players, like the mysterious new female head of the Beggar Clan, begin popping up left and right, leading toward the final battles, in which each character flashes his martial wares en route to finding Golden Lion Xie Xun (Lo Lieh) and the Dragon Sabre. The love story of Wu-ji and Zhou also shifts as Zhou morphs into an enemy. It all comes to a magnificent head when all the various clan heads gather at Shaolin for Xie's assembly. The fate of Xie, who was found earlier in this film, will be determined at Three Pine Peak by three long-white-haired monks who live inside trees; whoever can remove them from the trees—through combat, of course—will attain the Dragon Sabre and decide the fate of Xie. It is something that Zhou (the head of Er Mei), Zhao (the Mongolian princess), Shen Er (head of the Beggar Clan; played by Candy Wen Xue-er) and Wu-ji are intimately involved in attaining the Dragon Sabre. It's three women and one man locked in a fight that will determine the fate of the worlds of Wu Lin and Jiang Hu.

What made Jing Yong's *wuxia* novels intriguing were that he injected real historical characters into his stories, giving them a hint of truth. Prominently featured were Zhan San-feng, the founder of Wu Dung and creator of *tai chi*; the Ming Cult; and although a lesser Ming Cult character, the traitorous Zhu Yuan-zhang, who founded the Ming Dynasty. This was a reflection that even an insignificant man could make a difference, rise up and become the emperor.

This film features many of director Chu Yuan's trademarks: lots of characters, colorful sets, intricate stories, flowing costumes, many secret kung fu skills to be found and learned, and tons of short fights evenly spaced out to give the impression of wall-to-wall action. Cumulatively, the two *Heaven Sword and Dragon Sabre* films feature about 40 minutes of dueling (out of 195 minutes total) that happens over 70 fights. More than 80 percent of the fights are long shots, and they are often shot from behind a sheer curtain. This popular technique in Jiang Hu films adds a romanticized feeling to the action, but it also allowed stunt doubles to perform the fights. Actor Derek Yee's fight performance is dismal, which is surprising because in some of his earlier films (see *The Sentimental Swordsman*), he is formidable. But on the flip side, this was an exhausting long project for everyone involved, and with so many fights—regardless of how long they were—actors were always on set getting ready for the next one.

Titleography: *Heaven Sword and Dragon Sabre Part II*. Translation—*The Big Finale of the Tale of Heaven-Reliant and Dragon-Slayer*. In Chinese culture, the dragon is symbolic of the emperor, and heaven refers to the true emperor of China being the son of heaven, i.e., a Han Chinese. In the translated title, *Dragon-Slayer* is analogous to killing the evil Yuan emperor, and *Heaven-Reliant* is about having a reliable Han Chinese emperor in control. **MA Percentage: 24.21%** SHAW BROTHERS

HEERA

(1973—India) **141m. FCom:** S. Azim, Mansoor. **NOT/LOT:** None; **NOF/LOF:** 9/ 8m 52s. **D:** Sultan Ahmed. **C:** Sunil Dutt, Asha Parekh, Shatrughan Sinha, Farida Jalal, Helen, Mukri, Nasir Hussain, Kapitan.

He who lives by the snake gods dies by the snake gods. Despite all the different animal styles that have evolved in Chinese kung fu, no style has been created from the fighting movements of the ram—until now. Heera (Sunil Dutt), son of the local magistrate, is betrothed to Asha (Asha Parekh), the daughter of a greedy landowner who must allow the local villagers' cattle to feed on his land because of tradition. However, he changes his mind and wants the local magistrate to back him up on charging an extra feeding tax, but the righteous magistrate rules against him. The landowner breaks off the marriage and promises Asha to the local priest's drippy, slimy and shady son, Balwant (Shatrughan Sinha), who believes he was born to squeeze others' throats and to snatch everything that doesn't belong to him.

Balwant maliciously rapes and impregnates women, has his cobra god (who is a real cobra) kill the women, and then he moves on to his next lustful liaison. Now that Balwant is going to get Asha, he impregnates a beautiful maiden, Helen, which shames her into committing suicide. Unfortunately, the magistrate and villagers believe that Heera murdered her. Heera is exiled from the city for one year, during which time he learns about responsibility. Heera returns with a changed mind, but Balwant has not changed and is bent on destroying Heera and keeping Asha for himself.

In early Hong Kong kung fu films, fight instructors Liu Chia-liang and Tang Chia were considered the best fight choreographer pair in the industry. You could make a similar argument for Azim (a master of Indian blades) and his personally trained assistant, Mansoor as the best fight composer duo in India. Both were trained in *kilaripayit*, and they were the first thrill directors (as the position is often called in Indian film) to introduce the art into Indian action films and, more specifically, the enigmatic staff maneuvers of kilaripayit. This is the earliest film I have been able to track down that shows their experimentation with the cudgel maneuvers, as demonstrated by veteran actor Sunil (who was not versed in any fighting art). Later films starring top Indian action star Amitabh Bachchan, who had a better feel for the weapon, allowed for more creativity by Mansoor, who by the late 1970s branched out on his own.

What is unique about the fights in this film is that Heera adapts the fighting methods of his prize-winning ram that never loses a fight against any other of the village rams. Because of this, Heera becomes the ultimate head-butter and partakes in head-battering-ram fights with men twice his size and weight. Although the fights don't come close to what Hong Kong was doing at the same time, it is obvious that Azim taught his stuntmen to spin, flip or roll after being hit in order to amplify the power and dramatic look of each strike.

On a final "say what?!" comment, Chow Yun-fat is the spitting image of Sunil Dutt, even down to the body postures used in both these actors' early fight attempts. Unearthing these unpredictable moments is one reason that writing this book is a blast.

Titleography: As of this writing, no alternative titles could be found. **MA Percentage: 6.29%**

HERO OF THE WILD

大武士與小票客 (1977—Hong Kong) **90m. MAI:** Yuen Shen-yi, Yuen Biao, Yuen Kwei. **NOT/LOT:** 6/ 2m 58s; **NOF/LOF:** 21/ 25m 9s. **D:** Zhang Qi. **C:** Chen Hsing, Ding Hua-chong, Hwang Jang-lee, Lo Lieh, Doris Lung Chun-er, Yuen Kwei, Yuen Biao.

When kung fu men challenge each other to a fight to the death in the Jiang Hu world, it is not always about personal hate or revenge—often it amounts to a righteous hero vying for status in the kung fu underworld. Both fighters understand that it is simply the way of the lone wandering warrior and that it is nothing personal.

Traveling fighter Tu Ta-shan (Chen Hsing) challenges a fighter on the verge of retirement who, with his untrained son Hsiao Hu (Ding Hua-chong), is on a mission to destroy Ming traitor Nan Ba-ting (Hwang Jang-lee) and his organization. Nan and his gang are selling Chinese art to the Manchus, who are increasingly becoming a threat to security of the Ming Dynasty. Tu defeats the fighter, but before dying, the fighter beseeches Tu to complete his mission of killing the Ming traitors. Tu honors the request and also decides to teach Hsiao Hu kung fu so one day he can challenge Tu to a fight and avenge his father.

The rest of the film consists of Tu facing the increasingly powerful Ming traitors, fending off sneak attacks from the improving-his-martial-arts Hsiao Hu, and fighting Nan and a mysterious killer wearing a red devil mask in a final showdown.

Actor Chen Hsing does his usual tiger-claw-looking kung fu, complete with his typical arched back and skulking neck posture to make it look like he really knows the martial art—which is a common mistake made by many kung fu film stars in all decades. When it comes to the various kinds of actors in kung fu films, the real practitioners of kung fu (such as Chen Kuan-tai and the Liu family), those who are well-trained in martial arts movements (the Beijing Opera veterans) and actors who have had plenty of real fights (Jimmy Wong Yu, David Chiang), all understand the dynamics of proper guards. Notice that when Chen Hsing fights, the hand he is not using for blocking or striking hangs aimlessly by his side rather than in a proper tiger claw guard position. This is not to say he does not practice martial arts (his foundation is in karate), but because he is muscular and consequently has a big presence on-screen, it is easy to overlook his martial shortcomings. In actuality, the best fights in the film are the ones Chen is not in, such as on-screen cameos by fight instructors Yuen Biao and Yuen Kwei. (Some readers may know actor Yuen Kwei as Corey.) They add some needed spice to the fights. The action is further made delicious by the weapon work of actor Lo Lieh when he wields long-handled scimitars and Hwang Jang-lee when he uses a long-handled sword (*da dao*). (The da dao is different from a *guan dao*, which has a broader blade and a back spur.)

Titleography: *Heroes of Shaolin*; *Heroes of Shao Lin*; *Heroes of the Wild*; *Kung Fu Challenger*. Translation—*Big Heroic Fighter and the Insignificant Escort Guard*. There is nothing about Shaolin in this film, and the title *Hero in the Wild* probably comes from the wandering nature of the hero walking around in the wilds of China. The first four Chinese characters in the Chinese title reflect Chen Hsing's big hero part and Ding Hua-chong's insignificant part. The final three characters of the Chinese title (*xiao piao ke*) refer to the insignificant small-time guards who are part of security processions. You have seen kung fu films in which a band of guards escorts a prisoner, royalty or valuables: When they get attacked, it is the no-name actors who are all dressed the same that get killed easily. This convention is comparable to the landing parties in *Star Trek*: You know it is the nonfamous actors who are going to get vaporized by the aliens. **MA Percentage: 31.24%**

HEROES OF SUNG

龍虎會風雲 (1973—Hong Kong) **80m. FI:** Yuen Woo-ping, Yuen Cheung-yan. **NOF/LOF:** 35/ 16m 56s. **D:** Shen Chiang. **C:** Shi Szu, Lo Lieh, Chang Pei-shan, Lo Lieh, Richard Chan Chun, Yu Feng, Li Chia-qian, Tang Tien-xi, Chan Shen.

This film about the Song Dynasty concerns the delivery of some important royal seals. If the seals are not conveyed to the right people, the Song could find themselves singing, to borrow from Neil Diamond, a *Song Sung Blue*.

The film opens with Emperors Qin and Hui, the last two emperors of the Song Dynasty, being held prisoner by the invading Jin army. The emperors hand over two royal seals to loyal soldiers Jing Yue-feng (Fang Mien) and Meng Xi; they are disguised as Jin generals in order to get to see the emperors. The emperors explain that Prince Kang is heading south to the Huai River-Qin Ling Mountains line (a natural geographic boundary between northern and southern China). The prince needs the seals to establish the Southern Song Dynasty, as one seal proves he is the emperor and the other guarantees army support. Historically, the prince became known as the first emperor of the Southern Song Dynasty, Emperor Gao Zong.

On the way, Jing and Meng are injured and unable to continue, so Jing recruits his top two students, Wang Tian-long (Chang Pei-shan) and Fan Tian-hu (Lo Lieh), to carry a seal each. They are later joined by Meng's daughter Hong-er (Shih Szu) who carries another seal. (One of the three seals will turn out to be a fake.) However, the Jins get the wicked Wan Yan-he (Richard Chan Chun) and his wibbley wobbley swordswoman sister Wan Yan-nu (Li Chia-qian) to work for them. Yan-he steals Hong-er's seal right out from under her nose with his flying claw, or *fei zhua*. (The timeline is off here because the flying claw weapon did not appear until the Ming Dynasty.) Yan-he's biggest fear is that when Wang and Fan fight as a team, they use the Joint Hand Style, in which each takes his sword scabbard in one hand—Wang's is in his left hand, Fan's in his right—and crosses it with the other's so the two are locked together and fight while con-

In this film, Liu delves into the importance of family and also explores how that bond is strengthened when one's blood family and martial arts family are the same.

Extreme Chinese kung fu practitioner Ah To (Gordon Liu Chia-hui) is trapped in an arranged marriage with the beautiful but not so dainty extreme Japanese martial artist Kung Zi (Yuko Mizuno). Ah To is anxious about marrying a Japanese woman, but when their eyes meet, it is love at first sight and his fears are dispelled. When he learns that she is an expert in Japanese martial arts, his respect, admiration and love for her grow. The two have found an important common denominator, a solid foundation to build a life around. When Ah To and Kung Zi practice together, outsiders mistakenly think the two newlyweds are constantly fighting. As is typical with meddling from those who do not practice and therefore do not understand martial arts, these detractors spread rumors that Ah To is an abusive husband. After the same detractors plant the nasty seed that perhaps Kung Zi's martial arts are better than his, Ah To's ego is destroyed. For this husband and wife, the importance of whose martial arts are superior becomes an issue of national and martial arts pride. The marriage is soon on the rocks.

Kung Zi goes home to Japan and complains about Ah To to her *sensei* (Naozo Kato) and her *sempai*, or older karate brother, Takeno (Yasuaki Kurata). Takeno believes that Japanese should only marry other Japanese, and he takes advantage of her vulnerability by trying to woo her. The whole karate school decides it has been dishonored by Ah To's behavior and sends seven of its best martial artists to fight him.

Liu's fight direction is well planned when he tries to reveal the positive aspects of all the martial arts and weapons featured. As Ah To defeats each Japanese opponent (samurai sword versus Chinese *jian*, *naginata* versus Chinese spear, karate versus kung fu, *sai* versus short butterfly knives, ninja versus Chinese esoteric arts), it is really a study of how the simplicity of Japanese martial arts have historically evolved from the complexity of Chinese martial arts. Liu points out that keeping things simple does not always mean simple is effective and that sometimes simplification removes the richness of an art's history.

But on the other hand, Liu tap-dances around and ultimately indicates that it is not a matter of one country's martial arts being superior to another country's (though the film does have a stronger bias toward Chinese martial arts). Instead, it is the lineage between China and Japan that makes the countries like brothers. China and Ah To represent the "older brother," who, with great effort, is able to be victorious over his "younger brother" fighters from Japan. Liu's final point is also a comment that regardless of the violent histories between the two

nected. The plan is for Yan-nu to seduce the weaker Fan and force him to marry her. Then, due to filial piety rules, Fan will be forced to give Yan-nu the jade seal he carries, though Fan does not know if it is real or fake … or so he says. Eventually, the double-crossers get crossed and our heroes must cross their scabbards before they get crossed out by the Wans. If they can survive, they still need to deliver the seals to Prince Kang.

The wire work is rather funky in this film, but it is essential to point out that wire work was still in the experimental stage at the time. Choreographers were still discovering what they could get away with. There are a couple of yickety blickety shots that I had a blast trying to imagine how the fight instructors presented the ideas to the director, and how they went about figuring out how to shoot them. One example is when Wang and Fan do their Joint Hand Style in the final fight: They lock scabbards, and then their bodies spin like a helicopter blade, cutting down all those who stand in their way. Of course, the gag of cutting a body in two vertically is always a riot. But the blue light special stunt has to be when Wang grabs Fan and throws him feet-first at two guys. After Fan kicks them, he floats backward to Wang, his body still parallel to the ground. Wang then grabs Fan's hand and throws him backward. It all takes place in one awesome unedited shot. I envision a little cart with wheels that Lo Lieh had to lie flat on as they pushed and pulled it along the ground on either side of the camera with wires.

Titleography: As of this writing, no alternative titles could be found. Translation—*Dragon Meets Tiger, Moves the Wind and Clouds*. The Chinese title means that when a dragon meets a tiger, there will be a lot of cloud and wind movement—in other words, something big is going to happen. Of note, the last two characters of the Chinese titles, *fung yuin*, also serve as the title of Hong Kong's first special-effects-driven martial arts film, *The Stormriders* (1998). **MA Percentage: 21.17%** SHAW BROTHERS

HEROES OF THE EAST

中 華 丈 夫 (1978—Hong Kong) **103m. FI: Liu Chia-liang Wilson Tong. NOT/LOT: 13/ 9m 7s; NOF/LOF: 17/ 33m 20s.** D: Liu Chia-liang. C: Gordon Liu Chia-hui, Yuko Mizuno, Yasuaki Kurata, Ching Miao, Xu Hsao-chiang, Liu Chia-liang, Naozo Kato, Riki Harada, Tetsu Sumi, Manabu Shirai, NobuoYana, Yasutaka Nakazaki, Hitoshi Omae, Ou-Yang Sha-Fei.

As his reputation as a director grew, Liu Chia-liang began making films that mattered to him on a more personal level. His belief in the spiritual world and the importance of respecting the dead are reflected in *The Spiritual Boxer* (1975), a film that also warns against blindly accepting someone's appearance and shows how easy it is to take advantage of the ignorant. His lifelong devotion to the history and tradition of Shaolin martial arts is visible in *Challenge of the Masters* (1976). His reverence for his martial arts background in *hong jia* kung fu gave special meaning to *Executioners From Shaolin* (1977), which featured a portrayal of the art's founder, Hong Xi-guan, who was one of the 10 Tigers of Shaolin (and a distant relative of Liu's).

countries, China and Japan can still be a family working together for the good of Asia. In this film, that notion of good has to do with martial arts growth, which in Liu's view has always been a strong force in shaping both countries.

As the Japanese fighters begin to see that Ah To is a righteous and conscientious martial artist, the martial arts are seen not as a point of contention but as a part of their bond. Furthermore, when Ah To and Kung Zi reunite and work together as one, they overcome their differences and use those differences as strengths rather than weaknesses

Titleography: *Shaolin Challenges Ninja*; *Challenge of the Ninja*; *Shaolin vs. Ninja*. Translations—*The Chinese Husband* or *Brave Chinese Man*. *Chinese Husband* refers to Liu's husband character, as does *Brave Chinese Man*, which with the inferences of *Chinese* and *Brave* could explain the foundation behind the original English title, *Heroes of the East*. The various titles with *Shaolin* and *Ninja* play off the Chinese-versus-Japanese plotline by using two popular marketing words that sell in the West. **MA Percentage: 41.21%** SHAW BROTHERS

HEROES TWO

方世玉與洪熙官 (1973—Hong Kong) 91m. FI: Tang Chia, Liu Chia-liang. NOT/LOT: None; NOF/LOF: 41/ 31m 1s. D: Chang Cheh. C: Chen Kuan-tai, Alexander Fu Sheng, Fang Xin, Tong Yen-san, Wong Ching, Wu Chi-chin, Zhu Mu, Feng Yi.

Heroes Two was the first film that director Chang Cheh made about the heroes of Shaolin. In this movie, those heroes are Hong Xi-guan and Fang Shi-yu, two of the 10 Tigers of Shaolin. They are both students of Monk Zhi Shan, one of the Five Elders of Shaolin (the others being Wu Mei, Bai Mei, Feng Dao and Miao Xian, who is Shi-yu's grandfather). The historical Hong made his first cinematic debut in 1949 in *Hong Xi-Guan's Bloody Battle at the Forest Lui's Family*, but in most of his film appearances, the stories did not focus on Hong but instead centered on his association with the other 10 Tigers of Shaolin, particularly Fang.

Still from *Heros Two* © Celestial Pictures Ltd. All rights reserved.

As a team, Hong and Fang first appeared as part of a band of Ming rebels in *Seven Shaolin Heroes Venture Into O-Mei Mountain* (1950). They then fought each other over a bout of miscommunication in *The Fist Battle Between Fang Shi Yu and Hong Xi Guan* (1952), and their reconciliation as brothers against the Chings was featured in *Fang Shi Yu Comes to Hong Xi Guan's Rescue* (1956). In *Heroes Two* (1974), Chang Cheh cast Alexander Fu Sheng as Fang opposite Chen Kuan-tai as Hong. In the film, after the burning of Jiu Lian Shan Shaolin Temple, many Shaolin monks and fighters are on the run. Due to a series of events that do not make sense, Fang is tricked into fighting Hong, and he ends up handing over Hong to the Chings. However, he realizes his wrongdoing and rescues Hong from the Ching evildoers, headed by General Che Kang (Zhu Mu), who wants to meet Han fighters from Wu Lin just to see how good they are. Our heroes two will not disappoint him.

According to the film, Hong practices tiger kung fu and Fang practices crane kung fu. After they defeat the Four Red Robed Fighters from Tibet (guys dressed in shorts and wearing red cloaks), they have to combine their kung fu to defeat Ching leader Che, who uses phoenix fist (*zhu jia* kung fu of the Zhu family).

Although it is an art usually associated with the royal families of the Hakkas (a subgroup of Han Chinese), phoenix kung fu was created by two sisters named Zhu Miao-an and Zhu Miao-lian. Because the sisters were disciples of Liao Fa Shi Gu, a nun from Jiu Lian Shan, the foundation of the art is southern Shaolin in its origin. Some historians have noted that because of Ching persecution of anything Shaolin, phoenix kung fu was taught under the moniker of southern praying mantis kung fu, which naturally looks nothing like the praying mantis martial arts.

In reality, the creation of Hong Xi-guan's famed tiger crane form did not come about from his friendship with Fang Shi-yu, but by combining his skills with the crane martial arts taught to him by his wife, Fang Yong-chuin. Historically, Hong and Fang Shi-yu were students of Monk Zhi Shan (see *Shaolin Abbot*), so they may have at least heard of each other, so the film is incorrect when it depicts that Fang and Hong did not know each other.

Titleography: *Kung Fu Invaders*; *Heroes 2*; *Blood Brothers*; *Bloody Fists*; *Temple of the Dragon*. Translation—*Fang Shi-yu and Hong Xi-guan*. *Kung Fu Invaders* refers to the Chings. Fang and Hong are the eponymous blood brothers and the two heroes (or *Heroes Two*). *Bloody Fists* is a generic title, and *Temple of the Dragon* refers to the Shaolin Temple, the dragon being one of the tattoos a Shaolin monk would traditionally have on his arms if he chose to leave the temple. **MA Percentage: 34.08%** SHAW BROTHERS

HEROIC ONES, THE

十三太保 (1970—Hong Kong) 121m. FI: Liu Chia-liang, Liu Chia-rong, Tang Chia. NOT/LOT: 1/ 15s; NOF/LOF: 22/ 24m 27s. D: Chang Cheh. C: David Chiang, Ti Lung, Ku Feng, Wang Chung, Chen Hsing, Jin Han, James Nam Gung-fan, Lily Li, Chan Chuen, Cliff Lok, Bolo Yeung.

This film could have benefited from a bit more historical background. It opens in the waning years of the Tang Dynasty, and bandit Huang Chao has captured the capital, Chang An. Li Ke-yong (Ku Feng), ruler of the Sha Tuo state, is given the imperial title under special decree by the Tang emperor. Li leads an expedition against bandit Huang Chao by advancing his army to a place called He Zhong in order to join up with 28 town leaders.

One of those leaders is the powerful Zhu Wen (Chen Hsing), who sees all Li's 13 sons and troops drinking up a storm while visiting his castle headquarters. Zhu then voices doubt that they are capable of taking on Huang Chao. Zhu challenges Li and says that Li's most drunken son, Li Tsun-hsiao (David Chiang), could not even kill warlord Meng Cheih-hui (Bolo Yeung), who is currently killing up a storm outside the castle and challenging Li. Tsun-hsiao grabs his spear, swan-dives off the battlements and takes Meng out. Having won the challenge, Tsun-hsiao demands Zhu's imperial jade belt, which he reluctantly hands over. But that insult will come back to haunt the whole Li clan later.

Li orders nine of his sons, led by Tsun-hsiao and seconded by Shih Ching-zi (Ti Lung), to sneak into Chang An and agitate Huang Chao, but not commit any reckless acts. Yet Li's fourth son (Wang Chung) and his 11th son (James Nam Gung-fan) are jealous of Tsun-hsiao's popularity with Li, and on several occasions they do their best to screw things up in order to make Tsun-hsiao look bad. Even though they are deliberately jeopardizing the battle theater, Tsun-hsiao begs his father not to kill them, and Li complies.

Aware of Li and his sons' prowess as warriors, Huang Chao leaves Chang An. Li and his army take back the city. However, Zhu is still reeling over the loss of his royal jade belt and conspires with brothers four and 11 to kill Li and the rest. As the plan falls into place, Tsun-hsiao suffers a split "personality" in a totally unexpected scene, and it takes a lot of guts for Shih Ching-zi to keep going. The bloodshed is staggering. After the death of the first 500 enemy soldiers, I lost count, but during a 100-second fight scene, Tsun-hsiao harpoons 70 people. It is relentless and exhausting to watch. It must have also been an exhausting film for David Chiang.

Chiang, nicknamed "Elastic Double" from his stuntman years, was stretched to the limit in *The Heroic Ones*, not only because of all of his fights but also because of his costume. As was common, many of these films were shot in the middle of summer. The heat and humidity must have been extreme, but the real killer for Chiang was his fur costume with its wristbands and large headband.

It must've made Chiang sweat more than David Beckham playing soccer in a sauna. Plus, back then water was not on set for whenever someone was thirsty. Instead there was hot tea.

In Chinese families, it is common for each member to refer to the other as a number based on the order in which they were born, thus you hear the characters being called "brother 4" or "brother 11."

And now it's time for some historical clarity. The Tang Dynasty appointed non-Tang military governors called *Jie Du Shi* as a way to quell outside threats against China. The Sha Tuo tribe (aka the Sha Tuo Turks) was one group the Tang would employ to fight invaders. In real life, Li Ke-yong was a Sha Tuo Turk, and because Huang Chao and his rebels were a threat to the Tang, Li was given the title of Jie Du Shi in return for hunting down and killing Huang after he occupied Chang An. Jade-belted Zhu Wen was originally Huang's friend and ally but turned against him for love of money. Li defeated Huang during the Battle of Liangtianpo in A.D. 882, and after the fall of the Tangs, his son Li Tsun-shu founded the Late Tang Dynasty, one of the dynasties of the Five Dynasty and 10 Kingdom Periods of China. Zhu Wen was jealous of Li's powers and tried to kill him, but failed. Zhu went on to establish the Later Liang Dynasty during the same Five Dynasty period.

Several of the fights for actors David Chiang and Ti Lung are Chang Cheh's extensions of Jimmy Wong Yu's fights. At one point Jimmy Wong Yu was Chang's main man, and when Wong Yu left, his cinematic replacements were Ti and Chiang. So *Heroic Ones* has similar large-scale fights in which Chang had Ti and Chiang emulate the famous fights Wong Yu had in *Golden Swallow* (1967). For example, in one scene, Jimmy Wong Yu believably beats 100 swordsmen in a castle, and in another he protects the one he loves from a group of assassins while on the verge of death himself. In this film, Chiang has his "100 swordsmen" fight several times over, as if to outdo Wong Yu, and Ti has his near-death scene, only to come back to life to protect his father from a new group of assassins.

Titleography: *Shaolin Masters*; *Thirteen Fighters*; *13 Fighters*. Translation—*Thirteen Elite Bodyguards*. The last two characters of the Chinese title, *tai bao*, refer to a special high-ranking protective position, sort of like special forces. *Shaolin Masters* is an example of distributors using key words to draw audiences, even though the film has nothing to do with Shaolin. *13 Fighters* and *Heroic Ones* both refer to Li Ke-yong's sons. **MA Percentage: 20.41% SHAW BROTHERS**

HOT, COOL AND VICIOUS, THE

南拳北腿沾闆王 (1976—Hong Kong) 93m. MAI: Tommy Lee. NOT/LOT: 2/ 33s; NOF/LOF: 19/ 19m 43s. D: Lee Tso-nam. C: Wong Dao, Tan Dao-liang, Gao Fei, Sun Chia-lin, Jimmy Lung Fang, Tommy Lee, Wang Jue.

Sometimes revenge is not the best policy because forgiveness can pay off in the long run. Such is the life of the hero of this film: He learns that to forgive is the first step toward self-healing.

To atone for his mistakes and learn the art of healing, former inmate Lu (Tan Dao-liang) devotes his life to kicking crime in the butt when Mayor Yuen (Wang Jue) gives him the job as captain of security in his township. However, Yuen is secretly running a counterfeiting ring, and when his son Nan Shang rapes a local gal and kills her mother, Captain Lu must arrest Nan. Yuen fires Lu so he can't arrest Nan and then hires newly arrived kung fu fighter Bai Yu-ching (Wong Dao; actor Wang Jue's real son) to protect him. After Lu and Bai fight, they develop a respect for each other. When a revealed secret puts them on the

same side, they must battle Yuen's ultra-vicious albino assassin named White Hair (Tommy Lee) whose limping, praying mantis kung fu could "bug" them to death.

This is the first of two films Wong Dao and Tan Dao-liang would star in together in which each of these former tournament fighters would showcase their opposing talents: Tan's patented machine-gun-fast, hop-kicking *taekwondo* expertise; and Wong's taekwondo-kicking converted to northern Shaolin fist kung fu (as taught to him by choreographer Tommy Lee). However, neither actor was used to the other's on-screen fighting persona. This is most evident by Tan delivering kicks without belief, meaning both fighters were being too careful not to hurt each other. This is also clear in many of the other fights in the film, particularly the ones between Wong, Tan and fight choreographer Tommy Lee. The actors are often caught waiting for technique delivery, thus creating slow-paced fights.

Because of contract obligations, Wong and Tan would only do one more film together, *Challenge of Death* (1978), which was considered a sequel to this film.

Titleography: *The Hot, the Cool and the Vicious*. Translation—*Southern Fist Northern Leg Battle Yen Wang*. Both titles refer to Bai, Lu and White Hair, respectively. Bai hails from the south where styles of kung fu are known for their fist techniques and where the weather is hot. Lu represents the north where martial arts have more kicking maneuvers and where the weather is cooler. White Hair is the *Vicious* character or *Yen Wang*, which is the guardian of hell in Chinese mythology. **MA Percentage: 21.97%**

HOT POTATO

(1976—USA) 87m. SC: Pat Johnson. NOT/LOT: None; NOF/LOF: 13/ 10m 25s. D: Oscar Williams. C: Jim Kelly, George Memmoli, Geoffrey Binney, Irene Tsu, Judith M. Brown, Sam Hiona, Ron Prince, Hardy Stockmann.

The thing about a hot potato is that if you pick one up, chances are you will drop it. Maybe this film is more than a metaphor for the obvious behavioral response if you were to grasp onto this movie.

Jim Kelly is back as Black Belt Jones, who must battle the Men in Black River Formation. Villain Carter Rangoon (Sam Hiona) is the leader of Chang Lan, a small country somewhere in Southeast Asia. When he kidnaps June Dunbar (Judith M. Brown), a United States senator's daughter, and demands aid for his country, the government sends in Jones to rescue her. Helping Jones are Johnny Chicago (Geoffrey Binney), Pam (Irene Tsu) and Rhino (George Memmoli). But the subterfuge is deeper than expected because Rangoon has an ace in the hole: a prostitute named Leslie who is the spitting image of June and can pose for anyone trying to rescue her.

With a villain named Rangoon, you have to wonder if the story is somehow an allusion to the former capital of Burma, the country now known as Myanmar. (In 2006, the military government moved the capital to Naypyidaw.) And of course having Jones attack Rangoon's jungle stronghold riding in on an elephant could not possibly have anything to do with Hannibal, the famous African warrior of Carthage who marched war elephants against the Romans during the Second Punic War. Jones eventually secretly attacks Rangoon's primary headquarters, which culminates in a Rangoon-Jones romp and roll as our hero tries to save June from plummeting into a pit of tigers.

In the annals of arts film, *Hot Potato* may be construed as being at the low end of the spectrum. This is because for someone of Kelly's martial arts background and film experience, more should be expected if one's heart is into it. But on the other hand, it's possible Kelly's heart was not into this and other films, which might explain the lack of passion. And without passion, there is no interest or fun for the people who are doing what they are doing. This also doesn't just have to apply to martial arts actors, but anyone who does anything in life; do it for the passion and not the money. Although Kelly looks very distinguished with a brown Afro, most of his fights use repetitive combinations of high blocks for the attacker's punches followed by the same counter-reverse punches. In addition, each attacker comes in one at a time. Kelly also holds and wields his samurai sword like a baseball bat and avoids using kicks until one of the final fights. On the other hand, perhaps saving kicks until the end of the film was a conscious decision so the later fights would have something new to offer, which would be an intelligent choreographic move. However, when Kelly starts to do the Ali shuffle and Bruce

Lee-ish face during the final fight, it's time to toss in the towel.

When I saw this film in 1976, one scene stuck out in my mind, and it sticks with me to this day. One fight has Jones in a river surrounded by and fighting a group of short, skinny river ninjas—guys dressed in black with what look like drawstring bags over their heads. Jones poses back and forth in the direction of the ninjas, who jump in and out of line. The scene reminds me of those Shaolin films in which all the monks run around in circles or pose in a line as they set up their dreaded special formations in preparation to fight whoever is trying to get past them.

Titleography: As of this writing, no alternative titles could be found. **MA Percentage: 11.97%**

HUMAN TORNADO, THE

(1976—USA) **85m. FI: Uncredited. NOT/LOT: 2/ 42; NOF/LOF: 5/ 9m 23s.** D: Cliff Roquemore. C: Rudy Ray Moore, Lady Reed, J.B. Baron, Gloria Delaney, Herb Graham, Ernie Hudson, Howard Jackson.

Save the buzz and take out the fuzz. Martial arts movies were very popular with black audiences—and not just Bruce Lee films. Many other films found their way into the inner-city theaters where many white audiences would not tread … except me. These run-down-looking theaters reeked with passion for kung fu flicks, and actors like Rudy Ray Moore and his *Dolemite* films oozed it. In the vernacular of the times, "This cat Moore was outta sight."

The Human Tornado, a sequel to *Dolemite* (1975), has the loud-dressing funky fighter Dolemite (Rudy Ray Moore) dishing out street smarts and working to defeat an over-the-top white racist lawman (J.B. Baron) and some inept criminals trying to scare away with torture exotic dancers from black nightclub owner Queen Bee (Lady Reed).

What is unique about this martial arts comedy, if you will, is that it is an homage to and a parody of badly dubbed Chinese kung fu flicks—but it is not a spoof of Bruce Lee films. Lee was too respected by black audiences for that. That is not to say that *Fistful of Yen* (short martial arts flick within the 1977 film *Kentucky Fried Movie*) was disrespectful to Lee, because let's face it, the racist and stereotypical tones of that film were as loud as the Rolling Stones and Who concerts of that decade.

Human Tornado shows an understanding of what made kung fu films of that time appealing, and the film uses many of the same techniques: loud sound effects, switching of camera speeds, and editing that awkwardly splices images together. There's even the old trick of running a shot of a character jumping off a balcony in reverse, which makes it appear as if the character is jumping up high onto the balcony. In fact, Moore's overuse of contorted hand postures and circling the camera might actually be a nod to (or a knock on) the way David Carradine fought in the *Kung Fu* TV series. Ultimately, the film is a slice of life from a time you had to live to understand. But then that is what makes watching these films so intriguing because we can go back in time, relive the past and see how that affected the future.

Black Belt Hall of Fame member Howard Jackson lends some martial quality to the film. At the time (and even today), few probably realized that it was the first time an African-American or even an American, introduced a *tang soo do*-influenced fight scene into American-made martial arts films. Although you could argue that because Chuck Norris' *Slaughter in San Francisco* was a USA/Hong Kong co-production, then Norris was the first American to introduce tang soo do into an American-made martial arts film.

Titleography: *Dolemite II.* See above martialogy. **MA Percentage: 11.86%**

HUNTER IN DARKNESS

Yami No Karyudo (1979—Japan) **137m. FI: Uncredited. NOT/LOT: None; NOF/LOF: 10/ 10m 48s.** D: Hideo Gosha. C: Tatsuya Nakadai, Yoshio Harada, Ayumi Ishida, Keiko Kishi, Ai Kanzaki, Kayo Matsuo, Tetsuro Tanba, Sonny Chiba, Hajime Hana, Kôji Yakusho.

After starring in the exhausting Mas Oyama karate trilogy (see *Champion of Death, Karate Bear Fighter* and *Karate for Life*), Sonny Chiba had said what he wanted to say about the spirit of karate. So he traded in his karate *gi* for a samurai sword. For the remainder of the decade and throughout most of the rest of his martial arts film career, Chiba took on roles as samurai swordsmen. This is an interesting switch if you consider that toward the end of the 1970s, the *chambara* genre (samurai sword films) was on the decline. This is because all

the great samurai movie actors had run their successful courses while samurai TV serials were on the rise. *Hunter in Darkness* was Chiba's last chambara film of the decade.

Historically, in 1784 Edo (now Tokyo), near the end of the reign of the Tokugawa Shogun Ieharu (1760-1786), Japan was in the midst of the Great Tenmei Famine. A government official inside the walls of Edo had assassinated the son of the shogun's chief counselor. Ieharu's reign was rife with bribery and growing paranoia, and from the ashes of corruption arose a secret organization called the Hunter in Darkness.

This film opens with a highly respected one-eyed amnesiac assassin named Yataro (Yoshio Harada) bravely rising up from the depths of a river under a bridge; he cuts through the bridge and into a resting palanquin on the bridge's surface and kills the man inside. The man who hired Yataro to carry out the assassination is the dour and dynamic Gomyo (Tatsuya Nakadai), a man who wants to become a leading figure in the Hunter in Darkness. But in case you think Yataro is a Hunter in Darkness, then think it no more; an assassin for the Yakuza does not make the assassin a Yakuza. He's just a hired hit man for Gomyo.

Like any underground organization with supposedly upright officials in bed with it, there are some interesting nights of sleep. Lord Tanuma tells official Samon Shimengumi (Sonny Chiba) that if he can destroy the Kitamae Clan, he can become the governor of Ezo. Once Samon becomes the governor, he and Gomyo agree to form a partnership whereby Gomyo can run his shady business out of Ezo. Samon will get a major cut for looking the other way. However, what Samon and Gomyo don't know is that Yataro is the son of the head of the Kitamae Clan. In the past, during a twisted case of mistaken identity, Yataro accidentally killed his father. (Perhaps that is the stressor behind his lost memory.) Before his father died, he gave Yataro an important message. Yataro has since forgotten the message, but Samon is determined to find out what it was. On the Hunter of Darkness underground front, there are also major problems brewing. The various factions for and against Gomyo maneuver into place as he readies his bid to be the head Hunter of Darkness.

Secret societies like Hunter in Darkness operate in the shadows, and as such, all the major fight scenes in this film occur at night or in dark places. Although that fits the film's motif, it makes it impossible for the viewer to follow the action while swordsmen run around, scream and die in the dark. The fights are also shot with tight angles, making it difficult to enjoy the choreography. Or, to put it in a rhyming way: The danger of doing action in the dark opens the doors to the stuntmen getting a contusion during the confusion. However, the truth is more practical. Over the years while working in film, I have learned that the reason fights are shot like this is because they require less prep work and time to shoot correctly. During murky, chaotic fights, it's the sound effects—not the actors' skills—that sell the fights. You can see these fights are all about posing, clashing swords, tussling as the swords are connected, breaking apart from the tussle, then repeating.

Actor Tatsuya Nakadai offers some of the best poses in samurai film. (For the record, Toshiro Mifune has the best face.) Even when Nakadai is just standing with his sword or repositioning it, it looks like he's doing a lot. This is why the final fight is enjoyable. Because it is shot during the day (in a chicken coop, no less), we can clearly see the differing styles of fencing, poses and faces between Nakadai and Chiba. Although it is a short fight with very little action, it looks dynamic, as with each sword and body movement spooked chickens fly in and out of screen to give the fight more motion.

On a peculiar note, many female characters get killed in this film. I'm not sure what that means. Maybe it has something to do with the beauty of death, as compared to all the nondescript honor associated with *seppuku* (ritual suicide).

Titleography: *Hunter in the Darkness.* Translation—*Hunter of the Dark.* **MA Percentage: 7.88%**

IMPERIAL SWORD

聖劍風雲 (1977—Taiwan) **91m. KFI: Hsieh Hsing. NOT/LOT: 1/ 15s; NOF/LOF: 11/ 24m 25s.** D: Chen Zhi-hua. C: Roc Tien, Chia Ling, Zhang Yi, Miao Tian, Lung Fei, Hsieh Hsing, Yue Yang.

Saying a villain lacks manhood can have two meanings, and in this film, it is the lack of one that strengthens the other. The film begins with the assassination of an imperial judge by the head of the devious Hong Yang sect. In response, the deceased judge's daughter, Ling Fung (Chia Ling), secretly becomes a vigilante bent on recovering the Blood Rain Sword, which was stolen from the imperial treasury. She plans to use it to avenge her father and then make sure its power does not fall into corrupt hands. During her adventures, she meets Lee Fei (Roc Tien), a lone swordsman also in search of the sword. He wants to give it to the evil, albinolike eunuch Chao Pai (Zhang Yi) in return for his ransomed parents' lives.

Kung fu film heroine Chia Ling has often been branded as the Cheng Pei-pei of Taiwan. One difference is that Chia's kicks are better, thanks to her *hapkido* background. Chia was the first female kung fu star I worked with in Taiwan, and she only used the alias Judy Lee when she was at home in Florida. She also studied Chinese opera in Taiwan, so she is one of the few female stars with both types of cinematic martial arts training. Chia's experience is evident in her work: Her kicks look solid and realistic, and when she spins, strikes, parries and ducks, her motions have the grace of a dancer.

One of the typical double-crossing villains in this film employs a sword disguised as a belt wrapped around his gown. Historically, concealed weapons such as this one were popular with assassins because they could slip past a security checkpoint unnoticed. I have a sword like this, so if you ever see me in person, take another look at my belt.

The final showdown at a creaky windmill is very creative. The sun-hating villain awaits the heroes inside the mill, lurking in the shadows and waiting to launch a surprise attack. Flour sifts through the air and shafts of light stream in as windows are thrown open, and eventually a full barrage of light blasts the villain. The light-coming-through-the-cracks scene is reminiscent of the way Dracula is defeated by Van Helsing in several classic films. The choreography for Chia makes great use of her skills because she strikes a mesmerizing rhythm: cut, strike, spin, strike, cut, spin! Her earlier fights against multiple attackers achieve a similar choreographic cadence. At the climax of the windmill battle, just when it seems the heroes are about to vanquish the villain, he puts on his Gold Claw Gloves. Fortunately, Ling finally figures out the secret of the Blood Rain Sword, and the fight flows like blood.

Titleography: *The Brave in Kung Fu Shadow*; *Kung Fu Shadow*; *Glory Sword*. Translation—*Story of the Holy Sword*. The notion of the *Shadow* refers to the villain's evil activities and his sensitivity to light. **MA Percentage: 27.11%**

IMPERIAL SWORDSMAN, THE

大 內 高 手 (1972—Hong Kong) **86m. FI: Liang Shao-song. NOT/LOT: None; NOF/LOF: 27/ 28m 40s.** D: Lin Fu-ti. C: Shu Pei-pei, Yu Hui, Chuan Yuan, Ching Miao, Tung Li, Li Yung-zhong, Wong Chong-shun, Tang Di, Chan Shen, Lu Wei.

The Imperial Swordsman is a special film. Unlike the many Shaw Brothers *wuxia* productions of the early and mid-1970s that have few fight scenes, this film offers a lot of kung fu. Even though most of the actors did not practice martial arts, the total length of fight time clocks in at more than 28 minutes. Compare that to *The Jade Faced Assassin*, for example. (That martialogy discusses why early films often had fewer fights.)

The story begins when Fu Bing-zhong (Ching Miao) is accused by "friends" of conspiring with the Mongols to take over China. Lord Sun sends four imperial fighters to help special agent Yin Shu-tang (Chuan Yuan) infiltrate Fu's lair at Long Hu Mountain to find proof of his traitorous actions. However, Yin does not know the imperial fighters are there to help him. Instead, he thinks the four agents are assassins out to kill him. (When you're an agent, paranoia goes with the territory.) Based on his behavior toward them, the four are also unclear as to Yin's loyalty. A royal decree states that because Fu failed to guard the eastern border, he must return to the capital. Once Fu is in the capital, that gives Yin time to infiltrate Fu's lair. Then Yin can find evidence that Fu is a traitor. However, while escorting Fu back to the capital, Yin bonds with the seemingly righteous conspirator, and intrigue sprouts as combinations of the four fighters weasel in and out of Yin's favor, obscuring the truth.

Along with the obvious danger that goes with infiltrating Fu's gang of bloodthirsty swordsmen, Yin has to deal with four vicious giant men who guard Fu. Fittingly, "Fu" in Chinese can mean "good luck," but with a different tone it can also mean "rotten." Yin has to navigate that boundary carefully.

What is particularly engaging in this film is that actor Chuan Yuan plays his character more like a samurai than a Chinese swordsman. He walks and fights like a samurai, brandishing a 4-foot pole and eventually revealing that it has a sword hidden within. The fight choreography offers a thrilling blend of Chinese spins and Japanese slices, all beautifully accentuated with tight low-angle shots (like old samurai films) and subtle camera movements. Chuan fights with focused intensity, and though he wields his pole with wide, sweeping motions, the shots are tightly framed, and the results are crisp-looking weapon techniques. There is even a major character zipping around in what appears to be ninja garb, though it is essentially the traditional attire of Tang Dynasty assassins known as Forest Devils, which predated the ninja.

The film also makes use of some unique camera choreography. One sequence involves a peculiar upside-down camera maneuver shot from a bad guy's point of view as he jumps and flips; this is followed by a reverse angle looking back at his feet as he lands on a table. Another fight sequence presents an interesting long take with uninterrupted action: Yin runs into a cave corridor, fights multiple attackers and exits the frame. He is quickly followed by a second hero who runs into the same corridor, fights different attackers and leaves. Then a third hero follows suit. Finally, the camera pans over to another corridor, where the second hero is fighting yet another group of attackers. These sorts of creative shots bring a different sensibility and continuity to the fight scenes.

On a final note, the studio sets are truly remarkable, complete with underground moats, streams, dungeons and other water features. Yes, this is a fun film.

Titleography: As of this writing, no alternative titles could be found. Translation—*Imperial Palace Elite Fighter*. The titles reflect the lead character's ties to the imperial palace. **MA Percentage: 33.33%** SHAW BROTHERS

IMPOSTER, THE

七 面 人 (1975—Hong Kong) **91m. FI: Huang Pei-ji, Chan Chuen. NOT/LOT: 1/ 15s; NOF/LOF: 12/ 8m 24s.** D: Pao Hsueh-li. C: David Chiang, Chen Kuan-tai, Wang Chung, Danny Lee, Chen Ping, Shi Zhong-tian, Tong Lin.

This film was inspired by Tony Randall's performance in the Academy Award-winning *7 Faces of Dr. Lao* (1964), in which he plays an old Chinese man who himself plays six other characters. (The seven faces refer to Dr. Lao's own identity and his six alter egos.) Sir Run Run Shaw wanted to emulate the film and had David Chiang, arguably Shaw Brothers' most prolific actor at the time, play a similar character in *The Man of Seven Faces* (the Chinese title of this film).

Tseng Kan (Wang Chung) is trying to figure out a way to save his brother, Tseng Yung (Danny Lee), from the death penalty after being accused of rape, murder and robbery. Kan turns to upright hero Ge Liang (Chiang) for help. At the center of Ge's plan are his six secret identities. While incognito, Ge can wing, beg, gamble, calculate, fight, rope and dope the real culprits behind the crimes:

the cruel Captain Luo (Chen Kuan-tai), the gruesome Master Gao (Shi Zhong-tian) and the horrific Master Huang (Tong Lin).

The Imposter is more of a showcase of Chiang's acting range than it is a kung fu movie, and it only has about eight minutes of fighting. The fights themselves are shot and performed rather lazily. Even solid martial arts actors like Chiang and Chen engage in haphazard choreography using the heavy-hand technique, whereby one simply lays his open hand on slow incoming kicks and punches to create the impression of blocking. With camera speeds cranked down to 20-21 frames per second (which are then played back slightly sped up) the heavy hand is not so obvious. However, manipulating the camera speed can only help so much, and it won't hide a lack of energy. The final chase scene over hills and dales with Chiang on a motorbike and Chen on a horse does give at least the impression that nobody was intentionally horsing around on set, and Chiang does give a decent rendition of seven different characters. Unlike *7 Faces of Dr. Lao*, which won an award for outstanding makeup achievement, *Imposter*'s makeup is an underachievement.

Titleography: As of this writing, no alternative titles could be found. Translation—*Seven Face Man*. **MA Percentage: 9.51%** SHAW BROTHERS

INCIDENT AT BLOOD PASS

Machibuse (1970—Japan) **117m. FC: Kuze Ryu. NOT/LOT: None. NOF/LOF: 12/ 6m 20s.** D: Hiroshi Inagaki. C: Toshiro Mifune, Yujiro Ishihara, Ruriko Asaoka, Shintaro Katsu, Kinnosuke Nakamura, Chusha Ichikawa, Ichiro Arishima, Mika Kitagawa, Yoshio Tsuchiya, Jotaro Togami, Chieko Nakakita, Ryunosuke Yamazaki.

The one thing you never say to a samurai is, "Cut it out," because that may be your last request if it happens to be at the Kamaya Inn.

Toshiro Mifune plays a nameless ronin who is told something will happen at Sanshu Pass and he should go there. On his way, he rescues a woman from her abusive husband, escorts her to the pass and sets her up at the inn. In a vein similar to Hong Kong inn movies, an eclectic bunch of characters meet at the inn, and we eventually learn who the leader is, what the plan is (robbing a shipment of shogunate gold) and how they are going to pull it off. After the usual backstabbing and double-crossing, the hero exposes the truth.

As was typical in *chambara* (sword films) and *jidaigeki* (period films), this film has very little action and in actuality has no choreographic ideas to speak of. Besides what can only be described as an embarrassing boxing fight between Mifune and Yujiro Ishihara, there's a final three-minute battle that sees Mifune cross swords with Katsu for a brief moment. It's reminiscent of their fight in *Zatoichi Meets Yojimbo* (1970).

Because this film features several famous chambara actors known for outstanding samurai sword fights in the past, why is there is so little action in this and many other samurai movies? It is odd how history repeats itself and nobody notices it. Jidaigeki and chambara films of the 1970s portrayed how Japan resisted change and foreign influence, i.e., the fall of the Tokugawa shogunate. Yet the ultimate leader in Japan was the emperor, who accepted the West. It's ironic how the Japanese film industry was doing what their film plots were telling people not to do: oppose change and ignore Western influences. By this I mean that the Japanese stuck to their old filmmaking style, with long movies and little action. Furthermore, most directors resisted Western influence, except for the man known as the Emperor of Japanese Film, Akira Kurosawa. Kurosawa accepted advice from his favorite American director, John Ford, and perhaps that is why Kurosawa is Japan's best-known director. In fact, he set down the fight-limit guidelines to around 10 minutes of fighting per film, which he thought would give the genre space to grow (i.e., more action). Yet it didn't happen. Instead, filmmakers took the reigning film emperor's words literally and stuck to his guns.

A final note on *Blood Pass*: There is one neat and glorious moment in the final fight in which Mifune draws his sword like lightning and takes out seven samurai with seven strokes. Perhaps that was a metaphorical message in regard to the once-glorious heyday and international success of Kurosawa's *Seven Samurai* (1954), a moment in movie history that was fading into the relics of chambara time.

Titleography: *Ambush*; *The Ambush*; *Ambush at Blood Pass*; *Incident at Blood Island*; *Ambush at Blood Pass*; *Ambush at Blood Island*; *Incident at Blood Pass*; *The Yojimbo*; *Island*. Translation—*Ambush*. **MA Percentage: 5.41%**

INCREDIBLE KUNG FU MASTER, THE

醒目仔蠱惑招 and 肥龍功夫精 (1979—Hong Kong) **90m. MAD: Sammo Hung's Stuntmen's Association, Liang Jia-ren, Yuen Biao, Lam Ching-ying, Chen Hui-yi. NOT/LOT: 12/ 13m 35s; NOF/LOF: 23/ 28m 34s.** D: Joe Cheung Tung-cho. C: Sammo Hung, Stephen Tung Wai, Lee Hoi-san, Gao Fei, Huang Ha, Peter Chan Lung, Chung Faat, Mang Hoi, Addy Sung Gam-loi, Chen Hui-yi.

Imagine watching this film knowing nothing about Sammo Hung. Now imagine someone telling you that the way Hung's character teaches Stephen Tung Wai's character kung fu—with all the painful body contorting—was the same thing Hung went through when he learned Beijing opera. You would never believe it. If fact, it would be a lie, because Hung went through worse.

This is one reason why there are so few fantastic kung fu stars coming out of Hong Kong or anywhere else these days—because no one would dare submit himself to this sort of training. Stars like Hung did not do it for the money, they were sold into the livelihood by their parents. Working hard was a way to get less punishment and an opportunity to flip around onstage and bring face to one's *sifu*. I challenge any young contemporary martial artists to say they would go through this kind of commitment, and not for money or fame (and without suing their teacher).

Hung would admit this film is about the fights, about showing the audience the kind of training it takes to be that level of martial artist. (He would say that they are merely entertainers.) The film also debunks the traditional attitude that one should have only a single kung fu teacher in a lifetime and instead espouses the Bruce Lee philosophy of taking what is useful and discarding the rest.

The irony is that Lee had only one true sifu, Yip Man, and all his other theories about fighting and philosophy came from self-knowledge. Furthermore, most kung fu styles that exist today have evolved as a result of people mixing styles and movements they have learned or picked up from others over time. So ultimately, the notion of mixed martial arts is a very old idea.

This film opens with two brothers (in the familial sense and the kung fu sense), *wing chun* man Li Chin-fei (Huang Ha) and five animal stylist Li Chin-peng (Peter Chan Lung). After they rid the town of kung fu bully Yang Wei (Lee Hoi-san), Yang plants the seed of discord by telling each brother that one of them is better than the other. Their egos drive them apart, and the rift grows when Chin Fung (Gao Fei) sends one of his two sons to each of the opposing teachers. Chin vows that the son with better kung fu after two years will have his teacher rewarded with a lot of money.

Meanwhile, street moppet Ching wants to learn kung fu and runs into wandering winemaker Fei Jai (Hung), who tells him he should learn from both Li brothers. When the Lis find out what Ching is doing, they both boot him from their schools, and so Fei agrees to teach Ching. Fei's regimen is more painful than what Rocky went through while preparing to fight Apollo Creed in *Rocky* (1976). Two years later, the truth about Chin, his two sons and their motivations for learning kung fu from the Lis is revealed. It falls to Ching and Fei to save the day with some phenomenal slip-sliding fights, spear-wielding wizardry and head-butting brutality.

Titleography: *The Kung Fu Master*; *They Call Me Phat Dragon*. Translations—*Fat Dragon Kung Fu Soul* and *Awaken Eye Lad With Confusing Kung Fu Guile*. The title *They Call Me Phat Dragon* is a play on *They Call Me Bruce* (1982), *Enter the Fat Dragon* (another Hung picture, from 1978) and the slang term "phat." *Fat Dragon Kung Fu Soul* refers to Fei's peculiar way of teaching kung fu, and the *Awaken Eye* title refers to Ching's clever way of combining all the styles he learns into one. **MA Percentage: 46.83%**

INCREDIBLE PROFESSOR ZOVEK, THE

El Increible professor Zovek (1972—Mexico) **79m. FI: Uncredited. NOT/LOT: None; NOF/LOF: 2/ 2m 2s.** D: Rene Cardona. C: Zovek, Teresa Velázquez, Germán Valdés, José Gálvez, Nubia Martí.

Real-life folk hero Zovek was considered the Houdini of Mexico, an escape artist and amazing athlete known for performing incredible stunts. He once did 17,800 consecutive sit-ups (the final 200 while holding his secretary above his head), and another time he held eight motorcycles from speeding off by holding a bit in his teeth that was chained to the vehicles. He swam for eight hours straight and jumped rope for nine hours to raise money for the Red Cross. And he was a self-defense instructor for the Mexican military police.

Zovek plays himself in this movie, the first of a nine-film contract that keyed into his popularity. The film version of Zovek is a mind-reading hero who tries to foil a mad doctor's own mind-control powers. The doctor wishes to rule the planet and has put together a clan of strange creatures, including a deranged, fanged, muscle-bound cannibal; a horde of mutant dwarfs; and a monster whose face apparently became attached to the cell bars confining him. Although touted as a martial arts expert, Zovek is no cinematic fighter because his kicks and karate postures are weaker than butter on the surface of the sun. This is evident by his lack of balance; hip-leg angle before, during and at the end of the kick; and the foot position at the point of impact. But how could anyone pass up the opportunity to see such an inspirational figure zipping around on the big screen? Zovek died during the production of his second film, 1973's *Blue Demon y Zovek En La Invasión de Los Muertos* (*The Invasion of the Dead*).

Titleography: As of this writing, no alternative titles could be found. **MA Percentage: 2.57%**

INN OF EVIL

Inochi Bo Ni Furo (1971—Japan) **121m. FI: Uncredited. NOT/LOT: None; NOF/LOF: 5/ 4s 54s.** D: Masaki Kobayashi. C: Shintaro Katsu, Shin Kishida, Yosuke Kondo, Shigeru Koyama, Komaki Kurihara, Daigo Kusano, Shun Makita, Masao Mishima, Tatsuya Nakadai, Kanemon Nakamura, Ichiro Nakaya.

There's an inn on an island with only one way to get there, which is a footbridge from the riverbank. It's the Fukagawa Easy Tavern, where you can see the patrons' troubles are all the same and where everybody knows each other's name. Sound familiar? If you're thinking about the American TV show *Cheers*, you're right. But instead of sitting in a pub in Boston, we're in the Tokugawa period. And like on *Cheers*, each patron in this inn of evil has his or her place.

There's the owner and bartender, Ikuzo (Kanemon Nakamura), who is also head of a black-market ring that stores stolen goods from foreign ship heists. There's Ikuzo's main man and partner, Sadahachi (Tatsuya Nakadai), who is a former great samurai with a vendetta against the world. There's drunk Nameless the Wanderer (Shintaro Katsu), who drinks himself under the table. Then there's Officer Kanedo (Shigeru Koyama), who wants to give all the patrons of this inn of evil a paddy wagon ride to death. As you can see, even though the Easy Tavern was established in 1895, around the same time as the bar Cheers, the major difference between the two is in their different service mottos. Cheers welcomes people to a place where "everybody knows your name," while the Easy Tavern thinks more along the lines of "nobody leaves this place alive."

But that doesn't mean the less-than-savory patrons don't have heart. In the midst of their plan to rob a Dutch ship, a wimpy man foolishly storms into the tavern to say something to these thieving killers. The man is acting foolhardy because he wants to rescue his wife from a life of prostitution, but he knows that he's not a warrior and could never successfully fight the men who want his wife. Rather than kill this man, the patrons are moved to help him. They decide to go on a suicide mission to save his wife, as Sadahachi laments, "We give our lives for nothing." On the way to their deaths, the sword-swinging bar patrons face tons of sword-wielding cops. This film is more about the catharsis of characters than the adrenaline of an action sequence, and at the end of the day, anyone has the chance of being decent in an indecent world.

The final fight borrows the rope-snare idea seen in many Chinese *wuxia* films, in which the hero is trapped like a fly in a spider web of ropes. The cool difference here is that we see the trap unfold from Sadahachi's perspective when he looks at the policemen ensnaring him. The camera uses a kaleidoscopic multi-image special effect to show what each policeman looks like to him. That image looks like a fly's point-of-view shot, and each policeman looks like many policemen. And that's the buzz on this film.

Titleography: As of this writing, no alternative titles could be found. **MA Percentage: 4.05%**

INSTANT KUNG FU MAN

霎眼功夫 and 真假功夫 (1977—Hong Kong) **104m. MAD: Yuen Woo-ping, Yuen Kwei, Yuen Cheung-yan. NOT/LOT: 5/ 3m 55s; NOF/LOF: 19/ 31m 38s.** D: Dong Jin-hu. C: She Fei-yang, John Liu, Hwang Jang-lee, Yuen Yat-choh, Yuen Kwei, Jing Guo-zhong, Alan Hsu, Yuen Bao-huang.

When the wooden dummies in Shaolin's Luo Han Hall instantly turn to sawdust due to a termite infestation, it's a pretty good indication that this tale of double trouble and mistaken identities will have some silly antics. As an entomologist, I am compelled to note that the termites in this film are actually played

by fly maggots, which would not render the dummies into dust.

Xiao Fu (She Fei-yang) is a robber feared for his kung fu skills; Xiao Hu (She Fei-yang) is his smart but lazy non-martial-artist twin brother. Fu tells Hu to go to Shaolin and learn kung fu, but Hu ends up pulling a fast one on the monks with his clever bug trick. The temple then sends Monk Wu Kam (John Liu) to bring him back alive. Meanwhile, Fu steals some jewelry and double-crosses his partner in crime, Yi Lang (Hwang Jang-lee). After leaving the temple, Hu is mistaken for his brother and happily takes advantage of his fearsome reputation—until Yi Lang comes knocking on his head looking for revenge on Fu. As the ruse unravels, Yi finds that he is no match for the combined efforts of Fu, Wu and Hu.

Along with the classic twin mix-up gags, the film uses another familiar plot point: In the old days, good kung fu women fighters would only marry good kung fu men, so a successful suitor would have to beat such a woman in a fight. We see this again in *Two Wondrous Tigers* (1979) and Jet Li's *Fong Sai-yuk* (1993). In this film, when a young martial arts security guard (played by Yuen Yat-choh, younger brother of Yuen Woo-ping) believes Hu can be his kung fu teacher, it opens the doors for him to marry a kung fu woman he beats in a fight. Although the actress who plays the woman has the same last name as Yuen, they are not related.

Also of note is that when Liu fights, he does his usual three-arm technique, whereby he holds up his right leg with his right arm and uses it like a third arm. However, when Liu fights Hwang Jang-lee, a fellow dynamic *taekwondo* kicker (who is also predominantly right-footed), the choreography features both kickers using both feet. As a result, the action flows better and avoids looking like a kicking drill. The cumulative number of kicks thrown during their two fights will undoubtedly add up to more than all the kicks Chuck Norris delivered in his entire movie career. I'm not quite sure how to interpret this, but it sure sounds like there is something to be said about one's fight commitment to a film.

Titleography: *Kung Fu Man.* Translations—*Blinking Eye Kung Fu* and *Real and Fake Kung Fu. Instant Kung Fu Man* refers to the skilled Fu being mistaken for the harmless Hu: When Fu fights while thought to be Hu, it seems that Hu has learned kung fu in the blink of an eye. *Real and Fake Kung Fu* refers to the real kung fu of Xiao Fu and the fake kung fu of Xiao Hu. *Kung Fu Man,* although a generic title, is a shortened version of the original English title. **MA Percentage: 34.18%**

INTIMATE CONFESSIONS OF A CHINESE COURTESAN

愛奴 (1972—Hong Kong) **90m. FI: Xu Er-niu. NOT/LOT: 1/ 5s; NOF/LOF: 14/ 15m.** D: Chu Yuen. C: Lily Ho, Yueh Hua, Betty Bei Ti, Tong Lin, Fan Mei-sheng, Wan Chong-shan, Chan Shen, Fang Mian.

It's *My Fair Lady* with swashbuckling women, erotica, revenge, and a deadly game of cat and mouse. Yes, this old-style *wuxia* film from Shaw Brothers is shot with exquisite opulence and injected with surrealistic martial titillation and artful slaughter.

The hardcore Lady Chun deals in virgins, selling their chastity to the highest bidder, after which the girls become Chun's ladies of the night. The madam takes a special interest in the nubile young Ai Nu (Lily Ho) and becomes both her kung fu teacher and her lover. Ai Nu becomes an in-demand courtesan but also begins plotting a way out and exacting her revenge. That also sets off a heated battle of wits between Ai Nu and Constable Ji De (Yueh Hua), who is investigating a series of grisly murders. Ji knows it is Ai Nu who is unleashing her perfumed scents of terror on the all the men who took advantage of her—the highest bidder the first night, the second-highest bidder the next night, and so on—but he is constantly one step behind in his investigation and his sword-fighting abilities.

Any film that starts off with snow always captures my calm and reminds me of my martial arts training when I would run around barefoot in deep snow to usher the ancient Okinawan karate spirit into my psyche. Although this is an erotica film, the sword fights are well-choreographed, and considering that none of the actors came from a martial arts or swordplay background, the cast does a bang-up job.

Choreographer Xu Er-niu uses tight camera angles on the central fighter in each combat scene and has characters running in and out of frame to create a sense of mayhem. The focus is on the freneticism of the movements and emotions, not the precision of the sword techniques. The actors sell the fights with distraught and panicking faces rather than with crisp martial skills. As the film

Still from *Intimate Confessions of a Chinese Courtesan* © Celestial Pictures Ltd. All rights reserved.

progresses, the fights incorporate more tracking and spinning within individual shots, adding to the visual beauty and underscoring the hypnotic twist and turns of love and betrayal. The fights really turn it up when Chun's Deadly Finger kung fu starts poking holes in flying bodies, arms start flying and blood begins gushing.

Titleography: As of this writing, no alternative titles could be found. Translation—*Ai Nu*. The Chinese title, *Ai Nu*, is the film's title character. Literally translated though, the title means "Love Slave," which pretty much summarizes Ai Nu's life. The English title also refers to Ai Nu's place in life. **MA Percentage: 16.76%** SHAW BROTHERS

INTRIGUE OF THE YAGYU CLAN

Yagyu Ichizoku No Inbo (1978—Japan) **130m. FI: Uncredited. NOT/LOT: None; NOF/LOF: 16/ 11m 44s.** D: Kenji Fukasaku. C: Kinnosuke Nakamura, Sonny Chiba, Hiroki Matsukata, Teruhiko Saigo, Reiko Ôhara, Etsuko Shihomi, Kentaro Kudo, Jirô Chiba, Hideo Murota, Mayumi Asano, Hiroyuki Sanada, Ichiro Nakatani, Tetsuro Tanba, Toshirô Mifune.

As this film demonstrates, power struggles can tear apart even the closest families. In 1624, brothers Iemitsu and Tadanaga fight to become the third shogun of Japan and succeed their father, who has been assassinated. In the ensuing chaos, rising and falling clans clash, and alpha males Yagyu Tajima (Kinnosuke Nakamura) and Priest Gensinsai Ogasawa (Tetsuro Tanba) vie for personal glory. Only one man refuses to turn a blind eye and will do anything to patch things up, Yagyu Jubie (Sonny Chiba).

Films like this are not about creative choreography, but about blinding swordsmanship acuity. This is perfectly demonstrated in the long-anticipated final showdown between Tajima, who is Iemitsu's fencing teacher, and Gensinsai, who wants to be Tadanaga's fencing teacher. Each immaculate samurai swordsman wishes to be the head fencing instructor, depending on which brother becomes the next shogun. The actual fight lasts almost 90 seconds, but there is actually only one sword cut, one spray of blood and one death, which happens in a flash.

Another interesting fight takes place in Iemitsu's castle when a female assassin wielding a *naginata*—a long staff with a small, curved, *katana*-like blade at one end, often wielded by women—tries to kill Iemitsu. Of course, once Tajima draws his sword, the fight is swift and bloody.

Yagyu Clan features the fight debut of Henry Sanada and one of Etsuko (Sue) Shihomi's last performances, playing members of the Negoro clan. Sadly, though that clan was known for its double-weapon expertise with the *sai* and *tonfa*, this film offers no such fights worth discussing. The film also happens to be Fukasaku's first *chanbara* ("sword fighting") film, and although one of his favorite actors, Chiba, plays a somewhat minor character, his is the most memorable role, with his distinctive eye patch and tufted hairstyle. The film also spurred the creation of a highly successful TV show, *The Yagyu Conspiracy* (1978), featuring Chiba with his familiar trademarks.

Titleography: *Shogun Samurai*; *The Shogun's Samurai*; *The Yagyu Conspiracy*; *Yagyu Clan Conspiracy*. Translation—*Yagyu Clan of Intrigue*. As with Chinese films using "kung fu" or "Shaolin" in their titles, words Western audiences would recognize, Japanese film titles often included "samurai," "ninja" and "shogun" (undoubtedly due to James Clavell's 1980 novel, *Shogun: A Novel of Japan*). **MA Percentage: 9.03%**

INVINCIBLE ARMOUR

鷹爪鐵布衫 (1977—Hong Kong) **100m. KFI: Yuen Woo-ping, Hsu Hsia. NOT/LOT: 9/ 7m 51; NOF/LOF: 30/ 31m 33s.** D: Ng See-yuen. C: John Liu, Hwang Jang-lee, Tino Wong Cheung, Gao Fei, Yuen Kwei, Yuen Biao, Yuen Shun-yi, Lee Hoi-sang, Hsu Hsia, Cai Fu-gui, Jie Yuan   .

Although the practice of *chi gong* (*qigong*) has been around since China's Neolithic period (5000-3000 B.C.) as a means to strengthen *chi*, which in turn helps one's health, it was martial artists who realized that by reversing normal chi flow for a split-second (a technique known as *fa jing*), one could deliver a strike with incredible power. There were others who created ways of using chi to make their bodies resistant to punches, kicks and even weapon strikes, such as *da jing zhong* (big golden bell) and *tie bu shan* (iron shirt). Someone who was an expert in both striking and absorbing blows would be an almost unstoppable adversary; the only way to defeat such a fighter would be by finding his weak chi point on the body. When the chi point was struck the right way and at a specific time of day, it would drain the opponent's chi, like pulling out a plug, thus leaving the body open to even the weakest attack.

In this film, Ming General Chao Wu-fung (John Liu) has been framed for killing a national hero named Liu. The cruel, white-haired Minister (Hwang Jang-lee), an eagle claw and iron shirt expert, vows to capture and kill Chao at any cost. His plan to capture Chao is actually part of a larger plot to become emperor. While Chao is on the lam, a young teen whose father was killed by the Minister befriends him and teaches him iron finger kung fu, the only technique that can counter the iron shirt.

The English dub of the film says there are 108 acupuncture points, 32 of which can result in death when struck. Traditional theories of acupuncture state that there are actually 365 acupuncture points on the body (some say there are up to 10,000), 36 of which are considered death points. When Chao is trying to learn where these points are, giant red dots are superimposed on the villain to point some of them out. Fortunately, striking these points has to be spot-on, so although the real-life death points are in the vicinity of the red dots, they are not precise enough for those viewers hoping to learn the secret to killing someone with one blow.

A voice-over explains that eagle claw was invented during the Ming Dynasty. In fact, eagle claw martial arts were invented in 1259 by Song Dynasty General Yue Fei, who wanted to teach his troops a better way to fight the invading Jin. Inspired by watching an eagle fight, Yue brandished his thumbs, forefingers and middle fingers like the three-clawed talons of the eagle and developed flesh-tearing techniques. Yue also created a system of techniques known as the 108 Hands, which consists of grappling and pressure-point strikes. Perhaps the translated English script confused the 108 Hands with 108 acupuncture points.

Liu does his usual leg-stretching training sequences, using his rubbery limbs to their fullest advantage, and he has one really neat fight inside the House of Ancestors. He dispatches each attacker without looking at the opponent. The fight is short and sweet and reveals a flash of Liu's cool that he rarely shows with his usual endless kicking.

As in many other kung fu films, the villain in *Invincible Armour* has white hair. This detail is an allusion to the white-haired Monk Bai Mei, the traitor to the Ming and Shaolin whose devious behavior led to the destruction of the Jiu Lian Shan Shaolin Temple.

Titleography: *The Invincible Armour*. Translation—*Eagle Claw Iron Shirt*. **MA Percentage: 39.49%**

INVINCIBLE IRON PALM, THE

無敵鐵沙掌 (1971—Hong Kong) **69m. KFI: Chen Shao-peng. NOT/LOT: 2/ 2m 23s; NOF/LOF: 14/ 17m 36s.** D: Zhu Mu. C: Deng Guang-rong, Charlie Chin Chiang-lin, Ingrid Hu Yin-yin, Bai Ying, Jiang Nan, Zhu Mu.

This film offers fedora-*fu* in the halls of *Fist of Fury*. Brothers Hang Jia (Charlie Chin Chiang-lin) and Hang Tao (Deng Guang-rong) rescue a girl from being raped by a thug (Jiang Nan). When the lowlife admits the error of his ways and promises to clean up his act, the brothers let him go. Predictably, he runs back to his boss, Chen Jing (Bai Yin), and the two plan revenge against the brothers, with the added bonus of taking down their father's security business. Chen defeats the brothers using his special iron fist and 36 steps kung fu and shuts down the only form of law in the area.

Chen and his henchman open a brothel and casino. One of their scams involves accepting IOUs, then extorting more money from their clients when it comes time to pay up. Anyone who fails to capitulate will end up beaten and thrown in jail. The beautiful wife of one such borrower allows Chen's underling to have his way with her in order to pay off her husband's debts. From there, everything spirals out of control.

Meanwhile, the Hang brothers have begun training in special kung fu. Jia learns iron fist by pounding increasingly heavy sandbags and boiling his hands in cow urine, and Tao learns *ching gong* to make his kicks more powerful.

For reasons never explained, the two rejuvenated lads begin wearing fedora hats to all their fights as they clear a righteous path to take down Chen and his cronies.

There are several aspects of this film I really enjoy. When Tao is learning ching gong, that skill you see in the kung fu films that allows a man to run on treetops (*Crouching Tiger, Hidden Dragon* (2000) or leap high onto the roofs of buildings, he practices it in a way that is almost the correct way. (See *Master of the Flying Guillotine*.) Tao walks around the rim of a kiddie-pool-size bowl shaped like a watch glass (the bowl is only slightly concave).

There is also a noteworthy fight between Hang Tao and a group of bad guys. It's not so much that the quality of the fight is significant, but the setting is: The scene was shot on the same courtyard set where Bruce Lee would fight Robert Baker one year later. Baker played the Russian heavy Mr. Petrov in *Fist of Fury*. After that, the set was never used again in any other film.

Titleography: As of this writing, no alternative titles could be found. Translation—*Undefeatable Iron Sand Palm*. The film focuses on how Jia learns iron palm to defeat the villain. **MA Percentage: 28.96%**

INVINCIBLE SHAOLIN

南少林與北少林 (1978—Hong Kong) **101m. FI: Lu Feng, Robert Tai Ch-hsien, Liang Ting. NOT/LOT: 14/ 19m 27s; NOF/LOF: 19/ 22m 31.** D: Chang Cheh. C: Sun Chien, Lo Meng, Kuo Chue, Chiang Sheng, Lu Feng, Wei Bai, Wang Lung-wei, Sun Shu-pei, Chan Shen, Wang Ching-ho, Ching Miao.

Another dream film for Chang Cheh. There are no female leads, just pure male bonding and fighting kung fu men—his strengths as a filmmaker. Though not marketed as such, this film also marked the return of the cast of *The Five Venoms* (1978). (See martialogy.)

Up until nearly the end of Emperor Kang Xi's reign, the Shaolin enjoyed relative peace with the Ching authorities because they saved the Ching Dynasty from Russian invasion back in 1685. However, after Kang Xi died and Yong Zheng usurped the throne in 1723, the Shaolin were on increasingly shaky ground because Ming loyalists at Song Shan Shaolin upped their efforts to bring back the Ming, and this was a threat to the Chings. Through a series of events, Ching soldiers eventually attacked and razed Song Shan Shaolin Temple in 1736, which led to the sad and destructive fall of Shaolin but gave rise to numerous Shaolin legends that Chinese history and cinema have not forgotten. Based on the story, this film is probably set in the early 1730s, when Yong Zheng was preparing to destroy Shaolin. Under the guise of respect and honor, General Shu (Wang Lung-wei) enthusiastically invites three members from Northern Shaolin and three members of Southern Shaolin to compete with each other so he can admire their kung fu. He also says he would be interested in having the winners remain at his place to teach his men.

Shu purposely invites the best fighters of the north and only mediocre fighters from the south. Predictably, the northern fighters win. However, one of the southern students is accidentally killed during the friendly exhibition. The two surviving southerners understand the circumstances and must return home to report to their teacher about how the one student died and that it was an accident. But things go from bad to worse when Shu has them killed and lets news spread that the northerners did it. The three northern fighters—Xu Fong (Sun Chien), Yang Zhong-fei (Chiang Sheng) and Bao Shan-xiong (Lu Feng)—are suspicious of Shu's sincerity and decide to tread softly while continuing their own investigation.

Still from *Invincible Shaolin* © Celestial Pictures Ltd. All rights reserved.

The southerners feel they have been slapped in the face and send three more fighters. These fighters are also beaten by the northerners, and there are two more deaths. Now it is time to get dangerous as three southern students are chosen to undergo the most intensive of intensive training. Her Ying-wu (Kuo Chue) will learn *ching gong* and Shaolin pole, Zhang Cheng (Lo Meng) will learn praying mantis, and Mai Feng (Wei Bai) will learn *wing chun*. The three future heroes of Shaolin take a solemn vow of revenge against the northerners, and the gauntlet is thrown down.

After the success of showing Shaolin training in *The 36th Chamber of Shaolin* earlier in the year, Chang and his fight instructors were determined to tap into that spirit with their actors by creating some awesome training regimens for the three southern fighters. They would bring out subtle details about the arts not yet shown in film before. It is of note that Kuo Chue's character learns ching gong, like his characters in *Marco Polo* (1975) and *Shaolin Temple* (1976) did, a smart reflection of Kuo's real-life jumping abilities. As for Lo Meng, you will be lucky to see anything like praying mantis kung fu in his fights, which are all about highlighting his build and his tough arms. His fights therefore feature a lot of open-hand strikes and wrist-on-wrist blocks, though he eventually uses his fists more, including a great raucous body-ripping sequence that tears up the screen. Conversely, Sun Chien practices *taekwondo*, and his wrists aren't as tough as kung fu practitioners, so there is very little wrist contact in his fights. As a savvy viewer might expect, he usually kicks.

As I point out in other martialogies, using this team of actors from *Five Venoms* would in time lead to problems. Kuo Chue's pole fights are fast and smooth, and it was becoming evident that his overall weapon skills, toughness, gymnastic abilities and even his range of acting would make him the most successful of the *Five Venoms* actors. See *Crippled Avengers*, the group's next film together, for more.

Titleography: *Unbeatable Dragon*; *Shaolin Bloodshed*. Translation—*North Shaolin and South Shaolin*. *Invincible* refers to the Shaolin brothers uniting to defeat their Ching foes, thereby being invincible. *Unbeatable Dragon* is perhaps a metaphor for China. *Dragon* represents China and the *Unbeatable* refers to the Han Chinese (the Mings) and how they beat the Chings. **MA Percentage: 41.55%** SHAW BROTHERS

IRON BODYGUARD, THE

大刀王五 (1973—Hong Kong) **94m. FI: Liu Chia-liang, Tang Chia. NOT/LOT: None; NOF/LOF: 13/ 15m 30s.** D: Chang Cheh, Pao Hsueh-li. C: Chen Kuan-tai, Lily Li, Danny Lee, Yueh Hua, Lu Di, Tong Lin, Jiang Dao, Jiang Nan, Bei Di.

On June 11, 1898, young Ching Emperor Guang Xu invoked the Hundred Days Reform project. Enlisting the help of liberal-minded government members

Tan Si-tong, Kang You-wei, Liang Chi-chao, Lin Xu, Yang Rui, Yang Shen-xiu, Kang Guang-ren and Liu Guang-di, he proposed sweeping political, cultural and educational reforms. He wanted to show foreign powers that although China was weakened and defeated by Japan in the first Sino-Japanese War (1894-1895), it maintained strong national resolve. However, Guang Xu ruled under the influence of the conservative Empress Dowager Cixi, who used her power to ax the project, execute the eight reformists and put Guang Xu under house arrest until his death.

Based on real events, *The Iron Bodyguard* is about how one of the four leaders of the Grand Council (the Ching Dynasty's important policy-making body; Privy Council in the film), Tan Si-tong (Yueh Hua), developed a strong bond of brotherhood with the famous and highly respected martial artist (even by the Chings' estimation) Big Sword Wu Wang (Chen Kuan-tai). In the movie, Wu gave his life to fight corrupt Ching officials and save the lives of two of the important eight men who tried to help China with the Hundred Days Reform.

A lot goes on during the first fight between Tan and Wu because Yan Geng Iron Fist (Lu Di) and his three brothers attack Wu while he is finishing bedding a courtesan named Camomile (Bei Di). It is said Wu would walk a mile for his Camomile but only a few feet to defeat Yan. In the film, just as Tan is about to write a piece of poetry for the rich village elders, someone runs into the calligraphy moment yelling that Wu is in trouble. Tan, who always wanted to meet Wu, runs to the courtyard and joins the fight. As each fighter dispatches one of the Yan brothers, Tan expresses admiration for Wu's martial abilities. After the fight, Wu and Tan become instant blood brothers and agree to share a drink. When the elders ask Tan to finish his poem, he writes, "Feet stand on the big earth; hands hold the blue sky." The meaning is similar to the myth of Atlas, who holds the earth on his shoulders: With the upcoming reformations, Tan has a lot of weight on his shoulders. The poem also alludes to Tan's call for a new culture and a new way of thinking.

There is a clear difference in the fighting skills of Yueh, who was not a martial artist, and Chen, a legitimate martial arts actor. When Chen punches, his back remains straight and there is a definite sense of *fa jing* (the moment of focus of one's strike). In contrast, Yueh's back arches forward, and his arms merely go through the motions. Sometimes he simply lifts an arm into the final kung fu pose, and the stuntmen jump back at the right time to sell the attacks. During kicks, Chen's back remains straight and upright, while Yueh's feet seem to dangle in the air and lack any sort of spirit. In one novel fight scene, Chen's queue unbraids, so he sits down in front of a window and fights off Iron Fist while Camomile braids his hair.

In real life, Wu helped Kang You-wei and his student Lang Chi-chao to escape to Japan, while the other six reformists, Tan being the most prominent, were publicly executed September 28, 1898. Tan and the other five men beheaded became known as the Six Gentlemen of the Hundred Days Reform.

Titleography: *The Iron Body-Guard.* Translation—*Big Blade Wang Wu.* The title refers to the main character. **MA Percentage: 16.49%** SHAW BROTHERS.

IRON BUDDHA, THE

鐵羅漢 (1970—Hong Kong) 83m. FI: Sammo Hung, Han Kuo. NOT/LOT: 1/ 5s; NOF/LOF: 21/ 15m 32s. D: Yen Chun. C: Fang Ying, Ling Yun, Chen Hung-lieh, Wong Chung-shun, You Ching, Yu Hui, Fan Mei-sheng, Fang Mien, Gu Wen-zong, Yen Chun.

Once a villain, always a villain. But evildoers should beware the world of Jiang Hu, a martial arts realm outside of everyday society that has its own laws and a different sense of justice—one that is enforced by way of the sword.

When Master Liu Peng's (Fan Mei-sheng) Wind Chasing Knife thwarts voracious rapist Xiao Tien-zun (Wong Chung-shun), Xiao connivingly begs for mercy. Liu's two daughters implore him not to spare the criminal, but he relents and lets Xiao live. After giving his insincere thanks, Xiao leaves. He reappears three years later, rapes Liu's two daughters in front of him, kills Liu and proceeds to massacre all his students using the deadly Evil Poison Sword. Anyone cut or even pricked by the sword dies an agonizing death within two hours.

On that fateful day, one lone disciple, Luo Han (Ling Yun), is the only survivor because he was sidetracked saving Lady Peony (Fang Ying), the sister of a senior imperial guard, from being attacked by bandits. Although Luo Han saves her day, his crumbles when he finds his kung fu brothers dead and his kung fu sisters raped. He learns that the only way to defeat Xiao's Evil Poison Sword is to find the elusive Hu Long Sword, which is under the protection of the former head of the imperial guard, Wang Qi (Gu Wen-zong). Wang now lives a quiet life in the big city. Not knowing what Xiao looks like or where to find Wang, Luo must race to find the Hu Long Sword before Xiao finds him. What he doesn't realize is that Peony is the key to unlocking the mystery and helping him succeed.

In typical fashion for early Shaw Brothers films, the fights are short and somewhat evenly spaced out, giving the audience just enough action while masking the fact that most of the actors did not know how to fight or wield a sword. The actors' inexperience is evident in that most of them swing their swords like baseball bats, whether using one-hand or two-hand grips. The action is shot tightly and does not dwell on the actors' stances, and the editing is choppy to give the fights a somewhat lively appeal. Although kicks are usually delivered like pushes rather than crisp attacks, they do differentiate the fight choreography from Japanese samurai films, since it was rare for Japanese films in the early 1970s to have samurai characters throwing martial arts techniques beyond a few *jujitsu* flips or hand traps. Although some sword fights in Chinese films were influenced by Japanese films, it was important for Chinese filmmakers to distinguish their work in order to maintain face. Also notice that when the actors trampoline-jump in this film, their legs and feet dangle low and are not tucked up against the body; this is one way to recognize inexperienced leapers.

Titleography: As of this writing, no alternative titles could be found.

Translation—*Iron Buddha*. The title refers to the main character's name and his defining attribute: His name, Luo Han, means Buddha (although he is not an incarnation of Buddha), and he has a will of iron. **MA Percentage: 18.82%** SHAW BROTHERS

IRON-FISTED MONK, THE

三德和尚與舂米六 (1977—Hong Kong) **92m. AC: Sammo Hung. NOT/LOT: 6/ 7m 9s; NOF/LOF: 12/ 16m 20s.** D: Sammo Hung. C: Sammo Hung, Chen Hsing, James Tian, Zhu Qing, Wang Xia, Fung Ke-an, Casanova Wong.

Excuse the leap forward on this one, but when John Woo started filming his epic *Battle of Red Cliff* (2008) in April 2007, a film based on the Chinese literary classic *Romance of the Three Kingdoms*, Sammo Hung leaped into action and scooped Woo with the similarly themed *Three Kingdoms: Resurrection of the Dragon* (2008), which was shot, edited and released before Woo had time to breathe. As it turns out, the first time Hung scooped a major film production was with his directorial debut, *Iron-Fisted Monk*. When Shaw Brothers was quietly working on *The 36th Chamber of Shaolin*, a major production about Monk San De, former Shaw executive Raymond Chow and Hung jumped into the fray. Before anyone knew it, Hung shot, edited and released the San De-themed *Iron-Fisted Monk* six months before *36th Chamber*.

Zhuang Ming-liu (Sammo Hung), aka Luk in the English dub, tries to save his uncle from a malicious Manchu attack but fails. His uncle dies, and Monk San De (Chen Hsing) steps in to rescue Luk and sweep him away to the Shaolin Temple, where Luk learns kung fu. Before his time is up, Luk sneaks out of the Shaolin Temple to avenge his uncle's death. Luk arrives in a town where a mad rapist (Fung Ke-an) and his right-hand man, the meteor-ball-brandishing Ke Fu (Wang Xia), are planning to wreak havoc as the first step toward taking over the region. Luk teaches the locals kung fu and then teams up with San De to kill Ke Fu, send his hostile henchmen to hell, and use the gruesome Monkey Grabs Peaches maneuver to literally end on a high note and stop the rapist's reign of wicked behavior.

This film, like Hung himself, is a walking contradiction. While Hung is a rather large, portly man, he is more nimble than most men half his weight. *Iron-Fisted Monk* begins as a lighthearted martial arts comedy but takes a bleak turn into dark, heavy territory and features two incredibly violent rape scenes.

The film borrows a historical inaccuracy from Chang Cheh's *Shaolin Temple* (1976): Like Hu De-di in that film, Luk escapes Shaolin via a dog-made hole beneath a wall. (Documented escapes from Shaolin occurred by crawling out through a drainpipe.) Hung's own fight scenes are slow because he did not undercrank the camera (which would speed up the footage). He wanted to show the audiences how good and authentic his kung fu skills were, and viewers can appreciate his postures, hand positions and stances. Hung did, however, undercrank the camera for Chen Hsing's fights because (as has been mentioned before) his movements are slow and cumbersome, with bad posture and hunch-backed tiger claw hands. Undercranking these fights makes them watchable. Hung also used many different camera angles within the same fight, with some interesting camera transitions melting into a separate fight. These techniques are similar to what Yuen Woo-ping was experimenting with. On the whole, for a Sammo Hung production, there is not a large amount of martial arts in this film.

Titleography: As of this writing, no alternative titles could be found. Translation—*Monk San De and Zhuang Ming-liu*. These are the character names of Chen Hsing and Sammo Hung, respectively. **MA Percentage: 25.53%**

IRON MONKEY

鐵馬騮 and 鐵猴子 (1977—Taiwan) **91m. FI: Chen Mu-chuan. NOT/LOT: 17/ 12m 8s; NOF/LOF: 20/ 26m 23s.** D: Chen Kuan-tai. C: Chen Kuan-tai, Jin Gang, Wilson Tong, Shi Zhong-tian, Liang Chia-ren, Chi Kuan-chun, Sun Jia-lin, Ma Ji, Liu Yin-shan, Chen Mu-chuan, Li Ying, Viola Gu Yin.

Because of contract disputes with Shaw Brothers, Chen Kuan-tai got into directing. The head of Shaw Brothers, Run Run Shaw, was a shrewd business-man known for short-changing actors by playing on their desperation for work money. For example, when the studio was about to let superstar Lo Lieh go, the actor was so desperate to stay that he agreed to half his usual salary. But when it was Chen Kuan-tai's neck on the line, he left Shaw Brothers and gave himself the freedom to pursue his own acting career as well as to direct. Although perhaps not as successful as he had hoped, he made one film of great conse-quence: *Iron Monkey*, in which he plays the real-life martial arts champion of the

people Tie Ma-liu. For the first time, Chen was able to show his expertise in the two skills close to his heart: Monkey King Splitting and Deflecting Arm skills.

When General Ching (Jin Gang) rants that he wants to eradicate all Ming rebels, his witch hunt starts with Master Tie, the rebel leader. Tie's whole family is arrested, and his daughter becomes sex fodder for the Ming traitor who sold out one of her brothers. Just as all of this is happening, Tie's useless, gambling, nonmartial artist son, Tie Ma-liu (Chen Kuan-tai), stumbles home and tries to help his family. The Manchu officers brutally beat him, and his family members ignore Ma-liu for his own protection. That's because if they admitted to the Man-chus that he was there son, Ma-liu would have been arrested and sentenced to death. So before Ma-liu blurts out that these are his parents, a close family friend steps in and acts like he's Ma-liu's father by hitting Ma-liu and saying he is a worthless son for interfering with the Manchus doing their work.

After his parents and family are dragged away to be executed, Ma-liu runs away and vows to avenge them by killing General Ching. After aimlessly wandering the countryside, Ma-liu ends up at the Shaolin Temple. He wins over the heart of Bitter Monk (Chen Mu-chuan), who takes it upon himself to teach Ma-liu monkey kung fu. When Manchu soldiers come to the temple looking for fighters to be bodyguards for Ching, Ma-liu volunteers for the job even though it is against all temple rules; he's that determined to assassinate Ching. To gain the confidence of Ching's other protectors and increase his chances of getting close to the general, Ma-liu proves himself by beating up innocent people, including some of his fellow Shaolin kung fu brothers. But it works. Ching is im-pressed with Ma-liu's skills, dedication and ruthlessness. He brings Ma-liu in for an interview to be one of his bodyguards. Ma-liu's pain has its rewards because he can now have his day of reckoning with the general.

Suffice it to say, this is the most relaxed I have ever seen Chen Kuan-tai fight. He moves smoothly around the screen, as would be expected, since the kung fu he demonstrates is his style of styles. Even with transitions from high to low stances and vice versa, his posture remains constant and his body motions are fluid. Also, when Chen is using monkey skills in the film, the filmmakers don't undercrank the camera. This means that rather than artificially making him move fast, Chen was able to step things up a gear and be naturally fast. The best thing about his monkey styles is that he does them without having to act foolish, like actor Xiao Ho in *Mad Monkey Kung Fu* (1979; see martialogy).

The film's opening is excellent because Chen Kuan-tai makes the directo-rial decision to feature a real fight between a monkey and a hawk intercut with humans copying the movements. Chen explained to me that he had absorbed a lot of filmmaking skills while working at Shaw Brothers. After he read the *Iron Monkey* script, he was able to visualize the scenes and didn't need to have a script on set while shooting the film; it came out marvelous. For the aforementioned animal fight, there were no special effects or stock footage used. It was real. Chen recalled that they wasted a lot of footage trying to film a monkey and a hawk fighting. The animals were so uncontrollable that he just did tons of shots and selected the best ones later. There is also a scene in which Chen attacks a small monkey and it defends itself against his prodding and poking.

Interesting side note: Two years after being this film's fight choreographer, Chen Mu-chuan would land his first lead role as a drunken monkey kung fu stylist in *Monkey Fist, Floating Snake* (1979).

Several years ago, Chen Kuan-tai told me that he did *Iron Monkey* because it was about the heritage of his school of martial arts and his martial arts train-ing. As it turned out, he knew it was going to be a hit before it was released. This is because the movie only cost about 1 million Hong Kong dollars to make, but the distributors offered Chen 5 million for the movie.

Titleography: *Bloody Monkey Master*; *The Iron Monkey of Shaolin*; *School of Shaolin*. Translations—*Tie Ma-liu* and *Iron Monkey*. Tie Ma-liu is the lead character, and *Iron Monkey* is his nickname. **MA Percentage: 42.33%**

IRON OX, THE TIGER'S KILLER

鐵牛伏虎 (1974—Taiwan) **90m. KFI: Huang Fei-lung. NOT/LOT: 1/ 18s; NOF/LOF: 9/ 29m 17s.** D: Jin Sheng-en. C: Wang Guan-xiong, Zi Lan, Huang Fei-lung, Ceng Chao, Zheng Ji-ping, Zhou Ming-qing, Ma Chang, You Peng-shing.

If a tree falls in the forest and no one is around to hear it, does it make a sound? If a tree falls in the forest and was cut down by a lumberjack who used his hands to chop it down, should you be afraid of that man? The answer to both questions is yes.

Chan Ming-lung (Wang Guan-xiong) takes only three years to learn the secrets of his crippled master's kung fu from the two revered books of their style. He celebrates becoming the ultimate kung fu fighter by chopping down a stand of trees with his bare hands. But when Chan's master misinterprets the chumminess of Chan's girlfriend, Ellen (Zi Lan), with a former boyfriend, trouble follows. The ex-boyfriend is a member of the Five Tigers, a group headed by the town's police chief, Wong Chin-lao (Huang Fei-lung). Chan's master violently confronts the young man, who, along with his three friends, accidentally kills the man, which enrages Chan. One by one, the Five Tigers begin disappearing, leading to a heated investigation by Chief Wong, who suspects Chan has murdered the four tigers. Wong is long arm of the law, but Chan has his own idea of justice.

Like many independently made kung fu films prior to 1976, the fights in *Iron Ox, the Tiger's Killer* are full of arm flailing and windmill strikes, but choreographer Huang's use of tight and medium shots that fill the frame with action helps. The audience is forced to focus its attention on full-blown visuals of twisting and twirling upper bodies rather than Wang's sloppy kung fu and bad stances. (You can't see them because they are not in frame.) Shooting the fights this way also sets up a piece of photographic and choreographic genius.

Wang has an interesting fight on top of the famous Shaolin wooden posts (see *Secret of the Shaolin Poles* for a description) against one of the Five Tigers. There are just enough real shots of Wang on the tall posts to give the impression he is indeed fighting on them. To further sell the scene, much of the intricate choreography is actually performed with Wang on sheets of plywood atop the poles, which are carefully concealed out of frame and still leave the other poles visible. This is not to take anything away from Wang, because during the shots in which we can see him actually doing footwork and fighting on the posts, it looks as though the shoot was very windy, and that is no easy feat.

Titleography: *Angry Fist*. Translation—*Iron Cow (Ox)*, *Yielding Tiger*. The hero's anger comes from what he interprets as losing his girlfriend and his teacher's life to the Five Tigers gang, thus *Angry Fist*. Iron Ox refers to Chan, and the *Yielding Tiger* is Chief Wong: Chan's iron fist kung fu is as strong as an ox, and Wong is a member of the Five Tigers who is cautious and does not rush his judgments. **MA Percentage: 32.87%**

IRON SWALLOW

鐵 燕 (1978—Taiwan) **87m. FI: He Ming-xiao, Wang Yong-sheng. NOT/ LOT: 3/ 1m 27s; NOF/LOF: 21/ 20m 14s.** D: Zhang Pei-cheng. C: Chia Ling, Wong Dao, Ding Hua-chong, Wang Yong-sheng, Yee Yuan, Ou Li-bao.

A man has nothing to fear so long as his conscience is clear. On the surface, *Iron Swallow* plays like Cheng Pei-pei's *Golden Swallow* (1968). When *Golden Swallow* kills someone, she leaves a calling card: one of her signature darts. Her opponent Silver Roc uses a similar dart to frame her for murder in order to draw her out. In the same vein, Iron Swallow (Chia Ling) is also known for leaving a unique dart behind, and so in order to lure her into the open, the evil hit man Wu (Wang Yong-sheng) begins leaving a similar dart when he assassinates someone.

In this film, Tie Yin (aka Iron Swallow) goes on a rampage and attacks four prominent leaders in the world of Jiang Hu (a parallel world influenced by martial lore surviving by its own laws and code of ethics) for crimes they committed against her father a decade ago. The head of the foursome, Chu Xiao-tien (Yee Yuan), relocates his three maimed friends and hires a hit man to hunt down Tie Yin, all in order to hide the 10-year secret from his son, Tu Lung (Wong Dao), and his favorite kung fu student, Gou Fang (Ding Hua-chong). As more lies are exposed, the truth turns out to be more than Tu Lung and Gou Fang can bear. The two are forced into choosing sides, sides that will either make them work together or kill each other.

Iron Swallow makes use of some very creative camera work, such as circular tracking shots and the liberal use of slow motion during critical moments in the film. It all blends well with the overall visual style of the movie. Chia Ling's kicks are sharp, and most of the choreography by Wang Yong-sheng and He Ming-xiao keeps the fights within the tight confines of an invisible circle, where

the actors exchange blocks, ducks and strikes. It is very engaging and looks great on-screen. Chia Ling's opening fight is especially eye-catching: Her opponent gallops toward her on a horse, and as he leaps off the horse toward the camera, the camera swivels around in a continuous shot to follow the attacker into a short but sweet duel.

Titleography: *Shaolin Iron Eagle*. Translation—*Iron Swallow*. This is yet another example of an English title that sticks the word *Shaolin* into the title even though the film has nothing to do with Shaolin. The English title probably uses *Eagle* because it sounds more exciting than *Swallow*. **MA Percentage: 24.92%**

JADE FACED ASSASSIN, THE

玉 面 俠 and 絕 代 雙 驕 (1970—Hong Kong) **104m. FI: Han Guo. NOT/LOT: None; NOF/LOF: 17/ 10m 2s.** D: Yen Chun. C: Lily Ho, Gao Yuan, Ku Feng, Fan Mei-sheng, Chang Pei-shan, Pan Ying-zi, Irene Chen Yi-ling, Essie Lin Chia, Di Nuo, Luo Han, Yen Chun.

In the early and mid-1970s, as budgets increased and backlots became more extravagant on Shaw Brothers *wuxia* films, the fight scenes dwindled. To maintain the feeling that films were action-packed, fight scenes would be spaced throughout a film's duration. In *The Jade Faced Assassin*, for example, the story and visuals are downright awesome, but only 10 minutes are dedicated to swordplay and kung fu fight scenes. Films such as this could be produced more quickly because fight scenes take a long time and a lot of work to shoot, especially when the actors are untrained in martial arts. For example, stunt doubles might have to be inserted at just the right time. Also keep in mind that action shooting was usually done with one camera, often in extremely hot weather. So less fighting meant less hassle and a faster turnaround.

In this film, twins Siao Lu-er and Tse Xin-chan of the Chang Cheun Clan are separated at childhood to protect them from the evil Weird Four from Lao Shan. But Tse is pronounced dead, so hero Lian Lan-yan (Ku Feng) is reportedly given a special creed (mark of the clan) and told to give it to Siao when Siao is old enough to seek revenge. The plan goes awry when a group of villains in Happy Valley called the Tu Clan kidnap Siao and injure Lian beyond repair using the Deadly Palm Beauty, Smiling Sword, Thigh Eating Mouth and Heaven of Full Star skills. Lian is rescued by the Poison Scholar under the guise of doing medical experiments, which he claims will benefit the Tus later on.

Members of the Tu Clan are afraid of re-entering the Wu Lin world (the strict martial arts subdivision of the Jiang Hu underworld) because they have made so many enemies, but they devise a plan to teach Siao their aforementioned kung fu so she can lead them to glory. But as Siao grows up into a beautiful woman (Lily Ho), she defeats the Tus, thanks to the righteous advice of Lian, who still has bad *chi* flow and does not have his kung fu back. He tells Siao to leave Happy Valley and seek revenge against those who killed her parents and her twin. Dressed as a man, Siao wanders the Jiang Hu world with a heavy heart and a light sword to find the truth and the lost creed (the famous Nam Tin Seven Styles Sword book). As it turns out, Lian never had the creed, but once Siao finds it, the full truth will come out.

In the world of Wu Lin, one's kung fu can be measured by simple skills other than fighting, which is why one will see chopsticks, money and cups flying around and sticking into wood or candles, and furniture being sliced and diced. These were usually shot in those famous inn scenes, most notably in the Cheng

Pei-pei-starring *Come Drink With Me* (1966) and her fight at the village Inn.

In this film, Lian says he has bad chi flow and needs to get his kung fu back. This is actually a real phenomenon when someone gets injured by certain kinds of kung fu skills, skills that are intended to disrupt chi flow. (Chi is one's inner energy, life force or vital energy.) When that happens, one loses his or her kung fu abilities. Sometimes it can take years to build the chi back, at which point one can practice kung fu again.

Titleography: As of this writing, no alternative titles could be found. Translations—*Jade Faced Chivalrous Hero* and *Matchless Twin Heroic Beauties*. There is no assassin per se in the film. The Chinese titles are very romanticized, as was common for films based on wuxia novels. For the *Jade Faced Chivalrous Hero* title, the first two characters, translated as *Jade Face,* refer to the hero being good-looking and have nothing to do with any kind of gemstone. The final character, "xia," is the second character of "wuxia," thus saying the film is a period wuxia film. *Matchless Twin Heroic Beauties* also plays up the attractiveness of the twins. A remake of this story, *The Proud Twins* (1979), uses the novel's Chinese title as its own and stars Alexander Fu Sheng as one of the "beautiful twins." **MA Percentage: 9.65%** SHAW BROTHERS

JADE TIGER, THE

白玉老虎 (1977—Hong Kong) **100m. FI:** Tang Chia, Huang Pei-ji. **NOT/LOT: None; NOF/LOF:** 30/ 17m 34s. D: Chu Yuan. C: Ti Lung, Yueh Hua, Ku Feng, Lily Li, Fan Mei-sheng, Lo Lieh, Derek Yee, Shih Szu.

The modern world has been plagued by chemical warfare since at least World War I. Due to moral dilemmas and ethical questions, such weapons have been prohibited by international laws and treaties like the Geneva Protocol. Things are similar in the Jiang Hu world. Although clans vie for supremacy at nearly any cost, clans that use weapons of vicious poisons are considered to be dishonorable. In *The Jade Tiger*, for example, the bottom line to the whole story is about finding where an evil clan is making and stockpiling poison-based weapons in an effort to take over Jiang Hu.

It is Zhao Wu-ji's (Ti Lung) wedding day, and he is set to marry the love of his life, Qian Qian (Lily Li). The opposing Tang family arrives with 10,000 taels of gold—and it's not a gift for the bride and groom but a bounty for the head of Zhao Jian, leader of the Zhao Clan. The next day, Zhao Jian's most trusted assistant, Shang Guan-ren (Ku Feng), delivers Zhao's head to the Tang Clan and becomes an honored member of the Tangs. Wu-ji goes after Shang, but before he gets his revenge, he must force Shang to tell him where he hid a white jade tiger statue he stole because there is an important document inside it. An unnamed killer injures Wu-ji by keeping his eyes on him—yep, he literally takes his eyes out of his sockets and throws them at Wu-ji. As they explode, a child saves him and takes him to Hate Free Hall, a place where swordsmen go to leave the world of Wu Lin. The leader tells Wu-ji that hate is the most serious sickness. He says poison can take one life, but hatred poisons more lives.

His words are a portent of things to come. A half-crazed man (Lo Lieh) approaches Wu-ji in a restaurant, which forces him to go undercover as a Tang Clan supporter; that leads to Wu-ji being poisoned by a killer and rescued by a mysterious brother (Yueh Hua) and sister (Shih Szu). Wu-ji then has to forsake his fiancée in order to marry the sister and to keep his cover, which leads to double and triple crosses and turns Wu-ji's life upside down. It is a tragedy worthy of *Macbeth*, and Hate Free Hall may be Wu-ji's only chance for redemption.

In discussions with fellow screenwriters who are fans of kung fu cinema, one common gripe I've heard is that in many of these old films, particularly the *wuxia* movies dealing with Jiang Hu and Wu Lin (especially those by Chu Yuan), there is a lack of character development. In other words, we never learn more about each character beyond him or her being a hero or a villain. Part of the reason is that these old kung fu films are often based on novels or serialized comic book stories with rich histories, and they are well-known to the Chinese. For connoisseurs of these stories, there are many nuances inherent in the behavior, fighting styles, weapon choices and philosophies of the characters. When storytellers create red herrings and twists, many times out of left field, they often play on a Chinese audience's expectations of how a certain character should act, thus adding an element of surprise. That is why in this film, the hero can be naïve in one scene and then, though it appears to be out of character, be amazingly clever in another.

Titleography: As of this writing, no alternative titles could be found. Translation— *The White Jade Tiger*. **MA Percentage: 17.57%** SHAW BROTHERS

Still from *The Jade Tiger* © Celestial Pictures Ltd. All rights reserved.

JAGUAR LIVES

El Felino (1979—USA/Spain) **86m. AS:** Joe Lewis. **NOT/LOT:** 3/ 2m 27s; **NOF/LOF:** 5/ 4m 4s. D: Ernest Pintoff. C: Joe Lewis, Christopher Lee, Donald Pleasence, Barbara Bach, Capucine, Joseph Wiseman, Woody Strode, John Huston, Gabriel Melgar, Anthony De Longis.

Oh no—another world champion American martial artist tries his hand at doing a martial arts movie. Please excuse my brashness, but during the 1970s, the United States had too many world champion martial artists (a trend that spilled into the 1980s). According to karate magazines I read at the time, the martial arts world was pretty much limited to America, Japan, a few fighters from Europe and possibly a couple from Canada, hardly representative of the entire world.

Overall, 1979 world karate champion Joe Lewis—one of only five men to defeat possibly the best point fighter at that time, Chuck Norris—has a few moments of martial arts sparkle in his film debut as Jonathan Cross. Code-named the Jaguar, Cross travels the globe trying to break up a drug cartel headed by the secretive Esteban while also saving the world from the Scaramanga-esque clutches of Adam Caine (Christopher Lee, who played Bond villain Scaramanga in 1974's *The Man With the Golden Gun*) and searching out the truth about his best friend, Brett (Anthony de Longis, the Spanish swordsman who fought Jet Li in *Fearless* in 2006).

Christopher Lee had recently starred in David Carradine's *Circle of Iron* (1978) and was primed for his second martial-arts-influenced film. Years ago I had the chance to interview Lee; he was shocked that I knew he acted in these films. He also said that the young men doing the fighting were physically impressive and that he enjoyed doing a film genre that he was less traveled in. Also worth noting is that de Longis also starred in *Circle of Iron*.

Lewis' first kick combo in his first fight, although simple, is effective on film and looks reminiscent of some of Norris' kicking combos. However, Lewis' are faster and come across as more powerful. This is undoubtedly a consequence of this film being shot in 1979; the American filmmakers were starting to understand a little bit (and I mean a wee bit) about martial arts choreography. Perhaps his most sparkling moment is knocking two stuntmen off their motorcycles at the same time with a jumping split kick. This film also demonstrates the beauty of sound effects and close shots: You can wave a weapon in the air back and forth like a wagging stick and it looks and sounds cool, even if the moves are completely fake.

Yet Lewis and his *sai* made me sigh because unlike most Hong Kong films, the fights in *Jaguar Lives* seem to get worse as the movie goes along. In terms of choreography, the fights lack rhythm. Combatants do a few techniques, run to a new place, do a few more techniques, run to a new place, etc. And there is no fight payback, which is best exemplified by the final fight, during which the villain trips off a wall and plunges to his death. There is plenty of the actors flexing their muscles and posing for the camera rather than demonstrating their martial arts skills, which we all know they have in abundance. This film once again shows that just because someone is a real martial artist or even a champion, it does not mean he will be good on screen.

Titleography: As of this writing, no alternative titles could be found. **MA Percentage: 7.58%**

JEET KUNE THE CLAWS AND THE SUPREME KUNG FU

截拳鷹爪功 (1979—Hong Kong) **92m. MAI: Wong Mei, Da Xi-yan. NOT/LOT: 1/ 40s; NOF/LOF: 14/ 22m 17s.** D: Lee Tso-nam. C: Bruce Li, Ku Feng, Tong Yen-shen, Zhou Xiao-lai, Fang Ye, Hon Gwok-choi, Liu Hao-nian, Shan Guai.

With so many fists of fury flying around and so many Bruces punching and pounding the Japanese, it is no wonder China and Japan are still at odds over their pasts. In what appears to be the last installment of the *Fist of Fury* franchise, Chen Shen (Bruce Li) brings his brother Chen Chen's (Bruce Lee) altar back home from Shanghai to Macao in hopes of starting a new beginning. The Japanese martial arts school in Macao catches wind of Chen Shen's arrival and decides to settle the score against the Chen brothers for causing their school lose face in Shanghai. Also standing in Chen Shen's path is a new enemy, Shu Tang (Tong Yen-shen), a tough Chinese martial artist; the Japanese have convinced Shu Tang that Chen Shen is moving in on his girl.

Copycat Bruce Lee movies have always tried to convince the audience that their Bruce impersonators were comparable to the original, despite the obvious evidence to the contrary. One way to show off an impersonator's skill was through the standard kung fu training sequences. But the beauty of Bruce Lee was that it was not necessary to showcase his skills in this manner because he had nothing to prove. It was as clear as Kareem Abdul-Jabbar standing in a rice field that Lee was good. In terms of kicking, what separates Lee from his impersonators—and for that matter, all the other kung stars noted for leg work—is Lee's arm and hand postures used during the kicking process. When a star has to flail his or her arms away from the body during kicks instead of keeping them close to the body, it is a sign of poor balance. To the untrained eye, it's barely noticeable, but it is there.

What is curious about this film is that the lead Japanese fighter (Ku Feng) is not established in the movie as a cruel, ruthless and highly skilled martial artist, and he comes out of the blue at the end of the film to take on Chen Shen. Ultimately, this diminishes the importance of the duel. Perhaps realizing that three would not be a charm, director Lee Tso-nam caved in and had Li touch one of his bleeding wounds during the fight and lick the blood, as Lee does in *Enter the Dragon*. Even then it's obvious Li is no Lee.

Titleography: *Fist of Fury (Part) 3*; *Fist(s) of Fury III*; *Fist of Fury 2*; *The Fist of Fury (3)*; *Chinese Connection 3*. Translation—*Jeet Kune Eagle Claw Kung Fu*. Although the first two characters of the Chinese title are from the name of Bruce Lee's martial art (*jeet kune do*), there is no obvious eagle claw fighting in the film. Not wanting to get into all the various *Fist of Fury* explanations again (see *Chinese Connection 2*), I will note that the on-screen title of *Fist of Fury 3* has the numeral "3" superimposed onto the screen in a different font and color, almost as if it was made into a sequel by the distributors as an afterthought. The original release title is a play on the Chinese translation. **MA Percentage: 24.94%**

JONG-ARNG PAYONG

(1971—Thailand) **126m. FI: Uncredited. NOT/LOT: 1/ 1m 46s; NOF/LOF: 30/ 22m 14s.** D: Noi Kamolwatin. C: Sombat Methanee, Suthisa Pattanuch, Lee Ling Ling.

The spirit of *krabi krabong* shall pour in the rains of life to set the mind free, show clarity of loyalty and wash away treachery. Only a handful of Thai martial arts films are featured as martialogies, and the few films I was able to procure are undoubtedly not a full reflection of the rich martial arts culture of Thailand. Furthermore, I do not speak or read Thai, so my apologies for my lack of capturing any significant historical elements or even identifying the correct names of characters.

The film opens with a colorful and inspired festival at a riverside village featuring a Thai version of lion dancing, which is interrupted by a group of vicious vagabonds who attack the unsuspecting villagers. Three unrelated children—two boys named Pi Pet and Jin Hai and one girl—witness the senseless slaughter of their parents. These memories are pictures etched into their minds that become the seeds for brutal vengeance. Another little girl's mother survives but has an arm severed, which futilely grasps the sand as blood pools around it.

Time passes, but the thirst for revenge does not. Jin Hai (Suthisa Pattanuch) and the girl from the original three, now grown up, return from China having learned the way of the sword. They join the one-armed mother's daughter (Lee Ling Ling), a krabi krabong crusader for the downtrodden. Unfortunately, the other boy, Pi Pet (major 1970s Thai action star Sombat Methanee), who was the best friend of Jin Hai, somehow became the foster child of the bandit leader, so when his three brethren attack the bandit's bamboo jungle castle, Pi Pet fights them with the ferocity of a Thai tiger. Meanwhile, the bandits are planning to ambush the Royal Thai Army as they head off to war against Burma. The bandits aim their giant stolen cannons at the unsuspecting troops passing through the valley.

During a major skirmish, Jin Hai and Pi Pet chase each other into the jungle, miles away from the fort, where they cross steel in an epic krabi krabong-Chinese sword battle. The duel rages on for several days, through heat, mosquitoes and a torrential downpour. While they are sloshing around in the mud and puddles, bodies shivering from the cold, Pi Pet's memory returns. The four avenging children reunite, and with help of fellow villagers, they march on the bandit stronghold to quell the evil and to save the glorious army of the king of Thailand.

After watching more than 200 Shaw Brothers films, I was not expecting much from this film. To my utter surprise, it has some good choreography and stunts (albeit rudimentary) and a few unexpectedly gory deathblows. There is a lot of hand-held camerawork, mostly in close shots, mixed with quick pans and constant spins and movement by stuntmen in the background, which is similar to Hong Kong films. One major scene has the four heroes taking on a load of bandits in a two-minute sequence of individual shots with each shot lasting only a few seconds. Each shot simply shows one of the heroes killing a villain with just a single death strike. It is more dizzying than a bad music video that tries to fool us into thinking its stars can dance—except the Thai stars can fight … to a point. And the krabi krabong is interesting to watch, perhaps because it is so different from the usual samurai and Chinese sword fights.

Krabi krabong is a traditional Thai martial art with a 400-year history. It can be traced back to the ruins of Wat Putthai Swah, a sacred place with its foundation during Thailand's Ayutthaya period (1351-1767). Besides its open-hand skills being the predecessor for *muay boran* (a forerunner of *muay* Thai), krabi krabong, which roughly translates as "sword" and "stick," incorporates nine different weapons into the art. Perhaps the most recognizable is the krabi (or *daab*, a long-handled sword), most popularly shown in films as *daab song meu*, which has the user wielding a sword in each hand.

Titleography: As of this writing, no alternative titles could be found. **MA Percentage: 19.05%**

JUDGEMENT OF AN ASSASSIN

殺令 (1977—Hong Kong) **92m. FI: Tang Chia, Huang Pei-ji. NOT/LOT: None; NOF/LOF: 38/ 23m 37s.** D: Sun Chung. C: David Chiang, Tsung Hua, Ching Li, Michael Chan, Ku Feng, Gu Guan-zhong, Frankie Wei Hong, Liu Hui-ling, Ai Fei, Wang Lai.

Learning kung fu the old-fashioned way is a big part of the world of Jiang Hu, a sub-society that parallels the normal societies of the real world. It is about brotherhood between students and fellow martial artists, training not to fight, and the ultimate goal of learning to heal rather than hurt. Within the Jiang Hu world, there is a sub-community known as Wu Lin. There, martial inhabitants often vie to be the head fighter, swordsman or clan leader. They attain that position by adhering to the unwritten but respected ethical codes of righteousness, loyalty, chivalry and gallantry. However, there are those in the Wu Lin world who would forego the virtuous ways and try to gain power and position through deceit and violence. Wu Lin is a dangerous place, and many martial heroes would choose to roam these lands alone.

Judgement of an Assassin is a Wu Lin tale of competition, as clans fight to eliminate their rivals so that only one can enjoy the spoils of martial glory. When Yu Bao (Gu Guan-zhong) of the Sin Ha Clan is accused of wiping out the Golden Ax Clan, he is arrested and scheduled to be tried by the leaders of Wu Lin at Madam Fa Si-gu's (Wang Lai) estate, where she will preside over the trial. Yu is transported to the trial in a closed coffin covered in sharp spikes driven through the wood, the points sticking into Yu's blood-patched body.

To prevent violence at the trial, two famous martial fighters are hired: Golden Whip Man Ying-tai (Tsung Hua) and Swift Sword Hei Mo-le (David Chiang). We first see Hei flashing his perpetual smirking face while using his sword (with its handle attached perpendicularly at one end of the blade) to

induce a large blood spatter from an attacker. Yu explains to Hei that the Bai Du Clan wants to make war among the clans, and so the clan framed him. When Hei offers to remove the coffin spikes, one of the core sensibilities of Jiang Hu is revealed as Yu calmly says, "Honor comes before everything else; I will endure until my name is cleared." With that, Hei emotionally blurts, "I admire you. I must have you as my friend." That about says it all.

But at the trial, everything comes out in the open. Eventually, the real culprit shows his freaky face—it's Bloody Devil (Michael Chan), a man whose kung fu is so feared that he was banished from Wu Lin. He is back and more dangerous than before, and not even the combined efforts of Madame Fa, Old Hedgehog (Ku Feng) and Hei seem a match for him. In the end, something has to give, and that something is a flag.

Although many films use loud sound effects to bludgeon audiences into accepting false kung fu skills, in *Judgement*, loud sound effects are used during particular fights to make clear who the potent martial arts characters are in the film. Director Chu Yuan has a good eye for visuals, and his expertise of motion and vision meld effectively throughout the whole film, particularly with the intricate camera choreography of the fights.

Titleography: As of this writing, no alternative titles could be found. Translation—*Order for a Determined Kill*. The English title reflects the trial aspect of the film, and the Chinese title alludes to the assassination aspect. *Judgement* is spelled with an "e" because that is just the way it was released in Hong Kong. **MA Percentage: 25.67%** SHAW BROTHERS

KAALA SONA

(1975—India) **120m. AD: Ravi Khanna. NOT/LOT: None; NOF/LOF: 8/ 3m 21s.** D: Ravikant Nagaich. C: Feroz Khan, Parveen Babi, Prem Chopra, Danny Denzongpa, Farida Jalal, Imtiaz Khan, Helen.

If the Lone Ranger and his sidekick Tonto were in India, then it would be in this film. With cowboy looks and a gun in hand, Rakeesh (Feroz Khan) pursues his father's long-thought-to-be-dead killer, Poppy Singh (Prem Chopra), on horseback into the Wild West of India. Rakeesh partners up with Shera (Danny Denzongpa of Nepalese heritage), a native mountain man whose buckskin apparel, beaded headband and fringe hairstyle resemble the Chiricahua Apache Geronimo. The two become blood brothers and team up to free the enslaved plainspeople working in Singh's poppy fields, halt the drug trade and take down Singh, who looks and acts a bit like Quentin Tarantino's character from *Planet Terror* (2007).

Genre films inspired by American cowboy movies are known as spaghetti Westerns in Italy and noodle Westerns in Japan; India's version is the basmati Western. *Kaala Sona*, like many of the interesting Indian films in this book, has few fight scenes, but whenever Ravi Khanna is the action director, it is always worth the look. What helps to make the fights exciting is that the actors apply the same hyper energy seen in the song and dance choreography. And because these films all have an original music score, the rapid-fire drums and high-

pitched violin squeals add to the frenetic rush of action. In contrast, Hong Kong kung fu films often use the same soundtracks and recognizable musical cues, so fights from different films can appear overly repetitive.

The fights in *Kaala Sona* are replete with jumping front kicks, inside crescent kicks, flying side kicks, ax duels, kips, flips, rolls and a good smattering of *jujutsu*-like throws. The final fight is very energetic when the locals get into a brawl against Singh's henchmen. A woman uses a whip to entangle and hurl a baddie, a 5-year-old kid starts to throw his weight around, and the Walter Brennan-like village drunkard hits a few bad guys. Rakeesh's love interest, Durga (Parveen Babi), even starts whacking away during the fray with a pole and even pole-vaults herself into a man riding away on a horse. Then, out of left field, as Rakeesh is fighting Singh in what appears to be a dry, dusty area, the two leap off a cliff with sleds and speed down a snow-packed hill, where the final blow is dealt by an earthquake. Enough said?

Titleography: As of this writing, no alternative titles could be found. **MA Percentage: 2.79%**

KARATE BEAR FIGHTER

Kyokuskin Kenka Karate Burai Ken (1977—Japan) **87m. FI: Uncredited. NOT/ LOT: 5/ 2m 11s; NOF/LOF: 17/ 17m 52s.** D: Kazushiko Yamaguchi. C: Sonny Chiba, Eiji Go, Yutaka Nakajima, Etsuko Shihomi, Yumi Takigawa, Tetsuro Tanba.

Karate Bear Fighter is the second film in Sonny Chiba's trilogy and homage to his karate *sensei* Mas Oyama. (See *Champion of Death* and *Karate for Life*.) It follows Oyama (Sonny Chiba) as he challenges karate instructors, becomes a drunkard, gets heavily mixed up with the Yakuza, loses his karate spirit, fights a bear in order to help raise money for a little boy's sick father to receive treatment at a hospital, finds his karate spirit, takes on another bunch of vengeful and shady characters along the Ikebukuro seaside, and then moves on to part three of the film.

The plot is pretty cut-and-dry, but there are a few pivotal moments in the film worth detailing. The first occurs after a fight in a reed-infested area, when Oyama meets Gunji Uchiyama, a master of rod fencing. He teaches Oyama several philosophical lessons in life and about himself, which come to fruition later in the film. Later, when he fights the bear, Oyama ends up helping a little boy named Rintaro, who was born in a dump. His mother is dead, and his father is a drunk. Only Oyama is far from Tobacco Road—he is in Hokkaido. Rintaro's father needs money for medical treatment, and a rich man offers Oyama money if he can defeat a giant bear, which he does with a phenomenal eye poke that is unbearable to watch. The actor's bear costume is pretty convincing, and the fight was shot in such a way that it's only a few edits away from being believable. Although Rintaro begs Oyama to stay, Oyama must leave, as he must conquer his final demons in order to reach karate completion.

In terms of the karate aspects of the film, during the opening credits the real Oyama performs his style's *sanchin kata*. (See *Budo: The Art of Killing* for an explanation of this.) Chiba then fights a couple of karate students, and there is a very peculiar shot of Oyama breaking several slabs of ice. Why peculiar? The shot starts off in a wide angle, and we can plainly see Oyama as he winds up to break it; then the angle goes tight on the ice. In that shot, we no longer see Oyama's face, and the ice has obvious fissures, the exact breaking points of the ice when it is hit. On the cool side, the fights have fewer hand-held camera shots, no shaking (finally, thank goodness) and better camera-angle selection that reveals more real contact to bring out Oyama's view on contact during *kumite* (fights): heavy contact.

Chiba does one of his patented front-angle high-flying kicks (lacking in the first installment) that emphasize the skill and heroic nature of Chiba's Oyama. There is also a great unedited tracking shot in which Chiba fights three guys: They first move to the right for about 20 feet, then fight a bit, then move back to the original mark while still fighting. Bravo.

Titleography: *Kyokushin Karate Fist 2*. Translation—*Fighting Kyokashinkai Karate, the Ultimate Truth Brute Fist*. **MA Percentage: 23.05%**

KARATE FOR LIFE

Sora-te Baka Ichidai and *Karate Baka-Ichidai* (1977—Japan) **90m. FI: Uncredited. NOT/LOT: 2/ 1m 20s; NOF/LOF: 28/ 24m 37s.** D: Kazuhiko Yamaguchi. C: Sonny Chiba, Kojiro Hongo, Hideo Murota, Masaru Shiga.

In the venerable words of *sosai* (a martial arts style founder) Masutatsu Oyama, "A human life gains luster and strength only when it is polished and tempered." In Part 3 of Sonny Chiba's homage to his karate *sensei* (see *Champion of Death* and *Karate Bear Fighter*), Oyama (played by Sonny Chiba) gains that luster and strength through helping others. And even when he really needs the money, he does not sacrifice his spirit of karate honor and *budo* soul for the almighty yen.

This film is something of a cinematic rarity—especially for martial arts cinema—in that the final installment of the trilogy has the best fights. The first 10 minutes of the film feature a fight that is, in my opinion, the best pure karate fight I have ever seen in Japanese film, and possibly in all of karate martial arts cinema (though the fights in *Black Belt* (2007) are also good). It is certainly Chiba's best on-screen fight and possibly the longest sustained karate fight in Japanese martial arts film; it clocks in at approximately eight and a half minutes total.

Continuing the narrative from the second film, Mas Oyama's fame spreads. A good-hearted but naïve fight promoter approaches Oyama with the idea of taking on large Western opponents. Oyama does not realize that he and his new tag-team partner, Fujita (Kojiro Hongo), Japan's No. 1 judo practitioner, will be pitted against other people in pro-wrestling-like matches controlled by the Yakuza. When Oyama and Fujita refuse to lose and do serious damage to their opponents, the Yakuza set out to put them in their places, and the two friends must tag-team for real.

For me, the film was totally unexpected. It is movies like this that have made writing this book a pleasure. The opening fight, in which Oyama takes on 100 karate students without a break, is well shot. It uses mostly medium and wide angles so each martial arts technique is clearly shown. The fights also demonstrate the Japanese warrior maxim of "one strike, certain death." Close shots are used to emphasize certain techniques or the crunching force of Chiba's strikes.

Chiba makes good contact with the people he is blocking or striking, and each technique is delivered with true focus. He does not strike with excessive body motion, which action stars commonly do to give the impression of power. In a scene where oil is thrown all over the dojo's floor, there are no tricky or neat-looking balance routines like you would probably see in Hong Kong kung fu films. Chiba slides around as you would expect on an oil-slicked floor but uses martial techniques that blend in with the reality of the terrain. The oil-slick sequence is part of the violent *kumite* scene, and it is this complete opening fight sequence that puts this film into my top 20 must-see films of the 1970s.

But what starts as a great film eventually deteriorates due to the plot and some bogus subplots. The film's end features Oyama amid sparkly Lalo Schifrin music from *Enter the Dragon* (1973) in a mirrored chamber trying to figure out which reflection is the real person to strike. So although the ending may have been an homage to Bruce Lee, the movie turns into a snowstorm during the Summer Olympics—it is out of place.

Titleography: *Oyama's Lifetime of Karate.* **MA Percentage: 28.83%**

KARATE KILLERS, THE

怪客 (1973—Hong Kong) **87m. KFI: Chan Shao-peng. NOT/LOT: None; NOF/LOF: 24/ 35m 52s.** D: Bao Fang, Yeung Man-yi. C: Bai Biao, Tony Liu Junk-guk, Gao Gang, Xue Gu-yan, Ba Shan, Feng Yi, Shi Xiu, Du Wei-he.

The British Empire, which once spanned two thirds of the world, has been chastised for its presence in China and Hong Kong, but there is plausible evidence to suggest that the empire contributed to the establishment of the Republic of China because many Chinese patriots would find refuge in Hong Kong from Manchu death squads. This is one of the few Chinese films that recognize the British presence in Hong Kong as a detriment to the Manchus.

In this film with minimal dialogue, the head Manchu in Canton, An Kung (Gao Gang), is a horrendous human whose hair harries the republic duelists. (It's not so much that An Kung has a hair-brained scheme as hair gone mad.) He hunts down freedom fighter Wang Ye (Tony Liu Junk-guk in a rare role as a hero) and anyone else involved with the resistance and then lacerates them with his whipping and hammering hair. Meanwhile, pro-republic student Chang Fang (Bai Biao) has recently returned from America and wants to fight teacher Wang Ye to prove his superior martial skills, but Wang has retired from fighting. When An Kung wipes out Wang's kung fu school and patriotic students, Wang assumes Chang did it to get him to fight—and fight back he does. But just as the deathblow moment between Wang and Chang is about to occur, the moment is cut short when Wang's daughter screams that it was An Kung and not Chang who attacked the school. Wang and Chang unite to take on An Kung, but only Chang escapes with

his life and absconds to Hong Kong. An Kung fears the British in Hong Kong. He is promptly warned that his position means nothing to the British military, so he secretly enters Hong Kong to track down Chang. Although An Kung has plenty of dirty tricks up his sleeve, Chang is determined to take him to the cleaners.

The Karate Killers is unusual in that the fights are good at the beginning—firm and determined—with the hero looking sharp in his Bruce Lee-style white Chinese/Western-looking clothes, as seen at the beginning of 1972's *Fist of Fury* (aka *The Chinese Connection*). But the fights get sloppier over the course of the film. Some of the rapid-fire pacing of the action is quelled when the camera is undercranked (which creates a sped-up effect), making the fights look as fake as Richard Nixon's Watergate denial, made the same year this film was released. The seven-and-a-half minute finale is as relentless as it is tiring, with the combat sound effects being louder than usual in an attempt to convey the power of each strike. Steven Seagal movies often do this too. In both cases, the fights are like a candle in the wind, which if that song was performed by a kung fu star, might've been done by Elton Chong.

Titleography: *Stranger From Canton; Stone Cold Wu Tang; Hand of Death.* Translation—*Strange Person.* Although the hero supposedly practices karate (hence *Karate Killer*), there is no actual karate in the film. In addition, the movie is set in the early 1900s, but karate did not exist in Japan until 1912 (though it's possible he learned in Okinawa). The title might have been influenced by a film called *The Karate Killer* (1967), a spy movie derived from the *Man From U.N.C.L.E.* TV show. The Chinese title refers to Chang Fang, a Western-educated Chinese man (and therefore a *Stranger*). *Hand of Death* is a generic title that would work for nearly any martial arts film. The *Stone Cold* title is undoubtedly a namesake for the rap group Wu-Tang Clan. Some plot lines describe the film as being about a female Ching freedom fighter who poses as a prostitute to go behind enemy lines and fight the Japanese, which is wrong. The Chings never had freedom fighters against the Japanese, per se. That storyline sounds like *Spy Ring Kokuryukai* (1976). **MA Percentage: 41.23%**

KARATE KIBA

Karate Kiba (1976—Japan) **87m. FI: Uncredited. NOT/LOT: 8/ 3m 35s; NOF/ LOF: 10/ 3m 26s.** D: Simon Nuchtern. C: Sonny Chiba, Jiro Chiba, Etsuko Shihomi, Aaron Banks, Judy Lee, Bill Louie.

Sometimes a film comes along that leaves you scratching your head—especially if someone gets permission to use footage from one movie and then adds inconsequential footage of their own. I would love to think that if someone had cornered Sonny Chiba in a Los Angeles coffee shop, we'd learn the real story behind the making of this film. But at this moment, all we know is what we see. And what we see is a film with more holes than Swiss cheese.

The re-edited English version of *Karate Kiba*, released as *Viva Chiba the Bodyguard*, opens with a borrowed biblical verse from Ezekiel 25:17. The verse ends with, "And they shall know that I am Chiba the Bodyguard when I shall lay vengeance upon them!" Then we are suddenly in New York City, where a TV anchor is breaking the news of Salvatorre Rocco's murder and explaining how the drug kingpin's Japanese female companion has mysteriously disappeared. What follows next is plain UFO-in-Area-51 talk, meaning it's way out there and unclear as to why the film did this. American martial artists Aaron Banks and Bill Louie, playing themselves, argue about who is better, Sonny Chiba or Bruce Lee. They finally inform the viewer that Chiba is on a plane heading back to Japan.

Apparently, in this English version Chiba is himself, although in the Japanese version he plays a man named Kiba. Anyway, cut to the plane, where Chiba takes out a bunch of drug dealers. He lands, then boasts to the world that he vows to find and destroy the people who are spreading drugs to Japanese youth. He offers his services to anyone willing to share information about the ring of gangsters he wants to bring down. A mysterious woman (Judy Lee), who is unsurprisingly the lass from New York City, steps forward and gives Chiba information he can use to go after Yakuza gang boss Takagami. However, when a man shrouded by the dark shadow of the Mafia confronts Chiba and Chiba discovers the suitcase of a dead drug mule, the audience has to wonder whether he'll be the next dead mule or a triumphant thoroughbred.

As with his next film, *Golgo 13: Kowloon Assignment* (1977), this was something of a relaxation film, if you will. When I say relaxation film, I am referring to how martial arts stars occasionally take on a relatively undemanding film to recover from injuries in preparation for a movie that will require their all—heart, mind, body and soul. For Chiba in 1976, he was gearing up for a project comparable to Toshiro Mifune's *Samurai* trilogy about Miyamoto Musashi. In this case, it was a trilogy about Mas Oyama. (See *Champion of Death*, *Karate Bear Fighter* and *Karate for Life*.)

The fights make use of that bothersome shaky hand-held camera, and the choreography is basically bip, bap, boom (simple 1-2-3 rhythm) and one-punch kills to the face or body. There is one odd shot when Chiba and his partner, Rico, are running away from some mobsters who are shooting at them. Amid a storm of bullets, they leap over a car, but in the next shot, they are speedily driving away from the fight. With barely three minutes of fights in the film, the movie was truly a relaxation film for Chiba. Funny enough, Banks and Louie do the majority of the martial arts in this film.

Of note, the opening passage of Ezekiel 25:17 is spoken by Samuel Jackson in Quentin Tarantino's *Pulp Fiction* (1994). The actual biblical passage includes the final line, "My name is the Lord," as compared to in *Karate Kiba*, in which the last line is "I am Chiba the Bodyguard."

Titleography: *Viva Chiba the Bodyguard*. Translation—*Karate Fang*. **MA Percentage: 8.07%**

KARATE WARRIORS

Kozure Satsujin Ken (1973—Japan) **87m. FI: Uncredited. NOT/LOT: 1/ 40s; NOF/LOF: 16/ 17m 40s.** D: Kazuhiko Yamaguchi. C: Sonny Chiba, Akane Kawasaki, Akiko Koyama, Hideo Murota, Isao Natsuyagi, Tatsuo Umemiya.

The maxim of many a good martial artist should be, "If you lose your temper, you will lose the fight." This applies to anything you do in life, like your job or relationships, but it's also an important lesson in the codes of *budo* and *bushido*, which are lessons that Yakuza always seem to ignore.

In the film, wandering karate man Chieko (Sonny Chiba) abides by the code of budo (the martial way), while wandering warrior Mizuki (Isao Natsuyagi) clings to the code of bushido (the samurai way), which keeps him stuck in the past. So when the past (Mizuki) collides with the present (Chieko) it is the future (Mizuki's son) who can get damaged.

When the head of a local and powerful Yakuza gang dies, the sadistic Koriko takes over. He eventually gets sent to prison for his horrendous crimes and leaves his sons, Nishi and Iga, in charge. Drugs and money come between the brothers, and they form two separate gangs. The two wage war against each other, and the ultimate prizes will be money and control over the drug-trafficking trade. Then the crafty *karateka* Chieko—looking right out of Akira Kurosawa's *Yojimbo* (1961)— arrives in town and plays the two brothers against each other by offering his martial services to both sides. Also stepping into the mix is Mizuki, an old-school samurai soul living in the body of a 1970s assassin for hire. After Chieko seemingly pledges his loyalty to Iga, Mizuki is hired by Nishi to take him out. Yet the unknown variable that adds confusion to the final battle is Mizuki's little son because Chieko saves the son's life on several occasions and would feel distraught to have to kill the little boy's father. Mizuki is aware of his son's affection for Chieko, but due to his code of bushido, he must ignore it even while he recognizes that Nishi is an evil man. As mentioned in other martialogies, a samurai swears loyalty to his master, even if the master is a hardened criminal or a lowlife. This means the samurai must defend his master to the end because it is his *giri*, or obligation. Needless to say, it's a complicated situation for both warriors.

The most engaging fight of the film is when Mizuki and Chieko fight together to save Mizuki's son and fight each other during a Yakuza onslaught. Although the fight (like most in the film) is shot with a shaky hand-held camera that uses tight angles, the camera choreography works well to accent the simplicity of *kendo* and the sword-drawing art of *iaido*. Also adding beauty to actor Sonny Chiba's fights is the intelligent use of high-speed photography (slow motion) during his kicks, blocks and punches. The slow-motion techniques are also accented by a wind-like droning sound effect that does not make the techniques seem silly (like in many Korean films). The sound effects also add a different dimension to the magic of karate. For those of you who are into good technique, the slow motion clearly shows that Chiba spins his head to look at the target before his leg gets there when he does his spinning kicks. That's the proper way to do any kind of spinning kick. Also, the combination of doing real kicks—not just wimpy front or push kicks like those seen in pinky violence films—in conjunction with samurai sword techniques was new for Japanese martial arts films at the time. But the opposing ethical codes between Chieko and Mizuki are what makes this film dynamic because one code breeds life and the other death.

On the surface, a samurai could be called a martial artist, but the way of

bushido is not the way of budo. They are two separate ethical entities, which this film demonstrates (albeit sadly) in the end. The samurai-minded Mizuki must die in order to live, even if it means his son will become an orphan. His bushido code transcends family and friends. In contrast, the budo-minded Chieko fights to live because losing a battle is a lesson learned, and that lesson is not to lose a second time and to live to fight another day.

In a subtle nod to Japanese actress Myoshi Umeki, the first Japanese actor to make it in American TV, the film's final shot sees Chieko holding Mizuki's son in his right arm and walking along a wind-swept beach. It is the same heart-gripping shot seen during the opening credits of the TV show *The Courtship of Eddie's Father* (1969-1972), in which actor Bill Bixby carries child actor Brandon Cruz. *Eddie's Father* starred Umeki, and she was popular in Japan during the early 1970s.

Titleography: As of this writing, no alternative titles could be found. Translation—*Kozure Killing Fist Technique*. I have not seen the Japanese version, but maybe *Kozure* is Chiba's Japanese name in that version. **MA Percentage: 21.07%**

KASAM KHOON KI

(1977—India) **126m. FCom: Veeru Devgan. NOT/LOT: None; NOF/LOF: 7/ 5m 51s.** D: Ashok Roy. C: Jeetendra, G. Asrani, Prem Chopra, Farida Jalal, Jankidas, Amjad Khan.

Music and dance are so entrenched in Indian cinema that in this film, when the villain is going to wipe out all the heroes, he makes sure to kill a woman alongside them so they will have someone to dance for them in heaven. Music and dance are also associated with purity and innocence. Often in Indian movies, when the villain threatens to kill the beauty, he will order her to dance. If she is good, then he will spare her life. She typically starts off shy and worried, but as the beat progresses and her abilities flow smoother than the Ganges River on calm day, the villain becomes perturbed, knowing he must abide by his word. It is a beautiful sentiment.

Children Kishan (Jeetendra) and Ganga (Farida Jalal) are swept away by their mother from their rich, deviant father (Amjad Khan). When Ganga is old enough to marry, her future father-in-law requests a dowry of 25,000 rupees, which is up to Kishan to provide. Because he is the fight master of the village, Kishan is able to become a movie stuntman to raise the money. Ultimately, the marriage is part of a ruse by the father-in-law through which he keeps the money and sells Ganga to sex slave trader Prem (Prem Chopra), who poses as the groom and rapes her.

The heroic trio of Kishan, brother Gafoore (G. Asrani) and good friend Chandan search for Ganga and try to break up the sex trade ring. Along the way, they confront violent riffraff, dance their way into taking out three hired killers, expose the real big boss of the whole operation and eliminate the putrid Prem.

The film is full of illogical and odd fight sounds (boinging guitars, funny flute noises) and crummy postures. The stuntmen do clumsy 360-degree kicks and blindly leap out of cars and buildings. Some stunts use optical effects and are over-the-top hokey. But in some way, these fights are so wrong that they're just right. You can't help but smile at the campiness. The sequence in which the heroes take on the three assassins is rhythmically done to heavy drumbeats as the good guys dance around in traditional garb at a pool party. It is a pity that Indian films do not have more fight scenes because their choreographers are quite creative, and although they are martial arts fights in nature, they don't look or feel at all like Hong Kong kung fu flicks. In *Kasam*, I especially enjoyed the extreme-low-angle and in-your-face camerawork.

Titleography: As of this writing, no alternative titles could be found. **MA Percentage: 4.64%**

KID WITH THE GOLDEN ARM, THE

金臂童 (1979—Hong Kong) **81m. FI: Chiang Sheng, Lu Feng, Robert Tai Chi-hsien. NOT/LOT: 4/ 1m 45s; NOF/LOF: 29/ 23m 42s.** D: Chang Cheh. C: Sun Chien, Lo Meng, Pan Bing-chang, Kuo Chue, Lu Feng, Chiang Sheng, Wang Lung-wei, Wei Bai, Sun Shu-pei, Yu Tai-ping, Liu Jian-ming, Wu Hung-sheng, Yang Xiong, Liu Huang-shi, Sun Xin-xiang.

As mentioned in other martialogies (see *The Five Venoms*), some Shaw Brothers films, especially the ones that starred the Five Weapon Guys (four actors who were in *The Five Venoms*, plus one more), became popular in the United States. Some of their other Shaw Brother films after *Five Venoms* (1978) included *Invincible Shaolin* (1978), *Crippled Avengers* (1979), *Shaolin Rescuers* (1979), *The Daredevils* (1979) and *Magnificent Ruffians* (1979). I have also noted that the group experienced circumstances and issues that would test their unity. Yet *The Kid With the Golden Arm* is a special film for several reasons.

Director Chang Cheh was resolute toward the popularity of his *Five Venoms* and the plight of actor Wei Bai, so he gave the group one last hurrah. This film would turn out to be the last that the real Five Venom actors—Sun Chien, Lo Meng, Kuo Chue, Lu Feng and Wei Bai—would do together. The main reason for this last hurrah was because of Wei Bai's health. As it turned out for Chang, *Golden Arm* would also be the last he directed starring the Five Weapon Guys (actors Sun, Lo, Kuo, Lu and Chiang Sheng).

Compared to other Five Weapon Guys films, this movie focuses more attention on Sun as an actor and fighter, and it is clear that his character is the force behind the main plot twist and various red herrings in the screenplay and film. The film goes something like this: Iron Feet Yang Hu-yun (Sun Chien), head of the Hu Wai Security Bureau, is assigned to deliver 200,000 taels of gold as a much-needed relief fund for refugees suffering from a great famine. He is concerned about the area of Death Valley and the rising criminal activities of Silver Spear (Lu Feng), Iron Robe (Wang Lung-wei), Brass Head (Yang Xiong) and their leader, Golden Arm (Lo Meng), who is the new kid in Jiang Hu. However, at Yang's disposal are a host of do-gooders, including swordsman Li Chin-ming (Wei Bai); his fiancée, Heroine Leng (Pan Bing-chang); Long Ax Yan Jiu (Sun Shu-pei); Short Ax Fang Shi (Chiang Sheng); and drunken master Hai To (Kuo Chue). Despite having so many characters, interactions, subplots and back stories, the film is surprisingly easy to follow. And in case things get a little lost, there is an odd mini-synopsis by the villain Golden Arm in which to the sound of warbling oboe music in the background, he talks to himself and goes over the events that have transpired. It does not come across as forced and lends a different sort of charm to the film.

In terms of great famines in China, the worst happened between 1959 and 1961, with 20 million deaths resulting as part of Mao Zi-dong's Great Leap Forward. Other famous famines occurred during 1333-1337, 1850-1873, 1907 and 1936. Based on the costumes, this film is probably referring to the great famine of 1333-1337. And although the film's plot is based around a famine, the action will leave you full.

Compared to his previous four films with the Five Weapon Guys, Sun has twice as many fights in this film. In regard to choreography, though, as some of the Five Weapon Guys continued to star in films together, Sun did fewer and fewer fights, partly because of his lesser skill set. Like Lo Meng, Sun never worked as a fight instructor. Although fights in Five Weapon Guy films started becoming repetitive, since they were always fighting each other, *Golden Arm* mixes things up by returning to the Jiang Hu world. The film also brings in other fighting stars like Wang Lung-wei; brings back the fifth venom, Wei Bai; and also features for—the first time in any of these Five Weapon Guys films—a female combatant, actress Pan Bing-chang. Each of these elements adds a different dimension to the film. The importance of choreographer Robert Tai Chi-hsien

Still from *The Kid With the Golden Arm* © Celestial Pictures Ltd. All rights reserved.

throughout these films cannot be overstated. He ensured that fights scenes did not become too opera-like, and he had a unique eye when it came to choreography and camera placement. Some of the death visuals are uniquely cool and highly creative, such as the impale-two-insects-with-one-insect-pin skill, the corkscrew-sword wrench, and the squishy punch through the body. The fist sticking out of the body just hit by the squishy punch is totally a blood-coated rubber glove, but you'll love it anyway. I guess you could call it cheesy with syrup. (Syrup was often the base product used to create fake blood).

As was becoming more evident throughout the Five Weapon Guys' careers, Kuo Chue was the most versatile fighter and actor, capable of juggling comedy, drama and powerfully relaxed fighting. But the ultimate beauty of all the great martial arts talent in this film is that whenever anyone fights, the action is certain to be extremely smooth without being overly operatic. Because the actors were so familiar and comfortable working together, the camera angles and placements were not as crucial; regardless of the angle, the real contact of fists, arms and weapons was guaranteed, and so excessive coverage was not necessary.

Now back to the plight of Wei Bai. Undoubtedly because of the mental and physical stress of dealing with Tourette's syndrome, Wei Bai's kung fu is labored in *Golden Arm*. He leans forward at the waist too much during his fights, which throws his posture out of alignment. It is good that he uses a sword during his action set pieces because it limits having direct body contact with stuntmen—arms smashing on arms and legs, for example—which can lower the frequency of tics. His face clearly reflects the loss of confidence in his skills, but varying camera speeds hide it relatively well. Although by 1981 he had all but disappeared from the industry (barring a cameo in *Devil and the Ghost Buster* in 1988), Wei was able to pull off a decent performance in John Woo's *Last Hurrah for Chivalry*, which was shot at the same time as this film. The waning months of 1979 were a fitting and well-deserved last hurrah for Wei Bai.

Titleography: *Kid With the Golden Arms*. Translation—*Kid With the Golden Arm*. **MA Percentage: 31.42%** SHAW BROTHERS

KILL THE GOLDEN GOOSE

(1979—USA) **90m. FSC: Bong Soo-han, Ed Parker, Patrick Strong. NOT/LOT: 1/ 14s; NOF/LOF: 11/ 7m 42s. D: Elliot Hong. C: Ed Parker, Brad von Beltz, Bong Soo-han, Midori Arimoto, Seaward Forbes, Carlos Membrives, Branscombe Richmond.**

Hawaiian-born Ed Parker (aka Edmund Kealoha Parker), the founder and undisputed father of American *kenpo*, borrows from his roots in his first martial arts leading role as a dangerous hit man named Mauna Loa. He is hired by the Max Corporation to kill three of its business executives who are expected to testify in front of a U.S. Senate investigative committee concerning illegal defense contracts and alleged misconduct by the corporation. The only man in Mauna Loa's way is a police investigator nicknamed Captain Karate (Bong Soo-han), who apparently ended up marrying the only woman Mauna Loa ever loved.

The film naturally moves to the expected conclusive fight between two of the biggest influences on the direction of martial arts in America during the '60s and '70s, Parker's American kenpo versus Bong's Korean *hapkido*. At the end of the day, the fight is indeed worth the wait, as Parker and Bong were able to highlight several of their signature techniques. Sadly, the problem is that neither was particularly savvy with camera choreography and placement, leaving me feeling just a bit shortchanged by what could have been a truly great fight scene. I have to admit, I did enjoy seeing Parker go animalistic with rapid-fire attacks that look like he is fighting a swarm of Africanized honey bees while his silver hair maniacally flips and flops all over the place.

Titleography: *Kill the Golden Ninja*. The *Golden Goose* probably refers to Mauna Loa, and a different distributor added *Ninja* when that buzzword was popular. And with a name like Mauna Loa, he fights crazy like an out-of-control volcano. **MA Percentage: 8.81%**

KILLER, THE

大殺手 (1971—Hong Kong) **89m. FI: Yuen Cheung-yan, Yuen Wooping. NOT/LOT: None; NOF/LOF: 20/ 22m 47s. D: Chu Yuan. C: Chin Han, Tsung Hua, Wang Ping, Jiang Nan, Ching Miao, Yang Chi-ching, Ku Feng, Zheng Lei.**

Sometimes after major drug busts, police departments decide to show off their big catches in public. Doing so can backfire if the display does not act as a deterrent but instead makes criminals angry and determined. Furthermore, when a bust occurs, the drugs are usually put in storage, which can lead to trouble.

Perhaps officers should do what Inspector Ma (Chin Han) does: burn them. That way no one is tempted to do something stupid—except the criminals.

Reeling from one of Ma's fiery busts, sleazebag extraordinaire Chiao Zi-fei (Jiang Nan) decides to hire an assassin to get rid of all his other enemies. In that way he can claim innocence and not be blamed for the killings, because it was an assassin (who of course will disappear) who committed the murders. Meanwhile, the innocent but dense martial arts hero Hsieh Chun (Tsung Hua) returns home after a 10-year hiatus. He left to avoid being a third wheel to the growing love between Ma and the demure Yu Chiao (Wang Ping) when the three were street performers and Hsieh was a knife-throwing phenomenon. Hsieh is led to believe that local corrupt officials targeted Chiao and his gang, so he poses as an unknown killer and goes around dispensing kung fu justice to martial arts schools that support the corrupt authorities. Ma, now a powerful police inspector, is called in to find this mysterious killer. As the old love triangle rekindles, Ma discovers Hsieh's secret, and Hsieh thinks Ma is a corrupt official. To make matters worse, the two-faced Chiao adds one more piece of TNT to the mix: the leader of the Japanese drug cartel, a psychotic samurai warrior (Ku Feng) who kills with one stroke of his razor-sharp sword.

The Yuen brothers once again have their hands full dealing with actors who are not well versed in martial arts, as is evident when Tsung Hua uses a reverse grip on his pole weapon. He does so with both palms facing the same direction, making his skills look awkward. However, the empty-hand fights are filled with what used to be called "punch and crash" moments: When the hero hits someone, that person is sent crashing back or flipping into some brittle object such as wall décor, a window or a piece of furniture. It really adds to the power of the main fighter because the fight becomes a barrage of eye-pleasing visuals and lively sound effects. My hat is off to Tsung because there are several scenes in which he dismantles 10 attackers in a single, unedited shot. The scenes are similar to those of Taiwanese sensation Wen Chiang-long, though not as savagely intense.

Notice that actor Ku Feng holds his samurai sword like a baseball bat in many shots, which is incorrect. One hand should be against the *tsuba* (sword guard), and the other should be at the distal end of the *tsuka* (hilt). This error isn't surprising. When I made my first film in Taiwan, there were sword fights between Japanese samurai characters and Chinese swordsmen, and the techniques being used were similar. Fortunately, I had some *kendo* experience, and the choreographers were open to my suggestions to at least hold the swords correctly.

There is also a red-belt karate practitioner in the film. Not all karate styles have a red belt, but in essence, it represents one's advancement in wisdom, not skill. Only old *karateka* hold red belts, because wisdom comes with age rather than technique.

Titleography: *Sacred Knives of Vengeance*; *The Wandering Knight*. Translation—*The Killer*. The English titles are more interesting than the Chinese title. The film's hero is a knife-throwing expert seeking revenge, hence *Sacred Knives of Vengeance*. *Wandering Knight* is pushing it and is another example of a generic title that could work for many different films. **MA Percentage: 25.6%** SHAW BROTHERS

KILLER CLANS

流 星 蝴 蝶 劍 (1976—Hong Kong) 91m. FI: Yuen Cheung-yen, Tang Chia. NOT/LOT: None; NOF/LOF: 20/ 13m 21s. D: Chu Yuan. C: Tsung Hua, Chen Ping, Ku Feng, Yueh Hua, Lo Lieh, Fan Mei-sheng, Wang Chung, Ling Yun, Wang Xia, Danny Lee, Ching Li.

In the world of Jiang Hu—a sub-society of swordsmen, vagrants, beggars, transients and kung fu people who live by their own set of morals and exist outside the norm—many people come and go who have no names. To an assassin, names and fame mean nothing. Except, perhaps, in the name of love.

Draped in funeral black, but his heart still beating with life, assassin Meng Sheng-wen (Tsung Hua) is hired by a nameless bordello queen (Chen Ping) to take out the head of the powerful yet righteous Lung Men Society Clan, Sun Yu (Ku Feng). Sun Yu's only crime is killing rapists, murderers and bandits in the sometimes-lawless world of Jiang Hu. This makes him a target for shadowy men in black, so he has enlisted three unrivaled swordsmen to be his bodyguards. They are his stoic son, Sun Chien (Wang Chung); his foster son, the guarded Lu Hsiang-chuan (Yueh Hua), who is a master of 72 secret weapons hidden all over his body; and a serious killer fisherman named Han Tang (Lo Lieh), who rarely comes out into the public. (If Han Tang is forced to kill in the open, he smears his victim's blood on his face to hide his identity.) But this does not stop the treacherous chief of the Roc Clan (Wang Xia) from also plotting against Sun Yu.

News breaks that Sun Chien and Han have been mysteriously killed by an unknown swordsman, which opens the door for Meng to slip in. Because the Roc Clan is hot on Sun Yu's heels, he needs help fast, so the bordello queen arranges for Meng to be a bodyguard. As Meng makes his way to Sun Yu's lair, he is sidetracked in Butterfly Forest by the demure, poetry-spouting, puppy-eyed Hsiao Tieh (Ching Li). After several surreptitious rendezvous, they fall in love. Of course, Meng does not realize that she is the daughter of the man he must kill. She is also the former tragic love of his liquidator pal Yeh Hsiang (Ling Yun), who, after fighting bodyguard Han for three days and nights, was allowed to live. Yeh has since retired into misery and alcohol, but with the expectations of seeing Hsiao Tieh again and fighting with Meng, he sobers up.

A tsunami of distress, deception and death then envelops the clan. Bodyguard Lu kills the just-off-the-wagon Yeh, then traitorously turns around and throws poisonous darts into Sun Yu. Yu barely escapes and plunges into a deep well, where he hides out in hopes of getting well so that he can return, save his clan and kill Lu.

There is some nifty rope choreography when actor Yueh Hua is entangled in a web of ropes and lifted into the air. When doing choreography like this, the ropes are initially taut around the body, and so when a stuntman gets lifted into the air, he would often suffer rope burns. This is fine for the stuntmen (not really, but sadly they are pretty low on the totem pole of "who cares?"), but the filmmakers found it easier to suspend Yueh on a wire. In this way, the ropes can remain pretty loose because the actor is being lifted into the air by the wire and not the tight ropes, thus no rope burns. Han Tang fights using a fishing pole with a sword hidden inside and a windfire wheel (a circular weapon with a hole in the middle for grasping the weapon and flaring blades that look like fire in the wind), which he can pull out of his hat.

The best moment takes place during the final fight between actors Tsung and Yueh. In one unedited shot, Yueh spears Tsung, who blocks and exits stage right; then Tsung's stunt double attacks from behind the left side of the camera and Yueh blocks; Tsung runs behind camera to get to stage left and the stuntman rolls left out of frame, and then Tsung swishes back into camera stage left. I have done this maneuver on Chinese TV in Taiwan, and when the star would trip on his way to the other side, we would all have a good laugh. Director Tsui Hark pulls off a similar stunt well in *The Blade* (1995).

The Gu Long story this film is based on resurfaced as *Butterfly Sword* (1993).

Titleography: As of this writing, no alternative titles could be found. Translation—*Shooting Star Butterfly Sword*. The Chinese title refers to Meng's sword and technique. **MA Percentage: 14.67%** SHAW BROTHERS

KILLER ELEPHANTS

(1975—Thailand) 83m. FI: Uncredited. NOT/LOT: None; NOF/LOF: 3/ 6m 27s. D: Som Kit. **C:** Sombat Metanee, Alen Yen, Nai Yen Na, Chien Yu.

This movie is like a biker film, but with elephants. Sombat Metanee, one of the few Thai action stars of the 1970s, plays Kao Fei, aka Pa Sung, who pseudo-teams-up with Police Detective Chi Mee (Alen Yen) to take out the villainous Mao Tien. Mao, who wishes to prove he is top dog, is bent on killing Kao and wiping out his jungle village. Mao kidnaps Kao's pregnant wife to lure him into a trap, but his plans are foiled when Kao's pachyderm pals charge into Mao's compound, trample his goons, flip over cars and flatten every straw hut in sight in true *Tarzan Goes to India* (1962) style.

You might recognize many of the henchmen in this film as the poor flailers Bruce Lee wipes out in *The Big Boss* (1972; aka *Fists of Fury*), which was shot in Thailand. But the fights in this film lack direction and choreography. The actors don't have any idea how to pose in a fighting stance or how to space themselves out in relation to each other or the camera. Thus they all hunch their backs, and the lack of punch or kick extension detracts from what could have been some interesting fights. It seems a logical thought that if these stuntmen worked with Bruce Lee, they might have a better idea as to how to present the fight or even how to look good on camera. That would only happen if they took the time to learn from Lee, which based on what is seen on-screen, they did not. It is actually similar to American martial arts stars Jim Kelly and Bob Wall, who also worked with Lee. (Wall worked with Lee on two films). Based on what we see in the fights that they did in their subsequent American productions, they certainly lack any kind of Lee influence.

Sadly for *Killer Elephants*, there is no use of indigenous martial arts, though there is a brief clip of about 100 people demonstrating *krabi krabong* at the yearly Elephant Festival. Krabi krabong is a Thai martial art dating back about 500 years that utilizes weapons such as knives, swords, halberds, lances, staffs and shields. Its skills mirror the empty-hand movements of *muay boran*, the ancient and somewhat brutal foundation of *muay* Thai kickboxing. It is a pity no one thought of a way to work these native arts into this film. Thank goodness for Tony Jaa's *Ong Bak* films (2003 and 2009).

Titleography: As of this writing, no alternative titles could be found. **MA Percentage: 7.77%**

KILLER ELITE, THE

(1975—USA) 122m. SS: Whitey Hughes. NOT/LOT: 4/ 2m 4s; NOF/LOF: 2/ 1m 54s. D: Sam Peckinpah. **C:** James Caan, Robert Duvall, Arthur Hill, Bo Hopkins, Mako, Burt Young, Gig Young, Tom Clancy, Tiana Alexandra, James Wing Woo, George Cheung, Victor Sen Yung, Tak Kubota, Simon Tam, Kuo Lien Ying.

The Killer Elite is a label given to specific members of a private mercenary group called Com-Teg (Communications Integrity Associates) that is perhaps an offshoot of the CIA. Mike Locken (James Caan) and George Hansen (Robert Duvall) are members of this group of bodyguards and assassins, and while protecting a client, Hansen about-faces, kills the client, and shoots Locken in the arm and knee. After using martial arts as a powerful therapy to overcome his injuries and learning how to use his walking cane as a deadly weapon, Locken is assigned to protect Asian bigwig Yuen Chung (Mako) from a team of assassins lead by Hansen. Ultimately, the whole hit and protection scenario turns out to be subterfuge aimed toward finagling Locken and Hansen, the result of an internal power struggle between various leaders at Com-Teg.

When this film came out, the martial arts magazines gave it a lot of hype and press because it was the first big American film after *Enter the Dragon* that had A-list actors (Caan, Duvall) and an A-list director (Sam Peckinpah) attached to a story that had martial arts as part of the film's motif. Whether it was intentional or not, what made the film different from the martial arts point of view was that the lead character learned martial arts not so much for self-defense but to overcome physical disabilities after being shot in the arm and leg. The major disappointment to martial arts fans at the time was the film's big climax, a fight pitting Locken's band of good-guy mercenaries against the bad-guy ninjas and Yakuza. The finale was reported to feature Dan Inosanto (Bruce Lee's good friend and a top teacher of *jeet kune do*) doing fights. Although Inosanto was in it, at the end of the day, the film had very little martial arts action.

Titleography: As of this writing, no alternative titles could be found. **MA Percentage: 3.25%**.

KILLER METEORS, THE

風雨雙流星 (1976—Hong Kong) **94m. KFI: Chen Shen-yi. NOT/LOT: 1/ 22s; NOF/LOF: 8/ 11m 14s. D:** Lo Wei. **C:** Jimmy Wong Yu, Jackie Chan, Li Wen-tai, Chen Hui-lou, Lan Yu-li.

When you sign a contract in the Chinese film industry, you're obligated to abide by it, regardless of how big or small your cinematic stature is. Often that meant there was no way for martial arts stars under contract to avoid doing certain movies, even if they seemed destined to bomb. Director Lo Wei was a master of spotting talented actors and tying them to long-term deals with multi-film contracts. Once they agreed, opting out was not an option. *The Killer Meteors* was one film of many that Jackie Chan was essentially forced to be in, even if it is was just for a few moments.

Respected kung fu warrior Mi Wei (Jimmy Wong Yu), also known as Killer Meteor after his weapon of the same name, is as cool as ice even when faced with four assassins. Madam Phoenix (Lan Yu-li) hired the killers because she doesn't want Mi to obtain the antidote he was hired to find for her husband, Wa Wu-bin (Jackie Chan). Phoenix poisoned Wa as a means to control him. Mi is also a highly sought-after secret agent known for solving bizarre murder cases, and he is hired by Lord Fung to investigate a series of deaths that may somehow be related to some missing palace treasure.

As with any Gu Long-written screenplay, things come to a head at the film's end after numerous twists, red herrings and random surprises. Unlike Western screenplays in which clues foreshadow things to come and the ending makes sense, Gu just throws things out there that you would never have seen coming, even in retrospect. This aspect of Chinese films can be both charming and frustrating, but the bottom-line belief in Hong Kong kung fu cinema is that if the fights are good, the audience won't mind a silly story. The problem is that this film lacks good fights.

A novelist and screenwriter, Gu was one of the most prolific and influential scribes in the Hong Kong kung fu film industry of the 1970s; Ni Kuang was the other. Gu borrowed a page from Ni's *Flying Guillotine* and created a story about a weapon shrouded in mystery: the Killer Meteor. No one knows what it looks like because no one who has laid eyes on it has ever lived to tell the tale. Since this is one of Jackie Chan and Jimmy Wong Yu's less inspired films and there is very little action, much of the drama comes from the bagged weapon draped over Mi's shoulder. Those who are impatient to see what it looks like it can hit the fast-forward button.

Titleography: *Karate Death Squad*; *Jackie Chan Versus Wang Yu*. Translation—*Wind Rain and Two Shooting Stars* (*Meteors*). Writers like Gu Long create romanticized titles and character names for their kung fu movies that often include animals, emotions, elements, weather, behaviors and weapons, thus the beautiful Chinese title. English-language film distributors, in this case, don't seem to care about beauty or creativity. **MA Percentage: 12.34%**

KILLER OF SNAKE, FOX OF SHAOLIN

人鬼蛇狐大決鬥 (1978—Taiwan) **90m. FI: Liao Xiao-ming, Lin Man-hua. NOT/LOT: 1/ 20s; NOF/LOF: 11/ 32m 33s. D:** Man Wa. **C:** Carter Wong, Cheung Lik, Liu Ya-ying, Lin Man-hua.

In the Chinese mythos of snake and fox spirits, to be a mortal trapped between such powerful supernatural forces can lead to dealings with ghosts, spirits and fairies. Yuk Lin (Carter Wong) is unwittingly caught up in this world as he is called upon to rescue Wang Ku, a fox spirit in human form, from snake boy Tien Sing. The spiritual entity Ma Lung is also keeping an eye on Tien for using his snake-morphing powers to hurt Yuk, who is trying to live a true and noble life. Adding to the macabre mess is a long-haired green female ghost who asks Yuk to kill the man who raped and murdered her as a young girl. Just as the black magic and trickery of the spiritual world nearly kill Yuk, a Buddhist monk gives him a special book that holds the secret to defeating the inhabitants of Snake Hill and can help free the other wayfaring spirits from their limbos.

This is yet another Chinese kung fu film in which the actors are required to joyfully play with cobras and a variety of their wrapping relatives. Remember that these old films do not have special effects and that the filmmakers rely on realism when it comes to animal interactions. You can plainly see that these actors are chumming up to these deadly snakes Steve Irwin-style while trying to look calm and collected as the camera is rolling. I was once on the set of a Taiwanese kung fu film in which an actor had to literally bite the head off a chicken because he was playing a dangerous villain. Off-camera, he was freaking out about what he had to do, shaking like a leaf, but when the camera rolled, he was all business. I initially thought it was a special effect—a rubber chicken with fake blood—until the beheaded bird started running around the set. Flabbergasted does not begin to describe my reaction.

During the 1970s, when it was common for actors with martial arts experience to work with actors who had no training, slap choreography was popular. As this technique evolved, skilled fighting actors were able to punch out at full speed and stop their hands instantly upon contact with their opponents, giving the appearance of full-powered strikes. (This is where a lot of those short, quick, choppy movements seen in the choreography of later kung fu films are derived from.) Carter Wong was one of those martial-arts-trained actors who did slap choreography, but in this film, he looks unusually uncomfortable with the technique. Of course, this style of choreography is tougher with kicking, which is why proper distance between opponents, good camera angles and tough stuntmen are essential. I have the dislocated neck and hairline-fractured tailbone to prove it.

Titleography: As of this writing, no alternative titles could be found. Translation—*A Human Duels Against a Ghost, Snake and Fox*. There is no Shaolin in this film, but snakes, ghosts and foxes all show up. **MA Percentage: 36.54%**

KILLING MACHINE, THE

Shorinji Kenpo (1975—Japan) 86m. FI: Uncredited. NOT/LOT: 7/ 5m 35s; NOF/LOF: 21/ 11m 11s. D: Norifumi Suzuki. C: Sonny Chiba, Yutaka Nakajima, Makoto Sato, Naoya Makoto, Sanae Kitabayashi, Akiko Mori, Akira Oizumi, Hosei Komatsu, Koichi Sato, Genji Kawai, Junichi Tatsu, Etsuko Shihomi.

After the success of Sonny Chiba's biopics about Japan's historically important martial arts legend Morihei Uyeshiba (see *The Defensive Powers of Aikido* (1975)), Chiba focused on a second martial arts folk legend closer to home: Doshin So. So is the founder of *shorinji kenpo*, which translates to "Shaolin kung fu." It's an art in which Chiba holds a black belt.

The film opens with Doshin So (Sonny Chiba) as a Japanese spy shooting a roomful of Chinese soldiers during World War II. When he reports to his superiors, he learns that Japan has surrendered to the Allied forces. Returning to Osaka, So is depressed to see his countrymen being victimized by Yakuza, corrupt officials and occupying forces. Rather than become a sheep, he uses his Chinese Shaolin kung fu skills to become the shepherd. He takes it upon himself to protect the herd by standing up to the various Yakuza and American GI wolves who think they own the country. After hospitalizing some rambunctious GIs, So is sent to prison, where he befriends Otaki (fellow *Executioner* star Makoto Sato), a man searching for his wife after returning from the war. However, the prison warden tells So that because he injured Americans, he will likely be put to death. The warden arranges for So to escape and start life anew on the rural island of Shikoku.

Shikoku is no different from Osaka, but now So takes a more active role than ever by walking the streets dressed in a gray cape and teaching shorinji kenpo to aimless vets and local loafers, which he did not do in Osaka. So believes that learning shorinji kenpo is about building self-esteem. He wants to give the locals he teaches the confidence to fight back against Yakuza thugs. For example, when street combers Tomoda (Naoya Makoto) and Miho (Etsuko Shihomi) run into Yakuza after learning kenpo, Tomoda loses his arm. However, the two find peace and solace in their training and live on with determination. But after Otaki comes to Shikoku and joins So's ranks, things take a tragic turn. Otaki finds that his wife and child are alive, but his wife has remarried and is unable to leave her new husband. One day, as Otaki tries to protect a band of people from the Yakuza, some gangsters kill him. It is now time for a super shorinji kenpo showdown. With his gray cape blowing in the wind and a sense of calm in his wild eyes, So embarks on a mission of spiritual retribution, and it is time to turn the black market red.

In real life, Doshin So began practicing martial arts in 1929 while working as a topographer for the Japanese Imperial Army in Manchuria. He studied under *byahuren-monken kenpo* stylist Chinryo at the Taoist university Shi Fang Conghin. Chinryo eventually took So to Beijing and introduced him to his kung fu teacher, Bun Tai-so, who agreed to teach So the northern *shorinji giwa-monken* style of kenpo. (It translates to *shou din yi he men chuan* in Chinese, or "fist of righteousness and harmony" in English.) Several years later, So visited the former grounds of Song

Shan Shaolin Temple, which was burned down in 1736. He was made the 21st master of the giwa-monken style of kenpo at the site where the temple originally stood. When the Russian army entered Manchuria in 1945, members of the Chinese Hong Bang secret society smuggled So back to Japan. Observing the ravaged land and downtrodden people, So began teaching kenpo as a means to strengthen morale and a person's sense of morality. So also wanted to re-instill a sense of national pride in the Japanese through martial arts. In 1979, the Communist Chinese government invited So back to China to teach his Shaolin art. Unfortunately, he died and it never happened.

The choreography in this film is pretty snappy. This is also the first time a Japanese film shoots a fight in wide angle at normal speed and then instantly switches to slow motion within the same shot. Some good close-ups emphasize Shaolin *chin na* wrist-locking maneuvers, followed by the expected rolling flips of the opponents, which are also done in normal/slow-motion shots. One film critic notes that Chiba's gray cape emulates Clint Eastwood's spaghetti Western look, but in actuality, he is wearing the traditional shorinji kenpo training gear. There is one intense visual in the film when Chiba beats up a Yakuza rapist, cuts off his penis and tosses it to a dog in the street, which quickly devours it. That's one effective way to stop a rapist that should become standard in real life.

There are several talking points worth mentioning in the film. Sonny Chiba as Doshin So is offended when young girls are being forced to sleep with Chinese and Russian soldiers and vows to not let that happen. How quickly things are forgotten when the shoe is on the other foot. I am referring to the 200,000 or so Korean teens during World War II who were kidnapped and sent all over Asia to work as "comfort women" for the Japanese soldiers at their camps. But at least cinematically, So redeems himself when he is disgusted at the way Japanese people treat Koreans with malice and disrespect. So impresses upon the Japanese people that Japan is the Koreans' home, and they should be treated with dignity.

The messages in the film are quite clear, as reflected in two statements by So: "Strength and compassion must be together," and, "Overcoming one's weakness is the spirit of shorinji kenpo."

Titleography: As of this writing, no alternative titles could be found. Translation—*Shaolin Kung Fu*. The Japanese title is the name of the style So creates, and the English title reflects So's methodology of cleaning up the mean streets of Shikoku, although violently. **MA Percentage: 19.5%**

KING BOXER

天下第一拳 (1972—Hong Kong) 104m. KFI: Liu Chia-rong, Chan Chuen. NOT/LOT: 4/ 1m 29s; NOF/LOF: 30/ 21m 49s. D: Cheng Chang-ho. C: Lo Lieh, Kim Kee-joo, Chan Chuen, Chan Shen, Tien Fung, Wang Ping, James Nam Gung-fan, Bolo Yeung, Fang Mian, Tong Lin, Zhao Xiong, Gu Wen-zong.

How appropriate that the first Chinese kung fu film ever to play in the United States has the translated title *The Number One Boxer*. Try watching this film—or one of the hundreds of others that slow-boated to America back in the day—as if you were seeing it for the first time in the early 1970s. At that time, most of us were clueless as to what the genre was all about. We had no idea of the rich history of kung fu cinema, and we were not aware of just how similar all these

Still from *King Boxer* © Celestial Pictures Ltd. All rights reserved.

stories were. Try to remember how fresh these films were and how you were blown away to see a film that was like an American Western in which feet, fists and swords replaced guns. Recall those weird behavioral nuances that left you wondering what kung fu was all about.

In the film, Chao Chi-hao (Lo Lieh) is sent to learn kung fu from Shen Chin-pei (Fang Mian) by his injured master, Sung Wu-yang (Gu Wen-zong). Sung hopes that Shen can enter an upcoming martial arts tournament and defeat the local martial arts school run by the malicious Ming Dung-shen (Tien Fung), who also hires martial artist thugs like Japanese samurai mercenaries and the horrific headbutter Chen Lung (Kim Kee-joo) to do his evil deeds whenever he needs one done.

Upon Chao's arrival at Shen's school, Shen's star pupil shows his superiority by beating up Chao, which just makes Chao train harder. When Chen begins to butt heads with Shen and his students, Chao sticks his head into the mix and defends the honor of the school. Moved by Chao's bravery, Master Sung chooses Chao to learn his most prized secret kung fu skill, the Iron Palm. This makes Han Lung jealous, causing him to conspire with the rival school headed by Ming, to break Chao's hands and spirit. As Chao goes into seclusion, heals and then learns the Iron Palm in preparation for the martial arts tournament, Shen is killed by Ming's minions.

On his way to the tournament, Chao runs into Chen Lung, who has had a change of heart and realizes Ming is evil. Chen warns Chao that Ming's assassins are waiting for him down the path. As the two fight off the killers, Chen tells Chao to get to the tournament while he holds them off. At the tournament, Chao defeats Ming's top student. During the celebration, no one sees Ming kill Master Sung. Chao, now knowing that Ming was responsible for the deaths of his two kung fu teachers, decides it is time to use his Iron Palm Five Fingers of Death to take out Ming and the Japanese.

Watching this film back in the early '70s, I remember often hearing "brother" and "sister" and then seeing those two characters fall in love and hug in slow motion, not knowing these are terms used to identify kung fu school relationships rather than personal ones. Then there was the moral lesson that kung fu should be used for righteous purposes and not for hurting, which is the sort of message imparted in David Carradine's TV show Kung Fu. Most of us also never realized how much animosity and distrust there was between the Chinese and Japanese, but that message was underlined when Bruce Lee's Fist of Fury (1972) came to town. (Note: There were a lot of Chinese films that carried an anti-Japanese message, but King Boxer and Fist of Fury were the first two to bring the message stateside via film).

How ironic too that Lo Lieh is considered one of the all-time villains of kung fu films, but Western audiences were introduced to him as the good guy when his film The Stranger and the Gunfighter (1974) was released in America. Then there is the secret kung fu manual that can teach the right person how to make his kung fu more powerful and give him the tools to overcome evil. We also marveled at the incredible action and martial arts expertise of Lo Lieh and his Five Fingers of Death. I get chills reliving the emotions of that first viewing in Vestal, New York, like the first snowfall of winter that beckons a new time of year.

Today, it is cool to know from King Boxer that Iron Palm (enhanced in the film by making Lo Lieh's hands glow red) does exist, and unlike American superheroes, the things we see in Chinese martial arts films are attainable if a person is willing to sacrifice and dedicate oneself to training. Also memorable is the head-butting Chen Lung. With the proper training, one can actually build up calcium deposits on the front of the cranium to make one's skull hard as rock. We also see the righteousness of Chao, who refuses to use his Iron Palm to win the tournament because he only uses it when his life is in danger. Chan Shen's villain, Wang Hung-chieh, was so popular in the West that he was cast alongside Peter Cushing as the evil Chinese sorcerer in the Hammer Studios/Shaw Brothers production of Dracula and the 7 Golden Vampires (1974).

What also really struck me in the fights was the incredible height these fighters would flip from and fall flush on the hardwood floor, as dust would puff up from between the floorboards. And who can forget the borrowed squealing sound from the opening of NBC's TV show Ironside (1967-1975) marking the arrival of the Five Fingers of Death?

Titleography: Five (5) Fingers of Death; Hand of Death; Invincible

Boxer; Iron Palm; An Iron Man; King Boxer: Five Fingers of Death. Translation—The Number One Boxer in the World. The titles all logically fit certain aspects and plot lines of the film. **MA Percentage: 22.4%** SHAW BROTHERS

KING EAGLE

鷹王 (1970—Hong Kong) 80m. ASAB: Tang Chia, Yuen Cheung-yan. NOT/LOT: None; NOF/LOF: 16/ 11m 46s. D: Chang Cheh. C: Chang Pei-shan, Cheng Lei, Ching Miao, Li Ching, Ti Lung, Wang Kuang-yu, Chen Hsing, Wang Chung, Tung Li, Tong Yen-san.

In director Chang Cheh's world of Jiang Hu, men are men and women are women. For hero King Eagle Jin Fei (Ti Lung), who has retired from the affairs of Jiang Hu (see The Water Margin), there is no room for love with a woman, because a loner must continue to be a loner. He has no qualms leaving behind Jiang Hu, as is evident in his indifference when a dying man begs him to warn the Tien Yi Tong sect about fellow sect member Hung Sing-tien (Chang Pei-shan), who killed the sect's leader and wants to use the group for wrongful purposes. Under the Jiang Hu unwritten rules of being a knight-errant, he would have helped the dying man, but not anymore. Instead, Jin Fei does not lift a finger to help the dying man when Hung's men attack him. However, love somehow begins to weasel its way into his world when female fighter Yu Lin (Li Ching) helps Jin rescue a child. He finds it awkward to thank her because no one has ever done a favor for him before, let alone a woman; the situation has always been the reverse.

Yet Jin Fei still has a sense of righteousness when it is comes to affairs outside Jiang Hu, and he helps the weak. He still believes he has a duty to help those who cannot defend themselves, such as a waiter and his wife killed by Hung's men or a threatened child caught in the crossfire between rival swordsmen. After the honest and upright Yu Lin helps Jin, he bares his eagle's talons to return the favor by stopping Hung from destroying the Tien Yu Tong sect's good name. Jin joins Yu on her quest to stop Hung and his vicious assassins: Deadly Fingers Wen Hao Ba (Ching Miao); An Bing-er, who is Yu Lin's evil younger sister (Li Ching again); and Iron Shield Chief Chen Tang (Chen Hsing).

It was common in early kung fu films not to have a lot of fights. (See Vengeance of a Snow Girl (1971) for the reason why there were not a lot). However, the presence of even a few real martial talents, like in this film, elevates the level of realism and adds an extra dimension to the choreography. Actor Ti Lung's wing chun training and actor Chen Hsing's karate training—he does not do his usual tiger claw and hunchbacked posturing—give the fights an air of authenticity. The rhythm of the choreography and the weapon movements can be described as slash, thrust, slice and stab. There are no extended combinations in single shots, a style that would change drastically as the decade proceeded. Another element that helps this and other early kung fu films hold the audience's interest is the use of exotic weapons that add variety to the fight scenes.

Titleography: As of this writing, no alternative titles could be found. Translation—The Eagle King. **MA Percentage: 14.71%** SHAW BROTHERS

Still from King Eagle © Celestial Pictures Ltd. All rights reserved.

KING KUNG FU

(1976—USA) **94m. FI: Uncredited. NOT/LOT: None; NOF/LOF: 4/ 2m 33s.**
D: Lance D. Hayes. C: John Balee, Tim McGill, Billy Schwartz, Maxine Gray, Tom Leahy, Stephen S. Sisely.

Not your average monkey in a barrel, but a man in a gorilla suit in Wichita, Kansas, doing guerrilla filmmaking. When a Chinese gorilla named Jungle Jumper is too much to handle for his Caucasian master, he is renamed King Kung Fu (John Balee) and shipped to New York. Stopping in Wichita so the red-necks can gawk at him, King Kung Fu escapes, is pursued by two bumbling TV reporters, befriends a bustling bikini-clad babe named Rae Fay (Maxine Gray), joins a Wild West show, and becomes the target of a John Wayne-wannabe sheriff (Tom Leahy) and his deputy named Pilgrim.

Although this film was officially released in 1987, most of it was shot in the '70s, and it is stamped as a 1976 film. This is the plight of low-budget films bankrolled by the personal credit cards of producers—things are shot whenever there is time and money, and there are no police around to ask what's going on. As bad as this film is, it does offer some crude stop-motion photography, a decent John Wayne impersonation, one good spinning crescent kick by the gorilla with a subsequent flipping reaction by a stuntman, and an *escrima* baseball bat routine. Despite their limited resources, the filmmakers gave it their best shot, and that is always worth saying something positive about.

For better kung-fu-fighting gorillas, see *Shaolin Invincibles* (1977), and for what I think is one of the best gorilla-versus-human fight scenes on TV, check out Jim West (Robert Conrad) taking on a large ape in the "Night of the Simian Terror" episode of *The Wild Wild West* (1968).

Titleography: As of this writing, no alternative titles could be found. **MA Percentage: 2.71%**

KISS OF DEATH

毒女 (1973—Hong Kong) **94m. FI: Yasuyoshi Shikamura. NOT/LOT: 5/ 46s; NOF/LOF: 7/ 8m 11s.** D: Ho Meng-hua. C: Cheng Ping, Lo Lieh, Chan Shen, Jiang Dao, Fan Mei-shang, Hiu Siu-hung, Lin Wen-wei, Chen Ching.

In the 1990s, Western critics raved when femme fatale Fant-Asia films featured Anita Mui or Maggie Cheung doing high kicks in short skirts, all shot at a low angle to reveal their underwear.

These films were about women kicking men's butts in a male-dominated society, where spousal abuse was sadly accepted but kept behind closed doors. The reason for kicking butt was because females were good enough to do so; it wasn't just put in there to make a point or message about a woman's fighting ability. In this film, it is a well-choreographed moment. Shot in low angle, actress Cheng Ping executes a high kick and explicitly shows her underwear. It is not about female domination but about females standing up for themselves. This is a common theme for Cheng Ping's character in this, her film debut, and other films. (See *Big Bad Sis*.)

Simpleton factory worker Chu Ling (Cheng Ping) is an innocent everyday single woman living a humdrum life in Hong Kong. She returns home one evening and is confronted by five male rapists. She runs for her life through the maze of her apartment building, stairs seeming to wind away from the safety of her home, until she is trapped on the roof and raped and left for dead. Each man laughs sadistically, enjoying his powerful position over the downtrodden, helpless female. Chu's life is sent into a tailspin when she learns that her abdominal pains and bloody discharge are not symptoms of a pregnancy but of a deadly, incurable venereal disease known as Vietnam Rose, brought to Hong Kong by U.S. sailors on R&R excursions from Vietnam. She has been given the "kiss of death." But instead of this shy woman fading away into the cracks, she decides to fill in the cracks and create a few of her own by splitting and gutting the men who raped her.

Chu gets a job as a bar girl in nightclub run by Wong Ta (Lo Lieh), who is disabled but whose cane is deadlier than Kwai Chang Caine (David Carradine's character in *Kung Fu*). She shares her plight with Wong, and he shares his fighting knowledge with her. Once her training is complete, it is time for her to give the five men her own kiss of death in the form of a pair of razor-sharp scissors she meticulously hones. Her ultra-sharp tools of revenge make Lorena Bobbit seem tame by comparison.

The term "kiss of death" originated when Judas betrayed Jesus; he sealed the moment with a kiss in the Garden of Gethsemane. Elsewhere, the deadliest kiss known to mankind is from an insect known as the kissing bug: During the evening, it will feed on human saliva around the mouth and cause the debilitating Chagas disease, which affects approximately 20 million people in Central and South America as well as parts of the United States.

As is common in kung fu films, the lead actress in this film does not have a martial arts background, but her final fight works well thanks in part to camera choreography. The hand-held shooting at low angles brings out the brutality of her actions, and good extreme close-ups reveal animalistic revenge. Chen does one stunt that must have really hurt: As she somersaults over a table, she lunges into it and lands on her head, then rolls—ouch. The character Wong being a martial arts master is Ho's respectful statement to martial arts that even with a physical disability, a person can overcome it with kung fu. (See *Crippled Avengers*.)

Titleography: *The Kiss of Death*; *Vietnam Rose*. Translation—*Poisoned Woman. Kiss of Death* refers to the disease afflicting Chu, and *Poison Woman* refers to Chu herself. **MA Percentage: 9.52%** SHAW BROTHERS

KNIFE OF THE DEVIL'S ROARING AND SOUL MISSING, THE

鬼吼段魂刀 (1976—Hong Kong) **80m. KFI: Chen Shen-yi. NOT/LOT: 3/ 2m 14s; NOF/LOF: 29/ 19m 31s.** D: Lee Goon-cheung. C: Tan Doa-liang, Doris Lung Chun-er, Lo Lieh, Shao Luo-hui, Wan Chong-shan, Liu Ping, Tung Li, Tong Li.

In the dangerous world of Jiang Hu, you can never assume a fallen adversary is dead unless you check the body. Failing to do so could lead to the enemy's shocking return.

This film is set 20 years after a group of righteous swordsmen led by hero Shen Chia-hao vanquished the masked terrorist known as the Devil Swordsman, who was last seen pin-cushioned by sword jabs and sent rolling down a mountainside. Suddenly, these worthy warriors begin falling like leaves, the latest victim being Shen Chia-hao himself. Of course, everyone's worst fear is realized: The Devil Swordsman has returned from the grave, and this time it is personal.

The only way to defeat the clandestine killer is to attain the Sunshine Sword, which is kept in a safe haven at Shaolin Temple. To attain the sword, a person must prove himself worthy by fighting his way into the temple's inner sanctum. Shen's son (Tan Dao-liang), spurred on by his father's death and accompanied by fellow fighter Lady Han (Doris Long Chun-er), whose father was also a victim of the Devil Swordsman, comes up with a plan to send the villain back to Dante's inferno. But if they fail, everyone could be doomed to a horrible death.

What is most interesting about this film is that the first 28 fights all average out to be 33 seconds in length, which creates the sense of lots of action. When the fights are short and sweet, they also do not require as much detail to the action or much creativity. You might wonder why all films aren't made this way. The problem is that the lead actor can't get into a fighting groove and show off his wares on-screen in just 33 seconds, and that is ultimately what sells these films. But doing a film like this one is fine every now and then, and it also gives the actors—some of whom might be shooting several films at the same time—much-needed time to rest and recover. (See *Clans of Intrigue*.)

You will notice that actor Tan Dao-liang, who is known for kicking, does more weapon work in this film than usual. Although a distributor will tout this as a unique perspective for the movie—"For the first time ever, see Tan Dao-liang use a three-sectional staff!"—it is actually because he was injured. If you watch his stances carefully, you can see they are not as stable or solid as usual.

The Knife of the Devil's Roaring and Soul Missing also uses a little-seen weapon in kung fu films, the *er mei* (o-mei) piercer. Originating from Er Mei Mountain in Sichuan province during the Northern Song Dynasty (A.D. 969-1126), the piercer is a symmetrically tapered 1-foot metal rod with a sharp, pen-shaped metal point at either end. In the center of the rod is a ring attached to a swivel joint, which the user slides onto a finger. With a snap of the wrist, the weapon spins like an airplane propeller, which can fool or distract an attacker with its hypnotic twirling.

The fabled Er Mei Mountain is one of the Four Sacred Buddhist Mountains of China. It is also where the legendary Wu Mei, one of the Five Elders of Shaolin, hid after the destruction of Jiu Lian Shan Shaolin and eventually taught kung fu.

Titleography: *Thunderblade and Lightning* (*Lightening*) *Foot*; *Return of the Leg Fighter*. Translation—*The Ghost Roar Devil Breaking Knife*. Since *The Leg Fighters* (1980), which also starred Tan Dao-liang, was released on video in America first, the initial distributor renamed *The Knife of Devil's Roaring and Soul Missing* as *Return of the Leg Fighter* to capitalize on Tan's starring role. It was similar to the release order of Bruce Lee's *Enter the Dragon* and *Return of the Dragon*. Although *Return* was shot first, it was released after *Enter* and took its name from that film. **MA Percentage: 27.19%**

KNIGHT ERRANT

英 雄 本 色 (1974—Hong Kong) **89m. KFI: Shan Mao. NOT/LOT: 2/ 2m 48s; NOF/LOF: 15/ 32m 53s. D: Ding Shan-xi. C: Jimmy Wong Yu, Yasuaki Kurata, Lung Fei, Shan Mao, Eddy Ko, Wang Hao, Xie Jin-ju.**

Where do they find these people? Somehow Chinese kung fu films manage to track down incredibly talented individuals who give intense, amazing and sometimes bizarre performances. One of the weirdest exhibitions I have seen in any film is Dunpar Singh in *Kung Fu vs. Yoga* (1979). Coming in a close second is elderly actress Xie Jin-ju, who plays the disturbingly violent geriatric who teaches her three nephews killer karate so they can avenge the death of their father, which, based on her demented logic, led to their mother's suicide. She is unrelenting as she whacks these kids with a wooden pole until they bleed from the mouth, and she screams that this is a matter of revenge at all costs.

Now we skip to the past to see how that all happened: In 1937, during the Japanese occupation of Taiwan, a young Japanese officer tries to help unfairly treated Chinese prisoners, such as Lin Ming-chung (Wei Su). Unfortunately, he finds himself labeled a traitor and is forced to commit *hara-kiri*. In shame, the wife commits suicide too. As their three kids observe the horror, their grandmother takes over, and thus begins the kids' road to revenge.

Twenty years later, Lin's son Huo-shan (Jimmy Wong Yu) is a violent but good-hearted street fighter who is respected by the police. He sometimes snaps at the wrong time and takes justice into his own hands, then ends up having to pay his victims' hospital bills. Because of that, the family has no money for his blind sister's important eye operation. The three vengeful sons, now grown, arrive in Taiwan looking to avenge their father by spilling the blood of Lin's whole family, but Huo-shan steams into action like a grizzly bear on meth and kills them. He doesn't realize, however, that he is in no way prepared for the likes of the kimono-clad, karate-clobbering granny from Tokyo.

There is a certain kind of nuttiness about this film, and it is similar to an American slasher or horror film in that the sight gags are all about devising creative and bloody death scenes. Xie Jin-ju is no Suzy Wong or even a dragon lady—she is part Lee Marvin and part Bolo Yeung. In one training scene, while lying on the ground, she has some big bloke jumping up and down on her stomach while four others spread-eagle her limbs. One thing some fans might not know is that Jimmy Wong Yu is over 6 feet tall, and so he often has to fight using low stances to avoid towering over everyone and looking awkward. This is one of the few films in which Wong Yu's low-stance choreography is highly perceptible.

Titleography: *Dragon Fist*. Translation—*True Color of the Hero*. *Dragon Fist* is just a generic animal title, and there are no dragon styles in this film. Huo Shan's heart reflects a sense of righteousness that could make him something of a *Knight Errant*, and perhaps the title reflects his true colors as a hero. **MA Percentage: 40.09%**

KUNG FU

(1972—USA) **74m. TA: David Chow. NOT/LOT: 7/ 4m 52s; NOF/LOF: 5/ 3m 16s. D: Jerry Thorpe. C: David Carradine, Barry Sullivan, Albert Salmi, Benson Fong, Richard Loo, Keye Luke, Philip Ahn, Victor Sen Yung, Robert Ito, James Hong, Radames Pera, John Leoning, David Chow.**

David Carradine told me several years ago that one of his favorite lines as Shaolin priest Kwai Chang Caine was, "I don't seek to know all the answers, but to understand the questions." He felt the line captured the spirit of the philosophically esoteric and highly introspective ABC television program *Kung Fu*. This original made-for-TV pilot film of the same title first aired February 22, 1972, a day that changed millions of lives across America and the world.

For mainstream audiences in the West, *Kung Fu* was their first introduction to Shaolin kung fu in the most positive way imaginable. It was the true epitome of a martial artist who traditionally trains not to fight and learns to heal rather than hurt. It was a philosophy Carradine embraced and a notion that was in direct contrast to the rising popularity of the kung fu films that hit American shores around the same time as the *Kung Fu* pilot. Carradine also told me that from his perspective, it was important to show the true way of the Shaolin and kung fu and that the show created a balance between the violent kung fu films

and the peaceful calm of Caine. The show was an example of *yin-yang* balance.

Set in the 1870s on the Western frontier, *Kung Fu* follows the path of the half-Chinese, half-American kung fu priest Caine from Song Shan Shaolin Temple. Caine is on the lam for avenging the death of his blind teacher, Po, by killing the emperor's nephew. He also finds himself in the United States searching for his half-brother, Danny Caine. Along the way, he deals with racism, American bounty hunters and Chinese assassins. Historically, Ching Emperor Yong Zheng burned down Song Shan Temple in 1736, which means the show's timeline is off.

Carradine starred alongside Gordon Liu Chia-hui in Quentin Tarantino's *Kill Bill* films (2003 and 2004). Liu is the most recognized actor to portray a Shaolin priest in Asia, stemming from *The 36th Chamber of Shaolin* (1977), and much to his nature as a man and a martial artist, he acknowledges America's most famous Shaolin priest actor, Carradine. Liu has heartfelt joy for people like Carradine for what they have done for martial arts and martial arts cinema. Liu told me that he was impressed Carradine was going to be in *Kill Bill* and that it was important to tell Carradine how much he admired the show. In Liu's view, the series played an important part in teaching the people of the West to understand kung fu. He also added that Carradine played the role of what Liu thought a Shaolin priest truly was.

To me, the most memorable scene in this film takes place after Caine wanders through a desert and arrives at the town saloon for a drink. He gently asks for a glass of water and then empties the contents of a little bag into the water: medicinal herbs. It is shot in slow motion with that echoing, mystical, tin-pan sound so frequently used throughout the TV show (which ran from 1972 to 1975). Although the martial arts in the show were rarely good and Carradine's kung fu skills were more than a bit iffy, it never stopped me from watching it. When I was at SUNY Cobleskill, a time when there was only one TV per dorm, a friend and I would get to the TV room hours before the show began to reserve the TV. Back then, we were the only martial artists on campus, and because most people knew that, we were pretty much left alone for that one weekly hour. The classic moments from the show—such as snatching the pebble from the hand, *ching gong* walking on rice paper and Grasshopper learning the ways of the Shaolin—will always endure. But what's with the silk jacket Caine wears with the giant hand and ninja *shuriken* on the back?

Regardless of the mysterious circumstances surrounding the 72-year-old Carradine's death, as Caine would reflect upon death, "Each end brings a new beginning." Besides, life is not always about what a man leaves behind, but what a man leaves for the future, and in Carradine's case, that means an immense body of work, which over the years seemed to gradually move back toward his Caine alter ego. Even his Bill character in the *Kill Bill* films mirrored many of Caine's nuances and cadences.

Titleography: As of this writing, no alternative titles could be found. **MA Percentage: 10.99%**

KUNG FU FEVER

小 師 傅 與 大 煞 星 and 小 煞 星 與 大 師 傅 (1979—Taiwan) **76m. MAC: Chan Lung, Cheung Yum. NOT/LOT: 1/ 2m; NOF/LOF: 19/ 24m 50s. D: Kim Si-hyeon. C: Dragon Lee, Kim Kee-joo, Chui Man-fooi, Ron Van Clief, Ma Dao-zh, Shi Zhong-tian, Bruce Rhee, Huang Guo-liang, Tan En-mei.**

Warning: This is the only Bruceploitation film that proudly boasts a disclaimer at the film's beginning. "The story and characters are fictitious," it says. "No identification with actual persons, places, buildings and products is intended or should be inferred." Are you kidding? After this bold statement, the first shot is of the real Bruce Lee (in footage I have never seen) speaking on the phone to Miss Lu (Tan En-mei) about some secret book he wrote, which she is looking forward to reading. Then Lee suddenly dies. The next thing you know, Lee's top student in America, Ricky Chan (Dragon Lee), dressed in a yellow tracksuit with black stripes on the sides, is flying to Hong Kong to find this secret Finger Technique book before all the evil martial arts masters of the world get their hands on it. Meanwhile, a deranged schizoid (Ron Van Clief) believes he can become the best kung fu man in the world if he can kill Ricky in a one-on-one sparring match. But since he does not know how to find Ricky, he goes around killing Ricky's friends with a piano wire.

Just when it seems this film couldn't get any more outrageous, we are introduced to Ling Shao (Bruce Rhee), Bruce Lee's supposed best friend (yeah, right). The incredibly out-of-place Ling Shao is a flamboyant dandy who wears a pink scarf tied around his neck. He is first seen sitting under a beautiful elm tree in the middle of a lush meadow filled with grazing cattle. Next to him is a peculiar 46-inch oblong inflatable punching bag that sits on the ground; when struck, it pops back up (kind of like an oversize version of the early-'70s toys known as Weebles). I doubt even Tarantino could have come up with that one.

From certain camera angles, Dragon Lee probably looks more like Bruce Lee than all the other imposters, but his tendency to overdo Bruce's fidgety neck and head jerks and some of his poses is more disturbing than entertaining. The final fight is good for a laugh when the main villain's hands turn red during the fight. When he strikes someone, he burns a handprint onto their body, with the resulting perfect hand-shaped piece of burnt clothing sticking to his palm. It is a riot to watch. The rest of the fights are humorously lousy. Interestingly, there is some terrific outdoor scenery unlike anything else seen in other kung fu films of the 1970s.

Titleography: *Black Dragon Fever*. Translations—*Little Master and Big Malignant Star* and *Big Malignant Star and Little Master*. *Black Dragon* refers to Van Clief. *Big Malignant Star* (which refers to a jinx or a person who brings death and calamity) is coarse wording for Bruce Lee's untimely death, and the *Little Master* is Dragon Lee's character. **MA Percentage: 35.30%**

KUNG-FU INSTRUCTOR, THE

教頭 (1979—Hong Kong) **100m. FI: Tang Chia. NOT/LOT: 18/ 5m 9s; NOF/LOF: 26/ 23m 2s. D:** Sun Chung. **C:** Ti Lung, Wang Yu, Ku Feng, Chiu Ya-chi, Wang Lung-wei, Jiang Dao, Ai Fei, Tong Yen-san, Tien Ching.

It is the Hatfield-McCoy feud all over again—but kung-fu-style with the Zhous and the Mengs. The Hatfields and McCoys were feuding families in the late 1800s. The Hatfields lived on the Kentucky side of the Tug Fork River, and the McCoys lived on the West Virginia side. The feud erupted because of a hate crime resulting from the Hatfields fighting for the Confederates during the American Civil War and the McCoys fighting for the Union side. Coincidentally, *The Kung-Fu Instructor* takes place at about the same time.

In the film, a village is split in two, with the peaceful Zhous on one side and the violent Mengs on the other. There is an actual line demarcating whose side is whose. If any Zhou accidentally steps over the line, the Mengs cut off his legs as punishment. Meng chief Meng Er-da (Ku Feng) wants to take over the whole village, and his plan is to hire Wang Yang (Ti Lung), a famous kung fu instructor whose Shaolin pole-fighting skills are so amazing that he seems inhuman. When Wang politely refuses to teach Meng's men because he cannot leave his students, the Mengs frame him for rape and murder. They then offer him sanctuary from the Ching authorities in exchange for lessons. Even though he's forced to accept the offer and work for the Mengs, Wang still doesn't agree with their wicked ways. He's also outspoken about his disgust toward the village dividing line. To Wang, the line between righteousness and non-righteousness is clear, and he becomes more disappointed with his new students because they only want to learn how to fight and hurt others.

Unbeknown to all, Zhou Ping (Wang Yu) wants to learn kung fu so badly that

he is willing to sneak across the borderline, knowing full well that if he is caught, his limbs will be cut off. Secretly watching Wang from a tree-covered rooftop, Zhou (pronounced like "Joe") is eventually discovered. He quickly finds himself in the middle of Meng's men like a lone seal surrounded by a group of hungry sharks. Zhou finds himself in the midst of a "beating" frenzy, but our wee seal is more like a killer whale; he is not your regular Zhou. Wang is moved by his spirit and agrees to go over to Zhou's place and teach him. Meng Er-da is upset, hires an assassin to kill Wang and tells the Chings where Wang is hiding. Wang and Zhou hide in a secret place, where Wang vows to train Zhou in everything, stating that he is not the kind of teacher who holds back teaching things from a student.

In real life, a kung fu teacher would often hold back teaching a student everything for fear the student might one day try to take over the school and kill or beat up the teacher. Therefore, over time, many kung fu styles have slowly faded, as with each generation, another technique disappears.

The beauty of writing about films of a whole decade is that with a star like Ti Lung, who made films from 1970 through 1979, I can see how he grew and improved in martial arts. In this film, his kung fu stances, postures and skills have vastly improved, and his pole work is immaculate (as revealed through his stances and postures). The fights in this film with Ti Lung are slightly slow and methodical, so as to show the audience his abilities, thus the decision not to undercrank the camera during Ti's action. Director Sun Chung's Steadicam work also makes Ti's weapon work look more dynamic.

A theme in this film is that teaching kung fu is not always about money, but sometimes it is about finding a student who truly wants to learn kung fu no matter what the price. In these cases, the price is not money but commitment and loyalty. If a person asks a teacher to teach him, he has no say in what he will be taught. That is why some teachers do not charge money, because that way there is no obligation to compromise their principles on martial arts. It is not a business but a way of life, as kung fu instructor Wang Yang demonstrates in this film as he imparts the true martial arts knowledge to his only real student, Zhou Ping.

Titleography: As of this writing, no alternative titles could be found. Translation—*Kung Fu Instructor*. **MA Percentage: 28.18%** SHAW BROTHERS

KUNG FU VS. YOGA

老鼠拉龜 and 瑜珈功夫 (1979—Hong Kong) **75m. MAI: Chui Fat, Mang Hoi. NOT/LOT: 2/ 1m 13s; NOF/LOF: 25/ 39m 18s. D:** Chan Chuen. **C:** Qian Yue-sheng, Alan Hsu, Chan Chuen, Michelle Yim, Shan Guai, Paul Chang-chung, Fung Ke-an, Hui Tian-si, Dunpar Singh.

"Plenty good, plenty good." If you have seen this film, then you will get the quote. If you have not seen the film, get it and watch it because it has several of the most bizarre fights and training sequences I have ever seen. My hat goes off to the choreographers who made the utter weirdness of the film's combat look possible. I bought this film back in 1999 while filming a Christmas special for the CBS's *Martial Law* in which Sammo Hung was posing as Santa Claus in a mall. If that sounds wacky, which it was, it's nothing compared to this film.

Tiger (Qian Yue-shing in his only lead role) and Wu Shing (Alan Hsu) love kung fu, and that is about all they love to do. They constantly argue about whose kung fu dream is more realistic—Tiger beating up Wu or the other way around. To prove he is better, Tiger enters a street kung fu contest, and after he defeats three exceptional kung fu experts, he is dumbfounded to find out that first prize is the right to wed a beautiful lady named Ting (Michelle Yim). Tiger is not the most handsome lad on the planet, and after he and Ting are married in a traditional Chinese wedding ceremony, Ting is freaking out that she has to consummate the marriage. Her father comes up with the foolproof idea that Tiger must accomplish three quests before he can do the wild thing with Ting. First he must get a secret kung fu manual protected by a vicious fighting monk (Shan Guai). Second, he must obtain two jade buttons off the chest of a certain famous prostitute who happens to be a transvestite (Fung Ke-an). Finally, he must steal a rare ruby from the turban of the famous Indian yoga master Dal Bashir (Dunpar Singh).

With the help of his good pal Wu, Tiger accomplishes the first two quests. But then, as the Chinese say, the third quest becomes like a rat pulling a turtle (see titleography below), which leads to the last nine minutes of the film. This is when

Still from *The Kung-Fu Instructor* © Celestial Pictures Ltd. All rights reserved.

Wu and Tiger run into a man who can take his right leg, curl it up behind his back, put it on top of his left shoulder and kick Wu running toward him from the left side. Really. No special effects, real physical ability.

When I was working on *Martial Law*, my good pal Joey showed Sammo Hung this film, and even he was blown away. The funny thing is that a few years later, the actor and award-winning fight director Yuen De was visiting L.A., and when I told him about this movie, his face got all squinty. He was actor Dunpar Singh's double—although you can tell when it's him and not Singh. Yuen recalled that the filmmakers used a special kind of skin polish to make him look dark like Singh. The only problem was that it did not wash off, and so he was stuck with darker skin for several weeks after the shoot.

Titleography: As of this writing, no alternative titles could be found. Translation—*Rat Pulling Turtle*; *Yoga Kung Fu*. *Rat Pulling Turtle* refers to a Chinese saying that poses the following question: How can a rat pull a turtle with a piece of string? By using its mouth. But how can a rat pull a turtle with a piece of string when the turtle's head and legs are inside the shell? The saying applies when there is a job at hand with no apparent way to tackle it. It is like this book, for which I wanted to watch and write about every 1970s martial arts film—but how can I do that if these films are not available? **Percentage: 54.02%**

LADY HERMIT, THE

鍾 馗 娘 子 (1971—Hong Kong) 93m. FI: Liang Shao-song. NOT/LOT: 4/ 54s; NOF/LOF: 28/ 22m 39s. D: Ho Meng-hua. C: Cheng Pei-pei, Lo Lieh, Shih Szu, Wang Xia, Zhao Xiong, Chuan Yuan, Fang Mian.

Another early film that firmly establishes Cheng Pei-pei as the queen of kung fu movies, a title she has held since her first *wuxia* film, *Come Drink With Me* (1966). Ironically, this production co-starred 16-year-old Shih Szu, who was being groomed to be the next queen. And although she had her moment, time would tell that Shih did too many silly films, and that took away her royalty sensibility.

This movie's Chinese title, *The Female Zhong Kuei*, makes for a more interesting and symbolic take on the underlying plots of the film. Cheng Pei-pei portrays a Batman-like hero operating out of the Temple of Zhong Kuei. She is mild-mannered maid Liang Shu-shuang by day and secret swordswoman avenger Lady Hermit by night. She is trying to eliminate the Black Demon (Wang Xia) and his crooked Taoist priests, who are running a scam selling magic charms that supposedly protect the local villagers from the ghosts killing their families. In the evening, Black Demon's henchmen dress up as ghosts and kill non-believers, which sets off a buying frenzy for their protective magic.

Cui Ping (Shih Szu) arrives in town searching for Lady Hermit in hopes of becoming her student, not realizing maid Liang is the one she is looking for. Also, local martial arts hero Three Daggers Chang Chun (Lo Lieh) is in love with Liang, not knowing she is Lady Hermit. With Lady Hermit's health waning because of the lingering effects of an earlier attack by Black Demon using his deadly Shadow Less Claw technique, her identity is exposed to Cui and Chang. Lady Hermit adopts Cui to be her student and begins teaching her the Flying

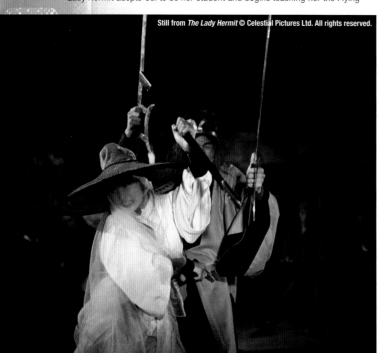

Still from *The Lady Hermit* © Celestial Pictures Ltd. All rights reserved.

Tiger skill, the only known kung fu in the world that can defeat the Black Demon. However, a love triangle soon develops between Liang, Chang and Cui, with Cui as the third wheel. Although her training is not complete, Cui stomps off with immature abandonment and challenges the Black Demon. When Cui's end is near, Lady Hermit arrives, and the two ladies must unite to save the day.

Back in A.D. 713, when Emperor Tang Shuin-tsong was sick, he dreamed that a little ghost stole his jade flute and a special pouch that belonged to his concubine Yang Gui-fei. (Yang Gui-fei was one of the four beauties of China; see *Dance of Death*.) Just as he was about to send the army after the ghost in the dream, a second, larger ghost with fuzzy hair and dressed in a blue gown appeared. It stopped the little ghost by gouging out its eyes and eating them. When Emperor Tang asked who the ghost was, it replied: "My name is Zhong Kuei. During the reign of Emperor Tang Gao-zu, after I failed my exams to become an official, I was so ashamed that I committed suicide. However, due to Emperor Tang Gao-zu's efforts, I was buried in a green gown, and for this I am eternally grateful. From that moment on, I vowed to get rid of all the evil spirits for the Tang Dynasty." When the emperor woke up, he was cured. He had a picture painted of Zhong Kuei and then told the world that Zhong Kuei was very powerful ghost that could get rid of evil spirits.

In *Lady Hermit*, Lady Hermit lives at Zhong Kuei temple and battles Black Demon and his gang of deadly "ghosts." In other words, she essentially becomes a female Zhong Kuei. I do believe that the eye-gouges in the film represent a subtle homage to the honorable ghost.

Titleography: As of this writing, no alternative titles could be found. Translation—*Female Priest Zhong Kuei*. See above martialogy. **MA Percentage: 25.32%** SHAW BROTHERS

LADY OF THE LAW

女 捕 快 (1975—Hong Kong) 86m. FI: Liang Shan-song, Ching Siu-tung. NOT/LOT: 1/ 53s; NOF/LOF: 15/ 12m 4s. D: Shen Chiang, Xiao Rong. C: Lo Lieh, Shih Szu, Chang Pei-shan, Yang Chi-ching, Chan Shen, Dean Shek, Tong Lin, Ou-Yang Sha-Fei.

In the West, we say that business is a dog-eat-dog world, but in the world of Jiang Hu, business is a sword-eat-sword world.

Before the Four Devil Spirits kill Jiao Tian-hao, the leader of the Yun Tong Security Company, Jiao gives his son, Yan-er, the coveted Flaming Dagger swordplay manual and orders him to practice for 10 years, then avenge his father's expected murder and bring honor back to the company. Just as Yan-er is also about to be executed, the most respected fighter in the Jiang Hu world, Madam White Brows, suddenly appears and saves him. Chief Chen Hua-tang (Yang Chi-ching), another hero of Jiang Hu, also arrives on the scene and is impressed with White Brows' handling of the situation. Madam White Brows uses her reputation and appeals to Chen to raise the boy as his own. She does not know that it was Chen who conspired to wipe out Jiao in order to eliminate his security business competition. However, Chen is so moved by her righteousness that he agrees to raise Yan-er. He also figures that this way he can keep his eye on Yan-er. In an instant, little Yan-er bonds with White Brows' child protégé, Leng Ru-shuang, and he vows the two will meet again.

Ten years later, the imbecilic Yan-er (Lo Lieh) is still being treated poorly by Chen, and Leng (Shih Szu) has become the feared Lady of the Law, who slashes all hardened criminals, especially rapists. Leng arrives at a local village to catch a serial rapist (and cuts off what needs to be cut off), and that villain happens to be Chen's son (Dean Shek). But Chen's son frames Yan-er for the dastardly crimes, and Yan-er must prove his innocence and defend himself against the hate-filled Leng. Luckily, she remembers fondly when they were kids and had that fleeting moment.

When Shih Szu co-starred with Cheng Pei-pei in *The Lady Hermit* (1971), it was considered to be the moment in which Pei-pei passed the mantle of the queen of kung fu to Shih because Pei-pei had hinted that she might soon retire. Three years and three movies later, Pei-pei married, retired and moved to the United States, and so Shaw Brothers cast who they thought was the next Pei-pei—Shih—in the Shaw/Hammer production of *Dracula and the 7 Golden Vampires* and then in *Lady of the Law* to cement her status. Unfortunately, things did not work out because lead swordswoman characters were losing their luster to solid male martial-arts-trained stars created by Liu Chia-liang and Chang Cheh, who were winning at the box office.

This film features Lo Lieh's best knife work in a crowd. He smoothly and effortlessly glides through a crowd of killers like a shark through a school of fish. Often in crowd fights, Lo can look awkward because, although he does practice some martial arts, his stances are weak and he can look off-balance, especially in wide-angle shots. But he really does a good job in this film. Also, the most memorable fight and sight gag in the movie takes place when Lo's character is about to be killed. He leans back, raises his feet up parallel to the ground, and then proceeds to fly backward—or forward; it's hard to say which one. As odd as it looks, it is rather neat on film. Then Lo continues the fight in a low crouched stance using some peculiar hacking maneuvers. I would guess this was conceived by fight instructor Ching Siu-tung, who quickly became known for off-kilter moves and techniques that seemed to make no sense but always achieved visual glory. This film's high-wire tightrope fight is pure unbalanced genius.

Titleography: As of this writing, no alternative titles could be found. Translations—*Female Sheriff* or *Female Vigilante*. The Chinese characters indicate that if the female works for the government, she is a sheriff, but if she works within the realms of the Jiang Hu world, she is a vigilante. The film is not clear on either one, so the English titles seem to cover both scenarios. **MA Percentage: 15.06%** SHAW BROTHERS

Still from *Lady of the Law* © Celestial Pictures Ltd. All rights reserved.

LADY PROFESSIONAL, THE

女殺手 (1971—Hong Kong) **80m. FI: Yasuyoshi Shikamura. NOT/ LOT: None; NOF/LOF: 1/ 3m 17s.** D: Kuei Chih-hung, Matsuo Akinori. C: Lily Ho, Zhang Pei-shan, Ching Miao, Wong Chung-shun, Chan Shen, Li Hao, Bolo Yeung, Jie Yuan, Yasuyoshi Shikamura.

No, that's not Agent 009 from the *Angel* films of the 1960s—*Angel With the Iron Fist* (1966) and *Angel Strikes Back* (1968)—but actress Lily Ho is back and she is taking "car" of business. This time she plays Ge Tian-li, an assassin who coolly kills her targets with a compact case that shoots darts into their necks and causes quite a stir. But she is no ordinary killer because she is only out to get the gang that extorted money from and killed her father.

However, during Ge's latest roller-coaster-ride hit, photographer Xiao Jiang (Huang Pei-shen) inadvertently takes her picture with one of those clunky, ancient Polaroid cameras. The model he's shooting recognizes Ge as the owner of the Rose Cafe, telling the audience that being an assassin is simply a side dish for her. Xiao senses that his meal ticket has arrived, and by using his contacts in the criminal world, he blackmails Ge into doing dirty deeds for two years. But eventually Ge pulls the plug on her business arrangement with Xiao after she successfully obliterates the snitch Shi Yun-pu (Chan Shen), who was about to expose a gold smuggling ring. She somehow escapes a long, bloody car-chase extravaganza complete with explosions and survives her car brake lines being cut as she swerves out of control down a hill. She now realizes that she is a liability to Xiao. So she goes after him and all the shady characters he associates with.

There is actually only one fight in this film. Three assassins—a bald, muscle-bound basher (Bolo Yeung); an equally bald bonker (Jie Yuan); and a slip-sliding, knife-wielding leaper (Yasuyoshi Shikamura)—corner Ge in a construction site at

night. Ge is tossed around like a little rag doll and yelps for help. But then she goes ballistic, and suddenly her weapons of choice are cement, rebar and cranes.

The film's finale reminds me of when I was a child suffering from cystic fibrosis: A nurse once asked me what my father did for a living. I quickly replied that he was a nun. Her eyes popped. I was simply recalling the time I was with my dad in some office, and when he was asked about his current employment, he said, "none." For Ge's last hit, she gets him at the airport while disguised as a nun. With the job finished, what do you suppose her next profession might be? None or nun?

Titleography: As of this writing, no alternative titles could be found. Translation—*Lady Assassin*. **MA Percentage: 4.10%** SHAW BROTHERS

LADY SNOWBLOOD

Shurayukihime (1973—Japan) **93m. FC: Hayashi Ikushiroo. NOT/LOT: 4/ 4m 7s; NOF/LOF: 7/ 11m 34s.** D: Toshiya Fujita. C: Meiko Kaji, Toshio Kurosawa, Sanae Nakahara, Noburu Nakaya, Yoshiko Nakada, Akemi Negishi.

A 20-year-old's take on vengeance is but a mask that pulls the wool over our eyes. When you see a 12-year-old girl standing naked in the cold, then see her flip over a *katana*-wielding priest, get her bicep sliced and utter not a squeal or a yelp—even while blood oozes down her arm—you know that this fledgling waif is going to be one dangerous woman.

After her mother dies giving birth to her in prison, Yuki (Meiko Kaji) is raised by a martial monk and criminal surrogate mother for one purpose: to wreak vengeance on the four crowing zealots who killed her father and pushed her mother down a destitute path of self-destruction and death. Yuki lives by a mantra, which she verbalizes as, "Forget joy, forget sorrow, forget love and hate, forget everything except vengeance." It is her destiny to kill.

Lady Snowblood is adapted from Kasuo Koike's *manga* comic book. (He is also known for his *Lone Wolf and Cub* series.) The film mimics the manga's sensibility. The story is split into four cinematic chapters, each intelligently shadowed by intrepid reporter Ryurei (Toshio Kurosawa; no relation to Akira Kurosawa). Ryurei's newspaper stories of Snowblood's assassinating adventures force two of the venomous villains to resurface and face the music. (In this case, that music is of the *shamisan*, the three-stringed Japanese lute.)

Kaji played a Yakuza samurai avenger in *The Blind Woman's Curse* (1970), but her steely eyes and sword-swishing role-play are more superbly displayed in the guise of Lady Snowblood. Her maverick *kendo* training culminates in better posturing and footwork and an increased awareness of choreography. Kaji effortlessly dodges and slices between the improved timing of the stuntmen's attacks.

Opening sequences of Yuki's *bokken* (wooden sword) training as a little girl quickly phase to older Yuki's controlled strikes. They then graduate to serious *katana* wielding as she slices through thick bamboo stalks, preparing the audience for the gushing fountains of arterial blood that are a mainstay of samurai films.

Yuki's vicious samurai blade is hidden within her innocent-looking bamboo umbrella. It is no wonder that Kaji draws her blade and fights using the same one-handed reverse sword grip and slicing maneuvers as Shintaro Katsu's Zatoichi character, whose sword was housed in a seemingly harmless blind man's walking cane. Also note that after killing her prey, Yuki doesn't clean her sword before re-sheathing it, a measure of her disdain and disrespect toward her victims.

It is no secret that several aspects of *Lady Snowblood* influenced Quentin Tarantino's *Kill Bill* films, right down to the intimate insertion of Lady Snowblood's theme song, "Flowers of Carnage," sung by Meiko Kaji herself, at the cranium-cutting climax in *Kill Bill Vol. 1*.

Titleography: *Lady Snowblood: Blizzard From the Netherworld*; *Blood Snow*; *Lady Snow Blood*; *Snow of Blood*. Translations—*Netherworld Snow Lady* and *Queen of the Snow God*. The English titles reflect the literal translation of the Japanese titles. The title *Blizzard From the Netherworld* accentuates the film's motif of raining blood and draws further on the harsh weather of snow blizzards. **MA Percentage: 16.87%**

LADY SNOWBLOOD 2: LOVE SONG OF VENGEANCE

Shurayukihime: Urami Renga (1974—Japan) **89m. FC: Hayashi Ikushiroo. NOT/LOT: None; NOF/LOF: 7/ 10m 54s.** D: Toshiya Fujita. C: Meiko Kaji, Yoshio Harada, Kazuko Yoshiyuki, Shin Kishida, Juzo Itami.

For fight choreographers, this film is about two fights, each of which is a single, unedited one-minute shot of absolute slaughter. Meiko Kaji returns as Yuki Kashima, the feared lone avenger Lady Snowblood. This time, she is not the devil of raw vengeance but an angel of righteousness. Wrapped in a warped purple umbrella, she unwittingly protects a man (Juzo Itami) from a corrupt government official (Shin Kishida) who has actually hired her to kill that man in return for a pardon for her murderous spree in the previous film. How Yuki cheats death in *Lady Snowblood* is a tale of guts, glory and arterial skullduggery that the filmmakers in this film chose to avoid.

Staying true to her cinematic history, Yuki keeps her sword hidden within her umbrella. Although it may seem ironic to camouflage her sword in a highly feminine object, in actuality it was illegal for a woman to openly carry a samurai sword. In a minor gaffe, this film takes place in 1905 but shows the brief appearance of an assassin flashing karate postures and kicks. Karate did not get introduced into Japan until 1912; it would have been more accurate to portray him as an Okinawan hit man.

On a quick scientific note, the black plague is spread by the bite of a flea, while the flea gets the bacteria by feeding on the blood of an infected rat. But then again, there are plenty of human rats in the Japanese government at the time this story takes place. This was essentially an extension of many Japanese filmmakers' views and lack of faith in the Japanese government during the decade in which these films were made.

The opening sword sequence is historically comparable to Bruce Lee's famous kicking sequence at the Japanese dojo in *Fist of Fury* (1972). As Yuki pays respects to her dead mentor, Priest Dokai, sunlight glints off two sword blades and alerts her. She is not alone—six assassins have interrupted her peace. What follows is a well-executed 60-second unedited wide-angle shot of Lady Snowblood briskly walking down a mountainside staircase while nonchalantly dispatching her attackers without breaking stride. It is great choreography that showcases Kaji's hard-practiced sword skills. As if this were not enough of an exhibition, at the end of the film, she does another 60-second unedited shot. This time, she takes out 11 attackers while being shot at by a handgun.

There is also a nod to Jimmy Wong Yu's *One Armed Swordsman* character in the guise of the one-armed *sai*-man killer. A sai is an Okinawan martial arts weapon believed to have its origins from the Indian *trishula* (a spear with a head like a trident) that the Malay shortened and modified into a weapon called a *tekpi*, which spread throughout Indo-China and probably found its way to Okinawa. It is basically a dagger-length pointed metal baton with two curved prongs that originate from the handle. The prongs were used to trap samurai sword blades during combat. The Japanese *jutte* is a single-pronged version of the sai, and the *manji sai* has the two curved prongs facing in opposite directions. In keeping with the history that many Okinawan weapons have their origins in farm tools, a theory exists that the sai was used to measure rice plants. Sounds "ex-sai-ting."

On an end note, this would turn out to be the last martial arts movie Kaji performed in. All I can say is that she did a bloody good job.

Titleography: *Lady Snowblood 2*; *Lady Snow Blood*; *Lady Snowblood: Grudge Love Song*. Translation—*Queen of the Snow God: Grudge, Love Song*. The titles reflect that this film is a sequel and about a character obsessed with vengeance. **MA Percentage: 12.25%**

LADY WHIRLWIND

鐵掌旋風腿 (1972—Hong Kong) **84m. FI: Sammo Hung. NOT/LOT: 2/ 2m 2s; NOF/LOF: 18/ 27m 46s.** D: Huang Feng. C: Angela Mao Ying, Zhang Yi, Bai Ying, Wu Ching-er, Liu Ah-na, Chien Yueh-sheng, Sammo Hung, Chin Nan-yi.

Who would have thought that a martial arts film would be named after the most famous American pornographic film of all time? *Lady Whirlwind*, the first kung fu film released in America to star a female lead (Angela Mao Ying), was renamed *Deep Thrust* after the 1972 porno movie *Deep Throat*, which starred Linda Lovelace. The distributors were quite insane, but the loud screaming of Mao Ying's character during her fights seemed to add to the mysterious allure of the film. The West had never heard kung fu women barking out such peculiar grunts and high-pitched yelps before. They even had the same voice actor who did the trailer for *Deep Throat* do the *Deep Thrust* trailer.

When Chinese patriot Ling Shi-hao (Zhang Yi) refuses to be part of a smuggling ring run by the big boss Tiao Da-niang (Liu Ah-na), she forces him to pay. Tiao is backed by a powerful Japanese gang headed by Tung Ku (Bai Ying), and Tung and his thugs beat the living daylights out of Ling, leaving him for dead. On a side note, it is rare in these kung fu films that the big boss is a ruthless female. This was the first film shown in the West with such a character, which no doubt added to the "dragon lady" stereotype.

Ling is found and nursed back to health by his eventual bride-to-be, Hsuang Hsuang (Wu Ching-er). Meanwhile, disgruntled debutante Tien Li-chun (Angela Mao Ying) is hell-bent on finding Ling and giving him an invitation to the grim reaper show because her sister committed suicide after Ling jilted her. After the Japanese beat Ling up once more, he goes into hiding. While on the run, he runs into a Korean herbalist. The good apothecary gives Ling a kung fu manual that reveals the secrets of the Tai Chi Palm. Meanwhile, Tien and Hsuang become friends, and Tien agrees not to kill Ling until after he has ended the whole sordid smuggling affair by foiling big boss Tiao and taking down Tung.

When you watch the fights, notice that Mao Ying's attacks and defensive moves are chest height and higher. This makes it easier for her to do techniques because of her *hapkido* background; at that time, she was not attuned to the influence of Beijing opera on fight choreography. Furthermore, her sweeping arm movements come across as more feminine, but her stalwart fighting look stems from her solid hand-posture guard positions. Although her whirlwind arm movements look like a windmill, she does not flail her arms. In fact, these arm sweeps would become part of her signature movements in other films.

Also interesting is that in the Chinese version of the film, when Ling is learning Tai Chi Palm, the voice-over does a good job explaining the concept of *fa jing*: When you strike an object, you reverse *chi* flow for a split second at the moment of impact. However, the training method shown in the film is not Tai Chi Palm but Iron Fist, whereby one strikes increasingly larger pieces of metal in a hot cauldron. The film also taps into the success of *King Boxer* (aka *Five Fingers of Death*) (1972) when, after successfully completing his Tai Chi Palm training, Ling's hands glow bright red.

Titleography: *Deep Thrust*. Translation—*Iron Palm, Tornado Leg*. The Chinese translation reflects the martial arts skills of Ling and Tien, respectively. *Lady Whirlwind* fits the whirlwind nature of Tien's tornado kicks, though she also uses whirlwind arm skills. **MA Percentage: 35.84%**

LADY WITH A SWORD

鳳飛飛 (1971—Hong Kong) **85m. FI: Han Ying-chieh, Xu Er-niu. NOT/ LOT: None; NOF/LOF: 11/ 24m 13s.** D: Kao Pao-shu. C: Lily Ho, Nan Kung-shun, Po Chin-hsien, Wang Hsia, Meng Yuen-wen, Ou-Yang Sha-fei.

The Chinese mind-set of honor and respect can be tough for Westerners to understand. In today's society, it is a no-brainer that you would never marry your fiancé if he had raped and killed your sister and then tried to kill your nephew in order to cover up his dastardly deeds. But the choice is not easy for swordswoman Fung Fei-fei (Lily Ho), who decides to spare the life of her fiancé, Lian Bao (Nan Kung-shun), so not as to anger her future in-laws or make them lose face.

However, when Lian Bao claims he did not know that the woman he raped and killed was her sister, which in his eyes makes everything OK, Fung decides to turn him in to the local magistrate, who happens to be his mother. Of course, she supports her child no matter what he has done and tries to slash Fung to bits and pieces.

Along with being the man who implemented the use of the trampoline into *wuxia* films and choreographed Bruce Lee in *The Big Boss*, fight instructor Han Ying-chieh created the postures and double-knife fighting method for Cheng Pei-pei's Golden Swallow character in the ultimate swordswoman film, *Come Drink With Me* (1966).

As a reflection of how slowly certain trends in fight choreography changed in Hong Kong and why Bruce Lee was a necessary shot in the arm for the martial arts film industry, Han is the perfect case study. Five years after *Come Drink With Me*, Han has Fei-fei's sister in this film fight with the same knives and in a similar fashion as actress Pei-pei. He also tackles Fei-fei's slice-and-dice mob sword fight like Jimmy Wong Yu in the sequel to *Come Drink With Me*, which is 1968's *Golden Swallow*. As with his older films, Han also has the character Fei-fei use a lot of broad underarm sword strikes, as if she were pitching a

Lee. His character continuously spouts off about Lee's combative philosophy, even to the point that the tournament sponsors compare him to Lee. This is also one of Ku Feng's best martial performances to date because choreographers Hsu Hsia and Yuen Cheung-yan perfectly mask Ku's limited martial arts training with quick bursts of technique. Then again, it's also worth noting that Ku's experience doing so many kung fu films made him a popular man at Shaw Brothers to teach novice actors the basic ways of kung fu fighting for film.

Titleography: *Soul Brothers of Kung Fu*; *Kung Fu Avengers*; *Incredible Dragon*; *Tiger Strikes Again*. Translation—*Being Forced*. *Dragon* and *Tiger* were two animals associated with Li, who starred in *Exit the Dragon, Enter the Tiger* (1976). He was the tiger who succeeded Bruce Lee, the dragon. *Soul Brothers* comes from the latest re-release under the Bad Azz Muthaz DVD label, which highlights Tom and Wei's partnership. *Last Strike* probably refers to the last deathblow of the film, and the Chinese title reflects Li's character being forced into a corner in which his only recourse is to fight. **MA Percentage: 39.32%**

LEGEND OF THE BAT

蝙蝠傳奇 (1978—Hong Kong) 101m. Fl: Huang Pei-ji, Tang Chia. NOT/LOT: None; NOF/LOF: 23/ 13m 29s. D: Chu Yuan. C: Ti Lung, Ling Yun, Chen Si-jia, Ai Fei, Zhuang Li, Liu Hui-ling, Xu Hsao-chiang, Yu An-an, Ching Li, Derek Yee, Gu Guan-zhong, Liu Yong, Yueh Hua, Wang Chung.

The concept of *yin* and *yang* is the Chinese philosophical tenet in which opposing forces are naturally interconnected and balanced. One cannot have all of one force without a bit of other. This interconnectivity is represented by the image of a circle that is half black and half white, and that is divided with an S-shaped line. There is a piece of black in the white and a piece of the white in the black. In the case of good versus bad, for example, nothing can be solely one or the other. Within the good there is a bit of bad, and within the bad there is a bit of good. When dealing with family clans in the world of Jiang Hu, an inherently good clan can disrupt the natural order, and *Legend of the Bat* investigates that little piece of black in the white.

After an auction on Bat Island in which a Japanese bidder wants the head of Chu Liu-hsiang (Ti Lung), Chu and his swordsman pal Yi Tien-hung (Ling Yun) arrive at Si Men Villa and encounter 12 dead martial artists and a man in white (Liu Yong) who has amnesia. In a restaurant, they run into swordsman Li Yu-han (Yueh Hua); his loyal wife, Liu Wu-min (Ching Li); and his father. Li wants to see if his father's lifelong devotion to the sword, the Wu Han Sword Array, is effective. As a personal favor, Li asks if he can test the array on Chu, because if it works it would give great face to his father's work. In martial arts, an array is not about one person or swordsman learning a technique but about a group of people or swordsmen learning a specific way to fight together as one. With great respect toward a man who has devoted his life to the sword, Chu agrees. However, even during friendly exchanges, things get out of hand as the swordsmen in the array try to kill Chu, but he is too good and demands to know why they are trying to kill him. The truth now comes out: It was not a friendly match after all. Lady Liu is dying from a disease that can only be cured by a special poppy from India that is on Bat Island, and Chu's head would have been payment for the poppy. Out of shame for the subterfuge, the father cuts off his own arm and asks Chu for forgiveness. In respect to the father's honesty and arm-lopping gesture, Yi and Chu decide to go to Bat Island to get the poppy to cure Lady Liu.

After fighting their way onto a floating house that transports them out to the ship heading to Bat Island, Chu and Yi board the boat, which is filled with a menagerie of mysterious customers. There is Lin Chi (Yu An-an), whose father built the mansion on Bat Island but has since disappeared, so she is going there to look for him, and Kao Chi-chung (Wang Chung), who is searching for a stolen black pearl.

While out at sea, a dead body is found on the boat. The film now becomes a murder mystery straight out of an Agatha Christie novel as more bodies start piling up, including those who were previously accused of the original murder. Suddenly, the boat explodes and only Lin, Kao, Chu and Yi survive. They drift in coffins and are picked up by a second boat that also fishes four naked women out of the water. Then they discover stowaways Li, Liu and the amnesiac man in white.

On Bat Island, the heroes find a cave of prisoners but get trapped inside the

softball. This technique would soon disappear from sword choreography. A few months later, Han worked with Bruce Lee, which forced Han to change his vision because Lee's fights influenced the growth of the genre and choreography. Han needed to change with the new times.

However, as is usual with these old stylized wuxia films, the use of exotic weaponry and the liberal insertion of non sequitur flips and soaring maneuvers always keeps things peculiarly captivating. Although Lily Ho's dance training makes her spins exceptionally smooth—thus the similarity with Pei-pei's movements—her lazy trailing hand adds a weak dimension to her martial reality.

Titleography: As of this writing, no alternative titles could be found. Translation—*Flying Phoenix*. The Chinese title is merely the main character's name, Fung Fei-fei. *Lady With a Sword* certainly reflects the film's motif. **MA Percentage: 28.49%** SHAW BROTHERS

LAST STRIKE

被迫 (1977—Hong Kong) 91m. MAD: Hsu Hsia, Yuen Cheung-yan. NOT/LOT: 8/ 9m 13s; NOF/LOF: 25/ 26m 34s. D: Wat Yat-wang. C: Bruce Li, Ku Feng, Ou-Yang Pei-Shan, Lo Meng, Carl Scott, Jiang Dao, Lee Hoi-san, Shao Yin-yin.

With his wannabe-Bruce Lee career in full swing but wearing thin, Bruce Li teamed up with upcoming Shaw Brothers star Lo Meng in his first major role. They play two illegal-immigrant kung fu brothers stuffed on a breadbox-sized boat with a girl they are both secretly vying to win. They land in Hong Kong to start a new life, where their martial righteousness gets them into fights and eventually leads them in opposite directions on the moral compass: Wei Lung (Li) goes north to good and Xiao San (Lo) plummets south to bad. As snide kung fu teacher Chin Shih-po (Ku Feng) lures Xiao to the dark side to do his dirty deeds, a rift grows between Wei and Xiao. When Wei tries to prevent the rift from growing, Chin has three hit men rape and kill Wei's girlfriend (the woman from the boat). In retaliation, Wei viciously truncates the trio and then beats Chin's prize kung fu disciple in a tournament at Madison Square Garden in New York.

Back in Hong Kong, as Wei continues to train and improve his kung fu skills, he adopts a young black man, Tom (Carl Scott), as his kung fu disciple. The name of the game of revenge escalates as Chin, still livid that Wei beat his best student in New York, sends more killers, including Xiao, after Wei. As Wei takes care of the killers and has it out with Xiao, Chin takes care of Tom.

When Wei arrives at Chin's abode for the final showdown, we see Tom hanging dead from a tree. The shot immediately calls to mind the image of a lynched African-American, like the photos from the American Deep South during the heyday of the Ku Klux Klan. It is either in bad taste or a powerful statement; I can't tell which one. A second ending was also shot and later released in which Tom was simply tied to a tree and released alive by Wei, after showing Chin die by an iron finger strike to the heart. This ending also reveals an X-ray shot of the hole in Chin's heart leaking blood, which was not shown in the original ending. Let us also not forget the *Rocky* theme music blaring during the opening credits.

Lo's street-fighting kung fu fakery impressed director Chang Cheh enough that after *Last Strike*, Chang cast him in a similar role in *Chinatown Kid* later that year. As this film moves along, not only do the street fights improve, but Li, who is usually dressed in shorts or a tracksuit, begins to fight more like Bruce

cave with them. In order to find their way out of the cave, under the guidance of Lin's found father, the heroes must traverse a dangerous maze of caves. Yet one by one, obstacles whittle them down to only three. These three make their way into Lord Bat's lair, where they find out that Bat is about upsetting the balance of things in nature and mankind as a means for him to become the best swordsman. Everything comes to a head during a dangerous battle in the dark, giving Bat the advantage.

Chu's action sequences in the film exemplify the balance of light and dark, yin and yang. In the beginning, the fights are shot with lurching overhead angles and close shots where there is clarity. But as the film moves along, the fights are fought in increasing darkness until the end of the film, when the final fight is shot nearly in darkness. However, there is a slice of light in the dark that reveals the death of the villain. That speck of bright light in the pitch black represents the driving force of yin-yang, where things can't all be dark or light, good or bad, but a bit of each in the other.

Titleography: *Clans of Intrigue 2*; *Bat Island Adventure*. Translation—*Unusual Tale of the Bat*. This is something of a sequel to *Clans of Intrigue* (1977), as Di Lung and Ling Yun reprise their roles from that film. **MA Percentage: 13.35%** SHAW BROTHERS

LEGEND OF THE BROKEN SWORD

折劍傳奇 (1979—Hong Kong) 83m. MAI: Chan Chuen. NOT/LOT: None; NOF/LOF: 22/ 32m. D: Ulysses Au Yeung-jun. C: Roc Tien, Tien Peng, Doris Lung Chun-er, Lin Yun, Wen Jiang-long, Yang Hui-shan, Elsa Yang.

To borrow from the 1977 song *The Things We Do for Love* (by the band 10cc), this film could be called *The Things Moms Do for Love*. In the film, a mother goes beyond protecting her daughter but is racked by sorrow and teeters on the edge of sanity as a result.

Lone swordsman Hu De-hua (Tien Peng) does not understand why weird assassins suddenly appear in his life and try to kill him. Adding to his trouble is the young lady Chang Si Si (Elsa Yang), who falls in love with Hu because he saves her from the vicious claw-and-chain clutches of the beastly Golden Bell Tang (Wen Jiang-long). Si Si eventually divulges that she has escaped from the enclosed Jiang Hu mountain encampment known as the White Cloud City and is looking for her father, Liu Yang (Lin Yun). What Si Si does not know is that Liu has locked himself within a vault at an undisclosed place so as not to be disturbed by the world of Jiang Hu and to avoid being found by his wife, Ching Yan-yan (Yang Hui-shan). Although the parents still love each other, they must remain apart because the two hold a secret that could hurt Si Si if it ever got out. In fact, for extra precaution, the mother disfigured herself beyond recognition so Si Si will never recognize her.

The other major problem for Si Si is that the rules of White Cloud City explicitly state that once you enter the city, you can never leave unless you die or defeat the 10 Elders of the City. She broke the rules, and now that she is recaptured and taken back to the city, there will be a steep price to pay. Hu decides that he must go to the city and save Si Si from a life of imprisonment. When he gets to the city, Hu learns that both Si Si and his destinies are being manipulated by some strange folks, and it is imperative that they get out of the

city fast. Standing in his way are wily assassins and 10 elder enforcers of doom, who shall determine whether they have a death together or apart.

The flying claw weapon (*fei zhua*) that Golden Bell Tang wields is an iron eagle claw attached to a long piece of rope or chain that appeared during the Ming Dynasty. Unlike a grappling hook, the flying claw was designed to grab the opponent's body on contact and rip away chunks of flesh.

Fight choreographer Han Ying-chieh was the first to use mini-trampolines, in the kung fu film *The Swallow* (1961). In order to recreate the leaping skills of kung fu heroes from *wuxia* novels (stories about kung fu heroes and knight-errant swordsmen), actors and stuntmen were taught to keep their legs in a crouched position while airborne (as if sitting over a toilet) so it looked like they were floating forward rather than falling down. This skill takes practice because the natural reflex from the moment of takeoff is to extend the legs in preparation for a landing. Good jumpers were able to remain in the crouching position until they landed or hit a second hidden mini-trampoline. The latter option further created the illusion of *ching gong*, which is a kung fu technique whereby practitioners could jump high and run atop objects like reeds, trees and flowers. Keep this in mind as you watch this and other films to see who really puts forth the effort.

Titleography: *Dressed to Fight*; *Raiders of the Dragon Blade*. Translation—*Legend of the Broken Sword*. *Dressed to Fight* means prepared to fight, as compared to being naked to fight. It's possible the title is a reference to the Brian De Palma film *Dressed to Kill* (1980), though the stories are in no way similar. Yes, this is a 1979 film and *Dressed to Kill* is a 1980 film, but remember that this film was undoubtedly released during the 1980s under the new title *Dressed to Fight*. In this film, the sword is a metaphor for the heart, and there are no actual broken swords. *Raiders of the Dragon Blade* sounds like a play on *Raiders of the Lost Ark* (1981), which infers when this English titled dub was released. **MA Percentage: 38.55%**

LIFE GAMBLE

生死門 (1978—Hong Kong) 95m. FI: Leung Ting, Lu Feng. NOT/LOT: 2/ 15s; NOF/LOF: 18/ 12m 39s. D: Chang Cheh. C: Alexander Fu Sheng, Kuo Chue, Lo Meng, Lin Chen-chi, Wang Lung-wei, Hui Ying-hong, Lee Yi-min, Lin Zhen-ji, Ku Feng, Shirley Yu, Lu Feng, Dik Wei.

No friendship lasts forever, and no enemy is perpetual. When Mo Jun-feng (Lo Meng) wants the most famous swordsmith in the Jiang Hu world, Qiu Zi-yu (Kuo Chue), to make a special set of seven daggers, Qiu denies who he is and claims to be just a simple blacksmith. Mo needs the weapons to kill four martial artist thieves who stole the touted King of All Jade pieces from Master Nan (Lee Yi-min), an upcoming and seemingly righteous nobleman. However, Chief Inspector Xiao (Ku Feng) and his aide, Xiao Hong (Hui Ying-hong), do not know who has the jade, so an assortment of thieves, assassins and other wrongdoers

are invited to a gambling party at Golden Lion Mao Kai-yuan's (Wang Lung-wei) lair as a way to find out who has the goods.

Meanwhile, Mao's in-house assassin, Yu Xiang (Alexander Fu Sheng), who is trapped by circumstantial loyalty to Mao, is instructed to prepare his throwing knives to kill whoever tries to escape the gambling den or whoever Golden Lion wants killed; it's a subterfuge so Mao can steel the jade. So as the gamblers arrive and begin playing what is a essentially a gambling game of death, the tension builds as real clues and fake clues reveal who is who. As the losers begin to pile up, so do the dead bodies. Qiu eventually admits that he is the famous swordsmith and delivers those special knives to Mo. But as one can imagine, the mo' we know the mo' trouble you can get into, as knives start flying around like vultures waiting to pounce on dying bodies.

The kung fu in this film is well-choreographed and makes liberal use of wide-angle side shots in which we can clearly see each combat skill, especially how each flip, kip and roll is specifically crafted and integrated. There is also lots of hand-held camerawork, which is probably the influence of director Chang, a firm believer in the visual power of hand-held shots. Another Chang-influenced fight piece is the knife duel between actors Alexander Fu Sheng and Lo Meng in which each must draw his knife gunfight-style to see who is faster. As previously noted, Chang was a fan of Hollywood Westerns, and his 1969 film title *Have Sword Will Travel* was influenced by Richard Boone's TV Western *Have Gun—Will Travel*.

A cultural note: Swordsmiths hold a special place in kung fu lore. Two of China's most famous swordsmiths were the husband-and-wife team of Gan Jiang and Mo Yeh from the Spring and Autumn Period of China (during the Eastern Zhou Dynasty, roughly 722-481 B.C.). They were famous for the twin *yin* and *yang* blades they made for King He Lu of the Wu state, which created the tomb legend of the Grave of Three Kings. In order to create more *chi* to make the furnace hot enough to melt the metal to make the swords, Mo and Gan cut off their hair and nails, put them into the furnace and use 300 hundred children to blow air into the bellows to stoke the flames. The resulting two swords became legendary.

Titleography: *Life Combat*. Translation—*Gate of Life and Death*. The English titles underscore the film's gambling and combative scenarios. The Chinese title refers to life and death being a gate we all enter and exit several times during our lives. It is also a metaphorical choice each character makes between living wrong or dying right, and how the character's reputation as a martial artist in the Jiang Hu world survives now or in the afterlife. **MA Percentage: 13.58%** SHAW BROTHERS

LIZARD, THE

壁虎 (1972—Hong Kong) **101m. FI: Yuen Woo-ping, Yuen Cheung-yan. NOT/LOT: 1/ 38s; NOF/LOF: 19/ 14m 33s.** D: Chu Yuan. C: Yueh Hua, Connie Chen Bao-zhu, Lo Lieh, Yang Chi-ching, Gu Wen-zhong, Ou-Yang Sha-Fei, Yue Feng.

This is as close to a Chinese Robin Hood as you will get. Bumbling, stuttering police officer Cheng Long (Yueh Hua) is nicknamed Brother Dumb by day, but by night, he changes into his alter ego, Wall Lizard. (The Chinese translation specifies that the lizard is one that climbs walls, as compared to a ground lizard.) Wall Lizard steals from rich Caucasians (while they are having sex, no less) and gives to the poor peasants. There is even a Maid Marian, You Xiao-ju (Connie Chen Bao-zhu), who pines to meet the Lizard because of his defiance of unjust laws and his defense of the downtrodden. By the way, this maiden knows kung fu, and instead of carrying water containers, she breaks them with her hands and feet.

But what Robin Hood legend would be complete without a conniving, vicious, cold-hearted Sheriff of Nottingham? In this film, that's the director of police, Chief Chen Can (Lo Lieh), who runs a prostitution ring and a crooked gambling house. Naturally, he is driving himself bonkers trying to capture and reveal the identity of the slippery Lizard.

In an effort to dethrone Chief Chen, the disguised hero plans to steal a valuable diamond necklace from a rich, flabby female getting married in a foreign consulate, and he intends to do it right under Chen's evil eye. As the robbery takes place, Pink Floyd's song *One of These Days* blasts in the background. This

Still from *The Lizard* © Celestial Pictures Ltd. All rights reserved.

song was popular in other kung fu films of the 1970s as well. The Lizard lives and gets away with the loot, only to find that his alter ego is the one getting the boot. Chen accuses Cheng Lung of being the Lizard, locks him up and throws away the key.

Maid Xiao-ju and her lovable grandfather (Yang Chi-ching) hatch a plan to free Cheng: She will pose as the Lizard, steal a valuable samurai sword from the Japanese ambassador, and then pin the robbery on Chen's slimy assistant. However, Chen disguises himself as the Lizard and shows up at Xiao-ju's place, tricking her and her grandfather into giving up their secrets.

It all comes down to a battle between Chen, Cheng and the hatchet men (popular henchmen in kung fu films set in the 1930s), as this lighthearted comedy gets inundated with knives, axes and blood, all in the name of keeping the Lizard legacy alive.

There are some standard choreography techniques used in this sort of film, though none are very exciting. The fights rely more on kicks and punches rather than weapons. Lo delivers punches like a fly swatter trying to whack a small lizard (which is appropriate, I suppose), and his kicks are more like pushes. It's a bit of a disappointment from the Yuen brothers, considering Lo's performance earlier that year in *King Boxer* (aka *Five Fingers of Death*). Connie Chen Bao-zhu uses slapping hands and hammer fists, and for kicks, she essentially raises her leg without putting much power beyond her moves. All these moves are easier for the actors to pull off because they require little balance and no flexibility. There is also less risk of injury, and the stuntmen only need to have average timing to sell the strikes.

Connie Chen was once considered one of Chinese cinema's biggest teen idols, and *The Lizard* was her last film. How appropriate that it was directed by Chu Yuan, who directed Chen in a similarly themed Robin Hood-esque film as a Lizard-like character in *Black Rose* (1965).

Titleography: As of this writing, no alternative titles could be found. Translation—*Wall Lizard*. **MA Percentage: 15.03%** SHAW BROTHERS

LONE SHAOLIN AVENGER

四大猛龍 (1977—S. Korea) **84m. MAI: Yang Wei. NOT/LOT: 2/ 55s; NOF/LOF: 17/ 24m 42s.** D: Cheng Kei-ying. C: Casanova Wong, Yang Wei, Lee Ying-ying, Chang Il-sik, Zhang Mang, Nam Chung-il, Elton Chong.

William Congreve wrote in his famous 1697 play *The Mourning Bride* that hell has no fury like a woman scorned. This film, however, suggests that hell has no place for a man scorned. Groom-wannabe Ma See-bing (Zhang Mang) and three of his henchmen kill the husband of the woman Ma wanted to marry. When the woman who jilted him commits suicide, Ma orders the rest of the family killed, but in the nick of time, her only child, Yen Chi-liang, is rescued by his uncle (Yang Wei). The uncle eventually teaches a grown-up Yen (Casanova Wong) the art of *taekwondo*. With a giant chip on his shoulder, Yen ventures out into the world to kill Ma. Yen also searches for the woman to whom he has been betrothed to since childbirth, a woman whose father was also killed by Ma and who can only be recognized by the other half of a jade amulet.

For many Korean martial arts stars trained in taekwondo, their earlier films often seem to have the requisite shot of breaking three boards with one flying kick. This display is also seen at many taekwondo demonstrations to show the authenticity of the kicks. That means several choreographic maneuvers are essentially recreations of kicking demos, which can make fights look too contrived. But what sets these Korean films apart from most Hong Kong films is pure audacity. In this film, for example, there are things like villains in Ku Klux Klan hoods and wacky wirework that looks like it was as much fun to set up and shoot as it was to watch. It's totally wrong-looking but was undoubtedly taken seriously by the filmmakers at the time of shooting.

The pace of the fights is slow, but what really hampers the overall look of the action is that throughout each shot, the camera remains static; it literally stands on its tripod in one place the whole time, without any pans, tilts, tracking or any kind of ambitious camera movement, as if the director of photography fell asleep. This also cramps the fights because without any zooms in or out, the spatial quality of the action is neutered and lifeless.

Titleography: *Bruce Against the Odds*; *The Mighty 4*; *The Mighty Four*; *Big Boss 2*; *Dragon Against the Odds*. Translation—*Four Big Vicious Dragons*. Yang Wei and Chang Il-sik were both designated Bruce Kong and Bruce Cheung Mong, respectively, which accounts for the use of *Bruce* and *Dragon* in the *Against the Odds* titles. The *Mighty Four* and Chinese titles refer to Ma See-bing and his three assassins. **MA Percentage: 30.5%**

LONE WOLF AND CUB 1

Kozure Ôkami: Kowokashi Udekashi Tsukamatsuru (1972—Japan) **82m. FC: Kusunoki Eiichi. NOT/LOT: None; NOF/LOF: 12/ 6m 20s.** D: Kenji Misumi. C: Tomisaburo Wakayama, Fumio Watanabe, Tomoko Mayama, Shigeru Tsuyuguchi, Matsuki Junai, Tomoo Uchida, Taketoshi Naito, Yoshi Kato, Yoshiko Fujita, Reiko Kasahara, Akihiro Tomikawa, Tokio Oki.

Films like *Seven Samurai*, *Yojimbo* and *Sanjiro* became classics with certain Western audiences because of the fiery spirit and emotions Akira Kurosawa could bring out in his actors, like Toshiro Mifune. These early viewers were not considered to be martial arts film fans but connoisseurs of foreign cinema. In contrast, viewers of 1970s Chinese kung fu films considered themselves fans of fun films with stylized violence. The *Lone Wolf and Cub* films transcended Kurosawa's quaint *chambara* (sword fighting) films and featured creative ways of killing with greater choreographic delights. These aspects appealed to kung fu film fans and made the *Lone Wolf and Cub* series a cult classic.

In Japan, *Lone Wolf and Cub* arrived just as the *Zatoichi* franchise ended. (see *Zatoichi at Large* or *Zatoichi at the Fire Festival*). The six-picture epic was adapted from the celebrated 1970 *manga* of the same name created and written by Kazue Koike with artwork by Goseki Komjima. It chronicles the life and adventures of the former shogunate executioner Ogami Itto and his 3-year-old son, Daigoro, across feudal Japan. Ogami is armed with his famous long-bladed *dotanuki* sword, a switch-bladed spear-like *naginata,* a regular *katana* and a marvelous menagerie of other menacing weapons hidden within Daigoro's cart. Incidentally, the cart does wheelies, skids and wobbles but, like the Weebles toy of the 1970s, it does not fall down. In the films, *Zatoichi* star Shintaro Katsu's older brother, Tomisaburo Wakayama, plays the lead role of Ogami. Wakayama was also a famous for the five-film *Wicked Priest* chambara series. (See *Wicked Priest Comes Back*.)

Some historical background: In the Tokugawa era, the shogun struggled to maintain his power. To keep his money and military, he issued high taxes on *daimyo* (military clan leaders). If anyone even thought about breaking an edict, the shogun could force the individual to commit *seppuku* (ritual suicide) and confiscate everything he or she owned. In order to see that the edicts were enforced, three groups were established. The first were spies, such as the Kurokawa Clan. The second were assassins and ninjas, such as the Yagyu Clan. The third were *kogi kaishakunin*, or executioners who worked for the shogun. In the *Lone Wolf and Cub* films, Ogami was the best of these executioners.

This first film in the epic opens in the Tokugawa era as best-of-the-best executioner Ogami heads home to be with his wife after a long day of beheading. He and son Daigoro (Akihiro Tomikawa, who only did these six films) visit a small graveyard shrine to pray for all the beheaded souls. Today's execution should never have happened: Ogami took the head of 5-year-old Lord Hirotada because his clan members could not bring themselves to make the cut. On their

way back home from the shrine, Ogami and Daigoro encounter blood, death and anger. Ogami's wife has been slaughtered by ninja sent by the shogun. While father and son stand in shock, Inspector Bizen (Taketoshi Naito) and his samurai squad conveniently happen along. He notices a death memorial with the shogun's crest on Ogami's family shrine, which suggests Ogami is praying for the shogun's death. The crest was in fact placed by the ninja to set Ogami up, and Bizen knows it is a ruse masterminded by the Yagyu Clan. Bizen attempts to arrest Ogami, but the executioner refuses to commit seppuku under false pretenses and disembowels Bizen and his bunch instead. Ogami knows his current life is over and that he must prepare to tread the *meifumando* (road to hell) as a *ronin* (masterless samurai). He offers little Daigoro the choice between a sword and a ball. If Daigoro chooses the sword, they will travel the path together; if he chooses the ball, he shall go be with his mother. You can guess which he chooses. This exact scenario is also played out in Jet Li's *The New Legend of Shaolin* (1994).

Yagyu Clan leader Retsudo has framed Ogami because he wants to seize Ogami's executioner position and hang his head on a wall for all to see. But the Yagyu Clan forgot that the better sword artist can't be stuck to a wall so easily. Just by looking at Ogami's solemn, stark, stoic face … well, in the words of Rod Stewart, "Every picture tells a story. Don't it?"

So the ronin and his be-carted rug rat leave the normal world behind to become assassins. The rest of the movie follows Ogami as he uses his patented *suio-ryu* sword to redden shores and create tsunamis of Yagyu blood. The first beach that Ogami's tsunami hits is Retsudo's son, in what the Yagyus would call the "edge of the waterfall fight." The movie ends with Retsudo earning another reason to kill Ogami and his son.

I must note that chambara films are often described as action-packed. Critics give the impression that the films feature nonstop blood, gore and great sword fighting. However, since the genre's inception in the 1950s, the average chambara samurai film has less than 10 minutes of fighting. The *Lone Wolf and Cub* series is no exception. Each of the six films barely averages 10 minutes of martial arts action. But when the fights are evenly distributed throughout the course of the film, it creates an impression in the audience that something is going on all the time. Chu Yuan's *Jiang Hu* films are probably the best movies that do this, but the *Lone Wolf and Cub* series is a close second.

What also sets the *Lone Wolf and Cub* series apart from other samurai and chambara movies and franchises is actor Tomisaburo Wakayama. His real-life martial arts skills add a strong air of authenticity to his sword fights and allow the choreographers to be more creative with the fight work. Wakayama's flair for spins and his good balance also add the illusion of power to his strikes, making the disembowelments more vicious and realistic. He not only freezes in solid stances but also smoothly breaks out of the stances into good rhythmic motion with more spins and poses. I love the short scene in which a seated Ogami kills two people. They sneak up behind him, but he catches them in the act with two crisp sword strikes—without looking.

Although there is still a modicum of close shots, they work because Wakayama's face is as stern as famous Japanese actor Toshiro Mifune's. There is also a welcome lack of shaky camerawork in the fights, so the excitement the viewer feels comes from the clarity of technique. Of course, the increased use of spurting blood and gore helps accent the fights' intensity too.

A few notes on Ogami's martial ways: Dotanuki is a Shinto-era sword-smithing school known for swords with broad blades that could cut through an opponent with a single slice. A regular *katana* could not cut through thick, healthy bone like that. *Suio-ryu* is a martial art founded by Mima Yoichizaemon Kagenobu in the early 1600s that includes *iaido* sword-drawing skills, naginata weapon-wielding skills and grappling.

Titleography: *Lone Wolf and Cub: Sword of Vengeance I*; *Sword of Vengeance*; *Lone Wolf With Child: Lend a Child, Lend an Arm*; *Babycart 1*. Translation—*Child and Expert for Rent*. With bad dubbing, a redone musical score and a restructured screenplay in which the character Retsudo is now the shogun, *Shogun Assassin* (1980) was a compilation of *Lone Wolf and Cub 1* and *2* put together by David Weisman and Robert Houston. **MA Percentage: 7.72%**

LONE WOLF AND CUB 2

Kozure Ôkami: Sanzu No Kawa No Ubaguruma (1972—Japan) **88m. FC: Kusunoki Eiichi. NOT/LOT: None; NOF/LOF: 12/ 8m 37s.** D: Kenji Misumi. C: Tomisaburo Wakayama, Kayo Matsuo, Akiji Kobayashi, Minoru Ohki, Shin

Kishida, Shogen Nitta, Kanji Ehata, Katsuhei Matsumoto, Akihiro Tomikawa, Izumi Ayukawa, Kôji Kobayashi, Maki Mizuhara, Ima Masaki, Reiko Kasahara.

The first film in this series introduced Ogami Itto (Tomisaburo Wakayama), the once-proud *kogi kaishakunin* (executioner for the shogun) who was framed as a traitor and whose wife was killed by Retsudo, the head of the Yagyu Clan, because he wanted to take over Ogami's position. Ogami and his son, Daigoro (Akihiro Tomikawa), have left the normal world behind to walk the figurative road to hell. Along the path, they become assassins for hire. For 500 gold pieces and a satisfactory explanation of who the target is and why he must be killed, the "lone wolf and cub" never fail to kill their sheep. However, at every turn in their road, Yagyu Clan assassins meet them, and each is more deadly than the last. But when you live with death for so long, the only thing worse than dying is dying alone. But despite all the death, this father and son have something to live for because they are not alone: They have each other.

Lone Wolf and Cub 2 opens with a samurai in a straw hat out to assassinate Ogami, but the samurai quickly learns there is an awful catch to his assignment when he tries to catch Ogami's downward sword slice in his hands. Rather than stopping the sword a few inches from his head, the straw-hat samurai stops the sword a few inches inside his head. SPLURT goes the samurai. A second man leaps out from behind the straw-hat man, only to be met with Ogami's spear. Ogami pins the second assassin like a butterfly in a display. The bug collection has just begun.

Elsewhere, the leader of the Kurokawa Clan, Ozuna, cautiously approaches a group of female Yagyu ninjas. He explains to their leader, Sayaka (Kayo Matsuo), that the Edo Yagyu are required to leave Ogami alone because he won the oft-talked-about "edge of the waterfall fight" in the first film. However, that edict does not apply to other Yagyu sects. Ozuna then makes a big mistake: He implies that Sayaka's sect is not qualified for the job of killing Ogami because its members are women. After a few quick slices, one of Ozuna's men goes to pieces. Ozuna correctly hires them at this point.

Meanwhile, Ogami is hired for his obligatory once-a-film assassination job. The man about to sell the Awa Clan's cloth-dying secrets to the shogunate must die. Standing in Ogami's way are the Awa Clan dyer's personal bodyguards, the Hidari brothers. Also known as the Gods of Death, the brothers are so feared that even the Yagyu Clan clams up in their presence. Clearly, this job will not be an easy one for Ogami. The brothers consist of Hand-Iron Claw Benma (Akiji Kobayashi), Flying Club Killer Tenma (Minoru Ohki), and Mailed Fist Kuruma (Shin Kishida) who has a mace-like club attached to his hand. To deal with the Gods of Death and the female ninjas, Ogami and his son will have to show their hands by rolling out a few cart tricks.

There are several great weapon bits in the film. The first is when Ogami throws a sword through two rooms and impales a ninja behind a wall. As the ninja slumps down and dies, the sword slowly cuts the wall in half and the bloody body falls out, showing the audience and the men who want to hire Ogami just how good he is. The second is when female ninjas literally pop up out of their clothes into the sky, leaving their street clothes on the ground to reveal them dressed in sexy undergarments. When Sayaka pops out of her clothes to reveal herself in a tight fishnet body stocking, Ogami breaks out his special pole weapon. With a flip of a hidden switch, the pole becomes a *naginata*, one of the core weapons of Ogami's *suio-ryu* martial arts. (See *Lone Wolf and Cub*.) The fight scene also plays right into actor Wakayama's expertise in *bo-jutsu*. The naginata is similar to the thin-bladed, long-handled Chinese *da dao* (a broadsword-size blade on a long pole) and was primarily used by the wives of samurai. Adding this weapon to the mix provides the choreographers a chance to give a different flavor to the film's action. Wakayama spins more than usual, as the nature of the weapon is to keep attackers at bay. His flair with the weapon looks good on camera, especially when the legs of the warriors he's cutting are left standing upright on the ground. This is a nod to one of the other battle field uses of the naginata: cutting off the legs of passing cavalry horses.

The fights against the Gods of Death introduce a beautifully morbid new dimension to blood fountains and showers of death. At the time the film was made, it was stuff the viewer probably had not seen before. The fights are shot in close-up, not to hide anything but rather to make sure the audience can see the brutality of each of the Hidari brothers' weapons. Battling one brother, Ogami splits the brother's hat and head vertically down to the neck, leaving the brother's face looking like an open-face flower with a blood-red stem. Another brother's blood

hisses out of his throat and blows away in a fine mist. It is not to be missed.

Oh yes, if you're wondering where Daigoro is during most of this, you haven't missed much. He's in his cart, watching the killing with the usual boredom kids have while their parents work. That's where you'll usually find him in the *Lone Wolf and Cub* movies. He does, however, get more active in later films.

Titleography: *Lone Wolf and Cub 2: Babycart at the River Styx*; *Sword of Vengeance Part II*; *Babycart 2*. Translation—*Perambulator (Pram) at the River of Sanzu*. *Shogun Assassin* (1980) was a compilation of *Lone Wolf and Cub 1* and *2*. *Sanzu* is a river that leads to one of three hells; it is comparable to the River Styx in Greek mythology. **MA Percentage: 9.79%**

LONE WOLF AND CUB 3

Kozure Ôkami: Shinikazeni Mukau Mubaguruma (1972—Japan) 87m. FC: Kusunoki Eiichi. NOT/LOT: None; NOF/LOF: 11/ 9m 43s. D: Kenji Misumi. C: Tomisaburo Wakayama, Go Kato, Yuko Hamada, Isao Yamagata, Michitaro Mizushima, Ichiro Nakaya, Akihiro Tomikawa, Sayoko Kato, Jun Hamamura, Saburo Date.

After the Yagyu Clan kills the wife of Ogami Itto and frames him for treason so that he loses his honored position as the shogun's executioner, Ogami (Tomisaburo Wakayama), turns his back on the normal world. Along with his wee son, Daigoro (Akihiro Tomikawa), who travels with him in a baby cart, Ogami becomes an assassin for hire. But in *Lone Wolf and Cub 3*, Ogami has a run-in with a *watari-kashi* (a samurai for hire) named Magomura Kanbei (Go Kato). In Magomura, Ogami sees a mirror image of himself: Magomura was also once a proud and honorable samurai, but now he is forced to do things that are not so honorable. In a series like this, there is little doubt that Magomura and Ogami's paths and swords will cross eventually.

Lone Wolf and Cub 3 begins with Ogami and Daigoro running into a young girl who was sold into sexual slavery. But she's not just any kind of sex slave—she has become part of the Yakuza-based flesh peddling organization known as Bohachi Mono. (See *Bohachi, Clan of the Forgotten Eight* for details as to who they are.) In order to save her from that life, Ogami puts himself in the middle of the mix and offers to go through the required *buri-buri* torture himself, which is given to anyone who wants leave the Bohachi Clan alive. Ogami endures the buri-buri and survives the painful ordeal without so much as a gasp, so the girl goes free and the fiery female Bohachi leader, Torizo (Yuko Hamada), is suitably impressed with his skills. She hires Ogami to kill a local corrupt deputy named Genba Sawatari for raping her sister. Catching wind of his impending doom, Genba waits for Ogami in the middle of the desert with warriors armed with swords and guns.

The film's penultimate fight is probably a reference to the Tokugawa shogunate's failed policy of isolationism. The anti-Tokugawan Ogami uses a makeshift Western machine gun hidden in Daigoro's cart to easily destroy 200 of Genba's Japanese-sword-wielding men. But for the final wave of attacks, mostly against Retsudo's Yagyu Clan killers, Ogami whips out his *naginata*. He proceeds to use the long-handled spear-like weapon with its slicing blade to bring it on in a huge battle royal. There are two interesting things to point out about Ogami using the naginata: First, the naginata is a weapon primarily used by females, so for Ogami to use such a weapon against the Yagyu assassins is an insult. Second, because the samurai viewed the naginata as a female weapon, the female user would have been considered a weaker opponent. This would explain why the Yagyu samurai attack with their swords raised above their heads. Their strategy is to create the illusion of an opening, which a lesser-trained fighter would take. But in the end, it's the Yagyu who get shocked by Ogami's charge. Zap! They take a short circuit to death. The final fight with Magomura is a one-on-one samurai duel, so Ogami breaks out his *dotanuki* (see *Lone Wolf and Cub*) in a final nod of respect to a fellow samurai.

Watari-kashi like Magomura are drifters, one class level above *ronin*. They were usually hired to accompany *daimyo* (feudal lords) on their required biannual trips to Edo, which the shogun implemented in order keep tabs on everyone. These roving watari-kashi remained loyal to these lords even if the lords were dishonorable or were doing wrong. It was all about serving the lord, no matter what. So when Magomura is supposed to kill a mother and daughter who are being raped by three of his lord's right-hand men, he does so. In Magomura's eyes, he is protecting his lord's honor with the murders; the women can't tell the authorities. On the other hand, Ogami sees the women's deaths as a way to shield them from a life of shame. In the eyes of both Magomura and Ogami, the women had to die. When the two meet and know of each other's reputations and Magomura asks for a duel, Ogami obliges out of respect but eventually calls it a draw because killing such a fine samurai talent would be waste.

The code of *bushido* (way of the samurai) says to do what is right by one's lord and not what is right in one's heart. The situation is similar to a soldier who must follow orders even if he knows them to be immoral. What originally made a ronin a ronin was his refusal to commit *seppuku* (ritual suicide) after the loss of his master or if ordered to do so by an authority figure. Therefore, samurai viewed ronin as men who turned their back on the code. But during the late Tokugawa period, there were a lot of ronin, so it became acceptable for ronin to uphold the code of bushido without having to blindly disembowel themselves to please their employers. Plus, a good swordsman would respect a good swordsman no matter what, which is why Ogami and Magomura consider each other samurai even though one is a ronin and the other is a watari-kashi.

Fun fact: If you watch the movie, you'll notice that Ogami uses rock-shaped arrows to direct prospective clients to his roving headquarters. This little code made of rocks was created by Ota Dokan (1432-1486). He was a real samurai warrior, Buddhist monk and military strategist notably known as the architect and builder of Edo Castle. He is also known for his eloquent death poem.

Titleography: *Lone Wolf and Cub 3: Babycart in Hades*; *Sword of Vengeance Part III*; *Lightning Swords of Death*; *Flying on the Wind of Death*; *Lupine Wolf*; *Baby Cart in Hades*; *Lend a Child*; *Lone Wolf and Cub: Baby Cart to Hades*; *Shogun Assassin 2: Lightning Swords of Death*; *Lend an Army*; *Baby Cart 3*. Translation—*Perambulator (Pram) Against the Winds of Death*. Since a compilation of parts from *Lone Wolf and Cub 1* and *2* was released as *Shogun Assassin*, *Lone Wolf and Cub 3* was released as *Shogun Assassin 2* and *Shogun Assassin 2: Lightning Swords of Death*. American distributors sure know how to confuse us and make us buy the same film numerous times. **MA Percentage: 11.17%**

LONE WOLF AND CUB 4

Kozure Ôkami: Oya No Kokoro Ko Ko Kokoro (1972—Japan) **89m. FC: Kusunoki Eiichi. NOT/LOT: None; NOF/LOF: 19/ 12m 16s.** D: Buichi Saito. C: Tomisaburo Wakayama, Yoichi Hayashi, Michie Azuma, Akihiro Tomikawa, Asao Koike, Tokugawa Yoshinao, Hiroshi Tanaka, Tatsuo Endo, Shin Kishida.

Ogami Itto (Tomisaburo Wakayama) and his son, Daigoro (Akihiro Tomikawa), whom Ogami still pushes around in a cart, are still on that road to hell. But the further they go, the more their past seems to slowly fade away. Like always, Ogami and Daigoro's lives revolve around survival, finding employment as hired killers and destroying the Yagyu Clan. The Yagyu Clan's only goal remains the same: to kill Ogami and his son.

At the film's beginning, a mysterious woman asks Ogami to assassinate a female street performer named Oyuki (Michie Azuma) because she poses a threat to the reputation of the feudal lord Kozuka Enki (Shin Kishida). Oyuki is like the titular character in Ray Bradbury's sci-fi novel *The Illustrated Man* in that her whole body is covered in tattoos; they include one of Witch Mountain and a flaming Kintaro (a red dragon) on her breast. The tattoos are one of her weapons. She uses them to shock and frighten people enough to make their hearts skip a beat or to arouse their imagination. She then uses that moment of weakness to strike with her vicious *kodachi* small-sword techniques. And in learning all that, the audience also learns that Oyuki's prime goal in life is to kill Enki and defeat his flaming sword.

Meanwhile, Retsudo (Tatsuo Endo), the head of the Yagyu Clan and the man who put the hit on Ogami's wife, has a new gambit. He orders his son Gunbei (Yoichi Hayashi) to search out and destroy Ogami. According to Retsudo, Gunbei has the best chance of killing Ogami because he is the only man who ever defeated Ogami in a fair duel. (Gunbei and Ogami fought when they vied for the position of executioner for the shogun.) Retsudo also believes that Ogami was only deemed the winner due to dubious circumstances. But because of those circumstances, Retsudo banished his son from the Yagyu Clan, never to be part of the clan again. But now he will welcome his son back to kill Ogami.

During this time, Ogami zeroes in on Oyuki. He meets her father, who is the head of Japan's nationwide guild of actors, puppeteers, comedians, dancers and storytellers. They are known as the Goumune Jindayua. Because Oyuki has made bad choices in life, Oyuki's father sadly accepts his daughter's fated death, but he silently revels in the knowledge that the famous Ogami will be the man to end her life. Before Ogami kills her, he and Oyuki have a heart-to-heart. She lets him know that she accepts the whole assassination ending,

and Ogami agrees to first let her complete her mission to kill Enki. It's a very *bushido*-like arrangement, and it shows that Ogami still retains some of his old self and honor. Eventually, Oyuki's moment of reckoning arrives and she faces Enki. Ogami's moment comes too, because he must now fight the only man who ever defeated him, Gunbei. Regardless of the outcome, an army of Yagyu killers awaits Ogami and Daigoro.

Kenji Misumi directed the first three *Lone Wolf and Cub* films, but Buichi Sato directed this installment. The difference in direction shows in the fights, the camera choreography and the actors' emotions. For example, it's immediately noticeable that Ogami shows more facial expression during his kills. Another example is the editing. In the first three films, fight sequences comprised individual techniques edited together, and when that happens, the fights lack rhythm. However, in this film there is a simple rhythm to the fights because the sword-fighting sequences look like extended exchanges of techniques and not choppy edits.

The final action sequence is perhaps a bit too much like the final action scene in *Lone Wolf and Cub 3*, in which the Yagyu Clan pops up all over a rock quarry and charges down the hill toward the lone Ogami. Machine-gun fire also erupts from Daigoro's cart. However, instead of just blasting groups of Yagyu into bullet-riddled corpses in an open area, this gun scene takes a different visual path when Ogami chases his opponents through narrow trenches—it looks like documentary footage commonly seen in World War I documentaries. The camera then tracks up the hill to follow Ogami wielding two long swords. On a quick historical note, Japan's most legendary samurai, Miyamoto Musashi, was famous for using a twin-samurai-sword fighting style. Perhaps this final fight by Wakayama was an homage to this great warrior.

If I might go out on a limb here, to me there is a very funny sequence in which Ogami is ambushed by mud-covered ninjas. After he disarms (and dislegs) them, he is left to be attacked by a bunch of torsos. It's like the scene is right out of *Monty Python and the Holy Grail* (1975). One of the ninjas even bites Ogami's leg. ("I'm not dead yet!")

Titleography: *Lone Wolf and Cub 4: Babycart in Peril*; *Sword of Vengeance IV*; *Babycart 4*; *Baby Cart in Peril*; *Lone Wolf and Cub: In Peril*; *Lone Wolf and Cub: Baby Cart in Peril*; *Shogun Assassin 3: Slashing Blades of Carnage*. Translation—*Heart of the Parent, Heart of the Child*. Since *Shogun Assassin* is combined footage from *Lone Wolf and Cub 1* and *2* and *Shogun Assassin 2* was *Lone Wolf and Cub 3*, that makes *Lone Wolf and Cub 4* the equivalent of *Shogun Assassin 3*. **MA Percentage: 13.78%**

LONE WOLF AND CUB 5

Kozure Okami: Meifumando (1973—Japan) **81m. FC: Kusunoki Eiichi. NOT/LOT: 2/ 1m 30s; NOF/LOF: 9/ 12m 5s.** D: Kenji Misumi. C: Tomisaburo Wakayama, Michiyo Ookusu, Akihiro Tomikawa, Shingo Yamashiro, Tomomi Sato, Akira Yamauchi, Hideji Otaki, Taketoshi Naito, Mawatara Hachiro, Fujio Suga, Rokko Toura, Koji Fujiyama.

Ogami Itto (Tomisaburo Wakayama) is still proving to be more than a handful for the Yagyu Clan and its head, Retsudo, a crazy-haired psychotic samurai whose sole purpose is to kill Ogami and his wee son, Daigoro (Akihiro Tomikawa). Ogami has left the normal world and journeys down the road to hell as a *ronin*, or assassin for hire. His only prerequisite for accepting a contract kill is to know the details behind the hit. But no matter where the Lone Wolf and Cub go, Retsudo and the Yagyus will always be their foes.

In this film, five men known as the Beasts of Hell stalk Ogami, but they also want to hire him. Before hiring Ogami, he must prove his worth, so each of the five warriors challenge him to a duel. If he defeats them, each dying Beast of Hell will give Ogami one fifth of his usual 500-ryo payment and part of the assassination story as to why the Beasts want someone dead. After losing to Ogami, one of the Beasts catches on fire. As he turns to ash, he calmly blurts his part of the story to Ogami, then dies. (Talk about being fired up to fight Ogami.) Five deaths later, the Beasts have earned Ogami's respect, and Ogami has earned 500 ryos of gold. Ogami accepts the Beasts' multi-mission to assassinate a bad-news Buddhist priest, seize a vital document and kill a child daimyo and his parents, all under the umbrella of saving face for the clan that employs the five Beasts.

But when Ogami faces the priest, the usually steadfast and cool ronin hesitates. For the first time, he fails to assassinate his target. Why? The answer might be fear. Nothing is cut-and-dry for Ogami, but in this instance, wetting his sword with the blood of a priest seems to faze him. With his reputation now at stake, Ogami's hellish road to redemption gets even more cluttered because of Retsudo and his killer clan and the hook-spear-wielding Kuroda Masked Clansmen, who were initially his allies but have turned against him.

The action sequences with the Kuroda Clansmen are shot in close-up with inserted shots of fighters getting speared with blood popping out of their wounds, but we never see any actual technique in wide angle. While you may surmise that keeping the Kurodas' art secret is a logical cinematic approach, the main reason you don't see wide-angle techniques is because none of the actors knew how to use the spear, and so the action was shot to hide that fact. But at least when the clansmen fight Ogami, the camera angles are carefully chosen so that you can still see Wakayama's obvious martial skills. During Ogami's other major battles—his *naginata* versus the Yagyu, his sword versus Kuroda swords—several of the fight routines are filmed in medium shot as the camera pans back and forth showing Ogami hacking everything in sight. It adds dynamic motion and energy to the fight, making Ogami look like a nuclear-powered human blender.

There's an important scene in this film that treads deeper into the character evolution of Ogami and Daigoro: The local police publicly flog Daigoro because he refuses to break a promise to a wayward lady pickpocket and turn her in to the police. Even after the lady admits she is the thief, Daigoro says nothing and feigns not knowing her. Ogami looks on with pride as Daigoro does not scream, cry or break his work under duress. To Ogami, Daigoro becomes a man after the flogging. The scene ends with father and son silently walking away hand in hand; Daigoro is no longer seated in his cart. The Ogami lineage is safe.

Throughout the series, Ogami kills like an unfeeling machine, almost like a Terminator. However, similar to how young John Connor is the Terminator's link to humanity, young son Daigoro is Ogami's last bastion of hope. With one more *Lone Wolf and Cub* film to go, it wouldn't have been surprising to see Ogami grunt, "*Kaette kimasu*" ... "I'll be back!"

Titleography: *Lone Wolf and Cub 5: Babycart In Lands Of Demons*; *Sword of Vengeance V*; *Tread Lightly on the Road to Hell*; *Road to Hell*; *Babycart 5*; *Shogun Assassin 4: Baby Cart at the River Styx*; *Baby Cart in the Land of Demons*. Translation—*Crossroads to Hell*. **MA Percentage: 16.77%**

LONE WOLF AND CUB 6

Kozure Ôkami: Jigoku E Ikuzo! (1974—Japan) **83m. FC: Kusunoki Eiichi. FI: Uncredited. NOT/LOT: None; NOF/LOF: 12/ 11m 40s.** D: Yoshiyuki Kuroda. C: Tomisaburo Wakayama, Akihiro Tomikawa, Junko Hitomi, Goro Mutsumi, Daigo Kusano, Jiro Miyaguchi, Renji Ishibashi, Ritsu Ishiyama, Minoru Ohki, Isao Kimura, Mayumi Yamaguchi.

You'd better watch out. You'd better not cry. You'd better not lower your sword, and I'm telling you why: Ogami Itto is coming to town. If you think this is a crazy beginning, you won't believe the almost Santa Claus ending of this film. But first, let's look at the plot to this final installment of the *Lone Wolf and Cub* series, in which Retsudo (Minoru Ohki), head of the Yagyu Clan, is laying the framework for the final downfall and death of Ogami (Tomisaburo Wakayama) and his son, Daigoro (Akihiro Tomikawa).

With five films and counting, the Yagyu Clan has still failed to kill Ogami and Daigoro. Retsudo himself has lost several sons to Ogami's patented *suio-ryu* wave-slashing stroke (see *Lone Wolf and Cub 1* through *4*). But Retsudo has one more son to go and throw at Ogami; it's his unnaturally outlandish bastard son, Hyoei (Isao Kimura). Retsudo banished Hyoei from the Yagyu Clan because of Hyoei's whimsical but sick tampering with the occult. In the fifth film, the audience learns that Ogami has one chink in his armor: things that deal with spiritual matters. Ogami was spiritually psyched out by a priest he almost failed to assassinate. Now Ogami is faced with getting physically manhandled by spirits when Hyoei raises three samurai from the dead. If Ogami's chink grows into a major chunk, then his road to hell will include a stop in limbo land because samurai sorcery will sink him into the quicksand of silence.

But after Ogami intelligently appeals to Hyoei's sense of samurai honor over mysticism, the bizarre gets weirder. The plot boils down to a moment of incestuous necrophilia in which Hyoei gets funky with his sister. And if that sounds like a disease, it probably should be because Retsudo cures it by sending the rest of his family to the netherworld. However, Retsudo has one more major pain in the butt to take care of, and it's not hemorrhoids. So rather than using aloe and an ice pack to calm his swelling ire, he breaks out his cold steel to put his No. 1 nemesis on ice.

So getting back to our Christmas carol: Get ready to die, or lose a limb, to be cut in half because it's just a whim. Ogami Claus is coming to town! In Yagyu town, hundreds of Yagyu assassins speed down a wintry wonderland on skis and toboggans while racing toward Ogami and Daigoro. Our wolf and cub pack themselves onto the baby cart and prepare for Mount Fuji fun by clashing with the crazy-looking but North Pole-appropriate white-haired Retsudo. Ogami and Daigoro maneuver over snow like Santa and his elf handling their sleigh on a stormy night. One part of the mountain battle is similar to a carnival bumper-car ride in which samurai Santa Ogami, with Daigoro, jockeys with Retsudo's men and a cannon-containing cart while speeding downhill. The foray features one man getting cut in half while zipping by on skis. His torso gets discarded, but his legs keep heading downhill on the skis—great balance, man. At the end of the holiday, the real gift for fans is a satisfying ending that's wrapped in tidings of Retsudo's discomfort and Ogami's joy.

The film's group fights mostly consist of a swing-and-slice style of samurai choreography in which an actor simply swings his sword and slices something, then the camera cuts to blood and guts getting strewn all over the place. Swing-and-slice fights are easier to arrange because the fight is choreographed for simplicity rather than intricacy. An actor just has to block an attack with one stroke and follow up with a swing to kill on the second stroke. Most samurai films like *Lone Wolf and Cub* are not as choreographically sophisticated as their Chinese counterparts, but the fights are simplistic because they're meant to be realistic. However, over the decade, simplification of choreography was replaced by more violent deaths and blood spurts.

This brings us to the ending of the Ogami saga. In the original *manga* (Japanese-style comic book) by Kazue Koike's, Ogami is fatally wounded in his final battle with Retsudo. His spirit leaves his body, which is a metaphor for Ogami giving up the ronin's road to hell for the actual afterlife one. Retsudo also intentionally lets Daigoro kill him by ramming a spear through his body. Embracing Daigoro with tears, Retsudo calls Daigoro the grandson of his heart. While different from the film ending, this is how Kazue Koike concluded his epic manga about the cycle of vengeance and hatred between the clans.

Trivia: Ogami fights three zombie fighters in this final *Lone Wolf and Cub* installment. In which film does Jimmy Wong Yu fight three zombie fighters? Hint: See the R section.

Titleography: *Lone Wolf and Cub 6: White Heaven In Hell*; *Sword of Vengeance VI*; *We're going to Hell*; *Babycart 6*; *Baby Cart 6: Go to Hell, Daigoro!*; *Lone Wolf and Cub: White Heaven in Hell*; *Shogun Assassin 5: Cold Road to Hell*. Translation—*Daigoro We're Off to Hell*. **MA Percentage: 14.06%**

LONG CHASE, THE

侠士行 (1971—Hong Kong) **81m. FI: Liang Shao-song. NOT/LOT: None; NOF/LOF: 18/ 16m 20s.** D: Ho Meng-hua. C: Li Ching, Yueh Hua, Lo Lieh, Chuan Yuan, Wang Xia, Peng Peng, Zhao Xiong, Luo Han, Tang Tien-xi, Li Xiao-cong.

It is amazing when you consider how conservative Hong Kong society was in the 1970s that directors such as Ho Meng-hua and Li Han-hsiang were able to avoid censorship with their adult-themed *wuxia* films, which wowed mainstream audiences. It was a reflection of their filmmaking prowess. Ho in particular went beyond many Shaw directors by not only delving into films that had adult situations, but also by tackling occult, science-fiction, horror, fantasy and monster movies, and he did so with exasperating efficiency and success. Despite his success, Ho's wuxia films have occasionally been overlooked because his style tends to be cut-and-dry and black-and-white, with no shades of gray between good and bad. Male bonding between kung fu or swordsmen archenemies represented Ho's affirmation of the virtuous power you can attain through life if you are a martial artist.

The Long Chase is a perfect example of Ho's notions of heroic bloodshed and virtue in the world of Jiang Hu. As the Chinese title states, the film is a study of the life and *Journey of a Swordsman*.

When King of the Flying Daggers Kou Yin (Yueh Hua) assassinates the evil Prime Minister Yan, he becomes an instant folk hero to the downtrodden. However, to Constable Fan Yi (Lo Lieh), he is a major pain. Under the threat of execution, Fan has five days to bring Kou in. Thus, the long chase begins, but the masked Kou manages to avoid Fan's initial effronteries. Further complicating Fan's mission is that he has no idea what Kou looks like. However, since they have crossed, he can recognize the way Kou moves.

While on the lam, Kou stumbles upon the injured hero Song Hua-long from Shantung, who was caught in an explosion set by bandits from Er Long Mountain. As Song dies in Kou's arms, he explains that his mission was to destroy the Er Long Mountain bandits, so he asks Kou to hand-deliver a special document to Judge Liu in the town of Hsuan Hua. Kou assumes Song's identity.

At the local Hsuan Hua inn, the owner's daughter Wang Hsueh-niang (Li Ching) praises the heroic deed of Kou ridding the world of Yan, unaware that Kou, under the guise of Song, is listening to her. However, when Fan arrives and recognizes Song's movements as Kou's, he bluntly accuses Song of being Kou. Wang steps in and saves him by acting like she and Song are old friends. Fan backs off but is not convinced. Kou and Wang fall in love.

Meanwhile, the head of the Er Long Mountain bandits, Ho Hsi-li (Wang Xia), celebrates the death of Song, but word gets back to him that Song is alive. He hires the Eight Freaks of Jiang Nan—curious villain names since the Seven Freaks of Jian Nan were exceedingly popular in Jing Yong's wuxia novel *The Legend of the Condor Heroes*—to help him fight Song. The bandits destroy the inn, kidnap Wang and kill her father.

Kou, who is madder than a wolverine in a buckeye patch, hands Song's document to Judge Liu, and the judge gives him 200 men to rescue Wang and attack the bandit's lair. Being a man of the law, Fan volunteers to help with the assault, and Kou accepts his brave offer. However, during the vicious battle, Ho and many bandits escape, and Kou is forced to expose his identity because he must climb a tall burning tower to rescue Wang. Fan admires his bravery and courage but still arrests him. Kou accepts his fate. But while en route back to the city, Ho and his hordes attack, which forces Kou and Fan to make one final stand together.

What I enjoy about these old wuxia films is how heroes or villains test each other's abilities. They do so based on *chi*, by way of the single-focused strike of reversed chi flow known as *fa jing*, and on *ching gong*, a jumping skill that has nothing to do with a person's chi. In *Long Chase*, for example, Fan throws five bowls at Kuo, and our masked vigilante reacts by catching one bowl on his fingertip, which spins and deflects the others skyward. The deflected bowls stick into the wooden ceiling like circular saw blades. At that moment, Fan and the audience know just how good Kuo and his chi are because he can put his chi into the bowls and make them not break when they stick into the ceiling.

The fight choreography style in the film is also dynamic and rhythmic, filled with spins and slashes. The camerawork incorporates smooth tracking shots to give added motion to the action. One great shot tracks behind a fighter played by a minor character, and this gives the viewer a sense of the fight from that person's perspective. It is like a point-of-view shot, but with real action and not just people jumping in and out of frame.

The film also uses "slashing in air" and "target practice" choreography. Slashing in air is when actors simply swing their swords in the air nowhere near their opponents. Undercranking the camera infuses danger into the fight. Target practice refers to an actor giving his opponent a target to aim and strike at; he places the sword in a specific spot, and the attacker hits the weapon without even bothering to try to hit the person. It is safer, but harder to do well. Again, undercranking the camera can help mask the true purpose of the technique.

Titleography: As of this writing, no alternative titles could be found. Translation—*Journey of a Swordsman*. **MA Percentage: 20.16%** SHAW BROTHERS

LUPIN III: STRANGE PSYCHOKINETIC STRATEGY

Rupan Sansei: Nenriki Chinsakusen (1974—Japan) **82m. SC: Kizoh Uni. NOT/LOT: None; NOF/LOF: 6/ 3m 4s.** D: Takashi Tsuboshima. C: Yuki Meguro, Kunie Tanaka, Shiro Ito, Arihiro Fujimura, E.H. Eric, Hideko Ezaki.

This film is one part *It Takes a Thief* (1968-1970), one part *From Russia With Love* (1963) and a dash of *Mission: Impossible* (1966-1973). Sir Mokkinat, who is introduced in the film while partially obscured and stroking his pet cat, is the head of the Macheronne Organization (shades of Ernst Stavro Blofeld and SPECTRE from the Bond franchise). This crime syndicate is bent on killing the greatest thief in the world, Lupin III (Yuki Meguro), so it can prevent him from rebuilding his father's famous empire. With Lupin out of the way, the syndicate could also go about stealing the mystical Darkened Clay Figure, which is known to possess psychokinetic powers born from an alien race. Lupin gets some help from his trusty aide, Daisuke Jigen (Kunie Tanaka), while simultaneously trying to win over the heart of Fujiko (Hideko Ezaki), whom he broke out of prison and did a jewelry heist with. While fighting off Sir Mokkinat's assassins, Lupin must also keep the dorky Inspector Zenigata at arm's length.

The fights are simple kicks, punches and a few flips. It's nothing too special, but the attack of the singing female rock stars is pretty unique in its setup, whereby Lupin eventually wins by a wiener, if you get my drift.

Titleography: As of this writing, no alternative titles could be found. Translation—*Lupin III: Chi Power, Detailed Strategy*. **MA Percentage: 3.74%**

MA SU CHEN

馬素貞報兄仇 (1972—Hong Kong) **75m. KFI: Chen Shih-wei. NOT/LOT: 1/ 1m 42s; NOF/LOF: 20/ 26m 35s.** D: Ding Shan-xi. C: Jimmy Wong Yu, Yen Nan-xi, Xue Han, Shan Mao, Chen Sha-li, Jiang Nan, Cai Hong, Yi Yuan.

Four months after actor Chen Kuan-tai's awe-inspiring performance as the real-life antihero gangster Ma Yong-zhen in Shaw Brothers' *The Boxer From Shantung*, Taiwanese filmmaker Ding Shan-xi, a director well-known for his historic sagas, cranked out an alternate version of Yong-zhen's story starring Jimmy Wong Yu, who was once the Shaw Brothers' biggest star. The film introduced audiences to the character Yong-zhen's heroic sister Ma Su-chen (played by rising Taiwanese kung fu star Yen Nan-xi) and showed how the two took down a major criminal gang in Shantung.

When the Japanese occupied China, they often killed Chinese, saying they had broken Japanese law. However, in the eyes of the foreign concessions, this was illegal. So if the Japanese wanted someone dead, they would hire Chinese criminals to either request Japanese help to kill that someone on their behalf or have the criminal just kill the person. In *Ma Su Chen,* it is the case of the latter. After Ma Yong-zhen kills a Japanese crime boss, Japanese hit men are subsequently sent to China to kill him—but they can only "legally" do so with the help of Shanghai crime boss Chao Chen-pai (Yi Yuan) and his gang of hatchet men. Chao promises to deliver Yong-zhen's head on a platter. We learn that Yong-zhen's gang killing spree was sparked by his love for two women, Tai Fung and Chao Fung. It is this love that puts him in harms way, because by going after Chao, Yong-zhen gets the ax treatment at Chao's Paradise Club. However, Yong-zhen pulls a disappearing act. Though he is presumed dead, his body is never recovered. Meanwhile, his scrappy sister, Ma Su-chen (Yen) arrives from Shanghai with an arsenal of kicks and punches and a thirst for vengeance.

The fights in the film follow what might be called the shake, rattle and flail rhythm, which Wong Yu thumps out as if following some imaginary drumbeat.

Still from *The Long Chase* © Celestial Pictures Ltd. All rights reserved.

But there is a compelling edginess to the fight scenes, which is apparent when Wong Yu defends himself against multiple attackers armed with razor-sharp axes. Add in one maniacal monk who fights with a large skull on a short stick that when he shakes it, it sounds like a "bone-ifide" chunky maraca, and that creepy shake, rattle and flail rhythmic trio is even more prominent. Listen for swathes of artists Emerson Lake & and Palmer's tune *Pictures at an Exhibition* and the old *Charlie's Angels* TV show music in the fight soundtrack.

In the final fight, hundreds of hatchet men wield flaming torches in the middle of the night. Director Ding has them constantly move during wide-angle and close shots, which creates a confusing set of visuals that can be difficult to concentrate on but which also convey the same frantic feelings Yong-zhen and Su-chen are experiencing as they dodge flames and hatchets.

Other films made in the 1970s that center around the Ma siblings are *The Avenger* (1972), *Brave Girl Boxer in Shanghai* (1972) and *Furious Slaughter* (1972).

Titleography: *Rebel Boxer*; *Bloody Struggle*. Translation—*Ma Su-chen Avenges the Feud Against Her Brother*. Jimmy Wong Yu often played rebel boxer characters, and a distributor aware of his cinematic background could easily justify *Rebel Boxer* as an appropriate title. *Bloody Struggle* is generic enough and could fit tons of other kung fu films. The main title *Ma Su Chen* is a different romanization of Ma Su-zhen, and the Chinese title summarizes the plot. **MA Percentage: 37.71%**

Still from *Mad Monkey Kung Fu* © Celestial Pictures Ltd. All rights reserved.

MAD MAD KUNG FU

怪招軟皮蛇 (1979—Hong Kong) **85m. MAD: Chien Yueh-sheng. NOT/LOT: 4/ 3m 15s; NOF/LOF: 14/ 28m 24s.** D: Ho Meng-hua, Yu Cheng-Chun. C: Cliff Lok, Peter Chan Lung, Lee Hoi-san, Yuen Xiao-tian, Jiang Dao, Zhang Zhao, Cheng Kang-yeh.

If you don't use your noodle, you might not end up rolling in the dough so much as rolling the dough. So in the ways of kitchen kung fu, using your noodle is something that one "kneads" to do.

Iron-head kung fu obliterator Lung Yung-feng (Lee Hoi-san) wants to butt heads with Beggar Zhu (Yuen Xiao-tian). In the English dub, Zhu is called Bamboo Stick. Zhu killed Lung's son because the son tried to forcibly marry Zhu's daughter. Lung's men then attack Zhu's student Kwan Chang-chi (Peter Chan Lung) while he is delivering a jade ring for the government. They also steal the ring thinking that Zhu will come out of hiding to help him. Instead, Kwan disguises himself as a beggar who knows no kung fu and also goes into hiding. But Kwan finds himself at the short end of the bamboo stick because local thugs pick on him. Along comes a noodle-vending good Samaritan (Cliff Lok) who clumsily defends Kwan using a bamboo stick. Kwan spreads the word that Bamboo Stick Zhu is in town, indicating that this dupe noodle-vendor is Zhu. Kwan figures that the ruse will take the heat off his teacher, the real Zhu. Only problem is that things will now get hot for the vendor. Kwan realizes that the vendor could never defend himself against Lung and his bronchial bad boys, so he teaches the oafish, bumbling vendor how to change his noodle-making skills into kung fu fighting abilities.

What happens next is a novel showdown between an ironman and a dough-boy, as the art of noodle making and the adage "no strings attached" take on a new meaning as strings and oodles of noodles flap and floop through the air. The film is called *Mad Mad Kung Fu*, but I think it should be called *Nutty Nutty Noodle Fu* because the way the noodles and bodies wrap around each other is just plain nutty.

This is yet another entry in the long line of Suexploitation films derived from Jackie Chan's *Drunken Master* (1978), with Yuen doing his usual red nose, big grin and gray hair routine. But instead of being a "boy" named Su, he's a drunk named Zhu. (Coincidentally, Johnny Cash's *Boy Named Sue* was a hit song in 1969.)

Titleography: *Old Dirty Kung Fu*; *Ol' Dirty Kung Fu*; *Drunken Master Slippery Snake*. Translation—*Strange Technique Soft Skinned Snake*. The noodle action scenes and the way the hero and the lead villain fight at the end are visually reminiscent of the way that male snakes intertwine during their territorial battles. Being a Suexploitation film, *Drunken Master* is an obvious inclusion into this film's title variations. I would guess that *Old Dirty Kung Fu* comes from beggar Zhu's look and lifestyle. **MA Percentage: 37.24%**

MAD MONKEY KUNG FU

瘋猴 (1979—Hong Kong) **110m. FI: Liu Chia-liang. NOT/LOT: 13/ 23m 22s; NOF/LOF: 20/ 24m 1s.** D: Liu Chia-liang. C: Liu Chia-liang, Hsiao Ho, Hui Ying-hong, Lo Lieh, Lin Hui-huang, Shen Xian, Lin Ke-min.

Monkey kung fu is a funny style, and the stylist's antics can make you laugh, "Ho, ho, ho." In a twist of linguistic irony, the mandarin Chinese word for monkey is *ho*. Although mention of monkey movements associated with kung fu can be traced back to the Han dynasty (206 B.C.-A.D. 220) and the Mi Hou Wu dance performed at the emperor's court was based on monkey movements, the "official" monkey style recognized as being solely and directly based on monkeys was created by Kou Sze in the late 1800s. During his 10-year sentence for murder in a prison in a forest, his cell window faced a colony of monkeys living in a batch of trees. After studying and observing their behaviors under different situations, Kou was able to distinguish different characteristics of individual monkeys and how they fought. He then categorized the monkey into five personality types: tall, wooden, lost, stone and drunken. However, it was during the late 1800s that kung fu man Lee Shao-hau recorded that monkeys were often timid when left alone, but when they were angry, they would become savage, mad and vicious. Thus, Lee Shao-hau created mad monkey kung fu, aka angry monkey martial arts.

Although director Liu Chia-liang's martial arts background is rooted in *hong jia* kung fu, several of his guilty-pleasure styles, if you will, were drunken style and monkey style. One of his favorite members of his *pai* (his cinematic martial arts group) was the Beijing-opera-trained Hsiao Ho, who specialized in playing the Monkey King Swuin Wu-kung. So it makes sense that *Mad Monkey Kung Fu* was the perfect project to feature Hsiao Ho in his first lead. His name even translates as "little monkey."

The film opens with drunk uncle Chan (Liu Chia-liang) unwittingly and boastingly demonstrating his drunken monkey kung fu skills to Chuen Shiang-yuan (Lo Lieh), who is purposely coaxing Chan into a trap that leads to him being accused of trying to rape Chuen's wife. In order to avoid prison and the death sentence, Chan must cripple his hands and hand over his daughter Xiao Hung (Hui Ying-hong) to Chuen. Ironically, the scene in which Lo Lieh cripples Liu's hands looks just like the scene in which Lo's hands are mangled in *King Boxer* (1971). Call it payback.

Alone on the street, Chan tries to make a living by having his pet monkey do tricks to earn money, but Chuen, who runs a protection racket, has his cronies kill the monkey, pushing him into a deeper depression. Fellow street person Little Monkey (Hsiao Ho) dresses up like a monkey to cheer up Chan. Although Little Monkey does not practice kung fu, he dares to stand up to Chuen's street thugs but is constantly beaten. Chan eventually decides to teach Little Monkey kung fu, who tries to use it and nearly becomes monkey brain food before Xiao Hung helps him escape.

Chan knows that it is time to learn mad monkey kung fu so that the normally timid Little Monkey can grow the beastly heart of the giant ape in *Mighty Joe Young* (1949), while still keeping the gentle nature of Judy the chimp in the TV show *Daktari* (1966-1968). They plan to go after the head banana, Chuen, who is the worst of the bunch.

What is most striking about the film's action is that actors Liu and Hsiao Ho do their fights with smooth, flowing movements and keep away from using the typical focused-strike look, where actors lock out their arms and tense their muscles in order to look powerful. It is a pity that Liu only did a handful of kung fu films as the lead because he is one of the few stars who could get away with doing anything on camera and be good at it. He never had to kick above the waist, do acrobatics, or take his shirt off to entertain.

Titleography: As of this writing, no alternative titles could be found. Translation—*Mad Monkey*. **MA Percentage: 43.08%** SHAW BROTHERS

MAGIC BLADE, THE

天涯明月刀 (1976—Hong Kong) 93m. FI: Huang Pei-ji, Tan Jia. NOT/LOT: None; NOF/LOF: 22/ 14m 8s. D: Chu Yuan. C: Ti Lung, Lo Lieh, Ku Feng, Tang Jing, Ching Li, Lily Li, Fan Mei-sheng, Chan Shen Gu Guan-zhong, Teresa Ha Ping, Liu Hui-ling, Xu Hsao-chiang, Ching Miao.

In Western chess, the board is divided into two sides, black and white, and white always moves first. One of the most famous opening moves is called the queen's gambit in which a player moves the pawn positioned in front of the king two spaces forward. The idea of this is to put the white queen in an attacking mode. But in the Eastern world of Jiang Hu, the swordsman Fu Hong-xue (Ti Lung) gets wrapped up in a chess match in which the players are real humans. He finds himself in a death gambit wherein all who try to oppose him will lose.

In *The Magic Blade*, the evil Lord Yu (Tang Jing) wants to be king of the Wu Lin world, the martial arts uberworld of Jiang Hu. (See *The Water Margin*.) To achieve his aims, Yu must posses the Peacock Dart. It is a coveted weapon and symbol of power, and whoever attains it, whether through bloodline or success in a fight, becomes the ruler of Wu Lin. In addition to this, Yu knows that he must kill two famous swordsmen to rule without having to look over his shoulder. His righteous opposition is Fu Hong-xue and Yen Nan-fei (Lo Lieh). Yu hires five assassins to kill Fu and Yen while Yu goes after the current holder of the Peacock Dart: Lord Chiu (Ching Miao). If Yu succeeds, then the martial arts world will be headed by such a cruel and ruthless man. He would throw Wu Lin and subsequently the world of Jiang Hu into chaos. Just imagine if Hitler were president of the world …'nuff said.

Just as rivals Fu and Yen are about to duel each other to see who is the better swordsman, two famous but unrelated-to-Yu assassins in Jiang Hu named Earth Evil and Wood Evil attack. But they are no match for Yen and Fu. However, to have two such famous assassins trying to kill them is a bad sign as Fu and Yen realize something is amiss. They eventually piece together Yu's plan

to get the Peacock Dart. So Fu and Yen set aside their differences and speed off to Peacock Mansion to help the holder of the dart, Lord Chiu, and help him prepare for Yu's onslaught.

During the raid and robbery on Peacock Mansion, Chiu shoots one of several darts from the Peacock Dart. A few colorful explosions later, the would-be thieves working for Yu are dead. As Fu and Yen arrive and Yu escapes, the dying Chiu entrusts the dart and his daughter Chiu Yu-cheng (Ching Li) to Fu.

Soon after, our heroes and Yu-cheng are on the road when those five assassins attack and fail to kill Fu and Yen. Yet amid the various melees, Lord Yu kidnaps Yu-cheng and holds her for ransom, which forces Fu to hand over the Peacock Dart. With the Peacock Dart now in Lord Yu's possession, things look bleak for Wu Lin. Can Fu still save the day? How many more assassins will they have to fend off? Will Lord Yu win the chess game and become king of the castle? Who will have the ultimate checkmate?

So what's with all the chess talk? One critical and highly creative scene is when Fu and Yen get caught up in a human Chinese chess match. It's a surreal moment in which Fu and Yen are pawns in the game of life. As they fight their way off the board, it turns out they are too tough for Lord Yu, not only on the board but also across it.

Screenwriter Ni Kuang was a fan of American Westerns, so it is no surprise that dead-eyed cool customer Ti Lung as Fu resembles Clint Eastwood's unshaven, gun-slinging, poncho-wearing character from the 1960s films *A Fistful of Dollars* and *For a Few Dollars More*. The major difference is that Ti Lung's weapon is more intriguing. It is a slender, machete-like sword blade with a *tonfa*-like swiveling handle that attaches to a long leather holster ominously tucked under his black poncho. What is especially ingenious about the weapon is that because it is not a normal sword, it does not limit Ti Lung to traditional kung fu stances, postures or sword techniques. The weapon's swiveling motion, which looks and sounds like a New Year's Eve noisemaker, also offers unique choreographic ways to block, counter and strike. Although the sound effects make it sound as if the sword spins on its handle, the weapon is solid, and it is Ti Lung's astute wrist work that sells the weapon's unique look and effectiveness.

A similar weapon is borrowed by Ti Lung's former cinematic partner and eventual staunch competitor David Chiang in a film released a year later. What film is that? Hint: In the J section. A neat note: One group of assassins lies on the ground waiting for Fu in the form of the Chinese character *jian*, which means "straight sword."

Western chess pieces are called pawns, knights, bishops, castles (rooks), kings and queens. In Chinese chess, the pieces are flat like checkers, move differently and have Chinese characters on them to distinguish which pieces are generals, mandarins, soldiers, elephants, horses, chariots and cannons. I have performed in human chess matches (a bishop with a pole) during which actors don costumes like chess pieces and move around on a giant chess board. When it's time for a piece to take another, we fight. It's one of those fun times when you can "chess-tise" someone without hurting his or her feelings.

Titleography: *The Moonlight Blade*. Translation—*The Edge of the Sky Bright Moon Sword*. In the Chinese title, the *Edge of the Sky* refers to Earth. All the titles are simply cool names for Fu's sword. **MA Percentage: 15.2%** SHAW BROTHERS

MAGNIFICENT, THE

龍形刀手金鐘罩 (1979—Hong Kong) 86m. MAC: Chen Shao-peng, Chan Sau-chung, Chan Chan-wa. NOT/LOT: 8/ 12m 43s; NOF/LOF: 26/ 38m 27s. D: Chen Shao Peng. C: Chen Hsing, Casanova Wong, Carter Wong, Doris Lung Chun-er, Dragon Lee, Liu Hao-nan, Li Fa-yuan, Tang Jin-tang.

In three words, I love snow. I used to practice martial arts in it, run in bare feet in it, and to me, I feel safe and calm when it snows. So when a film opens with a snow scene, it captures my attention not only because I love snow but also because I know calm things will soon change. It is like the old weather adage, the calm before the storm, and in this film, the storm is a metaphor for a violent nor'easter.

The film is set in the early days of the Republic of China, which was established in 1911. In the city of Nanjing, Sun Yat-sen was proclaimed the country's first provisional head. Yet there were powerful military leaders and fighters in

China who wanted to help the emperor regain his power and reinstate the Ching Dynasty. In a reversal of the common kung fu plot line in which Ming loyalists want to bring down the Ching, *The Magnificent* tells the tale of Ching loyalists attempting to overthrow the republic.

La Lan Ting Chio (Chen Hsing) is a powerful Ching general and frontiersman. He plans an uprising in the north in which he will use the influence of Ching official Lord Lou and Lou's family flag (crest) to gather support. So Sun Yat-sen loyalist Yan Chan-chin (Carter Wong), a stalwart commissioner for the republic, and his trusty assistant (Casanova Wong) must find La Lan and figure out a way to defeat his invincible golden-bell *chi gong* (*qigong*) technique before he sounds of their death knell.

It is a pity the filmmakers did not make more use of the snow while filming in South Korea, which would have given a moodier edge to the film. For the Bruceploitation fans out there, Dragon Lee is in the film for about 60 seconds. He howls and does a Bruce Lee impersonation, complete with the tight-lipped, neck-jerking head movement Dragon Lee is known for. Casanova Wong's *taekwondo* kicks are supple but powerful, which is in contrast to Hwang Jang-lee, whose kicks tend to be tight and powerful. The female knife thrower is a surprise because she keeps her blades hidden in tubers. But Chen Hsing is not a surprise because he does his usual hunched-back and neck-lurching kung fu postures.

There are two kinds of golden-bell chi gong: the little golden bell (*xiao jing zhong*) and the big golden bell (*da jing zhong*). They are not figurative bells that you wear over your body but are metaphoric bells. These skills can protect the body as if you are cloaked in a golden bell. The little bell skill prevents the body from being hurt by punches and kicks, and the big bell protects the body from weapon strikes. But neither gives the strength to break chains wrapped around your body.

According to the film, there are 379 acupuncture points, 36 of which are vulnerable to fatal strikes. With the help of Lord Lou's daughter (Doris Lung Chun-er), Yan Chan-chin studies the vital points of death and learns when and how to strike them. Usually, films show fighters practicing these techniques on dummies covered in dots. (See *Bruce and Shaolin Kung fu* (1978) or *Executioners of Shaolin* (1977).) In this film, Yan covers himself in dots and Lou's daughter attacks him, demonstrating what it's like to strike the death points on a moving opponent. There are actually 365 traditional acupuncture points while others say there are 400. These points are located along 12 meridians and eight extraordinary meridians. Of those points, 108 are for striking to cause injury or paralysis, and 36 of the 108 are death points.

Although La Lan is a fictional character, historically there were two leaders who tried to revive the Ching Dynasty: Yuan Shi-kai appointed himself the emperor in 1915, and in 1917, General Zhang Xun attempted to restore the abdicated Emperor Pu Yi to the throne. Both attempts failed. Side history note: After World War II, then-President Chiang Kai-shek of the Republic of China was defeated by the Communists, so Chiang set up the Republic of China on the island of Taiwan.

Titleography: *Dragon Master*. Translation—*Dragon Shape Blade Hand and the Golden Bell Shield*. The Chinese title refers to La Lan Ting Chio's two main kung fu skills: *Dragon* is one, *Golden Bell* is the other. I suppose with such skills, he could refer to himself as *The Magnificent*, a term reserved for the emperor, which La Lan aspires to be. **MA Percentage: 59.50%**

MAGNIFICENT BODYGUARDS

飛渡捲雲山 (1978—Hong Kong) **90m. FC: Yasuyoshi Shikamura, Jackie Chan. NOT/LOT: None; NOF/LOF: 24/ 23m 1s.** D: Lo Wei. C: Jackie Chan, James Tien, Bruce Leung, Wang Ping, Liu Ming, Wang Yun, Li Wen-tai, Yasuyoshi Shikamura, Fang Fang.

The irony about most martial arts film stars is that they either have limited training or don't practice martial arts at all. How they look on-screen depends on the fight choreographer. What makes the choreographer's job tough is when a producer or director insists on making the star look like something he or she is not. James Tien is an example of an actor with limited real martial arts training. However, because of his star stature and film experience, a producer like Lo Wei would want the fight choreographers to make Tien look like the next Bruce Lee. While Tien would never become anything akin to Lee, he does look decent in many of his films. But this says a lot more about the talent of the fight choreographers than of the stars.

Anyway, presenting the plot: The brother of a kung fu maiden Lady Nan

(Wang Ping) has three days left to live unless she can get him to a doctor. Of course, the doctor lives on the other side of Stormy Mountain, a place full of deadly robbers and ruthless killers that is headed by the King of the Mountain (Yasuyoshi Shikamura). The sister hires bodyguard Ting Chung (Jackie Chan) to be the head escort of her traveling party. Ting requests that he bring along some other bodyguards. They include the female Twin Pearl Sabres; a deaf kicker and lip-reader named Chang (Bruce Leung); and former cohort Tsang (James Tien), who says he's mainly there for the money. In reality, Tsang joins the traveling party because of a ruthless bandit named God of Darts he killed in the past. Now, God of Darts' lover Lady Liu is looking for revenge, and Tsang hopes to find and kill Lady Liu first. What better place to look for her than the heavily villain-populated land of Stormy Mountain? Before the company's departure, the Old Lady of the Ma Po Inn warns Tsang to beware of four people: the Scholar, the Monk, the Old Wolf and of course Lady Liu.

Upon their arrival to Stormy Mountain, the escort is eventually beset by each of the four don't-mess-with-me vagabonds, giving actors Chan and Leung ample screen time to demonstrate who the real martial-arts-trained stars are. These fights lead up to a twist so far-fetched that I'm led to believe the ending was probably created during the final days of shooting. When there is such a poor and cheap resolution to an intricate plot, it usually indicates that something—finances, egos, time, etc.—was falling apart on set. But the neat thing about this film is that the fight choreography did not fall apart at all.

In fact, what surprised me is that Jackie Chan's spry, nimble and smooth-fighting performance in *Magnificent Bodyguards* is more natural than most of his performances in the 1970s, including those in *Drunken Master* and *Snake in the Eagle's Shadow*. (Notice, however, that I did not say it's better.) By this I mean Chan does not use his recognizable rhythmic and bouncy choreography technique seen in the aforementioned two films and in his movies to come. Instead his rhythm is smooth, and his body does not bob up and down as a way to remember the rhythm of the fight movements.

During a neat film error, you can see the wires attached to Shikamura's body before he is hoisted up. What is cool about it is that he does a sequence of fight techniques prior to flying, which can be tough to do well while maintaining your balance before being hoisted up. It shows the competency of the actor, who is also one of the film's fight choreographers. As most people who have seen this film know, many of the fight techniques are shot in 3-D, which involves filming two images at the same time with two cameras standing side by side.

Titleography: *The Red Dragon, Master of Death, Eye of the Dragon*; *Magnificent Guardsmen*. Translation—*Flying Over the Clouds of Swirling Mountain*. The film is about bodyguards, so the titles with *Bodyguards* and *Guardsmen* fit. The other English titles are rife with generic words like *Dragon, Master* and *Death*. The Chinese translation refers to crossing over the area (*Swirling Mountain*; *Stormy Mountain* in the English dub) the traveling party goes through. **MA Percentage: 25.57%**

MAGNIFICENT RUFFIANS, THE

賣命小子 (1979—Hong Kong) **101m. FI: Kuo Chue, Lu Feng, Chiang Sheng. NOT/LOT: 9/ 3m 14s; NOF/LOF: 34/ 27m 18s.** D: Chang Cheh. C: Kuo Chue, Lu Feng, Lo Meng, Chiang Sheng, Sun Chien, Liao An-li, Wang Li.

During the Ching and other earlier dynasties, it was an honorable profession to be the head of an escort company (also known as a security company). Many a swordsman or martial artist would make his name not only in the world of Jiang Hu and its sub-society of Wu Lin in such a company, but also in the eyes of the government and the business sector. However, with the fall of the Ching Dynasty and the advent of modern weapons, security companies rapidly declined, leaving maybe one or two per city. With all these former martial artists and swordsmen out of a job, they became like *ronin*, masterless fighters looking for work from anyone willing to pay.

As you might imagine, competition was stiff. In this film, the conniving Yuan Ying-fei (Lu Feng) is a spoiled brat and a master of the Golden Sword Technique, which he uses with a huge golden *guan dao*. Yuan is losing business to the only other escort service in town. It's run by the righteous martial artist Guan Yun (Lo Meng), his mother and his sister. Yuan sets out to destroy Guan's company, take over his business and prove he is the best martial artist in town. After several failed attempts to buy the company, Yuan is only a moment away from violence when he sees Guan's sister and holds back. And each time Guan is about to fight, his mother stops him.

Yuan also revels in keeping his fighting skills sharp by inviting martial artists to his mansion under the guise of providing them with employment. He promises them jobs if they can defeat him, but he kills them if they fail. As you might imagine, Yuan has a high rate of unemployment. When word gets back to Yuan about a beautiful sword that was pawned at one of his pawnshops, he wants to meet the man who gave it up; he knows from the look of the sword that the martial artist must be good. Yuan learns of four starving martial artists: Zeng Qiao (Wang Li), He Fei (Chiang Sheng), Feng Jia-ji (Sun Chien) and master pole fighter Yang Zhu-feng (Kuo Chue). Yuan figures that if he can win them over, they would be happy to take out Guan and his company. After providing them with food, lodging and a place to take a communal bath (Chang Cheh taking his brotherhood motif to the extreme), Yuan asks them to confront Guan, and the four kung fu brothers happily comply.

Yuan's plan backfires when the four fighters bond with Guan because they share a common outlook on martial arts and life. Yuan hatches a plan to divide and conquer these five friends by framing pole master Yang for murdering Guan. As more bodies begin to pile up, Guan and Yuan comically dress up as ghosts in an effort to seek the truth. It is only a matter of time before Guan and Yang team up to take on Yuan in another of the Five Weapon Guys' extended fight finales. (See *Crippled Avengers*.)

As in *Shaolin Rescuers* (1979), actor Lu Feng brings the house down when he picks up his guan dao and fights with actors Chiang Sheng and Kuo Chue. As these Five Weapon Guys (Sun, Kuo, Lu, Lo and Chiang) matured, the action in their movies focused less on acrobatics and more on fighting. The camerawork incorporated more side angles and close-ups (especially during Lo Meng's fights) to show the solid wrist-on-wrist contact as well as the intricacy of the blocks and open-hand postures. The same held true for weapon action, with more close shots that clearly show solid weapon contact. The weapons buckle slightly on contact, proving that if the actors' timing was off and they missed a block, they would get hit and hurt, which must have happened a lot. I met Kuo Chue in Taipei after he had just completed filming and doing the choreography for *Masked Avenger* (1981), and his wrists were swollen masses with bruises up and down both arms. Again, Sun Chien had minimal action and contributions to the fights (as discussed in *The Daredevils* martialogy), but that would change in his next film, *The Kid With the Golden Arm* (1979).

Titleography: As of this writing, no alternative titles could be found. Translation—*Selling Life Young Men*. The Chinese title means that when a person works hard, he is basically selling his life for that job. This can refer to all the young men trying to find work as well as those who die trying to get work with Yuan. *The Magnificent Ruffians* refers to the four streetwise friends, who at first appear to be ruffians but turn out to be good men. **MA Percentage: 30.23%** SHAW BROTHERS

MAGNIFICENT WANDERERS, THE

江湖漢子 (1976—Hong Kong) 93m. FI: Hsieh Hsing, Chen Shen-yi. NOT/LOT: None; NOF/LOF: 19/ 14m 35s. D: Chang Cheh. C: David Chiang, Alexander Fu Sheng, Chi Kuan-chun, Lee Yi-min, Shan Mao, Yang Zhong-ming.

After the Ming Dynasty overthrew the Mongol-led Yuan Dynasty in 1368, the remnants of the Yuan fled back to Mongolia and kept the dream alive by establishing the Northern Yuan Dynasty. Neither the Ming nor the Yuan dynasties would recognize the legitimacy of the other's emperor as the ruler of China. Between 1368 and 1402, they went through periods of conflict and peace until a Mongol leader named Orug Temur Khan dethroned the Northern Yuan, making the Yuan Dynasty disappear for good.

This pseudo-comedy stars David Chiang as Tu Tie-xia, a famous fighter and Ming patriot from the world of Jiang Hu. The film takes place during this age of uncertainty when the Mings were in power but Mongols continued to invade the northern borders. Seeing the threat along some border village, Tu recruits a trio of martial arts misfits—Lin Shao-you (Alexander Fu Sheng), Shi Da-yong (Chi Kuan-chun) and Guan Fei (Lee Yi-min)—to help steal his gold back from his friends, who hid it. Some friends, huh? Meanwhile, two Mongol generals, Lu Bo-hua (Shan Mao) and Zhu Da-Cheng (Yang Zhong-ming), manage to nab the gold and proudly try to show it to the Mongol khan, but they find that the loot has been replaced by rocks. The khan demands that they find the real gold. In the name of laughter, the khan is portrayed like a dwarf in a tall inflatable robe with a goofy oversize hat to hide his face as he barks out orders with a speech impediment.

Tu and his mates get the gold back, but because they feel that they have not put the khan through enough, the four decide to disguise themselves as Mongols, ride into the enemy camp and take on the best Yuan martial artists just to see how good they are. Guan wins the *ching gong* contest (a technique that allows martial artists to jump high and run on top of grass) as he easily leaps from yurt to yurt. Tu out-shoots the Mongol archers with his gold pellet "arrows" and whacks people around with his bow. Shi wrangles and defeats two Mongolian wrestlers, and Lin spears four guys at once. Needless to say, the Ming Dynasty is safe because the four patriots escape the camp and join the Ming army, undoubtedly to give the Mongols plenty more trouble.

Titleography: *Magnificent Kung Fu Warriors*. Translation—*Jiang Hu Tough Guys*. Whenever a film with *Magnificent* in the title is about the recruitment of a fighter to do a job, one can't help but wonder if the title was inspired by the classic American Western *The Magnificent Seven* (1960). In this film, however, there are four fighters, and they are wandering the world of Jiang Hu, hence the Chinese title. **MA Percentage: 15.68%** SHAW BROTHERS

MAN FROM HONG KONG, THE

直搗黃龍 (1975—Australia/Hong Kong) 103m. FI: Sammo Hung. NOT/LOT: 3/ 1m 32s; NOF/LOF: 18/ 18m 31s. D: Brian Trenchard-Smith, Jimmy Wong Yu. C: Jimmy Wong Yu, George Lazenby, Yuen Kuei, Lam Ching-ying, Ros Spiers, Rebecca Gilling, Peter Armstrong, Roger Ward, Hugh Keays-Byrne, Frank

Thring, Sammo Hung.

It is the Far East versus the Land Down Under. In 1973, George Lazenby signed a four-picture contract with Golden Harvest, the first three of which were supposed to have Lazenby star with Bruce Lee (see *Stoner*). One of the films slated was *The Man From Hong Kong*, in which Lee would play a Hong Kong cop sent to Australia and would take on a drug kingpin called Wilton (played by Lazenby). After Lee's death, Jimmy Wong Yu was the other big star available to take the role of Inspector Fang Sing-lung of the Hong Kong Special Branch.

In the film, Fang arrives in Sydney to handle the extradition of Hong Kong drug courier Wen Zhan (Sammo Hung), who was arrested by Sgt. Morrie Grosse (Hugh Keays-Byrne) at Australia's most recognized natural landmark, Ayers Rock. Yet Grosse and his partner, Bob Taylor (Roger Ward), are of little help to Fang, who is something of a fish out of water. (The portrayal of the two white cops subtly reflects the racism toward Asians at that time in Australia.) Fang seeks help from the Australian reporter and hang-gliding expert Caroline Thorne (Ros Spiers). She teaches Fang how to hang-glide into Wilton's Hilton-like corporation building so he can shut him down.

On the surface, this film looks like a case of keeping up with the Joneses (or, I should say, with the Shaws). Golden Harvest was still in its infancy, its top box-office draw (Bruce Lee) had died two years earlier, and now it was doing co-productions with Australian film companies in hopes of cultivating some international appeal. But this film goes much deeper, socially and racially, than the Shaw Brothers films, and it is done in a way that only Jimmy Wong Yu could get away with, as discussed in the next two paragraphs.

Like the United States in the 1970s, Australia dealt with a lot of racial tension. Even Diana Ross was snubbed and prevented from doing a concert there based on pervading attitudes at the time. To have a lead Asian in an Australian film was really advanced thinking and a gamble. Still, the obvious racial slurs and indications by the two police characters and Wilton—Wilton to Feng: "Chinese make good houseboys."—show a darker side. The racially toned remarks do not slight Fang, and you do know someone will pay for them (and the respective villains do).

To really push the envelope, Jimmy Wong Yu has two steamy love scenes with two white Australian women, and it is Fang who is in charge as the dominant partner. To have kung fu actors like Bruce Lee or Jackie Chan in such scenes would have been a tougher sell for Chinese audiences because they are considered heroes in the eyes of the Chinese. They were thought of as being straight from the hallowed halls of Shaolin and were all about martial arts and purity in thought. But Wong Yu has always been a renegade in his own right and handily tackled the task.

The fights are of the smash, crash and bash variety. In one fight in a Chinese restaurant, Wong Yu truly whacks away at stuntman Peter Armstrong, and you can tell some of those kicks really landed. But then there is a touch of old-school, almost-*wuxia*-like martial arts when Fang brandishes his weapons amid a few well-placed floating skills that are believable because this man knows kung fu, and kung fu fighters do have some amazing (if unexplainable) skills.

In *Not Quite Hollywood*, a documentary about Australian exploitation films, director Brian Trenchard-Smith laments that Jimmy Wong Yu was a cantankerous sod on set. There were also complaints that Wong Yu brutally attacked Trenchard-Smith for real during a fight scene they had in an elevator. It is even said that Wong Yu crunched flies in his mouth before kissing one of the white women. Based on my experiences working in Chinese kung fu films, if these things did occur, it is all par for the course on a Hong Kong film set. However, I can well imagine that regardless of his star stature in film, Wong Yu was met with racial disdain and disrespect on the Australian set, perhaps most of the time behind his back, or snide remarks that many thought he would not have understood. I've seen this on American sets over the past decade toward the various Hong Kong actors working in the States. Furthermore, back in the day, racism was just as rampant in Australia as it was in America. The difference is that America openly spoke (and still speaks) about it. Also, being hit for real on a Chinese film set is nothing unusual. This was common in Bruce Lee films, but no one whined about it—instead it was a badge of honor.

Just ask Australian action star Richard Norton about his experience fighting Jackie Chan. Or ask me about my dislocated neck and the sword slash across my face that bled like Niagara Falls. It is just the way the films are—no gripes, you just do it and move on to the next scene, even if the blood is still not dried. I guess the documentary neglected to mention that Wong Yu almost died during the movie after a debacle with the hang glider. I wonder who was responsible for that? No wonder Jimmy Wong Yu clocked a few guys.

Titleography: *That Man From Hong Kong*. Translation—*Drive Straight Into the Enemy Strong Hold*. The Chinese title foreshadows Fang flying into Wilton's lair via hang glider. **MA Percentage: 19.47%**

MAN OF IRON

仇連環 (1972—Hong Kong) **94m. Fl: Liu Chia-liang, Chan Cheun. NOT/LOT: None; NOF/LOF: 11/ 21m 8s.** D: Chang Cheh, Pao Hsueh-li. C: Chen Kuan-tai, Ching Li, Tien Ching, Wang Chung, Tien Qing, Yang Chi-ching, Lu Di, Zhang Jing-po, Bolo Yeung, Zhu Mu, Jiang Dao.

Although this film is touted as a sequel to *The Boxer From Shantung*, (1975; see martialogy) it really is not. The movie begins with a brief discussion of how the just and fair gangster Ma Yong-zhen, played by Chen Kuan-tai, was brutally axed to death by a rival boss during an ambush at Qing Lin Tower. *Man of Iron* takes place 20 years after Ma's death and tells the story of a fictitious gangster, also played by Chen Kuan-tai, who is cast into a similar situation.

When cocky, low-level gangster Qiu Lian-huan (Chen) starts showing off his expert martial arts ability around Shanghai, he ends up teaching a lesson about manhood and respect to Yu Chow-kai (Tien Ching). Qiu also woos away Yu's girlfriend, Shen Ju-feng (Ching Li), by crashing into his living room on a motorbike. He then refuses to kowtow to Yu's nasty gangster father, Boss Yu Zhen-ting (Yang Chi-ching). Meanwhile, Zhen-ting's false friend and partner, Chang Gen-bao (Zhu Mu), takes advantage of Qiu's insolence and kills the Yu family. Chang blames Qiu for the crimes. He also claims that because he and Yu were good friends, which they weren't, then he is justified in sending out his gangs on a mission to dispose of Qiu. Chang's gangs go after Qiu with large knives that look like a cross between giant Philippine *balisong* knives and heavy-duty garden shears. But Qiu will not be slaughtered without a fight, so he shreds a few hundred of them.

An interesting bit of reality in the film is when Qiu uses a Raleigh bicycle to fight a slew of gangsters. The history of Raleigh bicycles began in 1887: Frank Bowden was so impressed by the bike he bought on Raleigh Street in Nottingham, England, that he offered to buy the business. He changed the company name to Raleigh Cycles in honor of the original address. The British introduced Raleigh bicycles into China before World War I. It is not clear whether the inclusion of a Raleigh in the film was intentional, but it is a pleasant surprise (for me and anyone else who is a fan of them) to see Chen Kuan-tai attack the

Still from *Man of Iron* © Celestial Pictures Ltd. All rights reserved.

thugs with the wheels of the bike. He also removes the bike chain and wraps it around his fist so he can take the rest of Yu Chow-kai's stooges out. Fun note: The leader of those stooges is played by actor Bolo Yeung, Shaw Brothers' muscle-bound bad guy and ruthless strong man of the inscrutable villain Han in *Enter the Dragon* (1973).

Although Chen does many helicopterlike arm movements, they are choreographed beautifully because each arm straight flail looks like it is an intended part of the action. Furthermore, Chen's expressive face, which is full of desperation, goes well with his powerful strokes. The final fight involves much more camera movement than the earlier fights. It adds to the frenetic pace and claustrophobia of being attacked by 30 or so wackos brandishing machetes, sticks and garden shears. It also leads to the kind of scene director Chang Cheh lives for: the long, painful, bloody demise of a hero who never gives up. It is truly something in the vein of the swan song of character Silver Roc, who is portrayed by Jimmy Wong Yu in *Golden Swallow* (1968).

Titleography: *Warrior of Steel*. Translation—*Qiu Lian-huan*. The translation is the title character's Chinese name. Although *Man of Iron* is rather generic, it does relate to Qiu's indomitable will because he refuses to back down from injustice. *Warrior of Steel* simply swaps one metal for another. **MA Percentage: 22.48%** SHAW BROTHERS

MAN WITH THE GOLDEN GUN, THE

(1974—UK/Thailand) **125m. SC: W.J. Milligan Jr. NOT/LOT: 1/ 35s; NOF/LOF: 7/ 4m 18s.** D: Guy Hamilton. C: Roger Moore, Christopher Lee, Britt Ekland, Hervé Villechaize, Soon Tech-oh, Yuen Qiu, Chan Yiu-lam, Chien Yueh-sheng.

I remember waiting in long lines with my father at the gas station during the oil crisis in 1973 to 1974. Mandatory gas rationing in upstate New York allowed only the purchase of $10 of gas at a time, and buying gas was based on the last number of your license plate—odd number bought on odd days of the month, while even numbers could buy gas on even days. If only we had secret agent James Bond to save us!

In this spy flick, Bond (Roger Moore) is thrust into international intrigue as the British government and the world's most deadly assassin, the three-nippled Scaramanga (Christopher Lee), vie for a missing miniature solex agitator, which can convert solar energy into electricity. Imagine that, a film about solar power in 1974. Ironically, decades later, people are again talking about our dependence on oil and the importance of alternative energy sources. Naturally during his tangles with Scaramanga, Bond faces other opponents who are masters in the arts of kung fu, karate, *krabi krabong*, sumo and Thai kickboxing

The fights in *The Man With the Golden Gun* are shot in a typical Western filmmaking fashion—a snail stuck in glue could move faster—and Moore generally acts like a nancy boy in a *gi*. The best scene is when a teen lass (Yuen Qiu; she also plays the landlady in *Kung Fu Hustle* (2005)) saves Bond's butt from Shu La (Chan Yiu-lam) and his karate cronies. The fight also features up-and-coming stuntman/actor Chien Yueh-sheng being clobbered and tossed off a bridge by Bond.

I dare say that for most of the Western audience, this film was their mainstream introduction to the Thai art of krabi krabong. Most people probably assumed it was Chinese kung fu because that was the standard at the time.

Krabi krabong is a weapon-based martial art native to Thailand, possibly with origins from the Yunnan people of Southern China. Many techniques are similar to the martial art weaponries of *silat* (Malaysia/Indonesia) and *banshay* (Burma; today Myanmar). It shows the possible further influence of Chinese martial arts in Southeast Asia. The krabi krabong weapon featured in this film is the *daab song mue*, a pair of swords wielded with one in each hand. Although primarily a weapon art, krabi krabong also uses empty-hand techniques that are mostly kick-based. Krabi krabong is the foundation of an older version of *muay boran* called *ling lom* (air monkey). Muay boran is of course the forerunner of *muay* Thai, which is considered a sport and has only been around since 1930.

What's interesting about all this is that although the ancient forms of Thai's martial arts are steeped in Buddhist notions, the ling lom aspect of muay boran has its foundation in the Hindu monkey god Hanuman. Traditional muay boran fights were actually dances to honor the story.

Titleography: As of this writing, no alternative titles could be found. **MA Percentage: 3.91%**

MANTIS FISTS AND TIGER CLAWS OF SHAOLIN

血海螳螂仇 (1977—Hong Kong) **93m. FI: Xu Er-niu. NOT/LOT: 1/ 1m 36s; NOF/LOF: 14/ 22m 55s.** D: Xu Er-niu, Zhang Sen. C: John Cheung, Dean Shek, Choi Chuk-guen, Cheung Lik, Shan Guai, Alan Hsu.

If you are a fan of Universal Pictures horror films of the 1950s—the classic mummy, Dracula, werewolf and Frankenstein flicks of yesteryear—then you will love *Mantis Fists and Tiger Claws of Shaolin*. It is one of those rare surprises in this book— along with *The Tongfather, Kung Fu vs. Yoga, Chinese Iron Man* and *The Fists of Vengeance*—that simply blew me away. It's not that these films have great kung fu fights, but it's the sheer audacity and creativity of these hidden gems.

The film opens with a pair of cartoon praying mantises rollicking around. After mating, the female eats the male while a voice-over explains that mantises are cannibalistic. The segment ends with the statement that this unsettling behavior is as disturbing as the movie itself.

The story begins, as many Hong Kong films do, with the rape of a beautiful young woman. Shuang Shuang (Choi Chuk-guen) is attacked in the forest where her screams are muffled by the trees, and the gang of men seems to get away with the crime. As the thugs celebrate their lewd victory, pieces of bamboo start flying through the air, and in Hollywood slasher style, these evildoers are impaled like insects pinned to a board for someone's bug collection.

Enter the hero, Bai Yung-feng (John Cheung). He swore to his dying mother that he would find his long-lost sister who was sold into prostitution. She is owned by the deranged sons of Hung Ching-piao (Dean Shek), who is an insane unrelenting, spear-wielding alpha male. As Bai rescues his sister and protects Shuang, he is severely wounded by Hung and his perverse progeny. One of the progeny is so perverse that apart from enjoying a rape or two, he wears a freaky jacket that is covered in a sheet of spikes.

Meanwhile, there is a government agent (Cheung Lik) snooping around the village investigating the gruesome killings that have plagued the area for years. Although he arrives in time to help Bai and his sister, the timid Shuang is not so fortunate. She gets raped two more times, which coincidentally sets off another round of savage bloodlettings in the village. What follows next gets more bizarre by the minute; this is certainly not your average kung fu film.

It is a welcome surprise to see how effective a villain actor Dean Shek is. For example, a scene in which he destroys a straw dummy with a spear could have been humorous but comes across rather dark and creepy. Yet the end is even darker and creepier. But what would you expect, after all, this is a horror film that is wrapped in rape, perverse progeny and insect kung fu.

The fights are choreographed very well and are full of shocking surprises. The restaurant brawl near the film's beginning that introduces Bai contains a unique head melon-smashing gag. Another memorable well-choreographed fight moment has actor John Cheung wielding a weapon that resembles a ghost-head broadsword (*gui tao dao*), which is a weapon rarely seen in kung fu films. Having a doctorate in entomology, I am compelled to point out that contrary to belief, cannibalism between mantises after copulation, except for one species of mantis, is not commonplace. But the end of this film takes mantis behavior to new heights, which make the ghost sword and melon look melancholy.

Titleography: *Mantis Fist*; *Mantis Fists & The Tiger Claws of Shaolin*. Translation—*Blood Ocean Praying Mantis Revenge*. The Chinese title makes perfect sense because the film is filled with oceans of blood and revenge at the hands of a mantis kung fu fighter. **MA Percentage: 26.36%**

MARCO POLO

馬哥波羅 (1975—Hong Kong) **108m. FI: Hsieh Hsing, Chen Xhen-yi. NOT/LOT: 9/ 15m 14s; NOF/LOF: 20/ 29m 32s.** D: Chang Cheh. C: Alexander Fu Sheng, Chi Kuan-chun, Tong Yen-san, Liang Chia-ren, Wang Lung-wei, Gordon Liu Chia-hui, Richard Harrison, Shih Tzu, Li Tong-chun, Carter Wong.

Many of director Chang Cheh's films are accounts of Chinese patriots fighting foreign invaders: the Japanese in *The Naval Commandos* (1977), European powers in *Boxer Rebellion* (1975) and the Chings in numerous Shaolin films, for example. This film has the Chinese trying to kick out the Mongolians as several Han assassins—in front of Marco Polo (Richard Harrison), no less—try to take out Kublai Khan (Li Tong-chun). They fail because of Khan's superior personal bodyguards: Abulahua, Caldalu and Dulldan (Gordon Liu Chia-hui, Liang Chia-ren and Wang Lung-wei). Fearing an uprising, Khan assigns Polo to be the inspector of Yang Zhao, a place where Chinese insurgents are known to live. He also orders Polo to suppress the Han rebels and warns Polo to beware of their special boxing techniques, which make their practitioners mentally unstable, leading them to do crazy things.

Polo sneaks into the city and fearfully observes four Han Chinese practicing special kinds of kung fu. Li Xiong-feng (Alexander Fu Sheng) practices iron palm, Zhou Xing-zheng (Chi Kuan-chun) practices iron shirt, Chen Jie (Kuo Chue) practices *ching gong* (light skills), and Huang Zong-han (Tong Yen-san) practices rock lifting and splitting. However, after Polo meets the head of the Chinese rebels and understands their plight, he tells them how they might be able to defeat the Mongolian killers on their trail and promises them that after their battle, he will leave China for good. With his chest swelling, Polo acknowledges the bravery of the Han Chinese and especially admires the strength of the Chinese women.

As you might expect, when our four Han heroes and three Mongolian maulers clash—especially considering the kung fu star power—the fights are controlled and evenly paced, and they flow relatively smoothly. A lot of the choreography focuses on the fighters slapping each other's arms and legs during throwing strikes and blocking the attacks, which is easier on the wrists and prevents the body from tensing up too much. The exception is the Fu Sheng and Liang Chia-ren fight, which uses a lot of rolling-arms combos. During the fights, their wrists heavily connect with each other's wrists or arms (essentially, bone on bone), which to someone with weak wrists would be incredibly painful. In fact, the rolling wrist way of fighting (imagine rolling a volleyball between your wrists in circles, making sure that the wrists stay connected to the ball) is one of Liang's specialties. Perhaps the big surprise of the film is Tong Yen-san's rock-splitting character, in that he just happens to have the biggest and most memorable heroic moment of all the stars. He powerfully pushes rocks over and through the city's walls, knocking the large pieces onto the charging Mongolians. He then uses a large concrete block to pummel and pulverize them into the ground before finally going out in a blaze of pin-cushioned, arrow-riddled glory, with blood squirting from him like a fireman's hose. It is a typical Chang Cheh heroic bloodshed moment in which his young heroes go down fighting to the bitter end.

Historically, explorer and trader Marco Polo (1254-1324)—accompanied by his father, Nicollo; his uncle Maffeo; and two Dominican friars—departed from the Venetian Republic in 1271 and traveled along the Silk Road. In 1274, they arrived at the Yuan Dynasty's capital city of Kanbaliq (now Beijing) and presented gifts from Pope Gregory X to Kublai Khan, the first emperor of the Yuan Dynasty and the grandson of Genghis Khan. Khan took a special liking to Polo, enjoying his storytelling so much that when Polo wanted to go home, he was not allowed to leave and instead was assigned to complete diplomatic missions for Khan. He was also appointed governor of one of China's largest commercial cities, Yang Zhou, in Jiangsu province. Between 1298 and 1299, Polo dictated his 17-year adventure to Rustichello da Pisaw while in an Italian prison in Genoa. Pisaw later published the book as *The Travels of Marco Polo*. Some historians debate the accuracy of Polo's accounts, refuting everything Polo did and accomplished. I guess they weren't into polo neck shirts and I'm sure we can count out water polo as their favorite sport, too.

Titleography: *Four Assassins*; *4 Assassins*. Translation—*Marco Polo*. **MA Percentage: 41.45%** SHAW BROTHERS

MAR'S VILLA

神 腿 (1979—Taiwan) **90m. AD: Stephen Dong Wei, Jia Kai. NOT/LOT: 6/ 4m 58s; NOF/LOF: 18/ 28m 2s.** D: Ding Chong. C: John Liu, Gao Fei, Dong Wei, Sun Yue, Wong Chi-sang, Jia Kai.

This "big gong" film—a movie that ends the opening credits with a loud, single gong sound—doesn't have anything to do with the Red Planet. Instead, it centers on the mostly old-school notion that one kung fu school might want to wipe out another kung fu school for simple reasons of honor, proving itself the best or because there can be only one martial arts studio in a particular area. Even when Bruce Lee opened up his first kung fu school, the teachers of other local schools tried to shut him down. They didn't take a legal path, but instead, they tried to prove that their fighting abilities were superior to his. If they had won, Lee might have bowed to them and closed his doors. In Mandarin, this challenge process is known as *ti guan* or "kicking down the school." (It's also the Chinese title of a great 1981 Shaw Brothers film directed by Liu Chia-liang called *Martial Club*.)

Mar's Villa opens with such a scenario. As the leader of the Fang Clan, Fang Gang (Gao Fei) challenges Ma Tian-lung (John Liu), who is head of the Magic Kick kung fu school, because, at the risk of sounding like a John Wayne cliché, the town ain't big enough for the two of them. Ma ends up killing Fang with his ultimate magic kicking skills. However, it is a hollow victory because Ma is deeply saddened that he took a human life. Unable to live with his grief, the distraught Ma hangs up his kicking shoes and marries his fiancee. But Fang's brother Kuai Yi (Gao Fei again) attacks Ma and mutilates Ma's legs, making him an utter cripple. This opens the doors for Fang's son (Dong Wei) to further torture Ma and who also tries to convince Ma's wife to be with him. Caged like a lab rat and turned into a groveling lunatic, Ma is saved by a loyal friend (Jia Kai), who nurses him back to health. Amid the familiar Dominic Frontiere score from Clint Eastwood's Western film *Hang 'Em High*, Ma trains, sprains and regains his magic kick to once again leg-split, rat-a-tat-roundhouse and strain-neck leap-kick his way to the top and rescue his wife. (The strain-neck-leap is what I call one of actor John Liu's signature kicking postures. When he does a flying side kick, his face and neck strain away from the direction of the kick to make it look like he's putting power into it. Thus, the term.)

With such great martial arts talents like John Liu, Gao Fei and Dong Wei (the kid who says, "Let me think," to Bruce Lee in *Enter the Dragon*), the choreography does deliver. Gao's solid stances and arm work are particularly good. Perhaps a problem with watching more than 500-plus martial arts films in rapid succession is that you quickly realize how certain actors do the same moves over and over in every film. Liu is one example. He always does splits; he stands still while holding his right leg up with his left hand usually from doing an inside crescent kick. Liu also finishes his barrages of similar kicks with the same low horse stance and hand guard, and he front-kicks his leg high to strike someone standing behind him. He is very good at what he does, but it gets old. Most people like Steven Seagal's first film, *Above the Law* (1988), because to most viewers in the West, *aikido* was new and so were his fights. But after the third film of the same old thing, Seagal's novelty quickly wore off. You will see and read that Liu was able to buck his own trend now and then, and it is those films that offer his most memorable martial arts performances. (See *The Dragon, the Hero* (1979).)

Titleography: *Mars Villa*; *Mar's Villa*; *Rocky Lee*; *Wu Tang Magic Kick*. Translation—*Magical (Godly) Legs*. The film has nothing to do with *Wu Tang*, though *Magic Kick* certainly makes sense. *Rocky Lee* is perhaps an attempt to tap into Bruce Lee's fame and Stallone's *Rocky* phenomena. After all, this film is about the comeback of a down-and-out martial artist. It seems *Mar's Villa* is a romanized misspelling of the lead character's name Ma, in association with his *Villa*. When the English dub says "It's Ma's Villa" or "It's Ma's School," it sounds like he's saying "Mar's." **MA Percentage: 36.37%**

MASTER AND THE KID, THE

俠骨柔情赤子心 (1978—Taiwan) **88m. FD: Liang Shao-song. NOT/LOT: 25s; NOF/LOF: 15/ 22m 42s.** D: Lin Fu-di. C: Yueh Hua, Wen Chi-ang-lung, Pan Ying-zi, Phillip Ko Fei, Chen Hsing, Weng Hsiao-hu, Ho Wai-hung.

Samurai flick *Lone Wolf and Cub* meets spaghetti-Western *Hang 'Em High* (1968) in Taiwan. The film opens with hero Nan Kung-sao (Yueh Hua) killing a Shaolin traitor named Ling Ger. As revenge for this killing, an unknown government official has assassins slaughter Nan's family. With a price of 1,000 *taels* of silver (88 pounds) on his head, Nan and the only surviving family member—his little nephew who travels with him in a baby cart—must evade those trying to collect the reward for his capture while trying to find out who wants them dead.

The familiar gong sound associated with the Shaolin Temple and heard at the film's beginning seems to indicate that the film could somehow be related to Shaolin folklore. As it turns out, it was a man named Ma Ling-ger who was responsible for setting off a sequence of events that led to the burning of the Song Shan Shaolin in 1736, but it is not clear in the film whether this is the same Ling-ger. Another Shaolin clue is that the master villain behind the assassinations is Ku Yen-fei (Chen Hsing), who hails from Luoyang, which is the prefecture-level city where the first Shaolin Temple was built in Henan province. As is common for most of actor Chen's films, he uses his tiger-claw kung fu training. He looks better on-screen when he is fully clothed because he has a tendency to hunch his back. When he is shirtless, his kung fu postures look awkward.

Something else that comes across a bit awkward in *The Master and the Kid* is the music. When soundtrack bites include Jean Michel Jarre's *Oxygene* (made popular in Asia by Jackie Chan's *Snake in the Eagle's Shadow*), the opening theme of *The Young and the Restless*, and the asynchronous tonal looping from the beginning of Pink Floyd's song *Echoes*, it can leave many viewers in the West scratching their heads looking for any sense of logic in these musical choices. Sometimes it seems that Taiwanese-made kung fu films do come off a bit more bizarre than even the bizarre Hong Kong-made films.

Yet one of the advantages of shooting Chinese period films or *wuxia*-style movies in Taiwan is that there are many more places to shoot outdoors than in Hong Kong. Hong Kong has a limited number of bamboo groves, rice paddies, forest areas and waterfronts devoid of buildings. The dense layout of the former British colony also limits the use of outdoor panoramas. Taiwan, on the other hand, offers plenty.

FYI: When productions shoot outside of Taiwan's capital city Taipei (the city where most production companies are located), they don't stay in hotels near the shoot area. Instead, they stay in Taipei and travel to and from the site each day. If there is an overnight shooting, the actors and crew stay on set and find a place to rest between shots. *Master and the Kid* was filmed during the summer, when temperatures in central Taiwan (and Hong Kong, too) can get into the triple digits and high humidity is commonplace. Filming fights during the day can be uncomfortable, exhausting and dangerous (plus not all actors are in shape). Under these conditions, imperfections in choreography are quite noticeable because there are not as many takes available, so outdoor chase scenes and fights often look disjointed. This film, however, has several moments of good, concise choreography emphasized by director Lin's use of bird's-eye-view shots and hand-held tracking shots and pans. The filming conditions must have been pretty severe because the final fight is short and lacks the traditional drawn-out gruesome death of the loser.

So when you consider the circumstances under which films like this are made, then add in freaky sound effects and off-the-wall music, these things can give Taiwanese-made kung fu films a certain unintentional charm. It just comes down to how much hokey stuff you're willing to overlook. Me, I don't even know what hokey means anymore, so I just watch everything.

Titleography: *Fury of the Shaolin Master*; *10 Commandments of Lee*; *One Man Army*; *Shaolin Master and the Kid*. Translation—*The Gentle Love of a Swordsman With an Innocent Heart*. Although no titles reflect the Chinese title, the film contains some elements associated with Shaolin. The studio Ground Zero released the film as *One Man Army*, so although it could be a generic title for any solo-hero kung fu film, perhaps someone was a fan of the Jerry Trimble film of the

same name. There is no Lee character or mention of commandments in the movie, but perhaps there is another English-dubbed version with an altered story line in which actor Yueh Hua's character is named Lee. **MA Percentage: 26.27%**

MASTER OF THE FLYING GUILLOTINE

獨臂拳王大破血滴子 (1976—Hong Kong) **89m. FC: Liu Chia-liang, Liu Chia-rong. NOT/LOT: 8/ 8m 36s; NOF/LOF: 25/ 39m 18s.** D: Jimmy Wong Yu. C: Jimmy Wong Yu, Jin Gang, Doris Lung Chun-er, Lung Fei, Chen Chien-po, Wang Young-sheng, Xue Han, Liu Chia-rong, Huang Fei-lung, Jimmy Lung Fong, Yu Song-zhao, Shan Mao, Wang Tai-lang, Shi Ting-gen, Jack Long, Kuo Chue, Sun Rong-zhi, Wang Li, Robert Tai Chi-hsien, Hsieh Hsin, Ma Jin-gu, Qi Hou-jiang, Jin Long, Su Zhen-ping, Hou Ba-wei, Zhang Yi-guai, Deng De-xiang, Ou Li-bao, He Wei-xiong.

Master of the Flying Guillotine is a sort of sequel to *One Armed Boxer* (1971) in that it features a character with the same handicap. It also notably has a large cast of martial arts superstars. Jimmy Wong Yu was a martial director's martial artist. In several of his directed films, there is a large cast of kung fu actors prominently featured, and they all do different kinds of martial arts. Wong Yu gave the actors the opportunity to flaunt their skills and show audiences the diversity and novelty of their martial ways. Take the beginning of this film, for example: It jumps off with 12 fights that run for 12 minutes and features 18 different styles of martial arts. I also want to point out that none of the fights feature Wong Yu, which clearly demonstrates that a Jimmy Wong Yu movie is not all about him. Respectfully, cheers.

In this film, when the blind anti-Ming assassin Fung Sheng Wu Chi (Jin Gang) hears that a one-armed fighter killed his two disciples, he leaves his mountain retreat and vows to avenge his students. Shaving his head and disguising himself as a lama Buddhist monk, Fung arms himself with the deadly and scary flying guillotine. (For the history behind the weapon, see *The Flying Guillotine.*) He vows to kill every one-armed fighter he meets.

Elsewhere, the anti-Ching one-armed boxer Liu Ti-lung (Jimmy Wong Yu) is invited to attend a martial arts tournament, but he chooses to be an observer. Right after Liu leaves the tournament, Fung shows up and beheads a one-armed fighter who turns out to be a fake; he really has two arms. He was living off Liu's reputation, and as a result he gets his head taken off. Several of the other tournament winners—a Thai boxer, a lama monk and an Indian fakir whose arms can grow 10 feet long—decide they want to assist Fung in his quest. Why? As is typical in many Chinese kung fu films, just because. Plot-wise, it sets up an array of cheeky encounters between them and Liu as he pinpoints the lama's weaknesses with popping furor, gives the Thai boxer a hot foot and twists the fakir's 10-foot arms into swizzle sticks.

As in *One Armed Boxer*, this film also has a lama monk character who can expand his body like a balloon. In the book *Tales of a Dalai Lama*, by Pierre Delattre, the 14th Dalai Lama describes a lama martial artist who stood in front of him and swelled up his body. I'm not sure if the lama technique is real. However, what is real and to me most impressive about this film is that Jimmy Wong Yu's character demonstrates to his students how to practice *ching gong*, which allows kung fu people to jump high and walk on top of reeds and bamboo trees. The real way to practice, as it appears in the film, is to start off with a wide-rimmed straw basket filled with bricks, then walk around the edge of the basket. Over the years, the practitioner removes one brick at a time, and the eventual goal is to be able to walk around the basket rim when the basket is empty. In actuality, in order for this training to work, it must be started by age 7 at the latest.

A cultural note: A fakir is an Indian god-man known for performing miracles, such as walking on hot coals, lying on a bed of nails and many other types of amazing feats. Many educated people in India consider fakirs to be fakes. They warn that fakirs prey on the country's religious superstitions.

One final note: This movie has the best cinematic musical shtick for a villain, one that's foreboding and dangerous-sounding. It's a short piece called *Super 16* by the band Neu. It should rank right up there with Darth Vader's theme from *Star Wars*. Even though *Super 16* sounds creepier, it is more difficult to hum or be played by college marching bands. (This is probably why it never received as much notoriety as John Williams' villainous score.) Quentin Tarantino used the Neu song as an homage to Jimmy Wong Yu in *Kill Bill Vol. I* (2003). Wong Yu has an incredible ear for using maniacal and unique music that is not generally used in other kung fu films. Take for instance the movie's opening theme, *Super*, also by Neu: I guess you could say that Jimmy Wong Yu "neu" what he was doing.

Titleography: *One Armed Boxer vs. The Flying Guillotine*; *One Armed Boxer 2*; *One-Armed Boxer 2*. Translation—*One Armed King Boxer Defeats the Blood Dripping Object*. See martialogy and *The Flying Guillotine*. **MA Percentage: 53.82%**

MASTER GUNFIGHTER, THE

(1975—USA) **121m. FI: Uncredited. NOT/LOT: 2/ 1m 5s; NOF/LOF: 7/ 4m 32s.** D: Frank Laughlin. C: Tom Laughlin, Ron O'Neal, Lincoln Kilpatrick, Geo Anne Sosa, Barbara Carrera, Victor Campos, Hector Elias, James Andronica, Richard Angarola, David S. Cass Sr.

After the success of *The Trial of Billy Jack* (1974), Tom Laughlin played what is essentially a Billy Jack-like hero during a different time and place in *The Master Gunfighter*. It's California around September 9, 1850, the day California became the 31st state, and instead of being a *hapkido* expert, Laughlin's is now a master of the samurai sword and a sharp-shooting gunslinger. Though he plays a different character, he uses the same cadences and line delivery as he reprises his signature pre-fight routine in which he would warn his opponent in detail of the upcoming doom that he would deliver with his foot, or in this film, his sword and gun.

The movie is adapted from the popular Japanese samurai film *Goyokin* (1969) and set in Southern California, near what is now Santa Barbara. In an attempt to prevent the U.S government from taking his land by force, the wealthy and wicked rancher Don Santiago (Richard Angarola) devises a plan to steal a government shipment of gold and deflect the blame to the local Chumash Indians. Furthermore, inducing the "legal" massacre of these Indians would also enable Santiago to steal their land. However, in his way is Santiago's estranged adopted son, Finley (Tom Laughlin), who also gets help from fellow fighter Paulo (*Superfly*'s Ron O'Neal).

Billy Jack's iconic black hat is replaced by a black straw hat that looks like a cross between a sombrero and one of those straw hats seen in samurai films that cover the face. Each time Finley is about to use his sword or guns, or the interesting combination of both at the same time, Laughlin is sure to give his patented fight setup dialogue, followed by lightning-fast sword slashes. The only problem is that we can't see what he's doing because each strike is filmed either in close-up or at night. We only see a body motion, hear a swishing sound of something being hit by the sword, and the resulting cut. One minor error is that Laughlin carries his samurai sword in its scabbard upside-down on his left hip. The blade should be facing up so he can make an instant cut while drawing the sword. Oh well, Laughlin studies hapkido, not *iaido*, the art of drawing and cutting with a *katana*.

Titleography: As of this writing, no alternative titles could be found. **MA Percentage: 4.64%**

MASTER OF KUNG FU, THE

黃飛鴻 and 黃飛鴻勇破烈火陣黃飛鴻 (1973—Hong Kong) **92m. FI: Yuen Cheung-yan, Yuen Woo-ping. NOT/LOT: 6/ 3m 38s; NOF/LOF: 18/ 13m 57s.** D: Ho Meng-hua. C: Ku Feng, Chen Ping, Wang Xia, Lin Wei-tu, Hsu Shao-hsiung, Chan Shen, Huang Kan.

Ku Feng was always a solid character actor, and although he was not a martial arts expert, he had an uncanny ability to adjust to any actor he fought with on camera. Because of this talent, he was one of the few non-martial artists assigned to teach new recruits the ins and outs of cinema fighting. *The Master of Kung Fu* was his first time as the lead martial arts character.

In the film, the smarmy, disrespectful foreigner Gordon procures a valuable jade collection with money earned from selling opium. He wants to find the most vicious kung fu killer in town to protect his assets and does so by organizing a fight competition between Mai Gen (Chan Shen) and the repulsive Li Tien-tao (Wang Xia). Li wins, kills Mai by using his Deadly Ghost Spirit Strike and steals the collection. Gordon blames all the other local kung fu teachers for stealing his jade and has them shot. Mai's friend Huang Fei-hong (Ku Feng) barely escapes with his life. He goes after Li to avenge Mai's death and to clear his own name and the names of all the other honest kung fu teachers.

Born in 1847, folk-hero Huang Fei-hong was a true reflection of the Confucian code. Apart from his phenomenal fighting skills, Huang was renowned for his chivalry, righteousness and "bone-setting" healing abilities. He eventually devoted all his time to running the Bao Zhi Lin Chinese herb clinic (which is

mentioned in the film) that was established and named by his father, Huang Chi-ying. A practitioner of *hong jia* (*hung gar*) kung fu, Huang was also an expert of several specialized techniques, such as the Iron Wire Fist and the No Shadow Kick. Although an integral part of this film, the No Shadow Kick was made famous by Tsui Hark's five *Once Upon a Time in China* films (1992-1994), which show actors Jet Li or Zhou Wen-zhuo as Huang flying sideways through the air kicking his feet as if he were riding a bicycle. In Hollywood circles, this became known as the Hong Kong Kick. In reality, nobody knows what the No Shadow Kick really looks like. It was apparently so fast that it did not leave a shadow. It is curious that these films chose to emphasize Huang's mysterious kicking abilities when you consider that hong jia kung fu emphasizes the fists. Huang died in 1924 at age 77 and was survived by his wife, Muo Gui-lan.

In regard to the fights in *Master of Kung Fu*, they are rather sloppy and uninspired. Most of the actors are either slow or off-balance. However, Ku is quite adept with the three-sectional staff, so his fights with that weapon are worth watching. Sadly, things go back down into the doldrums when characters Huang and Li fight atop the lips of large containers of water. It could have been spectacular but ultimately fails to deliver. Ku was never again cast as the main kung fu character in a film.

Titleography: *Shaolin Death Kicks*; *Death Kicks*. Translations—*Huang Fei-hong*; *Huang Fei-hong Bravely Defeats the Fierce Fire Tactic*. Huang Fei-hong is, as the title states, a *Master of Kung Fu. Death Kicks* refers to his fearsome No Shadow Kick. The Chinese titles refer to the title character and Huang battling the dreaded *Fire Tactic*. **MA Percentage: 19.11%** SHAW BROTHERS

MEN FROM THE MONASTERY

少林子弟 (1974—Hong Kong) **88m. FI: Liu Chia-liang, Tang Chia. NOT/LOT: 8/ 2m 41s; NOF/LOF: 30/ 18m 13s.** D: Chang Cheh. C: Chen Kuan-tai, Alexander Fu Sheng, Chi Guan-chun, Jiang Dao, Lu Di, Tong Yen-san, Wong Ching, Wu Chi-chin, Hu Che, Fung Ke-an, Deng De-xiang, She Tian-hung, Huang Pei-ji.

This is the first of five major films Chang Cheh made in honor of the Shaolin Temple—the others being *Heroes Two*, *Five Shaolin Masters*, *Shaolin Martial Arts* and *Shaolin Temple*. (See the movies' respective martialogies.)

Men From the Monastery recreates two important events that led to the divide between Wu Dung and the Shaolin Temple. The movie is essentially made up of four short films, each beginning with opening credits. The first three parts introduce Fang Shi-yu (Alexander Fu Sheng), Hu Hui-qian (Chi Guan-chun) and Hong Xi-guan (Chen Kuan-tai). The parts outline the events leading up to Part 4, which involves the burning of Jiu Lian Shan Shaolin Temple by Gao Jin-zhong (Jiang Dao). The finale erupts when all three heroes unite with several other fighters to take on key members of the Wu Dung School and Ching Dynasty fighters.

Part 1 opens with Shi-yu in the Luohan Hall of wooden dummies. Fang Dao-de (Lu Di) accuses Shi-yu of killing Monk Chen Guang. But in fact, it was Dao-de's assistant under his orders who actually committed the murder. Dao-de lies

Still from *Men From the Monastery* © Celestial Pictures Ltd. All rights reserved.

a chapter of Shaolin history.

So how does this film fare with history? Shi-yu killing Lei and Hu destroying the textile factory and defeating the Wu Dung fighters increased the rift between Shaolin and Wu Dung. What the film does not point out (keep in mind martial arts history is not 100-percent certain) is that Lei was the son-in-law of Li Ba-shan of the Wu Dung School. Li was the bodyguard of Chen Wen-yao, one of the men who devised the plan to burn down Song Shan Shaolin Temple. Lei's wife, Li Xiao-huan, convinced her father, Ba-shan, to seek revenge against Fang Shi-yu, who in turn sought the help of Monk San De and Tong Qian-jin to spur the retaliation.

As in the film, Hu attacked and destroyed the Brocade Hall textile mill to avenge his father and the multiple beatings Hu took as an adult. However, historically, Hu's father was killed when Hu was a child, and it was also at that time when Hu was badly beaten. Although the film does not mention it, one of the people Hu killed during the attack was Zhang Jin-hong, a second-generation student of Fang Dao-de. Although all the facts are not in the film, the tie-ins are.

Titleography: *Disciples of Death*. Translation—*Next Generation of Shaolin Heroes*. The Chinese title refers to the 10 Tigers of Shaolin, the next generation after the Five Elders of Shaolin. *Disciples of Death* and *Men From the Monastery* refer to the Shaolin warriors who fought the Wu Dung and Chings to the death. **MA Percentage: 53.82%** SHAW BROTHERS

MIGHTY ONE, THE

童子功 (1972—Hong Kong) 83m. FI: Zhang Yi-gui, You Tian-lung. NOT/LOT: 1/ 20s; NOF/LOF: 33/ 32m 29s. D: Joseph Kuo. C: Ivy Ling Po, Ling Yun, Liu Ping, Gao Ming, Lung Fei, Hsieh Hsing, Zhang Yi-gui, Shao Luo-hui

It is Jiang Hu time again. When all the swordsmen in the world are sleeping, thinking there is peace in this villa or that valley, this mansion or that fortress, this clan or that sect, there is still a quest to find this or that secret technique, this or that lost weapon, this or that extinct manual. In this case, villain Fang Yu-lung (Liu Ping) is sent on a mission by his boss, Dragon Valley Wang Fu-song, to find the missing fourth and fifth movements from the secret manual *The Mighty Power of Five Masters*. With it, Wang can rule the Jiang Hu world. Fang already has the first three movements in what he believes is Volume 1. Fang sends out the Five Lung (Dragon) Brothers to find Volume 2, which contains the last two movements.

When the Five Lung Brothers start harassing a married couple and take the wife away because Jiang Hu villains feel they can do what they want, a man in a large straw hat appears and dismantles them. Moments later, hearts flutter, including Fang's, as the knight-errant is none other than Water Knight Hsiang Kuei (Ling Yun), whose *chi* is so strong that he knows *xi xing da fa*, a technique whereby one can levitate objects and then draw them toward his outstretched hands. Although this technique was made popular in director Ching Siu-tung's *Swordsman II* (1992), it is also the premise behind George Lucas' concept of "the Force." A further similarity is that Hsiang is a master of the Light Sword. Is not that the way of the Jedi? I wonder if Lucas has a secret stash of Shaw Brothers films stuffed away in some closet. As some Jiang Hu swordsmen might

to subvert Shi-yu in the eyes of his teacher, Zhi Shan. Bai Mei (see *Executioners From Shaolin*) then appears as an ominous shadow cast against the wall—it's a metaphor for Bai Mei's shady character in Shaolin lore—and warns Dao-de that Shaolin is on to them. Bai Mei vows to kill Zhi Shan and tells Dao-de that the next time Dao-de fights Shi-yu, he must get Shi-yu to jump up and then stab him upward. We also see Shi-yu bathe in his legendary vat full of Chinese herbs and medicines that his mother forced him to sit in as a means to toughen his body. The implication of that is Bai Mei knows of a place where the herbs and medicine did not harden Shi-yu's body. As a foreboding of things to come, a fight breaks out between Shi-yu and one of Dao-de's students, Lei Lao-hu, who prepares to battle Shi-yu by practicing the Pile Formation. Also known as the plum-blossom formation, it is a collection of narrow 6-foot-tall posts placed in the ground and surrounded by short bamboo stakes. If Lei can push Shi-yu off the posts, he would fall onto the bamboo stakes and possibly land on his weak point and die. Lei fails.

Part 2 introduces Hu Hui-qian beginning with his father being killed by members of the Jin Lun School (ran by Wu Dung). Hu goes to their textile factory to seek revenge. Instead, he gets badly beaten and tossed into the river. He tries to get revenge several more times and is beaten each time. Shi-yu arrives on the scene, strikes up a friendship with Hu and takes him to Shaolin to train him to fight. After mastering Shaolin kung fu, Hu returns to the textile factory; his nostrils flare because he is a new man—a fighting machine! As would be expected, the Jin Lun students are so not afraid of the man, thinking that this time, they'll just put him out of his revenge-riddled mind and send him to the big textile factory in the sky. Oops. Yes, their faces take on that "oh, shit" moment when they realize it is they who have got the "runs."

Part 3 deals with Hong Xi-guan on the run while Ching soldiers are closing in. He manages to escape their tightening noose but then learns that the Shaolin Temple has been burned to the ground. Hong continues to recruit anti-Ching rebels, saying they must continue to fight. He meets up with Fang Shi-yu, Hu Hui-qian, Tong Qian-jin and a few others while Gao, Dao-de, and many Wu Dung and Ching fighters surround their secret hide-out. Only one man survives the final bloodbath, Hong Xi-guan. Three years later, *Executioners From Shaolin* begins where *Men From the Monastery* ends.

With Jiu Lian Shan Temple burning in the background, Part 4 is when all these three heroes meet with their various Ching villain counterparts in a final fight that will be the death for some, heartbreak for the survivors and the end of

Still from *The Mighty One* © Celestial Pictures Ltd. All rights reserved.

say, "May the chi be with you."

Later on, Fang tries out the first three movements from the secret manual on the old righteous man Ma, whom Fang accuses of hiding Volume 2, but things get more intense when Hsiang arrives to rescue Ma. When Fang turns his anger and his Three Mighty Powers special skill on the meddling Hsiang, an unknown, more powerful fighter leaps into the fray. It's swordswoman Hsiao Chu (Ivy Ling Po), and she's here to save Hsiang. The plot continues to thicken. As it turns out, Hsiang is her long lost brother. After Fang killed their father many moons ago, Hsiang and Hsiao got split up and lost contact over the years, but now brother and sister are back together and looking for some payback. Yes, this time it really is personal, and during a final fight on a cobblestone beach (an amazing combination), Fang finally realizes too late who Hsiang and Hsiao are. The finale is full of broken swords, levitating boulders and impalings, and the ending will rock the world of Jiang Hu.

There is a great wire gag in which a spear (on a wire) is shot horizontally toward actor Lin Yung in an inn. Lin Yung, also attached to a wire, is hoisted up out of the way at the last moment as the spear travels beneath his raised feet and sticks into the wall. The possibility of crossed wires in this gag is high, but it is pulled off without a hitch. The cobblestone beach scene is also impressive because cobblestone is a very difficult surface to fight on and the danger for spraining and twisting ankles is high. Also keep in mind that none of the actors are martial artists.

Titleography: *The Child's Efforts.* Translation—*Minor Kung Fu* (minor as in an underage child). The *Child* and *Minor* titles refer to Hsiang, who was badly wounded as a child. His scar reminds him of his mission and pushes him forward. *The Mighty One* refers to whoever can master the Mighty Power of Five Masters kung fu. **MA Percentage: 39.54%** SHAW BROTHERS

MING PATRIOTS, THE

中原鏢局 (1976—Hong Kong) 87m. FI: Liu Chia-liang, Liu Chia-rong. NOT/LOT: None; NOF/LOF: 27/ 27m 21s. D: Ulysses Au Yeung-jun. C: Carter Wong, Bruce Li, Chia Ling, Zhang Yi, Shan Mao, Lung Fei, Michael Chan, Chen Hui-lou, Roy Chiao Hung, Jimmy Lung Fong, Zhang Qin.

In *The Ming Patriots*, after the fall of the Ming Dynasty, a large Ming army under General Chao gathers in Kang Nan (aka Jiang Nan; a southern area of China) to await the arrival of the last princess of the Ming royal family in hopes that she will give spirit to their cause. Her crown jewels will be used to finance the struggle, but she is trapped in the capital. Her dire straights are compounded when the word is out that the vicious Prince Wang Shu (Zhang Yi) wants her assassinated and his ring around the city is closing in on her. She has nowhere to run and nowhere to hide. Enter Li Ti-lung (Bruce Li), owner of the Zhong Yuen Security Company, and an enchanting lady of the fist (Chia Ling), both of whom are willing to sacrifice their bodies, spirits and souls to deliver the princess, the crown jewels and the dead emperor's will to Chao. With the Ching army closing in and traitorous Chinese wanting to steal the jewelry, kill the princess and destroy the will, Li is on the verge of a game of death.

There are two great things about this movie: The first being that Bruce Li elicits a competitive acting exhibition the likes of which you will never see again. In his other films, Li is completely entrenched in copying Bruce Lee, but in this film, he actually seems like himself. It is probably the best fighting performance in Li's career.

The second highlight is a short spear-fighting cameo by Carter Wong in which his character tries to free the princess while fighting against the Ching hordes in and outside the palace. His spear seems to glide through the air as if in constant motion. As he runs around like a rabid wolverine, Wong's spear twirls, jabs and impales with sure-shot intensity and smooth continuity of motion. The best part of this sequence is a tracking shot in which Wong runs about 100 feet along the side of the palace moat while spearing Ching soldiers who flop into the water or retreat in feeble chaos. Truly, this is one of Wong's best weapon fight scenes ever.

The fights incorporate many medium and close shots, and unlike many American movies in which this sort of camerawork disrupts the energy, the camera choreography adds a new dimension of excitement because you feel the desperation in what the characters are doing—fighting to stay alive. The close shots use continuous, uncut transitions that flow between several opponents in sequence. The final Ming-Ching field battle marks the only time a kung fu film has played the soundtrack from *Zulu* (1964), a film based on the 1879 Battle

of Rorke's Drift in Natal, South Africa. Like the Mings, the Brits faced seemingly insurmountable odds: 140 British soldiers against 4,000 Zulu warriors.

One of the weaknesses of English dubbers is their unfamiliarity with Chinese history. According to this film's English voice-over, for example, Ming Emperor Chong Zhen died in the 16th century (i.e., the 1500s), when in fact he committed suicide in 1644.

On a fun cultural note: When Prince Wang takes a whiff from a snuff bottle, it gives him a momentary explosion of kung fu killing power. Snuff bottles came into vogue during the Ching Dynasty and usually contained tobacco powder. Smoking tobacco was illegal during the dynasty, but snuff was considered good for one's health. Elite fighters would add other powdered ingredients like ginseng to their snuff, so when they inhaled it, the ensuing burst of *chi (qi)* would make their strikes more powerful. In a similar though less narcotic vein, some Shaolin priests would wear beads during fights because they believed the jewelry gave them better chi power, and thus better fighting power. They also knew that with better chi flow came better health.

Titleography: *Revenge of the Patriots; Dragon Reincarnate.* Translation—*Zhong Yuen Escort Company* (as in escorting goods). Bruce Li is an actor who usually plays Bruce Lee (often times called the Little Dragon) or is associated with Bruceploitation films. The people who released this film as the *Dragon Reincarnate* (released under this title after Li's Bruceploitation movies became known) were probably indicating that Bruce Li in this film was a reincarnation (as in a different character) played by Bruce Li from his Bruceploitation films, thus the *Dragon* reference. Yes, it is a stretch, but it is a real possibility, too. **MA Percentage: 31.44%**

MONKEY KING WITH 72 MAGIC

新孫悟空72變; 孫悟空七十二變 and 猴王大戰天兵天將 (1976—Taiwan) 90m. KFI: Jin Wan-xi. NOT/LOT: 3/ 1m 54s; NOF/LOF: 8/ 9m 53s. D: Fu Ching-hua. C: Ding Hua-chong, Fan Dan-fung, Chen You-xin, Jiang Yang, Li Min-lang, Long Shao-fei.

If you saw Jet Li in *The Forbidden Kingdom* (2008), then you may recall that one of his characters in the film was Swuin Wu Kung, the Monkey King. This character is featured in the classic Chinese novel *Xi Yo Ji* (*Journey to the West*), written by Wu Chen-an in the 1500s.

This quirky low-budget version of the origins of the Monkey King introduces some of the gods and fairies in Chinese mythology (such as Guan Ying, Na Cha, Jade Emperor and Yang Chien) and explains how heaven and Earth were really created. It also explores how the Monkey King was born and became immortal and why he was put into suspended animation to rest for 500 years.

There are two major fights in the film. The first pits the Monkey King (Ding Hua-chong) against the god Na Cha (Fan Dan-fung) and his deadly steel rings. The second pits the Monkey King against the war god Yang Chien (Long Shao-fei) whose signature weapon is the three-pointed, double-bladed sword (*san jian liang ren dao*).

Although played by a woman in this film, Na Cha is indeed a male god. The legend of this god is featured in *Na Cha the Great* (1974) starring Alexander Fu Sheng and in the Communist Chinese animated feature *Nezha Conquers the Dragon King* (1979). (See their respective martialogies.) Also, for those of you who practice *tai chi*, the "monkey grabs peaches" technique stems from the Monkey King's naughty behavior during his time managing the heavenly peach groves.

Titleography: As of this writing, no alternative titles could be found. Translations—*New Swuin Wu-kong and His 72 Changes; Swuin Wu-kong and his 72 Changes; Monkey King Battles Heaven's Generals and Soldiers.* Swuin Wu-kung's name means "Light of the Meaning of Emptiness." The *Changes* refer to the Monkey King's 72 magical powers, or tricks, as the English title states. **MA Percentage: 13.09%**

MONKEY KUNG FU

出籠馬騮 (1979—Hong Kong) 90m. FI: Ching Siu-tung, Tony Leung, Hou Chao-sheng. NOT/LOT: 16/ 6m; NOF/LOF: 24/ 36m 6s. D: John Lo Mar. C: Ching Siu-tung, Hou Chao-sheng, Lin Hui-juang, Fong Ping, Huang Mei-mei, Chiang Cheng, Tony Leung, Yin Fa, Guan Feng, Lee Chun-wa, Huang Rong.

After being framed for murder, young Wei Chung (Ching Siu-tung) is sentenced to prison for three and a half years. His cellmate is a crazy old one-eyed man on death row. The old man is feared throughout the prison because he is a master of monkey kung fu. When the cocky Wei picks a fight with the old man,

Still from *Monkey Kung Fu* © Celestial Pictures Ltd. All rights reserved.

he quickly learns that life on death row can be more dangerous than death itself.

Surviving monkey kung fu attack after monkey kung fu attack, Wei eventually wins the respect of the elder simian mimicker because he's impressed with Wei's heroic personality, for putting up with his constant attacks and never backing down. The night before the old man's execution, he gives Wei a piece of wood and tells him to find the other half when he gets out of prison; if he does, he will understand its meaning.

Inmate Zhou (Hou Chao-sheng) befriends Wei, and while chained together during work detail, they escape. Zhou has the other wood piece, and once they combine the two pieces, the friends learn they have to do something and that something is to find the secret Gibbon Fist manual. It describes the White Drunken Monkey skill, which is the only way a person can defeat fighters from the Black Tiger clan, a clan that is trying to wipe out practitioners of the Zhou's monkey kung fu style. As it turns out, the inspector chasing the two fugitives also wants the book because he is actually the head of the Black Tiger clan.

It is neat to watch one of kung fu film's greatest fight directors, who even in his prime was rarely the star of a film, play the lead role of Wei. It is magnificent to see this side of his skills instead of the usual great choreography he does. Back in the day, Ching Siu-tung lived on the Shaw Brothers' lot since childhood and was trained in Chinese opera at its studios, so his choreography differed from Tang Chia and Liu Chia-liang, arguably Shaw Brothers' most successful fight-instructor tandem. They both went on to significant "solo" careers as fight instructors, Liu moving further along into becoming one of the most influential martial arts film directors of kung fu movies. Ching's style is evident in this film's entertaining fight sequences in the prison, in the bed and in the scene during which the two friends manipulate a muscle-bound ironsmith into chopping off their ankle chains with an ax.

Ching's trademark motion-filled tracking shots, which he often shot at 18 frames per second to increase the playback speed, appear intermittently in this film because he was not the head fight instructor. Ching is considered the "father of wire fu," and although this film does not have any, the following year in *The Sword* (1980), his spectacular wire choreography, which led to the over-the-top-frenetic label that Hong Kong's Fant-Asia films became known for in the years to come, would also elevate Hong Kong action films to new heights in the 1980s and even further in the 1990s. Incidentally, Ching was the first choice for brothers Larry and Andy Wachowski to choreograph the fighting in *The Matrix* (1999); Yuen Kwei was the second and Yuen Woo-ping was the third. Ching and Yuen Kwei turned the Wachowskis down because they believed they did not get

the proper respect.

Monkey Kung Fu is also a subliminal homage to the creator of monkey kung fu: Kou Sze, who during the mid-1800s was sentenced to 10 years in prison for murder and imprisoned in a forest on the outskirts of town. His cell window faced a wood of tall trees that harbored a colony of chattering monkeys. Fascinated by the simians' playful antics, Kou studied their behavior, paying particular attention to how the monkeys fought. He developed an unusual new hopping-and-squatting defense system and borrowed a number of maneuvering principles—including agility, grabbing, falling, lunging, light jumping and tumbling. Upon his release, Kou became known as the Monkey Master.

Titleography: *Stroke of Death*. Translation—*Legendary Fine Horse Is Out of the Cage*. *Stroke of Death* is a play on "stroke of luck"; Wei learns the stroke of death via a stroke of luck. The Chinese title suggests that something great will happen once the *Fine Horse Is Out of the Cage*, and in this film, it is the discovery of the White Monkey Drunken style to defeat the Black Tiger. **MA Percentage: 46.78%** SHAW BROTHERS

MR. NATWARLAL

(1979—India) **157m. AC: Veeru Devgun. NOT/LOT: None; NOF/LOF: 2/ 3m 20s.** D: Rakesh Kuma. C: Amitabh Bachchan, Rekha, Ajit, Amjad Khan, Rajni Sharma, Kader Khan, Indrani Mukherjee, Satyendra Kapoor.

This film is sort of a cross between Akira Kurosawa's *Seven Samurai* and Rob Reiner's film adaptation of *The Princess Bride*. Natwarlal (Amitabh Bachchan) is a Robin Hood-like hero who has lost his faith in goodness and humankind. As he battles the vicious underworld smuggler Vikram (played by chronic villain portrayer Amjad Khan), his hordes of enslaving *dacoits* (a Hindi term for robbers and villains), a giant of a man and a man-eating tiger, he eventually finds purpose in life with the help of the flute-playing Hindu god Krishna.

This film barely makes it into this book by 27 seconds. (*Good Guys Wear Black* is the cutoff point in terms of length for martial arts action time.) Perennial Indian action star Amitabh Bachchan steps away from the pole-fighting skills of *kalaripayit* and goes more with the jumping front kicks typical of David Carradine but done with about the same speed and intensity. However, it is the spiritual aspect of the story and the positive virtues that his character tries to attain during his journey that make this film captivating. In this sense, Natwarlal is almost like a Chinese *wuxia* hero wrapped in Indian stylism. Bachchan is a sharp-looking fellow with great screen presence, and apparently this is one of the first films in which he loops in his own singing voice during the standard song-and-dance routines associated with Indian films.

Titleography: As of this writing, no alternative titles could be found. **MA Percentage: 2.12%**

MURDER IN THE ORIENT

(1974—Philippines) **71m. FI: Uncredited. NOT/LOT: 2/ 1m 31s; NOF/ LOF: 9/ 5m 23s.** D: Manuel Songco. C: Ron Marchini, Leo Gong, Eva Reyes, Raymond, Jim Delon.

Sometimes a film comes along that raises two, no three, very important questions: Why was this film made? How did it get made? And is it possible that a local 5-year-old martial arts student choreographed the fights?

When the blades of two lost samurai swords are united, they form a treasure map revealing where two murderous Japanese soldiers buried $10 million of treasure during the Japanese occupation of the Philippines in World War II. This has the potential to be a pretty good story line with exciting samurai-style and karate-style fights, but instead, all that happens is people act and fight like pieces of wood. (I wonder whether anyone got a splinter.)

Oddly enough, the film stars legitimate martial artists like Leo Fong (who holds black belts in *taekwondo* and *arnis* and created his own style *wei kuen do*) and Ron Marchini (a successful tournament fighter and practitioner of *renbukai*). It is no wonder that martial artists and filmmakers in Asia guffawed at the state of martial arts and its so-called masters in the United States back in the 1970s.

Titleography: As of this writing, no alternative titles could be found. **MA Percentage: 9.27%**

MURDER OF MURDERS

玉蜻蜓 (1978—Hong Kong) **90m. AD: Lee Chiu. NOT/LOT: None; NOF/ LOF: 22/ 16m 42s.** D: Wu Ma. C: Chi Kuan-chun, Lo Lieh, Jin Gang, Yee Yuen, Miao Tian, Yin Bao-lian, Yueh Hua, Lee Chiu.

A dragonfly can go from 0 to 60 mph in one second, which is about the time it takes Pan Jin-fang (Lo Lieh) to secretly steal six valuable gems from a secure vaultlike room. But at the scene of the crime, he and the gem venders are found knocked out by a powerful gas, and the gems are nowhere to be found. Inspector Chao Zi (Jin Gang) can't pin anything on Pan, although he firmly believes Pan is the notorious thief Jade Dragonfly. But then Pan is poisoned at a local restaurant, and that complicates this mystery further. Adding to Chao's investigative headaches are the arrivals of Pan's kung-fu-fighting brother Yin-feng (Chi Kuan-chun) and Chao's detective rival Miao Tian-chi (Miao Tian). Soon it's a three-way race to find Pan's killer, the missing gems and the real Jade Dragonfly thief. Toss in the local Jiang Hu clan leader Tu Pa and everything is destined to go awry at a moment's notice.

As you might expect given actor Chi Kuan-chun's caliber of kung fu ability and cinema experience, his fights are spiffy and sharp. However, the best snippet of action is a short fight by actor Jin Gang at the film's beginning when the audience is introduced to his character, Inspector Chao Zi. As Jin casually walks toward the camera, he is attacked by many misfits, and without breaking stride, he sends them pining for the fjords. It is similar to the very neat and short spat actor Lo Lieh does when his Bai Mei character is introduced in Clan of the White Lotus (1979). The only difference between Chao and Bai is that Chao is rougher and strikes with more oomph. There is also a striking night fight in which actor Miao Tian uses a lamp attached to a long pole to fend off a balaclava-bearing blitzkrieger. This night fight starts with a novel close-up shot of someone's feet running backward toward an intercepting pair of feet, then the camera tilts up into a full-fledged fight.

An off-the-wall note: If you wonder what "pining for the fjords" means, then you've probably never been to Norway. It's a Norwegian colloquialism for "someone who is dying" or "thinking about death." When our times all come, it is something we can all "Afjord."

Titleography: The Massive. Translation—Jade Dragonfly. This film was based on the kung fu novel Jade Dragonfly written by Huang Yin. Like the phrase "best of the best," Murder of Murders places the murder in this film in the upper echelon of murders. I've no idea why it was renamed The Massive. Perhaps it has something to do with this being a huge case. **MA Percentage: 18.56%**

MURDER PLOT

孔雀王朝 (1979—Hong Kong) **90m. FI: Tang Chia. NOT/LOT: None; NOF/LOF: 44/ 17m 50s.** D: Chu Yuan. C: David Chiang, Ching Li, Wang Chung, Chen Ping, Danny Lee, Yu An-an, Lo Lieh, Ching Miao, Frankie Wei Hong, Liu Hui-ling.

When something is adapted from a novel written by Gu Long and takes place in the world of Wu Lin, you know there are going to be lots of characters. Then again, this film doesn't have even one-third the number of characters as The Water Margin, so there is hope.

In the world of Jiang Hu—a sub-world of beggars, transients, martial arts heroes and anti-government insurgents—there is a sub-community known as the world of Wu Lin. It is a world different from Jiang Hu in that all its inhabitants know martial arts. There are essentially two societies that have somewhat different kinds of people who occupy the same geographical area and, often, the same habitats. In the Wu Lin world, the complexity of relationships is exemplified by martial diversity, which is reflected in the structure of the various clans and sects. As in nature, the relationships that evolve can be characterized in five ways: competition, in which clans will vie against each other for whatever reason and death does not have to be the outcome; commensalism, in which only one clan can benefits from the relationship but neither does; parasitism, in which one clan is kept alive as long as necessary to hatch the other's plan, then wipes out the clan; mutualism, in which both clans benefit from the relationship; and predation or assassination. Murder Plot features all five interrelationships among the varying members of Wu Lin, though some are hidden more than others, like with the character Peacock King.

The Peacock King disappeared and was replaced by Happy King (Lo Lieh), the man responsible for the catastrophic 19-day bloodbath in which 900 heroes died at Zhang Bei Mountain while trying to get the 72 Technique kung fu manual. The expert swordsman Shen Lang (David Chiang), who wrote his fiancee Zhu Qi Qi (Ching Li) to explain that they would be married after he has completed a three- to five-year mission, attends a meeting of the Wu Lin leaders during which it is decided that they will hunt down and kill the Happy King before he invades the Central Territories. Qi Qi arrives in town looking for Shen, but

Jin Wu-wang (Wang Chung) traps her, the King of Beggars Panda (Danny Lee) and the mysterious Bai Fei-fei (Yu An-an) by striking them in specific parts of their bodies with his famous Ice Skill, which literally freezes them in their tracks. Witch Madam Wang (Liu Hui-ling) appears and asks Shen to protect Happy King because she wants Happy King to kneel down in front of her, thus admitting defeat to her. She also wants Happy King to endure a great loss of face while his kingdom crumbles and all the Wu Lin heroes take him down. Yet the Ice Skill cometh, and in typical wuxia-novel fashion, the film tries to condense the final chapters into 20 or so minutes.

The pacing of this film is amazing when you consider there are 44 fights, and each one is really short. Instead of having long fights with tons of story and exposition, director Chu Yuan spaces everything out evenly, so if you hit the fast-forward button, you might miss an engaging 10- to15-second sword fight. Filming short action sequences bodes well for actor David Chiang—compared to his fights in Shaolin Hand Lock (see martialogy), for example—as it does for most actors because it requires less energy and intense concentration. The most memorable sequence in this film is during actress Ching Li's opening fight. She walks across a doorway and blocks the attacks of three fighters without breaking stride. I have mentioned similar scenes of actors doing fights while walking and not breaking stride (see Clan of the White Lotus and Murder of Murders) and love them all. It is a tough move to do well and requires incredibly good timing from everyone involved.

Titleography: As of this writing, no alternative titles could be found. Translation—Peacock Kingdom. Murder Plot refers to Happy King's plan to kill all the Wu Lin heroes, and the Chinese title names the Jiang Hu place where everything about the film stems from and comes to a head. **MA Percentage: 19.81%** SHAW BROTHERS

MUTHERS, THE

(1976—Philippines) **101m. FI: Uncredited. NOT/LOT: None; NOF/LOF: 6/ 1m 56s.** D: Cirio H. Santiago. C: Jeannie Bell, Rosanne Katon, Trina Parks, Jayne Kennedy, Tony Carreon, John Montgomery, Sam Sharruff.

Black is beautiful, and so are the sista' martial arts pirates of the Philippines. There's no escrima, but this film is a screamer. Fresh from her blaxploitation blast in TNT Jackson (1975), Jeannie Bell explodes back onto the screen as Kelly, the femme fatale leader of a band of pirates. She is hired by a Filipino detective to infiltrate and investigate the cloaked activities on a mysterious island coffee plantation. Along the way, Kelly teams up with Marcie (former Bond girl Trina "Thumper" Parks), and they turn the jive-turkey plantation owner into turkey jerky.

This film barely makes the time requirement of this book. (See Good Guys Wear Black for minimum time requirement.) The martial arts scenes are short, hurried and probably shot in one take. But the film earns a few points: The use of light gymnastics is a nice addition, and there are some interesting uses of camera speed. Finally, despite the cast members' lack of martial arts experience, they at least give it the old college try, which is more than we can say about many American martial arts films made over the next several decades.

Titleography: As of this writing, no alternative titles could be found. **MA Percentage: 1.91%**

MY KUNG FU TWELVE KICKS

十二潭腿 (1979—Hong Kong) **87m. MAI: Bruce Leung, Tony Leung. NOT/LOT: 12/ 15m 34s; NOF/LOF: 6/ 20m 16s.** D: Do Liu-boh. C: Bruce Leung, Ku Feng, Lee Hoi-sung, Hon Gwok-choi.

You never know who knows kung fu, so respect everyone, including street beggars. This film focuses on Da Bien (Bruce Leung) learning kung fu from three masters who were soundly beaten and mutilated by Iron Skin master Kwai (Lee Hoi-sung). Kwai pummeled them because they refused to give him their secret tan tui manual. To avenge their pain, destroy Kwai, and give Da the abilities to get his revenge on the thugs who beat him up and killed his girlfriend, the three teachers reveal their secrets to Da.

Although tan tui is recognizable by its kicking techniques, its major influences come from three arts: northern praying mantis, chang chuan (northern long fist kung fu) and northern Shaolin. Furthermore, depending on what history you are attuned to, the founder of tan tui, which has deep roots in China's Hui Muslim community, was either infantry soldier Kun Lung Dai Shi, Shaolin Monk Xian Ji or the Muslim traveler Cha Shag Mir. The three masters who teach Da symbolize the three styles that form the foundation of tan tui. Knowing the movie's martial arts instructor Tony Leung as I do, each master pays homage to the three purported founders of the art, and it all culminates in the unifying principle of the three arts of tan tui kicks as taught to Da by *sifu* Wu (Ku Feng)—Wu is a street beggar who Da initially thinks is a no-good lazy bum.

The acting and comedy in this film are so forced and dreary that they look more like an afterthought, as if the fights were shot first and then the script was hurriedly put together around them (which is actually rather common). That said, the fights rock and the kung fu is superb.

Bruce Leung, known today for playing the frog villain in *Kung Fu Hustle* (2004), shows his wide range of exceptional martial arts talent as both a performer and a choreographer who specializes in the five animal styles. Although the fights draw on some of his earlier films as a Bruce Lee impersonator, Leung also reveals his physical prowess, which rivals Jackie Chan. This film taps into the success of Chan's teacher-student movies right down to using similar sound bites during the training sequences and many comparable comedy bits. Tan tui stylist and actor Chiang Cheng performs the opening tan tui sequence. As is common when fighting an enemy with powerful *chi* or some indestructible kung fu technique, the use of timing and precise striking is tantamount to success. For further explanation of this phenomenon, see *Executioners From Shaolin* (1977).

Titleography: *The Whirlwind Kicks*; *Incredible Master Beggars*. Translation—*12 Kicks of Tan Tui*. The Chinese title is close to the English title *My Kung Fu Twelve Kicks*, but the Chinese title can also be translated as *The 12 Lake Kicks*. In a sense, *The Whirlwind Kicks* describes Leung's kicking abilities, and *Incredible Master Beggars* describes the main protagonists. **MA Percentage: 41.91%**

MYSTERY OF CHESS BOXING

雙馬連環 (1979—Hong Kong) **90m. MAD: Ricky Cheng Tien-chi, Wang Chi-sheng, Wang Yong-sheng. NOT/LOT: 12/ 14m 48s; NOF/LOF: 18/ 28m 43s.** D: Joseph Kuo. C: Lee Yi-min, Jack Long, Yuen Xiao-tian, Wang Chi-sheng, Wang Yong-sheng, Ricky Cheng Tien-chi, Xiao Hu-dou, Long Guan-yu.

Sometimes the blatancy of rip-offs in Chinese films can really get under your skin, regardless of how creative the fight scenes are. Perhaps it is the danger of consecutively watching more than 550 films over an eight-month period, but when I see *Snake in the Eagle's Shadow* copycat movies aping Jackie Chan like Japanese macaques (monkey) at the Jigokudani spring in Nagano, I thank the DVD and VCR gods for the fast-forward button. Here we have yet another case of Suexploitation. (See *Dance of the Drunk Mantis*.)

Actor Yuen Xiao-tian once again plays another old, gray, mop-haired teacher who shows the hero-to-be Ah Bao (Lee Yi-min) how to defend himself without Ah Bao even realizing it. This is a choreography gag seen in Jackie Chan's *Snake in the Eagle's Shadow* in which Yuen's beggar kung fu character manipulates the movements of Chan's Chien Fu character to make the onlooker think Chien knows kung fu; but Chien doesn't know that it looks that way. The film *Dirty Ho* has an even more original souped-up version of this choreography stunt. (See their respective martialogies.)

Meanwhile, Ah Bao's elder students chastise and beat him, while the brutal Ghost Face Killer (Long Guan-yu) tries to wipe out all known stylists loyal to his archenemy Chiu Siu-tin (Jack Long). Of course, Ah Bao's father was assassinated by the Ghost Face Killer, which supplies the old reliable revenge motif.

Man, although that sounds just like the plot of *Snake in the Eagle's Shadow* to a tee, I must admit that the fights are actually very good and entertaining. The twist of using chess moves as a sort of anti-environmental way of defeating the five elements is unlike anything Jackie Chan ever did. What is also a little bit different is that Yuen comes across like an old vaudevillian (W. C. Fields, perhaps) with his juggling act, red face, large nose and jolly drunken demeanor. Furthermore, Ah Bao's main teacher is not Yuen's character but Chiu, who teaches Ah Bao the philosophy of chess while subliminally training him in ways to defeat the Ghost Face Killer's deadly Five Elements kung fu. The training looks like a movied-up version of *hsing-i* kung fu, though the film does not explicitly state it.

Titleography: *Ninja Checkmate*. Translation—*Double Chained Horses*, which is the name of a move in Chinese chess. *Checkmate* is logical considering that the strategy of the film's kung fu revolves around

chess, and of course, *Ninja* is just one of those generic non sequitur marketing words. **MA Percentage: 48.31%**

NA CHA THE GREAT

哪吒 (1974—Hong Kong) **90m. FI: Liu Chia-liang, Tang Chia. NOT/LOT: 1/ 1m 2s; NOF/LOF: 15/ 19m 35s.** D: Chang Cheh. C: Alexander Fu Sheng, Lu Di, Liu Jian-ming, Jiang Dao, Fung Ke-an, Li Zhen Biao, Li Yun-zhong.

This film launched the cheeky, lovable persona that Alexander Fu Sheng became famous for, a caricature that truly separated him from the whole stable of Shaw regulars and irregulars. He was the perfect choice to play Na Cha, a protection deity of Taoist mythology who is often depicted as an impish young trickster holding a flame-throwing spear in one hand and a golden hoop (aka a cosmic ring) around his right shoulder. Na Cha zips around the sky via a flaming wheel under each foot.

Interestingly, the Chinese invented a flamethrower lance in 200 B.C., which was a spear connected to a tube filled with gunpowder that spewed fire from the tip. This spear was the forerunner of the first cannon.

As legend has it, Na Cha was born 3,000 years ago, the third son of military commander Li Chi. When born, Na Cha was a ball of flesh. After his angry father struck the ball with his sword, Na Cha flew out, and although he instantly grew to adulthood, he had the mind and attitude of a child. Na Cha killed two demonic deities: rain god Third Prince Ao Bing and the *yaksha* (nature god) Li General Ao Bing's father, Ao Guang, who was Dragon King of the East Sea, kidnapped Na Cha's parents and demanded that Na Cha disembowel himself in order to save them. However, Na Cha was brought back to life and given great powers by the Taoist immortal Tai Yi. He used lotus blossoms given to him by the immortal Ran Dang to rebuild and reincarnate Na Cha into a warrior with great powers; this angered Na Cha's father, causing them to fight each other. Na Cha was superior to his father, so Ran Dang learned to control Na Cha by unleashing a purple cloud from his sleeve that could trap him inside a burning golden pagoda. Eventually, the Jade Emperor stepped in and united father and son into becoming heroic demon slayers.

If this sounds like a cool legend to you, imagine it filled with fight instructors Liu Chia-liang and Tang Chia's kung fu weapon choreography, and that pretty much sums up the film. The plot follows the legend closely, except that according to the film, Na Cha killed the gods Li Gen (Liu Jian-ming) and Ao Bing (Fung Ke-an) for trying to beat up a young man who was trying to stop Li and Ao from trying to rape the young man's fiancée. The other exception is that according

Still from Na Cha The Great © Celestial Pictures Ltd. All rights reserved.

to the legend, Na Cha and his father did not make peace and ended up at each other's throats for eternity. Now that would have made the film even longer.

The fights are below par compared to Fu Sheng's later films because he was still trying to find his weapon-choreography feet; he was not used to defending himself with and against a weapon, so his moves were jerky. The film opens with the oft-used red background in kung fu films, while actor Fu Sheng performs spear and gold ring routines and then a few spear fights. The red background and spear form were also used by Jackie Chan at the beginning of *Snake and Crane Arts of Shaolin* (1978). Throughout the spear form, Fu is filmed with close and medium shots so the audience cannot see his stances. But as the film progresses and as Fu becomes more attuned to the weapons, the audience sees more of his stances, though at this point the camera is undercranked to make Fu's movement quicker. The fights at the film's beginning use a bobbing pop-pop-pop rhythm. It is less noticeable by the film's end, which is a further indication that Fu was getting used to weapon choreography.

Other films specifically about Na Cha are *Nyasa Lad Against 7 Devils* (1966), *Na Cha and the 7 Devils* (the most well-known storyline about Na Cha) and nine Cantonese language films on Na Cha between 1949 and 1957, several of which starred Kwan Tak-hing as Na Cha. Kwan was an actor most famous for playing Chinese kung fu folk hero Huang Fei-hung in more than 80 films.

Titleography: As of this writing, no alternative titles could be found. Translation—*Na Jia (Cha)*. **MA Percentage: 22.91%** SHAW BROTHERS

NAVAL COMMANDOS, THE

海軍突擊隊 (1977—Hong Kong) **105m. Fl: Hsieh Hsing, Robert Tai Chi-hsien, Li Gu-ding. NOT/LOT: None; NOF/LOF: 10/ 8m 50s.** D: Chang Cheh, Pao Hsueh-li, Wu Ma, Liu Wei-bin. C: Liu Yong, Chi Kuan-chun, Ti Lung, Alexander Fu Sheng, David Chiang, Kuo Chue, Lu Feng, Chiang Sheng, Tong Yen-san, Shan Mao, Shih Tzu.

This film was a blast from the past for me: For some wide-angle shots of the Taiwanese Navy, which was under the Republic of China at the time, director Chang Cheh used real footage of the fleet. The reason for my nostalgia stems from when I was living in Taiwan in the late 1970s and early '80s. Whenever I went to see a kung fu film, everyone had to stand up and sing the national anthem while glory shots of the country's economic and military power flashed on the movie screen. They always used a stock shot of the U.S. 7th Fleet (with the Stars and Stripes clearly visible on one ship) as a representative of Taiwan's naval might.

In a flashback, graying Vice Adm. An Qi-bang (Liu Yong) tells the son of famous naval Captain Hu Jing-duan (Chi Kuan-chun) the story of how Hu, An and five brave Chinese navy men (Ti Lung, Kuo Chue, Lu Feng, Chiang Sheng and Tong Yen-san) pulled off a special mission in Jiang Yin, Jiangsu province. Thanks to their bravery and derring-do, they severely hurt the morale of the Japanese stationed in Shanghai during World War II. Their mission was to weave a torpedo boat past the Japanese blockade in Shanghai and up the mine-infested Yangtze River, then blow up the Japanese flagship called Izuma. However, after making it to the flagship, their boat gets sunk, but that's when the seven heroes take matters into their own hands and decide to storm the battleship. They receive a little help from Shanghai gangster Song Shan (David Chiang) and his aide, Xiao Liu (Alexander Fu Sheng), who provides weapons, distraction and two jade horses to successfully complete the mission.

In typical Chang Cheh fashion, this is a story of brotherhood in which all the eventual nine heroes become closer than any married couple. The movie is replete with heroic gestures of altruism, loyalty and courage, as each man goes out in a blaze of glory in the name of patriotism. Even when Song Shan is mortally wounded, he takes on the Izuma's best military fighter, champion karate master Hiroda (Shan Mao), and pronounces that even a wounded Chinese could defeat a Japanese. With Song Shan's last breath, Chiang pays homage to his Jian Nan character from *The Duel* (1971)—when he coughs into a clean white handkerchief, we see a few drops of blood left on it.

Although the Izuma never existed, the ship's name could have been inspired by the Imperial Japanese Navy's cruiser ship Izumi, an important warship made in England and purchased by Japan in 1894 during the First Sino-Japanese War. It was scrapped in 1912.

Although there are only a few fights in the film, there are a lot of single-strike deathblows once the Chinese heroes board the ship, which I don't count as fights. The short matchup between Alexander Fu Sheng and Chi Kuan-chun is

superb. Also, this was the last film that David Chiang, Ti Lung and Chang Cheh did together. Because Ti and Chiang's real-life relationship was faltering, their new Shaw Brothers contracts prevented them from appearing in the same shot or working at the same location at the same time.

Titleography: *Navy Descentors*. Translation—*Navy Commandos*. I can only assume that the alternative might be a misspelling for *Dissenters*, though the heroes do not disobey any orders. **MA Percentage: 8.41%** SHAW BROTHERS

NEVER GIVE UP

Yasei No Shomei (1978—Japan) **143m. Fl: Uncredited. NOT/LOT: 3/ 1m 1s; NOF/LOF: 4/ 3m 11s.** D: Junyo Sato. C: Ken Takakura, Ryoko Nakano, Hiroko Yakushimaru, Rentaro Mikuni, Isao Natsuyagi, Takahiro Tamura, Richard Anderson.

Reminding someone of the truth is the right thing to do, but doing it at the detriment of oneself is an act few are willing to go through with.

A former member of the American-trained secret Japanese Self-Defense Forces is dishonorably discharged for saving a little girl from an ax murderer. In civilian life, he becomes a life-insurance broker. He allows himself to get kicked around, insulted and beaten by thugs, until his former life emerges 10 years later, when it is time to protect the little girl again. He needs to keep her safe from not only a sleazy *kendo sensei* but also from the Self-Defense Forces that discharged him a decade earlier.

In terms of fighting, there's nothing new or flamboyant here, just a few kendo training shots, some basic karate kicks and army-style judo flips. It's not Ken Takakura at his best, even the limited fights he does in *Bright Red Flower of Courage* (see martialogy) and the *Abishiri Prison* movies in 1966 are better.

Titleography: As of this writing, no alternative titles could be found. Translation—*Wild of Light*. **MA Percentage: 2.94%**

NEW FIST OF FURY

新精武門 (1976—Hong Kong) **115m. Fl: Han Ying-chieh. NOT/LOT: 10/ 6m 13s; NOF/LOF: 16/ 20m 10s.** D: Lo Wei. C: Jackie Chan, Nora Miao, Chen Hsing, Liu Yi-long, Sun Lan, Liu Ming, Shi Ting-gen, Zheng Xiu-xiu, Han Ying-chieh.

This film marked Jackie Chan's second starring role, although his first was shelved until 1979. (See *Cub Tiger From Kwangtung*.) Lo Wei, who previously directed Bruce Lee in *Fist of Fury*, had Jackie Chan under his belt and attached to a multi-picture deal. Lo wanted to see if he could strike gold a second time, and so he had Chan star in *New Fist of Fury*.

Set during the Japanese occupation of Taiwan in 1911, the story revolves around Mao Li-er (Nora Miao, reprising her role from *Fist of Fury*), who is pining over the death of Chen Chen (Bruce Lee). The local Chinese inspector tells her that because of Chen Chen's furor, it is not safe for her to stay in Shanghai, so she absconds to Taiwan in hopes of drumming up anti-Japanese support on that island. Meanwhile, street thief Ah Lung (Jackie Chan) never steals from locals but somehow ends up getting his grubby hands on a box belonging to Li-er that has strong sentimental value for her; inside are Chen Chen's *nunchaku*. When Lung refuses to kowtow and join the Chinese traitors who work for the Japanese, he is beaten up. But as luck would have it, Li-er passes by to see him and the nunchaku lying in the gutter. She picks up Lung and the sacred weapon of Chen Chen, perhaps a metaphor for finding the next Chen Chen and his nunchaku. After he is nursed back to health, Lung learns kung fu at Taiwan's Ching Wu Men branch from teacher Hung (Han Ying-chieh) in hopes of fighting the Japanese. Li-er's pride and heart swell as she sees in Lung what she saw in Chen Chen: psychological projection in action.

However, the appointed Japanese governor of Taiwan, Okimura (Chen Hsing), is convinced that there are too many martial arts schools around, and he wants to change all their school names to align with his. All the Chinese heads of kung fu schools are ordered to appear at Okimura's school, and the only way they can avoid changing their school name is to defeat his top two fighters. As the Chinese lose face after face to the Japanese, Ah Lung stands up as the last bastion of hope for Chinese patriotism. After easily defeating the two Japanese *karateka*, Lung is beset upon by a screaming banshee in long black hair and in a kimono-like short dress, and she kicks the air out of Lung's lungs. It's Okimura's Amazonian daughter. To paraphrase the character Ah Gung from *Way of the Dragon*, "She's Japanese, he is Chinese." After Lung gets his breath back, he lands a barrage of flying drop kicks to her chest. Enter Okimura, who unleashes a *sai* attack. Luckily, one of the pieces of

Lung's three-sectional staff conveniently breaks off during their fight, leaving him with a makeshift *nunchaku*.

The types of skills that Chinese opera students, including Chan, seem to have difficulty with are karate- or *taekwondo*-style kicks, which Lo Wei should have figured out after Chan starred in *Cub Tiger from Kwangtung*. Although the struggle to do taekwondo kicks was obvious in *Cub Tiger*, Chan is able to differentiate himself from Lee in *Fist of Fury* by keeping away from doing Lee kicks and sticking to more Beijing opera-like kung fu skills. But for some insane reason, Lo has Chan do that cool slow-motion set of hand postures Lee did during his fight with Petrov, which makes the fight look more like a parody than homage, but that was not Lo's intention, since the film is dead serious in its demeanor and intention; as another anti-Japanese film featuring the Chinese hero defeating China's worst enemy. I actually thought this film's best fighting performance is by Zheng Xiu-xiu as Okimura's daughter. Her kicks are relatively solid and come across powerfully. It is unfortunate this turned out to be her only film.

Titleography: *Fists to Fight*. Translation—*New Ching Wu Men*. The Chinese title for the original *Fist of Fury* was *Ching Wu Men*, hence *New Ching Wu Men*. **MA Percentage: 22.94%**

NEW ONE-ARMED SWORDSMAN, THE

新獨臂刀 (1971—Hong Kong) **93m. FI: Liu Chia-liang, Tang Chia. NOT/LOT: 1/ 20s; NOF/LOF: 31/ 17m 10s.** D: Chang Cheh. C: David Chiang, Ti Lung, Li Ching, Ku Feng, Chen Hsing, Liu Gang.

When the Iron Triangle of director Chang Cheh and superstars David Chiang and Ti Lung meet the potent pair of fight instructors Liu Chia-liang and Tang Chia, we are talking about a quintet of talent that adds up to a single film that is 10 times better than many of its contemporaries. This is the last of the official *One-Armed Swordsman* franchise films made by Shaw Brothers. Jimmy Wong Yu and Shaw Brothers had a falling out over Wong Yu's joint venture with actor Shintaro Katsu in *Zatoichi and the One-Armed Swordsman* (1971). Then Shaw Brothers cast David Chiang, who along with Ti Lung, was considered to be Wong Yu's star-power replacement.

Twin-sword hero Lei Li (David Chiang) is so cockily confident with his swordsmanship that he agrees to cut off his arm and leave the world of Wu Lin if fellow hero Lung Yi-zhi (Ku Feng) can defeat Lei with his three-sectional-staff skills. However, Lei does not realize that Lung is not so heroic because Lung uses a secret weapon to defeat Lei, forcing him to lose the arm. This loss also opens the door for Lung to take over the Wu Lin world. After Lei is "disarmed," his world and body falling apart, he becomes a waiter in a restaurant and is treated like an outcast, only to have hero Feng Jun-jie (Ti Lung) come to his aid and bring him out of the doldrums. When Lung applies his wicked ways in the Wu Lin world and gets all *Pit and the Pendulum* on Jin with his giant, swinging, disemboweling blade, Lei runs rampant and literally single-handedly attacks Lung's Tiger Mansion Lair to find that an even more voracious villain awaits him—Chief Chan Chun-nam (Chen Hsing).

Still from *The New One-Armed Swordsman* © Celestial Pictures Ltd. All rights reserved.

The one-armed swordsman character first appeared in *One-Armed Swordsman* (1967) and later in the sequel *Return of the One-Armed Swordsman* (1969), both of which starred Jimmy Wong Yu. The characters are patterned after Yang Guo, the crippled protagonist in Jin Yong's serialized novel *Legend of the Brave Archer*, and after Hollywood star Chuck Connors' Jason McCord character from the NBC TV show *Branded* (1965) and its film version *Broken Sabre* (1965). Apparently, screenwriter Ni Kuang was a fan of Connors' TV show *The Rifleman*, and when *Branded* came out, it struck a nerve. In that series, McCord is wrongly accused of being a deserter, and when he's stripped of his rank, his commander breaks McCord's sabre in half, tossing the bottom half out the fort gate. As McCord stoically exits the fort with the gates closing behind him, he picks up the broken sabre, examines it, ponders his fate, then uses it as a weapon to fend off evil throughout the show's duration. There is a similar scene in the first *One-Armed Swordsman* in which Wong stares at his sword and ponders his fate.

I once asked Jimmy Wong Yu how he thought these films changed over the years. He shared that *One-Armed Swordsman* emphasized setting up the background story; *Return* devoted more time to the interrelationships of the characters, and more tricks were shown via weaponry and kung fu skills; and *The New One-Armed Swordsman* put more emphasis on the production, with many grand scenes. Wong Yu bore no animosity toward Chiang replacing him. In fact, five years later, they relived their one-armed characters in *One-Armed Swordsmen* (1976).

Titleography: *Triple Irons*; *The New One Armed Swordsman*. Translation—*The New One-Armed Swordsman*. *Triple Irons* refers to Ku Lung's secret three-sectional staff. **MA Percentage: 18.82%** SHAW BROTHERS

NEW SHAOLIN BOXERS

蔡李佛小子 (1976—Hong Kong) **95m. FI: Hsieh Hsing, Chen Shen-yi, Chen Jih-liang. NOT/LOT: 6/ 6m 48s; NOF/LOF: 23/ 22m 27s.** D: Chang Cheh, Wu man. C: Alexander Fu Sheng, Jenny Tseng, Wang Lung-wei, Liang Chia-ren, Wang Li, Shan Mao, Chen Hui-lou, Wang Qing-lung.

It is a sad state of affairs when someone tries to do a good thing and it comes back to bite them in the face. But as they say, no good deed goes unpunished. As it was becoming a popular trend at the time, this film opens with actor Alexander Fu Sheng demonstrating the film title's style of kung fu, *tsai lee fuo* (Cantonese *choy li fut*). By displaying the relevant movements that have been incorporated into the art from three contributing influences, it also gives the audience the heads-up of what martial art is being featured in the film.

Coach driver Zhong Jian (Alexander Fu Sheng) gets stabbed while saving Ms. Huang (Jenny Tseng, Fu Sheng's real wife) from the licentious lips of an amoral antagonist (Liang Chia-ren) who works for Feng Tian-shan (Wang Lung-wei), a man everybody in town is afraid to cross, including Zhong's kung fu teacher, Master Zhou (Shan Mao). Fearing retribution from Feng, Zhou kicks Zhong out of school but secretly introduces him to tsai lee fuo expert Monk Zhu, who is now a follower of Buddhist scripture. Initially, Zhu refuses to teach Zhong, but he pities him when he learns that every time Zhong tries to help someone, he gets in trouble. Feeling Zhong has the right heart, Zhu teaches him. This is similar to the real-life scenario of Chen Xiang trying to learn from Tsai Fu.

Meanwhile, the formidable Feng kills Zhou with his claw-hand attachment. It is similar to Vega's weapon in *Street Fighter* (1994), but in actor Wang Lung-wei's hands, it is much more deadly and impressive to watch. But Feng's fickled finger of fateful claw will have a major flaw if tries to make slaw out of Zhong Jian's paws. Zhong's training complete, it is time for Zhong to deliver Feng his own fickled finger of fate. Far-out.

The fights in the film are, in a word, great. It is especially eye-catching when the actors fight toward and then away from the camera within the same shot. It's even more impressive when it is a low-angle shot and the fighters completely fill the frame, allowing the audience to see and feel each technique. The level of expertise of these artists is most compelling when their cat stances are low, with the thigh of the hind support leg parallel to the ground and the front leg poised like a limp cat's paw with the toe or ball of the foot lightly touching the ground.

By 1836, Chen Xiang formally established tsai lee fuo while at Shaolin Temple by combining the skills he learned from Monk Tsai Fu and Li You-shan, then in homage to his first teacher and uncle Chan

Yue-hu, who was a monk at Jiu Lian Shaolin, he added on Fuo ("Buddha"). Although considered a southern style, tsai lee fuo combines northern kung fu's quick, agile footwork from Tsai and the south's long-arm techniques from Li. Chen taught tsai li fuo to his two sons—Guan-bo and An-bo—who according to the film, passed the art on to Chang Hong-sheng. The style's name then became known as Hong-sheng tsai lee fuo.

Titleography: *Demon Fist of Kung Fu*; *Grandfather of Death*; *Grandmasters of Death*; *Grand Masters of Death*; *The Choy Lay Fat (Tsai Lei Fuo) Kid*; *Mad Boy*; *Silly Kid*; *The New Shaolin Boxers*. Translation—*Tsai Lei Fuo (Choy Lay Fat) Lad*. Any title related to *Kid* or *Lad* is referring to Alexander Fu Sheng's character. *Grandfather* and *Grandmasters (Grand Masters) of Death* are undoubtedly about old Master Zhu's tsai lee fuo kung fu abilities, and *Demon Fist of Kung Fu* is probably in response to Wang Lung-wei's demonlike clawed hand. **MA Percentage: 30.79%** SHAW BROTHERS

Still from *New Shaolin Boxers* © Celestial Pictures Ltd. All rights reserved.

NEZHA CONQUERS THE DRAGON KING

哪 吒 鬧 海 (1979—People's Republic of China) 60m. FI: None. NOT/LOT: 1/ 35s. NOF/LOF: 3/ 2m 37s. D: Wang Shu-chen, Yim Jing-hin, Xu Jing-da.

Jet Li's *Shaolin Temple* (1982) is usually considered the first martial arts film made by Communist China. (Mao Ze-dong took over the country in 1949.) But if you want to get technical about it, the animated feature *Nezha Conquers the Dragon King* is the first Communist Chinese film that has martial arts in it. The various stories of the Chinese deity Nezha (aka Na Zha and Na Cha) and the antics with his kung fu ring, spear and fire-wheel feet have been featured in several earlier live-action and animated Chinese films (see *Na Cha the Great* and *The Story of Chinese Gods*). This version is a more fantastic retelling of director Chang Cheh's *Na Cha the Great*, except that this is the first film about Nezha that shows his legendary birth and his eventual three-faced reincarnation.

In the film, when Taoist priest Tai Yi arrives on the back of a white crane and feeds Nezha a speck of pollen, Nezha grows into full boyhood and is given a red scarf and a gold ring. (Immortal Taoists are known to ascend to or descend from the heavens on the backs of white cranes.) What follows is Nezha performing two intricate ribbon-and-ring rhythmic-gymnastic routines to Olympic-style music. This could be a nod by the filmmakers to point out that the athletic art of rhythmic gymnastics has its roots in ancient China, where martial arts and acrobatic street performers used rings and ribbons for dramatic effect. When Nezha becomes a young adult and fights the Dragon King and his minions, his fighting routines and spear-twirling forms are accompanied by Beijing opera music and take on a more pure martial arts flair.

Titleography: *Prince Nezha's Triumph Against Dragon King*; *Ne Zha Storming the Sea*; *Little Nezha Fights Great Dragon Kings*. Translation—*Ne Zha Stirs up the Sea*. **MA Percentage: 5.33%**

NOBLE WAR

Suk Kumpakan (1975—Thailand) 100m. FI: Uncredited. NOT/LOT: 1/ 25s; NOF/LOF: 6/ 3m 28s. D: Ne-ra-mitr, Seri Wungnaitum, Sompho Saengduen-chai. C: Unknown.

Using the *khon* style of traditional Thai dance theater, *Noble War* is a film adaptation of the ancient Hindu epic story of the *Ramayana*. (The Thai version of the *Ramayana* is called the *Ramakien*.) Khon Thai dance is a style of stage dance drama performed by nonspeaking dancers who convey their characters' emotions through stylized movement, and the relevant storytelling and expositions are told by a chorus positioned off to one side of the stage. The *Ramakien* is the most widely performed khon Thai dance. The colorful and extravagant costumes are steeped in strict traditions, and god and demon characters wear specific color masks so audiences can recognize them.

Based on 24,000 verses of Sanskrit, the legend of *Ramayana* has been orally passed down for 5,000 years. In A.D. 200, it was put into a written version by the poet Valkimi. It's an enchanting tale of undying love and loyalty in which the hero Ram (aka Ramayan) and his brother Lakshaman seek the Monkey King Hanuman to help them rescue Ram's wife, Seta, from the clutches of the dastardly King Ravan. As famous Indian film director Krishna Shah once shared with me, the *Ramayana* is a story of light against dark, good versus evil, and the core of the tale is about righteousness and Ram's attitude toward war. He doesn't wish to kill Ravan, and he gives him many options to avoid battle, but ultimately he must fight.

Curiously, Hanuman can fly, fight and change heights; he is similar to Swuin Wu-kung, the Monkey King featured in the Chinese classic novel *Xi Yo Ji* (*Journey to the West*), written by Wu Cheng 1300 years after Valmiki's version of *Ramayana*.

Although *Noble War* has only a few battles and fight scenes, it is a palatable parade of lush color, and the rudimentary wire work has actors flying around in unique khon and martial arts poses that are completely different from the postures seen in Chinese kung fu films. But what is also significant about the *Ramakien* is that the story aligns with the martial arts philosophy of fighting only as a last resort, and most importantly, it is uniquely intertwined with Thai martial arts.

Muay Thai has only been around since 1930. It is actually a watered-down version of a more vigorous and lethal form of the ancient martial art *muay boran*, which comes from an even older version of *pahuyuth* (systems of Thai martial arts) called *ling lom* (air monkey), which has its foundations in *krabi krabong*. What is interesting about all this is that although the ancient forms of pahuyuth are steeped in Buddhist notions, the ling lom aspect of muay boran has its foundation in the Hindu monkey god Hanuman. Traditional muay boran fights were actually dances to honor the *Ramakien* and the fights between the various deities involved, which of course include the hero Hanuman. Similar to Chinese kung fu, in which each technique of a form has a specific name, many muay boran maneuvers have names based on the fighting postures of the gods from the *Ramakien*.

Titleography: As of this writing, no alternative titles could be found. **MA Percentage: 3.88%**

NOT SCARED TO DIE

頂天立地 and 北派功夫 (1973—Hong Kong) 81m. FI: Yuen Cheung-yan. NOT/LOT: 1/ 30s; NOF/LOF: 15/ 19m 58s. D: Zhu Mu. C: Wong Ching, Jackie Chan, Yuen Qiu, Shen Zhi-hua, Li Wen-tai, Lung Zi-fei, Yuen Cheung-yan, Jiang Nan.

This film is set during the second Sino-Japanese war, which grew into a full-scale Japanese attack on China during World War II, during which hundreds of thousands of Chinese were killed. The plot concerns a group of Chinese patriots who resist Japanese aggression.

A Beijing opera troupe headed by Brother Tang (Wong Ching) travels around China performing patriotic plays. When a Japanese officer (Yuen Cheung-yan) tries to shut them down, a fight breaks out, some Japanese are killed, and the troupe becomes an enemy of the Japanese empire. Tang and his younger kung fu brother Xi Zi (Jackie Chan) are the main culprits the Japanese want to capture, and for most of the film, they successfully avoid being caught.

However, add in couple of Chinese traitors, a jealous woman and a sick old man who slows them down, and the Japanese soon have their way. Xi Zi is brutally murdered by Chinese patriots, and revenge now falls onto the lone shoulders of Brother Tang. In order to bring Tang out of hiding, the head Japanese officer (Lung Zi-fei) ups the ante by allying himself with the head of the Chinese traitors (Jiang Nan). They rape Tang's girlfriend, and then the officer orders his men to senselessly slaughter tons of Chinese women and children. The hate factor now boiling over, nothing can restrain Tang from going after all those who have wronged him and the Chinese people.

These kinds of anti-Japanese, low-budget Hong Kong films are not essentially about good fights but about how good the Japanese are beaten, whipped and killed. One of the peculiar drawbacks of Bruce Lee's *Fist of Fury* was that he had a good muscular body for fighting shirtless, and so when skinny Chinese martial arts actors tried to copy Lee's physicality on camera, it did not match up. These actors would then subsequently tense their muscles during fights trying to look cut like Lee but would instead end up looking slow, clumsy and actually thinner. There are several firsts in this film worthy of note. It is Yuen Qiu's first film. (See *Police Woman*.) It is the first hero lead for the Shaw Brothers regular villain actor Wong Ching. For Jackie Chan, who is sporting a military-style flat-top haircut, it is his first major fighting and speaking role.

Titleography: *Eagle's Shadow Fist*; (*In*) *Eagle Shadow Fist*. Translations—*Head Against the Sky and Standing on the Earth* and *Northern Style of Kung Fu*. The English titles that use *Eagle* are attempts to capitalize on the success of *Snake in the Eagle's Shadow*. *Not Scared to Die* is something the heroes yell in regard to fighting the Japanese. The first Chinese title is a metaphor meaning that someone is carrying the weight of the world on his shoulders and that the person is up for the task at hand. *Northern Style of Kung Fu* could refer to the performers being members of a Beijing opera troupe, so they probably use a northern style of kung fu against the Japanese. **MA Percentage: 25.27%**

NO. 37 PLOT, THE

三十七計 (1979—Taiwan) **76m. FI: Ricky Cheng Tien-chi. NOT/LOT: 3/ 6m 13s; NOF/LOF: 15/ 28m 14s.** D: Huang Guo-zhu. C: Hu Bu-le, Jin Long, Chen Hui-lou, Jia Kai, Jing Guo-zhong, Qi Hou-jiang, Zhang Peng-yi.

It's Jackie Chan meets Gordon Liu Chia-hui, on a different plane (maybe limbo), with 10 times the Chan silliness and then some, plus a cross-dressing grandmother. It's a movie in which 12 animals are better than five and a book of plots could probably be handier as a screenwriting tool than a way of kung fu.

In the Chinese kung fu film genre, in which the tireless carbon-copy mentality usually ratchets the industry into submission every 10 or so years, *The No. 37 Plot* duplicitously duplicates Chan's *Snake in the Eagle's Shadow* (1978) and subversively submerges Liu's *The 36th Chamber of Shaolin*, but it forgets to explicitly make the final point of the film, which leaves you with a bad taste after the movie. Not that the audience should be spoon-fed everything, but based on my experience working on Taiwanese films, things really do get lost in the making of their films. I remember one movie I did back in 1980 in which we shot two weeks' worth of fight scenes and then a script was put together around the fights. To this day, I still have no idea what the film was about or whether my character was good or bad (probably bad, since I got it at the end).

In this film, two bumpkin street hustlers, Chi Lai and Dung Fu (Hu Bu-le and Jin Long), live by a secret flimflam manual, *The 36 Plots*. One day, they unwittingly save a man's life, and he happens to be the last student of *hsing-i* kung fu master Shen Tsi-jia. The Five Animal Styles master Shi Hsia-ren (Jia Kai) wants to wipe out Shen and all his students to ultimately prove that his five animals are greater than Shen's 12 animals. Shen teaches Chi Lai and Dung Fu with the secret wish that they will defeat Shi and keep the art alive. If it sounds like *Snake in the Eagle's Shadow*, it is even more apparent when Shi looks the spitting image of Hwang Jang-lee and even fights like him.

Although Chinese folklore indicates that hsing-i and eagle-claw kung fu were created by Song Dynasty General Yue Fei in the 12th century, a more accepted version points to Ji Ji-ke (1620-1680) of Shanxi province as the founder. The art stresses that there should be harmony between the mind and a person's will, strength, limbs and breathing. The latter refers to the cultivation of your *chi* (*qi*), commonly referred to as "internal energy" in Western writings. There are three major styles of hsing-i; the Shan Xi method, the He Bei style and the Hernan School. The one utilized in this film, the original Shanxi school, explains the emphasis of the five elements (metal, wood, fire, wind, earth, water) as metaphors for the five stages of combat, in conjunction with 12 animal forms.

However, when all seems lost for our heroes, they combine the 12 animal forms with their 36 Plots to ultimately come up with the 37th Plot. That is not unlike *The 36th Chamber of Shaolin*, in which Monk San Te's idea of teaching kung fu to the layman adds another chamber to the already-existing 35 chambers of Shaolin.

If one were to adopt a silly meter for kung fu films, this film would be off the charts.

Titleography: *37 Plots of Kung Fu*. Translation—*37 Tricks*. **MA Percentage: 45.33%**

OATH OF DEATH

萬箭穿心 (1971—Hong Kong) **94m. FI: Chan Chuen, Liu Chia-rong. NOT/LOT: 4/ 1m 54s; NOF/LOF: 17/ 18m 45s.** D: Pao Hsueh-li. C: Lo Lieh, Tien Fung, Frankie Wei Hong, Ling Ling, Chang Pei-shan, Bolo Yeung, Wang Ping.

An old German proverb that first appeared in the medieval beast fable *Reynald the Fox* states, "Blut ist dicker als Wasser," or in English, "Blood is thicker than water." The proverb means family bonds are stronger than those of friendship. Occasionally, though, two or more friends may feel such a strong bond that they perform a blood oath, a ceremony in which they pledge loyalty to each other and mix their blood. Yet perhaps *Reynald* should have added, as *Oath of Death* shows, that blood is thicker than water, but not in the river of deceit.

The film is set during the waning years of the Song Dynasty (A.D. 960-1279). Three Song warriors—Jin Liang, Ma Ching-ting and Xiang Du-bu (Lo Lieh, Tien Fung and Frankie Wei Hong)—become blood brothers and vow to restore the Song and fight the Tartars (sometimes called Tatars) until the bitter end. Ma, the trio's newfound leader, exclaims, "With unity we can win." Ma's plan is to rescue Shabeilan (Wang Ping), the Tartar princess, from Fort Feng Lei, use her to get into the Tartar inner circle, then meet with other heroes to fight the Tartars from the inside. Ma believes that by becoming a general for the rising Yuan Dynasty and by supporting the Mongols, he and his brothers will be able to further destroy the Tartars. However, Jin and Xiang see how power is affecting Ma; at one point, Jin says he is becoming more ruthless than the Tartars. Living up to his now-notorious reputation, Ma assassinates Xiang and Xiang's wife and then goes after Jin, who barely escapes with his life.

Jin goes into hiding, begins extreme martial arts training and tries to figure out how to defeat Ma. His former friend uses a long, thick rope weapon, which he can make solid to use like a spear or change into a pliable, slashing,

Still from *Oath of Death* © Celestial Pictures Ltd. All rights reserved.

whiplike weapon. Jin's training sequences are bizarre to behold. He washes his face with rags dipped in boiling water, disfiguring himself. He heats a stick of wood in fire until the tip is red-hot, then sticks it in his mouth, leaving him with a raspy voice. He strikes his fingers against a tree until his hands are completely bloody and red. In fact, the shot looks just like the one in *King Boxer* (aka *Five Fingers of Death*), which was made one year later. Jim then perfects the Million Arrow Strike the Heart skill. And wait until you see why Jin ties one of his legs up to make it appear as though he has had a leg amputated and then jumps around like a frog on opium. (I would give you a hint, but that would totally ruin the awesomeness of the skill.) As you might imagine, the final fight between Jin and Ma is more far-out than Pluto.

Cultural note: The Tartars are a Turkic ethnic group inhabiting central Eurasia. They invaded China in the days of the Song Dynasty but were eventually defeated by Genghis Khan's Mongol Empire. In 1271, Genghis Khan's grandson, Kublai Khan, conquered China and established the Yuan Dynasty. He became the emperor of China in 1279.

Titleography: *Arrows of the Heart*. Translation—*Million Arrows Through the Heart*. *Oath of Death* refers to the blood oath the three friends make at the beginning of the film. *Arrows of the Heart* mirrors the Chinese title's literal translation, which alludes to the name of the kung fu skill Jin learns to fight Ma. However, the Chinese translation also refers to a proverb that says when one's heart is hurt like by an act of disloyalty or a jilted lover, it feels like being shot through the heart with a million arrows. **MA Percentage: 21.97%** SHAW BROTHERS

OILY MANIAC

油鬼子 (1976—Hong Kong) **84m. FI: Yuen Chung-yan. NOF/LOF: 5/ 5m 17s.** D: Ho Meng-hua. C: Danny Lee, Ku Feng, Wang Xia, Cheng Ping, Lily Li, Tong Lin, Angela Yu Chien, Hua Lun, Liu Hui-lin, Liu Hui-ru, Jiang Nan.

You have got to hand it to Danny Lee, an actor who truly set himself apart from all the other kung fu film stars. Yes, he did the usual kung fu films and *wuxia* movies, but then he had a weird stint during the mid-1970s when he starred in the insanely sane *Mighty Peking Man* (which doesn't feature martial arts), the insanely genius *Super Inframan* (which does feature martial arts) and the insanely insane *Oily Maniac*. In the film, he plays a disabled man who turns into a horrific, tar-covered kung fu fighting monster. This stint seemed to pigeonhole Lee as "not your typical martial arts star" at the time, which led to his groundbreaking cop characters in the 1980s.

Oily Maniac is based on a true story that occurred in Malaysia, and it begins at the creepy Coconut Oil Garden. Lee plays Sheng Yung, a lawyer with polio who works for the sleazy Hu Ly Fa (Wang Xia), who brokers scam deals and court proceedings to cheat good people out of their money and property. Sheng's mangled legs make Xiao Yue (Cheng Ping) hesitate to return his love and affection. Sheng is also worried that he won't be able to protect her. He doesn't realize that his co-worker Xiao Ly (Lily Li) loves him or that an evil plan is being hatched by Hu to trick Sheng's uncle Ah Ba (Ku Feng) into murder, which would make the landowner of Coconut Oil Garden rich while making the current workers on the land lose everything they have worked for.

Sheng visits Ah Ba on death row, where Ah rips off his shirt to reveal a magic spell that his shaman father tattooed on his back 20 years ago and shared the secret of before dying from an incurable disease. The warning says, "You can only use the spell to protect the less fortunate … but if you use it with wrong intent, you will die." In a moment of romantic weakness when Sheng loses all hope of winning over Xiao Yue and witnesses Hu's scheming, he takes the plunge into Malaysian folklore and becomes the Oily Beast of Coconut Oil Garden.

From this point, the film is filled with hilariously bad special effects. Once this oily beast beats the tar out of a bunch of deserving goons, the local police detective (Tong Lin) starts to take note of the garbled ramblings of monster sightings while things move to a finale of crude oil killings and tarmac terror. It's oil-*fu* versus sleaze-*dao* in that the film slides into a tragic love story between the beauties Xiao Yue and Xiao Ly and the beast.

Danny Lee shared with me several years ago that this was his first horror film and he relished the challenges, which included being picked up by a giant mechanical gorilla hand, stuffed into a tight red suit and mask, and covered in oil—and then fighting and sweating in that state all day. He also mentioned

that a lot of very cool and yucky scenes were cut out by the censors, so the film came across much less frightening. Fortunately, he was able to do scarier films in the future to get his horror fix.

Titleography: As of this writing, no alternative titles could be found. Translation—*Oily Monster*. **MA Percentage: 6.29%** SHAW BROTHERS

OKITA SOJI

(1974—Japan) **92m. NOT/LOT: 2/ 25s; NOF/LOF: 8/ 5m 31s.** D: Masanobu Deme. C: Masao Kusakari, Yukihiro Takahashi, Hosei Komatsu, Koji Takahashi, Masanobu Oki, Toshiyuki Nishida, Tsuruko Mano, Ichirô Araki.

In a nutshell, *Okita Soji* is a film that traces the growing friendships between Okita (Masao Kusakari) and his main pal, Kondo Isama (Yukihiro Takahashi). Both men are historically known as early members of the Tokugawa shogun's de facto police force known as the Shinsengumi. Okita was a captain under Kondo on that force. (For details and background on this police force, see the martial-ogy for *Shinsengumi*.)

Set during the waning years of the Tokugawa era (1863-1869), the film opens when young friends and fellow *tennen rishin-ryu* fencing stylists Okita and Kondo are dealing out some serious *bokken* (wooden sword) punishment to a gang of misfit swordsmen. Even with wooden swords, the friends easily pound the gang until they are tenderized like meat. When word gets out that the shogun, who is the commander in chief of Japan's army, needs bodyguards for his upcoming trip from Edo to Kyoto to meet with the emperor (Japan's supreme leader), Okita and Kondo sign up. In the process, they will make a name for their fencing school.

While on the road to join the shogun's forces, Okita and Kondo meet future members of the Shinsengumi. Their most notable new acquaintance is Serizawa Kamo, who can cut through a piece of armor with one slice. The film then follows how Okita and Kondo's friendship strengthens via the course of historical events that surround the famous Serizawa fire incident, the creation of the Roshigumi, the eventual evolution of the Shinsengumi, and the final fight in which Kondo and Okita are severely injured by bullets and cannon fire at the Battle of Toba-Fushimi during the Boshin War. (For you die-hard history buffs, and I mean die-hard, the *Shinsengumi* martialogy talks all about these events.) The audience then watches Okita slowly die from tuberculosis whiles he dreams about the good old days when he and Kondo were practicing fencing together. By the end of the film, I feel compelled to argue that Okita is probably the real last samurai and not Tom Cruise.

With a wee stretch of the imagination, you could possibly call this film the basis for Jackie Chan's famous *Drunken Master* (1978). Not because of the story, martial arts or fights but because both of the films depict real heroes— Huang Fei-hung in *Drunken Master* and Okita Soji in this film—in neo-'70s rocker hairstyles with bangs. It is no wonder that both of these characters exploded with success. In reality, Huang had a queue (required by Manchu law) and Okita had a topknot, which the samurai used to create space between the top of their head and their war helmet.

This movie is obviously a lower-budget affair, but that is a good thing because the fights are filmed in wide angle with just a few side-tracking shots when the heroes slice and dice their opponents. With minimal shot selection, fights are filmed faster, which saves time and money. They also look pretty good. Another major fight is shot in the dark, so the audience can only hear loud screams and the sound of someone getting de-limbed. It serves the film well because part of Okita's legend was his signature skill: the No Light Blade technique. He could slice through an attacker's neck at the left shoulder or right shoulder with one strike. This was difficult to see coming until it was too late. It's curious that Chinese legend Huang Fei-hong had a similar signature skill: the No Shadow Kick, which was so fast that it had no shadow. In a sense, that makes Huang and Okita martial brothers.

Titleography: *Okita Soji: The Last Swordsman.* **MA Percentage: 6.45%**

ONE-ARMED BOXER

獨臂拳王 (1971—Hong Kong) 89m. FI: Chen Shih-wei. NOT/LOT: 5/ 3m 49s; NOF/LOF: 44/ 31m 57s. D: Jimmy Wong Yu. C: Jimmy Wong Yu, Lung Fei, Ma Ji, Cai Hong, Tian Ye, Shan Mao, Guan Hong, Blacky Ko, Wang Yong-sheng, Xue Han, Zhang Yi-guai, Wu Dong-qiao, Pan Chun-lin, Hsieh Hsin.

After *One Armed Swordsman* (1967) became Shaw Brothers' first film to earn more than $1 million, Jimmy Wong Yu continued to portray his crippled alter ego in many other films. In his first directed film after leaving Shaw Brothers, Wong Yu returned to the one-arm motif, but instead of playing a swordsman, he played a one-armed boxer. The nature of the handicapped-hero film was to further expand on a new cinematic trend wherein the hero must undergo difficult kung fu training in order to defeat the villains. It became more in vogue later that decade, so you could say that Jimmy Wong Yu's concept really was before its time.

Yu Tien-lung (Jimmy Wong Yu) is a righteous martial arts student who projects the film into a state of war with his extracurricular battle over a birdcage. As trouble and conflict rise, audiences know that Tien-lung will lose his arm, but Wong Yu's direction orchestrates some beautiful red herrings that savor the moment of expected arm loss to build up the prospect of the inevitable. One cool scene has Tien-lung battling Korean hit men hired by the birdcage man inside a large mill that features giant interconnecting cogs. It is of course the perfect place for an arm to get jammed into the cogs and crunched to pieces. Several times the arm comes close to being trapped in a cog, but when will it happen? It's all about anticipation. (*Anticipation* also happens to be the title of a 1971 hit song by Carly Simon.)

Following the excruciating loss of a limb, Tien-lung undergoes equally painful training sequences to learn a secret technique for revenge. Armed with new and improved kung fu skills, Tien-lung is ready for the final showdown that takes place in a quarry. It is within this cage without walls that he will battle a wild menagerie of exotic fighters, such as an Indian yoga guru who runs around on his hands rather than his feet, a lama who swells up like a balloon, and a Japanese warrior who has vampire fangs. Why he has fangs is unclear, but suffice it to say, he doesn't suck as a fighter.

Because Jimmy Wong Yu is taller than his opponents, he uses low stances to maintain a smooth fight line—an imaginary line between the top of the heads of two opponents fighting on-screen. Fight choreographers prefer to have the heads at a similar height. Otherwise, the taller actor looks off-balance and tight when he punches and kicks shorter opponents because his strikes have to travel downward. However, like many tall actors, Wong Yu would tire out and his legs would look weak when he'd keep his stances low. In this movie, you can tell when this happens because he loses his straight posture. Fortunately, the sheer bizarreness of the characters he fights helps hide his fatigue. Seriously, which do you think the audience is going to notice more: wacky kung fu or Wong Yu's bad posture? It is pretty hilarious when the lama swells up like a balloon and Wong Yu uses the old fingers-popping-the-balloon technique. And speaking of crazy, how do you fight an Indian yogi who runs circles around you in a handstand and then viciously charges you by hopping on one finger? I can't quite put my finger on it, but I'm sure someone knows how to nail this yogi, which would make Tien-lung the one who is smarter than the average bear.

Jimmy Wong Yu once told me that before doing *One Armed Swordsman*, he argued with the movie's director, Chang Cheh, that his character should have his left arm removed because fighting with his left hand was difficult. However,

Chang convinced him that fighting with his left hand would convey how incredible his character's willpower was. Wong Yu then trained night and day, practicing everything with his left hand and arm. He also said that during the film his arm was tied behind his back, which made shooting even more difficult because he would lose his balance. Plus, how hazardous is an unprotected arm behind your back when your back gets slammed against a wall or you are knocked backward onto the ground? It's awkward and dangerous. When his arm was tied up, it was only released during the lunch hour, so he had to be tied up for more than eight hours a day for 40 days. When *One-Armed Boxer* was made, Wong Yu had the makeup people and some assistants untie him and massage his arm whenever possible throughout the day.

Titleography: *Chinese Professionals.* Translation—*One-Armed King Boxer. Chinese Professionals* may have something to do with the fighters being professional hit men (the Indian Guru, the Tibetan lama, the Korean kickers), but none of them are Chinese. **MA Percentage: 40.19%**

ONE ARMED SWORDSMEN

獨臂雙雄 (1976—Taiwan) 110m. MAI: Han Ying-chieh. NOT/LOT: None; NOF/LOF: 12/ 19m 7s. D: Jimmy Wong Yu, David Chiang. C: Jimmy Wong Yu, David Chiang, Lo Lieh, Zhang Yi, Lung Fei, Viola Gu Yin, Liu Meng-yan, Hong Liu, Hong Hua-liang.

In the 1970s, long before the dream team of Jackie Chan and Jet Li mon-eyed their way onto the green screen in *Forbidden Kingdom* (2008), there were three other matchups that studios were dying to get together on-screen: Bruce Lee and Sonny Chiba, Jimmy Wong Yu and Shintaro Katsu, and Jimmy Wong Yu and David Chiang. The first pairing was under negotiation when Lee died; the second eventually occurred, though with great loss to Jimmy Wong Yu (see *Zatoichi and the One-Armed Swordsman*); and the third happened in this film. When you consider that Shaw Brothers were constantly putting their top two to seven biggest kung fu stars in the 1970s in the same films, it's surprising it took them so long to pair Jimmy Wong Yu with Chiang. In fact, it is the only movie that these kung fu film legends did together.

In this film, word spreads that a masked one-armed swordsman is accused of committing 13 robberies, slaying innocent bystanders and killing Ching Chu-ying (Zhang Yi), a law officer who was also, incidentally, a one-armed swordsman himself. When two one-armed swordsmen named Fang Ping (Jimmy Wong Yu) and Li Hao (David Chiang) pass through the area, the locals accuse each of them of being the masked marauder. Fang and Li also accuse each other of being the killer, so they meet and agree to settle things with a duel to the death. However, through mutual adventures of combat against the Ghosts of Ying Shan, who wield wolf-teeth clubs, and the actual traitorous one-armed swordsman, Lai Su-wan (Lo Lieh), Fang and Li form a bond that disarms their accusers and leads them to unearth an evil plot to destroy the Shaolin Temple.

Even at the time it was made, *One Armed Swordsmen* was intended to be a throwback film featuring the set pieces that made earlier knight-errant films so popular. Chopsticks are thrown like knives; rapid sword-slicing motions in the air culminate in furniture and other objects falling apart; a villain breaks an abacus and shoots the pieces at a hero, who catches them under his hat and then reveals a neatly piled stack; a good guy tosses a bowl of wine in the air, kills a few baddies, then catches the bowl and continues drinking; and much more.

What is dynamic about the fight scenarios and weapon combat sequences is that Jimmy Wong Yu and Chiang are both naturally right-handed, and so it's quite impressive of them to pull off left-handed fight scenes, especially when Chiang must battle a Shaolin monk atop 10-foot posts. (*The Killer Meteors* and *Secret of the Shaolin Poles* feature similar fighting gags.) The fight in the chicken coop is just another great feather in the cap of this film. For about three minutes, you can tell that several people off-camera are throwing chickens on-screen, adding extra tension and danger to the fights. Occasionally, a chicken or two gets hit by a swinging sword, but they are not "fowl" balls, as none of them are hurt.

Of note, there is a DVD of the film going around that, for reasons unknown, automatically switches into insta-action mode after the first 12 minutes, showing only the film's fight scenes. The way to watch the complete film is to select one of each of the six chapters at a time.

Titleography: *One-Armed Swordsman.* Translation—*Two One Armed Heroes.* The titles all match the film. **MA Percentage: 17.38%**

ONE ARMED SWORDSMAN AGAINST NINE KILLERS

獨臂拳王勇戰楚門九子 (1976—Taiwan) **105m. MAI: Huang Guo-zhu. NOF/LOF: 19/ 17m 48s.** D: Hsu Tseng-Hung. C: Jimmy Wong Yu, Tsung Hua, Chen Hung-lie, Lo Lieh, Cho Kin, Lung Fei, Wan Shan

Actor Jimmy Wong Yu is up to his old one-armed tricks again. This is the fifth of eight films in which Wong Yu plays a one-armed hero. The major differences here are that it is his left arm and not his usual right arm that is missing, and this film is not a continuation of the original *One-Armed Swordsman* series. In fact, Jimmy Wong Yu plays a one-armed fighter and not a swordsman, and contrary to some synopses, the screenwriter is not Gu Long but Yao Ching-kang.

In the film, the famous one-armed fist fighter Liu Yi-su (Jimmy Wong Yu) is on the prowl to hunt down Chu Ji-zhu (Cho Kin), who is the head of the Chu Clan. In this case, the best defense is a good offense in that Liu decides to kill Chu before Chu finds and kills him. The only problem is that there are nine killers standing in Liu's way, and each successive kung fu fighter is better than the last. Although the number nine in Chinese numerology means good luck, it means bad luck to Liu in this movie. And part of Liu's luck of the draw is getting entrenched in a human Chinese chess match.

Chinese chess (*xiang qi*, which means "elephant game") may have originated during the Warring States period (476-221 B.C.); the strategy board game may have been linked to troop arrays modeled after Han Xin, the famous Chinese general. During the winter of 204-203 B.C., he developed a battle plan to attack Xiang Yu, the general who overthrew the Qin Dynasty. The game pieces are therefore named after Han's various battle implements, such as general, horse, chariot, cannon, soldier and elephant (there is evidence the Chinese used elephants in early warfare). The game piece Mandarin was added later on.

Chinese chess first played an important part in *The Magic Blade* (1976; see martialogy), in which actor Ti Lung had to fight his way out of a human chess match, a game played on a giant outdoor board set up in a clearing in the forest. In this film, although the human chess match motif can be a bit more dour than *Magic Blade*, for Western audiences, if they at least know the names of the chess pieces, the game makes a little bit more sense. Furthermore, having each player in the film yell out the names of the various chess moves also lets the Chinese audience knows what is happening in the film. When two fighters end up on the same place on the board, a fight ensues to see who must leave the game, and it is Liu who refuses to lose because the name of the game is death.

One of the most engaging assassins is played by actor Chen Hung-lie, who attacks Liu using an oversize broadsword that has a 6-foot-long, 12-inch-wide blade, which he snaps, crackles and whacks. It is fun to watch the whole "sworded" affair.

Titleography: *One Armed Against Nine Killers*; *One Armed Swordsman Annihilates the Nine Disciples of the Chu School*. Translation—*King of the One Armed Fist Bravely Fights Nine Fighters From Chu School*. What is a bit misleading about the titles is that the one-armed Liu annihilates 21 disciples. One is killed before the film starts, one is actually a group of four fan-wielding priests, one bunch comprises two assistant assassins, and one is a set of twins. Even if each group of fighters was considered to be one assassin, Liu still ends up fighting 14 killers. **MA Percentage: 16.95%**

PACIFIC CONNECTION, THE

(1974—Philippines) **102m. MAC: Mario Escudero, Remy Presas, Hiroshi Tanaka, Chi Qui Dcampo. NOT/LOT: 8/ 4m 46s; NOF/LOF: 16/ 17m 30s.** D: Luis Nepomuceno. C: Roland Dantes, Nancy Kwan, Guy Madison, Alejandro Rey, Gilbert Roland, Dean Stockwell, Hiroshi Tanaka, Elizabeth Oropesa, Fred Galang, Gloria Sevilla, Vic Diaz.

In 1521, Portuguese maritime explorer Ferdinand Magellan, the first Westerner to land on the Philippines, claimed the land in the name of Spain. Forty-four years later, Miquel Lopez de Legazpi defeated the leader of Cebu Island (then known as Sugbu) and established the first Spanish settlement of San Miguel there. For conquering the Kingdom of Maynila (now Manila), King Philip II of Spain rewarded Legazpi by appointing him the first colonial governor-general of the Philippines.

This film opens with a son and father practicing *arnis* (Filipino stick fighting) as the father shares the legend of a 100-year-old arnis master who will never rest until he has found a worthy successor. He explains that if a noble, right-hearted hero comes along, fate will have the master find him. Upon that, the father gives his son, Ben (Roland Dantes), half of a medallion and tells him the old master has the other half.

The moment is like a dream, but the dream fades as news spreads that the Philippines are now under Spanish rule and the new governor's sons, Allan (Gilbert Roland) and Miguel (Dean Stockwell; TV show *Quantum Leap*), are creating havoc. The sons stumble upon Ben's home, and when Allan makes advances at Ben's mother, arnis and swords clash as Ben and his father easily defeat Allan and Miguel. The cowards run to their father (Alejandro Rey; TV show *The Flying Nun*), who dishes out swift justice by killing Ben's father, raping and killing his mother, and sending Ben to Los Mananos by ship, where he will be put to death. However, the ship runs into a terrible storm, and while the ship is sinking, Ben kills the captain and several Spanish *conquistadores*. He is badly wounded and jumps ship. Washing up on an uncharted island, Ben is nursed back to health by Leni (Nancy Kwan). As you can guess, Ben runs into the old master (Guy Madison), who although blind, sees all. He says, "Blindness is only a position of the mind." The master agrees to teach Ben and tells him how to make arnis sticks that can withstand sword strikes, something he will need in preparation for the coming attack of the governor, his two sons and Mori (Hiroshi Tanaka; star of samurai movies like *Zatoichi Meets Yojimbo*, *Incident at Blood Pass* and two *Lone Wolf and Cub* films), a samurai whom the governor enlists from the Japanese government.

I found this film to be a total surprise on many levels. It features decent arnis stick fighting, some rudimentary disarming techniques, a few heaven six double-stick maneuvers and some *kali* knife skills. Although Roland Dantes is very muscular and it would have been easy to have him flex all over the screen and do the same stick skills as Bruce Lee's *escrima* fight in *Enter the Dragon*, he did not. In fact, this is part of what makes the film most impressive: During all the fights between different styles—arnis, Spanish fencing, samurai fighting—the fighters all stick to their respective ways of fighting.

After Chief Lapu Lapu killed Magellan with a Filipino *kampilan* dagger in 1521, natives were forbidden to carry swords. The Moros and Visayanns peoples combined their sword skills with Spanish sword skills and applied them to ratan sticks to create arnis/*escrima* and continued development of bladed weapons under the moniker kali. There are several scenes in the film that subtly reflect certain aspects of this history. Look for them when you watch this film.

Titleography: *Stickfighter, South Pacific Connection*. **MA Percentage: 21.83%**

PARVARISH

(1977—India) **155m. FI: Nishan. NOT/LOT: None; NOF/LOF: 2/ 2m 39s.** D: Manmohan Desai. C: Shammi Kapoor, Amitabh Bachchan, Vinod Khanna, Neetu Singh, Shabana Azmi, Kader Khan, Amjad Khan.

In the vein of James Bond, blood flows via dancing damsels, but instead of a suave, martini-toting super-spy, we have Amitabh Bachchan doing funky and flippy fights in *Parvarish*. Indian films often use motifs where children are somehow switched at birth or undergo some sort of trauma that influences their young psyche toward future wrongdoings. The movie's plot fits into this scheme wherein two kids are raised by the same parents, but one is not their son.

Along with his own newborn son, policeman Singh raises the son of the criminal Mangal (Amjad Khan) after the villain's wife dies during childbirth. The kids grow up like twins, but the audience is not told which is which, even when we see them in the classic from-child-to-instant-adulthood shot. Amit (Amitabh Bachchan) becomes an undercover policeman, and Kishan (Vinod Khanna) teaches blind people. Kishan also secretly works as a henchman for the outlandish, Dr. No-inspired Supremo (Kader Khan), who operates his criminal empire from a souped-up submarine. He also takes Mangal on as a partner when the man with "arrested" development is released from prison.

Mangal's criminal headquarters is right out of a Bond film and features a retractable walkway built over a deep quicksand pit, which has spiked walls that compress to give an iron-maiden effect for good measure. Adding to the lair's quirky charm is the backdrop of bright-red cellophane panels, where we can see the shadows of Indian go-go dancers digging the music. When Amit and Kishan dance their way into Mangal's hamlet of horror, the lair becomes an interesting set for the film's final squabble, quibble and quake. Despite the often-illogical fight editing, the short action sequences are farcically enjoyable. That final meeting of the kids and their parents on the deck of the submarine out at sea brings about a warm, fuzzy feeling that sews everything up faster than a Kimbo Slice getting decked in his first network-TV-aired MMA bout.

Titleography: As of this writing, no alternative titles could be found. **MA Percentage: 1.71%**

PETEY WHEATSTRAW

(1977—USA) **94m. FCO-CO: Howard Jackson. NOT/LOT: 11/ 1m 32s; NOF/ LOF: 9/ 7m 17s.** D: Cliff Roquemore. C: Rudy Ray Moore, Jimmy Lynch, Leroy Daniels, Ernest Mayhand, Ebony Wright, Steve Gallon, G. Tito Shaw, Brian Breye.

If you make a deal with the devil, you had better make sure you practice angel fu, and you better hope that halo above your head doesn't slip down and become a noose.

Weakling street urchin Petey Wheatstraw (Rudy Ray Moore) learns the secret ways of karate and how to use the *kama*, samurai sword and *nunchaku* from a vagrant named Bantu (Brian Breye), who turns out to be more of a black Kwai Chang Caine than a drunken hobo. As an adult, Petey becomes a famous stand-up comedian. But when he returns to Los Angeles to perform at a nightclub that rivals the newly mafia-supported black-owned comedy club, things get ugly. After Petey and his friends are gunned down on some church steps after a wedding, Petey makes a deal with the devil: If Satan brings Petey back to life to exact revenge on his murderers, Petey will marry Lucifer's daughter, the ugliest woman in the history of human- and inhuman-kind.

Moore's best fight scenes during the 1970s are in *The Human Tornado* (1976), so in that respect, this film is a giant step backwards. However, the sheer madness of this pseudo-horror film, which pits Petey against hordes of pink-leotard-wearing devil hit men, is so off-core that not even an apple a day can keep this irresistible movie away. As is usually the case with Moore's movies, the sound effects used during the fight scenes come right out of a typical Hong Kong kung fu film. It's a nice touch.

Titleography: *Petey Wheatstraw, the Devil's Son-In-Law*; *The Devil's Son-In-Law*. **MA Percentage: 9.38%**

PIRATE, THE

大海盗 (1973—Hong Kong) **96m. FI: Liu Chia-liang, Tang Chia. NOT/ LOT: None; NOF/LOF: 20/ 20m 43s.** D: Chang Cheh, Pao Hsueh-li, Wu Ma. C: Ti Lung, David Chiang, Tien Ching, Liu Gang, Tong Yen-san, Fan Mei-sheng, Yu Feng, Dean Shek.

One of Hong Kong's most famous and most feared pirates in history was Chang Pao-chai. He would rob British ships but was careful not to blatantly kill

Still from *The Pirate* © Celestial Pictures Ltd. All rights reserved.

British officers after boarding their vessels. After British officers complained to the Ching authorities, they put a price on Chang's head, and he became a target for bounty hunters and the government.

In this film, Chang's (Ti Lung) boat springs a massive leak after he successfully plunders a British ship, forcing him to make repairs at a coastal town run by corrupt officials in cahoots with the local shipbuilding-material supplier, Xiang You-lun (Tien Ching). Xiang secretly sabotages people's boats and small ships, which forces them to buy his goods at inflated prices. The poor fishermen are sometimes forced to sell their daughters to Xiang to get supplies. Chang is determined to undermine Xiang and distribute stolen money and booty to the help the fishermen. Meanwhile, Xiang's sister Hua Er-dao (Yu Feng) is a bounty hunter, and whenever local Ching officials capture a pirate, she bribes the officials into handing him over to her so she can collect the bounty from the Dutch East India Company; they then split the reward. Her next target is Chang. However, the province's commander in chief has sent the fair and just General Wu (David Chiang) into the area to investigate complaints of wrongdoings and to capture Chang, if possible.

Although some fights in *The Pirate* are effective, the finale boils down to repetitive sequences of splish-splashing in water. Ti Lung and David Chiang overemphasize their body motions to show power in the scene in which Chang and Wu fight from dawn to dusk. Though the fight does not succeed on a technical level, it does dramatize the conflict well. These two men, groaning from pure exhaustion, develop mutual respect for each other and even form a strong bond of brotherhood. In this respect, the fight tells the story it needs to tell, which is an important aspect of any good fight scene no matter if it is full of perfect technique or not.

And for you history buffs: Chinese pirates arose during the Yuan Dynasty around 1293 because Kublai Khan sent an expedition of 1,000 ships to Java to collect tribute from the last ruler of the powerful Malay island group kingdom of Singhasari. While the ships were en route, a rebel killed the kingdom's leader, Kertanegra. Kertanegra's son-in-law aligned himself with the arriving Mongols and killed the rebel, and his army then decided to attack the Mongols and force them to leave during a bad time for sea travel. Instead of risking death at sea from the monsoons, many marooned Chinese naval officers and their crews set up shop along Sumatran and Javanese river estuaries to protect themselves; they garnished food and provisions by robbing passing ships. They became highly touted pugilists and weapon experts, and their strength and ferocity coincided with increased shipping traffic associated with the maritime silk and spice routes.

Between 1802 and 1804, the most powerful pirates in Chinese history, Zheng Yi and his wife, Zheng Yi Sao, aka Ching Shih, formed a pirate coalition that grew to more than 10,000 men. Chang Pao-chai, the son of a fisherman, was kidnapped and adopted by Zheng Yi and Yi Sao. After Zheng Yi died, Yi Sao became the most feared pirate of the Chinese waters, becoming even more powerful than the Ching navy. She also married Chang, who eventually took over the family business. Chang mostly sailed the coastal waters of Canton, and it is reported he had 50,000 followers and possessed 600 ships. In 1810, Chang turned himself in to the Ching government and went on to be a high-ranking officer in the navy. After implementing anti-piracy achievements, he died in 1872. His wife was granted ladyhood, and he was survived by one son, Yu Lian. Chow Yun-fat's character Sao Feng in *Pirates of the Caribbean: At World's End* (2007) was inspired by Chang and Yi Sao.

Titleography: As of this writing, no alternative titles could be found. Translation—*The Famous Pirate*. Each title is fitting for the main character. **MA Percentage: 21.58%** SHAW BROTHERS

POLICE FORCE

警察 (1973—Hong Kong) **101m. FI: Liu Chia-liang, Tang Chia. NOT/LOT: None; NOF/LOF: 11/ 9m 22s.** D: Chang Cheh, Tsai Yang-ming. C: Alexander Fu Sheng, Lily Li, Wang Chung, Wang Xia, Wang Kuang-yu.

This is an example of what was known as a "relax and take it easy" film for kung fu actors. Because such a film has very little action, it required less time getting into the usual costumes, heavy makeup and prosthetics. It also gave the actors a chance to recover from nagging aches, pains and injuries. Finally, it presented the actors with an opportunity to hone their acting skills because they didn't have to portray the same mundane *wuxia* characters they were no doubt used to.

After winning a martial arts tournament, Liang Guan (Alexander Fu Sheng) is high on life and happy to be with his girlfriend, Shen Yan (Lily Li). Liang does not realize that a psychopath in the audience named Gao Tu (Wang Kuang-yu) fantasizes he is the victor with all the spoils. Snapping out of his daydream, Gao and his partner stalk Liang and Shen, trapping them out in the middle of nowhere. Gao threatens to hurt Shen at knifepoint and forces Liang to tape his own hands together. Liang offers the robbers all his money and whatever else they want, but they rebuff him and start playing around with Shen. Liang kills Gao's partner, but Gao flies off the handle, stabbing Liang five times and then fleeing the scene. Liang slowly bleeds to death. Shen gets away.

Liang's death motivates his best friend and martial arts training partner, Huang Gao-tung (Wang Chung), to join the police force. Three years later, he graduates at the top of his class. He is also an expert marksman and skilled in the ways of self-defense. Each day, Huang suffers the moral dilemma of wanting to seek revenge while trying to uphold the law. In his search for Gao, he constantly invades criminal hideouts, beats the thugs up, brings them in and has Shen look at them because she is the only witness who can identify Gao. Despite his efforts, Huang is unsuccessful. He also begins to fall in love with Shen and is forced to take bigger gambles, knowing that she won't be interested in him unless he can be a man and catch the killer.

Five years later, Huang is a powerful inspector. He gets a break while investigating the criminal activities of Sun Zuo-zhong (Wang Xia), when he finds out that Gao works for Sun. After capturing Gao and beating him within an inch of his life, Huang stops himself, realizing that he can use Gao to catch Sun. He hatches a plan to expose Sun, and it all comes down to a day on a yacht that ends up in international waters, where Huang's hands end up both literally and figuratively tied. Time is not on Huang's side because here comes Sun, making Gao's eve of destruction edge ever closer. But then, like any weather, Sun must come to an end. And it is Gao who will rain on Sun's parade.

Director Chang Cheh was the perennial silent politician because his contemporary films addressed problems in Hong Kong or praised parts of Hong Kong society. This film accentuated the pomp and circumstance of the Royal Hong Kong Police Force, and his positive portrayal certainly must have earned points with the British government.

Titleography: As of this writing, no alternative titles could be found. Translation—*Police*. **MA Percentage: 9.27%** SHAW BROTHERS

POLICE WOMAN

女警察 and 師哥出馬 (1973—Hong Kong) **71m. FI: Jackie Chan, Yuen Cheung-yan. FI: NOT/LOT: 1/ 1m 8s; NOF/LOF: 10/ 7m.** D: Zhu Mu. C: Yuen Qiu, Charlie Chin Chiang-lin, Bei Di, Hu Jin, Jiang Nan, John Cheung, Li Wen-tai.

So softly the superstars speak. I remember during my earlier conversations with Jackie Chan in the 1990s that he often pointed out why Hollywood fights are so stiff, have poor martial arts, are not creative and lack rhythm—all of which were totally true. It is perhaps a small case of humble pie that he doesn't point it out as much now, especially because movies like *Police Woman* are easily available to the mainstream audiences that showcase Chan's earlier martial arts and choreography, which are as bad as the rest of them. But Chan's saving grace was that he was able to grow and become the best, whereas many American stars shrunk and seemingly vied to be the worst.

When wayward beauty Hou Xiao-mei (Bei Di) ends up working for a not-so-beautiful gang headed by a cruel boss (Jiang Nan), she does everything in her power to get out, and that power rests with some incriminating photos she has of her boss, who wants them back at all costs. He orders his thugs, headed by a man with a large mole on his face (Jackie Chan), to retrieve them. Fleeing for her life, Xiao-mei jumps into a taxicab being driven by Chin Chen (Charlie Chin Chiang-lin), hides an envelope in the back seat, and then dies. Chin then becomes a target for the mob, and his only protection comes in the form of determined policewoman Hou Mei-hua (Yuen Qiu), the sister of Xiao-mei.

Although there are only seven minutes of fights in the film, believe it or not, Chan throws one of the best side kicks he's ever done. That's about the highlight of his fighting in this film, folks. Although when he is fighting Yuen Qiu, you can see the beginning development of his signature slightly knee-bent stances, which he uses in his contemporary fights to add desperation to the action. Yuen Qiu actually has good kicking postures and a decent grasp of basic judo techniques. Besides the significance of being an early Jackie Chan film (one he'd probably like to forget), this is also the debut movie as a lead for Yuen.

At age 7, as Kan Chia-fung, Yuen attended the same Beijing opera school

as Chan and was given the name Yuen Qiu by their opera *sifu*, Yuen Yu-jim. She went on to be a Bond girl in *The Man with a Golden Gun* (1974) and was a featured fighter in Lee Van Clief's *The Black Dragon's Revenge* (1975). Then, after starring in numerous Korean martial arts movies alongside Dragon Lee under the moniker of Phoenix Kim, she retired. More than 20 years later, she came out of retirement to star as the cigarette-smoking landlady in Stephen Chow's *Kung Fu Hustle* (2004).

Titleography: *Rumble in Hong Kong*; *Young Tiger*; *The Heroine*; *Here Come Big Brother*. Translations—*Police Woman* and *Elder Kung Fu Brother Coming Out* (i.e., facing a fight). *Rumble in Hong Kong* is a ploy to tap in to the success of Chan's *Rumble in the Bronx* (1995). *Heroine* and *Police Woman* make sense because the film's hero is a policewoman. *Young Tiger* is a late English title that sounds cool, and when you know Chan is in the film, it falls in line with all his other animal titles and may be assumed to be a fun film, though it is not. *Here Come Big Brother* is similar to the other Chinese title and refers to Chin Chen facing the mob. **MA Percentage: 11.46%**

POLICEWOMEN

(1974—USA) 100m. SC: Paul Nuckles. NOT/LOT: 1/ 2m 50s; NOF/LOF: 6/ 4m 46s. D: Lee Frost. C: Sondra Currie, Tony Young, Phil Hoover, Jeannie Bell, Laurie Rose, William Smith, Wes Bishop, Eileen Saki.

While foxy mammas in blaxploitation films took it to the Man with soul and flirtatious appeal, white Hollywood was not to be outdone and churned out minx mammas who reeked of blond ambition but lacked more "soul" than a pair of floundering flip-flops.

In this film, which has a sort *Charlie's Angels* TV vibe and music sense, Lacy Bond (Sondra Currie) is a guard at a female prison who foils part of a breakout led by Pam Harris (blaxploitation sensation Jeannie Bell; *TNT Jackson*). What everyone and their pet rock doesn't realize is that Bond is a karate expert who claws her hand a la James Bond but actually reverse-punches with the power of a wet noodle. After foiling the breakout attempt, Bond earns an undercover assignment to infiltrate a Mafia-like gang of female criminals who are secretly smuggling gold into the country to support their drug trade. As our heroine catfights her way into the organization, her heavy-metal mentality will be the kiss of death for the granny in charge.

I'd like to think the filmmakers gave the fights in this film their best shot, but judging from the excess of slow knee strikes and the poor quality of everything else—punches, kicks, flips, Irish rolls—I doubt it. On a positive note, it is refreshing to see Asian-American actress Eileen Saki cast as one of the evil gang members. Although her martial arts are as abominable as a snowman, her character does not speak with a stereotypical Asian-English accent. Cheers to that.

Titleography: As of this writing, no alternative titles could be found. **MA Percentage: 7.6%**

PROTECTORS, THE

鏢旗飛揚 (1974—Hong Kong) 62m. FI: Liu Chia-rong, Chan Chuen. NOT/LOT: None; NOF/LOF: 19/ 14m 57s. D: Wu Ma. C: Lo Lieh, Chang Pei-shan, Wang Xia, Yang Ai-hua, Chan Shen, Dean Shek, Chan Chuen, Wong Ching, Dong Cai-bao.

When a film features four hit men with names like Prince Spear, Flying on Grass, 1,000 Hands Buddha and Wu Yi Mountain, you should be prepared for the bizarre. Add in Lo Lieh as the hero, and we're back in the *wuxia* universe, where the Midas touch is not about a king or a goose but about a vagabond and a wall.

Chief Ling Xiao (Lo Lieh) of the Eagle Security Company finds satisfaction in a job well done; protecting and delivering large sums of money is all the compensation he needs. His partner, Chief Guan Wan-long (Chang Pei-shan), feigns righteous agreement until the woman he desires, Fang Yan-er (Yang Ai-hua), shows an interest in the sincere Ling. Biting his jealous tongue, Guan becomes prime bait for his former partner, Jin Bu-huan (Wang Xia), who convinces Guan to steal the next shipment of silver he and Ling are hired to deliver and then blame it on Ling. After Guan performs a *Mission Impossible*-style switcheroo, swapping the silver for bricks, Ling finds himself on the lam. Things look bad for Ling because Guan's sheepish grin is ram-tough while he pulls the proverbial wool over everyone's eyes.

At the peak of his career, Lo Lieh made 10 films a year, often working on up to four films on the same day. Even though this film contains only about 15 minutes of martial arts action, it's one in which you can tell Lo is using a double

during many of his fights. He did so not because he couldn't do the fights but because he often worked on several films at once. Lo's best fights are when he does group fights, because for him it is just about slashing and whacking in close shot. For minimal effort, one can come across on-screen as having high energy. The fact that he was the lead in this film while working on other films might also explain why *The Protectors* is such a short film.

Titleography: *The Flying Flag.* Translation—*Flying the Escort Flag.* Lo Lieh's character is the head of a security company, making him one of *The Protectors.* The Chinese title refers to the practice of a security company flying its colors while on the job. It was a source of pride. **MA Percentage: 24.11%** SHAW BROTHERS

PROUD TWINS, THE

絕代雙驕 (1979—Hong Kong) **105m. FI:** Tang Chia. **NOT/LOT: None; NOF/LOF: 42/ 26m. D:** Chu Yuan. **C:** Alexander Fu Sheng, Candy Wen Xue-er, Gu Guan-zhong, Wang Jung, Tang Ching, Wu Wei-kuo, Ao-Yang Pei-Shang, Meng Chiu, Yuen Bing, Ai Fei, Chan Shen.

With *Intimate Confessions of a Chinese Courtesan* (see martialogy), director Chu Yuan made his mark in the world of Jiang Hu. After Chu experimented with drama, opera, comedy and non-*wuxia* stories in *Web of Death* (1976), he re-entered the realms of Jiang Hu and Wu Lin. In fact, his next 16 films until the end of the decade, barring his last film of 1979 (*Forbidden Past*, a love story), were all *wuxia* films. All of Chu's wuxia films are good-looking movies with high production values. They are distinctly Chu's in that they employ his individual sense of photography, set design and color. He uses fog, gels, lighting and other techniques to set the mood, overall look and sensibility of the movies. Even the fights have a distinctive zing and swing to them. In terms of those fights, the single unifying factor for all 16 films since and including *Web of Death* is that the opera-trained Tang Chia was the fight choreographer. Seeing the way the fights were shot and choreographed leads to this discussion point: Whose fights today—or for the past 30 or so years—look like Tang's?

Based on a Gu Long novel of the same name, *The Proud Twins* is the second film made by Shaw Brothers telling the story of handsome twins separated at birth who learn kung fu from opposite sides of the tracks (1971's *Jade Faced Assassin* directed by Yen Chun, being the other). Hua Wu-tien (Wu Wei-kuo) learns from a princess in a posh palace, and the other brother, Jiang Xiao-yu (Alexander Fu Sheng), learns from 12 villains in a skuzzy town of bandits. As in *Jade Faced Assassin*, the rich twin is supposed to hunt down and kill the poor one, but they eventually meet, become good friends and find out the truth about who is really trying to take over the world of Jiang Hu. Although the stories in *Proud Twins* and *Jade Faced Assassin* are basically from the same novel, there are two major differences between the films. The twins in *Jade Faced Assassin* are female and there are only 10 minutes of fights. While in Chu's *Proud Twins*, the twins are male and there are 26 minutes of fighting. Chu's films often did not have many fights,

but because they were evenly spaced out throughout his films, it created the impression that there was a lot of action. Yet the unique factor of this Chu film compared to his others is that he devotes more screen time to the fights than in his other films. (Chu averages 15 minutes of action per film.)

Alexander Fu Sheng gives *Proud Twins* a completely different fight feel from the 1971 version. Also, everyone in this version wears flowing, gown-like costumes and uses swords, while Fu Sheng sticks out like a sore thumb in his short-sleeved brown-and-black Robin Hood-like costume. He mostly fights without a weapon and humorously acts like a kid in a candy store, though he is not as demonstrative as Jackie Chan.

Tang and Liu Chia-liang were stalwart fight instructor partners from the mid-1960s to the early 1970s, and their different training methods, sense of style and eye for martial arts created a much-needed balance. Tang's opera background and Liu's pure kung fu background always guaranteed traditional kung fu with acrobatics, spins and cool poses. As Liu got more into Shaolin-style films, in which the fights were more realistic (at least in terms of technique), Tang continued to make his mark doing wuxia-style films, eventually getting a second wind and finding a home with Chu Yuan. What was the other major difference between Tang and Liu? I once asked actress Cheng Pei-pei this exact question, and she succinctly told me that Tang worked well with actresses and had more patience. I also once asked actresses Anita Mui and Joey Wang who their favorite fight choreographers were and why. They both unequivocally answered Ching Siu-tung, because he had developed a great reputation of working well with actresses. He made them look good and was very patient with them. So, to rephrase an earlier question, who do you think is Ching Siu-tung's biggest influence in terms of fight directing?

Titleography: As of this writing, no alternative titles could be found. Translation—*Matchless Handsome Heroic Twins.* The titles rightly imply that the twins are handsome, proud and good fighters. **MA Percentage: 24.76%** SHAW BROTHERS

PROUD YOUTH, THE

笑傲江湖 (1978—Hong Kong) **92m. FI:** Tang Chia, Huang Pei-ji. **NOT/ LOT:** 1/ 19s; **NOF/LOF:** 9/ 19m 43s. **D:** Sun Chung. **C:** Wang Yu, Michael Chan, Shih Szu, Stanley Feng Tsui-fan, Wong Zhong, Ling Yun, Wu Hang-sheng, Ku Feng.

A well-rendered tale of good versus evil in the spirit of Jiang Hu, a parallel world influenced by martial lore surviving by its own laws and code of ethics outside the existing normal societies. Every two years, the righteous Sword Clans of the Five Mountains meet to appoint a leader to continue the vigilant battle against the ruthless Sun Clan, which also seeks to rule Jiang Hu.

Fledgling swordsman Nangong Song (Wang Yu) is a happy-go-lucky young man. He is full of life, cheer and respect for all, and he hopes to unite the good and the evil under the banner of peace and brotherhood. He joins the "old/ young" Bai Ying-ying (Shih Szu) on a journey of martial truth to save her father (Ku Feng) and duel the supposed evil master of the Twin Unicorn Horn Swords, Hao Jie-ying (Michael Chan). Hao turns out to be a benevolent and peaceful man, which further eggs on Nangong to bring about unity among the warring clans of Jiang Hu. Inspired by the lyrics of the late Hao's lamenting song of dying hope, *Last Sound of the Empty Valley*, Bai and Nangong solidify their duet of harmonious unity and perform their own music, a song about the treacherous truth of the solo man who is trying to orchestrate a takeover of Jiang Hu.

In this book's introduction, I describe how some films have single moments—sometimes single shots—that can make the whole film memorable for me. Although *The Proud Youth* is full of creative fight choreography (as one would expect, given the star power and director), one shot blew my mind. Director Sun, the first Chinese director to use a Steadicam in his films, sets up a continuous shot in which Wang Yu leaps toward camera; he lands on a mini-trampoline placed directly in front of the camera (unseen to the audience, below the lens), nails his mark, jumps completely out of frame and then lands back in frame 10 feet from the camera. I still have not seen a similar shot in any other film.

The scene in which Nangong learns the mysterious Nine Sword Style in the Chamber of Skeletons is also especially engaging. It leads to a confrontation with a secretive ringmaster of violence, and the two end up fighting on the slippery rocks of a waterfall. It was no doubt a difficult fight for the actors to tackle, but it is wonderfully executed and as engaging as watching a three-legged giraffe using its neck as a fourth leg. (If you're scratching your head, you're on the right track.) The red herring of the film turns out to be the character Si Ma Wu Ji, a freaky martial artist who practices the Plum Blossom Classics; the ultimate power of the technique shines through only after the practitioner castrates himself and becomes effeminate. It's interesting to note that Wu Mei, the only female among the Five Elders of Shaolin and a teacher of *wing chun*, practiced Plum Blossom Fist. A similar male-to-female transformation due to a secret technique is the impetus behind Brigitte Lin Ching-hsia's Dong Fang Bu Bai character in Ching Siu-tung's *Swordsman II* (1992). The difference here is that Si Ma Wu Ji is about as deadly as my grandmother knitting a sweater.

Also of note is that both of these characters—Si Ma Wu Ji and Dong Fang Bu Bai—have four Chinese characters in their names, something that most Chinese people no longer do. That is in part due to Emperor Chin Shi-huang, aka Chin Shi Huang Di. Because he was considered to be a tyrannical emperor and had a four-character name, most Chinese do not use four-character names so as not to be associated with the evil such a name could carry. It's sort of like having Hitler as a last name—chances are you would want to change it. Jet Li's character in *The Mummy 3: Tomb of the Dragon Emperor* (2008) was based on this emperor.

Titleography: As of this writing, no alternative titles could be found. Translation—*Laughing Proudly in the Jiang Hu World*. The English title fits the film and aligns well with the Chinese title. **MA Percentage: 21.78%** SHAW BROTHERS.

one of his most prized army leaders, but blood is thicker than water, and the commander's loyalty belongs to Ya-nei. So when Ya-nei tries to rape Lin's wife and Lin beats him up for the act, the commander and his other trusted friends conspire against Lin with a horrific plan.

Because Monk Lu also beat up Ya-nei, he tries to take the blame, but Lin cannot allow that to happen—though he tearfully appreciates the gesture. Lu leaves while Lin is invited to the commander's White Tiger Hall, so Lin sees this as an opportunity to clear the air. But it is a trap. At dinner, Lin is accused of trying to assassinate the commander and is beaten, tortured, forced to walk hundreds of miles to prison and is sentenced to execution upon arrival. Also, during his walk to the prison, the guards constantly beat Lin, boil his feet in water so he can't walk, step on his flayed feet and try to kill him. Yet when the head guard almost falls off a cliff, Lin rescues him. Lu Zhi-shen arrives and is appalled by the evil things the guards are doing to Lin, but Lin tells his friend not to kill them and to show mercy.

The head guard respects Lin so much that after arriving at the prison, he arranges better accommodations for Lin. Rather than being put in prison, Lin now gets to fend for himself, unshackled, at the prison fodder (or food storage) station located in the snowy wilderness. But it is all a setup by the head guard, as he and his men try to kill Lin by burning him alive as they set fire to his straw hut. What they don't know is that as the hut is burning down, Lin is not inside. When he returns and sees his "home" destroyed, Lin drops to his knees, looks to the heavens and screams, "Why torture me like this?" Eventually, his self-pity wanes, and he prepares his spear and his spirit to go after his enemies.

Lin arrives to prevent his wife from being raped by Ya-nei again, but Ya-nei is still able to kill her. The death scene of Ya-nei is superb. He tries to hide in a large bale of hay while the grief-stricken Lin drives his spear into it. Because Lin is one with his weapon, the spear channels his anger, and when he uses it, it forces Ya-nei's body to explode out of the hay pile with bursts of blood, snow and straw littering the ground. Next on Lin's hit list is the commander. After the groveling commander succumbs to Lin's fury, Lin heads off to the marshes of Liang Mountain to do battle against government corruption. A remake of this film, *All Men are Brothers: Blood of the Leopard*, garnished great success in 1993.

Of note in the film, the fights with the mad Monk Lu are edited with louder crashing sound effects to emphasize his power and the Herculean strength required to swing his monk's spade. Also, because Monk Lu drinks wine and eats meat, he is what is known in Shaolin circles as a mad monk. Before Emperor Li Shi-min (A.D. 599-649), second emperor of the Tang Dynasty, Shaolin monks were not allowed to consume meat or wine. However, after 13 Shaolin monks rescued Li from his father's enemies, he granted the monastery permission to eat meat and drink wine. Most monks chose not to, but some did, and it was thought that they became mad from the new habits. Jet Li's film *Shaolin Temple* (1982) is about how the Shaolin monks rescued Li Shi-min.

Titleography: As of this writing, no alternative titles could be found. Translation—*Lin Chung Escapes at Night*. *Pursuit* had several connotations: Monk Lu pursues Lin to protect him from the villainous guards, and Lin pursues justice. **MA Percentage: 15.04%** SHAW BROTHERS

PURSUIT

林沖夜奔 (1972—Hong Kong) 88m. FI: Bruce Liang, Liang Shao-song. NOT/LOT: None; NOF/LOF: 14/ 13m 14s. D: Cheng Kang. C: Yueh Hua, Fan Mei-sheng, Wang Chin-feng, Qin Pei, Gao Ming, Wong Chung-shun, Zhao Xiong, Yang Chi-ching, Li Hao.

This film's Chinese title, *Lin Chung Escapes at Night*, gives a bit more information than the English title by telling the audience the hero's name. Historically and in the film, Lin Chung was a student of famous Song General Yue Fei and one of the 108 Heroes of Liang Mountain, who bravely opposed the corrupt officials during the waning years of the North Song Dynasty (A.D. 907-960).

Pursuit is a story of brotherhood between Lin Chung (Yueh Hua; he played Lin in *The Water Margin*, made five months earlier), who is nicknamed Leopard Man because of his fierce eyes, and his good friend Lu Zhi-shen (Fan Mei-sheng). Also known as Flowery Monk, Lu is another of the 108 Heroes, and he swings a 63-pound monk's spade. Lin Chung's trusted friend Lu Qian (Qin Pei) serves and snivels at the feet of Gao Ya-nei (Gao Ming), who is the foster son of Commander Gao (Yang Chi-ching). Lin respects the commander and is

PURSUIT OF VENGEANCE

明月刀雪夜殲仇 (1977—Hong Kong) 88m. FI: Tang Chia, Huang Pei-ji. NOT/LOT: None; NOF/LOF: 42/ 19m 31s. D: Chu Yuan. C: Ti Lung, Liu Yung, Shih Szu, Lo Lieh, Paul Chang-chung, Derek Yee, Frankie Wei-hong.

After watching this film, it dawned on me that I have a new backdoor appreciation for Shaw Brothers films. I have mentioned elsewhere that the unknown world of Jiang Hu became tangible during the 1970s because audiences often saw the same sets repeated in these *wuxia* films. The use of the same cities and villages gives the world a sense of continuity and realism as different characters traipse in and out of familiar landmarks. And after watching every Shaw film of the 1970s, it is amazing to me how the filmmakers continued to innovate past the formulaic ways of the genre week after week with the same actors and production crews. The fight choreographers are especially impressive. Each week they would work on several films at a time, creating (for the most part) different fights and action looks for a group of movies that are essentially all about the same thing. It was hard work under intense pressure, heat and humidity. They would work 18-hour days, seven days a week and with no toilets, no water and no trailers. The only break they could count on was 30 minutes for a meal of watered-down rice, shredded pork, chicken feet and pig ears. No Western film studio could match these outlandish conditions and turn out such consistently good products. One bit of golden magic that the choreographers had in their bag of tricks was the use of exotic weaponry, and Ti Lung's weapon in this film is a perfect example, right down to the design, the style of wielding it, and the ever-important act of drawing and sheathing it.

Pursuit of Vengeance, a sort of sequel to *Magic Blade* (1976), opens with a lone swordsman dressed in black wandering the snow-covered lands of northern China. It is Fu Hong-xue (Ti Lung), who wears a *tonfa*-shaped sword holstered like gun on his right hip, which is a refined version of the weapon used by actor David Chiang in *Judgement of an Assassin* four months earlier. Fu arrives in town for a drink of goat's milk at a local tavern and becomes one of six men invited to Wan Mu Mansion. Each of the six men is accused of being the assassin who killed Chief Bai Tian-yu and 75 sub-leaders of the Shen Dao School on a snowy night 20 years ago.

On the night before Fu arrived in town for his goat's milk, someone killed 120 male and 78 female dogs, along with 1,000 chickens, so the Wan Mu Mansion assumes the killer is back in town to finish off the clan. Since all six invited guests are strangers who arrived in town on the night of the mass animal killings, logic dictates that one of the six has to be the assassin.

What follows is a fantastical martial arts version of *Clue* (1985), in which six guests are invited to a mansion and must cooperate with the staff to solve a murder mystery. There is no butler in *Pursuit*, but there is a maid (Shih Szu), and so most are made to pay with their lives as the guests whittle down. Adding to the confusion is a mysterious figure zipping around as the Man of 1,000 Masks, which turns the whole thing into more than a whodunit film. It is a series of follies in which facades falter and the frays lead to a final far-out fight.

Director Chu Yuan spaces out many short fights throughout the film, creating the illusion of lots of fighting. This would become a signature element of his style. His action scenes are made intense and kinetic by choreographers Tang Chia and Huang Pei-ji, who constantly direct stuntmen to run in and out of frame while the actors spin and hack. The focus is not so much on an individual fighter but on the fight as a whole. The scene with the maypole is very original and cool. The pole's draping ropes get twined with swords while Fu and two newfound allies trapped within the tightening and twisting cords quickly learn the ropes to swing for their lives.

Titleography: As of this writing, no alternative titles could be found. Translation—*Bright Moon Sword Seeks Revenge for Snowy Night*. The English title encapsulates the film's theme, while the Chinese title paraphrases the plot's revenge theme. **MA Percentage: 22.18%** SHAW BROTHERS II

RANGERS, THE

大小遊龍 and 大小游龍 (1974—Hong Kong) **92m. FD: Tommy Lee, Liang Shao-song. NOT/LOT: None; NOF/LOF: 22/ 23m 20s.** D: Hau Chang. C: Polly Kuan, Yasuaki Kurata, Jin Gang, Yeh Hsiao-yee, Ma Ji, Shao Luo-hui, Zheng Fu-xiong, Addy Sung Gam-loi.

The old nursery rhyme *Polly, Put the Kettle On* ("Polly, put the kettle on, we'll all have tea …") is believed to have originated when a father noticed how his daughters would chase away their brothers by pretending to start a tea party. If there were ever a rhyme called *Polly, Put the Kettle Kuan*, perhaps it would be like this film—the story of a daughter, Lin Jo-nan (Polly Kuan), who has her cup of tea when she chases away the evil salt smugglers who set her father up.

In reality, at the turn of the 20th century, the Ching government monopolized salt and tea trading to the point where prices were practically unaffordable. Soon salt and tea smuggling became a lucrative business for criminals. This film focuses on what happens when the local economy of a small village gets

"a-salted" by the salt smugglers. And this is where our story starts.

Lin Jo-nan's father is framed by salt smuggler Chang Piao (Yasuaki Kurata) and sent to prison, and Lin is constantly reminded that there is nothing she can do about it because she is a woman. So she disguises herself as a man (donning a Bruce Lee wig) and dresses her 10-year-old nephew as a niece, and they become a hit man and hit kid for Chang's smuggling competition, Ma Wing. After Lin foils his smuggling runs, Chang hires a brawny, overgrown lummox (Jin Gang) to trap the masquerading Lin and take her out. As Lin and the lummox go at it, Chang crashes the Ma Wing fight club to do some clobbering of his own. Of course, Lin's secret is revealed. Unfortunately for the bad guys, hell hath no fury like a woman suppressed. And the lummox is not a big goofy freak but an undercover agent who ends up trying to help Lin free her father and stop the salt smugglers before everyone dies of high blood pressure.

Kuan's fights consist of about 80 percent kicks, which is not a bad thing because she has reasonably good kicking form. Though she lacks power and throws her kicks in the air with no intention of hitting anybody, the stuntmen do a good job selling their reactions and flipping all over the place after they have been hit. This style of fight choreography is relatively safe for the stuntmen. It also means Kuan does not have to worry about pulling her kicks, and as a result, the fights look pretty smooth. Then when actor Yasuaki Kurata appears and injects his karate-style kicks into the action—snapping his legs to give a sense of his power like Bruce Lee did—the fights take on a more desperate tone for Kuan's character.

Titleography: *The Vigilantes*; *Lady Whirlwind and the Rangers*. Translation—Both translate as *Big and Little Wandering Dragons*. Lin and her nephew are the *Big and Little Wandering Dragons*. Rangers are a special kind of police officer, and there is a disguised character in the film who is one. Also, this film was released after the success of Angela Mao Ying's *Lady Whirlwind* (1972), and Polly Kuan's Lin character just kicks and kicks like Mao Ying did in that film. Ultimately, Lin takes matters into her own hand without approval from the law, which makes her and her nephew *Vigilantes*. **MA Percentage: 25.36%**

REAL BRUCE LEE, THE

(1973—Hong Kong) **99m. FI: None. NOT/LOT: None; NOF/LOF: None.** D: Larry Dolgin, Jim Markovic. C: Because this is a documentary, there is no main cast.

This is another documentary about Bruce Lee, but this one doesn't cover the usual stuff everyone knew about back in 1973. In a nutshell, it features early Bruce Lee footage from films he appeared in as kid and teen, then shows about an hour's worth of a South Korean Bruceploitation movie starring Lee impersonator Dragon Lee.

The filmmakers unearthed a collection of four early Bruce Lee films from when he was a child actor in Hong Kong. They amassed the archival footage of these films and edited together just the scenes with Bruce Lee in them and added dubbed English dialogue that undoubtedly was not translated from the original Cantonese. However, back then it was very interesting to see Lee as a child actor in *Kid Cheung* (1950; aka *The Kid*), *Bad Boy* (1951; aka *Infancy*), *Carnival* (1955; aka *An Orphan's Tragedy*) and *Orphan Sam* (1960). It would have been more compelling if the filmmakers had found out some interesting anecdotes about Lee's early years as an actor. For example, Lee would sleep right on the set until needed, then he would wake up, do his part and go back to sleep. It's also known that he used to love terrorize the actresses by running around with a pet praying mantis on his shoulder. Such insights would have given the film a bit more meaning.

After presenting some clips of Lee's funeral, the filmmakers discuss how Lee impersonators suddenly appeared, one of whom was Bruce Li. After a few minutes of film clips from Li's films, they get right into the meat of the movie: 66 minutes of a kung fu film starring a man they claim to have discovered deep in the heart of the Orient (South Korea). According to the film, he is the best Bruce Lee impersonator ever: Dragon Lee. I have to admit, how they got the clip must have been magic because this documentary was released in 1973 and the original Dragon Lee movie featured in this documentary, as described below, was not released until 1977.

Directed by Kim Si-hyun, the original 110-minute film was titled *The Last of Jung-mu Martial Arts Hall* (*Choihui Jeongmumun*). Its titleography includes *Dragon Lee Does Dallas*; *Real Bruce Lee*; *Dragon Bruce Lee*; *Ultimate Lee*; *The Last Martial Artist*; *The Last Fist of Fury*; *The Last of the Ching Wu School* and *Righteous Martial Party*.

Starring Dragon Lee, Lee Ye-min, Choi Min-kyu, Choi Hyeong-keun, Han Myeong Hwan, Kim Kee-joo, Kim Wang-kuk, Kwak Mu-seong, Ma Do-shik, Han Tae-il and Kwon Il-su, the movie rehashes Bruce Lee's *Fist of Fury*. In *Jung-mu Martial Arts Hall,* after senior student Dae-dong of the Ching Wu Kung Fu School is appointed head of the school, the Japanese kill him. Dae-dong's students then go out into the wilderness in search of the revered *taekwondo* master Keum-san (Lee Ye-min).

The lead Japanese fighter, the Chinese-hating Kuromasa, has a sole purpose in life, and that is to once and for all destroy the Ching Wu school. Meanwhile, when Hsiao Lung (Dragon Lee) finds out his teacher Dae-dong was killed by Kuromasa and his gang of martial arts killers, his mission is clear: kill Kuromasa and his cohorts and preserve the Ching Wu school.

Titleography: *Bruce Lee: The Little Dragon; The Young Bruce Lee.*

RED SUN

Soleil Rouge (1971—France/Italy/Spain) **112m. TA: Asukai Masaaki. NOT/ LOT: 2/ 32s; NOF/LOF: 7/ 3m 42s.** D: Terence Young. C: Charles Bronson, Ursula Andress, Toshiro Mifune, Alain Delon.

To borrow from ye olde English proverb: Red sky at night, shepherd's delight; red sky in the morning, shepherd's warning; red sun during the day, the sword will make you decay. So when the red sun sets in the American West, it's a metaphor for an East-West partnership as opposite sides of the ocean first battle against each other, then eventually battle for each other.

In the Wild West, a hard-nosed outlaw cowboy (Charles Bronson) and a traditional stubborn samurai (Toshiro Mifune) grudgingly team up to recover a gold ceremonial samurai sword intended as a gift from the emperor of Japan to the president of the United States. The sword has been stolen by a suave, ruthless gunslinger (Alain Delon) and his gang of bandits.

As I mentioned at the beginning of this book, martial arts films saved my life. I remember watching my first Chinese kung fu film ever, Bruce Lee's *The Big Boss* (aka *Fists of Fury*), at the V Drive-in in Vestal, New York, in 1972. I also recall the movie that preceded it: *Red Sun*, the first samurai film I ever saw. What a dynamic night.

What I find most fascinating about this film, besides the venerable mosquito-slicing scene, is the fight Mifune has with the Native American. The image of a Japanese samurai swordsman battling a Native American warrior is emblazoned on my mind forever. Sadly, no one else has bothered to pit an American Indian against a Japanese samurai. I would love to see or do a fight in a film today that brings out the spirit of both of these nations' fighting arts.

Little is known about Native American fighting arts. We know they made use of the spear, the bow and arrow, and the tomahawk. They are also steeped in spiritualism, with a great reliance on animals. The Seneca Indian tribe developed a form of body-hardening techniques that allowed them to withstand strong blows. Do they parallel Chinese kung fu's iron shirt body-toughening methods? Maybe. The Cherokees developed the throwing style of the tomahawk. The ritual martial arts of the Sioux Indians' "dog soldiers" focused on their long *teton* lances, but many of their secret techniques were lost after the Wounded Knee massacre. Unfortunately, martial arts films have not investigated these subjects much. Maybe one day.

Titleography: *The Magnificent Three.* Translation—*Red Sun. The Magnificent Three* refers to the addition of Ursula Andress to the Mifune-Bronson duo halfway through the film, but her magnificence is not a measure of her fighting skills, that is for sure. And it is also probably a film title nod to the *Magnificent Seven* (1960). **MA Percentage: 3.78%**

RESCUE, THE

血 洒 天 牢 (1971—Hong Kong) **79m. FI: Tang Chia, Yuen Cheung-yan. NOT/LOT: None; NOF/LOF: 14/ 15m 5s.** D: Shen Chiang. C: Lo Lieh, Shih Szu, Ling Ling, Bolo Yeung, Fang Mian, Chan Shen, Kim Jee-joo, Gu Wen-zong.

In the 1270s, Kublai Khan invaded China and established the Yuan Dynsty. During the year before Kublai Khan's invasion, the Southern Song Dynasty General Wen Tian-xiang, one of the three heroes of Song, led an army against him and was captured. When Kublai Khan offered him a position with the Yuan realm and asked him to convince the Song to lay down their arms, he refused and was subsequently imprisoned, tortured and put to death in 1283. During that time, he wrote *Song of Righteousness* and *Passing Ling Ding Yang*, which expressed his loyalty to China and the Song Dynasty and made him a powerful symbol of

patriotism and virtue.

According to legend, a handful of brave Song fighters broke into Celestial Prison in hopes of finding and rescuing General Wen. However, Wen was near death and knew he would slow the young fighters down, so he ordered them to take his books instead and make sure they did not die with him. This film tells the story of how swordswoman Bai Ya-er (Shih Szu); Le He-ru (Lo Lieh), who was secretly in love with her; and a team of daring Chinese patriots rescued Wen's words of wisdom. Only one man would survive, but that was enough. During future dark times in China, Wen's legacy would inspire stories of bravery and heroism against foreign invaders.

Although Bolo Yeung often played muscle-bound Jin or Mongol villains, in this film, he starts off as a bad guy but is persuaded to do right and becomes a hero. It is rare to have his character turn midway through a *wuxia* film, but he pulls it off with refreshing success and convincing fervor. His fights have a different flavor about them because the choreographers do not just focus on him being a cruel killer who can snap a man in two. His heroic stature is portrayed through longer shots of action and with different camera angles to reveal a warrior who ultimately gives all for his country.

The most memorable shot is when the character Le is in the prison fighting off the Mongol hordes and suddenly has to rescue the injured, unconscious Bai. He leaps toward her rather awkwardly, like an injured bird that can barely fly, which somehow seems to fit the film's crazy wire work. But once he drapes her limp body over his shoulder and runs along the prison's second-story balcony toward a window, there is a mesmerizing tracking shot in which he glides down the hallway; then there is a close-up in which it seems like Le is fly-walking toward camera. The remainder of the escape is equally engaging. Le's final heroic moment further demonstrates his love for Bai. When you see the film, you will understand what I mean when I say he adores her.

For posterity, the other two heroes of Song associated with the waning years of the Dynasty are Zhang Shi-jie and Liu Shou-fu.

Titleography: As of this writing, no alternative titles could be found. Translation—*Blood Spilled Heaven Prison.* **MA Percentage: 19.09%** SHAW BROTHERS

RESHMA AND SHERA

Reshma Aur Shera (1971—India) **158m. SAD: Ravi Khanna. NOT/LOT: None; NOF/LOF: 2/ 2m 37s.** D: Sunil Dutt. C: Waheeda Rehman, Sunil Dutt, Rakhee Gulzar, Vinod Khanna, Amitabh Bachchan, Ranjeet, Naval Kumar.

Romeo and Juliet comes to the deserts of India, where the sands of time are running out on a true forbidden love. Reshma (Waheeda Rehman) and Shera (Sunil Dutt) come together in an effort to end the enmity and hatred between their rival families, but ultimately, it's at the expense of themselves and their passion.

The film is shot like a classic cultural meditative National Geographic TV documentary. Ravi Khanna, one of India's most cinematically decorated fight/stunt coordinators, manages to weave Indian combative arts into Sunil Dutt's well-directed tapestry of Indian traditional wisdom within the first 15 minutes of the film, which features dance, song and fighting.

For the fights, first there is *pehlwani*, a synthesis of indigenous Indian wrestling styles dating back to 400 B.C. and Persian grappling arts introduced into India in the early 1500s during the Mughal Empire. Next is the use of the *shareeravadi* (a bamboo staff), which is one of the stick-fighting weapons of *silambam*, part of the southern style of *kilaripayit*. Dutt's silambam is rather crude in the film, but he does improve over his next several movies, as demonstrated in *Heera* (1973). The choreography also involves a sword fight using the *talwar*, the sword of choice used by practitioners of *gatka*, a Sikh Indian martial art created by Guru Nanak Dev in the late 1400s.

Titleography: As of this writing, no alternative titles could be found. **MA Percentage: 1.66%**

RETURN OF BRUCE

忠烈精武門 (1977—Philippines) **77m. MAD: Bruce Le. NOT/LOT: 3/ 1m 4s; NOF/LOF: 22/ 32m.** D: Joseph Kong Hung. C: Bruce Le, Meng Fei, Lo Lieh, James Nan Gung-fan, Cheung Lik, Chan Lau, Jiang Dao.

What do you get when you cross Bruce Lee, Ernst Stavro Blofeld from *You Only Live Twice* (1967), the kitten from *Way of the Dragon* (1973) and some low-end *escrima*? You get this film, featuring a criminal named Lin the Cat who carries the kitten from Bruce Lee's *Way of the Dragon*. When Lin dies, we see the hands of the spectral Mr. Matsuda (Jiang Dao) stroking the same kitten like a villain out of an old James Bond movie. And the film offers the most blatant Lee impersonation that I've seen in all of Bruceploitation-dom. Even Lee himself would probably do a double-take if he were to sit through this goofy yarn about a Chinese man named Bruce Wang (Bruce Le) trying to foil a smuggling ring with the help of a Korean policewoman in the Philippines.

Many Bruce Lee fans have seen certain photos of the legend with a beard and mustache, wearing red-tinted shades, a white jacket and a blue shirt. Well, that was really Le while on the set of *Return of Bruce*. From there, this film is just a collection of Lee-isms that pop up in a variety of fights. In one scene, Le rips someone's chest hair off and blows it out of his hand. In another, he stomps on someone—complete with a close-up of his face showing intense anger. And out of nowhere, with a fighting cameo that comes and goes in the blink of an eye, superstar Lo Lieh appears as a killer who bites the dust in less time than a humming bird's wings flap.

Sometimes fights use close-ups and turbulent camera movement to create a sense of intense action, thus making things look faster than they are or hiding bad technique, but this film could give you motion sickness. The fights are also peppered with too many shots of Le kicking or punching into the camera, usually followed by the reverse angle of someone falling away from the camera. Overusing these point-of-view shots gets tiresome quickly. It seems less like a unique visual ploy and more like a delay tactic to keep the cameras rolling and not lose the spirit of the fight while trying to come up with something new.

An unintentionally funny moment occurs when actor Cheung Lik does a decent white crane form, showing his deadly wing and beak attacks, and then when it comes time to fight, he uses pure karate. To the savvy onlooker, you might wonder what is the point of doing a great white crane form and then doing something completely different and unrelated in a fight. Therein lies the unintentional humor. The irony of it all hits home when Le, who up until now is doing a lot of kicks, suddenly breaks into white crane beaks and pokes out an opponent's eye or rips off an attacker's chest hair while squawking the mannerisms of Lee. If you watched this film while high on drugs, I guess you could call it killing two birds with one who is stoned.

Titleography: *Bruce's Return*; *Dragon Return*; *Ninja vs. Bruce Lee*; *Concord of Bruce*. Translation—*The Brave and Faithful to the Country From the Ching Wu School*. Any film in which the lead character looks or acts like Bruce Lee could have *Bruce*, *Dragon* or *Return* in the title, but where does *Concord* come from? Maybe it has something to do with a supersonic jet. The Chinese

title implies Le's continuation of his *Bruce and Shaolin Kung Fu* film, in which he was *Brave and Faithful to the Country* (of Korea) *From Ching Wu School*. The coincidence stretches further because although he was not fighting in Korea, the Korean reference is strong since he was from China and partnered with a Korean cop. **MA Percentage: 42.94%**

RETURN OF THE CHINESE BOXER

神拳大戰快鎗手 (1977—Hong Kong) **98m. AD: Hsieh Hsing. NOT/ LOT: 3/ 3m 37s; NOF/LOF: 20/ 31m 20s.** D: Jimmy Wong Yu. C: Jimmy Wong Yu, Lung Fei, Jin Gang, Zhang Yin-sheng, Xue Han, Tu Song-zhou, Gan De-min, Wang Yong-shen.

Here's Jimmy! This kooky kung fu flick directed by and starring Jimmy Wong Yu is as nutty as it is as fun. From a pure martial arts standpoint, actor Jimmy Wong Yu's non-weapon martial arts movies rarely show brilliant or exacting kung fu technique, but they are realistic in the sense that he always looks like he is fighting as if his life depends on it. What he lacks in precision, he makes up for with creativity by dreaming up bizarre villains, set pieces and fight scenarios.

When the traitorous Manchu General Tou makes a secret deal with the Tokugawa regime of Japan to give the Japanese a foothold in China, loyal Chinese strategists turn to General Kang Ta for help. They plan to offer him a beautiful woman and two antique Chinese swords in hopes that he will align himself against Tou. However, the Japanese entourage in China—rife with samurai, ninja, Thai boxers and Japan's No. 1 hired gun, Black Crane (Lung Fei)—will do whatever it takes to kidnap the woman and stop her from reaching Kang. Only one man can protect her, a man who can defeat everything the Japanese throw at him: the lone wandering fist fighter Sao Pai-lung (Jimmy Wong Yu).

It is plain to see that Wong Yu learned from working with Shintaro Katsu on *Zatoichi and the One-Armed Swordsman* (1971) because as the director of *Return of the Chinese Boxer*, he captures the essence of old Japan in the sets, costumes, hairstyles and even the samurai choreography at the beginning of the film. This also demonstrates the value of a talented director.

Wong Yu is one of the few Chinese directors who appreciate Japanese martial arts. He often has characters that show the spirit and tenacity of the art by giving the actors some latitude to do solid karate maneuvers. Along with creative skills, it was also essential for Wong Yu to make sure that the fighters didn't just look like guys in karate *gi* doing kung fu movements.

In this film, he features several Japanese arts and skills for the first time. In a death tournament scene in Japan, fighters brandish lethal versions of Okinawan karate weapons. Meanwhile, a secret society searches for a master assassin to send to China to do its cloak-and-dagger work, and his helpers end up being some of the tournament winners.

The martial arts in this film, and many others that Wong Yu directs, tend to come across as eccentric for the sake of an art's unknown danger—the secrets of the arts, if you will. This funkiness can make some fights look a tad unconventional, and these scenes are rather entertaining. There is a Chinese assassin who fights with lit sticks of dynamite, for example. And just when you think the Japanese have run out of assassins, they resurrect three zombies to attack fist fighter Sao with banshee-like screeching. Then there is the big showdown with the feared samurai Black Crane, who bursts into a warehouse carrying a large, fan-shaped gun with multiple barrels, undoubtedly influenced by the Japanese *Lone Wolf and Cub* series. But what does the Black Crane see? Fifty or so Sao dummies in various poses. Each time Black Crane shoots one, it falls to the ground and leaks steam all over the place. The scene is a hybrid of *The Wild Wild West* TV show and the mirror scene at the end of *Enter the Dragon*.

Titleography: *Samurai Terror*. Translation—*Miraculous Fist Fights Big Battle Against Fast Gunslinger*. The film is more like a sequel to *Master of the Flying Guillotine* (see that film's martialogy) because of the eclectic nature of the various fighters. The *Miraculous Fist* title refers to Sao's fighting ability and his showdown with the samurai Black Crane. *Samurai Terror* refers to Black Crane. Some Web sites also call this film *Invincible* and *Swift Shaolin Boxer*, which is incorrect. *The Swift Shaolin Boxer* (1978), aka *Invincible*, stars Angela Mao Ying and Barry Chan, with the translated Chinese title *Matchless In the World*. **MA Percentage: 35.66%**

RETURN OF THE 18 BRONZEMEN

雍正大破十八銅人; 少林寺十八銅人第 2 部 and
雍正大破銅人陣 (1976—Hong Kong) **94m. MAI: Cliff Lok, Chen Shao-peng. NOT/LOT: 17/ 7m 46s; NOF/LOF: 23/ 28m 41s.** D: Joseph Kuo. C: Carter Wong, Polly Kuan, Roc Tien, Huang Fei-long, O Yau-man, Lee Ting-gwan, Yuan Sen.

The Chinese titles of this film actually say this film is about 18 copper dummies, not 18 bronze men. And just as bronze is 88 percent copper and 12 percent tin, this film is about 12 percent true.

Emperor Kang Xi is near death, and his will states that Prince Ying Si will succeed him. However, when Prince Yong (Carter Wong) sees the will, he secretly alters it, adding certain calligraphy strokes to specific characters, so that he becomes the next emperor of China. Newly crowned, Yong is told that the Shaolin Temple is a hornet's nest for anti-Ching activity and asked what he wants to do about it. The film flashes back to young Prince Yong training at Shaolin and shows how those times influence his eventual decision to burn down the temple and kill all the monks. The beginning of the flashback is not made particularly obvious, so it's possible to misread the film as a story about Emperor Yong Zheng secretly entering the Shaolin Temple to learn kung fu in preparation to fight his enemies.

Shaolin law stipulates that any monk wishing to leave the temple must survive the famous Luo Han Hall of 108 Wooden Men test. In real life, the test takes place in a chamber created by monk Xin Yin at Jiu Lian Shan Shaolin Temple. This film depicts the wooden men as bronze (or copper) and locates them at Song Shan Shaolin Temple instead (two inaccuracies). According to the film, Emperor Yong Zheng was so angry at the abbot for not allowing him to finish his Shaolin training that it becomes his reason to order the temple destroyed and the monks slaughtered. In reality, the historical Yong Zheng never trained at Shaolin. The film's final words also reveal the creation of a new dangerous weapon: the deadly flying guillotine. (See *Flying Guillotine* (1975).) However, this weapon was never used against Shaolin, possibly because Yong Zheng died soon after the temple's destruction. (See *The Blazing Temple* (1976).) What the film does get right, though, is Yong Zheng making changes to the will.

The film's training sequences are very creative, especially the fights against the bronze men. Regardless of how cheesy they look (part of the film's charm), they still work. At the end of the day, the film's ultimate martial arts message is clear: If you want to learn Shaolin kung fu for personal gain (Yong Zheng wanted the revered dragon tattoos) or revenge (he also wanted to learn Ta Mo's 18 principles kung fu to defeat a romantic rival practicing *Ta Mo shen gong*), those are the wrong reasons, and bad karma will befall you. Incidentally, the above-mentioned styles of kung fu are real.

Titleography: *The 18 (Eighteen) Bronzemen, Part 2*. Translations—*Yong Zheng Breaks the 18 Copper Dummies*; *18 Copper Dummies of the Shaolin Temple Part 2*; and *Yong Zheng Breaks the Copper Dummy Trap*. As some of the titles indicate, the film is a sequel to *The 18 Bronzemen*. In this case, the common thread in the sequel is the bronze men and not the main character. It's possible the filmmakers stipulated 18 bronze men based on Yong Zheng's desire to learn Ta Mo's 18 principles of kung fu (i.e., one principle per bronze man).
MA Percentage: 38.78%

RETURN OF THE TIGER

(1977—Taiwan) **92m. KFD: Hsieh Hsing. NOT/LOT: 1/ 1m 17s; NOF/LOF: 21/ 29m 40s.** D: Jimmy Shaw Feng. C: Angela Mao Ying, Bruce Li, Zhang Yi, Lung Fei, Blacky Ko, Paul Smith.

It's Bruce at the shipyards—again. There are a string of Bruceploitation films in which Bruce Li has at least one fight at the docks, wherein he runs amid large metal cargo containers and finds an appropriate space to bash away at the enemy. It was never the central plot, just a popular scenario. So in *Return to the Docks*—I mean, *Tiger*—secret police investigator Chang Hung (Bruce Li) gets involved with two criminal gangs. One is headed by Sing Chi-sang (Lung Fe); Betty in *Kung Pow: Enter the Fist* (2002), the other by a Westerner, Big Paul (Paul Smith, a black belt in *taekwondo* and a former bodyguard and bouncer). Chang plays the two against each other to take them down for drug running.

The best fight scene is the opening brawl at a martial arts gym. Chang runs into a sticky situation, but his partner, Jane (Angela Mao Ying), dressed in a shiny silver jumpsuit and ski goggles, slaloms in to lend a hand.

Although the choreography in Mao Ying's fights is not particularly intricate (which was also the case when she appeared in Bruce Lee's films), she brings plenty of energy and sleek technique. She tears through bad guys like a combine harvester in a cornfield. She also performs her signature move made popular in *Enter the Dragon*, in which she winds up her arms, steps back, and blocks or avoids an attack. Li's finale against Smith is not too bad, considering that Smith probably had no idea what was going on. All of us foreigners getting our butts kicked by Chinese kung fu stars in movies were basically tossed into the fray without anyone showing us the ropes. Rather than focus on clean martial arts, kung fu director Hsieh Hsing (who was the fight choreographer I worked with on my first TV show for China Television in Taiwan) went for acts of strength, bludgeoning blows and a shocking ending. That added a certain level of creativity that Li's other contemporary Hong Kong films often times lacked.

Titleography: *Silent Killer From Eternity*. In a previous Bruceploitation film (*Exit the Dragon, Enter the Tiger*), Li plays a character called Tiger, so this film uses the old standby *Return of the (Something)* format in hopes fans might recognize Li. Though the title implies the film is a sequel or continuation, it is not. *Silent Killer From Eternity* has two plausible meanings: "Bruce Lee" is back from eternity to silently kill the bad guys, or the *Silent Killer* could be the drugs.
MA Percentage: 33.64%

RETURN OF THE STREET FIGHTER

Satsujin Ken 2 (1975—Japan) **82m. MAD: Masafumi Suzuki, Ken Kazama. NOT/LOT: 10/ 4m 41s; NOF/LOF: 15/ 16m 8s.** D: Shigehiro Ozawa. C: Sonny Chiba, Yoko Ichiji, Masashi Ishibashi, Claude Gagnon, Hiroshi Tanaka, Masafumi Suzuki, Etsuko Shihomi.

He's baaa-aaack, and this time it's personal. No, this is not referring to *Jaws* or even the return of independent assassin/bodyguard Tsurugi Takuma (Sonny Chiba), aka Terry Tsururgi in the English dub. It's the return of the larynx-lacking Tateki Shikenbaru (Masashi Ishibashi). In *The Street Fighter* (1974), Tsurugi ripped Tateki's throat to shreds and left him for dead. Sporting an electrolarynx voice replacement that makes his voice sound like a Cylon robot from *Battlestar Galactica* (1978), Tateki is out to battle Tsurugi and make him see stars.

The film setup is like *Street Fighter*. The Chicago Mafia-backed Yakuza want to kill *sensei* Kendo Masaoka (Masafumi Suzuki) because he plans to expose how they are extorting money from Asia's influential martial arts leaders to build the ultimate Asian martial arts center. The Yakuza want Tsurugi to kill Kendo, but he refuses. So the Yakuza hire an even cooler huddle of hit men to kill Tsurugi because he knows all about the plot to kill Kendo.

Seeing an eight-track tape deck in one of the characters' cars is certainly a '70s flashback, and Tsurugi has his own flashback when he has to face his arch nemesis, Tateki from *The Street Fighter*, again. Tateki returns with his gigantic *sai* (a large dagger-like weapon with two tines attached to the handle), which he uses to puncture and prong Tsurugi off a cliff, where he seems to plummet to his death. But while falling, Tsurugi recalls his father's dying words: "Trust no one … let no one beat you." He ends up surviving, but he needs time to recover. His Pippi Longstocking-looking assistant, Kitty Pinboke (Yoko Ichiji), helps him by hiding his whereabouts from the Yakuza. The Yakuza don't take kindly to that and kill her. Tsurugi recovers and vengefully rips, gouges and tears his way through the Yakuza ranks.

At the film's beginning, the Okinawan karate weapons *bo*, *nunchaku*, sai, *tonfa* and *kama* are demonstrated by various *karateka* to let the audience know what to expect in the fights. It is like the beginning of Chinese kung fu films when the heroes or villains perform their kung fu. Keep in mind that up until this point in Japanese film history, most audiences had not seen the power or danger of these weapons, so it was necessary to set them up so the audience could appreciate the choreography. It was also part of Chiba's effort to introduce these weapons into Japanese cinema, which up until then had mostly featured samurai swords.

Besides devoting 10 fewer minutes to fights than *Street Fighter*, *Return* uses more hand-held camerawork, albeit with less shakiness compared to earlier *chambara* (sword-fighting) films. This film also uses close shots of Chiba's hands while tracking and tilting the camera so we can see the intricacy of certain hand traps and subsequent throws. During what I call the "masseuse fight," we see what would soon become one of Chiba's signature techniques: During a front shot, Chiba leaps high above his opponent, kicks the guy in the face and lands.

Selling fights is also about trickery, and it can take practice to see the tricks. For instance, consider Jackie Chan in *Mr. Canton and Lady Rose* (1989), during the teahouse fight. When Chan's character slides down the spiral staircase, try to decipher if it is really Jackie or a double. During Chiba's masseuse fight, there's a shot in which Chiba seemingly flies over several people. However, if you watch the shadow on the curtain at the end of the shot, you can tell someone else is on the wire. But personally, I love the snow fight at the ski slope in which Tsurugi strikes the back of a hit man's head with so much power that his eye pops out, reddening the white ground. It is as gross as it is eye-catching.

Titleography: *Return of the Street Fighter.* Translation—*Killer Fist 2.* **MA Percentage: 25.39%**

RETURNED SINGLE-LEGGED MAN

Dol-a-on Oedali (1974—S. Korea) **88m. FI: Uncredited. NOT/LOT: None; NOF/LOF: 15/ 21m 48s.** D: Lee Doo-yong. C: Han Yong-cheol, Kwan Yung-moon, Jeong Ae-jeong, Lee So-yeong, Kim Mun-ju, Hwang Jang-lee.

Sometimes dubbed films are so bad that you can't help but watch. This film has it all: bad/rad fights, freaky sound effects (the characters sound like they are wearing clogs and walking around on hollow pottery), and weird camera speeds. Given the animosity between Korea and Japan (past and present), it is ironic that this movie uses music from old Japanese Yakuza films to set the tone and mood.

The film is set in the 1930s in Korea. When gangster Yong Cheol (Han Yong-cheol) wants to marry Hyang-suk, retire from being a gangster and get a fresh start, his adopted father and the gang's godfather, Wang Hae-rim, flails him into kimchi. After castigating Yong for even thinking of betraying the gang, Wang agrees to let him go if he does one more job: intercept a man carrying secret papers from the north and steal the attached gold shipment. What Yong doesn't know is that the deliveryman is Hyang-suk's brother and the payload is destined for the Cho Sun Independence Army to help fight the Japanese.

Yong steals the documents and kills the deliveryman but is then triple-crossed by Wang's Japanese right-hand man, the lunatic Yamamoto, who then kills Wang, takes over the operation for Japan and keeps the gold for himself. Filled with shame for killing Hyang-suk's brother, Yong drinks himself under the table, breaks his own leg, then gets captured and tortured by Yamamoto. Just when you think Yong does not have a leg to stand on, Korean independence fighter Kim Seung (Kwan Yung-moon) rescues him from Yamamoto's dungeon, and the two heroically unleash bad weather on Yamamoto and his followers with tornado kicks and hurricane footwork.

The fights suffer from the way they are shot, with tight camera angles made visually unappealing by rocking-and-rolling hand-held camerawork. But as is often the case, the fights get better as the film progresses, probably because the actors and stuntmen got into a groove and understood each other's timing. There are some good set pieces with actors doing up to 15 kicks in a single unedited shot. Very impressive.

This early film of actor Kwan Yung-moon really shows what weightlifting can do. Kwan is practically a beanpole at this stage in his career, but when you see him in Liu Chia-liang's *My Young Auntie* (1981), he is an ultra-muscular *chi gong* guy and still fights with the same intensity as he does in this movie.

Titleography: *Korean Connection.* Right on the heels of *The Chinese Connection*, except this time it is Korean. *Returned Single-Legged Man* refers to the hero fighting with a broken leg. **MA Percentage: 24.77%**

REVENGE OF KUNG FU MAO

大腳娘子 (1977—Taiwan) **104m. MAI: Shan Mao, He Wei-xiong. NOT/LOT: 5/ 3m 37s; NOF/LOF: 15/ 25m 40s.** D: Ding Shan-xi. C: Angela Mao Ying, Wong Dao, Jimmy Wong Yu, Min Min, Jin Gang, Li Jiang, He Wei-xiong, Shan Mao, Tie Ren.

Losing money at the horse races and having to explain it to your wife is bad enough, but imagine if your wife were someone like Angela Mao Ying—you might be too scared to ever come home.

This film begins innocently enough when two villages give money to Wang Wei-ying's (Angela Mao Ying) husband to buy a water pump so they can share water distribution. Unfortunately, the husband loses the money and more when he bets on horse races operated by a sexy woman who also owns the local gambling joints. The husband agrees to leave his struggling wife and child for the easy life and begins working as the rich lady's accountant. Meanwhile, the rich lady's henchmen plan to kill the villagers. The village elder (Min Min) teach-

es Wang and her brother Kang (Wong Dao) kung fu so they can help protect the village. By learning kung fu, Wang can also search for what she thinks is her lost husband in the dangerous underworld of gamblers and murderers.

There are two unique martial arts aspects in this film. It is the first time that a character, Wang Wei-ying, specifically learns *ban deng chuen* (bench kung fu), in which a piece of furniture becomes a weapon. The use of the bench is thought to have first been wielded as a weapon by southern martial artists in restaurants, and over the years it has appeared as a fighting prop in some 1970s films like *The Big Rascal.* (See martialogy.) However, Jackie Chan popularized the pugilistic pew as a weapon in *Young Master* (1980).

A second neat aspect of the film is the missing link in the evolution of whips. The most well-known whip weapon to kung fu practitioners is the soft whip, aka the nine-section whip (*jiu jian bien*), which comprises nine slender pieces of steel connected together to form a whip-like weapon. At the distal end of the whip is a steel knifepoint. The weapon was originally a solid iron weapon with nine vertebra-like sections fused together like a pagoda or a piece of bamboo, which was called a hard whip. Although the history is not clear, it seems that the transition stage, or missing link, between the hard and soft whips was a bullwhip-looking weapon consisting of nine long, thin, tightly connected metal sections. It is this whip that is featured in the film and used by one of the racehorse thugs.

Director Ding Shan-xi is known for his war films, but he is also a master of gut-wrenching, tear-jerking martial arts tragedies. He demands much more from his leads than just fighting abilities. In *Revenge of Kung Fu Mao*, Mao Ying is impressive with Shakespearean ranges of eloquence and heart-rending melancholy as she comes closer to learning the truth about her husband, but her eventual recovery is a triumph.

Titleography: *Big Foot Mama; Revenge of the Kung Fu Mao.* Translation—*Lady With Big Feet.* I worked with director Ding several times in Taiwan, and he explained to me how some Chinese films were given English titles. The literal translation mirrors the *Big Foot Mama* title (the insinuation being that the gambling lady is rich, i.e. has big feet), and *The Revenge of Kung Fu Mao* is merely playing on Angela Mao Ying's fame. For more on kung fu film titles, see the Introduction. **MA Percentage: 28.16%**

REVENGE OF THE SHAOLIN KID

古銅蕭 (1978—Taiwan) **90m. MAD: Li Chao. NOT/LOT: 3/ 3m 2s; NOF/LOF: 13/ 31m 44s.** D: Yu Han-hsiang. C: Chi Kuan-chun, Lo Lieh, Chia Ling, Chen Hsing, Mang Ling-ming, Wu Ma, Wei Hong, Jiang Qing-xia.

Until the mid-1990s, many top Hong Kong martial arts filmmakers firmly believed that it did not matter if the story was good or bad as long as the kung fu was fresh and entertaining. That's part of the reason why kung fu films of the 1970s created so many outlandish scenarios and apparatuses to train the determined student who wished to avenge his teacher, family or Shaolin Temple.

The *Revenge of the Shaolin Kid* is an example of such a film. It tells the tired tale of a child who sees his parents killed, learns kung fu, and returns as a strapping martial arts expert looking to defeat the villain and avenge his family.

So Lee Tian-jiao (Chi Kuan-chun) returns after 18 years to exact retribution for his father's murder at the hand of the traitorous Kim Men-zhen (Lo Lieh), the former Ming general who went to the dark side by joining the Chings. Of course, there is an even greater force of evil behind Kim: Dr. Lung Shi-tian, played by none other than the perennially hunchbacked tiger claw stylist Chen Hsing. The acting is a bit cheesy, so from the beginning of the film on, I recommend keeping your eyes glued to the screen and your thumb stuck to the fast-forward button.

Actor Chi Kuan-chun's kung fu is superb in this film (as it is in real life). One way good kung fu choreographers chose to accentuate a star's proven martial ability was to have him fight with one hand resting gently on the small of his back. It is actually very difficult to stay relaxed and keep the hand motionless while maintaining a straight-backed posture, especially when attacking and defending. But Chi does it effortlessly, even while in low crouches and high stances, and that is why the fights in this film are worth several viewings.

Titleography: *The Master of Death.* Translation—*Old Copper Flute.* The main English title reflects the story because the hero is rescued as a child and trained by a Shaolin monk. Ultimately, he becomes a *Master of Death*, though that sounds contrary to the Shaolin way. The translated Chinese title focuses on the cameo appearance of Chia Ling doing a Suexploitation routine in a gambling joint that really has nothing to do with the film. She seemingly fights with a flute, though the film does not mention if it is copper. **MA Percentage: 38.63%**

REVENGE OF THE SHAOLIN MASTER

冷刀染紅英雄血 and 江湖一盞燈 (1979—Hong Kong) 88m. KFI: Yuen Woo-ping, Yuen Cheung-yan. NOT/LOT: 1/ 38s; NOF/LOF: 30/ 30m 47s. D: Luo Zhen. C: Tan Dao-liang, Chen Hsing, Lung Fei, Zhang Fu-jian, Liu Shan, Cai Hong, Alan Hsu.

One sad thing about human nature is that after a disaster occurs, there are always people who want to take advantage of the situation. Take, for example, the greedy real-estate moguls who snatched up devastated beachfront hotels, resorts and properties destroyed by the 2004 tsunami that flooded the shores of Phuket, Thailand. Or consider the sleazy government officials stealing rice and money needed to help China's starving people during one of the country's worst droughts. At least in China's case, during real droughts, as depicted in this film, there are stories of heroic acts by handfuls of kung fu men who make these cowards cringe and think twice about exploiting others. This is the story of one such hero.

While en route to deliver money and rice to starving peasants in a severely drought-stricken area of China, Lin Cheng-hu (Tan Dao-liang) is attacked by a horde of bandits. He also finds that his security company pals are part of the greedy subterfuge when they turn against him and help the vagabonds steal the food. When high-ranking official Chin Chu (Cai Hong) hears of the atrocity, Lin is framed, beaten, tortured and sentenced to death after being forced to sign a confession for this vile act he did not commit. But this act of treachery is but a veil of deception by some higher heinous head, Yu Chin-pao (Lung Fei). As a few of Lin's faithful friends and his stout-hearted sister (Liu Shan) are losing the fight for his freedom, a lone Marshal (Chen Hsing) moseys into town. It is not the misty morn that villains should fear, but the Marshal's quick-draw claws of justice.

What separates the left-footed Tan from other great kicking martial arts film stars like John Liu and Hwang Jang-lee is that Tan is more attuned to mixing kung fu and opera-style choreography than many of his contemporaries. This doesn't mean the other kickers didn't know how to adjust to different fights, but Tan was more proficient in simultaneously combining kicks and weapon work with the flowing nature of operatic choreography. Furthermore, Tan's kicking posture is like Bruce Lee's; instead of leaning his back away in the opposing direction of the kicking foot like most big-screen kick fighters, he keeps his back upright. Because Yuen Woo-ping was trained in traditional kung fu and opera, he was able to adjust his choreography to match the skills of the talent. This film's fights lean more toward opera-style choreography, and this is why opera-trained actress Liu Shan was more adept at the fights. Along with some patented night fights, Woo-ping uses lots of extreme close-up camera angles and often snap-zooms back to show a cool pose or a subsequent sequence of moves. When done right, these camera techniques can be very dynamic.

Titleography: *Revenge of a Shaolin Master*. Translations—*Cold Sword Stained Red With Hero's Blood* and *One Lantern in the Jiang Hu World*. The title *One Lantern in the Jiang Hu World* refers to the notion of a righteous fighter in an unjust world who puts his life on the line to set things right. He is a beacon of hope, if you will. The film has nothing to do with Shaolin, so the English titles are nothing more than an attempt to attract an audience. *Cold Sword Stained Red With Hero's Blood* is an analogy to a cold, evil man (*Sword*) inflicting pain (*Stained Red*) on a righteous man (*Hero's Blood*). **MA Percentage: 35.7%**

RICA

Konketsuji Rika (1972—Japan) 92m. AD: Kikuo Watai. NOT/LOT: None; NOF/LOF: 10/ 11m 28s. D: Ko Nakahira. C: Rika Aoki, Kazuko Nagamoto, Masami Souda, Michi Nono, Fuminori Sato.

Let this film serve as a lesson to bullies out there: Be careful of the kid you pick on, because she might grow up to be bigger, smarter and tougher than you, and you might wind up paying for it.

Amerasian Rica (Rika Aoki), the bastard child of a mother raped by an American GI, is herself raped as a teen by her mother's boyfriend. She grows up to be a lean, mean, karate-fighting machine and becomes the head of an all-girl gang. She's not afraid to take on anyone, male or female, who messes with her and her girls. When Rica finds out that a low-level soldier of a local Yakuza family rapes, impregnates and abandons one of her girls, she is livid. On a beach and holding her friend's dying fetus in her hands, Rica vows vengeance and kills the Yakuza solider. For this, she is sent to reform school, where she quickly makes enemies with Reiko (Kazuko Nagamoto), the head girl thug.

Rica escapes from reform school. While on the lam from the authorities, the Yakuza and Reiko, she uncovers a plot to kidnap the girls in her gang and force

them into pornography before shipping them off to Vietnam to be prostitutes for American troops. As it turns out, Reiko and her girls are also targets for the same prostitution ring. After Rica saves her friends, Reiko and Reiko's girls from the same fate, they unite to take on the depraved Japanese gang leader and a sleazy American naval officer.

Considering that 200,000 Korean teens during World War II were kidnapped and raped by Japanese soldiers and sent all over Asia as prostitutes for the Japanese soldiers at their camps, there is a great deal of irony in this film. Historically, these enslaved women were known as "comfort women." It is something that the present Japanese government denies while the surviving 112 Korean comfort women are still demanding an apology.

In Japanese "pinky violence" films—so named because of the color of certain naughty body parts that were heavily censored in film by the government but were smartly hidden during the framing of nude shots—it's standard for the lead heroine to be raped, otherwise wronged, and sent to prison or reform school. It's also common for her to be a member of a girl street or motorcycle gang (though loners did exist). These films feature excessive nudity and females fighting in scanty costumes (or in the nude), but they led to great box-office success and gave a much-needed shot in the arm to Japan's crumbling film industry in the early 1970s. They created a genre of exploitation that was uniquely Japanese.

The fights in *Rica* appear to be thrown together with a piecemeal mentality. The action lacks any sense of authenticity, kicks are delivered with extremely bent legs (because everyone stands too close together due to no sense of spacing), and the only authentic karate moments are when lead actress Rika Aoki delivers some truly memorable power punches that look and feel authentic. For a Japanese woman, Aoki is a rather formidable presence, even towering over most of her male opponents. She has an edge similar to what Lucy Lawless brought to her role in the TV show *Xena: Warrior Princess*—the difference being that Rica also has a great right cross.

The final shot of the film, in which Rica is speeding down the highway on a white Harley Davidson motorcycle, is not only existential but also reflects her take-no-prisoners attitude and shows that she is "the man," so to speak. During the 1970s in Japan, to have a female caricature like that on a large American Harley was a shock to the status quo.

Titleography: *Rika the Mixed-Blood Girl*. Translation—*Rika the Mixed-Blood Girl*. **MA Percentage: 12.46%**

RICA 2: LONELY WANDERER

Konketsuji Rika: Hitoriyuku Sasuraitabi (1973—Japan) 85m. AD: Kikuo Watai. NOT/LOT: None; NOF/LOF: 10/ 10m 23s. D: Ko Nakahira. C: Rika Aoki, Ryunosuke Minegishi, Taiji Tonoyama, Mizuho Suzuki, Kaoru Hama, Masami Souda.

If you have the guts, you might survive in the world of delinquent girls and Yakuza gangs, or at least you will die as a respected adversary. One of the common lines in these "pinky violence" and Yakuza movies occurs when the hero boldly defies the opposing gang's elder. The leader, with a gravelly voice, will usually grunt, "You've got guts." This film, like its predecessor, shows that Rica (Rika Aoki) has more guts than a giant whale. This time she takes on an almost spy-like role when searching for her friend Hanako, who supposedly drowned on the party ship Tohoku.

Rica uncovers the sinking ship's mystery as a plot by rival Yakuza, dirty cops and an American crime mob all working together to cover up a prostitution ring and drug-smuggling operation. One Yakuza boss boldly rants that their crime is nothing compared to the environmental damage big businesses in Japan inflict on a daily basis. This is also a common theme in Japanese action and monster films of the decade. The arguments reflect the attitudes of Japanese youth in regard to the environment. (This trend started in *Godzilla* (1954), which addresses the effects of the atomic bomb.).

Rica 2 begins where *Rica* ends, with Rica flying down the road on her white Harley Davidson like a white knight out to save the teen girls of Japan. In this sequel, she becomes a superhero crime-fighter. Because she operates in cold climates, the filmmakers have her don a long, flowing cape that makes her look like Batgirl. She fights more male assassins and has to escape some sticky situations while trying to solve the mystery of the sinking ship and find Hanako.

Although Rica still uses her patented karate guard, the individual fights appear longer in this film because she ends up doing more tangles and tussles with her male opponents as compared to the freewheeling kicking in the first film. It is refreshing that the choreography includes snippets of basic *jujutsu* and judo combinations. The final fight in the Yakuza lair makes good use of the environment; Rica leaps off balconies and staircases and jumps over furniture while punching, kicking and trying to avoid bullets zipping all over the place.

And just when you think that maybe Rica has matured, in the middle of a fight she'll stop to blow a bubble with her gum, a reminder that she is still just a juvenile delinquent at heart.

Titleography: As of this writing, no alternative titles could be found. **MA Percentage: 12.21%**

RICA 3: JUVENILE LULLABY

Konketsuji Rika: Hamagure Komoriuta (1973—Japan) **85m. FI: Uncredited. NOT/LOT: None; NOF/LOF: 9/ 5m 14s.** D: Kozaburo Yoshimura. C: Rika Aoki, Jiro Kawarazaki, Taiji Tonoyama, Kotoe Hatsui, Reiko Kasahara, Masami Souda, Muneta Masami.

If a person is "bread" for the street, they are not always a loafer because when they are on a roll, the dough flows and things can become a piece of cake. In Rica's (Rika Aoki) case, she returns to her protectionist instincts when she uses two baguettes to dispel a gang of racist hooligans who are attacking a young girl because she is a Amerasian. She then teams up with another reform-school enemy (Muneta Masami) to save Japanese teens from being sold into a Hong Kong sex-slave operation.

Although Rica still fights using karate hand postures—her right and left crosses have become her signature strengths—the fight choreography in this third film has in fact dwindled when compared to the first two installments of the series. Except for the baguette fight, the other action bits are pretty flimsy and much shorter, which is probably the result of a new director opting not to use the same style of fight choreography. What made the first *Rica* film so successful was pitting Rica's street-fighting smarts and no-fear attitude against knife-wielding Yakuza thugs, but over the course of the sequels, she fights less, and the filmmakers rely more on her reputation than her fighting. Undoubtedly, the money shots in the film were saved for the spear-gun killings. Although they are rather gruesome scenes, Rica and her pals laugh at her sure-shot harpooning skills while dashing all over Yokohama in speedboats.

Titleography: As of this writing, no alternative titles could be found. **MA Percentage: 6.15%**

RIKISHA KURI

大車侠 (1974—Hong Kong) **97m. FI: Lin You-chuan. NOT/LOT: 16/ 15m 43s; NOF/LOF: 11/ 16m 9s.** D: Joseph Kuo. C: Wen Jiang-long, Zuo Yan-rong, Shi Zhong-tian, Liu Li-zu, Shao Luo-hui, Liu Ping.

Sometimes a taxi driver picks up a peculiar passenger who leads to lots of trouble. Such was the life of the old Chinese rickshaw man, especially when the customers were no-good Chinese lackeys collaborating with the Japanese prior to World War II.

Chinese kung fu comic book enthusiast, Mung Xiao-lung (Wen Jiang-long), constantly gets into fights when he sees good people being wronged. Although his heart is in the right place, he does not know his fist from his foot. So when he tries to teach a Chinese traitor a lesson about not cheating his fellow rickshaw runners, he gets pummeled like an American football quarterback who has no offensive line protecting him.

When elder Ping refuses to sell the Chinese meeting center Kim Moon Clubhouse to the local villainous authoritarian, some Japanese thugs (one of whom is played by Bruce Li) kill him, but not before Mung witnesses the truth. When he threatens to expose the evil Japanese plot to the foreign authorities, he becomes fodder for a frenzy of violence that kills his mother, uncle and girlfriend. Before his uncle succumbs to the Japanese death squad and its Chinese collaborators, Mung learns a few deadly kung fu techniques, as we see him do the old trick of thrusting his fingers through a large, heavy sandbag. If Mung pokes you in the eye, you are surely going to die, and so the pupil becomes the pupil destroyer.

Although the fights in this film are as slap-happy as they get, which is common in early kung fu films, I have to admire lead actor Wen Jiang-long's performance. Many times during this film, his character gets beaten like a dirty rug, and you can tell that Wen is really getting nailed. Regardless if stuntmen are holding back, when you are being hit from all

directions by four or five attackers during a 30-move set of choreographed kicks and punches, it has been my experience that usually about 10 of those strikes land. When you do this all day, it really adds up to some big-time bruising. When you watch Wen, you can tell that when a punch really lands, he just keeps going. During some of his beatings, I could not help but think of Jackie Chan getting whomped by Whang In-shik in *Young Master* (1980).

Titleography: *Rickshaw Man*. Translation—*The Big Rickshaw Man*. It's curious that this Chinese film uses the Japanese romanization *Rikisha Kuri* for "Rickshaw Man" in the initial English title; perhaps a respectful nod to Toshiro Mifune's 1958 film *The Kishira Man*, in which he plays a rickshaw man. **MA Percentage: 32.85%**

RIVALS OF KUNG FU

黃飛鴻義取丁財炮 (1974—Hong Kong) **93m. FI: Liang Shao-song, Li Gu-ding, Huang Han-jie. NOT/LOT: None; NOF/LOF: 14/ 15m 34s.** D: Wang Feng. C: Shih Zhong-tien, Lily Li, Shiek Khan, Yang Pan-pan, Ching Miao, Bruce Le, Tong Chung-san, Chan Shen.

Besides being famous for his skills with the *fei tuo* (a weapon consisting of a metal weight attached to a rope), Huang Fei-hung was renowned for his morality and his bone-setting abilities, which he practiced at his father's Bao Zhi Lin Chinese herb clinic. As a child, Huang was a martial arts street performer, and he eventually became Canton's best lion dancer, hence the nickname Lion King.

The lion dance is seen during Chinese New Year, special functions and at friendly competitions among martial arts schools. One version of lion dance history says that 2,000 years ago, when a Chinese village was being terrorized by a lion, the villagers used gongs, cymbals, drums and papier-mâché lions to scare the beast away. The villagers then set off firecrackers in celebration of the victory, which is why they are still used during celebrations featuring lion dancing today. Although firecrackers as we know them were not invented until the Tang Dynasty (A.D. 618-905), their predecessors arose 2,000 years ago when chunks of green bamboo burned as fuel in fires would eventually explode. Pockets of air and sap would be trapped in the plant's segments, and when heated, the air in the hollows would expand and pop.

There are two kinds of lions in these ceremonies: the northern lion (which looks like a Fu dog with long red, orange and gold hair); and the southern lion, which is featured in this film. Southern lions are multicolored and have a horn in the center of a large head along with big (sometimes springy) eyes. During lion dances, the lion stalks food (usually lettuce) and a *hong bao* (red envelope) full of money (which represents thanks for a blessing). The envelope is either dangled on a pole for the lion to chase or, when martial arts schools are competing, it can be hung 20 feet above the ground atop a tall platform. This Huang Fei-hung film centers around martial arts schools competing in lion dance competitions, a competition that erupts when someone is lion—I mean, lyin'.

In *Rivals of Kung Fu*, when Huang Fei-hung (Shih Zhong-tien) opens a new kung fu school in Canton, he is greeted with a lion dance, during which he puts $200 in the *hong bao*. When the rival kung fu school headed by master

Shen Chiu-kung (Shiek Khan) does a competitive lion dance, the hong bao has less money in it, which is cause for war for Shen. Philanthropist Chou Li-de (Ching Miao) offers Huang money and space so Huang can have 200 students. In return for this, Chou would like Huang to win the coveted Happiness and Prosperity trophy. The trophy goes to the lion dance winner at the annual Goddess Guan Ying Festival, and it is a prize Shen always wins. Huang politely declines his kind offer. To Huang, kung fu is personal. If he takes the money, he would be obligated to teach what his students want because they pay him the big bucks. Instead, a good teacher should carefully choose his students, not the other way around. In today's martial arts world, these virtues are quickly dying.

It was common for well-to-do men in China to carry around a bird in a birdcage everywhere they went, including restaurants. Such is the case with master Shen, but to Shen the bird represents fowl play. Shen is eating at a restaurant and being served by one of Huang's students, Ghost Seven-legs (Bruce Le). Shen accuses Ghost of killing his bird and demands $500 in restitution, or Ghost will be put in prison. Unable to afford Shen's extortion price, Huang agrees to help Chou for $500 in order to free Ghost and beat Shen for the lion dance prize. Huang wins the lion's prize, and it is also revealed that Shen lied about the dead bird. Justice is served.

The film introduces one of Huang's most loyal students, Butcher Wing (Tong Chung-san), who actor Sammo Hung magnificently plays in *The Magnificent Butcher* (1979). Other films with great lion dancing are Jackie Chan's *Young Master* (1980), Shaw Brothers' *Lion vs. Lion* (1981) and Tsui Hark's *Once Upon a Time in China III* (1993).

Titleography: As of this writing, no alternative titles could be found. Translation—*Huang Fei-hong Righteously Wins the Prize*. The English title refers to Huang and Shen's rival schools. **MA Percentage: 16.74%** SHAW BROTHERS

RIVER OF FURY

江湖行 (1973—Hong Kong) **80m. FI: Yuen Woo-ping, Yuen Cheung-yan. NOT/LOT: None; NOF/LOF: 3/ 7m 18s.** D: Chang Tseng-chai. C: Lily Ho, Danny Lee, Ku Feng, Tien Ching, Yang Chi-ching, Ou-Yang Sha-Fei, Fan Mei-sheng.

Although the Chinese title translates as *Visits in the World of Jiang Hu* (the oft-written-about sub-society in this book), the literal translation of *Jiang Hu of Rivers and Lakes* is more appropriate for this film. The story centers on a Chinese opera troupe that travels by boat up and down rivers performing at local villages and towns. Traditionally, this was how Cantonese opera spread: The opera productions would travel on red junks to the various opera houses along the waterways. Many famous anti-Ching Shaolin fighters, like Hong Xi-guan, would hide on these junks and teach kung fu to the various boat dwellers and performers.

In this film, Ye Zhuang-zi's (Danny Lee) father dies, and Ye is determined not to be like his old man, who was born, lived and died in the same place. Ye wants to go out and discover the world. At the docks, he runs into an old friend of his father's, helmsman Duo Bo (Ku Feng). The family friend agrees to take Ye under his wing and teach the eager lad the ways of the river. They end up sharing a boat with a Chinese opera troupe that stars diva Ge Yi-qing (Lily Ho). Ye and Ge fall in love and get engaged. As Ge becomes more famous, her mother demands a bigger dowry, which Duo arranges for Ye, provided that Ye will help him run errands in the form of drug deals. However, rich sleazebag master Liu (Tien Ching) enters the picture. Because he can arrange for the troupe to perform in bigger cities and theaters, Ge and her mother go ga-ga for him and break off the engagement to Ye.

When a drug deal goes awry and the police are looking for a culprit, Duo jumps ship with the money in his bag and leaves the anchor in Ye's hands. Confused and abused, Ye gets tagged with a two-year prison sentence for drug trafficking.

Two year later, Duo is an established gang boss with a mansion and Ge as his mistress. Unfortunately for him, Ye returns to town. With two years of pent-up anger over his mentor and fiancée's betrayal, Ye crashes Duo's party and unleashes a rage like no man or beast has ever seen before.

Actor Danny Lee's pugilistic bombardment matches his character's psychotic desperation, especially in the final fight when Ye demolishes Duo's digs. If looks could kill, actors Lee and Ku would successfully strike the death knell.

Their long, unbroken stares add intensity to an already intense fight, the faces further gasping with glare as the actors punch sparingly into the camera for close shots. Although Lee is not a trained stuntman, during the final fight, as Ku Feng tosses him around the various sets like a wet noodle, sloshing over furniture and slushing through doors, Lee does a bang-up job getting banged up.

Titleography: As of this writing, no alternative titles could be found. Translation—*Visits in the World of Jiang Hu*. See above martialogy. **MA Percentage: 9.13** SHAW BROTHERS

ROOTS OF EVIL

Die Brut des Bosen (1979—W. Germany) **85m. SS: Josel Martinez Chichilla. NOT/LOT: 8/ 4m 42s; NOF/LOF: 10/ 7m 39s.** D: Christian Anders, Antonio Tarruellas. C: Christian Anders, Maribel Martín, Dunja Rajter, Deep Roy, Fernando Bilbao, Ria Kemp, Wolfgang Schütte, José María Guía, Ichimi.

It is the Austrian Robin Shou/Bruce Lee meets the dwarf-giant duo from *Mad Max Beyond Thunderdome* (1985). In *Roots of Evil*, Frank Materns (Christian Anders) runs a successful karate and kung fu school in Madrid in memory of his karate teacher, *sensei* Takamura. Although it is a karate school, Materns wears a karate *gi* in one scene, is shirtless in another, and wears kung fu trousers and shoes in the next.

However, Van Bullock (Deep Roy), a dwarf, wants to open the biggest and best fighting school on the block, and Materns' Karate Academy is in the way. Van Bullock and his giant bodyguard, Komo (Fernando Bilbao), come up with a series of conniving plans to get their grubby hands on Materns' property. First they ask him nicely to move and offer to buy his school, but he declines. They politely ask him to be their sensei, and again Materns refuses. Then they try to extort him, set him up to sleep with a prostitute who plants drugs in his apartment, and get him arrested for drug dealing. After Materns gets locked up and sees the evil that Van Bullock is doing, he breaks out of prison with the help of his girlfriend and goes after Van Bullock. The police are hot on Materns' tail, and Materns learns that Komo killed Takamura. It is time for Materns to avenge his sensei's death and pay Van Bullock back for setting him up.

Anders looks like a white Robin Shou and tries to fight like Bruce Lee in his debut martial arts film. Like so many martial arts films made outside of Asia during this time, the focus seems to be on self-promotion of the star, his martial arts skills and trying to show off his physique. The fights are done one technique at a time with the same rhythm: punch … dramatic beat … punch … beat … flex muscles … beat … flex … scream … beat … death kick. Anders does do one interesting training sequence, though. Decked out in leather and looking like some sort of fetishist, he lies face down on the ground, and without using his hands, does some weird snapping motion that makes his whole body fly up 12 inches off the ground, which he repeats several times in a row. He looks like a click beetle.

Titleography: As of this writing, no alternative titles could be found. **MA Percentage: 14.53%**

SAVAGE FIVE, THE

五虎將 (1974—Hong Kong) **91m. FI: Liu Chia-liang, Tang Chia. NOT/LOT: 1/ 34s; NOF/LOF: 11/ 12m 17s.** D: Chang Cheh. C: David Chiang, Ti Lung, Chen Kuan-tai, Wang Chung, Danny Lee, Frankie Wei Hong, Wong Ching, Jiang Dao, Wang Bing Bing.

In the vein of Akira Kurosawa's *Seven Samurai* (1954), this tale begins when a group of bank robbers rumbles into a small, peaceful town with a stolen safe that needs to be opened. The lack of law in the area prompts the criminals to terrorize the townsfolk to the point where they can get away with anything, including rape, kicking people out of their homes for their own use, and beating up or even killing all who oppose them.

However, there are five fighters who refuse to give in and conspire to defeat the disruptive visitors. The only problem is that even though they have home-court advantage, the villagers constantly boo the five fighters because they are such an unlikely squad. The ragtag group consists of a rugged woodcutter (Chen Kuan-tai); his student, who is also the town blacksmith (Danny Lee); a kung fu street performer trying to overcome a serious illness (Wang Chung); a learned righteous alcoholic kung fu man (Ti Lung); and a chicken thief who, due to his past, must hide from the bandits (David Chiang). It would seem they have no chance against such superior opponents, but being the underdog is something these five heroes have been faced with their whole lives, and now is as good a time as any to go after the bad guys with tiger-like ferocity.

Still from *The Savage Five* © Celestial Pictures Ltd. All rights reserved.

Sadly, only one of the five survives the slaughter, and the villagers chastise him anyway, leading him to limp off into the wilderness alone.

Although there are not many fights in this film, there are some typical heroic moments for those who bite the proverbial dust (as one might expect from a Chang Cheh production). They are left gushing blood, their bullet-riddled bodies lying still, and the people they saved will eventually forget them. The fights, however, appear contrived because techniques are delivered one at a time with very few combinations. On the plus side, Ti Lung gets to show off some of his *wing chun* training, which over the years he used less and less of, eventually to the point that the chun wings were completely clipped.

The one shot that sticks in my mind is when one of the heroes is dying and he squeezes his wound, causing the blood to gush out. It reminded me of my death scene in my first film, *Flying Tiger and the Kung Fu Kids* (1980). After I got a bayonet in the heart, my good friend grabbed hold of my wound, causing the blood to flow freely. First aid is apparently something most kung fu characters know little about, except the *chi* healers, herbalists and bone-setter heroes in a number of *wuxia* films.

Titleography: *The Savage 5.* Translation—*The Five Elite Tiger Fighters.* **MA Percentage: 14.12%** SHAW BROTHERS

SAMURAI

Biance, il giallo, il nero, Il (1975—Italy/Spain/France) **108m. SC: Nazzareno Zamperla. NOT/LOT: None; NOF/LOF: 3/ 2m 55s.** D: Sergio Corbucci. C: Eli Wallach, Giuliano Gemma, Tomas Milian, Manuel de Blas, Jacques Berthier,

Romano Puppo, Nazzareno Zamperla, Hideo Saito.

Imagine *The Black and White Minstrel Show* (BBC TV, 1958-1978) recast as *The Yellow and White Detrimental Show.* A white actor in yellowface (Tomas Milian) plays a Japanese samurai wannabe and dung handler, Sakura, who reluctantly teams up with a happy-go-lucky, womanizing thief named Swiss (Giuliano Gemma) and an honest old sheriff nicknamed Black Jack (Eli Wallach). It's their mission to rescue a prize Japanese pony from a bunch of Native Americans (also played by white men). I imagine that someone back in the 1970s thought this was a hilarious idea and saw the film as more of a spoof of the Bronson-Mifune film *Red Sun* (1971) than a buffoonish commentary on Asians.

The disparaging portrayal of Sakura—complete with slanty eyes, freaky facial hair and a garbled Japanese-English accent (his "Japanese" is also gibberish)—is a prime example of the prevailing racial stereotypes of the time. It must have been painful for the Asian actors on set to watch Milian's performance, having to politely smile and play along while likely wanting to let loose with some real martial arts, rather than the clumsy karate fights the film features.

There is, however, one interesting maneuver. During one fight sequence, Sakura draws his samurai sword, runs at Swiss, plants the sword in the ground and uses it to vault himself into a flip. It is a pretty rudimentary move compared to what was being done in Hong Kong at the time, but that level of creativity was rarely seen in Western sword choreography.

Titleography: *Shoot First ... Ask Questions Later.* Translation—*The White, the Yellow, and the Black.* In Italy, *il giallo* are cheap crime and mystery paperback books that specifically have yellow book covers. Perhaps in this film, it is a humorous, albeit insulting metaphor that Sakura is the "yellow book cover" of the film. **MA Percentage: 2.7%**

SAMURAI

(1979—USA) **67m. FI: Uncredited. NOT/LOT: 3/ 1m 36s; NOF/LOF: 4/ 2m 1s.** D: Lee H, Katsin. C: Joe Penny, James Shigeta, Beulah Quo, Dana Elcar.

This made-for-TV movie takes a kitchen-sink approach to martial arts. Lee Cantrell (Joe Penny) is a lawyer by day and a samurai by night who battles a greedy land developer. The villain uses an earthquake machine to run out an elderly man who refuses to give in to threats or accept ridiculous offers on his property. The code of *bushido* is boiled down to a ninja-like costume, a karate *gi*, some fortune-cookie philosophy and a few 10-second fight scenes punctuated by piercing-but-unconvincing screams. In the words of *Star Trek* actor George Takei, "Oh my!"

Titleography: As of this writing, no alternative titles could be found. **MA Percentage: 5.4%**

SCANDALOUS ADVENTURES OF BURAIKAN, THE

Buraikan (1970—Japan) **103m. FI: Uncredited. NOT/LOT: None; NOF/LOF: 6/ 3m 2s.** D: Masahiro Shinoda. C: Tatsuya Nakadai, Suisen Ichikawa, Shima Iwashita, Tetsuro Tanba, Shoichi Ozawa, Masakane Yonekura, Kiwako Taichi, Fumio Watanabe, Hiroshi Akutagawa, Hisashi Igawa.

Based on a Kabuki play by Kawatake Mokuami, *The Scandalous Adventures of Buraikan* is about Naojiro Kataoka (Tatsuya Nakadai), an angst-driven man whose life's goal is to become a deranged actor and marry the most beautiful geisha, Michitose (Shima Iwashita). Why deranged? Well if the shoe fits ... he has the soul for it.

But standing in the way of Naojiro's dream is his mother. Because she sees her son as a mama's boy, there is no way she will allow him to marry a geisha. So what would any deranged actor do with that obstacle? He bludgeons his mother, wraps her in a bag and tosses her into the river without a smidge of guilt. As her body sinks in the water, Naojiro rises triumphant and free.

But nothing in life is free. A recurring theme in this movie is that death passes by a person at some point in life. The filmmakers make the theme real with a death mask that various characters end up wearing. One of these mask wearers is an old man who drags Naojiro's mother from the water. Death may have seemed to drag her to the bottom of the river, but the metaphorical death passed over her by dragging her back onto land alive. (She wasn't quite dead when Naojiro threw her into the river.) The old man takes the mother back to his house, where she befriends his daughter, Michitose. Eventually, she agrees to have her shocked-to-see-her-alive son marry Michitose. In her happiness, the mother forgives her son for trying to murder her. Wow. What a forgiving lady.

I wonder if Norman Bates from Alfred Hitchcock's *Psycho* (1960) might have learned something from this Kabuki play.

Elsewhere, Soshun Kochiyama (Tetsuro Tanba), a humble tea master and go-for guy for Chief Counselor Mizuno, listens to Mizuno's complaints about how he wants to lawfully eliminate all actors and all things fun. However, Soshun is a secret supporter of the arts and gathers a force of actors to act like staunch samurai to rebel against these outrageous laws and assassinate Mizuno. Part of Soshun's gang of pseudo-samurai and would-be assassins is Naojiro. To Naojiro, this attempt to kill Mizuno is a deranged plan but something right up his alley. As good actors, they do make headway and get close enough to almost kill Mizuno, but their heads get in the way because someone recognizes that the samurai are simply actors. It is a bad time to see if their fighting is as good as their prop swords.

Historically, after the death of Shogun Ienari, whose reign of power was considered an era of pleasure, excess and corruption, the new chief counselor, Mizuno Tadakuni (1793-1851), initiated the Tempo Reforms. These reforms were aimed at tightening moral standards and eliminating frivolous and wasteful activities like festivals, Kabuki and *noh* theaters, fireworks, private prostitution, pictures, actors and all other evil luxuries. Mizuno's plans were rejected by the country's *daimyo*, and Soshun was exiled until the death mask caught up to him.

Titleography: *The Buraikan*; *Outlaws*. Translation—*Notorious Outlaws*. **MA Percentage: 2.94%**

SCHOOL OF THE JUNG-MU FIGHTING TECHNIQUE, THE

Jeongmumun (1978—S. Korea) **88m. FI: Uncredited. NOT/LOT: 1/ 6s; NOF/ LOF: 14/ 26m 56s.** D: Nam Gi-nam. C: Bruce Pak, Cheong Nyong, Bae Su-chun, Lee Kang-jo.

This is what a bad martial arts film is all about. It stinks, but so does a nice piece of Gorgonzola cheese, and sometimes that's just what you're in the mood for.

The last of the Ching Wu students, Bai Fu (Bruce Pak), travels to Korea in search of his kung fu brother, Ching Lung (Bruceploitation actor Bruce Le's character in the *Bruce and Shaolin Kung Fu* films). Once they meet up, the brothers plan to join up with Po Su Pai, the head of the Korean resistance, to fight the Japanese occupation. However, High Priest Sha, leader of the cult-like local Japanese martial arts school, wants to kill Bai to avenge his samurai brother Xi Sha, whom Ching Lung killed in *Bruce and Shaolin Kung Fu 2*.

The film's pacing often drags; it feels like a quarter of the film is filled with shots of people walking through the Korean wilderness at tortoise speed. But when Bai Fu starts doing the Muhammad Ali shuffle, you know things are going to get interesting.

The fights are insanely wrong but crazy enough to get a giggle or two … hundred. The strikes clearly miss their opponents, people fall in the wrong direction after being punched, actors stand around like pieces of wood waiting for their cues to attack, and some stuntmen flip-flop on screen as if they did their stunt before the director said, "Action!" One memorable shot involves a stuntman falling off a balcony and onto a table that is supposed to break his fall, but he barely hits the table and lands awkwardly. Then there is Bai's room-length flying kick on a wire, which is to-die-for in a warped-but-good way. And let's not forget Sha's secret Chest Mirror technique. He wears the contraption the entire movie, but only during the final fight does the light reflect off it to blind Bai. Sha stands grinning for what seems like an eternity while Bai squints helplessly rather than stepping aside. Perhaps a pair of sunglasses would have helped.

Most of the fights employ *taekwondo* martial artists, resulting in hundreds of spinning, side and roundhouse kicks. It makes for a good comparison with other movie fights that use stylized karate kicks.

Many DVD rental sites maintain that this film uses clips from *Bruce and Shaolin Kung Fu* and that Sha wants revenge for the death of his martial arts brother Xi Sha. The thing is, though, Xi Sha died in *Bruce and Shaolin Kung Fu 2*. The exposition even features a clip of what we assume is Xi Sha's death. In reality, the clips added to this film are from *Bruce and Shaolin Kung Fu 2*, and the death scene is Bruce Le's character killing Mao Yi and General Kawasaki. (See *Bruce and Shaolin Kung Fu 2*). Of course, it could be another case of inaccurate dubbing. It would not be the first time a story was unwittingly changed by the dubbers who didn't fully understand what they were supposed to say. I have been there myself and accidentally did the same thing in the 1970s

when I dubbed kung fu films into English in Taiwan. However, since *Bruce and Shaolin Kung Fu 2* has also been released as *Bruce and Shaolin Kung Fu* that might explain the faux pas about Xi Sha's death. Is there no end to all of this Bruceploitation madness?

Titleography: *Return of Fist of Fury*; *New School of the Jung-mu Fighting Technique*. When it comes to Bruceploitation films, the *Fist of Fury* title had run the gamut, so it was time to start adding words like *Return* and *Revenge*. It would have been easier and less confusing to call this film *Bruce and Shaolin Kung Fu 3*. **MA Percentage: 30.72%**

SCORCHING SUN, FIERCE WINDS, WILD FIRE

烈日狂風野火 (1979—Taiwan) **93m. MAI: Chen Shen-yi, Jimmy Long Fang, Chen Shi-wei, Huang Guo-zhu, Jin Ming. NOT/LOT: None; NOF/LOF: 21/ 26m 57s.** D: Suen Chin-yuen. C: Angela Mao Ying, Lo Lieh, Dorian Tan Dao-liang, Zhang Yi, Tien Peng, Shi Ting-gen, Li Jiang, Ricky Cheng Tien-chi.

When a violet is attacked by herbicides, it can get stronger via nitrogen (chemical symbol N) mutation, making a violet change to violent.

History tells us that in December 1911, Sun Yat-sen became president of the Republic of China (modern-day Taiwan), but in a final effort to save the Ching Dynasty, the empress dowager appointed General Yuan Shih-kai to destroy the republic. However, Yuan wanted to be president of the republic, so he offered Sun a deal that if he (Yuan) was appointed president, then he would oust the Chings. Sun agreed. However, when Yuan's true plan to become emperor was revealed, many provinces ceded from the country, foiling his plans. When he died of kidney failure in 1916, China plunged into chaos as provincial warlords vied for power. With paranoia running high, Chinese civilians would hide their fortunes, thus setting up the all-important cinema plot point of secret treasure maps.

In this film, gun-runner and spooked warlord Tung (Zhang Yi) protects the whereabouts of his treasure while battling the righteous woman warrior Violet (Angela Mao Ying), who is trying to curb Tung's illegal activities and bring some semblance of peace to the fiefdom. A prison-buddy subplot develops when two convicts who are shackled together (Lo Lieh and Dorian Tan Dao-liang) escape the chain gang. They hope to hook up with the ethical southern rebels led by Pai Jing-sing (Tien Peng). It is a race to somewhere fast, and at the end of the Chinese rainbow of potted treasure, the kick of justice awaits whoever arrives first.

With its 21 fight scenes, the film moves at a steady pace until it suddenly breaks out into a swashbuckling extravaganza. An army lays siege to a castle, and the battle is complete with ramparts, ladders that scale walls, boiling oil being poured on enemies and rock pelting attackers. Plus, it's all set to the *Star Wars* soundtrack. It's reminiscent of the castle siege in the movie *Monty Python and the Holy Grail* (1975).

The fights in this film overuse leaping attacks and diving strikes. It's half goofy and half doofy that the opponents dive at each other from all distances, including from just two feet apart. Also, before the final death of an opponent on the ground, the fighters leap straight up into the air and punch down, even if they are already standing over the opponent. I'm reminded of fight choreographer Yuen De on the set of CBS's TV series *Martial Law*. He would astound the American stunt men by screaming, "Bigger reaction, bigger reaction!" He wanted over-the-top strikes to add more emotion and power to his fight scenes, which leaping attacks and diving strikes do.

The fights must have been grueling because many of them were shot outside on dirty, dusty roads, something I dreaded in my days in Taiwan. Back in the 1970s and early '80s we didn't used padding; if you had to bite the dust, do foot sweeps or otherwise touch the ground, hidden rocks in the dirt would inevitably slice, cut and scrape you into bloody shreds. Landing on your back or head on a jutting rock quickly ruined your day because being hurt was never an excuse for stopping a fight.

Titleography: *Any Which Way You Punch*; *Dragon Connection*; *Duel Under the Burning Sun*; *Scorching Sun, Fierce Winds, and Wild Fire*. Translation—*Vicious Sun, Piercing Winds, Wild Fire*. The English titles tap into the Chinese translation (one of them adding the obvious showdown word Duel) and reference Clint Eastwood's *Any Which Way You Can* (a title used when the film was distributed in the USA in the 1980s). *Dragon Connection* is probably a nod to Angela Mao Ying, who starred in Bruce Lee's *Enter the Dragon*; of course, one of Bruce's other films was *The Chinese Connection* (aka *Fist of Fury*). **MA Percentage: 28.98%**

SECRET OF CHINESE KUNG FU

鶴形伏虎鬥蚊龍 and 五形八拳 (1977—Taiwan) 87m. KFI: **Huang Fei-long. NOT/LOT: 3/ 4m 4s; NOF/LOF: 17/ 26m 41s.** D: Song Ting-mei. C: Lo Lieh, Si Ma-long, Lung Fei, Huang Fei-long, Jack Long, Wang Li, Blacky Ko, Xia Ling-ling.

Posture, posture, posture. One thing I have harped on in many martialogies is actors who hunch their backs, strain their necks, and let their arms flap in the breeze or dangle at their sides. Keeping the back straight and the nonstriking hand close to the body are two indicators that an actor really practices martial arts. If you carefully watch big-time martial arts film stars like Lo Lieh, Chen Hsing and Yueh Hua, their lack of true martial training is as obvious as NBA basketball star Wilt Chamberlain being out of place if he were cast as a Munchkin in *The Wizard of Oz* (1939).

This film is a perfect example of a star effortlessly fighting with great kung fu posture. Even if you were unfamiliar with martial arts, you would still recognize how star Si Ma-long just looks right when he effectively battles one or more attackers at a time, keeping his back perfectly straight the whole time. In fact, Si was so heavily touted as being the Taiwanese Alexander Fu Sheng that when Fu Sheng passed away, Si's career also abruptly ended.

The plot involves former cruel convict Kang Ho (Lo Lieh) returning to his seaside home village. He kills the owner of a local fish-canning factory and plans to take it over so he can use it as a front to smuggle drugs worldwide. However, after sailor Chang Chi (Si Ma-long) is rescued by local fisherwoman Yi Yi (Xia Ling-ling), Chang's white crane kung fu pecks away at Kang's plans, forcing the villain to hire Japanese karate experts and Thai kickboxers to deal with Chang.

The best fights are the ones between Si and the actors who play the Thai fighters (Blacky Ko and Jack Long) and one of the karate fighters (Wang Li); and all were legitimate martial artists up against a good kung fu man. As technique dictates, the battles against the Thai warriors are smoother, with more circular kicks and punches; against the Japanese *karateka*, the action looks more mechanical, but with a strange sense of fluidity that is not inherently obvious until Si fights Lo Lieh. The fights then basically run amok and become concoctions of facial strains and forced-power body motions. Lo's performance could be good or bad, depending on how busy he was and if the choreography was something his limited martial arts skills could handle. But then Lo Lieh is Lo Lieh. When he's on, he's as good as many legitimate martial artist, but when he's off, it's like running up Mt. Everest in bare feet. For this film, "Brrrrr."

Titleography: *Secrets of Chinese Kung Fu.* As of this writing, no alternative titles could be found. Translation—*Crane Forms Ready to Attack a Tiger Fights the Mosquito Dragon* and *Five Forms and Eight Fists.* The *Crane* and *Tiger* reflect Chang's martial abilities versus Kang's lesser (as in small, like a *Mosquito*) *Dragon* skills. For the *Five Forms and Eight Fists* title, *Five Forms* represent the five animal styles featured in some fights, and the *Eight Fists* are loosely being used by the undercover policeman. **MA Percentage: 35.34%**

SECRET OF THE DIRK, THE

大羅劍俠 (1970—Hong Kong) **77m. FI: Tang Chia. NOT/LOT: None; NOF/LOF: 24/ 16m 21s.** D: Hsu Cheng-hung. C: Ching Li, Zhang Yi, Shu Pei-pei, Tien Fung, Wang Xia, Ma Hai-lun, Cliff Lok, Zhao Xiong.

Whoever was involved in creating an English title for this film must have been Scottish or aware of Scottish weapons. That's actually not too much of a stretch when you consider the incoming governor of Hong Kong back in 1971 was the Glasgow-born Sir Murray MacLehose, later known as Lord MacLehose of Beoch. A dirk (or durk) is a dagger formerly worn by the Scottish Highlanders, and in this film, it is a special weapon that is representative of the Da Luo School.

When a corrupt general ravages a castle and orders it to surrender, the remaining soldiers use delay tactics in order to the give the women and children time to escape death. Two generals, Liu Hui-de and Liu Zong, escort the women and children to safety while also protecting the castle's precious treasure. But as time passes, the treasure is lost.

Years later, one of the survivors of the exodus, Miss Liu (Shu Pei-pei), who escaped with her three children, is attacked by the beastly Black Tiger Gang. She explains to her now-grown sword-fighting daughters, Ming Zhu (Ching Li) and Xiao Lan (Ma Hai-lun), and kung-fu-fighting son, Hsiao Ying (Cliff Lok) that the Black Tiger Gang is looking for the lost treasure. The only clue to the treasure's whereabouts is linked to a sword and a copy of a Buddhist scripture belonging to the family. Helping the good guys on their quest to find the treasure

Still from *The Secret of the Dirk* © Celestial Pictures Ltd. All rights reserved.

first is hero Zhou Ying-lung (Zhang Yi), a senior student from the Da Luo Sword School with a very special sword that can shoot blades from its handle or open up like fan.

When Zhou and the three Liu fighters are trapped and about to die at the hands of the gang leader, Wang Shan-hu (Tien Fung), Zhou's kung fu brothers show up with the symbol of their teacher's mark, the mysterious dirk. A fight breaks out with plenty of slicing and dicing, and it is up to Zhou and Ming Zhu to stop Wang and prevent the Black Tiger Gang from getting away with the treasure.

This is a kung fu film by story, but not necessarily by the fights, because the swinging-baseball-bat sword choreography looks similar to Western-style swashbuckling films. There is also a lack of creative camerawork, which accentuates the fights' simplicity. One curious bit of trivia about the film: When we first see the main villain, all that is visible is his arm resting on a chair while he feeds a large crow. It is a shot right out of *The Wild Wild West* TV show episode "The Night of the Winged Terror" (1969), in which the villain Tycho is seen with a large raven sitting on his wrist. I have been told that show was popular in Hong Kong in those days, and I cannot help but to wonder just how far its influence went.

Titleography: *Secret of the Da Luo School.* Translation—*The Da Luo Swordsman Hero.* The English title refers to the dirk, a dagger that is representative of the Da Luo School. There is no *Secret* within the dirk itself because the first clue for finding the treasure is etched on to the blade of General Liu Hui-de's long sword. Perhaps the person who created the English title did not notice this and assumed the message should have been on the dirk. Because the dirk represents the Da Luo School, it may also be a symbol for any member of that school, hence *Secret of the Da Luo School* (i.e. *Dirk*). **MA Percentage: 21.23%** SHAW BROTHERS

SECRET OF THE SHAOLIN POLES

方世玉大破梅花樁 (1977—Taiwan) **83m. AD: Liu Chia-liang. NOT/LOT: 3/ 3m 4s; NOF/LOF: 15/ 20m 10s.** D: Ulysses Au Yeung-jun. C: Meng Fei, Yasuaki Kurata, Tan Dao-liang, Zhang Yi, Liu Chia-rong, Doris Lung Chun-er, Zuo Yan-rong.

One of most famous legends in Shaolin folklore is Fang Shi-yu (Fong Sai-yuk in Cantonese). Fang was one of the legendary 10 Tigers of Shaolin, who learned kung fu from Zhi Shan at Jiu Lian Shaolin Temple in Fujian province.

Secret of the Shaolin Poles is the third of four films in which actor Meng Fei plays Fang. The others are *Prodigal Boxer* (1972), *Young Hero of Shaolin* (1975) and *Invincible Kung Fu Trio* (1978). Manchu bigwig Ma Yu-lung has it in for Fang because he killed many of Ma's top commanders and fighters in the ongoing Ming-Ching struggle. Ma imports Japan's top martial arts killer, Ryunokai Daisai (Yasuaki Kurata; the English dub renames the character as Dragon Lee) to challenge Fang to a fight to the death on Ma's Palm Flower Post Pattern. The basketball-court-sized pit features 6-foot-tall-by-6-inch-wide wooden logs looming over bamboo punji sticks and other deadly traps. In order to draw Fang out from hiding, Ma kidnaps Fang's mother and Ryunokai makes lewd sexual advances on Fang's girlfriend, Hsiang Zhun (Zuo Yan-rong). Ma's crippled kung fu brother, Chiu Mai (Tan Dao-liang), is sympathetic toward Fang's cause and begs Ma to forgive him. But Ma refuses even him.

Many different styles use post-pattern training, such as *ninjutsu* and *ba qua*. For about two years while I was studying *zi ran men* (the natural door), I practiced atop five 5-foot-tall posts in which one was positioned in the center of the four other corner posts. After an hour up on the posts, practicing kung fu movements on the ground suddenly feels light, and your stances feel incredibly firm.

Fellow producer-director in the 1970s, Ng See-yuen, was influenced by this modernized-looking version of the classic Shaolin hero when he envisioned Jackie Chan portraying the nontraditional version of Huang Fei-hong in *Drunken Master* (1978). Though both characters historically had the traditional queue hairstyle, these cinematic versions have long, floppy hair, with Meng Fei's Fang having a subtle queue. Meng's large fan used for fighting and his stylish long Chinese robe are also both used in Chan's *Young Master* (1980). The fighting atop posts was summarily copied later in the year in Jimmy Wong Yu's *Killer Meteor* and in Donnie Yen's 1993 version of *Iron Monkey*. (For more on queues, please get in line and see *Hand of Death* (1976)).

Titleography: *Story of Fang Shi-yu, Prodigal Boxer 2*. Translation—*Fang Shi-yu Easily Defeats the Palm Flower Post*. The implication behind the Chinese title is not just about victory, but about the importance of overcoming obstacles. The film is not really a sequel to *Prodigal Boxer*, per se. Although the same actor plays the same character, it is a different-looking Fang, the stories are not related, and there is no sense of continuation. **MA Percentage: 27.99%**

SECRET RIVALS, THE

南拳北腿 (1976—Hong Kong) **85m. KFI: Tommy Lee, Zhang Quan. NOT/LOT: 12/ 8m 45s; NOF/LOF: 22/ 21m 17s.** D: Ng See-yuen, James Nam Gung-fan. C: John Liu, Wong Dao, Hwang Jang-lee, James Nam Gung-fan, Lee Ye-min, Lu Hsiu-chen, Nam Chung-il.

The Secret Rivals was the breakout film for three relatively new important actors in the martial arts genre of the 1970s: John Liu, a flexible *taekwondo* specialist who kicks well only with his right foot; Hwang Jang-lee, a highly skilled taekwondo fighter known for powerful kicks who kicks well with both feet; and Wong Dao, a relatively proficient taekwondo stylist also well-schooled in *hong jia* kung fu who does no kicks in this film.

Sheng Ying-wei (Wong Dao) is sent to Korea to find Silver Fox (Hwang Jang-lee), who works for a Chinese warlord and has set up shop in Korea. Shao Yi-fei (John Liu) also wants to take down the coldhearted Silver Fox because he burned Shao's parents at the stake. Sheng unwittingly increases the rivalry between himself and Shao by not realizing that Shao is also vying for the affections of the warm-hearted Ching Chin-chin (Lu Hsiu-chen).

Actor Liu is prominently featured showing rubbery-leg flexibility, doing what became his signature sequences of splits, holding up his right leg with his right hand, and kicking hanging pots. During his fights, Liu never throws a combination of spinning kicks in which his left leg throws the last kick; that usually indicates that leg is weaker and also explains why in most films he avoids low static stances. Also listen for the music from the spaghetti Western *The Big Gundown* (1966) during his training sequences.

Not wishing to distract too much from Liu's kicking skills, the choreographers blended Hwang's kicking abilities with somewhat suspect-looking white crane hand gestures, but ultimately he looks different from Liu because he kicks well with both legs. His kicking is more balanced, and as a result he looks more powerful.

Although Wong's taekwondo is very good, he lacks the exacting kicking skills of Liu and Hwang, so the choreographers took advantage of his physique. Most of Wong's training scenes are more about letting Wong flex his muscles for the camera. But because all the other fighters in the film are trained in Korean martial arts (there is a lot of kicking in the film), the choreography can get a bit boring because it begins to look the same in each fight. Wong's posing comes across a lot like Bruce Lee, with similar facial expressions, hairstyle and use of *nunchaku*, and the same dubbed voice actor as Lee in *Fist of Fury*.

A note of interest: One of the problems of Chinese kung fu films with English subtitles is that often a character's Chinese name is subtitled as a translated name rather than a romanized name. So if you do not read or speak Chinese,

you would never realize that Silver Fox's name is actually Sheng Ying-wei. Even though the film character's name is sometimes romanized—e.g., the Chinese subtitle uses the Chinese characters for a name, and that name is romanized in the English subtitle, as in Sheng Ying-wei—it is the English subtitled translation of the name that becomes famous in the West. Thus, English names in the subtitles don't always match their Chinese name in the dialogue.

Titleography: *Enter the Silver Fox*; *Silver Fox Rivals*; *Secret Rivals: The Northern Leg and Southern fist*; *Secret Agents*; *Secret Envoy*. Translation—*Southern Fist, Northern Legs*. Hwang's Silver Fox look with white hair was popular with Hong Kong crowds. So when the character showed up in other films as a villain with white hair, English titles put *Silver Fox* in those film titles (even if his Chinese character's name was not Silver Fox). *Enter the Silver Fox* also borrows from Bruce Lee's *Enter the Dragon* title. Sheng and Shao are the *Silver Fox Rivals*. The Chinese title refers to the kung fu techniques of Shen and Shao, which are *Southern Fist* and *Northern Legs*, respectively. Southern styles of kung fu are known for their fists, and northern styles for kicking. **MA Percentage: 35.33%**

SECRET RIVALS, PART 2, THE

南拳北腿鬥金狐 (1977—Hong Kong) **78m. FI: Yuen Woo-ping. NOT/LOT: 11/ 9m 50s; NOF/LOF: 28/ 32m 17s.** D: Ng See-yuen. C: John Liu, Tino Wong Cheung, Hwang Jang-lee, Chen Yao-lin, Charlie, Yuen Kwei, Hsu Hsia, Gao Fei, Blacky Ko, Tu Song-zhao.

This film is an example of a studio wanting to do a sequel after killing off one of the main characters. The solution? A twin brother. When John Woo did the same with Chow Yun-fat's character in *A Better Tomorrow* (1986), many fans thought it was a chintzy move, but it is good to know that everyone might have a twin zipping around awaiting his or her call to revenge.

John Liu and Hwang Jang-lee return to the film that essentially put their movie careers on the map. Shao Yi-fei (John Liu) now unites with Sheng Ying-wu (Tino Wong Cheung), brother of Sheng Ying-wei from *The Secret Rivals*, to take on another precious-metal fox, the Gold Fox (Hwang Jang-lee), twin brother of Silver Fox (who was disposed of in the previous film). A robbery Silver Fox partook in that was mentioned in the first film becomes a plot device because Gold Fox, aka Jing Hu, finds a treasure map on his dead brother's body showing where the spoils are hidden. The problem is that Ying-wu has the Eight Diagram Medallion around his waist (given to him by his brother), and the medallion holds the key to the map's interpretation. Gold Fox sets out to avenge his brother's death by going after Ying-wu while also trying to retrieve the Eight Diagram Medallion, find the treasure and kill Shao.

Gold Fox uses an adaptation of the famed Er-mei sticks (see *Knife of the Devil's Roaring and Soul Missing*) but uses a larger version in which the swivel attaches to his hand and not his finger. Er-mei, aka E-mei or O-mei, is a mountain in Sichuan province and is the home to a Taoist nun sect of martial artists who created the Er-mei stick, a pointed rod that swivels 360 degrees on a ring that slides onto a finger.

The opening credits start with the final fight from *Secret Rivals* (not part of the fight count for this film), showing this film is a true sequel. Unlike *Secret Rivals*, which uses mostly Korean *taekwondo*-trained actors and stuntmen and thus has somewhat stilted choreography, Yuen Woo-ping's fights are oriented toward Chinese kung fu and have better kung fu appeal. But his creative effort falls short when he uses eight assassins split into two groups of four (one group against Shao, one against Ying-hu), which quickly falls into a sloppy disarray, especially in the long shots. There is also an iffy showing by actor Yuen Kwei, who once told me that he enjoys being behind the camera more than in front.

However, when the fights are filmed using medium angles, Woo-ping completely fills the screen with action. That's usually a good thing because we can see the techniques. But there are too many instances during the fights when the kicks and punches obviously miss their mark, which is something that Woo-ping's fight-directed films usually do not do; he's a stickler for making sure that a strike sells on the screen. The fights still move along at a good pace, but this is one of those films Woo-ping rarely speaks about. The fights also contain many instances of an actor doing the proverbial scream and then dashing into his next sequence of movements. Woo-ping moved away from using that device in later films. This film is also the first time we see actor John Liu kick the person behind him in the face with a front kick.

Titleography: *Secret Rivals 2: Revenge of the Gold Fox*; *Silver Fox Rivals 2*; *The Secret Rivals: Part II*; *Secret Agents II*. Translation—*Southern Fist and*

Northern Legs Battle the Gold Fox. See titleography of *Secret Rivals*. This is a true sequel, so *Secret Rivals 2* is appropriate. **MA Percentage: 54%**

SENTIMENTAL SWORDSMAN, THE

多情劍客無情劍 (1977—Hong Kong) **97m. FI: Huang Pei-ji, Tang Chia. NOT/LOT: None; NOF/LOF: 32/ 17m 28s.** D: Chu Yuan. C: Ti Lung, Ching Li, Yueh Hua, Derek Yee, Ku Feng, Fan Mei-sheng, Yu An-an, Ching Miao, Fung Ke-an, Xu Hsao-chiang, Wang Xia, Ai Fei, Yang Chi-ching, Chan Shen, Gu Guan-zhong.

The one thing viewers might not have realized about director Chu Yuan's labyrinthine stories set in the semi-mythical *wuxia* worlds of Jiang Hu and Wu Lin is that although they have lots of fights, screen time dedicated to the fights is always minimal. Chu makes the fights short and spaces them out to create the impression that there is a ton of action. And since most of Chu's films use fight instructors Tang Chia and Huang Pei-ji, the fights scenes often look very similar (barring the occasional use of interesting weaponry). As a choreographer, it does not surprise me. By this time in the 1970s, most choreographers in the Hong Kong industry had developed their own style of doing fights and using the camera. And as most people know by now, the choreographers usually set up the blocking and shot the fights without the directors being on set. Despite all that, *The Sentimental Swordsman* has a short fight at the 47-minute mark that is one of the most historically important fights in the annals of martial arts films. (More on that in a moment.)

Swordsman Li Hsin-huan (Ti Lung), aka Little Lee Flying Knife because he shoots knives from the tips of his fan, has been wandering for 10 years with his trusty sidekick, Chuan Jia (Fan Mei-sheng). He has remained outside the borders of China since he gave up his property to Long Xiao-yun in gratitude for saving his life. He also left his fiancée, Lin Xian-er (Ching Li), thinking she would marry Long.

Li also suffers from tuberculosis and drinks to deal with his pain and forget the love he left behind. He eventually decides to return home, not quite for love, but to catch the Plum Blossom Bandit, who has recently resurfaced and is killing many Wu Lin people. Li fears for Lin's safety.

On his way home, Li runs into another lonely soul roaming the snowy drifts of the north, Ah Fei (Derek Yee). The two exchange pleasantries and leave open the possibility that one day they may share a drink. Ah Fei stumbles on a security company under great duress attempting to deliver a package containing the Gold Thread Vest (Ching Emperor Yong Zhen, the man responsible for burning down Shaolin Temples, used to wear one of these for protection against assassins), which is ultimately left in Ah Fei's hands. Suddenly, everybody is trying to kill Ah Fei in order to get the vest because it is the only defense against the Plum Blossom Bandit's deadly darts.

Meanwhile, Li gets tricked into killing several swordsmen so evil factions

can accuse him of being the evil bandit; this sets up a battle between him and Ah Fei as well as the revelation about the true identity of the Plum Blossom Bandit. At the end of the day, it is neither the sword nor the dart that saves Li, but the cold, natural elements of nature.

And of course there's that famous fight scene: When I was learning fight directing from Yuen Bing on the set of Sammo Hung's CBS TV show *Martial Law*, I showed Yuen a Betamax copy of this film. Even though he had been a stuntman in the movie, he hadn't seen his work in about 20 years. At the critical moment, we froze the picture and he pointed out nine stuntmen attacking Derek Yee in a stockroom. It was the only time these stuntmen had all worked together on the same fight: Yuen Bing, Sammo Hung, Jackie Chan, Ching Siu-tung, Yuen Woo-ping, Yuen Cheung-yan, Yuen Biao, Yuen Hua and Yuen De. Wow.

Titleography: As of this writing, no alternative titles could be found. Translation—*Passionate Swordsman But Merciless Sword*. Both titles reflect who Li Hsin-huan is, but the Chinese title also tells how Li must fight. Two sequels were made, *Return of the Sentimental Swordsmen* (1981) and *Perils of the Sentimental Swordsman* (1982). **MA Percentage: 18.01%** SHAW BROTHERS

SEVEN COMMANDMENTS OF KUNG FU, THE

功夫七戒 (1979—Hong Kong) **84m. MAD: Hsiao Ho, Xiao Pei. NOT/ LOT: 7/ 6m 22s; NOF/LOF: 16/ 29m 56s.** D: Ke Shih-hao. C: Lee Yi-ming, Zhang Yi, Lung Fei, Gu Zheng, Jing Guo-zhong, Ma Jing-gu, Gu Zheng.

What I love about this film are the opening credits and a later scene in which the hero is practicing praying mantis kung fu amid large models of the insect. He copies the poses and devises a fighting strategy from those basic postures. I immediately identified with protagonist Xiao Ping (Lee Yi-ming) because I also studied the postures of the mantis and their uses in self-defense when I was working on an undergraduate research thesis at Cornell University in 1979. Of course, Xiao Ping wasn't trying to get his degree—he learned praying mantis kung fu as a means of avenging his teacher's death at the hands of his other mentor, the vicious Ho Chin-tin (Zhang Yi). This is another film drenched in Suexploitation—exploiting the Beggar Su character popularized by Simon Yuen Xiao-tian in Jackie Chan's *Drunken Master* (1979).

Similar to a praying mantis that kills ruthlessly, Ho teaches Xiao Ping to kill without regard and without mercy. Knowing that Ho will be waiting for him to seek revenge, Xiao Ping goes off into the forest on his own to do some extra training. He builds some elaborate giant straw praying mantises and begins to figure out how to kill. Despite his training, Xiao Ping is still a righteous lad. He just can't turn on the killer's instinct like a MMA fighter because his heart is full of mercy and compassion toward all people. But will this be his undoing?

According to Chinese history, around 1656 (although some believe it was as early as the 11th century, others in 1794), the Shaolin monk Wang Lung, dismayed after a recent combative loss, was studying his Buddhist texts when he was disturbed by the sound of a praying mantis attacking a cricket. Astonished by how easily the mantis defeated its prey, Wang began prodding the mantis with a piece of straw and observed how the insect jumped back and forth to escape harm and used its front legs to parry, then finally grasp and crush the straw. After years of studying the insect, Wang developed the 13 Arm and Hand Movements of the Mantis. My own collegiate research goal was to scientifically recreate Wang Lung's work. During the opening credits of this film, knowledgeable audiences will recognize actor Yi-min using the popular northern style of seven star praying mantis boxing along a series of seven connected points that look like a star constellation. (Note: There is also a southern style created by the Hakka people based on observations of a praying mantis attacking a bird.)

After logging hundreds of hours of videotaping myself poking at a mantis, having large predatory insects attack the mantis and watching mantises fight each other, I was able to identify 10 representative behavioral patterns employed by the mantis during attack, defense and provocation. I then figured out what a human could do to replicate its movements. A few years after receiving my degree at Cornell, while studying rice-pest management in Taiwan, I met a master of praying mantis kung fu. I could not resist sharing my research findings with him. By that time, I had put the 10 movements into a sequence representative of a form. His jaw dropped. He claimed that I had crudely performed 10 of the 13 basic hand and arm techniques created by Wang Lung. He called me the American Wang Lang. I joked that since Wang probably studied the larger, 5-inch-long Chinese mantis, *Tenedora aridifolia sinensis*, it might explain why I missed the other three movements observing the 2-inch European mantis, *Mantis religiosa L*.

Titleography: *Kung Fu Seven Warnings*; *The 7 Commandments of Kung Fu.* Translation—*Kung Fu Seven Forbidden* (i.e., things you should never do). The alternative English title and the Chinese title refer to the seven rules of fighting to live by, as told to Xiao Ping by his *sifu*, Lu Zi-hai. **MA Percentage: 43.21%**

SEVEN GRAND MASTERS, THE

虎豹龍蛇鷹 and 虎豹龍蛇鷹絕拳 (1978—Hong Kong) **95m. MAD: Yuen Kwei, Yuen Cheung-yan. NOT/LOT: 7/ 5m 44s; NOF/LOF: 24/ 31m 54s.** D: Joseph Kuo. C: Lee Yi-min, Jack Long, Alan Hsu, Lung Fei, Long Guan-wu, Yuen Kwei, Alan Hsu, Chien Yueh-sheng, Yan Nan-xi.

Over the centuries, many kung fu techniques and styles have disappeared or dwindled because teachers do not always pass on everything they know. A teacher might withhold a technique in case a student ever turns and tries to kill the teacher or take over the school with it. This way, the teacher always has a trick up his sleeve. Unfortunately, when the teacher dies, the technique dies with him.

In order to retire from fighting with a clear mind and to accept the accolades from the emperor as the best martial artist in Kiang Nan, Bai Mei kung fu master Shang Guan-cheng (Jack Long) must accept the challenges from seven grandmasters and defeat them. As Shang travels around the country to meet, greet and beat these mostly honorable kung fu men, a happy-go-lucky orphan named Hsiao Ying (Lee Yi-min) repeatedly begs Shang to teach him. A wayfaring stranger also encourages Hsiao's efforts in persuasion, but Shang is wary of taking on new students because when he was a student, his kung fu brother Ku Yi-fung (Alan Hsu) betrayed their teacher and stole three pages from *The 12 Strikes of Bai Mei*, a book entrusted to Shang.

After Hsiao saves Shang's life, Shang accepts him as a student and teaches him nine strikes of Bai Mei (three are missing). Hsiao turns on Shang and uses these skills against him because he thinks Shang killed his father. As you might guess, the wayfaring stranger is the evil man Ku, who is behind the murder plot and hopes to get his hands on the rest of the manual.

The fight choreography, kung fu actors and martial skills in *The Seven Grand Masters* are superb. Each style and weapon technique is clearly translated on-screen, and the actors move and fight just as one would expect according to their styles. Jack Long has an old face, and when he dons the right wig, he brings life to the old sifu Shang, with many years of injuries and fights behind him. The weapon sequence between Long and fight instructor Yuen Kwei, who plays the champion grandmaster of Hu Bei, is smooth. The ease of transitions between the various weapons also effectively reveals both actors' Beijing opera backgrounds. As is common in many kung fu films, when the 12 strikes of Bai Mei are being used, there is a voice-over explaining each movement.

In history, Bai Mei kung fu was created by one of the Five Elders of Shaolin, the white-eyebrowed priest-turned-Wu Dung (aka Wu Tang) Bai Mei. (see *Executioners From Shaolin* and *Clan of the White Lotus*). It is estimated that eventually 90 percent of the Ching army practiced Bai Mei. Because of this auspicious beginning, for about 100 years, people who practiced Bai Mei kung fu were considered traitors to China and the Shaolin.

Titleography: *The 7 Grand Masters.* Translations—*Tiger, Leopard, Dragon, Snake and Eagle* and *Tiger, Leopard, Dragon, Snake, Eagle and Unparalleled Fist.* The Chinese titles are based on the kung fu styles of the various grandmasters Shang faced, with the style *Unparalleled Fist* being his own. There are seven grandmaster characters in the film, although two are from the unparalleled fist school, so the second Chinese title makes better figurative sense. **MA Percentage: 39.6%**

SEVEN MAN ARMY

八道樓子 (1976—Hong Kong) **113m. FI: Chen Shen-yi, Hsieh Hsing. NOT/LOT: 6/ 4m 24s; NOF/LOF: 37/ 20m 56s.** D: Chang Cheh, Xiong Ting-wu, Wu Man. C: Ti Lung, David Chiang, Chen Kuan-tai, Alexander Fu Sheng, Lee Yi-min, Chi Kuan-chun, Wang Lung-wei, Gordon Liu Chia-hui, Liang Chia-ren, Bai Ying, Miao Tian, Ding Hua-chong.

In a weird way, *Seven Man Army* is a bit like the film *Marco Polo* (1975) set in World War II. Both films feature three Mongol villains (played by Wang Lung-wei, Liang Chia-ren and Gordon Liu Chia-hu); these actors also play the villains in Marco Polo) trying to kill Chinese patriots (played by Alexander Fu Sheng and Chi Kuan-chun, who are also in both movies). This film is also similar to Chang Cheh's *The Heroic Ones* (1970) in that (especially for Western audiences) it would have benefited from a bit more historical background as to the movie's

setup. The film opens stating that after the September 18 Incident (1931), Japan occupies three Chinese provinces with 200,000 soldiers, and on New Year's Day 1933 takes over Rehe. On April 21, 20,000 Japanese fiercely attack Gu Bei Kou at Ba Dao Lou Zi—the Chinese title. The English title of this film does not point that out, and the English subtitles in the film also fail to mention it.

Between January 1 and May 31, 1933, the Defense of the Great Wall campaign began (again started by Japanese, who after exploding hand grenades and shooting rifles, said it was the Chinese, thus the excuse to attack), which led to the Japanese capturing Inner Mongolia, Rehe and Manchukuo. Next for the Japanese was the siege at the Great Wall, specifically Gu Bei Kou, a strategically important section of wall located 62 miles from Beijing in the Yan Shan Mountains, which now brings us back to *Seven Man Army*.

Based on a true story of the wall's defense, the film is about how seven Chinese soldiers—Bai Zhang-xing, Wu Chan-zheng, He Hong-fa, Jiang Ming-kun, Pan Bing-lin, Chu Tian-cheng and Jia Fu-sheng, played by David Chiang, Ti Lung, Alexander Fu Sheng, Chen Kuan-tai, Lee Yi-min, Chi Kuan-chun and Bai Ying—held up 20,000 Japanese soldiers with simple guns, a few mortars and Chinese swords at Ba Da Ling (also known as Ba Dao Lou Zi), a section of Gu Bei Kou. For five days, the seven Chinese soldiers fooled the Japanese army into thinking the seven of them were thousands of Chinese soldiers defending the outpost. Prior to their deaths on the seventh day, the film recounts how each joined the army. The seven heroes also helped other Chinese forces safely retreat. Even the Japanese army respected the seven.

Doesn't this sound like the perfect setup for a heroic bloodshed film by Chang Cheh? Ding Shan-xi would probably have been a better directorial choice because this kind of film was his specialty, but as you can imagine, the film features scenes of thousands of Japanese soldiers charging the Great Wall with samurai swords and bayonets. It's all leading up to seven ultra-heroic moments when each Chinese soldier whips out his sword and goes ballistic. Chang returns to a classic scene from his film *Vengeance!* (1970), in which he intercuts slow-motion shots of Ti Lung's dying character with an actor dying on-stage during a Beijing opera performance. In *Seven Man Army*, shots of Lee Yi-min's Pan character dying a bloody demise on the battlefield are intercut with shots of Pan's character dying during a Beijing opera performance on-stage. It is righteous.

Some final historical notes: The September 18 Incident was the precursor to the Second Sino-Japanese War. Japan invaded China after accusing Chinese dissidents of blowing up a Japanese-owned railway in South Manchuria. Documented evidence, however, has proven that Japanese militarists actually set off the explosion. The Japanese government finally admitted involvement in August 2006.

However, an important World-War-II event the Japanese government refuses to admit is the Rape of Nanking. In December 1937, history clearly records that Japanese troops slaughtered 300,000 Chinese men, women and children and raped 20,000 Chinese women and girls. In the 2007 docudrama *Nanking*, several Japanese soldiers involved in the event are openly unapologetic about their behavior. According to the filmmakers, those soldiers have received death threats from Japanese people in Japan for their appearance in the film. The Japanese government has yet to make an official admittance of guilt, and the Chinese government continues to demand an official apology.

Titleography: *7 Man Army.* Translation—*Ba Dao Lou Zi.* Ba Dao Lou Zi is the name of the area of a section the Great Wall of China that the Japanese attack in this film. **MA Percentage: 22.42%** SHAW BROTHERS

SEVEN STEPS OF KUNG FU

七步迷蹤 (1979—Hong Kong) **84m. MAD: Wong Chi-sang, Tommy Lee. NOT/LOT: 9/ 6m 36s; NOF/LOF: 18/ 33m 4s.** D: Chester Wong Chung-gwong, Ding Chong. C: Ricky Cheng Tien-chi, Jia Kai, Chen Shan, Lung Fei, Tommy Lee, Lin Yi-wa, Wong Chi-sang.

The Chinese title, *The Seven Steps of Mi Zong*, best reflects this film's martial direction. *Mi zong* is a storied martial art for Huo Yuen-jia's Ching Wu Association. There are many legends surrounding how this style originated; I will share the story about the servant and the hole.

Hundreds of years ago, a servant wanted to learn kung fu from his housemaster, but the art was only taught secretly to family members at night. The servant watched them train through a small peephole, but he could only make out bits and pieces. He practiced what he saw and filled in the blanks with his own movements. When the students were beaten during kung fu challenges, the servant used his newly created hodgepodge of pugilistic prowess learned from secretly watching his teacher, and much to the surprise of everyone present, he bested his opponents. His skills were described as "lost track," and this is one of the fabled origins of *mi zong chuan* (kung fu). This story also inspired *Legend of a Fighter* (1982), in which Huo Yuen-jia secretly watches his father practice mi zong through a peephole, thus laying the foundation for Huo's Ching Wu Athletic Association.

Seven Steps opens with boyish hero Hsiao Hu (Ricky Cheng Tien-chi) leaping about on seven small, flat pans and trying to figure out how to use them to improve his abilities. His teacher, Li San-pei (Jia Kai), then arrives and warns him of impending doom. The traitorous Ching General Chu Chin-kung (Chen Shan) has assembled his shadowy Five Hands Gang to create subterfuge in the local town as a cover for his real plans: to sell out China by handing over a secret document to two lama priests. Hsiao Hu must up his training ante for the defense of the country, and he also has to figure out the identities of the Five Hands and retrieve the secret document from the two gorilla-sized lama fighters. Of course, he unites with his teacher for the final showdown with the traitorous white-haired general, who fights out of a very painful-looking side-split stance.

The archetypal white-haired villain is a historical nod to the Shaolin monk Bai Mei, one of the Five Elders of Shaolin. Bai Mei betrayed Jiu Lian Shan Shaolin Temple to the Manchus, who then razed it.

One of the training secrets of mi zong is toughening the knees. Today, this is done by folding your legs back so your heels touch your butt; then you grab the ankles, balance yourself on your knees and walk around on them as if you were on stilts. In the film, Hsiao Hu leaps around on his knees and is eventually able to crush fist-sized rocks by landing on them in this position. It is painful to imagine and to watch, and while it's probably not real, the filmmakers did a good job faking it.

Though he is tall and lanky, Ricky Cheng must have great leg strength and flexibility. In most of his fights, he remains in low stances or crouching postures to accommodate his short opponents. It's also worth keeping in mind that most of the shots probably had at least 10 or 15 takes, so his knees were under more stress than usual. When Cheng fights the two lamas, who are slightly taller than him, his fights become more flavorful and energetic. He flips and rolls off their bodies like a circus acrobat. One of the lamas is the 6-foot-2 actor Jing Guo-zhong, a guy I used to act with in Chinese kung fu soap operas back in the early 1980s.

Titleography: *Kung Fu of Seven Steps*; *Shaolin Raider of Death*; *Kung Fu of 7 Steps*; *Shaolin Raiders of Death*; *7 Steps of Kung Fu.* Translation—*The Seven Steps of Mi Zhong.* The only out-of-place title here is *Shaolin Raiders of Death*, as there are no Shaolin characters or even a mention of Shaolin, but the title could be a reference to the Chings, who are the enemies in this movie and raided the Shaolin Temple in real life. **MA Percentage: 47.22%**

SEX AND FURY

Furyo Anego Den: Inoshika Ocho (1973—Japan) **88m. FI: Uncredited. NOT/LOT: None; NOF/LOF: 7/ 8m 24s.** D: Norifumi Suzuki. C: Reiko Ike, Akemi Negishi, Ryoko Ema, Tadashi Naruse, Rena Ichinose, Rie Saotome, Christina Lindberg.

In the West, drinking and driving can lead to a backbreaking death on concrete; in Japan, drinking and samurai can lead to dissection by steel. But when the slicer is a female Yakuza, more than blood bites the bed on soft cushy pillows when your head lies on them … without the body attached.

Sex and Fury is an all-powerful, in-your-face "pinky violence" film (see *Rica* for a short discussion of the genre) that can only be described as beautifully demented. Its religious undertones are as daring as they are dangerous, and its heroine is as beautiful as she is deadly.

The film, set during the Meiji era in Tokyo, begins with Ocho (Reiko Ike) watching her undercover policeman father get assassinated by three stealth killers in the same vein of *Lady Snowblood* (1973). She grows up to be a pickpocket, master gambler and swordswoman bent on revenge, and she carries three *hanafuta* (playing cards that become a gambler's trademark) to identify the murderers. Each card has a distinctive tattoo etched onto it: a deer, a boar and a butterfly. During her journey of revenge, Ocho unwittingly gets caught up in a plot in which an English diplomat is trying to instigate an opium war in Japan.

Back in the early 1970s, having a Western female to do one's bidding in Japan would have given a man great face—even in today's Japanese society, a blonde American is considered a great trophy—so when director Suzuki cast Christina Lindberg, the June 1970 *Penthouse* Pet of the Month, to be the Western counterpart of Ocho in the film, Toei (the film distribution company) must have been pleased. Lindberg plays Christina, a spy for the English diplomat who not only has several tempestuous confrontations with Ocho, but also has a Japanese lover who is trying to assassinate the Yakuza boss the English diplomat is in cahoots with.

One of the most memorable and spellbinding scenes in the film is when Ocho is taking a bath and several Yakuza swordsmen storm into her bathroom, not aware of the grisly fate that awaits them. Ocho leaps out of the bath completely nude, swinging her sword back and forth and revealing beautifully embellished tattoos. Actress Reiko Ike uses a one-handed sword grip as she slices through these low-level hit men; this reflects both Ocho's confidence as a swordswoman and her disdain and disrespect toward the baddies, who do not deserve the use of her full skill level.

In the final fight, against better opponents, Ocho releases her fury fully and uses a two-handed grip. Each single blow is no longer just a horizontal slice to the midsection—she now deals solid, powerful vertical cuts that sever limbs and heads, spraying fountains of blood.

A few notes about samurai sword weights: The average weight for a 36-inch samurai sword is less than 2 pounds, and the average weight of the prop swords used in film is less than 1 pound. For parts of a fight requiring solid contact between two swords, a real sword with a blunt blade would be used. For general swishing, spinning and multi-attacker killing sprees in one shot, a fake sword would be used; it would likely be made light wood and painted silver. Either way, neither the real or prop swords would be particularly heavy.

Titleography: *Ocho*; *Sex & Fury.* Translation—*Elder Sister: Ochô Inoshika.* Ocho Inoshika's name translates into "a deer among wild boars," the boars being euphemisms for two of the killers she is looking for. The third killer would be, according to her name, out of bounds, which is explained in the film. *Sex and Fury* pretty much summarizes what is in the film, so it's an appropriate English title. **MA Percentage: 9.55%**

SEXY KILLER

紅粉煞星 and 毒后秘史 (1976—Hong Kong) **87m. FI: Huang Pei-ji. NOT/LOT: None; NOF/LOF: 7/ 6m 16s.** D: Sun Chung. C: Yueh Hua, Chen Ping, Tong Lin, Si Wei, Wang Xia, Tian Ching, Chan Shen.

The Shaw Brothers and sexploitation can often get opulent with such crass and sass, and with that come visuals that seek to reek. Given the success of Japan's "pinky violence" connection and America's blaxploitation, it was only a matter of time before *Sex and Fury* met *TNT Jackson* in Hong Kong. In this Shaw Brothers film, starlet Chen Ping sashays around topless while impaling and stabbing sleazebags—in slow motion, no less—and utilizing the room's grungy environment to full effect. Jackie Chan would be proud because he is the master of using a room's environment to bring out the most of his fights.

After its slick, James Bond-ish opening, *Sexy Killer* turns unnerving very quickly when sex-hungry villain Ma Yuan (Tian Ching) drugs, rapes and kills the innocent sister of Gao Wan-fei (Chen Ping), an undercover policewomen who has a bad reputation for crossing the line. Now she does more than cross the line—she erases it, draws a new one and crosses that one too. She then tracks down the local drug lord (Wang Xia), also a deviant. When Gao's only police ally, Deng Wei-pin (Yueh Hua), is double-crossed by his partner and Gao gets double-crossed by her four-timing boyfriend, the camel's back is about to break, and all it requires is the last straw. After Gao gets kidnapped by the baddies and pumped full of psychedelic drugs—snap!—there goes the last straw. Rather than become a demure begging addict, she goes bonkers and becomes a gun-toting mama and on a shooting spree. Imagine six floating Indian gurus who have learned to levitate in a room full of ceiling fans. If you can, then you are probably as high and freaked out as Gao.

The film channels the spirit of Pam Grier's *Coffy* (1973). As in quite a few Shaw Brothers kung fu films of the '70s in which directors were allowed to experiment with unique camera visuals and colors, the fights seem like a bit of an afterthought. And although the film has barely six minutes of fist pounding and punching passion, Chen's gruff grit holds the audience's attention like Shamu at SeaWorld. They both go over with a giant splash.

Titleography: *The Drug Connection*; *The Sexy Killer*. Translation—*Red Powder* (*Female Vicious*) *Jinx* and *Secret Story of the Toxic Queen*. Each title reflects various themes and plots of the film, but the Chinese titles are certainly catchier. **MA Percentage: 7.22%** SHAW BROTHERS

SHADOW BOXER, THE

太 極 拳 (1974—Hong Kong) **83m. FI: Yuen Woo-ping, Chen Tin-hung. NOT/LOT: 5/ 3m 17s; NOF/LOF: 20/ 21m 58s.** D: Pao Hsueh-li. C: Chen Wo-fu, Shih Szu, Frankie Wei Hong, Chan Shen, Yang Chi-ching, Wang Kuang-yu, Cheung Pak-ling.

Former Shaolin Monk Zhang San-feng created *tai chi chuen* in 1365. After leaving Shaolin Temple, Zhang came upon the Wu Dung Mountains during his travels. Awed by their majesty, he ended up living there and developed a new school of martial arts known as Wu Dung. (Modern audiences may be more familiar with the term as Wu Tang, as in the rap group Wu-Tang Clan.) As the legend goes, one day Zhang saw a crane fighting a snake. The snake used soft coiling motions to ward off the bird's attacks, and the crane used its wing to fend off the snake's strikes. Inspired, Zhang combined Taoist breathing exercises with these soft fluid, coiling self-defense moves and created the internal kung fu style *mien chuen* (aka cotton fist or soft fist). This would be the foundation of tai chi. Taoist monk Chiang Fa, aka Wang Zong-yue (it is common to change your name when starting a new life or spiritual beginning) taught mien chuen to Chen Wang-ting. Chen blended it with what he already new and created Chen tai chi, a way of tai chi that uses fast-slow and hard-soft movements; it is the perfect *yin-yang* combination. Wang-ting taught Chen Chang-ching, who then taught Yang Lu-chen. Yang made changes and created the Yang style of *tai chi*. Over time, three new styles of tai chi evolved: *wu*, *sun* and *wu/hao*.

Now to the film. Gu Ding (Chen Wo-fu) is a poor laborer who learns tai chi from master Yeung (Yang Chi-ching). He and his road-worker mates are cheated out of half their wages by their sleazy foreman, and the other half goes to line the pockets of boss Jin Dai-sing (Frankie Wei Hong). Soon Jin realizes that the only way he can be the baddest guy in town is by defeating Yeung. When Yeung refuses to fight, Jin turns to Yeung's student, the young man Gu. When Gu refuses to fight, Jin kills Yeung. But Gu stands steadfast. Tai chi honor and philosophy prevent Gu from getting even. Even when Jin violently beats him up and has a guy jump off a balcony and land on Gu's battered body, Gu still refuses to fight. (There are no tricks or stunt double for Chen—you can see he gets jumped on for real.) Only after Jin kills two more of Gu's best friends and rapes his girlfriend does he relinquish his battered moral compass and unleash his fury on Jin. The only problem is that Gu is not really using tai chi.

Writing this martialogy is not easy. Shortly after making this film, 24-year-old star Chen Wo-fu committed suicide. He never got to see the film. All the film's liner notes and many film reviews describe Chen as being a proponent of tai chi. Yet in the film, Chen's tai chi—my apologies here—is weak and disappointing.

The only other film about tai chi made during the 1970s that I could find is *Born Invincible*. Starring Carter Wong, it is more about *chi gong* (*qigong*) than tai chi, and the fights demonstrate no tai chi, not even a simple movement. I was also rubbing my head as to why the tai chi is so wrong in *The Shadow Boxer*, considering that Yuen Woo-ping was the choreographer. However, back then he did not know tai chi well. Eventually, he would learn it well enough to make Donnie Yen look great in *Drunken Tai Chi* 10 years later. The best tai chi moments in this film are when Yeung is explaining the philosophical tenets of tai chi while showing Gu five key movements, which he very awkwardly uses in the final fight. Chen's posture in the final fight is hunched, and during combat he uses excessive body motions and neck movements to look powerful. If he were doing the tai chi movements correctly, the power would have shone through without the posturing. Granted, it is a film, and certainly the choreographers require him to sell things, but even during the non-combative movements—flashing a few movements, striking a pose—his tai chi prowess is lacking. Again, my apologies for dissing Chen.

Although tai chi (really pronounced *tai ji*) is one of the most well-known martial arts in the world, it is probably the least understood. One misconception is that since the movements are slow, it doesn't take a lot of energy to perform. During the opening credits of this film, real-life tai chi expert Cheung Pak-ling demonstrates Yang tai chi. Note that Cheung's shirt is covered in sweat. Many practitioners and the average layman don't understand that if you do tai chi outside in the cold weather, you should sweat. This sweat is a result of chi flow. Another overlooked factor is that to do tai chi correctly and get its full health benefits, it is essential to practice chi gong in conjunction with tai chi. If not, doing tai chi is similar to swimming on land. Finally, although people are aware that tai chi is good for health and has spiritual and philosophical components, most are not aware that tai chi is an effective form of self-defense. If you don't embrace and practice all these aspects, then you can't completely understand tai chi.

Titleography: As of this writing, no alternative titles could be found. Translation—*Tai Chi Chuan*. The film equates part of tai chi's training to be like fighting a shadow, hence *Shadow Boxer*. **MA Percentage: 30.42%** SHAW BROTHERS

SHADOW BOXING, THE

茅山殭屍拳 (1979—Hong Kong) **96m. FI: Liu Chia-liang. NOT/LOT: None; NOF/LOF: 23/ 14m 51s.** D: Liu Chia-liang. C: Gordon Liu Chia-hui, Wang Yu, Cecilia Huang Hsing-hsiu, Liu Chia-rong, Lee Hoi-san, Xu Hsao-chiang, Wilson Tong.

This film is like an optical illusion: It is a full-blown Liu brothers production with excellent martial arts talent, but if you add everything up at the end, there's less than 15 minutes of actual fighting.

The film opens with an explanation of a peculiar phenomenon. In the old days, when someone died far from home and there was no way of transporting the body back, Mou Shan magic and corpse herders would be hired to re-animate the body with mantra or spells. The body would rise at night and follow the corpse herder by hopping.

Fan Zheng-yuan (Wang Yu) is learning the ways of corpse herding from master Chen Wu (Liu Chia-rong) while they prepare to hop a line of corpses to their various village homes for burial. When Chen Wu gets drunk and runs into some problems, it is up to Fan to finish the job. He elicits the help of his girlfriend, Fei (Cecilia Huang Hsing-hsiu). Meanwhile, police officer Xiang (Wilson Tong) is searching for Zhang Jie (Gordon Liu Chia-hui), a fugitive framed by the chief of police because Zhang can tie the crooked police chief to wrongdoings with local gang boss Zhou Qian-tai (Lee Hoi-san). Zhang decides to act like a zombie and blend in with Fan's corpse herd in hopes of evading the police until he can figure out a way to prove his innocence.

Because Zhou framed Chen for crimes he did not commit 10 years ago, Chen lost his kung fu school; that is why he drinks, gambles and hangs out with dead bodies. Fan, who is learning zombie-style magic fist kung fu from Chen, realizes that Zhang, an eagle claw expert, is not a zombie, and they decide to work together to set things right.

After a giant, almost yawning lull in the film, Gordon Liu breaks out some eagle claw kung fu and one can, for the moment, forget just how long it has been since the last fight. Another part of the film's shtick is that Fan is unable to use his magic fist techniques unless he or someone can read aloud the various mantras written on yellow pieces of paper that he has attached to various parts of his body. When they are read, he is able to invoke the spirit of the movement and translate it into defensive and offensive maneuvers. But when his clothes are ripped off, let's just say things get interesting.

Eagle claw kung fu is a traditional animal style that uses the movements and fighting methods of the eponymous bird. Its origins can be traced back to about 1250, when a Song Dynasty general, Yue Fei, was battling the Jins. One day, while watching an eagle fight, Yui noticed that it knew when to attack and retreat. He was fascinated by the efficiency with which the bird used its talons to grasp, crush and kill its enemy. Brandishing his thumbs, forefingers and middle fingers like the three-clawed talons of the eagle, Yui created 108 fighting strategies that focused on attack-and-retreat movements and incorporated joint locking, grappling, pressure-point strikes and flesh-tearing techniques.

Titleography: Spiritual Boxer, Part II. Translations—Mou Shan Zombie Style or Mou Shan Zombie Fist. Because Spiritual Boxer was directed by Liu Chia-liang and starred Wang Yu doing similar mantra-invoking kung fu skills, this film was titled Spiritual Boxer II. The Chinese title is the kung fu style master Chen teaches Fan. The Shadow Boxing may have something to do with zombie kung fu being dark and mysterious. The Chinese words for "shadow" and "eagle claw" also both have "ying" as their romanized spelling and subsequently sound similar. **MA Percentage: 30.42%** SHAW BROTHERS

SHADOW HUNTERS

Kage Gari (1972—Japan) **89m. SWC: Kuze Ryu. NOT/LOT: None; NOF/ LOF: 15/ 16m 13s.** D: Toshio Masuda. C: Yujiro Ishihara, Ruriko Asaoka, Ryohei Uchida, Mikio Narita, Tetsuro Tanba.

If you look at Chinese kung fu films over the decades, you'll see that there has been an incredible evolution in creative fight choreography. In comparison, Japanese chambara (sword fight) films have changed very little. This is mostly due to the fact that many Japanese fight choreographers were kendo practitioners, and as such, they tended to stay close to what they knew. There was no room to create innovative choreography beyond the traditional repertoire until a duet of films came out known as Shadow Hunters and Shadow Hunters 2: Echo of Destiny. The films are unique because they tried to break the mold in terms of chambara technique and choreography. The first installment, for example, has more than 16 minutes of sword fights; that is a lot of action for a chambara film prior to the 1980s.

The Shadow Hunters films take place during the Tokugawa era. Under increasing financial pressure, the shogunate is using dirty tricks to seize the properties and wealth of daimyo (feudal lords). To do so, the shogunate needs some sort of pretext, so it recruits an army of spies and ninjas called Shadows to dig up dirt. To counter the oppressive surveillance techniques, the daimyo rely on three Shadow Hunters—Moonlight (Mikio Narita), Sunlight (Ryohei Uchida) and de facto leader Muroto Jubei (Yujiro Ishihara)—to extinguish the darkness.

The Shadow Hunters' first mission is to stop a group of Shadows from delivering news to the shogun that the Izushi Clan is digging for gold on their own property's mountains. The Izushi Clan has an important document from

Tokugawa Ieyasu, the first Tokugawa shogun (1600-1616) that grants the clan permanent control of its fief. If the clan members can get this document to Edo and to the emperor, then the shogun can't take their wealth. The Shadow Hunters' task is to protect the courier from harm.

The opening fights for each Shadow Hunter set the stage for the novel action that follows. Moonlight always jumps before he slices or spins his body. He also ends his attacks with a jumping slice into the camera. Sunlight performs his opening fight from a seated position, which is unusual in chambara films. In earlier chambara films, a samurai might perform one or two strokes while seated to demonstrate his skill, but in this film, Sunlight performs a full-scale series of attacks. This is a challenge for the actor to showcase his expertise. With limited mobility, the actor can't use fancy sturdy stances or cool sword postures. The initial fight for Jubei incorporates a good rhythm of cut, blood, cut, blood. There are also single shots that end with Jubei dishing out some marvelous decapitated-head-impaled-on-bamboo gags. Most of the film's fights are shot at a wider angle than normal, and the director chose to avoid using too many close shots and shaky camera motions. The advantage of this is that we can see the technical skills of the actors.

The final fights for each of the three Shadow Hunters are also quite creative. Moonlight escapes an intricate series of mechanized bow-and-arrow traps while simultaneously hacking up ninjas. Dangling over a giant punji stick trap (a pit full of pointy bamboo sticks), Sunlight has to get back on solid ground while ninjas try to jab and stab him. Both these fights feature scenarios never before seen in chambara films, giving Shadow Hunters a unique feel. And Jubei? His fights are the exception in that they are the expected. Just as the audience always wants a cool gunslinger showdown in a Western, chambara audiences expect traditional choreography. The Jubei fight with the lead ninja, however, is still unique in that the baddie wields a giant kusarigama, which is a hand-held sickle-like weapon is attached to a long chain.

Whereas sanchin is an Okinawan breathing karate form used to strengthen one's ki, the fight choreography in Shadow Hunters was a breath of fresh sanchin air at a key moment in Japanese chambara film. Although this film would disappear into a conventional sequel, its 16 minutes of creative fights show why Shadow Hunters was truly unconventional.

Titleography: As of this writing, no alternative titles could be found. Translation—Shadow Hunters. **MA Percentage: 18.27%**

SHADOW HUNTERS 2: ECHO OF DESTINY

Kage Gari: Hoero Taiyo (1972—Japan) **89m. SWC: Kuze Ryu. NOT/LOT: None; NOF/LOF: 13/ 8m 18s.** D: Toshio Masuda. C: Yujiro Ishihara, Ryohei Uchida, Mikio Narita, Tetsuro Tanba, Junko Natsu, Yoshi Kato, Maki Carousel, Junko Miyashita, Mari Shiraki, Yoshio Aoki, Jiro Takagi.

The success of Echo of Destiny rallied the actors and filmmakers for this Shadow Hunters sequel. But a movie's success can be a curse because it can be difficult to mimic in the sequel.

The film is set during the Tokugawa era, and our three Shadow Hunters—Muruto Jubei (Yujiro Ishihara), Sunlight Nikko (Ryohei Uchida) and Moonlight Gekko (Mikio Narita)—are back to foil the corrupt shogunate. This time the shogun has his greedy and beady eyes on the Mori Igamori Clan's wealth. The clan members find themselves "canonized" by a shogunate government minister out to metaphorically blast them to kingdom come. This is how he plans to do it: The Igamori Clan had an actual cannon that they melted down to make newer and deadlier weapons. Because this is against the Tokugawa shogun's law, it's the pretext he needs to legally take their riches and land when he visits the clan. The Igamoris know this and hire the Shadow Hunters to escort a replacement cannon down a treacherous mountain before the shogun arrives. In their way are shogun-hired Shadow spies and ninja.

Featuring only half as much fighting as the first film, Echo of Destiny was not destined to echo the success of the first installment. The choreography lacks the creativity of the first film because of laziness or a tighter budget, and the originality is replaced by gorier, more over-the-top shots of severed bodies. The first Shadow Hunters created its own fight choreography niche and dared to go far beyond Akira Kurosawa's standard. (See Lone Wolf and Cub for details.) But in this sequel, the film melted back into the pot of gold that was the 1950s golden age of Japanese filmmaking. There was never a third film.

However, actor Ryohei Uchida's real-life expertise in kendo shines through. Even though he uses high, overemphasized sword swings and strikes, his movements still look good because his back and ending strike postures are firm and have a good martial line about them. I guess you could say that with the looming shadow of the cinematic axe, his character, Sunlight, still shone brightly, and his performance actually honored the film's Japanese title, *Roaring Sun*.

Titleography: As of this writing, no alternative titles could be found. Translation—*Shadow Hunters: Roaring Sun*. **MA Percentage: 9.33%**

SHADOW WHIP, THE

影子神鞭 (1970—Hong Kong) 78m. **FI: Xu Er-niu. NOT/LOT: None; NOF/LOF: 15/ 16m 28s. D:** Lo Wei. **C:** Cheng Pei-pei, Tien Fung, Wang Xia, Ku Feng, Lo Wei, Li Shou-chi. Gao Ming, Li Gu-ding.

Any film that begins with and continues a snow motif is something worth watching because it either means on-location shoots—usually South Korea in the winter, where star Cheng Pei-pei once told me everyone froze their butts off during shooting since back then they didn't have trailers or portable heaters—or elaborate sets in the studio where workers constantly tried to keep the snow from thinning. They would dump flakes all over the place, which would wisp away when someone walked by. It was a lot of effort to hold the look.

In the opening scene we catch a glimpse of Cheng Pei-pei's dynamic presence as Miss Yun snap, crackle and pops three ruffians known as the Serial Trio with her whip and then whips it out in time to save a wagon from tilting over. This distraction allows the Serials to skulk away. Arriving at the local Tavern, Yun sees the trio's horses and with a handful of whip-ass wrapped around her wrist, she stomps through the snow with Frosted Flake furor, creating her own Quisp and Quake in her wake. Entering the inn, she runs into the handsome, twinkle in his eyes Wang Jian-xin (Yueh Hua) who recognizes something about Yun's whipping boy attacks and asks her if she knows where Shadow Whip Fang Jian-xin is. She denies any knowledge and the fact that she handedly uses a whip like Shadow Whip is pure coincidence. Yun abruptly leaves as word quickly spreads that she runs a guesthouse with her Uncle (Tien Fung) at Red Pine Village

Still from *The Shadow Whip* © Celestial Pictures Ltd. All rights reserved.

Not befuddled by the obvious, Wang, along with various riffraff and Chief Hong Da-peng (Ku Feng), who are all looking for Shadow Whip, high-tail it over to the guesthouse. As it turns out, Shadow Whip stole 300,000 taels of jewels when he and Chief Hong worked for Xuan Wu Security, the agency that was protecting the jewels. Because Shadow Whip made Hong lose face, it is a matter of honor for Hong to find the jewels and Shadow Whip. Wang is looking for revenge against Shadow Whip for killing members of his family, and the other "*Star Trek*" who ruffians simply want the jewels. (*Star Trek*, because you can always tell which characters are going to die during the landing party.)

As it turns out, Yun's uncle is indeed the Shadow Whip, but only the Shadow Whip knows the truth as to who killed Wang's family and stole the jewels. The innocent Shadow Whip must now fight to remove this stain on his name by stopping those who point the finger of blame before it drives him insane. (Wow, that was a mouthful full of rhyme and reason.)

The action in the film as a whole is not particularly good, but do not despair, because actor Ku Feng stars in the most amazing whip movie ever made four months after this film. Here's a clue: It sounds like a bar on the dark side of

Jiang Hu and can be found in the B section.

Chances are that the bullwhip, which we tend to associate with the American West, was not used by the *wuxia* heroes or wandering swordsmen in the Jiang Hu or Wu Lin worlds. The Spanish Moors, who were North African Muslims, found their way to the Iberian Peninsula around A.D. 711 and are the probably creators of the bullwhip.

Titleography: As of this writing, no alternative titles could be found. Translation—*Shadow Magical Wonder Whip*. The translation is the name of the main character. **MA Percentage: 21.11%** SHAW BROTHERS

SHANGHAI JOE

Mio Nome è Shanghai Joe, Il. (1972—Italy) 98m. **MAI: Uncredited. NOT/ LOT: 2/ 1m 35s; NOF/LOF: 11/ 12m 44s. D:** Mario Caiano. **C:** Chen Lee, Klaus Kinski, Claudio Undari, Katsutoshi Mikuriya, Gordon Mitchell, Carla Romanelli, Piero Lulli.

A Japanese actor plays a just-off-the-boat Chinese immigrant in the Italian spaghetti-Western version of the American made-for-TV movie *Kung Fu* (1972). In the original American film, Shaolin priest Kwai Chan Caine is on the lam from the Chings and fights a renegade Shaolin monk out to assassinate him. In this adaptation, Fire Lotus Sect disciple Chin Hao, aka Shanghai Joe (Chen Lee), hides from the white slave trader Stanley Spencer (Piero Lulli), who rustles cattle and gleefully kills poor Mexican farmers. Chin must also face a renegade Fire Lotus master hired by Spencer. The opening fight is similar to the opening fight in David Carradine's *Kung Fu*, taking place in a bar where our non-whiskey-drinking hero is being bombarded with racist remarks.

Historically, in 1848, the first Chinese immigrants, one woman and two men, arrived in San Francisco aboard the American brig Eagle, which was part of the American fleet under Thomas MacDonough that defeated the advancing British fleet on Lake Champlain at the beginning of the War of 1812. In 1882, the U.S. government enacted the Chinese Exclusion Act, which prohibited Chinese immigrants from becoming naturalized citizens and banned the immigration of Chinese laborers to the United States. It is curious that the filmmakers set this film in 1882 because, if Chin were really to arrive in San Francisco from Shanghai, he would have been immediately sent back to China.

The Japanese DVD release of this film says that actor Chen Lee is Japanese but does not say what his real name is or why he acted under a Chinese name. Katsutoshi Mikuriya, who played the Fire Lotus assassin, was the owner of a Rome-based *taekwondo* school. It is no wonder the fights have a distinctive *taekwondo* flavor to them. In a flashback sequence, protagonist Chin Hao is seen practicing a taekwondo form while wearing a *dobok* in some shadowy temple.

One of the coolest moments in the American movie *Billy Jack* (1971) is when Billy methodically removes his socks and shoes before the fight in the park. Director Mario Caiano pays homage to that film by having Chin and the assassin remove their shoes before their final showdown. Another curious note about this intriguing film is that when Chin's girlfriend is sick, he frantically searches for an American doctor. But when Chin needs medical help, he uses acupuncture on himself. A final note: You've just got to love it when Chen Lee completely rips out the eye, optic nerve and all, from Klaus Kinski's eye socket. Keep your eyes open for the gag. Ouch!

Titleography: *My Name Is Shanghai Joe*; *The Dragon Strikes Back*; *The Fighting Fists of Shanghai Joe*; *To Kill or to Die*. Translation—*My Name Is Shanghai Joe*. Most immigrants who initially came to the United States were from Canton by way of Shanghai, and a common name for American servicemen in Asia was Joe. *The Dragon Strikes Back* is a later video release title, possibly using Dragon to invoke something Bruce Lee-ish. *To Kill or to Die* could be a generic title for any action film with death in it. Titles like these would often arise simply because they beat someone else to the punch. **MA Percentage: 14.61%**

SHAOLIN ABBOT

少林英雄榜 (1979—Hong Kong) **79m. FI: Deng De-xiang. NOT/LOT: 4/ 5m 32s; NOF/LOF: 27/ 20m 32s.** D: Ho Meng-hua. C: David Chiang, Lo Lieh, Lily Li, Hsu Shao-chiang, Gu Guan-zhong, Jiang Dao.

After the burning of Song Shan Shaolin Temple, two of the Five Ancestors of Shaolin, Hu De-di and Tsai De-zhong, and two of Tsai's students, Yung Zong and Zhi Kong, fled to Fujian province. They then established a new base of anti-Ching activities at Jiu Lian Shan Shaolin Temple. Zhi Shan, one of Zhi Kong's disciples, is considered to be one of the most fabled figures of all the Shaolin legends and the single most important individual in re-establishing Shaolin martial arts because most of his students became the next generation of Shaolin legends. While at Jiu Lian Shan, Zhi Shan also created the 35 Chambers of Shaolin, wherein each chamber represented a different level of physical, mental or spiritual training. *Shaolin Abbot* is based on parts of Zhi Shan's life.

Zhi Shan (David Chiang) is sent to Er Mei Mountain to find an ex-Ming general, Wu Chen, and acquire instructions for making guns and welding steel in order to create weapons to fight the Manchus. Shaolin monk Feng Dao-de (Gu Guan-zhong) overhears the plan and passes the information to the Manchus. While Zhi Shan is away, Emperor Yong Zhen orders his troops to burn down Song Shan Shaolin. After monk Bai Mei (Lo Lieh) hears that Shaolin is destroyed and only Zhi Shan has survived, Bai Mei takes it upon himself to hunt down Zhi Shan and kill him. Meanwhile, Zhi Shan recruits four fighters to train and help him prepare to battle Bai Mei and his evil Tibetan lama pal (Jiang Dao).

Still from *Shaolin Abbott* © Celestial Pictures Ltd. All rights reserved.

Actor Lo Lieh returns as the traitorous monk Bai Mei (see *Executioners From Shaolin* and *Clan of the White Lotus*), boldly displaying his iron shirt kung fu skill known as Golden Bell, which allows him to withstand vicious blows to the body. Of course, it is up to Zhi Shan to find and exploit the one spot where he is vulnerable.

The fights in this film are up and down, and compared to his performance in *Executioners From Shaolin*, Lo Lieh as Bai Mei is incredibly awkward. It's a testament to the importance of the fight choreographer: Liu Chia-liang, who directed and did the fight choreography in *Executioners*, has a unique talent for not only creating authenticity in his fights, but also making sure each actor fights to the best of his ability. That is not to say that choreographer Deng De-xiang is bad, it is just that he's not as good Liu. This is evident when you compare the

fighting performances of Lo Lieh and David Chiang in films that Liu and Deng choreographed. (For Chiang, compare his fights in the film *Shaolin Mantis*, which Liu Chia-liang directed and fight-directed.)

The Golden Bell skill Bai Mei exhibits is a real kung fu technique that can be practiced in any combination of three ways: by using the standing-post stance or hugging-a-tree stance, by using special toughening medicinal herbs, and by practicing *chi gong*. The ending of this film is different from what happened historically. After watching it and reading martialogies about the Shaolin Temple, see if you can figure out what is wrong and what is right.

In the film, the four fighters Zhi Shan recruits and teaches in preparation to fight Bai Mei are Li Jing-luin, Hong Xi-guan, Lin Xian-sheng and Gui Jue-qi. Although Li Xian-sheng and Gui Jeu-qi are fictitious characters, in reality Li Jing-luin was indeed a Shaolin monk, though Zhi Shan did not teach him. In fact, Li and Hong went on to become two of the legendary 10 Tigers of Shaolin, the other eight being Lian Ya-sung, Tong Qian-jin, Xie A-fu, Hu Hui-qian, San Te, Fang Shi-yu, Fang Xiao-yu and Fang Mei-yu. (Those last seven were Zhi Shan's students.)

Titleography: *A Slice of Death*; *Abbot of Shaolin*. Translation—*On the Honored List of Shaolin Heroes*. Zhi Shan was the abbot of Jiu Lian Shan Shaolin Temple and is considered one the most honored Shaolin heroes. *Slice of Death* is a play on this being a slice-of-life film about Zhi Shan, in which death is the operative end product. **MA Percentage: 33%** SHAW BROTHERS

SHAOLIN AVENGERS, THE

方世玉與胡惠乾 (1976—Hong Kong) **93m. FI: Hsieh Hsing, Chen Shen-yi. NOT/LOT: 15/ 6m 39s; NOF/LOF: 25/ 24m 43s.** D: Chang Cheh, Wu Ma. C: Alexander Fu Sheng, Chi Guan-chun, Tong Yen-san, Chen Hui-lou, Cai Hong, Lung Fei, Liang Chia-ren, Wang Lung-wei.

Because *The Shaolin Avengers* is a detailed remake of Chang Cheh's earlier film *Men From the Monastery* (1974), it is not considered one of his Shaolin classics. What is captivating is that each film uses the same leads for Fang Shi-yu and Hu Hui-qian (Alexander Fu Sheng and Chi Guan-chun) doing the same kinds of fights, but in this movie it is evident how each actor's martial arts have improved. Fight choreographer Hsieh Hsing kept the fights stylistically similar to *Monastery*, which was fight-directed by the kings of choreography at the time, Liu Chia-liang and Tang Chia. By the time this film was produced, Liu and Tang had split, and Hsieh had become Chang's go-to choreographer since *Marco Polo*.

In this film, after the burning of Jiu Lian Shaolin Temple, Hu Hui-qian, Fang Shi-yu and his older brother Fang Xiao-yu (Tong Yen-san) are fighting Fang Dao-de (Cai Hong) and swarms of Ching soldiers under the watchful eye of Wu Dung monk Bai Mei (Chen Hui-lou). As the battles buzz on, each of the three Shaolin heroes flashes back and reminisces about his training, family, friendships and reasons for fighting the Chings.

Shi-yu's story recalls (in more detail than *Monastery*) how Wu Dung fighter Lei Lao-hu (Lung Fei) destroys the Fang family altar after Lei kills Shin-yu's father. This in turn causes Shi-yu's mother, Miao Cui-hao, a student of Wu Mei (one of the Five Elders who taught Wing Chun kung fu), to put the late-teen Shi-yu through the rigors of Invincible Kung Fu. She immerses Shi-yu in wine baths. His whole battle with Lei on the *mei hua* posts is similarly featured in *Monastery*.

Shi-yu's brother Xiao-yu reminisces in his mind about the time he had to whip Shi-yu 999 times to get his blood to flow so that the pain-inducing herbs would get sucked in his body. Why did he have to do that? It's just the way it's done. But it tightens the bond between the two brothers rather than loosening it with anger. Now that they face death together, they audience feels greater sadness for them. (Although, nine is a lucky number in China, so 999 must be even luckier.)

Hu Hui-qian's multiple flashbacks mirror the events and fights from *Monastery* nearly beat for beat, except that the training is more detailed and the fights flow better. This is undoubtedly largely due to the fact that Chi had two more years of cinema fighting and kung fu training under his belt. Because of the added experience, he commits his martial movements as Hu with more belief, strength and refinement than before.

In *Monastery*, Fang Dao-de kills Shi-yu, but in this film, Shi-yu kills Dao-de, and Bai Mai and Shi-yu die after each inflicts a single blow on the other during a leaping, soaring, in-flight exchange. So what really happened in history? After Tsai De-zhong and Hu De-di, two of the Five Ancestors of Shaolin who

second message outlines fake Ming battle plans and is intended for Lo to capture, thereby diverting his troops away from the real attack. In order to get past enemy lines, Hong and several of his cohorts disguise themselves as zombies.

A few interesting things in the film: Lin initially fights using an old method of *dian xue* (or *dim mak*). In a sort of Three Stooges fashion, he strikes his opponents with finger flicks targeted at specific body parts and face areas. There is another moment (also seen in other films) in which an attacker runs straight up the back of his opponent with rapid kicking steps, then runs down the front of the same opponent in a similar fashion. The idea of this rapid-kick maneuver is to strike all the acupuncture points along the governing and conception vessels, which are the two acupuncture meridians located along the spine and the midline of the abdomen, respectively. There is also a nice shot in which Lo throws a sword past a retreating Ming fighter's neck and embeds it in a tree; when the fighter stops and turns toward Wong, he inadvertently runs his neck along the blade.

Titleography: *Legend of the Living Corpse*; *Shaolin Magnificent Armour*; *The Shaolin Brothers*. Translations—*Shaolin Brothers* and *Walking the Corpses in Xiang Xi* (the western central part of China). The *Living Corpse* refers to the fake ghost-jumping characters, while *Armour* refers to the Golden Garment that Lin is trying to recover from General Lo. Ironically, there is no mention of Shaolin in the film. Not even Lin and Lo's teachers are Shaolin monks. **MA Percentage: 20.12%**

SHAOLIN DEVIL AND SHAOLIN ANGEL

鐵首無情追魂令 and 鐵手無情追魂令 (1978—Hong Kong) **85m. KFI:** Dong Wei, Chan Chuen. **NOT/LOT:** 5/ 4m 38s; **NOF/LOF:** 23/ 22m 44s. **D:** Zhang Tong-zu. **C:** Chen Hsing, Wong Dao, Dong Wei, Hua Lin, Wang Hsieh, Chan Chuen, Cai Hong.

It just seems to be a universal truth that learning martial arts with bad intent will lead to a person's downfall as a martial artist and a human being. In this film, the seemingly righteous martial artist Wan Yi-fei's (Chen Hsing) goal in life is to be the leader of all fighters, and he believes the path to this end is to find the secret book of the ghost kung fu technique. Meanwhile, secret agent Han Hin (Wong Dao) is investigating a string of grisly murders by the Sign of Death murderer. The latest victim is Wang Fu, whose child Chen Wan (Dong Wei) refused to learn kung fu until after his father's murder. Yi-fei gets hold of the secret book and begins learning the ghost technique with the intent of defeating all fighters; the training involves some psychedelic-looking form of iron palm hands in a burning cauldren. Yi-fei becomes unhinged by his newfound power and grows increasingly evil. Chen and Han hook up with a Shaolin priest who teaches them Buddha strike in preparation for a final confrontation with the out-of-his-mind Yi-fei.

One of the unique weapons used in this film is the *bi guo*, a long-poled weapon with a hand on the end holding a calligraphy pen, usually at a right angle to the shaft. The nails of the fingers or the tip of the pen strike acupuncture points on the opponent's body. Wong Dao's character, Han Hin, also uses a neat weapon: a belt that unravels into a sword, which was originally created as a way to sneak a weapon into an official's heavily guarded palace to commit an assassination. Prior to the arrival of Han in the film, the fights seem slow-paced and too methodical. When he does appear, the camera is undercranked, making his fights amazingly quick and sharp, which conveys how skilled he is. When Han loses a fight, we know the bad guy must be great. Throughout the rest of the film, the fights are increasingly shot at normal speed, and the pace evens out to match Dao and Dong.

An interesting side note: My kung fu teacher in Taiwan once told me that his kung fu brother practiced a technique called poison fist, which must be trained with a pure heart. However, this man practiced with the idea of wanting to be a feared martial artist. After years of training, his hands became hard as iron, and people did fear fighting him. But as time passed, his hands turned black and then eventually withered into a mass of pulpy gray fingers. It was considered to be spiritual punishment for training with the wrong heart and mind-set.

Titleography: *Mask of Death*; *Kung Fu of Dammon Style*; *Shaolin Devil*

---

survived the destruction of the temple at Song Shan Monastery, established a new Shaolin temple at Jiu Lian Shan, it fell on the back of Monk Zhi Shan to keep the Shaolin martial arts alive. He carefully chose students he knew would excel in martial arts and also be responsible in keeping the arts alive into the next generation. Eight of Zhi Shan's most famous students, plus two other non-Zhi Shan students, collectively became known as the 10 Tigers of Shaolin. Shi-yu, Xiao-yu and Hu Hui-qian were three of them. According to some historians, Shi-yu died during the razing of Jiu Lian, and Bai Mei's real killer was Fang Dao-de, who feigned being a Wu Dung monk to get close to Bai Mei under the pretense of revenge.

Actor Cai Hong, who plays Fang Dao-de, has got to have one of the most torturous faces in all of kung fu film. He really looks agonizingly vicious and animalistic in each of his fighting roles. He is also quite prominent in *Five Shaolin Masters* (1974).

Titleography: *Incredible Kung Fu Brothers*. Translation—*Fang Shi-yu and Hu Hui-qian*. **MA Percentage: 33.73%** SHAW BROTHERS

SHAOLIN BROTHERS

少林兄弟 and 湘西趕屍 (1977—Hong Kong) **86m. MAI:** Huang Fei-long. **NOT/LOT:** None; **NOF/LOF:** 21/ 17m 18s. **D:** Joseph Kuo. **C:** Carter Wong, Tung Li, Tang Wei, Chin Meng.

In ancient China, it was believed that after a person died, he or she must be buried close to home. If a person died far from home, then his or her body had to be transported back as quickly as possible. Back then, the body was not shipped in a coffin. Instead it was herded back by Taoist priests known as corpse herders. They would enchant the body and march it home by making it jump like a kangaroo. During times of strife, it was not uncommon for a living person to act like one of these corpses in order to avoid being caught by the enemy. This film is based on a true story: Groups of Ming Loyalists tried to deliver important messages by posing as jumping ghosts in order to evade capture by the Chings.

Lo Lung-da (Carter Wong), a ruthless Ching general, asks his older kung fu brother Lin Yun-Chang (Tang Wei) to join his troops for a last major push to destroy the pro-Ming patriots. But when Lin refuses to join, Lo tries to kill him by throwing a poisonous needle at him, which is guaranteed to kill in a few hours. Lin escapes to his *sifu*, who temporarily saves his life and warns him that he has nine days to take revenge against Lo before the poison kills him. He must also destroy the secret Golden Garment (a vest that protects the wearer against weapon attacks), which Lo stole from the sifu.

Meanwhile, Hong Chun-jun (Tung Li), a Ming general, is assigned to deliver two messages. The first goes to the Ming high command, led by General Kuan Chen-ming, and outlines the complete military layout of the Ching army. The

Shaolin Angel; Shaolin Devil & Shaolin Angel. Translations—*Heartless Iron Head, Soul Chasing Sentencer* and *Heartless Iron Hand, Soul Chasing Sentencer.* The last character in both Chinese titles is pronounced *ling.* If you have ever seen a film in which an official sentences a man to death and does so by tossing down a long, triangular piece of wood with Chinese characters on it, that is called a ling. It is the same thing that Chinese ghosts with long tongues carry. *Mask of Death* refers to the Sign of Death assassin, who is introduced as a masked killer. *Dammon Style* is probably supposed to evoke the word "demon," or perhaps the character Damian from *The Omen* (1976). In either case, it would appear to be the result of someone who does not write or understand English well. *The Shaolin Devil & Shaolin Angel* title undoubtedly plays off the good-versus-evil scenario, with the ghost technique suggesting the devil's influence. **MA Percentage: 32.2%**

SHAOLIN HAND LOCK

十字鎖喉手 (1978—Hong Kong) **87m. FI: Tang Chia. NOT/LOT: 3/ 52s; NOF/LOF: 24/ 18m 14s.** D: Ho Meng-hua. C: David Chiang, Chen Ping, Lo Lieh, Michael Chan, Karen Yeh, Chan Shen, Hui Ying-hong, Dik Wei, Hsu Hsia, Brandy Yuen, Hui Tian-si, Ban run-sheng, Ringo Wong Chi-ming, Deng De-xiang.

As actor David Chiang moved past his prime and the slash, crash, flail and wail styles of fight choreography were coming to an end, discerning audiences began expecting more from fight scenes. The methods Chiang used in early fights started to lose their luster, and he had a difficult time changing his timing, movement and rhythm to blend in with the kind of precise fights being featured today. Though he would stick around for a few more years, his sheen on the screen was fading. Shaolin Hand Lock is one of the first films to show Chiang's difficulties in trying to do real, precise kung fu postures within staged fights. At the end of the day, he never threw in the towel and always gave it his best.

When Fang Yu-bao (Chan Shen), who hides long metal spikes up his sleeves, visits his old friend Li Bai (Dik Wei), a fight breaks out. Fang counters Li's famous *Shaolin Hand Lock*—a flip over the opponent's head that ends in a chokehold from behind—and stabs Li in the abdomen. Fang then kills Li's two present students, mistaking them for his son and daughter. When son Cheng Ying (Chiang) and daughter Meng Ping (Chen Ping) return home, Cheng pursues Fang to Thailand in order to find out who put the hit on his father. He learns that his father's old partner, Lin Hao (Lo Lieh), was the culprit.

With revenge on the brain and metal plates on his ribs (to prevent getting spiked during the hand-lock skill), Cheng launches his payback plan by becoming Lin's bodyguard, but Lin's current custodian of protection, Kun Shi (Michael Chan),

is openly suspicious of him. Soon after, Meng arrives in Bangkok looking to join the subterfuge, and everything spirals toward the final showdown with Lin.

The film spends a lot of time doing the travelogue routine in Thailand. It has too many speedboat chases through river pathways, but those elements do add authenticity to the setting: Audiences can tell the film was shot on location and not patched together from stock footage and shots in a Hong Kong studio.

The early fights are disjointed, with lots of arms flailing and too many hammer-fist strikes, which are easy to use in the controlled setting of a choreographed fight. The stuntmen are flat-footed and seem to be waiting for their cues to attack rather than looking for openings. This really distracts from the energy of the fight and was probably a result of using Thai stuntmen who were not attuned to the fighting styles.

Rather than being a barn burner, the finale flames out. The use of the environment feels forced, which is compounded by displaced wire work that interrupts the fight's pacing. For example, Chiang uses a tire swing to get up to the balcony and confront Lo, but it would have been faster and more logical to take the stairs. Of course, logic is one thing, but keeping up the fight pace is essential to maintain rhythm and audience interest.

Titleography: As of this writing, no alternative titles could be found. Translation—*Ten Words Throat Locking Hand.* The titles refer to the film's central kung fu technique, with the Chinese being a more accurate description of the maneuver. **MA Percentage: 21.95%** SHAW BROTHERS

SHAOLIN INVINCIBLE STICKS

棍王 (1979—Hong Kong) **87m. MAI: Tommy Lee. NOT/LOT: 8/ 7m 32s; NOF/LOF: 29/ 23m 33s.** D: Lee Tso-nam. C: Wong Dao, Zhang Yi, Jin Gang, Xia Guang-li, Jimmy Lung Fong, Cliff Ching Ching, Zhang Ji-long, Tu Song-zhao, Wong Chi-sang.

The pole position in this race of life is not about speed, but about family honor and being willing to truly appreciate who you are and where you came from.

When ultra-confident master pole fighter Chen Gu-yang's (Wong Dao) father is killed by the malicious Lu Tai-er (Zhang Yi), whose goal is to wipe out the Nine Stick Masters of the North, Gu-yang must, by tradition, take over the family mantle. But he can only do so after earning the right to carry the Chen pole by defeating his senior uncles. He fails miserably. With his ego destroyed and his kung fu embarrassed, Gu-yang is banished from the kung fu school and sent out into the cruel world to fend for himself. Unable to hold down a job, he is eventually befriended by street vendor Tai Li-lei (Jin Gang) and taken back to his home, where he falls in love with Li-lei's cousin Yu-Yu (Xia Guang-li). Through a series of gut-wrenching fights and emotional epiphanies, Gu-yang learns to appreciate his family's pole-fighting style. When Gu-yang hears of Lu's plan to wipe out the rest of his family and any other pole fighter in the province to become king of the poles, his training and heart go into overdrive.

In Chinese, the *guin* is just a plain, simple wooden pole (aka the *bo*, stick, staff or cudgel) and is considered to be the father of all martial arts weapons. It is one of the simplest and most fundamental weapons of self-defense in many cultures. In Chinese martial arts, the most common pole is about eyebrow height and can be made from various woods, such as bamboo, rattan, teak, white wax wood and oak (and for those with strong wrists, iron). Over time, the pole has branched into different manifestations, such as three-sectional staffs (see *The 36th Chamber of Shaolin*), lashing staffs, 18-foot-longs, rat-tail whipping poles, short batons and poles with iron tips, all of which are nicely featured in this movie.

Legend dictates that Shaolin monks are masters of the poles, and part of that folklore stems from the classic story of the 108 monks of Song Shan Shaolin Temple who saved China from the invading Russian army around 1664. (See *Shaolin Temple.*)

This film features some of actor Wang Dao's best fighting performances, especially his weapon skills. He makes a believable transition from bratty young man to well-honed master of the pole. His skill climaxes with a difficult fight scene in which he uses a basic pole against actor Zhang Yi and his long, rat-tail whipping pole deep within the tight confines of a lush bamboo forest. One can only imagine how wrecked their hands must have been from popping calluses and inadvertently whacking each other and bamboo trees

during the fight sequences.

Titleography: *Fist of Shaolin*. Translation—*King of Poles*. Both English titles stick in the word *Shaolin* to make the film more marketable in the West. **MA Percentage: 35.73%**

SHAOLIN INVINCIBLES

雍正命喪少林門 (1977—Taiwan) **90m. FI: Uncredited. NOT/LOT: 1/ 15s; NOF/LOF: 28/ 24m 56s.** D: Hau Chang. C: Carter Wong, Chia Ling, Tan Dao-liang, Chen Hong-lie, Yi Yuen, Doris Lung Chun-er, Jack Long.

This film based on a true story seems to stick to the path, until about halfway through, when two major questions erupt: What? Why?

According to the film, after Prince Yong changed his father's will and became Emperor Yong Zheng (Chen Hong-lie), he executed the families and friends of Lu Wang-chung and Yu Chiao. However, during the massacre, Yu's daughter Yu-niang (Doris Lung Chun-er) and granddaughter Lu Si-niang (Chia Ling) were rescued by a Shaolin priest. They learned the Lightning Eye Sword, and 10 years later, Yong Zheng was assasinated.

It has been postulated that a swordswoman named Lu Si-niang, the daughter of Lu Liu-liang (who was historically executed for literary crimes against the Chings), did indeed kill the emperor. An alternative version of the story says Yong died from an overdose of drugs he was using to gain immortality. A note on casting: Chia Ling was also featured as an unnamed female assassin who tried to kill Yong Zheng in *The Blazing Temple* (1976), so it is a nice touch to have her star as the assassin of an emperor in this film.

However, like many kung fu films, especially Taiwanese-made ones, poetic license takes on new meaning. Yong orders the official Lu Chen-gong (Yi Yuen) to hire personal bodyguards because Yong suspects the two women are coming after him and that they are aided by the Shaolin-trained warrior Kan Tien-chi (Carter Wong). Here is where the film goes off on a tangent: Yong decides who his bodyguards will be by fighting with them; if he is able to defeat them, he can trust them.

First up, he fights the Black and White Ghosts from Hell, who are also seen in numerous other kung fu films, such as *Forbidden City Cop* (1996). They usually appear with one fighter dressed in black, the other in white, both wearing tall pointed hats, and one of them sporting a long, dangling tongue. In Chinese folklore, they are known as Qi Ye (the one in black) and Ba Ye (the one in white). As the story goes, they were friends and generals. One day, when standing in a rainstorm, Ba Ye ran back to his house to get an umbrella, but he arrived back too late and found that his friend had drowned in the water (hence the black color). Ba Ye committed suicide in shame in order to be with his friend (thus the tongue sticking out). Legend says the two generals collect evil souls and bring them to the gates of hell to be punished.

The film's wackiness goes a step further when Zhong next fights a pair of full-grown male gorillas—yes, gorillas. Of course, these two silverbacks become the official bodyguards of the emperor of China. I think I read once that Ivan the Terrible, the Russian czar, had twin grizzly bears as bodyguards, so maybe it's not such a crazy idea after all.

Titleography: *The Thrilling Sword*. Translation—*Yong Zheng Died in Shaolin School*. You can believe Yong died in the Shaolin Temple in as much as you can believe he had gorillas as bodyguards. *Thrilling Sword* refers to learning Lightning Eye Sword fighting. **MA Percentage: 27.98%**

SHAOLIN KUNG FU

少林功夫 (1974—Taiwan) **92m. FI: He Ming-xiao. NOT/LOT: 2/ 1m 57s; NOF/LOF: 18/ 27m 36s.** D: Joseph Kuo. C: Wen Chiang-long, Liu Ping, Yi Yuen, Yee Hung, Yang Shan-shan, Tsang Chiu, Chan Chiu-ming, Tu Sung-zhao.

One of my surprise martial arts stars of the 1970s is the Taiwanese actor Wen Chiang-long. His early films are simply exhausting to watch because he is either being pounded into hamburger meat or pounding those who crossed him or his people.

In *Shaolin Kung Fu* (a name that has little to do with the film aside from a finger-strike technique with Shaolin origins), Wen revisits his popular caricature of a downtrodden rickshaw man who rises above his rascally rivals.

Lin Fung (Wen) is an honest, hardworking rickshaw puller who, against his blind wife's (Yang Shan-shan) begging wishes, gets into fights when the cause is righteous. For example, one of his fellow workers is unjustly beaten up by a maniacal rickshaw puller and bully (Liu Ping); the bully works for the sleazy rival

rickshaw company headed by Chu Tsao-pin (Yi Yuen). When Chu Tsao has had enough of Lin's meddling, his son Chu Tien-hai (Tsang Chiu) tries to rape Lin's blind wife, only to have Lin pull a wheelie on his head. He dies in the arms of his father. His heart filled with revenge and hatred, Chu Tsao kidnaps Lin's wife and lays a trap, knowing Lin will come looking for her. Chu Tsao's men pummel Lin and then try to rape his wife in front of him. She commits suicide, and Lin goes off his rocker. He is further flattened, stuck into a dungeon and tortured within an inch of his life. He finally escapes Chu Tsao's house of torture and hides in the mountains, where he learns a special kind of finger-piercing kung fu before coming back for revenge.

As Wen matured as an on-screen fighter, like in this film, he moved further away from trying to do more than 15 or so techniques per shot. Instead, he kept the shot sequences shorter and tighter. Opting to use more slapping choreography, which is easier on the actors and stuntmen, Wen also tried to add more focus and power to his strikes and blocks, which on one hand slows down the fight but on the other hand adds a new, interesting and partially welcome dimension to his fights.

He also has a dangerous fight on and around a series of cliffs in one of Taiwan's central rock quarries, where rolling down steep hills and losing footing on the loose shale rock can make fights a nightmare. It is all too easy to get injured with rocks sliding down and around you in the middle of a shot. Been there and done that, and it is not fun.

Titleography: *Shao-lin Kung Fu*. Translation—*Shaolin Kung Fu*. **MA Percentage: 32.12%**

SHAOLIN MANTIS

螳螂 (1978—Hong Kong) **102m. FI: Wilson Tong, Liu Chia-liang. NOT/LOT: 6/ 4m; NOF/LOF: 28/ 35m.** D: Liu Chia-liang. C: David Chiang, Cecilia Huang Chong-kuang, Liu Chia-rong, John Cheung, Xu Hsao-chiang, Wilson Tong, Frankie Wei Hong, Gordon Liu Chia-hui, Lee Hoi-san, Lily Li.

The martialogy for *Seven Commandments of Kung Fu* explains the origins of praying mantis kung fu and shares a story about how I recreated the history of the style for my undergraduate thesis at Cornell University. This martialogy will describe that process in greater detail, which is relevant because the heart of the film centers on how David Chiang's character, Wei Fung, invented praying mantis kung fu—much in the same manner I studied it in 1979.

The film is set during the early years of the Ching Dynasty, when the country was still beset by anti-Ching rebels trying to restore the Ming Dynasty. Under the threat of his parents being beheaded, Wei is ordered to infiltrate the Tien Clan as a tutor for Gi Gi (Cecilia Huang Chong-kuang), the daughter of clan chief Tien (Liu Chia-rong). Wei is ordered to gather proof that the clan is full of Ming loyalists and to retrieve a secret list of their underground contacts. Tien finds out that Wei works for the emperor, but Gi Gi has fallen in love with him. They are married instead. However, the lives of Wei's parents are still on the line, so he must get back to the emperor, forcing Gi Gi to chose between her husband and her family. She chooses her husband, and the only way they can leave is to pass the Five Posts. Each sentry point is guarded by a member of the family (Xu Hsao-chiang, John Cheung, Wilson Tong, Lily Li and Liu Chia-rong). Each of the five has deadly kung fu skills and will try to stop Gi Gi and Wei no matter what, even if that means killing them.

Wei is no match for Gi Gi's grandfather, and the old man tosses him easily into some tall grass. He begins lamenting his situation and flailing his arms in despair when he notices a praying mantis clinging to his arm. Wei calms down and has an idea: Maybe the secret to beating grandpa Tien lies in learning how to fight like the insect grasping his arm. After poking and prodding the creature, Wei devises praying mantis kung fu and returns to bug the Tiens.

When I was a student at Cornell, I watched hundreds of hours of video and identified 10 stereotypical behavioral patterns employed by mantises during attack, defense and provocation. I then adapted what I could to human movements. Mantises have a reaction time of $1/40^{th}$ of a second, so the first requirement for mantis stylists is be fast. I also noted that a mantis would slowly sway from side to side to give the effect of a moving shadow while stalking its opponents. This is why when a mantis stylist is crouched low or preparing his next set of movements, you will see him shaking or rocking in place. (I would be willing to bet, though, that when they learned the form, they did not know what the shaking was about.) Here is a list of the 10 strategies I noted: block; block and strike at the same time; grasp and pull back; push; grab and pull back; raise arms and strike; strike out fast; shuffle to side and block or strike; crush; and avoid.

This film demonstrates the importance of the fight director. Actor David Chiang is usually weak with his kung fu, and throughout the decade he did not improve. However, with Liu Chia-liang as his mentor and guide, Chiang gets better with each successive fight in this film. Liu also shoots each fight a different way. Take the first set of Five Posts fights for example. For Post 1, Liu uses many tight angles. Posts 2 and 3 use fast pans. Post 4 uses simultaneous tilts and pans to highlight individual moves, and Post 5 uses more tracking shots. The final fight cleverly removes the gore and lets the viewer's imagination take over. You see shadows on the wall, with one shadow spilling intestines. You might say that shot took a lot of guts.

To give an idea of Liu's drive on set, I will share a story told to me by his adopted kung fu brother Gordon Liu Chia-hui. He explained that his brother was and still is a perfectionist, and for one shot he had Gordon do the take over 40 times. He admitted that Liu was physically very tough and mentally frustrating. Gordon later made an excuse to leave the set so as not to disturb anyone else, and he cried and vomited.

Titleography: *Deadly Mantis*; *Deadly Shaolin Mantis*. Translation—*Praying Mantis*. Northern praying mantis kung fu was developed at the Shaolin Temple, so *Shaolin* is actually appropriate in this title. **MA Percentage: 38.24%** SHAW BROTHERS

SHAOLIN MARTIAL ARTS

洪拳與詠春 (1974—Hong Kong) 106m. FI: Liu Chia-liang, Tang Chia. NOT/LOT: 17/ 17m 33s; NOF/LOF: 21/ 18m 42s. D: Chang Cheh. C: Alexander Fu Sheng, Chi Kuan-chun, Gordon Liu Chia-hui, Irene Chen I-ling, Wang Lung-wei, Liang Chia-ren, Tong Yen-san, Yuen Man-zi, Yuen Xiao-tian, Feng Yi, Lu Di, Jiang Dao, Fung Ke-an, Liu Chia-rong, Tino Wong Cheung, Jiang Nan.

This is the third of director Chang Cheh's five major films made in honor of the Shaolin Temple, the others being *Heroes Two*, *Men from the Monastery*, *Five Shaolin Masters*, and *Shaolin Temple*. (See their respective martialogies.)

The film begins when the Ching (who are Manchu Chinese) and Shaolin martial artists (mostly Han Chinese) gather in honor of the kung fu god Guan Yu's birthday. Ching leader Wu Chung-ping (Jiang Dao) complains that the Shaolin martial arts initiator of the event is too young, and so the Chings demand to be the event's initiator. After the Shaolin argue that Guan is Han Chinese and it is

only proper to have a Han Chinese begin the worshipping ceremony, the Chings grow more antsy. The Shaolin martial artists therefore agree to break protocol and allow the Manchus to get involved in the opening. So the ceremony opens by having a Manchu and Han Chinese perform a kung fu demonstration using Guan Yu's legendary weapon, the *guan dao*.

But being that the Chings are inherently evil and always want to eliminate the Shaolin martial artists, it is no stretch of the imagination to believe that the Chings have ulterior motives for being part of the opening ceremony. The Chings start an all-out fight and then ruthlessly kill a Shaolin student. The Ching authorities say that since many were involved in the melee, it is hard to determine who started the fight.

The local head official orders Wu, with the help of three fearsome fighters (played by Wang Lung-wei, Liang Chia-ren and Feng Ke-an), to eliminate all martial arts schools in the area, starting with Shaolin. Four Shaolin students escape the bloodbath. Two students, Mai (Gordon Liu Chia-hui) and Ho (Tong Yen-san), are sent to train with King of the Eagle Claw for three months. The other students go into deep hiding. Li Yao (Alexander Fu Sheng) learns Hong Xi-guan's tiger crane kung fu, aka the Hong fist, from master Lung (Yuen Xiao-tian), while Pa Chung (Chi Kuan-chun) learns *wing chun* from master Liang (Feng Yi).

When, after three months of training, Mai and Ho attempt revenge against the Chings and fail, they are killed. This only feeds the fire of revenge as Li and Pa hunker down for three more years of intense training. Three years later, they have learned the necessary skills to avenge their Shaolin brothers and take on the Chings.

One of the most famous *wuxia* novels of all time was completed during the Ming Dynasty (1368-1644; Rennaisance period in Europe): *The Romance of the Three Kingdoms* (*San Guo Yan Yi*), it was initially compiled into novel form by Lo Guan-chung during the Yuan Dynasty. It takes place during the Three Kingdoms era between A.D. 220 and 265 and tells a compelling story of the blood brotherhood between Guan Yu, Zhang Fei and the leader of the Shu Kingdom, Liu Bei. Guan Yu (aka Guan Gong) was such a potent heroic figure that he attained deity status as the god of kung fu. He can be recognized by his red face, long black beard and weapon of choice, the guan dao (Guan's sword). As a kung fu god, he does not bless those who go into battle but those who observe the ways of righteousness and the code of brotherhood. (Incidentally, he was one of John Woo's boyhood heroes.) His guan dao, also known as the Green Dragon Crescent Blade, is said to have weighed between 100 and 200 pounds. Use of the weapon emphasizes strong slashes and spinning cuts as a result of adjusting to the momentum of the heavy blades during movement.

The fights in this film are about showing real traditional Shaolin kung fu, which up until this time was not always cinematically apparent, other than in flashes of choreography. Therefore, the fights appear a bit clumsy and slow in the beginning. However, because "real" kung fu was a relatively a new choreographic approach, the actors were still finding their kung fu footing. By the film's end, the actors are firing on all kung fu cylinders; their real movements flow better and don't look forced or contrived. Although many films before had shown minor training sequences in which the hero trains either on his own or with a mentor, the approach in this film adopted by choreographer Liu Chia-liang set the standard for the rest of the decade. At the movie's beginning, for example, Liu Chia-rong does a 98-second guan dao form with no fancy camerawork or undercranking, and he uses a real weighted guan dao. Without trying to look powerful, he lets the weapon's momentum do the form for him. Today, it is rare to see this on film or in live demonstrations because most people do fancy *wushu* movements with light guan dao that are easier to wield.

Titleography: As of this writing, no alternative titles could be found. Translation—*Hong Fist and Wing Chun*. See martialogy. **MA Percentage: 34.20%** SHAW BROTHERS

SHAOLIN RESCUERS

街 市 英 雄 (1979—Hong Kong) **101m. FI: Chiang Sheng, Lu Feng, Robert Tai Chi-hsien. NOT/LOT: 11/ 13m 8s; NOF/ LOF: 47/ 35m.** D: Chang Cheh. C: Bai Biao, Lo Meng, Lu Feng, Kuo Chue, Chiang Sheng, Sun Chien, Chan Shen, Jiang Nan, Cao Dao-hua, Wang Li, Yu Tai-ping, Gu Guan-zhong, Yang Xiong, Tan Zhen-dong, Liu Huang-shi.

This is another Five Weapon Guys film (see *Crippled Avengers*) and another of Chang Cheh's films about brotherhood and the Shaolin Temple. Compared to his earlier Shaolin films, *Shaolin Rescuers* moves forward with more fanciful choreography and more exotic weaponry. The film drifts away from traditional Shaolin kung fu and is more about entertainment. It reflects the attitude at end of the decade when more opera-trained kung fu stars got their chance to act alongside traditionally trained kung fu stars. In addition, more choreographers with opera backgrounds infused their skills and routines into fights. It is not unlike Jet Li's first film, *Shaolin Temple* (1982), in which the fight scenes were basically *wushu* practitioners doing the fight forms they had been performing for 10 years. The difference is that they were now wearing costumes and adding sound effects. What is a bit disconcerting is that director Chang had his younger kung fu actors look and act less like rugged, stalwart martial artists. Instead, he had them portray their characters as cute, innocent-looking adolescents.

The film opens with five members of the 10 Tigers of Shaolin—Hong Xi-guan, Monk San De, Hu Hui-qian, Li Jing-luin and Lian Ya-sung—fighting members of the Wu Dung. Only the severely wounded Hong Xi-guan (Bai Biao) escapes the clutches of Bai Mei's baddies. Meanwhile, the audience is introduced to three street-market bumpkins: bean-curd maker Chen A-jin (Lo Meng); waiter Yang Da-bao (Kuo Chue), who can use chopsticks and bowls with deadly efficiency; and dye-factory worker Zhu Cai (Sun Chien). Although Zhu practices kicking martial arts, he is no match when all of his mean kung fu brothers decide to gang up on him. During one such belligerent battle, Zhu is rescued by Chen and Yang. These three intrepid but rustic lads hide Hong Xi-guan from the Chings and Wu Dung leader Gao Zhing-zhong (Lu Feng). They put their necks on the line to sneak Hong medicine and nurse him back to health. As thanks for their patriotic acts, Hong teaches them special kung fu skills. Eventually, the four hook up with Hong's fellow Shaolin fighter Han Chi (Chiang Sheng) for a rip-roaring 15-minute Five Weapon Guys finale that features 17 continuous fight scenes and brings out the best fighting prowess in all the heroes and villains.

There are two especially impressive scenes, the first of which is when actor Sun Chien jumps up onto a courtyard wall of 4-foot *mei hua* poles and runs on top of them with ease and throws some well-balanced kicks. The other impressive sequence is when actor Lu Feng picks up his weapon of choice, the *guan dao* (a long-pole weapon with large blade at one end and spear point on the other). In a magnificent display, he fights all the good guys at once. His technique is so sharp that I'm surprised he didn't cut himself.

Although his *taekwondo* kicks are OK, Sun's limited martial arts training

made it difficult for him to do choreography with extensive acrobatics, weapon work, and certain fist-and-arm techniques. This is why Sun's camera time became increasingly short in his films, especially during the last fights when all the opera-trained fighters would be on-screen at the same time.

In regard to the film's opening, a few real-life notes: Monk San De was killed while defending Xi Chan Shaolin, the Shaolin Temple he established after the burning of Jiu Lian Shaolin. Furthermore, the 10 Tigers of Shaolin, except for San De, were not Shaolin monks but Shaolin-trained fighters loyal to the temple. It is often misinterpreted in many of these Chinese kung fu films that the Shaolin fighters battling with the various Ching and Wu Dung are Shaolin priests or monks, but they were not.

Titleography: *Avenging Warriors of Shaolin.* Translation—*Street Market Heroes.* The Chinese title refers to the main characters of Chen, Yang and Han. **MA Percentage: 47.66%** SHAW BROTHERS

SHAOLIN TEMPLE

少 林 寺 (1976—Hong Kong) **116m. FI: Hsieh Hsing, Chen Hsin-i. NOT/ LOT: 22/ 21m 32s; NOF/LOF: 15 / 28m 29s.** D: Chang Cheh, Wu Ma. C: Alexander Fu Sheng, Chi Kuan-chun, David Chiang, Ti Lung, Chue, Lee I-min, Tong Yen-san, Chiang Sheng, Shan Mao, Wang Lung-wei, Yueh Hua, Liu Yung, Shih Szu, Shan Mao, Wang Chung, Ku Feng, Lu Feng, Tsai Hong, Wei Hong, Lo Meng.

So many heroes, so little time. Since the Shaolin Temple is the fount for today's martial arts, this martialogy will be the foundation for several other Shaolin Temple films that will be referenced.

The year 1644 marked the fall of the Ming Dynasty, when foreign invaders from Manchuria established the Ching dynasty. Twenty years later, a Ming loyalist hiding in Taiwan sent a small army led by five young soldiers to Song Shan Shaolin Temple in Henan province; their mission was to learn Shaolin martial arts, stir up anti-Ching sentiment and wait. Twenty years after that, the Xilu people from the north invaded China, beating back Chinese forces to Tong Guan city in Hunan province. This would be comparable to Canada invading the United States at Minnesota and then driving American forces south to St. Louis, Missouri.

The Ching emperor issued an edict for help. In response, 128 monks from Song Shan Shaolin, armed with poles, went to Tong Guan, defeated the Xilu army and saved the country. The emperor offered riches and government positions as a reward, but the monks wished only to return to their temple and lifestyle. In order to prevent the emperor from losing face, they accepted an imperial jade seal as a reward. One version of the story says that in 1735, a government official named Deng Sheng was burning incense at the temple and was caught trying to steal the seal. He was then banished from the temple, and out of spite, he told Emperor

Yong Zheng that the Shaolin monks were planning subversive activities against the Ching. Under the guise of a peaceful visit to burn incense for the gods, the emperor ordered 3,000 soldiers to slaughter all the monks and burn the temple to the ground. However, five monks survived—those five young soldiers sent from Taiwan to Song Shan Shaolin some 60 years earlier. These five monks—Tsai De-zhong (Ti Lung), Li Shi-kai (Yueh Hua), Hu De-di (David Chiang), Fang Da-hong (Wang Chung) and Ma Chao-xing (Liu Yung)—became known as the Five Ancestors of Shaolin, and this film tells their story.

Director Chang Cheh and actors David Chiang and Ti Lung were known as the Iron Triangle of Hong Kong film in the early and mid-1970s because each of the films they worked on together was a solid hit. In this film, they bring to a close the story of the Five Ancestors. After the destruction of the temple, the Five Ancestors split up to spread kung fu. Hu De-di, Tsai De-zhong and two of Tsai's students, Yung Zong and Zhi Kong, fled south to Fujian province and established Jiu Lian Shan Shaolin Temple.

A few historical speaking points about the film: Some of the film's main characters—Hu Hui-qian, Fang Shi-yu and Hong Xi-guan (all of whom became members of the 10 Tigers of Shaolin) are seen training at Song Shan. Fang traverses the famous Luohan Hall of 18 Wooden Men (which should actually be 108), and Hu escapes from the temple via a dog tunnel to wreak revenge on the Chings who killed his father and beat him up as a kid. Furthermore, Buddhist nun Wu Mei, aka Ng Moi, who became one the Five Elders of Shaolin—her most famous student was Wing Chun—is featured as a philosophical sage to Hu De-di and Tsai De-zhong.

Still from *Shaolin Temple* © Celestial Pictures Ltd. All rights reserved.

In reality, none the 10 Tigers or Five Elders trained at Song Shan, and the famed Luohan Hall was one of the 35 chambers of Shaolin at Jiu Lian Shan. (Jackie Chan's film *Shaolin Wooden Men* reflects a better rendition of the Luohan Hall chamber.) The part in which Hu De-di escapes Shaolin borders on reality because although he was not at Song Shan, he did escape Jiu Lian Shan Temple by crawling out through a drainpipe.

Titleography: *Death Chamber*; *Death Chambers*. Translation—*Shaolin Temple*. The *Death Chamber* refers to the Luohan Hall of Wooden Men; the film says most who enter never exit it. It is a logical English title given that at the time of release, most Westerners would not be too familiar with the Shaolin Temple. Of course, this soon changed, and many films began to include the word "Shaolin" in their titles even though the films had nothing to do with it. **MA**
Percentage: 43.12% SHAW BROTHERS

SHAOLIN WOODEN MEN

少林木人巷 (1976—Hong Kong) **101m. FI: Jackie Chan, Tommy Lee. NOT/LOT: 18/ 16m 50s; NOF/LOF: 23/ 21m 3s.** D: Chen Zhi-hua. C: Jackie Chan, Jin Gang, Doris Lung Chun-er, Jiang Jin, Zhang Bing-yu, Wu De-shan, Liu Ping, Li Min-lang, Weng Hsiao-hu.

Producer Lo Wei finally realized Jackie Chan was not going to be the next Bruce Lee, but something different. He therefore gave Chan more freedom to experiment. In *Shaolin Wooden Men*, by combining the kung fu training of choreographer Tommy Lee with Chan's opera background, Chan amalgamated a whole new fighting look for himself. This style would further develop over his next six films, culminating with Chan's directorial debut in *Fearless Hyena* three years later. *Wooden Men* also represents Chan's first foray into drunken fist and snake kung fu, which were both styles that blew his career wide open two years later. (See *Drunken Master* and *Snake in the Eagle's Shadow*.)

Monks at Jiu Lian Shan Shaolin Temple all love Little Mute (Jackie Chan) because of his good nature and dedication to kung fu. So although he is not the best, several monks secretly try to expose him to Shaolin martial arts that other disciples are not privy to learn. One day, Mute stumbles into a secret cave and finds a wild-eyed man with long, shaggy gray hair and a loud, raspy voice like sand and glue. The man is also manacled to the cave's cold walls. It turns out he is the mad Shaolin monk Fat Yu (Jin Gang), who is imprisoned for life in the cave for practicing lion's roar kung fu. Mute treats Fat Yu with respect, getting him food and alcohol without anyone knowing, and Fat Yu begins teaching Mute powerful kung fu that stresses violence and showing no mercy. Sensing a change in Mute's attitude, one of the temple's kung fu nuns (Zhang Bing-yu) teaches Mute the eight steps of the snake kung fu. She emphasizes that killing and violence are not the way of Shaolin. Although it is not stated, the nun might be Wu Mei, one of the fabled Five Elders of Shaolin.

As Fat Yu continues to train Mute, we learn that he has ulterior motives. He wants Mute to deliver a message to the heads of the Green Dragon and White Tiger Clans telling them that he will soon unite with the clans and lead them to becoming the most feared clan in the world of Jiang Hu. The only way for Mute to deliver this secret message is to leave Shaolin, and the only way to leave Shaolin is to be able to traverse the venerated and dangerous Wooden Man Alley, which Fat Yu's skills enable him to do.

However, Mute learns just how evil Fat Yu is, and after Fat Yu escapes from the cave, the monks fear that the Shaolin Temple is in jeopardy because no one can defeat Fat Yu's lion roar. But word spreads that Mute has learned the eight steps of the snake from the nun, so there is hope. Another development is that Mute is not actually mute and only vowed to be remain silent until he found out who killed his father. We can all guess who the killer is, and the final fight takes on even more meaning.

In Stephen Chow's *Kung Fu Hustle* (2004), the cigarette-smoking landlady played by Yuen Qiu was a master of lion's roar kung fu. The style was created by the Tibetan monk Ah-Dat-Ta around 1440. Ah's kung fu, however, is not so much based around the physical act of sound so much as the philosophical implication of Buddha. When a lion roars, all will listen. When Buddha roars (or speaks), people will listen. However, during fighting, the loud roaring sounds are used to distract and disrupt an opponent's *chi*.

Historically, while at Jiu Lian Shan Shaolin temple, monk Zhi Shan's lead disciple, Xing Yin, developed a chamber known as the Luo Han Hall. It was a corridor that housed 108 wooden figures (some historians say 18) that could be mechanically maneuvered to attack anyone who entered the chamber. It was expected that when a student entered the Shaolin Temple, it was a lifelong commitment or that the student would stay long enough to complete the training cycle. For those who chose to leave before it was their time, they could only do so by successfully traversing the Luo Han Hall. However, most who entered the Hall left either dead or severely injured. In order to survive the ordeal, you really needed to be highly skilled and have a good reason to leave.

It is well-known that after this film, Jackie Chan disappeared for over a year because Lo Wei told him he was too ugly to be a leading man; he went to Japan for cosmetic eyelid surgery. After fully recovering and making a few more films for Lo, Chan was then borrowed by Seasonal Films producer Ng See-yuen to star in *Snake in the Eagle's Shadow*, the film that officially launched Chan into stardom. As painful as it might be to admit it, perhaps the crass Lo was right.

Titleography: *36 Wooden Men*; *Shaolin Wooden Men: Young Tiger's Revenge*; *Shaolin Chamber of Death*; *Wooden Man*. Translation—*Shaolin Wooden Men Alley*. Most of the titles are self-explanatory, except *Young Tiger's Revenge*. This title might be derived from Jackie's earlier film *Little Tiger From Canton* (an alternative title for *Cub Tiger From Kwangtung*) or from *Young Tiger*, an alternate title for *Police Woman*. Or perhaps it suggests a battle between a tiger and lion, i.e., the villain using lion roar kung fu. It is not clear where they got the number 36 from either. In Chang Cheh's *Shaolin Temple* (1976), the Luo Han Hall has 18 wooden men, so it's possible producer Lo Wei extrapolated 18 on each side of the alley, thus 36. **MA Percentage: 37.51%**

SHINSENGUMI

(1970—Japan) **122m. SWC: Takano Hiromasa, Kuze Ryu. NOT/LOT: 2/ 8s; NOF/LOF: 10/ 9m.** D: Tadashi Sawashima. C: Toshiro Mifune, Keiju Kobayashi, Kinya Kitaoji, Rentaro Mikuni, Yôko Tsukasa, Yuriko Hoshi, Kanemon Nakamura, Junko Ikeuchi, Kinnosuke Nakamura, Umenosuke Nakamura, Yumiko Nogawa, Takahiro Tamura, Katsuo Nakamura, Mita Kitagawa, Shinsuke Okimoto, Ichiro Nakaya, Ryohei Uchida.

While *Shinsengumi* had several pre-New Year's screenings, the official release date was January 1, 1970, and the movie turned out to be the biggest *jidaigeki* (period piece) film to focus on the Tokugawa era (1603-1868) of the 1970s. Serious history buffs will especially love this film. This is not Tom Cruise's *The Last Samurai* (2003) but a chronicle of true events as told by the Japanese. You'll find shades of a high-school history class in this martialogy, but at least there is no exam.

Shinsengumi stars Toshiro Mifune, Rentaro Mikuni, Keiju Kobayashi and Kinya Kitaoji as the important members of the titular Shinsengumi—Kondo Isama, Serizawa Kamo, Hijikata Toshizo and Okita Soji, respectively. These guys were originally a group of *ronin* who decided to live by an overly strict version of the code of *bushido* in order to eventually gain the status of samurai in the eyes of the shogun. They were a feared force of special police. Their primary mission was to fight anti-shogunate forces and protect the shogun unto the death. The film follows the rise and fall of the Shinsengumi. It begins with the arrival of U.S. Commodore Perry's black ships in Japan. It continues with the formation of the Roshigumi and explores how the Shinsengumi became an offshoot of that group. After a rollicking six-minute group sword fight, the film winds down and ends with the events that lead to the destruction and defeat of the shogunate forces as well as the demise of the Shinsengumi. Thank god for nutshells, but if you want more meat, here is the extended version. (For those who just want some kicks, jump to the end of the martialogy.)

When U.S. Commodore Perry's black ships arrived in Japan in 1853, it was the beginning of the end of the samurai and the shogunate. This is because Shogun Tokugawa Iemochi felt pressured to sign a treaty to open Japan's ports, which greatly angered Emperor Komei. The shogun was essentially the commander in chief of the Japanese army, and the emperor was the leader of Japan. (It's similar to how there is a prime minister and a monarch in England.) This led radical ronin from the Tosa and Chosu fiefs to assassinate prominent members of the shogunate—the administrative arm of the Tokugawa shogun. Other pro-Komei factions arose, chanting the slogan, "Revere the emperor, kill (or expel) the foreigner." This led to murders and violence in Kyoto, the emperor's capital and home city. In 1863, Shogun Iemochi responded to this violence and had samurai Kiyokawa Hachiro create and lead the Roshigumi, a band of 234 ronin.

On March 26, 1863, the Roshigumi—which included historically famous ronin such as Kondo Isami, Okita Soji, Serizawa Kamo, Hijikata Toshizo, Inoue Genzaburo, Tod Heisuke, Yamanami Keisuke, Nagakura Shinpachi, Niimi Nishiki and Harada Sanosuke, to name a few—left Edo for Kyoto. It's important to note that two days later, Kondo was in charge of arranging lodging for the members but accidentally forgot about Serizawa's group. In response to this perceived insult, Serizawa lost his temper and built a large bonfire outside the lodges in order to make Kondo lose face. This inane loss of cool by Serizawa was the seed of reckless behavior that would accompany him throughout his life. Anyway, the Roshigumi arrived in Kyoto on April 10 and set up shop in the village of Mibu.

But without warning and under the guise of expelling foreigners, Kiyokawa ordered the Roshigumi back to Edo because the Roshigumi leadership decided that they should now work for the emperor.

However, 13 ronin—including Kondo, Okita, Serizawa and Hijikata—defied the order and formed the Shinsengumi of Mibu. According to the film, the group got financial backing from Matsudaira Katamori of the Aizu Clan.

Living by what was considered an overly strict version of the bushido code even then, the Shinsengumi became a feared force, but it was also this strict code that led to their demise. The prime mission of this special police force was to fight anti-shogunate forces and protect the shogunate to the death. The original commanders of the Shinsengumi were Kondo, Serizawa and Niimi, but eventually the Shinsengumi split into three factions, and Kondo's and Serizawa's were the most relevant.

After receiving permission from the Aizu Clan to police Kyoto, the Shinsengumi, along with the Aizu and Satsuma clans, forced the Choshu Clan out of the imperial court during the Incident at the Royal Gate. In the process, the Shinsengumi created several powerful enemies: the Moro and Shimazu clans. Spies from the Roshigumi then infiltrated the Shinsengumi to look for weaknesses. Reckless actions by Serizawa and Niimi led to the assassination of Serizawa, and Niimi was forced to commit *seppuku*. Regardless of these growing problems, the Shinsengumi foiled the Kodaka Shutaro Clan's plan to burn the palace and kidnap the emperor during the Ikeda Mercantile Battle in 1864. That made the Shinsengumi instant celebrities to the general population. They were next involved in the Battle of Toba-Fushimi, a conflict between shogunate forces and the Choshu, Satsuma and Tosa alliance. It ended in defeat for the shogunate forces. As a result, the Meiji government forces captured and beheaded Kondo. The June 20, 1869, death of Hijikata Toshiz was the official end of the Shinsengumi.

The film's main fray takes place on land during the Ikeda Mercantile Battle, and it lasts for more than six minutes. Most of it is shot in the dark and within tight spaces and corridors to give the audience the claustrophobic feeling an enemy would have felt during a Shinsengumi sneak attack. Although the scene is very dark and you can barely see anything, the movie lights reflect the slashing steel swords at the right moments, creating a great sense of danger. Although great for the Shinsengumi's reputation, the Ikeda Mercantile Battle left one their younger heroes, Okita, wounded. Although he survived the battle, his injuries from that battle and a pre-existing condition left him with two years to live. Aware that his doom was imminent, Okita became an even more feared opponent because he had nothing left to lose. (For more on the life and times of Okita, see *Okita Soji*.)

Of interest, the film *Sword of Doom* (1966) is a fictional story about samurai Tsukue Ryunosuke (Tatsuya Nakadai), who is ordered by Serizawa to assassinate Kondo.

Titleography: *Shinsengumi: Assassins of Honor*; *Band of Assassins*; *The Shinsen Group*. Translation—*Newly Selected Group*. **MA Percentage: 7.49%**

SHOLAY

(1975—India) **188m. AC: Mohammed Ali, Gerry Crampton. NOT/LOT: None; NOF/LOF: 4/ 6m 9s.** D: Ramesh Sippy. C: Dharmendra, Sanjeev Kumar, Hema Malini, Amitabh Bachchan, Jaya Bhaduri, Amjad Khan, A.K. Hangal, Satyendra Kapoor.

Imagine *The Dirty Dozen* divided by six, or the *Seven Samurai* minus five. Whatever the math, stuff the results into a Sergio-Leone spaghetti Western complete with guitars, whistling, gunfire, bandits, train robbers and a no-armed swordsman … without the sword. This film is out of sight.

Two convicts, Veeru (Dharmendra) and Jai (Amitabh Bachchan; India's No.1 hero actor of all time), are recruited out of prison by retired police officer Singh (Sanjeev Kumar) to hunt down and bring in—alive—the most notorious murderer in the history of Northern India, Gabbar Singh (Amjad Khan; perennial bad cat of 1970s Indian cinema). Along the way, Veeru falls in love with the local village horse carriage driver, Basanti (Hema Malini), and the three join forces to protect the village and find Gabbar's mountain hideout. Basanti's weapon? Dancing.

In Indian films, when a woman gets captured or is a damsel is in distress, the villain never forces one of these beauties to have sex with him—he usually orders them to dance. That's when things can get freaky: As the song and dance routines break out, the body motions and musical rhythms seem to appease His Evilness or drive him to distraction, thus giving the hero time to fly into action.

The fights in this film look a bit overstaged, which is common in Indian films. Sometimes punches miss by a foot or so. But the final mauling in the mountain pits, which pits the thoroughly disarmed anti-hero (I wont give the name away) against the grumbling Gabbar, is not to be missed. The hero can only fight with kicks and head butts, but to be successful he needs to even the limb score, and that he does.

Sholay in Hindi means "fire," and we are not talking about losing a job, but a burning desire for revenge that makes this Indian curry Western as hot as the food of the same name and place.

Titleography: *Embers*; *Flames*; *Flames of the Sun*. Translation—*Fire*. Having several English titles reflects the success of this film outside of India (i.e., international distribution). *Flames of the Sun* seems to play off the spaghetti Western feel. **MA Percentage: 3.27%**

SINGING KILLER, THE

小煞星 (1970—Hong Kong) 104m. FI: Liu Chia-liang, Tang Chia. NOT/LOT: None; NOF/LOF: 9/ 4m 40s. D: Chang Cheh. C: David Chiang, Ti Lung, Tina Chin Fei, Wang Ping, Ku Feng, Stanley Fung Sui-fan, Dean Shek.

It is no secret in the Hong Kong film industry that director Chang Cheh was obsessed with iconic images of young men and the concept of brotherhood. In his work, male-male relationships are more important than male-female and female-female relationships. Chang was also a student of youth culture. His contemporary films investigated the subcultures of the various British youth movements in Hong Kong that appeared and disappeared in the three decades following the Korean War. If you are wondering about the unique costumes in *The Singing Killer*, they are the result of Chang integrating the British Teddy Boys subculture that began in London in 1953. Teddy Boys modeled their dress codes on the Edwardian era (the reign of King Edward VII, 1901-1910) and strived to differentiate themselves from mainstream culture with their fashion.

In the film, successful nightclub performer Johnny (David Chiang) is blackmailed into a jewelry heist by his bygone baddie associates, who are led by Big Brother (who has nothing to do with George Orwell's famous book *1984*). If Johnny cooperates, they will tell him where his long lost love, Lily (Wang Ping), is living. Things go awry when the simple robbery turns to murder, which Johnny gets framed for. The subterfuge grows when Johnny's two-faced manager obtains apparent video proof of Johnny's guilt, which brings up his thieving past and makes

Still from *The Singing Killer* © Celestial Pictures Ltd. All rights reserved.

him the obvious target for Detective Wang (Stanley Fung Sui-fan). As it turns out, Lily was working in the jewelry store the night of the heist, adding another twist.

The fights are nothing special, featuring the usual Chiang flail, his flipping his hair to one side and that peculiar yet subtle neck-craning tilt. But you have got to love the angst on Chiang's face when we are introduced to his character. Dressed in a golden Edwardian shirt and matching silk scarf, he looks rather uncomfortable banging the drums, strumming a guitar and singing on stage. I flash back to my English ladhood, hanging out at Forboys (a candy store in Tadley) and watching the Teddys go by.

Titleography: As of this writing, no alternative titles could be found. Translation—*The Little Jinx*. The title is referring to Johnny being an unlucky star. *The Singing Thief* might have been a more appropriate title, but Chang Cheh had already made a film with that title in 1969. **MA Percentage: 4.49%** SHAW BROTHERS

SISTER STREET FIGHTER

Onna Hissatsu Ken (1974—Japan) 86m. SC: Takashi Shirao. NOT/LOT: 8/ 7m 16s; NOF/LOF: 28/ 26m 14s. D: Kazuhiko Yamaguchi. C: Etsuko Shihomi, Emi Hayakawa, Sanae Ohori, Bin Amatsu, Sonny Chiba, Masashi Ishibashi, Tatsuya Kameyama, Ryoichi Koike, Hideo Kosuge, Akira Kuji, Toshio Minami, Kengo Miyaji, Hiroshi Miyauchi.

After watching this film, "eye" have to admit that "eye" have never seen so many eyes destroyed in one movie. There are gouged eyes, darts in eyes, knives and *kamas* (hand sickles) in eyes. There are more eye pokes in *Sister Street Fighter* than in a macular degeneration optometry clinic, and I should know, because my wife did 10 years of eye research at the David Geffen School of Medicine.

Actress Etsuko Shihomi got her first lead in this *Street Fighter* spinoff because her mentor, Sonny Chiba, was pleased with her martial arts development work as the first female member of his Japan Action Club. In the film, she plays the half-Japanese, half-Chinese Hong Kong detective Li Koryu, who is sent to Japan to investigate the disappearance of her brother and fellow *shorinji kenpo* practitioner, Li Mansai (Hiroshi Miyauchi). Mansai had infiltrated a drug-smuggling group in Hong Kong that has ties with Japan's Central Trading, and now he may be deader than a cow in a Kobe steakhouse, making his martial arts a mooo-t point.

To find her brother, Koryu seeks the help of her kenpo *sensei*. Her sensei promptly picks out his top student, Seiichi Hibiki (Sonny Chiba), to help Koryu get Yakuza boss Kakuzaki (Bin Amatsu). The only problem is that Kakuzaki has surrounded himself with a batch of violent villains who include seven female Thai kickboxers clothed in leopard skin, a banshee-screaming *nunchaku* nut, a karate-cutting killer, an intimidating black-hated bunch, and other weapon-wielding and unarmed assassins. And there is also the icy shorinji-kenpo-hating Inubashi (Masashi Ishibashi), who would think nothing of putting razor blades in his mother's coffee to give it a sharper flavor.

During her first few fights, Shihomi's postures and kicks are very reminiscent of famous Hong Kong superstar Angela Mao Ying. In particular, the way Shihomi kicks and positions her arms after a strike while waiting for the next opponent to attack is very Mao Ying-like. But during later fights in this film, Shihomi drops the Mao Ying look-alike postures and lets her karate background shine through. In an awesome fight scene, Shihomi twists an attacker's head 180 degrees. With his head on backward, the attacker walks down a staircase while spewing blood from his mouth. Koryu's final fight is an ocean side cliffhanging duel against the boss, who does the old *Enter the Dragon* iron-claw routine, which features a convoluted high-wire gag. Prior to fighting the Han wannabe, Koryu must chase him through a dark cave, and you've got to love the fake bats on strings that flutter around Koryu's head. But Koryu did not bat an eyebrow.

Hong Kong kung fu films often show stars doing martial arts during the film's opening credits. Similarly, *Sister Street Fighter* features Shihomi dressed in full shorinji kenpo attire (see *Killing Machine*) doing spinning kicks, twirling nunchaku and whirling *sai* (dagger-like weapons). It prepares the audience for the kind of martial arts the film will feature. This was also the first Japanese karate film to introduce a heroine during the opening credits. On a final note, Koryu's name is Tina Long in English dubs.

Titleography: *Female Fighting Fist in Danger*; *Lady Karate*; *Woman Certain Kill Fist*; *Lethal Fist Woman*. Translation—*Woman Deadly Technique Fist*. **MA Percentage: 38.95%**

SISTER STREET FIGHTER 2

Onna Hissatsu Ken: Kik Ippatsu (1974—Japan) **85m. FI: Uncredited. NOT/LOT: 8/ 11m 11s; NOF/LOF: 23/ 22m 7s.** D: Kazuhiko Yamaguchi. C: Etsuko Shihomi, Tamayo Mitsukawa, Michiyo Bando, Hisayo Tanaka, Hideo Murota, Kazushige Osone, Koji Fujiyama, Kôji Hio, Masashi Ishibashi, Yasuaki Kurata.

Thanks to the success of *Sister Street Fighter*, actress Etsuko Shihomi proved she could hold her own on-screen without having to fight naked, like in other pinky-violence films. So the studio decided to crank out another installment in a few months using the exact same formula, except this time there was no Sonny Chiba. Could Shihomi draw the same numbers with her name and fight skills alone?

In *Sister Street Fighter 2*, the daughter of a Hong Kong policeman, Birei (Hisayo Tanaka), goes missing. Heroine Li Koryu travels from Hong Kong to Japan looking for Birei. She does not know that the head of the diamond-smuggling sex-slave ring is under the protection of several karate-fighting bodyguards, including the Honidan brothers, who are led by Inoichiro (Masashi Ishibashi). Along the way, Koryu gets help from a male fighter named Shunsuke Tsubaki (Yasuaki Kurata), and the two pull out a few fight gems of their own to send the baddies to that great diamond mine below "ore" hell.

Similar to *Sister Street Fighter*, this film's opening credits feature Shihomi in *shorinji kenpo* gear doing kicking forms and weapon-training techniques with the *sai* and *nunchaku*. During the segment, she also introduces the audience to *jodo* sticks. (The art of jodo is a short-stick fighting system created in the early 1600s by the reputable swordsman Muso Gonnosuke Katsuyoshi.)

What gives Shihomi's fights a bit of edge over the first film is that she cocks her leg with nice balance and postures when she kicks. However, her weapon fights are slow and contrived because of her lack of weapon-fighting skills. Weapon fights are difficult for actors even if they know how to do correct weapon forms. It's easy to tell that Shihomi and her fellow actors are thinking too much about their movements by the hesitant ways they move. They also strike or block weapons with the same tense focus you see people use during a karate *kata*, which slows down the speed of the fight. Admittedly, a weapon is an extension of the hand, but a weapon fight is supposed to be more dynamic and not resemble a focused fist-and-kick drill.

The fights in this film are also shot overall like a rendition of Old MacDonald's farm: Here a camera shake, there a shake, everywhere a shake, shake. And like a kid's song that gets stuck in your head, you soon get tired of it. Camera zooms combined with shaky camera choreography can make you feel seasick, further creating the optical illusion of double vision. But on a humorous note, one character had no problem with it because Koryu literally nails a pair of glasses to that villain's head. What's also crazy is that the ingenious villains decided that the best way to smuggle illegal diamonds is to hide them in illegal drugs—two contrabands for the price of one, and possibly two stupid ideas for the crime of one.

Trivia: What new character nuance does Shihomi adopt for Koryu in this film that is similar to what a Sonny Chiba character does in another? Hint: It keeps doctors away. Or you can check out the martialogies in the E section to verify the answer.

Titleography: *Return of the Female Killing Fist*; *Sister Street Fighter: Hanging by a Thread*; *Lady Karate 2*; *Female Fighting Fist in Danger*; *Lethal Fist Woman: Hanging by a Thread*; *Sister Streetfighter 2*. Translation—*Woman Deadly Fist Technique: Critical Situation. Hanging by a Thread* refers to Koryu hanging by a rope while being tortured. The other titles reflect how the film is a sequel or describe that the lady with the wicked karate abilities is in some kind of trouble. **MA Percentage: 39.18%**

SISTER STREET FIGHTER 3

Kaette Kita Onna Hissatsu Ken (1975—Japan) **77m. FI: Uncredited. NOT/LOT: 2/ 2m 7s; NOF/LOF: 23/ 17m 29s.** D: Kazuhiko Yamaguchi. C: Etsuko Shihomi, Akane Kawasaki, Miwa Cho, Mitchi Love, Jiro Chiba, Rinichi Yamamoto, Masashi Ishibashi, Yasuaki Kurata.

Though there are four *Sister Street Fighter* films in this book, this is really the last *Sister Street Fighter* film of the series. Nope, you have not entered the *Sister Street Fighter* twilight zone. Technically, this is the last *Sister Street Fighter* film because it is the last time Etsuko Shihomi plays the *shorinji kenpo* and karate kick-butt babe Koryu. She's on the case to find another missing person. If you've been paying attention in the other installments, then you probably know the plot formula: Koryu will hook up with (but never romantically, of course) a

male fighter, and together they'll uphold the law and Batman and Batwoman some joker back to the nut house.

In this film, the apple-less Koryu travels from Hong Kong to Japan in search of missing person Shurei (Akane Kawasaki) and ends up tangling with the gold-smuggling, inscrutable, Han-inspired Oh Ryu Mei. (Han is the villain in *Enter the Dragon*.) Like any smart villain does in these martial arts movies, Oh surrounds himself with a harrowing horde of heavies. The horde is headed by Hebikura (Masashi Ishibashi). Think of the character as a hybrid of actor Lee Van Clief and a 1970s disco boy. After Koryu engages with her counterpart male protagonist, Go Kurosaki (Yasuaki Kurata), one can just about hear the villain scream "Oh-Oh." Although it sounds and reads like the echo of the villain's name, it is really about the double trouble Oh will be facing—not unlike Santa Claus screaming, "Oh-oh," if he gets stuck going down the chimney backwards.

Although the *Sister Street Fighter* films have virtually the same plot, the martial arts aspects tend to be different. Part of that difference also lies in the various fighting antagonists Koryu faces, (or more accurately defaces) with her kicks. Apart from the villain and Hebikura, Koryu takes on a black Japanese Shaka-like Zulu warrior who shakes things up. It was also just a matter of time before Bruceploitation hit Japanese film because male counterpart Go Kurosaki out-sticks and out-kicks a Japanese Bruce Lee look-alike who uses *nunchaku*. It is also worthy to note that with each successive film Shihomi stars in, her on-camera fights and karate skills improve. This is visible in her increasingly smooth spinning-kick combinations and her ability to sell power in her techniques by incorporating more snap to her punches and kicks. Live on, sister, because there is one more *Sister Street Fighter* to come.

Titleography: *Return of the Sister Streetfighter*; *Return of the Lethal Fist Woman*; *Sister Streetighter 3*. Translation—*Return of the Woman Deadly Technique Fist*. **MA Percentage: 25.45%**

SISTER STREET FIGHTER 4

Onna Hissatsu Godan Ken (1976—Japan) **77m. FI: Uncredited. NOT/LOT: 4/ 2m 21s; NOF/LOF: 16/ 12m 29s.** D: Shigehiro Ozawa. C: Etsuko Shihomi, Mitchi Love, Ken Wallace, Masafumi Suzuki, Masako Araki, Iwao Tabuchi, Yoshiki Yamada, Takanori Oya, Yoshihiro Igarashi, Masataka Iwao, Tony Cetera, Claude Gagnon, Hal Gold.

The trick with multiple sequels is to know when one should not be a sequel. This film is really not a sequel to *Sister Street Fighter 1, 2* or *3*, but its own movie. It has a different character, different plot line, and even a different way of fighting and choreography for star Etsuko Shihomi. I thought this was not a bad film. The fights are better than the other *Sister Street Fighter* movies, and the story is more intriguing. However, because it carried the *Sister Street Fighter* label, it did not get its proper due. If they changed the title to something like *Shinsengumi vs. Karate Babe*, it might have done better, especially because it would have given Shihomi some space between her dying franchise and a potential new one.

In this film, Kiku (Estuko Shihomi) is a karate teacher, and her traditionalist father is trying to marry her off to a proper Japanese gentleman. Whenever a prospective suitor drops by, Kiku gets out her karate suit, goes out the back door and escapes to the dojo to practice karate. Although she uses karate as an excuse to avoid personal matters, Kiku never avoids helping others with her karate. When her half-Korean, half-Japanese best friend Michi (Mitchi Love) needs her help to avenge the death of her half-black and half-Japanese brother, Kiku does not do a half-ass job but goes full steam ahead after the killer.

Using her karate abilities, Kiku poses as an extra on the set of a *chambara* (sword fight) film being produced by a film studio that acts as a cover for the international drug ring that killed Jim. After two smash-'em, bash-'em fights on the studio lot and a typical Penelope Pitstop-esque escape like from a Hanna-Barbera cartoon, she exposes the murderers and drug ring and "kikus" their butts while meeting Mr. Right (a young policeman with an old soul), thus making her dad happy.

The two main fights occur at the studio where Kiku is an extra. She is being chased by the crew and two stars from the film she is working on. The two stars are portraying true-life heroes Okita Soji and Kondo Isama. (Ding! Do those names ring a bell?) They attack her with prop samurai swords. This is actually an intelligent way to work some nice samurai fights into a contemporary film; fake-hero actors attack Kiku with traditional swordplay while she uses modern karate. Sure the fights start messy, with shaky camera movements and within the tight confines of the various film departments (makeup, costumes, props, etc.) of the film Kiku is working on. But as the fights progress, they occur in larger areas, which opens up the fight. At this point, there is no camera shaking, and the fights are shot using wider angles. We can now clearly see Shihomi's skills as she lets loose with kicking combinations that accent her fluid, tornado-like spinning kicks. On some occasions, they foolishly undercrank the camera, which is unnecessary. On a final note, each film of this series has progressively fewer fights, which is never a good thing for a martial arts film franchise. I'm sure Shihomi saw the end coming, but she still does some of her best fights in this the final installment.

The film is also unusual in that it touches upon on how tough life is for mixed-race children in Japan. But what is most amazing about this series is that the lead character and fighter is a woman who does not do any nudity—not once—throughout the entire series. Shihomi never got any more lead roles after her next (and last) film, *Dragon Princess* (1976). She again refused to abandon her principles of not being naked on camera. A true martial artist.

Titleography: *Sister Street Fighter: Fifth Level Fist*; *Fifth Level Fist*; *Lethal Fist Woman: Five Slashes*; *Sister Streetfighter 4*. Translation—*Woman Deadly Technique Fifth Level Fist*. *Fifth Level Fist* is a name of a technique. Also remember my title change proposal? So why *Shinsengumi vs. Karate Babe*? Historically, Okita Soji and Kondo Isama were important members of the Shinsengumi. (See *Shinsengumi* for details.) So Shihomi is the *Karate Babe*, and since she fought actors who were portraying these characters, that is the *Shinsengumi* half of the title. **MA Percentage: 18.81%**

SIX ASSASSINS

六刺客 (1970—Hong Kong) **79m. FI: Sammo Hung, Yasuyoshi Shikamura. NOT/LOT: None; NOF/LOF: 29/ 12m 50s.** D: Cheng Chang-ho. C: Ling Yun, Hsia Fang, Lily Li, James Nam Gung-fan, Gao Ming, Di Nuo, Tang Tian-xi, Zhang Jing-po, You Long, Yin Yi-feng, Chan Shen, Fang Mian, Chen Feng-chen.

Lord Zhen Guo Li Ming (Yin Yi-feng) is the Tang emperor's brother and a wicked oppressor of the subjects in his principality. He invades the peaceful bordering principality of Lord Ding Yuan (Chen Feng-chen), then robs and kills Ding Yuan and his family. Li Ming also orders his own border markers moved back in order to make it look as though Ding Yuan was encroaching on his property. Thus Li Ming is able to justify his savage behavior to the imperial authorities. After Li Ming lies and says he was avenging killings that Ding Yuan committed on his principality, the emperor decrees that all Ding Yuan's property and assets now belong to Li Ming. Ding Yuan's extended family and loyal soldiers will be disbanded and receive nothing, as punishment for Ding Yuan's supposed evil actions.

Incensed that Li Ming could get away with this immoral act, Lord Ruan Yi-cheng (Fang Mian) begs the righteous swordsman Mu Jun-jie (Ling Yun) to come out of retirement and happily married life to deal with this injustice by organizing a troupe of assassins to take out Li Ming and bring honor back to Ding Yuan's memory and family. After much deliberation, Mu is moved by the courage of five of Ding Yuan's loyal warriors, who plan to sacrifice their lives for their dead master's honor, and our six titular assassins are born! They hatch a plan to kill Li Ming who decides to travel through Ding Yuan's principality on his way to receive the emperor's royal decrees. Because he believes Ding Yuan's men are weak and cowardly, Li Ming feels confident in this arrogant act. To add salt to the wounds, Li Ming has Mu's wife brutally raped and killed as a warning for Mu not to try anything. Of course, this only steels Mu's resolve to take down Li Ming.

The film takes place during the time known as China's Dark Ages (A.D. 907-960) in a period called the Five Dynasties, which lasted between the fall of the Tang Dynasty and the formation of the Song Dynasty. Northern China split into five dynasties, and southern China split into 10 principalities. Murder, extortion and the Confucian code ran amok, which led to nationwide anarchy.

To hide the fact that actor Ling Yun did not practice martial arts—at the time, he probably did not know the difference between a sword and saxophone—the fights were broken down into one-step fights. Lin would simply block an attacker's strike and slice him with a sword, or to add a more rabid sense to the fights, he would block the attack of one opponent and slice an incoming opponent. This adds a nice rhythm to the fights and makes it easier for

Still from *Six Assassins* © Celestial Pictures Ltd. All rights reserved.

an inexperienced sword fighter to deal with multiple attackers.

Shooting the action tight hides mistakes and poor stances, and everything looks better with the liberal use of spins, kills and the actors nailing solid hero-shot poses. There's one creative and memorable moment that sees a sword re-bound off a tree and impale someone in the back while the fight continues as if nothing cool just happened. Keep in mind that this film was made in 1970 with mostly non-martial-artist actors, so everything is short and sweet. A remarkable 29 fights add up to just 13 minutes.

Titleography: *6 Assassins*. Translation—*Six Assassins*. **MA Percentage: 16.24% SHAW BROTHERS**

SLAUGHTER IN THE SNOW

Mushukunin Mikogami no Jokichi: Tasogare Ni Senko Ga Tonda (1973—Japan) **83m. SWC: Yuasa Kentaro. NOT/LOT: None; NOF/LOF: 10/ 7m 33s.** D: Kazuo Ikehiro. C: Yoshio Harada, Hajime Araki, Kai Ato, Takamori Gen, Toshio Hosoi, Renji Ishibashi, Kusuo Kita, Akiyoshi Kitaura, Tsutsui Koji, Natsuyagi Isao.

In this third and final installment of the *Trail of Blood* trilogy (see *Trail of Blood* and *Trail of Blood: Fearless Avenger*), the vengeful Jokichi (Yoshio Harada) is on the prowl for Yakuza boss Chuji. Chuji is the last of the three bosses (one boss killed per film) who were responsible for maiming Jokichi's hands and for the senseless slaughter of his wife and child. Jokichi carries a red sash, a memento from his wife's dead body, and three fingers on his right hand, which are the only mementos the three Yakuza bosses left him after cutting off his ring and pinkie fingers; that's also the reason Jokichi had to learn to sword-fight with his left hand. The crippled right is also a purposeful sick reminder left by the three bosses to torture and insult Jokichi. To our protagonist, his three remaining fingers remind him of the three bosses, while his two missing fingers remind him of his dead wife and child. But payback will soon be at hand.

Aware that Jokichi is near, Chuji hires Windmill Kobunji (Natsuyagi Isao) to murder him. Jokichi and Kobunji meet under strange circumstances for anyone to meet his would-be killer. Kobunji is under attack by vicious Yakuza because he tried to prevent Lady Oharu from being raped. After the fight, Kobunji collapses and uncontrollably coughs up blood; he has tuberculosis. Although Jokichi knows Kobunji is out to kill him, he helps the ailing Kobunji kill the Yakuza amid a whirlwind of blood and snow. Why rescue the man who wants to kill you? It's that code of *bushido*—honor your enemy if he is a true warrior.

After Jokichi nurses the wounded Kobunji back to health, he realizes Kobunji is just a sick samurai pining for Lady Oharu. Disillusioned by Kobunji's un-samurai antics, Jokichi abandons him to his own diseased devices. But Kobunji is actually one *onigiri* (rice ball) short of a bento box because he thinks Oharu is being held captive by the Yakuza boss Tozu. When Kobunji tries to rescue her, Tozu sends out his Yakuza army to kill him. Of course, Jokichi is in the wrong place at the wrong time again when he is forced into the trilogy's final fight, in which he takes on Tozu's terrors in a snow-covered field. It's no wonder this film is named *Slaughter in the Snow*.

But there is something wrong with this film that makes me feel it's "snow" good (a deja vu pun). Jokichi never gets to kill Chuji, and after killing Tozu's men, he just walks off into the "snowset." What gives? Perhaps the filmmakers thought a fourth film was in the making.

The final snow fight is the longest single fight in the trilogy and also the worst. As a film series moves along, the lead actor and the sword choreographer usually click and the action improves. But in the case of this trilogy, the fights don't get better. Why? Perhaps actor Yoshio Harada and choreographer Yuasa Kentaro just never clicked over the course of the trilogy because of the lack of action. But the techniques and skills of the actors come across more like pest-management specialists with fly swatters rather than master swordsmen with deadly tools. Yoshio has the right look of a hero, just not the *kendo* or *iaido* training to do the techniques well. On a final note, this could have been a better trilogy if they just condensed it into one movie, because it is really just about Jokichi killing the three men who wiped out his family.

Titleography: *Trail of Blood III*; *Homeless Mikogami Jokichi: The Sparks Fly at Dusk*. Translation—*Drifter Jokichi of Mikogami: Flash in the Twilight. Sparks Fly at Dusk* and *Flash in the Twilight* refer to the final snow fight. **MA Percentage: 9.10%**

SNAKE AND CRANE ARTS OF SHAOLIN

蛇鶴八步 (1978—Hong Kong/Taiwan) 95m. FI: Jackie Chan, Du Wei-he. NOT/LOT: 1/ 2m 30s; NOF/LOF: 39/ 22m 3s. D: Chen Zhi-hua. C: Jackie Chan, Nora Miao, Jin Gang, Jin Zheng-lan, Li Ying-guo, Liu Ya-ying, Miao Tian, Li Wen-tai, Tong Lin, Wang Yun, Liu Ping.

Jackie Chan zips around the world of Wu Lin, a subworld of martial artists that exists within the world of Jiang Hu. Eight important members of the Wu Lin world gather during the Mid-Autumn Festival to create a new martial art—the Eight Steps of the Snake and Crane—and the Nine Dragon Spear is to become the mark of their authority. But when the martial artists disappear without a trace, the Wu Lin world is sent into total disarray. However, one man has the coveted secret manual written by the fighters before their disappearance: Hsu Yin-fung (Jackie Chan).

Rather than keep the secret to himself, Hsu flaunts the manual in public, a ploy that is actually a sensitive subterfuge to draw out the killer of the eight martial artists. One by one, clans pop up out of the Wu Lin woodwork, all of which claim or feign honorable reasons for wanting the book, only to have Hsu's kung fu put them to the challenge. As the mystery grows, Hsu's skills increase, but he faces his greatest challenge from the Black Dragon Gang leader, Master Chin (Jin Gang), who wields his deadly knockout head butt.

In the final fight, Hsu uses *bao ding* balls (aka Chinese exercise balls, iron balls, Chinese medicine balls or *tai chi* balls) to defeat Chin. Created during the Ming Dynasty in Bao Ding, Hebei province, bao ding balls are held and rotated in orbit around one's hand as a means to strengthen the hands and fingers as well as to improve dexterity.

Dating back to the Shang Dynasty (1600-1046 B.C.), the Mid-Autumn Festival is an important Chinese holiday during which farmers celebrate the end of the summer harvest, and families and friends come together to respect the mythological "lady in the moon" and eat moon cake.

Fresh after shooting *Snake in the Eagle's Shadow* and learning new choreography from director/fight instructor Yuen Woo-ping, Chan took his choreography a big step forward in this film. His body shifts are more balanced, and he is never in the same stance long enough to slow the action down. His back is straighter than usual. What makes his choreography better is that although he keeps his techniques tight and his fists close to the body, he has good extension and limb elongation during technique delivery, which takes away the hunched look so often seen with many kung fu stars. Earlier fights in the film are com-

posed of side-angle medium shots, in which Chan and his opponent fill up the screen so there is nothing else to distract the viewer away from the kung fu. The most engaging fight in this film is when Chan battles Chin's three spearmen. The fight is pure danger as many of the spear jabs at Chan's head are shown in close shots, making sure we can see just how near he is to becoming a Chan kebab. In one instance, when a spearman pokes the spear right at Chan's face, Chan quickly leans toward the spear, then quickly shifts his head to the side at the last millisecond. It is very subtle yet hard to miss, and you know this sequence was shot more than once. Dude, no wonder he had that eye operation … accident.

Titleography: As of this writing, no alternative titles could be found. Translation—*Eight Steps of the Snake and Crane*. The Chinese title is the kung fu style created by the eight kung fu men at the film's beginning. **MA Percentage: 25.84%**

SNAKE CRANE SECRET

蛇鶴丹心震九州 (1978—Taiwan) 89m. FD: Lee Chiu. NOT/LOT: 11/ 8m 36s; NOF/LOF: 26/ 28m 39s. D: Wu Ma. C: Meng Fei, Meng Fei, Tan Dao-liang, Yang Hui-shan, You Tian-long, Fang Fang, Tung Li, Dean Shek.

Over the course of history, the subliminal enemy of one nation in one century might become the downtrodden punching bag of the same nation in the next century. Such is the case with Tibet, which for centuries was a staunch supporter of the Manchus who ruled over the Chinese and then pledged allegiance to the Republic of China leader Chiang Kai-shek after World War II. It is no wonder Communist China has little regard for Tibet and its autonomy. This film implicitly brings this tension to the foreground when the lead Ming traitor taps a lama fighter to help kill the Chinese patriots trying to save China from the Manchus (who established the Ching Dynasty in China).

With two brothers, two archetypal animal kung fu styles, two generations of fighters and two dynasties (the fading Ming and the rising Ching), this film is full of duals and duels. Ming traitor Hung Kung-shan (You Tian-long) kills the father of two brothers, who then become separated for 20 years. One son, Er Lang (Meng Fei), who supports the Ming cause, learns white crane boxing, and the other brother, a loyal Ching chief bodyguard (Tan Dao-liang), learns snake fist. They eventually meet again and find each other on opposite sides of the law. The Sun Moon fighters—the Chinese characters for "sun" and "moon" make up the character for the Ming—are trying to prevent Hung from getting a secret list of Ming loyalists, while the two brothers wrestle with their loyalties and brotherly love.

The snake and crane are two of the five animals styles of Shaolin martial arts that evolved from Ta Mo's observations of animals circa A.D. 520. The other are the fighting strategies of the dragon, tiger and leopard. However, it is important to note that the animal martial arts had also risen independently of Shaolin. For example, one style of white crane boxing is thought to have been created by Fang Chi-niang in the mid-1700s after she attacked a white crane and noticed how it evaded her jabs and pecked at the wood.

Dean Shek is effective in the film as a serious, scar-faced assassin—a far cry from his usual whining-idiot character, which is most closely associated with his role in Jackie Chan's 1978 films *Snake in the Eagle's Shadow* and *Drunken Master*. During the final showdown, you might think that Hung employs a Shaolin monk to fight the Ming heroes, but judging from the robes, the clothing and the absence of a completely bald head, the character is a lama Buddhist priest. The sound effects used when actor Meng Fei practices and fights using white crane kung fu are disturbingly distracting and make his serious combative ways look and sound sophomoric.

Titleography: *The Secret of the Snake and Crane*; *Secret(s) of the Dragon*; *Snake and Crane Secret*. Translation—*Snake Crane, Sincere and From the Bottom of the Heart, Shattered Nine States* (the nine states referring to the world). Although snake and crane kung fu are in the film, dragon is not. However, the Chinese dub implies that Hung practices dragon kung fu and that his goal is to take over the world (i.e., China). **MA Percentage: 41.85%**

SNAKE IN THE EAGLE'S SHADOW

蛇形刁手 (1978—Hong Kong) 97m. FI: Hsu Hsia, Yuen Woo-ping. NOT/LOT: 21/ 20m 49s; NOF/LOF: 18/ 25m 49s. D: Yuen Woo-ping. C: Jackie Chan, Yuen Xiao-tian, Hwang Jang-lee, Tino Wong, Dean Shek, Fung Ke-an, Peter Chan Lung, Hsu Hsia, Roy Horan, Charlie Chan-Yao-lin, Yuen Yat-choh, Jiang Jin.

Snake in the Eagle's Shadow is Jackie Chan's first real important film in the kung fu genre. The movie was so influential in the Hong Kong kung fu film industry that it was copycatted repeatedly, until the trend was exhausted. This film was also the progenitor to Suexploitation movies (see *Drunken Master*) via Yuen Xiao-tian's character, beggar Bai Chang-tien. Incidentally, though the film takes place toward the end of the Ching Dynasty, only the oafish lead villain characters have their hair in the queue required by Ching law.

The film opens with a dynamic fight between snake master Chao Chi-chih (Fung Ke-an) and eagle claw assassin Lord Shang Quan-ying (Hwang Jang-lee), whose goal in life is to wipe out all the snake kung fu stylists (a common rivalry theme often played out in the world of Wu Lin). Before Chao dies, he proudly says that he is not the last of the snake stylists and boasts that there are two more snake fighters alive: his teacher Bai Chang-tien and Chao's only son. Hearing that Chi-chih has been killed by Lord Shang, Bai disguises himself as a street beggar and searches for Chao's son.

Meanwhile, the orphaned-as-a-child Chien Fu (Jackie Chan) lives and works doing odd jobs. He is the janitor and dishwasher at a local kung fu school, where he is treated poorly, made fun of and looked upon as a whipping boy for smaller students eager to boost their egos. One day, as Chien walks the streets, he sees Bai being attacked by punks. Although he does not know how to fight, Chien bravely steps in to save the old man, who sneakily helps Chien defeat the thugs. The thugs eventually believe that Chien is an expert. Chien befriends Bai, takes him back to the kung fu school, and insists he sleep on his bed as he feeds and takes care of the old man.

A key scene: After a long day of being beaten up and picked on by the kung fu school's students, the downtrodden Chien lights up when Bai does juggling tricks with a bowl and then challenges Chien to take the bowl away. It is an endearing moment in which Chien's childlike wonder and innocence shine through, showing that regardless of the cruel world he lives in, there is hope in his life. That hope grows as Bai eventually decides to teach Chien snake fist kung fu as a means to defend himself from the unjust.

Eagle claw assassin Shang catches Chien fighting and recognizes the snake movements. He approaches Chien, pretends to be a student of Bai's and asks where he can find the old man. Chien is suspicious, but after getting trounced by Shang, who uses snake kung fu (thus "proving" he's Bai's student) and eagle claw skills, Chien agrees to put him in the loop. Chien is bothered by how easy it was for Shang to defeat him, so as he watches his pet cat kill a cobra, he creates a new form of kung fu: the snake fist combination cat's paw. He is not a moment to soon because Shang and his cohorts—one of them a Catholic priest (Roy Horan)—kill Chao's son. Just as they are about to finish off Bai, Chien arrives with his new snake and cat skills to overshadow Shang.

The actual origin of snake fist is relatively unknown, though it perhaps arose during the late Song Dynasty. The style evolved via copying the cobra, viper and python. The fighter's hands, fingers and legs represent the snake's head, tongue and tail, respectively. With the forefingers and middle fingers in a V-position, the viper consists of the two fingers aiming and striking at the arteries and veins, causing physiological damage by drawing blood. With the forearm held at a 90-degree angle to the upper arm, the wrist bent downward, and an open hand with fingers pointing at the opponent and thumb curled underneath the hand to maintain dynamic tension, the cobra hypnotically sways back and forth, then quickly strikes at the body's vital points. Hands and arms twisting and grappling around the opponent's arms and finishing with a vice-like grip to the throat or soft-tissue parts of the body are inspired by the twisting and asphyxiating power of the python.

The most common tactic of the snake fist demonstrates a principle from Sun Tzu's *The Art of War*. (For those who wish to know how to really say his name, it is prounced, "Soo-win Zi" and not like "Sun Zoo.") In it, Sun writes, "Attack with the head when the tail is attacked, attack with tail when the head is attacked, and attack with both the head and tail when the body is attacked."

Titleography: *Eagle's Shadow*; *Snake and the Eagle's Shadow*; *Bruce vs. Snake in Eagle's Shadow*; *Eagle Claw, Snake Fist, Cat's Paw*; *Snake Fist, Cat's Paw*; *Snaky Monkey*. Translation—*Snake Form Hooked Hand*. *Snake in the Eagle's Shadow* refers to the eagle stylist wanting to overshadow snake stylists—that is, to kill them. The use of *Eagle*, *Snake* and *Cat* in the titles is logical based on the film's various fighting styles. *Hooked Hand* in the Chinese title is in regard to the cat's paw and claws being hooked. *Drunken Master* has an alternate title with *Monkey* in it, so perhaps *Snaky Monkey* is a reference to that film. **MA Percentage: 48.05%**

SNAKE PRINCE, THE

蛇王子 (1976—Hong Kong) **90m. FI: Han Yi-sheng. NOT/LOT: None; NOF/LOF: 4/ 5m.** D: Lo Chen. C: Ti Lung, Lin Chen-chi, Wang Yu, Lin Wei-tu, Ching Miao, Fan Lei, Ko Ti-hua, Xu Hsao-chiang, Wu Hang-shen.

Say what? Yes, one of Shaw Brothers' biggest kung fu stars ever, Ti Lung, plays a 40-foot snake (one of three in the film). Ti Lung is the Snake Prince, who can devour people with a single bite but who also has a conscience. He chooses to marry the most beautiful girl in the local valley, Hei Qin (Lin Chen-chi), in return for diverting the mountain river toward the parched village farmlands to save their crops. After their snake-human wedding, the two consummate their marriage. During the act, Ti Lung gradually changes from a scaly humanoid into a giant snake. Hei Qin later lays a single giant egg, from which little snakes hatch and cry, "Mama, mama."

There's more, including a big village shindig full of rock 'n' roll music and a dance routine reminiscent of Michael Jackson's *Thriller* ... sort of. And when the stupid, jealous humans step out of line—who in their right mind would want to mess with a giant snake?—there is an all-out battle. When the giant snakes clash with the puny humans, this light fantasy turns ultra-gory, with blood and guts splattering across the screen. And at one point, Hei Qin's jealous sister decides to burn the baby snakes.

The film's few fights are filled with back-and-forth camera pans, and the action can be dizzier than a ride on the ill-fated SS Minnow from *Gilligan's Island*. This film is a herpetologist's nightmare that cannot be rivaled—until you see *Fangs of the Cobra*, at least.

Titleography: As of this writing, no alternative titles could be found. Translation—*Snake Prince*, the main character. **MA Percentage: 5.56%** SHAW BROTHERS

SNUFF BOTTLE CONNECTION

神腿鐵扇功 (1977—Taiwan) **84m. FC: Yuen Woo-ping. NOT/LOT: 26/ 9m 5s; NOF/LOF: 22/ 28m 3s.** D: Liu Li-li, Dong Jin-hu. C: John Liu, Hwang Jang-lee, She Fei-yang, Chien Yuen-sheng, Yuen Biao, Yuen Shen-yi, Gao Fei, Yuen Kwei, Roy Horan, Robert Kerver, Zhang Ji-ping.

Later in this martialogy, I will share one of the biggest Hong Kong secrets of actual fight choreography that goes beyond the obvious, which is about being creative and not thinking of any fight as being real. But first the plot.

After winning the Sino-Russian War (1887), Russia took control of most of Siberia, set up a puppet state in Mongolia and established a sphere of influence in Manchuria. According to this film, there are still factions in both countries who want the war to continue, among them the Russian General Tolstoy (Roy Horan) and the white-haired Ching General Shan Tung (Hwang Jang-lee), who practices the deadly Incredible Kick Iron Fan kung fu. When police inspector Xiao Ting-chien (John Liu) is secretly assigned to weed out the Ching traitor and the malicious maverick Russian general, his only clue is a snuff bottle his kung fu brother Gao (She Fei yang; some film reviews say actor Meng Fei plays Gao, but that's incorrect) pickpockets from Tolstoy. As it turns out, the matching snuff bottle is part of a recognition code used between Tolstoy and Shan Tung's second-in-command, Dao Guan (Gao Fei). A map of China's coastal defense system hangs in the balance, and it is up to Xiao to save the day.

Of historical note, snuff bottles came into vogue during the Ching Dynasty and usually contained tobacco powder. Smoking tobacco was illegal at the time, but snuff was considered good for one's health.

Although on paper the combination of Hwang Jang-lee and John Liu, two adept kickers, is exciting, they do not look as comfortable with each other as in their previous collaboration on *Secret Rivals* (1976). This is probably because the choreographers wanted to focus more on Hwang's iron fan work. But even that looks awkward because the smooth, flowing, somewhat balletic movements of the fan do not blend well with Hwang's high *taekwondo* stances. Hwang also tries to look powerful with the fan by using that jerking power-snap motion that taekwondo and karate practitioners use as a means of focusing their techniques (which is why their *gi* can snap so loudly). Apart from his usual super-flexible kicking, splitting and holding one-leg poses, Liu does some fantastic spear work while trying to accentuate his fighting stances with *mi zong* kung fu postures.

Also of note is when Dao Guan's personal bodyguard (Zhang Ji-ping) fights. It looks like he is thinking about the choreography rather than trying to look natural, and there is a reason for this. The secret to remembering choreography during fights is in the sounds of the fighters. You will notice that for each technique, fighters use their voices as cues to let their partners know they are about to attack, or the yells might be used to plot the movements and the cadence of the fights. The faster two fighters yell, the faster they learn to deliver the techniques. However, Zhang does not yell for each movement, and this explains why he looks like he's thinking about the choreography rather than going with the flow. This was one of the first things I learned while doing kung fu TV shows in Taiwan.

Titleography: *The Snuff Bottle Connection*. Translation—*God-like Legs and Iron Fan Kung Fu*. This title names the kung fu skills Hwang Jang-lee's character practices. *Snuff Bottle Connection* plays off the two bottles used as part of the secret code between the Russians and the Chings. **MA Percentage: 44.21%**

SOUL OF CHIBA

激殺! 邪道拳 / *Gekisatsu! Judo Ken* (1973—Japan/Hong Kong/Thailand) **89m. FI: Uncredited. NOT/LOT: 5/ 4m 6s; NOF/LOF: 22/ 19m 6s. D:** Chan Tung-man, Yukio Noda. **C:** Sonny Chiba, Etsuko Shihomi, Yasuyoshi Shikamura, Lung Chan, Fang Yuen, Tadashi Yamashita, Junichi Haruta, Kogenta Katayama, Hirofumi Koga, Bin Kurihara, Bolo Yeung, Naowarat Yuktanan.

This film is shocking, but not in the way you might think. *Soul of Chiba*, aka *Soul of Bruce Lee*, is actor Sonny Chiba's two-fold homage to Bruce Lee. First of all, Chiba and his Japan Action Club fighters shot this film in Thailand, the country where Lee shot his first film, *The Big Boss* (1971). The second reason will be revealed a bit later in the martialogy.

The film is set in Thailand, where student Mu Yu-tak (Sonny Chiba) seeks revenge for the murder of his Thai martial arts teacher, Chen Shin-kan (Fang Yuen), at the hands of Mu's martial arts brother Sam Wang (Yasuyoshi Shikamura). It is all somehow related to diamonds being smuggled into Thailand, which are being used to buy drugs bound for Hong Kong. Elsewhere, an undercover narcotics agent (Tadashi Yamashita) is matching wits with a drug boss whose hit squad is lead by former undercover cop Nepal (Bolo Yeung). Nepal wears a small Dick Tracy-style fedora hat and is mute because he had his tongue removed by a drug boss. According to the drug boss, he removed Nepal's tongue so he could never speak to his police colleagues or anyone else about the syndicate's inner workings. It seems, though, that Nepal could write about it if he wanted to.

Meanwhile, Mu's martial arts are about to get better than Wang's because he finds love and training with a local loom lady named Li Hua (Etsuko Shihomi). Here comes that "are you kidding me?" moment I mentioned earlier: Mu believes that the only way he can defeat Wang is to become as fast as greased lightning. Dressed in leather gear that makes him look like a guy from the Village People, Mu attaches electric wires to his body, connects himself to an electric generator and then cranks up the juice. What follows is a crazy shot of Chiba rapidly shaking his legs, arms and body in an ultra-spastic way that goes on as one unedited take for 70 seconds. Considering that the scene was shot at about 18 frames per second, Chiba must have been shaking in his britches for at least two minutes before taking a break. It has been widely reported that Bruce Lee would hook himself up to electricity as a way to quickly fatigue his muscles. It's said that Lee believed he would get an hour or so of workout in less than a minute this way—thus this is that second-fold homage to Lee mentioned earlier.

Some fight pieces are just plain entertaining in this film, like when Mu fights the Four Crazy Monkey Gods: four guys who work themselves into a simian frenzy and then leap, chatter and freak out like monkeys on meth. It is rather funny to see actual monkeys thrown at Chiba from behind the camera to amplify the existence of black-magic spirit possession, which is a reality in Thai spiritualism.

In other action, Tadashi Yamashita and Bolo Yeung brutally get it on with heavy-handed contact strikes; the cinematographer closely shoots their arms so you can see how they connect. There is a fight Chiba does toward the end of the film amid tall grass and on, around and by the side of a single-rope bridge, which is actually just a rope to hang onto when walking through water. But it is the last fight in which Chiba exhibits his smooth, relaxed and flexible martial arts skills. After this movie, Chiba would mostly use hard-edge karate skills and tension-breathing techniques to sell the power of his movements.

It was also difficult to nail down when this movie was

made. According to the various reported release dates, it came out in 1973, 1974 or 1977. However, based on the fight choreography, the physical and age appearances of Sonny Chiba and Bolo Yeung, the motif and storyline, and the cinematic signatures Chiba used in his karate-based films starting with *The Street Fighter* (1974), I am inclined to say that this is a pre-*Street Fighter* film and was made in 1973 or early 1974.

Titleography: *The Karate 2*; *Soul of Bruce Lee*. Translation—*Emotional Killing Outbursts! Unorthodox Way of Fighting*. Tadashi Yamashita starred in *The Karate* (released in the USA as *Bronson Lee, Champion*). The translated title seems to refer to Mu's unorthodox training method using electricity to generate electric-like killing outbursts of energy. **MA Percentage: 26.07%**

SOUL OF THE SWORD

殺絕 (1978—Hong Kong) **84m. FI: Tang Chia. NOT/LOT: 4/ 1m 19s; NOF/ LOF: 20/ 18m 51s. D:** Hua Shan. **C:** Ti Lung, Lin Chen-chi, Ku Feng, Xu Hsao-chiang, Yu Rong, Liu Hui-ling, Lily Li, Chan Shen, Lee Hoi-san, Jiang Han.

This film is as much about the soul of a sword as it is about the sole swordsman. The wandering swordsman is a recurring character in the world of Jiang Hu. He is a lone man whose mission in life is simply to be the best.

Part of this film's novelty for Western viewers, especially new enthusiasts of *wuxia pian* (the wuxia genre of films), was in exploring traditional swordsman lore. According to Chinese legend, each sword possesses a spirit that sings after it has tasted blood. The high-pitched (often overemphasized) "*shing!*" sound of a sword being drawn or wielded attempts to dramatize this point. In the opening of *Soul of the Sword*, the faceless swordsman Lu Tieng-gang, wearing his trademark hat and veil, trains with candles as we hear that distinctive sword sound reverberate through the room. It tells us that this sword has tasted blood and that it has a soul. This is why in wuxia films each sword has a name. It is not a weapon, but a living entity; it is not just an extension of the hand, it is the hand.

At the beginning of the film, Lu, the King of Swords, is about to duel a young swordsman who travels with a woman. Lu explains that because the young man cares for this woman and she is in his heart, the young man is destined to lose the fight. A true swordsman knows no emotion, and the wielder of the weapon should be free of hindrance. The outcome is settled just as Lu predicted: the young swordsman dies. But before he does, he asks to see Lu's face. Lu replies that the hat can only be removed after he dies—in other words, when he is defeated. Full of grief, the woman commits suicide.

A little boy witnesses the battle and now has a purpose in life: study the sword so he can defeat Lu and see his face. He grows to an adult (Ti Lung) and perfects his skills. He calls himself Nameless. With no credentials, he heads to Lu's villa, all the while haunted by the ghost of the woman he saw commit suicide years before. When he arrives at Lu's villa, Lu is not home. He is greeted

Still from *Soul of the Sword* © Celestial Pictures Ltd. All rights reserved.

by the kind Dr. Chui-I (Ku Feng), who after witnessing Nameless easily defeat the villa's expert swordsmen guards, invites him to stay at the villa. The doctor teaches Nameless about what life is and is not. Nameless begins a love affair with local shopkeeper Ho Lien (Lin Chen-chi), who looks just like the suicidal beauty and who is also being wooed by swordsman Yien (Xu Hsao-chiang). As Nameless and Ho's love grows, so do the jealous assassination attempts on Nameless by Yien. He is no match for Nameless, though at the pleadings of Ho, Nameless spares his life and won't kill him this time. Then Lu returns, and the showdown is set. Lu's words from that first encounter echo in Nameless' mind. Is Ho a hindrance? If so, what must he do to win? What is more important, love or the kill? These are questions not typically addressed in wandering swordsman films. There are also only three main characters, which is a departure from the usual wuxia films with intricate plots, red herrings and webs of many characters.

Based on Ti Lung's finger postures and stances, it is evident that Ti does not practice swordplay, which does not mean he does not sell it well. But this might be the choreographer's choice because the postures of Ti Lung's left hand—the hand not holding the sword—move between an open-hand posture or the correct two-finger posture, which looks like a Boy Scout salute. This shifting could mean that Ti's character's skills are not limited to one way of fighting or that Ti is not well-schooled in the sword. The fight in which Ti Lung slides on his back toward two rows of four swordsmen and then kips up onto his feet is a beautiful set piece. Other fights are shot with low-angle wide shots while incorporating camera pans giving similar fights a different perspective and creative appeal. The action extends the argument that camera choreography is of tantamount importance to fight choreography.

Titleography: As of this writing, no alternative titles could be found. Translation—*Kill All*. See martialogy. *Kill All* has a double meaning: To be the best, one must kill all challengers and also kill (i.e., end) all personal relationships. **MA Percentage: 24%** SHAW BROTHERS

SPIRITUAL BOXER, THE

神打 (1975—Hong Kong) **99m. FI: Liu Chia-liang. NOT/LOT: 8/ 5m 33s; NOF/LOF: 14/ 13m. 58s.** D: Liu Chia-liang. C: Wang Yu, Lin Zhen-ji, Chen Kuan-tai, Ti Lung, Jiang Yan, Shi Zhong-tian, Fung Ke-an, Lee Hoi-san, Wu Hang-shen, Ai Fei, Chan Shen, Jiang Han.

Toward the end of the Ching Dynasty, an aggressive martial arts Triad sect called the Righteous Fists of Harmony emerged, and their violent anti-foreign and anti-Christian mentality gave rise to the Boxer Rebellion (1898-1901), which had its origins in Shantung Province. The rebellion was also partially a response to Western religious meddling. Foreign Roman Catholics insisted that a local village temple important for spiritual purposes had been a church before Emperor Kang Xi banned Christianity 200 years ago and argued that it should be given back to the Catholics. The local court agreed, setting off the rise of the Boxers. The Boxers believed that through martial arts, *chi gong* (*qigong*) and prayer, they could stop Western bullets. Their fervor was further incited by the promise that millions of heaven-sent "spirit soldiers" would lead them to victory.

This whole perfunctory premise and the ensuing slaughter of innocents by the Boxers was a dark time in martial arts history. In a matter of years, the Boxers almost wiped out all the ethical codes and righteous moralities that had evolved throughout Chinese martial arts history—everything that the Shaolin and all their legends had worked for. Fortunately, their were new heroes like Huang Fei-hong who reminded China about the true path, and this is something that traditional kung fu stylists like director-actor-fight choreographer Liu Chia-liang never forgot. These new kinds of anti-Boxer Rebellion heroes would inspire this film as well as Liu's best martial arts film ever, *Legendary Weapons of Kung Fu* (1982).

The Spiritual Boxer opens with two Spiritual Boxers (Chen Kuan-tai and Ti Lung), fighters who allowed themselves to become possessed with kung fu spirits in order to become invincible warriors. They perform for the empress dowager and demonstrate their amazing kung fu powers. (A similar scene takes place in Chang Cheh's *Boxer Rebellion*.) For the climax of the performance, they invoke spirits to protect their bodies from Western rifle shots as they allow themselves to be shot at by the palace guards. Similar to historical reality, the audience is soon reminded that Spiritual Boxers were phony in that they could not

Still from *The Spiritual Boxer* © Celestial Pictures Ltd. All rights reserved.

stop bullets. The performers die. That brings us to a small village in the middle of nowhere where Triad boss Liu De-ruei (Shi Zhong-tian) is terrorizing the villagers. He runs a protection racket, acts as a loan shark and hands out kung fu beatings. Enter the clumsy but good-natured Hsiao Chien (Wang Yu), a student of a spirit invoker (similar to someone who does séances), which is different from a Boxer. When his teacher is too drunk to do the invoking and disappears while the police are looking for him, Hsiao has to take care of business.

Hsiao Chien's flimflam act consists of supposedly allowing traditional Chinese gods to possess his body, which he reveals by demonstrating the various martial arts associated with each god. Hsiao manages to con the villagers out of food and money until local kung fu ruffians associated with Triad boss Liu challenge him. On the run, he is saved by female street urchin Jin Lian (Lin Zhen-ji). After rescuing him, Jin does some behind-the-scenes trickery to help Hsiao, which makes Hsiao appear to be the real deal. After Hsiao takes on Liu with his newfound partner and bag of tricks, Liu's hold on the village wanes. Unfortunately, two dangerous killers who are also Liu's good buddies come to town. When Hsiao's spiritual world starts to crumble, his teacher returns and reminds him of the real kung fu abilities he learned through combining them with the gods' movements. Then the Triad fighters attack Hsiao. During the fight, his teacher yells out the gods' names, and Hsiao effortlessly defends himself using the Five Animal Gods (modeled after the Shaolin's Five Animal Styles) and the Five Elements Gods (emulating the Five Element Linking Fist of *hsing-i* kung fu).

Spiritual Boxer is an important film in the history of kung fu cinema for two main reasons. It was the first official kung fu comedy and introduced the idea of a teacher screaming out the names of kung fu movements to his pupil during a fight as a way to remind the student which technique to use. Most Western audiences associate this motif with Jackie Chan's *Drunken Master*, in which protagonist Huang's teacher yells out the names of the drunken gods to instruct him how to fight the lead villain. Secondly, this film marked the first time that a fight instructor (Liu Chia-liang) was given the chance to direct a movie. After this film was successful, it opened the doors for other kung fu choreographers to direct, to the point that it became the standard path for many kung fu filmmakers: red-trouser stuntman, assistant fight choreographer, fight choreographer (aka fight instructor or martial arts choreographer), fight director (or martial arts director) and, finally, film director.

Cultural note here: The term "Boxers" was coined by Western observers who equated the martial arts exercises practiced by these Chinese fighters to the training European pugilists went through.

Titleography: *Naked Fists of Terror*. Translation—*Supernatural Way of Fighting*. *Spiritual Boxer* and *Supernatural Way of Fighting* describe the hero's fighting style. *Naked Fists of Terror* is probably just a cool-sounding generic title that ultimately has little to do with the film. **MA Percentage: 19.71%** SHAW BROTHERS

SPIRITUAL KUNG FU

拳精 (1978—Hong Kong) **94m. MAI: Jackie Chan. NOT/LOT: 14/ 10m 31s; NOF/LOF: 16/ 27m 48s.** D: Lo Wei. C: Jackie Chan, James Tien, Wu Mensiu, Lee Tung-chun, Dean Shek, Li Wen-tai, Wen Li-peng.

Steven Spielberg axed the ending (see the titleography), but that doesn't take away the magic of the film. *Spiritual Kung Fu* is a genre-bending film that uses a martial arts backdrop to incorporate elements of sci-fi, horror and comedy.

A power-hungry vagabond (James Tien) wants to rule the kung fu clans, and to do so, his father steals *The Book of Seven Fists* from the hallowed library of Shaolin. Anyone who learns this secret art will be unbeatable, except against a hero who knows Five Star Fist kung fu. However, the Five Star manual has been missing for centuries. As the vagabond kills each clan leader, a meteor (a Fourth of July sparkler on a piece of string) hits the temple and awakens the five ghost protectors of the lost Five Star book. The goofy ghosts feel a kinship with smart-aleck non-monk disciple Yi Lung (Jackie Chan) and teach him Five Star Fist in order to save Shaolin and all the kung fu clans.

Though made in early 1978, the film was shelved and not released until after the success of Chan's *Snake in the Eagle's Shadow* (1978) and *Drunken Master* (1978). The film was director Lo Wei's answer to the Shaw Brothers smash hit *The Spiritual Boxer* (1975), which was actually the first purposely made kung fu comedy. Also, because of the curious success of the American TV show *Kung Fu* in Hong Kong, the blind monk character Wei Kong, was modeled after actor Keye Luke's blind character Master Po. He even has a soft spot for the meddling Yi Lung. The plot is also similar to the movie *The 36th Chamber of Shaolin* (1977). Yi Lung wishes to leave the temple to fight the clan killer, but he must prove to the Shaolin abbot that he is ready to leave. Yi Lung goes through a trial of combat and must choose a weapon to defeat other monks who are also armed with weapons. In *36th Chamber*, San Te chooses the monk's spade, the cudgel (pole) and his own invention, the three-sectional staff, for his trial by combat against the Shaolin Temple's master-of-arms priest, who uses butterfly knives.

In this movie, Yi Lung's weapon of choice is the *tonfa*, which ironically is not considered a traditional weapon of Shaolin. However, like most historical aspects of martial arts, many things are open to debate and interpretation. The tonfa is believed to have originated in China or Indonesia, but popular legend says it was brought to prominence in Okinawa during the times when the Japanese banned the use of swords and weapons on the island. Farmers began to use weapons derived from farm implements, and the tonfa was the wooden handle of a millstone that also doubled as rice huller.

Five Star Fist kung fu is based on the five animal styles of Shaolin, which date back to A.D. 520. The Buddhist monk Ta Mo was staying at Shaolin and devised a series of exercises called the 18 Buddhist fists. They were based on his observations of wild animals he encountered while traveling through the jungles from India to China. During 13th century although some historians argue the mid-1600s, Shaolin monk Zhue Yang along with fellow martial artists Li Sou and Bai Yu-feng improved upon Ta Mo's 18 movements to create the five animal styles of Shaolin: dragon, tiger, leopard, snake and white crane.

Titleography: *Karate Ghostbuster*. Translation—*Kung Fu Ghosts*. The Hong Kong English title mirrors the Shaw Brothers movie *The Spiritual Boxer*, and the American video release capitalizes on the success of *Ghostbusters* (1984). Official English-language releases in the states are required to remove the last 10 seconds of audio of the film because the original movie impinges on Spielberg's *E.T.* (1982). **MA Percentage: 40.76%**

STONER

鐵金剛大破紫陽觀 (1974—Hong Kong) 88m. **MAI: Sammo Hung, Chan Chuen. NOT/LOT: None; NOF/LOF: 16/ 16m 2s.** D: Huang Feng. C: Angela Mao Ying, George Lazenby, Whang In-shik, Takagi Joji, Sammo Hung, Jin Lou, Romanolee Rose, Samuel J. Peake, Hong Xing-zhong, Yang Wei.

In 1973, George Lazenby signed a four-picture contract with Golden Harvest. The first three films under the contract were to star Lazenby as Lee's partner in *Stoner* (at the time of the contract signing, it was called *The Shrine of Ultimate Bliss*), as Lee's enemy in *The Man From Hong Kong* and with Bruce Lee as an adversary in *The Game of Death*. His role in the last film, *A Queen's Ransom*, was yet to be determined. None of these films happened the way they were planned. Due to the bad press surrounding *Game of Death* and the fact that Lazenby was known to have met Lee for dinner the night he died, Lazenby was dropped from the project. At the same time, Shaw Brothers had its big stars, Ti Lung and David Chiang, starring in Hammer Films alongside the likes of Peter Cushing and Stuart Whitman. Then there was the sparkling Tamara Dobson shooting up Macao and Hong Kong in *Cleopatra Jones and the Casino of Gold*. Not to be outdone by Shaw Brothers' several successful

foreign co-productions, Golden Harvest went ahead with the other three films Lazenby was attached to.

The first, *Stoner*, was later released in the United States as *A Man Called Stoner*, borrowing the verbiage of Richard Harris' *A Man Called Horse* (1970). In *Stoner*, Lazenby ended up playing the character Lee would have played, and Angela Mao Ying was cast to play the character Lazenby would have portrayed.

When a rich man bids a lot money for the S.S. Wu Wang for scrap metal, the Hong Kong police are suspicious as to why he's willing to bid so much money on an old vessel making its final voyage from Thailand to Hong Kong. Similarly, Taiwan police have the same suspicion and send their top agent, Li Shao-hu (Angela Mao Ying), to Hong Kong to investigate. Meanwhile, Australian cop Stoner (George Lazenby) has been investigating the distribution of a new hallucinogenic drug that doubles as a mind-altering aphrodisiac, which his girlfriend overdosed on and died from; the syndicate that Stoner had been investigating targeted her. Stoner believes that Hong Kong billionaire Mr. Chin (Takagi Joji) is the ringleader. Stoner and Li eventually hook up, discover that a Taoist temple in Hong Kong is a front for drug manufacturing and distribution, and raid the place with guns blazing and feet flying.

Lazenby got the role of Bond in *On Her Majesty's Secret Service* (1969) because of his fighting ability. Although producer Raymond Chow had envisioned Lazenby and Lee fighting in this film, Mao Ying was a good replacement. Her final fight with Whang In-shik is filled with many spinning kick combinations. At several instances during the fight, it appears as though the actors are whipping their feet all over, with many kicks barely missing each other. It looks as if there was no actual choreography and the movements are not so much pre-planned retreats but instinctive moves to avoid being hit. Lazenby's fights are shot with tight angles, and he does flail and wind up before each strike, but undercranking the camera (thus speeding up the footage) helps sell his moves. It is curious that the undercranking is used for close shots rather than the normal long and medium wide-angle shots.

Titleography: *Shrine of the Ultimate Bliss*; *A Man Called Stoner*; *Hong Kong Hitman*. Translation—*Iron King Kong Defeats the Purple Sun Pagoda*. The Chinese title nicely keyed in on the expected recognition factor that Lazenby and Lee would have had associated with them from the pagoda in *Game of Death*. *Shrine of the Ultimate Bliss* refers to the drugs and where they were being made. **MA Percentage: 18.22%**

STORY OF CHINESE GODS, THE

封神榜 and 七彩封神榜 (1975—Taiwan) 85m. **FI: Uncredited. NOT/LOT: None; NOF/LOF: 14/ 22m 39s.** D: Zhang Zhi-hui. C: Because this is a cartoon, there is no main cast.

In many cases, you have to do some amazing things in your life to become a Chinese god. When such people die and ascend to heaven, they have to, for lack of a better way of describing it, apply for godhood. When an application is rejected, usually because the applicant feels he is more important and benevolent than he really is, things can go awry.

Without professing to be any sort of expert on Chinese gods, of which there are about 154 at last count, this film is based on the book *The Investiture of the Gods* (aka *The Creation of the Gods*), which was written during the Ming Dynasty by either Xu Zhong-lin (unknown-1566) or Lu Xi-xing (1520-1601).

The story and film tell the tale of the rise of the Zhou Dynasty at the expense of the Shang Dynasty. General Zhou, the last ruler of the Shang Dynasty, is a cruel man who enjoys lascivious debauchery. Because of this, his claim for immortality is rejected. When he decides to build an army of demons, evil spirits and wicked gods to wipe out mankind, priest Shen is sent down by the heavens to assist King Wu of the Zhou Dynasty in hopes of saving mankind and restoring a balance between heaven and earth. Both armies grow, and I'm sure someone knowledgeable about Chinese gods would have a field day recognizing the who's who of deities flying, fighting and morphing on-screen. It is probably a major disadvantage watching an English dub of this animated film because the names of most gods are either not mentioned or most certainly mispronounced. For example, Shen's name is said at least three different ways throughout the film, and I still don't exactly know who he really is. But I do have my thoughts on that.

I did recognize Zhou's adviser: Da Ji is a nine-tailed female fox spirit who can take on human form. Fox spirits are usually female and appear as young, beautiful women, and they can be good or bad. Da Ji is one evil babe, known for inventing nasty torture devices to use on righteous men. Her evil pal Fat Belly Guitar Pipa Jing (named after the Chinese-style lute) is also in the film. In terms of Shen, I would guess he's supposed to be the god Jiang Tai-gong because he was the one who led King Wu's army into battle. I also recognized Na Cha (thanks to the Chang Cheh's film *Na Cha the Great* (1974)), not because he was basically naked and wearing a bib to cover his naughty parts, but because he was zipping around on wheels of fire. But there are many I don't know, like the three big green giants with weapons that morph into snakes, spiders and *pipa*; the semi-nude unicorn kid; the flying human-eagle who spits knives; and the spirit guy who can take his head off and change into monsters. But the lead fighting god, the one with the third eye (which symbolizes enlightenment and signals that he has attained immortality) is the god who basically saves the day and kills all the evil gods. He is none other than Bruce Lee. I'm sure he wasn't in the Ming Dynasty novel, but his inclusion in the film shows the sort of reverence Lee attained in Chinese culture. The Lee character has a long final fight scene (about four minutes) in which he does what he does best: kick, punch and *nunchaku* evil into submission. He even does the slow-motion hand gesture from *Fist of Fury*.

Titleography: As of this writing, no alternative titles could be found. Translations—*List of the People Who Have Become Gods* and *The Seven Colors of the Rainbow, List of the People Who Have Become Gods*. The *Rainbow* refers to all the gods in the sky coming down to the earth. **MA Percentage: 26.65%**

STRANGER AND THE GUNFIGHTER, THE

El Kárate, el Colt y el Impostor / La Dove non Batte il Sole

龍虎走天涯 (1974—Italy/Spain/USA/Hong Kong) **107m. NOT/LOT: None; NOF/LOF: 5/ 8m 25s.** D: Antonio Margheriti (Dawson). C: Lee Van Clief, Lo Lieh, Wang Xia, Chan Shen, Patty Shepard, Femi Benussi, Karen Yeh, Julián Ugarte, Erika Blanc, Goyo Peralta, Al Tung.

An old Wild West gunslinger meets a young Far East kung fu fighter searching for treasure, and make no butts about it, the further they get behind, the faster they will find the treasure. Seeking Mr. Wang's fortune, rugged cowboy Dakota (Lee Van Clief) blows open four bank safes to find a woman's photo inside each one. When Mr. Wang gets blown up during the fourth explosion, Dakota is sentenced to be hanged for murder. As it turns out, the women are Wang's mistresses, and each has part of a treasure map tattooed onto her rear end. Back in China, several warlords wrathful over Wang's missing fortune send Wang's wayward warrior nephew Wang Ho-chien (Lo Lieh) to find the money. On the day Dakota is doomed to die, Ho arrives in the nick of time and saves him. Realizing that the babes' buttocks are the blueprint for bumping into the bounty, Dakota and Ho band together to find the mistresses of the missing moola. The plot device with the four female derrieres is borrowed from the USA/UK comedy film *Ooh ... You Are Awful* (1972).

After *King Boxer* (aka *Five Fingers of Death*) got international distribution, Lo Lieh was the most recognizable Chinese actor on the planet, at least for a few months until Bruce Lee came along. Keying in on Lo's notoriety and the luster of the spaghetti Western, Shaw Brothers cast Lo with veteran spaghetti Western actor Van Clief to create what was hoped to be a series of co-productions with European film companies.

Although the film did not do as well as hoped and Lo's international limelight dimmed, the film did set the table for two Shaw co-productions with England's Hammer Studios: *Dracula and the 7 Golden Vampires* and *Call Him Mr. Shatter*. In addition to acting like a stereotype, Lo performs some truly subpar fights. Besides the disrupting Moog synthesizer sound effect used when Lo jumps in slow motion, the fights are deathly slow, and the lack of undercranking reveals Lo's clumsy and off-balance martial arts abilities. It is actually rather sad because prior to this film, Lo had done some amazing fight scenes in other movies. On the other hand, this film reveals the importance of good fight instructors. Notice on the other hand (running out of hands) that Lo does the incorrect kung fu hand salute, which is supposed to be left palm over right fist, but he does it in reverse. A good fight choreographer would have also picked that up. But on a positive note: protagonist Ho is an expert acupuncturist, and the way the film describes the theory of acupuncture and *chi* (*qi*) is actually pretty clear.

Titleography: *Blood Money*; *Blood Money*. Translation—*Dragon and Tiger Travel to Far Away Places*. *Stranger* and *Dragon* in the titles refer to Ho, and *Gunfighter* and *Tiger* refer to Dakota. Blood money is money paid to a murder victim's next of kin, which is in line with the film's plot. **MA Percentage: 7.87%** SHAW BROTHERS

STRAY CAT ROCK: SEX HUNTER

Nora Neko Rokku: Sekkusu Hanta (1970—Japan) **85m. FI: Uncredited. NOT/LOT: None; NOF/LOF: 4/ 2m 3s.** D: Yasuharu Hasebe. C: Meiko Kaji, Rikiya Yasuoka, Tatsuya Fuji, Jiro Okazaki, Yoko Takagi.

Martial arts racism exists, and not just in America. The third film of the five-part *Stray Cat Rock* series pits Alley Cat gang leader Mako (Meiko Kaji) and her feline femmes fatales against the Eagles, a rival street gang that carries a heinous hatred toward "half-breeds"—those who are half-black and half-Japanese. It is one of Japan's shames (one it shares with Korea) that children of African-American servicemen fathers and Japanese (or Korean) mothers are discriminated against in some circles of society. As exploitive as these films are, arriving years before their Western blaxploitation counterparts, this film is a powerful cinematic statement about the underlying racism of Japanese society toward mixed-race couples. It is filmed with dogged self-belief and dangerous anti-government statements toward a topic that has haunted Japan since opening its doors to the West in 1868 at the isolated port of Kobe on Osaka Bay.

As one might expect from a film that pits an all-girl teenage gang against adolescent male hoodlums, the fights are influenced by karate and simple *kendo* techniques attached to the way of the knife. The fights are a bit haphazard and lack any sense of authentic martial arts technique, but the way they are shot creates intensity out of the choreography's simplicity.

Titleography: As of this writing, no alternative titles could be found. Translation—*Wild Cat Rock: Sex Hunter*. **MA Percentage: 2.41%**

STREET FIGHTER, THE

Gekitotsu! Satsujin Ken (1974—Japan) **91m. MAD: Masafumi Suzuki, Ken Kazama. NOT/LOT: 3/ 2m 6s; NOF/LOF: 21/ 26m 19s.** D: Shigera Ozawa. C: Sonny Chiba, Goichi Yamada, Yutaka Nakajima, Tony Cetera, Masafumi Suzuki, Masashi Ishibashi, Akira Shion, Osman Yusuf, Etsuko Shihomi, Jiro Chiba.

The neat thing about watching Japanese karate films after watching a ton of Chinese kung fu films is that for once the Japanese are the good guys. So instead of trying to kill the Chinese or destroy their martial arts schools, they are destroying the evil Yakuza. Enter Sonny Chiba, who gave Japanese karate films a different kind of fist of fury. Chiba brought Japanese karate center stage by sacrificing flair and artistry for more violence and brutality in the form of anti-hero Tsurugi Takuma the street fighter, aka Terry Tsurugi in the English dub..

In this first installment of the *Street Fighter* trilogy, the movie opens with Tsurugi breaking karate killer Tateki Shikenbaru, aka Junjoe (Masashi Ishibashi), out of prison. However, because Tateki's brother and sister can't completely pay for his services, Tsurugi launches one of the siblings out a four-story window. He sells the other sib as a sex slave to the inscrutable *Enter the Dragon* Han look-alike Rakuda Zhang.

Next up: A puppet Yakuza boss tries to hire Tsurugi to kidnap Sarai Hammett (Yutaka Nakajima), the heir to a billion-dollar oil fortune. Tsurugi turns down the contract for reasons not divulged (perhaps he enjoys giving the Yakuza grief), and the Yakuza put a hit on Tsurugi. Three Hong Kong hit men—a crazy blind swordsman, a bald hoodlum and a mad knife thrower—are put on his trail. Resentful that the Yakuza are yakking with Chinese Triads and the Chicago Mafia, Tsurugi approaches karate *sensei* Kendo Masaoke (Masafumi Suzuki) and offers to protect the teacher's niece Sarai. Of course, Kendo and Tsurugi need to exchange karate blows more powerful than a bullet train in order for Kendo to find Tsurugi trustworthy enough to protect his niece. But Yakuza puppet master Rakuda pulls the right strings and manages to kidnap Sarai. Tsurugi tries to rescue her, but he goes down faster than a sumo wrestler wearing iron shoes on thin ice. But Tsurugi's resolve to survive brings him back from the brink of death as he remembers his father's dying words: "Trust no one ... let no one beat you." Tsurugi storms the ship where Sarai is held hostage and where hired hit man Tateki is waiting for him. The ending becomes a free-for-all while Tsurugi shivers everyone's timbers and ends their peon lives.

When *Street Fighter* hit the American shores, kung fu film fans assumed Chiba would be a Japanese Bruce Lee. From the get-go, it was evident Chiba's character was not like Lee, such as when Tsurugi breaks Tateki out of prison or when Tsurugi hissingly grunts using heavy *sanchin*-style breathing (to strengthen *ki*) to subdue Tateki. So even though Chiba's performance was filled with over-the-top, perhaps Lee-inspired facial grimaces, Chiba was much more demonstrative than Lee. Certainly his sanchin and *shorinji kenpo*-inspired ultra-contorted finger and fist postures kept things from even remotely resembling a Lee film.

But what really cemented this film's cult status was its X rating, for extreme violence. The film shows an American getting castrated—which I'm sure had nothing to do with the U.S. presence in Japan—a villain getting his larynx violently ripped out, and the now-famous X-ray shot of someone's head collapsing under Tsurugi's hammerfist. Chiba's hunchbacked intensity blends well with the short duration of fights—short fights were a habit born from samurai films because filmmakers believed that real combative situations happened quickly.

Titleography: *Clash! Killer Fist*; *The Streetfighter*; *Sudden Attack: The Killing Fist*. Translation—*Direct Attack! Killer Fist*. The translated title refers to the directness of karate techniques in fights, *Street Fighter* relates to the brutal street-fighting style of Tsurugi, and the other English titles tap into the translation. The film's success spawned two sequels—*Return of The Street Fighter* and *The Street Fighter's Last Revenge*—as well as the four-film spinoff *Sister Street Fighter*. **MA Percentage: 31.23%**

STREET FIGHTER'S LAST REVENGE, THE

Gyakushi! Satsujinken (1974—Japan) **83m. FI: Uncredited. NOT/LOT: 3/ 3m 24s; NOF/LOF: 18/ 15m 5s.** D: Shigehiro Ozawa or Teruo Ishii. C: Sonny Chiba, Reiko Ike, Koji Wada, Tatsuo Endo, Akira Shioji, Tsuyoshi Otsuka, Frankie Black, Masafumi Suzuki, Etsuko Shihomi.

With this film comes the end of the *Street Fighter* trilogy (the second film being *Return of the Street Fighter*). Sonny Chiba dons the mask of Tsurugi Takuma, aka Terry Tsurugi in the English dubs, for one final curtain call. Yet this swan song is completely different from the first two installments because Tsurugi is a more likeable James Bond-esque character with *Mission: Impossible* tendencies rather than the vile anti-hero he once was.

Tsurugi is still tough as nails and still has a screw loose, and he strikes with thunderbolt power. In this film, we again see him use his karate tools of the trade to build up his reputation and tear down another Yakuza-Mafia partnership. When a labor dispute at a chemical manufacturing plant escalates into a riot, which the partnership uses to cover a heroin scheme, the Yakuza hire Tsurugi to run in and recover two cassette tapes under the protection of Mr. Owada. When the Yakuza double-cross Tsurugi with funny money, Tsurugi gets the last laugh as he pays them back with karate.

Yakuza assassin Kaho Huo (Etsuko Shihomi) steps in to stop the ultra-pissed Tsurugi with some karate of her own. Tsurugi eventually realizes that Kaho is an undercover cop working for a local assistant district attorney, so he steals back one tape from the Yakuza and plans to use it as a means to get his money. However, the assistant DA also wants to get his hands on the tapes—not for good but for his own evil plans. Tsurugi is now caught between the lawful and unlawful, which of course is dreadful and awful. When Tsurugi is defeated in a fight by the wimpy-looking assistant DA, he begins to question his martial training and mentality. After the required flashback wherein Tsurugi's father tells him to trust no one, it suddenly hits Tsurugi to do the opposite. He must trust someone, and that person is *sensei* Kendo Masaoka (Masafumi Suzuki). Kendo prepares Tsurugi for his final battle against the assistant DA's mysterious martial skills. It's a pseudo-wimp versus a debonair wild card. The final fight against Tsurugi's attorney nemesis is a recycled motif from the first film, which includes rain and a dockside battle.

What makes *Last Revenge* difficult to swallow is that the main villain easily defeats Tsurugi. It's unconvincing because the actor playing the assistant DA obviously had no martial arts skills and is also the weakest villain Tsurugi fights in all the *Street Fighter* films. There's no sense of danger about the man at all. I learned in Chinese kung fu films that trained martial arts actors dislike losing on-screen fights to nonmartial arts actors. But it is part of the job to do what you're told, and with Chiba's growing reputation and influence in the karate film industry, he recognized it was time to leave the franchise and move on.

On a final note: As Chiba was gearing up to play a series of historically important Japanese martial arts heroes like Mas Oyama, Morihei Ueshiba and Doshin So, he wanted to create an air of heroism in Tsurugi. So Tsurugi's usual ultra-nasty anti-hero caricature and over-the-top masochistic fighting style were toned down. Maybe Chiba losing a fight to a nonmartial artist and Tsurugi's trusting the sensei softened the audience's perception of Chiba and Tsurugi. Thus, perhaps these two things contributed to Chiba's Japanese martial arts hero epics being successful. Those are just my thoughts, though.

Titleography: *Street Fighter Counterattacks!*; *The Streetfighter's Last Revenge*. Translation—*Revenge! The Killing Fist*. **MA Percentage: 22.27%**

STREET MOBSTER

Gendai Yakuza: Hito-Kiri Yota (1972—Japan) **95m. FI: Uncredited. NOT/LOT: None; NOF/LOF: 8/ 3m 34s.** D: Kinji Fukasaku. C: Bunta Sugawara, Noboru Ando, Mayumi Nagisa, Asao Koike, Noboru Mitani, Nobuo Yana.

If you are pissed off at the Yakuza … well, don't be. When it comes to Yakuza films, actor Bunta Sugawara is to director Kinji Fukasaku as actor Chow Yun-fat is to director John Woo, in that both pairs created some of their genres' most memorable films. Before Fukasaku and Sugawara delved into the highly provocative and over-the-top ensemble casts in the *Battles Without Honor and Humanity* series that had tons of characters, *Street Mobster* was kept pretty simple, including the fights.

In *Street Mobster*, Okita (Sugawara) is fed up with all the arrogant posturing that local Yakuza thugs exhibit on the streets. He decides to organize his own band of mobsters to give those posers a run for their money. In one barroom brawl, while being reprimanded by a gang of Yakuza soldiers, Okita defiantly slouches on a sofa, ignores the thugs, then whips off his wooden *geta* (traditional Japanese wooden sandals) and proceeds to box with them while tossing in a few karate kicks and knife techniques. As is typical for Fukasaku—whether the scene is one-on-one or one-against-many—he rapidly moves and shakes the camera all around to convey the chaos of the fights.

Titleography: *Modern Yakuza: Outlaw Killer*. Translation—*Modern Yakuza: Outlaw Killer*. Okita lives on the street and is a thug, so *Street Mobster* is a logical title. **MA Percentage: 3.75%**

STRIKE AND SWORD

盲拳, 怪招, 神經刀 (1978—Hong Kong) **73m. FD: Feng Ke-an, Huang Ha. NOT/LOT: 1/ 39s; NOF/LOF: 18/ 22m 50s.** D: Luo Qi. C: Henry Yu Yung, Cai Hong, Zhao Me-bao, Cheung Lik, Liu Chia-yong, Liu Guo-cheng, Hon Gwok-choi, Huang Ha, Feng Ke-an.

In many Chinese kung fu films, when two characters are fighting in one place, they will suddenly break into a sprint, leap into the air and land in a completely different environment, where they continue to do battle. Why does this happen? Sometimes a fight can become tiresome for the actors or fight choreographers, and changing the scenery can re-inspire them. Another circumstance could be that the fight has been going on all day and the filmmakers are running out of light, so they need to stop and pick up somewhere else the next day. Look for clues like dried sweat stains on clothing or inconsistent blood makeup from place to place.

Strike and Sword has a fight scene in which the four heroes and the villain are battling inside a building, but when they exit, they end up in a giant, sprawling quarry in the middle of nowhere. Transitions like these can be a shock to the uninitiated audience's system—they're sort of like Dorothy stepping out of her black-and-white house into the colorful world of Oz, except in kung fu films, there is no setup.

Master Tsao Heng (Cai Hong) pines for the love of Ying Ying (Zhao Me-bao). He feels her love was taken away from him by another man, hero Plum Flower Meng Tian-yu (Henry Yu Yung). Tsao Heng orders his thug compatriots to kidnap Ying Ying, pillage the local village and bring any other available women to his lair to be sex slaves. When the gang kills an affable chicken street vendor, the vendor's son and two friends unite with Meng to hunt down Tsao's secret hideout, save the lasses and bring the villain to justice.

The music during the opening credits and the brutal finale plays like a Charlie Chaplin film—with bird calls, chiming bells, wolf whistles and boinging springs—even while the heroes repeatedly ram a villain's head into the side of a cliff. And yes, there is blood spurting all over too. Chinese and Western humor is indeed different. Earlier in the film, seemingly out of nowhere, a major fight breaks out amid a crowded duck crossing. As hundreds of ducks meander across a shallow stream, these guys are quacking—I mean cracking—heads. The smart fighters remember to duck at the right moment. All the fighters needed was some hoisin sauce to make a meal of it.

Titleography: *Kung Fu Means Fists, Strikes and Sword*; *Art of War*. Translation—*Blind Fist, Odd Technique and Nutty Sword*. The titles *Fists, Strikes and Sword* and *Blind Fist, Odd Technique and Nutty Sword* refer to the translated names of the three fighters who team up with Men Tian-yu. The *Art of War* title is an odd and possibly confusing choice because the film has nothing to do with Sun Tzu's (pronounced "soo-in zi") famous book on military strategy, which bears the same name. Also, the film should not be confused with the 1979 title *The Art of War by Sun Tzu*. **MA Percentage: 32.17%**

SUN DRAGON

豬仔血淚 (1979—Hong Kong) **86m. AC: Liang Shiao-sung. NOT/LOT: 6/ 7m 1s; NOF/LOF: 15/ 30m 19s.** D: Wa Yat-wang. C: Billy Chong, Louis Neglia, Ma Zung-de, Carl Scott, Joseph Jenning, Liang Shiao-sung.

Saguaro cacti invade Taiwan—the cardboard-looking ones, at least. Although I would rank this as a great fast-forward film—which means solid fights but really poor acting, especially by the foreigners—I also have some interesting background information about it. Watching the film, one could easily imagine it was filmed in the deserts of Arizona. As it turns out, a foreigner I knew who was in the movie once told me that the same three or four wooden saguaro cacti (the tall variety with bent arms) were randomly placed in many shots. Among the rugged terrain of central Taiwan, the cacti do a good job making things look like the deserts of the American Old West. When I first saw the film, I was convinced it was shot in the U.S. until the almost gratuitous rape scene (for some reason, many kung fu films have graphic ones) that takes place by a long suspension footbridge. It was the same footbridge where actor Barry Chan (aka Wei Zi-yuin) defeated me in my first TV kung fu soap opera show in Taiwan in 1980. In a weird way, that makes *Sun Dragon* a somewhat ambitious film. To paraphrase Dorothy from *The Wizard of Oz*, "We're not in Arizona anymore."

Billy Chong plays Sung Shao-chong, a Chinese immigrant in an American desert town who helps a downtrodden black man named Tom (Carl Scott). Tom learns a curious blend of *Sun tai chi*. (Note: Sun is the name of the founder of Sun tai chi.) He also learns leopard boxing from Sung's elderly master (Liang Shiao-sung). Carl and Sung then defeat the gang of racist thugs who killed Tom's parents.

Scott delivered the best martial arts performance by any foreign actor in Chinese kung fu films at that time, even outdoing Chuck Norris in *Way of the Dragon*. Speaking of Norris, Tom's final fight scene is against a Norris look-alike (Louis Neglia), who has the audacity to flash Tom a thumbs-down before the fight like he's judging a gladiator in the Colosseum. It is a pity Scott disappeared from the scene in 1980 after co-starring again with Chong in *Kung Fu Executioner*.

Chong's fights are an interesting mixture of Bruce Lee-style kicks and facial expressions peppered throughout with Chong's own physical prowess, but because of his hair and costume, you can't help but think of Jackie Chan's bumpkin character from his 1978 films *Snake in the Eagle Shadow* and *Drunken Master* instead.

Titleography: *Black Jim le Magnifique*; *Hard Way to Die*. Translation—*Piggy's Bloody Tears*. Because Tom learns a combination of Sun tai chi and leopard boxing, and Chong fights like the Little Dragon aka Bruce Lee, the *Sun Dragon* title fits. *Hard Way to Die* comes across like a blaxploitation title, which makes sense because of Scott's starring role. **MA Percentage: 43.41%**

SUPER FLY

(1972—USA) **93m. SC: Erik Cord. NOT/LOT: 1/ 1m 3s; NOF/LOF: 1/ 1m 3s.** D: Gordon Parks, Jr. C: Ron O'Neal, Carl Lee, Sheila Frazier, Julius Harris, Charles McGregor, Nate Adams, Polly Niles, E. Preston Reddick.

The 1970s were freaky times for those of us attending high school and college. I recall Black Panthers with machine guns surrounding the registrar's office at Cornell University. No school, not even an Ivy League university, was immune to the chaos of the times. This notion of black power led to the pervasiveness and popularity of blaxploitation films that at the time transcended race. And *Super Fly* is a chaotic film in which the hero is a strung-out cocaine dealer named Priest (Ron O'Neal) who wants to make one big final drug score, earn a million dollars for his efforts, and then live the good life in peace with his junkie girlfriend. There was no morality in this film. But when you consider that many blaxploitation films had heroes griping about racism and drugs because of the Man, they often ended in hypocrisy because the so-called heroes were just as violent and racist as the institutions they abhorred. Priest is refreshingly different because he determines his own fate and believes that his actions are a consequence of his own decisions. But to defeat the Man, he needs to become like the Man. No jive, man. Can you dig it?

This film barely makes the Chuck Norris *Good Guys Wear Black* cut. (See

that film's martialogy for explanation.) Out of nowhere, more than halfway into the film, Priest dons a karate *gi* with a yellow belt and spars with his instructor (E. Preston Reddick) on a small mat. I like that Priest does not wear a black belt, which so many others do in similar films. (Bo Svenson does in the 1976 film *Breaking Point*, for example.) In the brief scene, Priest rather innocuously flips, kicks, traps and punches his instructor. At the end of the film, when the head police detective and his henchfuzz pull one over on Priest, our hero uses the same techniques from his sparring session. It is pretty bad-looking, but at least the set up was there.

As a high school student in the early '70s, I rarely listened closely to music lyrics. But hearing the lyrics of Curtis Mayfield's song *Superfly* today adds a new dimension to something I was missing back then. If you give it a listen, you will hear what I mean.

Titleography: *Superfly*. **MA Percentage: 2.26%**

SUPER INFRAMAN

中國超人 (1975—Hong Kong) **85m. FI: Tang Chia. NOT/LOT: 1/ 10s; NOF/LOF: 18/ 21m 12s.** D: Hua Shan. C: Danny Lee, Bruce Le, Wang Xia, Liu Hui-ru, Yuan Man-zi, Lin Wen-wei, Dana.

Tokyo has Godzilla, and Hong Kong has Inframan. This film is an insane, souped-up Hong Kong version of Japan's *tokusatsu* genre of movies and TV shows, which are live-action productions that combine superhero characters and special effects. It is similar to such productions as *Ultraman*, *Grandizer*, *Kikaida* and *Kamen Rider* (there is even motorcycle action in *Super Inframan*), the major difference being that the wild and wacky kung fu fights of this Shaw film are vastly superior and really set it apart from its contemporaries. The costumes were provided by Ekisu Productions, which did many costumes for Toei Superheroes shows, and the three-green-eyed buggy creature looks right out of Sid and Marty Krofft's *H.R. Pufnstuf* TV show (1969-1971).

Still from *Super Inframan* © Celestial Pictures Ltd. All rights reserved.

Labeled as China's first tokusatsu-influenced superhero film, the movie opens with a giant Rodan-looking creature crashing onto a road in front of a bus full of children, setting off a chain of events such as earthquakes, volcano eruptions, fires and the fictional Mount Devil turning into a dragon head. (Rodan was a large flying reptile monster that was first seen in the 1956 Japanese *kaiju* (monster) film *Rodan*). Demon Princess Elzebub (Liu Hui-ru) announces to the world that she is the master of Earth and commands everyone to surrender or die. Professor Liu Ying-de (Wang Xia), head of the high-tech Research Center, theorizes that the princess is a human from an ice age 20 million years ago and that the only way to stop her, her marauding monsters and her troops of skeleton men is to use the BDX Project and transform high-ranking officer Lei Ma, aka Rayma (Danny Lee), into Inframan. Hopefully, his Thunder Fist attachments will be functional before the major push by the enemy, because if not, Earth will be lost.

I spoke to actor Danny Lee about his experience on the film about 10 years ago. He said that *Super Inframan* was one of the two strangest films he had ever made. (The other was the 1977 *Mighty Peking Man*, a Shaw film about a King Kong-like ape.) Lee added that *Super Inframan* had a lot of fight work involved, which was extremely tiring day after day. He said that he did indeed do all his own fights, except when he was just too plain tired and exhausted, at which point someone else would step in. Because the costume was tight and hot, he would change his underwear at least three times a day. The costume itself often ripped and had to be mended. The fights are filled with crazy wire work and covered from many different camera angles. It is everything that the American children's live-action show *Power Rangers* would have loved. It is also odd to see actor Bruce Le doing traditional kung fu techniques. As it turns out, *Inframan* is the last film Le did before playing real Chinese superhero Bruce Lee in various Bruceploitation movies.

During a fight with the skeleton army at the princess's lair, the stuntmen wear masks that, back then, were put together quickly without worrying if they fit or allowed for clear vision. You will notice when many stuntmen leap into the square pools of water, they painfully whack parts of their bodies into the sides of the concrete pits because the masks blocked their vision. Ouch.

Titleography: As of this writing, no alternative titles could be found. Translation—*Chinese Superman*. **MA Percentage: 25.14%** SHAW BROTHERS

SUPER WEAPON, THE

(1976—USA) 78m. TA: Ron Van Clief. NOT/LOT: None; NOF/LOF: None. D: Jim Sotos, Henry Scarpelli. C: Because this is a documentary, there is no main cast.

This film is an example of a kind of documentary that was popular in the 1970s and catered mostly to black audiences, for whom kung fu films were an event and not just a film. I recall that every time I saw a kung fu film in an inner-city Binghamton movie theater in upstate New York, it was standing room only. The audience would cheer, speak to the characters and pretty much imitate what was being said or done on screen.

The Super Weapon opens discussing the history of martial arts and does so with a true story that I have never seen used in any other martial arts documentary. The film talks about an Indian prince who created a self-defense method by jabbing needles into his slaves, recording the results and then developing strikes to attack those vulnerable areas. This prince's work dates back to 2600 B.C. The film continues with the story of Ta Mo, his 18 Luo Han fists and how they eventually led to the five animal styles of Shaolin kung fu.

Following the history, the documentary becomes a showcase for the founder of Chinese *goju* martial arts and a Hong Kong kung fu star considered by the film to the most dangerous man in America: Ron Van Clief, the Black Dragon. He is seen performing various *kata*, weapon and breaking demonstrations, and *ippon kumite* (one-step sparring), and he describes his martial arts style, *aiki-jitsu*. He then speaks about the philosophy of martial arts. As I was watching the film, I couldn't help but think that it felt like a video version of a Bruce Tegner book of self-defense (which I have three of).

The film also shows some intense kumite fights between some of Van Clief's students, which I enjoyed watching. It reminded me of my days back in the mid-'70s practicing Okinawan *goju-ryu* in Ithaca, New York. The documentary then becomes a spotlight for several good *karateka* as they describe their styles through demonstrations and forms. Here are the other martial artists featured in the film and their respective styles: George Mattson, *ueichi-ryu*; Jerry Gardner, violin player and *wing chun* practitioner; John Davis, *shotokan* and *jujutsu*; Musa Kumara, *aikido*; Louis Neglia (star of the film *Sun Dragon*); Charles Bonet (star of *Death Promise*), *shorin-ryu*, *bo*; John Blair; Elsie Roman, the only female, *nisi goju*; Frank Ruiz, knife-defense maneuvers; Alex Sternberg, shotokan; Thomas "LaPuppet" Carroll, shotokan; Pete Siringano, jujutsu, which features Bob Long really getting tossed around and injured; Byong Heong Park, *taekwondo*; and ending with a nifty *chi* (*qi*) demonstration in which jujutsu practitioner Frank DiFelice takes full-body strikes to the neck, solar plexus and groin. I like this documentary because it gives a good feeling and sensibility of what the growth and attitudes of serious martial artists were back in the 1970s and what martial arts meant to them.

Titleography: As of this writing, no alternative titles could be found.

SUPERCHICK

(1973—USA) 95m. SC: Eric Cord. NOT/LOT: 3/ 1m 29s; NOF/LOF: 1/ 31s. D: Ed Forsyth. C: Joyce Jillson, Louis Quinn, Thomas Reardon, Tony Young, John Carradine, Dale Ishimoto, Fuji.

Just as blaxploitation martial arts action was beginning to get noticed in Hollywood—with audiences reveling in ball-busting sisters taking on the Man or smarmy white trash—white filmmakers, not wanting to be outdone, began experimenting with karate and blondes. In both cases, it was not about how good the fights were but how curvy the heroines were.

Tara B. True (Joyce Jillson) is a drab brunette airline hostess by day and a philandering blond super-chick by night with beaus in Miami, New York and Los Angeles. She leads a life mixed with happy sexless sex, wild amazing sex and mile-high clubbing. When she is unwittingly duped into abetting some skyjacking criminals, she uses a first-class combination of karate kicks and judo throws while showing some skin to thwart them.

Some training sequences later in the film show Tara training at a karate *dojo* with two Japanese *sensei*. Though the scenes actually show basic judo throws, they do set up the final fight. And we can accept it when under duress, Tara lets out an exceptionally iffy barrage of chops, flips and kicks that look like neither but reflect the desired results … if that is really possible. Because the film has more martial arts action (if you can call it that) than Chuck Norris' *Good Guys Wear Black*, it squeaks its way into this book.

An interesting note: Jillson's real-life star power outweighs her thin acting career. Her successful syndicated astrology column opened the doors for her to become Nancy Reagan's personal astrologer.

Titleography: As of this writing, no alternative titles could be found. **MA Percentage: 2.11%**

SUPERMAN AGAINST THE AMAZONS

三超人與女霸王 (1975—Hong Kong/Italy/Mexico) 98m. SC: Franco Pasqueto. NOT/LOT: 1/ 3s; NOF/LOF: 16/ 13m 45s. D: Alfonso Brescia (Al Bradley). C: Yueh Hua, Karen Yeh, Aldo Canti, Marc Hannibal, Malisa Longo, Aldo Bufi Landi, Magda Konopka, Genie Woods.

Ignore that man behind the fire curtain. How on Earth did Yueh Hua, a major Shaw Brothers box-office draw, get roped into this film? That will likely remain a mystery. This is one of those movies that is so bad, it's good. Sort of.

When the new queen of the Amazons, Beghira (Magda Konopka), brutally kills all the other queen candidates, the next conquest for her tribe of battling beauties is to wipe out a nearby valley and learn the secret of sacred fire from the valley's immortal protector, Darma. In reality, Darma is merely a clever and eccentric Wizard of Oz-like magician who hides behind a curtain of fire and knows martial arts. (Darma also wears a green mask, chain-mail armor, a red cape and shorts.) At the film's beginning, Darma is training the heir to his pseudo-god throne, Aru (Aldo Canti), who fights better than Chuck Norris and does incredible flipping, jumping and high-falling stunts (similar to free running or *parkour*). When Darma dies at the hands of the Amazons, Aru enlists the help of two of Darma's "supermen" friends to fight Beghira and save the valley. They are a brawny black superhero from Africa named Moog (Marc Hannibal) and a lone sword master and kung fu expert from China, Chung (Yueh Hua). (It's political correctness in 1975!)

The fights are somewhat off-kilter, with such spectacles as women in bikinis and cloaks trying to do noodle-leg kicks while wearing plastic masks. And it is rather funny to see Chinese stuntmen dressed up as buxom Amazon women in skimpy outfits (like the Chinese stuntmen portraying the busty black Amazons in Jackie Chan's *Armor of God* (1987)) doing sword and fight choreography for Yueh Hua's action scenes. And Moog does a lion's roar just like the landlady in *Kung Fu Hustle* (2004). Also note that during the fight scenes, the filmmakers use the same sound effects as the typical Hong Kong kung fu films of the time period. One rather sage moment is the first appearance of the philosophical Chung, who is riding atop a water buffalo; it is similar to how the Taoist philosopher Lao Tzu is often depicted.

Titleography: *Amazons Against Superman*; *Amazons and Supermen*; *Barbarian Revenge*; *Return of the Barbarian Women*; *Super Stooges vs. the Wonder Women*; *Three Fantastic Supermen*; *Three Stooges vs. the Wonder Women*. Translation—*Three Supermen and the Amazon Queen*. With some mental tweaking here and there, the titles fit the notions and plots of the film. **MA Percentage: 14.08%**

SWIFT KNIGHT, THE

來如風 (1971—Hong Kong) **80m. FI: Liu Chia-rong. NOT/LOT: None; NOF/LOF: 21/11m 53s.** D: Cheng Chang-ho. C: Lo Lieh, Chin Han, Margaret Hsing Hui, Wong Chung-shun, Fan Mei-sheng, Fang Mian, Wang Xia, Tong Lin.

With patience, one can often find an old Chinese kung fu film that has directly influenced one of those exotic, gravity-defying Fant-Asia films popular from the early '80s through the mid-'90s. Fant-Asia describes novel martial arts *wuxia*-style films that uniquely combined science fiction, fantasy and horror with over-the-top martial arts choreography and high-wire stunts. For example, Yuen Woo-ping's *Iron Monkey* (1993) plays a lot like Cheng Chang-ho's *The Swift Knight*. Both films feature a masked hero trying to defy the Manchu emperor; a guarded friend who first doubts but ultimately helps the hero; a child who is an integral part of the plot; and a lovable, bumbling palace guard who takes it on himself to help the masked hero, even if it means risking his own life (Yuen Shen-yi in *Iron Monkey*, Fan Mei-sheng in *Swift Knight*).

In *Swift Knight*, the lewd and licentious Li (Wong Chung-shun; who is type-cast in these sleazy roles) takes a man's daughter away because he cannot pay his taxes. Li plans to have his way with her or perhaps sell her into prostitution. Luckily, the masked avenger Swift Knight—the alter ego of mild-mannered Lei Feng (Lo Lieh)—swoops in. He warns Li to return the girl, pay for her medical expenses and her family's living expenses, and burn up all the man's remaining IOUs, or else Li's life will end quickly. (As an aside, director Cheng lives up the road from where I am writing this book. I also wonder if this film was influenced by Bob Kane's Dark Knight comic books.)

Meanwhile, Prince Regent Jie hires the assassin in red, Zhu Pai of Hell (Wang Xia), to find and kill the poor maiden Xian Qin (Margaret Hsing Hui) and her baby. Incidentally, Lei Fung falls in love with Xian. In order to lure Swift Knight into the open, Zhu Pai of Hell slaughters innocent people and frames Lei for the murders. Secret service agent Liu Shuan-ping (Chin Han), who is disguised as a beggar, is also closing in on Swift Knight but feels something is awry. At this point, the film becomes like Danny Kaye's classic movie the *Court Jester* (1955), but bursts of laughter are replaced by bursts of arterial blood. Swift Knight must protect Xian and her baby from Zhu Pai because the child is the emperor's heir.

What is great about this film is that each fight is swift and to the point. The most engaging set pieces come from fight instructor Liu's character: He dresses like a Japanese street beggar, donning the wok-shaped Japanese Buddhist hat, and he fights like a samurai warrior, but he wields a Chinese sword. The mood, setups and scenarios mirror the typical beats seen in old Akira Kurosawa films but are infused with enough simple wire work to give the action a wuxia look and feel. As the Japanese say: So desu ne. And that's how it is.

Titleography: As of this writing, no alternative titles could be found. Translation—*Comes Like the Wind*. Although the Chinese title is the main character's name, his name's literal translation seems to be the impetus behind the English title. **MA Percentage: 14.85%** SHAW BROTHERS

SWORD OF THE MASTER

Maengsu (1979—S. Korea) **84m. FI: Uncredited. NOT/LOT: 1/ 47s NOF/LOF: 11/ 6m 23s.** D: Lim Won-sick. C: Lee Dae-yub, Sa Mi-ja, Hwang Hae, Do Kum-gong, Choe Bong, San Bang-won.

"Danger, Will Robinson, danger! This film is as phony as Dr. Smith's concern for the Robinson family!" So the robot (Dick Tufeld) from the TV show *Lost in Space* (1976-1968) might rant. This film is listed on several film and movie rental sites as a 1979 feature titled *Sword of the Master* that stars Sonny Chiba—wrong. It is actually the 1969 South Korean film *Maengsu* (aka *A Fierce Animal*), which stars Sa Mi-ja as a blind swordswoman trying to avenge her uncle's murder and find her long-lost mother, who abandoned her a child. During her travels, she learns the art of the Zatoichi-like blind swordsman technique from a mysterious master who is impressed with her spirit. The fights are mostly extreme close-up shots, slashing sword motions in and out of camera, with bodies dropping from strikes we do not see, and the blind swordswoman ending in a samurai-like pose. The fights are more about imagining the kill than actually seeing it.

Historically, when the samurai class arose in eighth-century Japan, the samurai code of ethics and sword style were similar to the code and single-edged sword design used by seventh-century Chinese Tang Dynasty swordsmen. One will note that the Korean swords in this film mirror the samurai sword in look and technique. It is conjectured that the Tang-backed Korean Silla people defeated the Japanese-backed Korean Temmu people using Tang swords, thus the Tang sword became part of Korean sword martial arts. It is also plausible that the samurai sword and its use were influenced by early Tang swords and swordsmen during this same time period.

Titleography: As of this writing, no alternative titles could be found. Translation—*A Fierce Animal*. **MA Percentage: 8.53%**

SWORDSMAN AND ENCHANTRESS

蕭十一郎 (1978—Hong Kong) **86m. FI: Tang Chia. NOT/LOT: None; NOF/LOF: 41/ 21m 24s.** D: Chu Yuan. C: Ti Lung, Ching Li, Lily Li, Candy Wen Xue-er, Xu Hsiao-chiang, Liu Yong, Gu Guan-zhong, Tang Jing, Shen Lao.

In the world of Swordsman and Enchantress, the Deer-Cutting Blade is the envy of all swordsmen and was created by Saint Xu Ru-zi, who spent a lifetime making the blade with nine kinds of steel. In the world of Wu Lin, it is considered a treasure that can break any other sword effortlessly. Xu believes that only two men are worthy of the sword: Lian Chen-bi (Liu Yong) of the Brocade Villa and Xiao Xi-lan (Ti Lung), a drifter in Jiang Hu.

While the blade is en route to Lian's villa, swordsman Xiao ambushes the escort and steals the sword. Four zombies arrive at the villa and demand the blade. Two are zombies of the West (dressed like mummies and carrying wolf claws), and two are zombie casters (one wielding giant cymbals, the other a wolf club). A freaky fight erupts, and that is just the beginning.

Then Xiao tries to kidnap Lian's wife, Chen Bi-zhen (Ching Li), but she is rescued by the real swordsman Xiao—Xiao Xi-lan. The imposter Xiao is a spunky young female named Lady Imp (Candy Wen Xue-er) who is up to no good. Shortly thereafter, she tries to frame the real Xiao for raping and killing Bi-zhen, only to have the real Xiao show up and save Bi-zhen again. He is injured in the process and escapes into a chasm with rivers and waterfalls. He ends up at a secret villa, where Bi-zhen takes care of him. Realizing they are falling in love, Xiao insists on taking her home, but it is too late. A jealous Lian flies off the handle and insists on dueling the injured Xiao. However, the honor code of Wu Lin prevents Lian from fighting an injured opponent.

Enter the self-professed "man junkie" Lady Fung (Lily Li), who nurses Xiao back to health. Lured by love, Bi-zhen returns to Xiao only for the two to be attacked by Lady Imp, who is the imposter Xiao. They barely escape by entering a forbidden yet mischievous mansion in the middle of a forest. This is where the film gets all *Wild Wild West* (the '60s TV show), and you'll see Mini-Me-like characters, Jiang Hu-style. The forbidden house becomes like the Eagles' song *Hotel California*, wherein you can check out any time you want, but you can never leave. The aptly named Puppet Mansion then strings our heroes along, until love pulls at their heartstrings to make the world a better place.

Twenty-five percent of the film is devoted to fighting, a rarity for Chu Yuan, whose films tend to have little action. There are several sequences in which Ti Lung does about 34 different moves per shot while wielding his spear with good straight-back postures. On the other hand, actor Liu Yong's move count per shot is

lower, and when he strikes he does so with a wobbly neck and hunched shoulders.

Two impressive shots: First, Ti Lung catches Lin's sword between his ankles and disarms him in slow motion. Second, in one swift, swashbuckling house-escape sequence, the whole fight moves in and out of every room in the house, up and down, and all around every balcony and porch of Lin's place, with smooth tracking shots and beautiful hand-held camerawork. It is much different from Chu's usual wuxia films, which make liberal use of long shots.

Titleography: As of this writing, no alternative titles could be found. Translation—*The Eleventh Man Xiao*. The Chinese title takes its name from Ti Lung's character and suggests that he is No. 11 of something, possibly an 11th son; the film does not make this clear. **MA Percentage: 24.88%** SHAW BROTHERS

SWORDSMAN AT LARGE

蕭十一郎 (1971—Hong Kong) **88m. FI: Wu Min-xiong. NOT/LOT: None; NOF/LOF: 13/ 17m 32s.** D: Hsu Cheng-hung. C: Margaret Hsing Hui, Tina Chin Fei, Frankie Wei Hung, Lu Ping, Bai Lin, Ke You-min.

When you consider China is a male-dominated society, it is such a powerful message in a 1971 Chinese film for a female character to use a whip as payback against male characters. Many films have their curiosities, and the opening scene of this film features Sammo Hung being killed by female warrior Fung shi-niang (Tina Chin Fei) after he and three of his cronies rape a woman. A scene like this can leave an indelible mark on a movie and even the actors in the scene. Perhaps this is why Sammo Hung's directorial debut six years later, *The Iron-Fisted Monk*, contains one of the most violent rape scenes witnessed in Chinese film up until that time.

In the old world of Jiang Hu, martial arts clans and sects constantly vie for control of their realms. In many stories, possessing some kind of hallowed sword bestows the power to do just that. All would bow to the owner of the sword, whether good or bad. Therefore, it is important that these powerful items not fall into the wrong hands. *Swordsman at Large* tells the story of Hsiao the Rambler (Frankie Wei Hung), a Robin Hood-like figure in search of one such revered weapon, the Deer Knife. It is written that whoever owns the Deer Knife will become the leader of the kung fu underworld. Hsiao's goal is to hand the sword to a righteous man or keep it hidden until a hero mightier in mind and spirit than he might arise. Along the way, many a kung fu flim-flam man assumes Hsiao's identity in an effort to defame him, to invoke fear among people or to fulfill their own greedy habits.

When asked why he doesn't do something about it, Hsiao tells the eventual love of his life, Shen Jiang-nan (Margaret Hsing Hui) in true knight-errant fashion: "I stand on my own principles. Why should I care about what other people do? As long as I haven't done any immoral deeds, why should I bother others? Isn't it best I go my own way?" His opposition is Happy King (Lu Ping), who wants the Deer Knife and Shen Jiang-nan.

One fight scene is filmed at dusk, and it is barely visible. Based on my old kung fu film days in Taiwan, I doubt this was intentional. When we shot outside, we did not always take lighting equipment with us (a generator could be hard to come by), and there were no big trucks full of equipment bringing up the rear. We shot using natural light until it was dark. But while your eyes would automatically adjust to the fading light, the camera wouldn't, and sometimes a director would stretch the shoot a bit too long, resulting in shots that were too dark.

A note about translating character names into English is that sometimes it can give a false impression. Two of the film's unique characters are Tai Chi, master of the 81 Techniques of Mystical Tai Chi Sword, and Flying Eagle (Bai Lin), guardian of the 18 Flying Eagle Techniques (she wears giant clawed gloves). One might think Tai Chi uses a tai chi chuan sword, but in fact he uses two single-grip moon swords. Also, watch out for Happy King's giant spiked shield in combo with the Deer Knife; they're a vicious stag to lock horns with.

Titleography: As of this writing, no alternative titles could be found. Translation—*Number 11 Son*. Although the film is about a swordsman (who really uses knives), *At Large* usually implies that someone or something bad is on the loose, so it is hard to decipher what the title creators at Shaw were thinking on this one. **MA Percentage: 14.26%** SHAW BROTHERS

SWORDSWOMEN THREE

江湖三女俠 (1970—Hong Kong) **95m. FI: Liu Chia-liang, Tang Chia. NOT/LOT: None; NOF/LOF: 19/ 13m 33s.** D: Shen Chiang. C: Lo Lieh, Essie Lin Chia, Shen Yi, Zhang Yi, Pan Ying-zi, Wong Chung-shun, Fang Mian, Yang Chi-ching.

Besides the Taoist nuns of Er Mei Mountain, it was uncommon to have more than one female be a major player in the world of Jiang Hu, which is part of a secretive underworld of martial artists, vagabonds, beggars and transients who had their own laws and codes of ethics that co-existed with the outside world. Like many Shaw Brothers directors, Shen Chiang was a student of *wuxia* films, and many Chinese directors I have met over the past 30 years were influenced by wuxia novels, specifically *The Water Margin* (1972). Out of that story's 108 Heroes of Liang Shan, there were only three females. It is not surprising that since Shen Chiang wrote this script, the three swordswomen can be seen as metaphors for the three Liang Shan heroines.

The three Han sisters, Lan-mei, Yu-Mei and Hsiao-lan (Essie Lin Chia, Shen Yi and Pang Ying-zi), are in charge of guarding the coveted Mighty Steel Sword. The weapon is so dangerous and powerful that no blood sticks to it after it has killed. Due to its magnetic surface, it attracts metal from within 10 feet when the user draws the sword, making any weapon duel moot. Whoever owns this sword shall rule over the realm of Jiang Hu.

Cocky swordsman Chu Tien-hsing (Lo Lieh) refuses to wait for the next official martial arts tournament and challenges the current No. 1 swordsman of Jiang Hu, Hsu Mu-liang (Yang Chi-ching). Hsu's son Chin-wu (Zhang Yi) says that if Chu can beat him, then Chu can challenge his father. Even though Chu fights dirty, Chin-wu prevails. But Chin-wu worries that because Chu is the fiancée of Yu-mei, one of the Mighty Sword guards, he might try to steal the sword anyway. As if on cue, Chu grabs the blade (with the help of his masked, knife-throwing female accomplice, Shadowless).

In the early years of kung fu films, most stars (male and female) did not practice martial arts. Shaw Brothers' actors were required to undergo cinema fight training, which is different from martial arts. However, to their advantage, most female stars usually had a background in Chinese dance that gave them a graceful edge over their male counterparts. It was easier to accommodate all the spinning that fight choreographers would insert into their fights. In this film, none of the actresses had either a martial arts or a dance background, which is probably why there are only about 13 minutes of fighting. The final battle between Chu and Hsu Chin-wu is entertaining, not because of their lax martial skills but because of the place of combat: a thick bamboo forest. Keep in mind that Chin-wu cannot use a metal sword, so he picks up whole bamboo trees and swings them at Chu. Chu not only slices them to bits, but he also chops down a large section of the forest, leaving thick, four-foot-high spikes jutting out all over the forest floor. It looks like Chin-wu has bitten off more than he can Chu.

Although the Chinese developed the mariner's compass about 4,500 years ago (a sliver of lodestone that floats on the surface tension of water), the term "magnet" is derived from a Cretan shepherd named Magnes. It was 4,000 years ago when Magnes found that the black lodestone rock his shoe nails stuck contained what became known as a magnetic property. The mineral was subsequently called magnetite. But who used magnetite in their swords first? Perhaps the Chinese? It is in their literature.

Titleography: As of this writing, no alternative titles could be found. Translation—*Three Swordswomen of Jiang Hu*. **MA Percentage: 29.88%** SHAW BROTHERS

TASTE OF COLD STEEL, A

武林風雲 (1970—Hong Kong) **79m. AS: Xu Er-niu. NOT/LOT: 2/ 31s; NOF/LOF: 11/ 23m 10s.** D: Yueh Feng. C: Zhang Yi, Chen Hung-lieh, Shu Pei-pei, Essie Lin Chia, You Ching, Wu Ma, Ku Fung, Wong Chung-shun, Xu Er-niu, Hong Liu, James Tien.

To borrow from Jimi Hendrix, "Purple haze is in my eyes, excuse me while I kiss the sword." Someone was either asleep on this film or they knew what they were doing because the traditional kung fu salute has messages attached to it, and the way you present it can mean life or death. Do the salute right and you

do not have to fight; do the salute wrong and it may be your swan song.

The foundation for the kung fu salute—arms held out in front of you, right fist resting against a left open palm or a left palm covering the right fist—originated during the beginning of the Ching Dynasty, when Ming loyalists would use the salute as a sign of recognition. When someone reversed the hand position (right open hand over left fist) that was cause for a fight to the death. At the beginning of *A Taste of Cold Steel*, the snotty Prince Lu (Chen Hung-lieh) arrives at the funeral of Master Gan, not to pay respects but to lay claim to the revered Violet Light Sword because whoever owns the sword can lead the world of Jiang Hu.

When Prince Lu approaches the coffin and Master Gan's three daughters (You Ching, Shu Pei-pei and Essie Lin Chia), he salutes them with his left fist covered by his right palm. A fight quickly ensues. Either the director purposely used the insulting hand gesture, or the actor did not know the correct way to do the salute and it was never noticed (an all-too-common occurrence).

Over the past few years, Hollywood films that use martial arts have been shooting fights using tight shots and shaking the camera to hide actors' lack of fighting skills and to add a sense of motion, all under the guise of bringing the audience into the action so they can feel it more. Early use of this method was featured in *Rocky II* (1979). However, when this style of filmmaking is overdone, as in *The Bourne Supremacy* (2004) and *Batman Begins* (2005), it can make viewers dizzy. In fact, this shooting method is old hat.

Several fights in *Cold Steel* use similar techniques—but not to cover up a lack of fighting ability. Instead, they're used as a cheaper replacement for optical effects. Every time a character draws the Violet Light Sword, it shines purple and the light envelops the wielder. It was a tricky effect to pull off when the sword changed hands midway through a fight. Two things were done: Someone was wriggling around on the ground with black light shining on the sword, and/or someone was on a platform with a spotlight covered with a purple gel. Keeping the camera tight on the sword user while rocking the camera hid these things very well and also brought the audience into the fight—and all nine years before *Rocky II*.

James Tien's Taoist monk character, who literally appears out of nowhere, is injected into the movie to remind us that one should learn kung fu to protect the weak and the poor rather than bully innocent people. As it did then, this message often falls on deaf ears these days.

Titleology: As of this writing, no alternative titles could be found. Translation—*Story of Events That Happen in the Martial World*. Violet is considered a cool color, and tasting steel is a metaphor for those who live and die by the sword. **MA Percentage: 29.88%** SHAW BROTHERS

TATTOO CONNECTION, THE

鱷魚頭黑煞星 and 鉅鑽風雲 (1978—Hong Kong) **90m. FC: Bruce Leung. NOT/LOT: None; NOF/LOF: 19/ 19m 27s.** D: Lee Tso-nam. C: Tan Dao-liang, Jim Kelly, Chen Hsing, Li Hai-ji, Norman Wingrove, Bobby Cannavarro, Zheng Fu-xiong, Jiang Dao, Bolo Yeung, Zheng Shu-ying.

Many Bruce Lee-aping contemporary films feature a fight scene at the docks, where walls of stacked shipping crates create a modern-day Roman amphitheater of death. In place of vicious lions are gangsters and thugs. But in *The Tattoo Connection*, one of the lions is a man of conscience. Dong Hao (Tan Dao-liang) harbors the Christian virtue of forgiveness and often convinces his belligerent Triad leader, Boss Lok (Chen Hsing), to spare the lives of his underlings who have screwed up. But that is about to change.

When Lok steals a large, priceless diamond, ex-CIA operative Lucas (Jim Kelly) is sent to Hong Kong by the diamond's insurance agency to find the gem. Word spreads in the underworld that Lucas is in town, so Lok assigns his No. 1 fighter and bodyguard, Dong Hao, to protect the diamond until it can be sold to an American buyer who is already lined up. Lucas and Dong's worlds intersect, setting up a clash of the legs.

Because Bruce Leung personally understood how detrimental to an acting career Lee-look-alike pictures could be, he prevents Kelly from being forced to do one in this film. Furthermore, Kelly's action is mostly shot with tight camera angles and undercranked camera speeds, both of which successfully hide Kelly's habit of not extending his kicks during his fights. Although Kelly's fights often have him moving backward using the same one-hand blocking combination he used in *Enter the Dragon* to block several punches at the same time, he is much smoother in this film compared to his other post-*Enter the Dragon* films. While Kelly mostly uses his right leg for kicking, Tan uses both legs, which stylistically separates their on-screen kicking skills. When Kelly has a final big break-a-neck strike or a slow strangling chokehold, you can tell he wanted to go all "Lee face" but Leung stopped that, which gave Kelly a new persona and fight look that he was able to hold onto a little bit in his final martial arts productions. Lastly, Kelly was able to get it on with Bolo Yeung in this film, something that some fans had hoped for in *Enter the Dragon*.

Titleography: *Black Belt Jones 2: Tattoo Connection*; *Black Belt Jones 2*. Translations—*Crocodile Head and Black Jinx* and *Tale of the Huge Diamond*. Before you get all heated up over the insinuation of Jim Kelly being the *Black Jinx*, it could also mean in Chinese that every time one fights with him, they will lose. *Crocodile Head* refers to the vicious nature of Boss Lok. *Tale of the Huge Diamond* basically sums up the plot. *Black Belt Jones 2* is banking on the popularity of *Black Belt Jones*, even though the film is not actually a sequel. The *Tattoo* aspect refers to the eagle tattoo found on the shoulders of the gang members under Lok's leadership. **MA PERCENTAGE: 21.61%**

TAXI DRIVER

的士大佬 (1975—Hong Kong) **94m. FI: Yuen Cheung-yan, Chan Chuen. NOT/LOT: 1/ 25s; NOF/LOF: 9/ 8m 3s.** D: Pau Hsueh-li. C: David Chiang, Wang Chung, Shi Zhong-tian, Lin Zhen-ji, Tong Lin, Liu Hui-ru, Yang Ze-lin, Wu Chi-chin.

Chen Guang (David Chiang) is part Hirsch, part Danza, part DeNiro and part DeVito in this film, which itself is part *Taxi Driver* (1976) and part NBC television show *Taxi* (1978-83). Chen fights, makes decisions, tries to save young girls from themselves and is the go-to guy whenever there is a problem. The film uses the example of a taxi driver to tell the story of Hong Kong—not the Pearl of the Orient side that tourists romanticize about but the seamier side of this former postage stamp colony. Chen navigates through the overcrowded streets and apartments of Hong Kong while he gets sucked into delivering babies, fighting petty thieves, saving his friend To Fat (Wang Chung) from the belligerent drivers of a rival taxi company, and avoiding lascivious prostitutes who set up taxi drivers to be beaten up and robbed.

While trying to pursue the girl of his dreams, Li Ching (Lin Zhen-ji), Chen gets carjacked by three men wearing stockings on their heads. They force him to drive the getaway car when they rob a bank, and security cameras spot Chen's face loud and clear. After the police quickly identify him as the prime suspect, it is up to him to find and capture the thieves before the cops come knocking. Thanks to a little help from his cabbie friends, Chen proves taxing for the cops, and at the final showdown with head robber Ma Shang-long (Shi Zhong-tian), Chen gives the villain his most expensive fare ever: a paddy wagon ride to prison.

As with many films of the early '70s, the fights are collections of flailing arms and feet, and actors noodle their kicks at each other with as much power as a hammer being used by a 2-year-old. Part of the problem was that kung fu fight choreographers were not proficient in creating believable fights with martial arts in a modern setting, opting to leave technique behind and assume brawling infused with kicks would be fine. There is a short sequence with actor David Chiang practicing kung fu in a park that plainly shows his lack of good martial arts training while he does front stances with an overly bent trail leg and a horse stance as wobbly as his wavering knees. It is worth noting that just because an actor does not seriously practice martial arts, that doesn't mean they can't fight on camera. Chiang was known for getting into real street brawls (as was Jimmy Wong Yu). On many occasions, those experiences translated well on screen, but not in this film.

Titleography: As of this writing, no alternative titles could be found. Translation—*The Big Brotherly Taxi Driver*. Tough translation. There is no such word as "taxi" in Chinese, so the first two characters are used because they sound like "taxi." The second two characters literally translate as "big brother," but the inference is not about gangs or a family member, but of a hillbilly sort of young man. (Note: In American folklore, a hillbilly is stereotypically ignorant or a country bumpkin who knows nothing, but the Chinese version of a hillbilly, as in this film's title, is neither. Instead it is someone you can go to for advice because his life as a hillbilly gives him a unique perspective on life.) **MA Percentage: 9.01%** SHAW BROTHERS

TEN BROTHERS OF SHAOLIN

十大弟子 (1979—Taiwan) **86m. MAI: Tommy Lee. NOT/LOT: 15/ 2m 20s; NOF/LOF: 25/ 18m 35s.** D: Ding Chong. C: Chia Ling, Wong Dao, Zhang Yi, Huang Fei-lung, Gao Fei, Liu Li-zu, Liang Chia-ren, Dong Wei, Liu Yi-lung, O Yau-man, Jia Kai.

The stories of the legendary 10 Tigers of Shaolin or the 10 Tigers of Canton probably influenced this movie because there are no historic heroes in the annals of martial arts fighters known as the 10 Brothers of Shaolin. Regardless, it is a story of how one female fighter named Lu Shao-hua (Chia Ling), five Shaolin monks and five Shaolin-trained non-monks headed by Ji Yong (Wong Dao) come together for an important mission. They unite to protect an important Ming loyalist, Kung Chu-chang, during his journey to White Stone Tower and to prevent him from falling into the hands of the malicious Manchu commander, Kong Ching-ho (Zhang Yi).

Because the film features a number of "running away from trouble" scenes, many of the 10 brothers fall victim to Kong or to his right-hand man, Commander Tsao (Liang Chia-ren). Meanwhile, any hint of a love affair between Shao-hua and Ji Yong quickly dissolves when she bravely states, "My country comes first before love." This is a true Confucian concept that is intertwined within Chinese society. It guarantees subservience to the real master of an individual: the government.

This being a Shaolin film, there is the expected Ming-versus-Ching conflict and the requisite Shaolin monk traitor, who in this film recognizes the error of his ways and mutilates his head with a monk's cudgel as penance. This traditional weapon, also known as a Shaolin scepter, looks like the frame of a Chinese lantern on the end of a pole. It is used during religious ceremonies as a symbol of the presence of heavenly guardians, but because it is made of steel, it doubles as an effective means of self-defense. It was usually only carried by the abbot of Shaolin Temple.

An unusual sequence for this kind of film ebbs between the movie's tidal waves of bloody violence after Shao-hua kills Kong's son. Apart from the obvious vengeful filleting of Shao-hua by Kong's superior kung fu, there is a three-minute sequence of Kong lamenting the loss of his son. While a re-looping shot of his dramatic anger echoes on the screen, we are forced to see the softer side of the ruthless, murdering Kong. For a moment, we might even feel sorry for him. But that moment soon fades when Ji Yong and the four surviving brothers of Shaolin come clamoring for revenge. They prepare to make Kong look and feel like a quivering bowl of raspberry Jell-O.

Perhaps the most bothersome thing in this film is when the English dub refers to the martial arts of the Shaolin monks as "Chinese karate." That goes to show that the dubbers often had no idea what they were dubbing about.

Titleography: *Warriors of the Sacred Temple*. Translation—*Ten Elder Disciples*. Indeed the English titles match the notion of 10 fighting men or warriors being from the sacred Shaolin Temple. **MA Percentage: 24.32%**

TEN TIGERS OF SHAOLIN

廣東十虎 (1978—Hong Kong) 84m. FI: Liang Shao-song. NOT/LOT: 11/ 1m 18s; NOF/LOF: 32/ 34m 32s. D: Wei Hai-feng. C: Bruce Leung, Huang Yuan-shen, Hon Gwok-choi, Bai Biao, Larry Lee, Michelle Yim, Shan Guai, Han Yi-sheng.

In the Shaw Brothers version of *Ten Tigers of Kwantung* (1979), the cast is a veritable who's who from the Shaw stable of actors. This weaker version comes across more like a "who's that" because many of the actors are not as well-known, and cumulatively, their martial arts are weaker. If you're wondering why we're talking about Tigers from Kwantung instead of Shaolin, the simple answer is the English title is wrong. The Chinese title correctly lets on that this film is about the 10 Tigers of Kwantung, a band of heroic fighters from Canton (Canton means Kwantung in Cantonese), whereas the 10 tigers of Shaolin are 10 completely different heroes who learned their martial arts at the Shaolin Temple. Whenever possible, the 10 Tigers of Kwantung—Lu A-tsai, Tan Ji-her, Tie Zhi-chen, Tie Qiao-san, Su Qi-er, Li Ren-chao, Su Hei-hu, Huang Cheng-ke, Huang Ying-lin (the group's leader) and Huang Chi-ying (Huang Fei-hung's father)—give the Manchus a run for their money, and this movie is no different.

This film is a story about how one Manchu official, Yun San-piao (Huang Yuan-she), tries to make them pay for it. He attempts to crash the wedding of one of the 10 Tigers, Su Qi-er (Hon Gwok-choi), and to kidnap both Su's wife, Chu Sang (Michelle Yim), and the wife of Huang Ying-lin's (Bai Biao) friend Ah Pei. It's all an effort to split up the 10 Tigers so Yun and his Manchu marauders can take them out one by one.

The main Tigers featured in this film are the bumbling Su Qi-er, who provides comic relief; Huang Ying-lin, who wields a walking cane; Huang Chi-ying (Larry Lee); and Lu A-tsai (Bruce Leung), who aptly demonstrates Lu's patented eight diagram pole skills.

One of the problems with a film that tries to feature too many main characters in an extremely linear story is how to bring out everyone's martial arts abilities. That requires solid, well-planned choreography and should feature the skills that each Tiger is historically known for. However, in this film, rather than spend time with each individual character, the movie waits until the final fight when all 10 Tigers battle Yun, his top kung fu protectors and the rest of his allies at the same time. Each Tiger ends up mixing and matching his skills with one or several opponents at a time. The fights break down into generic segments only to eventually have one or two Tigers break away from the pack for some one-on-one fights with the lead villains. This is why the film statistically has more fights than most kung fu films made during the 1970s—a whopping 32 different fights. But it is not the film with the greatest length of martial arts in terms of film time. Although there are flashes of good martial technique from some of the stars (Leung, Lee and Bai), the desperation of the historic time they are recreating is more like desperation to save the film's story, which is rather weak to begin with considering the importance of the real 10 Tigers of Shaolin.

Titleography: *10 Tigers of Shaolin*. Translation—*Ten Tigers of Kwantung*. **MA Percentage: 42.66%**

THAT MAN BOLT

(1973—USA) 103m. SC: Erik Cord. NOT/LOT: 3/ 1m 51s; NOF/LOF: 7/ 5m 2s. D: Henry Levin, David Lowell Rich. C: Fred Williamson, Byron Webster, Miko Mayama, Teresa Graves, Masatoshi Nakamura, John Orchard, Jack Ging, Ken Kazama, David Chow.

Who is the man that can shut down the door of a crime? Bolt! Can you dig it? Who's the cat with the clout when there's crime to be locked out? Bolt! Right on. The success of *Shaft* (1971), arguably the first blaxploitation flick, set the coolness standard for a new generation of black cinematic heroes. (I hope the late Isaac Hayes would forgive my paraphrasing his classic 1972 Academy Award-winning best original song, *Shaft*.) Although Bolt is modeled after solid dudes like Bond, Flint, Lee and Shaft, actor Fred Williamson's black cat does not quite have the same soul.

Bolt is hired by some sort of international British intelligence syndicate to deliver a briefcase filled with $1 million. The case is from Hong Kong and is headed to Mexico City via Los Angeles as part of a plan to reveal who is behind an international drug and prostitution ring. Although I am a fan of blaxploitation films, this book is first and foremost about martial arts. That said, the fights in this film are awful.

I could have sworn the bouts are shot in slow motion, but believe me, they

are not. It is worth noting that this movie features several legitimate martial artists: former California State Judo Champion David Chow, World Professional Light Heavyweight Karate Champion Mike Stone and Japan Kickboxing Champion Ken Kazama, who plays Spider, an assassin trained in the Chen Fu Buddhist Monastery by the same old monk who taught Bolt. Although the fights deserve no further mention, it is interesting that the filmmakers got Shaw Brothers film legend Li Yun-zhong to play the head of the Chen Fu school.

Titleography: As of this writing, no alternative titles could be found. The title is clearly influenced by James Coburn's *Our Man Flint* (1966). **MA Percentage: 6.88%**

THEY CALL HER ONE EYE

Thriller: En Grym Film (1974—Sweden) 104m. SC: Jan Kreigsman. NOT/LOT: 6/ 3m 15s; NOF/LOF: 1/ 4m 10s. D: Bo Arne Vibenius. C: Christina Lindberg, Heinz Hopf, Despina Tomazani, Per-Axel Arosenius, Solveig Andersson.

Rape, molestation and forced prostitution, is there no cure? Maybe. Beware, you purveyors of these wicked acts against the innocent because, when things get patched up in the blink of an eye, you evildoers are going to die.

Little Swedish milkmaid Frigga, aka Madeleine, was raped as a child, and the trauma has turned her into a mute. As a teen, she is tricked and forced into heroin addiction and prostitution. But when adult Frigga (Christina Lindberg) learns that her despicable, manipulative pimp, Tony (Heinz Hopf), has had her parents killed, she decides that enough is enough. She learns how to shoot a rifle and drive a car, and she trains in the deadly art of karate. Her desire for revenge against Tony and the sex-starved johns she has had to endure is compounded when, in an agonizing and gory scene, Frigga's left eye is gouged out by Tony with a scalpel as punishment for scratching the face of a customer she shunned.

As one might expect from a lifetime nonpractitioner of martial arts, Lindberg's on-camera *shotokan* training sequences are similar in intensity to a squirrel eating acorns in an oak tree void of predators. It is tough to choreograph a fight scene with someone who has noodle arms and legs and make her look deadly. However, director Vibenius circumvented this by draping Lindberg in a long-sleeved, body-length leather jacket to hide the meek-looking limbs that come with Lindberg's build. He also intelligently shot the film's only martial arts fight, in which Lindberg takes on two policemen, in slow motion. When the cops are dispatched, blood slowly spews from their mouths in long, curling red ribbons. It is very effective and made even more memorable by the mournful music, which sounds like Akira Ifukube's orchestration at the end of *Godzilla* (1954). This may not be as crazy as you think.

Just as Godzilla is walking underwater toward Dr. Serizawa, who is preparing to unleash his deoxygenating pellet into the water as mankind's final hope to destroy the monster, so is Frigga womankind's final hope to destroy a different kind of monster. The music is also perhaps a nod to Lindberg's starring role in the Japanese film *Sex and Fury* (1973). The music electronically whines at a monosyllabic hum that draws out like the blood trailing from the dying policemen's gaping mouths.

Frigga's matching eye patch and jacket ensemble is thought to have inspired Darryl Hannah's character Elle Driver in Quentin Tarantino's *Kill Bill* films (2003-2004).

Titleography: *Hooker's Revenge*. Translation—*Thriller: A Cruel Picture*. If the shoe fits, wear it. **MA Percentage: 7.13%**

36TH CHAMBER OF SHAOLIN, THE

少林三十六房 and 少林卅六房 (1977—Hong Kong) 111m. FI: Liu Chia-liang. NOT/LOT: 18/ 45m 51s; NOF/LOF: 7/ 15m 17s. D: Liu Chia-liang. C: Gordon Liu Chia-hui, Lo Lieh, Wilson Tong, Lee Hoi-sung, Liu Chia-rong, Hua Lin, Hon Gwok-choi, Yuen Xiao-tien.

Director Liu Chia-liang's films often deal with authentic martial arts training, technique and virtues. *The 36th Chamber of Shaolin* is such a film, based on the true story of Monk San De (Te), one of the 10 Tigers of Shaolin from Jiu Lian Shan Shaolin Temple. (See *Executioners From Shaolin*.)

It is fitting that San De's name means "three virtues." I once asked Gordon why Liu Chia-liang cast him in the film, and he said because Liu Chia-liang saw him as a good student who was obedient and had a good attitude—three virtues.

Gordon also told me how one day he and Liu Chia-liang were returning home after shooting *Challenge of the Masters* (1976). The director saw a waterfall and watched the water hit a round rock, noticing how it created a halo effect above the rock. This created an image in Liu Chia-liang's mind of a bald monk training in the rain. That was the inspiration behind the opening shot of this film.

This was an important film in martial arts cinema history because it was the first to open the doors to the secret martial arts training methods of the ancient Shaolin Temple. Prior to San De's arrival, the temple had 35 chambers, with each representing a spiritual, mental or physical form of training. The story focuses on student Liu Yu-de, who escapes Manchu execution and seeks asylum in the Jiu Lian Shan Shaolin Temple in hopes of learning martial arts. Through hard training, we witness how Liu Yu-de becomes Monk San De; by his desire to teach Shaolin kung fu to laypeople, the 36th chamber of Shaolin is created.

The film also demonstrates how San De invented the three-sectional staff and used it to stop the Manchus. In reality, the three-sectional staff was invented in A.D. 360 by the first emperor of the Song Dynasty, Chao Hong-yin. At the time of the staff's invention, Chao was just a bodyguard for the Royal Family and was an expert of the wooden staff (aka the *guin* or *bo*). In the old days, your weapon was a reflection of who you were, so if it broke, it was a sad occasion. One day, Chao was attacked. To defend himself, he hit his opponent on the head, breaking the top third of his pole. He had a blacksmith link the broken ends with two iron rings. During another fight, the pole broke again, and once more, two iron rings connected the broken ends. Thus the three-sectional staff was invented, and it proved valuable in warfare because wielders could break the legs of horses to bring down powerful cavalrymen.

Still from *The 36th Chamber of Shaolin* © Celestial Pictures Ltd. All rights reserved.

The film also depicts San De teaching kung fu to the legendary real-life heroes Hong Xi-guan, Tong Qian-jin and Lu A-tsai. Although in reality these three men learned kung fu from Zhi Shan (one of the Five Elders of Shaolin), director Liu Chia-liang was giving a nod to the fact that their lives were intertwined with San De's.

Historically, San De, Hong Xi-guan and Tong Qian-jin were all members of the 10 Tigers of Shaolin. Also, as history tells, when Tong was under the watch of San De, Tong snuck out of the Jiu Lian Shaolin Temple with a stolen pass. This was punishable by death, and so San De sent Lu A-tsai after Tong to kill him. Yet when Lu found him, he was so moved by Tong's righteousness that he let him live. Eventually, Tong was allowed to seek refuge from the Chings at Xi Chan Shaolin Temple in Canton, which is the temple San De established.

One final note: Gordon shared with me that the bamboo/water scene took two weeks to complete, and by the end of that time, he had actually learned how to ski across the water as the film depicts.

Titleography: *Master Killer*; *Disciples of Master Killer*; *Shaolin Master Killer*; *The Thirty-sixth Chamber.* Translation—Both titles are different ways of writing *The 36th Chamber of Shaolin.* Whoever came up with *Master Killer* either did not understand the tenets of the Shaolin Temple (not to kill) or was creating a name-appearance contradiction, like when somebody 7 feet tall would be nicknamed Shorty. As mentioned in my introduction, using words such as "Shaolin," "master," "killer," "disciple" and other similar words was common in movie titles. **MA Percentage: 55.08%** SHAW BROTHERS

THUNDERBOLT FIST, THE

霹靂拳 (1972—Hong Kong) **86m. FI: Liang Shao-song. NOT/LOT: 7/ 6m 2s; NOF/LOF: 22/ 22m 37s.** D: Chang Yi-hu. C: Shih Szu, Chuan Yuan, Wang Chin-feng, James Nam Gung-fan, Fang Mian, Tong Lin, Li Gu-ding, Kim Kee-joo, Chen Fung-chen, Yukio Someno.

The Japanese are coming! The Japanese are coming! … Again. When the Japanese threaten to usurp a Chinese village to prove their superiority, they want to do so honorably by defeating the village's top kung fu man, Fang Ping-bai. According to the unwritten rules of *da lei tai* fighting competitions, the winner's request must be honored. After Fang beats the head Japanese fighter, Gu Gang (James Nam Gung-fan), the not-so-honorable Japanese fighters stab Fang in the back with a samurai sword. Before dying, Fang tells his young child, Tie-wa, to train in kung fu in the mountain with his old friend Gin Chi (Kim Jee-joo), who lives with his daughter, Die Er. Before leaving, Tie-wa bids farewell to his betrothed, Feng Niu. She is told to bury Tie-wa's father and hide his secret Thunderbolt Fist kung fu manual.

After many year of training, Tie-wa (Chuan Yuan) comes down from the mountains seeking revenge for his father. He finds that his fiancée has married his good friend Da Xiong (Tong Lin). Da mistakenly believes Tie-wa wants to move in on his wife and attacks Tie-wa, who takes the punishment, knowing that he could hurt Da but also understanding his stupid behavior. Gu Lan (Chen Fung-chen), the son of Gu Gang, asserts his father's control over the village by beating the living daylights out of Da. Tie-wa saves his friend, but Gu and his gang beat the dying daylights out of Tie-wa, maiming and burning his right arm.

As we can guess, it is time to learn the powerful Thunderbolt Fist technique. Even though he only has one arm, Tie-wa whips it in wide circles like tornado, ready to beat the Japanese into a whirlwind of submission.

One of the problems with watching early kung fu films is that the training scenes aren't as well integrated into the story as in later films (such as numerous Jackie Chan films). The idea in early films was to give the audiences enough information so they could accept that the hero would be ready to tackle the bad guy. Even though that villain beat him earlier in the film, the hero now has attained the missing skill that will make the difference. It is sort of like comparing the wire work of the 1970s to the '80s,'90s and 2000s—there really is no comparison.

As this film progresses, the fights get better. That's probably because the actors got used to working with each other and began to get a better sense of timing and familiarity with each other's fighting movements. The same thing probably happened with the choreographer and actors. During the big finale, Shih Szu (as the grown up Die Er) does some very good reverse-grip sword work (a rarity in kung fu films of the era), and everything is shot tighter to add more tension to the swishing and slashing. There is also the eventual showdown between Tie-wa and Gu Lan. A particularly memorable image in the film is a close shot on a samurai sword that tracks across the screen only to get blocked by Die Er; then the camera pulls back as the fight then immediately opens up into a vicious sword sequence. Very dynamic indeed.

Titleography: As of this writing, no alternative titles could be found.

223

Still from *The Thunderbolt Fist* © Celestial Pictures Ltd. All rights reserved.

Translation—*Sound of Thunder Clap Style* or *Fist*. The English and Chinese titles both describe the film's secret kung fu skill. **MA Percentage: 33.31%** SHAW BROTHERS

THUNDERKICK, THE

一網打盡 (1973—Hong Kong) **90m. FI: Liu Chia-rong, Chan Chuen. NOT/LOT: None; NOF/LOF: 13/ 32m 2s.** D: Teddy Yip. C: Larry Lee, Yukio Someno, Huang Pei-ji, Lau Tai-chuen, Bolo Yeung, James Nan Gung-fan.

The way of the *karateka* is to be mindful of one's manners and to act with humility. But sometimes, in order to help the defenseless people around you, it is time to crack open the *gi*, let go of the *chi* and fight for what's right.

When it comes to the criminal world in early kung fu films, each movie usually has one opium den, brothel or casino that the hero has to shut down for the good of the townsfolk. Otherwise, the weak-minded would smoke, sex or gamble away their lives, leaving their families to suffer the consequences. When a film has all three evil elements lurking in the shadows of backstreet China, the plot is pretty predictable, and you might want to keep your thumb on the fast-forward button. This film does offer some rip-roaring fights starring Okinawan karate stylist Larry Lee as Chi Sing. Against his begging mother's wishes to stop fighting, Chi Sing takes on the three maniacal owners of the respective three houses of evil (the gambling den, opium parlor and brothel). The final fight is an exhausting showdown clocking in at almost 9 minutes, and it features another legitimate karate stylist, Yukio Someno.

One of the biggest differences between traditionally trained karate stylists and Beijing opera actors is that most opera folks are unable to deliver authentic side kicks and roundhouse kicks. Watching Jackie Chan's films, for example, you will notice he rarely does a side kick, and his roundhouses are more often parts of spinning combinations rather than single, damaging thrusts. Suffice it to say, Larry Lee has firm kicks, and compared to many *taekwondo* actors, he uses fewer spins and more straight kicks. Lee also uses a lot of open-hand techniques for slapping, blocking, chopping and parrying; doing so reduces the risk of injuries when working with actors who are not trained in martial arts.

Lee also exhibits his expertise with a traditional Okinawan straight-styled *tonfa* (from which the modern side-handled police baton is derived). It is thick board with a rounded edge and a handled mount, and the forearm-length section of the weapon is flattened. Originating from the wooden handle used to turn the millstone that would grind grains and rice, the tonfa is an example of an agricultural tool morphing into a weapon. This movement began after Sho Shin, the Okinawan king (1477-1526), implemented a ban on weapons in hopes of quelling violence and assuring stability in a country recovering from civil war. After Japan annexed Okinawa in 1879 and Japanese samurai freely roamed the land, the weapon ban was even more heavily enforced, so farmers and former Okinawan noblemen (who were allowed to carry weapons throughout Sho Shin's ruling) now turned to farming tools as weapons.

Titleography: *Survival of the Dragon*; *The Thunder Kick*; *Dragon From Shaolin*. Translation—*One Web Hit All Completely Gone*. After Bruce Lee's films,

many titles were released using *Dragon* in alternative English titles. The original English title has nothing to do with anything dragon-like, or even Shaolin. The English title is just using those generic words to attract a buyer. The hero does have powerful kicks, so *Thunderkick* is appropriate, and the Chinese title reflects how with one hit (as in "all in one go") the hero takes out the brothel, opium den and casino in a single swift strike. **MA Percentage: 35.59%**

TIGER'S CLAW

二龍爭珠 (1974—Hong Kong) **80m. MAI: Chen Shao-peng. NOT/LOT: 1/ 21s; NOF/LOF: 13/ 27m 15s.** D: Ng Tin-chi. C: Cliff Lok, Shiek Khan, Yang Wei, Lin Ching, Lisa Lui Yau-wai.

To borrow from Paul Simon's 1972 hit *Mother and Child Reunion*, "On this strange and mournful day, when the father and child reunion is only a fight away."

Cocky combatant Shen Yi-wu (Cliff Lok, with a Bruce Lee haircut) searches all over to prove he is the best fighter. He defeats his opponents, but he should be careful to avoid sharp objects because they might pop his swelling head. One day he overhears some townsfolk say he could never defeat Tiger Ko (Shiek Khan), the aging former great fighter who is serving a life sentence for a bum rap. Tiger was convicted of killing his former best friend, Hu Liu-er (Yang Wei), who tried to frame Tiger for a crime he did not commit. Hu figured with Tiger in prison, he could get his lustful hands on Tiger's wife. Shen mock-rapes his kung fu sister to get into prison and fight Tiger. Tiger agrees to fight Shen after he can escape prison and find out what happened to his wife. Tiger learns that the child his wife bore after he entered prison was not Hu's but his own—and we can guess who the son is. Unaware of who Tiger might be, Shen is determined to destroy Tiger to prove he is the best. Although Tiger finds his long-lost wife and learns the truth as to who Shen really is, the torn-up-inside Tiger is still obligated to fight Shen to the death.

It's a rare event when actor Shiek Khan plays the good guy. In this film, his hair-and-beard combination is reminiscent of Spock's evil facsimile from the original *Star Trek* episode "Mirror Mirror". The audience is reminded that Shiek played Mr. Han in Bruce Lee's *Enter the Dragon* (1973) because the soundtrack from the film blares every time he fights.

The English dub first says Tiger has been in prison for 10 years, but later, when the real story is out, the dubbers change the prison sentence to 20 years, thus making Shen's age logical for the film. It's another example of how when films get dubbed, plot points are often missed, and we dubbers had to make things up as we went along, because once we dubbed a line, there was no going back.

Shiek uses the same bobbing fighting rhythm he used as Han in *Enter the Dragon*. That speaks to the nature of his film experience (bobbing fights were popular in the '50s and '60s), but it somehow fits his character because his skulking posture looks like a tiger stalking its prey. Though the fights are fast and furious, the kung fu looks sloppy, which is surprising for someone of Cliff Lok's abilities. The fights also use a lot of slapping choreography for blocks and strikes rather than fists and good martial arts hands.

The main reason to use slap choreography is that it is easier to remember and less likely to lead to injury, which can be particularly important for inexperienced and older actors. You might also notice these kinds of fights when solid kung fu practitioners fight Korean or Chinese *taekwondo* stylists. These practitioners are not known for extensive arm-toughening methods and can have a painful time fighting someone who practices traditional *wing chun* or *hong chuan* kung fu. That's been my experience, at least.

Titleography: *Shaolin Tiger Claw*; *Shaolin's Tiger Claws*. Translation—*Two Dragons Fight for the Pearl*. In many Chinese films, the titles are often metaphors. In this film, the dragons are the father and son, and the pearl is being the best fighter. There's nothing to do with Shaolin here, though. And since Shiek's character is called Tiger, it is logical enough to toss in Claw, which implies Shiek is using tiger claw kung fu (which he sort of is). **MA Percentage: 34.5%**

TIGRESS OF SHAOLIN, THE

痳瘋怪拳 and 痳瘋怪拳 (1979—Hong Kong) **93m. FI: Huang Ha, Chen Di-ke. NOT/LOT: 10/ 13m 56s; NOF/LOF: 26/ 21m 46s.** D: Luo Chi. C: Liu Chia-yung, Hui Ying-hong, Lin Hui-huang, Chen Chien-po, Huang Ha, Tang Jin-tan, Chen Di-ke, Wang Ching-ho, Chiang Chen, Liu Jiu-yi.

It is said that a leopard cannot change its spots, but someone with leprosy can change his boils, and this film boils down to whether the hero can learn the hand-contorted 10 secret ways of the "odd leprosy fist," which is also the Chinese title of the film.

After Xiao San's (Liu Chia-yung) father dies, Xiao gets a letter of recommendation to learn kung fu from Meng Peng at the Tibetan-run Zhen Nan Clinic, which is really a front for Meng's smuggling business. Arriving in town, Xiao, aka Ah San ("Ah" is a Chinese term of endearment), has an odd run-in with Drunk Shrimp (Huang Ha), learning that his monkey kung fu is no match for sotted seafood.

Ah San soon discovers that the clinic makes money by beating people up and charging them an arm and a leg for healing, sort of like a lung doctor prescribing smoking to his patients. When Ah San refuses to partake in the scheming, he is apparently beaten to death (though he fakes his demise) and tossed into the river. But he is saved just barely by Xiao Hong (Hui Ying-hong). Finding work in a dilapidated restaurant, he gets into a silly fight with Little Rat. They eventually become pals and work at a grocery store. Meng pops back into the picture when his men frame the owner for drug trafficking and then behead him. Feeling Xiao and Little Rat might expose him, Meng sets out to kill them. On the lam from Meng and his Tibetan hit men—headed by Ji (Lin Hui-huang), who dresses like a Native American with sunglasses and fights with a giant steel comb—Ah San seeks help from a Shaolin monk, Hai Zhuang (Chiang Chen) who teaches him eight diagram pole fighting.

Still from *The Tigress of Shaolin* © Celestial Pictures Ltd. All rights reserved.

Ah San next learns leprosy fist from Xiao Hong's wacky godmother (Liu Jiu-yi), while picking up extra movements from her godfather, the Drunk Shrimp. Ah San is now ready to take on Meng and Ji, who arrive at the final fight inside giant coffins that walk around like boxes with feet.

There are no such martial arts as leprosy fist or drunken shrimp, but my hat is off to the filmmakers for their creativity. Actress Hui Ying-hong's stances, postures and hand positions are firm, which are a reflection of her real-life kung fu training. When main actor Liu Chia-yung uses the butterfly swords (aka butterfly knives) during the opening credits, the footage is shot at 18 frames per second to make his movements super-fast. Yet for the kung fu and spear training sequence, the film is shot at 20 frames per second. In reality, he does the movements slowly, making sure that the postures, stances and technique are perfect, so when we watch the film it looks like he is doing everything sharp, crisp and smooth. It is odd how the filmmakers chose to do the butterfly swords too fast and everything else looking normal-speed. These varying uses of camera speed cast doubt on skill levels and film continuity.

Although Chia-yung looks good, there is ultimately nothing special about his kung fu. At least, there is nothing that makes him stick out from everyone else, which is perhaps why he never attained the heights of his famous kung fu film-

maker uncles, Liu Chia-rong and Liu Chia-liang. A few months after *Tigress* was made, Chia-rong revisited leprosy kung fu in *Fists and Guts* (1979).

Historically, Yang Wu-lung created eight diagram pole fighting during the Song Dynasty (A.D. 969-1279). Wu-lung was a member of the famed Yang family, notably known for the Yang Women Warriors (see *14 Amazons*) and the family's exceptional spear techniques. Of note, Gordon Liu Chia-hui portrayed Wu-lung in the Shaw Brothers film *The Eight Diagram Pole Fighter* (1983).

Titleography: As of this writing, no alternative titles could be found. Translation—*Odd Leprosy Style. Tigress of Shaolin* refers to the wild godmother who cleans dishes at Shaolin and teaches Ah San leprosy fist king fu. **MA Percentage: 38.39%** SHAW BROTHERS

TNT JACKSON

(1974—USA/Philippines) **67m. MAI: J. Lo, Tan Siu-tong, Boni Uy. NOT/LOT: 4/ 1m 51s; NOF/LOF: 15/ 12m 16s.** D: Cirio H. Santiago. C: Jeannie Bell, Stan Shaw, Pat Anderson, Ken Metcalfe, Chiquito, Imelda Ilanan, Leo Martinez.

Cirio Santiago, one of the pioneers of blaxploitation, directs Jeannie Bell as the explosive TNT Jackson. She's a "one-mama massacre squad" (as the tag line says) headed to Hong Kong in search of her long-lost brother, Stag. Upon her arrival, she investigates Stag's last known whereabouts and is attacked by some thugs, but she shows them no mercy. She befriends Chinese kung fu fighter and bar owner Joe (Chiquito) and learns that Stag got caught up with some drug dealers, who are also under investigation by an undercover agent. The criminals' internal squabbling could mean it's the right time for TNT to strike.

Like actress Reiko Ike, who was samurai-swording nude in *Sex and Fury* (1973), Bell does some topless slugging. Glimpses of her nude flash on-screen as she turns on the light to nail someone, then clicks it off to hide in the dark, repeating until all the thugs have been dropped like bad habits.

TNT Jackson was one of the first American films to introduce audiences to the Filipino *balisong* knife. First documented in the 1710 French book *Le Perret*, the balisong knife (also known as the butterfly knife) may be so named after the place of its invention in the Batangas province of the Philippines. Dating back to A.D. 800, the balisong knife carries the label of an ancient escrima weapon and was considered to be a popular Filipino utility knife during the late 1500s. It was made popular in the United States after island-hopping American soldiers returned home from the Pacific after World War II. It is essentially a folding pocketknife in which the blade is hidden within grooves in the handles (like the wings of a butterfly that fold up when it is at rest).

This film also marks the first martial arts confrontation between a black female and a white female on-screen, though it is a clumsy and awkward one. It is interesting that Bell modeled many of her fighting postures after Diana Rigg's character Emma Peel from the British television show *The Avengers* (1965-1968). The most intriguing sequence is the final showdown, in which TNT battles the newly crowned drug kingpin Charlie (Stan Shaw) in a karate fight laced with kicks, rolls and mis-hits. What is so exceptional about this routine is that it was shot from a wide-angle bird's-eye view, a la Hong Kong's Chang Cheh, and done in one continuous 27-second take during which Bell and Shaw (no stunt doubles) exchange 17 consecutive strikes. That has to be some kind of American record to have martial arts actors exchange so many fight techniques in a single take. Bravo for blaxploitation.

Titleography: *Dynamite Jackson; Dynamite Wong and TNT Jackson.* **MA Percentage: 21.07%**

TO KILL A JAGUAR

絕 不 低 頭 (1977—Hong Kong) **90m. FI: Yuen Woo-ping, Yuen Cheung-yan. NOT/LOT: None; NOF/LOF: 13/ 11m 20s.** D: Hua Shan. C: Ling Yun, Liu Yong, Tsung Hua, Nora Miao, Wang Lung-wei, Chan Shen, Fan Mei-sheng, Jin Lou, Liu Jian-ming, Frankie Wei Hong.

In real life, jaguars and monkeys are natural enemies. But with a wicked stretch of the imagination, it is curious that in this film the anti-hero is named Jaguar and his girlfriend/downfall partner is Bobo, maybe named after one of

the world's smartest apes, who first appeared in 1952 as a backup feature in DC Comics' *Rex the Wonder Dog*.

The film is set in the Bund during the 1920s, when the alluring Bobo (Nora Miao) arrives in Shanghai to look for her lost father. She is immediately beset by gangsters because she is caught in the middle of a gang fight between Jaguar (Tsung Hua) and Wu Bui (Wang Lung-wei) over some stolen merchandise. Both say the goods belong to their respective bosses, Boss Kam (Frankie Wei Hong) for Jaguar and Cheung Sam (Fan Mei-sheng) for Wu. Jaguar wins the day, the merchandise and Bobo's heart, and it turns out he and Bobo were childhood friends. They fall in love, which sends them through an open door they can never close.

When Cheung Sam opens a casino in the Bund's French concession, Boss Kam sends Jaguar to shut it down. He's confronted by Cheung's bodyguard, the super-cool Ko Tang (Ling Yun), who is deadlier than deadly and faster than fast with his silver Luger (a handgun invented by Germany's Georg J. Luger in 1898). Yet they become friends, and as their friendship grows, Ko tells Jaguar about how he saved a righteous man from prison, and Jaguar reciprocates by telling Ko about his best childhood friend. However, when Ko suddenly dies, the man Ko once saved, Luo Lieh (Liu Yong), comes to town to avenge his death. Luo doesn't realize that the man who killed Ko is his best childhood friend, Jaguar, and at one time they both vied for the affections of Bobo. It's a wicked triangle with vexed vertices of love, friendship and vengeance.

Although there are not many fights in this movie, they are filled with ax-hacking and plenty of backstabbing (literal and figurative). The fighting duo of the Yuen brothers introduces close, low-angle shots that really bring the action to the fore—it's practically 3-D. The action is further enhanced by a quick editing style that would become common in the 1980s, especially in Fant-Asia films.

Cultural note: The Bund developed in the 1860s in Shanghai's International Settlement, an extraterritorial zone of British and American influence not governed by Chinese laws. The word "Bund" is of Anglo-Indian origin, meaning "embankment on the waterfront." The Huangpu River divides the Bund into two sections: Pu Dong and Pu Xi ("east of river" and "west of river"). Members of Shanghai's criminal underworld quickly learned that if they lived within the Bund's jurisdiction, they were immune to Chinese prosecution. So long as no foreigners got hurt, the powerful Chinese gangs could grow unhindered by Chinese law.

Titleography: As of this writing, no alternative titles could be found. Translation—*Never Lower the Head*. In English, the title character is named Jaguar (though he does not practice any kind of leopard, tiger or jaguar kung fu), and several people are trying to kill him. The Chinese title refers to the notion that one must never admit defeat or bow to someone else; Jaguar does not, and that ultimately leads to his demise. **MA Percentage: 12.59%** SHAW BROTHERS

TO KILL WITH INTRIGUE

劍花煙雨江南 (1977—Hong Kong) 98m. **KFI:** Chen Shen-yi, Jackie Chan. **NOT/LOT:** 3/ 1m 5s; **NOF/LOF:** 14/ 23m 56s. D: Lo Wei. C: Jackie Chan, Hsu Feng, Yu Ling-lung, Chen Shen-yi, Wang Jue, Ma Ji, Yu Ling-lung, Tong Lin, Jiang Qing-xia, Chen Hui-lou.

That buzzing noise you hear is not the air conditioning—it's the attack of the Killer Bee Clan! This is one of only a few *wuxia* films in which Jackie Chan plays a lead character. (His appearance as a street vendor trying to catch his friend's cheating wife in the Shaw Brothers erotic film *The Golden Lotus* does not count.)

Headed by the mysterious veiled Ting Chan-yen (Hsu Feng; Taiwan's answer to Hong Kong's Angela Mao-ying), the Killer Bees fly into the palace of Lord Lei Chi-feng and sting everyone to death. Only Lord Lei's son Hsiao Lei (Jackie Chan) is spared because Chan-yen wants Hsiao Lei to experience the pain she has felt since Lord Lei killed her whole family 15 years ago. The next thing you know, Hsiao Lei and Chan-yen are having wild sex together (the only steamy love scene Chan has had in film). But when Chan-yen hears Hsiao Lei humming his fiancée's name, she disappears from the nest, leaving lone drone Hsiao Lei in the hive. He is suddenly awakened by the Bloody Rain Gang, who mistaken him for their assassination target. Hsiao Lei prevails, although he also earns another lifelong enemy, and the only way he can defeat the gang's leader is if he learns some secret kung fu skills from his new honey, Chan-yen.

Although some of the martial arts action is good, the bulk of Chan's fights have too many flips and rolls. His empty-hand work is also awkward because Chan was in the middle of developing his patented low, wide-stance defending posture, which became more prevalent in his later *wu da pian* films (a genre he created). The lead villain practices iron shirt *chi gong* (*qigong*), and Hsiao Lei has to figure out his weak point. For an in-depth discussion of this, see *Executioners From Shaolin* (1977) or *Born Invincible* (1978).

There are two exotic weapons of note in this film. The first is the snake spear, also called a flame blade. It features a wavy-bladed point that increases the wound's surface area. The second is a gigantic headed cudgel, a weapon used to crush an attacker's body with one single blow. Ironically, one of the most enduring visuals I recall from this film is when Chan fights the lead villain on a raised grassy knoll that looks like a large baseball pitcher's mound surrounded by a two-foot high wall.

Titleography: As of this writing, no alternative titles could be found. Translation—*The Sword, the Flower, and the Smoke and Rain on South Beach*. When kung fu novelists wrote screenplays, the titles were all about beauty and creating a sense of adventure and intrigue; even if the title did not always reflect the story, it always reflected the mood. **MA Percentage: 25.53%**

TONGFATHER, THE

大惡寇 (1974—Taiwan) 92m. **FI:** Yu Tian-lung, Wang Yong-sheng. **NOT/LOT:** None; **NOF/LOF:** 12/ 29m 28s. D: Roc Tien. C: Roc Tien, Tian Hao, Yi Yuan, Pan Zhang-min, Wang Yong-sheng, Chen Hung-lieh.

Imagine Orson Welles bringing Humphrey Bogart and *The Man From U.N.C.L.E.* to kung fu films. There are great kung fu films and there are disappointing kung fu films—and then there is this film, a total surprise. This is one of the most outstanding kung fu films I have ever seen, not because of the fights (which are bizarrely effective and entertaining), but because of two things that no other Taiwanese-made kung fu film has ever done. Keep in mind that *The Tongfather* was made in 1974.

Right from the opening scene, this thing has Mickey Spillane noir written all over it. Each shot looks like something out of a hardboiled black-and-white thriller. Director Roc Tien has created a film more electrifying than a hair dryer tossed into a bathtub. If that weren't enough, it takes only a few minutes to realize the English dubbing is excellent; it makes you wonder why all kung fu films aren't done this way. As you watch more intently, it hits you—all the actors are speaking English. That's right, although the voices are dubbed, you can tell each actor is speaking his lines in English (probably with a really bad Chinese accent, but nonetheless in English).

That is the beauty of shooting without sound. Once I was working on the Shaw Brothers production *The Battle for the Republic of China* (1980) as the speech coach for an actor who had to do a major speech in English. Instead of having him memorize the lines, I yelled out the lines in English from behind the camera, and he simply repeated them. During post, I dubbed in his lines in English.

Tongfather is a brutal yarn about two Taiwanese undercover agents (Roc Tien and Tian Hao) sent to Hong Kong to take down the powerful Triad and Yakuza bosses peddling opium and other vices.

One of the most powerful scenes I have seen in a long time is when the head of the Chinese Triads (Chen Hung-lieh) proves his loyalty to the Yakuza boss by calmly breaking his own leg while having a conversation with him. When the Yakuza boss asks his right-hand man to take the Triad boss home, he replies with hypnotic calm, "I'll manage it alone, thank you." He then crawls out of the office on his stomach, dragging his dangling leg over the rough surface. It is as gripping as pair of rock-climbing shoes on flypaper.

Tien delivers his lines with Humphrey Bogart-esque grunts and glares. He also displays fighting savvy while staying as confidently cool as TV spy Napoleon Solo. His straight-laced posture and barrages of superb look-away kicks—just before the moment of impact when kicking someone's face, he looks in the opposite direction—are alive with voodoo magic. They are startlingly swanky, and it is a real pity that Tien never made a sequel or another film that rivals the technical cinematic accomplishment of this one.

Titleography: *Hands of Death*; *Notorious Bandit*. Translation—*The Big Bad Bandit*. The title *The Tongfather* smartly combines references to Francis Ford Coppola's successful *The Godfather* (1972) and the San Francisco Chinese Triad family known as the Tongs. The literal translation of the Chinese title fits, and *Hands of Death* could be used for any kung fu film. **MA Percentage: 32.03%**

TOUGH GUY

下南洋 (1974—Hong Kong/Philippines) **87m. MAI: Bai Biao, Liu Hao-nian. NOT/LOT: None; NOF/LOF: 24/ 17m 4s.** D: Tony Liu Jin-guk. C: Bai Biao, Ron Van Clief, Gao Gang, Chen Lou, Liu Hao-nian, Tang Guo-shi, Tony Liu Jin-guk, Yu Tou-yun, Jorge Estraga, Nancy Veronica.

The two best on-screen fight performances by non-Asians in Hong Kong kung fu films during the 1970s were Carl Scott (*Sun Dragon;* 1979) and Ron Van Clief, founder of the Chinese *goju* system of martial arts. In this, Van Clief's debut film, he plays a member of a quartet of martial arts fighters who seemingly harass Chinese dockworkers trying to make an honest living in the Philippines.

Simpleton farmhand Tai Yu (Bai Biao) wants to be rich like his kung fu brother and childhood martial arts rival Chi Fu-shi (Liu Hao-nian), who found his fortune working in the Philippines. Tai arrives in the Philippines and becomes a target for pickpocket Xiao Mao (Chen Lou). Tai catches Xiao, but his righteous and benevolent character, which comes from proper kung fu training, dictates that he befriend the down-on-his luck Xiao; he even invites him to share his minuscule apartment. After Tai becomes a dockworker and begins paying the bills, Xiao still steals Tai's money and his only true treasure, a pair of kung fu shoes his mother made for him before he left rural China. Tai finds Xiao being beaten up by street gamblers, who have sucked Xiao's stolen money dry and claimed the shoes for their own. Tai fights like a man possessed to get his shoes back, after which he accepts the loss of his money and insists that Xiao stay with him and turn his life around. This is the old way of martial arts, specifically the way of the Shaolin, to believe that everyone has good in them.

When a fight breaks out at the docks, Tai's skills shine through and the head boss hires Tai to be the supervisor, but he has Tai sign a contract he is unable to read. Still, he trusts his wormy boss. Yet after Black Man (Van Clief) returns and accuses Tai of selling out the Chinese by working for the foreigners, it strikes a chord as Tai finds out that the boss in not exporting tobacco but drugs. Tai tries to quit, but he is under contract, and if he were to walk off the job, that would make his word meaningless. Xiao steals the contract but ends up paying with his life, a price too steep for Tai and his newfound friend Black Man. When the dust settles, the Filipino boss brings in Tai's hostile and arrogant kung fu brother, Chi Fu-shi, to kill Tai. Tai has never defeated his kung fu brother before, and it tears him up inside to have to even think about fighting his childhood pal.

The whole film challenges the basic tenets of martial arts when it comes to integrity, morality and how one deal with others, whether they be a friend, foe or someone less fortunate. Although director Liu's message is in your face, the violent reverse of the point is also abundantly clear.

Van Clief's kicks are also in your face, or at least the face of his opponents. The choreographers made sure that he fully extends each kick, making them sharp and snappy, which is a good combination to have on film.

Titleography: *Black Dragon*. Translation—*Travel Down the Southern Sea.*

Tough Guy is a rather generic title; certainly *Black Dragon* fits the Van Clief bill better. The Chinese title refers to Tai Lin traveling across the South China Sea to the Philippines. **MA Percentage: 19.62%**

TRAIL OF BLOOD

Mushukunin Mikogami No Jôkichi: Kiba Wa Jiki Tetsu Ita (1972—Japan) **87m. SWC: Yuasa Kentaro. NOT/LOT: None; NOF/LOF: 13/ 9m 6s.** D: Kazuo Ikehiro. C: Yoshio Harada, Katsuo Nakamura, Ryunosuke Minegishi, Etsuko Ichihara, Ryoko Nakano, Asao Uchida, Akifumi Inoue, Bunta Sugawara.

Trail of Blood is the first of three films that make up the *Trail of Blood* trilogy. As logical as that sounds (three films in a trilogy), it's really illogical because the filmmakers could easily have tightened three mediocre films into what could have been one of the best *chambara* (sword fight) movies of all time. Instead, the filmmakers str-e-e-etched this thing out, diluted the story's place in samurai movie history and perhaps diminished the performance of Yoshio Harada, who plays the titular character, Jokichi of Mikogami. Although he lacked good swords skills and postures to match the hero persona, Harada had the perfect face of a dour samurai warrior destined to die a slow, traveling death.

After the injured *ronin* Jokichi of Mikogami resolves to let life pass him by, he arrives at an inn and meets the beautiful Kinu, who attentively tries to heal his wounds. He is dumbfounded that someone is willing to take care of him and not the other way around, because as a wandering swordsman, he finds that people are always asking him for help. The flame of love is lit, a love that plays a bit like Hong Kong film director Chang Cheh's film *King Eagle* (1971). Anyway, local Yakuza strongman Oyabun arrives at the inn, and Kinu resists his sexual advances. Jokichi also defends her honor and ousts Oyabun out the open door. But Oyabun's Yakuza senior, Boss Chogoro, vows revenge for Oyabun's loss of face. Wow—when was the last time your boss stood up for you when you tried to abuse someone? Something is wrong in this world if that ever happens. But then again, it's no wonder because there is a lot of wrongdoing in this world.

Taking the smart road, Jokichi retires from fighting and runs off with Kinu. They marry and have a child, and Jokichi becomes a craftsman. However, three years later, the Yakuza find Jokichi, Kinu and their kid. Because Jokichi will not fight them, the Yakuza cut his ring and pinky finger from his right hand and mangle his left hand so he can never fight or do crafts again. But that is not enough for the bad guys. The three Yakuza bosses—Kyubei, Chogoro and Chuji—rape and kill Kinu and then kill Jokichi's son. Revenge and blood-and-guts hatred are nothing compared to the pain and agony Jokichi unleashes on the Yakuza over this and the next two films, *Trail of Blood: Fearless Avenger* and *Slaughter in the Snow*. With three baddies to kill and three films, I bet you can guess what the crux of each plot is.

There's a nod to a Chinese kung fu film star and a character he played in this film just begging to be revealed. Since Jokichi's right hand is maimed beyond repair by villainous Yakuza, he has to learn to fight with his left (albeit crippled) hand. This essentially makes Jokichi the Japanese version of the one-armed swordsman, a film character made famous by Hong Kong actor Jimmy Wong Yu in the 1967 kung fu film *One Armed Swordsman*. Because fighting with just a left hand can be a difficult thing for an actor to do, the fights in this film are devoid of real choreography. Lacking even the basic straight-backed posture of any *kendo*-trained martial artist, actor Yoshio's fights consist of him striking a single opponent, dashing away and in many cases stumbling over himself.

For an in-depth discussion on why chambara films have so little fight action, see the martialogies for *Zatoichi Meets Yojimbo* and *Lone Wolf and Cub*.

Titleography: *Trail of Blood: The Ripping Fangs*. Translation—*Drifter Jokichi of Mikogami: Fang Ripping. Trail of Blood* refers to Jokichi leaving a trail of blood behind him on his mission of vengeance. I'm not sure what the *Ripping Fangs* metaphor means, but it could refer to Jokichi's anger or perhaps how the remaining fingers of his right hand look like a set of fangs. **MA Percentage: 10.46%**

TRAIL OF BLOOD: FEARLESS AVENGER

Mushukunin Mikogami no Jôkichi: Kawakaze Ni Kako Wa Nagareta (1972—Japan) **80m. SWC: Yuasa Kentaro. NOT/LOT: None; NOF/LOF: 9/ 9m 57s.** D: Kazuo Ikehiro. C: Yoshio Harada, Ryunosuke Minegishi, Atsuo Nakamura.

The is the second installment of a film trilogy about the *ronin* Jokichi of Mikogami (Yoshio Harada). Even though his name might make pre-adolescents titter, Jokichi is a ronin on the road of revenge with several hand conditions:

The right hand is missing several fingers, and the left is so crippled that he can barely hold onto to anything, never mind fight. Nevertheless, he teaches himself to use a sword.

To catch you up on where this sequel picks up, it's important to know that three Yakuza bosses—Kyubei, Chogoro and Chuji—are hunting retired ronin Jokichi because he shamed one of their men, who was trying to rape a woman. The bosses break Jokichi's left hand and remove the ring and pinkie fingers from his right hand. But wait! There's more: They also rape and murder Jokichi's wife and kill his son. In the first movie, Jokichi goes on a hunting spree and successfully catches up with and kills Kyubei. In this movie, Jokichi stalks Chogoro, but his moment to strike doesn't come easily.

Chogoro is in Itako, which is the home base for the Eight Yakuza Bosses of Tanto. To avoid becoming a permanent enemy of the whole Yakuza brotherhood, Jokichi must earn their respect, plead his case and ask for the head of Chogoro. His plea is met with a steel-slashing reply instead, and several Yakuza swordsmen attack him. Just when all seems lost, one of the head bosses, Juzaboro, stops his brethren. He respects Jokichi's courage, and in return for Juzaboro's help, Jokichi agrees to find the boss's runaway daughter, Oyuki. After that subplot ends with Juzaboro being angrier than 10,000 bees in a bonnet, Juzaboro still gives Jokichi his blessing to go after Chogoro.

The fights are actually sloppier than the first film in that they are slower-paced and actor Yoshio Harada's stances are off-balance. However, the final fight in this film features a unique camera angle rarely seen in a *chambara* (sword-fight) film. It is a high-angle (or bird's-eye-view) shot that reveals the danger of Jokichi's situation while he stumbles all over the place trying to gain some semblance of balance. However, in this instance, being off-balance is something done on purpose to make us feel the inherent danger that comes with being more susceptible to a fatal strike. But when Harada gets ready to do some serious sword poses, postures and strikes, he is still off-balance, and that was probably not planned.

As the final fight moves on, continued camera coverage is relegated to close shots, which slow the fight down. Instead of having the usual pacing, like the quick bursts of sword strikes we see Toshiro Mifune's *Miyamo Musashi* trilogy (1954-1956), the fights rumble along with one technique, a pause, another technique, a pause, two slashes, a pause, etc. With fights like this, there is always a pause for concern.

Titleography: *Fearless Avenger*; *Trail of Blood II*. Translation—*Drifter Jokichi of Mikogami: A River Wind Flows Past*. Jokichi is certainly a *Fearless Avenger*, and *A River Wind Flows Past* could represent his journey of vengeance. It also could have something to do with the fights he has near, by and in a river. **MA Percentage: 12.44%**

TRIAL OF BILLY JACK, THE

(1974—USA) **173m. KA: Bong Soo Han. NOT/LOT: 3/ 56s; NOF/LOF: 10/ 11m 12s.** D: Tom Laughlin. C: Tom Laughlin, Delores Taylor, Victor Izay, Teresa Kelly, Russell Lane, Geo Anne Sosa, Lynn Baker, Riley Hill, Sparky Watt, Rolling Thunder, Gus Grey Mountain, Sacheen Little Feather, Bong Soo Han.

Billy Jack (1971) ends after a climactic shootout with the police, after which the title character surrenders, and amid protests from defiant crowds, the law carts him off. In this sequel, Billy Jack (Tom Laughlin) is sentenced to four years in prison. In the meantime, the Freedom School, an experimental school located on a Native American reservation in Arizona that caters to troubled youths and teen runaways, grows as Jean Roberts (Delores Taylor; Laughlin's wife) introduces some advanced thinking into the curriculum. The students can now express their views on the government and bash state politicians via their privately owned TV station and newspaper, and the school also brings in master Han (Bong Soo Han) to speak about and teach *hapkido*. But once again, the voices of the close-minded conservative attitudes of the nearby town are louder than ever, and they now have larger political clout and a deeper hatred for liberalism and Native Americans. After Billy Jack is released from prison, he also becomes a target for violence; redneck ruffians are out to beat him to a pulp, and corrupt law enforcement officials want him dead. When the ploys of these high-ranking government officials fail, they bring in the National Guard to quell Jean, the school, all the students and Billy Jack once and for all.

It had been three years since *Billy Jack*, and it is evident that Laughlin's hapkido skills improved and he no longer required a double for most of the martial arts sequences. We first see Han teaching Jean basic hapkido kicks

when Billy Jack arrives home after being released from prison. Han and Billy Jack immediately bond because they both demonstrate to each other their advanced hapkido walking cane skills. Similar to *Billy Jack*, there is one fight in which we got to see director Laughlin's intelligent use of the setup. He has Billy Jack explain to a group of cowboy townies out to teach him a lesson how a little girl could break the knee of a large, obnoxious cowboy. What follows is Billy Jack taking out three cowboys with three right-legged kicks without putting his right leg on the ground. He then puts his right foot down and does a right hook kick on a fourth attacker coming from behind. It is done in wide angle in one shot with no loud sound effects and no undercranking of the camera. It looks pretty good. The other major fight sees Han and Billy Jack removing their shoes and socks before taking on a larger group of rednecks at a political dinner that features the town's rich folks denigrating a Native American as part of their after-supper entertainment. Billy Jack and Han give them their just deserts. It's a pity Laughlin didn't do more fights in these Billy Jack films, but it seems appropriate that a film about non-violence with too much violence could detract from the messages he was sharing with audiences.

The disturbing finale centers around the National Guard opening fire and killing unarmed students, a scene inspired by the horrific Kent State shootings. On May 4, 1970, students at Kent State University in Ohio were shot at by the National Guard in response to protesting against the American invasion of Cambodia. The guardsmen fired 67 bullets, killing four and wounding nine. Some of the student casualties were merely walking to their next class and never made it.

The popularity of this film spawned another sequel, *Billy Jack Goes to Washington* (1977), which was a major flop. It did, however, feature a 50-second fight scene in which Billy Jack and Jean—in bare feet—take on a bunch of FBI thugs. Laughlin reprised his Billy Jack character battling child pornographers in *The Return Of Billy Jack* (1985), but the movie was never completed.

Titleography: As of this writing, no alternative titles could be found. **MA Percentage: 7.01%**

TRIANGULAR DUEL

鐵三角 (1972—Taiwan) **96m. KFI: Lin You-chuan. NOT/LOT: 8/ 4m 35s; NOF/LOF: 25/ 29m 13s.** D: Joseph Kuo. C: Wen Chiang-long, Yan Nan-xi, Jiang Nan, Miao Tian, Liu Ping, Shi Zhong-tian, Cai Hong, Bruce Li, Wu Dong-qiao.

After Bruce Lee ripped karate, judo and essentially anything that had to do with Japanese martial arts in *Fist of Fury* (aka *The Chinese Connection*), the karate-trained Taiwanese director, Joseph Kuo, immediately took it upon himself to defend the honor of Japanese martial arts (which all originated in China anyway) to show that just because an art had the Japanese label, they all ultimately had the same virtues. Kuo took a risk with this film, considering he released it months after Lee's *Fist of Fury* enveloped Chinese audiences worldwide with outward anti-Japanese sentiment and a sense of Chinese nationalism.

Kuo cast Taiwan's new martial arts golden boy, Wen Chiang-long, in his first major role, and the stage was set for something peculiarly special. Wen plays rickshaw boy Kang Luen, an energetic youth wishing to join the new local martial arts school and learn karate and judo from a Chinese karate master, Tien Kin (Jiang Nan). Tien agrees to teach Kang only if he promises not to fight because that is not what karate is about.

Meanwhile, Tien is invited to join the local Chinese martial arts consortium and gracefully declines. In response, the chairman of the organization (Liu Ping) and his ratty and natty adviser, Liu Kei-fang (Miao Tian), hire three men known as the Iron Triangle—a Korean iron kick killer, a Japanese iron palm pulverizer and a Chinese iron shirt mangler—to destroy the school and kill Tien. Before that, Kang tries to defend the honor of the school and gets in a fight, after which he is banned from fighting for one year. As his world crumbles around him, he endures several beatings from others who challenge him; he even gets chastised by his karate brothers for not fighting back. The stalwart Kang continues training and waiting for his year of abstinence from fighting to end. When that happens, things get as explosive as crocodiles attacking water mines.

Iron palm is not a martial arts style, but a conditioning method used by several disciplines. Exercises commonly include striking increasingly hard objects or thrusting one's hands into urns filled with increasingly large heated iron pellets. Secret liniments or ointments are applied to the hands after each training session. Other methods of iron palm also involve practitioners using their *chi* to make the training more effective. I am not familiar with techniques specifically called iron kick, but there are methods used for toughening the shins to make one's kicks potent. Iron shirt is, again, a martial arts technique that uses stances, herbs and chi gong to make the body resistant to strikes.

Overall, the fights in this film are sloppy, which is unusual for actor Wen Chiang-long, whose freneticism usually cancels out the awkwardness of his action. However, being that this is his first lead, you still can't help but admire the sheer endurance in his fight against actor Cai Hong. They end up fighting in a deep mud pool for about three minutes—punching, kicking and choking each other while covered in sludge. Consider that this fight probably took at least two days to shoot, and imagine being covered head-to-toe in mud for that long. When the fight switches into a lake, you can see the guarded joy in their faces as they leap into the water, knowing the dirty work is over.

Titleography: As of this writing, no alternative titles could be found. Translation—*Iron Triangle*. The Chinese title is the name of the group of three killers in the film, who all practice some form of an iron kung fu technique. **MA Percentage: 35.21%**

TRILOGY OF SWORDSMANSHIP

群英會 (1972—Hong Kong) **107m. FI: Chui Hing-chun, Liang Shao-song, Tang Chia, Liu Chia-liang. NOT/LOT: None; NOF/LOF: 39/ 20m.** D: Yueh Feng, Cheng Kang, Chang Cheh. C: Yueh Hua, Shih Szu, Tian Ching, Gao Bao-shu, Lo Lieh, Lily Ho, Tsung Hua, Jin Han, Chen Yan-yan, Bolo Yeung, Ti Lung, David Chiang, Li Ching, Ku Feng, Tong Yen-san, Wang Chung, Wu Chi-chin, Zheng Lie, Chen Hsing, Wang Kuang-yu.

Inspired by Jimmy Wong Yu's *The Gallant* (1972), which features three unrelated kung fu shorts within a film, *Trilogy of Swordsmanship* is a collection of three swordsmen stories. Due to their short running times, the films are relatively simple in terms of story and structure.

The first installment, *The Iron Bow*, deals with being a worthy successor to ancestral greatness. Beautiful kung fu maiden Ying Ying (Shih Szu) plans to honor her dead father's wishes by marrying only a man who can draw the string of the deceased's inhumanly heavy iron bow and shoot down a bird. When the magistrate's sleazy son, master Shi (Tian Ching), demands Ying Ying's hand, her mother (kung fu film director Gao Bao-shu, a rarity in the genre) challenges him to fulfill the iron-bow challenge. Shi gives a weak attempt and fails, but the passerby hero Kuang (Yueh Hua) does shoot down the bird. Shi runs off and vows revenge. And even though it's love at first sight for Ying Ying, she still spear-fights Kuang to make sure his kung fu is good. When Shi returns for revenge against Kuang, Ying Ying takes on Shi and his backup, the muscle-bound Polar Bear (Bolo Yeung), in order to give Kuang time to escape because the magistrate has trumped up charges to arrest him. Ying Ying kills Shi, then flees the city with her family in search of Kuang. Although the spear fights with Ying Ying are slow, they are beautifully shot and truly show actress Shih Szu's precise technique. Undercranking the camera would have demeaned her efforts because the movements would have come out fast, and when that happens, you'd miss the real skill of the movements. Therefore, the slower camera speed helps to glorify her growing prominence as a female kung fu star. One odd thing in this short is that although Kuang shoots down the bird, he does not use the iron bow, and thus we don't see him draw the bow.

The second part of the movie, *The Tigress*, is about swashbuckling bandit Pang Xun (Lo Lieh), who searches for high-priced courtesan Shih Chung-yu (Lily Ho) in order to hear her play the *pipa*, a lute-like instrument. When she snubs him, he leaves scorned and says that in the future she will beg to play for him. Meanwhile, Minister Li (Jin Han) wants Pang captured. A recent chance was missed because the man on the job, General Wang Xing-yu (Tsung Hua), was bedding Shih. Just when Wang is to be beheaded for his failure, Shih negotiates a stay of execution. If she and Wang can capture the notorious Pang within three days, Wang will be free to go, and Li will respect prostitutes and admit that Shih is a good sister (an upright lady). If she fails, then all bets, and heads, are off. Though it takes some comedic turns, this short film ends on an exceedingly tragic note when Shih plays her pipa for Pang because it is the last time he will hear any music.

The final short, *White Water Strand*, is a mini-sequel to Chang Cheh's *The Water Margin* (1972), which is a story about how 108 Heroes of Liang Shan defied the corrupt Song Dynasty government. Xu Feng-ying (Li Ching) and Hua Feng-chun (Zheng Lie) are descendants of the Liang Shan heroes. They try to rescue Xu Shi-ying (Ti Lung), son of the famous 108 Hero Golden Lander

Xu Ning, from the treacherous government official Luo Tian-yi (Ku Feng). Luo escorts Xu to his execution. In passing, another 108 Hero, Mu Yu-ji (David Chiang), unwittingly helps Luo because he thinks Luo is under attack by ruthless bandits. Realizing the error of his ways, Mu helps Xu but then gets captured by Luo. Luo arranges a public execution of Mu to strike fear into the hearts of the Chinese people. The message is not to impede the Jin invasion of China. Xu and his fellow Liang Shan descendants plan to rescue Mu, then head south to tell the emperor the Jins are coming. In his fights, Luo wields a Spiderman-web-looking weapon with bells attached around the outer edge, and it's fascinating. The last heroic bloodbath is showered with some interesting sight gags. The most amusing for me is when Mu flies completely through the frame, but in the background, during some packed pugilism. The split-second maiden voyage of David Chiang Airlines from one side of the screen to another was a riot, and I watched it repeatedly.

And an interesting side note: Shaw Brothers continued this three-vignette idea with a string of erotica films throughout the decade.

Titleography: As of this writing, no alternative titles could be found. Translation—*A Collection of Hero Tales*. **MA Percentage: 18.69%** SHAW BROTHERS

Still from *Trilogy of Swordsmanship* © Celestial Pictures Ltd. All rights reserved.

TWELVE GOLD MEDALLIONS, THE

十二金牌 (1970—Hong Kong) **101m. FI: Xu Er-niu, Sammo Hung. NOF/LOF: 15/ 10m.** D: Cheng Kang. C: Yueh Hua, Chin Ping, Ching Miao, Chiao Chiao, Wang Xia, Wong Chung-shun, Gu Wen-zong, Ku Feng, Yang Chi-ching, Zheng Wen-jing, Li Yun-zhong.

Twelve Gold Medallions (referred to in the film as 12 Golden Plaques) maps the true events that eventually led to the tragic ending of the founder of eagle claw and *hsing-i* kung fu, General Yue Fei. The story revolves around the signing of the Treaty of Shaoxing between the Jins and the 10th emperor of the Song Dynasty, Gao Zong. After signing the treaty, Gao Zong became the first emperor of the Southern Song Dynasty. As history shows, the Jins invaded northern China in 1126, took Kai Feng (the capital city) and exiled the current Song Dynasty emperor, Qin Zong, to Manchuria. General Yue fought the Jins and was planning to retake Kai Feng but was stopped by Gao Zong. Gao Zong feared that if Yue Fei were able to take back Kai Feng, Qin Zong might reclaim the throne, and

Gao would lose his power and position. Obviously, this is something he didn't want to happen. The only way to remain emperor would be for Qin Zong to die or never be rescued, and the only way to prevent the rescue would be to have Yue Fei stop his march on Kai Feng. So under the advice of his adviser Chin Hui, Gao Zong deviously sent out 12 edicts on golden medallions ordering Yue to return to the new capital where Gao Zong was situated. Therefore, if at least one medallion got through to Yue, Gao Zong would remain in power.

This film is about how true patriots of China, led by Wavering Sword Miao Lung (Yueh Hua)—so named because he had a sword flexible enough to double as a belt, thus giving the appearance that he was unarmed—thought that preventing Yue from marching on Kai Feng was a grave mistake. Miao Lung assembles a ragtag group of chivalrous swordfighters who pledge to intercept and kill the mercenary messengers and retrieve the gold medallions.

Standing in Miao Lung's way is his kung fu teacher, Jin Yan-tang (Ching Miao). The Song Dynasty official Qin Hui Chin Hui (Li Yun-zhong) promises Jin Yan-tang great power if Jin can kill Miao Lung and his patriots, which would prevent them from retrieving the medallions. One of Miao Lung's fellow patriots is his fiancée, Jin Suo (Chin Ping), who also happens to be Jin Yan-tang's daughter. But not even that will stop Jin Yan-tang, as is evident when he ruthlessly kills his eldest daughter when she voices support for her younger sister Jin Suo. Adding to the dilemmas, Miao Lung recruits Old Man Master Wen (Gu Wen-zong). Wen is an old friend of Jin Yan-tang, and Miao Lung hopes Wen can convince Jin to stop trying to kill Miao Lung, Jin Suo and the other patriots. There is a bond of kinship between teachers and students that is as strong as any notion of filial piety, so it is an agonizing prospect for Miao Lung to have to fight and kill his teacher. But Jin Yan-tang has no problem trying to kill Miao Lung. Why? Because the Confucian code dictates that country comes first, while friends and family come second. For Jin Yan-tang, getting back the medallions for Quin Hui at any cost is worth more than his students, family and friends.

In the film, as in reality, one medallion does get through to General Yue Fei, thus at the end of the day, Miao Lung and his patriots fail. On receiving his order, Yue Fei stopped his march on Kai Feng to free the former emperor and returned to the capital of the new Southern Song Dynasty, Lin An, where upon his arrival, the devious Chin Hui Qin Hui trumped up charges of treason and disobedience against Yue. He had Yue arrested, put in prison and executed. In 1141, after Gao Zong signed the Treaty of Shaoxing, China was split in two: To the north was the Jin Dynasty, and to the south was the Southern Song Dynasty. It has been

written that while in prison, Yue wrote several important books on martial arts. These books became the impetus for several important films made by Shaw Brothers in the 1970s, namely the *Heaven Sword and Dragon Sabre* and *Brave Archer* series. Another version of Yue's demise states that he was ambushed and killed on his way home to Lin An. In 1162, Emperor Hsiao Tsung of the Southern Song recognized Yue's heroic efforts and reinstated his name and honor in the annals of time with a proper burial.

Although there are few fights, the film's action is more about showing the awesome *chi* skills of each character, thus emphasizing that it was indeed a power struggle that was not just of politics, but of kung fu skills. But the most interesting highlight is when Miao Lung uses a special piece of jewelry to suck poison out of Jin Suo's wound. Recent discoveries show that certain kinds of jewelry can act as a detox method to suck out a person's bad chi, which can arise out of injury, disease, mental and emotional issues, and poor diet. They also show how if you balance the body's chi, you can improve your health.

The final duel between all levels of kinship, friendship and respect is a commentary on China's politics at the time the film was made. What people were doing in Communist China during the Cultural Revolution was turning on friends and relatives. They would report them as dissidents to the government. Those dissidents would then be sent to re-education camps to perform hard labor. **Titleography:** *Twelve Gold Medallions*. Translation—*Twelve Golden Medallions*. They are not really medallions but gold-colored plaques, each with a handle and a character written on it. **MA Percentage: 9.90%** SHAW BROTHERS

TWO GREAT CAVALIERS

雌 雄 雙 煞 (1978—Taiwan) 94m. FI: Guan Hong, Liang Jia-ren. NOT/LOT: 2/ 7m 37s; NOF/LOF: 23/ 31m 37s. D: Yang Jing-chen. C: Angela Mao Ying, John Liu, Liang Chia-ren, Wen Chiang-lung, Shi Zhong-tian, Chen Hsing, Jing Guo-zhong.

Get your kicks on Route 66—or make that Fung Wan Village. By the late 1970s, the popularity of the *guo shu pian* genre of martial arts films (created at Shaw Brothers by Chang Cheh and Liu Chia-liang) and the increasingly athletic and comedic film style popularized by Jackie Chan was gaining ground. Lower-budget fly-by-night independent productions tried to make quick bucks by signing big out-of-contract studio names. They would have the fight instructors put the heroes in bizarre circumstances and give villains some dreaded, unbeatable kung fu skills.

Enter actor Chen Hsing, playing a freaky green-handed villain whose fighting strikes make the sound of a ricocheting bullet; Angela Mao Ying, the cute Bruce Lee all-star actress who always pouts and scowls; Liang Chia-ren, who fights with great posture and metronomic glee; and John Liu, who does the same fantastic kicks, kick-holds and splits in every film. Two of these actors shall become the Two Great Cavaliers. Who, you might say? Hint: See the Chinese translated title below and work backwards.

Two Great Cavaliers follows the usual Ming-Ching dynastic template, with a maniacal Manchu assassin (Chen Hsing) killing all Ming loyalists who refuse to hand over a secret list of Chinese patriots. Hero Song (Liang Chia-ren) is poisoned by the dreaded green-hand strike, and only O Yang-Chung (John Liu) knows the cure. However, he's retired from fighting and wants to get married. When Hsiao Mei (Angela Mao Ying) begs him to return with her to Fung Wan Village to help Song, he refuses and then has to throw about 1,000 screen kicks before he's left alone.

The fights overuse a relatively common choreographic presentation: The main fighter's body takes up center frame and faces camera while attackers come in from all angles to be blocked and struck by the hero, who scarcely looks at the incoming strikes. It is a way to show kung fu superiority because the hero does not have to pay attention to where the attacks are coming from and simply defends against them intuitively.

It is also part of the persona created by years of kung fu films wherein four to eight actors statically stand during a five-to-10-minute dialogue scene, spew out words and get to the next fight. By having characters act in this manner, it actually adds excitement to the fights because of all the excessive motion of the actors in combat is in direct contrast to the monotonous, stand-at-attention line delivery.

Another common element in cheaper films is the actors having more leeway to deliver their favorite techniques and flash certain poses, which is why you might notice Liu doing the same poses after every sequence of kicks.

Furthermore, before starting a fight, the combatants usually strike a pose after a rapid-fire exhibition of intense shadow-boxing. In most cases, especially for veterans of kung fu films, they end up improvising something either before the camera starts or when the director calls for action. This is why you occasionally see an actor simply flailing his arms wildly before freezing in a stance with contorted finger or arm postures.

Titleography: *Blade of Fury*; *Deadly Duo*; *The Two Great Cavaliers*. Translation—*Male Female Ferocious Fighting Pair*. *Deadly Duo* and *Two Great Cavaliers* fit the bill of the literal Chinese translation, but *Blade of Fury* is out of bounds because none of the main characters fight with a sword or knife. It's another example of how words were used to attract an audience, even if they didn't fit the film. **MA Percentage: 41.74%**

TWO WONDROUS TIGERS

出閘虎 (1979—Hong Kong) 87m. AD: Wilson Tong. NOT/LOT: 3/ 1m 29s; NOF/LOF: 20/ 36m 42s. D: Zhang Sen. C: John Cheung, Gao Fei, Yang Pan-pan, Meng Chiu, Charlie Chan Yao-lin, Tiger Yang Cheng-wu, Peter Chan Lung.

In the old days, when you wanted to get married, all you had to do was defeat the bride in a fight and she would be yours, no questions asked. This actually brings up an interesting scenario. In the dregs of Chinese society, as in other societies worldwide, it is commonly acknowledged that a husband can strike his wife. It should not be acceptable, but it is part of the culture. You've got to wonder if a film like *Two Wondrous Tigers* either creates or imprints this mind-set behind the societal ill of beating women.

Some martial arts films give you the sense that a bunch of actors got together as an excuse to practice their kung fu rather than out of passion for what they were doing. It's in films like this that stories and plots are of little value and many of the fights are mundane; they're just there to fill up time. Keep in mind, back then there were no storyboards or training for weeks before shooting. Actors would show up on set and put fights together on the spot. If director felt like doing a fight, he would go grab a meal or take a nap and let the fight director do what he wanted.

This film begins with two lads who practice tiger claw kung fu: Tiger (John Cheung) and Ko (Gao Fei). They have an inane fight over a *cha xiao bao* (a pork bun), then decide to become friends and answer an advertisement of the Yang family: Whoever can defeat their daughter Ah Mei (Yang Pan-pan), her older sister (Meng Chiu) and their older brother (Charlie Chan Yao-lin) in a fight can win money and Ah Mei's hand in marriage. Tiger and Ah Mei really do fall in love, but the local king of thugs, Master Ma (Tiger Yang Cheng-wu), wants to kidnap Ah Mei so she can bear him a son.

There is an interesting fight between actor John Cheung and action director Wilson Tong. It's a battle of the big cats, pitting Cheung's tiger claw against Tong's leopard fist (a style not often used in film).

Leopard fist has its foundations in monk Ta Mo's 18 Buddhist Fists exercises, which were based on his observations of wild animals he encountered while en route from India to China. During the mid-1600s, Shaolin monk Zhue Yang (along with fellow martial artists Li Sou and Bai Yu-fen) improved upon Ta Mo's 18 movements to create the five animal styles of Shaolin (dragon, tiger, snake, white crane and leopard). The main fighting philosophy of leopard boxing, which often uses a half-closed fist, is, "Why block when you can hit?" The art is about utilizing a hit-and-run strategy. It is one of the few styles that often simultaneously blocks and strikes at the same time.

Ah Mei is very skilled with the spear. Since her family name in the movie is Yang, perhaps the film is also a nod to the famed spear-wielding women warriors of the Yang family. The final fight is marvelous: In order for the newlywed Tiger to consummate his marriage to Ah Mei, he must fight her again to win the next prize. It's similar to the bedroom scene in *Executioners From Shaolin* (1977) and adds new meaning to the notion of fighting for the woman you love.

Titleography: *The Two Wondrous Tigers*. Translation—*Tiger Coming Out of the Dam*. The Two Wondrous Tigers are the two main protagonists, and the *Tiger Coming Out of the Dam* refers to actor John Cheung's character becoming a man and falling in love, the dam being a metaphor for the gushing out of Tiger's love that can be taken two ways. **MA Percentage: 43.89%**

ULTIMATE WARRIOR, THE

(1975—USA) 94m. SC: Pat Johnson, Reggie Parton. NOT/LOT: None; NOF/ LOF: 8/ 4m 7s. D: Robert Clouse. C: Yul Brynner, Max von Sydow, Joanna Miles, William Smith, Richard Kelton, Stephen McHattie.

New York City's Twin Towers still exist in this film's post-apocalyptic 2012 world wherein plagues have wiped out everything that can grow except man's ability to grow meaner and nastier. After a string of martial arts films intended to be martial arts films, director Robert Clouse did this film, and without realizing it, Yul Brynner came across like one of Hong Kong's top martial arts film stars of all time, Gordon Liu Chia-hui.

In the decaying city, two rival factions—one led by the benevolent Baron (Max von Sydow) and the other by the violent Carrot (William Smith)—vie for the city's dwindling food and water supplies. Yet the key to changing the balance of power can be found in the ruins of a New York City's public library. It's not found in a book on technology or some philosophical or religious text, but within a man called Carson (Yul Brynner). Depending on who you are, he is either a feared or a respected lone warrior. This fighting machine of a man stands outside the library and waits to help one group at the expense of hurting the other. He is won over by Baron, not just for his sense of righteousness and fair play but also because he has a good supply of cigars. In order to save mankind and his pregnant daughter, Baron asks Carson to escort his daughter and a bag of disease-resistant vegetable seeds out of the city and head south to North Carolina, where it is said there exists a large area of habitable land, perhaps man's last hope for survival. Blocking their escape is Carrot. As the confrontation comes to head, either Carrot will become sliced and diced or Carson will.

What impresses me most about Brynner's knife and empty-hand fights is that regardless of whether he is punching, kicking or wielding a knife, he has the straightest back posture of any American martial arts star I have ever scene. This is the reason why on-screen, Liu and Brynner look similar.

Titleography: As of this writing, no alternative titles could be found. **MA Percentage: 4.38%**

VALLEY OF THE FANGS

餓狼谷 (1970—Hong Kong) 86m. FI: Liu Chia-rong. NOT/LOT: None; NOF/LOF: 14/ 18m 6s. D: Cheng Chang-ho. C: Li Ching, Lo Lieh, Fan Mei-shang, Chen Liang, Wang Kuang-yu, Wei Ping-ao, Cheng Lei, Wang Xia, Chen Yan-yan, Li Peng-fei.

A real swordsman asks not for the return of his favors, and a benevolent person always begets kindness. With age-old philosophical tenets such as these, it is no wonder many Westerners look to the East for a spiritual peace or guidance. When was the last time you did something without the expectation of gain? It would be a beautiful thing if more people were like this film's hero, Yu Ju-lung (Lo Lieh), who selflessly helps a family trying to save its father from corrupt officials, and does so just because it is the right thing to do.

Valley of the Fangs is set during the Ming Dynasty, when the wicked Prime Minister Jia Shou-dao tries to dupe the boy emperor—possibly Emperor Wanli, who ascended the throne at age 9 and was the only boy emperor during the era—and uses his rank and power to oppress the people. Only Imperial Academy senior lecturer Song Yuan dares to rebel and expose Jia. An angered Jia tells Song, "You're in trouble," when Jia manipulates the boy emperor into imprisoning and torturing Song. However, Song was such a highly respected lecturer that the late emperor gave him an Iron Shield of Pardon, which is a get-out-of-jail-free card, so to speak. Even if he commits a felony, he can be a free man. However, the pardon must be delivered to the current emperor in order for it to be honored. Aware of this, Jia orders General Master Gao (Wang Xia) to kill Song's wife (Chen Yan-yan) and daughter (Li Ching) and retrieve the order. The daughter disguises herself as a traveling *pipa* (a four stringed lute-like instrument from the Qin Dynasty, circa 215 BC) performer with the shield hidden inside the instrument. The daughter and mother run into a group of Gao's goons but are saved by righteous swordsman Yu Ju-lung. Yu falls in love with the daughter's singing voice and takes it upon himself to escort her and her mother to deliver the shield.

However, as Gao ups the ante, Yu and his party are forced to seek refuge in the Valley of the Fangs, where Lord Cheng (Li Peng-fei) is under Imperial Order to build a large kiln. When a group of hard-nosed workers find out that they are trying to free the highly respected Song, they do all they can to fend off Gao and his grollied greeblies. But Yu and only Yu can prevent their funeral fires.

In early films, stars were often instructed to just swing their swords like madmen and try not to think about the choreography too much, which put the onus on the stuntmen to hit their marks. Several fights in this film use this method. Also, movies such as this one employ kung fu foolery in that there are scenes that are more about having fun with the fu rather than making a star look like an expert. Such scenes bring the *wuxia* characters to life, hence the flying bits and the use of cutlery gags. After Bruce Lee, it was tough for actors to outdo him and what he brought to the screen, but wuxia films worked because they were of a different genre. This film also includes some completely out-of-place comedic relief during a vicious battle in which the women put a string of firecrackers in a goon's trousers; when they explode, the guy flies through the air.

Titleography: As of this writing, no alternative titles could be found. Translation—*Hungry Wolf Valley*. The English title sounds like the film should have a snake motif, but the *Fangs* refer to wolf fangs. **MA Percentage: 21.05%** SHAW BROTHERS

VENGEANCE!

報仇 (1970—Hong Kong) **98m. FI: Tang Chia, Yuen Cheung-yan. NOT/LOT: 4/ 3m 55s; NOF/LOF: 10/ 12m 51s.** D: Chang Cheh. C: David Chiang, Ti Lung, Ku Feng, Wang Ping, Wang Chung, Cliff Lok, Hsu Hsia, Chen Hsing.

When a film is super, all you need to do is add a "P" to it to make it supper. And *Vengeance!* is a satisfying noir-ish feast of blood, gore, spurt and artery fights.

This is the fourth film that the Iron Triangle (David Chiang, Ti Lung and Chang Cheh) did together. The first three films were made in the '60s, with *Vengeance!* being the first in the '70s. Director Chang Cheh delves into the world of Beijing opera, which was in essence the foundation for the fanatically far-out Hong Kong stuntman industry so prominently featured in the daring stunts of the 1980s and 1990s.

In this film set in China during 1925, Kuan Yu-lo (Ti Lung) is a dignified lead in a Beijing opera troupe. His malicious murder is planned during a mahjong match between a band of gang members, one of whom has his desiring eyes on Kuan's wife. This all leads to an operatic conclusion when Kuan's relentless avenging-angel-of-death brother, Hsiao Lo (David Chiang), swoops into town on air-route retribution.

Beijing opera originated in 1790, specifically at the birthday celebration of the kung fu Emperor Chien Lung. (Parts of his life are vividly depicted and portrayed by actor Liu Yong in four films made by Shaw Brothers during the 1970s.) For his 70th birthday, Chien Lung invited Chinese opera entertainers

from around the kingdom to come to Beijing and perform their respective styles. Chien Lung then chose the top performers and commissioned them to stay in Beijing to work together to create a new style of opera. This gave further rise to the operatic term "red trousers" (*hong ku zi*), which the acrobats and supporting fighter characters wear during an opera performance, and it is also the name of their occupation.

Because the red trousers in opera were associated with beginning opera students, and most of the early stunt fighters and fighting extras in kung fu films were recruited from opera schools, rookie stuntmen since the 1950s on are typically called red trousers as well. Thus the red trousers were the progenitors and foundation of Chinese martial arts cinema as we know it. Of interest: The first Chinese film ever made, *Ding Jun Shan* (1905), starred Tan Xin-pei, China's top Beijing opera performer at the time. As time passed, more opera stars and red trousers became martial arts stars, fight choreographers and film directors. Jackie Chan, Ching Si-tung and Sammo Hung, to name a few, were all originally red trousers in opera and in film.

Besides being the color of pants Beijing opera students wore during training and performances, the term "red trousers" also symbolically describes the indentured servitude of kids who were bound by contract and often forced to painstakingly live and train at Beijing opera schools. In fact, *Red Trousers: The Life of the Hong Kong Stuntmen* (2003) was an award-winning documentary that director/actor Robin Shou and I worked on. It discusses the history and livelihood of Hong Kong stuntmen.

Back to the movie! During a bombastic moment of bravado and grandeur in which the line between opera fantasy and operatic reality is as clear as the weapons of mass destruction found in Iraq, Chang intercuts an opera performer's onstage and over-the-top expressionistic demise with Kuan's bloody, agonizing death; it's also all highlighted with eye-gouging grossness. The final fight with Hsiao Lo dressed in pure white is a perhaps a metaphorical proclivity of director Chang and his vision of the angel of death. Basically, if you die a hero, then you can become an angel of death.

His snow-white costume is smattered with blood, and wide-angle camera shots beautifully reveal the effect of all the hidden pouches that explode blood-red on cue. Sprayed with slow-motion exasperation and defiled doom, hand-held camera shots visually add more life and energy to the action sequences. The energy and life is further accentuated by having the stuntmen be in constant motion, even if they are not directly involved in the fight during the shot. The most glorious shot is the pure fountain of blood erupting from Chiang's white suit.

Titleography: *Kung Fu Vengeance*. Translation—*Vengeance*. How appropriate for a kung fu film to have a title that reflects a major theme in many kung fu films. *Kung Fu* was added to one title to make sure you know it is a kung fu film. **MA Percentage: 17.11%** SHAW BROTHERS

VENGEANCE OF A SNOW GIRL

冰天俠女 (1970—Hong Kong) **117m. FI: Xu Er-niu, James Tien. NOT/LOT: None; NOF/LOF: 18/ 14m.** D: Lo Wei. C: Li Ching, Yueh Hua, Paul Chang Chung, Tien Fung, Ku Feng, Chiao Chiao, Wong Chung-shun, Niu Niu.

To rephrase the famous speech from Shakespeare's *Richard III*: Now is the winter of our discontent, made glorious by this daughter of the Phoenix Sword, and all the clouds that lowered upon our house in the deep bosom of the ocean buried.

Similar to the hunchback Richard in Shakespeare's play, Shen Ping-hong (Li Ching) is a cripple. And although she too broods upon her handicap—in this case, her useless legs—she uses her Phoenix Sword, which is hidden within one of her two large green crutches, to rise above the clouds. She tackles the winter head on by heading to the northern Chinese lands of ice and the snow in an attempt to bring back her own summer through treachery, murder and manipulation.

When Shen witnesses the murder of her parents as a child by four swordsmen led by Lord Gao Hung the Sword Wizard (Tien Fung), she ends up as a cripple. She returns 10 years later to seek revenge against the now-elderly slayers of her family, only to fall in love with Lord Gao's son Gao Tien-ying (Yueh Hua). After Shen hears the truth from Lord Gao about how and why her parents were killed, she is still required by filial piety to complete her vengeful path, regardless of the reason. And even though Shen learns how to use her father's Phoenix Sword from the Two Old Hermits of Min Hill, she is no match for the Sword Wizard. Being the upright man he is, Lord Gao tells Shen that the only way she can defeat him is if her legs are healed. He tells her that if she can retrieve the

Heat Resistant Armor from the Prince of Ping Nan, then she can use it to enter Nan Hai Volcano to retrieve the Magic Pearl. Then all Shen needs to do is go to the Snow Fields of the North and sit in the Heat Fountain to heal her legs. She accepts Lord Gao's suggestion, and Tien-ying quickly volunteers to accompany her. Thus the adventure begins. However, of the other surviving members of the original four swordsmen who killed her family, the fading sheen of Golden Warrior Tung (Ku Feng) will do anything to kill Shen and even kill Tien-ying.

One important thing to keep in mind with these old films and the actors in them is that the usual length-of-time ratio of fights to drama is very low because the actors did not know or practice martial arts. If there were too many fights, the actors would burn out or run the risk of injury. Also, due to the endurance factor and the limited number of takes a director would risk to run his stars through, fights would often look sloppy. A way around that was to undercrank the camera and shoot with tight angles.

That being said, one has to really take their hat off to lead actress Li Ching, who had no martial arts experience whatsoever but does a standup job of sword fighting. This is especially apparent when the choreographers try to tap into her Chinese dance abilities so that her swordplay mirrors the techniques traditional female Chinese dancers use to move their flowing, long-sleeved costumes. The fact that Li Ching also has to act and move like someone who is disabled while struggling with two crutches further reflects on her strong talent for action performance.

Titleography: *A Daughter's Vengeance*; *Vengeance Of A Snowgirl*. Translation—*Icy Sky Female Hero*. Both English and Chinese titles match well with the film's title character and impetus for life. **MA Percentage: 11.97%** SHAW BROTHERS

VENGEFUL BEAUTY, THE

血芙蓉 (1977—Hong Kong) **78m. FI: Tang Chia. NOT/LOT: None; NOF/ LOF: 25/ 19m 45s.** D: Ho Meng-hua. C: Yueh Hua, Lo Lieh, Xu Hsao-chiang, Chen Ping, Shao Yin-yin, Frankie Wei Hong, Wang Lung-wei, Lin Hui-huang.

After Ching Emperor Kang Xi died, Emperor Yong Zheng usurped the throne in 1722 with a couple of pen strokes by changing a few characters on his father's will and proving, once again, that the pen is mightier than the sword. But that did not stop him from using the sword too. He went ballistic, and because he feared the Shaolin, he ordered the destruction of the Shaolin Temples and the slaughter of all Shaolin monks, students and supporters of anything remotely tied to Shaolin. Yet Yong Zheng did not stop there. He was afraid of the politicians and scholars who surrounded him, so he had his most trusted military men and weapon

designers create a special weapon known as the flying guillotine, He used it to assassinate his enemies. Since no one who saw the weapon lived to talk about it and all the wielders were eventually put to death, it is still unknown as to what the historical weapon really looked like. However, director Ho Meng-hua came up with a possible design for the weapon in *The Flying Guillotine* (1974). That film starred Chen Kuan-tai as Ma Tang, a former guillotine assassin who saw the emperor for the sick man he was and quit the military. Ma then created a weapon to counter the guillotine because the emperor sent waves of assassins to silence him. But as legend has it, Ma disappeared and Yong Zheng continued to kill anyone who was a threat to his security or who could expose his secret weapon. Which brings us to *The Vengeful Beauty*.

In a film that was intended to be *Flying Guillotine III*, the beheading blade returns for a final cut at Shaw Brothers, and director Ho Meng-hua returns as the director and heads the franchise off in a different direction. The film begins when a masked vigilante known as the Bloody Hibiscus (Chen Ping) goes around killing Ching death squads, who are killing upright Han Chinese citizens accused of reading and writing subversive books.

Meanwhile, the conscientious Ching policeman Han Tien-de arrests a killer, but he does not know his detainee is one of Yong Zheng's assassins on the prowl. Yong Zheng (Frankie Wei Hong) catches wind that the assassin is being interrogated. Afraid the assassin may divulge his secret, thus impairing his delusions that he is a benevolent emperor of the people, Yong Zheng orders chief hatchet man Jin Gang-feng (Lo Lieh) to execute Han and his pregnant wife, Rong Qiu-yan (Chen Ping).

While Jin's assassins go the policeman's home, Jin proudly tells the emperor that the policeman and Rong are dead. However, Rong is out visiting her Wu Dung kung fu teacher's grave, where she bumps into her older kung fu brother Wang Jun (Yueh Hua). They reminisce about their kung fu training and past history, and she affirms her love for her husband—only to return home to have her life bloodily turned upside down. What Jin does not know is that his assassins have killed the husband of the Bloody Hibiscus—cue ominous music.

When Jin finds out Rong is still alive, he is livid. There is no way he is going to admit to the emperor that he lied, so Jin orders his three adult children—Ren-ting (Lin Hui-huang), Biao (Wang Lung-wei) and Shao-zhi (Shao Yin-yin)—to find Rong and decapitate her. On her way to find refuge with her uncle, Rong runs into former guillotine assassin Ma Sang (Xu Hsao-chiang), and he has Ma Tang's original counter-weapon, which looks like an iron umbrella without the material attached between the ribs. She also runs into Wang. As the three are on the lam together, a love triangle develops between Rong, Wang and Ma. It makes their heads spin and also makes them easier targets for Jin's children. After Shao-zhi pulls the wool over everyone's eyes and uses her feminine wiles to do the nasty on Ma, Rong responds in kind by unleashing her own kind of nasty on Shao-zhi, in the form of a deadly kung fu weapon. The topless Shao-zhi stumbles through the woods in slow motion, heaving and slashing her weapon through the air before crumpling onto the forest floor, defeated.

Once Jin's two sons also fail in killing Rong, it is Jin's turn at the chopping block. To show his love for Rong, Ma decides to confront Jin alone. Meanwhile Rong goes into labor and is attacked from all directions by more assassins sent by Jin. Rong struggles to keep it together but starts bleeding from the belly. Her baby is in trouble. Wang has his own troubles too, as his past with women catches up with him. Ma arrives at Jin's headquarters and begins to annihilate Jin's bodyguards, but when he attacks Jin, the villain performs his ultra-secret kung fu skill. With a last-ditch effort, Jin goes quintuplet on Ma. He turns from one badass Jin into to five badass Jins, giving new meaning to the term "high-five." This mass confusion of five Jins turns out to be more than a handful for Ma until Bloody Hibiscus appears. With her patented knife now elongated into a spear, Rong assures Jin that he has made the wrong choice.

You can't help but think that perhaps this film was influenced by Junko Fuji's *Red Peony Gambler* film series (1968-1972). After all, they both feature women warriors named after red flowers. Furthermore, director Ho Meng-hua had just finished a string of films with actress Chen Ping in which she played a gambler known as Red Peony.

In any case, there are some interesting fights in this film that use a lot of rolls on the ground rather than flips in the air. There is also a very creative wide-angle bird's-eye-view tracking shot of Rong fighting a bunch of assassins in a bamboo forest.

There is also a very intelligent bit of sleight-of-hand that director Ho did in regard to the Ma Sang character. Recall from the opening paragraph that Yong Zheng usurped the throne in 1722 by using a pen and changing the name on his father's will to make it look like he was the heir to the emperor. (Imagine if Yon Zheng was supposed to be the emperor, but someone added a G to make "Yon" look like "Yong." Ta-da, Yong is the emperor.) In this film, Ho does something similar. With a few magic strokes of his pen, lead hero Ma Tang from Ho's original *Flying Guillotine* film is changed to hero Ma Sang. In the words of rap group Cypress Hill, "Insane in the membrane. Insane in the brain!"

Titleography: *Bloody Hibiscus*. Translation—*Bloody Hibiscus*. The titles all refer to the protagonist. **MA Percentage: 25.32%** SHAW BROTHERS

VILLAGE OF TIGERS

惡 虎 村 (1973—Hong Kong) **78m. Fl:** Xu Er-niu. **NOT/LOT: 2/ 12s; NOF/ LOF: 22/ 29m 45s. D:** Yueh Feng, Wang Ping. **C:** Shu Pei-pei, Yueh Hua, Wang Xia, Karen Yeh, Chan Shen, Wu Hu, Tung L.

Although *The Water Margin*, one of the most famous *wuxia* novels, was finished during the Ming Dynasty (1368-1644), the wuxia people were historically considered important warriors who were graced with unquestionable loyalty to the ministers they served during the Spring and Autumn Period (770-476 B.C.). During the Warring States period (475-221 B.C.), famed Han Dynasty historian Si-ma Chien (145-86 BC) praised the wuxia gallants who altruistically opposed tyranny. During the Tang Dynasty (A.D. 618-907), wuxia prose gained prominence because fighters took on mythical qualities in which heroes and villains could sit opposite each other and fight with their minds as astral spirits, the winner returning to his body alive, the loser destined to roam the spirit world. With the influence of the novel *The Water Margin*, where the 108 Heroes were known as the Stars of Destiny, it became common that wuxia clans and sects would have romanticized names, which is the impetus for this film about a group of vagabonds known as the Village of Tigers, who according to Kellogg's anti-Tony the Tiger, are not "Grrreat!"

The Village of Tigers, led by Hu Jiao (Wang Xia), is looking to kill righteous swordsman Luo Hong-xun (Yueh Hua), and when they trap him in an inn, then as was popularly presented with an angst of humorous seriousness in the 1970s hit TV show *Hogan's Heroes* (1965-1971), "Back to zee vall, heads vill role." The problem is that the Tigers roll the wrong head; they kill Sword of Southern Style, who is related to the powerful Ba Family, which is headed by the psychotic matriarch Grandma Ba (Wu Hu). To cover their butts, the Tigers blame it on Luo, who now becomes the Ba Family's target. At the top of the vengeance food chain is whip woman Jiu Gu-niang, aka 9th Miss (Shu Pei-pei), who's just waiting to find missing-link Luo. Adding to the confusion over Luo's guilt, a traitor in the midst of the Ba family makes Luo look like the perfect scapegoat. Just as things are looking bad for Luo, the person with the poison has the brew that is untrue when Luo becomes the lad with sword who is not bad. What do I mean by all that? Basically, it is tiger-hunting time, and it is the village of Ba that is feeling feline because Luo and Jiu shall skin them alive. Yuck, that would be a freaky looking tiger rug.

The movie's choreography style is a perfect example of a hit, crash and roll. The sets, in several instances, are rooms full of break-away furniture in which each stuntman gets a chance to strut, fret and smash himself about the stage. And unlike the poor player in Shakespeare's *Macbeth*, who is heard no more, these low-paid stuntmen get to be heard from again and again. The actor simply does his fighting technique, and then each of his reactions is a separate shot, so we get to see the stuntman roll over a table, break a table, land on a table or knock over a table. With shooting the stunts at 20 to 22 frames per second, it makes the stunts look and feel more realistic.

For a 1973 film, this movie has a lot fights that also feature some great high leaps and trampoline stunts with good high-knee form to create the feeling of *ching gong*, the skill that gives fighters the ability to leap high and run on top of bamboo tress. But some of the grand gags are weirdly cute, like Shu Pei-pei's helicopter kick, wherein her body rises, hovers, then spins around in midair while her severed enemies spray blood in all directions. Then there's the far-out visual of when a whip slides a body along the ground, which strangely enough looks oddly normal and makes you think that if you had a whip, you could easily do the same thing. Let's also not forget the well-orchestrated rope web scene, which is always a tricky thing to choreograph correctly—it really shows the good measure in the old days of a choreographer's creativity. Notice that because Yueh Hua does not know how to kick, the choreographers have him do low kicks and high crescent kicks because they require the least amount of flexibility.

Titleography: As of this writing, no alternative titles could be found. Translation—*Village of Evil Tigers*. Both titles refer to the name of the villainous gang of the film. **MA Percentage: 38.4%** SHAW BROTHERS

VILLAINS, THE

土匪 (1973—Hong Kong) **81m. FI: Uncredited. NOT/LOT: None; NOF/LOF: 8/ 5m 19s.** D: Chu Yuan. C: Yueh Hua, Shih Szu, Bei Di, Chen Hong-lieh, Jin Fung, Ching Miao, Dean Shek, Chan Shen.

When it is brother vs. brother, who suffers more? The family or the family name? It is a choice of family secrecy or family honesty, but to sacrifice one for the other is a choice we can only hope to never have to make. But it is a choice the Feng family must make because blood isn't always thicker than water.

The film is set in China's post-warlord era, circa 1929. After Miss Lin's (Shih Szu) father dies, she is sent to live with her father's rival, an official named Feng (Ching Miao), whose wife had a thing for Lin's father but was not rich enough to allow her parents to give him her hand in marriage. This history already causes a rift between Feng and Lin, and Feng sternly blurts that this is a traditional Chinese family so there is no free love or gender equality. In other words, she is now their housekeeper and basically has no freedom. However, she falls in love with Feng's oldest son, Zheng-er (Yueh Hua), a lawyer in the making. Feng disapproves because he favors his younger, trouble-making, brothel-visiting, fight-prone son, Fang-feng (Chen Hong-lieh). After Fang-feng weasels his father into kicking Zheng-er out of the house and out of his will, Fang-feng rapes and impregnates Lin.

When Feng discovers that Lin is pregnant and refuses to believe it is Fang-feng's child, he beats Lin up until she lies and says the baby belongs to Zheng-er's loyal servant. Feng kicks them both out, only to have Fang-feng hunt them down and kill the servant. Fang-feng now becomes a fugitive of the law and organizes a group of bandits that violently pillages the countryside. Feng realizes he has made an error and sends for Zheng-er to return. He has since become a government commissioner, and his first assignment is to stop Fang-feng before he kills Lin, murders his brother, and completely destroys the family name and reputation.

Titleography: As of this writing, no alternative titles could be found. Translation—*Bandits*. Both titles refer to the Fang-feng, the villainous son who becomes a ruthless bandit. **MA Percentage: 6.56%** SHAW BROTHERS

VOYAGE OF EMPEROR CHIEN LUNG, THE

乾隆下揚州 (1978—Hong Kong) **93m. FI: Tang Chia, Huang Pei-ji. NOT/LOT: None; NOF/LOF: 18/ 14m.** D: Li Han Hsiang. C: Liu Yong, Jiang Nan, Hui Ying-hong, Lee Gwan, Yueh Hua, Lun Gu-jun.

The Voyage of Emperor Chien Lung is the third of four films by Shaw Brothers that star Liu Yong as the kung fu Emperor Chien Lung. Liu was one of the Ching Wu students in Bruce Lee's *Fist of Fury*. Ching Emperor Chien Lung was famous for dressing like a commoner and secretly visiting Chiang Nan in Jiang Su province (in the southern part of China) to learn about his subjects and expose the various kinds of corruption that were being dealt out by devious Ching Dynasty officials. Historically, Chien Lung was also the emperor responsible for commissioning the creation of Beijing opera schools, which of course became the foundation for today's Hong Kong kung fu fight choreography and some of the industry's top stuntmen and martial arts filmmakers, like Jackie Chan, Sammo Hung and Ching Siu-tung. (See *Vengeance!*)

The film starts with Chien Lung enjoying himself in a battle of wits with Minister Er Rong-an (Jiang Nan) and Treasurer Liu Yung (Lee Gwan). He also loves to listen to his two advisers squabble among themselves and vie to outdo each other in the eye of the emperor. After Liu is able to weasel famous painter Zheng Xie-qiao (Yueh Hua), who has retired from painting, to paint and sign four paintings for Chien, the emperor is impressed and awards Liu with a special royal gown, which he proudly swaggers in before the jealous Er. (Note: Growing up in a life of poverty, the real Zheng was a Ching official in another city in China, where he resigned after being criticized for building a shelter for the poor. He then used the angst of this past to create marvelous paintings of orchids and bamboo. Settling in Jiangsu, he became known as one of the Eight Eccentrics of Yangzhou province.)

After the painting incident, Chien Lung sits with Liu while disguised as a simple restaurant patron. They sit at a table for the "emperor" of the local village, a smarmy and pudgy brat named Zhang Ya-dong (Lun Gu-jun), whose father is the governor. Zhang

puts the moves on the beautiful, innocent and engaged Phoenix (Hui Ying-hong), as he and his cohorts rudely suggest that after spending one night with Zhang, that will all change. This angers Chien Lung, and he screams, "Don't you respect the law?" Zhang orders his men to beat up Chien. While Chien beats the daylights out of Zhang's men, Phoenix does some neat little kung fu moves that subtly help Chien.

As is typical for these Chien Lung films, the fights are short with nothing really special about them; in this case, they are barely over the minimal time to be included in this book.

Of note, if you are ever in a Chinese restaurant and see someone tapping their forefinger on the table while their tea is being filled, that is a habit that stems from Chien Lung's secret visits. When Chien Lung would pour tea for one of his ministers, who of course knew it was Chien Lung, they could not openly say, "Thank you, your highness." instead, they would tap their finger on the table as a sign of thanks.

Titleography: As of this writing, no alternative titles could be found. Translation—*Chien Lung Visits Yangzhou Down South. Voyage* in the English title refers to a journey and has nothing to do with Chien Lung traveling by boat, but it sounds more adventurous than "visit" or "trip." In the Chinese title, *Yangzhou* is the city in Jiangsu province that Chien Lung visits. **MA Percentage: 2.96%** SHAW BROTHERS

WATER MARGIN, THE

水滸傳 (1972—Hong Kong) **119m. FI: Liu Chia-liang, Tang Chia, Liu Chia-rong, Chan Chuen. NOT/LOT: 2/ 30s; NOF/LOF: 28/ 20m.** D: Chang Cheh. C: David Chiang, Ti Lung, Lily Ho, Ku Feng, Tetsuro Tanba, Toshio Kurozawa, Chin Feng, Yueh Hua, Hu Wei, Yang Ze-lin, Wang Chung, Fan Mei-sheng.

The Water Margin is based on the novel of the same name—as a novel, it has also been titled *Shui Hu Zhuan, All Men Are Brothers* and *Outlaws From the Marsh*. It is one of the most famous *wuxia xiao shu* (wuxia novels) of all time. Completed during the Ming Dynasty (1368-1644), it tells the stories of the 108 Heroes, who lived in the Liang Shan Marshes and bravely opposed corrupt officials during the waning years of the North Song Dynasty (A.D. 907-960). It is also a typical story that defines the world of Jiang Hu (see *All Men Are Brothers*).

Wuxia prose gained prominence during the Tang Dynasty (A.D. 618-907), when stories began to romanticize wuxia heroes, combining altruism, exceptional martial arts skills and magical powers. The nature of wuxia literature can be gleaned from the meaning of the Chinese characters 武俠. The first Chinese character is *wu*, which means "martial" or "military" and is two characters combined. Those two characters are *zhi* (止) and *ge* (戈), which mean "stop" and "fight," respectively. (It is like the compound word "filmmaker," which consists of the two separate words "film" and "maker.") Philosophically, this would imply that it takes fighting to stop fighting. (This is a paradigm further reflected during the rise of the Shaolin Temple.) Although *xia* may loosely be translated

Still from *The Water Margin* © Celestial Pictures Ltd. All rights reserved.

as "chivalrous hero," it is more a concept than a title. Anyone with virtue—righteousness, loyalty, courage, truthfulness, honor—could be described as xia. Wu with xia therefore involves virtuous people who accomplish good deeds via their fighting abilities and their codes of ethics, which are developed out of superior martial skills.

In addition to these wuxia characteristics, *The Water Margin* existed as part of an oral tradition long before it appeared in any formal compilation. When put on paper, the characters in these stories typically took on exaggerated, mythical characteristics. The final author of *The Water Margin* is unknown, though writers such as Shi Nai-an and Lo Guan-chung are believed to have contributed to the final work.

Depending on which version of the book you read, director Chang Cheh's movie version of *The Water Margin* covers Chapters 60 to 67. Many films about Jiang Hu are crowded with characters, and this film is an extreme example. One of the basic rules of screenwriting is to limit the number of main characters to three or four in the first act of the screenplay (typically 17 to 23 minutes). This film introduces 19 characters in the first two minutes. The 108 or Liang Shan Heroes are concerned about the city of Zheng Tou, and they also find that their founding father, Chao Gai, has been killed by Golden Spear Shi-wen-gong (Toshio Kurozawa). To make matters worse, the emperor orders the death of the Liang Shan Heroes, whom he considers to be bandits. Regardless of the negative situation in Zheng Tou, the heroes agree to avenge Chao Gai's death and attack the city because of their code of honor.

The only way they can defeat Golden Spear is if they can recruit Jade Unicorn Lu Chun-ji (Tetsuro Tanba; *Intrigue of the Yagyu Clan* (1978)) and his adopted son, the great musician and wrestler Yen Ching, aka Xiao Yu (David Chiang), to unite in battle. An elaborate plan to coerce Yen Ching and Lu into helping out the 108 Heroes involves Clever Star Wu Yung (Chin Feng) posing as a fortuneteller. The temperamental Black Whirlwind Li Kuei (Fan Mei-sheng) accompanies him as his mute assistant, and it's ironic because Li Kuei's big mouth always gets him into trouble. Under the guise of a threat—which is really an empty threat because the 108 Heroes are righteous men and respect Yen Ching and Lu—they tell Yen Ching he will die unless he helps the Liang Shan Heroes.

Yen Ching sees through the plan and confronts the rambunctious Li Kuei, who mouths off and gets thrown around like a rag doll by Yen Ching's wrestling skills. When government soldiers storm Lu's house—having been tipped off by his adulterous wife, who wishes to see her husband imprisoned—he does not turn in Clever Star or Li, but instead gets thrown in jail for abetting criminals Yen Ching escapes. The 108 Heroes attempt several rescues that fail, and Fearless One Shih Hsiu (Wang Chung) is captured after one such try. The day for Lu and Shih's execution arrives, but Welcome Rain Sung Jiang (Ku Feng), the newly appointed leader of the 108 Heroes, finally succeeds in rescuing them.

The fate of the city and the 108 Heroes comes down to five kung fu duels pitting good guys Li Kuei, Shih Hsiu, Magic Sword Wu Sung (Ti Lung), Leopard Man Lin Chong (Yueh Hua) and Tigress Lady Hu San-niang (Lily Ho) against five of Golden Spear's best fighters. Golden Spear faces off against Lu and Yen Ching in a final showdown. Adding to the drama is the revelation that Golden Spear is Lu's younger kung fu brother. The two trained under the same teacher, and Lu's Jiang Hu code of ethics gets in his way, perhaps to the detriment of all the 108 Heroes. Only time will tell.

Considering the film's length, the fight time in *The Water Margin* is pretty short, but the focus is on the stories of brotherhood and all the relationships between the various characters (and there are a lot of them). One might expect the soundtrack to feature traditional lamenting Chinese music, but it is filled with Ennio Morricone spaghetti Western blurbs, churning organ grinds, 1970s guitar riffs and melodies that recall early Yes songs. The whispering "chica-chica-chaaa" used during some of actor David Chiang's special moments is quite memorable. Of all the characters, though, most critics and fans find Fan Mei-shang's rendition of Li Kuei most engaging; it's accentuated by the gruff emotion of Fan's Chinese voice dubber. Fan used the Li Kuei caricature in other films, such as *Five Tough Guys* (1974).

Titleography: *Outlaws of the Marsh*; *Seven Blows of the Dragon*; *Waterside Story*. Translation—*Waterside Shore Biography* (*Water Margin*). See the above martialogy. *Seven Blows* refers to the seven heroes in the final duels: Li, Shih, Wu, Lin, Hu, Lu and Yen Ching. **MA Percentage: 17.23%** SHAW BROTHERS

WAY OF THE BLACK DRAGON

黑煞 (1978—Hong Kong) 88m. MAD: Billy Chen Hui-yi. NOT/LOT: None; NOF/LOF: 16/ 16m 56s. D: Chan Chue. C: Carter Wong, Cecilia Wong, Ron Van Clief, Chen Lou, Charles Bonet, He Hsiang.

Despite the title, this film is neither blaxploitation nor Bruceploitation. Bill Eaton (Ron Van Clief) teams up with righteous husband-to-be Chen (Carter Wong) to rescue his fiancée, Allison (Cecilia Wong), from the clutches of prostitution and from becoming a drug mule. I guess anytime a black cop character like Eaton teams up with a Chinese cop character like Chen, people will see parallels between this film and Jackie Chan's *Rush Hour* franchise, and will begin to infer that *Rush Hour* was influenced by the film. Whether that is true or not, the next distributor could certainly lay claim that *Way of the Black Dragon* is the original *Rush Hour*.

One thing admirable about Van Clief is that unlike some of his contemporaries (Jim Kelly, for example), he resisted trying to become the black Bruce Lee. He declined to do fight scenes or use body postures that looked even remotely like something Lee would do. In my first Taiwanese kung fu film, the studio labeled me as the American Bruce Lee, and that backfired. I was so preoccupied trying not to imitate Lee that my performance suffered.

There are several fights in this film in which Van Clief does a great job of looking very nonchalant when he is being attacked. It is bordering on the great Lo Lieh fight at the beginning of the *Clan of the White Lotus* (see its martialogy), in which Lo effortlessly defends himself against several strikes while walking forward without breaking stride or the natural rhythm of his movements—very smooth indeed.

The film also demonstrates an innocuous-looking stunt: getting knocked off a boat into the water. It might look easy, but that doesn't mean it's safe. If the body of water is one of the various bays or harbors of Hong Kong or the Dan Shui River of Taipei, things can get risky. The water is very polluted, and swallowing a mouthful could make a person sick for weeks. It is also essential not to inhale the water. Even though that sounds like a no-brainer, many novice stuntmen will reflexively inhale water. So once the stuntman resurfaces, it is imperative to spit even if he's only got a few drops of saliva in the mouth. Flipping into the water at any speed can force water into the stomach through the nose, which is just as bad as swallowing. Keep that in mind the next time you see a stuntman taking the plunge into the murky waters of Hong Kong Harbor.

Titleography: *Black Dragon*, *Black Strike*. Translation—*Black Vicious Fighter*. The *Black* in each title is representative of Van Clief, and *Black Dragon* is meant to suggest that he is the black Bruce Lee. **MA Percentage: 19.24%**

WAY OF THE DRAGON

猛龍過江 (1972—Hong Kong) 90m. MAI: Bruce Lee, Little Unicorn. NOT/LOT: 6/ 4m 1s; NOF/LOF: 9/ 20m 3s. D: Bruce Lee. C: Bruce Lee, Nora Miao, Chuck Norris, Bob Wall, Little Unicorn, Whang In-shik, Wei Ping-au, John Benn, Tony Liu Yung.

The return of the *nunchaku*, and this time it is double trouble. In this film set in Italy, Lee plays Tang Lung, a country bumpkin from Hong Kong sent to Rome to work at his uncle's restaurant. Once there, however, he ends up fighting the Mafia.

Lung uses two nunchaku and a pole to mow his way through the wimpy hoards of mob hit men, and eventually three karate killers are hired to lessen Lung's life. Though the Japanese and American top fighter are karate characters in the film (played by Korean actor Whang In-shik and Chuck Norris, respectively), in reality Whang and Norris both practice Korean martial arts. Lee originally planned to face Joe Lewis in the iconic Colosseum fight, but the two had a falling out. Norris took Lewis's place, resulting in Norris' best fight scene to date. Several years after Lee's death, Norris told *Inside Kung-Fu* magazine that if Bruce had let him choreograph the fight, it would've been better. After numerous B-movies and a highly successful TV show, Norris has yet to deliver a superior fight scene.

Lee's potential as an innovative and influential filmmaker is apparent throughout the film. The Colosseum fight, for example, intercuts shots of a kitten toying with a rock, which mirror the dynamic of the duel. Lee also uses sound creatively, accenting moods and emotions with percussion instruments and uttering his patented battle screams (which have sadly been mimicked ad nauseam, thus cheapening the mythology). Note that the musical cue used when Norris gives Lee a thumbs-down at the Colosseum is borrowed from Sergio Leone's famous Western *Once Upon a Time in the West* (1969).

Way of the Dragon also draws on Lee's own life for inspiration, including his time spent as a waiter at a Chinese restaurant in Oakland and his teaching a lesson to an American stuntman by knocking him 15 feet backward with one kick. The actor Wu Ngan, who is holding the air shield that Lee kicks back in the film, was a childhood friend of Bruce's and a male servant in the Lee household when Bruce was growing up in Hong Kong. The film as a whole also reflects the racism Lee was exposed to while living in Hong Kong and America and working in Hollywood.

Lee's fights were symbolic messages that Chinese people inside and outside America did not need to be subservient. They also showed that the little Asian man could stand up to the big powers. It is no wonder people cheered when Lee beat the cruel Japanese, did in the proud Russian and, in this film, disposed of the arrogant Japanese karate fighter and the silent, sneaky American Kudo Colt (Norris). It is ironic that none of the white bad guys beaten in any of Lee's films were British characters, considering the first brunt of racism Lee faced was while living in Hong Kong when it was a British colony.

Titleography: *Return of the Dragon.* Translation—*Powerful Dragon Crosses the River.* The film was released in the United States after Lee's *Enter the Dragon*, which the *Return of the Dragon* title attempted to capitalize on. Many fans at the time mistakenly believed it was a sequel. *Powerful Dragon* is a metaphor for Tang Lung because he travels to another country, or *Crosses the River*, which is a metaphor for the sea or ocean. **MA Percentage: 26.74%**

WAYS OF KUNG FU, THE

身形拳法與步法 (1978—Hong Kong) **90m. MAI: Li Chao, Alan Hsu, Liu Jun-hui. NOT/LOT: 12/ 14m 5s; NOF/LOF: 22/ 22m 35s.** D: Li Chao. C: Liang Chia-ren, Meng Fei, Tsung Hua, Chi Kuan-chun, Ma Chang, Le Chao, Yu Tien-lung, Cliff Ching Ching.

Everything you do in life can be translated into kung fu training—it all depends on your point of view. Renegade Shaolin monk Wu Tak (Cliff Ching Ching) returns to the Shaolin Temple and uses his advanced skills for nefarious purposes. He becomes the abbot and uses the monastery as a cover for jewelry heists, knowing that no one would suspect a Shaolin monk to be a master thief. Meanwhile, bumbling loser Ta Kung (Chi Kuan-chun) is sent away by the previous abbot (who is ailing) in hopes he will avoid Wu Tak's wrath. Though Ta Kung has no interest in learning kung fu, he does so without realizing it by carrying out simple tasks for master Shang King (Liang Chia-ren), such as chopping wood, taking water from the well and ringing out laundry. And while Ta Kung also

learns kung fu is not meant for hurting others, he enthusiastically grasps that when someone is in danger, kung fu can be righteously handy.

In a sort of *Drunken Master* rip-off, the downtrodden Ta Kung also learns drunken style from a beggar with messy gray hair (Yu Tien-lung). The beggar also has another student (Meng Fei), and together the student and Ta Kung face the wicked Wu Tak. A policeman (Tsung Hua) who has spent his entire life trailing Wu Tak also joins them in bringing the treacherous monk down.

The training scenes feature actor Liang Chia-ren as a teacher doing what he does best: demonstrating kung fu with correct posture, perfect hand positions and spot-on stances. These sequences might appear slow compared to the rest of the film, but director Li Chao was willing to sacrifice speed to avoid sloppy martial arts. In fact, it was this performance by Liang that caught the eye of Sammo Hung, which led to his casting Liang as the *wing chun* teacher in *Warriors Two* (1978). His training sequences in that film are shot similarly so you can clearly see his true wing chun postures.

We see evil monk Wu Tak using a small steel ring when he fights, as well as a lashing staff—a long pole with a short flail end. Legend says the lashing staff was invented by the first emperor of the Song Dynasty, Chao Hong-yin, after his pole broke into two pieces during a fight and the parts were reconnected with iron rings. As it turns out, the long piece of the pole broke again, which he also reconnected, thus inventing the three-sectional staff. (See *The 36th Chamber of Shaolin.*)

Titleography: As of this writing, no alternative titles could be found. Translation—*Body Posture Fist Work and Leg Method.* Ultimately, from a physical standpoint, actor Liang Chia-ren is the epitome of the three martial attributes (at least in the film), as he demonstrates proper posture, fist work and leg method during the kung fu training scenes. **MA Percentage: 40.74%**

WEB OF DEATH, THE

五毒天羅 (1976—Hong Kong) **87m. FI: Tong Chia, Yuen Cheung-yan. NOT/LOT: None; NOF/LOF: 18/ 8m 16s.** D: Chu Yuan. C: Yueh Hua, Lo Lieh, Ching Li, Ku Feng, Wang Xia, Angela Yu Chien, Wang Chung, Lily Li, Ching Miao, Chan Shen.

What kind of spider shoots webs with crackling spitfire colors, smoking explosions and loony lightning? The dreaded Five Venom Spider, a mystical tarantula encased in what looks like an old-style English street lantern. When a user opens the lantern, the spider's silk streams high into the air and forms a large web capable of killing any person or crowd of people the web falls onto and covers. Because of this destructive danger, Chief Hong of the Five Venom Clans (Wang Xia, in a rare non-villain role) has the weapon hidden in a secret location. The Five Venom Clans are a subset of five clans of martial artists and swordsmen that exist in the Jiang Hu world. The clans are Toad, Centipede, Spider, Scorpion and Snake.

However, Snake Chief Liu Shen (Lo Lieh) is distraught over the Five Venom Clans' waning respect and fame in the Wu Lin world. He plots to attend the year's martial arts tournament at Wu Dung Mountain during Zhong-Chio Jie (the Mid-Autumn Festival) and take the currently unlocated Five Venom Spider with him to ensure victory over all competitors. Chief Hong forbids it, but Liu defies him. Liu and Centipede Chief Chio Xin (Lily Li) hatch a plan to spread the word about the weapon's existence. The logic is that because this is such a deadly weapon, good-hearted and righteous swordsmen will feel they must find it before the wrong person does. Of course, Liu's wrong hands will be at hand at the right moment.

Elsewhere, senior Wu Dung Clan member Fei Ying-xiang (Yueh Hua), who does not belong to any Five Poison Clan, saves the life of spunky beggar girl Hong Su-su (Ching Li), who is actually Chief Hong's daughter. Su-su then helps Fei find the spider. Through a series of double- and triple-crosses, accidental poisonings, and wrongful accusations, Fei and

Still from *The Web of Death* © Celestial Pictures Ltd. All rights reserved.

Su-su fall in love, and Liu manages to get his grubby hands on the spider. Drunk with visions of grandeur, he sidesteps the tournament, kills Chief Hong, and then goes around pickling all who oppose him. The martial arts world's only hope is the power of the Nether Flower, which blooms once every 10 years, and the only person known to know where to find it was Chief Hong—but there is another. Who is it, and is it too late?

Seeing as how a tarantula plays one of the film's villains, it's worth asking just how deadly such spiders are in real life. Though fearsome-looking, tarantulas are in fact relatively harmless. Their bites are not lethal to humans (unlike, say, black widows, Brazilian wandering spiders, brown recluse spiders or Australian funnel-web spiders). Also, their barbed hairs (called urticating hairs), which the spider literally kicks off its body, can cause mild irritation. Bee stings are worse.

The Mid-Autumn Festival (aka the Moon Festival) is an important Chinese holiday dating back to the Shang Dynasty (1600-1046 B.C.), the era when Stonehenge was built and Moses led the Israelites out of Egypt. Farmers celebrate the end of the summer harvest, and families and friends come together to honor the mythological "lady in the moon" by eating moon cake. Yum.

Titleography: As of this writing, no alternative titles could be found. Translation—*The Five Venom Silk Sky Trap*. The Chinese title refers to the weapon everyone wants and its horrifying web of death. **MA Percentage: 9.5%** SHAW BROTHERS

WICKED PRIEST COMES BACK

Gokuaka Bozu: Nembutsu Sandan Giri (1970—Japan) **94m. FI: Uncredited. NOT/LOT: None; NOF/LOF: 13/ 12m 32s.** D: Takashi Harada. C: Tomisaburo Wakayama, Bunta Sugawara, Ichiro Nakaya, Yuki Jono, Tatsuo Endo, Shinichiro Mikami, Yuriko Mishima, Eizo Kitamura, Toshiaki Minami.

In Shaolin culture, a monk is called "mad" if he chooses to eat meat and drink alcohol. Somewhat similarly in Japanese culture, a priest is called "wicked" if he chooses to drink alcohol, gamble and mess around with women. How about that—one can be a Buddhist monk, have his cake and eat it too, so to speak.

Before his fame was cemented in the *chambara* (sword-fighting) film series *Lone Wolf and Cub*, Tomisaburo Wakayama played the wicked priest Shinkai in five films between 1968 and 1971. However, only the last two were made in the 1970s: *Wicked Priest Comes Back* and *Wicked Priest: Wine, Women and Swords*. His character walks a fine line between licentious overindulgence and defending the downtrodden—he does the latter to atone to the heavens for the former. With a walking stick that houses a hidden sword, Shinkai roams Japan during the Meiji period (1868-1912). A running subplot of the series is Shinkai's anticipated duel to the death with his former friend and now-bitter foe Ryutatsu the Whipmaster (Bunta Sugawara). Shinkai blinded his former pal with a finger poke to the eye in *Wicked Priest* (1968). Aside from that subplot, each movie is a stand-alone narrative.

This film, the fourth in the series, opens amid a beautiful snowscape with Shinkai on his way home to Nogata to pray at his mother's grave. He is attacked suddenly by Yakuza, and he paints the white snow blood-red. Three surviving attackers skulk off. Arriving at a gambling den, Shinkai meets an old childhood pal, Takegoro (Ichiro Nakaya). But times have changed, and so has his chum. Takegoro is in the midst of an argument because he is trying to use expired money for gambling bets. As things escalate, Takegoro takes out a large shotgun. Shinkai gets Takegoro out of the mess because the casino's Yakuza owner, Old Lady Karuda, takes a liking to him. She agrees to let Takegoro off the hook if he cuts off his pinkie. Takegoro doesn't just cut it off, instead he blasts it off with a shotgun. Obviously, times have changed. Takegoro leaves the den in pain and in a huff—so much for childhood friends.

Shinkai arrives home to find two rival Yakuza gangs, the Godawara and Ryuo, vying to control the river workers. Shinkai convinces the Godawara to help the workers in return for his fighting services. The Ryuo hire Takegoro to kill Shinkai because they learn that it was Shinkai who killed their boss in the opening snow-fight scene. Although Shinkai defeats Takegoro, Shinkai is badly beaten by the Ryuo. However, Old Lady Karuda saves his live and nurses him back to health. Meanwhile, the two gang bosses agree to kill Shinkai. During the fight between Shinkai and the gangs, Shinkai is blinded by an explosion that was meant to kill him.

The next thing you know, the blind Shinkai gets all Zatoichi (see *Zatoichi Meets Yojimbo*) against the gangs. But he falters. The darkness of no eyesight turns bleaker when Ryutatsu shows up to kill Shinkai. Yet in a moment of Chris-

tian benevolence (Ryutatsu turned Catholic after losing his eyesight), Ryutatsu decides to fight alongside Shinkai and help him to defeat the Yakuza. The film's final shot is peaceful and dream-like, but like a dream, it will fade into the next and final film of the series. Actor Bunta Suguwara also portrayed Ryutatsu in *Blind Yakuza Monk* (1970).

Although the choreography is sloppy, the use of slow motion, limited camera movement and attention to camera angles make the fights look real. In this film, the bad choreography is OK because it is about the fighting rather than making Shinkai look like some supreme master. After all, Shinkai suddenly becomes blind, so realistically his fighting skills need to suffer. There is also a great over-the-shoulder shot of the blind Shinkai stumbling through the Yakuza gangs' headquarters. The camera then switches to an angle on Shinkai's head as he walks and kills at the same time, using one technique at a time—very effective-looking.

A few final fun facts: Lady Karuda's teeth are pitch-black. This practice is known as *ohaguro*, which is when a married woman in a time before the Meiji era dyed her teeth black. The ritual of cutting off one's pinkie was an act of atonement or a way to pay off gambling debts and is known as *yubitsume*. It is a popular trope in Yakuza films. In addition, the reason it was such a powerful gesture of atonement is that the pinkie has the tightest grip on the hilt of a samurai sword. Without the pinkie, a samurai's grip is weaker. In the Yakuza world, a missing pinkie also shows a greater dependence on needing protection from one's boss. Finally, notice that when Shinkai fights in the snow, Wakayama and the combatants are in bare feet, which shows a lot about their discipline as actors. It reminded me of the time when I was practicing Okinawan *goju ryu* in Ithaca, New York, where during driving snowstorms, our *dojo* of six students would go out jogging for a few miles dressed in just our *gi* and in bare feet. Brrr.

Titleography: *The Killer Priest Comes Back*. Translation—*Wicked Priest Triple Slice Pilgrimage*. **MA Percentage: 13.33%**

WICKED PRIEST: WINE, WOMEN & SWORDS

Gokuaku Bozu - Nomu Utsu Kau (1971—Japan) **89m. FI: Uncredited. NOT/LOT: None; NOF/LOF: 13/ 11m 5s.** D: Buichi Saito. C: Tomisaburo Wakayama, Bunta Sugawara, Takashi Shimura, Kyosuke Mashida, Toru Abe, Fumio Watanabe, Takuzo Kawatani.

Wicked priest Shinkai (Tomisaburo Wakayama) is a lovable, pseudo-oafish character who was able to scrounge out five films. Yet the fourth was perhaps too similar to the film character Zatoichi, which might have been too much of a good thing. (See the *Zatoichi* martialogies.) After the *Wicked Priest* films, Wakayama ditched his jolly, fun-loving monk character and portrayed a psycho samurai in the following year's first installment of the six-film *Lone Wolf and Cub* series.

This final *Wicked Priest* film opens with Shinkai pleasuring a bunch of prostitutes to the point of exhaustion. A miffed Yakuza brothel owner tears into the room and catches Shinkai in his underwear, or a flapping-in-the-wind loincloth to be exact. Disrupted from his swell time, Shinkai bops the bozos and flees the brothel before the police arrive, while clinging to his loincloth for dear life. Shinkai finds shelter with a group of squatters in the old Dunghill Mansion owned by a once-proud samurai who is now a demented geriatric. For reasons not explained in the film, the old samurai believes Shinkai is an incarnation of Japan's most famous samurai, Miyamoto Musashi.

Meanwhile, two rival Yakuza bosses are posing as legitimate businessmen. They convince the upright head of the transportation service, Wajima (Takashi Shimura), that he should let them raze Dunghill Mansion to help the economy. Shinkai has become friends with Wajima and the Dunghill Mansion residents, and he helps Wajima realize that the businessmen are actually Yakuza. After Wajima refuses to give the Yakuza the necessary permits to destroy the mansion and build their company, the head of the local police, who is on the Yakuza payroll, fixes things in the Yakuza's favor. They not only get their permits, but the deed to the mansion too.

In retaliation, Shinkai and his new girlfriend (a Buddhist nun he had sex with earlier on) disguise themselves as the secretary of the army and his female aide. They try to steal back the deed but are exposed in the process. Although they retain the deed, the Yakuza are perturbed that Shinkai is becoming part neuroscientist and part entomologist—that is, he has a lot of nerve to bug the Yakuza. The Yakuza send over hit men to kill Shinkai and Wajima, and Wajima ends up dead. Shinkai and Wajima's son vow to avenge Wajima's death.

Wakayama is one of the few famous samurai actors in the late 1950s to early 1970s who seriously practiced martial arts beyond what was required in school. An exceptional judo teacher, he was also well-trained in *kendo, iaido, bo-jutsu* and *shorinji kenpo*. As the *Wicked Priest* and *Lone Wolf and Cub* films progressed, the fights drew on his wealth of martial skills. In this film, although he uses simple techniques, Wakayama shows good presence without a weapon in the opening fight. Using just his pole in another fight, he again uses simple techniques with short bursts, which makes timing easier for the stuntmen doing their weapon clashes. Bo-jutsu doesn't use fancy twirling skills like the Chinese pole, thus comparing pole fights between Chinese and Japanese films is ludicrous. The final fight of the film is the long-awaited duel between Shinkai and Ryutatsu the Whipmaster. (See *Wicked Priest Returns* for details on this character.) It's basically karate versus judo mixed with one-punch-destruction exchanges that are complimented by blood squirts from every orifice. It is a dessert of a fight in the desert—a sweet ending to the film series.

Titleography: *Wicked Priest: Blessed Virgin Killer*; *Bloody Priest*. Translation— *Wicked Priest: Wine, Women & Swords*. **MA Percentage: 12.45%**

WILD BUNCH OF KUNG FU

老頭拳頭大饅頭 (1979—Hong Kong) 86m. MAI: Guan Zheng-liang. NOT/LOT: 4/ 3m 23s; NOF/LOF: 12/ 18m 41s. D: Guan Zheng-liang. C: Yuen Xiao-tian (Simon), Fong Ching, Amy Tao, Fan Dan-fung, Long Xuan, Sun Lan, Lung Tian-hsiung.

Actor Yuen Xiao-tian once again dons the gray wig, garbage-dump hat and scruffy clothes to ignore his AA meetings and drink himself into another Suexploitation saga. This is the worst of the lot—films that use the Beggar Su character from Jackie Chan's *Drunken Master* (1978). It has an overdone premise, waning passion, and a lack of any creative fight choreography or skilled martial artists in the film. Quality goes out the window, as quantity enters through the door.

Non-kung-fu-fighting shepherd Big Dumpling (Fong Ching) catches two thieves eating one of his sheep, but they beat him up, drag him through town and humiliate him. At the peak of toiletry and alcoholic humility in a restaurant, Dumpling is saved by drunken Liu (Yuen Xiao-tian). Liu introduces Dumpling to fellow sot Yu, who looks like a thin Santa Claus with a short Pippi Longstocking queue. The two wine-guzzling martial arts masters take it upon themselves to teach Dumpling how to fight. After learning how to do back flips and snap a towel, the still-non-kung-fu-fighting shepherd uses his body weight and dough-making abilities to kill the lamb-eating thieves and their big boss, a raucous man who raped Yu's granddaughter and killed the brother of Yu's future son-in-law.

Sadly, the fights are about as interesting as watching sheep eat grass. There's not much to write home about, which is why this part of the beggar franchise is in foreclosure and needs house renovation to make the sale.

Titleography: *Against Kung Fu Rascal*; *Against Rascals With Kung Fu*. Translation—*Old Man Fists Fight Big Buns*. The Chinese title suggests the character's nickname should be Big Bun rather than Big Dumpling. The *Wild Bunch of Kung Fu* title is inspired by the Western *The Wild Bunch* (1969); instead of a film about an aging group of outlaws looking for one last big score, we have a bunch of aging kung fu masters trying to even the score. The *Rascals* referred to in the alternate titles are the sheep-eating thieves. **MA Percentage: 25.66%**

WINGED TIGER

插翅虎 (Hong Kong—1970) 87m. FI: Liu Chia-liang, Tang Chia. NOT/LOT: 1/ 8s; NOF/LOF: 10/ 12m 54s. D: Shen Chiang. C: Angela Yu Chien, Chen Hong-lieh, Tien Fung, David Chiang, Shen Yue-ming, Luo Han, Wei Ping-ao, Tang Tian-yi, Tong Tin-hei, Zheng Lei, Fang Mian, Ching Miao, She Bao-chin.

Another film trapped in the esoteric alternate world of Jiang Hu, which is a sub-society of martial artists, beggars, vagrants, vagabonds and wandering heroes who live according to a distinct set of morals, rules and ethics. Within Jiang Hu, there exists the Wu Lin world, which is a microcosm of martial artists and swordsmen. It is kind of like the world of sports: It is not a physical place but exists within the normal world. Its inhabitants live by a different set of rules, but instead of athletes, they're martial artists. And while members of the sports world vie for prized trophies that signify their team is the best, those in Wu Lin often vie for a prized weapon or a secret kung fu manual.

Winged Tiger Deng Fei (Zheng Lei) and Underworld King Yin De-ling are rivals in Wu Lin. They are like the Charles Barkley and Reggie Miller of Wu Lin (if Wu Lin were the NBA). Before he passed away, the Underworld King wrote

a prized kung fu manual and split it in half. He gave one half to his Yin Clan family members and the other to Winged Tiger's clan. If the knowledge of the manuals were ever combined, Wu Lin would be plunged into chaos. The wise but deceased king assumed his students would never unite the manual, but that was a fatal mistake.

The news is out that Winged Tiger is on his way to marry Underworld's King's sister Yin Cai-fa (Angela Yu Chien), and that spells t-r-o-u-b-l-e. That's because if Cai-fa and the Winged Tiger marry, chances are the two halves of the secret kung fu manual will unite and plunge the Wu Lin world into doom. The chief of Hua Shan of the Eight Schools asks the righteous and superior swordsman, Guo Zhou-ru (Chen Hong-lieh), to stop the marriage and retrieve the halves of the manual so that everyone in the Wu Lin world may benefit from their contents. Guo happens to be a great mimic of people's voices. He learns how to fight and speak like Winged Tiger, even copying his secret heel spikes and leaping skills. When the two meet in the wilderness, in what had to have been an eye-opening fight on-screen for the audience back in 1970, Guo defeats Winged Tiger, assumes his identity and heads off to the Yins. The future of the world of Wu Lin is now in Guo's hands.

The wire work in this film is so bad and illogical that it is good. With pendulum-like hangs, sweeping flying gags and suspended-animation freeze maneuvers, I could hardly wait for the next one just to see what choreographers Liu Chia-liang and Tang Chia would try to get away with. In terms of camerawork, they also used several well-placed Dutch angles, which did not become popular in fight scenes until the 1980s. Dutch angles are shots with the camera slightly tilted to one side so the horizon is at an angle to the bottom of the frame. They were popular with German cinematographers during World War II—Dutch shots of Hitler really added to his creepiness—and were called Deutsch angles (meaning German angles). Back then everyone thought the word was "Dutch."

Based on the time the film was made, there was a unique hand-held camera shot in one scene. It follows Guo in close-up from behind during a group fight. The audience sees the back of his shoulder throughout the shot while he moves through his attackers. Most hand-held camera shots moved around, in and out of the fight scene, and rarely hovered over the shoulder of an actor. The final fight has overly cool close-ups, tracking shots and more hand-held shots that are just too good to be bad, although several are way off-speed. Odd lighting also adds a sense of mystery to the action.

Titleography: As of this writing, no alternative titles could be found. Translation—*Winged Tiger*. **MA Percentage: 14.98%** SHAW BROTHERS

WITHERED TREE

Kogarashi Monjiro (1972—Japan) **91m. FI: Uncredited. NOT/LOT: None; NOF/LOF: 7/ 7m 20s.** D: Sadao Nakajima. C: Bunta Sugawara, Tsunehiko Watase, Goro Ibuki, Saho Sasazawa, Rinichi, Yamamoto, Asao Koike.

Withered Tree is a film based on true events. It's about Kogarashi Monjiro (Bunta Sugawara), a man who is wrongly accused and sent to a remote penal colony on Miyake Island. The colony is also home to a very active volcano, Mount Oyama, and that makes the living conditions worse. Kogarashi and four other inmates build a makeshift raft and plan to escape whenever Mount Oyama erupts. (Historically, that eruption occurred in 1835.) Only Kogarashi survives. He sets out to discover who framed him and who has been trying to kill him since returning.

The opening fight is inundated with extreme close shots using a hand-held camera, which makes the action bothersome to watch. When the actors strike with their swords or knives, they use excessive windups to swing their swords as if they're baseball bats. Strike three, the fight is out. However, there is one fight that is shot in the rain, which seems to be a popular motif in many Japanese martial arts films. It not only reflects that certain calm and serenity one should get from being a good samurai or martial artist, but cinematically, the rain adds to the film's mood and takes away some of the dizzying edge of the hand-held shooting angles.

Although the final fight at the seaside uses wild swinging swords, there is a 50-second sequence shown as a single unedited shot of Suguwara as Kogarashi running on a beach and then sprinting into the water. The intensity of the fight increases as Sugawara purposefully and violently splashes in the ocean to create fountains of spraying water. The actual choreography is minimal, with each man dying by a simple single strike as the antagonist steps into frame. But you get a sense of how tiring a real fight would be against so many attackers. In reality, Sugawara does not need to act tired because running on the beach in water without a break while trying to remember the choreography and swing the sword on cue is exhausting. The tricky thing about these extended unedited sequences is if the fight looks bad on camera, it would have been immediately re-shot so the actor doesn't lose the rhythm and pacing of the scene. So when you watch this scene, imagine having to do it at least four or five times in a row. Talk about running on empty.

In writing this book, I've come to realize how many of the stories in these films mirror each other or borrow elements from each other. Here's what I mean: A year later, the American-French film *Papillon* came out. It's not a martial arts film, but it is about two men who escape from a penal colony on an island. The only differences are that the penal colony is French and the island is called Devil's Island. Intelligent filmmakers who follow Asian cinema know that this borrowing also happens between movies in the East and West. For example, Quentin Tarantino's *Reservoir Dogs* (1992) and George Lucas' *Star Wars* (1977) were greatly inspired by *A Better Tomorrow 2* (1987) and *Hidden Fortress* (1958), respectively.

Titleography: As of this writing, no alternative titles could be found. **MA Percentage: 8.06%**

WITS TO WITS

狼 狽 為 奸 (1974—Hong Kong) **95m. AD: Yuen Woo-ping. NOT/LOT: None; NOF/LOF: 13/ 15m 22s.** D: Wu Ma. C: Henry Yu Yung. Wu Ma, Shiek Khan, Wang Chen.

Here we go: Pu is after Pai, who becomes friends with Ku; Pai and Ku are played by Wu and Yu, and the action director is named Woo but has no relation to the director, who is Wu. The classic comedic duo of Abbott and Costello would have had a *Who's on First?* field day if they knew about Chinese last names.

With Captain Pu on their tails, con artists Ka Ku (Wu Ma) and Pai Xing-lang (Henry Yu Yung) team up with a crafty casino boss (Shiek Khan) to steal a load of gold from a local bank. However, as the heist goes down and the police surround the bank, only a first-class flim-flam man will be able to fool the other conman's con.

Yuen Woo-ping's action directing limits each actor's number of techniques to fewer than 10 per shot, and his subtle camera movements are refreshingly unique. He often starts on one fight sequence before panning to another already in progress within the same shot. The fights are filled with pans and tilts, and most takes are either close or medium shots, which brings the viewer into the

action. Yuen shoots in a way that does not give the sense that he is hiding something so much as adding something. The tight framing also accentuates the claustrophobic feel of the fights, making the action feel desperate and life-threatening. Of particular note is that there is little to no music during the fight scenes, which forces the viewer to listen to the fights. As a result, they sound better, which enhances the realism to make them look better.

Titleography: *From China With Death*; *Dirty Partners*. Translation—*Wolf and Another Kind of Wolf Do Evil Things Together*. The English title *From China With Death* is a play on the James Bond film *From Russia With Love*. The heroes are con men, so *Dirty Partners* is appropriate. The Chinese translation just means that there are two evil guys who are in cahoots with each other. **MA Percentage: 16.18%**

WOLVES, THE

Shussho Iwai (1971—Japan) **131m. FI: Uncredited. NOT/LOT: None; NOF/LOF: 8/ 10m 38s.** D: Hideo Gosha. C: Tatsuya Nakadai, Noboru Ando, Kyoko En-ami, Komaki Kurihara, Toshio Kurosawa, Hisashi Igawa, Isao Natsuyagi, Tetsuro Tamba, Kunie Tanaka.

While some principled gangs might claim there is honor among thieves, their use of deception is ultimately a business decision. At the end of the day, the instigators of dishonor can always argue that duplicity is simply in their nature.

The death of Emperor Taisho on Christmas Day, 1926, marks the end of the Taisho period in Japan and the beginning of the Showa period. With this new era comes a slew of pardons from the government, several of which are for Yakuza gangsters from the Enoki-ya gang. Two of those pardoned are Seji Iwahashi (Tatsuya Nakadai) and Tstomu Onodera (Toshio Kurosawa). Onodera, against Yakuza law, has fallen in love with the boss's daughter, Aya. He and Iwahashi had been serving 10-year sentences at Abashiri Prison on the northern island of Hokkaido for murders committed against the opposing Kan'non-gumi gang during a skirmish over the blowing up of a railroad building. When they return to gangland life, things have changed. Their boss has mysteriously died, and Aya is now betrothed to the head of the Kan'non-gumi gang as a peace offering. But Iwahashi soon learns that the new boss of the Enoki-ya gang and Aya's fiancé from the Kan'non-gumi gang plotted the murder of the old Enoki-ya boss. They also sent Iwahashi's best friend, Gunjiro Ozeki (Noboru Ando, son of a famous real Yakuza boss) to kill the old boss.

Iwahashi and Ozeki do not clash, but rather discuss life in prison and the effects of the Great Kanto Earthquake, which Iwahashi avoided while serving time. While Ozeki laments that he must move away to Shimauchi (in Nagano), he and Iwahashi devise a way to save face—a plan that ultimately comes back to threaten them like a voracious pack of wolves.

The film's first 10 minutes have been lauded for their typical crippling fingers of intense violence, even though there are actually 78 seconds of flesh-ripping sword and *tanto* knife choreography. The film's fight scenes are more or less mired in tussles and wide-thrusting motions. However, the over-the-top emotions and grunts exhibited by the major fighters add a certain dynamism to the action.

As a historical side note: The Great Kanto Earthquake on the Kanto Plain of Honshu Island (which includes Tokyo and Yokohama) occurred in 1923 and measured 8.3 on the Richter scale. (The 1994 Northridge earthquake in California measured 6.7.) It lasted about 10 minutes and claimed 142,000 lives. One of the most prominent structures to survive the quake in Tokyo was the Imperial Hotel, built by American architect Frank Lloyd Wright. One of the tragedies of the quake was the mass murder of about 6,600 ethnic Koreans by vigilante mobs because the newspapers accused Koreans of using the disaster to commit arson, robbery and poisoning of the drinking water.

Titleography: As of this writing, no alternative titles could be found. Translation—*Prison Release (Promotion) Celebration*. Many of the Yakuza characters in the film come across like the proverbial wolves in sheep's clothing, acting like a friend until one's neck is vulnerable. **MA Percentage: 8.12%**

WONDER WOMEN

(1973—USA/Philippines) **81m. AC: Eric Cord. NOT/LOT: None; NOF/LOF: 5/ 1m 58s.** D: Robert Vincent O'Neill. C: Nancy Kwan, Ross Hagen, Maria De Aragon, Roberta Collins, Tony Lorea, Sid Haig, Vic Diaz.

Sadly, this film reflects the plight of Asian-American actors in the 1970s. It is denigrating that someone with the pedigree, training and experience of Nancy

Kwan would have to resort to playing a mad doctor who kidnaps world-class athletes, removes their body parts, and transplants them onto or into the rich and famous. Even now in the 2000s, Asian-American actors still fall prey to racial stereotyping, which predominantly portrays men as kung fu fighters, Yakuza gangsters or computer geeks, and women as seductive dragon ladies, attentive Suzie-Wong types, or the "Oriental" woman with long, beautiful hair. Just ask the producers of the 1972 *Kung Fu* TV show why they did not want to cast Bruce Lee as Kwai Chang Caine.

Regardless of how bad the martial arts are in a film, if it falls within the Chuck Norris gauge (see *Good Guys Wear Black*), it makes it in this book. To say the fights are bad in this movie would be an understatement, so the best thing to do is not have much of a statement. It is worth noting that the action coordinator, Erik Cord, did do several short martial-arts-influenced fights in other 1970s films. He even worked with *Black Belt* Hall of Famer Fumio Demura in the *Island of Dr. Moreau* (1977), which did not contain any martial arts action.

Titleography: *Chinese Puzzle*; *The Deadly and the Beautiful*; *Women of Transplant Island*. All the titles fit the film except *Chinese Puzzle*. That title, which suggests the film has a mystical edge, may have been conceived because of Kwan's involvement or because of the "mystique of the Orient" mentality. Nice try … not. **MA Percentage: 2.42%**

WONDERMAN FROM SHAOLIN

金 虎 門 and 陰 陽 十 八 翻 / Keum Ho-moon (1979—S. Korea) **82m. MAI: Hui Tian-si. NOT/LOT: 7/ 3m 28s; NOF/LOF: 16/ 25m 42s.** D: Godfrey Ho, Kim Seon-gyeong. C: Casanova Wong, Eagle Han Ying, Kim Jeong-Ran, Elton Chong, Hyeon Kil-su, Cui Min-kui, Hui Tian-si.

Talk about lost in translation. This film really mixes up some historical facts. For example, the English-dubbed version explains that the Mongolians invaded northern China at Shandong (Shantung) province in 1231, which is like saying the Canadians invaded America by crossing the northern border of Virginia.

There was never a Shaolin Temple in Shandong. However, with a leap of faith, perhaps the Korean filmmakers were cognizant that in 1231 Ogedai Khan ordered General Sartaq to invade Korea as part of a plan to take over China. The invasion was temporarily quelled when monk Kim Yun-su killed Sartaq during the Battle of Ch'oin-son by shooting an arrow into his eye. If that invasion had been successful, then the Mongols, known for their navy, might have sailed across the Yellow Sea from Korea and landed on the shores of Shandong province. Yes, it is a stretch, but as martial artists know, stretching is part of our training.

Anyway, Il-kong (Hyeon Kil-su) attempts to weasel his way into the Shaolin Temple to steal an important gold statue of Buddha and take over the monastery for the Mongol leader. (In 1231, that would be Ogedai Khan.) Il-kong shaves his head and vows subservience to the temple's leader, Priest Wong (Cui Min-kui). Wong's second new disciple is So-sun (Casanova Wong), who is apparently mute and mentally disabled but saves a young maiden from lascivious looters. The maiden gives So-su a secret kung fu manual to learn the Fire Fist as a means to defeat Il-kong's wicked Wind Blade Chi technique. Il-kong promises power and riches to three powerful fighting monks if they join the Mongols, kill Priest Wong and steal the gold statue.

The three monks who join Il-kong use weapons such as the monk's cudgel, flying dove knives (a rare weapon thought to be of Mongolian origin) and nine-teeth hook knives (the number of teeth being representative of long life).

The film employs "hand place" choreography, which was popular in Korean martial arts movies and low-budget Chinese kung fu films. The defender puts his hands in a position for the attacker to aim at with punches or kicks, so when the attacks are done slowly, it looks like the defender is placing his hands on the incoming strike. Or it looks like the defender can reach out toward the slow incoming attack and place his hands on the attacker's legs or arms. Adjusting the camera speed, removing certain frames during editing (which sometimes makes the fights look jerky), or looping in loud and occasionally bizarre sound effects can make the fights look relatively smooth and convincing.

Titleography: *Magnificent Wonderman*; *Magnificent Wonderman From Shaolin*. Translations—*Golden Tiger Gate* and *The Yin Yang 18 Flips*. After Il-kong takes over the Shaolin Temple, he replaces the temple sign with a sign that reads "Golden Tiger Gate." So-sun is the eponymous *Wonderman*, though the use of *Shaolin* in the title is not derived from either of the Chinese titles. There are no gymnastics or flipping skills in the film, so the second Chinese title is a mystery. **MA Percentage: 35.57%**

WORLD OF DRUNKEN MASTER, THE

酒 仙 十 八 跌 (1979—Hong Kong) **86m. MAI: Yuen Cheung-yan. NOT/LOT: 8/ 10m 19s; NOF/LOF: 24/ 30m 36s.** D: Joseph Kuo. C: Yuen Xiao-tian, Jack Long, Lung Fei, Long Guan-wu, Chen Hui-lou, Lung Tien-hsiang, Lee Yi-min, Tu Song-zhao, Jeannie Chang, Yu Song-zhao.

No AA meeting for these masters, just a grand old get-together to discuss kung fu and *sifu* and to fight over the only woman either of them ever loved.

According to the film, the legendary Wu Song (see *Delightful Forest*) created the drunken style of kung fu 1,000 years ago based on movements handed down from the Eight Immortals. (See *Drunken Master* for details on these Eight Drunken Gods.) Wu Song, who is famous for killing a tiger with his bare hands, was one of the 108 Heroes who fought against corruption during the Song Dynasty (A.D. 960-1279). In the real world of drunken masters, one of the other famous true-life martial artist heroes of China associated with the drunken style is one of the 10 Tigers of Canton, Su Qi-er, also known as Beggar Su.

In this cinematic world of drunken masters, two old kung fu brothers, Beggar Su (Yu Song-zhao) and Fan Da-pei (Jack Long), meet during the twilight of their years to end a lifelong squabble about whose fault it was that their sifu, Chang Seventh (Chen Hui-lou, the old man in *Kung Pow: Enter the Fist*), and his daughter, Yu Lu (Jeannie Chang), both died. In the middle of their drunken turmoil, they smell the ambrosia of their passion (wine) and instead decide to have a drink together and reflect on the past.

In a flashback, two young grape salesmen, Su (Lee Yi-min) and Fan (Long), are caught stealing grapes from a vineyard. Their punishment is to work in a winery, which predictably leads to the habit of them making and drinking wine. The mischievous youths also resent Tiger Yeh's (Lung Fe; Betty from *Kung Pow*) protection racket, which drains the local villagers dry, so they fight off collecting agents only to get beaten to a pulp. Chang Seventh teaches them drunken kung fu to even the odds. This sets off Tiger Yeh on a mission to destroy the winery, the winery's employees, Seventh Chan, Chan's daughter and his two now-lovable staggering kung fu winos—lads who refuse to whine but never refuse the wine.

Actor Jack Long's face lends itself well to the character of the young and old Fan; as the older version, he requires just a touch of makeup and white hair. Thus many of his roles cast him as an old kung teacher. His real-life buddy Lee Yi-min, who plays the younger Su, often purposely played a humorous, Jackie Chan-type bumpkin for Hong Hua Films. Long and Lee Yi-min's fights are not as good as in their previous film together, *The Seven Grandmasters* (1978). The drunken movements are too clean and too precise, and the fights look methodical and contrived rather than like sets of smooth-flowing movements. One highlight is a voice-over that points out the various 18 Falls of the Drunken Gods during a fight scene so the audience can see what drunken kung fu movements look like and how they are applied in combat.

Historically speaking, Wu Song was not a practitioner of the drunken arts, though a Buddhist version of the origin of drunken kung fu does tell that the art was indeed created during the Song Dynasty by a martial artist named Liu Chi-tsan.

Titleography: *Drunken Dragon*; *World of the Drunken Master*. Translation—*The 18 Falls of the Drunken Gods*. The English titles tap into the obvious popularity of Jackie Chan's *Drunken Master* (1978), which is a no-brainer because Yuen Xiao-tian reprises his beggar alter ego in the film's opening credits. *Drunken Dragon* provides a tidy bit of alliteration that rolls off the tongue and incorporates the film's theme of the animal styles of kung fu, though only a snake stylist appears in this film. **MA Percentage: 47.58%**

YOUNG AVENGER, THE

小 毒 龍 (1972—Hong Kong) **81m. FI: Xu Er-niu. NOT/LOT: 1/ 51s; NOF/LOF: 18/ 16m 44s.** D: Yueh Feng. C: Shih Szu, Yueh Hua, Chen Yen-yen, Fan Mei-sheng, Tong Lin, Wu Ming-cai, Tang Di, Li Xiao-cong, Chan Shen, Wu Ming-cai, Xu Er-niu, Hu Wei.

The more one watches *wuxia* films that deal with the world of Jiang Hu, the smaller Jiang Hu gets, and at the Shaw Brothers studio, this was not an accident. If you watch a lot of these old films, the sets become familiar, so much so that in the old days audiences would equate the sets with certain famous films. Having the same sets show up in other movies made the world of Jiang Hu more tangible and real—as if you could truly expect to find all these different heroes and villains running around in this familiar world. The characters would logically end up, at least in cinema, in the same Jiang Hu places, but under different circumstances.

So what are the circumstances the heroes face in this chapter? The film begins with Li Bao-zhu (Shih Szu), who is the assassin Xiao Du Lung, feared even in criminal circles. We meet her while she is finishing her current job—to kill the Tung brothers. We are left wondering how such a beautiful lass became a stone-faced killer.

Flash back 10 years earlier, when one of the legendary Four Heroes of Jiang Nan, Li Kui (Tong Lin), who is master of the Piercing of the Dragon Sword, is confronted by the hunchback Liu Tuo (Fan Mei-sheng), who laments that Li Kui killed his brother 20 years earlier. The brother, however, was an evil ne'er-do-well who deserved to die. Liu is willing to forego challenging Li Kui to a duel if Liu can learn his swordplay. Li Kui admits he has put those days behind him and has forgotten the skill, but when Liu attacks, Li Kui easily defends himself. Li Kui shows mercy, the classic trait of a retired Wu Lin (that part of the Jiang Hu world in which martial artists and swordsmen reside) swordsman, but Liu sneakily hits Li Kui with a deadly iron palm strike. Liu vows to practice hard and come back in 10 years to kill Li Kui, not knowing that his iron palm has fatally injured Li Kui.

Still from *The Young Avenger* © Celestial Pictures Ltd. All rights reserved.

It is worth noting that many wuxia films feature heroes and villains from Jiang Nan. Historically, Jiang Nan a culturally rich area of China with good agricultural lands and a good economy. Many martial arts heroes hailed from there, and where there are heroes, there are powerful villains.

Before he dies, Li Kui sends his young daughter, Li Bao-zhu, to one of his fellow Four Heroes: Mad Monk (Chan Shen). He tells his daughter that she must learn his Piercing of the Dragon Sword skill in order to avenge his death in 10 years by hacking the hunchback to hell. Now 10 years later, Bao-zhu is back in town dressed like a boy, swaggering her assassin reputation, when she picks a fight with Iron Fan Chen Shih-lun (Yueh Hua), who comes to realize Bao-zhu is his cousin. Embarrassed to the point of tears for trying to hurt her cousin as well as having a sense of coming home, Bao-zhu dresses like a lady for the rest of the film.

Because of Bao-zhu's presence, her enemies are arriving and killing people in the village. Furthermore, the loathsome Liu is salivating in the wings with a hoard of heavies ready to destroy the village. Bao-zhu insists on leaving, but cousin Chen and the villagers agree to go one-for-all and all-for-one against Liu. There are shades of *Seven Samurai* when the village joins in the bashing of the invading villains, culminating in a finale of blood-and-guts gore with eye-gouging grossness.

Worthy of mention is a shot during the final fight when lead actress Shih Szu is supposed to storm through a tall, two-door wooden gate; her butt gets stuck in the doorway. It is rather humorous. Again, as is typical in these early wuxia films, there are not many fights, but they are shot with exceptional camera

precision and laced with smooth tracking shots and hand-held helming.

Titleography: As of this writing, no alternative titles could be found. Translation—*Xiao Du Lung* (*Little Poisonous Dragon*). The name of Bao-zhu's alter ego. **MA Percentage: 21.71%** SHAW BROTHERS

YOUNG LOVERS ON FLYING WHEELS

電單車 (1974—Hong Kong) **99m. FI: Liu Chia-rong, Liu Chia-liang. NOT/LOT: 4/ 1m 40s; NOF/LOF: 10/ 8m 27s. D: Ti Lung. C: Ti Lung, Cheng Ke-wei, Helen Ko, Jiang Nan.**

I can only imagine that when Shaw Brothers offered Ti Lung, one of its biggest stars and moneymakers, the opportunity to direct his first film with the company's best screenwriter, Ni Kuang, and two of the top fight choreographers in the business (the Liu brothers) at his disposal, the studio probably thought it had just come up with yet another cash machine. What they ultimately produced was a film about a man, Song Da (Ti Lung) who wanted to impress a girl, Ye Wei (Helen Ko), by buying a motorcycle so she would not have to take the bus. As we would say in the 1970s, "That was heavy, man," adding in a joke term from today, "Not!"

Song hopes to win a martial arts tournament; first prize is a motorcycle. After he loses, he borrows money from a loan shark, buys a bike and takes his girl on a ride. Unfortunately, the bike breaks down, it starts to rain, the girl gets wet, and the relationship ends. Of course, Song's bike gets stolen and the loan shark wants his money back, but Song cannot afford it. The loan shark and his gang beat him up, and Song pays them back by selling his blood (a rare type). On the good news front, Song gets a new girlfriend, Yu-mei (Chen Ke-wei). But the bad news is that her father hates him because he is a motorcycle beatnik. Something has to give, and it does in a positive way when Song uses his kung fu on the loan shark and wins the acceptance from Yu-mei's father. Sorry for the laundry-list film description. Perhaps it's a sign that the movie was hung out to dry.

Ti Lung, with a Bruce Lee haircut and a whopping eight minutes of fights, may not have taken full advantage of the talent he had at hand, but it is never an easy thing to jump from superstar martial arts actor into directing yourself with the expectation of success. (Just ask Tony Jaa about how things went on his directorial debut, *Ong Bak 2*, released in 2009). After the film flopped like an undercooked pancake, Ti was given one more chance to prove his kung fu mettle (see *Young Rebel*). Similar to his kung fu film counterpart David Chiang, whose directorial debut four months earlier with *Drug Addict* was also not a pure martial arts film, Ti wanted to distance himself from what he was known for and explore a new direction. It was a daring move, but in retrospect perhaps not a smart one.

Titleography: As of this writing, no alternative titles could be found. Translation—*Motorbike*. Even though the Chinese title is more accurate, it doesn't sound as exciting as the English, which suggests you might be sitting down to see a bizarre kung fu film. **MA Percentage: 10.22%** SHAW BROTHERS

YOUNG PEOPLE

年輕人 (1972—Hong Kong) **118m. FI: Tang Chia, Liu Chia-rong. NOT/LOT: 5/ 2m 37s; NOF/LOF: 10/ 8m 56s. D: Chang Cheh. C: David Chiang, Ti Lung, Chen Kuan-tai, Irene Chen I-ling, Agnes Chen Mei-ling, Wang Zhong, Bolo, Wu Ma, Wong Ching.**

What do you get when you mix three of Shaw Brothers' biggest kung fu stars of 1972 in a film in which one plays the drums, one kicks butt and one is a baseball hero? And if you add one prolific Hong Kong martial arts film director and sprinkle in some good old American folk songs, like Carole King's *You've Got a Friend* (1971) and Joni Mitchell's *The Circle Game* (1966)? How about if you stir in a 20-minute basketball game, a martial arts tournament and a 20-minute go-kart race? And top it off with a woman who falls in love with each of the three actors but gets no one, while the three boys get each other? I am not quite sure what to call the result, but it's another of Chang Cheh's films about the youth of Hong Kong—in this case college students. It's a film with no plot, direction or back story. Instead, it's just a romp-and-roll, feel-good brotherhood movie with respect for *mei hua* kung fu and an ending dance number that features the cha-cha with ma-ma-martial arts dips and bops.

Historically, *mei hua chuan* (plum flower fist) was founded by Monk Feng Ke-shan, who was killed in 1814 during an anti-Ching uprising. One of his most famous students was one of the Five Elders of Shaolin, Wu Mei, a Buddhist nun. After moving to Er Mei Mountain in Sichuan province, Wu Mei taught mei hua kung fu to a lady named Wing Chun. Although historians and *wing chun* practitioners have varying accounts on how wing chung kung fu was created, most versions agree that Wing Chun is the founder and namesake of the art. And, of course, the style was a stepping stone for Bruce Lee's art without fighting, *jeet kune do*. (Note: Mei hua's forerunner was *mei hua jie chuan* (plum flower fast fist), which consisted of five methods and 48 forms.)

One of the problems Bruce Lee created for other action stars was that he had a great build. Subsequently, many kung fu stars would rip off their shirts during fight scenes to reveal muscles that were not so grandiose. In an effort to look muscular, the actors would flex and tense their muscles during a fight, which made the fights look tense and slow. In this film, director Chang Cheh would shoot the fights either in slow motion or at a wicked 18 frames per second to hide the muscle-tensing done by the actors. It is a bit weird to use such extremes of camera speed in a film with so little action because it creates an uneven tempo and does not allow the audience to adjust to the circumstances. But at the end of the day, this film's nine minutes of fighting are not about the fights.

Titleography: As of this writing, no alternative titles could be found. Translation—*Youth*. **MA Percentage: 9.79%** SHAW BROTHERS

YOUNG REBEL, THE

後生 (1975—Hong Kong) 99m. FI: Liu Chia-rong, Chan Chuen, Huang Pei-ji. NOT/LOT: 6/ 2m 7s; NOF/LOF: 17/ 12m 55s. D: Ti Lung. C: David Chiang, Ti Lung, Ming Ming, Wen Wen, Yuen Xiao-tien, Feng Yi, Jiang Nan, Jiang Dao.

David Chiang riffs on revenge as Xiang Rong, a simpleton delivery boy who is constantly taken advantage of, treated like dirt, beaten up and hung out to dry. But one day, bully Shi (Jiang Dao) and his gang push Xiang too far, and Xiang snaps and whacks the gang, but they are too much for him. This leads to a wild bicycle chase that reaches its climax when Xiang and his good buddy Gen Lai (Ti Lung) tar and feather the gang. In order to help Xiang defend himself, Gen introduces Xiang to his *wing chun* teacher. But Xiang's impetuous nature erupts, and although he quickly becomes a lethal fighter, he loses control of his temper constantly and gets kicked out of the school.

Still from *The Young Rebel* © Celestial Pictures Ltd. All rights reserved.

One day, while making a delivery to a local gang-run karate school headed by Mr. Tou, Xiang has a run-in with Tou's students. After Xiang beats up all the students due to misplaced anger and ego, Tou takes a liking to him and hires him as muscle to beat up his rivals. When the money starts pouring in and Xiang gets in too deep, Tou orders him to kill his major competitor, Boss Long, or else Xiang's mother will die. After some two-faced double-crossing, Xiang ends up getting the short end of the stick. But similar to the fabled Monkey King's hair that grows into a long pole to be used as a weapon, Xiang's short stick grows into a weapon—one that's filled with "shear" energy in that it is a deadly pair of gardening shears. After trimming away at Tou, Xiang unleashes a barrage of Tony Jaa-like elbows and slap-happy choreography. (Tony Jaa is the contemporary Thai action star known for elbow strikes.) But the fight doesn't end until Tou finds himself stepping on wooden planks, which he quickly learns isn't that great of an idea when wearing spiked track shoes. Because of the awkwardness, Tou gets a point "plank" look at Xiang's size-8 kick.

After all the killings and violence, Xiang sees the error of his ways and submits himself to the long arm of the law and the law of martial arts; he will never again fight unless he has to. Xiang returns to his wing chun kung fu teacher to apologize and have one more lesson, but none is needed. He has learned the idea of the full circle, and though he will now be living in a cellblock, martial arts will be his freedom no matter where he is.

As discussed in other martialogies, there is some debate whether a real person named Wing Chun existed. There are also plenty of stories and controversy surrounding the development of the wing chun martial arts style, each with their own unique history. One story says that a nun named Wing Chun first learned martial arts under Zhi Shan, one of the Five Elders of Shaolin. When Zhi Shan's student Hong Xi-guan returned from Canton, he told Zhi how narrow the streets were in Canton. Northern Shaolin martial arts are characterized by broad sweeping motions, which may not be useful in confined spaces, so Hong and Zhi set out to develop stances and hand techniques that could generate similar power within the confines of a "four-brick tile" space. Since these techniques were perfected within the monastery's Wing Chun Hall, the style (named after a nun named Wing Chun) was called wing chun. Another story says that Zhi Shan consulted with Hong's wife, Fong Wing Chun, and the style was named after her.

After two unsuccessful runs as a director—this film and *Young Lover of Fly Wheels* (1974)—superstar Ti Lung hung up his director's shoes and got back to kicking in front of the camera.

Titleography: *The Rebel Youth*. Translation—*Naïve Youths*. All titles indicate off-the-path youths who try to find their way down the road of teenage life. **MA Percentage: 15.19%** SHAW BROTHERS

ZAKHMEE

(1975—India) 143m. FI: Gulab Azim. NOT/LOT: None; NOF/LOF: 7/ 6m 17s. D: Rajah Thakur. C: Sunil Dutt, Asha Parekh, Rakesh Roshan, Reena Roy, Tariq, Helen, Johnny Walker, Imtiaz.

What is Jackie Chan's *Project A* (1983) set doing in a 1975 Indian film? Part of the beauty of film is that inspiration comes from many different and unknown directions. In *Heera* (1973), actor Sunil Dutt takes on a man-eating tiger. And although this film is not a sequel, he battles another tiger in *Zakhmee*, and this time it's personal.

Dutt plays Anand, an innocent man who is wrongly sentenced to prison for the murder of his business partner. In reality, he witnessed the business partner's murder at the hands of the cruel mobster Tiger. Fearing for his family, Anand accepts the prison sentence until he instinctively saves his cellmate from the prison's feared "alpha-mate" killer. Upon beating him to a pulp, Anand looks to the proverbial divine skies for intervention and laments, "The desire of dying is now within ourselves; we have to see the strength in the hands of a murderer." And with that, he escapes prison to clear his name and wreak vengeance against the crime syndicate that has now kidnapped his family and threatens them with unspeakable atrocities.

Indian action films like this one are very long and are not written as a way to show or promote Indian martial arts. In fact, reviews I have read about Indian films usually focus on the song and dance sequences, how famous the music became, and the dancing abilities of the actors. It is no wonder that in this film, for example, the first fight occurs 90 minutes in. Watching Indian films for the martial arts truly takes patience and time.

During the 1970s, Hong Kong fight directors often had a difficult time transitioning between traditional kung fu- or *wuxia*-style fights and contemporary brawls, making the action look slovenly. Although there is no use of *kalaripayit* martial arts in this film, fight instructor Gulab Azim smoothly switches from traditional martial arts scenarios to modern action. Regardless of the time period of the film, Dutt's signature move, the head butt (which I call the Dutt Butt), works well, and that comes down to how Azim makes it fit. Seriously though, the final fight scene in the villain's mountaintop chalet, especially the large open room with opposing staircases to a balcony that creates an amphitheater-looking stage, really looks like the *Project A* set in which Jackie Chan goes to his enemy's home. What is also novel about the *Zakhmee* fight is the out-of-nowhere and totally unexpected scene in which a woman (Reena Roy), a true rarity in Indian films, come flying through a large window on a motorcycle. She drives up and down the staircases while taking out the baddies. This in turn creates enough distraction for protagonist Anand to chase the head gangster into a cellar, wherein he not only defeats the man but takes on a handful of the villain's cronies to flip, roll and crash into objects all over the basement.

What is also weird is that the older Dutt gets in real life, the more he looks and moves like Chow Yun-fat. Or maybe it is the older Chow Yun-fat gets, the more he looks like Dutt.

Titleography: As of this writing, no alternative titles could be found. **MA Percentage: 4.39%**

ZANJEER

(1973—India) **145m. FI: Ravi Khanna. NOT/LOT: None; NOF/LOF: 5/ 9m 6s.** D: Prakash Mehra. C: Amitabh Bachchan, Jaya Bhaduri, Pran, Om Prakash, Ajit, Bindu, Iftekhar, Keshto Mukherjee.

Sometimes the knight in shining armor who rides in on a white horse is not a righteous hero. India's biggest action star of the 1970s (maybe of all time), Amitabh Bachchan, polishes his deep baritone voice and sultry, piercing eyes for a film about tainted pharmaceuticals and what it takes for his character, Inspector Vijay Khanna, to take down the life-sucking empire of the villainous Mr. Teja (Ajit).

What is most heartfelt and virtuously endearing about *Zanjeer* is the strong bond of friendship and brotherhood Vijay develops with gambling den owner Sher Khan (Pran). When Vijay becomes the new policeman on the block, constantly being transferred due to his honest take and no-nonsense approach, Vijay goes to Khan's gambling den and voices his opinions on how gambling hurts the layman. Because Khan is considered an upright citizen by the law and locals, he does not take kindly to Vijay's words. The two men rock, roll, fly kick, punch, tire and still attack until neither has the energy to stand. Khan is impressed by Vijay's upright nature and offers his hand of respectful friendship, but Vijay refuses unless Khan disbands his gambling dens. To Khan, money is not as important as trustworthy friends, so he agrees to stop his business. The two shake hands with the understanding that each would die for the other as blood brothers. It is the foreboding moment of the film.

These old Indian movies really play like old kung fu films, whether it be the notion of brotherhood, the righteous hero or the philosophical beckoning that guides the protagonist when times get rough. With *Zanjeer*, there is even the classic "oh shit" moment when the villain realizes that he did not kill the entire innocent family of his good-guy nemesis, as the now grown-up survivor Vijay points it out to the now-crapping-in-his-britches villain before mopping the floor with him. These grand moments are effective in any good film.

Titleography: As of this writing, no alternative titles could be found. **MA Percentage: 6.28%**

ZATOICHI AND THE ONE-ARMED SWORDSMAN

獨臂刀大戰盲俠 / *Shin Zatoichi: Yabure! Tojin-ken* (1971—Hong Kong/Japan) **104m. FI: Uncredited. NOT/LOT: 2/ 33s; NOF/LOF: 13/ 11m 58s.** D: Hsu Tseng-hung, Yasuda Kimiyoshi. C: Jimmy Wong Yu, Shintaro Katsu, Wong Ling, Zhang Yi, Yuko Hama, Masato Kagawa.

This is the film that almost destroyed Jimmy Wong Yu's career. During the 1990s, the biggest kung fu film dream team that captured the imagination of Western and Eastern audiences was the continually rumored pairing of Jackie Chan and Jet Li, which became an eventual reality with *Forbidden Kingdom* (2008). The martial arts film dream teams of the early 1970s were Bruce Lee and Sonny Chiba, and Jimmy Wong Yu and Shintaro Katsu, with only the latter becoming a reality.

In Jimmy Wong Yu's third incarnation as the one-armed swordsman Fang Gang (changed to Wang Gang for this film because of copyright issues with Shaw Brothers), he teams up with Japanese cinema legend Shintaro Katsu, who reprises his role of Zatoichi, the blind swordsman. Though the movie is more whimsical than tough-minded, it is still arguably one of the best Sino-Japanese films ever made.

It is the old wrong-place-at-the-right-time story, in which Fang, as a wandering Chinese swordsman in Japan, is wrongfully accused of slaughtering a Japanese family and becomes a hunted man. The final fight is the result of a language barrier; Fang believes Zatoichi is his enemy because he misinterprets something that Zatoichi does and vice versa, leading each hero to think the other is the villain. Naturally, with two cultures, two legendary cinematic heroes and two big stars, something had to happen, and it did.

Jimmy Wong Yu told me several years ago that because he and Katsu were hot movie stars, the film's deal included having two endings, one for the Japanese audience and one for the Southeast Asian audience. Jimmy Wong Yu lost in the Japanese version, but Katsu lost in the Southeast Asian one.

But how did this film hurt Wong Yu's career? As it turns out, the Chinese producer who brokered the deal was with Golden Harvest, which created a legal battle with Shaw Brothers and put Wong Yu in the middle. Wong Yu also shared with me that Shaw Brothers went to court in Japan at the same time to sue Golden Harvest for infringement of the copyright over the One-Armed Swordsman character. However, when Wong Yu told the Japanese judge that he was in Japan as a tourist, the court threw out the case, and Shaw Brothers threw out Wong Yu, forcing him to shoot films stealthily and carefully. He could not work openly.

Because the film used Japanese sword choreographers, Katsu's fights had the typical Zatoichi look: sudden bursts of a few techniques, pauses, stares, his ears listening for a clue, then further flurries of backhanded-sword-grip slashing fury. On the other hand, Wong Yu's fights look disjointed because the Japanese choreographers tried to capture the smooth circular fights seen in hiss previous *One-Armed Swordsman* movies. (See *The New One-Armed Swordsman* for discussion.) However, they were unable to bring that luster to this film, and its lack is most evident during long shots. The fights look painfully awkward because the Japanese stuntmen were not used to Wong's style of movement. Because of that, it is no wonder this film has very little action, like the other Katsu-starring *Zatoichi* films,.

And even though each version of the film's ending closes with Wang Gang and Zatoichi lamenting, "If only we could understand each other," at least this movie got made, and Wong Yu got to play other one-armed characters and still went on to become a screen legend.

Titleography: *The Blind Swordsman Meets His Equal*; *Zatoichi 22*; *Zatoichi Meets His Equal* (Match); *Zatoichi Meets* (and) *the One Armed Swordsman*. Translation—*One Armed Swordsman Battles a Blind Hero*. It is intuitive how these titles were derived. **MA Percentage: 9.5%**

ZATOICHI AT LARGE

Zatoichi Goyo-tabi (1972—Japan) **88m. FC: Kusunoki Eiichi. NOT/LOT: None; NOF/LOF: 8/ 5m 43s.** D: Kazuo Mori. C: Shintaro Katsu, Rentaro Mikuni, Hisaya Morishige, Etsushi Takahashi, Naoko Otani, Osamu Sakai.

Zatoichi is a portly, pudgy, blind traveling massage therapist created by novelist Kan Shimozawa. Despite his physical handicap, Zatoichi has the discipline to endure ridicule. But when one crosses the same line with his relatives, friends or women he befriends, the hidden sword in his cane swishes out, slices, kills and is back in the scabbard before the assailant can say, "Za—." For details on this character and comments on samurai choreography, see *Zatoichi Meets Yojimbo*. Each each film is a stand-alone story.

In *Zatoichi at Large*, a woman is once more the center of Zatoichi's conscientious good nature. After delivering the baby of a dying woman and leaving the baby with its aunt, Zatoichi is accused by the newborn's 7-year-old brother of killing his mother. The brother thinks this because he sees Zatoichi standing over his bloody and dying mother. As is also standard for many Zatoichi films, Zatoichi somehow incurs the wrath of a Yakuza boss. In this film, it's Boss Tetsugoro (Rentaro Mikuni), who has just arrived in town to set up shop. However, Tetsugoro is aware of Zatoichi's Yakuza ties and warns him not to mess around in his underground affairs, which include plans to take over the village. Like in any film, when a character is told not to do something, it's pretty much guaranteed he will do it anyway. That is screenwriting 101.

After Zatoichi refuses to comply via some rather nifty emphatic sword-slashing skills, Tetsugoro is ultra-peeved. He's enemy No. 1. Meanwhile, when the dead mother's husband arrives home and hears his son rant about who killed his mother, Zatoichi makes enemy No. 2. Next, after Tetsugoro's men beat the *sarashi* (a white cloth samurai and Yakuza wrap around their midriffs) off Zatoichi's body, old retired police officer Tobei rescues him. When Zatoichi tells Tobei about Tetsugoro's plans, Tobei stands up to Tetsugoro and gets killed. The onus of Tobei's death falls onto Zatoichi via Tobei's warrior-age son—enemy No. 3. As Zatoichi tries to clear his name of each murder, the flaming wrath of Tetsugoro's desire to torch Zatoichi becomes so hot that he literally sets Zatoichi on fire. Although engulfed in flames and under a conflagrated attack by Tetsugoro and his Yakuza, it is Zatoichi who gets all pyromaniacal and burns them straight to hell.

Similar to the inn scenes we see in Chinese kung fu films in which the *chi* or skills of a fighter could be measured by the little gimmicky things the warrior could do with chopsticks, money and cutlery, *chambara* (sword-fighting) films have similar moments. In this film, Zatoichi is attacked by some of Tetsugoro's men, and he unsheathes his sword, blocks the incoming sword into the ceiling, cuts a *tatami* mat in half, cuts his assailants' clothes off their bodies, then re-sheaths his sword in less than a few seconds. What also makes the fights in this film a bit more enjoyable is that there is less camera shaking during the action, which at the time was a popular but dizzying camera technique.

However, the not-so-bloody final fight is a composite of a few sword techniques performed within several shots but edited to look like a continuous fight. After each clash of swords, there are moments of posing and pauses followed by another quick barrage of techniques. But the way Zatoichi incorporates a large puppet head and ladder into the fight give a new meaning to ventriloquism.

Titleography: *Zatôichi 23*; *New Zatoichi Story: Official Trip*. Translation—*Zatoichi Arresting Journey*. Later in the film, Zatoichi is arrested by a local official. **MA Percentage: 6.50%**

ZATOICHI AT THE BLOOD FESTIVAL

Shin Zatoichi Monogatari: Kasama No Chimatsuri (1973—Japan) **87m. FC: Kusomoto Eiichi. NOT/LOT: None; NOF/LOF: 6/ 5m 43s.** D: Kimiyoshi Yasuda. C: Shintaro Katsu, Yukiyo Toake, Eiji Okada, Kei Sato, Yoshio Tsuchiya, Shiro Kishibe, Rie Yokoyama, Tatsuo Endo, Takashi Shimura.

Jesus said the meek shall inherit the earth, and if Zatoichi were real, he would certainly be up there to collect a few votes for the humblest man. (For details on this character and a discussion of samurai fight choreography, see *Zatoichi Meets Yojimbo*.) On the surface, Zatoichi is a rotund, mild-mannered, blind masseur who wanders Japan during the Tokugawa period. In this final film stop for the 1970s, with a flip of his coin, he moseys toward his childhood home and bumps into a young lady. She was raised by the same women who raised him. He also bumps into childhood chum Shinbei (Eiji Okada), whose return to the village is less than savory.

Zatoichi's home village of Kasama is in debt and needs to pay off a large fine to the local magistrate, who is also illegally doubling his tax take on local farmers. Shinbei bails out the villagers, and they feel indebted to him. What they don't know is that Shinbei is using his apparent act of kindness to take over their land, which includes a lucrative quarry of Inada floral stone. According to the lord of the treasury in Edo, if the villagers lack the correct deed for the land, Shinbei is well within his rights to use the land for whatever purpose because he paid the villager's fines. Shinbei knows there are no deeds because the land traditionally belongs to the villagers, but this natural right is not recognized by the Tokugawa regime. After Zatoichi finds out about the magistrate's illegal actions and Shinbei's devious plans, he threatens to expose them. For the last time during the 1970s, Zatoichi becomes a target for death, which sets up the final fight scene in the final Zatoichi film of the decade, which in reality turns out to be the longest single fight scene of the 1970s *Zatoichi* films. Bravo.

The film uses the kind of visual style that was popular in the *Lone Wolf and Cub* films. In one fight scene, there is a low-angle wide shot with Zatoichi facing the camera. When people sneak up behind him, he rapidly slices and cuts behind himself to nail the assailants before they realize they have just been killed. For the record, that was recorded as one of the six fights in my fight statistics for this film. The scene lasts two seconds.

Compared to other Zatoichi films, the fights were shot better than usual because they're not as dark (i.e. shot under brighter light), don't use as many tight

angles and don't incorporate shaky-cam techniques. The choreography consists of stab-and-slice combinations with the occasional block. In many of Zatoichi's fights, the choreography is crafted to keep Zatoichi from having to block a lot of strikes. Instead, his opponents strike first, which makes more sense given Zatoichi's heightened senses. Using this type of fighting style made it easier for the stuntmen, who only had to worry about hitting their strike marks (where the sword needed to be) and then remember to announce out their arrival with a blood-curdling yell (a cue for Katsu to react). Katsu knew where the strike was supposed to be, and all he needed to do was spin toward the voice and slice. The stuntmen then just had to stand and wait for the bloody reaction and squirt shot—a samurai film's liquid fountain for success. Good night, Zatoichi, see you in 17 years (1989).

Titleography: *A New Tale of Zatoichi: Blood Festival of Kasama*; *Zatoichi 25*; *The Blind Swordsman's Conspiracy*; *Zatoichi at the Blood Fest*; *Zatoichi's Conspiracy*; *New Zatoichi Story: Blood Festival in Kasama*. Translation—*New Zatoichi Conspiracy: Blood Festival in Kasama*. **MA Percentage: 6.57%**

ZATOICHI AT THE FIRE FESTIVAL

Zatoichi Abare Himatsuri (1970—Japan) **95m. FC: Kusunoki Eiichi. NOT/LOT: None; NOF/LOF: 12/ 7m 46s.** D: Kenji Misumi. C: Shintaro Katsu, Tatsuya Nakadai, Reiko Ohara, Masayuki Mori, Peter, Kô Nishimura, Ryutaro Gomi, Yukio Horikita, Jun Katsumura.

How can a man have the eyes of an eagle when he's blind as a bat? If he's Zatoichi, he just does.

Zatoichi is a short-haired, portly, blind masseur whose walking cane is a deadly sword, which he uses with great restraint. However, if push comes to shove and his life or someone he deems worthy of his protection is in danger, he becomes quite unrestrained. For details on Zatoichi and notes on *chambara* samurai choreography, see *Zatoichi Meets Yojimbo*. With 21 films in the franchise, Shintaro Katsu took over the production reigns of the series. (Remember that each film is a stand-alone story.) Becoming the producer gave Katsu a stronger say in the Zatoichi films' emotional and visual content.

The opening of this film explains that a man unified the chiefs of eight provinces of the Kanto District Yakuza in the 1830s to create a single powerful entity and used underground taxes and protection money to finance his newly formed gang. That man is Dark Imperial Lord Yamikubo (Masayuki Mori), Shogun of the Underground.

Zatoichi saves a woman bought by Yamikubo's men at a mistress auction. While under Zatoichi's watchful protection, her jealous *ronin* husband (Tatsuya Nakadai) kills her because he believes she deserves to die for sleeping with Zatoichi (which she did not do). The deranged masterless samurai also plans to kill anyone who slept with his wife like, as the ronin says, "Snipping a chrysanthemum." Zatoichi's plight in this film sees him on the constant lookout for Yamikubo and the jealous ronin, both of whom want him dead.

After a major failed attempt by Yamikubo's men to kill Zatoichi in a bathhouse, Yamikubo yammers with more venom than a pit of rattlesnakes. With a somewhat James Bond-ish appeal, Yamikubo and his men corner Zatoichi and poke at him with long flaming spears while he is trapped on a small circular platform in the middle of a pond that is lit on fire (hence the film's title). Even if Zatoichi can even survive this grueling ordeal, the jealous ronin still waits in the wings wanting to whack and hack Zatoichi into mulch.

The scene with Zatoichi in the bathhouse is precious. In the middle of a soothing bath, a bunch of Yamikubo Yakuza leap up from under the water and attack the disarmed Zatoichi. Because they are in a bathhouse everyone is naked—talk about fleshing out the characters. Although we can say the fight is literally a blood bath, it is how Zatoichi prevents the audience from seeing his naughty parts while fighting that makes this a humorous set piece.

The fights are composed of quick combinations of kills that are completed within several swipes and are much smoother than the fights in earlier Zatoichi films. This could be because Katsu was now in charge of production. He also began using a different fight choreographer, and by this time Katsu's feel of the blade was second nature. There is one amazing sequence that features the standard bit in which Zatoichi takes out as many opponents as possible with a few slices in one unedited shot. He kills five men with eight strokes while protecting a beautiful woman and cutting down a tree. Five men and one tree done quickly is a visual reverie.

But the final stare-down with actor Tatsuya Nakadai is the reason Western audiences took to Japanese samurai films decades before taking to Chinese kung fu films. These scenes were reminiscent of Wild West movie showdowns, in which the main villain and hero face off for that short gun battle. Plus, in the West, the perception and belief that the Japanese had learned how to make movies from Hollywood played into the Western ego. This perception is akin to the old imperialistic powers' belief in the "white man's burden" attitude, which in this case could be called Hollywood's white man's burden, a delusion that still exists today.

Titleography: *Blind Swordsman's Fire Festival*; *Zatôichi 21*; *Zatoichi Goes to the Fire Festival*; *Zatoichi at the Fire Festival*; *Zatoichi: The Festival of Fire*; *Zatoichi's Fire Festival*. Translation—*Zatoichi's Violent Fire Festival.* See above martialogy. **MA Percentage: 8.18%**

ZATOICHI IN DESPERATION

Shin Zatoichi Monogatari: Oreta Tsue (1972—Japan) **95m. FI: Uncredited. NOT/LOT: None; NOF/LOF: 7/ 5m 33s.** D: Shintaro Katsu. C: Shintaro Katsu, Kiwako Taichi, Kyoko Yoshizawa, Yasuhiro Koume, Katsuo Nakamura, Asao Koike, Joji Takagi, Masumi Harukawa, Yoshihiko Aoyama.

Zatoichi is a slightly chunky, visually impaired masseur who can stop anyone in the blink of an eye with the sword hidden in his cane. For more information on the character Zatoichi, see *Zatoichi Meets Yojimbo.*

Often cited as one of the worst Zatoichi films, *Zatoichi in Desperation* begins with our hero trying to give money to an elderly *shamisen*-carrying woman on a bridge. (The shamisen is a Japanese three-stringed lute.) As she steps forward to take the money, she trips and falls off the bridge to her death. Zatoichi learns that she was trying to raise money in order to buy her daughter out of a local brothel. Zatoichi uses his insane hearing abilities to win money at a local gambling house headed by Yakuza boss Mangoro Kagiya (Asao Koike) to buy the woman's freedom. Kagiya's reaction to this is that he wants Zatoichi to become human sashimi. Of course, Kagiya fails, but the freed girl's raw story about how her little brother was killed by hooligans and her fishing village was wiped out sinks the film into a total downer. The final fight does not feature either a villain worthy of Zatoichi's skills or that lone highly skilled *ronin* who forces Zatoichi to stretch his own abilities.

As the film franchise was winding down in the 1970s (one more to go with 1973's *Zatoichi at the Blood Festival*), so did the amount of screen time devoted to sword fights. The fights in this film are mostly shot under dark conditions, which was often a plausible way of extending Zatoichi's blindness to the audience. The audience has to struggle to figure out what is going on, just like Zatoichi. When everything is shot close-up (usually with the camera focused on someone's face) or at various other tight angles, the fights look darker than usual. There was no credited fight choreographer for this film, which might indicate that Katsu choreographed the fights. If this was the case, it might explain why the fights look the way they do: rough and poorly shot. It would seem logical to think that Katsu was a good fight choreographer because he fought a lot on-screen, but such was not necessarily the case.

Although this movie was the penultimate *Zatoichi* film for the decade, Katsu reprised his role one last time in *Zatoichi* (1989).

Titleography: *Zatôichi 24.* Translation—*New Zatoichi Conspiracy: Broken Cane.* The *Broken Cane* is a metaphor for Zatoichi's sad spirit for most of the film. **MA Percentage: 5.84%**

ZATOICHI MEETS YOJIMBO

Zatoichi to Yojinbo (1970—Japan) **115m. FC: Yuasa Kentaro. NOT/LOT: None; NOF/LOF: 14/ 7m 7s.** D: Kihachi Okamoto. C: Shintaro Katsu, Toshiro Mifune, Ayako Wakao, Osamu Takizawa, Masakane Yonekura, Shin Kishida, Kanjuro Arashi, Toshiyuki Hosokawa, Shigeru Kôyama.

Perhaps the most popular *chambara* (sword-fight film) character of all time is the gruff, dumpy, short-haired, blind masseur and sword master Zatoichi. He was a Yakuza of sorts who wandered the backlands of Japan during the Tokugawa era (1603-1868), also known as the Edo era. He usually made money from gambling, mostly because he needed it to help someone. Because he was blind and a masseur, Zatoichi was considered a non-person and, therefore, it would have been legal for any samurai to cut him down just for kicks. His non-entity status also meant that he was not allowed to carry a *katana* (samurai sword). Instead, he carried a formidable sword hidden in his humble walking cane. When he whipped the sword out, he wielded it using a reverse grip (like

when one holds a dagger and uses it to stab downward). With a cane sword as a sharp as his remaining senses, Zatoichi was not as blind as others might have thought. For a man who lost his sight, he had a lot of vision.

Actor Shintaro Katsu appeared as Zatoichi in 26 films between 1962 and 1989. Six of those films were made in the 1970s. In sticking with Kurosawa's action blueprint, each film barely averaged seven minutes of fighting. The largest amount of fighting occurs in *Zatoichi and the One-Armed Swordsman*, and most of that action stemmed from Jimmy Wong Yu's involvement. Also, due to Kurosawa's importance in the chambara genre, it is appropriate that one of Kurosawa's greatest actors, Toshiro Mifune, appeared as one of Kurosawa's most famous chambara characters in the first of these 1970s films: a *yojimbo*, which literally means "bodyguard." Like all the Zatoichi films, *Zatoichi Meets Yojimbo* is a stand-alone story.

This film opens with several thugs running through a field during pouring rain. Zatoichi kills two of the baddies, but his sword breaks, forcing him to find a swordsmith in a familiar village. But things aren't as tranquil as Zatoichi assumes. The Yakuza boss Masagoro, who is the son of "nicer" Yakuza boss Ya-suke Eboshiya, offers yojimbo Sassa Daisakka (Toshiro Mifune) 100 ryos of gold for Zatoichi's head on a silver platter. Zatoichi often has run-ins with Yakuza, so it is not uncommon for them to want him dead. But during their initial encounter, the yojimbo is flabbergasted by how well Zatoichi wields his steel blade. Eventually, he learns that his blind adversary is a righteous, honorable and trustworthy man, totally worth his metal. However, Masagoro is a suspect in the theft of shogunate gold, and Sassa is actually a spy sent by the shogun to find it. Adding to the mix is Eboshiya's other son, the famous 9-Headed Dragon Kuzuryu, who arrives in town under the guise of protecting his father but whose real goal is to find the gold. As the three lead their family tree toward sure destruction, the yojimbo and Zatoichi agree to work together to find the missing gold before everything becomes dust in the wind.

What is positive about this film's fights is that they are shot with good light. Many Zatoichi films feature night fights or other fights in the dark. The purpose of this cinematic decision was to create a blind feeling for the audience. In fact, Zatoichi would often cut candles to even the playing field. This film also features a classic fight sequence that appears in many samurai pictures: A character, usually the hero, runs through a group of samurai warriors and hacks them down with as few strokes as possible in one unedited shot. In this film, it is one of the villains who hacks down five men with four strokes in five seconds. Talk about a stroke of bad luck for those guys.

Japan's most influential filmmaker, Akira Kurosawa, is rightly considered the father of chambara. Because Kurosawa emphasized character development over action, his films had few samurai sword fights, and when they occurred, they were short and consisted of a series of quick slices and blood spurts. There were several reasons for this: His films were about the spirit of *bushido* rather than the action, and the short fights fit the notion that a real fight would be similarly brutal and quick. During action scenes, actors like Toshiro Mifune, Tatsuya Nakadai and Katsu relied on posing, stances and intense glares to make the fights more emotional. This focus on emotion is also why the actors' technical use of the sword is the same from movie to movie—they draw their sword, slice, cut and stab, then pause emotionally before putting it away. Samurai films would generally feature less than 10 minutes of action per movie. This set them apart from Chinese kung fu films, which placed a more important role on the fights. By setting this standard for fight choreography, it gave the genre an incredible amount of space to grow, that growth being directly related to the on-screen time devoted to sword fights and action. The whole irony is that because he was Kurosawa, filmmakers followed his lead, and in terms of on-screen fight time, nothing changed.

Hong Kong was churning out tons of films each year (up to 500 during the 1950s). That could tap into China's incredibly rich cultural martial arts history and heritage. This required Chinese choreographers to have a wide knowledge of martial arts and weapons. In Japan, however, while there are many differing styles of swordplay, they all tend to look the same to the average viewer. So samurai film choreographers only worried about simple sword and *naginata* (a spear-like weapon) fighting; trying to have the audience recognize each style of fencing was not the goal. Thus fights in Japanese films tended to look the same, which makes the notion of having few fights and keeping them short an extremely smart move on the part of the filmmakers. Many swordfights are over in seconds, which requires minimal choreography but maximum impact, so the lead-up to a fight can take a long time to create the impression of a long action sequence. If an audience is used to few fights being the norm, then there is not an expectation for more. Also, it saves the studios money. In terms of shooting, samurai fights are easier to set up and block because they are less complex and require the actors to memorize fewer movements per camera shot.

Of noteworthy interest, before and during World War II in Japan, *kendo* was a required course in school, and instructors used it to encourage the fighting spirit and instill a sense of national pride in students based on Japan's samurai warrior past. Many of the samurai film actors during the golden age of Japanese cinema were already well-trained in kendo and the art of samurai swordplay. Therefore, most samurai actors already had a knack for the sword. It was now just about the actor putting that look of the sword onto film. Actors like Toshiro Mifune, Shintaro Katsu, Tatsuya Nakadai, Tomisaburo Wakayama and Raizo Ishikawa had both.

Titleography: *Zatôichi 20*; *Zatoichi vs. Yojimbo*. Translation—*Zatoichi and Yojimbo*. **MA Percentage: 6.19%**

THE BEST 20 MARTIAL ARTS FILMS OF THE 1970S BEFORE AND AFTER THE BOOK WAS WRITTEN

Note: For the "Best" films listed for "After the Book," the best does not always imply that they have the best fight scenes but that there is something very special in the movies that really stuck with me. (See the Preface.)

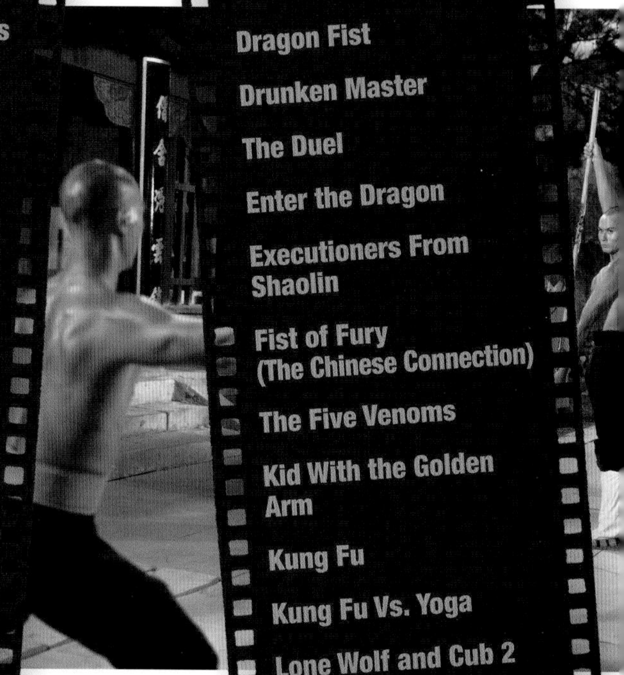

AFTER

The Avenger

Big Land Flying Eagles

Black Tavern

Brothers Five

Chinese Iron Man

Defensive Power of Aikido

Drunken Master

Executioner From Shaolin

Fist of Fury (The Chinese Connection)

The Fists of Vengeance

The Gallant

Karate for Life

Kung Fu Vs. Yoga

Mantis Fists and Tiger Claws of Kung Fu

Secrets of Chinese Kung Fu

The Seven Grandmasters

Snake in the Eagle's Shadow

The Pacific Connection

The 36th Chamber of Shaolin

The Tongfather

BEFORE

The Big Boss (Fists of Fury)

Billy Jack

Born Invincible

Buddhist Fist

Clan of the White Lotus

Dragon Fist

Drunken Master

The Duel

Enter the Dragon

Executioners From Shaolin

Fist of Fury (The Chinese Connection)

The Five Venoms

Kid With the Golden Arm

Kung Fu

Kung Fu Vs. Yoga

Lone Wolf and Cub 2

Snake in the Eagle's Shadow

The 36th Chamber of Shaolin

Warriors Two

The Thought of Bruce Lee's Game of Death

INDEX OF TALENT ALIASES

Please see "Rules of the Name 2" in the KEY TO THE MARTIALOGIES section for an explanation about the formatting used for the aliases. If you see a name that looks misspelled, it probably is. When Chinese actors are credited in romanized English, the names are spelled differently based on which romanization is used. Sometimes whoever writes the romanized names spells them incorrectly, thus crediting the actor with a misspelled name, which creates a "new" English romanized name for the actor. For example:

Sun Lan: Suen Lam / Suen Laam / Sum Nam / Sung Lam / Sun Luan / Sun Lna / Sun Nan. Sun Lna should be Sun Lan, but because it appeared as Sun Lna in one of his films, it is now one of his alternative names. Another example: **Jiang Ming:** Kong Ming / Kiang Ming / Kiavg Ming.

Obviously, Kiavg Ming is misspelled in romanization.

Sometimes an actor's nickname or character name appears in the credits. Liang Chia-jen has been dubbed Beardy in the credits of an alternative title of one of his films, thus it is on his list of alternative names. Furthermore, although many Chinese actors have English names, distributors created some names without the actor's knowledge, such as "Corey" and "Kara" in Corey Yuen Kwei and Kara Hui Ying-hong, respectively. Even the character name Bolo for actor Yeung Tze (listed as Yeung, Bolo) has become Yeung's most recognized name, so it is now his "real" name. Other circumstances in which names pop up for whatever reason abound, but I am sure you get the gist of things.

Names are listed surname first, given names second.

A: Actor; **AT:** Actress; **D:** Director; **F:** Fight Choreographer. The talent's listing is only based on their work during the 1970s.

Ai Fei: Ngaai Fei / Ai Ti. **A**

Au-Yeung Jun. Ulysses: Ou Yang-jun. **D, A**

Ba Shan: Ang Saan / Anthony Pa San / Leung Tung / Ba San / Anthony Leung / Bar San / Bar Shan. **AT**

Bachchan, Amitabh: Amitabh Harivansh Srivastav. **A**

Bae Su-cheon: Pooi Sau-chin / Pei Shou-qian / Pooi Sau-chin / Bae Sun-cheon. **A**

Bai Biao: Pai Piao / Jason Pai Piao / Baak Biu / Pia Piao / Pak Piu / Pai Piau / Pak Biao / Pak Bill / Jason Pai Piow. **A, F**

Bai Ying: Pai Ying / Baak Ying / Baak Ying-git / Pak Ying / Y. Pe / Bae Ying / Pai Ing / Bair Ing. **A, F**

Baker, Robert: Bob Baker. **A**

Bao Fang: Baau Fong / Pao Fong / Pau Fong / Bow Fong / Fong Pao / Pau Jihuan **A, D**

Bei Di: Betty Tei Pei / Betty Pei Ti / Booi Dai / Pei Dee / Betty Pei / Betty Pei Ti / Booi Dai / Han Bai-chou / Pei Ti. **AT**

Bell, Jeannie: Jeanie Bell / Jeanne Bell / Jean Bell. **AT**

Ban Run-sheng: Baan Yun-sang / Baan Ma-chai / Zebra Pan / Pang Yuen-sang / Pan Yung-sheng / Ban Yueng-san. **A**

Cai Fu-gui: Choi Foo-gwai / Tsai Fu-kwei. **A**

Cai Hong: Choi Wang / Tsai Hung / Choi Hung / Tsai Houng / Teai Hung / Tsai Hon / Glenn Choi / Choi Yue. **A**

Cai Zhong-qiu: Choi Chung-chau / Tsoi Chung-chow / Choi Chung-chao. **A**

Canavarro, Bobby: Bobby Ming / Ka Wa / Ga Hua. **A**

Carradine, David: Dave Carradine. **A**

Ceng Chao: Tsang Chiu / Chang Chiu / Tsang Chi / Tsang Chao / Cheng Chao. **A**

Chan, Barry: Wai Ji-Wan / Wei Zi-yun / Wei Tze-yung / Wai Chi-wan / Hwai Zi-yuen / Wai Tze-wen / Cheung Hang / Zhang Heng / Wei Tzi-yung / Wai Tzu-yun / Wei Tzu-yun. **A**

Chan Chan-wa. **A, F**

Chan Chue: Chen Tzer / Chen Chih / Chen Cho. **D**

Chan Chuen: Chen Quan / Chen Chuan / Chan Cheun / Chen Chuen / K. C. Chan / Chan Chun. **A, F, D**

Chan Chun, Richard: Chan Chun / Chen Jun / Chen Chun. **A**

Chan, Jackie: Sing Lung / Cheng Long / Chen Yuen-lung / Chan Kong-sang / Chen Yuan-lung / Cheng Lung / Fang Shi-long / Sing Lung / Jacky Chan / Jackie Chen / Chen Wen-lung / Chan Yuen-lung. **A, F, D**

Chan, Michael: Michael Chan Wai-man / Chan Wai-man / Chen Hui-min / Bruce Chen / Raymond Chan / Chen Hui-ming / Charlie Chan / Chen Huey-miin / Weiman Chan / Chen Wei-man / M. Chan / Chen Wei-min / Chan Wai-mang. **A, F**

Chan Lung, Peter: Chan Lung / Chen Long / Chen Lung. **A, F**

Chan Sau-chung. A, F

Chan Shen: Chim Sam / Zhan Sen / Jim Sum / Chan Yi-cheng / Chan Sheng / Chan Cheng / Zhan Sen. **A**

Chang Cheh: Zhang Che / Cheung Chit / Cheung Kit / Chang Che / Chang Cheuh / Chang Chueh / Chang Yik Yan / Chin Chien / Cheh Chiang. **D**

Chang Il-sik: Bruce Cheung Mong / Cheung Mong / Zhang Mang / Chang Mang. **A**

Chang Chung, Paul: Cheung Chung / Zhang Chong / Cheung Chung / Cheung Chown / Chang Chung. **A, D**

Chang Pei-shan: Cheung Pooi-saan / Zhang Pei-shan / Cheung Pi-shan. **A**

Chang Pin: Cheung Ban / Zhang Bin / Chang Zhen-wu. **A**

Chang Tseng-chai: Cheung Chang-chak / Zhang Zengse / Chang Tseng-chai / Chang Tsung-che. **D**

Chen Bi-feng: Chan Bik-fung / Chen Pi-Feng / Chen Bi-feng. **AT**

Chen Chien-po: Sham Chin-bo / Sam Chim-boh / Cen Qian-po / Sham Tsim-Po / Po Chai. **A, F**

Chen Ching, Lily: Chan Jing / Chen Jing / Chan Ching. **AT**

Chen Di-ke: Chan Dik-hak / Chan Shing-gwok / Chen Ti-ko / Chan Tik-hak / Chen Ti-ke. **A**

Chen Feng-chen: Chen Feng-zhen / Chan Fung-chan / Jin Bong-jin. **A**

Chen Hong-lieh: Chen Hung-lie / Chan Hung-lit / Golden Chen Hung-lieh / Chen Hon-lei / Chan Hung-lik. **A**

Chen Hong-min: Chan Hung-man / Chen Hung-min / Chen Hung-man / Cheng Hung-min / Chen Hon-ming / Chen Hung-men / Chen Hsiung-min. **D**

Chen Hsiao-hao: Chin Siu-ho / Qian Xiao-hao / Chen Hsiao-hao / Chien Hsiao-hao / Chin Siu-hao. **A**

Chen Hsing: Chan Sing / Chen Xing / Chen Sing / Chen Shing / Chen Hsing / Chen Shen / Chan Xing / Chen Xing / Cheng Sheng / Cheng Shing / Chan Sheng. **A, F**

Chen Hui-lou: Chan Wai-lau / Chen Hui-lou / Chen Wai-lau / Chen Wei-lo / Chen Hui-lui / Cheng Hwei-lou. **A**

Chen Hui-yi: Billy Chan Wui-ngai / Chan Kooi-ngai / Chan Kooi-aau / Ah B / Chan Wai-yee / Chan Wu-ngar / Bee Chan / Chan Ngai / B. Chan / Chan Fu-yee / Chan Wui-kan. **A, F**

Chen Jin-han: Chan Gam-hon. **A**

Chen Jih-liang: Yan Yat-leung. **F**

Chen Kuan-tai: Chen Guan-tai / Chan Goon-taai / Chan Goon-tai / Chen Kwan-tai / Chan Koon-tai / Chan Kuan-tai / Chen Kung-tai / Ah-Tai / Chen Guan-tay, Chan Kun-tai. **A, F, D**

Chen Liang: Chan Leung. **A**

Chen Lieh: Chen Hong-lie / Chan Hung-Lit / Chan Hung-Lit / Golden Chen Hung-Lieh / Chen Hon-Lei / Chan Hung-Lik / Chen Hong-lie / Chen Hong Lieh. **A**

Chen Ling-wei: Chan Ling-wai. **A, F**

Chen Lou: Chan Lau / Chen Liu / Chan Liu / Chan Bo-tak / Peter Chan. **A**

Chen Mu-chuan: Chan Muk-chuen. **A, F**

Chen Ping: Cheng Ping / Chan Ping. **AT**

Chen Qi-qi: JoJo Chan Kei-kei / Chan Kei-kei / Chan Chi-chi / Jo Jo Chan. **AT**

Chen Sen-lin: Chan Sam-lam / Chan Dan. **A**

Chen Sha-li: Sally Chen Sha-Li / Chan Qui-lee / Chan Qui-lee / Shirley Chen / Chen So-li / Cheng Sa-li. **AT**

Chen Shao-peng: Chan Siu-pang / Chan Siu-paang / Chan Shiu-peng / Chen Shu-pang / Chan Siu-tang / S. P. Chan. **A, F, D**

Chen Shen-yi: Chan San-yat / Chen Hsin-i / Chan Tin-tai / Siu Ying-go / Hsiao Ying-ko / Siao Ying-go / Hsiao Ying-ke / Chen Hsin-ie, / Chan Chan. **A, F**

Chen Shih-wei: Chan Sai-wai / Chen Shi-wei / Chan Sai-Wai. **F, A**

Chen Si-jia: Chan Si-Gaai / Chen Szu-chia. **AT**

Chen Yan-yan: Chan Yin-yin / Chan Yan-yan / Chen Yen-Yen. **A**

Chen Yao-lin, Charlie: Charlie Chan Yiu-lam / Chan Yiu-lam / Chen Yao-lin. **A**

Chen You-xin: Chan Yau-san / Chen You-hsin / Chan Yat-san / Chen Yu-hsin / Chen E-hsin. **A, D**

Chen Zhi-hua: Chen Chi-hwa / Chan Jeung-wa / Chen Zhi-hua / Chan Jeung-wa / Chen Chih-hua / Chen Che-hwa / Chan Chi-wah / Chen Jyh-hwa / Chi Chi-hwa / Chen Chih-hu / Charlie Chen. **D, A**

Cheng Chang-ho: Jeng Cheong-who / Jeong Chang-hwa / Chung Chang-wha / Chang Chang-ho / Cheng Chang-wha / Chung Chang-hwa / Chung Chang-haw. **D**

Cheng Kang: Ching Gong / Cheng Gang / Chin Kong / Ching Kong / Cheng Gang. **D**

Cheng Kang-yeh: Jeng Hong-yip / Zheng Kang-ye / Cheng Hong-yip / Alan Cheng / Cheng Kang-yip / Jocky Cheng. **A**

Cheng Kei-ying: Jeng Kei-ying / Zheng Qi-ying / Jeng Kei-ying / Cheng Chi-ying / Tommy Cheng / Cheng Kei / Cheng Ki-ying / Keith Cheng. **D**

Cheng Lei: Cheng Lui / Jeng Lui / Zheng Lei. **A**

Cheng Pei-pei: Jeng Pooi-pooi / Zheng Pei-pei / Cheng Pui-Pui / Betty Cheng / Regina Yuan. **AT**

Cheng Tien-chi, Ricky: Chien Tien-chi / Ching Tin-tsz / Cheng Tien-tzu / Ching Tin-chi / Chin Tien-chi / Shing Tien-che. **A, F**

Cheung Ching-ching: Chang Ching-ching / Zhang Qing-qing. **AT**

Cheung, John: John Cheung Ng-long / Cheung Ng-long / Zhang Wu-lang / John Chang / Chang Wu-lang / Cheung Wu-long. **A, F**

Cheung Lik: Zhang Li / Nick Cheung / Wai Lung / Cheong Lieh / Chang Lee / Chang Li / Chang Lieh. **A, F**

Cheung Ling, Pearl: Pearl Chang / Chang Ling / Chang Lin / Pearl Zhang Ling / Zhang Ling. **AT**

Cheung Tung-cho, Joe: Cheung Tung-jo / Zhang Tong-zu / Joe Cheung / Cheung Tung-joe / Cheung Tung-jo / Joseph Cheung / Chang Tung-jo / Cheung Ton-cho. **D**

Chi Kuan-chun: Qi Guan-jun / Chik Goon-gwan / Chi Kuan-chung / Chik Goon-gwan / Chi Kuan-jiun / Chik Kun-kwan / Chi Kian-chun / Chi Kuan-chan. **A, D**

Chia Ling: Ga Ling / Jia Ling / Ga Ling / Judy Lee / Judy Lei / Kar Ling / Chia Ning. **AT**

Chiang Cheng: Kong Jing / Jiang Zheng / Kong Ching / Kong Kwok-keung / Kong Keung. **A**

Chiang, David: David Chiang Da-wei / Geung Daai-wai / Jiang Da-wei / Chiang Da-wei / John Keung / John Chiang / John Chang / John Kiang / Keung Tai-Wai / Yan Wei / Keung Dai-wai / Garth Lo / Chiang Ta-wei / Yen Wei. **A, D**

Chiang Ming: Kong Ming / Kiang Ming / Jiang Ming.

Chiang Sheng: Jiang Sheng / Kong Sang / Chiu Gong-sang / Chao Gang-sheng / Chao Kang-Sheng / Chiang Shang / Chiu Kang-seng / Kwong Sang / Chian g Sheng / Chao Kon-sen. **A, F**

Chiao Chiao: Lisa Chiao Chiao / Chiu Gaau / Jiao Jiao / Chiu Kao / Lina Chiao / Jiu Kau / Gloria Chel / Tsiu Kau. **AT**

Chiao Hung, Roy: Kiu Wang / Qiao Hong / Kiu Wang / Chiao Hung. **A**

Chiba, Sonny: Sonny Chiba Shinichi / Shin'ichi Chiba / Shinici Chiba / Sonny J. J. Chiba / Sony Chiba / Rindo Wachinaga / Qian Ye Zhen Yi / Chin Yip Chan Yat / Sadaho Maeda. **A**

Chien Yueh-sheng: Chin Yuet-Sang / Qian Yue-sheng / Tom Chin / Chen Yue-sang / Chen Yiet-san / Chin Yuet-sun / Chien Yu-Sheng / Chin Yuet-san / **A, F, D**

Chin Chiang-lin, Charlie: Chun Cheung-lam / Qin Xiang-lin / Chin Hsiang-lin / Charlie Ching / Ching Hsiang-lin. **A**

Chin Chun: Gam Gwan / Jin Jun / Kam Kwan. **A**

Chin Feng: Gam Fung / Jin Feng / Kam Fung / Gam Fung / King Feng. **A**

Chin Han: Gam Hon / Jin Han / Kam Hon / King Han / Bi Ren-xu. **A**

Chin Fei, Tina: Gam Fei / Jin Fei. **AT**

Chin Lung: Gam Lung / Jin Long / Chu Din-miu. **A, F**

Chin Meng: Chun Mung / Qin Meng. **AT**

Ching Ching, Cliff: Ching Ching / Cheng Qing / Ching Chen. **A**

Ching Li: Cheng Lee / Jing Li. **AT**

Ching Miao: Cheng Miu / Jing Miao / Tsen Miao / Tseng Miao. **A**

Chiu Chun: Zhao Chun / Cho Chun. **A**

Cho Kin: Cao Jian / Tsao Chien / Tso Kin / Cho Gin / Chou Kin / Tsao Chin. **A**

Choi Chuk-guen: Sai Zhu-juan / Sarina Sai. **AT**

Chong, Billy: Billy Zhuang Quan-li / Billy Chong Chuen-lei / Chong Chuen-lei / Willy Dohzan / Willy Doxan. **A**

Chong, Elton: Jeng Chan-dut / Zheng Zhen-hua / Jeong Jin-hwa / Elton Wong. **A**

Chow A-Chi, Artis: Chow A-ji / Zou Ya-zi / Chou Ya-tsu / Tzou Ya-tzu. **D**

Chu Chi-ling: Chiu Chi-ling / Zhao Zhi-ling / Chiu Chi-ling / Chau Chi-ling. **A**

Chu Yuan: Chor Yuen / Choh Yuen / Chi Yau / Chun Yue / Chin Yu / Cho Yuan / Chor Yun. **D**

Chuan Yuan: Chuen Yuen / Hong Ga / Kang Chia / Chuan Yun. **A**

Chui Fat: Chui Faat / Xu Fa / Tsui Fat / Chang Yu / Cheung Yau / Chui Yau / Chui Siu-hung. **A, F**

Chui Man-fooi, Martin: Chui Man-fooi / Cui Min-kui / Choi Min-kyu / Tsui Wen-kuei / Chui Man-kwai / Marty Chiu / Marty Chui. **A, F**

Chung Faat: Zhong Fa / Chung Fa / Chung Fat. **A**

Clouse, Robert: Go Lok-shut / Gao Luo-si. **D**

Cord, Erik: Eric Cord. **A, F**

Cui Fu-sheng: Chui Fook-sang / Tsui Fu-sheng / Tsui Fo-sheng / Chui Fu-shen / Chui Fox-sang / Chu Fook-san. **A**

Cui Min-kui: Martin Chui Man-fooi / Chui Man-fooi / Choi Min-kyu / Tsui Wen-kuei / Chui Man-kwai / Marty Chiu / Marty Chui / Jim Choi. **A, F**

Dai Liang: Tai Leung / Daai Leung / Day Liang / Tai Liang. **A**

Da Xi-yan: Dai Sai-aan / Big Little Eye / Ta Hsi-yen / Sung Gam-shing / Sung Lai / Tai Siu-un / Ta Sei-en / Sung Kam-sing / Addy Sung. **A, F**

Dana: Daan Loh / Dan Na / Tsen Shu-yi / Sam Suk-yee / Cen Shu-yi / Dana Tsen / Danna / Shum Shuk-yee. **AT**

Deng De-xiang: Dang Tak-cheung / Tang Tak-cheung / Teng Te-hsiang / Teng Tak-tseung / Dang Wai-kuen / Teddy Deng / Tang Te-hsiang. **A, F**

Deng Guang-rong: Alan Tang Kwong-wing / Dang Gwong-wing / Alan K.W. Tang. **A, D**

Di Nuo: Chai No / Chak Lok. **A**

Dik Wei: Dik Wai / Dick Wei / Tu Lung / Tsu Chi-lung / Tiu Lung / Tao Lung / De Wai / Tu Chi-lung / Ti Wai / Dei Wei / Dyi Wei / C. L. Tu / Tao Chi-lung / Tu Ji-long / Chui Gat-lung / Di Wei. **A**

Ding Chong: Ting Chung / Ding Chung. **A, D**

Ding Hua-chong: Ding Wa-chung / Ting Wa-lung / Ting Hua-chung / Ting Hwa-chung. **A**

Ding Shan-xi: Ting Shan-his / Ding Sin-saai / Ting Shan-si / Tung Shan-si / Ting Sing-si / Ting San-see / Tin Sin-si / David Ting / Ting Hsien-hsia / Ting Shan-hsien / Dang Seu-sai / Ding Sin-sai / Ting San-shi. **D**

Dobson, Tamara: Tamara. **AT**

Dong Cai-bao: Tung Choi-bo / Dung Choi-bo / Tung Tsai-pao. **A**

Dong Jin-hu: Dung Gam-woo / Tung Kan-wu / Richard Tung Chin-hu / Dong Jan-woo. **D, A**

Dong Wei: Stephen Tung Wai / Dung Wai / Stephen Tung / Tung Wei / Tung Yun-wei / W. W. Tung / Wong Wai-Wan. **A, F**

Du Shao-ming: To Siu-ming / Do Siu-ming / Tu Shiao-ming / To Shiao-ming. **A**

Du Wei-her: To Wai-wo / Do Wai-who / Du Wei-her / Tu Wei-ho. **A, F**

Etsuko Shihomi: Sue Shihomi. **AT**

Fan Dan-fung: Faan Daan-fung / Fan Dan-feng / Fan Tang-fong. **AT**

Fan Mei-sheng: Faan Mooi Sang / Fan Mui-Sang / Fan Mui-sheng / Fang Mui-san / Fan Mui-sung. **A, D**

Fang Fang: Fong Fong. **AT**

Fang Long-xiang: Fong Lung-seung / Fang Loong-hsiang / Fang Long-shiang / Fang Long-hsiang. **D**

Fang Mian: Fong Min / Fang Mien / Fong Min. **A**

Fang Ye: Fong Yau / Fang Yeh / Fong Yei / Fun Yie / Fang Yen / Fong Yeh / Fong Yam. **A, F, D**

Fang Ying: Fong Ying / Ngai Fong-nay. **AT**

Feng Jing-wen: Fung Ging-man / Feng Ching-wen / Fung King-man. **A**

Feng Yi: Fung Ngai / Feng I / Fung Yien. **A**

Fong Ching: Fong Jing / Fang Zheng / Fang Jung. **A**

Fu Ching-wa: Fu Jing-wa. **D**

Fuji Junko: Sumiko Fuji / Junko Terashima. **A**

Fujita Toshiya: Fujita Shigaya. **D**

Fu Sheng, Alexander: Fu Shen / Foo Sing / Cheung Fu-sheng. **A**

Fung Ke-an: Fung Hak-on / Fung Hak-on / Feng Ke-an / Feng Ko-an / Fung Hark-on / Fung Yuen / Fung Ku-on / Fung Kin. **A, F**

Fung Sui-fan, Stanley: Fung Sui-faan / Feng Cui-fan / Feng Tsui-fan / Fung Tsui-feng / Fung Tsui-fan / Fung Tsiu-fan / Fong Sue-fan / Feng Shui-fan / Fung Sui-fann / Fong Chu-fang / Fung Shiu-fan / Fung Shu-fan / Fung Shiu-kan. **A**

Gao Bao-shu: Kao Pao-shu / Go Bo-shu / Kao Pau-shiu. **AT, D**

Gao Chiang: Ko Keung / Kao Chin / Go Keung / Kao Chiang / Miu Si-shing / Mo Sa-seong / Roger Mao / Richard Kao. **A**

Gao Fei: Phillip Ko Fei / Go Fei / Ko Fei / Philip Ko / Phillip Kao / Ko Fai / Kao Fei / Ko Fei-lap / Ko Fee / Philip Kau / Ko Kwan / Phillip Koh. **A, F**

Gao Gang: Thompson Kao Kang / Go Gong / Ko Kong / Thomson Kao Kan. **A**

Gao Li: Gao Lap / Gou Laap / Kao Li. **D**

Gao Ming: Go Ming / Kao Ming / Go Fung. **A**

Gao Yuan: Kao Yuen / Ko Yuen / Kao Yuan / Kao Yung / Jiang Jia-qi / Kaw Yeong. **A**

Gao Zhen-peng: Ko Jan-pang / Go Jan-paang / Kao Cheng-peng. **A**

Gam Fook-man: Gam Fook-maan / Jin Fu-wan / Chin Fu-wan / Chin Fook-wang. **A, F**

Gan De-men: Kon Tak-mun / Gon Tak-moon / Chen Ti-men / Kon Tak-moon / Chien Tak-mun. **A, F**

Ge Pao: Ko Pao / Got Baau / Got Pau / Joseph Kuo / Got Hiu-chung. **A**

Griffith, James: Jim Griffith. **A**

Gu Guan-zhong: Goo Goon-chung / Ku Kuan-chung / Koo Kwan-chung / Ku Kung-chung / Guh Guan-jong / Gu Kwoon-ching. **A**

Gu Wen-zong: Goo Man-chung / Ku Wen-chung / Ku Wen-tsung / Ku Wan-chung / Koo Man-Chung / Ku Un-chung. **A**

Gu Zheng: Goo Chang / Goo Chang / Ku Jeng. **A**

Guan Cong: Kwan Chung / Gwaan Chung / Kuang Chorng. **A**

Guan Feng: Kwan Fung / Gwaan Fung / Kuan Feng / Guan Dong / Kwan Tung. **A**

Guan Hong: Kwan Hung / Gwaan Hung / Koun Hong / Robert Kwan / Kwan Tak-hung. **A**

Guan Shan: Gwaan Saan / Kwan San / Kwan Shan / Kuan Shan. **A, D**

Guan Zheng-liang: Gwan Jing-leung / Gwaan Jeng-leung / Kwan Ching-leung / Gwaan Jing-leung / Kwan Ching-liang. **A, F, D**

Guo Wu-xing: Kwak Mu-seong / Gwok Miu-sing / Tony Kwok / Kwok Miu-Sing / Alain Ko / Kwok Chung-sit / Kuo Wu-Sing. **A**

Guo Xiao-zhuang: Gwok Siu-chong / Kuo Shu-chuan / Kok Shie-jong. **AT**

Ha Ping, Teresa: Ha Ping / Xia Ping / Hsia Ping / Teresa Ha. **AT**

Han Hsiang-chin: Hon Seung-kam / Han Xiang-qin / Han Hsian-chin. **AT**

Han Kuo: Hon Gwok / Han Guo. **F**

Han Myeong-hwan: Hon Ming-woon / Han Ming-huan. **A**

Han Su: Hon Siu / Han So / Hon So. **A**

Han Yi-sheng: Hon Yee-sang / Hon Yee-san / Hon Ye-sang. **A, F**

Han Ying: Hon Ying / Eagle Han Ying / Kim Young-ll / Gam Ying-yat / Chin Ying-I / Charlie Hyun. **A, F**

Han Ying-chieh: Hon Ying-git / Han Ying-jang / Han Yin-jen / Han Ying-kit / Han Ying-jie. **A, F, D**

Harada Riki: Takeshi Yamamoto / Yakeshi Yamamoto. **A**

Hao Lu-ren: Hao Li-jen / Kok Lee-yan / Kok Lee-yan / Ho Lee-yan / Ho Li-jei. **A**

Hau Chang: Hou Zheng / Ho Chang / Hou Cheng / Hou Tseng / Hou Ching. **D**

He Ming-xiao: Ho Ming-hiu / Hoh Ming-hiu / Her Ming-shiao / Ho Ming-hsiao. **A, D**

Heung Wah-keung, Charles: Heung Wa-keung / Xiang Hua-jiang / Shiang Hwa-chiang / Charles W. K. Heung / Hsiang Hwa-chiang. **A**

Ho Fan: Hoh Faan / He Fan. **A, D**

Ho, Godfrey: Godfrey Ho Jeung-keung / Hoh Jun-sing / Wallace Chan / Ho Jang-cheon / Alton Cheung / Tommy Cheung / Ho Chi-chiang / Ho Chi-keung / Ho Chieh-chiang I Ho Chih-ciang / Daniel Clough / Antonin Gasner / Martin Greenfield / Godfrey Hall / Zhi Jiang-he / Benny Ho / Chi-Mou-ho / Ho Chun-sing / Fong Ho / Larry Hutton / Godfrey Ho Chi-kung / Ho Chih-kuang / York Lam / Bruce Lambert / Charles Lee / Frank Lewis / Jerry Sawyer / Victor Sears / Felix Tong / Robert Young / Albert Yu. **D**

Ho, Lily: Lily Ho Li-li / Hoh Lee-lee / He Li-li / Ho Lee-lee. **AT**

Ho Meng-hua: Her Mung-hua / Hoh Mung-wa / Ho Meng-ga / Homer Gaugh / Horace Mengwa. **D**

Ho Wai-hung: Hoh Wai-hung, He Wei-xiong, Ho Wei-hsiung. **A**

Hon Gwok-choi: Han Guo-cai / Korea Nation Village / Korean Village / Han Kuo-tsai / Hon Kwok-choi / Hon Kok-choi / Han Kwok-choi / Han Guo-cai. **A, F**

Hong Hua-lang: Hung Fa-long / Hung Dut-long / Hung Hwa-lang. **A**

Hong Liu: Hung Lau. **A**

Hong Xing-zhong: Hung Sing-chung / Hung Hsing-chung / Hung Shin-chung / Hun Hsin-chung. **A**

Horan, Roy: Lu Yi-shi. **A**

Hou Ba-wei: Hau Pak-wai / Hau Ang-wai / Hou Po-wei / Ho Bou-wei / Hau Park-wai. **A, F**

Hou Chao-sheng: Hau Chiu-sing / Hau Sau-seng / Hou Chao-sheng. **A**

Hsia Fang: Ha Faan / Chen Rong-mei. **AT**

Hsiao Ho: Siu Hau / Xiao Hou / Siu Hau / Hau Yiu-chung / Hau Chi-chung / Hsiao Hou / Xiao Hou. **A, F**

Hsieh Hsing: Che Hing / Xie Xing / Tse Hing. **A, F**

Hsing Hui, Margaret: Ying Wai / Xing Hui / Ying Wai / Mergaret Hsing Hui. **AT**

Hsu Alan: Alan Chui Chung-san / Chui Chung-san / Xu Zhong-shen / Alan Tsui Chun-sun / Choi Chung-san / Hsu Chung-sin / Tsui Chung-san / Tsui Chung-shun / Xu Zhong-xin / Chung San / Hsu Chung-hsin / Chui Kong-shinn / Chui Jong-shinn / Chu Chung-sen. **A, F**

Hsu Cheng-hung: Hsu Tseng-Hung / Chui Chang-wang / Xu Zeng-hong / Sui Jang-hung / Hsu Tsan-Hong / Zer Jun-hoon / Hsu Tsan-hon / Tsu Tsan-hong. **D**

Hsu Chin-liang: Chui Chun-leung / Xu Jin-liang / Chui Chun-leung / Tchii Ching-long. **D**

Hsu Feng: Chui Fung / Xu Feng / Tsui Fung / Xu Feng / Chu Feng / Chee Fung / Shu Feng / Hsu Fung / Shyu Feng. **AT**

Hsu Hsia: Chui Ha / Xu Xia / Chui Pak-lam / Xu Bo-lin / Tsui Ha / Hsu His. **A, F**

Hsu Tseng-hung: Chui Chang-wang / Xu Zeng-hong / Chui Chang-wang / Sui Jang-hung / Hsu Cheng-hung / Hsu Tsan-hong / Zer Jun-hoon. **D**

Hsu, Tyrone: Tyrone Hsu Tien-yung / Chui Tin-wing / Xu Tian-rong / Chu Tien-yun / Chi Tin-wing / Shu Tien-jung. **D, A**

Hu Jin: Woo Gam / Hu Chin / Hu Gin / Hu Jing. **AT**

Hu Wei: Woo Wai / Charlie Hu. **A**

Hu Yin-Yin, Ingrid: Woo Yan-yan / Hu Yin-yin / Fu In-in. **AT**

Hua Lun: Wa Lun / Hua Lin / Chan Tin-lun / Chen Tien-lun / Hwa Lun. **AT**

Hua Shan: Wah Bo-fat / Wah San / Wah Shan / Hwa San / Wa Saan. **A, D**

Huang Chong-kuang: Chester Wong Chung-Gwong / Wang Chung-kong / Wong Chung-kwong / Wang Chung-kuang / Wang Tsung-kwan. **A, D**

Huang Feng: Wong Fung / Hwang Feng / Wang Feng / Hung Feng. **A, D**

Huang Fei-long: Wong Fei-long / Wong Fei-lung / Wong Lung / Nam Siu-foo / Huang Fei-lung. **A, F, D**

Huang Guo-liang: Wong Kwok-leung / Wong Gwok-leung / Wan Lung. **A**

Huang Guo-zhu: Wong Gwok-chue / Huang Kuo-chu / Huang Kou-ju / Wong Kwok-tso. **A, F, D**

Huang Ha: Wong Gwong / Wang Hai / Wong Ha / Wong Hai / Wang Hsia / Wang Ha / Huang Hsia. **A, F**

Huang Han-jie: Huang Han-chieh / Wong Hon-git / Wong Hon-kit. **F**

Huang Hsing-hsiu, Cecilia: Cecilia Wong Hang-sau / Wong Hang-sau / Huang Xing-xiu. **AT**

Huang Jun: Wong Jun / Huang Chun. **A**

Huang Long: Wong Lung / Huang Lung. **A, D, F**

Huang Mei: Wong Mei / Wong Mooi / Wong Hung / Wong Ga-hung / Wong Mui / Wang Mei. **A**

Huang Pei-ji: Wong Pau-gei / Huang Pei-chih / Wang Pei-chi / Huang Pei-chi. **A, F**

Huang Wei-wei: Wong Mei-mei / Huang Mei-Mei. **AT**

Huang Xing-xiu: Cecilia Wong Hang-sau / Wong Hang-sau / Huang Hsing-hsiu. **AT**

Huang Yi-long: Wong Yat-lung / Huang I-lung / Wang I-lung / Wang Yi-lung / Wang Ye-lung. **A**

Huang Yuan-shen: Wong Yuen-san / Tony Wong / Wong Yuen-sung / Wang Yuen-sun. **A, D**

Hui Bat-liu: Hu Bu-le, Shiu Bu-lai. **A**

Hui Man-yu: Hui Man-yui / Hu Wen-rui / Luk Gwo / Liu Ge / Hu Wen-rui. **A**

Hui Tian-si: Austin Wai Tin-ci / Wai Tin-tsz / Hui Tien-chi / Siu Sei / Wei Tien-tzu / Hui Tien-sze / Jacky Yuen / Austin Wai. **A, F**

Hui Ying-hong: Kara Hui Ying-hung / Wai Ying-hung / Carol Wai / Hui Ya-hung / Wei Ying-hung. **AT**

Hung, Sammo: Hong Jin-bao / Hung Gam-bo / Sammo Hung Kam-bo / Samo Hung Kam-bo / Hung Ching-pao / Hung Chin-pao / Chu Yuen-lung / Chu Yuan-lung / Samo Hung Kam-po / Sammu Hung / Hong Kam-po / Hun Ching-pao. **A, F, D**

Hwang Jang-lee: Wong Jing-lei / Huang Zheng-li / Wong Ching-lee / Huang Cheng-li / Huong Cheng-li / Wong Ching-lei / Wang Chang-li / Wong Cheng-lee / Wang Cheng-li / Wang Jang-li / Wang Jia-le / Wang Jang-lee / Huang Tai-chu / Wang Chang-li / Silver Fox / Huang Jing-lee / Jason Hwang / Hwang Jeong-ri / Hwang Jeong-li / Wong Cheng-ll / Hwang Jeong-ri / Huang Jang-lee / Wan-Chung-lee / Wang Chang-lee / Wong Cheng-lee / Wong Cheng-li / Wong Chung-li / Wong Zheng-lieh / Wang Chin-li / Wang Ching-lee / Wang Ching-Li / Wong Cheng-li / Wong Cheung-li / Wong Tsing-lee. **A**

Hyeon Kil-Su: Yuen Gat-chue / Xuan Ji-zhu / Bob Yuen / Charlie Hyung / Charlie Hyun / Hyun Kill-soo. **A**

Jang Il-ho: Chang Yi-hu / Cheung Yat-Woo / Zhang Yi-hu. **D**

Jia Kai: Ga Hoi / Chai Kai / Chia Kai / Chen Chai-kai / Chan Ga-hoi / Chia Hai / Chan Kar-hoi / Gary Cho / Ka Hoi. **A, F**

Jiang Bin: Kong Ban / Ching Pin / Kung Bun / Chiang Pin / Jiang Bin. **A, D**

Jiang Dao: Kong Do / Chiang Tao / Chang Tao / Tony Kong / Kong Tao / Kong Tau / Kung Tau / Chiang Dao. **A**

Jiang Han: Keung Hon / Chiang Han / Wan Hei / Yin His. **A**

Jiang Jin: Chiang Kam / Cheung Gam / Chiang Chin. **A, F**

Jiang Ke-xin: Queenie Kong Hoh-yan / Kong Hoh-yan / Chiang Ko-hsing. **AT**

Jiang Long: Kong Lung / Kong Long / Chiang Lung. **A**

Jiang Ming: Kong Ming / Kiang Ming / Kiavg Ming. **A** (note: sometimes in a film the Chinese name is even mispealt in romanization, but that is the way the credit reads)

Jiang Nan: Chiang Nan / Geung Naam / Geung Nam / Keung Nam / Xiang Nam. **A**

Jiang Qing-xia: Kong Ching-ha / Chiang Ching-shia / Virginia Chiang / Chiang Ching-hsia / Kong Ching-hai / Chang Ching-ha. **AT**

Jiang Yang: Kong Yeung / Chiang Yang / Walter Kong Yang. **A**

Jie Yuan: Gai Yuen / Gaai Yuen / Che Yuen / Hsieh Yuan / Chieh Yuan / Jie Yuan / Tsze Yuen. **A, F**

Jin Feng-ling: Gam Fung-ling, Chin Feng-ling / Kam Fung-ling. **AT**

Jin Han: Chin Han / Gam Hon / Kam Hon / King Han / Bi Ren-Xu. **A**

Jin Gang: Kam Kong / Gam Gong / King Kong / Chin Kang / Kum Kong / Kam Kang. **A**

Jin Lou: Gam Lau / Chin Lu / Chin Lu-ming / Gam Lau-ming / Jin Lu. **AT**

Jin Sheng-en: Gam Sing-yan / Cheng Sheng-en / Tit Hon / Tien Han / Chin Chao-pai / Kam Chiu-pak. **A, D**

Jin Wan-xi: Gam Man-hei / Gam Maan-hei / Chin Wan-his / Kin Wan-see / Chin Wan-che. **A, F**

Jin Zheng-lan: Gam Ching-lan / Kim Jeong-ran / Kim Ching-lan / Kim Chin-lan. **AT**

Jing Guo-zhong: Ching Kuo-chung / Ging Gwok-chung / Yin Kwok-chung / Jin Gno-jong. **A**

Kaji Meiko: Ohta Masako. **AT**

Ke Jun-xiong: O Chun-hung / Oh Jun-hung / Ko Chun-hsiung / Ka Chuen-hsiung / Kuo Chuan-hsiung / Ko Tsun-hsiung / Koo Chuan-hsiung. **A, D**

Ke Shih-hao: Got Si-ho / Ger Shih-hou. **D**

Kei Ho-chiu: Qi Hao-zhao / Kei Gei / Kei Kei/ Howard Ki. **A**

Kelly, Jim: James Kelly. **A**

Kim, Bobby: Robert W. Kim / Ang Bei-gam / Gam Sing-lung. **A**

Kim Jeong-ran: Gam Ching-lan / Jin Zheng-lan / Kim Ching-lan / Sally Chan / Chen Sha-li. **AT**

Kim Kee-joo: Gam Kei-chu / Jin Qi- zhu / Chin Chi-chu / Kim Ji-joo / Kam Chi-ku / Kim Kee-chu. **A**

Kim Si-hyeon: Gam Shut-hin / Jin Shi-xian / Kao Ke / Liu Yueh-lin. **D**

Kim Tai-chung: Tong Lung / Tang Long / Kim Tai-jong / Tung Lung. A

King Hu: Woo Gam-chuen / Hu Jin-quan / Wu Kam-chuen / Frankie Gam Chuen / Hu King-chuan / King Chuan/ Hu Jing-chuan / Hu Chin-chuan / King Ho. **D**

Ko, Blacky: Blacky Ko Sau-leung / Oh Sau-leung / Ke1 Shou-liang / Yuan Lung / Siu Hak / Ko Shau-liang / Kou Shou-leung / Ko Shou-liang / Or Sau-leung / Darkie Kor / Blackie Ko / Cylon Or / O Sou-Leung. **A, F**

Ko, Eddy: Eddy Ko Hung / Go Hung / Gao Xiong / Kuo Hsiung / Eddie Ko / Lin Su / Lam Sam / Kuo Hung / Lin Sheng / Kao Hung/ Lin Sun. **A**

Kong Hung, Joseph: Kong Hung / Jiang Hong / Joseph Velasco / **D**

Ku Feng: Gu Feng / Kuk Fung / Chen Si-wen / Guk Fung / Gok Fung / Kok Fung / Ku Fang / Kuo Fung / Hu Feng / Guu Feng. **A**

Kuan, Polly: Seung Goon Leng Fung / Polly Shan Kwan / Polly Shang Kuan / Polly Shang Kuan Ling Feng / Polly Kwan / Polly Shang-Kwan Ling-Fong / Polly Shang Kwan Ling Feng / Polly Shian Kuan / Shan Kwan Ling Fung / Sun-Kuan Rin-Feng / Shang-Guan Ling-Feng / Shan-Kwon Ling-Fung / L. F. Shankuan / Shang-Kuan Ling-Fung. **AT**

Kuei Chih-hung: Gwai Chi-Hung / Gui Zhi-hong / Kuei Cheh-hung / Kwei Chi-hung / Siu Kwai / Kuei Chi-hung. **D**

Kuo Chue: Phillip Kwok **/** Guo Zhen-feng / Phillip Kwok Chun-fung / Guo Zui / Gwok Jan-fung / Kuo Chui / Philip Kwok / Jun Kwok / Kuo Chue / Kwok Tsu / Kuo Tsui / Kuo Chu / Guo Zui. **A, F**

Kuo, Joseph: Joseph Kuo Nan-hong / Gwok Naam-wang / Guo Nan-hong / Kao Non-hung / Kwok Nan-hung / Kuo Nan-hung / Joseph Poon / Kong Bing-ham / Chang Ping-han / P. S. Chiang / Chiang Ping-han. **D**

Kurata Yasuaki: Chong Tin Biu Chiu / Cang Tian Bao Zhao / Shoji Kurata / Bruce Lo / Shoji Karada / Akira Kurata / Chong Ti Bo-Chu / Chaua Tieng Pao Chao / Tung Choi-po / David Kurata / Y. Kurata / Yasuki Kurata / Yusaki Kurata / Yusuaki Kurata / / Tsang Tyan / Kurata Yoshiaki. **A**

Kurozawa Toshjo: Sin Lung / Qian Nong. **A**

Kwan Yung-moon: Kuen Wing-man / Quan Yong-wen / Kuan Yung-wen / Kuen Wing-man / Chuan Yung-wen / Kun Wing-man / Sam Kuen / Kwon Yeong-mun / Kuen Man-yung / Kwon Young-moon / Kwan Young-moon / Kuan Yung-Moon / Kwan Yung-Wun. **A**

Kwon Il-su: Kuen Yat-chu / Quan Yi1-zhu. **A**

Lam Ching-ying: Lam Jing-ying / Lin Zheng-ying / Lam Cheng-Ying / Lin Cheng-Ying / Park Chung-ying / Lim Chen-ying. **A, F**

Lam, Meg: Meg Lam Kin-ming / Lam Gin-ming / Lin Jian-ming / Lin Jian-min / Lum Ken-ming / Lin Chien-ming. **AT**

Lan Yu-li: Lily Lan Yu-li / Laam Yuk-lee / Nan Yu-li / Nam Yuk-lee. **AT**

Lau Tai-chuen: Lau Daai-chuen / Liu Ta-chuan. **A**

Law Ma, John: Law Ma / Luo Ma / Lo Mar / John Lomar / Law Chau-woo / Lo Chau-wu. **D**

Le, Bruce: Huang Chien-lung / Huang Kin-lung / Lu Xiao-long / Lui Siu-lung / Lui Siu-lung / Wong Kum-hung. **A, F, D**

Lee, Bruce: Li Xiao-long, Bruce Lee Siu-lung, Lee Lung, Little Dragon Lee, Yam Lee, Siu-lung Lee, Xiaolong Li, Lee Siu-lung, Lee Jun-fang. **A, F, D**

Lee Chiu: Li Chao / Li Zhao / Le Chao / Lee Ying-Chiu. **A**

Lee Chiu-jun, Max: See Foo-jai / Seefu Chai / Bye Foo-chai / Marloon Lee / Shi Fu-zi / She Fu-tsai / She Fe-tsai. **A, F, D**

Lee Chun-wa: Lee Chun-hwa, Lee Chung-wah. **A**

Lee, Danny: Li Hsiu-hsien / Li Hsiu-shien / Li Hsui-hsien / Danny Li Hsiu-hsien / Danny Li Sau-yin / Li Xiu-xian / Li Sau-yin / Danny Lee Sau-Yin / Lee Sau-yin / Lee Shou-hsien / Lee Hsiu-hsien / Lee Siu-yin / Danny S. Y. Lee. **A**

Lee, Dragon: Gui Lung / Ju Long / Gui Lung / Bruce Lei / Keo Ryong / Guh Ryong. **A**

Lee Goon-cheung: Li Kuang-tsang / Li Guan-jang / Li Kou- chang. **A, D**

Lee Gwan: Lee Kwan / Li Kun / Li Kuen / Li Chuan / Li Quin / Lee Quinn. **A**

Lee Hang: Lee Bing-hung / Nelson Lee / Li Heng. **A**

Lee Hoi-san: Li Hai-sheng, Lee Hai-sheng, Lee Hoi-sang, Li Hai-shen. **A**

Lee Kang-jo: Roman Lee Kang-jo / Lee Hong-joh / Li Kang-zhu / Lee Hong-joh. **A**

Lee, King: King Lee King-chue / Lee King Chue / Li Qing-zhu / Ging Chue / Ching Chu / Jing Zhu / Lee King-chu / Li King-chu / Li Ching-chu. **A**

Lee Kwan: Lee Gwan / Li Kun / Li Kuen / Li Chuan / Li Quin / Lee Quinn. **A**

Lee, Larry: Larry Lee Gam-kwan / Lee Gam-kwan / Li Jin-kun / Li Chin-kun / Lee Kam-kwun. **A, F**

Lee, Tommy: Gam Ming / Jin Ming / Chin Ming / Lee Gam-ming / Li Chin-ming / Li Ming-wen / Lee Ming-man / Kam Ming / Ming Chai. **A, F, D**

Lee Tso-nam: Lee Chok-laam / Li Tso-nan / Lee Chu-nan / Lee Tso-an / Li Jok-nam / Do Liu-boh / Du Lu-bo. **D**

Lee Tung-chun: Li Tong-chun / Li Tung-Chun. **A**

Lee Xiao-ming: Lee Siu-ming / Li Xiao-ming / Li Hsiao-ming. **A, F**

Lee Ye-min: Lee Wan-man / Li Yun-min / Lee Wan-man. **A**

Lee Yi-min: Lee I-min / Lee Aau-man / Li Yi-min / Simon Lee / Lee Ngai-man / Li Yi-min / James Lee / Lee Gong / Li I-min / Li Yi-man / Lee Siu-tung. **A, F**

Lee Ying-Ying: Li Ying-ying. **AT**

Lei Cheng-gong: Raymond Lui Shing-gung / Lui Shing-gung / Lui Gung / Lei Kung / Lui Wai-man. **A, F, D**

Leung Ting: Liang Ting. **A, F**

Leung, Tony: Tony Leung Siu-hung / Liang Xiao-xiong / Hsiung Kuang / Alex Leung Siu-Hung / Leung Mau-Hung / Liang Shao-Hung. **A, F**

Li, Bruce: Bruce Li Shao-lung / Hoh Chung-diy / He Zong-dao / Ho Chung-dao / James Ho Chung-tao / Bruce Ho Chung-tao / Lee Shaio-lung / Bruce Ho Chung-To. **A, D**

Li Ching: Lee Jing / Li Jing / Li Chin. **AT**

Li Fa-yuen: Lee Fat-yuen / Lee Faat-yuen. **A**

Li Gu-ding: Lee Ka-Ting / Lee Ga-ding / Lee Kay-Ting / Lee Ga-ding / Steve Lee / Li Chia-ting / Dick Lee / Li Jia-ding. **A, F**

Li Chao: Lee Chiu / Li Chao / Li Zhao / Le Chao / Lee Ying-Chiu. **A, F, D**

Li Chao-jun: Max Lee Chiu-jun / Lee Chiu-jun / See Foo-jai / See-fu Chai / Bye Foo-chai / Marloon Lee / Shi Fu-zi / She Fu-tsai / She Fe-tsai. **D**

Li Chia-hsien: Lee Ga-sai / Lee Ga-sai / Li Jia-qian / Li Chia-chien / Jessie Lee. **AT**

Li Han-hsiang: Lee Hon-cheung / Li Han-xiang / Li Han-chiang / Lee Han-chiang / Lee Han-cheung / Richard Lee. **D**

Li Hao: Lee Ho / Lee Hiu. **A, F**

Li Jian-xiong: Lai Kim-hung. **A**

Li Jiang: Lee Keung / Li Chiang. **A, F**

Li Kun: Lee Kwan / Lee Gwan / Li Kuen / Li Chuan / Li Quin / Lee Quinn. **A**

Li Li-Hua: Lee Lai-Wa / Lee Lai-Wah / Teresa Li/ Li Li-hwa. **AT**

Li, Lily: Lily Li Li / Lee Lai-li / Li Li-li / Lee Li-li / Li Lai-lai / Lee Lai-lai. **AT**

Li Long-yin: Lee Lung-yam. **A**

Li Min-lang: Lee Man-long / Li Ming-long / Li Ming-lang. **A**

Li Peng-fei: Lee Pang-fei / Lee Paang-fei / Li Peng-fei / Li Ping-fei. **A**

Li Qing-zhu: King Lee King-chue / Lee King-chue / Ging Chue / Ching Chu / Jing Zhu / Lee King-chu / Li King-chu / Li Ching-chu. **A**

Li Shou-chi: Lee Sau-kei / Li Shou-qi / Li Shao-chi / Lee Suk-kei. **A**

Li Su: Lee Siu / Lee Siu / Lee Sok. **D**

Li Tong-chun: Lee Tung-chun / Li Tung-Chun. **A, F**

Li Xiao-cong: Lee Siu-chung / Li Shao-shung. **A**

Li Xiang: Lee Seung / Li Hsiang / Maria Lee / Lee Sheung / Stella Lee. **AT**

Li Xiao-tian: Michael Lai Siu-tin / Lai Siu-tin / Li Shiao-dien / Hugo Lai / Li Hsiao-tien. **A**

Li Yun-zhong: Li Yung-zhong / Lee Wan-chung / Li Yun-chung / Li Ying-chung / Li Wen-chung. **A**

Li Wen-tai: Lee Man-tai / Lee Man-taai / Li Man-tai. **A**

Li Zhen-biao: Li Chen-Piao / Lee Jan-biu. **A**

Li Zhen-hua: Lee Jan-wa / Lee Lung-wa / Le Lung-hua. **A**

Li Zhi-lin: Lee Chi-lun / Li Ching-luen / Julie Lee **AT**

Liang, Bruce: Bruce Leung Siu-lung / Liang Hsiao-Lung / Liang Shao-Lung / Liang Xiao-Long / Leung Shi-Lung / S. L. Lieung. **A, F**

Liang Chia-ren: Leung Kar-yan / Leung Ga-yan / Liang Gu-ren / Beardy / Leung Ka-yan / John Liang Chia-jen / The Postman / Leung Chia-lun / Liang Chia-jen / Leung Kir-yan / Carlton Leung / Bryan Leung / Leung Ka-yin. **A, F**

Liang Lan-si: Nancy Leung Laan-si / Leung Laan-si / Leung Lan-sze / Liang Lan-szu / Frances Leung. **AT**

Liang Shao-hua: Leung Siu-wa. **A**

Liang Shao-song: Leung Siu-chung / Liang Shao-sung / Liang Shao-soong / Liang Shao-tsung. **A, F**

Liao Chiang-lin: Karl Liao Chiang-lin / Liu Kong-lam / Liao Jiang-lin / Liu Kong-lam. **D**

Liao Xiao-ming: Liu Hok-ming / Liu Hor-ming / Liao Hsuen-ming. **A, F**

Lin Bing: Lam Bing / Lam Bing / Lin Bin / Lin Pin. **D**

Lin Chen-chi: Lam Jan-kei / Lin Zhen-ji / Lam Chun-chi / Lam Ging-kei / Lin Ching-chi. **AT**

Lin Chia, Essie: Lam Ga / Lin Jia / Lam Ka. **AT**

Lin Ching-hsia. Brigitte: Lam Ching-ha / Lin Qing-xia / Venus Lin / Lam Ching-ha / Lin Ching-ha / Lin Ching-tsia / Lam Cheng-ha / Brigette Lin / Bridget Lin / Lin Chin-Hsia. **AT**

Lin Feng-chiao, Joan: Lam Fung-giu / Lin Feng-jiao / Joan Lim / Lam Fung-giu / Lin Kwong-qiao. **AT**

Lin Fu-ti: Lam Fook-Dei / Lam Fook Dei / Lin Fu-di. **D**

Lin Guang-rong: Lam Gwong-wing / Lam Kwong-Wing / Lam Kong-wing. **A**

Lin Guo-xiang: Lam Gwok-cheung / Lin Kuo-chiang / Lin Kuo-hsiang / Lin Kuo-shiang / Lam Kwok-cheung / Lin Kock-hsiang / Lin Kwok-shieung / Lam Kwok-cheng. **D**

Lin Hsiao-hu: Lam Siu-foo / Lin Xiao-hu / Lin Shao-fu. **A**

Liu Huang-shi: Lau Fong-sai / Lau Kwong-shi / Daai Baak-oui / Liu Kwong-shi. **A**

Lin Hui-huang: Lam Fai-wong / Lin Huei-huang. **A**

Lin Jiao: Lam Kau / Lam Gaau / Lin Chiao / Lin Yu-cheng / Lin Chia / Lam Kout. **A**

Lin Ke-ming: Lam Hak-ming / Ke Ming / Lam Hak-ming / Lam Hark-ming / Hart Lam. **A, F**

Lin Man-hua: Lam Moon-wa / Albert Lam / Lam Moon-wah / Lam Mun-wah / Silver Lam / Lin Mang-hwa. **A, F**

Lin Wei-tu: Lam Wai-tiu / Li Wei-tu. **A**

Lin Wen-wei: Lam Man-wai, Eddie Lam Man-wai. **A**

Lin Yi-wa: Lam Yi-wa / Eva Lin I-wa / Lam I-wa / Lin Hsiu-feng. **AT**

Lin You-chuan: Lam Yau-chuen / Lin Yu-Chuan. **F, A**

Lin Zhen-ji: Lam Jan-kei / Lin Chen-chi / Lam Chun-chi / Lam Ging-kei / Lin Ching-chi. **AT**

Ling Po, Ivy: Ling Boh / Ling Po / Ling Bo / Siu Guen / Jun Hai-tang / Lvy Ling Po / Xiao Juan. **AT**

Ling Yun: Ling Wan / Ling Lung-sung. **A**

Liu Chia-hui, Gordon: Lau Ga-fai / Liu Gu-hui / Lau Kar-fei / Lau Ga-fai / Lau Kir-fai / Lau Kar-fai / Liu Jia-hui / Lau Ka-fei / Liu Chia-fai / part of Liu Brothers / Master Killer. **A, F**

Liu Chia-liang: Lau Kar-Leung, Kung Fu-Leung, Gung Fu-Leung, Kung Fu-Liang, Lau Ga-Leung, Liu Chia-Liung, Liu Ka-Liang, Lau Ka-Leung. **A, F, D**

Liu Chia-rong: Lau Kar-wing / Lau Ga-wing / Liu Gu-rong / Bruce Lau / Liu Chia-yung / Lau Ga-wing / Lau Ka-wing. **A, F, D**

Liu Chia-yung: Liu Gu-yong / Lau Ga-yung / Jimmy Liu / Lau Kar-yung / Sammy Lau Kar-yung / Lau Kar-yun / Lau Ka-yun / Liu Chia-hsiung. **A**

Liu Chuan-hua: Lau Chuen-wa / Liu Tsung-Hwa. **AT**

Liu De-kai: Alan Lau Tak-hoi / Lau Tak-hoi / Roy Liu / Liu Teh-kai / Liu Te-kai. **A**

Liu Gang: Lau Gong / Liu Kang / Lau Kong. **A**

Liu Guo-cheng: Lau Kwok-shing / Lau Gwok-shing / Liu Kuo-cheng. **A**

Liu Hao-nian: Lau Hok-nin / Lin Ho-nien / Mang Foo / Lau Hok-nien / Lau Hok-lien. **A, F**

Liu Hao-yi: Hilda Liu Hao-yi / Lau Hiu Yi / Lau Hiu-yi / Liu Hau-yi. **AT**

Liu Hui-Ling: Lau Wai-ling. **AT**

Liu Hui-ru: Terry Lau Wai-yue / Lau Wai-yue / Terry Liu / Liu Hui-yu / Liu Hui-ju. **AT**

Liu Jian-ming: Jamie Luk Kim-ming / Luk Kim-ming / Jimmy Luk Kim-Ming / Lu Jian-min. **A**

Liu Jun-guk, Tony: Lu Chin-ku / Tony Lo Chun-guk / Liu Jun / Tommy Loo Chun / Lu Chun-ku / Loo Chun-kok / Lu Chun / Lo Chun-gok / Lu Chun-ku / Lo Chun-cook / Tommy Loo Chung. **A, D, F**

Liu Jun-hui: Lau Jun-Fai / Lau Chong / Lau Fei / Lau Chun-fai / Wynn Lau / Lau Fai. **A, D**

Liu Lan-ying: Lau Lan-ying / Lau Laan-ying / Parwana Chanajit / Lui Ran-in. **AT**

Liu Li-li: Lau Lap-lap / Lily Liu. **AT, D**

Liu Li-zu: Lau Lap-cho / Lau Laap-jo / Liu Li-tsu. **A**

Liu Liu-hua: Lau Luk-wa / Liu Lu-hua. **AT**

Liu Meng-yan: Lau Mung-yin / Liu Meng-yin. **AT**

Liu Ping: Lu Ping / Kei Fung / Lin Lu / Qi Feng / Nu Ping. **A**

Liu Ta-chuan: Lau Tai-chuen / Lau Daai-Chuen. **A**

Liu Tan: Lau Dan / Lau Daan / Liu Dan / Danny Lau / William Liu Tan / Lau Tan / Lu Tan. **A**

Liu Ya-ying: Lau Nga-ying / Lau Wai-ying. **AT**

Liu Yi-long: Lu I-long / Lu Yat-lung. **A**

Liu Yong: Tony Liu / Lau Wing / Tony Liu-yong / Anthony Lau / Liu Wing / Liu Yun. **A**

Liu Wu-chi: Lau Ng-kei / Liu Wi-qi / Liu Wu-chih. **AT**

Lo Chen: Law Chun / Luo Zhen / Lo Jun / Li Meng-fei / Lo Chuen. **D**

Lo Lieh: Law Lit / Luo Lie / Lo Liee / Luo Lie / Wong Lap-dat / Joe Lee / Law Lik / Law Lit / Ro Re / Ro Rye / Lao Lit / Lo Lei / Luo Lieh / Law Lieed / William Lowe. **A, D, F**

Lo Mar, John: John Law Ma / Law Ma / Luo Ma / Lo Mar / John Lomar / Law Chau-woo / Lo Chau-hu / Lo Chau-wu / Lo Hsiu-hu / Lo Chiu-hu / Lu Mar. **D**

Lo Meng: Luo Mang / Lo Mang / Johnson Law / Turbo Law / Ramone Law / Law Mong / Lo Mona / Lo Wang / Law Mon / Lo Mong-law / Kwan-lam. **A, F**

Lo Wei: Law Wai / Luo Wei / Luo Wei / Law Wai / Lo Wai. **A, D**

Lok, Cliff: Goo Lung / Gu Long / Koo Lung / Ku Lung / Gam Tung / Chin Tong / Chin Tung / Lung Goon-ting / Lung Kuan-ting / Kan Tung / Kam Tung. **A, D**

Long Guan-wu: Mark Lung Goon-mo / Lung Goon-miu / Mark Long / Lung Kuan-wu / Loong Koon-mo / Long Guan-wun / Dragon Lung. **A**

Long, Jack: Jack Lung Sai-ga / Lung Sai-ga / Long Shi-gu / Lung Shih-chia / Wang Chiang / Wong Keung / Lung Si-kar. **A, F**

Long Shao-fei: Lung Siu-fei / Lung Siu-fai. **A**

Long Xuan: Lung Suen / Lung Chuan / Lung Hsuan. **A**

Lu Chin-ku: Tony Liu Jun-guk / Tony Lo Chun-guk / Liu Jun / Tommy Loo Chun / Tommy Loo Chung / Lu Chun-ku / Loo Chun-kok / Lu Chun / Lo Chun-gok / Lu Chun-ku / Lu Chung-lu / Lu Jun-gu / Lo Chun-cook / Lo Chun-ku / Liu Jun-guk / Tony Liu / Tony C.K. Lo / Lui Jun-go. **A, F, D**

Lu Di: Lo Dik / Lu Ti. **A**

Lu Feng: Luk Fung / Chue Luk-fung / Chu Qi-xue / Chu Lu-feng / Lu Chu-feng / Luk Fung. **A, F**

Lu Hsiu-chen: Lui Sau-ching / Lu Xiu-zhen / Lui Sau-ching / Yeo Su-jin. **AT**

Lu Qi: Law Kei / Luo Qi / Law Chi / Lo Kei / Lo Ke / Luo Chyi / Law Kee / Law Gei-sek / Gei Sek / Lo Chi-shih / Lo Kai-shi / David Lo / Luo Qi / Lo Chi. **A, D**

Lu Wei: Liu Wai / Lo Wai / Lo Wa. **A**

Lun Gu-jun: Lun Ga-chun / Lun Chia-chun / Yan Jing-yat. **A**

Lung Chun-er, Doris: Doris Lung Chun-erh / Lung Gwan-ngai / Long Jun-er / Lung Chung-erh / Mabel Lung / Lung Gwan-yi / Doris Chen / Lung Kun-yee / Lung Juen-er / Lung Chun-ern / Long Gin-erh / Long Jiun-er. **AT**

Lung Fei: Long Fei / Chow San-kwai / Loong Fei / Leroy Lung. **A, F**

Lung Fong, Jimmy: Long Fang / Lung Fong / Jimmy Lee / Lee Kin-man / Li Chien-min / Lee Kin-ming. **A, F, D**

Lung Tien-hsiang: Lung Tin-cheung / Long Tian-xiang / Lung Tung-sheng / Lung Tin-cheung / Lung Tien-sheng / Lung Tien-shiang. **A**

Luo Han: Law Hon. **A**

Luo Jiang: Law Keung. **A**

Luo Qi: Law Kei / Law Chi / Lo Kei / Lo Ke / Luo Chyi / Law Kee / Law Gei-sek / Gei Sek / Lo Chi-shih / Lo Kai-shi / David Lo / Luo Qi / Lo Chi. **A, D**

Luo Zhen: Law Chun / Lo Chen / Lo Jun / Li Meng-fei / Luo Zhen / Lo Chuen. **D**

Ma Chang: Ma Cheung / Ma Tsan. **A, F**

Ma Chi-ho: Mak Chi-Who / Matsuo Akinori / Mai Chih-Ho / Ma Chi-Ho / Mai Zhi-he. **D**

Ma Dao-zhi: Ma Diy-chik / Ma Do-shik. **A**

Ma Hai-lun: Helen Ma Hoi-lun / Ma Hoi Lun. **AT**

Ma Ji: Ma Kei / Ma Chi. **A**

Ma Jin-gu: Ma Chin-ku / Ma Chiu-ku / Ma Gam-guk / Xiao Kao-shan / Siu Ko-san / Hsiao Kao-shan / Ma Kim-kot / Lam Chun-fung. **A, F**

Ma Zong-de: Ma Chung-tak / Ma Shung-tak. **A**

Maka, Karl: Mak Ga / Mai Jia / Carl Mak / Mak Kar / Kar Mak / Kais Mak. **A, D**

Mang Hoi: Maang Hoi / Meng Hai / Randy Mang Hoi / Meng Hoi / Mung Hoe / Man Hoi / Mount Hoi / Mon Hai. **A, F**

Mansoor, A: Mansoor. **F**

Mao Ying, Angela: Mao Ying / Maau Ying / Mao Fu-ying / Mao Fook-jing / Miao Ying / Mou Ying. **AT**

Mars: Feng Sing / Huo Xing / Huo Hsing / Fwa Sing / Fu Sing / Cheung Wing-faat / Chiang Wing-faat. **A**

Meng Chiu: Kitty Meng Chie / Maang Chau / Meng Qiu / Mang Chau / Cheryl Meng / Mon Chun / Mang Gwan-ha. **AT**

Meng Ding-ge: Mang Ding-goh / Maang Ding-goh / Meng Ting-ge / Martin Ting. **A**

Meng Fei: Mang Fei / Maang Fei / Menq Fei / Mong Fei. **A**

Mi Xue: Michelle Yim / Mai Suet / Mi Hsueh / Michelle Mai Shuet / Micelle Mei Suet / Michelle Lai / Mi Hsuen / Mei Shu / Mai Sit. **AT**

Miao, Nora: Miu Hoh-sau / Miao Ke-xiu / Nora Miao Ke-hsiu. **AT**

Miao Tian: Miu Tin / Miao Tien / Wiao Tien / Miao Tin. **A**

Mun Yiu-wa: Man Yiu-wah / Man Yu-wah / Sai Mon Yiu Wa. **D**

Nam Chung-il: Nam Chung-yat / Naam Chung-yat / Nan Zhong-yi. **A**

Nam Gi-nam: Nam Ki-nam. **D**

Nam Gung-fan, James: Naam Gung-fan / Nan Gong-xun / Nan Kung-hsun / Lam Kung-fun / Nan Kon-fun / Alberto Golango / Lan Kung-hsun. **A, D**

Nan Gong-xun: James Nam Gung-Fan / Naam Gung-fan / Nan Kung-hsun / Lam Kung-fun / Nan Kon-fun / Alberto Golango / Lan Kung-hsun. **A, D**

Neglia, Louis: Liu Yee Si Baak Ga / Lu Yi Shi Bai Jia. **A**

Norris, Chuck: Law Lai-si / Luo Li-shi. **A**

Ng See-yuen: Ng Sze-yuen / Ng See-yuen / Woo Se-yuen / Wu Sy-yeuan / Ng Tse-yuen. **D**

Ng Tin-chi: Wu Tian-chi / Ng Tien-tsu. **D**

O Yau-man: Ke You-min / Ho Yu-ming / Lung Siu / Lung Se / Ko You-ming. **A, D**

Ou Li-bao: Au Lap-bo / Au Laap-biu / Au Li-pao / Oliver / Ou Li-pao. **A**

Ou-Yang Pei-Shan: Au Yeung Pui San / Au Yeung Pui Saan / Susanna Au-Yeung / Auyang Pei-Shan / Au-Young Pui-Sun / Au-Yeung Pooi-Saan. **AT**

Ou-Yang Sha-Fei: Au Yeung Qui Fei / Oyang Sha-Fei / Auyang Siao-Fei / Au-Yeung Sha-Fei / Au-Yang Sa-Fay / O-Yang Sha-Fei / Au-Yang Sha-Fei / Au-Yeung Sha-Fai / Auyan Sar-Fa / On-Yang So-Fei. **AT**

Pak, Bruce: Cheong Nyong / Cheong Ryong. **A**

Pan Ying-zi: Poon Ying-chi / Pan Yin-tze / Pan Yan-tze / Pan Ying-tzu / Violet Pan ying-zi / Poon Yin-chi / Poon Ying-chi. **AT**

Pan Yue-kun: Poon Yiu-kwan / Pan Yao-kun / Poon Baak-bye / Pan Yao-kwan. **A, F**

Pang Bing-chang: Helen Poon Bing-seung / Poon Bing-seung / Pan Ping-chang / Pang Ping-chang / Poon Bing-shen / Pan Ping-shang / Helen Pou / Portia Poon. **AT**

Pao Hsueh-li: Pao Hsieh-Li / Pao H. L. / Bou Shur-Li / Bau Hsieh-Lee / Baau Hok-Lai / Pao Hsuen-Li / Li Hsieh I Pao Xueh-li. **D**

Park Dong-ryong: Pok Tung-lung / Piu Dung-lung / Po Dong-long. **A**

Peng Gang: Peng Kong / Paang Gong / Peng Kang / Johnny Pang / Pang Kang / Pang Kong / Pan Kong / Pang Yin-cheung / Peng Hsien-chang. **A, F**

Qian Yue-sheng: Chin Yuet-sang / Chien Yueh-sheng / Tom Chin / Lisp Guy / Chen Yue-sang / Chien Yue-sang / Chen Yiet-san / Chin Yuet-sun / Chien Yu-sheng / Chin Yuet san. **A, F**

Qin Pei: Paul Chun Pui / Chun Pooi / Chin Pei / Paul Chin / Paul Chiang / Paul Chin Pei / Chin Pui / Chiu Pui / Chin Pey. **A**

San Kuai: San Gwaai / Shan Guai / San Kwai / San Kuei / Lau Wing / Shan Kuai / Shan Qu. **A, F**

Sanada Hiroyuki: Duke Sanada / Harry Sanada / Henry Sanada / Hiroyuki Shimosawa. **A**

Santiago, Cirio: Leonard Hermes / Cirio H. Santiago / Luis Nepomuceno. **D**

Saxon, John: Juen Saat-shun / Juen Saat-shun. **A**

Scott, Carl: Carl R. Scott. **A**

Sen Chin-yuen: Sun Kam-yun. **D**

Shakamura Yashiyusha: Luk Cheun / Lu Chuan / Luk Chuen / Lu Chuen / Yafli Yoshi Shikamura / Yagli Yoshi Shikamura / Chuen Taai Cheung / Lu Cun Tai Xiang / Yasuyoshi Shikamura / Luk Chuen Taai Cheung / Lu Chuen Tai Hsiang. **A, F**

Shan Guai: San Kuai / Saan Gwaai / San Kwai / San Kuei / Lau Wing / Shan Kuai / Shan Qu. **A, D**

Shan Mao: Saan Maau / San Mao / Su Mau / Shan Mou / Saan Maau. **A, F**

Shao Luo-hui: Shaw Luo-hui / Siu Law-fai / Siu Law-fai / Show Lo-fai / Mooi Fong-yuk. **A**

Shao Yin-yin: Siu Yam-yam / Shaw Yin-yin / Susan Shaw / Siu Yin-Yin. **AT**

Shaw Feng, Jimmy: Siu Fung / Shao Feng / Siu Fung / Shaw Fung James. **D**

She Fei-yang: Yip Fei-yang / Yip Fei-yeung / Lee Yuen-hing / Yip Fai-yang / Yeung Ping-on / Yang Ping-an. **A**

She Tian-hang: Stephan Yip Tin-hang / Yip Tin-hang / Yeh Tien-heng. **A**

Shek, Dean: Sek Tin / Shi Tian / Shih Tien / Dean Saki / Charlie Shek / Shik Tien / Shih Tieh / Sheck Tien / Shik Tin. **A**

Shen Chiang: San Kong / Shen Jiang / Shen Kang / Shen Kiang / Sun Kwong / Shen Yuang / **D**

Shen Lao: Shum Lo / Sam Liu. **A**

Shen Xian: San Sin / Sheng Se / Hsin Hsien / Sheng Hsien / Sen Sian / Yu Yuen-yin. **A, F**

Shi Di: Shut Dik / Sze Ti. **D**

Shi Feng: Sek Fung / Shih Feng / Shih Fong / Shih Rong. **A**

Shi Ting-gen: Shih Ting-ken / Shut Ting-gan / Shi Ting-kan / Shi Shing-gung / Shi Cheng-kung / Se Ting-kin / Siu Shut / Shao Shih. **A**

Shi Xiu: Sek Sau / Bill Chan / Bill S. S. Chan / Shek Sau / Chan Sek-Sau. **A**

Shi Zhong-tian: Shut Chung-tin / Shih Chung-tien / Shih Chung-tieng / Wa Hon / Hua Han / Shih Chun-tien / Se Chun-tin. **A**

Shiek Khan: Sek Gin / Shi Jian / Sek Gin / Shih Kien / Sheck Kin / Shih Chien / Shek Kin. **A, F**

Shih Jun: Sek Jun / Dan Juan / Shi Jun / Shih Chun / C. Shih. **A**

Shih Szu: Shi Si / Lei Qiu-si / Szu Szu / Shin Szu / Si Si. **AT**

Shihomi Etsuko: Sue Shihomi. **A**

Shu Pei-pei: Shu Pooi-pooi / Shu Pui-pui. **AT**

Si Wei: Si Wai / Szu Wei / Antonio Ho. **A**

Si Ma Hua Long: Shut-Ma Wa-Lung / Ssuma Hua-lung / Seema Wah-lung / Sze-Ma Wah-Lung / Szema Wah-lung. **A**

Si Ma-long: Sze-Ma-lung / Shut Ma-lung / Yang Kong / Yang Kuang / Shut Ma-lung / Shaking Eagle. **A**

Someno Yukio: Leung Yau Hang Hung / Liang Ye Hang Xiong / Leung Yau Hang Hung / Someno / Yukio Fomeno / Yim Yau / Ran Ye / Jan Yeh / Leung Yeh. **A**

Song Ting-mei: Sung Ting-mei. **D**

Su Chen-ping: So Chan-ping / Su Zhen-ping / So Chan-Ping / Percy So Jin-ping. **A, F, D**

Su Yuan-feng: So Yuen-fung / So Fung / Charliema Hsu / Charliema Tsu / So Yuk-fung. **A**

Su Zhen-ping: Su Chen-ping / So Chan-ping / Percy So Jin-ping. **A**

Sun Chien: Suen Gin / Sun Jian / Suen Gin / Suen Jian-yuan / Sun Kin. **A**

Sun Chung: Sun Zhong / Tung Ming-shan / Suen Chung **D**

Sun Jia-lin: Suen Ga-lam / Suen Ga-lam / Sun Chia-lin / Karin Sun. **AT**

Sun Lan: Suen Lam / Suen Laam / Sum Nam / Sung Lam / Sun Luan / Sun Lna / Sun Nan. **A**

Sun Rong-zhi: Sun Jung-chi / Suen Wing-chi / Suen Wing-gat / Suen A-gat / Sun Wing-che / Sun Rong-ge. **A, F**

Sun Shu-pei: Suen Shu-pau / Sun Su-po / Sun Su-pei / Sun Su-pai. **A, F**

Sun Xin-xiang: Sun Hsin-shiang / Suen San-cheung. **A, F**

Sun Yue: Suen Yuet / Sum Yuen / Sun Yuen / Sun Yeuh / Sun Yuih / Sun Yueh / Sung Yueh. **A**

Sung Gam-loi, Addy: Big Little Eye / Ta Hsi-yen / Sung Gam-shing / Sung Lai / Tai Siu-un / Ta Sei-en / Sung Kam-sing / Dai Sai-aan. **A, F**

Tai Chi-Hsien, Robert: Dai Che / Daai Chit / Tai Chi-tsien / Tai Chi-hsien / Tai Che / Tai Chi / Tai Yee-tin / Tai Chit / Tai Kei-Yin / Tai Yee-yin / Tai Chi-yen / Robert Tai. **A, F, D**

Tanba Tetsuro: Tetzuro Tamba / Daan Boh Chit Long / Dan Bo Zhe Lang. **A**

Tan Dao-liang: Dorian Tan Tao-liang / Taam Diy-Leung / Flash Legs / Delung Tam / Delon Tan / Bobby Ming / Delon Tam / Tan Tao-Leong / Tan Tao-liang / Dorian Tan / Delon Tanners / Bruce Tan. **A, F**

Tan Zhen-dong: Tony Tam Jan-dung / Taam Jan-dung / Tan Chen-tu / Tam Jun-tao / Tam Dung / Tan Dong / Taam Jan-diy / Tam Chun-to / Tan Chun-to / Tam Chun-tung / Tony Jam. **A**

Tanba, Tetsuro: Tetsuro Tamba. **A**

Tang, Alan: Alan Tang Kwong-wing / Dang Gwong-wing / Deng Guang-rong / Alan K. W. Tang. **A, D**

Tang Chia: Tong Gaai / Tang Jia / Tang Ji. **A, F**

Tang Jing: Tang Ching / Tong Jing / Tong Ching / Tan Chin / Tang Qing. **A**

Tang Di: Tang Ti / Tong Dik / Tong Dick / Tang Dih / Tang Dei. **A, D**

Tang Jin-tang: Tong Kam-tong / Tong Gam-tong / Mulo Chiba / Ma Lung / Tang Chin-tang. **A, F**

Tang Tian-xi: Tong Tin-hei / Tong Tien-chi / Tong Ti-he. **A**

Tang Wei: David Tong Wai / Tong Wai. **A**

Ti Lung: Di Lung / Dick Loong / Tommy Ti Lung / Dick Loong / Din Lung / Di Long / Tommy Tam / Tam Fu-wing / Tam Wing / Ti Long / Dik Lung. **A, D**

Tian Ching: Tian Qing / Tin Ching / Tien Ching / Tien Chun-sheng / Tien Cheen / Tin Ceng. **A**

Tian Hao: Tin Hok / Tien Ho. **A**

Tian Ming: Tin Ming / Tien Ming / Tieng Ming. **A**

Tian Ye: Tin Yau / Tien Yeh / Tieng Yeh / Tin Yaiu / Tien Yue / Joe Tin / Tian Ye / Tin Yieh. **A**

Tien Fung: Tien Feng / Tin Fung / Tian Feng / Chang Chin / Tien Fong. **A, D**

Tien, James: James Tin Jun / Tian Jun / Paul Tien / James Tien Chun / James Tyan / Tin Chuen / Tien Chein / Chan Man / Chen Wen. **A, F**

Tien Ni, Tanny: Tim Lei / Tian Ni / Tan Nei / ''Tanny'' / Tanny Chu / Tien Ni / Tien Nei / Tin Lian. **AT**

Tien, Roc: Tin Paang / Tian Peng / Tien Peng / Tin Pang / Tien Pong. **A, D**

Ting Pei, Betty: Ding Pooi / Ding Pei. **AT**

Tong Lin: Tung Lam / Tung Lin. **A**

Tong Tin-hei: Tang Tian-xi / Tong Tien-chi / Tong Ti-he. **A**

Tong Wai, David: Tong Wai / Tang Wei. **A**

Tong, Wilson: Wilson Tong Wai-shing / Tong Wai-shing / Tang Wei-cheng / The Foot Doctor / Tang Wei-cheng / Tong San / Tang Wei-shang / Tang Shan. **A, F, D**

Tong Yen-san: Bruce Tong Yim-chaan / Tang Yan-can / Tang Yen-tsan / Tong Yim-chan. **A**

Tong Yim-chaan: Bruce Tong Yim-chaan / Tang Yan-can / Tong Yen-san / Tang Yen-tsan / Tong Yim-chan. **A**

Tove, Birte: Bik Dai Do Foo / Bi Di Du Fu. **AT**

Tsai Yang-ming: Choi Yeung-ming / Cai Yang-ming / Tsai Yi-ming. **D**

Tsang Chiu: Chang Chiu / Ceng Chao / Tsang Chi / Tsang Chao / Cheng Chao. **A, F**

Tsang, Eric: Eric Tsang Chi-wai / Chang Chi-wai / Ceng Zhi-wei / Eric Tseng / Chen Chih-wei / Tseng Chi-wei / Tseng Chih-wei / Zeng Zhi-wei. **A, D**

Tsang Kong, Kenneth: Chang Kong / Ceng Jiang / Tsang Koon-yet / Kent Tsang / Ken Tsang / Tsang Chiang. **A**

Tsang Ming-cheong: Chang Ming-cheong / Ceng Ming-chang / Chang Ming-ceong / Siu Kong-tung. **A**

Tseng, Jenny: Yan Lei / Zhen Ni (Jenny) / Jenny Cheng / Yan Lei / Chen Ni / Jenny Yan / Jenny Yen. **AT**

Tsui Hark: Chui Hak / Xu Ke / Mark Yu / Tusi Hark / Shyu Keh. **D**

Tu Song-zhao: Yu Chung-chiu / Chui Chung-chiu / Yu Chung-hei / Yu Song-chao / Yu Sung-chao / Chui Chung-chiu / Chester Yee / Yu Chon-chiu. **A, F**

Tsung Hua: Chung Wa / Zong Hua / Hsung Hua / Chung Hwa / Tsuan Hua / Chung Hua. **A**

Tung Li: Dung Lik / Dong Li / Tung Lik / Hong Wa / Kang Hua / Alex Tang Lec. **A**

Tung Shu-yung: Charles Tung Shao-yung / Dung Shiu-wing / Dong Shao-yong / Charles Tung, Jr. / Dung Shiu-wing / Tung Hsiao-Yung / Tung Shao-yung. **D**

Unicorn, Little: Siu Kei-lun / Xiao Qi-lin / Unicorn Chan / Unicorn. **A, F**

Van Clief, Ron: Lung Yuin Chi Li Fu / Ron van Cliff. **A**

Velasco, Joseph: Joseph Kong Hung / Kong Hung / Jiang Hong. **D**

Wall, Bob: Robert Wall / Luo Ba-wo / Law Bat-wing. **A**

Wan Chong-shan: Man Chung-san / Maan Chung Saan / Wen Chung-Shan / Wan Chung-shan / Marlon Man. **A**

Wan Shan: Maan Saan / Wang Shan / Man San. **A**

Wang Chi-sheng: Wong Chi-sang / Wong Aau-sang / Wang Qi-sheng / Wang Chi-Sang / Wang Ki-san / Wang Ki-sen / Wang Chin-sheng / Wang Che-san. **A, F**

Wang Chin-feng: Wong Gam-fung / Wang Ching-Feng / Huang Chin-feng. **AT**

Wang Ching-ho: Wong Ching-ho / Wong Ching-hiu / Wang Qing-he / Wang Chin-ho / Wang Qing-he. **A**

Wang Chung: Wang Zhong / Wong Chung / Wong Chun. **A**

Wang Feng: Wong Fung. **D**

Wang Guan-xiong: Wong Goon-hung / Wang Kuan-hsiung / Frank Wong / Champ Wang / Wong Gwan-sheong / Wong Kwan-hsiung / Wang Kwn-shong. **A**

Wang Hao: Wong Ho. **A, D**

Wang Jue: George Wang Jue / Wong Gok/ Wang Kuo / Wang Chueh. **A**

Wang Jung: Wong Yung / Wang Rong / Wang Yung / Jeff Wong. **A**

Wang Kuang-yu: Wong Gwong-yue / Wang Guang-yu / Lin Tsung / Lam Chung / Lin Tsong / Wong Kwong-yue / Wang Kwong-yu. **A**

Wang Lai: Wong Loi. **AT**

Wang Li: Wong Lik / Wang Li / Wang Lieh / Wong Ming-fai / Wang Ming-hui. **A**

Wang Lung-wei: Johnny Wang Lung-wei / Wong Lung-wai / Wong Loong-wai / Wong Wai / Wong Lun-wai / Wang Lung-wai. **A**

Wang Ping: Wong Ping / Wang Pin. **AT**

Wang Qing-liang: Wang Chiang-liang / Wong Hing-leung / Wang Ching-liang. **A, F**

Wang Re-ping: Wong Yeuk-ping / Wong Yeuk-ping / Wang Jo-Ping / Wong Chak. **A, F**

Wang Tai-lang: Wong Taai-long / Wong Tai-long / Wang Tai-long / Wang Chiang / Wong Keung / Wang Tai-liang. **A, F**

Wang Tian-lin: Wong Tin-lam / Wang Tien-lin / Wong Tin-Lam / Wang Tin-lam / Wang Tin-Lin. **D**

Wang Xia: Wang Hsieh / Wong Hap / Wang Hsia / Wong Shai / Wong Hap / Wang Hack / Wang Chi / Wang Ya. **A**

Wang Yong-sheng: Wong Wing-sang / Wang Yung-hseng / Wang Yung-shang. **A**

Wang Yu: Wong Yue / Wong Yu / Young Wong-yu / Yung Wong-yue. **A**

Wat Yat-wang. D

Wen Xue-er, Candy: Man Suet Ngai / Wen Xue-er / Man Suet-Yi / Wen Hsueh-erh / Man Suet-yee. **AT**

Wei Bai: Wai Pak / Wai Baak / Wei Pai / Wei Pei / Mooi Kwok-shing / Mooi Gwok-shing. **A**

Wei Hai-feng: Ngai Hoi-fung / Wei Hoi-feng / Wei Hai-feng / Ye Hoi-fung. **D**

Wei Hong, Frankie: Wai Wang / Wei Hong / Wei Hung / Frankie Wei Hung / Ng Ban / Frankie Wei Hua / Wu Dong-ru / Xiao Lin / Wu Bin. **A**

Wei Ping-ao: Ngai Ping-ngo / Yue Ping-Au / Wei Ping-Ou / Paul Wei / Wei Ping-Aou / Yi Ping-O / Newton Wei. **A**

Wen Jiang-long: Man Kong-Lung / Wen Chiang-long / Jackie Wen / Wen Chiang-lung / Min Chiang-lung / Jackie Wen Chiang-long. **A, F**

Weng Hsiao-hu: Yung Siu-foo / Weng Xiao-hu. **A**

Whang In-shik: Huang Ren-zhi / Wong Yan-chik / Whong In-sik / Wong In-sik / Whang Ing-sik / Hwang In-shik / Whong Inn-sik. **A, F**

Wong, Carter: Carter Wong Ka-Tat: Wong Ga Daat / Huang Gu-da / Patrick Wong / Carter Huang / Wang Chia-ta / Huang Cha-ta / Carter Hwang / Hwang Chia-ta / Huang Chia-daa / Huang Chia-da. **A, D**

Wong, Casanova: Jut Saat-fat / Ka Sa-fa / Ca Sa-fa / Wang Ho / Chia Sa-fu / Chia Che-fu. **A**

Wong Chi-ming, Ringo: Wong Chi-ming / Huang Zhi-ming / Wong Chi-ming / Jimmy Huang / Wang Chih-ming. **A, F**

Wong Chi-sang: Wong Aau-sang / Wang Qi-sheng / Wang Chi-sheng / Wang Ki-san / Wang Ki-sen / Wang Chin-sheng / Wang Che-san. **A, F**

Wong Ching: Wang Qing / Wang Ching / Wang Ching-lung / Wong Ching-lung. **A**

Wong Chung-shun: Wong Chung-shun / Huang Zong-xun / Huang Chung-hsin / Huang Chung-shun / Huang Chuang-shun / Huang Chung-hsing / Huang Tsung-shun / Huang Zong-xun / Wang Chung-hsin / Don Wong **A**

Wong Dao: Don Wong-tao / Don Wong / Wong Diy / Wang Dao / Wang Tao / Wong Tou. **A**

Wong Cheung, Tino: Wong Cheung / Wang Jiang / Wang Chiang / Chan Tin-lung / Chen Tien-long / Wong Cheong. **A**

Wong Mei: Wong Mooi / Huang Mei / Wong Hung / Wong Ga-hung / Wong Mui / Wang Mei. **A, F**

Wong, Tino: Tino Wong Cheung / Wong Cheung / Wang Jiang / Wang Chiang / Chan Tin-lung / Chen Tien-long / Wong Cheong. **A**

Wong Yu, Jimmy: Jimmy Wang Yu / Wang Zhcng-quan / Wong Jing-Kuen. **A, F, D**

Wong Yuen-san: Wong Yuen-san / Huang Yuan-shen / Tony Wong / Wong Yuen-sung / Wang Yuen-Sun. **A, D**

Woo. John: Ng Yue-sam / Wu Yu-sen / Wu Yu-sheng / Wu Yu-shen / Wu Yao-shen / John Y. S. Woo / John Y. Woo / Ng Yue-sum. **A, D**

Wu Chi-chin: Ng Chi-yam / Wu Chi-qin / Wu Chih-ching / Wu Chi-ching. **A**

Wu Chia-xiang: Ng Ga-seung / Ng Ka-seung / Wu Chia-hsiang / Wu Chia-shiang / Wu Chia-shang / Wu Gu-xiang. **A, D**

Wu Dong-qiao: Ng Tung-kiu / Ng Dung-kiu. **A, F**

Wu Hang-sheng: Ng Hong-sang. **A**

Wu Ma: Ng Ma / Fung Ng-ma / Wo Ma / Wuu Ma / Feng Wu-ma / Fung Wo-ma. **A, D**

Wu Min-xiong: Mo Man-hung / Wu Man-sheung / Wu Min-hsiung / Yu Min-sheong / Wu Ming-sheong / Wu Ming-hsiung / Jimmy Wu. **A, D**

Wu Ming-cai: Ng Ming-choi / Yuen Ting / Ng Ming-toi / Ming Tsai / Wu Ming-tsai. **A, F**
Wu Wei-kuo: Ng Wai-kwok / Wu Wei-guo. **A**
Wu Wen-su: Mo Man-sau. **AT**

Wu Yuan-jun: Ng Yuen-Jun / Patrick Wu Yuan-chun. **A**

Xia Guang-li: Ha Kwong-li / Ha Gwong-lee / Hsia Kwan-li / Shar Kung-li / Shiah Guang-lih. **AT**

Xiao Hu-dou: Siu Foo-dau, Hsiao Hou-Tao. **A**

Xia Ping: Teresa Ha Ping / Ha Ping / Hsia Ping / Teresa Ha. **AT**

Xiang Hua-jiang: Charles Heung Wah-keung, Heung Wa-keung, Shiang Hwa-chiang, Charles W. K. Heung, Hsiang Hwa-chiang. **A**

Xiang Ling: Heung Ling / Shang Lang. **D**

Xiao Hu-dou: Siu Foo-dau, Hsiao Hou-Tao. **A**

Xiao Huang-long: Siu Wong-lung / Siu Wong-lung / Hsiao Huang-lung / Wong Siu-lung. **A, F**

Xiao Pei: Siu Pui / Siu Pau / Shiao Po. **F**

Xiao Rong: Stanley Siu Wing / Siu Wing / Siao Wing / Hsiao Yung. **D**

Xie Jin-ju: Tse Gam-guk / Che Gam-guk. **AT**

Xiong Ting-wu: Hung Ting-miu / Hsiung Ting-wu / Hsiang Ting-wu. **D**

Xu Er-niu: Simon Chui Yee-ang / Hsu Erh-niu / Simon Hsu. **A, F**

Xu Hsao-chiang: Xu Shao-qiang / Norman Chu Siu-keung / Tsui Siu-keung / Chui Siu-Keung / Tsui Shui-Keung / Chiu Siu-keung / Hsu Shao-chiang. **A**

Xu Song-hao: Chui Chung-hok / Tsu Sung-hok / Tsu Song-hao / Hsu Sung-ho / Tsui Fook-bo. **A, F**

Xue Gu-yan: Nancy Sit Ka-yin / Sit Ga-yin / Nancy Siu. **AT**

Xue Han: Sit Hon / Hsieh Han / Hsueh Han / Shit Hong / Shih Han / Sit Hong / Hsued Han / Xue Han / Shu Hong. **A**

Yan Nan-xi: Nancy Yen Nan-see / Yin Naam-hei / Yin Nam-hei / Yan Nan-his / Yian Jue-jue / Yan Nan-see / Yen Nan-his. **AT**

Yang Cheng-wu, Tiger: Yeung Shing-ng / Yang Cheng-wu / Yeung Shing-ng / Tiger Yeung / Paul Yang. **A**

Yang Chi-ching: Yeung Chi-hing / Yang Zhi-qing / Yang Chih-ching / Yang Chih-chin / Yang Tse-ching / Yan Chih-ching. **A**

Yang Fan: Yeung Fan / Sherman Yang Feng / Yang Fang. **D**

Yang Hui-shan: Elsa Yeung Wai-san / Yeung Wai-saan / Yang Hui-sang / Queenie Yang / Linda Young / Yang Hui-san. **AT**

Yang Jing-chen: Yeung Jing-chan / Yang Ching-chen / Yeung Ching-chan / Yang Ching-cheng. **A**

Yang Jing-jing: Yeung Jing-jing / Yang Ching-ching / Yeung Ching-ching / Yiang Ching-ching / Yang Tsing-tsing. **AT**

Yang Kwan, Peter: Yeung Kwan / Yang Qun / Yang Chun / Peter K. Yang / Yeung Kwun / Yeung Kwan / Yang Chuan / Yang Qun. **A, D**

Yang Lun: Yeung Lun / Yang Shu-sheng / Yeung Shu-sing. **A**

Yang Pan-pan: Sharon Yeung Pan-pan / Yeung Paan-paan / Pamela Yang / Sharon Yang. **AT**

Yang Su: Yeung Siu / Young Su. **D**

Yang Wei: Yeung Wai / Bruce Kong / Yan Wei. **A, F**

Yang Xiong: Yeung Hung / Yang Hsiung / Ma Tze-pang / Yang Song / Yang Xiun / Yang Ni-chiu. **A**

Yang Yang: Yeung Yeung. **A, D**

Yang Ze-lin: Yeung Chak-lam / Yang Tse-lin / Yeung Chak-sam. **A**

Yasuda Kimiyoshi: On Ting Gung Yee / An Tian Gong Yi. **D**

Yasuyoshi Shikamura: Luk Chuen / Luk Chuen Taai Cheung / Lu Cun Tai Xiang / Luk Chuen / Luk Chuen Taai Cheung / Lu Chuen Tai Hsiang/ Shika-mura Lu Chuan. **A, F**

Yeh Hsiao-yee: Yip Siu-yee / She Xiao-yi / Yip Siu-yik / Yeh Hsiao-I / Yeh Shao-i. **A**

Yee, Derek: Derek Yee Tung-sing / Yi Dung-sing / Er Dong-sheng / Erh Tung-sheng / Yee Tung-shing / Derek T. S. Yee. **A**

Yee Hung: Yi Hong. **AT**

Yee Yuen: Yi Yuan / Yi Yuen / I Yen / Yik Yuen / I Yuan / Yue Yuen / Yee Yuan / Ye Yuan. **A**

Yeh, Karen: Karen Yip Leng-chi / Yip Leng-chi / She Ling-zhi / Karen Yeh Ling-chih / Yeh Ling-tzu / Ho Pik-yu / Yip Leng-chi. **AT**

Yeh Yung-tsu: Teddy Yip Wing-cho / Yip Wing-jo / She Rong-zu / Ip Wing-cho / Ip Wing-tso / Yeh Jung-chu / Yeh Jung-tsu / Yeh Rong-chio / Yeh Yung-tsao / Yip Wing-cho / Yeh Yung-cha / Yeh Tsung-tsu / Ye Rong-zu / Teddy Yip. **A, D**

Yen Chun: Yan Jun / Yim Chun / Yim Jun / Yen Chuan. **A, D**

Yen Shi-kwan: Yam Sai Goon / Ren Shi-guan / Yan Yee-kwan / Yen Si-kuan / Yam Sai-kun / Jen Shin-kuan / Jen Shih-kuan / Yin Sai-quen / Yam Sai-koon. **A**

Yen Yu-lung: Aan Yuk-lung / Yan Yu-long / Ngan Luk-lung. **F, A**

Yeung, Bolo: Bolo Yang / Bolo Yeung Sze / Yang Sze / Yeung Shut / Yang Szu / Bolo Yung / Yeung See / Yeung Shut / Yang Si / Bolo Yeung Tse / Yan Si / Yang Si / Yeung Tze. **A, F, D**

Yeung Man-yi: Yeung Maan-yi / Yang Man-yi / Yeo Ban-yee. **D**

Yi Lui, James: Yi Lui / Yi Lei / I Lei / Yi Loi / Eric Yee / Yee Lau. **A, D**

Yi Yuan: Yee Yuen / Yi Yuen / I Yen / Yik Yuen / I-Yuan / Yue Yuen / Yee Yuan / Ye Yuan / Ye Yuen. **A**

Yim, Michelle: Mai Suet / Mi Xue / Mi Hsueh / Michelle / Mai Shuet / Micelle Mei-suet / Michelle Lai / Mi Hsuen. **AT**

Yin Bao-lian: Pauline Wan Bo-lin / Wan Bo Lin. **AT**

Yin Fa: Wan Faat / Wan Fat. **A**

Yin Yi-feng: Wan Yat-fung. **A**

Yip Leng-Chi, Karen: Yip Leng-chi / She Ling-zhi / Karen Yeh Ling-chih / Yeh Ling-tzu / Ho Pik-yu / Yip Leng-chi. **AT**

Yip, Teddy: Teddy Yip Wing-Cho / Yip Wing-jo / She Rong-zu / Ip Wing-cho / Ip Wing-tso / Yeh Yung-tsu / Yeh Jung-chu / Yeh Jung-tsu / Yeh Rong-chio / Yeh Yung-tsao. **A, D**

You Ching: Yau Ching / You Qing / Cheung Yung-yung / Yu Ching. **AT**

You Long: Yau Lung / Yu Lung / Yau Ling / Yau Shung-git / Yu Chung-chieh / Yiu Lung. **A**

You Peng-sheng: Yau Pang-sang / Yau Paang-sang / Yau Chung-wai / Chung Wai / Yau Ping-sang. **A**

You Tian-lung: Yu Tien-lung / Yau Tin-lung / You Tian-long / Yau Tin-lung / Henry Liu Tien-lung / Lau Tien-lung / Lau Tin-lung / Yu Tian-long / Lau Tin-fook. **A**

Yu An-an: Candice Yu On-on / Tsui On-on / Chui On-on / Yu De-ying / Yu On-on / Candy Yu. **AT**

Yu Cheng-Chun: Wat Jing-chun. **D**

Yu Chien, Angela: Yue Sin / Yu Qian / Yu Seen / Angel Yu Chien / Yen Zhi-ling. **AT**

Yu Feng: Yue Fung. **AT**

Yu Fung-chi, Florence: Florence F. C. Yu. **D**

Yu Han-hsiang: Yu Hon-cheung. **D**

Yu Hui: Yue Wai / Shirley Hui / Yu Hai / Jeanette Yu. **AT**

Yu Rong: Yue Wing / Yu Yung. **A**

Yu Ling-lung: Yuk Leng-lung / Yu Ling-long. **AT**

Yu Song-zhao: Yu Chung-chiu / Chui Chung-chiu / Yu Chung-hei / Yu Song-chao / Yu Sung-chao / Chui Chung-chiu / Chester Yee / Yu Chon-chiu. **A, F**

Yu Tien-lung: Yau Tin-lung / You Tian-long / Yau Tin-lung / Henry Liu Tien-lung / Lau Tien-lung / Lau Tin-lung / Yu Tian-long / Lau Tin-fook. **A, F, D**

Yu Tien-lung: Yau Tin-lung / You Tian-long / Henry Liu Tien-lung / Lau Tien-lung / Lau Tin-lung / Yu Tian-Long / Lau Tin-fook. **A, F, D**

Yu Tou-yun: Yue Tau-wan / Ma Chao / Chui Tau-wan / Yu Tau-wan / Lau Wan. **A**

Yu Yung, Henry: Yue Yeung / Yu Yang / Bruce Ly / Kenny Kung / Shue Jia-ian. **A**

Yuan Chiu-feng: Yuen Chau-fung / Yuen Qiu-feng / Yuen Chow-fung / Yuen Chiu-feng / Yuen Hsiu-feng. **D**

Yuan Sen: Yuen Sam / Yuen Sum / Yuen Shen. **A**

Yue Yang: Ngok Yeung / Yo Yang / Yueh Yang. **A**

Yueh Feng: Griffin Yueh Feng / Ngok Fung / Yue Feng / Yueh Fung. **D**

Yueh Hua: Ngok Wa / Yue Hua / Yo Hua / Ngok Wah / Yuei Hwa / Yao Hua/ Yueh Hwa / Elly Yuen Hua / Elliot Ngok Wa / Leung Hok-hwa / Elliot Yue / Liang Leh-hua / Elly Leung. **A**

Yuen Bing: Yuen Bun / Yuen Ban / Yuen Pih / Yuen Pun / To Chau-kwan / Tiu Chow-kwan / To Chow-kwan / Yuan Pin / Yuan Bin. **A, F**

Yuen Biao: Yuen Biu / Yuan Biao / Ha Ling-chun / Yan Piao / Yuen Bill / Ha Ling-chan. **A, F**

Yuen Bao-huang: Yuen Biu-wong / Yuan Bao Huang / Yuen Po-wong. **AT**

Yuen, Brandy: Brandy Yuen Jan-yeung / Yuen Jan-yeung / Yuan Zhen-yang / Yuen Chun-wei / Yuen Chen-wei / Yuen Jan-wai / Yuen Cheung-yeung / Yuen Ching-wei / Yuen Chun-yeung / Yuen Chun-yong. **A, F**

Yuen Cheung-yan: Yuan Xiang- ren / Yuan Hsiang-ren / Yuan Hsian-jen / Yuen Chong-yan / Yuen Cheong-yan / Yuen Cheung-yen / Yuan Hsiang-ten / Yuan Hsiang-yen / Yuan Chang-jen / Yuan Shyang-ren / Yuen Cheng-yan. **A, F**

Yuen De: Yuen Tak / Yuan De / Yuan Te / Richard Hung / Chiang Lin / Hung Cheung-tak / Yuen Tat. **A, F**

Yuen Hua: Yuen Wah / Yuen Wa / Yuan Hua / Wong Yuen-wah / Yu Wah / Yuan Hua / Sam Yung / Yung Gai-chi / Yung Kai-chi. **A, F**

Yuen Kwei: Corey Yuen Kwai / Yuen Fooi / Yuan Kui / Don Yuen / Cory Yuen / Yuan Kuei / Yuen Kuei / Yuen Fui. **A, F**

Yuen Man-zi: Yuen Man-tzu / Yuen Maan Chi / Yuen Man-chi. **AT**

Yuen Qiu: Yuen Chau / Yuan Qiu / Gam Ga-fung / Lam Sau / Lin Xiu / Lin Siu / Lin Hsiu / Phoenix Kim / Kan Chia-fong / Kan Chia-feng. **AT**

Yuen Shen-yi: Yuen Shun-yi / Yuen San-yee / Yuan Shen-yi / Ugly Yuen / Eagle Yuen / Sunny Yuen / Yuen Hsun-yi / Armstrong Yuen / Yuen San-yee / Yuen Shun-yee / Yuan Hsin-yi / Steven Yuen / Yuen Shun-I. **A, F**

Yuen Woo-ping: Yuen Wo-ping / Yuen Who-ping / Yuan He-ping / Yuen Ho-Ping / Peace Yuen / Yuan Ta-yean / Yuan Ta-yen / Yuen Dai-an / Yuen Woo-pang / Yuan Ho-ping / Yuan Her-ping / Yuan He-ping. **A, F, D**

Yuen Xiao-tian: Simon Yuen Siu-tin / Simon Yuen / Simon Yuan / Yuen Siu-tin / Yuan Xiao-tian / Yuen Hsiao-tien / Yuan Hsiao-tien / Yuen Hsiao-tieng / Yuen Siu-tien / Yuan Hsiao-tieng / Yuen Shui-Tin / Yin Siu-tin. **A, F**

Yuen Yat-Choh: Yuan Ri-chu / Yuen Yat-Chor / Simon Yuen Jr. **A**

Yung Yuk-yi: Rong Yu-yi / Yung Yuk-yee / Yung Yuk-i. **AT**

Zhan Long: Chim Lung. **A, F**

Zhang Bing-yu: Cheung Bing-yuk / Chang Ping-yu / Chang Pin-Yu / Cheung Bing-yue. **AT**

Zhang Fu-jian: Cheung Fook-gin / Chang Fu-chien. **A**

Zhang Guo-zhu: Chang Kuo-chu / Jeung Gwok-chyu / Cheung Gwok-chue / Cheong Kwok-chu / Cheung Kwok-chu. **A**

Zhang Ji-long: Peter Chang / Cheung Gai-lung / Peter Chen / Cheung Gai-lung. **A, F**

Zhang Ji-ping: Chang Chi-ping / Cheung Gei-ping / Cheung Kei-ping / Cheung Goon-lung / Chang Kuan-lung / Cheung Gee-ping. **A**

Zhang Jie: Cheung Git / Cheung Chieh. **D**

Zhang Jing-po: Cheung Ging-boh / Chang Ching-po / Cheung Wang / Chang Hung. **A, D**

Zhang Peng: Cheung Paang / Cheung Paang / Chang Pang / Cheung Fook-gan / Chang Peng / Cheng Ping. **A, F**

Zhang Qi: William Cheung Kei / Cheung Kei / Chang Chi / Cheung Kay / William Chang Key / Cheung Kei / Chang Chee / William Chang Kee/ Janq Chyi. **D**

Zhang Qing-qing: Cheung Ching-ching / Chang Ching-ching. **A**

Zhang Quan: Richard Cheung Kuen / Cheung Kuen / Chang Chuang / Chang Chuan / Richard K. Cheung. **A, F**

Zhang Sen: Cheung Sam / Chang Sum / Cheung Sum/ Chang Shen. **D**

Zhang Tai-lun: Cheung Taai-lun. **A**

Zhang Tong-zu: Joe Cheung Tung-cho / Cheung Tung-jo / Joe Cheung / Cheung Tung-joe / Cheung Tung-jo / Joseph Cheung / Chang Tung-jo / Cheung Ton-cho. **A, D**

Zhang Yi: Cheung Yik / Chang Yi / Cheung Yik / Cheung I / Chang I / Zhang Bo-shen. **A**

Zhang Yi-dao: Bruce Lai / Chang Yi-tao / Cheung Yat-diy / Cheung Yat-dao / Phillip Cheung / Bruce Lai / Jang Il-do / Chang Yi-chu. **A**

Zhang Yi-gui: Cheung Yee-kwai / Cheung Yee-gwai / Cheung I-kuei / Chang I-kuai. **A, F**

Zhang Yin-sheng: Emily Cheung Ying-chan / Cheung Ying-chan / Emily Chang / Chan Ying-cheng / Chang Yng-Jen. **AT**

Zhang Zhi-chao: Cheung Chi-chiu / Richard Chen (2), Chang Chi-Chao, Stewart Cheung, Zhang Zhi-Chao. **D**

Zhang Zhao: Cheung Hei / Cheung Chiu / Cheung Hay / Cheung Hey. **A**

Zhang Zong-gui: Cheung Chung-Kwai / Tong Cheung / Cheung Chung-kai / Chang Chung-kai / Chang Tzong-guey / Cheung Chung-qu. **A, F**

Zhao Xiong: Chiu Hung / Chao Hsiung / Lam Kin-chuen. **A**

Zheng Fu-xiong: Cheng Fu-hung / Jeng Foo-hung / Cheng Fu-hsiung / Cheung Fu-hung / Tsang Fu-hung / Zheng Fu-xiong. **A**

Zhong Guo-heng: Chung Gwok-hang / Chung Gwok-hang / Chong Kuo-hong. **D**

Zhou Ming-qing: Chow Ming-ching. **A**

Zhou Run-jian: Danny Chow Yun-gin / Chow Yun-gin / Chiao Feng / Chou Jen-chien / Chow Yun-chi / Kiu Fung / Chou Yun-kin / Chow Yun-kin. **A, F**

Zhou Shao-dong: Sherman Chow Shiu-dung / Chow Shiu-dung / Chou Shao-tung. **A**

Zhou Xiao-lai: Chow Siu-Loi / Jau Siu-lai / Chou Hsiao-lai. **A**

Zhu Qing: Chu Ching / Jue Ching. **AT**

Zhu Ke: Chu Ko / Jue Haak / Jue Hak / Ju Hak-wing / Chu Ke. **A**

Zhu Mu: Jue Muk / Chu Mu / Jue Muk / Chu Muk / Cheung Ji / Hdeng Tsu. **A, D**

Zi Lan: Chi Laan / Tsi Lan / Chi Lan / Tzu Lan. **AT**

Zuo Yan-rong: Joh Yim-yung / Tso Yen-yung. **AT**

COMPLETE MARTIAL ARTS FILM REFERENCE
LIST BY COUNTRY: 1970 – 1979

Key: FR–France; HK–Hong Kong; INDO–Indonesia; IT–Italy; JA–Japan; ME–Mexico; PH–Philippines; SK–South Korea; SP–Spain; TH–Thailand; TU–Turkey; UK–United Kingdom; USA–United States of America; AU–Australia; **Bold**–Titles; **Nonbold**–Alternative Titles as found in the titleography of a martialogy. **Note on co-productions:** Alternative titles will only be included with the country that appears first in this movie list. So for **Supermenler** – 1979 (IT/SP/TU), its alternative titles will only be listed in Italy. Also, although *Supermenler* counts as a film for Italy, Spain and Turkey, in the final tally of all films made during the 1970s, it will only be counted as one film. For Chinese films, when possible, the original language film title of a movie will have a romanized English title in parenthesis after the main English title. All films that have a martialogy will have a symbol to denote that as well as the corresponding page number.

HONG KONG – TAIWAN

Abbot of Shaolin – (see Shaolin Abbot)
Action Tae Kwon Do – 1972
Adventure, The – 1972
Adventure in Denmark – 1973
Adventure of Heaven Mouse – (see Snake in the Crane's Shadow)
Adventure Sandstorm – (see The Adventure)
Adventurer, The – (see Money Trip)
Adventures of Emperor Chien Lung, The – 1977
Adventures of Shaolin – 1978
Against Drunken Cat's Paws – (see No-one Can Touch Her)
Against Kung Fu Rascal – (see Wild Bunch of Kung Fu)
Against Rascals with Kung Fu – (see Wild Bunch of Kung Fu)
Agency, The – (see Master Samurai)
All Men Are Brothers – 1973
Along Came a Tiger – (see Along Comes a Tiger)
Along Came the Tiger – (see Along Comes a Tiger)
Along Comes a Tiger – 1977
Along Comes the Tiger – (see Along Comes a Tiger)
Amazon Against Superman – (see Superman Against the Amazons)
Amazons Vs. Superman – (see Superman Against the Amazons)
Amazons and Supermen – (see Superman Against the Amazons)
Ambush – 1972
Ammunition Hunters, The – 1971
Amsterdam Connection – 1978
Amsterdam Kill. – 1978
Angry Dragon – 1973
Angry Fist – (see Iron Ox, the Tiger's Killer)
Angry Guest, The – 1972
Angry Hero, The – 1973
Angry River – 1970
Angry Tiger – 1973
Annoyed Guest, The – (see The Angry Guest)
Anonymous Heroes, The – 1971
Any Which Way You Punch – (Scorching Sun, Fierce Winds, and Wild Fire)
Ape Girl – 1979
Arrows of the Heart – (see Oath of Death)
Arson: The Criminals, Part III – 1977
Art of War – (see Strike and Sword)
Art of war by Sun Tzu – 1979
Arts of the Snake and Crane – (see Snake and Crane Arts of Shaolin)

Assassin – 1976
Asssassin – (see Secret Rivals)
Assassin, The – 1971
Assassin, The – (see Return of the Assassin)
Assassin, The – (see The Bodyguard)
Assault of Final Rival – 1978
Assault: The Criminals, Part IV, The – 1977
Assignment – 1976
Association, The – 1975 (SK)
Attack of the Kung Fu Girls – (see None But the Brave)
Attack to Kill – (see A Dead Rivalry)
Avenger, The – 1972
Avenger, The – (see Kung Fu Infernos)
Avengers – (see Blood and Guts)
Avengers Handicapped – (see Crippled Avengers)
Avenging Boxer – 1979
Avenging Dragon – (see Two Graves to Kung Fu)
Avenging Eagle, The – 1978
Avenging Ninja – (see Zen Kwun Do Strikes in Paris)
Avenging Warriors of Shaolin – (see Shaolin Rescuers)
Awaken Fist, The – (see The Awaken Punch)
Awaken Punch, The – 1973

Back Alley Princes – (see Back Alley Princess)
Back Alley Princess – 1973
Back Alley Princess in Chinatown – (see Chinatown Capers)
Bad Guys Wear Black – (see Black Belt Karate)
Badge 369 – (see Supremo)
Bamboo Brotherhood – 1973
Bamboo House Of Dolls, The – 1973
Bamboo Trap – 1979
Bamboo Women's Prison – (see The Bamboo House of Dolls)
Bandits, The – 1971
Bandits From Shantung – 1971
Bandits Prostitutes & Silver – (see The Damned)
Bandits, Prostitutes and Silver – (see The Damned)
Barbarian Revenge – (see Superman Against the Amazons)
Bastard, The – 1973
Bat Island Adventure – (see Legend of the Bat)
Battle in Red Temple – (see The Story in Temple Red Lily)
Battle of Guningtou, The – 1979
Battle of Shaolin – (see The Damned)
Battle Wizard, The – 1977
Battles with the Red Boy – 1972
Beach of the War Gods – 1972
Beauty Heroine – 1973

Bedeviled – 1975
Begging Swordsman, The – 1970
Behind Bruce Lee – (see Bruce Lee – True Story)
Belles of Taekwondo – (The Dragon Tamers)
Best of Shaolin Kung Fu – 1976
Bewitched Princess, A – 1970
Big Bad Sis – 1976
Big Boss, The – 1971
Big Boss of Shanghai – 1979
Big Boss 2 – 1979
Big Boss II – (see Big Boss 2)
Big Boss Part 2, The – 1976
Big Brother – 1974
Big Brother Cheng – 1975
Big Brother Tong Shan – (see The Big Boss)
Big Family, The – 1976
Big Fellow, The – 1973
Big Fellow, The – (see Super Inframan)
Big Fight, The – 1972
Big Foot Mama – (see The Revenge of Kung Fu Mao)
Big Holdup, The – 1975
Big Land Flying Eagles – 1978
Big Leap Forward – 1978
Big Rascal, The – 1979
Big Risk, The – 1974
Big Showdown, The – 1974
Big Wheel – (see Rikisha Kuri)
Black and White Swordsman – (see Black and White Swordsmen)
Black and White Swordsmen – 1971
Black and White Umbrellas – 1971
Black Belt, The – 1973
Black Belt Jones II – (see The Tattoo Connection)
Black Belt Jones 2: Tattoo Conection – (see The Tattoo Connection)
Black Belt Jones II): Tattoo Conection – (see The Tattoo Connection)
Black Belt Karate – 1979 (INDO)
Black Dragon – (see Way of the Black Dragon)
Black Dragon – (see Tough Guy)
Black Dragon, The – 1973
Black Dragon Fever – (see Kung Fu Fever)
Black Dragon vs. Yellow Tiger – (see Tiger from China)
Black Dragon's Revenge, The – 1975
Black Enforcer, The – 1972
Black Friday, The – 1973
Black Guardly – (see The Cannibals)
Black Guide – 1973
Black Guide – (see Chinese Hercules)
Black Hercules Vs. Yellow Tiger – (see Men of the Hour)

Black Hurricane – 1970
Black Jim Le Magnifique – (see Sun Dragon)
Black List – 1972
Black Magic – 1975
Black Panther – 1973
Black Panther of Shaolin, The – (see Bamboo Trap)
Black Strike – (see The Way of the Black Dragon)
Black Tavern, The – 1972
Black Terminator – (see Black Samurai)
Blade of Fury – (see The Two Great Cavaliers)
Blades of Emotion – (see Sentimental Swordsman)
Blade Spares None, The – 1970
Blazing Temple, The – 1976
Blind Boxer – 1972
Blind Fist of Bruce – 1979
Blind Fists – (see Blind Boxer)
Blind Hero Fighting Evil Wolf – 1972
Blind Swordswoman – (see Golden Sword and the
   Blind Swordswoman)
Blind Swordsman Meets His Equal, The – (see
   Zatoichi Meets the One-Armed Swordsman)
Blind Swordsman Vs. White Wolf – (see Blind Hero
   Fighting Evil Wolf)
Blind Swordsman's Revenge, The – 1974
Blood and Guts – 1971
Blood and Rose – 1975
Blood & Rose – (see Blood and Rose)
Blood Avenger – (see Bamboo Brotherhood)
Blood Boxer – (see Ma Su Chen)
Blood Brothers – 1973
Blood Brothers – (see The Heroic Ones)
Blood City – (see The Last Days of Hsin Yang)
Blood Dragon – (see Beach of the War Gods)
Blood Fingers – (see Brutal Boxer)
Blood Hero, The – (see Bloody Hero)
Blood Leopard – (see Blood of the Leopard)
Blood Money – (see Stranger and the Gunfighter)
Blood of the Dragon – (see Desperate Chase)
Blood of the Ninja – (see Desperate Chase)
Blood on his Hands – (see Edge of Fury)
Blood on the Sun – (see The Big Fight)
Blood Pact – (see 36 Crazy Fists)
Blood Revenge – 1974
Blood Start – (see The Boxer's Last Stand)
Blooded Treasury Fight – 1979
Bloodfisted Brothers – (see Militant Eagle)
Bloody Avengers – (see Boxer Rebellion)
Bloody Duel: Life & Death – (see Bloody Fight)
Bloody Hibiscus – (see Vengeful Beauty)
Bloody Escape, The – 1974
Bloody Fight – 1972
Bloody Fists – (see The Heroic Ones)
Bloody Fists, The – 1972
Bloody Hand Goddess – 1970
Bloody Hero – 1976
Bloody Money – (see Stranger and the Gunfighter)
Bloody Monkey Master – (see Iron Monkey)
Bloody Ring – 1973
Bloody Struggle – (see Ma Su Chen)
Blows and Pillows – 1972
Boatman Fighters, The – (see Cheung Po Chai)
Bod Squad – (see Deadly Angels)
Bod Squad, The – (see Virgins of the Seven Seas)
Bodyguard, The – 1973
Bold Brothers – (see The Invasion)
Bold Face, Heart and Blood – (Showdown at Cotton
   Mill)

Bold Three, The – 1972
Bolo – 1977
Bolo: The Brute – (see Bolo)
Bone Crushing Kid – 1979
Born Invincible – 1978
Born of Fire – 1974
Boxer From Shantung, The – 1972
Boxer From the Temple, The – 1979
Boxer in Shanghai – (see Brave Girl Boxer in
   Shanghai)
Boxer King of Chaozhow – (see The Greatest Thai
   Boxing)
Boxer Rebellion – 1975
Boxer Who Kills, The – (see The Fist That Kills)
Boxers, The – 1972
Boxers, The – 1973
Boxers of Loyalty and Righteousness – 1972
Boxer's Adventure – (see Wild Bunch of Kung Fu)
Boxer's Adventure – 1979
Boxer's Adventure – (see Militant Eagle)
Boxer's Last Stand, The – 1976
Boxing Wizard – (see Peculiar Boxing Tricks and the
   Master)
Bravado of a Lady Fight – (see Bruce Lee's Ways of
   Kung Fu)
Brave and the Evil – 1971
Brave Archer, The – 1977
Brave Archer Part II, The – (see The Brave Archer 2)
Brave Archer 2, The – 1978
Brace Girl Boxer From Shanghai – (see Brave Girl
   Boxer in Shanghai)
Brave Girl Boxer in Shanghai – 1972
Brave in Kung Fu Shadow – (see Imperial Sword)
Brave in Kung Fu Shadow, The – (see Imperial
   Sword)
Brave in the Kung Fu Shadow – (see Imperial Sword)
Brave Lion, The – 1974
Brave Man, The – (see Cheung Po Chai)
Bravest Fist – 1974
Bravest One – 1975
Bravest Revenge, The – 1970
Breaking Swords of Death – (see The Deadly Break-
   ing Sword)
Breakout from Oppression – 1973
Broken Blade – (see Relentless Broken Swords)
Broken Oath – 1977
Broken Sword – 1971
Bronze Girls of Shaolin – (see The 18 Bronze Girls
   of Shaolin)
Bronze Head and Steel Arms – 1972
Brotherhood – 1976
Brothers, The – 1973
Brothers, The – (see Dragon and Tiger)
Brothers, The – 1979
Brothers Five – 1970
Brothers Two – 1974
Bruce Against Iron Hand – (see Bruce and the Iron
   Finger)
Bruce Against Snake in the Eagle's Shadow
   – 1979
Bruce and Shaolin Kung Fu – 1978
Bruce and Shaolin Kung Fu 2 – 1978
Bruce & Shao-Lin Kung Fu – (see Bruce and Shaolin
   Kung Fu 2)
Bruce and the Iron Finger – 1979
Bruce and the Shaolin Fist – (see Bruce and Shaolin
   Kung Fu 2)

Bruce, D-Day at Macao – (see Little Super Man)
Bruce, D-Day at Macau – (see Little Super Man)
Bruce has Risen – (see Deadly Strike)
Bruce, Hong Kong Master – (see Hong Kong Super-
   man)
Bruce is Loose – (see Green Dragon Inn)
Bruce in New Guinea – (see Bruce Li in New Guinea)
Bruce, Kung Fu Girls – 1975
Bruce Takes Dragon Town – 1974
Bruce the Super Hero – 1979
Bruce Vs. Black Dragon (see Bruce and Shaolin
   Kung Fu)
Bruce Vs. Snake in Eagle's Shadow – (Snake in the
   Eagle's Shadow)
Bruce's Deadly Finger – 1976
Bruce's Deadly Fingers – (see Bruce's Deadly
   Finger)
Bruce's Fingers – (see Bruce's Deadly Fingers)
Bruce's Return – (see Return of Bruce)
Bruce Le's Greatest Revenge – 1978
Bruce Lee Against Supermen – 1975
Bruce Lee Battle to Death – 1977
Bruce Lee – A Dragon Story – 1974
Bruce Lee: A Dragon Story – (see Bruce Lee's
   Deadly Kung Fu)
Bruce Lee Fights Again – (see Big Boss 2)
Bruce Lee – His Last Days – (see Bruce Lee and I;
   1975)
Bruce Lee – His Last Days, His Last Nights – (see
   Bruce Lee and I; 1975)
Bruce Lee and I – 1975
Bruce Lee & I – (see Bruce Lee and I)
Bruce Lee & I – (see Fist of Unicorn)
Bruce Lee Superdragon – (see Bruce Lee: A Dragon
   Story)
Bruce Lee Superstar – (see Legend of Bruce Lee)
Bruce Lee, Star of Stars – (see Exit the Dragon,
   Enter the Tiger)
Bruce Lee Story, The – (see Bruce Lee: A Dragon
   Story)
Bruce Lee the Little Dragon – (see The Real Bruce
   Lee)
Bruce Lee – The Invincible – (see Bruce Li – The
   Invincible)
Bruce Lee, the Man and the Legend – 1977
Bruce Lee: The Man, the Myth – (Bruce Lee – True
   Story)
Bruce Lee, the Star of All Stars – (see Exit the
   Dragon, Enter the Tiger)
Bruce Lee – True Story – 1976
Bruce Lee Vs. Supermen – (see Bruce Lee Against
   Supermen)
Bruce Lee Vs. The Iron Dragon – (see Bruce and the
   Iron Finger)
Bruce Lee, We Miss You – (see Dragon Dies Hard)
Bruce Lee We Miss You – (see Bruce Lee A Dragon
   Story)
Bruce Lee's Deadly Kung Fu – 1976 (Important
   Note: see BLDKF's martialogy)
Bruce Lee's Fist of Vengeance – (see Bruce Le's
   Greatest Revenge)
Bruce Lee's Greatest Revenge – (see Bruce Le's
   Greatest Revenge)
Bruce Lee's Iron Finger – (see Bruce and the Iron
   Finger)
Bruce Lee's Secret – (see Bruce Lee's Deadly Kung
   Fu)

Bruce Lee's Ways of Kung Fu – 1979 (SK)
Bruce Li in New Guinea – 1978
Bruce Li in Snake Island – (see Bruce Li in New Guinea)
Bruce Li the Invincible Chinatown Connection – (see Bruce Li – The Invincible)
Bruce Li, Superdragon – (see Bruce Lee: A Dragon Story)
Bruce Li, Superdragon – (see Dragon Dies Hard)
Bruce Li's Iron Finger – (see Bruce and the Iron Finger)
Bruce Li's Jeet Kune Do – (see Bruce Lee's Deadly Kung Fu)
Bruce Li's Magnum Fist – (see Magnum Fist)
Brutal Boxer – 1972
Brutal Revenge – (see Fighing Ace)
Buddha Assassinator – 1979
Buddhist Assassinator – (see Buddha Assassinator)
Buddhist Fist – 1979
Buddhist Shaolin Avengers – (see The Awaken Punch)
Budo Wing – (see Butcher Wing)
Buffalo Hsiung – (see Assignment)
Bullet Ballet – (see The Magnificent Gunfighter)
Burning Shaolin Temple – (see The Blazing Temple)
Butcher Wing – 1979
Butterfly 18 – 1979
Butterfly Murders, The – 1979
By Hook and By Crook – 1978
By Hook & By Crook – (see By Hook and By Crook)

Call Him Mr. Shatter – 1974 (UK)
Call Me Chivalry – (see Ninja Swords of Death)
Call Me Dragon – 1974
Call To Arms – 1972
Cannibals, The – 1972
Canton Challenge – (Showdown at Cotton Mill)
Cantonen Iron Kung Fu – 1979
Cantonese – 1978
Captive – 1971
Casino, The – 1972
Cavalier, The – 1978
Challenge – (see Drunken Master)
Challenge Me Dragon – (see Fighting Dragon)
Challenge of Death – 1978
Challenge of the Dragon – 1974
Challenge of the Masters – 1976
Challenge of the Ninja – (see Heroes of the East)
Challenger, The – 1979
Champ of Champs – (The Crane Fighters)
Champion, The – 1973
Champion of Champions, The – 1972
Champion of the Boxer, The – 1972
Champion on Fire – (see Fury in Storm)
Chang Gang, The – (see Assault of Final Rival)
Chang Shang-Fon Adventures – (see Adventure of Shaolin)
Chaochow Guy – 1972
Chase, The – 1971
Chase, The – 1978
Chase Step by Step – (see Dragon and Tiger, 1974)
Chasing the Dragon – (see Fists of Dragons)
Cheeky Chap, The – 1979
Cheung Po Chai – 1975
Child's Efforts, The – (see The Mighty One)
China Armed Escort – 1976
Chinatown Capers – 1974

Chinatown Kid – 1977
Chinese – 1972
Chinese, The – (see Cantonese)
Chinese Acupuncturist, The – 1975
Chinese Acupuncture Kung Fu – (see Chinese Kung Fu and Acupuncture)
Chinese Amazons – 1975
Chinese Amazons, The – (see Chinese Amazones)
Chinese Boxer, The – 1970
Chinese Boxing – 1974
Chinese Chien Chuan Kung Fu – (see Legend of Bruce Lee)
Chinese Connection, The – (see Fist of Fury)
Chinese Connection 2 – 1977
Chinese Connection 3 – (see Jeet Kune the Claws and the Supreme)
Chinese Dragon, The – 1973
Chinese Enforcers, The – (see Chinatown Capers)
Chinese Gods – 1975
Chinese Godfathers – 1974
Chinese Goliath – (see Big Boss 2)
Chinese Hercules – 1973
Chinese Iron Man – 1973
Chinese Kung Fu – (see The Dumb Ox)
Chinese Kung Fu – 1974
Chinese Kung Fu Against Godfather – 1974
Chinese Kung Fu and Acupuncture – 1973
Chinese Mack, The – (see Martial Arts)
Chinese Mechanic – (see The Chinese Dragon)
Chinese Professionals – (see One-Armed Boxer)
Chinese Samson – (see Writing Kung Fu)
Chinese Superior Kung Fu – 1975
Chinese Superman – (see Super Inframan)
Chinese Tiger – 1974
Chinese Vengeance – (see Blood Brothers)
Chinese Whimsy, The – 1974
Ching Wu and Shaolin Kung Fu – (see Bruce and Shaolin Kung Fu)
Ching Wu and Shaolin Kung Fu Part 2 – (see Bruce and Shaolin Kung Fu 2)
Ching Wu & Shaolin Kung Fu II – (see Bruce and Shaolin Kung Fu 2)
Chin Sha Yen – 1977
Chiu Chow Kung Fu – 1973
Chivalrous Inn – 1977
Chivalrous Killer – (see Heaven Sword and Dragon Sabre)
Chivalrous Knight – (see Chinese Godfather)
Chivalrous Robber Lee San – 1972
Chivalry of Conspiracy – (see Lu Hsiao Fury)
Chivalry, The Gunman and Killer, The – 1977
Choi Lee Fat – 1970
Choy Lay Fat Kid, The – (see The New Shaolin Boxers)
Choi Lee Fat Kung Fu – 1979
Choi Lee Fut Strikes Again – 1970
Chow Ken – 1972
Chu Chow Kung Fu – (See Chiu Chow Kung Fu)
Chuck Norris Vs. the Karate Cop – (see Yellow Faced Tiger)
Circle of Iron – 1979
Clan Of Amazons – 1978
Clans Of Intrigue – 1976
Clans on Intrigue 2 – (see Legend of the Bat)
Clan of Righteousness – 1979
Clan Of The White Lotus – 1979
Claw of the Tiger – (see Tiger's Claw)

Cleopatra Jones & the Casino of Gold – 1975 (USA)
Cleopatra Jones Meets the Dragon Lady – (see Cleopatra Jones & the Casino of Gold)
Clones of Bruce Lee – 1977
Clutch of Power – 1977
Cobra Girl – (see Fangs of the Cobra)
Cold Blade – 1970
Cold-Blooded Eagles – (see The Avenging Eagle)
Cold Wind Hands – 1972
Colossus of the Congo – (see the Mighty Peking Man)
Cool Wind Hands – (see Cold Wind Hands)
Comet Strikes, The – 1971
Concrete Jungle – 1974
Condemned, The – 1976
Conman and the Kung Fu Kid – (see Wits to Wits)
Conspiracy – 1975
Conspiracy of Thieves – 1975
Countdown in Kung Fu – (see The Hand of Death)
Countdown to Kung Fu – (see The Hand of Death)
Cover Girl Models – 1975
Crack Shadow Boxers – 1978
Crane Fighter, The – 1979
Crane Fighters, The – (see The Crane Fighter)
Crash the Bottle – (see Supermen Against the Orient)
Crazy Acrobat – 1974
Crazy Boy and Pop-Eye – 1979
Crazy Couple – 1979
Crazy Group, The – 1975
Crazy Guy, The – 1975
Crazy Guy with Super Kung Fu – 1978
Crazy Guy with the Super Kung Fu – (see Crazy Guy with Super Kung Fu)
Crazy Instructor, The – 1974
Crazy Nuts of Kung Fu – 1974
Crazy Partner – 1979
Crimes are to be Paid – 1972.
Criminal, The – 1977
Criminals, The – 1976
Criminals 2: Homicides, The – (see Homicides – The Criminals Part II)
Criminals 3: Arson, The – (see Arson: The Criminals Part III)
Criminals 4: Assault, The – (see Assault: The Criminals Part IV)
Crimson Charm, The – 1970
Cripple Lee Become Immortal – 1976
Crippled Avengers – 1978
Crippled Heaven, The – (see The Crippled Masters)
Crippled Heroes – (see Crippled Avengers)
Crippled Masters, The – 1979
Cruel Killer – 1971
Cruelty Goddess – (see Bloody Hand Goddess)
Crush – 1972
Crystal Fist – 1979
Cub Tiger from Kwangtung – 1973
Cute Foster Sister – 1979

Damager – (see Chinese Kung Fu and Acupuncture)
Damned, The – 1977
Dancing Kung Fu – (see The Cavalier)
Dance of Death – 1971
Dance of the Drunk Mantis – 1979
Dance of the Drunken Mantis – (see Dance of the Drunk Mantis)
Dangerous Chase – (see Desperate Chase)

Daredevil, The – (see Flight Man)
Daredevils, The – 1979
Daredevils of Kung fu – (The Daredevils)
Dare you touch me – (see Bruce Takes Dragon Town)
Dark Alley – 1972
Darkest Sword, The – 1970
Daughter's Vengeance, A – (see Vengeance of Snow-Maid)
Dead Rivalry, A – 1976
Deadly Angels – 1977
Deadly Buddhist Raiders – (see The Bloody Fists)
Deadly Breaking Sword, The – 1979
Deadly Bunch – (see Furious Slaughter)
Deadly Chase – 1973
Deadly Challenger – (see Challenge, The)
Deadly China Doll – (see The Opium Trail)
Deadly Confrontation – 1979
Deadly Duo – (see The Two Great Cavaliers)
Deadly Duo, The – 1971
Deadly Fists – (see Revenge of the Iron Fist Maiden)
Deadly Fists Kung Fu – 1974
Deadly Hands of Kung Fu – (see The Dragon Lives Again)
Deadly Knives, The – 1972
Deadly Kick, Flash Legs – (see Shaolin Deadly Kicks)
Deadly Kung Fu Factor – (see The Delivery)
Deadly Kung Fu Lady Fu – (see Deadly Silver Spear)
Deadly Mantis – (see Shaolin Mantis)
Deadly Mission – (see Incredible Kung-Fu Mission)
Deadly Rivalry, A – (see A Dead Rivalry)
Deadly Shaolin Kick – (see Shaolin Deadly Kicks)
Deadly Shaolin Mantis – (see Shaolin Mantis)
Deadly Strike – (see Breakout from Oppression)
Deadly Silver Spear – 1977
Deadly Silver Spear – (see Silver Spear)
Deadly Snail vs. Kung Fu Killers – 1977
Deadly Strike – 1978
Deadly Three – (see Enter the Dragon)
Deaf and Mute Heroine, The – 1971
Death Beach – (see The Bloody Fists)
Death Blow – 1973
Death Challenge – 1977
Death Chamber – (see Shaolin Temple)
Death Chambers – (see Shaolin Temple)
Death Comes in Three – 1973
Death Duel – 1977
Death Duel, The – 1972
Death Duel of Kung fu – 1979
Death Duel of Mantis – 1978
Death Duel of Silver Fox – (see Demon Strike)
Death Duel of the Mantis – (see Death Duel of Mantis)
Death for Death – (see Big Rascal)
Death Kick – (see The Master of Kung Fu)
Death of Bruce Lee – (see The Black Dragon's Revenge)
Death on the Docks – 1973
Death Player – 1973
Death Stroke – (see Butcher Wing)
Death Trap – 1974
Decisive Battle, The – 1972
Debt of Crime, A – 1975
Deep Thrust – (see Lady Whirlwind)
Deep Thrust: The Hand of Death – (see Lady Whirlwind)
Delightful Forest – (see The Delightful Forest)
Delightful Forest, The – 1972

Delinquent, The – 1973
Delivery, The – 1978
Demon Fist of Kung Fu – (see The New Shaolin Boxers)
Demon Strike – 1979
Demons in Flame Mountain, The – 1978
Descendant of Wing Chun – 1979
Desperate Avenger – 1975
Desperate Chase – 1971
Desperate Chase 2 – 1971
Desperate Crisis – 1974
Desperate Killer – 1978
Desperados, The – (see The Mighty Couple)
Destroyer, The – (see The Hero)
Destroyers – (see The Magnificent Ruffians)
Destroyers of the 5 Deadly Venoms – (see The Magnificent Ruffians)
Devil and Angel – 1973
Devil & Angel – (see Shaolin Devil and Shaolin Angel)
Devil Force – (see The Tiger Jump)
Devilish Killer – 1971
Devil's Mirror, The – 1972
Devil's Owl, The – 1976
Devil's Treasure, The – 1973
Devils to Worry – (see Sorrowful to a Ghost)
Devil Strikes – 1977
Devil Woman – (see Evil Snake Girl)
Dirty Half Dozen, The – (see Hustler Squad)
Dirty H – 1979
Dirty Kung Fu – 1978
Dirty Partners – (see Wits to Wits)
Dirty Tiger and Crazy Frog – 1978
Discharged, The – 1977
Disciples Of Shao Lin – (see Disciples of Shaolin)
Disciples Of Shaolin – 1975
Disciples of Shaolin – (see Call To Arms)
Disciples of Death – (see Men From the Monastery)
Disciples of Master Killer – (see the 36th Chamber of Shaolin)
Dog King and Snake King – 1974
Double Crossers, The – 1978
Double Double Crosser – (see A Dead Rivalry)
Double Hands of Fury – (see The Two Cavaliers)
Dowager Empress – (see The Empress Dowager)
Dracula and the 7 Golden Vampires – 1974 (UK)
Dragon and Tiger, The – (see Bamboo Brotherhood)
Dragon and Tiger – 1973
Dragon and Tiger – 1974
Dragon and Tiger Joint Hands, The – 1973
Dragon and Tiger Ways – (see Tiger Vs. Dragon)
Dragon and the Hero – (see Dragon, The Hero)
Dragon and the Tiger Kids – 1979
Dragon and the Tiger Kids, The – (see Dragon and the Tiger Kids)
Dragon Blows – 1974
Dragon Bruce Lee 2 – (see Big Boss 2)
Dragon Connection – (Scorching Sun, Fierce Winds, and Wild Fire)
Dragon Den – 1974
Dragon Devils Die – (see Blooded Treasury Fight)
Dragon Dies Hard – 1977
Dragon Dies Hard, The – (see Bruce Lee – A Dragon Story)
Dragon Fighter – (see Struggle Through Death)
Dragon Files – (see The Man From Hong Kong)
Dragon Files, The – (see The Man from Hong Kong)

Dragon Fist – 1978
Dragon Fist – (see Chow Ken)
Dragon Fist – (see Knight Errant)
Dragon Force – (see Big Rascal)
Dragon Force Operation – 1976
Dragon Forever – (see The Hand of Death)
Dragon From Shaolin – 1975
Dragon From Shaolin – (see The Thunderkick)
Dragon Fury – 1974
Dragon Gate – 1975
Dragon Kid – 1975
Dragon Lee – (see Kung Fu Fever)
Dragon Lee Fights Again – (see Big Boss 2)
Dragon Lives – (see He's a Legend; He's a Hero)
Dragon Lives, The – (see He's a Legend; He's a Hero)
Dragon Lives Again, The – 1977
Dragon, the Lizard and the Boxer, The – 1977
Dragon Master – (see The Magnificent)
Dragon Missile, The – 1976
Dragon Never Die – (see Kung Fu 10th Dan)
Dragon of the Swordsman – 1978
Dragon on Fire – (see The Lama Avenger)
Dragon on Fire – (see Enter Three Dragons)
Dragon on Fire – (see The Dragon, the Hero)
Dragon the Great – (see The Dragon, the Hero)
Dragon, the Hero, The – 1979
Dragon, the Odds – (see Crazy Boy and Pop-Eye)
Dragon Reincarnate – (see Ming Patriots)
Dragon Snake, The – (see The Champion of Champions)
Dragon Squad – (see Four Real Friends)
Dragon Story, A – (see Bruce Lee's Deadly Kung Fu)
Dragon Strikes Back, The – (see Shanghai Joe)
Dragon Swordsman – (see Dragon of the Swordsman)
Dragon Tamers, The – 1975
Dragon, Tiger, Phoenix – (see Dragon Vs. Needles of Death)
Dragon, Tiger and Phoenix – (see Dragon Vs. Needles of Death)
Dragon Vs. Needles of Death, (The) – 1976
Dragon Vs. Needles of Death, The – (see Dragon Vs. Needles of Death)
Dragon Warrior – (see The Big Rascal)
Dragon Zombies Return – (see The Zodiac Fighters)
Dragon's Claws – 1979
Dragon's Executioner – (see Chinese)
Dragon's Fatal Fist – (see Invincible Kung Fu Trio)
Dragon's Hero – (see Enter the Invincible Hero)
Dragon's Snake Fist, The – (see The Crazy Instructor)
Dragon's Vengeance – (see The Chinese)
Dragoneer 5: The Indomitable – (see Golden Dragon Silver Snake)
Dragoneer 4: The Dynamite – (see Dynamite Shaolin Heroes)
Dragoneer 13 – The Significant – (see Enter the Invincible Hero)
Dreaming Fists with Slender Hands – 1979
Dream Sword, The – 1979
Dressed to Fight – (see Legend of the Broken Blade)
Drinking Knight, The – 1970
Drug Addicts, The – 1973
Drug Connection, The – (see The Sexy Killer)
Drunk Fish, Drunk Frog, Drunk Crab – 1979
Drunk Master – (see Drunken Master)
Drunk Monkey – (see Drunken Master)

Drunk Shaolin Challenges Ninja – (see Heroes of the East)
Drunken Arts and Crippled Fists – 1979
Drunken Dragon – (see Drunken Arts and Crippled Fists)
Drunken Dragon – (see World of the Drunken Master)
Drunken Fighter, The – (see Five Superfighters)
Drunken Fist Boxing – (see Drunken Master)
Drunken Fist Boxing – (see Story of the Drunken Master)
Drunken Master – 1978
Drunken Master, The – (see Drunken Master)
Drunken Master Part 2 – (see Dance of the Drunk Mantis)
Drunken Master Part 2: Dance of the Drunk Mantis – (see Dance of the Drunk Mantis)
Drunken Master and Boxing Wizard – (see Peculiar Boxing Tricks and the Master)
Drunken Master Slippery Snake – (see Mad Mad Kung Fu)
Drunken Master Strikes Back – (see Peculiar Boxing Tricks and the Master)
Drunken Monkey – (see Monkey Kung Fu)
Drunken Monkey – (see Monkey Fist, Floating Snake)
Drunken Monkey in the Tiger's Eyes – (see Drunken Master)
Drunken Monkey Kung Fu Guy – (see Desperate Killer)
Drunken Swordsman – (see The Idiot Swordsman)
Dual Flying Kicks – 1978
Duel, The – 1971
Duel at Forest – (see Dragon Fury)
Duel at Tiger Village – 1978
Duel For Gold – 1971
Duel in Forest – (see Dragon Fury)
Duel in the Desert – 1977
Duel in the Tiger Den – 1972
Duel of Fist – 1971
Duel of Fists – (see Duel of Fist)
Duel of Harbour – (see Chinese Hercules)
Duel of Karate – (see To Subdue Evil)
Duel of Karate Guy – (see To Subdue Evil)
Duel of Master – (see Duel at Tiger Village)
Duel of the Brave Ones – 1978
Duel of the Dragons – 1973
Duel of the Dragons – (see Of Cooks and Kung Fu)
Duel of the Dragons – (see The Lama Avenger)
Duel of the Iron Fists – (see The Duel)
Duel of the Masters – (see Chinese Kung Fu (not The Dumb Ox))
Duel of the Shaolin Fist – (The Duel)
Duel of the Seven Tigers – 1979
Duel of the 7 Tigers – (see Duel of the Seven Tigers)
Duel Under the Burning Sun – (Scorching Sun, Fierce Winds, and Wild Fire)
Duel with Devil – 1971
Duel with the Devils – 1977
Duel with Samurai – 1971
Dumb Ox, The – 1974
Dwarf Sorcerer, The – 1974
Dynamite Brothers – 1973
Dynamo – 1978
Dynasty – 1977
Dynasty of Blood – (see Blood Brothers)

Eagle Claw and Butterfly Palm – (see Eagle's Claw and Butterfly Palm)
Eagle Claw Vs. Butterfly Palm – (see Eagle's Claw and Butterfly Palm)
Eagle Fist – (see Eagle's Claw)
Eagle Claws Champion – (see On the Back Street)
Eagle Claw, Snake Fist, Cat's Paw, Part 2 – (see Drunken Master)
Eagle King – 1979
Eagle Shadow Fist – (see Not Scared to Die)
Eagle's Claw – 1977
Eagle's Claw, The – 1970
Eagle's Claw and Butterfly Palm – 1978
Eagle's Claw Champion – (see On the Back Street)
Eagle's Claw, Snake's Fist, Cat's Paw – (Snake in the Eagle's Shadow)
Eagle's Shadow – (see Snake in the Eagle's Shadow)
Eagle's Shadow Fist – (see Not Scared to Die)
Eagle's Showdown – (see Descendant of Wing Chun)
Ebony, Ivory, and Jade – (see She Devils in Chains)
Eccentric Person, An – (see Peculiar Boxing Tricks and the Master)
Edge of Fury – 1978
Eight Dragon Sword, The – 1971
Eight Escorts – 1979
Eight Hundred Heroes – 1975
800 Heroes – (see Eight Hundred Heroes)
Eight Immortals – 1971
Eight Masters – 1977
8 Masters – (see Eight Masters)
Eight Peerless Treasures – (see Eight Escorts)
Eight Strikes of a Wild Cat – 1976
8 Strikes of the Wildcat – (see Eight Strikes of a Wild Cat)
Eight Swordsmen in Kwong Nan – (see The Greatest Plot)
18 Amazons – (see Bruce Lee's Ways of Kung Fu)
18 Bronze Girls of Shaolin, The – 1978
18 Bronzemen – 1976
18 Bronzemen, The – (see 18 Bronzemen)
18 Bronzemen Part 2, The – (see Return of the 18 Bronzemen)
18 Bronzemen 3 – (see Eight Masters)
18 Claws of Shaolin – (see Eighteen Jade Arhats)
Eighteen Claws of Shaolin, The – (see Eighteen Jade Arhats)
18 Claws of Shaolin, The – (see Eighteen Jade Arhats)
18 Deadly Arhats – (see Eighteen Jade Arhats)
18 Deadly Strikes – (see 18 Fatal Strikes)
18 Disciples of Buddha – 1970
Eighteen Fatal Strikes – 1978
18 Fatal Strikes – (see Eighteen Fatal Strikes)
18 Fatal Strikes – (see Fangs of the Cobra)
Eighteen Jade Arhats – 1978
Eighteen Jade Arhats, The – (see Eighteen Jade Arhats)
18 Jade Pearls – (see Eighteen Jade Arhats)
18 Jades – (see Eighteen Jade Arhats)
Eighteen Riders for Justice – (see Eighteen Swirling Riders)
18 Riders for Justice – (see Eighteen Swirling Riders)
Eighteen Shaolin Brave Men – (see Eighteen Swirling Riders)

18 Shaolin Brave Men – (see Eighteen Swirling Riders)
18 Shaolin Disciples – 1975
18 Shaolin Disciples – (see Shaolin Kung Fu Mystagogue)
Eighteen Shaolin Riders – (see Eighteen Swirling Riders)
18 Shaolin Riders – (see Eighteen Swirling Riders)
Eighteen Swirling Riders – 1977
18 Swirling Riders – (see Eighteen Swirling Riders)
18 Women Fighters of Murim – (see Bruce Lee's Deadly Kung Fu)
8th Wonder of Kung Fu – (see 13 Style Strikes)
Emperor Chien Lung – 1976
Emperor Chien Lung And The Beauty – 1979
Emperor of the Filthy Guy – (see Filthy Guy)
Emperor's Tomb Raiders, The – (see Imperial Tomb Raiders)
Empress Dowager's Agate Vase – 1974
End of the Wicked Tigers – 1976
End of Wicked Tiger – (see End of the Wicked Tigers)
End of the Black – 1973
End of the Black, The – (see End of the Black)
Enter the Dragon – 1973
Enter the Deadly Dragon – (see Dragon Lee Vs. the 5 Brothers)
Enter the Fat Dragon – 1978
Enter the Game of Death – 1978
Enter the Invincible Hero – 1977
Enter the Panther – (see Conspiracy)
Enter the 7 Virgins – (see Virgins of the Seven Seas)
Enter the Silver Fox – (see Secret Rivals)
Enter the Whirlwind Boxer – (see Young Hero of Shaolin)
Enter Three Dragons – (see The Lama Avenger)
Enter Three Dragons – 1978
Escape, The – 1972
Escape to High Danger – 1973
Escaped Convict, The – 1974
Escaper, The – 1973
Eternal Conflict – (see Odd Couple)
Eternal Conflict, The – (see Dance of Death)
Eunuch, The – 1970
Eunich of the Western Palace – 1979
Everlasting Chivalry – 1979
Ever Victorious Hall – 1973
Evil Karate – 1971
Evil Snake Girl – 1974
Evil Slaughter – (see Murder Masters of Kung Fu)
Excelsior – 1973
Executioners From Shaolin – 1976
Executioners of Death – (see Executioners from Shaolin)
Executioners of Shaolin – (see Executioners from Shaolin)
Exit the Dragon, Enter the Tiger – 1976
Extreme Enemy – 1971
Eye of the Dragon – (see Magnificent Bodyguards)

Fabulous Protectress, The – 1970
Face Behind Mask, The – 1977
Face Behind the Mask, The – (see The Face Behind the Mask)
Fai & Chi: Kings of Kung Fu – (see Kung Fu Vs. Yoga)
Fairy, the Ghost and Ah Chung, The – 1979

Fairy Wife – (see, The Fairy's Bride)
Fairy's Bride, The – 1971
Fangs Of The Cobra – 1977
Fantastic Magic Baby, The – 1975
Farewell Buddy – (see The Young Dragons)
Farewell To A Warrior – 1976
Fascinating Avenger Girl – 1974
Fast Fists, The – 1972
Fast Fists, The – (see Chow Ken)
Fastest Fist, The – (see The Fast Fists)
Fatal Claws, Deadly Kicks – (see The Woman
   Avenger)
Fatal Needles and Fatal Fists – (see Fatal Needles
   Vs. Fatal Fists)
Fatal Needles Vs. Fatal Fists – 1978
Fast Sword, The – 1971
Fatal Flying Guillotines – 1977
Fatal Kicks in Kung Fu – (see The Thunderbolt Fist)
Fatal Strike – (see Brother Two)
Fate of Lee Khan, The – 1973
Fearless Duo – 1978
Fearless Fighters – 1971
Fearless Golden Dragon – 1974
Fearless Hyena – 1979
Fearless Kung Fu Elements – 1978
Fearless Master Fighter – (see Fearless Duo)
   Fearless Young Boxer – (see Avenging Boxer)
Female Chivalry – 1975
Female Fugitive – 1975
Ferocious Brothers – 1972
Ferocious Monk From Shaolin – (The Furious Monk
   From Shaolin)
Ferocious to Ferocious – 1973
Fierce Among Strong – 1975
Fierce Fist – 1976
Fierce Fist, The – (see Fierce Fist)
Fierce One – (see Jaws of the Dragon)
Fight, The – (see Knockabout)
Fight – 1979
Fight for Shaolin Tamo Mystique, The – (see Fight
   for Survival)
Fight for Survival – 1977
Fight Out of Hell Gate Shaolin Hellgate – (see
   Heaven and Hell)
Fighter with Two Face, The – (see Fists of Dragons)
Fighting Ace – 1979
Fighting Dragon – 1975
Fighting Justice – (see Ape Girl)
Fighting Dragon Vs. Deadly Tiger – (see Call Me
   Dragon)
Fighting of Shaolin Monks – (see Shaolin Monk)
File of Heroes – 1974
Filial Girl at the Icy Valley, The – 1970
Filial Son – 1975
Filthy Guy – 1978
Finger Of Doom – 1971
Fingers of Death – (see Master With Cracked
   Fingers)
Fingers That Kill – 1972
First Sword in the Middle-Land – 1971
Fist and Guts – 1979
Fist Fighter – (see Valley of the Double Dragon)
Fist for a Fist – (see Triumph of Two Kung Fu Arts)
Fist of Dragon – (see Fists of Dragons)
Fist of Dragons – (see Fists of Dragons)
Fist of Fire – 1975
Fist of Fury – 1972

Fist of Fury 2 – (see Chinese Connection 2)
Fist of Fury 2 – (see Jeet Kune the Claws and the
   Supreme Kung Fu)
Fist of Fury Part 3 – (see Jeet Kune the Claws and
   the Supreme Kung Fu)
Fist of Fury 3 – (see Jeet Kune the Claws and the
   Supreme Kung Fu)
Fist of Justice – (see Bolo)
Fist of Legend II – (see TheBodyguard)
Fist of Legend 2: Iron Bodyguard – (see The
   Bodyguard)
Fist of Legend II: Iron Bodyguards – (see The
   Bodyguard)
Fist of Shaolin – 1973
Fist of Shaolin (see Shaolin Invincible Sticks)
Fist of Shao-Lin – (see Fist of Shaolin)
Fist of Unicorn – 1973
Fist of Vengeance – (see Little Super Man)
Fist That Kills, The – 1972
Fist to Fist – 1973
Fist to Kill – (see Sunset in the Forbidden City)
Fist Too Fast – (see The Legendary Strike)
Fistful of the Dragon – (see Chinese Connection 2)
Fists and Guts – (see Fist and Guts)
Fists for Revenge – 1974
Fists from Shaolin – (see Fist of Shaolin)
Fists, Kicks and the Evils – 1979
Fists, Kicks & the Evils – (see Fists, Kicks and the
   Evils)
Fists Like Lee – (see Along Comes a Tiger)
Fists of Bruce Lee – 1979
Fists of Death – (see Rage of the Wind)
Fists of Dragons – 1977
Fists of Fear, Touch of Death – 1977
Fists of Fury – (see The Big Boss)
Fists of Fury Part 3 – (see Jeet Kune the Claws and
   the Supreme Kung Fu)
Fists of Fury 3 – (see Jeet Kune the Claws and the
   Supreme Kung Fu)
Fists of Fury 3, The – (see Jeet Kune the Claws and
   the Supreme Kung Fu)
Fists of Fury in China – (see Chinese Kung Fu
   Against Godfather)
Fists of Glory – (see The Big Boss)
Fists of Shaolin – (see Fist of Shaolin)
Fists of Shaolin – (see Shaolin Invincible Sticks)
Fists of Vengeance – (see The Deadly Knives)
Fists of Vengeance – (see Of Cooks and Kung Fu)
Fists of Vengeance, The – 1973
Fists of Vengeance – (see Green Jade Statuette)
Fists of the Double K – (see Fist to Fist)
Fists of the White Lotus – (see Clan of the White
   Lotus)
Fists to Fight – (see New Fist of Fury)
Five Barriers, The – (see Rivals of the Silver Fox)
Five Deadly Venoms, The – (see The Five Venoms)
5 Deadly Venoms, The – (see The Five Venoms)
Five Devil Ghost, The – 1971
Five Elements of Kung Fu – (see Adventure of
   Shaolin)
Five Fingers of Death – (King Boxer)
5 Fingers of Death – (King Boxer)
Five Kung Fu Daredevil Heroes – 1977
5 Kung Fu Daredevil Heroes – (see Five Kung Fu
   Daredevil Heroes)
Five Masters of Death – (see Five Shaolin Masters)
5 Masters of Death – (see Five Shaolin Masters)

Five Pretty Young Ladies – (see Bruce, Kung Fu
   Girls)
Five Shaolin Masters – 1974
5 Shaolin Masters – (see Five Shaolin Masters)
Five Superfighters – 1979
Five Tiger Generals – (see The Savage Five)
Five Tough Guys – 1974
Five Venoms, The – 1978
Flaming Swords – (see Strife for Mastery)
Flash Challenger – (see Ferocious to Ferocious)
Flash Legs – (see Shaolin Deadly Kicks)
Flight Man – 1973
Fly Dragon Mountain, The – 1971
Flyer and Magic Sword – (see Hooded Swordsman)
Flying Claw Fights – (See No-one Can Touch Her)
Flying Dragon Cat – (see The Dragon Missile)
Flying Dragon Execution – (see The Dragon Missile)
Flying Dragon Mountain – (see Fly Dragon Mountain)
Flying Fingers of the Unknown – (see Shaolin Iron
   Claws)
Flying Flag, The – (see The Protectors)
Flying Guillotine, The – 1974
Flying Guillotine 2 – 1977
Flying Guillotine II – (see Flying Guillotine 2)
Flying Man of Ma Lan – (see Flight Man)
Flying Masters of Kung Fu – (see Revengeful
   Swordswoman)
Flying Over Grass – 1970
Flying Swallow – (see Ninja Swords of Death)
Flying Sword and the Smart Kid – (see Flying Sword
   and the Smart Lad)
Flying Sword and the Smart Lad – 1970
Flying Sword Lee – 1979
Flying Swords Girl – 1970
Flying Tiger, The – 1973
Flying Wheels – (see Deadly Chase)
Follow the Star – 1978
For Your Fists Only – (see Kung Fu Attraction)
For Whom to be Murdered – 1978
Forbidden Killing – 1970
Force of Bruce Lee's Fist – (see Fist of Unicorn)
Force 3 From Shanghai – (see Snake in the Crane's
   Shadow)
Forced to Fight – 1971
Forest Duel – (see Dragon Fury)
Forest Duel 2 – (see Dragon Fury)
Four Assassins – (see Marco Polo)
Four Hands of Death – 1977
Four Invincibles – 1979
Four Real Friends – 1974
Four Riders – 1972
Four Shaolin Challengers, The – 1977
Fourteen Amazons, The – (see The 14 Amazons)
14 Amazons, The – 1972
14 Demons – (see No-one Can Touch Her)
Fox and Hounds – (see Kung Fu Master Named
   Drunk Cat)
Fox Bat – (see Foxbat)
Foxbat – 1977
Freedom Strikes a Blow – (see Chinese Hercules)
Friends – 1973
From China with Death – (see Wits to Wits)
From the Highway – 1970
From Hong Kong with Love – 1975
Fugitive, The – 1972
Full Moon Scimitar – 1979
Funny Kung Fu – 1978

Funny Man and the Boxer – (see The Guy!! The Guy!!)
The Furious – 1974
Furious Avenger, The – 1974
Furious Dragon – 1973
Furious Jumpboxer – (see The Furious Avenger)
Furious Killer – 1973
Furious Imposter, The – (see The Furious Avenger)
Furious Monk From Shaolin, The – 1974
Furious Slaughter – 1972
Furious Ultimatum – (see The Righteous Fist)
Fury – (see The Boxer's Last Stand)
Fury in Storm – 1974
Fury of Black Belt – (see The Awaken Punch)
Fury of King Boxer – (see The Fast Fists)
Fury of Shaolin Fist – (see Chivalrous Robber Lee San)
Fury of Shaolin Master – (see Master and the Kid)
Fury of the Black Belt – (see The Awaken Punch)
Fury of the King boxer – (see Chow Ken)

Gallant, The – 1972
Gallant Boxer – (see The Gallant)
Gallant Duo, The – (see The Last Duel)
Gallantry King, The – 1977
Gambling for Gold – 1973
Gambling for Head – 1975
Gambling Syndicate, The – 1973
Game of Death, The – 1973/1978 – (USA)
Game of Killers – 1979
Game of Killers, The – (see Game of Killers)
Game of the Dragon – (see Bruce Li – The Invincible)
Games Gamblers Plays – 1974
Gangbusters Kung Fu – (see He has Nothing but Kung Fu)
Gangsmen Tavern – (see Chivalrous Inn)
Gathering of Heroes, A – 1973
Gee and Jor – 1978
Gecko Kung Fu – 1972
General Stone – 1976
Generation Gap, The – 1973
Ghost, The – 1972
Ghost Hill, The – 1971
Ghost Story, The – 1979
Ghostly Face – 1973
Ghostly Face, The – 1972
Ghost's Sword – 1971
Ghost's Revenge, The – 1971
Girl Boxer – (see A Girl Fighter)
Girl Called Tigress, A – 1975
Girl Fighter, A – 1972
Girl Named Iron Phoenix – 1973
Girl of the Night – 1972
Girl with the Skillful Hands – (see Heroine)
Glory Sword – (see Imperial Sword)
God Wears a Black Belt – (see Inheritor of Kung Fu)
God father of Hong Kong, The – (see Dragon Force Operation)
Godfather of Hong Kong, The – (see The Mandarin)
Godfather Squad, The – (see Little Godfather of Hong Kong)
Godfather's Fury – 1978
Gold Connection, The – 1979
Gold Cyclone Whirlwind – (see The Hurricane)
Gold Snatchers – 1973
Golden City – (see Kung Fu Brothers in the Wild West)
Golden Dragon Silver Snake – 1979
Golden Headed Eagle – 1970

Golden Key – 1978
Golden Killah – (see Golden Mask)
Golden Knight – 1970
Golden Leopard's Brutal Revenge – (see Valley of the Double Dragon)
Golden Lion, The – 1973
Golden Lotus, The – 1974
Golden Mask – 1977
Golden Nun – 1977
Golden Peacock Castle – 1977
Golden Seal, The – 1971
Golden Sun – (see Dragon Dies Hard)
Golden Sword and the Blind Swordswoman – 1970
Golden Triangle – 1975
Goliathon – (see The Mighty Peking Man)
Good and the Bad, The – (see Tiger Vs. Dragon)
Good, Bad & Loser – (see The Good, the Bad and the Loser)
Good, the Bad and the Loser, The – 1976
Goodbye Bruce Lee: His Last Game of Death – 1975
Goodbye Bruce Lee! – (see The New Game of Death, 1977)
Goose Boxer – 1978
Gourd Fairy, The – 1972
Grand Father of Death – (see The New Shaolin Boxers)
Grand Passion, The – 1970
Grandmasters of Death – (see The New Shaolin Boxers)
Great Assassin – (see Night of the Assassins)
Great Boxer – 1972
Great Boxer, The – 1971
Great Chase, The – (see Prominent Eunuch Chen Ho)
Great Chinese Boxer, The – 1975
Great Dragon Boxer – (see The Black Dragon)
Great Duel, The – 1971
Great Escape, The – (see The Escape)
Great General – 1979
Great Hero – (see Magnum Fist)
Great Heroes, The – (see Hero of the time)
Great Highwayman – 1970
Great Hunter – 1976
Great Justice, The – 1979
Great Soldiers Wins a General – (see Militant Eagle)
Greatest Duel of the Red Eagle – (see Seven Men of Kung Fu)
Greatest Plot, The – 1977
Greatest Thai Boxing, The – 1973
Green Dragon Inn – 1977
Green Jade Statuette – 1978
Green Jade Statuette, The – (see Green Jade Statuette)
Growling Tiger – (see Tiger from China)
Gui Shou Long Hu Dou – 1972
Guillotene, The – (see The Dragon Missile)
Guy!! The Guy!!, The – 1974
Guy With Secret Kung Fu, The – 1978
Gym Kata Killer – 1978

Half a Loaf of Kung Fu – 1978
Hammer of the Gods – (see The Chinese Boxer)
Hand, The – 1973
Hand Cuffs – (see The Handcuff)
Hand of Death – 1976
Hand of Death – (see King Boxer)

Hand of Death – (see The Karate Killers)
Handcuff, The – 1979
Handlock – (see Shaolin Handlock)
Hand of Death, The – (see Hand of Death)
Hands of Death – (see The Tongfather)
Han's Island – (see Enter the Dragon)
Hapkido – 1972
Hap Ki Do – (see Hapkido)
Happy Forest – (see The Delightful Forest)
Harbour Dragon and Tiger Fights – 1975
Hard as a Dragon – (see The Tiger Jump)
Hard Man In Danger – 1973
Hard Way to Die – (see Sun Dragon)
Hawk's Fist – (see Shaolin Iron Claws)
He has Nothing but Kung Fu – 1977
He Heals and Kills – 1971
He Walks like a Tiger – 1973
He Who Never Dies – 1979
He's a Legend, He's a Hero – (see He's a Legend; He's a Hero)
He's a Legend, He's a Hero – (see The New Game of Death; 1977)
He's a Legend; He's a Hero – 1976
He's a Legend; He's a Hero – (see Bruce Lee's Deadly Kung Fu)
Heads for Sale – 1970
Heaven And Hell – 978
Heaven and Hell Shaolin Hellgate – (see Heaven and Hell)
Heaven & Hell Gate Shaolin Hellgate – (see Heaven and Hell)
Heaven Sword and Dragon Sabre – 1978
Heaven Sword And Dragon Sabre Part II – (see Heaven Sword And Dragon Sabre 2)
Heaven Sword And Dragon Sabre 2 – 1978
Heavenly Sword – (see Unparalleled Judo Knife)
Heinous Fiend, The – 1974
Hell Cats – (see The Hot Box)
Hell's Wind Staff – (Dragon and the Tiger Kids)
Hell'z Windstaff – (Dragon and the Tiger Kids)
Hellfighters of the East – (see Four riders)
Hellfire Angel, The – 1979
Hellgate – 1970
Here Come Big Brother – (see Police Woman)
Hero – 1976
Hero, The – (see Hero)
Hero Kan Feng Chih, The – (see The Cavalier)
Hero From Shanghai – 1977
Hero of Shanghai – (see Hero from Shanghai)
Hero of Chiu Chow, The – 1973
Hero of Kwantong – (see Hero of Kwantung)
Hero of Kwantung – 1974
Hero of the Earth – (see The Champion of Champions)
Hero of the Time – 1979
Hero of the Waterfront – (see Hero of Chiu Chow)
Hero of the Wild – 1977
Hero Tattooed with Nine Dragons – 1977
Hero Tattooed with 9 Dragons – (see Hero Tattooed with Nine Dragons)
Hero's Blood – 1970
Hero's Tear, A – 1978
Heroes Behind Enemy Lines – 1975
Heroes Behind the Enemy Lines – (see Heroes Behind Enemy Lines)
Heroes of Shaolin – (see Hero of the Wild)
Heroes of Shao-Lin – (see Hero of the Wild)

Heroes of Shaolin Part 2 – 1977
Heroes of Sung – 1973
Heroes of the East – 1978
Heroes of the Late Ming Dynasty – 1975
Heroes of the Wild – (see Hero of the Wild)
Heroes of the Underground – 1976
Heroes Two – 1973
Heroic Defenders, The – 1977
Heroic Event – (see Magnificent Wanderers)
Heroic Figure – (see Men of the Hour)
Heroic Ones, The – 1970
Heroine – 1975
Heroine, The – (see None But the Brave)
Heroine, The – (see Police Woman)
Heroine in the Dust – 1972
Heroine Kan Liam Chu – (see Heroine Kan Lian Chu)
Heroine Kan Lian Chu – 1976
Heroine Susan, the Sister of the Shantung Boxer – 1973
Her Vengeance – 1971
Hill Fortress – 1973
Himalayan, The – 1977
Him Sim Ba Dna – (see The Furious Avenger)
His Name is Nobody – 1979
His Sabre is Matchless – (see Broken Sword)
Ho's Thungz & Scrillaz – (see The Damned)
Homeboy – (see Black Fist)
Homicides – The Criminals Part II – 1976
Honey Moon Killer, The – 1975
Honeymoon Killer – (The Honeymoon Killer)
Hong Kong Cat – (see Super Kung Fu Kid)
Hong Kong Cat Named Karado – (see Super Kung Fu Kid)
Hong Kong Connection – (see Black Guide)
Hong Kong Face-Off – (see Fist to Fist)
Hong Kong Hitman – (see Stoner)
Hong Kong Karate Hatchet Men – (see Duel of the Brave Ones)
Hong Kong Superman – 1975
Hooded Swordsman – 1971
Horse Boxing Killer – (Cute Foster Sister)
Hot Blood – 1977
Hot Box, The – 1972
Hot, Cool and Vicious, The – 1976
Hot, the Cool and the Vicious, The – (see The Hot, Cool and Vicious)
Hot Dog Kung fu – (see Writing Kung Fu)
Hot Pursuit, The – 1974
Hsao Li's Fly Knife – (see Flying Sword Lee)
Hsueh Kang Crashed the Flower Lantern Festival –1970
Huang Fei-Hong: Bravely Crushing the Fire Formation – 1970
Huge Brother – 1972
Huge Brothers – (see Huge Brother)
Hung Boxing Kid, The – (see Disciples of Shaolin; 1975)
Hung Kid Boxing, the – (see Call To Arms)
Hunted, The – 1970
Hunter, The – (see Great Hunter)
Huo Yuanjia, the Brave Hero – (see The Great Boxer).
Hurricane, The – 1972

I Love You Bruce Lee – (see Bruce Lee & I)
I'am Chinese – (see Unsubdued Furies)
I'll Get You One Day – 1970

Idiot Swordsman, The – 1979
Idle Swordsman – (see The Idiot Swordsman)
Image of Bruce Lee – (see Storming Attacks)
Immortal Warriors – 1979
Imperial Sword – 1977
Imperial Swordsman, The – 1972
Imperial Tomb Raiders – 1973
Impetuous – 1972
Impetuous Fire – 1973
Imposter, The – 1975
Imprudent Iron Phoenix, The – 1973
In Eagle Dragon Fist – (see Dragon Fist)
In Eagle Shadow Fist – (see Not Scared to Die)
In Hot Pursuit – (see The Hot Pursuit)
In the Beginning – 1979
Incredible Dragon – (see Deadly Strike)
Incredible Dragon – (see Last Strike)
Incredible Kung Fu Brothers – (see Shaolin Avenger)
Incredible Kung Fu Master, The – 1979
Incredible Kung-Fu Mission – 1979
Incredible Master Beggars – (see My Kung Fu Twelve Kicks)
Incredible Three – 1978
Incredible 3 – (see Incredible Three)
Infernal Street – 1973
Inframan – (see Super Inframan)
Inheritor of Kung Fu – 1973
Innocent Lust – 1977
Insanity Being – 1972
Inspector Karate – (see Number One Iron Man)
Instant Kung Fu Man – 1977
Internal Conflict – (see Odd Couple)
Intimate Confessions ofA Chinese Courtesan – 1972
Intrique, The – (see The Old Master)
Intruder at White Lotus Temple – 1971
Invasion, The – 1972
Invincible – (see The Swift Shaolin Boxer)
Invincible, The – (see Bruce Li – The Invincible)
Invincible, The – 1972
Invincible Armour, The – 1977
Invincible Boxer, The – 1973
Invincible Boxer, The – (see King Boxer)
Invincible Bruce Lee – (see Bruce Lee Fights Back From The Grave)
Invincible Eight – 1971
Invincible Enforcer – 1979
Invincible Hero, The – (see Mean Streets of Kung Fu)
Invincible Iron Palm, The – 1972
Invincible Killer – 1978
Invincible Killer, The – (see Invincible Killer)
Invincible Kung Fu – (see Ruthless Revenge)
Invincible Kung Fu Brother – (see Shaolin Avenger)
Invincible Kung Fu Trio – 1974
Invincible Monkey Fist – 1978
Invincible One – (see Disciples of Shaolin; 1975)
Invincible Shaolin – 1978
Invincible Shaolin Kung Fu – (see Butterfly 18)
Invincible Super Chan – (see Forced to Fight)
Invincible Super Chan, The – (see Forced to Fight)
Invincible Super Guy – 1976
Invincible Sword – 1971
Invincible Swordswoman – 1977
Invisible Terrorists – 1976
Iron Body-Guard – (see Iron Bodyguard)
Iron Bodyguard – 1973
Iron Bridge Kung Fu – 1979

Iron Buddha, The – 1970
Iron Bull, The – 1973
Iron Claw – (see Iron Fisted Eagle's Claw)
Iron Dragon Strikes Back – (see The Gold Connection)
Iron Fan and Magic Sword – 1971
Iron Finger – (see Bruce and the Iron Finger)
Iron Fist Adventures – (see The Adventure)
Iron Fist Boxer – (see Peculiar Boxing Tricks and the Master)
Iron Fist, Eagle Claw – (see Iron Fisted Eagle's Claw)
Iron Fist Pillage – (see The Duel)
Iron Fisted Eagle's Claw – 1979
Iron-Fisted Monk, The – 1977
Iron Fisted Warrior – (see Cantonen Iron Kung Fu)
Iron Fists – 1977
Iron Fists – (see Fists of Vengeance; 1973)
Iron Hand – (see Enter the Dragon)
Iron-Hand Boxer, The – (see Cantonen Iron Kung Fu)
Iron Head – (see The Crazy Instructor)
Iron Maiden – (see The Legendary Strike)
Iron Man – (see Chinese Iron Man)
Iron Man, An – (see King Boxer)
Iron Man, The – 1974
Iron Monkey – 1977
Iron Monkey of Shaolin, The – (see Iron Monkey)
Iron Monkey 2 – (see Duel at Tiger Village)
Iron Monkey II – (see Duel at Tiger Village)
Iron Monkey Strikes Back – (see Duel at Tiger Village)
Iron Ox, the Tiger's Killer – 1974
Iron Palm – (see King Boxer; 1972)
Iron Profligates – 1974
Iron Punch Contest – 1973
Iron-Punch Contest – (see Iron Punch Contest)
Ironside 426 – 1977
Iron Swallow – 1978
Iron Swallow – (see Shaolin Iron Claws)
Ironic Hero – (see Number One Iron Man)
Island of Hell – (see Hell's Gate Island)
Island of Horrors – (see Hell's Gate Island)
Island of Virgins – 1978

Jackie Chan Versus Wang Yu – (see The Killer Meteors)
Jade Claw – (see Crystal Fist)
Jade Faced Assassin, The – 1970
Jade Killer – (see Eighteen Jade Arhats)
Jade Tiger, The – 1977
Japanese Connection – (see A Tooth for a Tooth)
Jaws of the Dragon – 1976
Jeet Kune the Claws – (see Chinese Connection 2)
Jeet Kune the Claws and the Supreme Kung Fu – 1979
Judgement Of An Assassin – 1977
Judicial Sword – 1975
Jumping Ash – 1976

Karado: The Kung Fu Flash – (see Super Kung Fu Kid)
Karate Bomber – (see Half a Loaf of Kung Fu)
Karate Cop – (see Yellow Faced Tiger)
Karate Death Squad – (see The Killer Meteors)
Karate Frightmare – (see Kung Fu Rebels)
Karate From Shaolin Temple – 1976
Karate Ghosbuster – (see Spiritual Kung Fu)
Karate Killers – 1973
Karate King – (see The Champion)

Karate on the Bosphorus – 1974 (TU)
Karate 2, The – (see Soul of Chiba)
Kendo – (see The Tiger Jump)
Kickmasters – (see When Taekwondo Strikes)
Kick of Death – (see One Foot Crane)
Kick of Death – (see Prodigal Boxer)
Kickmaster – (see When Taekwondo Strikes)
Kid in Pier, The – (see Chinese Hercules)
Kid With The Golden Arm, The – 1979
Kid's Ace in the Hole – (see Fighting Ace)
Kidnap – 1974
Kidnap in Rome – 1976
Kill Factor – (see Death Dimensioin)
Killer, The – 1971
Killer Bs – (see The Woman Avenger)
Killer Clans – 1976
Killer Dragon Returns – (see Duel with the Devil)
Killer Fist – (see Shaolin Kung Fu Mystagogue)
Killer Fists – (see Shaolin Kung Fu Mystagogue)
Killer from Above – 1977
Killer from Shantung – (see Boxer of Shantung)
Killer Hillz – (see Lung Wei Village)
Killer Hillz – (see 72 Desperate Rebels)
Killer Meteors, The – 1976
Killer of Snake, Fox of Shaolin – 1978
Killer Priest – (see Shaolin Monk)
Killer Snakes, The – 1974
Killer's Game – (see Green Jade Statuette)
Killers On Wheels – 1976
Killing of a Chinese Bookie – (see Dynamite Brothers)
King Boxer – 1972
King Boxer, The – 1971
King Boxer: Five Fingers of Death – (see King Boxer)
King Boxers – (see The King Boxer)
King Eagle – 1970
King Gambler – 1976
King of Boxers, The – (see The King Boxer)
King of Kung fu – (see Walks like a Tiger)
King of Kung Fu – (see He's a Legend; He's a Hero)
King of Kung Fu – (see Enter the Game of Death)
King of the Boxers – (The Big Boss)
King's Sword, The – 1970
Kings of Blade and Sword – 1970
Kings of Kung Fu, The – (The Daredevils)
Kiss Of Death – 1973
Kiss Of Death, The – (see Kiss of Death)
Knife of the Devil's Roaring and Soul Missing – 1976
Knight, The – (see Struggle with Death)
Knight Errant – 1974
Knockabout – 1979
Kung Fu Ace – (see Fighting Ace)
Kung Fu Arts – (see Raging Tiger Vs. Monkey King)
Kung Fu Arts: Horse, Monkey, and Tiger – (see Raging Tiger Vs. Monkey King)
Kung Fu Arts – (see Raging Tiger Vs. Monkey King)
Kung Fu Attraction – 1976
Kung Fu Avengers – (see Last Strike)
Kung fu Brothers, The – (see The Brothers)
Kung Fu Brothers in the Wild West – 1973
Kung Fu Challenger – (see Hero of the Wild)
Kung Fu Commandos – (see Incredible Kung-Fu Mission)
Kung Fu Conspiracy – (see The Big Risk)
Kung Fu Crusher – (see Bone Crushing Kid)
Kung-fu Daredevils – (see 5 Kung Fu Daredevil Heroes)

Kung Fu Doctor's Martial Arts – (see Chinese Kung Fu and Acupuncture)
Kung Fu Expert – (see Dirty Kung Fu)
Kung Fu Fever – 1979
Kung Fu Gangbusters – (see He has Nothing but Kung Fu)
Kung Fu Genius – 1979
Kung Fu Girl – (see None But the Brave)
Kung Fu Girls – 1978
Kung Fu: The Head Crusher – (see Tough guys)
Kung Fu Hell Cats – (see Five Tough Guys)
Kung Fu Hercules – (see Fatal Needles Vs. Fatal Fists)
Kung-Fu Inferno – 1974
Kung-fu Instructor, The – 1979
Kung Fu Invaders – (see Heroes Two)
Kung-fu Kid, The – 1977
Kung Fu Kids – (see Dreaming Fists with Slender Hands)
Kung Fu Killers – (see The Angry Guest) (USA)
Kung Fu Killers – (see Two Assassins of Darkness)
Kung Fu King – 1973
Kung Fu Leung Strikes Emmanuelle – (see Zen Kwun Do Strikes in Paris)
Kung Fu Mama – 1973
Kung Fu Man – (see Instant Kung Fu Man)
Kung Fu Massacre – (see The Big Showdown)
Kung Fu Master – (see The Incredible Kung fu Master)
Kung Fu Master Named Drunk Cat – 1978
Kung Fu Mean Fists, Strikes and Swords – (see Strike and Sword)
Kung Fu Monks – (see The Monk)
Kung fu of Dammon Style – (see Shaolin Devil and Shaolin Angel)
Kung Fu of Seven Steps – (see Seven Steps of Kung Fu)
Kung Fu of 7 Steps – (see Seven Steps of Kung Fu)
Kung Fu of Tae Kwon Do – (see Valley of the Double Dragon)
Kung Fu on Sale – (see Kung Fu Sale)
Kung Fu on the Bosphrus – (see Karate on the Bosphorus)
Kung Fu Phantom – (see Phantom Kung fu)
Kung Fu Powerhouse – (see One by One)
Kung Fu Punch of Death – (see Prodigal Boxer)
Kung Fu Queen – (see The Avenger)
Kung Fu Revenger – (see The Guy!! The Guy!!)
Kung Fu Sale – 1979
Kung Fu Seven Warnings – (see Seven Commandments of Kung Fu)
Kung Fu Shadow – (see Imperial Sword)
Kung Fu Stars – 1975
Kung-Fu Sting – (see Million Dollars Snatch)
Kung Fu Strongman – (see The Dumb Ox)
Kung Fu Superman – (see Little Superman)
Kung Fu 10th Dan – 1974
Kung Fu of 10th Dan – (see Kung Fu 10th Dan)
Kung Fu Rebels – 1978
Kung Fu Terminator – (see Cute Foster Sister)
Kung Fu: The Invincible Fist – (see Tiger Vs. Dragon)
Kung Fu: The Invisible Fist – (see Tiger Vs. Dragon)
Kung Fu the Punch of Death – (see Prodigal Boxer)
Kung Fu Trouble Maker – (see Kung Fu Rebels)
Kung Fu Vengeance – (see Vengeance!)
Kung Fu Vs. Yoga – 1979
Kung Fu Warlords – (see The Brave Archer)

Kung Fu Warlords 2 – (see Brave Archer 2)
Kung Fu Warrior – 1979
Kung Fu Warrior, The – (see Kung Fu Warrior)
Kung Fu's Hero – 1973
Kung Fu Vengeance – (see Vengeance)
Kung Fu-ry! – (see Yellow Killer)

Lady Constable – 1978
Lady Constables – (see Lady Constable)
Lady Blood Boxer – (see Snake Girl Drop In)
Lady Exterminator – 1977
Lady Hermit, The – 1971
Lady Iron Monkey – (see Ape Girl)
Lady Karate – (see Spy Ring Kokuryukai)
Lady Killer, The – 1978
Lady Kung Fu – (see Hapkido)
Lady of Steel – 1970
Lady of the Law – 1975
Lady Professional, The – 1971
Lady Whirlwind – 1972
Lady Whirlwind and the Rangers – (see The Rangers)
Lady with A Sword – 1971
Lama Avenger, The – 1979
Land of the Brave – 1974
Lantern Festival Adventure – 1977
Lantern Street – 1977
Lantern Street, The – (see Lantern Street)
Last Battle of Yang Chao, The – 1976
Last Challenge of the Dragon – (see The Big Family)
Last Days of Hsian Yang, The – (see Last Days of Hsin Yang)
Last Days of Hsin Yang, The – 1979
Last Duel, The – 1972
Last Fist of Fury – (see Bruce Li in New Guinea)
Last Hurrah for Chivalry – 1979
Last Judgement, The – 1979
Last Message, The – 1976
Last Strike – 1977
Last Tiger from Canton – (see Cub Tiger from Kwangtung)
Last Tiger of Canton – (see Cub Tiger from Kwang-tung)
Law Don – 1979
Lawman, The – 1979
Layout – (see Hero from Shanghai)
Lee Lives Within – (see Showdown at the Equator)
Lee's Younger Days – (see Mysterious Heroes)
Left Hand of Death – 1974
Legend of All Men are Brothers – 1977
Legend of Bruce Lee – 1976
Legend of Mother Goddess, The – 1975
Legend of the Assassinator – (see Night of the Assassins)
Legend of the Bat – 1978
Legend of the Broken Sword – 1979
Legend of the Living Corpse – (see Shaolin Brothers)
Legend of the Mountain – 1979
Legend of the Seven Golden Vampires – (see Dracula and the 7 Golden Vampires)
Legend of the 7 Golden Vampires – (see Dracula and the 7 Golden Vampires)
Legend of the Tiger – (see Tiger Love)
Legendary Fok, The – (see The Great Boxer)
Legendary Hero Fok – (see The Great Boxer)
Legendary Strike, The – 1978

Let Them Fight Each Other – (see Dirty Tiger and Crazy Frog)

Li, the Magic Blade – (see Flying Sword Lee)

Life and Death – 1977

Life Combat – (see Life Gamble)

Life Gamble – 1978

Life for Sale – 1973

Lion That Roars, The – (see The Roaring Lion)

Lion's Heart, The – 1972

Little Adventurer – 1975

Little Boxer King – (see The King Boxer)

Little Godfather – (see Little Godfather from Hong Kong)

Little Godfather from Hong Kong – 1974

Little Hero – (see The Bastard)

Little Hero – 1978

Little Hero – (see Little Super Man)

Little Killer, The – (see The Singing Killer)

Little Super Man – 1975

Little Tiger from Canton – (see Cub Tiger from Kwangtung)

Little Tiger from Kwantung – (see Cub Tiger from Kwangtung)

Living Buddha Chikung – 1975

Living Sword, The – 1971

Lizard, The – 1972

Lonely Killer – 1975

Long Chase, The – 1971

Lost Samurai Sword – (see The Lost Swordship)

Lost Swordship, The – 1977

Love and the Sword – (see The Samurai)

Love Competition – 1976

Love of the White Snake – 1978

Lovely Female Fighter – (see The Comet Strikes)

Lu Hsiao Fury – 1976

Lucky, Lucky – 1974

Lung Kuen Siu Chi – 1975

Lung Wei Village – 1978

Lut Tau Lung Foo Dau – 1975

Ma Su Chen – 1972

Macho Man – (see Big Rascal)

Macho Man – (Duel in the Tiger Den)

Mackoman – (see The Big Risk)

Mad Boy – (see The New Shaolin Boxers)

Mad Killer – 1971

Mad Mad Kung Fu – 1979

Mad Monk, The – 1977

Mad Monkey Kung Fu – 1979

Mad Monk Strikes Again, The – 1978

Mad Monkey – (see Mad Monkey Kung Fu)

Mad World of Fools, A – 1974

Madboys in Hong Kong – (see Killers on Wheels)

Magic Blade, The – 1976

Magical Power of Fan Li Wa – 1971

Magic Curse, The – 1977

Magic Palm – 1971

Magic Ring – 1976

Magic Swords – (see Sword of Heaven and Hell)

Magnificent, The – 1979

Magnificent Acrobats – (see The Daredevils)

Magnificent Bodyguards – 1978

Magnificent Butcher, The – 1979

Magnificent Chivalry – 1971

Magnificent Duo – 1977

Magnificent Guardsmen – (see Magnificent Bodyguards)

Magnificent Gunfighter, The – 1970

Magnificent Gunfighters – (see The Magnificent Gunfighter)

Magnificent Kung-Fu Warriors – (see Magnificent Wanderers)

Magnificent Ruffians, The – 1979

Magnificent Sword, The – (see The Sword Hand)

Magnificent Swordsman – (see Swordsman with an Umbrella)

Magnificent 3 – 1979

Magnificent 3, The – (see Magnificent 3)

Magnificent 2 – 1974

Magnificent Wanderers – 1976

Magnum Fist – 1978

Majesty Cat, The – (see Ninja Swords of Death)

Man Beyond Horizon, A – 1972

Man Called Stoner, A – (see Stoner)

Man Called Tiger, A – (see The Man Called Tiger)

Man Called Tiger, The – 1972 (AU)

Man From Hong Kong, The – 1976 (AU)

Man From Hong Kong, That – (see The Man From Hong Kong)

Man of Iron – 1972

Man on Police Gazette – 1973

Manda The Snake Girl – (see Evil Snake Girl)

Mandarin, The – 1973

Mandarin Magician – (see Bloody Ring)

Mandarin Magicians – (see Bloody Ring)

Manhunt – 1978

Many Faces of a Diamond – 1972

Mantis Combat – 1978

Mantis Fights Cock – (see Death Duel of Mantis)

Mantis Fist – (see Mantis Fists and Tiger Claws of Shaolin)

Mantis Fist Fighter – (see Thundering Mantis)

Mantis Fists and Tiger Claws of Shaolin – 1977

Mantis Fists & Tiger Claws of Shaolin – (see Mantis Fists and Tiger Claws of Shaolin)

Mantis in the Monkey's Shadow – (see Phantom Kung Fu)

Mar's Villa, The – 1979

Marco Polo – 1975

Mars Villa – (see The Mar's Villa)

Martial Arts – 1974

Martial Hero – 1972

Martial Hero of Southern Frontier – (see Martial Hero)

Martyrs, The – 1977

Marvellous Fists – (see Cub Tiger from Kwangtung)

Marvelous Kung Fu – 1979

Marvelous Kung Fu, The – (see Marvelous Kung Fu)

Marvelous Stunts of Kung Fu – 1979

Mask of Death – (see Shaolin Devil and Shaolin Angel)

Massacre Survivor, A – 1979

Massive, The – (see Murder of Murders)

Master & the Boxer – (see 36 Crazy Fists)

Master and the Kid – 1978

Master Killer – (see The 36th Chamber of Shaolin)

Master Killers – (see Kung Fu Brothers in the Wild West)

Master of Death – (see Revenge of the Shaolin Kid)

Master of Death – (see Magnificent Bodyguards)

Master of Death – (see Fighting Ace)

Master of Jeet Kun Do – (see Bruce Lee's Deadly Kung Fu)

Master of Kung Fu, The – 1973

Master of the Flying Quillotene – 1976

Master with Crack Fingers – (see Cub Tiger from Kwangtung)

Master with Cracked Fingers – (see Cub Tiger from Kwangtung)

Masters of Kung Fu – (see Revengeful Swords-woman)

Masters of the Iron Arena – (see Men of the Hour)

Match for Tiger and Dragon – (see Bamboo Brother-hood)

Matchless Conquerer, The – 1971

Mean Drunken Master – (Iron Bridge Kung Fu)

Mean Streets of Kung Fu – 1973 (The invincible Hero)

Men From The Monastery – 1974

Men of the Hour – 1977

Men on the Hour – (see Men of the Hour)

Merciful Sword, The – 1971

Method Man – (see Avenging Boxer)

Middle Kingdom's Mark of Blood – 1979

Mighty Couple, The – 1971

Mighty One, The – 1972

Might Peking Man – 1977

Militant Eagle – 1978

Million Dollars Snatch – 1976

Ming Dynasty – (see Dynasty)

Ming Patriots, The – 1976

Mission Kiss & Kill – 1979

Mission Impossible – 1970

Money Crazy – (see The Pilferer's Progress)

Money Tree – 1973

Money Trip – 1979

Monk, The – 1975

Monk's Fight, The – 1979

Monkey Comes Again – 1971

Monkey Fist – 1974

Monkey Fist, Floating Snake – 1979

Monkey King with 72 Magic – 1976

Monkey Kung Fu – 1979

Monkey Kung Fu – (see Monkey Fist, Floating Snake)

Monkey Kung Fu – (see Five Superfighters)

Monkey in the Master's Eyes – (see Bone Crushing Kid)

Monkey Love – (see Raging Tiger Vs. Monkey King)

Moonlight Blade: Vengeance on a Snowy Night – (see Pursuit of Vengeance)

Moonlight Sword and Jade Lion – 1977

Mortal Combat – (see Crippled Avengers)

Mr. Big – 1978

Mr. Boo – (see The Private Eyes)

Mr. Funnybone – 1976

Murder Masters of Kung Fu – 1973

Murder of Murders – 1978

Murder Plot – 1979

Muscle of the Dragon – (see The Dragon, The Hero)

Mutiny on the High Sea – 1975

My Kung Fu Master – 1978

My Kung Fu Twelve Kicks – 1979

My Life's on a line – 1978

My Life's on the line – (see My Life's on a line)

My Millionaire Sister – (see Secret of My Millionaire Sister)

My Name Called Bruce – 1978

My Son – 1970

Mysterious Footworks of Kung Fu – 1978

Mysterious Heroes, The – 1977

Mysterious Killer in Town – (see Psychopath)

Mystery of Chess Boxing – 1979
Myters, The – (see The Martyrs)

Na Cha and the Seven Devils – 1973
Na Cha the Great – 1974
Naked Comes the Huntress – 1978
Naked Fist of Terror – (The Spiritual Boxer)
Naked Fist Fighter – (The Spiritual Boxer)
Naughty! Naughty! – 1974
Naval Commandos, The – 1977
Naval Descentors – (see The Naval Commandos)
Negotation – 1977
New Fist of Fury – 1976
New Game Of Death, The – 1975
New Game Of Death, The – 1977
New One-Armed Swordsman, The – 1971
New Prodigal Boxer – (see Secret of the Shaolin
   Poles)
New Shaolin Boxers, The – 1976
Night of the Assassins – 1979
Night Of Devil's Bride – 1975
Nine Golden Knights – (see Golden Knight)
99 Cycling Swords – (see Lung Wei Village)
Ninja Avengers – (see Fury in Storm)
Ninja Checkmate – (see Mystery of Chess Boxing)
Ninja Fist of Fire – (see The Fist that Kills)
Ninja Heat – (see Black List)
Ninja Kids – (see The Young Dragons)
Ninja Killer – (see Fearless Fighters)
Ninja Killer – (see Karate on the Bosphorus)
Ninja Massacre – (see Secret Message)
Ninja Swords of Death – 1978
Ninja Terminator – (see Black List)
Ninja Thunder Kicks (Thunderkicks) – (see Revenge
   of the Shaolin Master)
Ninja Warlord – 1973
Ninja Wolves – 1979
No One Can Touch Her – 1979
No. 37 Plot, The – 1979
Noble Ninja – (see The Chivalry, The Gunman and
   Killer)
None But the Brave – 1973
North and the South Chivalry, The – 1977
Notorious Ex-Monk, A – (see Shaolin Ex-Monk)
Notorious Ones – 1972
Notorious Bandit – (see Tongfather)
Not Scared to Die – 1973
Number One, The – (see Warriors Two)
Number One Iron Man – 1973

Oath Of Death – 1971
Octagon force – (see Yoga and Kung Fu Girl
Odd Couple – 1979
Of Cooks and Kung Fu – 1979
Oily Maniac – 1976
Ol' Dirty Kung Fu – (see Mad Mad Kung Fu)
Ol' Dirty Stikes Back – (see Peculiar Boxing Tricks
   and the Master)
Old Dirty Kung Fu – (see Mad Mad Kung Fu)
Old Master, The – 1979
On the Back Street – 1974
On the Blackstreet – 1974
On the Waterfront – 1972
One Arm Against the Dragon Gate – (see To Crack
   the Dragon Gate)
One Arm Vs. Nine Killers – (see One-Armed Swords-
   man Against Nine Killers)

One Armed Against Nine Killers – (see One Armed
   Swordsman Against Nine Killers)
One Armed Swordsman Against Nine Killers
   – 1976
One Armed Swordsman Annihilates the Nine Dis-
   ciples of Chu School – (One Armed Swordsman
   Against Nine Killers)
One Armed Swordsmen – 1976
One Armed Swordswoman – 1974
One-Armed Boxer – 1971
One-Armed Boxer 2 – (see Master of the Flying
   Quillotene)
One-Armed Boxer II – (see Master of the Flying
   Quillotene)
One-Armed Boxer Vs. the Flying Quillotene – (see
   Master of the Flying Quillotene)
One-Armed Boxer Vs. the Master – (see Master of
   the Flying Quillotene)
**One-Armed Chivalry Fights Against One-
   Armed Chivalry** – 1977
One-Armed Swordsmen – (see One Armed Swords-
   men)
One-Armed Vs. The Red Devil – (see The Great
   Duel)
One by One – 1973
One Day I will Get You – (see I'll Get You One Day)
One Foot Crane – 1979
108 Heroes – (see All Men are Brothers)
One Man Army – (see The Master and the Kid)
One Way Only – 1979
One Who Broke Down the Dragon Party, The – (see
   To Crack the Dragon Gate)
Only the Brave Stands – (see Challenge of the
   Dragon)
Operation Dragon – (see Enter the Dragon)
Operation Iron Man – (see The Association)
Operation Regina – (see A Queen's Ransom)
Operation White Shirt – 1973
Opium Trail, The – 1973
Orthodox Chinese Kung Fu – 1977
Outlaw of the Forest – (see The Delightful Forest)
Outlaws of the Marsh – (see The Water Margin)
Owl, The – 1974

Pai Yu Ching – 1977
Paid with Blood – 1970
Paris – 1974
Paris Killers – (see Paris)
Patriotic Heroine – 1971
Patriotic Knights – 1971
Payment in Blood – 1973
Payoff – 1979
Peculiar Boxing Tricks and the Master – 1978
Peculiar Fist Kid – (see Drunken Arts and Crippled
   Fists)
Peerless Swordsman, The – (see Death Duel)
Peking Man – (see The Mighty Peking Man)
Phantom Kung Fu – 1978
Phantom Lute, The – 1975
Phantom Madam Peach Blossom – 1975
Pilferer's Progressions – 1978
Pirate, The – 1973
Point the Finger of Death – (see One-Armed Chiv-
   alry Fights Against One-Armed Chivalry)
Poison Rose and the Bodyguard – 1979
Police Force – 1973
Police Woman – 1973

Pork Chopper – (see Young Hero of Shaolin)
Pretended Rebel, A – (see Ninja Wolves)
Princess and the Toxicant – 1977
Princess and Toxicant, The – (see Princess and the
   Toxicant)
Private Eye – 1973
Private Eyes, The – 1976
Prodigal Boxer – 1972
Prodigal Boxer 2 – (see Secret of the Shaolin Poles)
Prodigal Boxer 2 – (see Young Hero of Shaolin)
Prodigal Son – (see The Gallant)
Professional Killer, The – (see The Assassin)
Prominent Eunuch Chen Ho – 1978
Protectors, The – 1974
Proud Horse in the Flying Squad – (see Duel in the
   Dessert)
Proud Twins, The – 1979
Proud Youth, The – 1978
Psychopath – 1978
Pursued – 1970
Pursuit – 1972
Pursuit Of Vengeance – 1977

Qigong Master – (see Chinese Kung Fu and
   Acupuncture)
Queen Bee, The – 1974
Queen Boxer – (see Chase Step by Step)
Queen Boxer – (see The Avenger)
Queen Hustler – 1974
Queen of Fist – (see Kung Fu Mama)
Queen's Ransom, A – 1977
Quick Cutting without Knife – (see Choi Lee Fat
   Kung Fu)

Rage of the Wind – 1973
Rage of Wind, The – (see Rage of the Wind)
Rage of the Master – (see The Hero)
Rage of the Tiger – (see The Hero)
Raging Tiger Vs. Monkey King – 1978
Raiders of the Dragon Blade – (see Legend of the
   Broken Sword)
Raining in the Mountain – 1979
Rainny Night's Killer – 1974
Rangers, The – 1974
Rascal Billionaire, The – 1978
Rat Catches, The – 1974
Rats, The – 1973
Real Bruce Lee, The – 1973
Real Man, A – (see Fearless Fighters)
Rebel Boxer – (see Ma Su Chen)
Rebel of Shaolin – (see Shaolin Traitor)
Rebel Youth, The – (see The Young Rebel)
Reckless Cricket – 1979
Red Beard – 1971
Red Boy – (see Fantastic Magic Baby)
Red Clothes Lama – (see Shaolin Red Master)
Red Dot Chivalry – (see Middle Kingdom's Mark of
   Blood)
Red Dragon, The – (see Magnificent Bodyguards)
Red Phoenix – 1979
Red Shaolin Master – (see Shaolin Red Master)
Red Tasseled Sword, The – 1975
Re-Enter the Dragon – (1978)
Relentless Broken Blade – 1979
Relentless Broken Swords – 1979
Rendezvous of Warriors, The – 1973
Renegade Master – 1977

Renegade Monk – (see Shaolin Ex-Monk)
Rescue, The – 1971
Return of the Assassin – 1973
Return of the Barbarian Women – (see Superman Against the Amazons)
Return of the Chinese Boxer – 1977
Return of the Dead – 1979
Return of the Dragon – (see Way of the Dragon)
Return of the 18 Bonzemen – 1976
Return of the Five Deadly Venoms – (see Crippled Avengers)
Return of the 5 Deadly Venoms – (see Crippled Avengers)
Return of the Kung Fu Dragon – 1978
Return of the Leg Fighter – (see Knife of the Devil's Roaring and Soul Missing)
Return of the Panther – (see The Dumb Ox)
Return of the Scorpion – (see Duel of the Seven Tigers)
Return of the Secret Rivals – (see Filthy Guy)
Return of the Tiger – 1976
Return of the Tiger – 1977
Return of the Valuables – 1975
Return to China – (see Not Scared to Die)
Revenge Dragon, The – (see Dragon Force Operation)
Revenge is Sweet – 1974
Revenge of Fist of Fury – (see The Death Duel)
Revenge of Fury – (see The Death Duel)
Revenge of Kung Fu – 1977
Revenge of Kung Fu – (see The Death Duel)
Revenge of Kung Fu Mao – 1977
Revenge of a Shaolin Master – 1979
Revenge of the Black Dragon – (see Black Dragon's Revenge)
Revenge of the Dragon – (see Shaolin Chastity Kung Fu)
Revenge of the Dragon – (see Way of the Dragon)
Revenge of the Dragon – (see The Duel of the Brave Ones)
Revenge of the Gold Fox – (see Secret Rivals 2)
Revenge of the Iron Fist Maiden – 1973
Revenge of the Lady Warrior – (See No-one Can Touch Her)
Revenge of the Patriots – (see Ming Patriots)
Revenge of the Shaolin Kid – (see Shaolin Hand Lock)
Revenge of the Shaolin Kid – 1978
Revenge of the Shaolin Masters – (see Revenge of the Shaolin Master)
Revengeful Swordswoman – 1979
Revenger, The – (see The Gallant)
Rickshaw Man – (see Rikish Kuri)
Rickshaw Puller – 1974
Rider of Revenge – 1971
Righteous Fist, The – 1972
Right Overcomes Might – 1978
Rikisha Kuri – 1974
Rivals Of Kung Fu – 1974
River Of Fury – 1973
Roar in the Woods – 1975
Roaring Kung Fu Fighter – (see Sleeping Fist)
Roaring Lion, The – 1972
Rocky Lee – (see Mar's Villa)
Rotary Kicks – 1973
Rover's Fast Swords – (Wanderer with Nimble Knife)
Royal Family – (see Eunich of the Western Palace)

Royal Fist – (see Showdown)
Royal Monks – (see Disciples of Shaolin 1975)
Rumble in Hong Kong – (see Police Woman)
Ruthless Revenge – 1979

Sacred Knives of Vengeance – (see The Killer)
Samruai, The – (see Samurai; 1979)
Samurai, The – 1979
Samurai Blood, Samurai Guts – (see Blood and Guts)
Samurai Terror – (see The Swift Shaolin Boxer)
Samurai Vs. Swordsmen – 1971
Savage Five, The – 1974
Savage 5, The – (see The Savage Five)
Savage Killers – 1976
Saviour Monk – 1975
Saxon – (see Foxbat)
Scandalous Warlord, The – 1979
School of Chivalry – (see Fist of Fury)
School of Shaolin – (see Iron Monkey)
Scorching Sun, Fierce Winds, and Wild Fire – 1979
Screaming Tiger – 1979
Sea Gods and Ghosts – 1977
Seaman No. 7 – 1972
Seaman Number Seven – (see Seaman No. 7)
Secret Agent Chang Jiang No. 1 – 1970
Secret Agents – (see The Secret Rivals)
Secret Agents II – (see The Secret Rivals Part 2)
Secret Envoy – (see The Secret Rivals)
Secret in the Mist, The – 1974
Secret Message – 1979
Secret of Bruce Lee – (see He's a Legend, He's a Hero)
Secret of Chinese Kung fu – 1977
Secret of Kowloon Town – 1977
Secret of My Millionaire Sister – 1971
Secret of Shaolin Kung Fu – (see Butterfly 18)
Secret of the Buddhist Fist – (see Buddhist Fist)
Secret of the Dirk, The – 1970
Secret of the Dragon – (see Snake Crane Secret)
Secret of the Shaolin Poles – 1977
Secret of the Snake and Crane, The – (see Snake Crane Secret)
Secret of the Water Technique – (see Legend of All Men are Brothers)
Secret Rivals, The – 1976
Secret Rivals II – (see The Secret Rivals Part 2)
Secret Rivals 2, The – (see The Secret Rivals Part 2)
Secret Rivals Part 2, The – 1977
Secret Rivals, The: The Northern Leg and Southern Fist – (see The Secret Rivals)
Secret Shaolin Kung Fu – (see Butterfly 18)
Secrets of Chinese Kung fu – (see Secret of Chinese Kung fu)
Secrets of the Dragon – (see Snake Crane Secret)
Sensual Pleasures – 1978
Seizure Soul Sword of a Blind Girl – 1970
Sentimental Swordsman, The – 1977
Seven Blows of the Dragon – (see The Water Margin)
7 Blows of the Dragon – (see The Water Margin)
Seven Blows of the Dragon II – (see All Men Are Brothers)
7 Blows of the Dragon II – (see All Men Are Brothers)
Seven Coffins, The – 1976

Seven Brothers Meet Dracula – (see Dracula and the 7 Golden Vampires)
7 Brothers Meet Dracula – (see Dracula and the 7 Golden Vampires)
7 Brothers & a Sister Meet Dracula – (see Dracula and the 7 Golden Vampires)
Seven Commandments of Kung Fu – 1979
7 Commandments of Kung fu – (see Seven Commandments of Kung Fu)
Seven Grand Masters – 1978
7 Grand Masters – (see Seven Grand Masters)
Seven Indignant – 1973
Seven Indignant Killers – 1977
Seven Knights, 8 Banners – (see Seven Men of Kung Fu)
Seven Kung Fu Assassins – (see All Men Are Brothers)
Seven Magnificent Fights – (see Seaman No. 7)
Seven Man Army – 1976
7 Man Army – (see Seven Man Army)
Seven Men of Kung Fu – 1978
Seven Soldiers of Kung Fu – (see All Men Are Brothers)
7 Soldiers of Kung Fu – (see All Men Are Brothers)
Seven Spirit Pagoda –1976
Seven Steps of Kung fu – 1979
Seven to One – 1973
72 Desperate Rebels – 1978
72 Desperate Rebels, The – (see 72 Desperate Rebels)
Seventy Two Hours in Green Town – (see Tiger From Hong Kong)
72 Hours in Green Town – (see Tiger From Hong Kong)
Sex Desire Monk – (see The Monk)
Sex Life of Bruce Lee, The – (see Bruce Lee and I; 1975)
Sexy Killer – 1976
Sexy Killer, The – (see Sexy Killer)
Sexy Invite Sixty Two – (see Marvelous Stunts of Kung Fu)
Shadow Boxer, The – 1974
Shadow Boxin' – (see The 36 Deadly Styles)
Shadow Boxing, The – 1979
Shadow Girl – 1971
Shadow of the Snake Wizard – (see Bruce and Shaolin Kung Fu)
Shadow of the Tigers – (see Duel of the Seven Tigers)
Shadow Whip, The – 1970
Shanghai boxer – (see Brave Girl Boxer in Shanghai)
Shanghai Beach – (see The Big Rascal)
Shanghai Killers – (see The Chase)
Shanghai Lil and the Sunluck Kid – (see The Champion)
Shaolin, The – (see Shaolin Avenger)
Shaolin Abbot – 1979
Shaolin Archer – (see Brave Archer)
Shaolin Archer 2 – (see Brave Artchers 2)
Shaolin Avengers, The – 1976
Shaolin Bloodshed – (see Invincible Shaolin)
Shaolin Boxer, The – 1974
Shaolin Boxers, The – (see The Shaolin Boxer)
Shaolin Brothers – 1977
Shaolin Challenges Ninja – (see Heroes of the East)
Shaolin Chamber of Death – (see Shaolin Wooden Men)

Shaolin Chastity Kung Fu – (see Revenge of the Dragon)
Shaolin Daredevils – (The Daredevils)
Shaolin Deadly Hands – (see Shaolin Invincible Guy)
Shaolin Deadly Kicks – 1977
Shaolin Death Kick – (see Cub Tiger from Kwangtung)
Shaolin Death Kicks – (see The Master of Kung Fu)
Shaolin Death Squad – (see Shaolin Kids)
Shaolin Death Squads – 1977
Shaolin Devil and Shaolin Angel – 1978
Shaolin Devil & Shaolin Angel – (see Shaolin Devil and Shaolin Angel)
Shaolin Devil, Shaolin Angel – (Shaolin Devil and Shaolin Angel)
Shaolin Drunken Monkey – 1979
Shaolin Ex Monk – 1978
Shaolin Executioner – (see Executioner from Shaolin)
Shaolin Hand Lock – 1978
Shaolin Hellgate – (see Heaven and Hell)
Shao-Lin Hero Chang San Feng – (see Adventure of Shaolin)
Shaolin Heroes – 1979
Shaolin Heroes, The – (see Shaolin Heroes)
Shaolin Incredible Ten – (see 10 Shaolin Disciples)
Shaolin Invincible Guys – 1978
Shaolin Invincible Sticks – 1979
Shaolin Invincibles – 1977
Shaolin Iron Claws – 1978
Shaolin Iron Eagle – (see Iron Swallow)
Shaolin Iron Eagle – (see Shaolin Iron Claws)
Shaolin Iron Finger – (see Renegade Master)
Shaolin Kids – 1977
Shaolin Kickboxer, The – (see Iron Fists)
Shaolin King Boxer, The – (see Iron Fists)
Shaolin Kung Fu – 1974
Shao Lin Kung Fu – (see Shaolin Kung Fu)
Shaolin Kung Fu Master – 1978
Shaolin Kung Fu Mystagogue – 1977
Shaolin Long Arm – (see Chinese Kung Fu; 1974)
Shaolin Magnificant Armor – (see The Shaolin Borthers)
Shaolin Magnificent Kicks – (see Chivalrous Inn)
Shaolin Mantis – 1978
Shaolin Martial Arts – 1974
Shaolin Master and the Kid – (see Master and the Kid)
Shaolin Master Killer – (see The 36th Chamber of Shaolin)
Shaolin Masters – (see The Heroic Ones)
Shaolin Monk – 1977
Shaolin Plot, The – 1977
Shaolin Quickdraw – (see Fury in Storm)
Shaolin Raider of Death – (see Seven Steps of Kung Fu)
Shaolin Raiders of Death – (see Seven Steps of Kung Fu)
Shaolin Red Master – 1978
Shaolin Rescuers – 1979
Shaolin Saints – (Boxers of Loyalty and Righteousness)
Shaolin Silver Spear – (see Deadly Silver Spear)
Shaolin Swallow – (see Chin Sha Yen)
Shaolin Tamo Buddhist Monk – (see Shaolin Monk)
Shaolin Temple – 1976
Shaolin Temple – (see Seven Spirit Pagoda)

Shaolin Thief – (see Thief of Thieves)
Shaolin Tiger Claw – (see Tiger's Claw)
Shaolin Tough Kid – (see Shaolin Red Master)
Shaolin Traitor – 1977
Shaolin Traitorous – (see Traitorous)
Shaolin Vengeance – (The Furious Monk From Shaolin)
Shaolin Vs. Lama – (see Unique Lama)
Shaolin Vs. Ninja – (see Heroes of the East)
Shaolin Warrior – (see Thou Shall Not Kill…But Once)
Shaolin Wooden Men – 1976
Shaolin Wooden Men…Young Tiger's Revenge – (see Shaolin Wooden Men)
Shaolin's Born Invincible – (see Born Invincible)
Shaolin's Tiger Claws – (see Tiger's Claw)
Shaolin's Tough Kid – (see Goose Boxer)
Sharp Fist of Kung Fu, The – 1975
Shatter – (see Call Him Mr. Shatter)
She'd Hate Rather Love – 1971
She'd Hate Rather Than Love – 1(see She'd Hate Rather Love)
Shogun Avenger – (see The King Boxer)
Shogun Massacre – (see Buddha Assassinator)
Shogun Saints – (see Boxers of Loyalty and Righteousness)
Showdown – 1972
Showdown at Cotton Mill – 1978
Showdown at the Equator – 1978
Showdown of the Master Warriors – (see Death Duel of Kung Fu)
Shrine of Ultimate Bliss, The – (see Stoner)
Silent Guest from Peking, The – 1975
Silent Killer from Eternity – (see Return of the Tiger) Bruce Li
Silly Kid – (see The New Shaolin Boxers)
Silver Fox Rivals – (see Secret Rivals)
Silver Fox Rivals 2 – (see The Secret Rivals Part 2)
Silver Hermit From Shaolin Temple – (see Silver Spear)
Silver Hermit Meets the Bloody Fangs of Death – (see Silver Spear)
Silver Spear – 1979
Silver Maid – 1970
Silver Fox Masters –(see Killer from Above)
Simple-Minded Fellow, The – 1976
Singing Killer, The – 1970
Single Fighter – 1974
Sister of Shangtong – (see Heroine Susan, the Sister of the Shantung Boxer)
Six Assassins – 1970
6 Assassins – (see Six Assassins)
Six Heroic Figures – (six Kung Fu Heroes)
Six Kung Fu Heroes – 1977
60 Second Assassan – (see My Life's on a Line)
Skillful Fighter – (The Spiritual Boxer)
Skyhawk, The – 1974
Slash: Blade of Death – (see The Chase)
Slaughter in San Francisco – (see Yellow Faced Tiger)
Sleeping Dragon – 1974
Sleeping Fist – 1979
Slice of Death – (see Shaolin Abbot)
Smart Cavalier – (see The Cavalier)
Smart Kung Fu – (see The Cavalier)
Smugglers – 1973

Snake and Crane Arts of Kung Fu – (see Snake and Crane Arts of Shaolin)
Snake and Crane Arts of Shaolin – 1978
Snake and the Eagle's Shadow – (Snake in the Eagle's Shadow)
Snake Crane Secret – 1978
Snake-Crane Secret – (see Snake Crane Secret)
Snake Deadly Act – 1979
Snake Fist, Drunken Step – (see Snake Deadly Act)
Snake Fist Dynamo – (see The Crazy Instructor)
Snake Fist Fighter – (see Cub Tiger from Kwangtung)
Snake Fist of a Buddhist Dragon – 1979
Snakefist Vs. the Dragon – (see Snake in the Monkey's Shadow)
Snake Girl, The – 1974
Snake Girl Drop In, The – 1974
Snake in Eagle's Shadow 3 – (see The Damned)
Snake in the Crane's Shadow – 1978
Snake in the Eagle's Shadow – 1978
Snake in the Eagle's Shadow 2 – (see Snaky Knight Fight Against Mantis)
Snake in the Eagle's Shadow 3 – (see The Damned)
Snake in the Monkey's Shadow – 1979
Snake Killer – (see The Killer Snakes)
Snake Prince, The – 1976
Snake Queen – 1974
Snake Shadow, Lama Fist – 1976
Snake Shadow Rivals – (see Fierce Among Strong)
Snake Woman's Marriage – 1975
Snake's Fist, Cat's Paw – (see Snake in the Eagle's Shadow)
Snaky Knight Fight Against Mantis – 1978
Snaky Monkey – (see Snake in the Eagle's Shadow)
Snuff Bottle Connection – 1977
Soldiers of Darkness – (see Eunuch of the Western Palace)
Son of Yellow Dragon – 1974
Son of the Dragon – (see Son of Yellow Dragon)
Sons of Wu-Tang – (see Clutch of Power)
Sorrowful to a Ghost – 1970
Soul Brothers of Kung Fu – (see Last Strike)
Soul Collector – (see Heroic Ones)
Soul of Bruce Lee – (see Soul of Chiba)
Soul of Bruce Lee, The – (see Soul of Chiba)
Soul of Chiba – 1974 (TH/JA)
Soul of Samurai – (see Impetuous Fire)
Soul of the Sword – 1978
Special Hand – (see Psychopath)
Spirits of Bruce Lee – (see Angry Tiger)
Spiritual Boxer, The – 1975
Spiritual Boxer Part 2 – (see The Shadow Boxing)
Spiritual Boxer II – (see The Shadow Boxing)
Spiritual Fists – (see Boxer Rebellion)
Spiritual Kung Fu – 1978
Spy Ring Kokuryukai – 1976
Sting of the Dragon Master – (see When Taekwondo Strikes)
Stomp, The – (see Secreet Message)
Stone Cold Wu Tang – (see The Karate Killers)
Stoner – 1974 (AU/USA)
Storming Attacks – 1978
Stormy Sea, The – 1976
Stormy Sun – 1973
Story in Temple Red Lily – 1979
Story of Daisy – 1972
Story of Fong Sai Yuk – (see Secret of the Shaolin Poles)

Story of Punishment – (see All Men are Brothers)

Story of Thirty-Six Killers – (see Thirty Six Killers)

Stories of the Assassinators – (see Night of the Assassins)

Stories of the Assassinators: Part 1 (about Chuan Chu) – (see Night of the Assassins)

Story of the Chinese Gods – 1975

Story of the Dragon – (see Bruce Lee's Deadly Kung Fu)

Story of the Drunken Kung Fu – (see Story of the Drunken Master)

Story of the Drunken Master – 1979

Strange Bedfellows – (see Mad World of Fools)

Strange Skill – 1978

Strange People – (see Mad World of Fools)

Strange Swordman of Dark Night – (see The Devil's Treasure)

Stranger, The – (see The Gallant)

Stranger and the Gunfighter, The – 1974 (SP/IT/USA)

Stranger from Canton – (see Karate Killers)

Stranger From Shaolin – 1977

Stranger in Hong Kong – (see Cub Tiger from Kwangtung)

Street Gangs of Hong Kong – (see The Delinquent)

Strife for Mastery – 1977

Strike and Sword – 1977

Strike 4 Revenge – (see Four Riders)

Strike of Death – (see The Hand of Death)

Strike of Mantis Fist – (see Death Duel of Mantis)

Strike of the Thunderkick Tiger – 1978

Striking Fist – (see Duel of Fist)

Stroke of Death – (see Monkey Kung Fu)

Strong Eastman – 1973

Strong Justice, The – (see Kung Fu Infernos)

Struggle – (see Duel of the Brave Ones)

Struggle for Avengence – 1971

Struggle Karate – 1971

Struggle Through Death – 1979

Struggle With Death – 1976

Succabare – (see Princess and the Toxicant)

Sun Dragon – 1979

Sunset in the Forbidden City – 1976

Super Boxer – 1971

Super Chan – (see Forced to Fight)

Super Dragon – (see Dynasty)

Super Dragon – (see Super Power)

Super Dragon – (see Dragon Dies Hard) Bruce Li

Super Dragon Vs. Superman – (see Bruce Lee Against Supermen)

Super Dynamo – (see Chinese Kung Fu (not The Dumb Ox)

Super Inframan – 1975

Super Kung Fu Fighter – 1978

Super Kung Fu Kid – 1974

Super Man Chu – (see Stormy Sun)

Super Man Chu: Master of Kung Fu – (see Stormy Sun)

Super Manchu – (see Stormy Sun)

Super Power – 1979

Super Riders Against the Devil – 1976

Super Riders V3 – 1975

Super Riders with the Devil, The – (see Super Riders Against the Devil)

Super Stooges Vs. The Wonder Women – (see Superman Against the Amazons)

Superdragon – (see Legend of Bruce Lee)

Superdragon: The Bruce Lee Story – (see Bruce Lee, A Dragon Story)

Superdynamo – (see Chinese Kung Fu)

Superfighters, The – (see Five Superfighters)

Superfist – (see Super Power)

Superfist – 1976

Supergirl of Kung Fu, The – 1975

Supergirl Kung Fu Chiu Chow – (see Chiu Chow Kung Fu)

Superman Against the Amazons – 1975 (IT/ME)

Supermen Against the Orient – 1974

Superpower – (see Super Power)

Superstar, The – (see Bruce Lee and I)

Superior Youngster – (see Super Kung fu Kid)

Supremo – 1974

Survival of the Dragon – (see The Thunderkick)

Swift Knight – 1971

Swift Shaolin Boxer, The – 1978

Sword, The – 1971

Sword Hand, The – 1971

Sword for a Killer, A – 1970

Sword of Heaven and Hell – 1979

Sword of the Wind Chimes – 1977

Sword on Fire – 1971

Sword Renounced, A – (see The Blind Swordsman's Revenge)

Sword Shot at the Sun – 1979

Sword with the Windbell – (see Sword of the Wind Chimes)

Swordsman and Enchantress – 1978

Swordsman at Large – 1971

Swordsman, Protector, Assassin – (see The Chivalry, The Gunman and Killer)

Swordsman with an Umbrella – 1979

Swordswomen Three – 1970

Taekwondo – (see Valley of the Double Dragon)

Taekwondo Heroes – (see When Taekwondo Strikes)

Tai Chi Shadow Boxing – (see The 36 Deadly Styles)

Tantinum Blade – (see Shaolin Devil and Shaolin Angel)

Taste Of Cold Steel, A – 1970

Tattoo Connection, The – 1978

Tattooed Dragon, The – 1973

Tattooed Dragon Connection – (Hero Tattoed with Nine Dragons)

Taxi Driver – 1975

Teahouse, The – 1974

Temple of the Dragon – (see Heroes Two)

Ten Brothers of Shaolin – 1979

Ten Commandments of Lee – (see The Master and the Kid)

Ten Fingers of Death – (see Cub Tiger from Kwangtung)

Ten Fingers of Steel – (see Screaming Tiger)

Ten Magnificent Killers – 1977

10 Magnificent Killer – (see Ten Magnificent Killers)

Ten Tigers of Kwan Tung – (see The Tigers of Kwantung)

Ten Tigers of Kwangtung – (see The Tigers of Kwantung)

Ten Tigers of Shaolin – 1978

10 Tigers of Shaolin – (see Ten Tigers of Shaolin)

Terminal Impact – (see Duel of the Seven Tigers)

That Man From Singapore – (see Life For Sale)

These Hands Destroy – (see Phantom Kung fu)

They Call Me Phat Dragon – (see The Incredible Kung fu Master)

They Call Him Mr. Shatter – (see Call Him Mr. Shatter)

They Call Him Bruce Lee – 1979

Thief of Thieves – 1974

Third Sword, The – 1978

13 Evil Bandits – (see No-one Can Touch Her)

13 Fighters – (see The Heroic Ones)

13 Golden Nuns – 1977

13 Style Strikes – 1979

13 Worms – 1971

37 Plots of Kung Fu – (see The No. 37 Plot)

36 Crazy Fists – 1977

36 Deadly Styles – 1979

36 Deadly Styles, The – (see 36 Deadly Styles)

Thirty Six Killers – 1971

36 Snap Kicks – (see 36 Tan Tui)

36 Sword Guards – 1971

36 Tan Tui – 1972

36 Wooden Men – (see Shaolin Wooden Men)

Thirty Sixth Chamber, The – (see The 36th Chamber Of Shaolin)

36th Chamber Of Shaolin, The – 1977

This Time I'll Make You Rich – 1974

Those Kung fu Men from Peking – (see Silent Guest from Peking)

Thou Shall Not Kill...But Once – 1975

Thou Shalt Not Kill – (see The Living Sword)

Thousand Mile Escort – 1976

Thousand Mile's Escort – (see Thousand Mile Escort)

Thousand Years Fox – 1971

Three Avengers, The – (see The Lama Avenger)

3 Avengers, The – (see The Lama Avenger)

Three Donkeys – (see Crazy Guy with the Super Kung Fu)

Three Fantastic Supermen in the Orient – (see Supermen Against the Orient)

Three Shaolin Musketeers – 1978

Three Stooges Vs. the Wonder Women – (see Superman Against the Amazons)

Three Supermen Against the Orient – (see Supermen Against the Orient)

Three Supermen Vs. the Orient – (see Supermen Against the Orient)

Three Swordsmen – (Three Shaolin Musketeers)

Thrilling Sword, The – (see Shaolin Invincibles)

Thunder kick, The – (see The Thunderkick)

Thunder Storm – 1970

Thunderstorm Sword – (see Thunder Storm)

Thunderblade and Lightening Foot – (Knife of the Devil's Roaring and Soul Missing)

Thunderblade and Lightning Foot – (Knife of the Devil's Roaring and Soul Missing)

Thunderbolt – 1971

Thunderbolt Fist, The – 1972

Thunderfist – (see Death Blow)

Thunderkick, The – 1973

Thundering Mantis, The – 1979

Tiger – 1972

Tiger – 1973

Tiger and Crane Arts – (see Savage Killers)

Tiger & Crane Arts – (see Savage Killers)

Tiger and Crane Fists – (see Savage Killers)

Tiger and the Dragon – 1971

Tigers at Top – 1975

Tiger at the Top – (see Tigers at Top)
Tiger Boxer – 1973
Tiger Claw Death Kick – (see Dragon Dies Hard)
Tiger Force – 1975
Tiger from Canton – (see Martial Hero)
Tiger from China – 1974
Tiger from Hong Kong – 1974
Tiger Jump, The – 1974
Tiger Jungle – 1976
Tiger Love – 1977
Tiger Love, The – (see Tiger Love)
Tiger of Northland – 1976
Tiger of the Northland – (see Tiger of Northland)
Tiger Over Wall – 1979
Tiger Over the Wall – (see Tiger Over Wall)
Tiger Strikes Again – (see The Last Strike)
Tiger, Tiger, Tiger – 1975
Tiger Vs. Dragon – 1972
Tiger's Claw – 1974
Tiger's Kong Fu – (see Tiger Love)
Tiger's Love – (see Tiger Love)
Tigers of Kwantung, The – 1979
Tigress Of Shaolin, The – 1979
To Catch an Eagle by the Claw – (see Dragon of the
    Swordsman)
To Crack the Dragon Gate – 1970
To Kill a Jaguar – 1977
To Kill a Mastermind – 1979
To Kill or to die – (see Shanghai Joe)
To Kill with Intrigue – 1977
To Subdue the Devil – (see Duel of Karate)
To Skin a Tiger – 1972
To Subdue the Devil – (see Duel of karate)
Tongfather, The – 1974
Tooth for a Tooth, A – 1973
Tormentor – 1973
Tornado – (see Twister Kicker)
Tornado of Chu Chiang – (see Tornado of Pearly
    River)
Tornado of Pearl River – 1974
To Subdue Evil – 1971
To Subdue the Devil – (see To Subdue Evil)
Tough Duel – 1972
Tough Guy – (see Duel at Tiger Village)
Tough Guy – 1974 (PH)
Tough Guy – 1972
Tough Guy – (see Kung Fu's Hero)
Tough Guys – (see Tough Guy; 1972)
Tough Kung Fu Kid – (see By Hook and By Crook)
Toughest Guy, The – (see Secret Agent Chang Jiang
    No.1)
Tournament, The – 1974
Trail of the Dragon – 1974
Traitorous – 1976
Traveling Swordsman of Thunder – (Dragon of the
    Swordsman)
Treasure Castle – 1972
Triangular Duel – 1972
Trilogy Of Swordsmanship – 1972
Triple Irons – (see The New One-Armed Swords-
    man)
Trouble Maker Coming – (see Kung Fu Rebels)
Triumph by Two Kung Fu Fists – (see Triumph of
    Two Kung Fu Arts)
Triumph of Two Kung Fu Arts – 1977
True Master – (see Deadly Silver Spear)
Trust and Brotherhood – 1972

Twelve Gold Medallions, The – 1970
Twelve Kung Fu Kicks – (see My Kung Fu Twelve
    Kicks)
Twister Kicker – 1974
Two Assassins of Darkness – 1977
Two Assassins of the Darkness – (see Two Assas-
    sins of Darkness)
Two Cavaliers – 1973
Two Dragons Fight Against Tiger – 1974
Two Graves to Kung Fu – (see Inheritor of Kung Fu)
Two Great Cavaliers – 1978
Two Great Cavaliers, The – (see Two Great Cava-
    liers)
Two in Black Belt – 1978
Two Kids with Gut – (see Bravest One)
Two Tigers, The – 1973
Two Tricky Kids – (see Ruthless Revenge)
Two Wonderous Tigers – (see Two Wondrous Tigers)
Two Wondrous Tigers – 1979
Tycoon, The – (see Big Boss of Shanghai)

Unbeatable Dragon – (see Invincible Shaolin)
Unconquered – 1970
Unconqueror Man, The – (see Man on Police
    Gazette)
Undeated Sword – 1970
Underworld – (see Black Guide)
Unforgettable Heroine – 1975
Unicorn Fist, The – (see Fist of Unicorn)
Unicorn Palm – (see Fist of Unicorn)
Unique Lama – 1978
Unparalleled Judo Knife – 1971
Unsubdued Furies –1973
Unsung Heroes of the Wilderness – 1971

Valiant Ones, The – 1975
Valley of the Double Dragon – 1974
Valley of the Fangs – 1970
Vengeance! – 1970
Vengeful Beauty, The – 1977
Vengeance of a Snow Girl – 1970
Vengeance of a Snow Maid – 1970
Vengeance of a Snowgirl – (see Vengeance of a
    Snow Girl)
Vengeful Beauty, The – 1977
Venom Warriors – (The Daredevils)
Venturer, The – 1976
Verdict, The – (see The Criminal)
Vietnam Rose – (see Kiss of Death)
Vigilantes, The – (see The Rangers)
Villains, The – 1973
Village of Tigers – 1973
Village of the Tigers – 1974
Village on Fire – (see The Awaken Punch)
Virgins of the Seven Seas – 1974 (WG)
Virgins of the 7 Seas – (see Virgins of the Seven
    Seas)
Voyage of Emperor Chien Lung, The – 1978

Wander Man, The – (see Kung Fu 10th Dan)
Wanderer with Nimble Knife – 1979
Wanderers Fast Blade – (Wanderer with Nimble
    Knife)
Wanderer's Fast Blade – (Wanderer with Nimble
    Knife)
Wandering Dragon – 1978
Wandering Swordsman, The – 1970

Wang Yu, King of Boxers – (see Screaming Tiger)
Wang Yu The Destroyer – (see The Hero)
Wang Yu's 7 Magnificent Fights – (see Seaman
    No. 7)
Warrior of Steel – (see Man of Iron)
War of the Boundary – 1979
War of the Zodiacs – (see The Zodiac Fighters)
Warriors, The – (see Warriors Two)
Warriors of the Sacred Temple – (see Ten Brothers
    of Shaolin)
Warriors Two – 1978
Water Clan Master – (see Legend of All Men are
    Brothers)
Water Margin, The – 1972
Water Margin 2 – (see All Men Are Brothers)
Waterside Story – (see The Water Margin)
Way of the Black Dragon – 1978
Way of the Dragon – 1972
Way of the Tiger, The – 1973
Ways of Kung Fu, The – 1978
Ways of Kung Fu – (see Bruce Lee's Ways of
    Kung Fu)
Web Of Death, The – 1976
Well Of Doom, The – 1974
When the Lion Roars – (see The Lion's Heart)
When Tae Kwon Do Strikes – (see When Taekwondo
    Strikes)
When Tae Kwon Do Strikes – (see When Taekwondo
    Strikes)
When Taekwondo Strikes – 1973
When Tough Guys Meet – (see The Big Risk)
Whiplash – 1974
Whirlwind Kicks, The – (see My Kung Fu Twelve
    Kicks)
White Butterfly Killer, The – 1976
White Lotus – (see Intruder at White Temple)
White Ninja – (see Militant Eagle)
Widow Takes Revenge, The – 1971
Wild Bunch of Kung Fu – 1979
Wild Dragon Lady – 1976
Wild Tiger – 1973
Wily Match, The – (see Four Hands of Death)
Wing Chun Big Brother – (see Bruce Lee's Deadly
    Kung Fu)
Winged Tiger, The – 1970
Win Them All – 1973
Winner, The – 1979
Winner Takes them All, The – 1975
Wits to Wits – 1974
Wolf Boxer – (see Ninja Wolves)
Wolf Fang Creek – (see The Venturer)
Wolf Girl – 1974
Woman Avenger, The – 1979
Woman of the Hour – 1977
Women Soldiers – (see Chinese Amazons)
Wondering Knight, The – (see The Killer)
Wooden Man – (see Shaolin Wooden Men)
World Champion – (Hero Tattooed with Nine Dragons)
World of Drunken Master – 1979
World of the Drunken Master – (see Drunken Arts
    and Crippled Fists)
World of the Drunken Master, The – (see World of
    Drunken Master)
World War of Kung Fu – (see The Big Fight)
Wrath of the Sword – 1970
Writing Kung Fu – 1979

Wu Tang Ho's, Thugs & Scrilllah – (see The Damned)
Wu-Tang Magic Kick – (see Mar's Villa)
Wu Tang Matrix – (see Men of the Hour)
Wu-Tang Msytagogue – (see Shaolin Kung Fu Mystagogue)

Yellow Faced-Tiger – 1974 (USA)
Yellow Killer – 1972
Yoga and Kung-Fu girl – 1979
You are Wonderful – 1976
Young Avenger, The – 1972
Young Bruce Lee – (see Legend of Bruce Lee)
Young Bruce Lee – (see The Real Bruce Lee)
Young Dragons, The – 1975
Young Hero of Shaolin, The – 1975
Young Hero of Shaolin II – (see Chinese Iron Man)
Young Flying Hero – 1970
Young Illusionist – 1979
Young Lovers – 1979
Young Lovers On Flying Wheels – 1974
Young Master, The – 1979
Young People – 1972
Young Rebel, The – 1973
Young Tiger, The – (see Police Woman)
Young Tiger, The – 1973
Young Tiger's Revenge – (see Shaolin Wooden Men)

Zatoichi and the One-Armed Swordsman – 1971 (JA)
Zatoichi: Attack! Chinese Sword – (see Zatoichi and the One-Armed Swordsman)
Zatoichi the Blind Swordsman – (see Golden Sword and the Blind Swordswoman)
Zatoichi the Blind Swordswoman – (see Golden Sword and the Blind Swordswoman)
Zatoichi Meets His Equal – (see Zatoichi and the One-Armed Swordsman)
Zatoichi Meets his Match – (see Zatoichi and the One-Armed Swordsman)
Zatoichi Meets the One-Armed Swordsman – (see Zatoichi and the One-Armed Swordsman)
Zatôichi 22 – (see Zatoichi and the One-Armed Swordsman)
Zatoichi Vs. the One-Armed Swordsman – (see Zatoichi and the One-Armed swordsman)
Zatoichi Vs. White Wolf – (see Blind Hero Fighting Evil Wolf)
Zen Kwan Do Strikes in Paris – (see Zen Kwun Do Strikes in Paris)
Zenkwando Strikes in Paris – (see Zen Kwun Do Strikes in Paris)
Zen Kwun Do Strikes in Paris – 1979
Zodiac Fighters, The – 1978

JAPAN

Adventures of Kosuke Kindaichi, The – 1979 (Kindaichi KosukeNo Boken)
Aftermath of Battles Without Honor & Humanity –1979 (Sono Go No Jingi Naki Tatakai)
Akumyo: Notorious Dragon – 1974 (Akumyo: Shima Arashi)
Alleycat Rock: Crazy Riders 71 – (see Stray Cat Rock: Wild Measures 71)
Alleycat Rock: Machine Animal – (see Stray Cat Rock: Machine Animals)

Alleycat Rock: Sex Hunter – (see Stray Cat Rock: Sex Hunter)
Alleycat Rock: Wild Jumbo – (see Stray Cat Rock: Wild Jumbo)
Alleycat Rock: Female Boss – (see Stray Cat Rock: Female Boss)
Ambitious, The – 1970 (Bakumatsu)
Ambush, The – (see Incident at Blood Pass)
Ambush at Blood Island – (see Incident at Blood Pass)
Ambush at Blood Pass – (see Incident at Blood Pass)
Ambush, The: Incident at Blood Pass – (see Incident at Blood Pass)
Assassin, The – 1970 (Yakuza Deka: Marifana Mitsubai Soshiki)
Assassination of Ryoma, The – 1974 (Ryoma Ansatsu)
Assassins of Honor – (see Band of Samurai)
Assassins Quarry – (see Professional Killers: Baian is Quicksand)
At the Risk of my Life – (see Inn of Evil)
Attacks! The Street Fighter's Last Revenge – (see The Streetfighter's Last Revenge)

Baby Cart at the River Styx – (see Lone Wolf and Cub 5)
Baby Cart in Hades – (see Lone Wolf and Cub 3)
Baby Cart in Peril – (see Long Wolf and Cub 4)
Baby Cart in the Land of Demons – (see Lone Wolf and Cub 5)
Babycart 1 – (see Lone Wolf and Cub 1)
Babycart 2 – (see Lone Wolf and Cub 2)
Babycart 3 – (see Lone Wolf and Cub 3)
Babycart 4 – (see Long Wolf and Cub 4)
Babycart 5 – (see Lone Wolf and Cub 5)
Babycart 6 – (see Lone Wolf and Cub 6)
Baby Cart 6: Go to Hell, Daigoro! – (see Lone Wolf and Cub 6)
Bad Name's Breaking of Territories – (see Akumyo: Notorious Dragon)
Bad Reputation: Invading the Turf – (see Akumyo: Notorious Dragon)
Bakuhatsu! Boso Zoku – 1975 – (Chiba Baku-hatsu! Boso Zoku)
Bakuto Kirikomi-Tai – 1971
Bandit Vs. Samurai Squad – 1978 (Kumokiri Nizaemon)
Bandits Vs. Samurai Squadron – (see Bandit Vs. Samurai Squad)
Band of Assassins – (see Band of Samurai)
Band of Ninja, A – (see Iron Castle)
Band of Samurai – 1970 (Shinsengumi)
Battle Cry – 1975 (Tokkan)
Battles Without Honor and Humanity: Deadly fight in Hiroshima – 1973 (Jingi Naki Tatakai: Hiroshima Shito Hen)
Battles Without Honor and Humanity: Death Match in Hiroshima – (see Battles Without Honor and Humanity Deadly fight in Hiroshima)
Battles Without Honor and Humanity 2: Deadly fight in Hiroshima – (Battles Without Honor and Humanity: Deadly fight in Hiroshima)
Beast Must Die, The: Mechanic of Revenge – (see The Beast Shall Die)
Beast Shall Die, The – 1974 (Yajû Shisubeshi: Fukushû No Mekanikku)

Beat '71 – (see Stray Cat Rock: Wild Measures 71)
Big Boss in a Silk Hat – 1970 (Shiruku Hatto No O-Oyabun)
Big Boss in a Silk Hat: The Short-Mustached Bear – 1970 (Shiruku Hatto No O-Oyabun: Chobi-HigeNno Kuma)
Black Cat's Revenge – (see The Blind Woman's Curse)
Blind Karate Man, The – (see Za Karate)
Blind Swordsman's Conspiracy, The – (see Zatoichi at the Blood Festival)
Blind Swordsman's Fire Festival – (see Zatoichi at the Fire Festival)
Blind Woman's Curse, The – 1970 (Kaidan Nobori Rryu)
Blind Yakuza Monk – 1970 (Hitokiri Kannon-Uta)
Blizzard from the Netherworld – (see Lady Snow-blood)
Blood Snow, Lady Snow Blood – (see Lady Snow-blood)
Blood Vendetta – 1971 (Gyaken Nitsu Sakazuki)
Bloodshed – (see Demons)
Bloody Priest, The – (see Wicked Priest: Wine, Women & Swords)
Bodyguard, The – (see Karate Kiba)
Bodyguard Kiba – 1973 (Bodigaado Kiba: His-satsu SankakuTobi)
Bohachi, Clan of the Forgotten Eight – 1973 (Bohachi Bushido)
Boryokudan sai buso – 1971
Boryoku gai – 1974
Boryoku senshi – 1979
Bôsô panikku: Daigekitotsu – 1976
Boss with the Samurai Spirit – 1971 (Kapone No Shatei Yamato Damashi)
Bounty Hunter - Volume 4 – 1975 (Shokin Kasegi)
Brave Red Flower of the North – (see Bright Red Flower of Courage)
Bright Red Flower of Courage – 1970 (Nihon Jokyou-den, Makkana Dokyoban)
Bronson Lee, Champion – 1978 (Za Karate 3: Denko Sekka)
Brutal Tales of Chivalry 7 – 1970 (Showa Zankyo-den: Shinde Morai Masu)
Brutal Tales of Chivalry 8 – 1971 (Showa Zankyo-den: Hoero Karajishi)
Buraikan, The – (see The Scandalous Adventures of Buraikan)

Champion of Death – 1975 (Kenka Karate Kyokushinken)
Cherry Blossom Fire Gang – (see Red Cherry Blos-som Family of Kanto)
Chimimoryo: A Soul of Demons – 1972 (Yami No Naka No Chimimoryo)
Chivalrous Woman – 1971 (OnnaTtoseinin)
Chi-Zome No Daimon – 1970
Clash! Killer Fist – (see The Streetfighter)
Code of the Forgotten Eight – (see Bohachi, Clan of the Forgotten Eight)
Conspiracy of the Yagyu Family – (see Intrigue of the Yagyu Clan)
Crazy Raid on Shimuzu Port – 1970 (Kureji No Nagurikomi Shimizu Minato)
Crimson Bat: Oichi: Wanted, Dead or Alive – (Crim-son Bat: Wanted Dead or Alive)

Crimson Bat: Wanted Dead or Alive – 1970
Crossroads to Hell (literal English title) – (see Lone Wolf and Cub 5)

Daidatsugoku – 1975
Dasso Yugi – 1976
Dawn of Judo – (see Sanshiro Sugata)
Day of the Apocolypse – (see G.I. Samurai)
Deadly Fight in Hiroshima – (see Battles Without Honor & Humanity: Deadly fight in Hiroshima)
Death Match – (see Swords of Death)
Death of the Shogun – (see The Shogun Assassins)
Defensive Power of Aikido, The – 1975 (Geki-tosu! Aikido)
Delinquent Girl Boss: Blossoming Night Dreams – 1970 (Zubeko Bancho: Yume Wa Yoru)
Delinquent Girl Boss: Unworthy of Penance – (see Delinquent Girl Boss: Worthless to Confess)
Delinquent Girl Boss: Worthless to Confess – 1971 (Zubeko Bancho: Zange No Neuchi Mo)
Demon Pond – 1979 (Yasha Ga Ike)
Demon Spies – 1974 (Oniwaban)
Demons – 1971 (Shura)
Detective Doberman – 1977 (Doberman Deka)
Devil's Island, The – (see Hell's Gate Island)
Doberman Cop, The – (see Detective Doberman)
Dragon Princess – 1976 (Hissatsu onna kenshi)
Dragon Princess – (see Demon Pond)
Drenched Swallow – 1978
Drifting Gamber, The – 1970 (Bakuchi-uchi: Nagaremono)
Duel at Ezo – (see Duel at Fort Ezo)
Duel At Fort Ezo – 1970 (Ezo-yakata No Ketto)
Duel in the Wind – 1971 (Kaze No Tengu)
Duel of Swirling Flowers – 1971 (Nihon jokyo-den: ketto midare-bana)

Echo of Destiny – (see Shadow Hunters 2)
Edo Secret Police, The – 1979 (Omitsu Doshin: Edo Sosamo)
Elder Sister: Ochô Inoshika – (see Sex and Fury)
End of the Samurai – (see The Ambitious)
Errance – 1973 (Matatabi)
Evil Woman's Diary – 1970 (Onna Gokuakucho)
Evil Yakuza Vs. Mamushi Brothers – (see Gokudo Vs. Mamushi)
Executioner, (The) – 1974 (Chokugeki! Jigo-ken)
Executioner 2, (The) – (see Karate Inferno)
Executioner II, The – (see Karate Inferno)
Executioner II, The: Karate Inferno – (see Karate Inferno)

Fall of Ako Castle, The – 1978 (Ako-Jo Danzetsu)
Fearless Avenger – (see Trail of Blood: Fearless Avenger)
Female Fighting Fist in Danger – (see Sister Street Fighter)
Female Ninja Magic – 1974 (Kunoichi Ninpo: Hyakka Manji-Garami)
Female Ninja Magic: 100 Trampled Flowers – (see Female Ninja Magic)
Female Ninjas: In Bed with the enemy – 1976 (Kunoichi Ninpo: Kannon Biraki)
Female Yakuza Tale – (see Female Yakuza Tale: Inquistion and Torture)

Female Yakuza Tale: Inquisition and Torture – 1973 (Yasagure Anego Den Sokatsu Rinchi)
Festival in Kasama – (see Zatoichi at the Blood Festival)
Fifth Level Fist – (see Sister Streetfighter 4)
Fighter's Last Revenge – (see The Streetfighter's Last Revenge)
Firebird, The – (see The Phoenix)
Firebird: Daybreak Chapter – (see The Phoenix)
Fire's Bird – (see The Phoenix)
First Generation: Top Fighters – 1970 (Kenka Ichidai: Dodekai Yatsu)
5 Kamen Riders Vs. King Dark – (see Kamen Rider X: The Five Riders Vs. King Dark)
Five Wolves – (see The Last Swordsman)
Flower of the Winter – 1978 (Fuyu No Hana)
Flying At 'Ya Android Kikaider – 1973 (Tobidasu Jinzo Ningen Kikaida)
Flying from the Movie Screen: Inazuman – 1974
Flying on the Wind of Death – (see Lone Wolf and Cub 3)
Fort Ezo – (see Duel at Fort Ezo)
47 Blades Of Vengeance – (see The Fall of Ako Castle)
Furyo Bancho Boso Bagi-Dan – 1970
Furyo Bancho Detatoko Shoubu – 1970
Furyo Bancho Ichimou Dajin – 1972
Furyo Bancho Ikkaku Senkin – 1970
Furyo Bancho Kuchi Kara Demakase – 1970
Furyo Bancho Yarazu Buttakuri – 1971

Gakusei Yakuza – 1974
Gambler Family – 1970 (Bakuto-ikka)
Gambler: Foreign Opposition – (see Sympathy for the Underdog)
Gambler: Mercernary Army – (see Sympathy for the Underdog)
Gambler With a Bad Reputation – 1970 (Fudat-suki Bakuto)
Gamblers in Okinawa – (see Sympathy for the Underdog)
Gambler's Sudden Attack – 1971 (Bakuto Kirikomi-tai)
Gangster Cop – (see Yakuza Deka)
Gang Vs. Gang: The Red and Black Blues – 1973
Gendai ninkyô-shi – 1973
Gendai yakuza: sakazuki kaeshimasu – 1971
Girl Boss Blues: Queen Bee's Challenge – 1973 (Sukeban Burusu - Mesubachi No Chosen)
Girl Boss Blues: Queen Bee's Counterattack – 1971 (Sukeban Burûsu: Mesubachi No Gyakushû)
Girl Boss: Escape from Refrom School – 1973 (Sukeban: Kankain Dasso)
G.I. Samurai – 1979 (Sengoku Jieta)
G-Men – 1973 (Yakuza Tai G-Men)
Godfather: Ambition – (see Godfather of Japan)
Godfather, The: Ambition – (see Godfather of Japan)
Godfather, The: Resolution – (see Godfather of Japan: Final Chapter)
Godfather of Japan – 1977 (Nippon No Do Yabohen Japanese)
Godfather of Japan: Final Chapter – 1978 (Nihon No Don: Kanketsu Hen)
Go for Broke – (see Battle Cry)

Go! Go! Kamen Rider – 1970
Gokudo Comes Back – 1970 (Gokudo Kamagasaki Ni Kaeru)
Gokudo Comes back to Kamagasaki – (see Goduko Comes Back)
Gokudo Criminal – 1970 (Gokudo Kyojo Tabi)
Gokudo Criminal Record Plight – (see Gokudo Criminal)
Gokudo of Kamagasaki – 1973 (Kamagasaki Gokudo)
Gokudo Vs. Delinquent Boss – 1974 (Gokudo Vs. Furyo Bancho)
Gokudo Vs. Mamushi – 1974 (Gokudo Vs. Mamushi)
Gokudo's Notorious Reputation – 1972 (Gokudo Makari Touru)
Golgo 13 – (see Golgo 13: Kowloon Assignment)
Golgo 13: Kowloon Assignment – 1977 (Golgo 13: Kuron No Kubi)
Goranger: Fire Mountains Last Explosion – 1975
Goranger: The Blue Fortress – 1975 (Himitsu Sentai Gorenjā: Aoi Daiyōsa)
Goranger The Bomb Hurricane – 1976
Goranger The Movie – 1975 (Himitsu Sentai Goranger)
Goranger: The Red Death Match – 1976 (Himitsu Sentai Gorenjā: Makka Na Mosingeki!)
Guillotine Island – (see Hell's Gate Island)

Hakuchyu No Shikaku – 1979
Hanuman and the 6 Ultramen – (see The 6 Ultra Brothers Vs. the Monster Army)
Hanuman Pob Jed Yodmanud – (see The 6 Ultra Brothers Vs. the Monster Army)
Hanzo the Razor: Sword of Justice – 1972 (Goyokiba)
Hanzo the Razor: The Snare – 1973 (Goyokiba kamisori Hanzo Jigoku Zeme)
Hanzo the Razor: Who's Got the Gold? –1974 (Goyokiba Oni No Hanzo: Yawahada Koban)
Haunted Gold – (see Hanzo the Razor: Who's Got the Gold)
Haunted Life of a Dragon-Tattooed Lass, The – (see The Blind Woman's Curse)
Haunted Samurai, The – (see Duel in the Wind)
Heart of a parent, Heart of a child – (see Long Wolf and Cub 4)
Hell is Man's Destiny – (see Brutal Tales of Chivalry 7)
Hellworms – 1979 (Jigoku No Mushi)
Hell's Gate Island – 1977 (Gokumon-To)
Himiko – 1979
Hiroshima Jingi: Hitojichi Dakkai Sakusen – 1976
Hito-kiri Yota: Kyoken San-Kyodai – 1972
Hokuriku Proxy War – 1977 (Hokuriku Dairi Sensou)
Homeless, The – 1974 (Yadonashi)
Homeless Mikogami Jokichi the Sparks Fly at Dusk – (see Slaughter in the Snow)
Honor of Japan – 1977 (Nihon No Jingi)
Hoodlum Soldier – (see Yakuza Soldier: Fuse)
Hunted, The – (see Duel in the Wind)
Hunter in Darkness – 1979 (Yami No Karyudo)
Hunter in the Dark – (see Hunter in Darkness)

New Abashira Prison: A Pledge of Honor Invites the Storm – 1972 (Shin Abashiri Bangaichi: Arashi Yobu Danpu Jingi)

New Battles Without Honor & Humanity 1 – 1974 (Shin Jingi Naki Tatakai)

New Battles Without Honor & Humanity 2: Head of the Bossman – 1975 (Shin Jingi Naki Tatakai: Kumicho No Kubi)

New Battles Without Honor & Humanity 3: Last Days of the Boss – 1976 (Shin Jingi Naki Tatakai: Kumicho Saigo No Hi)

New Female Prisoner: Cell X – 1977 (Shin Joshuu Dasori: Tokushu-Bô X)

New Female Prisoner Scorpion: #701 – 1976 (Shin Joshuu Dasori: 701-Gô)

New Fraternal Honor – 1970 (Shin Kyôdai Jingi)

New Tale of Zatoichi: Blood Festival of Kasama – (see Zatoichi at the Blood Festival)

New Zatoichi Story: Blood Festival in Kasama – (see Zatoichi at the Blood Festival)

New Zatoichi Story: Broken Stick – (see Zatoichi in Desperation)

New Zatoichi Story: Official Trip – (see Zatoichi at Large)

Nora-Neko Rock: Wild Jumbo – (see Stray Cat Rock: Wild Jumbo)

Nihon Boryoku-Dan: Kumicho Kuzure – 1970

Nihon Boryoku-Dan: Koroshi No Sakazuki – 1972

Nippon Dabi Katsukyu – 1970

Ochô – (see Sex and Fury)

Ogin: Her Love and Faith – (see Love and Faith)

Okinawa: The Ten-Year War – 1978 (Okinawa Ju-Nen Senso)

Okinawa Yakuza War – 1976 (Okinawa Yakuza Senso)

Okita Sôji – 1974

Okita Soju – The Last Swordsman – (see Okita Soji)

Okoma: The Orphan Gambler – (see Chivalrous Woman)

One Way Passage to Death – 1970 (Gendai Ninkyo Kyodaibun)

Orphan Gambler 1, The – (see Chivalrous Woman)

Outlaw Killers: Three Mad Dog Brothers – 1972

Outlaws – (see The Scandalous Adventures of Buraikan)

Pandemonium – (see Demons)

Path of a King – 1971 (Nihon Yakuza-Den: Sôchiyô e No Michi)

Phoenix, The – 1978 (Hi No Tori)

Poison Gas Terror – (see Yakuza Deka: Poison Gas Affair)

Police Tactics – (see Battles Without Honor and Humanity 4: Police Tactics)

Power of Aikido, The – (see The Defensive Power of Aikido

Prison Gate Island – (see Hell's Gate Island)

Prison Release Celebration – (see The Wolves)

Professional Killers – 1973 (Hissatsu Shikakenin)

Professional Killers: Baian is Quicksand – 1973 (Hissatsu Shikakenin: Baian Arijigoku)

Professional Killers: Spring Snow Needle Death – 1974 (Hissatsu Shikakenin: Shunsetsu Shikake-Bari)

Proof of a Man – 1977 (Ningen No Shômei)

Proxy War in Hokuriku – (see Hokuriku Proxy War)

Queen Bee Strikes Again – (see Girl Boss Blues: Queen Bee's Counterattack)

Queen Bee's Challenge – (see Girl Boss Blues: Queen Bee's Challenge)

Razor, The: Sword of Justice – (see Hanzo the Razor: Sword of Justice)

Razor 2: The Snare – (see Hanzo the Razor: The Snare)

Razor 3: Who's Got the Gold? – (Hanzo the Razor: Who's Got the Gold)

Red Cherry Blossom Family, The – (see Red Cherry Blossom Family of Kanto)

Red Cherry Blossom Family of Kanto – 1972

Red Peony: Execution of Duty – 1972 (Hibotan Bakuto: Jingi Tooshi Masu)

Red Peony Gambles her Life – (see Red Peony: Here comes Oryu)

Red Peony Gambler 5: Oryu Returns – (see Red Peony: Here Comes Oryu)

Red Peony: Here comes Oryu – 1970 (Hibotan Bakuto: Oryu Sanjo)

Red Peony: Request for your Life – 1971

Red Silk Gambler, The – 1972 (Hijirimen Bakuto)

Return of the Female Killing Fist – (see Sister Streetfighter 2)

Renegade Ninjas – (see The Shogun Assassins)

Restoration of meiji, the – (see The Ambitious)

Resurrection of the Golden Wolf, The – 1979 (Yomigaeru Kinrô)

Return of the Desperado – (see Gokudo Comes Back)

Return of the Lethal Fist Woman – (see Sister Streetfighter 3)

Return of the Sister Street Fighter – (see Sister Streetfighter 3)

Return of the Streetfighter – 1975 (Satsujin Ken 2)

Return to Jelucia – (see Message From Space)

Rica – 1972 (Konketsuji Rika)

Rica 2: Lonely Wanderer – 1973 (Konketsuji Rika: Hitoriyuku Sasuraitabi)

Rica 3: Juvenile Lullabay – 1973 (Konketsuji Rika: Hamagure Komoriuta)

Rika the Mixed-Blood Girl – (see Rica)

Road to Hell – (see Lone Wolf and Cub 5)

Rupangu-To No Ritsugun Nakano Gakko – 1974

Ryotatsu the Whip Master – (see Blind Yakuza Monk)

Saburai – The Way of Bohachi – 1974 (Saburai Bohachi Bushido)

Saigo No Tokkôtai – 1970

Samurai Adviser – 1978 (Tono Eijir No Mito Komon)

Samurai, Part VI – (see Swords of Death)

Sanshiro Sugata – 1970

Scandalous Adventures of Buraikan, The – 1970 (Buraikan)

Secret Detective Investigation: Net in Big Edo – 1979 (Omitsu Ddoshin o Edo Sosamo)

Scorpion: Grudge Song – (see Female Prisoner 701 Scorpion Grudge Song)

Secret Task Force Goranger – (see Goranger the Movie)

Sengoku Rock: Female Warriors – (see Naked Seven)

Seven Naked Samurai – (see Naked Seven)

Sex and Fury – 1973 (Furyô Anego Den: Inoshika Ochô)

Sex & Fury – (see Sex and Fury)

Shadow Hunters – 1972 (Kage Gari)

Shadow Hunters 2 – 1972 (Kage Gari: Hoero Taiyo)

She-Wasp's Challenge – (see Girl Boss Blues: Queen Bee's Challenge)

Shinsen Group, The – (see Shinsengumi)

Shinsengumi – 1970

Shinsengumi: Assassins of Honor – (see Shinsen-gumi)

Shocking! Defiant Fist – (see The Soul of Bruce Lee)

Shogun Assassin 2: Lightening Swords of Death – (see Lone Wolf and Cub 3)

Shogun Assassin 3: Slashing Blades of Carnage – (see Lone Wolf and Cub 4)

Shogun Assassin 4: Baby Cart at the River Styx – (see Lone Wolf and Cub 5)

Shogun Assassin 5: Cold Road to Hell – (see Lone Wolf and Cub 6)

Shogun Assassins, The – 1979 (Sanada Yu-kimura No Bouryaku)

Shogun's Samurai, The – (see Intrigue of the Yagyu Clan)

Showa Zankyo-Den: Hoero Karajishi – 1971

Showa Zankyo-Den: Yabure-Gasa – 1972

Shogun Samurai – (see Intrique of the Yagyu Clan)

Shogun's Samurai – (see Intrique of the Yagyu Clan)

Side with Duty – (see Red Peony: Execution of Duty)

Silence – 1971 (Chinmoku)

Sister Street Fighter – 1974 (Onna Hissatsu Ken; Onna Hissatsu Kenshi)

Sister Street Fighter 2 – (Sister Streetfighter 2)

Sister Street Fighter 3 – (Sister Streetfighter 3)

Sister Street Fighter 4 – (see Sister Streetfighter 4)

Sister Street Fighter: Fifth Level Fist – (see Sister Streetfighter 4)

Sister Streetfighter: Hanging by a Thread – (see Sister Streetfighter 2)

Sister Streetfighter 2 – 1974 (Onna Hissatsu Ken: Kik Ippatsu)

Sister Streetfighter 3 – 1975 (Kaette Kita Onna Hissatsu Ken)

Sister Streetfighter 4 – 1976 (Onna Hissatsu Godan Ken)

6 Ultra Brothers Vs. the Monster Army, The – 1974

Slaughter in the Snow – 1973 (Mushukunin Mikogami No Jokichi: Tasogare Ni Senko Ga Tonda)

Sniper 13 – (see Golgi 13: Kowloon Assignment)

Snow of Blood – (see Lady Snowblood)

Soft-Boiled Goro – (see Useless Creature Fighting Man's Life)

Sonny Chiba's Dragon Princess – (see Dragon Princess)

Soul of Chiba – 1974 (Gekisatsu! Judo Ken) (TH/HK)

Soul to Devils, A – (see Chimimoryo: A Soul of Demons)

Star Rangers – (see Goranger the Movie)

Zatoichi Meets Yojimbo – 1971 (Zatoichi Vs. Yojimbo)

Zatôichi 20 – (see Zatoichi Meets Yojimbo)

Zatôichi 21 – (see Zatoichi at the Fire Festival)

Zatôichi 22 – (see Zatoichi Meets the One-Armed Swordsman)

Zatôichi 23 – (see Zatoichi at Large)

Zatôichi 24 – (see Zatoichi in Desperation)

Zatôichi 25 – (see Zatoichi at the Blood Festival)

Zatoichi: The Festival of Fire – (see Zatoichi at the Fire Festival)

Zatoichi Vs. Yojimbo – (see Zatoichi Meets Yojimbo)

Zatoichi's Conspiracy – (see Zatoichi at the Blood Festival)

Zatoichi's Fire Festival – (see Zatoichi at the Fire Festival)

Zero Woman: Red Handcuffs – 1974 (Zeroka no onna: Akai wappa)

SOUTH KOREA

Action Episodes – 1971 (Hwalgeugdaesa)

Angry Dragon – (see Dragon Lee Vs. 5 Brothers)

America bangmunggaeg – (see Visitors in America)

At The Risk Of Life – 1975 (Sasaenggyeoldan)

Badge of a Man, A – 1973 (Sana-i Hunjang)

Best Disciple, The – 1976 (Sujeja)

Best of the Best, The – 1970 – (see Two Sword Masters)

Best Player of High School, The – 1978 (Gogyo Godanja)

Betrayer, A – 1974 (Baesinja)

Big Boss 2 – (see Lone Shaolin Avenger)

Big Brother of Dangsan – 1977 (Dangsandae-hyeong)

Big Opponent, The – 1977 (Daejeogsu)

Billy Jang – 1974 (Billijyang)

Black Dragon – 1975 (Heuglyong)

Black Dragon Fever – (see Kung Fu Fever)

Black Dragon River – 1976 (Heuglyonggang)

Black Hawk – 1972 (Heugmae)

Black Knight, The – 1974 (Heugmusa)

Black Leopard – 1974 (Heugpyo)

Black Mark of Shaolin – (see Heuk-Pyo of Shaolin Temple)

Black Spider – 1975 (Heuggeomi)

Black Sword – (see The Treasure Regained)

Black Swordman – 1972 (Heuggaeg)

Blind Swordman – 1974 (Jug-Janggeom)

Blind Swordsman, The – 1971 (Maeng-in Daehyeobgaeg)

Blood of the Leopard – 1972

Blood Relations – 1976 (Pisjul)

Blood Treasury Fight – 1979

Bloody Fist – 1973 (Hyeolgwon)

Bonecrushers – (see The Manchu Boxer)

Brand – 1974 (Nag-in)

Bridge of Death – 1974

Bruce Against the Odds – (see Lone Shaolin Avenger)

Bruce Lee Fights Back from the Grave – (see Visitors in America)

Bruce Lee's Ways of Kung Fu – 1979 (Mulim 18 Yeogeol) (HK)

Burning Jungmu Martial Arts Hall, The – 1977 (Bulta-Neun Jeongmumun)

Burning Shaolin Temple, The – (see Shaolin Temple on Fire

Burning Solim Temple – (see Shaolin Temple on Fire)

Camellia Man, The – 1979 (Dongbaegkkoch Sinsa)

Chaser, The – 1979 (Chugyeogja)

Chase Without Tomorrow – 1976 (Naeileobsneun Chugyeog)

Close Kung Fu Encounters – (see Great Escape)

Code Named Tokyo Expo 1970 – (see Operation Tokyo Expo '70)

Code-Named Tokyo Expo – (see Operation Tokyo Expo '70)

Combat of Three Kingdoms – 1972 (Samgug-daehyeob)

Cross Hands Martial Arts – 1978 (Sibjasugwon)

Dalmasingong – (see Grandmaster of Shaolin)

Dangerous Hero, A – 1974 (Wiheomhan Yeon-gung)

Dangsan Martial Arts – 1979 (Dangsanbigwon)

Dark Glasses – 1971 (Gemeun Angyeong)

Dark Night in Tokyo – 1970 (Donggyeong Mujeongga)

Dark Swordsman – (see The Devil's Treasure)

Deadly Angels – 1977 (Yeoshintam) (HK)

Deadly Kick, The – 1976 (Gugje Gyeonchal)

Deadly Kick, The – (see Deadly Roulette)

Deadly Roulette – 1976 (Gugje Gyeonchal)

Death Fist of Shaolin – (see Four Clans of Death)

Den of Bandits – (see Wonderman from Shaolin)

Devil's Assignment, The – 1973

Disarmament – 1975 (Mujanghaeje)

Divine Martial Arts of Dharma, The – (see Grand-master of Shaolin)

Don't Look Back – 1979 (Dwidol-a Boji Mala)

Double Cross – (see The Double Crossers)

Double Crossers – 1976

Double-Edged Sword – 1970 (Ssanggeom)

Dragon Against the Odds (see Lone Shaolin Avenger)

Dragon Bruce Lee – (see The Last of Jung-mu Martial Arts Hall)

Dragon Force – (see Horim Temple Daetong-Gwan)

Dragon from Shaolin – (see Four Clans of Death)

Dragon King – (see Wang Yong)

Dragon King 2 – (see Wang-ryong)

Dragon Lee Does Dallas – (see The Last of Jung-mu Martial Arts Hall)

Dragon Lee Vs. the 5 Brothers – 1978 (Odaejeja)

Dragon Lee Vs. the Five Brothers – (see Dragon Lee Vs. the 5 Brothers)

Dragon Magic Sword, The – 1970 (Doglyong-mageom)

Dragon's Snake Fist, The – 1979

Dragoneer 4—The Dynamite – (see Dynamite Shaolin Heroes)

Duel at the So-Rim Temple, A – 1975 (Solimsa-ui Gyeoltu)

Duel in Nang San – 1972 (Nangsan-ui Gyeoltu)

Duel in Tae Bak Mountain – 1973 (Taebaeksanui Gyeoltu)

Duel of the Tough – (see Mu-rim Battle)

Dynamit Shaolin Heroer, The – (see Dynamite Shaolin Heroes)

Dynamite Shaolin Heroes – 1978 (Solimsa Mokryeondosa)

8 Grandmasters – (see The Eighth Head)

18 Amazons, The – (see Bruce Lee's Ways of Kung Fu)

Eighteen Women Fighters of Murim – (see Bruce Lee's Ways of Kung Fu)

Eighth Head, The – 1973 (Paldaejangmum)

8th Head, The – (see The Eigth Head)

8th Leader – (see The Eighth Head)

Enforcer, The – 1971 – Cheolsumujeong

Enlightened Buddhist Named Mok-ryeon – (see Dynamite Shaolin Heroes)

Enter the Invincible Hero – 1977 (Heugpobigaeg)

Escape – 1970 (Samsib-yuggye Julhaenglang)

Eumyangdo – 1971

Ferocious Dragon Rage – 1977 (Maenglyong-noho)

Fierce Dragon – 1979 (Maenglyong-aho)

Fierce Animal, A – 1969 (Maengsu) (see Sword of the Master)

Fight Between Flying Tigers, A – 1978 (Biho-sangjaeng)

Fighter with Miraculous Martial Arts – 1978 (Singwonbigaeg)

Fights Against Keum-Kang – 1971(Yonghotu-geumgang)

Final Facedown in Cheonma Mountain – 1971 (Cheonmasan-ui Gyeoltu)

Fist of Hercules – (see Jum-mu Fighting Skills)

Five Barriers, The – (see Rivals of the Silver Fox)

Five Brothers, The – (see Dragon Lee Vs. the 5 Brothers)

5 Brothers, The – (see Dragon Lee Vs. the 5 Brothers)

Five Commandments – 1976 (Ogye)

Five Daggers – 1971 (Daseosgae-ui Dangeom)

Five Disciples, The – (see Dragon Lee Vs. the 5 Brothers)

Five Fighters – 1971 (5 In-ui Geondaldeul)

Five Murim Swordsmen – 1979 (Mulim-ogeol)

Five Young Fighters – (see Five Fighters)

Flying Dragon in the Dark Night – 1971 (Heukya Biryongdo)

Flying Dragon's Gate – 1977 (Bilyongmun)

Flying Il Ji-mae, The – 1978 (Nal-euneun Iljimae)

Four Brave Dragons – (see Lone Shaolin Avenger)

4 Brave Dragons – (see Lone Shaolin Avenger)

Four Clans of Death – 1978 (Sadaetong-uimun)

Four Fierce Dragons – (see Lone Shaolin Avenger)

4 Fierce Dragons – (see Lone Shaolin Avenger)

Four Infernos to Cross – (see Horim Temple Daetong-Gwan)

4 Infernos to Cross – (see Horim Temple Daetong-Gwan)

Four Iron Men – 1977 (Sadaecheol-in)

4 Iron Men – (see Four Iron Men)

Four Masters – 1977 (4 In-ui Sillyeogja)

44th Street, New York – 1976 (Nyu Yog 44 Beonga)

Freedom Fighter: Koo Byeon-Shin – (see Righteous Fighter, Koo Byeon-shin)

From Bangkok with Orders to Kill – (see The Yellow Killer)

Gate of Life or Death – 1977 (Sasaengmun)

General in Red – 1973 (Hong-uijanggun)

Golden Belt, The – (see The Best Disciple)

Chain, The – (see Zanjeer)
Chakravyuha – 1978
Chalte Chalte – 1976
Charas – 1976
Chor Machaye Shor – 1974

Dark Horse – 1973 (Chupa Rustam)
Dharam Karam – 1975
Dharam Veer – 1977
Dharmatma – 1975
Dil Kaa Heera – 1979
Dillagi – 1978
Do Chor – 1972
Do Jasoos – 1975
Do Shikaari – 1979
Don – 1978
Dus Numbri – 1976

Embers – (see Sholay)

Flames – (see Sholay)
Flames of the Sun – (see Sholay)
Food, Clothing, and Shelter – 1974 (Roti Kapada Aur Makaan)
Free – (see Azaad)
5 Rifles – 1974

Ganga Ki Saugand – 1978
Girl Without a Name – (see Anamika)
Gol Maal – 1979

Hamare Tumhare – 1979
Hanky Panky – (see Gol Maal)
Haseenon Ka Devata – 1971
Haathi Mere Saathi – 1971
Hatyara – 1977
Hear Pheri – 1976
Heart and the Wall, The – 1978 (Dil Aur Deewaar)
Heera – 1973
Himalay Se Ooncha – 1975
Himmat – 1970
Hot Spices – 1972 (Garam Masala)
Hum Kisise Kum Naheen – 1977
Hum Tere Ashiq Hain – 1979
Humjoli – 1970

Independent – (see Azaad)
Inkaar – 1977

Jangal Mein Mangal – 1972
Jawab – 1970
Jay-Vejay: Part II – 1977
Johny Mera Naam – 1970
Jurmana – 1979
Jwar Bhata – 1973

Kaala Aadmi – 1978
Kaala Sona – 1975
Kala Dhandha – (see Black Mail)
Kahani Kismat Ki – 1973
Karmayogi – 1978
Kasam Khoon Ki – 1977
Kasauti – 1974
Keemat – 1973
Khel Khel Mein – 1975

Laala Aadmi – 1978
Laila Majnu – 1976

Labyrinth, The – (see Chakravyuha)
Loafer – 1973
Love Sublime – 1978 (Satyam Shivam Sundaram)

Maa Aur Mamta – 1970
Maha Chor – 1976
Manchali – 1973
Maryada – 1971
Man Ki Aankhen – 1970
Mastana – 1970
Master of Kadawung, The – 1971 (Tuan Tanah Kedawung)
Mera Gaon Mera Desh – 1971
Mera Rakshak – 1978
Mischief – (see Dillagi)
Mother – 1976 (Maa)
Mr. Natwarlal – 1978
Muqabla – 1979
My Village, My Country – (see Mera Gaon Mera Desh)

New Day, New Night – 1974 (Naya Din Nai Raat)

Parvarish – 1977
Phandebaaz – 1978
Phir Kab Milogi – 1974
Pran Jave Par Vachan Na Jaye – 1974
Pratiggya – 1975
Preetam – 1971
Purab Aur Pachhim – 1970

Rakhwala – 1971
Raja Rani – 1973
Reshma Aur (and) Shera – 1972
Roop Tera Mastana – 1972
Roti – 1974

Sabse Bada Rupaiya – 1976
Sachaa Jhutha – 1970
Samadhi – 1972
Sarkari Mehmaan – 1979
Sawan Bhadon – 1970
Sazaa – 1972
Shaque – 1976
Sharafat – 1970
Sholay – 1975
Shor – 1972
Sign of Marriage – (see Suhaag)
Suhaag – 1979
Suhana Safar – 1970
Surakshaa – 1979
Sworn Promises, The – 1978 (Kasme Vaade)

Thief of Baghdad – 1977
Train, The – 1970
Trimurti – 1974
Truth and Falsehood – (see Sachaa Jhutah)
Tum Haseen Main Jawan – 1970
Two Shades of Blood – 1979 (Lahu Ke Do Rang)

Warrant – 1975
Wife's Servant – 1972 (Joroo Ka Ghulam)

Yaadgaar – 1970

Zakkhmee – 1975
Zanjeer – 1973

INDONESIA

Balada dua jagoan – 1979
Beranak Dalam Kubur – 1972
Birth in the Tomb – 1972 (Beranak Dalam Kubur)
Black Belt Karate – 1977 (Karate Sabuk Hitam) (HK)
Black Magic Terror – (see Black Magic 3)
Black Magic 3 – 1979
Bloody Vengeance – 1977
Bruce Li – The Invincible – 1978 (HK)

Dance of Death – 1976
Duel in Taekwando – 1977

Ghostly Face – 1972

Karate-A-Bali – (see Ghostly Face)
Kera sakti – 1977
Kung Fu Karateka – 1978

Pembalasan si pitung – 1972
Pembalasan Siptung Jiih – 1977

Queen of Black – (see Black Magic 3)

Special Silencers – 1979

ITALY

Dragon Strikes Back, The – (see Shanghai Joe)

Fighting Fists of Shanghai Joe, The – (see Shanghai Joe)

Hercules Against Karate – (see Schiaffoni e karate)
Hercules Vs. King Fu – (see Schiaffoni e karate)

Karamurat, la Belva Dell'Anatolia – 1976 (TU)
Karamurat – (see Magic Man)

Il Mio Nome è Shanghai Joe – (see Shanghai Joe)
Il Ritorno Di Shanghai Joe – (see Return of Shanghai Joe)

Magic Man, The – 1976 (TU)
Mr. Hercules Against Karate – (see Schiaffoni e karate)
My Name is Shanghai Joe – (see Shanghai Joe)

Questa Volta Ti Faccio Ricco! – 1974

Samurai – 1975 (Il Bianco, Il giallo, Il nero) (SP/FR)
Schiaffoni e karate – 1973

Red Sun – 1971 (SP/FR)
Return of Shanghai Joe – 1975 (WG)

Shanghai Joe – 1972
Stranger and the Gun Fighter, The – 1974 (Là Dove Non Batte il Sole) (SP/USA/HK)
Supermenler – 1979 (SP/TU)
Superman Against the Amazons – 1975 (ME/HK)
Supermen Against Godfather – (see Supermenler)

Three Superboys Strike Again, The – (see Uc Kagitcilar)

To Kill or To Die – (see Shanghai Joe)
Tre Supermen Contro il Padrino – (see Supermenler)
Tutti Per Uno…Botte Per Tutti – (1973)

Uc Kagitcilar – 1976 (Che Carambole) (TU)

MEXICO

Incredible Professor Zovek, The – 1972
Increíble profesor Zovek, El – (see The Incredible Professor Zovek)

Superman Against the Amazons – 1975 (IT/HK)

PAKISTAN

Final Challenge – 1977 (Aakhri Muqabala)

PEOPLE'S REPUBLIC OF CHINA

Little Ne Zha Fights Great Dragon Kings – (see Nezha Conquers the Dragon King)

Ne Zha Conquers the Dragon King – (see Nezha Conquers the Dragon King)
Ne Zha Storming the Sea – (see Nezha Conquers the Dragon King)

Nezha Conquers the Dragon King – 1972

Prince Ne Zha's Triumph Against Dragon King – (see Nezha Conquers the Dragon King)

PHILIPPINES

Agency, The – (see Master Samurai)
Ahas Sa Pugad Lawin – 1979
Alamat Ni Julian Makabayan, Ang – (see A Peasant's Legend)
Alat – 1975
American Beauty Hostages – (see Ebony, Ivory and Jade)
Ang Pagbabalik Ni Harabas at Bulilit – 1977
Anino Ng Araw – 1975
Apat Na Bagwis – 1972
Apat Na Patak Ng Dugo Ni Adan – 1971

Bagsik at Kamandag ni Pedro Penduko – 1974
Bamboo Gods and Iron Men – 1974
Bandolera – 1972
Banta Ng Kahapon – 1977
Batong Buhay, Mga – 1970
Batwoman and Robin – 1972
Batwoman and Robin Meet the Queen of the Vampires – 1972
Beloy Montemayor – 1976
Bertong Suklab – 1976
Bionic Boy – 1977
Bionic Boy II – (see Dynamite Johnson)
Bitayin Si… Baby Ama! – 1976
Black Kung Fu – (see Bamboo Gods and Iron Men)
Black Valor – (see Savage!)
Bodyguard, The – 1977
Boxer – 1972
Bruce Liit – 1978
Bruce's Return – (see Return of Bruce)

Captain Barbell Boom! – 1973
Cleopatra Wong – 1978

Chinese Puzzle – (see Wonder Women)
Concord of Bruce – (see Return of Bruce)

Dakpin… Killers for Hire – 1979
Daluyong at Habagat – 1976
Day of the Bullets – (see Daluyong at Habagat)
Devil's Angels – (see Pay of Die)
Devil's Three – (see Pay of Die)
Devils Three: The Karate Killers – (see Pay of Die)
Dimasalang – 1970
Dirty Dozen – (see Hustler Squad)
Dirty Hari – 1972
Dragnet – 1973
Dragon Fire – 1974
Dragon Returns – (see Return of Bruce)
Dugo at Pag-Ibig Sa Kapirasong Lupa – 1975
Durugin Si Totoy Bato – 1979
Dynamite Jackson – (see TNT Jackson)
Dynamite Johnson – 1978
Dynamite Wong and TNT Jackson – (see TNT Jackson)

Ebony, Ivory, and Jade – 1976
El Vibora – 1972
Elias, Basilio at Sisa – 1972

Female Big Boss – (see Cleopatra Wong)
Fight, Batman, Fight! – 1971
Fly Me – 1973
Foxfire – (see Ebony, Ivory, and Jade)
Foxforce – (see Ebony, Ivory and Jade)
Fung Ku – 1973

Game of Death, The – 1974
Guadalupe – 1971
Gulapa: Ang Barakong Mayor Ng Maragondon – 1977

Habang Ako'ng Batas – 1971
Harabas' Angels –1979
Hit and Run – 1975
Holdup – 1979
Hostage: Hanapin si Batuigas – 1977
Hot Potato – 1976 (USA)
Hulihin Si… Tiagong Akyat – 1973
Hunted, The – 1970
Hustler Squad – 1976

Ibilanggo Si… Cavite Boy – 1974
Ikaw… Ako Laban Sa Mundo! – 1976
Iking Boxer – 1973
Iligpit Si… pretty boy – 1977
Invencibles Del Karate, Los – (see Master Samurai)
Isa Para Sa Lahat, Lahat Para Sa Isa – 1979
Isla de Toro – 1972

Jess Lapid Story, The – 1978

Kapitan Eddie Set: Mad Killer of Cavite – 1974
Karateka Boxer – 1973
KINGPin – 1973
Kontra Hari – 1971
Kumander Erlinda – 1972

Lagot Kung Lagot – 1972
Lalaki… Ang Alamat… Ang Baril, Ang – 1979
Laruang Apoy – 1977

Legend of Julian Makabayan, The – (see A Peasant's Legend)
Leon at Ang Daga, Ang – 1975

Magic Fighters – 1975
Mandawi – 1971
Mars Ravelo's Captain Barbell Boom! – (see Captain Barbell Boom!)
Master Samurai – 1974
Maynila – 1979
Mean Business – (see Pay of Die)
Mulawin – 1976
Murder in the Orient – 1974
Muthers, The – 1976
Mystical World of Pedro Penduko – 1973

Nardong Putik – 1972
Nasa Lupa Ang Langit at Imperyno – 1978
Ninja Vs. Bruce Lee – (see Return of Bruce)
No Tears for the Brave – 1974
Nueva Ecija – 1973
Nueva Viscaya – 1973

Pacific Connection, The – 1975
Pagbabalik Ni Harabas at Bulilit, Ang – 1977
Panther, The – 1973
Pay or Die – 1979
Peasant's Legend, A – 1979
Pedro Penduko – (Mystical World of Pedro Penduko)
Pepeng kulisap – 1979
Peter Pandesal – 1977
Pipo – 1970
Policewoman – 1974
Pulang lupa – 1971
Putol Na Kampilan – 1972

Return of Bruce – 1977
Return of the Bionic Boy, The – (see Dynamite Johnson)
Return of the Dragon – 1974
Revenge of the Lady Fighter – 1973 (Buhawi)

Sa Kamay Ng Tatlong Takas – 1971
San Cristobal – 1972
San Diego – 1970
Savage! – 1973
Savage Sisters – 1974
Shadow of the Dragon – 1973
She Devils in Chains – (see Ebony Ivory and Jade)
Sinong kapiling? Sinong kasiping? – 1977
Sino si Boy Urbina – 1979
South Pacific Connection – (see The Pacific Connection)
South Seas – 1974
South Seas Massacre – (see South Seas)
Special Squad, D.B. – (see Holdup)
Stickfighter – (see The Pacific Connection)
Super Gee – 1973

They Call Her Cleopatra Wong – (see Cleopatra Wong)
They Call Him Bruce Lee – 1979
They Call Him Chop Suey – 1975
Technician, The – (see Savage!)
Tidal Wave and West Wind – (see Day of the Bullet)
Time for Dying, A – (see Pipo)
T.N.T. Jackson – 1974 (USA)
Tough Guy – 1974 (HK)

The Ultimate Guide to Martial Arts Movies of the 1970s

Trionic Warrior – (see Bionic Boy)
Trubador – 1972
Tsikiting Master – 1979

Udyok – 1971

Women of Transplant Island – (see Wonder Women)
Wonder Women – 1973 (USA)

SPAIN

Jaguar Lives – 1979 (El Fino) (USA)

Red Sun – 1971 (IT/FR)

Samurai – 1975 (IT/FR)
Supermenler – 1979 (IT/TU)
Stranger and the Gun Fighter, The – 1974 (El Kárate, El Colt Y El Impostor) (IT/USA/HK)

SWEDEN

Hooker's Revenge – (see They Call Her One Eye)

They Call Her One Eye – 1973
Thriller: En Grym Film – (see They Call Her One Eye)

THAILAND

Aussawin Darb Khyyasit – 1970

Born to Fight – 1978 (Gerd Ma Lui)

Choom Pae – 1976

Giant Thai Idol Yuk Wud Jaeng – 1973 (Ta Tien)
Gold – 1973

Hanuman Vs. 5 Kamen Riders – 1974
Hanuman Vs. 7 Ultraman – 1974

Janbogu Esu To Jaianto – (see Jumborg Ace & Giant)
Jong-arng Payong – 1971
Jumborg Ace & Giant – 1974 (Yuk Wud Jaeng Pob Jumborg A)

Khun Suek – 1976
Killer Elephants – 1976

Man with the Golden Gun – 1977 (UK)
Mars Men – 1974 (Yuk Wud Jaeng Wu Jumborg A)

Noble War – 1975 (Suk Kumpakan)

Operation Black Panther – 1977 (Yeh Nuat Sua)

Soul of Chiba – 1974 (JA/HK)

Thao huay Lai liew – 1975

Warlord, The – 1976

TURKEY

Alin Yazisi – 1972
Altay'dan Gelen Yigit – 1977
Aslan Adam – 1975 (Kilic Aslant)

Baba Kartal – 1978
Babalarin Babasi – 1975
Babanin Evlatlari – (see Mettetemi In Galera)
Babanin Sucu – 1976
Battal Gazi'nin Intikami – 1972
Battal Gazi'nin Oglu – 1974

Cemil – 1975
Cemil Donuyor – 1977

Dayi – 1974
Deli Yusuf – 1975

Fatihin Fedaisi Kara Murat – 1972

Hakanlar Carpisiyor – 1977
Heart of a Father – 1979 (Insan Avcisi)

Iki Arkadas – 1976
Insanlari Seveceksin – 1979
Instanbul Gang – 1979 (Kriminal Porno)

Justice – 1977 (Adalet)

Kaplanlar Aglamaz – 1978
Kara Murat Denizler Hakimi – 1977
Kara Murat Devler Savasiyor – 1978
Kara Murat Olum Emri – 1974
Karamurat, la Belva Dell'Anatolia – 1976 (IT)
Karamurat: The Sultan's Warrior – 1973 (Karamurat: Fatihin Fermani)
Karate on the Bosphorus – 1974 (Karate Instanbulda) (HK)
Kilic Bey – 1978
Kuskun Cicek – 1979

La Polizia Brancola Nel Buio – 1975
Lion Man – (see Aslan Adam)
Lionman – (see Aslan Adam)
Lionman and the Witchqueen – (Lionman II: The Witchqueen)
Lionman II: The Witchqueen – 1979

Magic Man, The – 1976 (Kara Murat Seyh Gaffar'a Karsi) (IT)
Maglup Edilemeyenler – 1976
Man Without Tomorrow – 1976 (Yarinsiz Adam)

Olum Gorevi – 1978

Raid, The – 1977 (Baskin)

Savulun Battal Gazi Geliyor – 1973
Sevgili Oglum – 1977
Sold Man – 1977 (Satilmis Adam)
Supermenler – 1979 (IT/SP)

Tek Basina – 1976
Three Superboys in the Snow, Thre – 1977 (Mettetemi In Galera)
Tuzak – 1976

Vurgun – 1973

Uc Kagitcilar – 1976 (IT)

UNITED KINGDOM

Call Him Mr. Shatter – 1974 (HK)

Diamonds are Forever – 1971
Dracula and the 7 Golden Vampires – 1974 (HK)

Live and Let Die – 1973

Man with the Golden Gun – 1977 – (TH)
Moonraker – 1979 (FR)

Pink Panther Strikes Again, The – 1976 (USA)

Return of the Pink Panther – 1975
Revenge of the Pink Panther – 1978 (USA)

Spy Who Loved Me – 1977

USA

Avenging Godfather – (see Disco Godfather)

Bare Knuckles – 1977
Billy Jack – 1971
Billy Jack Goes To Washington – 1977
Black Belt Jones – 1974
Black Eliminator – (see Death Dimension)
Black Godfather – 1974
Black Samurai – 1977
Black Terminator – (see Black Samurai)
Breaker! Breaker! – 1977
Breaking Point – 1976
Budo: The Art of Killing – 1979

Cannonball – 1976
Carquake – (see Cannonball)
Circle of Iron – 1978
Cleopatra Jones – 1973
Cleopatra Jones & the Casino of Gold – 1975 (HK)
Cindy Jo & the Texas Turnaround – (see Breaker! Breaker!)

Deadly and the Beautiful, The – (see Wonder Women)
Death Dimension – 1978
Death Dimensions – (see Death Dimension)
Death Force – (see Fighting Mad)
Death Journey – 1976
Death Machine – (see Death Machines)
Death Machines – 1976
Death Promise – 1977
Devil's Express – 1976
Devil's Son in Law, The – (see Petey Wheatstraw)
Disco Godfather – 1979
Doc Savage the Man of Bronze – 1975
Dolemite – 1975
Dolemite II – 1976
Dynamite Brothers – 1974
Dynamite Brown – (see Dynamite Brothers)

Ebony, Ivory & Jade – 1976 (PH)
Enter the Dragon – 1973 (HK)
Enter the White Dragon – (see Death Promise)

Fighting Black Kings – (1976)
Fighting Mad – 1978

286

Fistfull of Yen – 1977
Force of One, A – 1979
Foxy Brown – 1974
Freeze Bomb, The – (see Black Samurai)
Freeze Bomb – (see Death Dimension)
Friday Foster – 1973

Game of Death, The – 1973/1978 (HK)
Golden Needles – 1974
Good Guys Wear Black – 1978

Hot Potato – 1976 (PH)
Human Tornado – (see Dolemite II)

Icy Death – (see Death Dimension)

Jaguar Lives – 1979 (SP)

Kentucky Fried Movie – (see Fistful of Yen)
Kill Factor – (see Death Dimension)
Kill the Golden Goose – 1979
Kill Golden Ninja – (see Kill the Golden Goose)
Killer Elite – 1975
Killing of a Chinese Bookie – (see Dynamite Brothers)
King Kung fu – 1976
Kung Fu – 1972

Master Gunfighter, The – 1975
Mean John Burrows – 1976
Men of the Dragon – 1974

Pay-Off Time – (see Death Promise)
Petey Wheatstraw – 1977
Pink Panther Strikes Again, The – 1976 (UK)

Revenge of the Pink Panther – 1978 (UK)

Samurai – 1979
Samurai – 1975 (IT)
Seven – 1979
Silent Flute – (see Circle of Iron)
Slaughter – 1972
Slaughter's Big Rip-Off – 1973
Slumfighter – (see Death Promise)
Stoner – 1974 (AU/HK)
Stranger and the Gun Fighter, The – 1974 (HK/IT/SP)
Strongest Karate – (see Fighting Black Kings)
Stud Brown – (see Dynamite Brothers)
Sudden Death – 1977
Super Weapon – 1976
Superchick – 1973
Super Fly – 1972

Take a Hard Ride – 1975
That Man Bolt – 1973
Three the Hard Way – 1974
T.N.T. Jackson – 1975 (PH)
Trial of Billy Jack – 1974

Ultimate Warrior – 1975

Warrior, The – 1979
Warrior Within – 1976
Wild Wild West Revisited, The – 1979
Women in Cages – 1971
Wonder Women – 1973 (PH)

Yakuza, The – 1975 (JA)
Yellow Faced Tiger – (1974) (HK)

WEST GERMANY

Return of Shanghai Joe – 1975 – (IT)
Roots of Evil – 1979 (Die Brut des Bosen)

Virgins of the Seven Seas – 1974 (Karate, Küsse, Blonde Katzen) (HK)

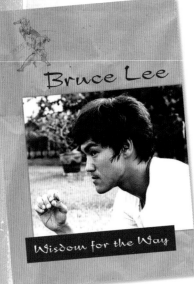